THE HANDBOOK OF
SOCIAL
RESEARCH
ETHICS

THE HANDBOOK OF SOCIAL RESEARCH ETHICS

Editors

DONNA M. MERTENS
Gallaudet University

PAULINE E. GINSBERG
Utica College

Copyright © 2009 by SAGE Publications, Inc.

All rights reserved. No part of this book may be reproduced or utilized in any form or by any means, electronic or mechanical, including photocopying, recording, or by any information storage and retrieval system, without permission in writing from the publisher.

For information:

SAGE Publications, Inc.
2455 Teller Road
Thousand Oaks, California 91320
E-mail: order@sagepub.com

SAGE Publications Ltd.
1 Oliver's Yard
55 City Road
London EC1Y 1SP
United Kingdom

SAGE Publications India Pvt. Ltd.
B 1/I 1 Mohan Cooperative Industrial Area
Mathura Road, New Delhi 110 044
India

SAGE Publications Asia-Pacific Pte. Ltd.
33 Pekin Street #02-01
Far East Square
Singapore 048763

Printed in the United States of America

Library of Congress Cataloging-in-Publication Data

The handbook of social research ethics/Donna M. Mertens, Pauline E. Ginsberg [editors].
    p. cm.
Includes bibliographical references and index.
ISBN 978-1-4129-4918-7 (cloth)

   1. Social sciences—Research—Handbooks, manuals, etc. 2. Research—Moral and ethical aspects—Handbooks, manuals, etc. I. Mertens, Donna M. II. Ginsberg, Pauline E.

H62.H24565 2009
174.'90014—dc22   2008010387

Printed on acid-free paper

08 09 10 11 12   10 9 8 7 6 5 4 3 2 1

Acquiring Editor:	Vicki Knight
Associate Editor:	Sean Connelly
Editorial Assistant:	Lauren Habib
Production Editor:	Sarah K. Quesenberry
Copy Editor:	QuADS Prepress (P) Ltd.
Typesetter:	C&M Digitals (P) Ltd.
Proofreader:	Vicki Reed Castro
Indexer:	Kay Duscheck
Cover Designer:	Gail Buschman
Marketing Manager:	Stephanie Adams

CONTENTS

Preface ix

Acknowledgments xv

SECTION I. HISTORY AND PHILOSOPHY 1

1. Social Science Research Ethics: Historical and Philosophical Issues 5
   Karen Strohm Kitchener and Richard F. Kitchener

2. Research Ethics in the Postmodern Context 23
   Joshua W. Clegg and Brent D. Slife

3. Feminist Perspectives on Research Ethics 39
   Mary M. Brabeck and Kalina M. Brabeck

4. Critical Race Theory: Ethics and Dimensions of Diversity in Research 54
   Veronica G. Thomas

5. Philosophy, Ethics, and the Disability Community 69
   Martin Sullivan

6. Transformative Research and Ethics 85
   Donna M. Mertens, Heidi M. Holmes, and Raychelle L. Harris

SECTION II. PERSPECTIVES ON ETHICAL REGULATION — 103

7. Governmental Regulation in Social Science — 107
   Linda Mabry

8. The Role of Institutional Review Boards: Ethics: Now You See Them, Now You Don't — 121
   Richard Speiglman and Patricia Spear

9. Researching Ourselves Back to Life: Taking Control of the Research Agenda in Indian Country — 135
   Joan LaFrance and Cheryl Crazy Bull

10. Ethical Practices in Qualitative Research — 150
    Yvonna S. Lincoln

11. Ethical Perspectives in Program Evaluation — 170
    Amanda Wolf, David Turner, and Kathleen Toms

SECTION III. ETHICS AND RESEARCH METHODS — 185

12. On Ethics in Sociolegal Research — 189
    Richard Schwartz

13. Experiments, Quasi-Experiments, and Ethics — 198
    Melvin M. Mark and Chris Gamble

14. The Ethics of Data Archiving: Issues From Four Perspectives — 214
    David Johnson and Merry Bullock

15. Ethnography: Constitutive Practice and Research Ethics — 229
    Anne Ryen

16. Covenantal Ethics and Action Research: Exploring a Common Foundation for Social Research — 243
    Mary Brydon-Miller

17. Research Ethics and Peacemaking — 259
    Colin Irwin

SECTION IV. ETHICAL ISSUES IN RESEARCH PRACTICE — 275

18. Cultivating Self as Responsive Instrument: Working the Boundaries and Borderlands for Ethical Border Crossings — 279
    Hazel Symonette

19. The Ethics of the Researcher-Subject Relationship: Experiences From the Field — 295
Peggy Gabo Ntseane

20. Maintaining Indigenous Voices — 308
Fiona Cram

21. Ethical Issues in Cross-Cultural Psychology — 323
David Matsumoto and Caroline Anne Leong Jones

22. Partnership Ethics — 337
Linda Silka

23. Visual Representation of People and Information: Translating Lives Into Numbers, Words, and Images as Research Data — 353
Julianne H. Newton

24. Use and Misuse of Quantitative Methods: Data Collection, Calculation, and Presentation — 373
Bruce L. Brown and Dawson Hedges

SECTION V: ETHICS WITHIN DIVERSE CULTURAL GROUPS — 387

25. Conducting Ethical Research and Evaluation in Underserved Communities — 391
Katrina L. Bledsoe and Rodney K. Hopson

26. Indigenous African-Centered Ethics: Contesting and Complementing Dominant Models — 407
Bagele Chilisa

27. Research Ethics and Sensitive Behaviors: Underground Economy — 426
Divya Sharma

28. Epistemological Domination: Social Science Research Ethics in Aotearoa — 442
Helen Moewaka Barnes, Tim McCreanor, Shane Edwards, and Belinda Borell

29. An Ethical Agenda in Disability Research: Rhetoric or Reality? — 458
Colin Barnes

30. LGBTQ: Protecting Vulnerable Subjects in *All* Studies   474
    Sarah-Jane Dodd

31. Involving Minors in Research: Ethics and
    Law Within Muticultural Settings   489
    Luis A. Vargas and Margaret E. Montoya

32. Ethical Research With Older Adults   507
    Karen Szala-Meneok

SECTION VI. CONCLUSIONS AND FUTURE DIRECTIONS   519

33. Research Ethics in Transnational Spaces   521
    Robert Stake and Fazal Rizvi

34. Privacy and New Technologies:
    The Limits of Traditional Research Ethics   537
    Nicholas C. Burbules

35. Graduate Training in Responsible Conduct of
    Social Science Research: The Role of Mentors and
    Departmental Climate   550
    Celia B. Fisher, Frederick J. Wertz, and
    Sabrina J. Goodman

36. Social Research Attuned to Deliberative Democracy   565
    Kenneth R. Howe and Heather MacGillivary

37. Frontiers in Social Research Ethics: Fertile Ground
    for Evolution   580
    Pauline E. Ginsberg and Donna M. Mertens

Author Index   614

Subject Index   635

About the Editors   653

About the International Advisory Board Members
and Contributors   655

PREFACE

As ethical lapses on a grand scale appear in the media, it heightens our awareness of the importance of addressing ethics in all dimensions of our lives. As social science researchers and evaluators, we have a shared responsibility to be informed as to history of applied research ethics and participate in a challenging agenda for the future. This *Handbook* provides an understanding of that history and expands the ethical frontiers that confront social scientists in the new millennium. It emphasizes understanding of those ethical issues that arise in the theory and practice of research within the technologically advancing and culturally complex world in which we live. In the process, contributors also examine ethical dilemmas that arise in the relationship between research practice and social justice.

Given the complexity and urgency of ethical matters in social research, this volume is designed to address the following goals:

- Identify salient contemporary ethical issues in social science research
- Locate those issues historically, theoretically, and methodologically
- Define and explore the role(s) of ethics in research from multidisciplinary, multicultural perspectives
- Make explicit the differing ethical emphases entailed by differing research traditions
- Locate ethical concerns within research practice
- Elucidate the relationship between good ethical practice and good research practice

Our intent is to explore the topic of social science research ethics in ways that acknowledge evolving understandings and questions about the relationship between ethics and research. This *Handbook* is intended to clarify the role of ethics within the social science research community[1] and the constituencies we serve, as well as to encourage debate about issues that merit continued discussion. Examples are provided that explore how ethical practice, as it is manifest in different disciplines, cultural and geographic settings, and research perspectives, makes contributions to a broader and deeper understanding of ethics in research. This volume explores the meaning of good ethical practice by engaging eminent scholars in the process of providing insights into difficult questions and engaging the reader in assessing their relevance to research practice. Are there universal ethical principles? Should the research community accept cultural relativism as a stance? What are the boundaries that define ethical and unethical practice once differing research perspectives, assumptions, and practices are taken into account? What are the differences in descriptions of an ethical relationship between the researcher and the individuals who participate in the research, when research is done using traditional experimental psychology as contrasted with non-Western, innovative participatory approaches?

♦ The Scope of the Handbook

Despite the varied theoretical underpinnings and ethical differences associated with different methodological and discipline-based approaches, many individual researchers combine the use of quantitative and qualitative methods, while still others participate in cooperative research efforts that partner investigators who were trained in different methods and who identify with multiple disciplines. Professional associations' codes of ethics for U.S.-based professional associations are rooted in the human subjects protection measures that appeared in the Belmont Report (Shadish, Cook, & Campbell, 2002). Lincoln and Denzin (2000) recognized that many scholars who use qualitative methods have contributed to understanding ethics in research when it is considered from the perspective of the gendered, historically situated, interacting individual. The ethical issues shift as previously silenced voices enter the discourse. For example, feminists and critical race researchers have articulated an ethical perspective that refocuses and redefines previous ontologies, epistemologies, and methodologies (Lincoln & Denzin, 2000, p. 1048). Shifts in ethics also arise when researchers are taken into new areas of investigation triggered by demographic shifts such as the aging boomer population in North America and increased worldwide migration, new theoretical developments, such as positive psychology, resilience theory and appreciative inquiry, and new technologies such as increasing miniaturization and the expanding reach of the Internet. The field of research ethics has not yet reached the point of clearly defining differences, similarities, and implications of different methodological approaches, different populations, emerging social trends, and emerging theory development in the various disciplines.

Using contributors' assumptions as starting points for thought, we hope that the framework used in this *Handbook* will help clarify thinking and that tensions identified will result in dialogue leading to improved approaches to the ethical conduct of research. Researchers should be aware of their philosophical, theoretical, and discipline-based assumptions (i.e., their functional paradigms) as these influence their approach to research. Thus, ethical issues associated with quantitative, qualitative, and mixed methods are included, and the viewpoints of various research perspectives are incorporated into the descriptions of ethical issues. The intent is to provide as full a picture as possible of what is considered to be "good" and "ethical" research methodology from a variety of perspectives by examining approaches to ethics across topical concerns, methodologies, and disciplines. This informs researchers of a diversity of ways in which ethical issues are addressed, and it is hoped that this will lead to insights that will improve potential solutions to ethical dilemmas they face.

In doing this, we are the first to acknowledge that there is some unevenness in representation. Applied researchers outnumber those whose research is better described as "basic." Although we have sought geographic diversity, our contributors are overwhelmingly North American. Several topics that we had hoped to include and thought to be important to a contemporary handbook are absent. These include ethics of research in crisis situations, where authors we attempted to recruit expressed interest but were pulled from one crisis to the next without sufficient time to prepare a manuscript, and ethical issues in research when religious faith is a variable, for which we solicited a chapter, but it was not forthcoming. We had originally anticipated including two additional chapters examining professional codes, one comparative, across professions and issues, and the other examining the position of a single professional organization with regard to cultural competency. Both sets of authors found the work difficult, however, and were unable to complete it for this edition. We apologize for these omissions in profound awareness that the volume is not comprehensive in this respect, as well as with regard to other topics that are important to contemporary ethical thought.

Our paramount purpose is to present and explore debates and issues that relate to ethics within socially responsible research. In this matter, we are in accord with Kitchener (2000) who indicated that having a code of ethics governing professional behavior is not sufficient to resolve ethical dilemmas. Rather, inherent contradictions and gaps in codes of ethics, as well as complexities that require a deeper understanding of contextual variables, suggest a need for a handbook of social research ethics that situates them within the broader context of historical and philosophical thought (Section I)[2] and examines the regulatory aspects of ethics from a variety of perspectives (Section II). Moreover, we are acutely aware that it is the interface between thought and praxis that continually pushes the boundaries of our understanding of ethics beyond regulations and codes. To explore this interface, we first focus on research methods in education and the social sciences, primarily, but not exclusively, anthropology, psychology, and sociology, where contributors use varied methodological approaches (e.g., experimental designs, laboratory experiments, and participatory action research; Section III). We then focus on ethical concerns that arise in more specific research contexts (e.g., privacy concerns and partnership ethics) and more recent innovations (e.g., peace polling and participatory evaluation; Section IV). Contributors discuss ways in which their practice of research influences and is influenced by ethical issues. Widening our lens, we then draw back to look at how research questions and populations are themselves influenced by the broader culture. The penultimate section of the *Handbook* (Section V), therefore, examines those ethical issues brought to the table by researchers' interactions with groups that have, by virtue of geography, number, or condition, been excluded in the past from inclusion in the research agenda and/or, if regarded as objects of research, who have been excluded from appropriate ethical consideration grounded in their culture, values, and history. Finally (Section VI), we look toward the future in terms of preparation of new researchers and ethical implications for a changing world. Abstracting from contributors' offerings, we identify trends and emerging issues in the concluding chapter.

Several factors support the rationale for undertaking this *Handbook* at this time. These include

- Increased amount of social research being undertaken
- Increased range of individuals/groups/ institutions undertaking social research

- Increased understanding that some issues (e.g., sampling and random assignment) formerly defined primarily as methodological have strong ethical components[3]

- Increased demand from policy and legislative bodies for evidence-based research as justification for decision making at all levels of policy and practice

- Concerns about research design and use of research data that are narrowly defined and may support a specific political agenda

- National/international/disciplinary concerns about professional standards and responsibilities

- Need to have appropriate safeguards that preserve the reputation of researchers and the institutions for which they work as well as research participants

- Increased demands for respect and justice by researched communities, geographic, ethnic, and those made vulnerable by virtue of number, physical condition, and/or power differentials

Each of these factors has led to growing debate about the role of ethical concerns within social research as reflected in the literature over the past few years.

◆ Audience

Like many research handbooks, this one is geared to the interests of social science scholars working in the social research realm throughout the world. We expect the complete *Handbook* to serve as a comprehensive resource text for those specializing in the scholarship and practice of research. The text is likely to be of particular interest to faculty teaching research methodology courses, as well as to members of institutional review boards. Emerging researchers, university-based and independent scholars and researchers, graduate student researchers (including thesis and dissertation writers/researchers) particularly, but not exclusively, constitute those for whom this *Handbook* is designed to provide guidance in their advanced studies. We especially see it as relevant to those scholars struggling with contemporary and future societal factors and demands for improved ethical practice in research. As a handbook that focuses on the history, philosophy, and practice of research, this is designed to serve as a text for graduate classes aimed at understanding ethical implications at various decision points in the research process. A smaller potential readership comes from among theoretical ethicists whose primary work sites are in the university, social activists, and those who may serve on institutional or organizational ethics boards for medical and social service organizations.

◆ Organization

The organizational table included in this Preface provides a list of major topics addressed by the *Handbook*'s contributors and indicates, using the names of the first authors, those chapters in which each topic appears as a substantive component. For those chapters with a primary focus on the topic, the author's name is in bold print.

Individual chapters articulate a range of perspectives, processes, and issues associated with social science research, each grounded in and informed by ethical practice. We find that the expertise of each chapter's author(s) frequently resulted in the chapters reflecting a somewhat different direction from that which we expected, but we are delighted and encouraged by this divergence. In our feedback to authors, we have made a consistent point that their emphasis must be on ethical issues involved in the research described rather than on providing intricate details of a specific research theory, methodology, instrument, or setting and have been rewarded by a high level of abstract thought thoroughly grounded in concrete examples. The following table of topics may prove especially useful for those who teach ethics in social research settings.

Topics Addressed and Relevant Chapters[4]

Topic	Relevant Chapters
Action research	**Brydon-Miller**
Afrocentrism	**Chilisa, Ntseane, Bledsoe**
Aging	**Szala-Meneok**
Children	**Vargas**
Codes of ethics	Brabeck, Lincoln, Kitchener, Mabry, Schwartz, Stake
Confidentiality	Brabeck, Burbules, Chilisa, Cram, Dodd, Ginsberg, Johnson, Kitchener, Moewaka Barnes, Matsumoto, Sharma, Szala-Meneok, Vargas
Cross-cultural comparisons	Bledsoe, Chilisa, Cram, **Matsumoto**, Moewaka Barnes, Ntseane, Sharma, Wolf
Culture	Bledsoe, Chilisa, Cram, Ginsberg, LaFrance, Matsumoto, Mertens, Moewaka Barnes, Ntseane, Ryen, Sharma, Stake, Symonette, Thomas, Vargas
Data management and display	**Brown**, Irwin, **Johnson**, Matsumoto, Newton
Deafness	**Mertens**, Sullivan
Disability/ableism	**Barnes**, Mertens, **Sullivan**
Emancipatory paradigm	Barnes, Sullivan
Empowerment	Barnes, Brabeck, Brydon-Miller, Silka, Sullivan
Ethical review panels	LaFrance
Ethnocentrism	LaFrance, Matsumoto
Ethnography	**Ryen**, Schwartz, Stake
Evaluation research	**Wolf**, Ginsberg
Feminism	**Brabeck**, Thomas
Gender	Brabeck, Dodd, Ryen, Thomas
Globalization	**Burbules, Stake**
Government regulation	**Mabry**, Speiglman, Johnson
History of ethics in research	Brabeck, Clegg, Kitchener
Human rights	Johnson, Speiglman, Sullivan, Mertens
Indigenous peoples	**Chilisa, Cram, LaFrance**, Lincoln, **Moewaka Barnes, Ntseane**, Vargas, Mertens
Informed consent	Brabeck, Cram, Chilisa, Kitchener, Matsumoto, Ntseane, Sharma, Szala-Meneok, Vargas
Institutional review boards (IRBs)	Kitchener, LaFrance, Lincoln, Mabry, Moewaka Barnes, Ntseane, **Speiglman**, Stake, Vargas
International issues	Irwin, **Mabry, Sharma**, Johnson
LGBTQ	**Dodd**
Mentoring	**Fisher**
Mixed methods	Bledsoe, Brabeck, Mertens
Partnerships	LaFrance, Mertens, **Silka**, Sullivan, Vargas
Philosophy of social science	**Clegg, Kitchener**, Lincoln, Mertens, Sullivan, Thomas
Postmodernism	**Clegg**
Power	Brydon-Miller, Irwin, LaFrance, Ntseane, Moewaka Barnes, Barnes, Bledsoe, Cram, Silka, Mertens, Ginsberg, Chilisa, Ryen

(Continued)

(Continued)

Topic	Relevant Chapters
Qualitative research	**Lincoln**, Newton, **Ryen**, Szala-Meneok
Quantitative research	**Brown, Mark, Irwin**
Race	Bledsoe, Cram, LaFrance, **Thomas**
Reciprocity	Brabeck, Ryen, Sullivan
Resilience	Brabeck
Self	Cram, Ryen, **Symonette**
Social justice	Brabeck, Lincoln, Mertens
Technology	**Burbules**, Stake, Johnson
Theory	**Brabeck, Clegg, Howe, Kitchener, Lincoln, Thomas**, Mertens
Transformative paradigm	**Mertens**, Sullivan
U.S. law	Mabry, Speiglman, Vargas

◆ Notes

1. References to social science research and the social science research community in this proposal are inclusive of both basic and applied social research. The area of program evaluation is also included in this volume with specific focus in several chapters; however, much of what is written has applicability in both research and evaluation.

2. See especially Chapter 1 with regard to the philosophical subdiscipline of ethics itself, while later chapters in Section I relate social science research ethics to key concepts in the philosophy of social science. This being said, it is important to note that this volume is not expected to supplant a thorough examination of social science research ethics from a philosophical point of view. Rather, our concern is to recognize that social science research ethics are grounded in Western philosophical tradition.

3. A comparison of the index of Cook and Campbell's (1979) *Quasi-Experimentation: Design and Analysis Issues for Field Settings* with that of its successor, Shadish, Cook, and Campbell's (2002) *Experimental and Quasi-Experimental Designs for Generalized Causal Inference* will bear this out as will a comparison of chapter 5 in the original with chapter 4 in the later work.

4. Chapters are identified by the name of the first author. Bold print for author names indicates that in this chapter, the topic is a major theme.

◆ References

Cook, T. D., & Campbell, D. T. (1979). *Quasi-experimentation: Design and analysis issues for field settings.* Skokie, IL: Rand McNally.

Kitchener, K. S. (2000). *Foundations of ethical practice, research, and teaching in psychology.* Mahwah, NJ: Lawrence Erlbaum.

Lincoln, Y. S., & Denzin, N. K. (2000). (Eds.). *Handbook of qualitative research* (2nd ed.). Thousand Oaks, CA: Sage.

Shadish, W. R., Cook, T. D., & Campbell, D. T. (2002). *Experimental and quasi-experimental designs for generalized causal inference.* Boston: Houghton Mifflin.

ACKNOWLEDGMENTS

We wish to express our thanks to our families who have seen rather too much of our backs hunched over our computers since we joined forces on July 4, 2005, and have seen a few events alleged to be family picnics turn into handbook discussions. They have been patient, sometimes beyond belief, and at times have invested this project with nearly as much importance as we ourselves have done. Thanks also go to the support staff and graduate students from Gallaudet University, Glenda Mobley, Martina Smidova, Heidi Holmes, and Peggy Prosser, who found time to squeeze in handbook activities among all their other responsibilities. Thanks also to the chairs of Gallaudet's Department of Educational Foundations and Research, Thomas Kluwin and Barbara Gerner de Garcia, for their support.

We also want to thank our authors and advisory board members. Advisory board members include Rodney Hopson, Ricardo Millett, Michael Patton, Mel Mark, Luis Vargas, Helen Simons, Fiona Cram, Colin Irwin, Cliff Christians, Brent Slife, Bagele Chilisa, Lisa Schwartz, Jennifer Greene, and Janice McLaughlin (some of whom did double duty as contributors). Altogether, you have taught us a tremendous amount, not only about diverse approaches to research ethics, but also about writing, providing constructive feedback, and showing grace under pressure. For those who were our friends and colleagues before we began this undertaking, we relished the opportunity to enrich our relationships with you. Many of you were strangers to one or both of us when this project began and, although we still may not have met face-to-face, we feel as if you have widened our circle of friends. Thank you for sharing your concerns and pleasures with us—and for persisting in the project through illnesses and injuries, loss and infirmity of dear ones, job changes and promotions, holidays and vacations. Many are the times we enjoyed virtual long-distance celebratory glasses of wine, twirls around the office or living room floor, and panoramas of mountains and seacoasts that were conveyed through your e-mails and telephone calls.

Finally, we want to thank SAGE Publications for the consistent guidance and support of the editorial staff. We had heard bad things about changing editors in midstream and were initially apprehensive when Lisa Cuevas left for greener pastures and Vicki Knight took her place. We need not have worried! Not only did the benefits of editorial faith in the project and quick responses to our inquiries continue, but so did the highly productive working lunches and the unerring selection of exceptional restaurants.

Donna M. Mertens

Pauline E. Ginsberg

♦ Publisher's Acknowledgments

SAGE Publications gratefully acknowledges the contributions of the following reviewers:

Gail Dummer, Michigan State University

Michael Kalichman, University of California–San Diego

Mike Peddle, Northern Illinois University

Thomas Schwandt, University of Illinois–Urbana-Champaign

Joan Sieber, California State University Hayward

Daniel Walsh, University of Illinois–Urbana-Champaign

SECTION I

HISTORY AND PHILOSOPHY

In this section, we lay the foundation of the *Handbook* with chapters that historically and philosophically situate ethical concerns in the practice of social science research. The focus in this section is on the various theoretical positions and approaches taken by those who contemplate the meaning of ethics in social science research. The organization of the section is roughly historical. That is, a chapter on basic philosophical foundations anchors this section, with chapters describing more recent influences following.

In the first chapter, "Social Science Research Ethics: Historical and Philosophical Issues," Kitchener and Kitchener examine the philosophical roots of ethics in research from the perspectives of Kant, J. S. Mill, Hegel, and others. They provide a model of ethics that draws from four areas: "(1) *Descriptive ethics* studies how people actually behave and what ethical values they actually hold. This area belongs to empirical social science. (2) *Normative ethics* is concerned with the questions: How should an individual behave; what properties are valuable or good? (R. Kitchener, 2008). (3) *Meta-ethics* asks questions about the meaning of ethical words, the logic of justifying moral decisions, the reality of moral properties, and so forth. (4) Finally, *applied ethics* uses principles and insights from normative ethics to resolve specific moral issues in concrete and particular settings (e.g., medical ethics, business ethics). Social science research ethics is thus an example of applied ethics" (K. Kitchener, 2000; pp. 5–6, this volume). Their model includes five levels of ethics: particular behavior, ethical rules, ethical principles, ethical theory, and meta-ethics (concerned with the meaning and justification of ethical statements).

In Chapter 2, "Research Ethics in the Postmodern Context," Clegg and Slife describe the postmodernist movement as one that brings to the foreground the question of whether ethics is foundational to the *telos* of the research enterprise or a foundationless, relativistic extra consideration. This chapter addresses the question of whether there is a substrate of ethical commitments that underlies or ought to underlie all social science research. Of the many candidates for these postmodern "family resemblances" (Wittgenstein, 1953/2001, as cited by Clegg & Slife), they selected four categories of relevance: particular (not generalizable; but particular stories), contextual (recognition of specific, situated variables as essential to meaning making), value laden (interpretation that makes values explicit), and other-focused (multiple interpretations that make power relations explicit).

Following the philosophical chapters, the volume turns to various theoretical frameworks that enhance our search for the meaning of ethics in research, beginning with Brabeck and Brabeck's chapter on feminist theory ("Feminist Perspectives on Research Ethics"). They critique the development of ethics based on men as the normative human beings. Feminist perspectives can be credited with the inclusion of women in the research agenda and with their greater inclusion among social science practitioners. They focus on feminist scholars' contributions to research ethics as they apply to all stages of the research process, from selection of research topics to the language in which results are communicated.

Despite differences and debates, across feminist theories there is general agreement on the broad, central themes that define feminist ethics. Five central themes are identified by Brabeck and Brabeck (Chapter 3, this volume). These are "the assertions that women and their experiences have moral significance, all discriminatory distortions must be critiqued, power dynamics must be analyzed and action directed at achieving social justice is required" (p. 50).

Feminists advocate for making visible and challenging the bases of discriminatory distortion, including gender, race, class, sexual orientation, culture, age, ability, linguistic status, and other relevant dimensions. Power dynamics are examined in all contexts, especially between the researcher and participants. Feminist ethics requires social action to bring about social justice. Brabeck and Brabeck provide examples of the ethical tensions that arise through an application of feminist theory in the study "of the help seeking and strategies to survive abuse employed by 75 women of Mexican origin who had experienced intimate partner abuse" (Brabeck & Guzman, in press, as cited in Chapter 3, p. 43, this volume).

In Chapter 4, Thomas extends the theoretical insights from feminist theory by integrating them with critical race theories ("Critical Race Theory: Ethics and Dimensions of Diversity in Research"). She reviews the ethical issues that have surfaced through the application of critical race and its intersection with feminist theory examined from historical, philosophical, and pragmatic perspectives. Through the lens of critical race theory, she examines ethical issues in research that are related to discrimination and oppression and the researcher's responsibility to address such issues in pursuit of social justice.

As feminist perspectives made sexism visible and critical race theory made racism visible in social science research, so the disability community identified able-ism. In "Philosophy, Ethics, and the Disability Community" (Chapter 5), Sullivan focuses on the philosophical and historical scholarship of disability scholars that contributes to debates that further understanding of ethical issues. He raises questions about the control of the research, with specific reference to who is doing the research, the prior knowledge on which the research is based, and the "why" of the research as crucial bases to deciding if the research is ethical or not. His "chapter reviews those debates by focusing on the emergence of the disability rights movement and disability studies, the reconceptualization of *disability* and its implications for disability research, the development of the emancipatory research paradigm," and potential partnerships that might emerge from adopting a transformative stance in disability research (Chapter 5, p. 70, this volume). The emancipatory research paradigm is political in nature, firmly rooted in the social model of disability, and focuses on "exposing oppressive, disabling structures and changing them to extend the control disabled people have over their own lives" (Chapter 5, p. 73, this volume).

Mertens, Harris, and Holmes (Chapter 6) take the implications of disability, feminist, and critical race theories to a higher level of abstraction with their presentation of the philosophical and historical contributions of the transformative paradigm to research ethics in their chapter, "Transformative Research and Ethics." The writings of scholars who work within the domain of social transformation and human rights raise issues related to ethics in research that allow for an enhanced examination of established research ethics codes in the interest of contributing to a philosophically grounded approach to transformation toward improved social justice. The transformative paradigm emphasizes the need to examine critically the basic beliefs that researchers bring with them to guide their decisions about what variables are important to consider and how and from whom data are collected in an ethical manner. In the context of educational, social, and psychological programs, many of the programs studied by social science researchers are intended to serve people "who have been pushed to the margins on the basis of race/ethnicity, language, indigenous/immigrant status, education level, disability, age, religion, socioeconomic status, and other contextually dependent variables. Issues of discrimination and oppression are commonly associated with those characteristics that are connected with the focus of such programs and policies. For researchers who are aware of the historical and political factors that surround program participants, . . . power issues associated with greater privilege in society" constitute an apparent ethical tension that needs to be addressed (Chapter 6, p. 86, this volume). To that end, this chapter elucidates the transformative paradigm with its accompanying philosophical assumptions as a way of examining the underlying beliefs that define the role of the researcher as one who works in partnership for social change and who challenges the status quo.

1

SOCIAL SCIENCE RESEARCH ETHICS

Historical and Philosophical Issues

◆ Karen Strohm Kitchener and Richard F. Kitchener

The ethics of social science research is a relatively new field, emerging only in the middle of the 20th century. Although there have been several books written on the topic (e.g., Diener & Crandall, 1978; Kimmel, 1988, 1996; Reynolds, 1979, 1982; Sieber, 1992), there is no unanimous consensus about its fundamentals. What is the ethics of social science research about?

◆ **Ethics**

Ethics can be conceived to consist of several areas. (1) *Descriptive ethics* studies how people actually behave and what ethical values they actually hold. This area belongs to empirical social science. (2) *Normative ethics* is concerned with the questions: How should an individual behave; what properties are valuable or good? (R. Kitchener, 2008). In short, whereas descriptive ethics studies the "is" side of the is-ought distinction, normative ethics studies the "ought" side. (3) *Meta-ethics* asks questions about the meaning of ethical words, the logic of justifying moral decisions, the reality of moral properties, and so forth. (4) Finally, *applied ethics* uses principles and insights from normative ethics to resolve specific moral issues in concrete and particular settings (e.g., medical ethics, business ethics). Social science research ethics is thus an example of applied ethics (K. Kitchener, 2000).

Traditionally, ethical positions have been divided on questions of normative ethics and of what normative ethical principles one should follow. Of course, everyone has his or her own personal values and norms, but the question is, "Which values or norms should be relied on in making a decision? Which personal moral norms and values are really good or adequate ones to hold? Which ones are rationally defensible?"

For example, researchers need to be tolerant when studying how and why people act as they do (American Anthropological Association [AAA], 2006). But this does not necessarily mean that researchers should agree with the values of the people or culture they are studying. Furthermore, there are some values social scientists ought not to hold—for example, torturing research participants or sexually exploiting them. In short, the basic normative question is "What are the ethical values that social scientists ought to hold, and how can they be justified?"

♦ Social Science Research Ethics

In the context of social science research, there are two fundamental ethical questions: What is the ethically proper way to collect, process, and report research data? How should social scientists behave with respect to their research subjects? (The second question has received the most attention.)

There appear to be three sources for answers to these questions: professional codes of ethics, federal guidelines, and general ethical principles.

First, virtually every social science has a professional code of ethics (AAA, 2006; American Political Science Association, 1998; American Psychological Association [APA], 2002; American Sociological Association [ASA], 1999). Many social scientists appear to think that such codes of ethics are sufficient for answering the ethical questions that arise when they conduct their research since these codes prescribe and proscribe certain values and ways of acting. But ethical questions remain: Are such codes themselves ethically justified? What happens when one belongs to more than one professional society and one finds conflicting advice from these divergent codes? Furthermore, issues arise that the codes do not cover. For example, take the issue of doing research on sexually transmitted diseases and discovering that a subject has AIDS but has not disclosed this to his partner nor is he using condoms. Considering that the sexual partner is placed at risk, the researcher is confronted by the potentially lethal consequences of the subject's behavior. In cases like these, sociologists are urged to balance the promise of confidentiality with other obligations in their ethical code (ASA, 1999). Often it is unclear, as it is in the above case, whether or how ethical codes apply.

It would be reassuring if ethics codes solved all such conflicts, but they don't. As the profession develops, new situations and arenas of research arise. Since ethics codes are revised only periodically, new ethical challenges remain unaddressed until the next revision. Consequently, social science researchers need to understand the foundational ethical principles on which their professional codes stand, how to apply these in concrete situations, and how to critically evaluate their own conclusions.

A second source of ethical rules is found in federal guidelines (see Chapter 7, this volume). These federal mandates specify what is permissible and what is not. But again, are the federal guidelines warranted from an ethical point of view? What happens when such guidelines conflict with professional codes of ethics or one's personal value system?

Finally, there are ethical principles. Even if one does not believe in common or universal moral principles, there are several widely cited accounts of general ethical principles that govern biomedical research, psychiatric ethics, and psychology. In addition, there are general accounts of ethical principles governing social science research. These principles can be used to answer ethical questions arising in research, even if the more narrowly formulated professional codes of ethics and professional guidelines do not. At least, that is what we argue: The social sciences need a general set of ethical principles governing their behavior. We suggest a five-level model, involving particular behavior, ethical rules, ethical principles, ethical theory, and meta-ethics.

◆ Historical Overview

Before suggesting such a model, however, we need to briefly address the issue of why social scientists are (or should be) concerned about research ethics. What has happened historically to engender such interest on the part of the various social scientists, professions, and governmental agencies?

The contemporary concern with the ethics of social science research has several historical roots: (1) as an extension of biomedical ethics, which was a reaction to the Nazi atrocities uncovered during the Nuremberg Trials; (2) as an indigenous moral concern within several of the social sciences, a concern that partly was fueled by controversial cases in the social sciences; and (3) as a general (philosophical) concern about research ethics.

BIOMEDICAL ETHICS AND FEDERAL REGULATIONS

As noted above, one of the most important historical antecedents of social science research ethics was biomedical research ethics. First, there was the Nuremberg Code of ethics, which set forth morally acceptable and unacceptable conduct with regard to medical research with humans. Next, there were several, now famous, cases of controversial biomedical research that came to public attention (Katz, 1972): the Thalidomide Drug Tragedy (in 1961), the Jewish National Hospital cancer study (in 1965), the Willowbrook hepatitis study (in 1966), and the Tuskegee syphilis study (in 1972). Subsequently, it was disclosed that there was controversial research performed by the U.S. Government and universities funded by it—the notorious radiation studies, the MKULTRA studies, and so forth. The upshot of this development was the creation of a set of federal guidelines for research on humans. The first was set forth in a report of the Surgeon General of the Public Health Service in 1966 (PPO #129). This, in turn, led to the establishment of institutional review boards (IRBs) in 1971 and 1974. The 1974 National Research Act authorized the National Commission for the Protection of Human Subjects in Biomedical and Behavioral Research to formulate the ethical principles that should govern the conduct of biomedical and behavioral scientists performing research on humans—the Belmont Report (1978). (See Childress, Meslin, & Shapiro, 2005.)

How does this history relate to social science ethics? From the beginning (1966), the behavioral sciences were included in the guidelines—first in the Surgeon General's revisions (in 1966 and 1969) to his original 1966 comments and then in the Department of Health, Education, and Welfare (now the Department of Health and Human Services) guidelines in 1968, 1971, 1974, 1979, 1981, and 1984.

It has always remained unclear, however, what *behavioral science* meant in this context and precisely what kind of research was considered to be ethically debatable. Was it the result of the deception studies of the 1960s, the biomedical studies involving behavioral control (e.g., psychosurgery;

drug studies; behavioral modification programs performed on prisoners, veterans, children, the mentally committed, and the aged), and/or a national concern about data banks and the invasion of privacy? These questions have never been thoroughly examined.

INTERNAL ETHICAL DELIBERATION

Insofar as social scientists received funding from the government, they were required (at least initially) to abide by the federal guidelines set forth in IRB procedures. A second source underlying the emergence of a social science research ethics involved the internal history of the various social sciences. Beginning in the 1940s, several social sciences became aware of the need to develop a set of ethical rules to govern their disciplines. This need was magnified as a result of the recognition of several controversial social science research studies: the 1953 Wichita Jury Trial (Katz, 1972), the 1960 Smallville USA study (Vidich & Bensman, 1960), Milgram's (1974) study of obedience, the Project Camelot (Horowitz, 1967), the New Jersey Negative Income Tax Program from 1968 to 1972 (Kershaw & Fair, 1976), 1970 Tearoom Trade study (Humphrey, 1975), and Zimbardo's prison study (Zimbardo & White, 1972). These studies stimulated social scientists to reflect on the ethical foundations and implications of their research methods. Partly as a result of this, most social sciences formulated professional codes of ethics.

PHILOSOPHICAL ETHICS

Third, several individuals saw the need for a general set of ethical principles that would cover social science research. The Belmont Report (1978), for example, set forth the principles of beneficence, justice, and respect, providing the philosophical basis for federal guidelines concerning institutional review. It was, however, directly tied to biomedical ethics and said virtually nothing about the social sciences. The most famous attempt to construct a set of general ethical principles governing biomedical research was made by Beauchamp and Childress (1979). Although the Belmont Report and Beauchamp and Childress provided basic sources for constructing a general account of biomedical ethics, neither spoke directly about social science research ethics. Many books have been written about the ethics of a particular social science, the most frequently is psychology. Most of these are focused on ethical issues in clinical and counseling psychology, with psychological research being given a much less central role. Anthropology has produced fewer general works on the ethics of anthropological research and sociology virtually none.

What then about a general account of social science research ethics, one applicable to all social science research? Although there have been several books that have attempted to do this (e.g., Diener & Crandall, 1978; Kimmel, 1988, 1996; Reynolds, 1979, 1982; Sieber, 1992), what is lacking in most of these accounts is an adequate philosophical foundation. In most of these works, for example, there are discussions of confidentiality, informed consent, deception, harm, and so on, and there is the mandatory ritual in many of them of citing standard philosophical theories of ethics—Kantianism, utilitarianism, virtue ethics, and so forth. But, with the exception of K. Kitchener (1984, 2000), how these theories relate to issues, say, of deception was not clearly spelled out, so that the connection between these abstract ethical theories and practical issues is not very apparent. Several of these general accounts, many of the specialized works, and at least one professional code of ethics indicate the need for middle-level ethical principles—for instance, principles of autonomy, nonmaleficence, or beneficence. This would suggest a tripartite level of ethical theory, something that Beauchamp and Childress (1979) explicitly adopted and an approach that several other general accounts of ethical theory adopted—for example, Fox and DeMarco (1990) and Resnik (1998). Given the prevalence of this approach, we believe that it is sufficiently widespread to be termed "the standard or received model"; others call it *principlism*. Here, we explicitly adopt this model (K. Kitchener, 2000), which was partially adopted in the 2002 revision of the American Psychological Association Code of Ethics. We believe that, with suitable revisions and qualifications, it has the potential to become the standard model for general social science research ethics.

◆ A Five-Level Model of Ethics

With the goal of providing a basis for ethical decisions, the material that follows first distinguishes between two planes of moral thinking: the immediate plane and the critical evaluative plane (Hare, 1981). Second, it suggests that the ethics codes and more general ethical principles such as "do no harm" constitute the foundations for the critical evaluative level of reasoning. Last, it offers suggestions for decision making when ethical principles conflict.

The model has five levels: The lowest level is that of *particular behavior (action) and ordinary moral judgment*. The second level is that of *ethical rules*, which govern the decisions and actions of the first level and begins the critical evalauative level. Each profession has its own set of rules by which its members may educate new professionals and, in some cases, judge the action of researchers as ethical or unethical. The third level is *ethical principles*. These are more general than moral rules and, in turn, provide the justification for them. The next level is that of *ethical theory*. Here are the traditional theories of normative ethics, theories of obligation that propose a general account of how one ought to act and what things are worthwhile or good: utilitarianism, deontology, virtue theory, contractarianism, natural law theory, natural rights theory, perfectionism, the ethics of care, and so forth. Finally, at the fifth level is *meta-ethics*, exploring the meaning of ethics.

Figure 1.1 diagrams this model. At the lowest level, judgments and actions are

Figure 1.1   A Model of Ethical Decision Making

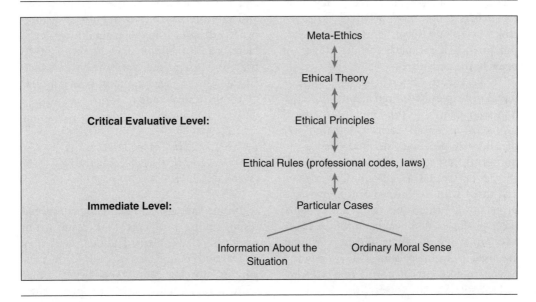

based on information about the problem and our ordinary moral sense. Our ordinary moral sense is based on a combination of what we have learned about being moral over a lifetime and our moral character. In ideal circumstances, it predisposes us to act in morally appropriate ways and leads to sound ethical choices, but in ambiguous or confusing cases, it may not. When ordinary moral values fail to provide guidance or when called on to evaluate or justify ordinary moral judgments, the components of the critical evaluative level can be called on to help in decision making. The critical evaluative level is composed of four tiers of increasingly general and abstract forms of justification. If the first tier does not provide insight for the issue at hand, the second can be consulted, and so on.

Ethical rules, such as those stated in the ethical codes, comprise the first tier. These ethical codes are grounded in foundational ethical principles, which comprise the second tier. The problems stemming from the inadequacy of professional codes may sometimes be resolved by reference to these higher-level principles. Principles are more general and fundamental than ethical rules or cases; foundational ethical principles may thus provide a more consistent framework within which cases may be considered. In other words, they may help researchers think about what to do when ethics codes are silent. Furthermore, they can provide a rationale for the choice of items in the code itself.

While slightly different sets of foundational principles have been suggested, those that seem central to thinking about ethical problems in social science research are beneficence (do good), nonmaleficence (do no harm), respect for persons (individuals should be treated as autonomous agents, and those with diminished autonomy need protection), justice (be fair), and fidelity (keep promises, don't lie, be faithful). These five principles articulate distinctions that are used in ordinary moral discourse and articulate core ethical norms that are central for social science research.

On the other hand, foundational principles themselves may conflict and offer contradictory moral advice. Researchers might be faced with deciding whether to break the confidence of a participant to protect the physical well-being of someone affected by the participant's behavior. The facts of the case may be clear, but the social science researchers' ordinary moral sense might fail them. At the first step, the critical evaluative level, the decision may be grounded in the ethical codes that give the researcher permission to break confidence in order to protect others from harm. If asked, this rule might be justified by the principle of allowing no harm to come to others.

If someone challenges this judgment and points out that breaking confidence destroys trust and forces the social science researcher to break a promise, such as to keep information confidential, social science researchers must be prepared to reason further about the problem. Ethical theory could be consulted, and a decision might be justified on the basis of something like the Golden Rule: In other words, act in such a way toward others as you would wish them to act toward you or others you love. The decision might also be made from a utilitarian perspective of doing the least amount of avoidable harm.

Finally, conflicts about ethical principles and ethical theory may require a higher-order reflection on the meta-ethical level. Here, considerations may be brought to bear to assist in the clarification of which ethical theory seems more relevant and plausible in this context.

LEVEL 1: THE IMMEDIATE LEVEL OF MORAL REASONING (PARTICULAR CASES)

People have ethical beliefs and emotional responses to problems that result from what they have learned about what they ought and ought not to do from their parents, teachers, and society. In other words, individuals have an immediate, prereflective response to an ethical situation based on the sum of their prior ethical knowledge and experience. In addition, as they grow older and become more educated, they begin to develop the capacity to reason about their moral beliefs. As that capacity matures, their ability to understand moral problems becomes more complex (Rest, 1983). Thus, prior learning and the complexity of their reasoning provide the foundation for their ordinary moral sense. This ordinary moral sense is, for example, the basis on which a professional is outraged when a researcher seriously abuses a research subject.

However, there is a second component of the immediate level of moral reasoning that is often ignored in discussions of moral decision making—assessment of the information available. An erroneous understanding or misperception of the events that are occurring and their consequences for the people involved can, and often does, lead to poor moral choices.

Ordinary Moral Sense

As already noted, under ideal circumstances, an individual's moral character provides the foundation for her ordinary moral sense and includes her beliefs about her ethical responsibilities. These immediate moral beliefs are critical to everyday ethical actions. In fact, as researchers develop their designs, their moral character may be more important than a particular set of ethical rules or principles. Under most circumstances, for example, a researcher does not need to be told that he or she should not fabricate results. It is an ethical assumption that is an intrinsic part of what it means to do research. In other cases, for example, when deciding whether to continue an experiment in light of ill effects to a participant, there may be little time for conscious and explicit reflection.

It is to our ordinary moral sense (common morality) that, we believe, some are referring to when they suggest that in the face of difficult ethical decisions, people should fall back on their own moral values or conscience. However, it is not difficult to establish that our conscience may not be sufficient. As already noted, in some cases the situation may be so unusual that one might have no sense of what direction to take. But, in addition, the ordinary moral sense of some people cannot be trusted to lead to good ethical decisions. In other words, not everyone has moral intuitions that lead to defensible ethical choices. We would never argue, for example, that Hitler's ordinary moral sense was as valid as that of Martin Luther King.

As professionals mature, consider the ethical problems that they encounter in research, and critically reflect on them, their ordinary moral sense and common morality ought to become more sophisticated. Those moral values they learned as they were growing up and through their professional education will be supplemented by a deeper understanding of both their professional roles and their obligations. However, for this to occur, they must engage in thoughtful reflection on the ethical problems they face and on the underlying moral values that can enlighten their decision making. Some of this can be done by reading and understanding the professional code of ethics and using the code as a way to expand their ordinary moral standards.

Information About the Situation

To act ethically, social science researchers also need clear information about the situation. Relevant information may range on a continuum from some that is quite clear-cut to some that is open to interpretation. Sometimes researchers make ethical errors because their understanding of specific circumstances or details about the issue is incomplete or erroneous.

LEVEL 2: ETHICAL RULES

For social science researchers, the first resource in evaluating tough ethical decisions ought to be their ethics codes. They attempt to bring together the cumulative wisdom of the profession about acting morally when doing research. Basically, they formulate a set of action guides researchers must follow and ideals that researchers should strive to follow. These rules should provide answers to many of the everyday ethical questions that social science researchers have and provide a standard against which others, both in the profession and outside it, can judge their actions. For some social sciences, for example, anthropology, the code serves the function of socializing and educating new individuals into the field. For others, for example, psychology and sociology, the codes are also used to adjudicate claims of unethical behavior. Generally, the rules establish a threshold of behavior below which the conduct of research should not fall.

While one might wish that an ethics code embody a "moral point of view," other forces may act to shape it. For example, the development of ethics codes was partially driven by the need to protect professions from federal regulation.

Typically, codes address issues such as the standards of confidentiality, the nature of informed consent, the privacy of information gathered, limits on deceiving participants, risk-benefit evaluation, and dual relationships with participants. On the other hand, codes fail to address important ethical concerns such as issues of truth telling and promise keeping.

Despite the criticisms, ethics codes continue to make an important contribution when social scientists are struggling to identify how to be ethical when doing research. They provide one level of ethical justification for taking or not taking certain actions, allow the profession to reprimand those who transgress beyond its guidelines, and can promote a sense of professional trust and loyalty. To return to a point made earlier, firm moral rules, such as those explicated in the professional codes, are particularly important when social science researchers are tempted by their own weakness or by the weakness of others.

LEVEL 3: ETHICAL PRINCIPLES

We have argued that when researchers' ordinary moral sense fails them, they may need to critically evaluate their decisions. The first step in this critical evaluation involves ethical rules. But when rules are inadequate or unclear, researchers ought to turn to ethical principles, such as nonmaleficence and beneficence, to help them frame the issue from a moral point of view. The principles suggest that each person and each problem that the social scientist is evaluating ought to be considered from a perspective that would offer respect for people's rights and dignity, including their privacy, confidentiality, and autonomy, and that each relationship into which a social science researcher enters should be characterized by integrity, including being honest and fair. Similarly, they suggest that when social science researchers enter into professional relationships, high priority should be placed on contributing to the welfare of those who might benefit from their work and avoiding harm to others.

Ethical principles act as general norms that provide a rationale for the moral rules in ethics codes. These principles—nonmaleficence, beneficence, autonomy, fidelity, and justice—are derived from the common morality that undergirds the practice of social science. When social scientists are conducting research ethically, these are the implicit principles they share. Similarly, they appear to be the principles that tacitly guided the practice of ethical social science researchers prior to the writing of the first ethical codes. In this sense, they provide the foundation or justification for all subsequent codes, including the current ones. If, for example, a standard was written that advocated or led to injustice, we could judge it to be a poor standard.

Nonmaleficence

Nonmaleficence means "Do not cause others harm." It finds its roots in the history of medical practice. Although popularized as *primum non nocere* (above all, do no harm) and attributed to the Hippocratic Oath, it does not occur there in that form or in other places in the Hippocratic corpus. Instead, the sentiment of not harming patients can be traced back to ancient times and has been recognized by modern ethicists as central to medical ethics.

In general, the duty to not inflict harm on others includes neither inflicting intentional harm nor engaging in actions that risk harming them. In other words, it forbids certain kinds of activities, in contrast to the principle of beneficence, which suggests that there are certain positive obligations, such as helping others.

The principle of nonmaleficence need not be considered absolutely binding if it is in conflict with other moral principles, such as in the case of self-defense, where one's own right to life is being violated. On the other hand, many ethicists (Beauchamp & Childress, 2001; Frankena, 1963; Ross, 1930) suggest that, all other things being equal, not harming others is generally a stronger ethical obligation than benefiting them. Returning to the concept of role obligations, if the focus of psychology or sociology is to promote human welfare, harming another would not only prevent achieving of this goal, it would also thwart it. In other words, if social science researchers must choose between harming someone and benefiting them, the stronger obligation could be summarized as "Help others, but at least do not harm them."

The problem with the standard "Do no harm" is that the concept of harm is vague and ambiguous. What constitutes harm, for example, when distinguishing the discomfort and stress that are frequent temporary side effects of participating in research from the long-term harm that sometimes is the outcome? The principle of nonmaleficence leads to ethical concerns such as how much discomfort is justifiable in research and whether it is justifiable to use high-risk research procedures.

Beauchamp and Childress (2001) pointed out that the concept of harm needs to be distinguished from the justification of harm, meaning that just because harm occurs does not mean that it is morally wrong. Sometimes harm may be justifiable although regrettable. The short-term harm or discomfort that sometimes accompanies research can probably be justified, especially if the participant entered the study freely and was informed of the risks. As a result, it is unlikely to be defined as unethical.

The position taken here is that as the risk and magnitude of potential harm increase, ethical prohibitions and limits on the research procedure also increase. However, the risk of harm must also be balanced with other ethical principles.

Beneficence

Beneficence means to do good or benefit others. The purpose of social science research is to contribute to the health and welfare of others by increasing our knowledge. In fact, most codes explicitly state that the goal is to promote the welfare, understanding, and protection of the individuals and groups under study.

The principle of beneficence has two aspects (Beauchamp & Childress, 1989). The first requires acting in ways that further others' well-being. For example, the Preamble of the Ethical Principles of the Psychological Code of Conduct begins with the assumption that the profession will "develop a valid and reliable body of scientific knowledge based on research" and that research is used to "improve the condition of both the individual and society."

The second characteristic of beneficence obligates researchers to balance the potentially beneficial consequences of an action against the potentially harmful ones (Beauchamp & Childress, 2001). Unfortunately, in a world as complex as it is today, there is often a price to pay for accruing benefits. This issue may be most familiar to social scientists who work with IRBs. They must evaluate whether the benefits that may follow from a proposed research project outweigh the possible negative consequences of the research.

Doing good for others, just like not harming them, has its limits. Many people want the freedom to choose their own course for their lives even if others do not think that their choice is a good one. If beneficence was accepted as the primary ethical principle, a scientist could always trump an individual's wishes as long as the scientist were acting in the person's best interests, even if it meant deceiving him or her.

Respect for Persons

This principle is based on the assumption that others should be treated as autonomous individuals. Autonomy means self-rule "while remaining free from both controlling interference by others and personal limitations, such as inadequate understanding, that prevent meaningful choice" (Beauchamp & Childress, 2001, p. 58). Generally, autonomy has been understood to include both freedom of action, doing what one wants to do with one's own life as long as it does not interfere with similar actions of others, and freedom of choice, making one's own judgments. It has two aspects. First, it includes the right to act as an autonomous agent, to make decisions, to develop values, and so on. The second follows from a reciprocal responsibility. If people wish to be treated autonomously, they must treat others in the same way. This reciprocity presumes a fundamental respect for the rights of others to make choices even when their beliefs may appear to be mistaken, unless their choices infringe on the rights of others.

In psychology, respect for autonomy as a moral principle has sometimes been confused with autonomy as a personality construct. Feminist authors such as Gilligan (1982) have, for example, suggested that as a personality type, autonomy is conceptualized as separateness and individuation. They argue that it may be a characteristic of the development of many men but not of women. The development of many women is characterized by a greater concern for attachment and relationship. Similarly in the multicultural literature, authors (particularly in anthropology) have argued that an emphasis on autonomy reflects a bias toward an individualistic perspective that may not be appropriate in collectivist cultures (Christakis, 1996).

The commitment to informed consent in social science research derives from respecting autonomy. By requiring social scientists to inform research participants about aspects of the research that might influence their willingness to participate, it safeguards their right to make choices about their own life.

Autonomy, and therefore informed consent, assumes that individuals are competent to make decisions. Macklin (1982, p. 337) pointed out that, on the one hand, it would be ethically unacceptable to violate individual freedom and interfere in others' lives against their will if they are competent. On the other hand, it would be equally unacceptable to allow "harm, destruction, or even death to befall an innocent helpless human who is unable to make a reasonable choice." Thus, social scientists have a particularly strong obligation to protect people who may not be fully competent by phrasing consent in a way that is intelligible.

It should be noted that there are no absolute criteria, including psychological or legal ones, for determining competence. Age plays a critical role because in the average person it is closely linked to cognitive development and cognitive decline (see Chapters 31 and 32, this volume). This is an important consideration for social scientists who work with adolescents and college students since they may not be fully competent to choose to participate in research even though legally they may be of age.

Fidelity

The principle of fidelity is at the core of the fiduciary relationship between social science researchers and research participants.

The Oxford English Dictionary offers a helpful description: it involves the qualities of faithfulness or loyalty and, second, of honesty and trustworthiness.

The principle of fidelity seems especially critical in the social sciences because issues such as honesty and promise keeping are basic to trust. While trust is vital to all human relationships, it is particularly vital to the researcher-participant relationship. This relationship involves an implicit contract that sets up certain role obligations for each. As an example, research may be invalidated if students believed that scientists made a practice of lying to them. Similarly, if research participants made a habit of falsifying the information that they gave to scientific investigators, social science research would be for the most part impossible. Lying, deception, and failure to be trustworthy have serious consequences for all professionals. They destroy faith in the researcher and in the benefits that social science can offer to the public. If lying and deceit were perceived as the norm, research participants would ultimately be suspicious of the professional's motives and would feel no obligation to be truthful in turn. This is one reason why deception in research is so ethically troublesome (Diener & Crandall, 1978). Furthermore, it breaks the researchers' responsibility to be truthful.

Although confidentiality and informed consent can be understood as deriving from the rights of autonomous persons, they can also be understood as obligations that researchers incur when they enter into relationships with research participants based on fidelity. Contracts between researchers and consumers typically include the promise of confidentiality. Failure to keep that promise destroys the trust necessary for human, much less professional, relationships.

Justice

The principle of justice has less to do with the individual relationship between the social science researcher and the research participant and more to do with how to distribute goods and services in the human community. This is a deeply critical social issue since science has been criticized for focusing on white males as participants and then assuming the results to generalize to women and people of other races and color.

Issues of justice arise, according to some philosophers, because in society there are conflicts of interest over limited goods and services and because human benevolence is limited. As a result, to live together with minimal strife, people must develop rules and procedures for adjudicating claims and distributing goods and services in a fair manner. The problems associated with proportioning goods and services are called issues of distributive justice. In social science, they involve at a minimum how the benefits and burdens associated with the social science research ought to be distributed—in this case, how the information derived from the research is used and how the burden of participating in the research is shared. It is based on the principle of justice that most social science research codes forbid social science researchers to unfairly discriminate based on characteristics such as age, gender, race, ethnicity, national origin, religion, and so on.

There are those who may ask why social science researchers should be concerned with issues of justice at all. In answering the question, Rawls (1971) argued that reasonable people must be committed to justice by the fact that they are engaged with others in activities designed to promote their common interests. If they expect others to be fair and respect their interests, they must treat others fairly in return. He suggests that a concern with fairness is a requirement of people engaged in a society that assumes social cooperation.

Generally, social scientists ought to have a commitment to being "fair" that goes beyond that of the ordinary person. It would be inconsistent with the commitments of social science research to focus their efforts only on particular groups, such as the white middle class, and condone or promote unfair treatment of others.

LEVEL 4: ETHICAL THEORY

About the first three levels, there is considerable agreement in the standard model (see Figure 1.1): ethical rules (e.g., informed consent, confidentiality, privacy, dual relationships, and conditional deception) ground particular moral decisions; and ethical principles (e.g., autonomy and beneficence) ground moral rules. Such a view is found in the Belmont Report (1978), Beauchamp and Childress (2001), K. Kitchener (2000), and many others. But it is at the next level—ethical theory—that advocates of the standard model disagree. Originally, Beauchamp and Childress (1979, p. 5) suggested that ethical theories (e.g., utilitarianism, deontology) ground ethical principles, both in the sense of justifying them and in providing guidelines when ethical principles conflict (although in their latest publication [Beauchamp & Childress, 2001], they no longer hold this view). This view is also present in our model and in several other versions, although once again it remains unclear precisely how ethical theory relates to ethical principles; our own view is that ethical theory does not algorithmically entail ethical principles but rather functions as an heuristic aid in reflecting on ethical principles.

Although individuals may disagree about the precise justificatory role ethical theories play, there is widespread agreement that higher-order theoretical principles are useful and sometimes necessary in moral reasoning. But which ethical theories are necessary and/or sufficient in relation to the lower-level ethical principles such as autonomy and beneficence? Here there is room for considerable disagreement. For reasons of space, certain views will be excluded from discussion. *Ethical egoism* (one should always act to benefit only oneself) has not seemed to be a viable ethical principle to most ethical theorists. The same is true of theological ethics (one should act as God or scripture mandates). Several individuals have advanced "anti-ethical theory" views: Nietzsche's perfectionism, Marx's socioeconomic account of class morality, and Freud's psychoanalytic account of ethical principles. These accounts, although interesting, are not directly relevant to social science research ethics and have not been particularly influential in the field. The same can be said for postmodernist ethics (see Chapter 2, this volume).

Historically speaking, *natural law theory* (*natural rights theory*) is the view that ethical obligations, moral standards, and one's rights are somehow a part of the natural order (including the nature of the person). There is an objectively existing moral order, either as a part of human nature or (indirectly) as given to us by God. Human nature is essentially rational (and/or social) and hence provides the basis of morality and our natural human rights. Natural law theory and natural rights theory are closely related and are still prevalent in the thinking of many people (e.g., in the Nuremberg Code).

In ancient times, natural law theory was opposed to the radical social conventionalism of the Sophists and Skeptics. A less radical form provided the basis for *contractarianism*, the view that moral standards, human rights, and justice are based on the hypothetical agreement individuals are assumed to make to certain kinds of social, political, and moral norms or conventions. There are two contemporary versions of this view. The most famous modern representative was Thomas Hobbes (1651/1994), who set forth the modern version of the social contract model, a hypothetical account (or thought experiment) of the emergence of social norms. According to Hobbes, humans originally can be imagined to exist in a state of nature, in which their behavior is governed by pure self-interest. In such a state, life would be "solitary, poor, nasty, brutish and short" as individuals compete for scarce goods. Individuals would come to see the advantage of forming larger social groups and creating institutions such as the government and the law, whereby individuals would agree to give up some of their rights in exchange for a more secure life where a sovereign power would provide security.

A second version of this view is sometimes called (Kantian) *contractualism* (Rawls, 1971). Rawls's *original position* was similar to Hobbes's, but Rawls suggests constraints that operate to restrict one's agreement. One of these is that of the *veil of ignorance*, in which one does not know what position one would occupy in society and one then chooses what norms of justice should exist in society. Rawls assumes that it would be rational for individuals to choose those norms that are, in fact, fair and just. This position is thus a combination of contractarianism and the Kantian universalizability principle. Given the centrality of issues of human rights and of justice in contemporary social science research ethics, a view like Rawls's has been deeply influential.

An ethical theory that has always been important is *virtue theory*. According to Aristotle (1989), moral humans are those who have good character. They have developed their innate moral faculties as a result of practice, a good family and social environment, and feedback from other morally good agents. To become good, one must learn how to act in a morally proper way, thereby creating appropriate moral traits (or virtues) such as wisdom, honesty, courage, bravery, and so on. Our function as human beings is to become rational individuals, thereby attaining a state of well-being and flourishing. This occurs, Aristotle insisted, only if one has a proper social and political setting; if one does, then one can be expected to make good judgments in one's life and hence be trusted. This was the assumption made by most individuals during the 1960s about physicians and the kind of research they performed: They could be trusted to behave in a morally proper way because they are virtuous. However, as a result of biomedical research in the first half of the 20th century, in Nazi Germany and in the United States, this assumption was questioned. Consequently, external ethical review was mandated, encapsulated in current codes of ethics, governmental regulations, and external review by IRBs.

According to *utilitarianism* (Bentham, 1789/1996; Mill, 1861/1979), the moral acceptability of an action is determined by its consequences. If the results are good (e.g., are pleasurable or bring happiness), these results determine if the action is right. However, one has also to consider the negative consequences of the action for everyone involved. One calculates the positive and negative consequences for everyone, which determines the goodness of the action. This at least is the view of *act-utilitarianism*—that action is morally right that produces the greatest good for the greatest number of individuals. Later, a second version was proposed: *rule-utilitarianism*—that action is morally right that is an instance of a general rule, the establishment of which would produce the greatest good for the greatest number of individuals.

As many have pointed out, some version of utilitarianism underlies cost-benefit analysis, of making sure that the benefits of the research outweigh the negative consequences or harm produced by it. Such a position also seems to lie behind the principles of beneficence and nonmaleficence.

If utilitarianism is one of the pillars of modern research ethics, the other is *deontology*. The deontologist claims that the moral correctness or incorrectness of an action is determined by inspecting the inherent properties of the envisioned action or rule. If it does not have these properties (e.g., if it is not universalizable), then one ought not to do it.

The most famous deontologists were Immanuel Kant and W. D. Ross. Kant's (1781/1964) deontology rests on his famous *Categorical Imperative*: Always act in such a way that one could will the maxim of one's action to become a universal law of human conduct. A second formulation of the categorical imperative was as follows: Treat humanity, whether others or yourself, always as an end and never merely as a means. In short, one should never exploit people but treat them as intrinsically valuable.

Clearly, much of the current thinking about research ethics is explicitly based on something like a Kantian deontology: Respect people's rights, treat them as autonomous agents, don't deceive them, and so on, are explicitly Kant-inspired ethical principles.

Another deontological theory is the approach of W. D. Ross (1930). According to Ross, there are several kinds of ethical duties we have that emerge as a result of encountering certain kinds of personal and social situations. These he called *prima facie duties*; these obligations can only be overridden by other ethical considerations. For example, moral principles like those proposed earlier are neither absolute nor relative, but they are always relevant. They can be overturned only when there are other ethical duties that outweigh them. This view underlies *principlism* (Beauchamp & Childress, 2001; Belmont Report, 1978) and the model adopted here.

Finally, there has arisen a feminist ethics, sometimes called the *ethics of care*, which has influenced our model. According to this view (e.g., Gilligan, 1982; Noddings, 1984), one's ethical obligations are one's duties to particular types of people—for instance, to family members. One's duty is to care for them, look after their welfare and well-being, and nurture their growth and development. Although this view is critical of abstract ethical rules and principles, it should remind researchers that they have some obligation to care for research participants.

These theories of ethics represent most contemporary approaches to a philosophy of ethics. Some of these are more relevant to social science research ethics than others are, and some of these are more familiar to the general public. For most of the 20th century, the major contenders were deontology and utilitarianism, but in the 1960s, virtue theory became a strong third candidate. Since then, there has emerged a plethora of competing views about the nature of ethical obligation.

So far, we have mentioned four levels of ethical behavior and decision making. As we proceeded through this list, the discussion became more and more abstract, hence removed from the nitty-gritty of ethical decision making. And yet, such a model is part of the standard view. One could also argue that it is implicitly present in the Belmont Report (1978) and in the ethical stance to be found in the published volumes of many national commissions. However, our last level—the level of meta-ethics—is not explicitly present in these accounts, although it is implicitly in them and one that is necessary to add to the standard model.

LEVEL 5: META-ETHICS

The subject matter of meta-ethics concerns questions *about* ethical theory; it is not concerned with ethical theory itself. Fundamentally, it is concerned with the meaning and justification of ethical statements. Although this has rarely been pointed out, biomedical and social science ethics have debated issues in meta-ethics for decades. The questions that are at the center of this discussion include the following.

First, is there a single ethical theory (e.g., utilitarianism) or ethical principle (e.g., nonmaleficence) that is adequate for social science research ethics, or are there many ethical stances that are valuable and should be retained? Most individuals seem to assume a pluralism, in which all the various ethical approaches have something to offer when it comes to thinking about matters ethical.

Second, since not all these ethical theories are simultaneously compatible but rather conflict, which one should guide our ethical reflection? Utilitarianism might recommend a cost-benefit approach, whereas deontology might propose that one should never violate an individual's privacy. Since different ethical theories conflict, how should one decide which one to follow? Currently, there are several approaches to this question. A *rankings* approach suggests that the various ethical theories need to be ranked in importance and weighted; for example, deontology is higher than utilitarianism. A *balancing* approach claims that all the approaches are valuable and, in a given situation, must be balanced to get the best overall combination.

A third issue concerns the question of the appropriate method to use in applied ethics. If particular cases are at the bottom and abstract general principles are at the top, then the question is whether one proceeds in a top-down fashion or in a bottom-up fashion. In the top-down approach, one begins with abstract ethical theory (or principles) and then proceeds to apply these principles to concrete cases, most typically by a deductive process (*deductivism*). A somewhat related top-down approach is *specificationism* (Richardson, 1990), which proceeds by taking a general ethical norm and making it more specific by incorporating more and more details about the why, when, how, and so on, until the specified norms lead to a directive about the particular case at hand. (One can also combine specification with balancing.)

On the other hand, one can also proceed in an inductive manner. *Inductivism* was the method employed by the APA in generating its code. One begins with judgment about particular cases and then proceeds to induce a general summary statement covering these cases. In this approach, a general ethical principle or theory is just a convenient summary of what has already been decided.

More radical than inductivism is *particularism*. Being opposed to ethical theory and hence denying the existence and need for general ethical principles or theory, particularism argues that one makes an ethical judgment or decision after looking at all the details of a particular case. There is no reason to think that another particular case will have any property of sufficient ethical importance to warrant a general connection between such cases. Everything is decided on a case-by-case basis. Hence, particularism denies ethical rules, ethical principles, and ethical theory.

A position closely related to particularism is *casuistry* (Jonsen & Toulmin, 1988): One engages in ethical reasoning by first looking at a particular case. These cases, if sufficiently important, are taken to be paradigm cases. One can then classify these various paradigm cases in a taxonomy and proceed to reason by analogy from them to new cases. Casuistry does not deny the importance of some ethical principles but insists that inferential principles involve reasoning by analogy between particular cases.

The standard model in bioethics and in social science research ethics is *principlism*, according to which there are several midrange ethical principles that are "freestanding" and individually warranted—for instance, autonomy and beneficence. This cluster of ethical principles is self-sufficient and not in need of justification by higher-order ethical theory; however, these principles do justify lower-level ethical rules—for example, confidentiality. When there is a conflict between such ethical principles, one may appeal to ethical theory as a useful heuristic aid in making an ethical decision about how to resolve such a conflict, but ethical theory does not deductively support a univocal decision about which principle takes preeminence.

Principlism seems to be the dominant view in bioethics and the behavioral sciences, being present in the Belmont Report (1978) and explicitly advocated in Beauchamp and Childress (2001). It is also advocated by K. Kitchener (2000), Sales and Folkman (2000), Sieber (1992), and Steininger, Newell, and Garcia (1984), among others. It is explicitly present in the 2002 revision of the APA code, which marks a radical change from previous versions, and is not present in other codes of ethics.

There are at least two alternatives to principlism: (1) the existence of a set moral rule with no higher-order set of ethical principles and (2) the existence of ethical theory and a set of ethical rules. We could diagram the possibilities as in Figure 1.2.

We believe that each of these approaches can be found among the national commissions established by the federal government in the decades since the 1970s. As noted previously, we argue for the last option.

◆ Conclusion

No one has yet written a comprehensive history of social science research ethics, nor has anyone written a theoretical account of the ethics of social science research that is both sensitive to the empirical, scientific details of this area and grounded in an adequate philosophical theory. Although we do not feel that our approach sufficiently does these things, we do hope we can stimulate others to reflect on these issues and to work on producing an up-to-date and comprehensive account of the historical and philosophical issues surrounding the ethics of social science research. Such a project, in our view, would involve a discussion of several collateral issues, ones that have yet to be thoroughly considered: What is the value of social science knowledge? How does one compare this value with the value of behaving in a morally adequate way during the research enterprise? What is the appropriate method or methods to use in social science research? Is there a unified method applicable to all the social sciences, or must one be content with a radical pluralism in the methodology of the social sciences? Are the social sciences value laden and, if so, in what sense? Is this quality of being value laden compatible with claiming objectivity in the social sciences? And so forth.

While we wait for such an account, we must be content with something much more restrictive—a sketchy and admittedly incomplete model of social science research ethics. Although we recognize the inadequacies of our model and its shortcomings, we nevertheless believe that it provides the beginnings of a plausible account of the ethics of social science research.

◆ References

American Anthropological Association. (2006). *Code of ethics*. Arlington, VA: Author.

American Political Science Association. (1998). *Principles of professional conduct*. Washington, DC: Author.

American Psychological Association. (2002). *Ethical principles of psychologists and code of conduct*. Washington, DC: Author.

American Sociological Association. (1999). *Code of ethics*. Washington, DC: Author.

Aristotle. (1989). *Nicomachean ethics* (W. D. Ross, Trans.). Oxford, UK: Oxford University Press.

Beauchamp, T. L., & Childress, J. E. (1979). *Principles of biomedical ethics*. Oxford, UK: Oxford University Press.

Beauchamp, T. L., & Childress, J. E. (1989). *Principles of biomedical ethics* (3rd ed.). Oxford, UK: Oxford University Press.

Beauchamp, T. L., & Childress, J. E. (2001). *Principles of biomedical ethics* (5th ed.). Oxford, UK: Oxford University Press.

Figure 1.2 Models of Principlism and Alternatives

		Ethical theory	Ethical theory
	Ethical principles		Ethical principles
Ethical rules	Ethical rules	Ethical rules	Ethical rules
Particular action	Particular action	Particular action	Particular action

Belmont report: Ethical guidelines for the protection of human subjects of research. (1978). Washington, DC: Government Printing Office.

Bentham, J. (1996). *An introduction to the principles of morals and legislation* (J. H. Burns et al., Eds.) Oxford, UK: Clarendon Press. (Original work published 1789)

Childress, J. F., Meslin, E. M., & Shapiro, H. T. (Eds.). (2005). *Belmont revisited: Ethical principles for research with human subjects.* Washington, DC: Georgetown University Press.

Christakis, N. A. (1996). The distinction between ethical pluralism and ethical relativism: Implications for the conduct of transcultural clinical research. In H. Y. Vanderpool (Ed.), *The ethics of research involving human subjects: Facing the 21st century* (pp. 261–280). Frederick, MD: University Publishing.

Diener, E., & Crandall, R. (1978). *Ethics in social and behavioral research.* Chicago: University of Chicago Press.

Fox, R. M., & DeMarco, J. P. (1990). *Moral reasoning: A philosophic approach to applied ethics.* New York: Holt, Rinehart & Winston.

Frankena, W. (1963). *Ethics.* Englewood Cliffs, NJ: Prentice Hall.

Gilligan, C. (1982). *In a different voice.* Cambridge, MA: Harvard University Press.

Hare, R. (1981). The philosophical basis of psychiatric ethics. In S. Block & P. Chodoff (Eds.), *Psychiatric ethics* (pp. 31–45). Oxford, UK: Oxford University Press.

Hobbes, T. (1994). *Leviathan* (E. Curley, Ed.). Indianapolis, IN: Hackett. (Original work published 1651)

Horowitz, I. L. (Ed.). (1967). *The rise and fall of Project Camelot: Studies in the relationship between social science and practical politics.* Cambridge: MIT Press.

Humphrey, L. (1975). *Tearoom trade: Impersonal sex in public places* (Enlarged ed.). Chicago: Aldine.

Jonsen, A., & Toulmin, S. (1988). *The abuse of casuistry.* Berkeley: University of California Press.

Kant, I. (1964). *Groundwork of the metaphysics of morals* (H. J. Patton, Trans.). New York: Harper & Row. (Original work published 1781)

Katz, J. (1972). *Experimentation with human beings.* New York: Russell Sage Foundation.

Kershaw, D., & Fair, J. (1976). *New Jersey income-maintenance experiment.* New York: Academic Press.

Kimmel, A. J. (1988). *Ethics and values in applied social research.* Newbury Park, CA: Sage.

Kimmel, A. J. (1996). *Ethical issues in behavioral research.* Cambridge, MA: Blackwell.

Kitchener, K. S. (1984). Intuition, critical evaluation and ethical principles: The foundations for ethical decisions in counseling. *Counseling Psychologist, 12,* 43–55.

Kitchener, K. S. (2000). *Foundations of ethical practice, research, and teaching in psychology.* Mahwah, NJ: Lawrence Erlbaum.

Kitchener, R. (2008). Moral philosophy. In W. A. Darity (Ed.), *International encyclopedia of the social sciences* (2nd ed.). New York: MacMillan.

Macklin, R. (1982). Refusal of psychiatric treatment: Autonomy, competence, and paternalism. In R. B. Edwards (Ed.), *Psychiatry and ethics* (pp. 331–390). Buffalo, NY: Prometheus.

Milgram, S. (1974). *Obedience to authority: An experimental view.* New York: Harper & Row.

Mill, J. S. (1979). *Utilitarianism* (G. Sher, Ed.). Indianapolis, IN: Hackett. (Original work published 1861)

Noddings, N. (1984). *Caring.* Berkeley: University of California Press.

Rawls, J. (1971). *A theory of justice.* Cambridge MA: Harvard University Press.

Resnik, D. B. (1998). *The ethics of science.* London: Routledge.

Rest, J. (1983). Morality. In J. Flavell & E. Markham (Eds.), *Manual of child psychology: Vol. 4. Cognitive development* (pp. 520–629). New York: Wiley.

Reynolds, P. D. (1979). *Ethical dilemmas and social science research.* San Francisco: Jossey-Bass.

Reynolds, P. D. (1982). *Ethics and social science research.* Englewood Cliffs, NJ: Prentice Hall.

Richardson, H. S. (1990). Specifying norms as a way to resolve concrete ethical problems. *Philosophy and Public Affairs, 19,* 279–310.

Ross, W. D. (1930). *The right and the good.* Oxford, UK: Clarendon Press.

Sales, B. D., & Folkman, S. (Eds.). (2000). *Ethics in research with human participants.* Washington, DC: American Psychological Association.

Sieber, J. E. (1992). *Planning ethically responsible research.* Newbury Park, CA: Sage.

Steininger, M., Newell, J. D., & Garcia, L. T. (1984). *Ethical issues in psychology.* Homewood, IL: Dorsey Press.

Vidich, A. J., & Bensman, J. (1960). *Small town in mass society.* Garden City, NY: Doubleday.

Zimbardo, P. G., & White, G. (1972). *The Stanford prison experiment* [Slide-tape show]. Stanford, CA: Stanford University.

2

RESEARCH ETHICS IN THE POSTMODERN CONTEXT

◆ Joshua W. Clegg and Brent D. Slife

Discussing a topic as broad and as frequently misunderstood as postmodernism requires some organizing principle, some general definition. Yet postmodernism makes such broad generalizations problematic at the outset. From the postmodern viewpoint, any definition of anything, including the definition of postmodernism itself, is a value judgment, with ethical and even political implications. Another problem in defining postmodernism is that postmodernists (whoever these undefined entities are) resist the closed "totalizing" conceptions of things. They view such conceptions as inappropriate reductions of the real—stereotypes of the rich experience of whatever is being conceived or defined.

Postmodernism is not, then, best understood in conceptual terms at all; it is perhaps best understood by engaging in practices that are postmodern, rather than conceptualizing things as postmodern. Consequently, this entire chapter (and perhaps this entire volume) could be construed as the modernist project of summarizing the unsummarizable, and thus conflicting with the very spirit of postmodernism. Any conception of postmodernity would have to be pluralistic, rarely unitary, and perhaps even poetic. Still, we remain committed to making this chapter understandable to the modern thinker and coherent within the underpinnings of this book, which implies some dedication to a clear organization.

Consequently, we begin by outlining some of the major movements and figures in postmodern philosophy. We follow this with a discussion of four postmodern ethical/philosophical commitments, which we frame not as conceptual foundations but as Wittgensteinian (1953/2001) "family resemblances." These four resemblances, which include the *particular*, the *contextual*, the *value laden*, and the *other*, are then contrasted with modernist commitments. True to the rich, particular, and contextualized values of postmodern theorists, we illustrate and explicate these contrasting commitments in terms of particular examples from existing research traditions.

Much of this discussion will appropriately concern what would traditionally be considered "methodological" issues. However, we caution the reader that one of the primary lessons of a postmodern approach to research ethics is that every research activity is an exercise in research ethics, every research question is a moral dilemma, and every research decision is an instantiation of values. In short, postmodernism does not permit the distinction between research methods and research ethics.

♦ The Postmodern Context

Postmodern thought is something of an antithesis to the thesis of modernism—different sides of the same coin. Some of the specific characteristics of both modernism and postmodernism are outlined below, but in general, this dichotomy centers on the dialectic between a generally naturalistic, positivistic, and realist worldview (modernism) and its antithesis in a critical, constructivist, or interpretivist worldview (postmodernism). In its historically explicit form, this dialectic is essentially a 20th-century phenomenon, but its roots reach back into the Enlightenment and perhaps before.

Of the most essential modernist themes, naturalism, probably boasts the oldest pedigree. Naturalism, or the notion that the world and everything in it can be explained in terms of natural, material, and narrowly empirical processes, had advocates among the pre-Socratic philosophers (e.g., Democritus). There were, of course, any number of antinaturalist philosophers in the Western intellectual tradition, particularly among the mystical or hermetic and early Christian philosophers. It was not until the Enlightenment, particularly in the 18th and 19th centuries, that the theme of naturalism was wedded to a broader intellectual and cultural positivism, or a general belief in the social, empirical, and theoretical power of science to ask and answer the basic questions of reality. This marriage permitted the modernist worldview to be fully forged as a culturally powerful antithesis to various premodern mystical, feudal, or otherwise centralized worldviews.

However, the rise of an unambiguously naturalistic worldview was not unopposed by influential thinkers. Nearly every major philosopher of the Enlightenment era was interested in and supported the development of a naturalistic philosophy, but there were many who also advocated a kind of metaphysical counterpoint to strictly empirical or material accounts. Descartes (1641/1996), for example, produced an elaborately mechanistic (and naturalistic) account of the human organism while also postulating a purely metaphysical realm of the mind (*res cogitans*). Even in Britain, the home of the most stridently empiricistic philosophers, thinkers in the tradition of Berkeley (1710/2004) or Reid (1764/2005) cast doubt on the unproblematically realist approach to philosophy.

Notwithstanding these currents of dissent, the postmodern view as a whole could not develop until modernism itself was fully fledged by the dramatic successes of the industrial age, or what Polkinghorne (2005) called "technification" (p. 5). Modernism as a generally dominant Western worldview reached its zenith only in the late 19th and early 20th centuries, and this is precisely when the forces of postmodernism began to gather. The successes of industrial technology began to meet its excesses, and the positivist worldview received both the praise and the blame. Philosophers and scientists began to question the monolith of materialistic and naturalistic science, and that dissent would eventually be labeled (not unproblematically) "postmodernism." The gathering force of postmodern philosophy was, in some sense, the natural dissenting extension of the modernist worldview and so, like Western philosophy in general, is typically divided into an Anglo-American tradition and a Continental European tradition.

ANGLO-AMERICAN POSTMODERNISM

In the Anglo-American tradition, the primary thematic contexts for postmodernism have been philosophy of language and philosophy of science. Philosophy of language in the 20th century made a radical "shift from a focus on meaning as reference to a focus on meaning as use," and this was "a change revolutionary enough to mark the shift from modern to postmodern in philosophy of language" (Murphy, 1997, p. 23).

Alfred North Whitehead was one of the first who began to question a fully realist and objectivist philosophy (i.e., meaning as reference). In his later writings, Whitehead (1925) asserted that "process rather than substance is the most basic reality. Substance, in fact, is an abstraction from the processes of experience" (p. 90). For Whitehead, the generalized categories of "existence" were not the fundamental realities but were essentially perceiver dependent. In this way, Whitehead delineated a pivotal theme of postmodernism—its rejection of the modernist division of the subjective and objective in favor of a perceiver-dependent or interpreted reality.

Ludwig Wittgenstein, another influential Anglo postmodern philosopher, claimed that "meaning depends on the role language plays in a system of conventions, both linguistic and nonlinguistic, of practices, performances, 'forms of life'" (Murphy, 1997, p. 24), a claim that has had profound implications for postmodern philosophy. In Wittgenstein's later work, language almost completely abandons its objective and rationalist roots and replaces them with particular forms of everyday life. Again, meaning is viewed more as a particular social function ("use") than as a reference to an objective reality. Other philosophers in this tradition include Gilbert Ryle (1900–1976) and J. L. Austin (1911–1960).

This shift from substance to process and from the abstract or universal to social convention and everyday life was mirrored in the Anglo-American philosophy of science. Thomas Kuhn (1996), for example, asserted that change in science was not the product of systematic empirical or rational progress but was, rather, the result of radical paradigm shifts in scientific epistemology. For Kuhn, then, science had to be understood culturally and socially. W. V. Quine (1908–2000) also eschewed a view of science founded entirely on a system of empirical and rational facts. Philosophers such as Imre Lakatos (1922–1974) and Paul Feyerabend (1924–1994) further elaborated this nonfoundationalist approach to the philosophy of science.

The Anglo-American tradition of postmodernism also included ethical philosophers such as Alasdair McIntyre (1984)—who argued that ethics had to be understood within its social and historical context—and, to some extent, philosophers in the American pragmatist tradition. American pragmatism, beginning with William James (1842–1910), John Dewey (1859–1952), and Charles Sanders Peirce (1839–1914), was by no means a unitary tradition, but in general, pragmatists replaced a realist picture of the world with one that centers meaning in functional relations. This tradition was at least partly a postmodern one in that it undermined the modernist worldview. As Richard Rorty (1991) argued, pragmatists believe that the epistemology that underlies science is not a "privileged method," and they deny "that the results of the natural sciences suffice to give meaning to our lives" (p. 75).

Generally, then, Anglo postmodernism reacts to Anglo modernism by emphasizing the interpreted and social over the objective and rational. The modernist considers the objective and the rational to be essentially uninterpreted and universal, whereas the postmodernist views even these "foundations" of modernism as context and perceiver dependent. For many modernists, this sort of context and perceiver dependence raises the specter of radical relativism, and some see chaos and nihilism as the eventual result (Capaldi & Proctor, 1999). As we will see, however, this kind of relativism is not inevitable in postmodernism. The absence of a modernist grounding of ideas, such as objectivism and foundationalism, does not mean the absence of grounds altogether. As we will describe, postmodern grounds include, to name a few, the particular, the contextual, and the value laden.

CONTINENTAL EUROPEAN POSTMODERNISM

The Continental European strain of postmodernism began to take shape with a systematic reconceptualization of subjectivity, beginning in the Austro-German tradition. Immanuel Kant (1781/1998) set the agenda for this reconceptualization when he reaffirmed and systematized the subjective-objective dichotomy in terms of the noumenal, or independent and unknowable reality, and the phenomenal, or the interpreted, knowable reality. This reduction of human knowledge to human experience paved the way for what Wilhelm Dilthey (1883/1988) would later call "human science" conceptions of knowledge.

The phenomenological tradition was perhaps the most prominent of these human science approaches. Hegel (1770–1831) pioneered the philosophical investigation of the phenomenal, but it was Edmund Husserl (1900/1999) who turned phenomenology into a systematic investigation of human experience. For Husserl, this was a radical enterprise that explicitly undermined naturalistic conceptions of science. He claimed, following the logic of his teacher Franz Brentano (1838–1917), that experience is always intentional—always an experience of something. This may seem like a deceptively simple premise, but it has radical implications. Unlike the modernist notion of an independent and isolated "object," this intentionality implies that experienced objects are irreducibly composed in both perceiver and perceived. Under Husserlian phenomenology, purely objective (uninterpreted) reality is an incoherent notion.

The students of Husserlian phenomenology extended this basic logic into an elaborate and robust challenge to the modernist worldview. Martin Heidegger (1927/1962), for example, argued that all meaning, including the meanings of research findings, is fundamentally interpretive. All knowledge, in this sense, is developed within a preexisting social milieu, ever interpreting and reinterpreting itself. This perspective, usually called hermeneutics, was systematically applied to the social sciences by Hans Georg Gadamer (1960/1989). He argued that because the social sciences (like other sciences) build their interpretive assumptions into their methods (including their scientific methods), they necessarily reproduce their theoretical assumptions in their professional treatments and empirical findings.

Other students of Husserlian phenomenology radically redefined the nature and scope of meaning, and thus the human sciences. The analysis of Maurice Merleau-Ponty (1964), for example, demonstrated important differences between the conventional category of "body" and the phenomenological meaning of embodiment. He claimed, in fact, that all higher-order intellectual meaning was derivative of the concrete experience of our embodiment. Jean-Paul Sartre (1943/1956) even more radically redefined all meaning in terms of the radically free human agent. Emmanuel Levinas (1961/1969) was another phenomenologist who redefined meaning, this time in terms of the ethical. Later students of both phenomenology and hermeneutics—for example, Paul Ricoeur (1913–2005), Charles Taylor (1931–)—further developed this tradition into a nonnaturalistic and nonpositivist approach to research and the social sciences.

Another influential strain of Continental postmodernism emerged from France and was concerned primarily with the deconstruction of social meanings, including institution, power, and politics. Jacques Derrida (1930–2004), Jean-Francois Lyotard (1924–1998), and Michel Foucault (1926–1984) are some of the more prominent figures in this tradition. In postmodern approaches to the human sciences, Foucault (1972) is especially influential, given that many of his works deal explicitly with the institutions of psychology and psychiatry. This tradition of deconstructing power has also been influential in much of postmodern feminist psychology. Feminist theorists such as Jane Flax (1990) or Evelyn Fox-Keller (1982) have drawn on the rhetoric of power relations developed in the French tradition.

In general, then, like Anglo-American postmodernists, Continental postmodernists reject an objectivist and rationalist view of science. For thinkers in the Continental tradition, the "objective" categories of science are objects of human experience and thus depend on the values, perspectives, and context of the researcher. For these reasons, Continental postmodernists move away from general and abstract conceptions of science and move toward particular research contexts and concrete researcher-participant relationships.

♦ Family Resemblances: Research Ethics in the Modern and the Postmodern

As noted in the introduction, we are committed to some degree of organization and clarity in this chapter, but we are also wary of an overly systematic presentation of postmodern philosophy. Consequently, Ludwig Wittgenstein's (1953/2001) notion of family resemblances will serve as a fairly malleable "organizing principle" for our discussion of postmodern ethics. Wittgenstein used the analogy of apparent similarities among members of the same family to describe a unity that does not necessarily depend on a coherent, universal underlying structure. Likewise, we employ the notion of family resemblance because there is no coherent, unitary tradition that could be called postmodern and yet there is a general set of similarities that, though they often derive from entirely different logics, nevertheless characterize a general ideological trend that could be called postmodern. It is our hope that this approach to the topic will be true to the nonreductive, nontotalizing spirit of postmodernism, while at the same time providing accessibility to those readers unfamiliar with it.

Of the many candidates for postmodern family resemblances, we selected four that we will treat below: particular, contextual, value laden, and other focused. These four were selected for two reasons. First, we judged them to be those most directly related to social science research and, second, they provide instructive contrasts with modernist research ethics. However, these resemblances do not lead to a set of postmodern ethical guidelines per se. Such an outcome would be inconsistent with the nonreductive, nonfoundationalist sensibilities of the postmodernist. Postmodern thought provides us not with clear-cut answers to the problems of research ethics but, rather, with challenging, instructive, and transforming dialogues that help us think about the ethical implications of research.

Our discussion of family resemblances will also extend beyond the boundaries of what have been traditionally (i.e., in the modernist tradition) considered ethical issues. Research ethics from the postmodern perspective is not separated from the goals and procedures of the research enterprise itself (like it often is in modernist research). For this reason, we discuss postmodernist themes as they apply not just to conventional (modernist) ethics but also to research practices in general. In drawing comparisons between the research practices of modernists and postmodernists, we hope to illuminate many of the hidden values of both approaches to inquiry. We also hope to make clear some of the ethical implications of a postmodernist approach to research without reducing these to a set of ethical principles or guidelines.

PARTICULAR

Modern

From the traditional modernist worldview, the primary function of research is not to discover findings that pertain only to the particular (situation or population) but to uncover the generalizable, if not universal, laws (or principles). Examples of this span the history of psychology: 19th-century psychophysicists sought the universal laws of perception; behaviorists, perhaps the quintessential modernist psychologists, sought the explanation of all "psychological" phenomena in terms of a single, basic mechanism—for example, operant conditioning; even movements such as Gestalt psychology, whose antagonism to reductionistic psychology was explicit, still understood psychological science as the pursuit of universal, general principles. The Gestaltist Kurt Lewin (1931/1999), for example, characterized a mature (or "Galilean") psychology as one that recognizes that "every psychological law must hold without exception" (p. 52).

To discover the universal and unchanging, the methods of the social sciences have properties intended to reveal these laws and principles, such as replication, standardization, and reliability. For the modernist, psychological law and its principles must hold in every situation, and thus we need not take the particulars of the situation into account. The particular case is considered an instance of the universal law, and likewise, the particular individual is essentially a concrete instance of general abstract phenomena, such as law, principle, and theory. For the modernist, the individual, or individual case, is of interest only in its relation to these abstractions and not as a particular or unique phenomenon.

This insistence on abstract universals is chronicled in Jerome Kagan's (1998) book *Three Seductive Ideas*. In it, Kagan asserted that many psychologists do not find it

> terribly important to specify the agent being studied, whether rat, monkey or human, or the context in which the subject acts, whether laboratory, natural habitat, work-place, or home, because broad conclusions can be drawn regardless of the agent and context. (p. 1)

The modernist focus on the general is evident in essentially every subdiscipline of 20th-century psychology (Slife, Reber, & Richardson, 2005), but a particularly clear instance of this phenomenon is the theory and research on intelligence, a topic Kagan treats at length. According to Kagan (1998), there has been little empirical success in substantiating the notion of a universal concept that could be labeled "intelligence." Nevertheless, the undifferentiated and unspecified term is employed at all levels of psychological discourse. As Kagan argued, "The descriptor 'intelligent' is frequently found in sentences that are indifferent to the age and background of the person (or sometimes the animal species) or the evidential basis for the assignment" (p. 52).

Not surprisingly, the modernist focus on abstract generalizations has migrated into the general discussion on research ethics. The very term *research ethics* suggests a generalized set of rules for dealing with the ethical implications of research. In the social sciences, we often approach the question of research ethics in an essentially bureaucratic manner, developing handbooks, professional guidelines, and review boards whose purpose is to engender, if not legislate, adherence to general codes of conduct. In modernist research, research ethics is not a particular set of concrete dilemmas but a general set of rules meant to apply to all (or at least most) research situations.

Postmodern

From the postmodern perspective, we do not live in the realm of the abstract and general, hence their relevance to us is limited. We live instead in the concrete and particular—a particular place at a particular time, which is our primary nexus of meaning making. This means that the personal and narrative are valued over the abstract and universal. Abstract principles (e.g., concepts, ideas) are still important, but concrete particulars are more fundamental. Postmodernists do not seek a universal set of truths, nor do they subscribe to an independent or objective knowledge-advancing tradition. To the postmodernist, science is one of many cultural objects that "are not only enrooted in the incontrovertible presence of this perceived world" but are "also the achievement of a cultural activity, of a cultural life of which science, considered subjectively as human work, is a part" (Ricoeur, 1965, p. 168).

The primary methodological implication of the postmodern denial of objectivity and universality is that while "the mainstream tradition has focused almost exclusively on problems of standardization" (Mishler, 1986, p. 233), psychological research inspired by postmodern traditions has focused more on the understanding of particular lives. These traditions have focused on particular stories because, as Taylor (1992) argued, "we grasp our lives in a narrative. . . . In order to have a sense of who we are, we have to have a notion of how we have become" (p. 47).

Within the contemporary social sciences, there are innumerable interpretive investigations whose intent is to narrate particular lives, but let us consider one especially rich example. In an article in *Qualitative Inquiry*, Arthur Bochner (1997) narrated an event from his own history as a way of illuminating multiple levels of psychological knowledge. He told of being awakened in a hotel room and informed of his father's death. In the article, Bochner narrated his actions, thoughts, and feelings following this revelation. He used this narrative to discuss grief and dying, psychological method and theory, and the method of personal narrative itself. When, for example, he compared psychological literature on death and dying with his own experience, he concluded that the academic world is "long on conceptualizations and short on details; long on abstractions, short on concrete events; long on analysis, short on experience; long on theories, short on stories" (p. 424).

From within a very particular context, Bochner (1997) drew a number of conclusions about social science methods, and this practice reflects the postmodern approach to "data." As Bochner put it,

> We do not turn stories into data to test theoretical propositions. Rather, we link theory to story when we think with a story, trying to stay with the story, letting ourselves resonate with the moral dilemmas it may pose, understanding its ambiguities, examining its contradictions, feeling its nuances, letting ourselves become part of the story. (p. 436)

From this postmodern perspective, the notion of "generalization" in inquiry is more from concrete parts to concrete wholes rather than from concrete instances to abstract generalities.

Bochner's (1997) story also highlights another ethical tension between modernist and postmodernist approaches to research. Insofar as a tradition holds to "a reverent and idealized view of science that positions science above the contingencies of language and outside the circle of historical and cultural interests" (p. 422), research practices themselves will meet with little broader social control. Under the modernist worldview, the special status of the "scientific" easily leads to that circumstance where "psychologists too often use their warrant of expertise not only to manipulate variables but also to manipulate people and their lives" (p. 422). There is a kind of monolithic power inherent in the universalism of the scientific mythos, and a postmodern understanding of research ethics would likely begin in the deconstruction of that power.

Practical Implications

Again, the practical implications of a postmodernist conceptualization of research would likely never be put into simple guidelines or an ethical code. However, the postmodern "family resemblance" of emphasizing the *particular* does imply, as opposed to modernist research, greater emphasis on what is unique in each situation and the individual. As such, the postmodernist would likely move away from testing thin theoretical propositions and move toward the richer and thicker accounts encompassed in a narrative. Similarly, the instrumental use of science—where universals, power, and expertise are viewed as the means to various social ends—would be eschewed in favor of less certainty and more humility about knowledge and its use. If we take the particular as a fundamental research value, ethical research has less to do with an attempt to reason about ethical research practices and more to do with an uncertain researcher perpetually struggling with the obligations and responsibilities of a particular situation, to a particular community, and to a particular participant.

CONTEXTUAL

Modern

Because generalizable principles and laws are the *telos* of modernist research, traditional theory and method have attempted to remove all possible contingency from both theoretical models and particular research findings. In modernist methods, "truth was to be found through method, by following general rules of method that were largely independent of the content and context of the investigation. Any influence by the person of the researcher should be eliminated or minimized" (Kvale, 1996, p. 61).

Theories and findings are thus only considered universally valid if they are free from any contingent context. In this sense, when the modernist is attempting to discern general social science principles, much of culture, history, relation, and subjectivity are primarily sources of error variance.

The acontextual nature of modernist theory is explicit and unambiguous in most contemporary psychological traditions. Personality theory has nearly always sought to describe the psyche as an abstract and context-less type; learning researchers obsessively attempted to remove all contextual factors in their animal research (e.g., using rats from the same genetic stock, raised in the same environment, and subjected to precisely identical conditions). Indeed, the modern symbol of the scientist—the laboratory—is significant because of its context-less representation of the modern subject of science. The justification for such context-independent research procedures lies in the modernist notion that general knowledge comes from predictable events and that this predictability can only be ensured in the absence of all confounding contextual factors.

Because context-less results were so fundamental to psychological research in the 20th century, a great many programs of research could be employed as exemplars. Here, we will consider the research of Daniel Kahneman and Amos Tversky—work widely considered to be one of the great successes of contemporary social science research. Tversky and Kahneman (1983) summarized the basic conclusion drawn from a large portion of their work: "People do not normally analyze daily events into exhaustive lists of possibilities or evaluate compound probabilities by aggregating elementary ones. Instead, they commonly use a limited number of heuristics, such as representativeness and availability" (p. 294). The language used in this statement is instructive in its reflection of the acontextual ideal of modernist research. First, this statement represents a conclusion about "people" outside of any special context, as if this extra-contextual condition actually occurs and is possible. Second, reduction to a "limited number" of heuristics in "common use" would be pivotal to any research program, because reduction to context-less fundamentals is the sine qua non of modernist investigation. There is little discussion here, for example, of the changing use of heuristics depending on the context or situation involved. Indeed, the ability to talk without (or at least across) contexts is an essential goal of modernist research. It is that very ability that qualifies the statement as knowledge (possibly even truth).

Tversky and Kahneman's (1983) approach to reporting their findings reflects and embodies this acontextual ideal. In one study, the participants are considered fully described by the phrase "a group of 88 undergraduates at UBC" (p. 297). Research subjects are discussed in terms of general categories—for example, "naive" or "sophisticated" (p. 300), and the behaviors of subjects are discussed only in general or aggregate terms—for example, "the numerous conjunction errors reported in this article illustrate people's affinity for nonextensional reasoning" (p. 308). Like the vast majority of modernist research, for Tversky and Kahneman, essentially every statement that could be considered representative of general knowledge will not (and, in fact, should not) contain any unique contextual content.

This way of valuing acontextual knowledge is clearly reflected in the modernist discourse about research and research ethics (e.g., ethical principles). Just as ethical codes are designed to apply to all particular individuals (see the previous section), they are also constructed to apply across contexts (and not to take the uniqueness of contexts into account). Just as modernists assume that there is some independent set of verifiable facts, they also assume that there is some independent (though perhaps more difficult to define) set of acceptable ethical codes.

Postmodern

The postmodern perspective holds that meaning is always embodied, situated, and inseparable from its surrounding context. For the postmodernist, the personal and the public are inseparable parts of the same whole, and "any attempt rigorously to eliminate our human perspective from our picture of the world must lead to absurdity" (Polanyi, 1974, p. 3).

For a postmodern researcher, then, procedures and findings are enriched by context and impoverished, even misunderstood entirely, by laboratory sanitization and numerical representation. This approach to research, most clearly embraced by the qualitative or interpretive traditions, asserts that "if participants are removed from their setting, it leads to contrived findings that are out of context" (Creswell, 1998, p. 17). Even more, enriching contexts are considered integral elements of all research findings. Discussing interviews, for example, Steinar Kvale (1996) asserted that "the interview takes place in an interpersonal context, and the meaning of the interview statements depends on this context" (p. 44). Contexts, in this sense, are not just "variables" that "interact" with the subject of interest; they are necessary for understanding the subject of interest itself. From the postmodern perspective, even traditional biological laboratory science can be undermined by its focus on inert bodies—with all their passive, inanimate connotations—and enriched by a focus on embodiment as lived, contextualized, and animate (see Merleau-Ponty, 1964).

Phenomenological research is an example of a tradition that explicitly advocates and integrates a detailed description of the research context into the results. In a study by Philip Welches and Michael Pica (2005), for example, the authors provide a rich array of contextualizing information. Their article, which analyzes the experiences of nine men who had been admitted to a psychiatric hospital for being a danger to self or others, provides a detailed case study for each of the participants, including relevant personal details and excerpts from the interview interactions themselves. The contexts of the interview situations as well as some of the relevant behaviors of the participants are also described in a way that shows how integral they are to the understanding of the study's findings.

This sort of "thick" description also provides a necessary context for understanding and evaluating the conclusions drawn by the researchers. The interpretive categories developed by Welches and Pica (2005), contrary to most modernist research, served to "classify common themes" (p. 49) and not to draw general conclusions about abstract psychological processes. As in most phenomenological research, the authors' goal was to develop a general descriptive account of a specific kind of situation and not an abstract model of psychological or social functioning.

We recognize, of course, that the modernist may see no way to build "general" knowledge from such contextualized analysis. For the postmodernist, however, the contextualization of the subject matter situates it in the whole of knowledge (e.g., the culture, the era) and thus provides knowledge transfer through context and not through its elimination (as in the modernist tradition).

Practical Implications

The practical implication of the *contextual* for a postmodern research ethic is, in some sense, straightforward: The researcher does not attempt to eliminate—whether through laboratory or control—context from the investigation or its results. Instead, the postmodern researcher values the importance of context (e.g., situation, history, embodiment, possibilities) for understanding the meaning of the results and for situating them in the broader context of the discipline or culture.

The postmodern researcher also values the uniqueness and autonomy of research participants and is thus wary of removing contextual (including unique and personal) factors through laboratory and procedural controls. For the postmodernist, the use and presentation of knowledge is a primary ethical consideration—one in which the research participant is intimately concerned, and so the modernist attempt to eliminate the unique contexts of research participants appears dangerously egocentric.

VALUE LADEN (INTERPRETIVE, PERSPECTIVAL)

Modern

The pursuit of natural or social laws also requires that knowledge claims be free from bias, prejudice, and personal or subjective values. For the modernist, "goods or 'values' were understood as projections of ours onto a world which in itself was neutral" (Taylor, 1992, p. 53). It is for precisely this reason that, for the modernist, "scientific statements ought to be value-neutral; facts were to be distinguished from values, and science from politics" (Kvale, 1996, p. 62).

Traditional methods thus attempt to build impersonal, blinded, and mechanical procedures that minimize personal nuance, bias, or interpretive slant. For the modernist, bias is bad, and the "objective" world provides a value-free picture of reality. As Howard Kendler (2004) phrased it, "Empirical results are value-free. Raw data do not imply any moral judgment" (p. 122), and it is the role of science "to provide unbiased information" (p. 123). For the modernist, the scientific method provides a bridge between the subjective realm of the scientist and the objective realm of nature and, thus, provides supposedly value-neutral, objective information about the world.

This objectivist perspective has put the research of positive psychology in an interesting position. This movement attempts to discern and promote "the highest qualities of civic and personal life" (Seligman, 1998), yet the modernist philosophy of social science says that this seemingly value-laden task should be conducted in a value-free manner. Indeed, the main leader of this movement, Martin Seligman (1998), considers positive psychology to be a superior approach to other sources of optimal human functioning, because those other sources are "too subjective... dependent on faith or... dubious assumptions; they lacked the clear-eyed skepticism and the slow cumulative growth that I (and Csikszentmihalyi) associated with science" (p. 7).

Consequently, positive psychologists cannot draw from moral traditions or disciplines that discuss the nature of a good or flourishing life. All they believe they can do is classify "the strengths that every major subculture in America today values positively" (Seligman & Csikszentmihalyi, 2001, p. 90). In other words, their work is an empirical polling of what other people think are "the highest qualities of civic and personal life." The essential point here is that, even when studying human values, the modernist espouses a value-free approach to research, and it is this very distinction between hard fact and subjective value that makes "research ethics" a consideration separate from scientific knowledge.

Postmodern

For the postmodernist, the subjective and objective are inseparable and together constitute any given meaning. In this sense, all meaning—all experience—is inherently and inescapably interpretive, and bias is not only inevitable but also a basic element of all knowledge practices. H. G. Gadamer (1960/1989), in fact, argued for the essential importance of prejudice in all research. As Richardson, Fowers, and Guignon (1999) framed this argument,

> Prejudices are not external impositions that constrain our ability to be free and rational subjects. On the contrary, having a "horizon" or framework of prejudgments is what first makes it possible for us to think and act in intelligible ways. (p. 230)

Bias and *prejudice* are often pejorative terms in our modernist culture, so the more common terminology in postmodern philosophy is *value* or *value laden*. To say that all knowledge is biased is to claim that any meaning-making activity is directed by values and interpretive contexts. Fact and value are inseparable because the postmodernist sees a "fundamental moral orientation as essential to being a human interlocutor" (Taylor, 1992, p. 29). Taylor (1992) stated it even more strongly: "We cannot do without some orientation to the good" (p. 33).

For the postmodernist, then, value and bias are fundamental and, indeed, the primary impetus for research (e.g., the selection of a research topic). As such, bias and value should not be avoided or eliminated but made as explicit and transparent as possible: "The important thing is to be aware of one's own bias" (Gadamer, 1960/1989, p. 269). Although full value transparency in research is perhaps impossible, the postmodern ideal is to make one's own assumptions, historical context, and value stances explicit in reports of research findings.

A study of working-class girls conducted by Sandra Jones (2001) should serve as an exemplar of this approach to research. Jones, who explicitly aligns herself with feminist and critical theory, observed, interviewed, and analyzed biographical information concerning 10 female academics who grew up in the working class. Her approach to this research included the assumption that "the researcher is the research instrument" (p. 147), and so, when evaluating interview data, it was "important to ask who is listening and what is the nature of listener's relationship with the speaker" (p. 147).

To help identify her values as a researcher, Jones provided information about her own childhood context among the working class and discussed some of the effects of her powerful position as researcher. Jones also made explicit many of her research values. She talked about how she is sensitive to power relations and so strove for equity in research situations. She discussed her belief that research participants should be approached in dialogue, and so she provided participants with copies of transcripts and drafts of her interpretations.

Finally, Jones incorporated her values and influence into the presentation of her research findings. When she quoted the participants, she included her own dialogue in the excerpts. She also narrated her own reactions to the included excerpts as well as how she came to her subsequent interpretations. The main point here is that the author tried to make the values of her investigation as explicit and as integrated into the research findings as possible, and this practice helps the reader understand how those values influenced the findings.

From the postmodern perspective, values are just as influential in modernist findings; they are just not acknowledged. Researcher values are integral to all kinds of research, and the need to recognize and incorporate these influences is an ethical imperative. This is the reason, as mentioned at the outset, why there is no hard distinction between research ethics and research per se. Even the most basic research activities are situated within an evaluative context and carry very concrete ethical implications.

Practical Implications

The value-ladenness of social science research has many ethical implications from the viewpoint of a postmodern. First, we need to recognize that there is no escape from this value-ladenness—the assumptions and philosophies underlying research often involve values that frequently remain unexamined in modernist research. Second, we should identify these values as much as possible before, during, and after engaging in research. We do this to understand their potential impact and to be open to their replacement in the service of the topic of study. Perhaps even more important, we do this to serve the particular individuals or groups affected by the study. Third, such values are integral to the meaning and use of any study's results, so these should be taken explicitly into account in presenting, reporting, or applying the research in question. In short, values and their explicit discussion are of primary importance at every stage of social science research.

OTHER-FOCUS

Modern

The "other" of the social sciences is generally conceived of as an impersonal subject because the generalized, decontextualized, and unbiased ideal of modernist research requires a research participant whose values, projects, and idiosyncrasies do not interfere with the claims of science. The ideal subject is thus impersonalized and reduced—an object in the sense of any other natural thing.

This notion of a manipulated, controlled, and objectified subject is fairly endemic to modernist research, and the social science vocabulary for describing research participants well illustrates this phenomenon. Although *observer* was the most frequently used participant term in late-19th- and early-20th-century psychology, the increasingly objectivist inclination of (particularly American) psychology was accompanied by an increasing use of the term *subject*. The historian of psychology, Kurt Danziger (1990), argued that this terminology was borrowed from French psychiatry, where its earliest known use was to refer to corpses used for anatomical dissection. The use of such a term makes sense from the modernist viewpoint because it implies a kind of clinical distance and almost inanimate or passive status, much as any other "subject" matter (e.g., cells, structures).

In contemporary psychology, *subject* continues to be a common term. In fact, Henry Roediger (2004), while president of the Association for Psychological Science, argued strenuously for a return to the exclusive use of the "subject" terminology because it better fit his conception of the research subject. For him, "the college student is the ideal experimental animal" (p. 46), an animal he compares with drosophila, the fruit fly that has been the subject of so many genetic studies. It makes sense that he would prefer *subject* to *participant* because his research topics, like so many in psychology, concern presumed universal properties—learning and memory—rather than unique, particular individuals.

Terms other than *subject* have begun to see significant use in the social sciences. In the last two versions of the APA style manual, for example, the shift to *participant* has been explicitly encouraged. It could be argued that the terminological shift to *participant* signals a kind of drift from the hard modernist worldview in American psychology, and there may be some truth to this argument. However, Gary VandenBos (the executive director of publications and communications for APA) describes this shift as largely political and legal: "'Subjects' implies that these are people who are having things done to them, whereas 'participants' implies that they gave consent" (Carey, 2004). There is really no suggestion that one treats a participant differently than a subject; the change has more to do with legal consent. In any case, whether they are participants or subjects, the ultimate goal of the modernist is to systematically control them and their values and context.

Postmodern

When postmodernists hear the kind of "control" discourse found in modernist research, they often consider it a vocabulary of power and dominance, a consideration most notably connected with the work of the postmodernist Michel Foucault. Modernity's instrumentalized and reduced research subject is understood more as a means to solidify the power of those who conduct research than as a means to discern generalized principles. For the postmodernist, in fact, all "disciplines constitute a system of control in the production of discourse" (Foucault, 1972, p. 224), including any particular postmodernist discipline.

This sensitivity to power relations is a hallmark of many postmodern approaches to research, and it entails a concomitant sensitivity to how researchers subject research participants to their projects. As Foucault (1972) argued, "We must conceive discourse as a violence that we do to things, or, at all events, as a practice we impose upon them" (p. 229). It is not surprising, then, that the status of the participant is extremely significant to the postmodern researcher. The particularity of the valuing other is not a research confound but is, rather, the starting place for all meaning-making activities. The values, projects, and idiosyncrasies of the research participant constitute both an ethical imperative and the foundational knowledge relation. As such, a primary imperative of postmodernist research is "to do research 'with' rather than 'on' people" (Burman, 2001, p. 260).

An excellent example of this approach to research is Michelle Fine's four-year study on the impact of a college-in-prison program at Bedford Hills Correctional Facility (Fine et al., 2001). The impact of an other-focused approach to research is immediately apparent in the author line of the book, where there are 11 names listed. The multiplicity of authors stems from the fact that, in addition to graduate student researchers, Fine recruited participant observers from among the female inmates she was studying. These women conducted interviews, took field notes, and met as a research team every few weeks to compare findings. True to the other-focused ideal, the research reports generated from this study are rich with participant narratives.

Fine's design made her project an essentially communitarian one, where research interpretations are not the province of merely the privileged researcher but also of those for whom researchers presume to speak. These kinds of methods aim to provide a research environment where "the respondents become active agents, the creators of the worlds they inhabit and the interpreters of their experiences" (Marecek, Fine, & Kidder, 2001, p. 34). While many postmodernists recognize that asymmetrical power relations are perhaps inevitable in many aspects of research, they nevertheless seek to make power relations as explicit as possible and reveal rather than obscure the unique constructive contexts of research participants.

Practical Implications

The other-focus of the postmodernist has important ethical implications for researchers. The first is undoubtedly that we need to have greater sensitivity to the power relations of many research settings and relationships. For many postmodernists, the subjectification and objectification of persons, and even animals, is a kind of violence that should never be tolerated. The researcher should do research *with* people, including making participants co-investigators, rather than *on* people.

Second, postmodernists recognize that data interpretation is unavoidable in any kind of research, regardless of the methods used, and that such interpretation is the province, not simply of the "author" but also of a community of researchers, participants, and readers. Philosophers of science have long understood how data underdetermine these interpretations, allowing for alternative interpretations that usually go unmentioned in research reports (Curd & Cover, 1998). For the postmodernist, reports and presentations should avoid misleading language, such as "the data indicate," and should discuss instead the many data interpretations available as well as the reasons for the interpretations favored by researchers and the participants producing the data.

♦ Conclusion

We have argued that the postmodern turn points toward a research tradition that is interpretive, particular, contextual, value laden, and other focused—that is, in fact, thoroughly ethical in its character. Research methods are not essentially amoral—as in many modernist understandings, with ethics as a separate consideration. Research from the postmodern perspective is rife with values, assumptions, and perspectives that need to be identified and incorporated explicitly in the "findings." There is no moment in the conceptualization, design, execution, or presentation of research that is not inescapably and fundamentally ethical. As Kvale (1996) argued, "Ethical decisions do not belong to a separate stage . . . but arise throughout the entire research process" (p. 110).

Because the postmodernist sees research as an inherently ethical enterprise, the notion of a separate, postmodern ethical code is problematic. If the postmodernist is to talk about research ethics, it could only be a discussion about a kind of praxis or, perhaps, even a way of being: "Moral research behavior is more than ethical knowledge and cognitive choices; it involves the person of the researcher, his or her sensitivity and commitment to moral issues and action" (Kvale, 1996, p. 117). For the postmodernist, all research activity is fraught with moral and ethical issues. As such, scientific investigations require not a set of general solutions to such issues but a very particular commitment to both an insistent ethical self-examination and an unflinching sensitivity to our relation with the other.

♦ References

Berkeley, G. (2004). *A treatise concerning the principles of human knowledge*. Whitefish, MT: Kessinger. (Original work published 1710)

Bochner, A. P. (1997). It's about time: Narrative and the divided self. *Qualitative Inquiry, 3*(4), 418–438.

Burman, E. (2001). Minding the gap: Positivism, psychology, and the politics of qualitative methods. In D. L. Tolman & M. B. Miller (Eds.), *From subjects to subjectivities: A handbook of interpretive and participatory methods* (pp. 259–275). New York: New York University Press.

Capaldi, E. J., & Proctor, R. W. (1999). *Contextualism in psychological research? A critical review.* Thousand Oaks, CA: Sage.

Carey, B. (2004, June 15). The subject is subjects. *The New York Times.* Retrieved April 30, 2008, from http://query.nytimes.com/gst/fullpage.html?res=9501E5D61030F936A25755C0A9629C8B63

Creswell, J. W. (1998). *Qualitative inquiry and research design: Choosing among five traditions.* Thousand Oaks, CA: Sage.

Curd, M., & Cover, J. A. (1998). *Philosophy of science: The central issues.* New York: W. W. Norton.

Danziger, K. (1990). *Constructing the subject.* Cambridge, UK: Cambridge University Press.

Descartes, R. (1996). *Meditations on first philosophy* (J. Cottingham, Trans.). Cambridge, UK: Cambridge University Press. (Original work published 1641)

Dilthey, W. (1988). *Introduction to the human sciences* (R. J. Betanzos, Trans.). Detroit, MI: Wayne State University Press. (Original work published 1883)

Fine, M., Torre, M. E., Boudin, K., Bowen, I., Clark, J., Hylton, D., et al. (2001). *Changing minds.* New York: The City University of New York Graduate Center.

Flax, J. (1990). *Thinking fragments: Psychoanalysis, feminism, and postmodernism in the contemporary West.* Berkeley: University of California Press.

Foucault, M. (1972). *The archaeology of knowledge* (A. M. S. Smith, Trans.). New York: Harper Colophon Books. (Original work published 1969)

Fox-Keller, E. (1982). Feminism and science. *Signs, 7*(3), 589–602.

Gadamer, H. G. (1989). *Truth and method* (J. Weinsheimer & D. G. Marshall, Trans.). New York: Crossroad. (Original work published 1960)

Heidegger, M. (1962). *Being and time* (J. Macquarrie & E. Robinson, Trans.). San Francisco: Harper Collins. (Original work published 1927)

Husserl, E. (1999). Logical investigations (J. N. Findlay, Trans.). In D. Welton (Ed.), *The essential Husserl: Basic writings in transcendental phenomenology.* Bloomington: Indiana University Press. (Original work published 1900)

Jones, S. J. (2001). Embodying working class subjectivity and narrating self: "We were the hired help." In D. L. Tolman & M. B. Miller (Eds.), *From subjects to subjectivities: A handbook of interpretive and participatory methods* (pp. 145–162). New York: New York University Press.

Kagan, J. (1998). *Three seductive ideas.* Cambridge, MA: Harvard University Press.

Kant, I. (1998). *Critique of pure reason* (P. Guyer & A. Wood, Trans.). Cambridge, UK: Cambridge University Press. (Original work published 1781)

Kendler, H. H. (2004). Politics and science: A combustible mixture. *American Psychologist, 59*(2), 122–123.

Kuhn, T. (1996). *The structure of scientific revolutions* (3rd ed.). Chicago: University of Chicago Press.

Kvale, S. (1996). *Interviews: An introduction to qualitative research interviewing.* Thousand Oaks, CA: Sage.

Levinas, E. (1969). *Totality and infinity* (A. Lingis, Trans.). Pittsburgh, PA: Duquesne University Press. (Original work published 1961)

Lewin, K. (1999). The conflict between Aristotelian and Galilean modes of thought in contemporary psychology (D. K. Adams, Trans.). In M. Gold (Ed.), *The complete social scientist: A Kurt Lewin reader* (2nd ed., pp. 37–66). Washington, DC: American Psychological Association. (Original work published 1931)

Marecek, J., Fine, M., & Kidder, L. (2001). Working between two worlds: Qualitative methods and psychology. In D. L. Tolman & M. B. Miller (Eds.), *From subjects to subjectivities: A handbook of interpretive and participatory methods* (pp. 29–41). New York: New York University Press.

McIntyre, A. (1984). *After virtue* (2nd ed.). Notre Dame, France: University of Notre Dame Press.

Merleau-Ponty, M. (1964). *Primacy of perception* (W. Cobb, Trans.; J. Edie, Ed.). Evanston, IL: Northwestern University Press.

Mishler, E. G. (1986). The analysis of interview narratives. In T. R. Sarbin (Ed.), *Narrative psychology* (pp. 233–255). New York: Praeger.

Murphy, N. (1997). *Anglo-American postmodernity: Philosophical perspectives on science, religion, and ethics*. Boulder, CO: Westview Press.

Polanyi, M. (1974). *Personal knowledge: Towards a post-critical philosophy*. Chicago: University of Chicago Press.

Polkinghorne, D. (2005). *Practice and the human sciences: A case for a judgment-based practice of care*. Albany: SUNY Press.

Reid, T. (2005). *Essays on the active powers of the human mind: An inquiry into the human mind on the principle of common sense*. Whitefish, MT: Kessinger. (Original work published 1764)

Richardson, F. C., Fowers, B. J., & Guignon, C. B. (1999). *Re-envisioning psychology: Moral dimensions of theory and practice*. San Francisco: Jossey-Bass.

Ricoeur, P. (1965). *History and truth* (C. A. Kelbley, Trans.). Evanston, IL: Northwestern University Press.

Roediger, R. (2004). What should they be called? *APS Observer, 17*(5), 46–48.

Rorty, R. (1991). *Objectivity, relativism and truth: Philosophical papers I*. Cambridge, UK: Cambridge University Press.

Sartre, J. P. (1956). *Being and nothingness: An essay on phenomenological ontology* (H. Barnes, Trans.). New York: Philosophical Library. (Original work published 1943)

Seligman, M. (1998). President's column: Positive social science. *APA Monitor, 29*(4), 2–5.

Seligman, M. E. P., & Csikszentmihalyi, M. (2001). "Positive Psychology: An Introduction": Reply. *American Psychologist, 56*, 89–90.

Slife, B. D., Reber, J., & Richardson, F. (2005). *Critical thinking about psychology: Hidden assumptions and plausible alternatives*. Washington, DC: American Psychological Association Press.

Taylor, C. (1992). *Sources of the self*. Cambridge, MA: Harvard University Press.

Tversky, A., & Kahneman, D. (1983). Extensional versus intuitive reasoning: The conjunction fallacy in probability judgment. *Psychological Review, 90*(4), 293–315.

Welches, P., & Pica, M. (2005). Assessed danger to others as a reason for psychiatric hospitalization: An investigation of patients' perspectives. *Journal of Phenomenological Psychology, 36*(1), 45–73.

Whitehead, A. N. (1925). *Science and the modern world*. New York: Macmillan.

Wittgenstein, L. (2001). *Philosophical investigations* (E. Anscombe, Trans.). London: Blackwell. (Original work published 1953)

3

FEMINIST PERSPECTIVES ON RESEARCH ETHICS

◆ Mary M. Brabeck and Kalina M. Brabeck

In this chapter, we review the feminist philosophical work that articulates a feminist ethical framework. We describe two debates within this literature that have relevance for feminist ethical research. We then discuss five themes identified in the feminist ethical literature.[1] We apply those five themes to a feminist research project to illustrate what is gained from applying feminist ethics to research.

◆ *The Philosophical Foundation of Feminist Ethics*

Feminist ethicists claim, in Jean Bethke Elshtain's words, that "feminism without ethics is inconceivable" (1991, p. 126). According to Elshtain, feminist consciousness (M. Brabeck & Brown, 1997) and the feminist enterprise itself involve political, activist agendas to achieve social justice and improve women's lives. This moral position has implications for feminist researchers. Feminist ethicists expose the individual and institutional practices that have denied access to women and other oppressed groups and have ignored or devalued women. Feminist researchers are obligated not only to adhere to ethical guidelines for research (e.g., American Psychological Association, 2002) but also to ask, How does the research contribute to enhancing the conditions of women, and all oppressed people?

Like all ethical theories, doing feminist ethics involves examination of the nature, consequences, and motives of action (Baier, 1994; Cole & Coultrap-McQuin, 1992; Noddings, 1984; Shogan, 1988). However, a feminist ethical framework also provides a critique of moral philosophy as largely a male enterprise. That is, our understanding of women and their experiences has developed under a patriarchy that privileges male insights, beliefs, and experiences (Lerner, 1986). Often, the rigid, narrow roles that women are assigned are transformed into pervasive caricatures that fail to capture the complexity of women's experiences. Thus, feminist ethicists call for eradication of the misrepresentation, distortion, and oppression of women resulting from a historically male interpretation of women's experiences. Ethical feminist researchers are required to apply their skills to correct distortions of oppressed and marginalized people, to illuminate the experience of those who have been described from a deficit model, and to challenge prevailing epistemologies and methodologies (Andolsen, Gudorf, & Pellauer, 1985).

Furthermore, feminist ethicists (Noddings, 1984; Ruddick, 1980) call for careful attention to women's experiences (mothering, caring for others, women's friendships, etc.) to inform ethical thought and action. From a feminist ethical research stance, a researcher is compelled to ask the following questions: Whose voices are left out of the research? What populations are ignored in the study of the phenomenon under investigation? Which experiences are not given scholarly attention?

Of course, feminist thought is not unitary. There are multiple feminisms, including liberal Marxist, radical, relational, and postmodern, and disputes exist among feminist scholars. (See, e.g., Eisenstein, 1981; Enns, 1993; Tong, 1989, 1993, for discussions of different feminisms and feminist ethics.) Some of these disputes are especially relevant to defining and practicing feminist ethics in research. Here, we will discuss two disputes of particular relevance: first, the claim of gender differences in the ethics of care and, second, radical feminism's separatist stance.

Carol Gilligan (1982) originally claimed the ethic of care as a moral orientation that could be identified by examining the experiences of women and girls through listening to their responses to the ethical dilemmas they face. Gilligan claimed that the experiences of subordination and inequality that circumscribe the lives of women and girls give rise to a moral self grounded in human connections and characterized by concern for others. Gilligan emphasized the differences between men and women. She identified a unique "feminine self" and characterized the associated values as the "feminine voice." In contrast to the feminine voice, Gilligan claimed that the masculine voice is socialized to be concerned with abstract rules of justice. In decision making, women invoke the ethic of care, and men invoke the ethic of justice.

Gilligan's theory in part rests on a critique of Kantian moral theory, which posited abstract moral reasoning as the pinnacle of human thought. In contrast, Gilligan claimed that women's subjective knowledge is a "different" but equally valid moral lens. Her claims about women's ethic of care challenged the ideas of individualistic moral choice derived from Kantian moral imperatives.

Gilligan and other relational feminist theorists (e.g., Noddings, 1984; Ruddick, 1980) have identified the processes of attention and reflection as critical to the ethical process. These ethicists emphasize the values of empathy, nurturance, and caring over or in addition to justice, rights, and moral rules. Some of these feminist theorists (e.g., Noddings, 1984; Ruddick, 1980) see the mother-child relationship as paradigmatic and foundational for the development of a relationship-based morality, instead of a rights-based morality. Instead of claiming that humans are autonomous, separate, independent, and rational in their decision making, they recognize human interdependence on one another, the connections among people, and the responsibility for one another that each of us who claims to pursue an ethical life embraces.

Relational theory has a history that can be traced back to at least Hume's (1817) moral theory. Hume claimed that to be a good person one must go beyond only using reason and deepen one's feelings for others. He believed that moral sentiment leads us to choose good and to avoid evil and that moral sentiment is innate and based on feelings rather than on reason alone. Since moral sensibility is innate, we all have the capacity for compassion, apprehension of the morally good, and care for the welfare of others. Thus, the claims that subjectivity and values from human relationships, rather than reason alone, can be the basis for moral action, have a long historical foundation. However, the empirical evidence for Gilligan's claim about gender differences in care and justice is not found to the extent that Gilligan and colleagues originally asserted (e.g., M. Brabeck, 1989; Walker, 1984, 1986, 1989; Walker, deVries, & Trevethan, 1987).

Gilligan's relational theory and the debates surrounding it are instructive for ethical researchers in a number of ways. Gilligan's claim regarding gender differences in moral reasoning comes out of concerns that women's experiences were being ignored in most research on ethical decision making. Lawrence Kohlberg's (1969) theory dominated the field at the time, and his original study (Colby, Kohlberg, Gibbs, & Lieberman, 1983) was based on an all-male sample at Harvard College. Gilligan claimed that when she listened to girls and women in moral judgment interviews, she found that their concerns were different from the concerns of boys and men. She insisted that this difference should be valued. Gilligan and other feminist writers (Flax, 1990; Miller, 1976; Noddings, 1984) argued that the qualities associated with women must be as fully valued as those associated with men. What society calls woman's passivity may be thought of as peacefulness (Bell, 1993; Flax, 1990).

A woman's maternal work may be associated with the ethic of care or beneficence (Noddings, 1984). A woman's attention to particularities might be thought of as concern for the welfare of others (Gilligan, 1982). These qualities may in fact be claimed as human moral attributes that all ought to aspire to develop. Thus, attending to the concerns of girls and women can help us understand and more fully describe the *human* condition. This insight ought to direct the attention of ethical feminist researchers to the concerns of women and girls and other underrepresented groups in the questions that they ask and should guide them to consider the value of those concerns as they discuss the implications of their findings. Such an enterprise is consistent with other social movements seeking to achieve social justice.

However, some feminist researchers (e.g., Hare-Mustin & Marecek, 1990; Lott, 1990) have pointed out that the "women equals care, men equals justice" dichotomy is dangerous because it maintains women as subordinate and fails to attend sufficiently to the diversity among women, relegates women to the private sphere and men to the public, essentializes gender differences, and privileges men (Applebaum, 1997; Houston, 1989, 1990). Bernice Lott (1990) described the potential problem of Gilligan's dualistic theory of care:

> Although the picture of the cooperative, caring, person-oriented adult woman drawn by the newer proponents of a feminine-masculine dichotomy is different from, and more positive than, the earlier negative portraits associated with Freud or Erikson, both visions have in common a focus on traits, stable personality components that are presumed to predispose to particular ways of behaving across situations. (p. 89)

Instead of affirming the intrinsic value of the ethic of care for women, one might, in the pursuit of social justice, instead advocate that the oppressive structures that relegate women to the private and men to the public sphere be changed. Society needs people who are both caring and just to create moral communities. Hence, ethical feminist researchers must not only seek to identify the differences between groups (i.e., women vs. men) but also investigate the differences within groups (i.e., within subgroups of women). Moreover, ethical feminist researchers must contextualize those differences within oppressive social structures to avoid essentializing and reinforcing hierarchical positions of power (M. Brabeck, 1996; Spelman, 1988).

A second dispute within feminist theory relevant to ethical research involves the work of radical feminists (e.g., Daly, 1978, 1984; Marks & de Courtivron, 1981; Raymond, 1986). Radical feminists view women's attributes, moral sensibilities, and affective relational skills as innately different from men's, and many see these differences as arising from biologically based experiences, such as women's ability to give birth and nurse. For radical feminists, women's values and virtues are unique to women and not available to men. Thus, to build an adequate moral domain for women, theorists must pay attention to the subjectivities of women that arise from their unique experiences (Andolsen et al., 1985).

Radical feminists claim that women may not be able to dismantle patriarchy but they can save themselves through feminist-womanist ways of knowing, doing, and being that are separate from males and the masculine. They denounce patriarchal attempts to label, and thereby assert power over, women through determining limits to, and the boundaries of, women's experience and knowledge. They reject assertions of "objective truth" and "the good" since they are irredeemably masculine in their construction. Radical feminists eschew the tools of science and scientific inquiry as tools that distort women's realities. In their place, they promote deconstructing previous knowledge claims and positioning women's subjective ways of knowing as normative (Harding, 1987; Harding & Hintikka, 1983).

A number of feminist theorists recognize the valuable critique of patriarchy offered by radical feminists but view separatism as counterproductive. They argue (Spelman, 1988) that engagement in oppressive structures is necessary to achieve the feminist social justice agenda (Applebaum, 1997). Furthermore, if women's valuable and unique subjectivities have developed within patriarchy, how then can we separate the "true" nature, ethics, or epistemology of women's ways that are not touched and distorted by patriarchy? In fact, embracing women's innate, biologically determined subjectivity as "women's ways of knowing" may simply reinforce stereotypes about women as closer to nature than men (Hare-Mustin & Marecek, 1990).

However, some feminist researchers have called attention to the value of using the tools of patriarchy to support the feminist agenda of achieving social justice (Hare-Mustin & Marecek, 1990). These researchers point to the important roles that quantitative, qualitative, and action-oriented methodologies play in investigating the lives of girls, women, and all marginalized groups. They problematize empirical methods and the epistemologies on which they are based, even as they continue to employ them. They call for diversity of epistemologies and methods in knowledge development (Harding, 1987; Nielsen, 1990). If the question involves determining the differences among groups, establishing the psychometric properties of instruments, or testing hypotheses, quantitative research methods are essential. Recent multivariate methods allow for the study of complex relationships among multiple determinants of behaviors that move well beyond simple questions of differences between men and women. If the research goal is to explore a new population, to develop item content for a measure, to contextualize empirical results, or to illuminate individuals' stories, qualitative, participatory methodologies are called for.

Social justice agendas, such as empowering marginalized groups, have been advanced through sophisticated and rigorous participatory research methods. For example, feminist researchers (e.g., Brydon-Miller, 2001; Maguire, 1987) have argued that participatory action research (PAR) engages researchers and community members as equal participants; combines popular, experiential knowledge with that of an academic, "rational" perspective; and seeks to empower people through collective action aimed at radically transforming society (K. M. Brabeck, 2003). When the central issue involves social action directed to a specific community-defined problem, PAR is the most obvious choice of methodology. Feminist researchers are thus open to a wide diversity of methods, some of which were developed within patriarchy, for asking questions. However, the feminist researcher needs to be aware of the epistemological assumptions behind each method when interpreting the research results and discussing the limitations of any individual study. Radical, separatist theories, which assume the essential and innate nature of women, may also create a false universalism that claims that women share a "common nature" regardless of race, ethnicity, class, or attributes that influence how their identities are constructed (Sparks & Park, 2000; Spelman, 1988). To dispute this, many researchers have looked for intragroup differences among women and have found that men and women from the same ethnic, socioeconomic, language, age, and disability groups have more in common than women from different social groups (Spelman, 1988). These researchers have exposed the many intersecting social identities among women and have furthered our understanding of women and their enormous diversity.

◆ Themes of Feminist Ethics and Application to Research

Despite differences and debates, across feminist theories there is general agreement on the broad, central themes that define feminist ethics. Five common themes have been identified from feminist ethics (M. M. Brabeck, 2000):

1. Women and their experiences have moral significance.

2. Attentiveness and subjective knowledge can illuminate moral issues.

3. A feminist critique must be accompanied by a critique of all discriminatory distortions.

4. Feminists engage in an analysis of the context and the power dynamics inherent in any context.

5. Feminist ethics require action directed at achieving social justice.

Each of the five themes of feminist ethics is elaborated below, and the implications for ethical research are discussed. (See also M. M. Brabeck & Ting, 2000.) To do so, we draw from a recent research project conducted by the second author (K. Brabeck, 2006). We briefly describe her study of the help seeking and strategies to survive abuse employed by 75 women of Mexican origin who had experienced intimate partner abuse (K. Brabeck & Guzman, in press). At each stage of the research process, the researcher had to make ethical choices that had an impact on her study. We first briefly describe the study and then discuss how each of the five themes of feminist ethics informed her work. Although we do not offer a solution to every issue the researcher faced, we identify how the feminist ethical lens informs ethical responses.

DESCRIPTION OF THE RESEARCH STUDY

The study aimed, first, to document how battered Mexican origin women act to survive abuse and, second, to explore whether sociocultural variables were associated with help seeking. Help seeking was defined as the use of formal (e.g., shelter) and informal (e.g., family) sources, as well as the personal strategies (e.g., locking oneself in a room) that women use to survive abuse. Sociocultural variables included two cultural variables—machismo (belief in traditional gender roles, male dominance, and female passivity) and *familismo* (valuing family obligation, cohesion, and reciprocity)—and four sociostructural variables—income, education, English proficiency, and immigrant status.

The participants included 75 women of Mexican origin over the age of 18 who had experienced some form of physical, psychological, or sexual abuse from a heterosexual partner. They were recruited with the help of local agencies serving immigrants and battered women. Data were collected via semistructured interviews by the principal investigator, who is Spanish-speaking. The instruments used included the Machismo subscale of the Multiphasic Assessment of Cultural Constructs—Short Form by Cuéllar, Arnold, and González (1995) and the Brief Familismo Scale by Buriel and Rivera (1980). Both instruments had been developed, normed on, and translated into Spanish by persons of Mexican origin. The participants also responded to a series of items assessing frequency and perceived effectiveness of overall and specific sources of formal and informal help as well as personal strategies to survive abuse. Finally, the participants responded to four open-ended questions regarding perceived barriers to help seeking, perceived effective strategies, and suggestions for improving services for battered women of Mexican origin. The open-ended questions were analyzed using textual analysis. All questions and consent forms were translated and back-translated by two bilingual Mexican American graduate students and pilot tested with a small sample prior to commencing the study.

Results from this study indicated that the participants sought help more than once from several formal and informal help sources; some (e.g., shelter and family) were perceived as more effective than others (e.g., lawyer and partner's family). Findings further demonstrated that the participants engaged in several personal strategies to survive abuse; some (e.g., maintaining a relationship with God) were rated more effective than others (e.g., placating the batterer). Analyses showed that women with higher levels of *familismo* sought informal help more frequently than those with lower levels. Results also indicated that women with only grade school education, no English language skills, and undocumented status sought formal help less frequently than women who were not constrained by these barriers. Textual analysis of four open-ended questions suggested why particular help sources and strategies were or were not effective, illuminated the participants' strengths, and provided suggestions for improving services to this group of women.

Results from this study have been submitted to a journal (K. Brabeck & Guzman, in press) and presented at professional conferences. In addition, the results were presented in oral and written formats to the community agencies that assisted in the recruitment of participants.

APPLICATION OF FEMINIST ETHICS TO THE RESEARCH STUDY

In this section, we apply each of the five themes of feminist ethics to the research described above.

1. *Women and their experiences have moral significance.*

As previously discussed, practicing feminist ethics requires researchers to attend to women's experiences in order to better understand the complexities of and the diversities among women and members of marginalized groups. First, in complying with this mandate, the principal investigator drew on her clinical experiences and the experiences of her clients in the formulation of the research questions. In addition to reviewing the research literature, personal, lived experience gathered in clinical sessions from previous clients of Mexican origin who had experienced intimate partner abuse informed the research questions and the design of the study.

Second, the feminist researcher must be careful to represent the experiences of participants as authentically as possible. Therefore, the researcher used published measures that had been developed, normed, and translated for populations of Mexican origin (the *Machismo* subscale of the *Multiphasic Assessment of Cultural Constructs—Short Form* by Cuéllar & González, 1995, and the *Brief Familismo Scale* by Buriel & Rivera, 1980). Where questionnaires were developed, interviews with battered women of Mexican origin and with domestic violence/immigrant agency service workers, along with a review of the literature, were used. As previously noted, all instruments were translated into Spanish and back-translated into English by two bilingual Mexican American graduate students to ensure linguistic and cultural accuracy. All measures were pilot tested prior to the study. However, the researcher interrogated herself repeatedly throughout the process whether the measures and the methods captured the complex and multi-faceted reality of abused women of Mexican origin.

Third, the researcher chose to focus the project on women who are marginalized. The majority of the participants (97%) were mothers and 63% of the participants were undocumented immigrants. Sixty-one percent of the participants did not speak English. The median of years in school was nine. Because so many participants reported no income at all, the median monthly income was $0.00 (the mean monthly income was $335.36, SD = $498.94). All participants were women of Mexican origin, and all had been in an abusive relationship. Fourth, the researcher chose to focus on differences among women of a particular subgroup, as opposed to differences between groups (i.e., Latinas and Caucasian women or women and men). The researcher sought to examine how various demographic and experiential factors affected the help-seeking behavior of the women in the study.

Given that feminist research ethics requires attentiveness to diverse women's voices and needs, one issue the researcher faced was how to address the needs of Latinas who were not of Mexican origin and did not qualify for the research project (e.g., women from Puerto Rico, El Salvador, or other countries). Because they were not of Mexican origin, women in need of money could not earn the $10 that the women of Mexican origin were offered in compensation for participation. This inspired some feelings of resentment among the former. This dilemma is an example of negotiating the needs of people while maintaining scientific rigor by focusing on only one group. This negotiation was particularly difficult because the researcher was a graduate student operating without substantial financial support and therefore unable to provide funding to all women who wanted to be part of the study but did not meet the participation criteria.

Another issue that came up during the study involved whether participants who wanted their names to be used in the reporting of qualitative results should have their names published. Who has the privilege of deciding this question? Ethical codes, such as the American Psychological Association's (1992) *Ethical Principles of Psychologists and Code of Conduct*, mandate confidentiality. However, what if a woman wants to use her name and feels that using her name is empowering? Should she be able to do so? The researcher is in a position to understand that for safety reasons, confidentiality should be maintained. Participants who are unsophisticated in published research may not realize that, at a later date, they may wish to have the cover of confidentiality in a publicly available report. However, this raises the problem of paternalism (or parentalism[2]) and puts the researcher in the position of undermining participants' autonomy. The ethical feminist researcher needs to consider all these issues carefully.

2. Attentiveness and subjective knowledge can illuminate moral issues.

In placing greater value on women's experiences than on preordained categories (e.g., right and wrong, good and evil), a framework of feminist ethics values grounded knowledge, or the knowledge derived from lived, and often subjectively known, experience. This stance is both a response to the hegemony of objective rational science and an attempt to stay close to the experience as it has been fully lived by the participant.

To be attentive to participants' subjective experience requires the researcher to take the research participants' points of view and to integrate that knowledge into the research process so that results reflect both scientific conclusions (what can be determined but may be outside the participant's experience) and personal integrity (what only the participant can know).

In an attempt to include the cognitive, affective, sociocultural, and subjective realities of women's experiences, the researcher chose to use a qualitative research method—open-ended questions. Each participant was encouraged to speak in her language of choice (Spanish or English) and to tell her story in her own words. In addition, the researcher chose to use standardized measures and subject them to quantitative analysis, in order to examine questions that can be statistically tested.

A dilemma that the feminist theme, attention to women's subjective experiences, posed for this researcher was "How does a white, graduate-educated, upper-middle-class, bilingual but English-dominant, American woman 'take the perspective' of her participants?" Feminist standpoint theorists have offered a way out of this dilemma (Hartsock, 1987). By grounding claims to women's virtues in women's lives and the unique particularities of each woman's experiences, standpoint theory can account for differences among women as well as between men and women. Moral adequacy, then, depends on paying attention to the particularities of individuals' and a community's narratives while examining these particularities in light of their unique sociocultural contexts; entering into their perspectives; and asking, How is a person's life affected by bigotry, prejudice, and other distortions? Humility and constant self-interrogation were required by the researcher as she examined how her own biases entered the study; this process is discussed further below under Theme 4.

Ideally, the researcher should involve the women participants in the research findings. This researcher provided a summary of the research results to the clinics, and through the clinics to the women. She offered to meet with the staff and allowed the staff access to the data as a way to give the information to the participants. It would have been better to be able to show the women the results of the study, discuss the data with them, and get feedback before the final version of the study report was completed. This would have helped the women articulate their subjectively known experience better, and they would have been given an opportunity to correct any biases the researcher might have introduced into the study. Time and life circumstances (the researcher left the area where the study was conducted) prohibited this. She hopes, in the future, to directly involve participants in the design of research goals, the development of the methodology, and the interpretation of results; this approach is similar to PAR (K. Brabeck, 2004).

A second problem the theme of attentiveness to subjective experience raises concerns informed consent. As noted in the discussion above, a question the ethical feminist researcher had to address was "How can one safeguard confidentiality and maintain the safety of participants while not being parentalistic?" On the one hand, the autonomy of each person and respect for that autonomy requires that each person knowledgeably and freely agree to participate in the study. However, women who are undocumented and in abusive relationships are vulnerable. To some degree, their experience has negatively affected their well-being, resulting in depression (Cascardi & O'Leary, 1992), low self-esteem (Sackett & Saunders, 1999), feelings of self-blame (Clements & Sawhney, 2000), heightened stress and anxiety (Trimpey, 1989), and even posttraumatic symptoms and posttraumatic stress disorder (Jones, Hughes, & Unterstaller, 2001). All these mental health outcomes can affect thought processing and decision making. Can an undocumented mother who is in an abusive relationship garner enough autonomy and self-efficacy to give fully informed consent? Might not a woman who has been abused want to please the researcher and out of such motivation give her consent? Might not the money (a very small amount of $10) be a subtle source of coercion for women who have no income? How is a researcher to know that a woman fully understands the research project and fully consents to participate? How should the consent be obtained? If participants sign a document, are they "at risk" if an abusive partner is stalking them? There are no easy answers to these questions, but they ought to be raised by an ethical researcher.

The stance of the researcher regarding the abuse also presents a dilemma. Should a woman be "counseled" out of the relationship if she desires to remain within it, when, from the researcher's perspective, the abusive relationship is fundamentally patriarchal and damaging to her well-being? If the participant's subjective reality, likely affected by psychological abuse, keeps her in the abusive relationship, what ought the ethical researcher's stance be? Scholars and researchers in the domestic violence field remind us that abused women exert agency and resistance in a myriad of ways besides the obvious act of leaving. As Mahoney (1994) observed, "The popular concept that treats agency in women as synonymous with exit from a violent relationship must be challenged to make comprehensible the many ways women assert [them]selves in response to violence" (p. 73). Hence, in her exploration of help seeking, the researcher included investigation of the myriad of personal strategies that women employ to protect themselves and their children in the context of abuse—for example, hiding oneself, saving money, or placating the abuser to deescalate the level of violence (Davies, Lyon, & Monti-Catania, 1998; Lempert, 1996). Respect for women's autonomy and a deeper understanding of what survival and resistance mean require giving women the ultimate choice in the decision to remain in an abusive relationship.

3. A feminist critique must be accompanied by a critique of all discriminatory distortions.

Feminist ethicists assert that analysis of gender oppression illuminates oppression and dominance over other groups. However, feminists caution against focusing on gender oppression alone, thereby often privileging the experiences of Caucasian, heterosexual, middle-class women over those of women of color, lesbians, poor women, and any women who live outside the North American and North European dominant contexts. An ethical feminist critique of sexist distortions of reality, therefore, must be accompanied by a critique of racist, classist, homophobic, and other distortions. While gender has been located at the intersection of other important loci of oppression (e.g., ethnicity, culture, class, age, sexual orientation, ability, linguistic status), for most women, gender is not the most salient variable on which they experience interpersonal and sociopolitical oppression.

Out of ethical concerns for social justice and liberating all oppressed people, feminists embrace human diversity as a requirement and foundation for ethical action. A feminist ethical framework also requires that researchers work for individuals' empowerment as an ethical imperative and strive to reduce the effects of sexism, racism, classicism, homophobia, ageism, and anti-Semitism on selves and others. The goal of feminist ethics is not simply to show that women are oppressed as a group but to rid the world of all oppression.

In line with this theme, the feminist researcher in the study under discussion sought to highlight both the sociocultural barriers faced as well as the multiple signs of resiliency demonstrated by a marginalized group of women (i.e., of Mexican origin, Spanish-speaking, of lower-socioeconomic status). At all steps of the process, the researcher had to focus on the multiple points of oppression (immigrant and, for some, undocumented status; lack of formal education; poverty; ethnicity, race, and position as non–English speakers or second-language learners) rather than on gender alone. By examining intragroup differences, as opposed to comparing women with men or Mexican women with Anglo women, the researcher sought to more fully identify the multiple and intersecting characteristics of the participants. The researcher aimed to highlight the ways in which participants' various identities, of which gender is only one, intersected to shape their resources, options, and hence responses to abuse. For example, limited education resulted in limited job opportunities, information, and understanding of domestic violence, legal rights, and available services. Immigrant status limited the women's opportunities because of lack of English proficiency as well as undocumented status. The participants described fearing that shelter workers or police officers would not speak Spanish, complicating their efforts to be understood, particularly if the batterer did speak English. Many women explained how batterers used the women's undocumented status to threaten and intimidate them into silence, particularly if the women believed that they would be deported and hence separated from their children. Aspects of women's cultural identity also shaped responses to abuse in both positive and negative ways. A high value placed on family reciprocity and cohesiveness (i.e., *familismo*) emerged as a strength with regard to informal help seeking. Participants who appeared to have a greater self-in-belonging identity perceived greater options and support from friends and family.

Religious identity also intersected with help seeking and survival. For some women, faith and prayer were an important strategy for daily survival. Many women described religious officials as helpful in connecting them to other services. At least one participant, however, had a different experience: She was told by her priest to "take it" because that's "what a wife does." Hence, religious identity both illuminated and stifled options. The interview data indicated that traditional gender roles and values of machismo and *marianismo* (i.e., women's value through suffering) limited women's options through providing a rationale and a mandate for women to silently suffer abuse for the sake of their husbands and children (although quantitative data did not yield similar results in this study). The lack of empirical evidence to support this qualitative finding most likely is accounted for by the restricted range of scores; that is, since the majority of participants in the current study had already left their abusers one or more times and many had sought help at least once, it is likely that they had developed more liberal attitudes toward gender roles than women who had not sought help and who had remained with their abusive partners (Vera, 2002).

Finally, women's identity as mothers was a theme throughout the interviews. The participants reported feeling both empowered by motherhood to create a better life for their children as well as constricted by it—that is, staying because of their ability to provide for their children independently from the abuser. Hence, importance was given to the multiple, often intersecting and sometimes conflicting, social identities of the participants. In formulating the discussion and conclusions, the researcher also needed to identify the positive aspects of the experiences and qualities of the participants.

Importantly, both qualitative and quantitative data indicated that the majority of women in this study sought help from a variety of sources and also engaged in a myriad of personal strategies to survive abuse on a daily basis. This finding contradicts stereotypes of these women as submissive, passive victims and presents them as active, determined survivors who defy numerous and formidable obstacles to protect themselves and their children. Moreover, as previously mentioned, the cultural value of *familismo* was identified as a strength, in that women with higher levels of this value reported more help seeking from informal help sources.

4. *Ethical practitioners should engage in an analysis of context and the power dynamics inherent in that context.*

Because a feminist analysis reveals the power hierarchies inherent in each particular situation, practicing feminist ethics requires a researcher to critique the ways in which one's own positions in power hierarchies affect one's perceptions and moral sensitivities. This self-critique and analysis of power relationships is a prerequisite to developing knowledge in all ethical psychological practices. Postmodernism (Foucault, 1972) has challenged the assertion of absolute objectivity and insisted on viewing the critical analysis of all knowledge as historically and politically situated. Postmodernism offers important tools for analyzing power and powerful methods for deconstructing how "woman" has been constructed under patriarchy (Derrida, 1982). Both feminists and postmodernists recommend that researchers interrogate ways of knowing and inherent power hierarchies that affect what is accepted as "knowledge."

However, if realities are only constructions arising out of specific contexts, then no universal experience may be claimed. Hence, no universal truth or moral absolute exists, and it becomes difficult to talk about moral arguments against oppressive acts or decide on ethical action required of ethical feminist practitioners. While agreeing that the hegemony of any single narrative ("text") should be questioned, feminists point out that postmodernism may lead to radical relativism. Postmodernists who reject all narratives also reject a narrative that provides a theoretical explanation for forces such as sexism and patriarchy (Lerner, 1986). Self-interrogation of how a white middle-class researcher's own positions in the hierarchy of power within any context affects one's perceptions and moral sensitivities is basic to feminist ethical research. The researcher in the study under discussion worked with a Latina supervisor and mentor, who helped her check her perspectives and assumptions.

A dilemma involving power hierarchies arose regarding how to recruit participants. Is it ethical to ask agency employees and caseworkers to assist in recruitment? Might the power differential between helper and helpee cause women clients to feel coerced to participate? There were similar ethical dilemmas regarding where to interview participants. Many participants asked to be interviewed at agencies; the researcher considered the implications of conducting research on help seeking in the place where a woman receives services and asked, How might this venue influence her to respond in a more desirable way? She carefully considered the impact (including safety of the researcher) of conducting research in the home versus the clinic and allowed participants to choose the venue.

Because the researcher was Spanish-speaking, she was often approached with requests from agency staff that she assist with impromptu translations. For example, a client arriving at a shelter required a basic orientation, and sometimes Spanish-speaking staff were not available. A dilemma arose over negotiating the potential dual relationships that ensued: If she acted as both translator and researcher, how might the power dynamics inherent in both relationships shape subsequent interactions? Finally, the researcher had to constantly guard against assuming that her reality was shared by the participants. Staying close to their experience (Theme 1) and recognizing that identifying subjective knowledge (Theme 2) helped the researcher address the power differentials inherent in the research project.

5. Ethical psychological practice requires action directed at achieving social justice.

Feminist ethics are concerned not only with what ought to be but also with how to bring what is more in line with what ought to be (Smith & Douglas, 1990). Any ethical feminist approach to research, therefore, must include social justice action to achieve equity for women within existing political, economic, and social structures. When structures are not amenable to equity, they must be altered to be more just. Individual moral action is not sufficient to address structural wrongs, even when one embraces feminist virtues and ethics. The ultimate ethical feminist goal is to enhance the human condition and create a more just and caring world. This means that feminist ethical researchers must use knowledge and the process of generating knowledge as tools to bring about individual, familial, communal, educational, institutional, legal, and social change.

In the present example, the researcher purposely chose to use multiple methodologies. The quantitative analyses were designed to give agency staff the "hard numbers" that would help in their applications for federal and private funding and grants. The interview was designed to give the participants an opportunity to give voice to their lived experience. However, the researcher had to confront the question "What is the direct benefit of the research to the participants?" Beyond the abstract "value of knowing they may help other women in similar circumstances," how might these women and others like them benefit from the study? The participants were given monetary compensation for their participation, an acknowledgement that their time was worth something. Although this was not a formal counseling experience, the participants were also offered support and validation of their stories by a clinician who spoke their language. Some research (e.g., Lykes, Brabeck, Ferns, & Radan, 1993) has shown that telling one's stories in the service of helping others (*Nunca mas*) is a source of help in itself. When appropriate, the participants were provided with further information—that is, regarding the Violence Against Women Act (VAWA) and the fact that police and emergency room staff would not ask them about their legal status, and at times they were given information to access services—that is, legal or shelter—that thus far they had not used.

Giving back to agencies and staff was another important consideration. The investigator had developed a relationship with community agencies over time. Before beginning the research, she had worked as a supervised volunteer counselor at a shelter and as a volunteer at a legal agency conducting psychological evaluations of immigrant women applying for residency under the VAWA. Building relationships with, and giving back to, the institutions and agencies that are "in the trenches" and "on the frontline" of making what is more in line with what ought to be is an important role for the feminist researcher.

◆ Conclusions

In conclusion, a feminist ethical framework informs research through the assertions that women and their experiences have moral significance, subjective knowledge can illuminate moral issues, all discriminatory distortions must be critiqued, power dynamics must be analyzed, and action directed at achieving social justice is required. As our case study demonstrates, viewing research through the lens of feminist ethics exposes several ethical issues that might otherwise go unnoticed. This illustrates the contribution of feminist ethics to the challenge of patriarchal assumptions, the inclusion of different "ways of knowing," the respect for participants, the embrace of marginalized groups, and the integrity of the research.

◆ Notes

1. The philosophical underpinnings of the five themes of feminist ethics, described in this chapter, are discussed more fully in M. M. Brabeck (2000). This volume was the product of a task force of the APA Society for the Psychology of Women. The book has been used in continuing education courses offered by the APA since 2002.

2. Karen Kitchener (2000) noted that the term *parentalism* denotes the same behavior as *paternalism*, without perpetuating the gender-linked terminology of "paternalism." Clearly, the connoted behavior is one in which both men and women engage.

◆ References

American Psychological Association. (1992). Ethical principles of psychologists and code of conduct. *American Psychologist, 47*, 1597–1611.

American Psychological Association. (2002). Ethical principles of psychologists and code of conduct. *American Psychologist, 57*(12), 1060–1073.

Andolsen, B. H., Gudorf, C. E., & Pellauer, M. D. (1985). *Women's consciousness, women's conscience: A reader in feminist ethics*. Minneapolis, MN: Winston Press.

Applebaum, B. (1997). Good liberal intentions are not enough! Racism, intentions and moral responsibility. *Journal of Moral Education, 26*(4), 409–421.

Baier, A. (1994). *Moral prejudices: Essays on ethics*. Cambridge, MA: Harvard University Press.

Bell, L. A. (1993). *Rethinking ethics in the midst of violence: A feminist approach to freedom*. Lanham, MD: Rowman & Littlefield.

Brabeck, K. (2004). Testimonio: Bridging feminist and participatory action principles to create new spaces of collectivity. In M. Brydon-Miller, P. Maguire, & A. McIntyre (Eds.), *Travelling companions: Feminisms and participatory action research*. Westport, CT: Greenwood Press.

Brabeck, K. (2006). Exploring battered Mexican-origin women's help-seeking within their socio-cultural contexts (Doctoral dissertation, The University of Texas at Austin, 2006). *Dissertation Abstracts International*. Retrieved April 6, 2008, from ProQuest Digital Dissertations database. (Publication No. AAT 3246884).

Brabeck, K., & Guzman, M. (in press). Frequency and perceived effectiveness of battered Mexican-origin women's strategies to survive abuse. *Violence Against Women*.

Brabeck, K. M. (2003). Participatory action research. In J. R. Miller, R. M. Lerner, L. B. Schiamberg, & P. Anderson (Eds.), *Human ecology: An encyclopedia of children, families, communities, and environments*. Santa Barbara, CA: ABC-Clio.

Brabeck, M. (1989). *Who cares? Theory, research and educational implications of the ethic of care*. New York: Praeger.

Brabeck, M. (1996). The moral self, values and circles of belonging. In K. F. Wyche & F. J. Crosby (Eds.), *Women's ethnicities: Journeys through psychology* (pp. 145–165). Boulder, CO: Westview Press.

Brabeck, M., & Brown, L. (with Christian, L., Espin, O., Hare-Mustin, R., Kaplan, A., Kaschak, E., Miller, D., Phillips, E., Ferns, T., & Van Ormer, A.). (1997). Feminist theory and psychological practice. In J. Worell & N. Johnson (Eds.), *Shaping the future of feminist psychology: Education, research and practice* (pp. 15–35). Washington, DC: American Psychological Association.

Brabeck, M. M. (Ed.). (2000). *Practicing feminist ethics in psychology*. Washington, DC: American Psychological Association.

Brabeck, M. M., & Ting, K. (2000). Feminist ethics: Lenses for examining ethical psychological practice. In M. M. Brabeck (Ed.), *Practicing feminist ethics in psychology* (pp. 17–35). Washington, DC: American Psychological Association.

Brydon-Miller, M. (2001). Education, research, and action. In D. L. Tolman & M. Brydon-Miller (Eds.), *From subjects to subjectivities: A handbook of interpretive and participatory methods* (pp. 76–89). New York: New York University Press.

Buriel, R., & Rivera, L. (1980). The relationship of locus of control to family income and familism among Anglo- and Mexican-American high school students. *Journal of Social Psychology, 111*, 27–34.

Cascardi, M., & O'Leary, K. D. (1992). Depressive symptomatology, self-esteem, and self-blame in battered women. *Journal of Family Violence, 7*(4), 249–259.

Clements, C. M., & Sawhney, D. K. (2000). Coping with domestic violence: Control attributions, dysphoria, and hopelessness. *Journal of Traumatic Stress, 13*(2), 219–240.

Colby, A., Kohlberg, L., Gibbs, J., & Lieberman, M. (1983). A longitudinal study of moral judgment. *Monographs of the Society for Research in Child Development, 48*(1–2, Serial No. 200).

Cole, E. B., & Coultrap-McQuin, S. (Eds.). (1992). *Explorations in feminist ethics: Theory and practice*. Bloomington: Indiana University Press.

Cuéllar, I., Arnold, B., & González, G. (1995). Cognitive referents of acculturation: Assessment of cultural constructs in Mexican Americans. *Journal of Community Psychology, 23*, 339–356.

Daly, M. (1978). *Gynecology: The metaethics of radical feminism*. Boston: Beacon Press.

Daly, M. (1984). *Pure lust: Elemental feminist philosophy*. Boston: Beacon Press.

Davies, J. M., Lyon, E., & Monti-Catania, D. (1998). *Safety planning with battered women: Complex lives/difficult choices*. Thousand Oaks, CA: Sage.

Derrida, J. (1982). Différance. In *Margins of philosophy* (pp. 3–27). Chicago: The University of Chicago Press.

Eisenstein, H. (1981). *Contemporary feminist thought*. Boston: G. K. Hall.

Elshtain, J. B. (1991). Ethics in the women's movement. *Annals of the American Academy, 515*, 126–139.

Enns, C. Z. (1993). Twenty years of feminist counseling: From naming biases to implementing multifaceted practice. *The Counseling Psychologist, 21*, 3–87.

Flax, J. (1990). *Thinking fragments: Psychoanalysis, feminism and postmodernism in the contemporary West*. Berkeley: University of California Press.

Foucault, M. (1972). *The archaeology of knowledge*. Oxford, UK: Routledge.

Gilligan, C. (1982). *In a different voice: Psychological theory and women's development*. Cambridge, MA: Harvard University Press.

Harding, S. (Ed.). (1987). *Feminism and methodology*. Bloomington: Indiana University Press.

Harding, S., & Hintikka, M. B. (Eds.). (1983). *Discovering reality: Feminist perspectives on epistemology, metaphysics, methodology and philosophy of science*. Boston: D. Reidel.

Hare-Mustin, R. T., & Marecek, J. (Eds.). (1990). *Making a difference: Psychology and the construction of gender*. New Haven, CT: Yale University Press.

Hartsock, N. C. (1987). The feminist standpoint: Developing the ground for a specifically feminist historical materialism. In S. Harding (Ed.), *Feminism and methodology* (pp. 157–180). Bloomington: Indiana University Press.

Houston, B. (1989). Prolegomena to future caring. In M. M. Brabeck (Ed.), *Who cares? Theory, research and educational implications of the ethic of care* (pp. 84–100). New York: Praeger.

Houston, B. (1990). Caring and exploitation. *Hypatia, 5*(1), 115–120.

Hume, D. (1817). *A treatise of human nature*. London: Thomas & Joseph Allman.

Jones, L., Hughes, M., & Unterstaller, U. (2001). Post-traumatic stress disorder (PTSD) in victims of domestic violence: A review of the research. *Trauma, Violence and Abuse, 2*(2), 99–119.

Kitchener, K. (2000). *Foundations of ethical practice, research, and teaching in psychology*. Mahwah, NJ: Lawrence Erlbaum.

Kohlberg, L. (1969). Stage and sequence: The cognitive-developmental approach to socialization. In D. A. Goslin (Ed.), *Handbook of socialization theory and research* (pp. 347–480). Chicago: Rand McNally.

Lempert, L. (1996). Women's strategies for survival: Developing agency in abusive relationships. *Journal of Family Violence, 11*(3), 269–287.

Lerner, G. (1986). *The creation of patriarchy.* New York: Oxford University Press.

Lott, B. (1990). Dual natures of learned behavior. In R. T. Hare-Mustin & J. Marecek (Eds.), *Making a difference: Psychology and the construction of gender* (pp. 65–101). New Haven, CT: Yale.

Lykes, M. B., Brabeck, M. M., Ferns, T., & Radan, A. (1993). Human rights and mental health among Latin American women in situations of state sponsored violence: Bibliographic resources. *Psychology of Women Quarterly, 17,* 525–544.

Maguire, P. (1987). *Doing participatory research: A feminist approach.* Amherst, MA: Center for International Education.

Mahoney, M. (1994). Victimization or oppression? Women's lives, violence, and agency. In M. Fineman & R. Mykitiuk (Eds.), *The public nature of private violence: The discovery of domestic abuse* (pp. 59–92). New York: Routledge.

Marks, E., & de Courtivron, I. (Eds.). (1981). *New French feminisms.* New York: Schocken Books.

Miller, J. B. (1976). *Toward a new psychology of women.* Boston: Beacon Press.

Nielsen, J. M. (Ed.). (1990). *Feminist research methods: Exemplary readings in the social sciences.* Boulder, CO: Westview Press.

Noddings, N. (1984). *Caring: A feminine approach to ethics and moral education.* Berkeley: University of California Press.

Raymond, J. (1986). *A passion for friends.* Boston: Beacon Press.

Ruddick, S. (1980). Maternal thinking. *Feminist Studies, 1,* 342–367.

Sackett, L. A., & Saunders, D. G. (1999). The impact of different forms of psychological abuse on battered women. *Violence & Victims, 14*(1), 105–117.

Shogan, D. (1988). *Care and moral motivation.* Toronto, Ontario, Canada: OISE Press.

Smith, A. J., & Douglas, M. A. (1990). Empowerment as an ethical imperative. In H. Lerman & N. Porter (Eds.), *Feminist ethics in psychotherapy.* New York: Springer.

Sparks, E. E., & Park, A. H. (2000). The integration of feminism and multiculturalism: Ethical dilemmas at the border. In M. M. Brabeck (Ed.), *Practicing feminist ethics in psychology* (pp. 203–224). Washington, DC: American Psychological Association Press.

Spelman, E. (1988). *Inessential woman: Problems of exclusion in feminist thought.* Boston: Beacon Press.

Tong, R. (1989). *Feminist thought: A comprehensive introduction.* Boulder, CO: Westview Press.

Tong, R. (1993). *Feminine and feminist ethics.* Belmont, CA: Wadsworth.

Trimpey, M. L. (1989). Self-esteem and anxiety: Key issues in an abused women's support group. *Issues in Mental Health Nursing, 10*(3/4), 297–308.

Vera, S. (2002). Attachment and context in Latinas' termination of abusive relationships. *Dissertation Abstracts International, 68*(5). (Doctoral dissertation, Boston University). Retrieved April 6, 2008, from ProQuest Digital Dissertations database. (Publication No. AAT 3015608).

Walker, L. J. (1984). Sex differences in the development of moral reasoning: A critical review. *Child Development, 55,* 677–691.

Walker, L. J. (1986). Sex differences in the development of moral reasoning: A rejoinder to Baumrind. *Child Development, 57,* 522–526.

Walker, L. J. (1989). A longitudinal study of moral reasoning. *Child Development, 60,* 157–166.

Walker, L. J., deVries, B., & Trevethan, S. D. (1987). Moral stages and moral orientations in real-life and hypothetical dilemmas. *Child Development, 58,* 842–858.

4

CRITICAL RACE THEORY

Ethics and Dimensions of Diversity in Research

◆ Veronica G. Thomas

Critical theories are frameworks aimed at challenging and destabilizing established knowledge with the goal of raising consciousness of social conditions and promoting emancipatory values such as equity, social welfare, justice, mutuality, and political liberty (e.g., Fay, 1987; Hammersley, 2005). Proponents of this approach have articulated ways of thinking about, describing, and collecting knowledge and social constructions. They have also addressed oppression and the political fabric of society, both of which have ethical and methodological concerns for researchers. Critical researchers consider moral and ethical issues within the context of their work through an examination of the historical problems of domination, alienation, social struggles, and how social inequities arising from racism and other forms of oppression continue to privilege certain groups and disadvantage others. Discrimination and oppression, in their various forms, are deeply embedded societal conditions that have ethical implications through challenging our stance on issues such as human rights, liberty, freedom, democracy, and justice for all.

Historically, racism and sexism rendered individuals who were not members of the dominant group (i.e., white males), at best, as invisible and nonexistent for the purposes of understanding and describing human behavior (Brown, 1995). When people of color and women were studied, they were often seen as "deviant" from the norm. Still today, understanding the behaviors, motivations, attitudes, and outcomes of diverse populations continues to pose a formidable challenge, with explicit ethical implications for researchers. Critical race theory (CRT), as a form of oppositional scholarship, challenges the experiences of white males as the normative standard and grounds its conceptual framework in the experiences of people of color. CRT and research embedded within this perspective are intimately linked to issues of ethics and social justice, in large part, by seeking to access previously silenced knowledge about social reality, emphasizing a deeply contextualized understanding of social phenomena, illuminating restrictive and alienating conditions, and promoting resistance and struggle to rectify oppressive conditions. Further, the underpinnings of CRT, and research methodologies particularly consistent with the CRT paradigm (e.g., participatory action research, community-based research, qualitative research, feminist research), provide guidance for identifying the ethical responsibilities of investigators who are conducting research in marginalized communities and offering strategies that might facilitate, rather than limit, social justice research (Halse & Honey, 2005; Manzo & Brightbill, 2007).

This chapter discusses CRT and how it can be used as a lens for conducting more valid and ethical research in diverse communities. The author begins by briefly tracing the philosophical and theoretical roots of CRT, from its origins in the 20th-century Frankfurt School to recent analysis that aimed at delineating interconnections among the economic, political, social, and cultural dimensions of society. A discussion of CRT, including critical race feminism (CRF), as an epistemological and methodological stance follows. The author concludes by articulating ethical responsibilities, through the lens of critical race, when studying marginalized populations.

♦ Philosophical and Theoretical Roots of Critical Theories

While many contemporary critical theorists and researchers would not likely describe themselves as Marxists, knowledge of the outgrowth of critical theory provides rich contextual information for better understanding of this theory. The historical roots of critical theory are grounded in the Western European Marxist tradition. The philosophy of Karl Marx (1818–1883), a Prussian philosopher, political economist, and revolutionary, promoted the notion that philosophers and researchers should not only seek to interpret social reality but also aim to make positive social change. Marx's emphasis on critiquing existing ideologies, coupled with the practice of social revolution, was the catalyst for the development of a number of related perspectives, including critical theory, which opposed the dominant social order of society. In his 1937 classic essay, "Traditional and Critical Theory," Max Horkheimer (trans. 1972) described "critical theory" as a social theory oriented toward critiquing and changing society as a whole, in contrast to traditional theory, which is oriented mostly to simply describing, understanding, or explaining phenomena. From the 1930s through the 1960s, critical theory was on the cutting edge of social theory, and it distinguished itself through its critique of positivism, arguing that the positivist sciences were instrumental in reproducing existing social relations and obstructing social change. Critical theory called for a critical approach to social analysis that would detect existing social problems and promote social transformation. It represented an ambitious attempt to understand modern society through an interdisciplinary approach, integrating philosophy, political economy, history, psychoanalysis, sociology, and cultural theory. In essence, critical theorists of the Frankfurt School considered themselves revisionists who sought to both understand society and make it more rational and just. Ethical considerations for first-generation critical theorists within the Marxist tradition were generally subordinated to political and class issues, while racism and discrimination of people of color were not meaningfully addressed.

In the late 1960s, Jürgen Habermas redefined critical theory in a way that freed it from a direct tie to Marxism or the prior work of the Frankfurt School. In Habermas's epistemology, critical knowledge was conceptualized as knowledge that enabled human beings to emancipate themselves from various forms of domination through self-reflection. Habermas's work embraced psychoanalysis as the paradigm of critical knowledge. This perspective considerably expanded the scope of what was considered as critical theory within the social sciences, which currently includes a vast array of approaches (e.g., world systems theory, feminist theory, postcolonial theory, CRT, performance studies, transversal poetics, queer theory, social ecology, the theory of communicative action, structuration theory, and neo-Marxian theory). As critical theory and methods evolved in this country, they were not tied to a particular disciplinary field but, instead, drew ideas from various academic disciplines. Contemporary critical theorists (e.g., Bohman, 1991; Habermas, 1996) argue that that this form of social inquiry takes a "dual perspective," with dual methods and aims. Here, critical perspectives are viewed as simultaneously explanatory and normative; that is, they are adequate both as empirical descriptions of the social context and as practical proposals for social change. This dual perspective has been consistently maintained by critical theorists in their debates about social scientific knowledge, whether it is with regard to the positivism dispute, universal hermeneutics (study of interpretation), or micro- or macrosociological explanations.

Critical theory illuminates how scientific research has traditionally focused on the instrumental values of control and domination at the expense of embracing the emancipatory values of justice, mutuality, and autonomy—all of which have ethical implications. Proponents of critical theory challenge taken-for-granted conditions and look to find more equitable alternatives to existing social conditions (Bell, 1995; Crenshaw, 1989, 2002; Ladson-Billings, 2005; Wing, 1997a, 1997b, 2000). In this respect, critical theory can play a significant role in calling for the conduct of more just and inclusive research in culturally complex communities through squarely addressing power interests and studying how research can be used to challenge (instead of support) the status quo. As newer forms of critical theory emerge related to racism (CRT) and sexism (critical feminist theory), and the intersection of the two (e.g., CRF), these perspectives are positioned in a discourse of emancipation and liberation and as a methodological and epistemological tool with ethical underpinnings designed to expose the ways in which race (and racism), gender (and sexism), and the interaction of these and other dimensions (e.g., class, sexual orientation, disability) have unjustly affected the lives of people of color and women. Critical research is ethically motivated via its interest in exposing prevailing oppressive social and power structures and its aim to emancipate and empower disenfranchised people (Brooke, 2002; Hirschheim & Klein, 1994).

CRITICAL RACE THEORIES: ADDRESSING DIMENSIONS OF OPPRESSION

CRT draws from and extends the parameters of the early generations of critical theory. However, the early generations of critical theorists have also been criticized for their failure to deliver emancipation for oppressed groups (Ellsworth, 1989) and their denial of their own practices that continued to marginalize and silence oppressed populations (Tuhiwai Smith, 1999). As such, CRT significantly expanded the domain of critical theory by explicitly centering social inequities arising from institutional racism, sexism, and the interactive effects of sexism and racism (and oftentimes class) within their discourse. Critical race approaches are deeply grounded in an interdisciplinary knowledge base (e.g., law, ethnic studies, women studies, psychology, anthropology, sociology, history) that seeks to better understand the life experiences of marginalized people and challenges researchers to examine their own values and ethical responsibilities for the facilitation of social change.

Solórzano (1997) described CRT as a framework or set of basic perspectives, methods, and pedagogy that seeks to identify, analyze, and transform those structural and cultural aspects of society that maintain the subordination and marginalization of people of color. As a movement beginning in the 1970s, CRT had its origin in the law in response to the failure of Critical Legal Studies (CLS) to adequately address the effects of race and racism in American jurisprudence. CLS, a radical movement of predominantly white male legal academics that emerged in the 1970s, included postmodern critiques of individualism and hierarchy in modern Western society. Drawing from European postmodernist thought and focusing on the deconstruction of concepts such as justice, neutrality, or the "reasonable man," CLS did not focus attention on racism, which was also typical of Marxian approaches, where attention to class overshadowed other issues.

While people of color, white women, and others were attracted to CLS because it challenged orthodox ideas about the inviolability and objectivity of laws that oppressed individuals for centuries, these same supporters also recognized that CLS excluded the perspectives of people of color and women and generally were not able (or willing) to expand their analyses beyond the worldview of progressive white male elites (e.g., Bell, 1992; Delgado, 1988; Wing, 1997a, 1997b, 2000). From a fierce critique of the role of U.S. law in sustaining the hegemonic system of white (male) supremacy, a strand of critical race scholarship emerged with the writings of the legal scholars Derrick Bell (then at Harvard University) and Allen Freeman (University of New York at Buffalo). At that time, both Bell and Freeman were deeply concerned about the slow process of racial reform in this country and that the gains made by the civil rights laws of the 1960s were quickly being eroded in the 1970s. Bell, Freeman, and other scholars (e.g., Crenshaw, 1989, 2002; Crenshaw, Gotanda, Peller, & Thomas, 1995; Delgado, 1984, 1988; Delgado & Stefancic, 2001) contend that CLS could not offer strategies for social transformation because it failed to incorporate race and racism into the analysis. This error was made evident by CLS scholars through their ignoring the histories of those oppressed by institutionalized racism and not listening to the lived experiences of marginalized people. Inspired by the writings of early scholars, W. E. B. DuBois, the African American activist, historian, and sociologist, in 1903 argued that the problem of the 20th century is the problem of color. CRT holds that race and racism lie at the nexus of American life. From an ethical standpoint, ignoring racism and oppression at the individual, institutional, and cultural levels, especially when studying the lives of people of color, implicitly and explicitly violates the set of ethical principles as defined by the Belmont Report (National Commission for the Protection of Human Subjects in Biomedical and Behavioral Research, 1978), of beneficence, justice, and respect for people, in part by compiling a faulty knowledge base that results in a distorted understanding of the lives of people under investigation.

There are several major tenets of CRT, all of which have implications for what researchers value and perceive as "good" and as their own ethical responsibility for addressing unequal relations of power, advocating social justice, challenging the dominant hegemonic paradigms, and opening up new spaces for decolonized knowledge production. One principal tenet is that race and racism are timeless, endemic, and permanently entwined within the social fabric of American society (Bell, 1992, 1995; Lawrence, 1995; Solórzano, 1997). Furthermore, critical race scholars argue that racism is not an aberrant but, instead, the natural order of American life, the usual way business is conducted in this society, and a common everyday experience for most people of color. They also view race as a socially constructed phenomenon rather than a biologically determined reality. In other words, race is what a society articulates it to encompass. A second major tenet of CRT is "Whiteness as property," meaning that given the history of race and racism in this country and the role that U.S. jurisprudence has played in reifying conceptions of race, the notion of whiteness can be considered a "property interest" functioning on three levels—the right of possession, the right of use and enjoyment, and the right to transfer (C. I. Harris, 1995). Interest convergence, a third tenet of CRT maintains that early civil rights legislation provided only basic rights to African Americans, rights that had been enjoyed by whites for centuries and only inasmuch as these rights converged with the self-interest of whites (Bell, 1980). A fourth tenet of CRT is the critique of liberalism, which lodges harsh criticisms on the three basic notions that have been embraced by liberal legal ideology—colorblindness, neutrality of the law, and incremental change—none of which takes into consideration the persistence and permanence of racism and the construction of people of color as Other (Crenshaw, 1988). A fifth CRT tenet, having direct implications for knowledge production, is counterstorytelling (Matsuda, 1995), which from a critical race perspective, entails a method of telling a story that aims to cast doubt on the validity of accepted premises or myths, especially ones held by the majority (Delgado & Stefancic, 2001).

By the 1980s and 1990s, there were other significant legal scholars who contributed to CRT. Most notable among these include Richard Delgado and Kimberle Crenshaw. These scholars, similar to the position of their predecessors, argue that persons of color speak from an experience framed by racism, which, in turn, gives them a voice that is different from the dominant culture and one that deserves to be heard (Crenshaw, 1988, 1989; Delgado, 1988). CRT continued to evolve from its early focus on African Americans and the impact of the law on black-white American relations to examining how issues related to the law and immigration, national origin, language, globalization, and colonization relate to race (Parker, 2004). Additionally, it has moved beyond the legal discipline to include fields such as education, ethnic studies, and political science. Most notable is the development of a CRT of education (Dixson & Rousseau, 2006; Ladson-Billings, 2005; Ladson-Billings & Tate, 1995) and the use of CRT as a lens for understanding and addressing issues such as educational inequities, school discipline and hierarchy, tracking, IQ and achievement testing, controversies over curriculum and history, the treatment of African American students (particularly African American males), and institutionalized stereotyping (DeCuir & Dixson, 2004; Duncan, 2002; Lynn, 1999; Lynn, Yosso, Solórzano, & Parker, 2002).

Although critical race analyses originally focused primarily on race, the writings in this area stress that oppressions are neither neatly divorceable from one another nor amenable to strict categorization (e.g., Crenshaw, 1989; A. P. Harris, 1997; King, 1988; Matsuda, 1992). Now, CRT encompasses other dimensions including feminism (FemCrit), Queer Crit, Asian Crit, Latino critical studies (Lat-Crit), TribalCrit, CRF, and critical white studies in its effort to address racism and its accompanying oppressions beyond the black/white binary. CRF, which is discussed below, is an extension of feminist theory (see Chapter 3, this volume) and CRT, with an explicit emphasis on situating the unique status of women of color due to their intersecting race and gender status. It is grounded in the contributions of various black feminist scholars (e.g., bell hooks, Audre Lorde, Patricia Hill Collins) who challenged binary thinking (women or black) and sought to move scholarship to a fuller integration of the manner in which race and gender function together in structuring social inequities (especially for African American women).

Critical Race Feminism

The term *critical race feminism* stems from the primary legal traditions from which it derives, including CLS, CRT, and feminist jurisprudence. From its origin, CRF has been anti-essentialist, arguing for a deeper understanding of the lives of women of color based on the multiplicity of their identities (Caldwell, 1995; Hua, 2003; Wing, 1997a, 1997b). Similar to critical race theorists, critical race feminists emphasize that race is a constant part of normal transaction in everyday social interactions and people are part of a racial economy. Additionally, CRF attempts to integrate the way race and gender function together in structuring social inequality (Dua, 1999), and it is advanced by diverse groups of women of color, including "Third World" women, black women, and indigenous women. These women vigorously challenge the assumptions of the Western/white women's movement that all women share some universal characteristics and suffer from universal oppressions that can be understood and described by a group of predominately white, Western-trained women academics (Tuhiwai Smith, 1999). Furthermore, Tuhiwai Smith (1999) pointed out, from a CRF perspective, that the interlocking relationships among race, gender, and class make oppression of black women and other "women with labels" a complex sociological and psychological condition. As such, race and racism produce differences among various groups of women, which, in turn, challenge the notion of a common experience of gender oppression or universal global sisterhood and solidarity.

CRF has been characterized by three central tenets within North American feminism: (1) bringing into feminist theorizing an analysis of the interconnection of race/racism with gender and other oppressions, (2) arguing for the notions of social difference and multiplicity within feminism, and (3) offering a distinctive and different feminist epistemology (Hua, 2003). Furthermore, CRF, according to Hua (2003), seeks to reclaim feminism by speaking of racism, colonialism, and neocolonialism. This is done by critically examining how women of color are "othered," subjugated by various brutal histories such as slavery, colonization, genocide, lynching, racism, sexism, classism, homophobia, and globalized exploitation of labor.

In the 1980s, CRF was deeply influenced by scholars such as bell hooks (1984, 1995) and Audre Lorde (1984), who both criticized white liberal feminists on ethical and moral grounds for failing to recognize their racial and class biases and privileges. Their work, as well as other critical race feminist discourse in this country (e.g., Guy-Sheftall, 1995; Hill Collins, 1990), was framed predominately from a white-black perspective. The limitations of a white-black dichotomy in CRF and efforts toward promoting multicultural feminism and global CRF are discussed (Hua, 2003; Shohat, 1998; Wing, 2000). Hua (2003) stressed that contemporary CRF permits us to move beyond the black-white discourse and provides a more open and contested epistemological space to include not only black feminists but also other colored feminists, mixed-race feminists, as well as "white" feminists who are engaging in critical race analyses. Global CRF is a strand of CRF that embraces perspectives from international and comparative law, global feminism, and postcolonial theory (Wing, 2000).

CRF, like CRT, has implications for research and how researchers view their ethical responsibility in knowledge production and improving the position of women of color within society. Michele Fine (2006) coined the phase *contesting research*, which is quite relevant to a critical race and critical feminism stance. "Contesting research" is work aimed at interrupting dominance; emphasizing a commitment to centering marginalized voices; and advocating that people, especially those who have experienced historic oppression, hold deep knowledge about their lives and experiences and should help shape the questions and frame the interpretations of research. This perspective argues that an ethical obligation of researchers is to foreground and advocate for the perspective of historically excluded groups, working from the inside out and creating opportunities for the production of new knowledge and the development of new theory (Cahill, 2007; Fine, 2006; Torre & Fine, 2006).

◆ Foregrounding Ethical Considerations in Critical Race Theory Research[1]

Ethics is concerned with attempts to formulate the principles and codes of moral behavior. It seeks to provide guidance in relation to what is morally right and wrong. Clearly, the philosophical foundations of CRT perspectives, ethics, and research methodology are intricately linked. Engaging in research within a CRT paradigm is explicitly ethical in nature to the extent that we view racism, sexism, and other forms of oppression as inherently "bad" and issues of equity, democracy, social justice, and inclusiveness as serving the common good. At the cornerstone of CRT work is making visible the notion that Western civilization is created around reproducing inequity for nondominant groups of people (Crenshaw et al., 1995) and that these inequities have long-standing ramifications for the individual and collective behavior and social outcomes of oppressed people.

Ethical decisions arise throughout the entire research process from study conceptualization and design; data gathering, analysis, and synthesis; data interpretation and report writing; and dissemination of findings. Ethical responsibilities take center stage when conducting research with diverse populations and historically disenfranchised groups. While some ethical considerations are quite obvious (e.g., doing physical harm to participants), other ethical issues may be more subtle (e.g., the right of researchers to impose their ideology on the people being studied, unequal power relations between the researcher and the researched, the right of oppressed individuals to help shape research questions and interpretations, the lack of input from research participants about how knowledge generated from studies of their lives should be used, the right of the people researched to the data generated and the benefits accruing from the research, how institutions privilege traditional forms of research and devalue other kinds of knowledge). These subtler ethical challenges, which CRT paradigms address, need to be made explicit in research in the social and behavioral sciences.

The critical researcher has an ethical responsibility to assess his or her own values, beliefs, and prejudices, which can and do influence various aspects of the research process in a myriad of ways, such as informing (a) what questions the researcher asks and ultimately does not ask, (b) what issues the researcher illuminates and ultimately minimizes, (c) which research approaches are used and privileged and which are dismissed, (d) what data are collected and what data are ultimately overlooked, (e) how interpretations are made and whose interpretations are held in high and low esteem, (f) what conclusions are drawn and what conclusions are not considered, and (g) how results are presented and to whom they are disseminated (Thomas & McKie, 2006). Researchers are often face with a myriad of ethical dilemmas when conducting research with marginalized populations that require them to be critical of their own positionality and reflexivity and the power relations involved (Cahill, Sultana, & Pain, 2007). Writings related to devising transformative and culturally responsive approaches to evaluations yield insights into conducting more ethical and socially just research with diverse population and are consistent with CRT perspectives. (See writings by Frierson, Hood, & Hughes, 2002; Mertens, 2003; Thomas & Stevens, 2004; Thompson-Robinson, Hopson, & SenGupta, 2004.)

Two dimensions of ethics are often referred to in scientific discourse: procedural ethics and ethics in practice (Guillemin & Gillam, 2004). Procedural ethics includes those mandated by institutional review boards (IRBs) to ensure that the study's procedures adequately deal with the ethical concerns of informed consent, confidentiality, right to privacy, deception, and protection of participants from harm. Ethics in practice, or situational ethics, relates to concerns involving the unpredictable, often subtle, yet ethically important periods that arise while conducting the research. Scholars conducting work within the CRT tradition argue that research, as a construct, has long been a power-oriented, Western cultural practice whereby people of color have been, in the name of research, inappropriately labeled, physically and mentally harmed, and stereotyped (Tuhiwai Smith, 1999), all of which are inherently unethical (i.e., disrespectful of people, non-beneficent, and unjust) and potentially irreversibly harmful. IRBs, entrusted with ensuring the ethical conduct of research, have been charged by scholars pushing for antiracist research methodologies with inappropriateness and the use of traditional ethics review procedures based in positivism, which separates thought from action and subject from object and assumes that research should and can be value-free (Chavez, Duran, & Baker, 2003). Acts of institutional racism are perpetuated when IRBs work to legitimate and justify a set of practices that are considered dominant by marginalized communities instead of encouraging knowledge to come from the community and be defined in ways that may be different from the dominant cultural norms (Grégoire & Yee, 2007). Furthermore, it has also been argued that IRBs generally give emphasis to assessing risks to individuals without paying attention to risks to communities (Minkler, 2004), a condition that has ethical implications for research focusing on marginalized communities.

There have been attempts to approach ethics from an antiracism stance in an effort to deepen the dialogue and inform solutions to ethical conflicts that arise from dominant ways of thinking about and organizing research. These approaches argue for IRBs to serve as a catalyst for encouraging research participants to be creators of knowledge and resistors of oppressive research (Grégoire & Yee, 2007). One notable example of such an approach includes work carried with or in collaboration with the Access Alliance Multicultural Community Health Centre, a community health center that serves immigrants and refugees in Toronto, Canada. The Access Alliance has developed a statement of four values (i.e., community benefit, capacity building, collaboration and inclusion, equity and dignity) and principles that draw from an antiracist framework and community-based participatory research. Not satisfied with traditional IRBs, Access Alliance has established its own Research Ethics Committee, which works to ensure that the research is consistent with both accepted ethical standards and the four values established by Access Alliance. (For additional information on the Access Alliance Multicultural Community Health Centre, check out www.ccph.info.)

In addition to the two aforementioned dimensions of ethics, a third type of ethics, referred to as relational ethics (Ellis, 2007), is consistent with a CRT paradigm. Ellis (2007) described relational ethics as doing what is necessary to be true to one's character and responsible for one's actions and their consequences on others. Relational ethics recognizes and values mutual respect, dignity, and connectedness between researcher and the researched and between researchers and the communities in which they live and work.

◆ Ethical Research Responsibilities Grounded in Critical Race Theory

Research grounded in CRT recognizes, from an ethical as well as a methodological standpoint, the importance of attending to issues of race, gender, institutional power dimensions, and status throughout the entire research process. In doing so, critical methodologies offer a framework for insights into an analytical perspective for (a) identifying the important research issues in more inclusive and just ways, (b) framing more inclusive questions and asking them in more just ways, (c) reviewing relevant literature, (d) collecting and analyzing data in ways that give "voice" to research participants, and (e) forming conclusions and recommendations from the evaluations that promote equity and social justice. Solórzano and Yosso (2002) put forth five tenets of a CRT methodology that have ethical implications for research: (1) placing race and its intersectionality with other forms of subordination at the center of research; (2) using race in research to challenge the dominant scientific norms of objectivity and neutrality; (3) having research connected with social justice concerns and potential praxis with ongoing efforts in communities; (4) making experiential knowledge central to the study and linking the knowledge to other critical research and interpretive perspectives on race and racism (and other forms of oppression); and (5) emphasizing the importance of transdisciplinary perspectives that are based in multiple fields for enhancing an understanding of the effects of racism and other forms of discrimination on persons of color.

A researcher's unwillingness to engage with those who occupy different social positions silences the voices of individuals who do not have access to the tools of knowledge production (Shope, 2006), and such research is devoid of critical analysis and ethical consideration of the interests of the individuals under examination. Grounding research in the experiences of people of color creates a space for an absent person and his or her experiences that can ultimately form a counterpoint to hegemonic narratives (Ong, 1995; Smith, 1990). Critical race methodology seeks to come to know individuals' reality by asking them about it. Furthermore, critical methodology explicitly acknowledges the interactive relationship between researcher and participants (Guba & Lincoln, 1994). Race and racism, gender and sexism, intersectionality, and the ethical responsibility of researchers to appropriately capture the lived experiences of the researched are in the foreground in research design, data collection and analysis, and interpretations from a CRT perspective. Critical theorists argue for extending what counts as research to be more inclusive of differing methodologies and writing genres. This includes the use of personal narrative, diaries, and poetry. They demonstrate unconventional ways of thinking about, doing, and writing research (Quaye, 2007). Critical race theorists argue that it is only through hearing the stories and having access to the experiential knowledge of those who are victimized by inequities that we can better understand the socially ingrained and systemic forces at work in their oppression (Pizarro, 1998). Critical research methodologies foreground important issues that have ethical implications for working with diverse groups, such as privileging subjectivity; attending to the importance of race, ethnicity, gender, class, and other often dismissed factors as central elements of individuals' lived experiences and realities; avoiding exploitation of research participants as subjects and objects of knowledge; and empowering the disenfranchised through social research (Fonow & Cook, 2005; Ladson-Billings, 2005; Tuhiwai Smith, 1999).

The cornerstone of critical methodology is reflexivity. This requires an awareness of the researcher's contribution to the construction of meanings throughout the research process and acknowledgment of the impossibility of remaining totally detached from the subject matter under study (Nightingale & Cromby, 1999). Reflexivity also stresses the importance of exploring the ways in which a researcher's involvement with a particular study influences, acts on, and informs such research. Two types of reflexivity are relevant: personal reflexivity and epistemological reflexivity. Personal reflexivity involves reflecting on the ways in which our own values, ethics, experiences, interests, beliefs, political commitments, wider aims in life, and social identities shape the research; here, researchers think about how the research may have affected and possibly changed them as individuals and as researchers. On the other hand, epistemological reflexivity entails researchers reflecting on the assumptions (e.g., about the world, about knowledge) that they make in the course of the research and the implications of such assumptions for the research and its findings. Reflexivity requires investigators to ask several important questions that have both ethical and methodological implications for both individuals and their communities, such as: (a) How has the research question been defined and might limit what can be found? (b) How have the design of the study and the method of analysis constructed the data and the findings? (c) How might the research question be investigated differently? (d) To what extent would this different way of investigating the research question give rise to a different understanding of the phenomenon under study? (Willig, 2001).

CRT, QUALITATIVE, QUANTITATIVE, AND MIXED-METHODS PERSPECTIVES

Critical methods do not simply embrace one type of research methodology. While qualitative types of methods are often more suitable to the critical theory ontology of documenting historical realism or virtual reality shaped by social, political, cultural, economic, ethnic, and gender values crystallized over time (Guba & Lincoln, 1994), critical theorists are not uniformly opposed to the use of quantitative and mixed-methods perspectives. For example, Ladson-Billings (2003), a scholar who has used CRT to explicate new epistemological perspectives on inequality and social injustice in education, did not advocate that CRT is the only way to research the racialized subject, noting that researchers may want to reach into their methodological tool kit for various quantitative approaches and analytic techniques such as multiple regression and structural equation modeling. Ladson-Billing did, however, stress that researchers should use these analytic approaches with the full knowledge of what those tools can and cannot do and what "truths" these tools illuminate and what "truths" are simultaneously occluded by them.

Critical research is participatory in nature such that research participants are active in the construction of knowledge about their lives and the researchers attempt to be more transparent about their roles (Fonow & Cook, 2005). Participatory research has significant implications for refocusing researchers' ethical commitments. Participatory ethics builds on the long-standing traditions of grassroots social movements, activism, critical race and feminist theories, and the work of social justice advocates who strive to address unequal power relations and challenge the dominant hegemony (Cahill et al., 2007). Additionally, a key feature of participatory ethics is the presumption of engaged scholarship, of doing research informed by an "ethic of care" involving a deep respect for relationships and humanity (Ellis, 2007). Case study research, from a CRT perspective, requires researchers to move beyond a simple description of phenomena to systematically investigating a problem within a real-life context and answering questions of "How?" and

"Why?" instead of simply "What?" (Smith-Maddox & Solórzano, 2002).

Mixed-methods research, sometimes described as experimental methodological pluralism, is also a strategy that can be of value to critical researchers. This methodological approach is still evolving and is variously defined (Johnson, Onwuegbuzie, & Turner, 2007), with the broader descriptions characterizing mixed methods as an approach that allows inclusion of the issues and strategies surrounding methods of data collection (e.g., questionnaires, interview, observations) and methods of research (e.g., experiments, ethnography), and related philosophical issues (e.g., ontology, epistemology, axiology; Greene, 2006). As researchers increasingly acknowledge that no single method can capture the whole and complex reality, mixed-methods research is becoming more common. Mertens (2003, 2007) discussed the potential strength in combining qualitative and quantitative methods and how the intersection of culturally competent mixed methods and social justice have implications for the role of the researcher and the choice of specific paradigmatic perspectives. Critical mixed methodologies, which are inherently transformative in nature, provide a mechanism for addressing the complexities of research in culturally complex and diverse settings that can provide a basis for empowerment, social change, and social justice.

◆ Conclusions

CRT is part of a larger transformative paradigm that has implications for a research approach that expands researchers' explicit responsibilities for dealing with a myriad of ethical issues, including addressing racism and other forms of oppression; considering differential power imbalances and privileges between researchers and the researched; broadening conceptualizations of what counts as knowledge; expanding considerations of harm to include communities (not just individual harm); and working to promote social justice, equity, and democracy. An important theme of all CRT perspectives is that of "voice scholarship" or "naming" one's own reality. In this paradigm, the use of parables, chronicles, stories, counterstories, poetry, fiction, and revisionist histories is also a legitimate form of data collection for knowledge generation. Critical approaches shift the research lens away from deficit views of individuals of color to more asset-based and empowering approaches. It is the responsibility of critical race researchers to choose their ethical value commitments of working toward a just society; operating within inclusive and empowering epistemological frameworks and methodologies; and allowing their social justice values to inform the scope, design, conduct, and dissemination of their research. Some argue that critical theories and their resultant research are inherently ethically motivated given that their two main areas of interest, power and emancipation, are intrinsically ethical considerations. Critical research seeks to expose the weaknesses and contradictions within a particular area (Wilson, 2003); address issues of power, empowerment, and emancipation (Ulrich, 2001); and generate a knowledge base that can make a positive (and just) difference in the lives of the individuals and communities under study.

CRT researchers have in their toolbox a vast array of analytical tools to engage their scholarship, with due consideration to issues of justice, ethics, and validity. Therefore, a critical epistemology does not require researchers to adopt one particular methodological tool. It does, however, necessitate that the researcher engage in critical reflection on the use of various methods of analysis and interpretation and the adoption of an explicit ethical stance on the means and ends of the research. All critical research methods, whether they are qualitative, quantitative, or mixed methods, must be planned and implemented with a critical epistemology that helps shape the identification of the topic for study; the type and nature of the research questions posed; and the consideration of how a variety of macro and micro factors (e.g., subjectivity, race, ethnicity, gender, class, and intersectionality, as well as historical, sociocultural, and political factors) influence the knower as well as knowledge production and have explicit ethical implications. CRT approaches have much promise for exposing and strengthening diverse communities by yielding invaluable information that allow members of these communities to tell their stories in a contextualized fashion rather than have the stories re-created by others devoid of shared lived experiences.

◆ Note

1. Yosso (2005). For the remainder of this chapter, reference to CRT is inclusive of CRF, which was an outgrowth of CRT and feminism analyses.

◆ References

Bell, D. (1980). *Brown v. Board of Education* and the interest-convergence dilemma. *Harvard Law Review*, 93, 518.
Bell, D. A. (1992). *Faces at the bottom of the well: The permanence of racism.* New York: Basic Books.
Bell, D. A. (1995). Racial realism. In K. Crenshaw, N. Gotanda, G. Peller, & K. Thomas (Eds.), *Critical race theory: The key writings that formed the movement* (pp. 302–312). New York: New Press.
Bohman, J. (1991). *New philosophy of social science: Problems of indeterminacy.* Cambridge: MIT Press.
Brooke, C. (2002). What does it mean to be "critical" in IS research? *Journal of Information Technology*, 17, 49–57.

Brown, L. S. (1995). Cultural diversity in feminist therapy: Theory and practice. In H. Landrine (Ed.), *Bringing cultural diversity to feminist psychology: Theory, research, and practice* (pp. 143–161). Washington, DC: American Psychological Association.
Cahill, C. (2007). Repositioning ethical commitments: Participatory action research as a relational praxis of social change. *ACME Editorial Collective.* Retrieved January 13, 2008, from www.acme-journal.org/vol6/CC.pdf
Cahill, C., Sultana, F., & Pain, R. (2007). Participatory ethics: Politics, practices, and institutions. *ACME Editorial Collective.* Retrieved January 13, 2008, from www.acme-journal.org/vol6/CCFSRP.pdf
Caldwell, P. (1995). A hairpiece: Perspectives on the intersection of race and gender. In R. Delgado (Ed.), *Critical race theory: The cutting edge* (pp. 267–277). Philadelphia: Temple University Press.
Chavez, V., Duran, B., & Baker, Q. (2003). The dance of race and privilege in community-based participatory research. In M. Minker & N. Wallerstein (Eds.), *Community base participatory research for health* (pp. 81–98). San Francisco, CA: Jossey-Bass.
Crenshaw, K. W. (1988). Race, reform, and retrenchment: Transformation and legitimation in anti-discrimination law. *Harvard Law Review*, 101, 1331–1387.
Crenshaw, K. W. (1989). Demarginalizing the intersection of race and sex: A black feminist critique of antidiscrimination doctrine, feminist theory and antitrust politics. *University of Chicago Legal Forum*, 139–167.
Crenshaw, K. W. (2002). The first decade: Critical reflections, or "a foot in the closing door." In F. Valdes, J. McCristal Culp, & A. Harris (Eds.), *Crossroads, directions and a new critical race theory* (pp. 9–31). Philadelphia: Temple University Press.
Crenshaw, K., Gotanda, N., Peller, G., & Thomas, K. (Eds.). (1995). *Critical race theory: The key writings that formed the movement.* New York: New Press.
DeCuir, J. T., & Dixson, A. D. (2004). "So when it comes out, they aren't that

surprised that it is there": Using critical race theory as a tool of analysis of race and racism in education. *Educational Researcher, 33*(5), 26–31.

Delgado, R. (1984). The imperial scholar: Reflections on a review of civil rights literature. *University of Pennsylvania Law Review, 132,* 561–578.

Delgado, R. (1988). Critical legal studies and the realities of race: Does the fundamental contradiction have a corollary? *Harvard Civil Rights–Civil Liberties Law Review, 23,* 407–413.

Delgado, R., & Stefancic, J. (2001). *Critical race theory: An introduction.* New York: New York University Press.

Dixson, A., & Rousseau, C. K. (2006). *Critical race theory in education: All God's children got a song.* New York: Routledge.

Dua, E. (1999). Introduction. In E. Dua & A. Robertson (Eds.), *Scratching the surface: Canadian anti-racist feminist thought* (pp. 7–31). Toronto, Ontario, Canada: Women's Press.

DuBois, W. E. (1903). *The souls of black folk: Essays and sketches.* Chicago: A. C. McClurg.

Duncan, G. (2002). Beyond love: A critical race ethnology of the schooling of adolescent black males. *Equity & Excellence in Education, 35*(2), 131–143.

Ellis, C. (2007). Telling secrets, revealing lives: Relational ethics in research with intimate others. *Qualitative Inquiry, 13*(1), 3–29.

Ellsworth, E. (1989). Why doesn't this feel empowering? Working through the repressive myths of critical pedagogy. *Harvard Educational Review, 59*(3), 297–324.

Fay, B. (1987). *Critical social science: Liberation and its limits.* Ithaca, NY: Cornell.

Fine, M. (2006). Contesting research: Rearticulation and "thick democracy" as a political project of method. In L. Weis, C. McCarthy, & G. Dimitriadis (Eds.), *Ideology, curriculum, and the new sociology of education: Revisiting the work of Michael Apple* (pp. 145–166). New York: Routledge.

Fonow, M. M., & Cook, J. A. (2005). Feminist methodology: New applications in the academy and public policy. *Signs: Journal of Women in Culture and Society, 30*(4), 2211–2236.

Frierson, H. T., Hood, S., & Hughes, G. B. (2002). Strategies that address culturally responsive evaluation. In *The 2002 user-friendly handbook for project evaluation* (pp. 63–73). Arlington, VA: National Science Foundation.

Greene, J. C. (2006). Toward a methodology of mixed methods social inquiry. *Research in the Schools, 13*(1), 93–98.

Grégoire, H., & Yee, J. Y. (2007, Winter). Ethics in community-university partnerships involving racial minorities: An anti-racism standpoint in community-based participatory research. *Partnership Perspectives, 4*(1), 70–77. Retrieved January 13, 2008, from http://depts.washington.edu/ccph/pdf_files/PP-W07.pdf

Guba, E. G., & Lincoln, Y. S. (1994). Competing paradigms in qualitative research. In N. K. Denzin & Y. S. Lincoln (Eds.), *Handbook of qualitative research.* Thousand Oaks, CA: Sage.

Guillemin, M., & Gillam, L. (2004). Ethics, reflexivity, and "ethically important moments" in research. *Qualitative Inquiry, 10,* 261–280.

Guy-Sheftall, B. (Ed.). (1995). *Words of fire: An anthology of African-American feminist thought.* New York: New Press.

Habermas, J. (1996). *Between facts and norms.* Cambridge: MIT Press.

Halse, C., & Honey, A. (2005). Unraveling ethics: Illuminating the moral dilemmas of research ethics. *Signs: Journal of Women in Culture and Society, 30*(4), 2141–2162.

Hammersley, M. (2005). Should social science be critical? *Philosophy of the Social Sciences, 35*(2), 175–195.

Harris, A. P. (1997). Race and essentialism in feminist legal theory. In A. K. Wing (Ed.), *Critical race feminism: A reader* (pp. 11–17). New York: New York University Press.

Harris, C. I. (1995). Whiteness as property. In K. Crenshaw, N. Gotanda, G. Peller, & K. Thomas (Eds.), *Critical race theory: The key writings that formed the movement* (pp. 357–383). New York: New Press.

Hill Collins, P. (1990). *Black feminist thought: Knowledge, consciousness, and the politics of empowerment.* Boston: Unwin Hyman.

Hirschheim, R., & Klein, H. K. (1994). Realizing emancipatory principles in information systems development: The case for ethics. *MIS Quarterly, 18,* 83–109.

hooks, b. (1984). *Feminist theory: From margin to center.* Boston: South End Press.

hooks, b. (1995). Black women: Shaping feminist theory. In B. Guy-Shetfall (Ed.), *Words of fire: An anthology of African American feminist thought* (pp. 270–282). New York: New Press.

Horkheimer, M. (1972). Traditional and critical theory. In *Critical theory: Selected essays* (pp. 188–243; M. J. O'Connell et al., Trans.). New York: Herder & Herder. (Original essay published 1937)

Hua, A. (2003, May 2–3). Critical race feminism. In *Pedagogy and practice.* Canadian Critical Race Conference 2003, University of British Columbia, Vancouver, Canada.

Johnson, R. B., Onwuegbuzie, A. J., & Turner, L. A. (2007). Toward a definition of mixed methods research. *Journal of Mixed Methods Research, 2,* 112–133.

King, D. (1988). Multiple jeopardy, multiple consciousness: The context of a black feminist ideology. *Signs: Journal of Women in Culture and Society, 14,* 42–72.

Ladson-Billings, G. (2003). It's your world, I'm just trying to explain it: Understanding our epistemological and methodological challenges. *Qualitative Inquiry, 9*(1), 5–12.

Ladson-Billings, G. (2005). The evolving role of critical race theory in educational scholarship. *Race Ethnicity and Education, 8*(1), 115–119.

Ladson-Billings, G., & Tate, W. F. (1995). Toward a critical race theory of education. *Teachers College Record, 97*(1), 47–68.

Lawrence, C. R. (1995). The id, the ego, and equal protection: Reckoning with unconscious racism. In K. Crenshaw, N. Gotanda, G. Peller, & K. Thomas (Eds.), *Critical race theory: The key writings that formed the movement* (pp. 235–257). New York: New Press.

Lorde, A. (1984). *Sister outsider: Essays and speeches.* Freedom, CA: Crossing Press.

Lynn, M. (1999). Toward a critical race pedagogy: A research note. *Urban Education, 33,* 606–626.

Lynn, M., Yosso, T. J., Solórzano, D. G., & Parker, L. (2002). Critical race theory and education: Qualitative research in the new millennium. *Qualitative Inquiry, 8*(1), 3–6.

Manzo, L., & Brightbill, N. (2007). Towards a participatory ethics. In S. Kindon, R. Pain, & M. Kesby (Eds.), *Connecting people, participation and place: Participatory action research approaches and methods* (pp. 33–40). London: Routledge.

Matsuda, M. J. (1992). When the first quail calls: Multiple consciousness as jurisprudential method. *Women's Rights Law Reports, 14,* 297.

Matsuda, M. J. (1995). Looking to the bottom: Critical legal studies and reparations. In K. Crenshaw, N. Gotanda, G. Peller, & K. Thomas (Eds.), *Critical race theory: The key writings that formed the movement* (pp. 63–79). New York: New Press.

Mertens, D. M. (2003). Mixed methods and the politics of human research: The transformative-emancipatory perspective. In A. Tashakkori & C. Teddlie (Eds.), *Handbook of mixed methods in social and behavioral research* (pp. 135–164). Thousand Oaks, CA: Sage.

Mertens, D. M. (2007). Transformative paradigm: Mixed methods and social justice. *Journal of Mixed Methods Research, 1*(3), 212–225.

Minkler, M. (2004). Ethical challenges for the "outside" researcher in community-based participatory research. *Health Education & Behavior, 31*(6), 684–697.

National Commission for the Protection of Human Subjects in Biomedical and Behavioral Research. (1978). *The Belmont report: Ethical principles and guidelines for the protection of human subjects of research.* Rockville, MD: National Institutes of Health.

Nightingale, D. J., & Cromby, J. (Eds.). (1999). *Social constructionist psychology: A critical analysis of theory and practice.* Buckingham, UK: Open University Press.

Ong, A. (1995). Women out of China: Traveling tales and traveling theories in postcolonial feminism. In R. Behar & D. A. Gordon (Eds.), *Women writing culture* (pp. 350–372). Berkeley: University of California Press.

Parker, L. (2004). Commentary: Can critical theories of or on race be used in evaluation research in education? In V. G. Thomas & F. I. Stevens (Eds.), *Co-constructing a contextually responsive evaluation framework: The talent development model of school reform* (New Directions for Evaluation, No. 101, pp. 85–93). San Francisco: Jossey-Bass.

Pizarro, M. (1998). "Chicana/o power!" Epistemology and methodology for social justice and empowerment in Chicano communities. *Qualitative Studies in Education, 11*(1), 57–80.

Quaye, S. J. (2007). Voice of the researcher: Extending the limits of what counts as research. *Journal of Research Practice*, Article M3. Retrieved May 1, 2007, from http://jrp.icaap.org/index.php/jrp/article/viewArticle/60/81

Shohat, E. (Ed.). (1998). *Talking visions: Multicultural feminism in a transnational age.* Cambridge: MIT Press.

Shope, J. H. (2006). "You can't cross a river without getting wet": A feminist standpoint on the dilemmas of cross-cultural research. *Qualitative Inquiry, 12*(1), 163–184.

Smith, D. (1990). *The conceptual practices of power.* Boston: Northeastern University Press.

Smith-Maddox, R., & Solórzano, D. G. (2002). Using critical race theory, Paulo Friere's problem-posing method, and case study research to confront race and racism in education. *Qualitative Inquiry, 8*(1), 66–84.

Solórzano, D. (1997). Images and words that wound: Critical race theory, racial stereotyping, and teacher education. *Teacher Education Quarterly, 24*(3), 5–19.

Solorzano, D. G. & Yosso, T. J. (2002). Critical race methodology: Counter-storytelling as an analytical framework for education research. *Qualitative Inquiry, 8*(1), 23–44.

Thomas, V. G., & McKie, B. (2006). Collecting and utilizing evaluation research for public good and on behalf of African American children. *Journal of Negro Education, 75*(3), 341–352.

Thomas, V. G., & Stevens, F. I. (Eds.). (2004). *Co-constructing a contextually responsive evaluation framework: The talent development model of school reform* (New Directions for Evaluation, No. 101). San Francisco: Jossey-Bass.

Thompson-Robinson, M., Hopson, R., & SenGupta, S. (Eds.). (2004). *In search of cultural competence in evaluation* (New Directions for Evaluation, No. 102). San Francisco: Jossey-Bass.

Torre, M. E., & Fine, M. (2006). Participatory action research (PAR) by youth. In L. Sherrod (Ed.), *Youth activism: An international encyclopedia* (pp. 456–462). Westport, CT: Greenwood.

Tuhiwai Smith, L. (1999). *Decolonizing methodologies: Research and indigenous peoples.* London: Zed Books.

Ulrich, W. (2001). A philosophical staircase for information systems definition, design, and development. *Journal of Information Technology Theory and Application, 3*(3), 55–84.

Willig, C. (2001). *Introducing qualitative research in psychology: Adventures in theory and method.* Buckingham, UK: Open University Press.

Wilson, M. (2003). Rhetoric of enrollment and acts of resistance: Information technology as text. In E. Wynn, E. Whitley, M. Myers, & J. DeGross (Eds.), *Global and organizational discourse about information technology* (pp. 225–248). Dordrecht, The Netherlands: Kluwer Academic.

Wing, A. K. (Ed). (1997a). *Critical race feminist: A reader.* New York: New York University Press.

Wing, A. K. (Ed.). (1997b). Introduction. In *Critical race feminist: A reader* (p. 106). New York: New York University Press.

Wing, A. K. (Ed.). (2000). Introduction. In *Global critical race feminism: An international reader* (pp. 1–23). New York: New York University Press.

Yosso, T. J. (2005). Whose culture has capital? A critical race theory discussion of community cultural wealth. *Race Ethnicity and Education, 9*(1), 69–91.

5

PHILOSOPHY, ETHICS, AND THE DISABILITY COMMUNITY

◆ Martin Sullivan

As feminist perspectives identified sexism in social science research, so the disability community identified able-ism. The concern of the disability community with issues of informed consent among those whose physical, sensory, intellectual, and/or psychological condition limits their ability to comprehend the risks and benefits of participation in research and/or to communicate consent or lack thereof has also informed social science research ethics as they affect other vulnerable groups such as children and prisoners. This chapter focuses on the contribution of disability scholars to the understanding of ethical issues in research.

◆ **Introduction**

It can be argued that the essence of social research is about getting to know and understand "how and why things are as they are" in society. It differs from a mere "finding out" about the social from, say,

---

AUTHOR'S NOTE: I would like to thank Donna Mertens and the three anonymous reviewers for their constructive comments on various drafts of this chapter. Responsibility for its final content rests with me.

a newspaper, insofar as research involves a systematic, purposive effort to find out more about a particular social phenomenon to understand it better. Indeed, much of what we know about the society in which we live is the product of serious research. Serious research generally has an institutional setting—university, college, polytechnic, research center—and involves a community of scholars, which over time, has established appropriate ways—an ethics—of doing research as well as an accumulation of knowledge on the subject, which often acts as the springboard for further research. Another outcome, a side effect as it were, is that the researcher becomes the bearer of all that institutional power and authority, which places him or her in a powerful position in the research relationship.

Since social research involves human individuals and groups, the ways in which they are positioned within research is extremely important for their own protection and for what we as a society come to know about those individuals or groups. In terms of protection, there is an asymmetrical power relationship between the researcher and the researched, between the knower and the (to be) known: Does the research have scientific merit? Is it intrusive and potentially harmful to the researched? Is there any reciprocity between the researched and the researcher? Is there any payback for the researched as individuals or as a group? These are some of the questions that must be asked to protect the subjects of research. And then, if we accept that a great deal of what we know about individuals and groups is a product of research, social research must be seen as producing certain groups and individuals in certain ways for social consumption and understanding. In other words, one set of questions will produce a population in a certain way while another set of questions will produce it in a totally different way. So who is doing the research, the prior knowledge on which the research is based, the "why" of the research, and who controls the research become crucial questions in deciding if the research is ethical or not.

Nowhere more so than in disability studies have the questions on what constitutes ethical research been so hotly contested. This chapter reviews those debates by focusing on the emergence of the disability rights movement and disability studies, the reconceptualization of disability and implications for disability research, the development of the emancipatory research paradigm, debates around it, and the emergence of other approaches to disability research, questions around impairment, and who should do disability research. In highlighting these debates, this chapter will provide a genealogy of the contribution disability scholars have made to the understanding of ethical issues in social research.

◆ The Emergence of the Disability Rights Movement in the Late 20th Century[1]

Following the examples set by the civil rights and women's liberation movements of the 1960s and 1970s, disabled people throughout the Western world began to speak out for themselves and organize to assert more control over and in their lives. Up to this point, organizations for disabled people had been mostly dominated and controlled by parents and professionals and functioned as charities. This was especially true of the larger, nationwide organizations, which reflected the conventional wisdom of the time that disabled people were the tragic victims of circumstance and deserved the pity and care of the able-bodied and able-minded. Throughout Western society such wisdom had resulted in disabled people being removed from their communities and dumped in large, impersonal institutions that were run along medical lines and provided the most basic of services. Toward the end of the 1960s, this view began to be challenged, first in the area of intellectual disability[2] by normalization theory as developed by nondisabled academics (see Nirje, 1969; Wolfensberger, 1972) and then by disabled people themselves who in their reconceptualization of disability gave the world the social model of disability (see Oliver, 1990b; Union of the Physically Impaired Against Segregation [UPIAS], 1976).

Normalization theory was aimed at "making available to all mentally retarded people patterns of life and conditions of everyday living, which are as close as possible to the regular circumstances and ways of life of society" (Nirje, 1969, cited in Shakespeare, 2006, p. 22). Wolfensberger's approach to normalization—social role valorization—became dominant in the United States (and influential in many more countries) and presented a radical critique of the medicalization of intellectually disabled people and the death-making tendencies of long-stay hospital care and institutionalized service provision in the community. A concerted campaign to deinstitutionalize intellectually disabled people and to resettle them in their communities where they could lead normal lives followed. It was in this context that People First, a self-advocacy group for intellectually disabled people, formed in Oregon in 1973. The group formed as the direct result of a group attending a conference in Canada, which was purported to be for "people with mental retardation" but turned out to be dominated by professionals (Shoultz, 1997). People First groups have sprung up around the world providing the spaces where intellectually disabled people can develop leadership and assertiveness skills and become confident in their abilities as self-advocates.

At Berkeley, California, physically impaired disability activists founded the first center for independent living in the United States in 1972 (deJong, 1979). These activists adhered to the belief that the barriers they faced to exercising their citizenship were more the product of social attitudes than their individual impairments (Bowe, 1978; Hahn, 1985). This social understanding of disability provided the theoretical basis on which the disability rights movement in North America adopted the notion of people with disabilities as belonging to a minority group that was systematically discriminated against in ways which denied members their civil and individual rights. Street-level politics, sit-ins, demonstrations, and other means of confrontation subsequently became the modus operandi for Americans with disabilities in their struggle for antidiscrimination legislation, which would guarantee them their individual rights (Anspach, 1979). Direct action resulted in Section 504 of the Federal Rehabilitation Act in 1973, which prohibited discrimination in federally funded services, and the Americans With Disabilities Act of 1990, which banned discrimination against Americans with disabilities.

In the United Kingdom, activists adopted a more explicitly structural analysis of disability in which the distinction between (biological) impairments and (social) disability was far more sharply drawn and which allowed disability to be recast as social oppression (Shakespeare, 2006). This social model of disability provided the theoretical underpinnings for the first course in disability studies in the United Kingdom in 1975 at The Open University.

This brief history alerts us to two features of the disability rights movement that have implications for disability research: first, the ontological variations between the movements in the United Kingdom and the United States and, second, the diversity within the disability community. The question of diversity, especially in terms of impairment, is of ubiquitous concern for disability researchers as different forms of impairment not only necessitate different approaches and methodologies but also generate different subcultures in which disability assumes different meanings and which call for a more nuanced approach to research. In short, the disability community is a heterogeneous and culturally complex community. Researchers need to keep this in mind. While this chapter focuses mainly on developments within disability research within the United Kingdom, it does consider ethical research with people with physical, intellectual, sensory, and psychiatric impairment.

◆ The Social Model, Disability Studies, and Disability Research

The social model of disability was developed by disabled people themselves and has become the underpinning justification for the disability rights movement. Its principles were first articulated in November 1975, when the UPIAS and The Disability Alliance met to discuss the Fundamental Principles of Disability.[3] The separation of *impairment* and *disability* lies at the heart of the model, with impairment having to do with the body and disability the negative social response to impairment. From this perspective, disability was not something individuals had but the exclusion imposed on impaired people in societies designed for and by able-bodied people; disability, in other words, was social oppression. The social model of disability thus constituted an epistemological break with the hegemonic individual (medical) model, where to have an impairment was to be disabled and dependent; it signaled a break with, and the need to change, perceptions of disability as a personal problem of individuals who should properly seek medical intervention for cure, amelioration, or care; it signaled a break with welfarism and dependency creating policies and services, and heralded disabled people as self-determining subjects rather than tragic victims. The "personal tragedy theory" (Oliver, 1990b), which underpins the individual medical model, had become the conventional wisdom and resulted in social policies, which tried to compensate these victims for the tragedies that had befallen them—policies that do things to and for disabled people rather than support them to do things for themselves.

Within the United States, disability studies/activists have largely followed a minority group model rather than the structural, social oppression model of their U.K. counterparts. For British writers, many with backgrounds in Marxism and materialism, merely joining the game as it was, was not enough. Their agenda was to create a new, nondisabling society in which not only impaired people would be emancipated but also others such as workers, women, blacks, gays, and lesbians. Notwithstanding the differences in perspective, both U.S. and U.K. disability activists and academics were redefining who they were and proclaiming, "We are not your passive, tragic recipients of care but active, self-determining subjects who demand our rights to be included as free and equal citizens." Such a proclamation had, still has, and always will have ethical implications for those social researchers undertaking disability research.

The social model of disability also provided the ontological basis for the emerging field of disability studies within sociology, especially in the United Kingdom. Because the social model directs attention to what disabled people experience in common rather than their differences (i.e., their impairment categories), the focus of disability studies became not people with impairments and their personal stories but a structural analysis of the disabling society; of the dependency creating services rather than enabling practice; of disabled people's very high rates of unemployment, poverty, homelessness, and marginalization; and of the disability rights movement's struggle for civil and individual rights.

It was only a matter of time before questions of epistemology and the ethics of disability research began to be asked. In particular, the what, how, and who of disability research fell under the spotlight. The origins of the debate lie in an article by Paul Hunt in 1981 titled "Settling Accounts With Parasite People" (see Hunt, 1981; Oliver, 1990b). Here, Hunt pointed out the oppressive consequences of research done by the objective, detached, and balanced social scientist on disabled people living in institutions. Such research, he claimed, changed nothing for people living in the institutions who were struggling within oppressive management regimes. All it did was to advance the careers of the researchers by "presenting themselves to the powers that be as indispensable in training 'practitioners' to manage the problem of disabled people in institutions" (cited in Oliver, 1990b, p. 9). In short, for Hunt, the researchers' detachment was death inducing because it meant that they didn't side with the residents in their struggle. In any event, the ethical debate sparked off by Hunt led to a new orthodoxy in disability research—the emancipatory paradigm—to which we now turn our attention.

♦ Emancipatory Disability Research: Its Genesis

What constitutes disability research? Who should be doing it? How should it be done? The motivations for doing disability research, its effectiveness, and so on were some of the points of debate that followed on from Hunt's article. In the early 1990s, a national conference on disability research was held in Britain followed by a special edition of *Disability, Handicap & Society* (1992, Vol. 7, No. 2), which reported on the conference. Here, Mike Oliver argued that disability research has been dominated by the positivist research paradigm, which views disability as an individual problem to be cured or alleviated in some way. He noted, however, that in recent times positivist approaches to the social world had been challenged by a new interpretive paradigm, which sees all knowledge as socially constructed and a product of a particular time and place. From this perspective, disability is a social problem requiring education, attitude change, and social adjustment on the part of both abled and disabled people. While Oliver conceded that the interpretive or constructivist paradigm was an advance on positivism, it did not go far enough and only amounted to changing the rules of the game and not the game itself. He criticized both positivist and interpretive approaches for placing disabled research subjects in an inferior position to researchers and for producing research that disabled people had experienced as alienation from the process and from themselves, both collectively and individually. He proposed a new paradigm for disability research—the emancipatory paradigm—in which the social relations of research production would be fundamentally changed. For Oliver, emancipatory research would be nonexploitative, nonalienating, and more relevant for disabled people. In short, emancipatory disability research would be far more ethical research.

First, emancipatory research was not about merely investigating the world but about changing it. Hence, the new research paradigm was to be political in nature, and firmly rooted in the social model, and its focus was to be on exposing oppressive, disabling structures and changing them to extend the control disabled people had over their own lives.

Second, the main reason for the alienation of disabled people from the research process was the lopsided power relationship between the researcher and the researched, in which the researcher had all the control over what was researched and how it was researched. Under these conditions, disabled research subjects were treated as passive objects, mere data sources for expert researchers to collect and analyze, after which they would move on. In other words, the research was producing researchers in particular ways—as scientific, decisive, dynamic, the knowers—and the researched (disabled people) in particular ways—as passive, dependent, inferior, the known. This had to change, for once disabled people decided to empower themselves, the research method needed to facilitate this empowerment had to be determined by them. This meant that researchers had to put their skills at the disposal of disabled people to use in whatever way they choose. In this act, the social relations of research production are fundamentally changed with control over the process being passed from the researcher to the researched. The research participants now have a role in deciding the what, the how, and the when of the research process.

Under these social relations, reciprocity is possible with researchers revealing as much about themselves as the researched. But the task of emancipatory research is not about helping individuals understand themselves better but "endeavouring to collectivize the political commonality of individual experiences" (Stone & Priestly, 1996, p. 706)—or, in other words, to build the disability movement's collective understanding of disability as a basis for action.

Oliver (1992) argued that this self-understanding is a pathway to empowerment because it allows "a redefinition of 'the real nature of the problem'" (p. 112). From this perspective, a different agenda for disability research emerges:

> It is not disabled people who need examining but able-bodied society; it is not a case of educating disabled and able-bodied people for integration, but of fighting institutional disablism; it is not disability relations which should be the field for study but disablism. (p. 112)

While Oliver focused on what constituted ethical social relations between the researcher and the researched in disability research, Gerry Zarb (1992) focused on what he termed the material relations of research production and how these could affect the social relations of research. The material relations include the funding agencies that have the potential to influence the direction and character of the research, the policy makers who control the resources for research, and the large research institutions, which dominate "contract" policy research. Zarb's is a useful discussion as it raises serious, ethical questions about the funding of disability research: Who is funding it? Why are they funding it? What do they want to find out about disabled people? For what intents? Who will profit? To what effect on disabled people?

Jenny Morris (1992) in her contribution to the debate focused on feminist theory and methodology (as did Lois Keith in hers). Morris argued that while disability research had a lot to learn from feminist theory and methodology, feminist research had failed to apply its basic principles to disability with the subjective reality of disabled women having found no place in mainstream feminist work. She challenges feminism to begin correcting this by asking if the oppression of disabled women is of interest to disabled women only and to begin including research in which gender issues intermesh with disability. In this instance Morris is drawing our attention to the broader problem of the invisibility of disability and disabled people in research generally. She is also addressing the issue of who should be doing disability research in terms of the role of nondisabled researchers. Both these issues are addressed below.

Morris (1992) had some quite pertinent things to say about the kind of disability research she would like to see undertaken and, in doing this, argued that disability research has a lot to learn from the feminist principle of making the personal political. Hence, the personal, subjective experience of disability, "of being in pain, of physical and intellectual limitations," is a valid topic for research; it is political and emancipatory insofar as it "assert[s] the value of our lives" (p. 164) and contributes to personal liberation. For Morris, research on personal aspects of disability is equally important to that on social barriers because together they uncover the complexity of the personal and public aspects of disability and confirm to disabled people that

> our anger is not about having "a chip on your shoulder," our grief is not "a failure to come to terms with disability." Our

dissatisfaction with our lives is not a personality defect but a sane response to the oppression we experience. (p. 163)

Such research is emancipatory for Morris (1992) because it stands in stark contrast to the vast majority of disability research, which "does anything other than confirm the oppressive images of disability." In short, research that positions disabled people in this way cannot be called ethical; it is unethical.

Morris's piece is also important for drawing attention to the debate emerging in disability studies between those with a background in materialism and those with one in feminism. The former (e.g., Finkelstein, 1976; Oliver, 1990b, 1992; Zarb, 1992) argue that the focus should remain solely on the public reality of material, disabling barriers and their removal, while the latter (e.g., Crow, 1996; Keith, 1992; Morris, 1989, 1992) argue that the subjective experience of disability places the personal and private at the very heart of the theoretical concerns and political action of disability studies. Materialists fear that experiential accounts run the risk of re-medicalizing disability, while feminists argue that they provide a powerful way of understanding the world as a precondition for changing it. These debates are important not only for setting the research agenda in disability studies but also for drawing attention to the fact that the explanatory adequacy of the social model has always been contested within disability studies.[4]

Notwithstanding, without explicitly mentioning ethics or ethical research, *Disability, Handicap & Society* (1992, Vol. 7, No. 2) provided the blueprint for ethical disability research as defined and determined by disabled people. It was to adhere to the new emancipatory paradigm as outlined by Oliver; it was to be enabling not disabling, reflexive, and self-critical, and politically committed but rigorous, so as not to deteriorate into propaganda (Barnes & Mercer, 1997).

♦ Emancipatory Research: Contradictions in the Field

Four years later a seminar was held at the University of Leeds in which leading disability researchers in the United Kingdom reflected on the extent to which their research in the interim could be described as emancipatory or not. The various papers were edited and published as *Doing Disability Research* (Barnes & Mercer, 1997). The collection gives accounts of how researchers reconciled the theoretical purity of the emancipatory research paradigm with the practicalities of maintaining intellectual and ethical integrity in their research.

Equally important, *Doing Disability Research* draws attention to the pervasive diversity within the disability community and how this diversity demands a nuanced approach to research rather than a "one size fits all" emancipatory approach. The particularities of doing research with people with intellectual disability, with survivors of the psychiatric system, and with Deaf people are briefly considered below in an attempt to illustrate this point in relation to diversity of impairment within the disability community.

The title of Oliver's (1997) contribution "Emancipatory Research: Realistic Goal or Impossible Dream?" points to his disillusionment about ever achieving the dream of emancipatory disability research under the conditions of late capitalism, in which the vast majority of funding for large-scale primary research goes to work based on the individual medical model of disability. He believes that the best we can get under these conditions is participatory and action research, and while these forms of research are about improving the existing material and social relations of research production, they are not about challenging and ultimately eradicating them. Moreover, Oliver was convinced that despite the honorable intentions of participatory research, "we as researchers gain, but mostly at the expense of those whose lives we have researched" (p. 26) because researchers are deeply implicated in the structures, which maintain the current oppressive relations of research production.

For Oliver, this does not mean that all disability research is unethical and must stop. Rather, it is about researchers being reflexive and honest about the contribution their research practice makes to upholding or undermining the current oppressive social and material relations of research production. And in the end, whether one's research is emancipatory or not can only be judged in hindsight according to Oliver. He hopes that one day in the future when disabled people have emancipated themselves, some will look back and see the book he wrote with Jane Campbell (Campbell & Oliver, 1996) "as having made a small contribution to that emancipation" (Oliver, 1997, p. 29).

Other contributors raised a number of the practical difficulties they had encountered in trying to carry out research based in the emancipatory paradigm. These included the following:

- The material relations limiting research to a participatory mode (Zarb, 1997)
- The difficulties in applying the model to groups with other than physical and sensory impairment, such as psychiatric system survivors (Beresford & Wallcraft, 1997) or people with learning difficulties (Booth & Booth, 1997)
- The role of nondisabled researchers (Lunt & Thornton, 1997; Priestly, 1997; Stone, 1997; Stone & Priestly, 1996)
- Who owns the research (Priestly, 1997; Shakespeare, 1997)
- How to go about "taking the lead from disabled people" and how to maximize their involvement in research and researcher accountability to disabled people (Beazley, Moore, & Benzie, 1997)

Each of these practical difficulties has implications for doing not only ethical disability research but ethical social research generally. These difficulties and their ethical implications are discussed below before a consideration of the transformative paradigm, as developed by Mertens (2003, 2005, 2007), for doing ethical disability research. But before that, Tom Shakespeare's contribution to *Doing Disability Research* throws into sharp relief some of the difficulties associated with the emancipatory research paradigm as developed by Oliver (1992) and Zarb (1992).

In reflecting on *The Sexual Politics of Disability: Untold Desires* (Shakespeare, Gillespie-Sells, & Davies, 1996), which he coresearched and cowrote with two others, Shakespeare (1997) was adamant that the authors retained choice and control over the process, not the research subjects. In their defense, the three identify as disabled people and only one as an academic. Their reasons for researching and writing the book lay somewhere in between personal ambition and political commitment (p. 178). They used a variety of methods to collect the data and had a commitment to the individuals involved rather than the social scientific community or a particular methodology. Personal accounts were included in the book not only to give the participants the chance to speak for themselves but also to meet the target length, which the publisher had set. Shakespeare (1997) doesn't "really care" if the research is emancipatory or not. He would "rather follow my own intellectual and ethical standards, rather than trying to conform to an orthodoxy" (p. 185). But he believes that the research does adhere to the social model of disability, which underpins the emancipatory research paradigm. And while participants exercised a degree of control insofar as many wrote their own accounts and their priorities influenced the format and scope of the final text, Shakespeare was not prepared to let others control what he wrote or dictate the appropriate stance to take. While the authors were broadly accountable to their research participants, Shakespeare would not want to be accountable to anyone other than his publisher or his conscience.

So blindly adhering to some methodological orthodoxy is more dodgy ethically for Shakespeare (1997) than remaining "faithful to the participants, by which we meant basic ethical commitments not to misrepresent, betray confidentiality, or distort" (p. 182). He went on to reject Oliver's assertion that disability research is only justifiable if it has as its goals policy interventions to improve the lives of disabled people or social analysis for political goals. Shakespeare argued that different forms of social research may be more or less applied or pure and more or less applied to the needs of particular groups within the disability movement. Hence, "we need to have a range of models for the connection between [disability] theory and practice" (p. 187).

In making this statement, Shakespeare reflects the position many of the contributors to *Doing Disability Research* (Barnes & Mercer, 1997) found themselves in when trying to deploy the emancipatory paradigm in the field in its purest sense. All found that they had to make some compromises to complete their research. But these compromises did not mean the abandonment of ethical disability research; rather, it meant that researchers were guided by the spirit of the emancipatory paradigm rather than straitjacketed by its law. All justified these compromises by insisting that the theoretical and practical motivation for their research was the social model of disability and, therefore, ethical. It is interesting to note the change in emphasis in the latest edited collection from Barnes and Mercer (2004) on disability research. Here, the emphasis is on implementing the social model in disability research rather than doing emancipatory research per se (only one of the 13 titles mentions emancipatory disability research).

So in keeping with Shakespeare's assertion that we need a variety of models for disability research and the apparent "softening" of the emancipatory research paradigm, are there any other paradigms, which promote ethical disability research in terms of the way it positions people with disability? Yes, there is one: the transformative paradigm.

◆ The Transformative Paradigm for Social Research

The transformative paradigm forms an umbrella for a group of researchers who were concerned with issues of pluralism and social justice and were dissatisfied with the interpretive paradigm in which a relatively small but powerful group of "expert" constructivist researchers were working with relatively powerless research subjects (Mertens, 2005). This group contained critical theorists, participatory action researchers, racial and ethnic minorities, feminists, Marxists, and persons with disability (Mertens, 2005). While the transformative paradigm shares a lot with the emancipatory paradigm insofar as they both seek the emancipation of their research subjects, they part company on a number of points.

First, the transformative paradigm recognizes that there are many points of difference (gender, ethnicity, class, disability, sexual orientation, age, etc.) that are used to facilitate or refuse access to resources and rights. Hence, transformative disability research seems to be more explicitly geared than emancipatory research toward uncovering how class, gender, ethnicity, age, and other demographic characteristics intersect with disability to produce disadvantage. In this sense, transformative disability research seems to be more inclusive.

Second, emancipatory research assumes that research subjects are conscious of their situation and ready to take leadership in their struggle. Mertens (2007, p. 212), however, argued that transformative research is more than just a matter of handing leadership over to the research subjects; there is an element of the researcher being a "bit of a provocateur" who "recognizes inequalities and injustices," "possesses a shared sense of responsibility," and works humbly with the community to transform its situation.

Third, a far more systematic approach is provided within the transformative paradigm with its emphasis on the use of mixed methods for data collection. By using both quantitative and qualitative methods, the cultural complexity and diverse needs of disability community members can be accommodated.

Finally, there is the question of tone. The emancipatory paradigm is explicitly concerned with the social oppression of disabled people and, consequently, cannot help but generate a climate of "them" and "us." The transformative approach emphasizes social justice for minorities and a "together with" climate in which structures of power can be challenged to transform lives.

Hence, from a transformative-emancipatory perspective it is possible to review some of the practical difficulties that those working within the emancipatory paradigm encountered and the solutions they arrived at. While both difficulties and solutions have implications for carrying out ethical disability research, they also contain lessons for the practice of ethical social research generally.

♦ Ethical Disability Research and the Problem of Impairment

We have seen how disability studies was, and continues to be, based on the social model that separates impairment and disability and concentrates on the commonalities of the disability experience. In turn, this has engendered a sense of homogeneity across the disability community and a one-size-fits-all orthodoxy to disability research, namely the emancipatory paradigm. In practice this has proved to be problematic when taking the reality of impairment into account, especially when researching learning disability, deafness, and psychiatric system survivors.

LEARNING DISABILITY

John Swain (1998) reflected on the changing political and social context of people with learning disabilities as they shift from large institutions to community care. He noted the importance of research to inform policy makers on the success or otherwise of this shift and whether it could be done better. In this context, it is important to listen to people with learning difficulties on what they have to say about living in the community, their social networks, relationships, risk taking, and instances of abuse, especially sexual abuse. Swain used this paper to "highlight some of the impenetrable ethical dilemmas" (p. 4) that arose when researching the sexual abuse of people with learning difficulties. These include the following:

1. "Don't people have a right to unexamined lives?" Should one undertake this research or not?

2. *Respect:* This involves the issues of communication and control of the process; the use of open-ended questions, which assumes the collection of data to be constructed through the interviewer and interviewee (p. 16) when the latter may lack the intellectual sophistication; the possibility of unintended deception (p. 17); ownership and control of the data on private concerns, especially in publication.

3. *Informed consent:* This involves the issues of capacity to be informed and to consent; for example, open-ended questions may follow lines neither the researcher nor research subjects expect (p. 20); the notion of "informing" is simplistic because

explaining is an interactive process involving "a sharing of understandings or agendas" (p. 22); given that researchers exert overt and covert pressures on research subjects knowingly and unknowingly, the overarching problem is if consent is given voluntarily or not[5] (p. 22).

4. *Privacy:* This involves the fact that confidentiality can be ensured but not anonymity—the more the biographical information released, the greater the possibility of recognition.

5. *Safety:* This involves consideration that remembering events may cause distress and a counseling relationship may develop on which the research subject becomes dependent.

6. *Exploitation:* This involves what occurs when the concerns of the researcher predominate those of the research subjects; for example, the need to publish may open the data to less sympathetic secondary analysis.

Tim and Wendy Booth draw attention to several additional practical and ethical dilemmas involving communication that they encountered in their research on the children of parents with learning difficulties. These included inarticulateness, temporality, the reticence of young people, and poor recall (see Booth & Booth, 1997, pp. 136–139). In this situation, the ethical imperative on the part of the researcher is to include their stories in the research so that they are not further disempowered and violated by being made invisible. This means that the researcher must work harder to get participants' stories and to develop methods of reporting to include them in the research findings.

DEAF RESEARCH

A section of the deaf community here in Aotearoa New Zealand do not identify as disabled but as Deaf people, as members of a linguistic minority. Deaf from birth, they are fluent in New Zealand Sign Language and enjoy a flourishing Deaf culture. Others who chose not to belong to Deaf culture are categorized as hearing impaired, may be profoundly deaf or hard of hearing, may have become deaf later in life, do not sign but use a combination of lip reading and oral communication, and identify as deaf and disabled (Knowlton, 2006). Ethical research with Deaf and deaf people requires a prior understanding of this diverse and politically complex community as well as having an interpreter on hand to facilitate communication.

PSYCHIATRIC SYSTEM SURVIVORS

Ethical research of psychiatric system survivors is also fraught within the emancipatory paradigm primarily because the survivors' movement has, according to Beresford and Wallcraft (1997), developed independently of the disabled persons' movement and does not wholly subscribe to the social model of disability. Traditional research on survivors has been highly medicalized, involved a lot of drug company research, and, consequently, objectified and pathologized mental health service users. In response, the survivors' movement developed "user-led" rather than emancipatory research, which focused on

- the concept of "crisis" or distress rather than mental illness;
- social or spiritual models of understanding distress rather than medical ones;
- hearing voices and other devalued perceptions being seen as having a number of possible explanations rather than as manifestations of psychotic illness;
- psychiatric treatments sometimes described as abuse or torture rather than medical treatment; and

- medical and psychiatric concepts and labels often regarded as damaging, stigmatizing, unhelpful, or inappropriate (Beresford & Wallcraft, 1997, pp. 78–80).

♦ Who Controls?

The question of who controls disability research is central to the emancipatory paradigm, in which researchers are expected to hand total control of the process to their disabled research subjects. This has proved a sticking point for researchers (see Beazley et al., 1997; Priestly, 1997; Shakespeare, 1997), given that (1) the material relations (requirements of funding bodies, etc.) militate against handing complete control of the process over to participants; (2) it has the potential to seriously jeopardize researchers' personal and academic integrity (e.g., successfully completing that master's or Ph.D.); and (3) sometimes, it is not possible to determine which group of disabled people to hand control to (Stone, 1997; Stone & Priestly, 1996).

Not all agree with Oliver's (1992, 1997, 1999) and Zarb's (1992) rejection of participatory research as parasitic and oppressive to disabled people. Indeed, Stone and Priestly (1996) argued that their theoretical and political commitment to the social model involves transferring "a degree of control to disabled people" and that this does not run counter to the goals of emancipatory research (p. 711). As noted earlier, the conclusions of researchers at the 1996 Leeds Seminar (Barnes & Mercer, 1997) seem to be providing a backdoor entry for participatory research into the emancipatory paradigm. No such problem exists in the transformative paradigm, which provides an umbrella for a variety of methods, including participatory research.

Participatory research involves collaboration with participants to varying degrees in refining the research question, selecting participants, formulating questions, providing focus groups for analysis of data, writing up results, dissemination of results, and action based on results. Cocks and Cockram (1995) suggested that Oliver and Zarb have underestimated the potential for the collective action of participatory action research to empower oppressed groups. Other variants of participatory research, such as "collaborative learning," are also potentially empowering as lay and academic concepts and theories are integrated to provide a collective view of the world (Mercer, 2004).

Collaborative, participatory research seems entirely ethical and appropriate when it comes to undertaking research with people with severe learning difficulties. Here, the reality is that only "a degree of control" will ever be transferred to these research subjects, given the nature of their impairment. Few have access to the written word, and as we have seen, many struggle with the spoken word as well. This means that people with learning difficulties will require support to conduct meaningful research, which in turn places a huge ethical responsibility on their collaborator researchers to maintain the integrity of what they have to say, to faithfully communicate their experiences in an acceptable way to the research community, and to not assume a dominant role in the research process if it is to be truly participatory (Chappell, 2000) and ethical.

When compared with the research based on the normalization principle in the 1970s and 1980s (see Chappell, 1992, 2000), the emancipatory outcomes of participatory research for people with learning difficulties become obvious. In the former, research was for an audience of service providers and planners and focused overwhelmingly on services with normalization as the yardstick against which quality issues were measured. In participatory research, people with learning difficulties have acted as research advisors, interviewers, and life historians (Goodley, 2000; Goodley & Moore, 2000; Johnson & Traustadottir, 2005; Knox, Mok, & Parmenter, 2000; Ward & Simons, 1998) and, in so doing, have come to be seen as reliable informants and the "best authority on their own lives, experiences, feelings and views" (Stalker, 1998, cited in Mercer, 2004, p. 126). These are clearly emancipatory gains for people with learning disabilities as a result of participatory and collaborative research with them.

◆ Who Benefits and Who Should Do Disability Research?

Oliver's (1999) renunciation of disability research because he has been the main beneficiary, gives pause for thought. If investigatory social research is as exploitative and parasitic as he asserts, where does it leave us as disability researchers, let alone ethical disability researchers? Well first, along with Shakespeare (1997), I reject Oliver's assertion that his research has not been emancipatory for disabled people. Certainly he has benefited personally and professionally but so, too, have the thousands of disabled people who have read his work and had their consciousness altered as a result to become proud of whom they are and enabled to become forceful activists for disability rights and to campaign for a better deal for all disabled people.

A similar question arose out of identity politics and asked whether only disabled researchers can do emancipatory, ethical disability research. The argument was that just as white males benefit from the racist and patriarchal society, able people benefit from ablist and disabling society, so they are part of the problem. This argument is countered by the recognition that both disabled and nondisabled researchers are equally capable of undertaking unethical and exploitative research. From my perspective this renders being impaired as neither necessary nor sufficient for conducting ethical disability research.

I think that the questions of who benefits and who should do disability research are red herrings when it comes to doing ethical disability research. What is important is researchers having a commitment to research informed by the social model of disability: they are committed to advancing the aims of the disability movement, use nonexploitative methods, are academically rigorous, and widely disseminate findings in accessible forms for use in the struggle against oppression (Stone & Priestly, 1996, p. 715).

◆ Invisibility

A major concern of disabled people has been their invisibility in social research generally. For example, see Morris's (1992) mention of the invisibility of disabled women in earlier feminist writing. I feel particularly "dissed" when the variables for age, ethnicity, and gender are included but not disability. Research shows that 1 in 5 (20%) has a disability for six months or longer here in Aotearoa New Zealand and that similar figures obtain in the United Kingdom and the United States. One could argue that for social researchers not to plan for disability in their research means that their findings are always partial and always skewed and that the ethical basis of their work is questionable at the very least.

◆ Some Conclusions

This chapter has considered the ethics of disability research via a review of debates within the disability rights movement and disability studies on the how, what, and why of disability research. The social model of disability, which separates impairment (biological aspects) from disability (oppressive social response to impairment), provided the foreground for these debates. Positivist/postpositivist research is deemed oppressive and unethical because it locates disability in individuals and positions disabled people as data objects (the disabled) to be known, manipulated, and exploited for scientific and personal advance. The interpretive/constructivist paradigm is an advance, but it still leaves powerful "experts" in control to interpret what disabled people are saying and then say it for them. The emancipatory paradigm, as developed by disabled academics (and owing a lot to feminism), adheres to the social model and proposes to hand complete control of the research process to disabled people themselves. The practical difficulties that emerged in the field around issues of control do not arise in the transformative paradigm of research, however. Disability research in the transformative paradigm would cleave to the social model and be aimed at the positive transformation of disabled peoples' lives but would not be bound to hand complete control of the process to the research subjects. The current state of the debate is that the social model of disability provides the ontological and epistemological basis for ethical disability research.

The prime lesson that social researchers can learn from the debate disability scholars have had about what constitutes ethical disability research is to think carefully about the way in which their research subjects are positioned within their research. And, as Oliver (1999) reminds us, it is in our labors that we not only produce social and material goods but that we also produce ourselves. There is an added dimension for social researchers and that is that we are actually producing those we research. This places a huge burden of responsibility on us to do this in a manner that enhances our humanity and that makes us collectively and individually more fully human.

◆ Notes

1. See Braddock and Parish (2001) for a good starting point to an institutional history of disability in Western society from antiquity to the 21st century.

2. Learning difficulties, learning disability, and intellectual disability will be used interchangeably in this text as opposed to the oppressive category *mental retardation*.

3. The social model itself is more closely associated with the work of Mike Oliver (1990a, 1990b), Vic Finkelstein (1976, 1980), and Colin Barnes (1990, 1996).

4. Throughout the 1980s and 1990s, materialist variants of the social model were in the ascendancy in disability studies in the United Kingdom, but more latterly, with the growing influence of postmodernism and post-structuralism, accounts of disability as an embodied experience have become more common.

5. I would argue that these concerns apply equally in the majority of cases where informed consent is sought.

◆ References

Anspach, R. R. (1979). From stigma to identity politics. *Social Science and Medicine, 134*, 755–763.

Barnes, C. (1990). *Cabbage syndrome: The social construction of dependency*. London: Falmer Press.

Barnes, C. (1996, August). The social model of disability: Myths and misconceptions. *Coalition*, pp. 27–33. Retrieved January 8, 2007, from www.leeds.ac.uk/disability-studies/archiveuk/Barnes/Coaliton.pdf

Barnes, C., & Mercer, G. (Eds.). (1997). *Doing disability research*. Leeds, UK: The Disability Press.

Barnes, C., & Mercer, G. (Eds.). (2004). *Implementing the social model of disability: Theory and research*. Leeds, UK: The Disability Press.

Beazley, S., Moore, M., & Benzie, D. (1997). Involving disabled people in research: A study of inclusion in environmental activities. In C. Barnes & G. Mercer (Eds.), *Doing disability research* (pp. 142–157). Leeds, UK: The Disability Press.

Beresford, P., & Wallcraft, J. (1997). Psychiatric system survivors and emancipatory research: Issues, overlaps and differences. In C. Barnes & G. Mercer (Eds.), *Doing disability research* (pp. 66–87). Leeds, UK: The Disability Press.

Booth, T., & Booth, W. (1997). Making connections: A narrative study of adult children of parents with learning difficulties. In C. Barnes & G. Mercer (Eds.), *Doing disability research* (pp. 123–140). Leeds, UK: The Disability Press.

Bowe, F. (1978). *Handicapping America*. New York: Harper and Row.

Braddock, D. L., & Parish, S. L. (2001). An institutional history of disability. In G. L. Albrecht, K. D. Seelman, & M. Bury (Eds.), *Handbook of disability studies* (pp. 11–68). Thousand Oaks, CA: Sage.

Campbell, J., & Oliver, M. (1996). *Disability politics: Understanding our past, changing our future*. London: Routledge.

Chappell, A. (1992). Towards a sociological critique of the normalisation principle. *Disability, Handicap & Society, 7*(1), 35–51.

Chappell, A. (2000). Emergence of participatory methodology in learning difficulty research: Understanding the context. *British Journal of Learning Disabilities, 28*, 28–43.

Cocks, E., & Cockram, J. (1995). The participatory research paradigm and intellectual disability. *Mental Handicap Research, 8*, 25–37.

Crow, L. (1996). Including all our lives: Renewing the social model of disability. In C. Barnes & G. Mercer (Eds.), *Exploring the divide: Illness and disability* (pp. 55–72). Leeds, UK: The Disability Press.

deJong, G. (1979). Independent living: From social movement to analytic paradigm. *Archives of Physical Medicine and Rehabilitation, 60*, 435–446.

Finkelstein, V. (1976). Comments on the discussion between the Union and Disability Alliance on 22 November 1975. In *Fundamental principles of disability*. London: UPAIS. Retrieved January 8, 2007, from www.leeds.ac.uk/disability-studies/archiveuk/finkelstein/UPIAS%20Principles%202.pdf

Finkelstein, V. (1980). *Attitudes and disabled people*. New York: World Rehabilitation Fund.

Goodley, D. (2000). *Self-advocacy in the lives of people with learning difficulties*. Buckingham, UK: Open University Press.

Goodley, D., & Moore, M. (2000). Doing disability research: Activist lives and the academy. *Disability & Society, 15*(6), 861–882.

Hahn, H. (1985). Towards a politics of disability: Definitions, disciplines and policies. *Social Science Journal, 22*(4), 87–105.

Hunt, P. (1981, May). Settling accounts with the parasite people. *Disability Challenge, 1*, 37–50.

Johnson, K., & Traustadottir, R. (2005). *Deinstitutionalization and people with intellectual disabilities: In and out of institutions*. London: Jessica Kingsley.

Keith, L. (1992). Who cares wins? Women, caring and disability. *Disability, Handicap and Society, 7*(2), 167–175.

Knowlton, M. (2006). *The Deaf way: Exploring key attributes of support workers in the Deaf community*. Unpublished MSW (Applied) social work research report. School of Sociology, Social Policy and Social Work, Massey University, Palmerston, North New Zealand.

Knox, M., Mok, M., & Parmenter, T. R. (2000). Working with the experts: Collaborative research with people with an intellectual disability. *Disability & Society, 15*(1), 49–61.

Lunt, N., & Thornton, P. (1997). Researching disability employment policies. In C. Barnes & G. Mercer (Eds.), *Doing disability research* (pp. 108–122). Leeds, UK: The Disability Press.

Mercer, G. (2004). From critique to practice: Emancipatory disability research (pp. 118–137). In C. Barnes & G. Mercer (Eds.), *Implementing the social model of disability: Theory and research*. Leeds, UK: The Disability Press.

Mertens, D. M. (2003). Mixed methods and the politics of human research: The transformative-emancipatory perspective. In A. Tashakkori & C. Teddlie (Eds.), *Handbook of mixed methods in social and behavioral research* (pp. 135–164). Thousand Oaks, CA: Sage.

Mertens, D. M. (2005). *Research and evaluation in education and psychology* (2nd ed.). Thousand Oaks, CA: Sage.

Mertens, D. M. (2007). Transformative paradigm: Mixed methods and social justice.

Journal of Mixed Methods Research, 1(3), 212–225.

Morris, J. (1989). *Able lives: Women's experience of paralysis.* London: The Women's Press.

Morris, J. (1992). Personal and political: A feminist perspective on researching disability. *Disability, Handicap & Society, 7*(2), 157–166.

Nirje, B. (1969). The normalization principle and its human management implications. In R. Kugel & W. Wolfensberger (Eds.), *Changing patterns in residential services for the mentally retarded* (pp. 179–195). Washington, DC: President's Committee on Mental Retardation.

Oliver, M. (1990a, July). *The individual and social models of disability.* Paper presented at the Joint Workshop of the Living Options Group and the Research Unit of the Royal College of Physicians on People with Established Locomotor Disabilities in Hospitals. Retrieved January 8, 2007, from www.leeds.ac.uk/disability-studies/archiveuk/Oliver/in%20soc%20dis.pdf

Oliver, M. (1990b). *The politics of disablement.* Basingstoke, UK: Macmillan.

Oliver, M. (1992). Changing the social relations of research production? *Disability, Handicap & Society, 7*(2), 101–114.

Oliver, M. (1997). Emancipatory research: Realistic goal or impossible dream? In C. Barnes & G. Mercer (Eds.), *Doing disability research* (pp. 15–31). Leeds, UK: The Disability Press.

Oliver, M. (1999). Final accounts and the parasite people. In M. Corker & S. French (Eds.), *Disability discourse.* Buckingham, UK: Open University Press.

Priestley, M. (1997). Who's research? A personal audit. In C. Barnes & G. Mercer (Eds.), *Doing disability research* (pp. 88–107). Leeds, UK: The Disability Press.

Shakespeare, T. (1997). Researching disabled sexuality. In C. Barnes & G. Mercer (Eds.), *Doing disability research* (pp. 177–189). Leeds, UK: The Disability Press.

Shakespeare, T. (2006). *Disability rights and wrongs.* London: Routledge.

Shakespeare, T., Gillespie-Sells, K., & Davies, D. (1996). *The sexual politics of disability: Untold desires.* London: Cassell.

Shoultz, B. (1997). *The self-advocacy movement.* Retrieved January 8, 2007, from http://soeweb.syr.edu/thechp/selfadvm.htm

Stone, E. (1997). From the research notes of a foreign devil: Disability research in China. In C. Barnes & G. Mercer (Eds.), *Doing disability research* (pp. 207–227). Leeds, UK: The Disability Press.

Stone, E., & Priestly, M. (1996). Parasites, pawns and partners: Disability research and the role of non-disabled researchers. *British Journal of Sociology, 47*(4), 699–716.

Swain, J. (1998). *Public research, private concerns: Research into the lives of people with learning difficulties.* Retrieved April 7, 2007, from www.leeds.ac.uk/disability-studies/archiveuk/swain/REsearch%20ethics.pdf

Union of the Physically Impaired Against Segregation. (1976). *Fundamental principles of disability.* London: Author.

Ward, L., & Simons, K. (1998). Practing partnership: Involving people with learning difficulties in research. *British Journal of Learning Disabilities, 26*(4), 128–131.

Wolfensberger, W. (1972). *Principles of normalization in human services.* Toronto, Ontario, Canada: National Institute on Mental Retardation.

Zarb, G. (1992). On the road to Damascus: First steps towards changing the relations of disability research production. *Disability, Handicap & Society, 7*(2), 125–138.

Zarb, G. (1997). Researching disabling barriers. In C. Barnes & G. Mercer (Eds.), *Doing disability research* (pp. 49–66). Leeds, UK: The Disability Press.

6

TRANSFORMATIVE RESEARCH AND ETHICS

◆ Donna M. Mertens, Heidi M. Holmes, and Raychelle L. Harris

What are the ethical implications of pouring millions of dollars into research and producing volumes of articles on critical social problems such as HIV/AIDS or literacy if the epidemics of disease and illiteracy are escalating? Chilisa (2005) suggested that ongoing research that fails to address the problem effectively from the researched's frame of reference perpetuates conditions that violate human rights and impedes progress toward social justice. Hence, pathways to strengthening the ethical character of research include funding, conducting, disseminating, and using research based on philosophical positions that create space for knowledge systems that recognize "local language and thought forms as an important source of making meanings of what we research . . . Given the HIV/AIDS epidemic in Sub-Saharan Africa, the need for diversity in research epistemologies has become not a luxury of nationalism of the African Renaissance, but rather an issue of life and death" (p. 678).

The intransigence of social problems and the need to examine critically the philosophical assumptions that undergird the ethics of research do not arise only in developing countries. Witness the difficulties in the United States with regard to provision of educational, psychological, and social services to the poor and people with disabilities or those who are from racial or ethnic minority groups. How is it that blacks in the

United States are more than four times as likely as whites to be diagnosed with schizophrenia? Blow et al. (2004) suggested that diagnostic measures developed primarily with white patients in mind do not automatically apply to other groups. How is it that males, especially those from minority ethnic and racial groups, are diagnosed as having disabilities in much greater numbers by a ratio of about 2 males for every 1 female (U.S. Department of Education, 2004)? Yet, at the same time, girls from all ethnic groups may be underidentified as having certain disabilities because the indicators are manifested differently for females and for males. Therefore, girls with undiagnosed disabilities are not receiving the supportive services necessary to succeed in school and life (Mertens, Wilson, & Mounty, 2007), while minority children with disabilities all too often experience inadequate services, low-quality curriculum and instruction, and unnecessary isolation from their nondisabled peers (Losen & Orfield, 2002).

Another example of discrimination and oppression in the United States was made visible through the differential aftermath of the devastation caused by Hurricane Katrina, which pounded the Gulf Coast states in August 2005. Elliott and Pais (2006) conducted a survey of over 1,200 hurricane survivors to examine the influence of race and socioeconomic class on evacuation timing, emotional support, housing, employment, and plans to return to their pre-storm communities.

> Results reveal strong racial and class differences, indicating that neither of those dimensions can be reduced to the other when seeking to understand responses by survivors themselves. This intersection renders low-income black home owners from New Orleans those most in need of targeted assistance as residents work to put themselves and the region back together. (p. 295)

This introductory commentary brings to the surface the need to examine critically the basic beliefs that researchers bring with them to guide their decisions about what variables are important to consider and how and from whom the data are to be collected in an ethical manner. In the context of educational, social, and psychological programs, many of the people the programs are intended to serve are the ones who have been pushed to the margins on the basis of race/ethnicity, language, indigenous/immigrant status, education level, disability, age, religion, socioeconomic status, and other contextually dependent variables. Issues of discrimination and oppression are commonly associated with those characteristics that are connected with the focus of such programs and policies. For researchers who are aware of the historical and political factors that surround program participants, the need to consider power issues associated with greater privilege in society is apparent.

In this context, where intransigent social, educational, health, economic, civil, and environmental conditions result in violations of human rights on a daily basis, the ethical conduct of research demands attention to a full array of complexity. The use of a lens of transformation provides researchers with the means to address explicitly issues of human rights and social justice. To that end, this chapter elucidates the transformative paradigm with its accompanying philosophical assumptions as a way of examining the underlying beliefs that define the role of the researcher as one of working in partnership for social change and challenging the status quo.

The transformative paradigm (Mertens, 2005, 2007, 2009) is a framework of belief systems that directly engages members of culturally diverse groups with a focus on increased social justice. Being firmly rooted in a human rights agenda, the ethical implications of research are derived from the conscious inclusion of a broad range of people who are generally excluded from the mainstream in society. Such research strives to extend the meaning of traditional ethical concepts to reflect more directly ethical considerations in culturally complex communities. Power issues in terms of determining research focus, planning, implementation, and use are also examined from a transformative stance based on axiological assumptions related to respect for communities that are pushed to the margins and recognition of the resilience that rests within community members.

To be quite blunt, the usefulness of research as a means to social transformation is not a universally agreed on concept. Gustavsen (2006) questioned the potential role of research for social transformation: "If we really want to become involved in socially significant practical action with demands for long time horizons, for relating to numerous actors and engaging in highly complex activities, perhaps the notion of linking such involvement to research as traditionally conceived is futile" (p. 25). He concluded that an unsettling of the status quo of research is needed; that is, research needs to be transformed to engage in a purer form of democracy that will support the development of social relationships that embody a principle of equality for all participants.

One of the major principles underlying transformative approaches to research is the belief in an often overlooked strength in communities that are rising to the challenge of addressing seemingly intransigent problems. When theoretical perspectives such as resilience theory, positive psychology, feminist theory, and critical race theory are used to frame a study, then a deliberate and conscious design can reveal the positive aspects, resilience, and acts of resistance needed for social change. Ludema, Cooperrider, and Barrett (2001) argued that research and evaluation have largely failed as instruments for advancing social-organizational transformation because they maintain a problem-oriented view rather than focusing on the strengths of a community. Historically, research and evaluation have had a deficit-based orientation, such that the "problem" was derived from deficits found in the people whom the program was designed to help. They proposed turning away from such a deficit-based view and looking instead at what is positive. The basis for social change is seen as emanating from an unconditional positive question that reaffirms the life-giving and life-sustaining aspects of organizational existence. Important exceptions to deficit-based programs and research provide examples of resilience-based strategies, such as the Communities that Care System (Hawkins & Catalano, 2003; Chapter 22, this volume).

◆ Transformative Paradigm

A paradigm is a set of metaphysical constructs associated with specific philosophical assumptions (basic beliefs) that describe a person's worldview and serves to guide the organized study of that world (Denzin & Lincoln, 2005). Bawden (2006) asserted that evaluators (and social researchers, by implication) have a responsibility to critically examine their worldviews because they influence choices, either consciously or unconsciously. He commented,

> If indeed, as Stufflebeam (2001) argues, any evaluation is a study that is designed and conducted to assist some audience to assess an object's merit and worth, then explicit attention must be paid to foundational assumptions about the nature of worth and value, and to how these can come to be known in any given contextual situation, if it is to be an ethically defensible practice. (p. 38)

There are four basic belief systems that are relevant to defining a paradigm in a research context, with assumptions associated with each belief system:

1. *Axiology:* Assumption about the nature of ethical behavior

2. *Ontology:* Assumption about the nature of reality

3. *Epistemology:* Assumption about the nature of knowledge and who can know what by what means

4. *Methodology:* Assumption about appropriate approaches to systematic inquiry

The axiological assumption asks, What is considered ethical or moral behavior? In transformative terms, the question is asked, How can research contribute to social justice and the furtherance of human rights? Ontologically speaking, how do we know what is real? In this chapter, this question is not asked about physical objects, such as a desk in a room, but rather about a determination of the reality associated with socially constructed concepts, such as literacy or health. The transformative ontological question asks, Whose reality is privileged in this context, and what is the mechanism for challenging perceived realities that sustain an oppressive system? The epistemological question asks, What is the nature of knowing, and what is the method for knowing the nature of reality and the means for generation of knowledge (Fonow & Cook, 2005)? It brings up questions about who can know what and how the knower relates to what would be known. If I am to genuinely know the reality of something, how do I need to relate to the people from whom I am collecting data? The knower is the researcher, and the would-be-known is the participant in the study. Should I be close to the participants so that I can really understand their experiences, or should I maintain a distance between myself and the participants so that I can be "neutral"? This question raises concerns about the definition of objectivity as it is operationalized in a research context. Methodologically, choices go beyond quantitative, qualitative, or mixed methods to how to collect data about the reality of a concept in such a way that one feels confident that one has indeed captured that reality and done so in an ethical manner.

♦ Axiological Assumption

The transformative paradigm places priority on the axiological assumption as a guiding force for conceptualizing subsequent beliefs and research decisions. Hence, this assumption is examined from a number of different perspectives. A historical and contemporary view of social justice is defined in terms of distributive justice. Theories of ethics are identified that are commensurate with the transformative paradigm. Declarations of human rights provide insights into the meaning of social justice. Codes of ethics are evolving in professional associations and from indigenous peoples that are compatible with the transformative paradigm's axiological assumption. And the implications of regulatory concepts of ethics are examined from the transformative perspective.

DISTRIBUTIVE JUSTICE

Aristotle's concept of social justice as distributive justice includes the idea that justice is achieved through the equitable allocation and distribution of benefits (Reisch, 2002). In contrast to contemporary views of distributive justice, Aristotle applied his principle of equity in terms of sharing resources only within the hierarchical social stratum of the time, such that only men of property in Athens would come under the distributive justice principle. Political and social revolutions in the late 18th century linked justice to equality and human rights. However, continued oppression by the rich and powerful throughout history indicates that the idealized notion of equality and human rights for all is not a reality.

Rawls (2001) raised the issue of the need to establish an imperative to act for the furtherance of social justice, which was, up to that time, missing in others' discussions of the topic. He asserted in his maximin theory that every person has an equal right to personal liberty and that social and economic equality demands that the need of the least advantaged be given priority and the principle of equal opportunity be applied to all available positions.

In contemporary writings about social justice, the attainment of social justice is linked with the goals of social diversity and "with challenges to the normative power structure and the oppression it produces" (Hyde, 1998, cited in Reisch, 2002, p. 348). Reisch noted that a social justice approach may involve unequal distribution of resources. However, unequal distribution of resources would be justified only if such inequalities served to advance the least advantaged groups in the community (Franklin, 1998; Isbister, 2001). The pursuit of social justice by researchers requires acknowledgment of the political dimensions of research contexts and working cooperatively with community members to clarify goals. Although Reisch (2002) was writing about social justice in the context of social work, his comments have applicability to understanding the meaning of social justice in a transformative research context as well:

> A social justice perspective also contains the imperative of challenging prevailing assumptions about power, privilege, and various forms of oppression in the theories that underlie current policies, programs and methods.... This requires us to advocate for the elimination of those policies that diminish people's sense of control over their lives... Simultaneously, we need to work for the expansion of those programs that enable people to exercise personal freedom by... making them feel like integral and valued parts of society. These goals reflect a potential synthesis of the historic division between individual and collective well-being at the heart of debates over social justice and may provide the basis for its attainment in an increasingly diverse and conflict-ridden world. (p. 351)

THEORIES OF ETHICS

Simons (2006) identified rights-based and social justice theories of ethics that are commensurate with the transformative axiological assumptions. Rights-based theories justify their actions on the basis that every person must be treated with dignity and respect and that the avoidance of harm must be the primary principle. The social justice theory of ethics takes the rights-based theory to a group or societal level (House, 1993), leading to an awareness of the need to redress inequalities by giving precedence, or at least equal weight, to the voices of the least advantaged groups in society. The implicit goals of inclusion of those who have been denied access to power are an accurate representation of their viewpoints, as well as support for the less advantaged in terms of their being able to take the role of an active agent in social change.

HUMAN RIGHTS DECLARATIONS

The transformative paradigm is firmly rooted in a human rights agenda much as it is articulated in the United Nations (UN) Universal Declaration of Human Rights (1948). Although the declarations of the UN are situated in a multilateral context, they provide guidance in understanding a basis for transformative work nationally as well as internationally. Human rights is a globally relevant issue; "developed" countries are not exempt from violations of human rights.

The UN's declaration is based on the recognition of the inherent dignity and of the equal and inalienable rights of all members of the human family, including the rights to life, liberty, security of the person, equal protection under the law, freedom of movement, marriage with the free and full consent of the intending spouses, ownership of property, freedom of thought and religion, freedom of opinion and expression, peaceful assembly, participation in governance, work in just and favorable working conditions, and education. Importantly for this text, Article 25 reads,

> Everyone has the right to a standard of living adequate for the health and well-being of himself [sic] and of his [sic] family, including food, clothing, housing and medical care and necessary social

services, and the right to security in the event of unemployment, sickness, disability, widowhood, old age or other lack of livelihood in circumstances beyond his [sic] control. (UN, 1998)

The UN Universal Declaration contains language indicating that everyone is entitled to these rights, without distinction of any kind, such as race, color, sex, language, religion, political or other opinion, national or social origin, property, birth, or other status. However, the UN recognized that the Universal Declaration did not result in enjoyment of the rights contained therein for all people. They noted that specific attention would need to be given to groups that were not being afforded these rights based on race, disability, gender, age, political standing, or status in the workforce. Consequently, they approved the following:

- The International Convention on the Elimination of All Forms of Racial Discrimination in 1969, which affirms the necessity of eliminating racial discrimination throughout the world in all its forms and manifestations and of securing understanding of and respect for the dignity of the human person.

- The Declaration on the Rights of Disabled Persons (UN, 1975), which assures them the same fundamental rights as their fellow citizens, no matter what the origin, nature, and seriousness of their handicaps and disabilities. The UN subsequently developed and approved the Convention on the Rights of Persons With Disabilities in December 2006 (UN, 2006a).

- The Convention on the Elimination of All Forms of Discrimination Against Women (UN, 1979), which provides the basis for realizing equality between women and men through ensuring women's equal access to, and equal opportunities in, political and public life—including the right to vote and to stand for election—as well as education, health, and employment.

These were followed by the Convention on the Rights of the Child (UN, 1990a) and the International Convention on the Protection of the Rights of All Migrant Workers and Members of Their Families (UN, 1990b). After 20 years of debate, the UN finally approved the Declaration of the Rights of Indigenous Peoples (UN, 2006b). Subsequently, the UNICEF, with the endorsement of the International Organization for Cooperation in Evaluation and the International Development Evaluation Association, prepared a report based on a meeting of 85 evaluation organizations that maps the future priorities for evaluation in that context. This excerpt captures the emphasis on human rights:

> Within a human rights approach, evaluation should focus on the most vulnerable populations to determine whether public policies are designed to ensure that all people enjoy their rights as citizens, whether disparities are eliminated and equity enhanced, and whether democratic approaches have been adopted that include everyone in decision-making processes that affect their interests. (Segone, 2006, p. 12)

PROFESSIONAL AND INDIGENOUS CODES OF ETHICS

In addition to guidance on human rights issues from international bodies, codes of ethics from relevant professional associations and organizations provide guidance for researchers and evaluators as to what constitutes ethical practice (see Chapter 7, this volume). These codes of ethics have been critically reviewed and revised to reflect a greater concern for principles that are reflective of the axiological assumptions of the transformative paradigm. The American Evaluation Association (AEA) modified its guiding principles to include an explicit principle related to the role of cultural competency in ethical evaluation practice. The American Psychological Association (APA) revised its ethics code in 2002, strengthening protection of people in research that involves deception (Fisher, 2003). Ethics in psychology has also been extended by Brabeck's (2000) application of feminist principles in psychology (see also Chapter 3, by Brabeck & Brabeck, this volume).

Two subgroups of the APA[1] also developed multicultural ethical guidelines for research. The implications for research methods derived from the guidelines that are most relevant to the transformative paradigm read as follows:

> Related to the research question is choosing culturally appropriate theories and models on which to inform theory-driven inquiry... Psychological researchers are encouraged to be aware of and, if appropriate, to apply indigenous theories when conceptualizing research studies. They are encouraged to include members of cultural communities when conceptualizing research, with particular concern for the benefits of the research to the community. (APA, 2002, p. 3).

The Guidelines for Research in Ethnic Minority Communities contains the following description of the researcher's ethical responsibilities:

> As an agent of prosocial change, the culturally competent psychologist carries the responsibility of combating the damaging effects of racism, prejudice, bias, and oppression in all their forms, including all of the methods we use to understand the populations we serve... A consistent theme... relates to the interpretation and dissemination of research findings that are meaningful and relevant to each of the four populations[2] and that reflect an inherent understanding of the racial, cultural, and sociopolitical context within which they exist. (APA, 2000, p. 1)

Interestingly, the APA endorses the role of the psychologist as an agent of prosocial change; this is reflective of the axiological assumption of the transformative paradigm that ethical research is defined by its furtherance of social justice and human rights, all the while being cognizant of those characteristics associated with diverse populations that impede progress on these fronts.

Researcher guidelines are also available from indigenous communities that provide insights into the ethical grounding of research (see Cram, 2001; Chapter 20, this volume). Researchers from the Sign Language community[3] adapted the Māori Terms of Reference to their own specific context (Harris & Holmes, 2007; Harris, Holmes, & Mertens, in press). The complexity of the Deaf[4] community as a cultural and linguistic minority includes dimensions such as levels and type of hearing loss, parental hearing status, access to and ability to benefit from auditory enhancing technologies, language usage based on signs and/or voice, and use of visually accessible sign languages. Their ethical guidelines, Sign Language Communities Terms of Reference, are commensurate with the transformative paradigm. Representative guidelines of particular significance to Sign Language communities include the following:

- Research involving the Sign Language community has to be done "by Deaf, for Deaf and with Deaf."

- Instead of using spoken language and providing interpreters for Deaf members, research projects should mandate sign language as the primary language of research teams, interpreters should be provided for hearing people who do not know sign language, and bilingual publications in sign language and the majority language should be accepted and encouraged.

- There should be increased emphasis on confidentiality because of the compactness of the Sign Language community and because the visual nature of sign language requires documentation through video (as opposed to audiotapes or transcribed interviews), making it difficult to preserve anonymity.

REGULATORY CONCEPTS OF ETHICS

The transformative paradigm pushes the regulatory principles of respect, beneficence, and justice on several fronts. Respect is critically examined in terms of the cultural norms of interaction in diverse communities and across cultural groups. Consent is obtained with full awareness through appropriate culturally competent means. It includes self-awareness in relationship to community. (See Chapter 26, this volume, in which the author, Chilisa, explains the African ethical principle of *umbuntu*; Chilisa & Preece, 2005.) Beneficence is defined in terms of the promotion of human rights and increase in social justice. An explicit connection is made between the process and outcomes of research and furtherance of a social justice agenda.

COMMENSURATE THEORIES

The theoretical and axiological thinking of critical theorists, feminists, and other human rights advocates has much to offer in the consideration of ethical principles in research. The ethical principles underlying feminist, critical, postcolonial, and indigenous theories are commensurate with the axiological assumptions of the transformative paradigm (see Chapters 4, 9, 20, and 26, this volume).

♦ Ontological Assumption

The ontological assumption of the transformative paradigm holds that reality is socially constructed; however, it does so with a conscious awareness that certain individuals occupy a position of greater power and that individuals with other characteristics may be associated with a higher likelihood of exclusion from decisions about the definition of the research problem, questions, and other methodological aspects of the inquiry. Ontological assumptions rooted in positivist philosophy have been criticized by many groups who have been pushed to the margins in the scholarly decolonization literature. A critique from Native American communities notes that

> production of meaning from a Eurocentric perspective does not capture any "truth" of Native and tribal lives but also infiltrates Native lifeworlds in the form of "epistemic violence." (Spivak, 1988, p. 126, as cited in Duran & Duran, 2000, p. 96)

> Social scientists have been rewriting tribal canonical texts (i.e., ritual) via anthropology and other disciplines since first contact and therein have produced meaning that has changed and distorted tribal understandings or forced them underground. Clinical psychology as well as research-oriented psychology is extremely narrow-minded. The assumptions of these fields are based on a utilitarian worldview. . . . Western empirical research is based on the illusion of objectivity, with a transhistorical, transcultural orientation. It operates within an a priori essentialist Cartesian model of a unified, rational, autonomous subject, the construction of which is problematized in the work of French poststructuralism and German critical theory. (Duran & Duran, 2000, p. 96)

The ontological assumption asks the question, What is real? In a research context, researchers identify variables and measure aspects of those variables in an attempt to look for objective truth, what is real within some level of defined probability, or truth as defined within a complex cultural context. A transformative lens focuses the ontological question on an explicit acknowledgement that reality is socially constructed and that specific characteristics associated with more or less power determine which version of reality is accepted as "real." Power issues pervade the choice of variables and their definitions, determining what is "researchable." Power is implicit in decisions about which interpretation of reality is accepted. This point is illustrated in the power associated with explanations of the achievement gap between minority and majority students (e.g., based on either race or hearing status) in the United States.

O'Connor and Fernandez (2006) described the results of a National Research Council (NRC) report that explored the assumptions associated with the relationship between poverty and the overrepresentation of minority youth in special education. They provided a critique indicating that this explanation oversimplifies the concept of compromised development associated with being poor and underanalyzes the effect of culture and the organization of schools that situate minority youth as academically and behaviorally deficit, thus increasing the probability that they will be placed in special education. They noted that the NRC recognizes that children in high-poverty districts are exposed to a higher degree of teacher bias and have lower funding, which is necessary to reduce class size and attract qualified teachers. However, the NRC concludes that these variables contribute to the incidence of disability. O'Connell and Fernandez described a different reality based on the evidence:

> It is schools and not poverty that place minority students at heightened risk for special education placement. . . . [T]here is nothing about poverty in and of itself that places poor children at academic risk; it is a matter of how structures of opportunity and constraint come to bear on the educational chances of the poor to either expand or constrain their likelihood of achieving competitive, educational outcomes (O'Connor, 2002). Disproportionality, then, is the structured probability with which minority youth are more likely to be "documented" as disabled. (p. 10)

People who wrote the legislation in the United States about education for people with disabilities based national policy on a reality that assumes that D/deaf/hard-of-hearing students placed in mainstream settings are more successful at academics than those placed in a residential environment. Administrators and local school district board members encourage parents of D/deaf/hard-of-hearing children to place their children in mainstream settings under the assumption that these represent the least restrictive environment for them (Individuals With Disabilities Education Improvement Act, reauthorized 2004). However, Deaf and hard-of-hearing students in residential schools achieve as much as or more than those in mainstream environments (Marschark, Lang, & Albertini, 2002). The social abilities of Deaf and hard-of-hearing students in residential schools are higher than those of students at public schools because they have Deaf role models, full access to direct communication, and peer interaction. Nevertheless, most D/deaf students in mainstream settings are placed in self-contained classrooms with minimal social interaction with hearing peers and often little to no interaction with other deaf students. Some of them work 1:1 with a special education teacher who may not know anything about Deaf culture, sign language, or teaching D/deaf children.

Ladson-Billings (2006) made a similar argument in her explanation of the "achievement gap" when minority and disadvantaged students are compared with their white and privileged counterparts. She explained that a significant amount of research on poor, African American, Latina/o, American Indian, and Asian immigrant students has led to very few solutions. A long history of educational research gives privilege to the explanation that race/ethnicity and/or poverty is to blame for the lack of academic achievement. Should researchers explore the historic, economic, sociopolitical, and moral debt in the United States that results in poor opportunities for quality educational experiences for those pushed to the margins? What is required is a serious investigation of the costs of segregation and the costs of equitable funding and to use research and evaluation to understand that "a cumulative effect of poor education, poor housing, poor health care and poor government services create a bifurcated society that leaves more than its children behind" (Ladson-Billings, 2006, p. 10).

◆ Epistemological Assumption

The epistemology of the transformative research paradigm queries the nature of knowledge and who can know what about whom, leading to questions about the nature of the relationship between researcher and participant. Transformative epistemology is characterized by a close collaboration between researchers and participants of a study, whether they are community leaders or members of organizations. Communication is achieved by the use of participants' language of choice. The research purpose, design, implementation, and utilization are developed and implemented with appropriate cultural sensitivity and awareness. Researchers require collaboration with the host(s) of the community, not necessarily the leaders but people of the community. The relationship is interactive and empowering. It requires that trust be built through observance of appropriate cultural norms.

The epistemology of the postpositivist stance is reflected in the early work of Campbell, in which he envisioned an experimenting society that would lead to incremental reform as knowledge was gained through random assignment to alternative treatments (Campbell & Stanley, 1966). This approach included the notion that researchers should be value neutral to produce scientifically valid knowledge. Christians (2005) criticized this postpositivist notion that "a morally neutral, objective observer will get the facts right" (p. 148). He asserted that ethical behavior must be cognizant of the "power relations associated with gender, sexual orientation, class, ethnicity, race, and nationality" (p. 148).

The inherent danger of paradigms and the prevailing hegemonic discourse in the academic field prevents us from realizing that there are multiple truths. Not only that, false information can easily be perpetuated by those in power. For instance, in *Psychology of Deafness*, Myklebust (1964) claimed that D/deaf people were more immature; had increased emotional problems; were more naive and primitive; were inferior in physical coordination; exhibited marked retardation in language; were only able to complete concrete tasks; and were schizophrenic, maladjusted, belligerent, subhuman, isolated, paranoid, neurotic, suspicious, psychotic, dependent, and depressed. He also claimed that D/deaf males were effeminate and D/deaf females were masculine. At that time, Myklebust was a hearing researcher who did not meaningfully involve D/deaf people in his research. The majority of the research in the Deaf community is done by hearing people (Lane, 1999). Academic power is achieved through controlling academic discourse and by devaluing the discourses of the underrepresented, such as D/deaf people. Research in the field of D/deaf education typically focuses on the abilities D/deaf people lack rather than the abilities D/deaf people have. That in itself is oppressive (Erting, 1992; Evans, 2004; Lane, 1999). A "D/deaf-as-deficient" focus is a way for people in power to keep control of academic knowledge and maintain their positions of power.

What do we gain or lose in our struggle for ethical behavior by allowing the perspectives of feminists, critical theorists, postcolonialists, and others who are steeped in multivocal and cross-cultural representation to raise questions and proffer different bases of what is accepted as real in the ethical domain? What do we gain by having these conversations at the borders and intersections of ethics in research and evaluation?

In the transformative paradigm, the issues of understanding culture and building trust are paramount. There are complications associated with this assumption. For example, suppose a researcher is studying people who do violence to gays or lesbians or studying a white supremacist group. What does it mean to understand culture and build trust in such a context? This is one of the many tensions that surfaces in transformative work. A partial answer comes from an understanding of the notion of privilege and the interrogation of unearned privilege. Kendall (2006) explained,

> The superiority of whiteness is a social construct, created by some white men but in all our names. This construct informs both the past and the present and affects each of our lives daily. All of us who are white receive white privileges.... We can use them in such a way as to dismantle the systems that keep the superiority of whiteness in place. One of the primary privileges is having greater influence, power, and resources.... As white people, we keep ourselves central, thereby silencing others.... If we look at race in North America as only a Black-white construct, we miss the true purpose of the system. We must be aware of how the power holders oppressed all people of color to shape the country as they wanted it. Racism is one of several systems of oppression. Others are class, sexism, heterosexism, the institutionalized primacy of Christianity, and able-bodiedism. These systems work toward a common goal: to maintain power and control in the hands of the wealthy, white, heterosexual, Christian, able-bodied men. Examining the intersections is essential to understanding the intentional and finely crafted nature of the system. Finally, this system is brilliant but not impervious to change. We can dismantle it if we know it well and work together toward that goal.

Researching from a transformative stance necessitates working from a multiplicity of vantage points. Kendall (2006) reminded us that studying "whiteness" as a metaphor for power that oppresses is a necessary part of understanding discrimination and oppression, thereby making visible the tensions associated with relationships between researchers and communities, especially when the research focuses on oppressive societal systems.

Building trust and relationships while engaging in critical self-reflection expands thinking around the traditional concept of objectivity in research. As a challenge to the "status quo" of research, Heron and Reason (2001) asked questions such as

> Isn't it true that people can fool themselves about their experience? Isn't this why we have professional researchers who can be detached and objective? The answer to this is that certainly people can and do fool themselves, but we find that they can also develop their attention so they can look at themselves—their way of being, their intuitions and imaginings, their beliefs and actions—critically and in this way improve the quality of their claims of knowing. We call this "critical subjectivity"; it means that we don't have to throw away our personal, living knowledge in the search for objectivity, but are able to build on it and develop it. We can cultivate a high-quality and valid individual perspective on what there is, in collaboration with others who are doing the same. (p. 149)

EPISTEMOLOGY AND INDIGENOUS PEOPLES

Gordon (1990) wrote about the need for African American epistemology in educational theory and practice. Wright (2003) supported the notion of understanding epistemology within the context of the African American experience when he cited the work of Scheurich and Young (1997, 1998) on "coloring epistemologies," Delgado Bernal (1998) on Chicana feminist epistemology, Ladson-Billings (2000) on an "ethnic epistemology," and Dillard (2000a, 2000b) on an "endarkened feminist epistemology" (p. 198).

Dillard's (2000a, 2000b) endarkened feminist epistemology is based on the intersection of race, gender, nationalism, and spirituality. She used a sociocultural identity rather than a biological conception of race and gender. She explicitly acknowledged research as a political and utilitarian tool associated with an obligation to the black community and as an intervention to disrupt the white, hegemonic research paradigm. She spoke of "research as a responsibility answerable and obligated to the very persons and communities being engaged in the inquiry" (Dillard, 2000b, p. 663). She called for a "transformation at the epistemological level if education research is to truly change or transform" (Dillard, 2000b, p. 663). The concept of endarkened feminist epistemology brings with it a change in the role of the researcher to that of a supportive and reflective activist in the community, as well as one who challenges the prevailing research establishment.

Audism and the Deaf Experience

When, where, and how did the paradigm of D/deaf people as deficient emerge? This paradigm can be traced back many centuries when the definition of language was directly associated with speech and civilized behavior and any other forms of communication were considered savage and restricted to animals. The historical analysis of this deficit paradigm is an important topic discussed in detail by other researchers (Bauman, 2004; Branson & Miller, 2002). In research ethics with the Deaf community, this deficit paradigm takes the form of audism. Audism is a term that was originally coined and defined by Humphries (1977) as "the notion that one is superior based on one's ability to hear or behave in the manner of one who hears" (p. 12). Humphries continued by explaining that not only is audism perpetuated by hearing people toward D/deaf people, but it also occurs between D/deaf people, where, for instance, a D/deaf person oppresses another D/deaf person by expecting the same behavior expected from hearing people.

◆ Methodological Assumptions

Methodological assumptions involve the philosophical basis for making decisions about appropriate methods of systematic inquiry. Inclusion of a qualitative dimension is critical in transformative research as a point of establishing a dialogue between researchers and community members. Mixed-methods designs can be considered in order to address the information needs of the community. However, methodological decisions are made with a conscious awareness of contextual and historic factors, especially as they relate to discrimination and oppression. Thus, the formation of partnerships between researchers and the community is an important step in addressing methodological questions in research (see Chapter 22, this volume).

Research in the transformative paradigm is a site of multiple interpretive practices. It does not have a specific set of methods or practices of its own. This type of research draws on multiple strategies, methods, and techniques emanating from different theories and approaches. The methodological assumptions associated with the transformative paradigm are commensurate with approaches such as participatory research, action research, and feminist research and, as such, provide a philosophical framework to integrate research and evaluation for social transformation. Richardson and St. Pierre (2005) used the concept of crystallization as a guiding principle because of the inclusion of different perspectives, such as fiction, field notes, and scientific articles. Researchers get more out of their research study by listening and valuing each member's "voice" through crystallization, not limited to three sides, as in triangulation, but maximized through several possible approaches. There is not one "correct" way of approaching the study but several different points of view.

Transformative ethical considerations need to occur at multiple points in the research process, from discussions of basic beliefs and paradigmatic stances to the establishment of the focus of the research and in all subsequent decisions regarding methods; sampling; and data collection, analysis, and use. For example, sampling needs to be reframed to reveal the dangers of the myth of homogeneity, to understand which dimensions of diversity are important in a specific context, to avoid additional damage to populations by using labels such as "at risk" that can be demeaning and self-defeating, and to recognize the barriers that exist to being part of a group that can contribute to the research results. The transformative paradigm also leads us to reframe data collection decisions to be more inclined to use mixed methods, while at the same time being consciously aware of the benefits of involving community members in data collection decisions, assessing the appropriateness of methods with a depth of understanding of the cultural issues involved, building trust to obtain valid data, designing modifications that may be necessary to collect valid data from various groups, and linking data collection to social action. Methodological questions with ethical implications include the following:

- What are the important dimensions of diversity to include in research in order to give accurate and appropriate representation to groups that have been pushed to the margins of those with more privilege in society?
- What is the ethical responsibility of the researcher to identify and appropriately address those dimensions of diversity?
- What is the ethical cost of ignoring or inappropriately representing the dimensions of diversity in research?

Methodological issues for working within a framework that promotes social justice, dimensions of diversity, and cultural competency are discussed further in many chapters in the methodological section of this *Handbook*.

♦ Conclusions: Social Action

The authors raise questions that require continued discourse with members of oppressed groups. Several questions need to be addressed in transformative research—for instance, What are the challenges associated with establishing an ethical relationship in research, and what are the ethical strategies for determining ownership of the research data and results? The researcher, participants, and community members need to discuss who has the power and how the balance of power can be shifted to support those with less power.

The transformative paradigm emphasizes the need for trust between researcher and participants; many challenges arise in developing a trusting relationship. Researchers need to examine critically the risks and roles for themselves when conducting research in culturally complex communities, especially when they are in direct engagement with members of culturally diverse groups with a focus on increased social justice. Helpful insights come from critiques in scholarly literature from Africa (Chilisa, 2005) and New Zealand (Smith, 2005).

Language and communication are also considered as challenges when research is conducted with communities that do not use the dominant language. If the dominant language is the language of the oppressor, then researchers and participants need to establish which language(s) is (are) used in research team meetings, in the field, in e-mail correspondence, in field notes, and in personal journals. This should be discussed explicitly among the research team members and participants. The team needs to agree on when it is okay to use the majority language and when is it not. Earlier in this chapter, when the issue of language was raised, it was asserted that the language used should be the one selected by the participants. Of course, in many studies, not all participants use the same language—another challenge.

Another challenge that transformative researchers might experience is the publication and dissemination of findings.

Academic power and knowledge are critical to publish scholarly work successfully. Gilmore and Smith (2005) argued that the academic genre not only involves knowing the rules of academic writing but also includes insider knowledge about creating and disseminating that knowledge. To exercise academic power, one must know how to write according to the paradigm of the field—in other words, one must be cognizant of the beliefs of the people involved in controlling the knowledge of the field. However, strict adherence to the limits of disseminating research knowledge through the lens of academia blinds us to "alternative explanations or perceptions of the same phenomena" (Grushkin, 1998, p. 182). This blindness promotes hegemonic control of what information may or may not enter the field. Transformative researchers are not exempt from this need for critical self-reflection.

For instance, until recently, academic journals in the social sciences frowned on citing "experience" and continue to show explicit preference for citing "research literature" (Gilmore & Smith, 2005). Gilmore and Smith argued for indigenous voices, saying that the experience of other community members should be valued, by placing the underrepresented's voices on an equal footing with citations of research literature. For example, in the case of the Deaf community, primacy should be given to Deaf people's experience and perspective. This may necessitate that publications be bilingual (in print English and video-based sign) and made accessible to community members first before the rest of the world. After all, it is their information to begin with, and it is about them as a community.

In conclusion, researchers and participants working together in a collaborative manner need to address challenges throughout the research process. We need to consider the challenge of respecting the ownership of knowledge by a community, then publishing and disseminating for the majority language and culture. One might, therefore, ask, Why does the world know about research first in a language that is not the community's language? Why make the language of the oppressor superior? From a transformative stance, researchers working with community members and coresearchers operate with a conscious awareness of the nature of challenges to ownership, power, and communication among outsiders and insiders of the researched community. A quote from bell hooks (1993), a critic of white supremacist capitalist patriarchy, illustrates the transformative point of view: "If we want a beloved community, we must stand for justice, have recognition for difference, without attaching difference to privilege" (p. 10).

The transformative researcher feels a moral imperative to challenge the status quo for the purpose of contributing to a more just society.

◆ Notes

1. The Council of National Psychological Associations for the Advancement of Ethnic Minority Interests (CNPAAEMI) is made up of the presidents of the five national ethnic/racial minority professional associations, Asian American Psychological Association, Association of Black Psychologists, National Hispanic Psychological Association, Society for the Psychological Study of Ethnic Minority Issues (Division 45 of APA), and Society of Indian Psychologists, and the president (or his or her designee) of the APA (2002). The CNPAAEMI published Guidelines for Research in Ethnic Minority Communities (APA, 2000), and the APA's Joint Task Force of Division 17 (Counseling Psychology) and Division 45 (Psychological Study of Ethnic Minority Issues) published Guidelines on Multicultural Education, Training, Research, Practice, and Organizational Change for Psychologists (APA, 2002).

2. The APA developed guidelines for four specific groups: Asian American/Pacific Islander populations, persons of African descent, Hispanics, and American Indians.

3. Sign Language communities refer to people whose primary experience and allegiance is with Sign Language as a cultural component of the Deaf community and culture. However, all researchers who conduct research in Sign Language communities should be conscious about the complexity of deaf people and the Sign Language community. The capitalization of the term, *Sign Language* signifies a cultural group, similar to African Americans and the Jewish community.

4. The American Heritage Dictionary of the English Language, Third Edition, (1992) defines *Deaf* as "of relating to the Deaf or their culture" and *deaf* as the "lack of hearing sense." Ladd (2003) elaborated on the lowercase deaf terminology, which refers to people who wish to retain their membership and primary experience with the cultural majority. The authors try their best to keep the distinction clear throughout the paper.

◆ References

American Psychological Association. (2000). *Guidelines for research in ethnic minority communities*. Washington, DC: Council of National Psychological Associations for the Advancement of Ethnic Minority Interests.

American Psychological Association. (2002). *Guidelines on multicultural education, training, research, practice, and organizational change for psychologists*. Washington, DC: Author.

Bauman, H. (2004). Audism: Exploring the metaphysics of oppression. *Journal of Deaf Studies and Deaf Education, 9*, 239–246.

Bawden, R. (2006). A systemic evaluation of an agricultural development: A focus on the worldview challenge. In B. Williams & I. Imam (Eds.), *Systems concepts in evaluation: An expert anthology* (pp. 35–46). Washington, DC: American Evaluation Association.

Blow, F. C., Zeber, J. E., McCarthy, J. F., Valenstein, M., Gillon, L., & Bingham, C. R. (2004). Ethnicity and diagnostic patterns in veterans with psychoses. *Social Psychiatry and Psychiatric Epidemiology, 39*(10), 841–851.

Brabeck, M. (Ed.). (2000). *Practicing feminist ethics in psychology*. Washington, DC: American Psychological Association.

Branson, J., & Miller, D. (2002). *Damned for their difference: The cultural construction of deaf people as disabled: A sociological history*. Washington, DC: Gallaudet University Press.

Campbell, D. T., & Stanley, J. C. (1966). *Experimental and quasi-experimental designs for research*. Skokie, IL: Rand McNally.

Chilisa, B. (2005). Educational research within postcolonial Africa: A critique of HIV/AIDS research in Botswana. *International Journal of Qualitative Studies in Education, 18*, 659–684.

Chilisa, B. & Preece, J. (2005). *Research methods for adult educators in Africa*. Cape Town, South Africa: Pearson/UNESCO.

Christians, C. (2005). Ethics and politics in qualitative research. In N. Denzin & Y. Lincoln (Eds.), *Handbook of qualitative research* (3rd ed., pp. 139–164). Thousand Oaks, CA: Sage.

Cram, F. (2001). Rangahau Maori: Tona tika, tona pono—The validity and integrity of Maori research. In M. Tolich (Ed.), *Research ethics in Aotearoa New Zealand* (pp. 35–52). Auckland, New Zealand: Pearson Education.

Denzin, N., & Lincoln, Y. (Eds.). (2005). *Handbook of qualitative research* (3rd ed.). Thousand Oaks, CA: Sage.

Dillard, C. (2000a). *Cultural considerations in paradigm proliferation*. Paper presented at the annual meeting of the American Educational Research Association, New Orleans, LA.

Dillard, C. (2000b). The substance of things hoped for, the evidence of things not seen: Examining an endarkened feminist epistemology in educational research and leadership. *Qualitative Studies in Education, 13*, 661–681.

Duran, B., & Duran, E. (2000). Applied postcolonial clinical and research strategies. In M. Battiste (Ed.), *Reclaiming indigenous voice and vision* (pp. 86–100). Vancouver, Canada: University of British Columbia Press.

Elliott, J. R., & Pais, J. (2006). Race, class, and Hurricane Katrina: Social differences in human responses to disaster. *Social Science Research, 35,* 295–321.

Erting, C. (1992). Deafness and literacy: Why can't Sam read? *Sign Language Studies, 75,* 97–112.

Evans, C. (2004). Literacy development in deaf studies: Case studies in bilingual teaching and learning. *American Annals of the Deaf, 149,* 17–27.

Fisher, C. B. (2003). *Decoding the ethics code: A practical guide for psychologists.* Thousand Oaks, CA: Sage.

Fonow, M. M., & Cook, J. A. (2005). Feminist methodology: New applications in the academy and public policy. *Signs, 30*(4), 2211–2236.

Franklin, J. (Ed.). (1998). *Social policy and social justice: The IPPR reader.* Malden, MA: Polity Press.

Gilmore, P., & Smith, D. (2005). Seizing academic power: Indigenous subaltern voices: Metaliteracy and counternarratives in higher education. In T. McCarty (Ed.), *Language, literacy, and power in schooling* (pp. 67–88). Mahwah, NJ: Lawrence Erlbaum.

Gordon, B. (1990). The necessity of African-American epistemology for educational theory and practice. *Journal of Education, 172,* 88–106.

Grushkin, D. A. (1998). Why shouldn't Sam read? Toward a new paradigm for literacy and the deaf. *Journal of Deaf Studies and Deaf Education, 3,* 179–204.

Gustavsen, B. (2006). Theory and practice: The mediating discourse. In P. Reason & H. Bradbury (Eds.), *Handbook of action research* (pp. 17–26). London: Sage.

Harris, R., & Holmes, H. (2007, November). *Transformative evaluation in deafness: Learning from indigenous peoples.* Paper presented at the annual meeting of the American Evaluation Association, Baltimore.

Harris, R., Holmes, H., & Mertens, D. M. (in press). Research ethics in sign language communities. *Sign Language Studies.*

Hawkins, J. D., & Catalano, R. F. (2003). *Investing in your community's youth.* South Deerfield, MA: Channing Bete.

Heron, J., & Reason, P. (2001). The practice of cooperative inquiry: Research "with" rather than "on" people. In P. Reason & H. Bradbury (Eds.), *Handbook of action research* (concise paperback ed., pp. 144–154). London: Sage.

hooks, b. (1993). A revolution of values: The promise of multi-cultural change. *Journal of the Midwest Modern Language Association, 26*(1), 4–11.

House, E. (1993). *Professional evaluation: Social impact and political consequences.* Newbury Park, CA: Sage.

Humphries, T. (1977). *Communicating across cultures (deaf-hearing) and language learning.* Unpublished doctoral dissertation, Union Graduate School, Union Institute, Cincinnati, OH.

Isbister, J. (2001). *Capitalism and justice: Envisioning social and economic fairness.* Bloomfield, CT: Kumarian Press.

Kendall, F. E. (2006). *Understanding white privilege.* New York: Routledge.

Ladd, P. (2003). *Understanding deaf culture: In search of deafhood.* Tonawanda, NY: Multilingual Matters, Ltd.

Ladson-Billings, G. (2006). From the achievement gap to the education debt: Understanding achievement in U.S. schools. *Educational Researcher, 35,* 3–12.

Lane, H. (1999). *The mask of benevolence: Disabling the deaf community.* San Diego, CA: DawnSignPress.

Losen, D. J., & Orfield, G. (Eds.). (2002). *Racial inequity in special education.* Boston: Harvard Education Press.

Ludema, J. D., Cooperrider, D. L., & Barrett, F. J. (2001). Appreciative inquiry: The power of the unconditional positive question. In P. Reason & H. Bradbury (Eds.), *Handbook of action research* (concise paperback ed., pp. 155–165). London: Sage.

Marschark, M., Lang, H., & Albertini, J. (2002). *Educating deaf students: From research to practice.* New York: Oxford University Press.

Mertens, D. M. (2005). *Research and evaluation in education and psychology: Integrating diversity with quantitative, qualitative and mixed methods* (2nd ed.). Thousand Oaks, CA: Sage.

Mertens, D. M. (2007). Transformative paradigm: Mixed methods and social justice. *Journal of Mixed Methods Research, 1*(3), 212–225.

Mertens, D. M. (2009). *Transformative research and evaluation.* New York: Guilford Press.

Mertens, D. M., Wilson, A., & Mounty, J. (2007). Gender equity for people with disabilities. In S. Klein, C. Dwyer, L. Fox, D. Grayson, C. Kramarae, D. Pollard, & B. Richardson (Eds.), *Handbook for achieving gender equity through education* (pp. 583–604). Mahwah, NJ: Lawrence Erlbaum.

Myklebust, H. (1964). *The psychology of deafness.* New York: Grune & Stratton.

O'Connor, C., & Fernandez, S. D. (2006). Race, class, and disproportionality: Reevaluating the relationship between poverty and special education placement. *Educational Researcher, 35,* 6–11.

Rawls, J. (2001). *Justice as fairness: A restatement.* Cambridge, MA: Belknap Press of Harvard University Press.

Reason, P., & Bradbury, H. (2006). Introduction: Inquiry and participation in search of a world worthy of human aspiration. In P. Reason & H. Bradbury (Eds.), *Handbook of action research* (concise paperback ed., pp. 1–14). London: Sage.

Reisch, M. (2002). Defining social justice in a socially unjust world. *Families in Society, 83,* 343–354.

Richardson, L., & St. Pierre, E. A. (2005). Writing: A method of inquiry. In N. Denzin & Y. Lincoln (Eds.), *Handbook of qualitative research* (3rd ed., pp. 959–978). Thousand Oaks, CA: Sage.

Segone, M. (Ed.). (2006). *New trends in development evaluation* (Issue #5). Geneva, Switzerland: UNICEF Regional Office for CEE/CIS and IPEN. (www.unicef.org/ceecis/resources_1220.html)

Simons, H. (2006). Ethics in evaluation. In I. Shaw, J. Greene, & M. Mark (Eds.), *The Sage handbook of evaluation* (pp. 243–265). London: Sage.

Smith, L. T. (2005). On tricky ground: Researching the native in the age of uncertainty. In N. Denzin & Y. Lincoln (Eds.), *Handbook of qualitative research* (3rd ed., pp. 85–107). Thousand Oaks, CA: Sage.

United Nations Organization. (1948). *Universal declaration of human rights.* Retrieved February 25, 2008, from www.un.org/Overview/rights.html

United Nations Organization. (1975). *Declaration on the rights of disabled persons.* Retrieved February 25, 2008, from www2.ohchr.org/english/law/res3447.htm

United Nations Organization. (1979). *Convention on the elimination of all forms of discrimination against women* (CEDAW). Retrieved February 25, 2008, fromwww.un.org/womenwatch/daw/cedaw/text/econvention.htm

United Nations Organization. (1990a). *Convention on the rights of the child.* Retrieved February 25, 2008, from www2.ohchr.org/english/law/crc.htm

United Nations Organization. (1990b). *International convention on the protection of the rights of all migrant workers and members of their families.* Retrieved February 25, 2008, from www.un.org/millennium/law/iv-13.htm

United Nations Organization. (2006a). *Convention on the rights of persons with disabilities.* New York: Author. Retrieved March 21, 2007, from www.un.org/esa/socdev/enable/rights/ahc8adart.htm

United Nations Organization. (2006b). *Declaration of the rights of indigenous peoples.* Retrieved March 21, 2007, from www.un.org/esa/socdev/unpfii/en/declaration.html

U.S. Department of Education. (2004). *The facts about . . . investing in what works.* Retrieved October 25, 2004, from www.ed.gov/nclb/methods/whatworks/whatworks.html

Wright, H. K. (2003). An endarkened feminist epistemology? Identity, difference and the politics of representation in educational research. *Qualitative Studies in Education, 16,* 197–214.

SECTION II

PERSPECTIVES ON ETHICAL REGULATION

What constitutes ethical regulation? At its least formal, it may consist of nothing more than professor to student, senior researcher to junior researcher, or peer to peer communication of the way things are done by word and by example. Are participants and colleagues treated with respect? Are disagreements resolved by negotiation, by fiat, or by some combination of the two? How are tasks apportioned? Are research methods transparent, consistent with discipline standards, and up-to-date? Are suggestions and inquiries welcomed or waved aside? Is the work of all acknowledged or only that of some? At its most formal, ethical standards have become rules, adherence to which is required and lack of adherence to which may become the stuff of lawsuits censure, expulsion from professional organizations, or loss of licensure. In between, one finds written codes of ethics that are stated in generalities and in specifics, those that self-identify as advisory and those that do so as mandatory, those that are explicitly limited to certain populations and/or settings and/or methodologies and/or funding sources and those that pertain across the board. As the degree of explicitness and formality of ethical codes varies, so does the means by which they are honored and enforced.

The six chapters in this section examine six variations in formality, explicitness, and enforcement. Linda Mabry's "Governmental Regulation in Social Science" (Chapter 7) examines the role of governmental regulation in social science research. Its benefits and limitations are placed in the context of both professional and institutional regulation and of transnational and international organizations.

Focusing particularly on the United States, Richard Speiglman and Patricia Spear take a hard look at a principle source of ethical gatekeeping, institutional review boards (IRBs). In Chapter 8, "The Role of Institutional Review Boards: Ethics: Now You See Them, Now You Don't," they review the history and intended function of IRBs, contrast that with their current processes and procedures, and ask a series of questions regarding the effects of their apparent "net-widening" and "mission creep" on the research process.

While IRBs constitute the most common source of formal ethical oversight in the United States, other entities are increasingly becoming concerned about the effects of research on their members, clients, students, staff, and normal operations. Many school districts and social agencies, for example, have found it necessary to develop policies and procedures limiting access of researchers and specifying the types of research that they will and will not accommodate. Normally, their concerns are consistent with IRB and professional standards but are expanded to include concerns about demands of research that divert staff time from service delivery and clients'/members'/students' time and energy from other activities. In other words, while IRBs examine the risks and benefits of the proposed research, these entities are also concerned with the opportunity costs of participation and ask whether the agency's or group's benefits from the proposed research will outweigh the cost to the entity itself.

"Researching Ourselves Back to Life: Taking Control of the Research Agenda in Indian Country" by Joan LaFrance and Cheryl Crazy Bull (Chapter 9) looks at these issues from the point of view of indigenous communities, particularly those of North America. (See also related chapters in this volume by Barnes, McCreanor, Edwards, & Borell [Chapter 28], Chilisa [Chapter 26], Cram [Chapter 20], and Ntseane [Chapter 19], which discuss indigenous concerns in Botswana [Chapters 19, 26] and New Zealand [Chapters 20, 28].) LaFrance and Crazy Bull describe the formalization and nature of research review processes developed by tribal communities in the United States to counter "a long history of intrusive studies that have built the reputations of anthropologists and other researchers but brought little more than the loss of cultural ownership and exploitation to Indian people" (Chapter 9, p. 135). Both what is to be studied and how it is to be studied are germane. The chapter concludes with discussion of the ethical issues that arise when indigenous value systems and ways of knowing meet Western scientific tradition.

Yvonna Lincoln's "Ethical Practices in Qualitative Research" (Chapter 10) discusses the rationale for "phenomenologically oriented research within a new ethical framework" that emphasizes persons, contexts, and global sensibilities based on criteria of authenticity and relationships among self/other, self/community, and self/culture (p. 150). The roles of culture and a global perspective as well as their implications for reporting are discussed from a philosophical and theoretical perspective. As such, the chapter provides a counterpoint between the very specific chapters that precede and follow it.

Concluding this section of the *Handbook*, the reader moves away from Lincoln's abstract analysis to Amanda Wolf, David Turner, and Kathleen Toms's chapter, "Ethical Perspectives in Program Evaluation," which reports the perspective of program evaluators—for example, applied social researchers likely to use a mix of qualitative and quantitative methods—regarding the ethical considerations they bring to their work. Responses of evaluators in North America and Australasia to Q-sort materials show shared values with regard to evaluator integrity and independence but diverge somewhat with regard to the meaning of those characteristics in practice. The authors ask what the implications of their findings are for the development of ethical standards for evaluation that are shared across cultural and national boundaries. The reader who reads the chapters together might want to expand their inquiry and consider the question of whether the principles Lincoln limns might also be applicable to mixed methods or even quantitative ones.

7
GOVERNMENTAL REGULATION IN SOCIAL SCIENCE

◆ Linda Mabry

The pursuit of scientific inquiry can be instrumental to the governance of a nation, but government attempts to harness social science through regulation raise a number of considerations. This chapter explores government's interest in social science, its interest in ethical research practice, and issues regarding the regulation of social research and evaluation in an internationalizing context.

◆ Government Interest in Social Science

Government interest in social science reflects, in part, the type and purpose of the government. The variety of forms of government that have existed across time defy a single, simple articulation of government purpose, but perhaps it can be safely said that internal stability and protection from external threats are general aims since these aims can be seen across a broad spectrum of types from popular, self-governing regimes to corrupt, self-interested regimes. Many modern governments have pursued (or have claimed to pursue) economic and social benefits for their citizens, for example, by attempting to secure favorable strategic and trade positions among nations and to provide or sustain social services and legal rights. In such pursuits, information is always important: Can we protect ourselves from our neighbor's weaponry? Are our manufacturing technologies optimal? How can we both exploit and sustain our natural resources? What infrastructure, trade practices, or training could increase our standard of living? What do we need to know to gain or to maintain advantage?

Academia serves society by providing a means for collecting, analyzing, and conveying information and by providing for education to ensure the continuing availability of information. Both the so-called "hard sciences," such as physics and geology, and the "soft" or social sciences, such as economics and program evaluation, have contributed information useful to government. In return, the value of the academy to society is concretely demonstrated by public support, especially by government expenditures for research and higher education. In self-governing societies, the expertise and independence of the academy is, like the investigative and communicative function of a free press, positioned to reveal and correct government misuses. But neither independence nor government appreciation of the information gained through disinterested inquiry are guaranteed, as has been painfully illustrated by official disregard, manipulation, and silencing of scholars and the press and by recurrences of book burning across history. Such action manifests the negative impact of governmental regulation of research. Can the impact be good?

CREATING AND SUSTAINING THE RIGHTS AND PROTECTIONS OF CITIZENS

Efforts toward rational improvement of society are discernible across cultures and time: in the promeritocracy establishment of civil service exams in 2000 BCE China, in the move toward one-person-one-vote democracy in 500 BCE Greece, in the use of statistics in Napoleonic France. In our own time, the progeny of these and other efforts can be seen in varied enterprises such as clinical pharmaceutical trials, research on sustainable agriculture, and studies of the effectiveness of educational initiatives. Many kinds of research and evaluation win public funding because they promise societal benefit, implying this logic:

Social research ➔ Information
➔ Societal improvement.

The benefits of social science have never been equally available to all citizens, however, even when their collective resources have sponsored research. At times, some persons have paid dearly for benefits accrued by others. In perhaps the most horrific example, organ transplant recipients have benefited from knowledge gained in torturous Nazi medical experiments. This and other inhumane episodes demonstrate the need for a research ethos in which there is simultaneous *extraction of information from participants* and *protection of participants* from adverse consequences of the extraction along these lines suggested at the bottom of this page.

Such logic displays a positive role for government in regulating research to protect the welfare of citizens during the pursuit of information intended to improve their lives. Protection of citizens, however, can be a euphemistic mask for paternalism

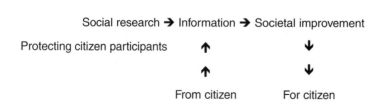

or suppression. Among the murky issues raised by governmental regulation of research are questions regarding how much regulation is helpful, which aspects of research can be usefully regulated by government, and whether government regulation is sufficient to prevent research from benefiting some citizens at the expense of others or from benefiting citizens by exploiting non-citizen residents and citizens of other nations.

DIFFERENCES IN GOVERNMENTAL PURPOSES FOR SCIENTIFIC INQUIRY

Different types of governments have different uses for research. For example, Biblical accounts of the military superiority of the ancient Hittites suggest that their government focused research on the development of armaments, as did Cold War adversaries during the 20th century and as do the so-called rogue nations today. Some governments show more interest in research related to capacity building, medical advancements, economic productivity, and social welfare. Some governments favor research that supports their preferred ideologies, sponsoring research that may be skewed from the outset by the type of questions posed and neglecting research focused on alternatives. Differing governmental appetites and interests regarding research have consequences for public funding and, to the extent that the means of publication and communication are government controlled, for dissemination of research results.

Whether and how government should regulate social science begs at least two questions: How much government (or government regulation) is optimal? Who governs and for the benefit of whom? The question of how much government or government regulation is desirable is a matter of long-standing controversy. On one side, political and economic philosophers from Adam Smith (1776/2003) to Milton Friedman (1962) have argued for the least possible government and regulation, a view evidently not shared by Chairman Mao Zedong, General Augusto Pinochet Ugarte, or King Abdullah bin Abdul Aziz Al Saud.

Monarchies, dictatorships, and despotic and totalitarian regimes established for the purpose of empowering and enriching certain individuals as well as oligarchies, plutocracies, and fascist and imperialist regimes established for the purpose of empowering and enriching certain groups are more likely to institute tight government control of research to support and protect their own interests rather than those of their citizenries. Many aspects of research might be subject to oversight by such governments. Research focused on justifying government policy is more likely to be encouraged, for example, and research that highlights policy alternatives or countervailing perspectives—such as critical ethnographies, feminist research, and stakeholder-oriented evaluations—is more likely to be barred.

At the other end of the continuum, a laissez-faire policy regarding research, or failure to adopt a formal policy regarding research, offers maximum freedom of focus and conduct for researchers. However, such a policy (or lack of policy) would tolerate studies with little societal utility and no protection of citizens who may, knowingly or unknowingly, serve as sources of information. It would tolerate, for example, the research conducted by Laud Humphreys (1970) on furtive homosexual activity, a study in which those observed in public places were unaware that their activities were being documented for research and publication.

Protection of citizens from research-related harm is most probable in self-governments such as democracies, representative democracies, or parliamentary systems where, in addition, greater interest in research intended to benefit the population is also most probable. To continue with the example above, four years after Humphreys published his research, his government, that of the United States, instituted legal protections for the human subjects of research, including the requirement that they be informed about research purposes and methods, that they consent in advance to their participation, and that they be protected from undue risk (see Chapter 8, this volume).

Support for research conducted in the interest of citizens is moderated by their diversity and degree of empowerment. Conflicting citizen interests inevitably result in competing advocacies, and those empowered by the electorate, by wealth, by historical tradition, or by other means are well positioned to establish and fund research in their own interests. For example, only relatively recently have women's health issues as a research focus moved toward parity with men's health issues, more or less corresponding chronologically with moves toward gender parity in income and electability. Those citizens in positions of governmental power enjoy disproportionate advantage. For example, stem cell research in the United States (but not elsewhere in the world) was constrained by the George W. Bush administration in deference to the President's ideology and that of his conservative constituents (see Dale, 2001), and research documenting possible signs of global warming was distorted and suppressed (see Max, 2007), ostensibly because of the administration's ties to industry, to the point that

> from the perspective of the public or policymakers, scientific debate and political debate on many environmental issues already have become indistinguishable. Such cases of conflation limit the role of science in the development of creative and feasible policy options. In many instances, science—particularly environmental science—has become little more than a mechanism of marketing competing political agendas. (Pielke, 2006, p. 28)

In a politically charged research environment, government may favor not only certain research but also certain researchers. By way of illustration, on the topic of global warming, David Bellamy of Great Britain or Bjørn Lomborg of Denmark, who have dismissed or minimized global warming (Leake, 2005; Lomborg, 2001), might be favored by governments refusing to sign the United Nations' (UN) Kyoto Protocol to limit greenhouse gas emission; members of the Union of Concerned Scientists, which supports pollution control and development of renewable energy to address global warming, might be favored by signatory governments.

The political stew also involves a variety of partisan positions. Libertarians, for example, might reject regulation of research, while liberals might encourage a wide range of research, especially if participating citizens are legally protected from harm; conservatives might favor a more limited array of topics and the constraints implied by the notion of small government.

◆ Government Regulation of Scientific Inquiry

REGULATING SCIENTIFIC INQUIRY FOR ETHICAL REASONS

Even where governments are similarly committed to the protection of citizens, different roles are suggested by the variety of ethical frameworks that might be valued. To note just a few, *utilitarian* ethics provide a justification for research that may be helpful to many even if harmful to a few (Mill, 1863/1891); *relational* ethics prioritize reciprocity and mutual support between researcher and subject, disallowing the casualties tolerable from a utilitarian position (see Flinders, 1992); *transformative* ethics encourage addressing local issues and empowering the disenfranchised in the process and dissemination of research (Mertens, 2005).

Whether government is the appropriate locus of regulation for research ethics, or other aspects of research, should take into consideration the availability of other means for ensuring appropriate and competent social science, for example, the agency of individual researchers and the institutions and professional organizations with which they affiliate themselves.

Individual Responsibility for Research Ethics

Social scientists might, of course, assume individual ethical responsibility toward persons from and about whom they collect information. While many researchers and evaluators exercise great care, the record of practice includes disturbing instances, such as the Humphreys study, of some acting on ethics their colleagues have disapproved. John Van Maanen (1973), in another example, merely observed police behavior in "a rather brutal encounter in which . . . a black homosexual was severely beaten" (p. 52) and later reflected,

> I was party to much discrediting information regarding the legality and propriety of police actions . . . it was clear that I had moral choices to make regarding my conduct. . . . I kept my mouth shut. And, after a short time, I was too vulnerable to legal sanction, for I had not reported what I heard or saw. (Manning & Van Maanen, 1978, p. 341)

Because of their interest in protecting access to sources of information, avoiding observer effects that might invalidate findings, and protecting their research agendas, unregulated social scientists might give too little priority to ethical conduct.

Institutional Regulation of Research Ethics

Uneven as individual self-monitoring has proven, regulation of research ethics by universities and other research groups, institutions that require research conduct and dissemination, invites similar difficulty. In Van Maanen's case, his prestigious position at the Massachusetts Institute of Technology (MIT) suggests that he was rewarded for his controversial study of "rookie cops."

In contrast, the case of Stanley Milgram may indicate a degree of institutional censure. As a student at Yale University in 1961, Milgram conducted obedience experiments in which participants, assigned the role of "teachers," were instructed by white-coated researchers to administer electric shock to "learners," whom they had briefly met but could not see during the experiments, if the learners responded incorrectly to word-pair items. When the "teachers" administered what they believed to be (but were not) electric shocks, the "learners" (actually actors) simulated pain vocalizations, leading the researcher to conclude, "Stark authority was pitted against the subjects' strongest moral imperatives against hurting others, and, with the subjects' ears ringing with the screams of the victims, authority won more often than not" (Milgram, 1974).

The psychological impact on the "teachers," who discovered their willingness to override their own principles of conduct and inflict pain on others, may have been lastingly harmful. Milgram was denied tenure at Harvard but became a full professor at the City University of New York, suggesting something of the range of actual institutional responses to questionable ethical practice by researchers.

Professional Regulation of Research Ethics

Associations organized by social scientists from different institutions have demonstrated interest in encouraging ethical practice but little capacity to compel it. While ethical codes and principles have been established by professional associations whose members engage in social science, adherence is often merely implied by voluntary membership rather than enforced. The American Sociological Association's

(1997) *Code of Ethics* offers an example, while the American Psychological Association (2007) explicitly decoupled its *Ethical Principles of Psychologists and Code of Conduct* from civil liability. The *Code of Ethics* of the National Association of Social Workers (1996) does mention sanctions for unethical behavior but also that they are to be exacted by an external body:

> When necessary, social workers who believe that a colleague has acted unethically should take action through appropriate formal channels (such as contacting a state licensing board or regulatory body, an NASW committee on inquiry, or other professional ethics committees). (Standard 2.11.d)

Another complication is suggested by the multiple memberships of researchers belonging to different professional associations whose ethical expectations are unaligned. The American Anthropological Association, for example, acknowledges that its members may also be affiliated with other organizations, that they may engage in multidisciplinary research efforts, and that multiple ethical codes can complicate interpretations of ethical practice.

Even in the absence of overlapping codes, whether an instance of research conduct upholds or violates ethical standards is subject to interpretation, and judgments may differ. The complicated contexts of application require balancing and prioritizing among the specific provisions of ethical codes (House, 1995), and sometimes it is not possible to adhere to each provision simultaneously (Mabry, 1999). For example, the American Evaluation Association's (2004) *Guiding Principles* urges evaluators to report fully the merits and shortcomings of programs and, simultaneously, to show respect for persons—although the evaluation may reveal inadequate performance by some program personnel. Guidance for balancing these aims is attempted in the admonition to "reduce any unnecessary harms that might occur, provided this will not compromise the integrity of the evaluation findings" (Principle D.3). In addition, perplexed evaluators are urged to confer with experienced colleagues.

A final, and insurmountable, problem with relegating regulation of research ethics to professional organizations is that researchers unaffiliated with either institutions or professional organizations cannot be bound, even loosely, by the ethical expectations of these groups. One attempt to address this problem can be seen in the attempt by the National Council on Measurement in Education to extend the reach of its code beyond its own members by explicitly encouraging nonmembers who engage in educational assessment activities to follow its ethical expectations, but the organization does not monitor conformance even of its members.

Government Regulation of Research Ethics

The proliferation of professional codes of ethics underscores the need for ethical social science, but the variability of individual, institutional, and professional ethics provides, at best, uneven protection of citizens serving as information sources for social scientists. These variations, the limitations on enforceability of institutional and professional ethics, and the growth in cross-institution and interdisciplinary projects suggest that if ethical research practice is to be ensured, not just stated, a means of ensuring compliance may be necessary. Because it has such means, the regulation of research ethics has inexorably fallen to government.

Can even well-intentioned governments be trusted with research ethics? Consider a thread of U.S. history. Between 1932 and 1972, U.S. Public Health Service physicians misled nearly 400 impoverished African American men into a false belief that they were receiving medical care when, in fact, the research goal was to collect data from them regarding their worsening cases of syphilis, especially autopsy data (J. H. Jones, 1993). Two years after the end of the study, in 1974, government protection of human subjects was statutorily required by the National Research Act, and five years after that, the U.S. Department of Health, Education, and Welfare adopted as policy the *Belmont Report* (National Commission for the Protection of Human Subjects of Biomedical and Behavioral Research, 1979). Drawing on the Nuremberg Code developed during trials of Nazi war criminals, the *Report* calls for respect for persons, beneficence, and justice as ethical principles to guide research conduct and urges that risks be minimized, estimated in advance, and subjected to review and that participation by human subjects be informed and voluntary. Thus, government regulation had the force of law. It has also had fiscal incentives: "Federal funds administered by a department or agency may not be expended for research involving human subjects unless the requirements of this policy have been satisfied" (U.S. Department of Health, Education, and Welfare, 2000, p. 117). And it had mechanisms for oversight and formal approval: Institutional review boards (IRBs) have been established to examine proposals to conduct research involving human subjects (see Chapter 8, this volume). For the eight survivors of what came to be called the Tuskegee Experiment, a presidential apology came 25 years later, when President Bill Clinton, on May 16, 1997, called the research an "outrage to our commitment to integrity and equality for all our citizens," a commitment that, by then, could be enforced.

The continuing story includes complicating variations in the interpretation and application of the federal regulations. The variability among IRBs' interpretation of legal requirements has been documented (Stair, Reed, Radeos, Koski, & Camargo, 2001) and lamented. Taking an example based on personal experience as illustration, the IRB at Indiana University disallowed all action research in education until the end of the 1990s, while the same type of research was routinely approved at Washington State University. The Indiana IRB justified its stance by saying that the students of a teacher-researcher would have no real opportunity to choose not to participate, hence the IRB viewed such proposals as coercive.

Moreover, social scientists have not always agreed with IRBs, some objecting to restrictions they considered unreasonable (see Begley, 2002) and evaluators objecting to restrictions they considered obstructive to accuracy and validity (see Oakes, 2002). Recently, IRBs have been criticized as purveyors of an anachronism:

> IRBs are institutional apparatuses that regulate a particular form of ethical conduct, a form that may be no longer workable in a trans-disciplinary, global and postcolonial world.... [although it is] the dominant bio-medical ethical model that operates in many North American universities today ... [a] utilitarian ethical model. (Denzin, 2003)

REGULATING OTHER ASPECTS OF SCIENTIFIC INQUIRY

The difficulties involved in government regulation of research ethics portend problems for government regulation of other aspects of social science: research focus, methods, practitioners, findings. The importance of managing research findings has been more obvious to governments than that of regulating ethical practice, as the earlier example of global warming suggested. Government may not only use research to support favored policies but may also exploit discrepant findings by different researchers, delay action by calling for more research, and influence the direction of social science inquiry.

The determination of research topics has been susceptible to government influence through the allocation of public funds to dedicated research centers and to governmental investigative bodies—for example, the U.S. Government Accounting Office, which undertakes studies for Congress.

Government funding can also influence the direction taken by independent researchers and private research groups through the establishment of grant categories and criteria, and it can channel funds to sympathetic researchers and think tanks. An idealist might hope that public funding could protect social science from dependence on wealthy individuals, well-funded foundations, and other private sources capable of veering research focus in questionable directions, but ideological battles regarding studies of the human genome and the medical use of embryonic stem cells reveal the possibility that governments, too, might obstruct or swerve research focus inappropriately.

Less likely is government control of research methods. However, recently in the United States, the Department of Education, in regulations flowing from the No Child Left Behind legislation (2001), established funding priorities favoring experimental, quasi-experimental, and other quantitative research designs. Although researchers objected vigorously (e.g., Berliner, 2002; Eisenhart & Towne, 2003; Erickson & Gutierrez, 2002; Feuer, Towne, & Shavelson, 2002; Pellegrino & Goldman, 2002; Viadero, 2007), the priority was later extended from educational research to educational evaluation: "The Secretary [of the U.S. Department of Education] considers random assignment and quasi-experimental designs to be the most rigorous to address the question of project effectiveness" (U.S. Department of Education, 2005, p. 3586).

The damage to social science has been articulated by practitioners, including, in evaluation, the following:

> Flexibility in methods choice and serious consideration of alternative design options are not luxuries [but, rather, a responsibility that] has traditionally belonged to the evaluator. It is that responsibility that undergirds evaluative credibility. (Chelimsky, 2007, p. 31)

> Proclaiming almost any single design as the best in any or all program contexts, without adequate attention to what is happening in the real world, is unlikely to be wise, a thought that is almost an evaluation cliché. (Datta, 2007, p. 50)

The government's willingness to ignore the objections of researchers was mirrored by its willingness to override evaluators' responses to its proposed funding priority for evaluation methods. Although individual and organizational opposition to the proposed priority outnumbered support by a margin of approximately 10:1, the Department of Education nevertheless "determined that the comments did not warrant changes" to its proposal (U.S. Department of Education, 2005, p. 3586). Such a dismissive attitude toward invited professional input demonstrates the capacity for ill-conceived unilateralism in government regulation of the methods of social science (see also Mabry, 2008).

BEYOND GOVERNMENT

As social science is increasingly transcending national borders, the limits of government regulation are becoming clearer. Government can regulate research to protect its own vulnerable populations and distinct ethnic groups, as IRBs in the United States take special consideration regarding research conducted on Native American reservations, where there are sovereign tribal rights. But how is the government of one country to ensure competent, sensitive practice by its social scientists when they are working in another country with an unfamiliar culture? What oversight is possible when multinational research teams disperse to sites in different countries?

International and Transnational Research Ethics

In the aftermath of World War II, ensuring ethical research practice across national borders was attempted when Nazi doctors were tried as war criminals. The resulting Nuremberg Code first formalized many of the protections now required by U.S. IRBs—for example, that "all unnecessary physical and mental suffering and injury" should be avoided, that the consent of human subjects to participate in research "is absolutely essential," and that "the degree of risk to be taken should never exceed that determined by the humanitarian importance of the problem to be solved by the experiment" (International Military Tribunals, 1949).

The Declaration of Helsinki in 1964 urged informed consent, voluntary participation, and optional withdrawal from medical research projects. It contrasted slightly with the Nuremberg Code's utilitarian language regarding "the humanitarian importance of the problem," proclaiming instead that "considerations related to the well-being of the human subject should take precedence over the interests of science and society" (World Medical Association General Assembly, 1964).

In the continuing effort, the UN has also attempted to address issues in international and transnational research. UN documents regarding human rights in general offer some basic guidance. For example, the International Covenant on Civil and Political Rights (UN General Assembly, 1966) provides that

> everyone shall have the right to freedom of expression; this right shall include *freedom to seek, receive and impart information and ideas of all kinds, regardless of frontiers* [italics added], either orally, in writing or in print, in the form of art, or through any other media ... subject to certain restrictions, but these shall only be such as are provided by law and are necessary. (Article 19)

Specific research areas have been considered in the UN's codifications—for example, research on human cloning:

> Promotion of scientific and technical progress in life sciences should be sought in a manner that safeguards respect for human rights and the benefit of all, mindful of the serious medical, physical, psychological and social dangers that human cloning may imply for the individuals involved. (UN General Assembly, 2005)

Working in concert with other organizations, the UN has attempted to curb potential exploitation of impoverished countries and their citizens regarding research related to the HIV/AIDS pandemic:

> Vaccines may be conceived and manufactured in laboratories in one country (sponsor country or countries), usually in the developed world, and tested in human populations in another country (host country or countries), often in the developing world. (Joint United Nations Programme on HIV/AIDS [UNAIDS], 2000, p. 7)

> Efforts must be made ... to ensure that the risks participants take are justified by the benefits they receive by virtue of their participation in the research. A key means by which to protect participants and the communities from which they come is to ensure that the community in which the research is carried out is meaningfully involved in the design, implementation, and distribution of results of vaccine research. (UNAIDS, 2000, p. 9)

The UN's broad view of ethics can be seen in this encouragement of community participation in research design and conduct and in its adoption of principles intended to guide legislation in member countries regarding electronic data storage:

> Information about persons should not be collected or processed in unfair or unlawful ways, nor should it be used for

ends contrary to the purposes and principles of the Charter of the United Nations. (UN General Assembly, 1990)

Every country shall designate the authority which, in accordance with its domestic legal system, is to be responsible for supervising observance of the principles set forth. (UN General Assembly, 1990)

When the legislation of two or more countries concerned by a transborder data flow offers comparable safeguards for the protection of privacy, information should be able to circulate as freely as inside each of the territories concerned. If there are no reciprocal safeguards, limitations on such circulation may not be imposed unduly and only in so far as the protection of privacy demands. (UN General Assembly, 1990)

Where international law cannot be brought to bear, the unenforceability of guidelines promulgated by international groups is frequently self-acknowledged in wordings such as these:

It is *hoped* that this document will be of use to potential research participants, investigators . . . It *suggests* standards. (UNAIDS, 2000, p. 5 [italics added])

[The Helsinki Declaration] standards as drafted are *only a guide* to physicians all over the world. Physicians are not relieved from criminal, civil and ethical responsibilities under the law of their own countries. (World Medical Association General Assembly, 1964 [italics added])

Even unenforceable guidelines, however, have sometimes influenced the enforceable regulatory policies of governments. For example, the Nuremberg Code and the Helsinki Declaration influenced the *Belmont Report* in the United States and subsequent legislation requiring review of research plans to ascertain and minimize potential risks to human subjects.

Research and Evaluation by International and Transnational Organizations

Oversight difficulties proliferate not only in situations involving multiple and overlapping governmental jurisdictions but also in research conducted or commissioned by international and transnational organizations such as the World Bank.

Operating on an assumption that "investment in education can contribute to economic growth" (Psacharopoulos & Woodhall, 1991, p. 21), the Bank has been criticized for its limited view of education "in stark contrast with such other agencies as UNESCO, whose educational concerns remain conceptually broad" (P. W. Jones, 1992, p. 224). The Bank's interest in "economic analysis of investment choices [that] may help determine investment priorities in education" (Psacharopoulos & Woodhall, 1991, p. 10) focuses its practice of educational evaluation on quantifiable indicators at the expense of detailed data regarding critical contexts and processes (see Banerjee, Deaton, Lustig, Rogoff, & Hsu, 2006; P. W. Jones, 1992; World Bank Independent Evaluation Group, 2006). Constrictions to the practice of research and evaluation results in an overemphasis of test scores (World Bank Independent Evaluation Group, 2006) and dangerous overgeneralizations of findings (P. W. Jones, 1992).

The impact of the Bank's impact evaluations for borrower countries has included implementation of prohibitive user fees for education and social services, promotion of private schooling, and other loan conditions that "have a harmful impact on poor people, increasing their poverty not reducing it, by denying them access to vital services" (Kovach & Lansman, 2006, p. 3). The Bank's loan conditions were questioned by some of its own 180 shareholding member countries, who called a conference on the subject in 2006 in Oslo, Norway (see Solheim, 2006). Even an internal Bank report charged that the Bank's programs do not emphasize learning outcomes. A significant risk of such programs is that their focus on quantitative growth can overshadow improvements in educational quality and outcomes, including student learning outcomes. (World Bank Independent Evaluation Group, 2006, p. 26)

Tens of millions of children in the developing world—primarily girls, the poor, and other disadvantaged groups—remain out of school; hundreds of millions drop out before completing primary school, and of those who do complete it, a large proportion fail to acquire desired levels of knowledge and skills, especially in the poorest countries. (World Bank Independent Evaluation Group, 2006, p. xiii)

The Bank has persisted in its focus and methodology for decades despite recognized "chronic implementation failures" (P. W. Jones, 1992, p. 253) in the 1960s to 1970s, "fail[ure] to respect borrower differences [in defining] critical issues facing world education" (p. 223) in the 1980s, and "jeopardising public commitments to educational quality" (p. 249) in the 1990s. The Bank's evident unwillingness to correct its approach to design, data collection, and analysis reveals an ethical dimension of methodology. The gap in ethical regulation by government or international governing structures is also visible.

♦ Gaps and Issues

To move toward the future, it is helpful to recall that mid- to late-20th-century efforts to create international protections for research participants lacked the means of enforcement necessary to ensure their ethical treatment. Similar efforts by professional associations of social scientists, suffering similar limitation, have suggested a need for governments to protect their citizens from adverse consequences. Although government regulation of social science has proven necessary to ensure ethical treatment of human subjects, their regulatory structures have been controversial with social scientists, who have protested vagaries in the interpretation and application of regulations, reviews of research plans that have drifted into nonethical aspects of investigation, and failures of regulatory bodies to distinguish appropriately between research and evaluation. Such controversies may be inevitable when those who do not practice research attempt to regulate it, lacking as they necessarily must the nuanced understandings of practitioners. But controversy would be inevitable even if social scientists themselves could enact and enforce regulation.

Moreover, the agendas of governments may spawn policies that misdirect the focus and methods of social science, manipulate findings, and permit exploitation of citizens—linking back to initial international and transnational concerns. Like the ethical codes of professional associations, the principles advanced by international bodies are limited in their enforceability. As the UN did in its code for electronic data, international groups may call on member nations to enact legislation in accordance with the group's principles, but compelling compliance is another matter. So, like nonregulatory expectations in national contexts, the aspirations articulated by international groups have proven insufficient to ensure appropriate international research and evaluation practice. Moreover, even where member nations do comply with common principles, differences in their adopted articulations of expectations can create labyrinths of variations obstructing enforcement, especially for social science projects located in multiple countries.

Also, gaps may remain regarding assurance of the cultural competence of researchers and evaluators. The diversity arising from social scientists' different national backgrounds and from variations in practice within and among their social science subdisciplines may exacerbate those gaps. What constitutes appropriate data collection, for example, depends on community norms at the research site, the expectations of the research approach (different for critical ethnography and program evaluation, for example), the social scientist's embodiment of the moral expectations of his or her national and professional milieux, and other considerations. Where outsiders impose conditions in the interests of their own projects, human subjects with little experience of social science may be vulnerable to culture shifts they cannot anticipate, risks unlikely to be understood even if informed consent procedures are scrupulously followed.

As if these pros and cons regarding regulation of social science were not enough to cause paralyzing ambivalence, a deep ontological issue remains: Regulations and their enforcement create climates of compliance antithetical to the curiosity that drives research and to the freedom that promotes discovery; that is, regulation can obstruct the social value, the raison d'etre, of social science.

History suggests incapacity to develop and balance regulations regarding ethics in social science that are simultaneously unambiguous, universal, and enforceable. In the chronology of attempts to do so, a role for government regulation has sometimes been seen and implemented. Understanding the appropriate parameters for government's contribution to ensuring that social science is truly socially beneficial is complicated by the internationalizing of research and evaluation. The point that has been reached in the development of ethical safeguards is fraught with worrisome complexities and dilemmas. Social scientists, their institutions and professional associations, governments, and international and transnational organizations, all bearing responsibilities relevant to ethical practice, need to commit to a continuing struggle to strive for the best ethics of which all are capable.

◆ References

American Evaluation Association. (2004). *Guiding principles for evaluators*. Fairhaven, MA: Author. Retrieved July 5, 2006, from www.eval.org/Publications/GuidingPrinciples.asp

American Psychological Association. (2007). *Ethical principles of psychologists and code of conduct*. Washington, DC: Author. Retrieved July 5, 2006, from www.apa.org/ethics/code2002.html

American Sociological Association. (1997). *Code of ethics*. Washington, DC: Author. Retrieved July 5, 2006, from www2.asanet.org/members/ecoderev.html

Banerjee, A., Deaton, A., Lustig, N., Rogoff, K., & Hsu, E. (2006). *An evaluation of World Bank research, 1998–2005* (Report No. WB18913). Washington, DC: World Bank.

Begley, S. (2002, November 1). Review boards pose threat to tough work by social scientists. *Wall Street Journal*, p. B1.

Berliner, D. C. (2002). Educational research: The hardest science of all. *Educational Researcher, 31*(8), 18–20.

Chelimsky, E. (2007). Factors influencing the choice of methods in federal evaluation practice. In G. Julnes & D. Rog (Eds.), *Informing federal policies on evaluation methodology: Building the evidence base for method choice in government sponsored evaluation* (New Directions for Evaluation, No. 113, pp. 13–33). San Francisco: Jossey-Bass.

Dale, J. (2001). Science, ideology and profit: The stem-cell research controversy. *Socialism Today, 60*. Retrieved July 10, 2006, from www.socialismtoday.org/60/stem_cell_row.html

Datta, L. (2007). Looking at the evidence: What variations in practice might indicate. In G. Julnes & D. Rog (Eds.), *Informing federal policies on evaluation methodology: Building the evidence base for method choice in government sponsored evaluation* (New Directions for Evaluation, No. 113, pp. 35–54). San Francisco: Jossey-Bass.

Denzin, N. K. (2003, April). *IRBs and the turn to indigenous research ethics*. Paper presented at the conference on Human Subject Protection Regulations and Research Outside the Biomedical Sphere, College of Law, University of Illinois Champaign–Urbana.

Eisenhart, M., & Towne, L. (2003). Contestation and change in national policy on "scientifically based" education research. *Educational Researcher, 32*(7), 31–38.

Erickson, F., & Gutierrez, K. (2002). Culture, rigor, and science in educational research. *Educational Researcher, 31*(8), 21–24.

Feuer, M. J., Towne, L., & Shavelson, R. J. (2002). Scientific culture and educational research. *Educational Researcher, 31*(8), 4–14.

Flinders, D. J. (1992). In search of ethical guidance: Constructing a basis for dialogue. *Qualitative Studies in Education, 5*(2), 101–115.

Friedman, M. (1962). *Capitalism and freedom*. Chicago: University of Chicago Press.

House, E. R. (1995). *Principled evaluation: A critique of the AEA Guiding Principles* (New Directions for Program Evaluation, No. 66, pp. 27–34). San Francisco: Jossey-Bass.

Humphreys, L. (1970). *Tearoom trade: Impersonal sex in public places*. Chicago: Aldine De Gruyter.

International Military Tribunals. (1949). *Trials of war criminals before the Nuremberg Military Tribunals under Control Council Law No. 10* (Vol. 2, October 1946–April 1949). Washington, DC: Government Printing Office. Retrieved July 10, 2006, from www.csu.edu.au/learning/ncgr/gpi/odyssey/privacy/NurCode.html

Joint United Nations Programme on HIV/AIDS. (2000, May). *Ethical considerations in HIV preventive vaccine research* (04.07E). Geneva, Switzerland: Author. Retrieved February 1, 2007, from http://pre.ethics.gc.ca/english/links/links.cfm

Jones, J. H. (1993). *The Tuskegee syphilis experiment*. New York: Free Press.

Jones, P. W. (1992). *World Bank financing of education: Lending, learning and development*. London: Routledge.

Kovach, H., & Lansman, Y. (2006, June). *World Bank and IMF conditionality: A development injustice*. Brussels, Belgium: European Network on Debt and Development (Eurodad). Retrieved November 10, 2006, from www.globalpolicy.org/socecon/bwi-wto/wbank/index.htm

Leake, J. (2005, May 15). Wildlife groups axe Bellamy as global warming "heretic." *Times*. Retrieved February 10, 2006, from www.timesonline.co.uk/tol/news/uk/article522744.ece

Lomborg, B. (2001). *The skeptical environmentalist: Measuring the real state of the world*. Cambridge, UK: Cambridge University Press.

Mabry, L. (1999). Circumstantial ethics. *American Journal of Evaluation, 20*(2), 199–212.

Mabry, L. (2008). Consequences of NCLB on evaluation purpose, design, and practice. In T. Berry & R. Eddy (Eds.), *Consequences on NCLB on educational evaluation* (pp. 21–36). New Directions for Evaluation (No. 119). San Francisco: Jossey-Bass.

Manning, P. K., & Van Maanen, J. (1978). *Policing: A view from the street*. New York: Random House.

Max, A. (2007, April 6). International group issues global warming report. *Live Science*. Retrieved April 10, 2007, from www.livescience.com/environment/070406_ap_GW_report.html

Mertens, D. M. (2005). *Research and evaluation in education and psychology: Integrating diversity with quantitative, qualitative, and mixed methods* (2nd ed.). Thousand Oaks, CA: Sage.

Milgram, S. (1974). *Obedience to authority: An experimental view*. New York: Harpercollins.

Mill, J. S. (1891). *Utilitarianism* (11th ed.). London: Longmans, Green, & Co. (Original work published 1863)

National Association of Social Workers. (1996). *Code of ethics*. Washington, DC: Author. Retrieved July 5, 2007, from www.socialworkers.org/pubs/code/default.asp (Revised 1999)

National Commission for the Protection of Human Subjects of Biomedical and Behavioral Research. (1979). *The Belmont report* (Department of Health, Education, and Welfare Publication Nos. (OS) 78–0013 and (OS) 78–0014). Washington, DC: Government Printing Office.

No Child Left Behind Act. (2001). Public Law No. 107–110, 107th Congress, 110 Congressional Record 1425, 115 Stat. (2002).

Oakes, J. M. (2002). Risks and wrongs in social science research: An evaluator's guide to the IRB. *Evaluation Review, 24,* 443–478.

Pellegrino, J. W., & Goldman, S. R. (2002). Be careful what you wish for—you may get it: Educational research in the spotlight. *Educational Researcher, 31*(8), 15–17.

Pielke, R. A. (2006). When scientists politicize science. *Regulation, Spring,* 28–34. Retrieved April 5, 2007, from http://sciencepolicy.colorado.edu/publications/search.html?searchString=when+scientists+politicize+science&selectedMetadata%5B%5D=2432&action=Search&goInto=&toClose=

Psacharopoulos, G., & Woodhall, M. (1991). *Education for development: An analysis of investment choices.* New York: Oxford University Press.

Smith, A. (2003). *An inquiry into the nature and causes of the wealth of nations.* New York: Bantam Books. (Original work published 1776)

Solheim, E. (2006, November 28). Welcome speech. Oslo conference on [World Bank loan] Conditionality, Oslo, Norway. Retrieved February 1, 2006, from www.regjeringen.no/en/dep/ud/About-the-Ministry/Minister-of-International-Development-Er/Speeches-and-articles/2006/Welcome-speech-at-the-Oslo-Conference-on-Conditionality.html?id=436990

Stair, T. O., Reed, C. R., Radeos, M. S., Koski, G., & Camargo, C. A. (2001). Variation in institutional review board responses to a standard protocol for a multicenter clinical trial. *Academic Emergency Medicine, 8*(6), 636–641.

United Nations General Assembly. (1966, December 16). *International covenant on civil and political rights.* New York: Author.

United Nations General Assembly. (1990, December 14). *Guidelines for the regulation of computerized personal data* (Resolution 45/95). New York: Author.

United Nations General Assembly. (2005, March 8). *United Nations declaration on human cloning* (Resolution 59/280). New York: Author.

U.S. Department of Education. (2005, January 25). Scientifically based evaluation methods (RIN 1890-ZA00). *Federal Register, 70*(15), 3586–3589.

U.S. Department of Health, Education, and Welfare. (2000, October 1). *Code of federal regulations* (Title 45, Part 46, Subpart A, Section 46.122 (45CFR46.122), revised). Washington, DC: Government Printing Office.

Van Maanen, J. (1973). *Working the street: A developmental view of police behavior* (MIT Working Paper #671-83). Cambridge: Massachusetts Institute of Technology.

Viadero, D. (2007, April 18). AERA stresses value of alternatives to "gold standard." *Education Week, 29*(33), 12–13.

World Bank Independent Evaluation Group. (2006). *From schooling access to learning outcomes: An unfinished agenda. Evaluation of World Bank support to primary education.* Washington, DC: Author. Retrieved with summary on April 10, 2007, from www.worldbank.org/oed/education

World Medical Association General Assembly. (1964). *Declaration of Helsinki: Ethical principles for medical research involving human subjects* (Document 17.C). Helsinki, Finland: Author. Retrieved July 6, 2007, from www.wma.net/e/policy/b3.htm (Revised 1996)

8

THE ROLE OF INSTITUTIONAL REVIEW BOARDS

Ethics: *Now You See Them, Now You Don't*

◆ Richard Speiglman and Patricia Spear

> *As a principal investigator, you have multiple and possibly conflicting responsibilities to the IRB, the research subjects, and the sponsor.*
>
> —IRB study approval letter to the first author
>
> *As IRBs expand their responsibilities, terminology that might have been very clear in its original context is strained or ambiguous when applied to new areas, leading to imprecision and unreasonable regulatory burden as well as inappropriate regulation and restriction.*
>
> —Center for Advanced Study, 2005, p. 4

Under federal regulation, institutional review boards (IRBs), also often called independent ethics committees (IECs), are mandated reviewers of all U.S. federally funded research involving human subjects, whether *conducted* in the United States or in other countries.[1] Institutions in the United States often conduct non–federally funded as well as federally funded research. Depending on decisions made at each institution, the same IRB may be required to review both federally funded and non–federally funded research. Foreign institutions receiving U.S. federal funds for research involving human subjects must establish IRBs meeting U.S. Department of Health and Human Services (DHHS) standards for reviews of projects funded in their countries.

IRB mandates and activities have historically been driven by concern for the ethical conduct of research. However, other concerns also influence IRB behavior and may dilute the focus on ethics or challenge scholars' abilities to perform quality research. In this chapter we review the history of IRBs in the United States, including consideration of ethical and nonethical foci, and applicable federal regulations. The chapter discusses how IRBs are constituted, what they review, and why the review process is relevant to social and behavioral science research involving human subjects. In addition to core legal and historical documents and published materials that address ethics and IRBs, the chapter also relies on our experiences as researcher and IRB member and as institutional grants administrator also responsible for IRB operations. Common themes in the chapter are the distinctions—and conflicts—among an IRB's concern for and support of not only the protection of research subjects and the ethical conduct of research but also academic freedom and freedom of expression, institutional risk management, and a focus on regulatory compliance. The chapter also touches on some of the issues that have arisen in the last few years about the relevance and reach of IRB review to nonmedical research projects. It concludes with an expression of optimism that IRBs themselves are now becoming the object of research efforts.

◆ Origin of IRBs in the United States

Prior to World War II, there were no agreed-on ethical guidelines or established rules regulating research involving human subjects. Whatever research of this type—including clinical trials of pharmaceuticals—was done, was accomplished with as much or as little ethical oversight as the researchers felt appropriate. In most cases, trials and experiments were conducted on populations with little or no ability to accept or reject inclusion. Prisoner populations were most common, and other populations such as orphans and minorities were also subjects in clinical trials.

Following World War II, when the Nuremberg war crime trials revealed the terrible abuses inflicted on concentration camp prisoners by the Nazis in the guise of biomedical research, world revulsion led to a convening of experts under the aegis of the World Medical Association at Helsinki, Finland.[2] The resulting document, "Ethical Principles for Medical Research Involving Human Subjects," was adopted by the World Medical Association in 1964 (revisions and clarifications as recent as 2002) and was the basic international document on ethical principles for a number of years. However, the document focused on clinical medical research, not on behavioral and social science research.

Unethical experimentation took place not just abroad and not just in concentration camps and prisons, and it was carried out not just by obscure, independent researchers. The Tuskegee study in the United States, run from 1933 until its exposure in 1972, was conducted by the U.S. Public Health Service (PHS) on untreated poor blacks with and without syphilis in Alabama, with the rationale that effects of modern treatment ought to be compared with effects of no treatment. Even when effective treatments became available in the 1940s, treatment was denied to the men in this study who were infected.[3]

According to one text, initial steps toward regulation of human research in the United States were evident in 1953. In that year, the National Institutes of Health's (NIH's) "Clinical Center" began to oversee human experimentation at the NIH intramural campus in Bethesda, Maryland, by reviewing protocols "to avoid 'unusual hazards' to subjects before proceeding with experiments" (Shamoo & Resnik, 2003, p. 198). In 1965, the National Advisory Health Council issued the first United States prior review requirements for the use of human subjects in proposed research, and in 1966, the U.S. Surgeon General extended the prior peer review requirement to all NIH-funded research making use of human subjects (Shamoo & Resnik, 2003).

The discovery of and publicity about the Tuskegee study became emblematic of highly unethical research and the lack of federal assurance of ethical research even by its own practitioners. It led to the creation in 1974 of the National Commission for the Protection of Human Subjects of Biomedical and Behavioral Research. The Commission's charge included "to identify the basic ethical principles that should underlie the conduct of biomedical and behavioral research involving human subjects and to develop guidelines which should be followed to assure that such research is conducted in accordance with those principles" (Steneck, n.d., p. 43). The Commission studied the issues for several years and produced the *Belmont Report* in 1979. The report "attempts to summarize the basic ethical principles identified by the Commission in the course of its deliberations" (National Commission for the Protection of Human Subjects of Biomedical and Behavioral Research, 1979). This report for the first time included behavioral research in its definition and also tried to define the boundary between practice and research. It established the ethical principles of respect for persons, beneficence, and justice for study participants,[4] and for the first time informed consent in language understandable to participants was required, which would include a discussion of the balance between risks and benefits to the subjects and a statement that participation was voluntary. This code of ethical research practice was adopted in 1979 and is the cornerstone on which later guidelines and policies have been built.

For a number of years after the *Belmont Report*'s adoption, each federal agency that supported or conducted research involving human subjects had its own policies and procedures to regulate this research. By the end of the 1980s, much more research was being conducted with federal resources. An overabundance of regulations among different agencies led to the development of a codified regulation, which was adopted in 1991: The Federal Policy for Protection of Human Subjects, usually known as the Common Rule because, as of 1991, it had been accepted by and applied to research involving human subjects supported or conducted by approximately 16 federal agencies. At the DHHS, the Office for Human Research Protections (OHRP) "supports, strengthens and provides leadership to the nation's system for protecting volunteers in research that is conducted or supported by the U.S. Department of Health and Human Services (HHS)" (OHRP, 2006).

When the OHRP was established, it took on a new role as educator to IRBs in a broad way, providing guidance on the interpretation of the Common Rule. In its previous form as Office for Protection from Research Risks, it had conducted regional and national meetings for IRB professionals and researchers, but as OHRP, it expanded this role considerably and now not only provides training but has also become one of the institutions advocating for the idea of certification for IRB professionals and credentialing of IRBs.[5] At this time, there are at least two independent organizations providing examinations for certification of IRB professionals and also for credentialing IRBs themselves. IRB professionals are divided over both these activities, some favoring the additional work and examination, which they feel may make them more valuable to their institutions, and others believing that this effort is simply a reaction to the problems of the late 1990s (described below), that those issues have been resolved, and that the IRB system is working fine without additional examinations and certifications, which are seen to be self-serving and unnecessary.

The Common Rule can be read on the OHRP Web site and is often referred to as

45 CFR 46, its designation in the Code of Federal Regulations (DHHS, 2005). It has been amended over the years and now includes a definition of research, detailed information on projects exempt from research, as well as sections on the treatment of special populations including children, pregnant women and fetuses, and prisoners.[6] It is presumed that all researchers who include human participants in their research are familiar with the requirements of 45 CFR 46 and reflect on potential ethical questions, whether at the stage of study design, data collection, or reporting of findings.[7] For those reading this *Handbook*, the primary regulatory source will be 45 CFR 46.

◆ Organization and Behavior of IRBs

Application of the regulations at 45 CFR 46 to human subjects research projects is implemented by means of an IRB review. Every federally funded research project that includes human participants must be reviewed either by an IRB established at the grantee institution or by an independently established IRB. Furthermore, each institution conducting research supported with federal funds must register with the OHRP by filing a duly constituted Federal-Wide Assurance, which documents the institution's intent to comply with the 45 CFR 46 regulations.[8] At the institution's discretion, it may also elect to apply the same federal regulations to non–federally funded research.

WHAT IS AN IRB?

An IRB is a committee set up to review all—or all federally funded—research that includes human participants.[9] It must consist of at least five members, at least one of whom must be a nonscientist and at least one of whom must be from outside the institution with the IRB. Although, as we discuss below, IRBs experience competing priorities, the main task of an IRB "is to ensure that research is conducted in an ethical manner so that the welfare of subjects is protected" (Penslar, 1995, p. 99).

WHAT DOES THE IRB REVIEW?

The IRB reviews the scientific merit of the project, through the project's protocol, and the mechanism and contents of the consent procedure and documents that ensure ethical treatment of research participants (subjects). Primary scientific review may be conducted by others, such as an academic department or funding agency, but as noted in *Institutional Review Board: Management and Function*,

> Even when scientific review is not designated as an institutional IRB responsibility, IRBs must feel confident that the scientific merit of the protocol justifies a risk/benefit determination. (Amdur & Bankert, 2002, p. 147)

The IRB's job is to protect research participants by (a) making sure that the research is valid, (b) ensuring that the risks are minimized or balanced by benefits or potential benefits, and (c) ensuring that potential participants are given information relevant to making an informed decision about participating in the research and about the choices involved in doing so. The review process includes making sure that, if appropriate, a federal Certificate of Confidentiality is in place before the project begins, to protect sensitive information from disclosure.[10] The process also includes making sure that research instruments such as questionnaires are phrased so that participants can understand them and also that they are appropriate to the culture of participants. In some cases where the research is conducted in another country, there will be requirements for review by people who understand the culture where the project will be implemented. Additionally, IRBs are to determine that selection of subjects is equitable and recruitment is ethical.

Not infrequently, a focus of concern is the appropriate financial or other compensation, payment, or incentive for participation. This turns out to involve a potentially complicated calculus, including reflection on the degree of coercion, if any, introduced by the payment. A recent journal article on the matter points out that there is little empirically based knowledge of how such incentives actually operate and raises the question of whether the culture of the study population and risk-benefit ratio should contribute to determination of the appropriate payment level (Ripley, 2006).

WHAT DOES THE RESEARCHER HAVE TO DO?

"Researchers are responsible for obtaining appropriate approval before conducting research involving human subjects" (Steneck, n.d., p. 39) if (a) the project is defined as *research*, (b) human subjects are involved, and (c) the project is not exempt from review. For these purposes *research* is an activity "conducted with the intention of drawing conclusions that have some general applicability and uses a commonly accepted scientific method" (Steneck, n.d., p. 39). *Human subjects* are living individuals concerning whom identifiable, private information is secured.

For projects meeting these criteria, the researcher needs to write a protocol describing the research (often adapted from the grant application to the funding agency), the need for the research, research methods, the study population, and methods for evaluating the research. He or she needs to include whatever documents will be used for subject recruitment and all consent forms and instruments to be used. The IRB is to review all this material and request additional information if anything is unclear.

WHAT ARE THE IRB'S OPTIONS?

The IRB can approve the entire package, ask questions about or require modifications to the research protocol or associated materials such as consent documents, or disapprove the entire study. Additionally, an IRB is authorized to stop a project that is ongoing if it determines that there are significant problems with the study. There is no provision for appeal if a study is disapproved by an IRB.

WHAT IS NOT WITHIN THE IRB'S PURVIEW, AND WHAT PROCEDURAL REQUIREMENTS ARE KEY?

Exempt projects involve research that is of very low perceived risk, including among other examples in the social sciences, commonly accepted educational research, research involving educational tests, research relying only on data publicly available or data not identified with particular individuals, and research relying on survey procedures or observations of public behavior if subjects' identities are not recorded and subjects are not put at risk because of the research (45 CFR 46.101(b)). Finally, research conducted or approved by federal department or agency heads is exempt from review. However, as one IRB Web site notes, "the exemption is from IRB review but is not from ethical conduct or, where needed, appropriate consent" (Independent Review Consulting Inc., 2002, p. 3.2.1). Significantly, though, it is the IRB, not the individual researcher, who is to determine that a project is exempt from IRB review. Not subject to review are projects with goals that are entirely therapeutic. Student educational projects "designed to teach research methods and techniques . . . may not be considered research" (Shamoo & Resnik, 2003, p. 200).

Expedited review may be accomplished through review by fewer than the full board of reviewers. Research activities eligible for expedited review are limited to those in specific low-risk categories that present no more than minimal risk to the subjects. Below we consider how substantial a proportion of social science research may be included in the low-risk category. Candidates for expedited review include research involving materials collected for nonresearch purposes and research on individual or group characteristics or behavior. Methods might include survey, interview, oral history, focus group, and program evaluation, among others. The fact that a project is expedited does not affect the relevant requirement for informed consent or its waiver. Expedited review may also be used to request minor modifications for studies that have already secured approval. Full board review is used for all other applications.

♦ Crisis of Confidence

A series of adverse events in human subjects research projects in the late 1990s and into the early years of the new century led to heightened sensitivity on the part of the federal office charged with oversight of human subjects research and IRBs. In particular, the death of a young man, Jesse Gelsinger, after participation in a gene therapy clinical trial, greatly energized the regulatory community and caused OHRP to pay closer attention to the oversight of IRBs and clinical trials. A number of IRBs were closed down temporarily when irregularities were discovered, and the IRB community in general was put on notice that additional scrutiny would be the norm in the future.[11] What is significant for this discussion, however, is that these dramatic interventions did not concern projects in the realm of social science.

At the same time, and perhaps as a result of the heightened awareness and concern about human subjects in research, in 2002, a new committee was formed to replace the relatively new National Human Research Protections Advisory Committee, which itself had been instituted in 2000 as part of the response to the Gelsinger death, to try to address some of the then-perceived problems. The new committee, The Secretary's Advisory Committee on Human Research Protections (SACHRP), was moved to DHHS, where OHRP also resided. SACHRP was to address "issues and topics pertaining to or associated with the protection of human research subjects" (OHRP, 2007). SACHRP was initially tasked with paying particular attention to "special populations, such as neonates and children, prisoners, and the decisionally impaired; pregnant women, embryos, and fetuses; individuals and populations in international studies; populations in which there are individually identifiable samples, data, or information; and investigator conflicts of interest." In addition, the Committee was given responsibility to review selected activities of the OHRP and other HHS offices and agencies, including the granting of waivers and oversight of IRBs.

♦ Net-Widening, Mission Creep, and Other Problems

In reaction to research scandals, primarily in biomedicine, ethical codes and regulatory guidelines proliferated in the second half of the 20th century. While at first the regulations did not seem to apply to social sciences, "the language used in research ethics frameworks suggested that their provisions applied to all research involving humans" (Israel & Hay, 2006, p. 143). This process has involved what critics term *mission creep* (Center for Advanced Study, 2005, p. 2) and *net-widening*. How did this happen, and what are the implications?

It appears that the regulatory net was thrown wide because of institutional conservatism and threat of illegitimacy and/or financial vulnerability. Again, as described by Israel and Hay (2006), these developments transpired with little input from social scientists and little understanding that social and medical sciences are quite distinct:

> As a result, regulation of research ethics in many countries is now underpinned by an unsettling combination of biomedical research and institutional risk minimization models. In particular, social scientists have faced problems with regulatory practices associated with informed consent, confidentiality, beneficence and various research relationships and, not surprisingly, an adversarial culture has emerged between researchers and regulators. (pp. 143–144)

While the current application of regulation to social science research has its share of defenders, it has also attracted several vocal critics. In the pages that follow, we summarize several arguments related specifically to IRBs and behavioral and social science research. (a) Much IRB activity has to do not with protection of subjects or promotion of ethics but instead with institutional risk management. In a related manner, too much IRB activity concerns relatively trivial documentation rather than confrontation of seriously threatening areas of research. (b) The proportion of social research considered *covered* by IRBs should be limited. (c) Academic freedom and freedoms of association and expression have unnecessarily been limited. An unintended consequence of the above is researcher self-censorship and corresponding difficulty in securing funding to support research activities in certain topical areas or using particular research methods. We end this discussion with a few notes on interventions that have been suggested to contribute to more balanced application of regulation.

1. *Institutional Risk Management and Bureaucratic Documentation and Other Enforcement Practices.* IRBs are institutional entities. As such, their operations exist within the context of institutional priorities (e.g., reputation, endowment, and staff), deference to which may or may not have much of an ethical dimension or prioritize the protection of human subjects. Accordingly, it is argued, net-widening or mission creep and a focus on documentation rather than content and institutional risk management rather than ethics exacerbate the problem (Center for Advanced Study, 2005)[12]:

> vetting research through IRBs is thought to protect the university by filtering out overtly or unjustifiably risky research protocols.
>
> Yet there is almost no experience of litigation in social science or humanities research involving human subjects. (p. 11)

While the IRB may provide a venue for constructive feedback, "in many institutions and in a great number of countries, social scientists have felt that the processes adopted by research ethics committees have been excessively bureaucratic and arbitrary" (Israel & Hay, 2006, p. 137).[13] Committees can be slow to respond, lack necessary expertise to make appropriate judgments, or simply prove unresponsive to researchers' real problems. This process has been criticized as involving a misallocation of resources to the relatively risk free rather than truly risky projects. And one side effect of the completion of documentary regulations is the imposition of a significant burden on researchers and, in turn, on IRB members.

One scholar, political scientist Malcolm Feeley, in his 2006 presidential address to the Law and Society Association, has criticized his IRB's concern with "the remotest risk" and the resultant withholding of approval or requirement of "significant research modifications in order to preempt speculative harms. In short, in the name of minimizing risks, IRBs subject researchers to petty tyranny" (Feeley, 2007, p. 765).

2. *Definition of Social Research Considered Covered.* Not all research is covered research requiring prior IRB approval. IRBs have a responsibility to provide exemption when appropriate. However, some researchers believe that IRBs are not doing so and instead are insisting on carrying out full reviews even when not required. Requiring unnecessary or excessive review, perhaps because of a concern with lawsuits and potential program shutdowns, can result, although this violates principles espoused in the Belmont Report, in the inappropriate handling of projects with minimal risk as though they were consequential.

Increased workload for IRB staff, volunteer members, and researchers follows. But another outcome is the appearance if not the reality of lack of trust with researchers to carry out research ethically without oversight, despite the fact that it is the researchers who have to implement human subjects protections. More important is the difficulty experienced by IRBs in focusing on legitimate procedures and important cases with the greatest risk for harm.

For example, the question is raised, What about two people talking, one of whom intends to write about the conversation? Why would IRB involvement be required? What if the conversation took place ten years prior to a decision to author a research paper that included reflection on the conversation? What about a faculty member's reflecting on years of teaching and wanting to write about it? Professors have been told they may not do so, absent documentation of students' informed consent. When does *practice*—of teaching, for example—become *research?*[14]

Critics of contemporary IRB behavior point to problems arising from what is described as the uncritical expansion of responsibility from the biomedical realm to those of the social sciences and humanities:

> As IRBs expand their responsibilities, terminology that might have been very clear in its original context is strained or ambiguous when applied to new areas, leading to imprecision and unreasonable regulatory burden as well as inappropriate regulation and restriction. (Center for Advanced Study, 2005, p. 4)

Examples include constraints on historians conducting oral history interviews in the area of Holocaust memories, procedural constraints on social surveys making them impossible to conduct, and members of preliterate tribes asked to sign consent forms.

The limitation inherent in the assumption that ethical research as promoted by IRB involvement is brought to the foreground in a consideration of ethnographic research. A team of experienced ethnographers assessing why ethics committees do not work well for fellow ethnographers concludes that many ethics committees fail to understand the epistemological assumptions underlying the work of ethnography (Tolich & Fitzgerald, 2006). As an early-career sociologist writing about his ethnographic field work explained, "Hanging out raised ethical issues both in the field and in the academy" (Dohan, 2003, p. 242). His data collection method involved hanging out in Latino neighborhoods in San Jose and Los Angeles, something very difficult to write up fully in advance in a protocol. Dohan's point is that informed consent presented problems both in the field work and at the university with the IRB. As he noted, while one might want to secure informed consent from all persons crossing the researcher's field of view, in practice, social norms may prohibit it, it may be impossible, and in some cases, it could have negative consequences for "informed" community members already in the researcher's company and appearing to be "sponsors" of the research. Turning from concern with the field to that of the IRB, Dohan (2003) wrote,

> Hanging out also raised certain ethical issues in the academy. Relative to my concern about informed consent and protection of human subjects in the field, however, I find the ethical issues raised

by the academy to be irrelevant, at best, and perhaps even misguided. The Institutional Review Board (IRB) that ultimately approved my research plans had originally asked that I obtain written documentation of informed consent from anybody who participated in this study. Ultimately, the IRB granted a waiver of this requirement. (p. 243)

According to Feeley (2007), a special problem with IRB regulations and ethnographic research is found in the fact that while IRBs require that their approval be granted *prior* to initiation of research "we [qualitative researchers] often don't know we have started our research until after it is begun" (p. 768). He went on,

> Prior IRB approval may feasibly be required for biomedical tests or questionnaire-based research, but it poses severe problems for other types of research whose beginnings are often discerned retrospectively, and whose nature often leads researchers to revisit their field notes to investigate questions not formulated at the offset. (p. 768)[15]

A related problem arises with reference to journalism professors and their obligation to comply with IRB regulations, while print or other media journalists face no requirements beyond professional ethical guidance (and concern about potential legal consequences):

> We recommend focusing on those areas of research that pose the greatest risk, such as biomedical research, while removing or reducing scrutiny of many fields within the social sciences and humanities that pose minimal risk. Some fields, such as journalism and ethnography, and methods, such as oral history, have their own, well-established sets of ethical guidelines and appeal procedures. In addition, they pose virtually no risk to the subjects. (Center for Advanced Study, 2005, p. 3)

3. *Academic Freedom and Freedoms of Association and Expression.* Feeley and The Center for Advanced Study also raise the critique to a higher level. In the latter's words, the power of the IRB compromises academic freedom and also

> most of what is done by human interaction in the social sciences and the humanities involves nothing more than speech: a conversation, a questionnaire. To be required to secure a permit before one can have a conversation is the antithesis of freedom of expression or inquiry. (Center for Advanced Study, 2005, p. 17)

Feeley (2007) went so far as to suggest that First Amendment and academic freedom protections, long-term values of research projects, are being forgotten in the benefit-harm equation. In his critique of IRBs, Feeley charged that they "have taken on the form and function of censorship boards, and as such the universities that embraced them uncritically indulge community standards rather than provide researchers with a shield against them" (p. 766). Furthermore, he noted, some argue that the process amounts to prior restraint, in conflict with Constitutional protections of free expression, resulting in a chilling effect.

Both "upstream" and "downstream" effects result from what Feeley considers to be overly conservative IRB behavior. In the case of the former, he believes that researchers may "learn" to engage in self-censorship by scaling back on the content and/or methods of "difficult" projects or abandoning them altogether. Use of alternative, less optimal methods or suboptimal sampling strategies can compromise data and scientific quality, and hence the potential value of research, themselves outcomes of ethical import. Downstream effects might include limited funding availability for certain study designs and the endangerment of research areas and methodologies altogether. In short, he believes, important research may not be undertaken if a lesson learned by researchers from their IRB experience is to stick to "easy" projects.

♦ Suggestions for Resolution of the Problems

The history and contemporary reality presented above has resulted in a system that is described by critics both inside and outside the regulatory agency as "in crisis," "compromised," or "at risk" and in loss of respect among some of the people whom IRBs are intended to regulate.[16] One distressing result of overly engaged IRBs is that their credibility is undermined, and some researchers are reported to evade, circumvent, or ignore committees or their requirements or shop for "better" committees. Other reactions are equally unpleasant: For example, subjects are encouraged to ignore informed consent forms prior to signing them, or it is suggested that they sign consents with fictitious names in cases where greater risk is associated with signing the form than with not signing.

With increasing regulation and bureaucratization of IRBs, Israel and Hay (2006) concluded, "Research ethics regulators have achieved the seemingly impossible. They have given ethics a bad name" (p. 143). On the other hand, both OHRP and the organization Public Responsibility in Medicine and Research (PRIM&R) have a much more positive approach to the value of IRBs and of their roles in general. OHRP's mission has been stated earlier in this chapter, and PRIM&R, which sees itself (regardless of its name) as representing both social science and medical research practitioners, "is dedicated to advancing the highest ethical standards in the conduct of research" by, among other means, developing educational and certification programs for those engaged in the review and conduct of research (PRIM&R, 2007).

Several suggestions have been made. If translated into social research fields, the *Belmont Report*'s distinction between *practice* and *research* in the biomedical realm may prove to provide a starting point for conversation.

Noting that "confidentiality is the nub of regulatory concern" for social science research, The Center for Advanced Study's (2005) white paper suggests dealing with confidentiality

> without involving the machinery of IRB research review and approval at all.... The institution could (and should) promulgate a rule prohibiting the public disclosure of all harmful, personally identifiable information in which the public has no interest unless the person concerned has given consent or in response to lawful process.... [other harms] are harms of a significantly different order, predominantly temporary in their impact, more continuous with the risks "encountered in everyday life," and, we suggest, beyond the proper scope of the IRB.... outside of the broad protections of informed consent and confidentiality, their predicted likelihood in any particular case is incalculable in advance. IRBs have no reasonable way to assess these harms. (p. 13)

Dohan (2003) and Tolich and Fitzgerald (2006) suggested the use of different guidelines and review formats for qualitative and ethnographic research, with Tolich and Fitzgerald suggesting that some responsibility for ethics review shifts to journal editors and thesis review boards. However, at this point in time, these are only suggestions for dealing with the intersection of the IRB and social science research. The reality is that OHRP requires IRB review and oversight of all nonexempt federally funded research involving human participants. Reaching consensus on changes to the type of review required or to establish what body (if any) should review these types of projects will take time and reflection.

We do not suggest that completely removing scrutiny for minimal-risk social/ behavioral science projects is appropriate.

However, recognition of and respect by OHRP for existing ethical guidelines and procedures in other fields that involve research with human subjects, as noted above, might provide an avenue for discussion and, ultimately, agreement on the types of review that would be appropriate. And the other organizations/fields need to understand OHRP's position as well, rather than simply criticizing its work. While this process of dialogue and discussion will not be quick, it should begin, so that in time there can be agreement on the types of review and approval required for different kinds of research involving human subjects. To this end, discussant organizations should include OHRP, to be sure, but also a variety of other organizations under whose umbrellas research is conducted, including journalistic, psychological, sociological, judicial, historical, and others whose experience will inform the discussion.[17] Convening these various organizations and encouraging a dialogue aimed at developing procedures that do protect subjects from harm, yet do not insist on unreasonably burdensome procedures, would seem to be a timely and important activity given the concerns raised by social and behavioral science researchers. It appears, from discussion on the IRB Forum, an online discussion mechanism among IRB professionals and researchers, that a number of professionals associated with IRBs and other agencies and institutions as well as a number of officials at OHRP share these concerns and, we hope, would be willing participants in discussions of the issues (IRB Forum, 2007).

♦ Conclusion

In terms of the critical perspectives we reviewed, a liberal worldview emerged: The statements from Feeley and The Center for Advanced Study, among others, present a liberal critique based on constitutional rights, just procedures, and other factors. Respect for the status quo, together with a determination to improve education of IRB members as well as researchers and to provide guidance on the Common Rule, is well expressed by OHRP itself in its mission statement and by PRIM&R in its materials.

But another look at the ethics of IRBs emerges from the critical stance of a scholar engaged in action research. From that perspective, IRBs were created and continue to function in a legalistic fashion and with increasingly complicated documentation and other requirements, "in an attempt to instill ethical values on otherwise amoral research practice" (Brydon-Miller, Chapter 16, this volume). Ironically, from Brydon-Miller's perspective, the trajectory to protect human subjects is currently defined by a highly specific focus on *informed consent* and other documents rather than a more penetrating examination of the ethical implications of the *research itself*.

Without question the appearance, development, and presence of IRBs have resulted in a broader concern with and understanding of ethical issues by researchers associated with universities and other institutions. But the ethic of human subjects protections may have resulted in compromises to other ethics; in particular, standards for legality and the "rule of law." As a result, according to Feeley (2007), because of rights violations one "cannot accord them [IRB practices] the fidelity that law requires" (p. 771).

The Illinois White Paper suggests that institutions avoid the filing of assurances that they will apply the Common Rule to all research under their auspices. Institutions "can (and should) then create an internal set of guidelines that commit to the highest ethical standards. Under this approach, however, local research can be overseen in more flexible and appropriate ways" (Center for Advanced Study, 2005, p. 20). Feeley's (2007) comments, however, suggest that this approach leaves something to be desired:

> If ethical standards are important, they should be applied to research without regard to particular sources of funding. And if there is an effective enforcement mechanism already in place to vet larger-scale projects that are funded by prestigious sources, it makes sense to apply that mechanism to other research as well. (p. 765)

We conclude this chapter by reflecting on our experiences—as researcher, as IRB administrator, and as IRB members, our reading of the literature cited here, and our involvement in the IRB Forum and other discussions. Without question, focus on the ethics of research in the United States has been promoted by IRBs and the federal regulations by which they and researchers are guided. At the same time, researcher discontent with IRB worldview assumptions and with routine IRB procedures is strong and demands change. One subtheme, concerning the effectiveness of the IRB system, could, and may soon, be informed by research-based findings. We look forward to procedural and even epistemological reform emerging from the new *Journal of Empirical Research on Human Research Ethics* and hope that broader attention still to the ethical implications of "research itself" will follow.

◆ Notes

1. All references to IRBs should be read to include IECs as well.

2. The Nuremberg Code, adopted as an ethical code for human subjects research, assumed that research was medical in nature, failed to refer to an oversight body, and was not binding on researchers (*Trials of war criminals before the Nuremberg Military Tribunals under Control Council Law No. 10*, 1949).

3. There were also studies, without informed consent, of the effects of radiation on hospital patients, children, and soldiers.

4. As summarized by Penslar (1995),

> Respect for persons means treating others as autonomous agents . . . having rights and the freedom of self-determination. . . . Beneficence towards human subjects means that research should be for the good of the subject (if not directly, then indirectly through benefiting society), and that possible benefits are maximized and risks are minimized. . . . Justice means that benefits and harms are to be distributed fairly [throughout society]. (p. 99)

5. When Office for Protection from Research Risks changed to OHRP, it moved from NIH to DHHS to reduce the possibility of conflict of interest since, as well as all the other IRB responsibilities, the office provides oversight to NIH activities.

6. The National Bioethics Advisory Committee, appointed by President Clinton in 1995, addressed, in addition to human cloning, embryonic stem cell research, and gene therapy research, research on people with mental disorders (Shamoo & Resnik, 2003).

7. Some other federal agencies have additional requirements for research funded by them, including the FDA (21 CFR 50 and 21 CFR 56). These regulations, however, will only rarely be an issue for behavioral and social science researchers.

8. Additionally, the PHS requires every institution with PHS funds to have in place procedures for handling allegations of scientific misconduct.

9. The institution that is host to the research determines the breadth of coverage of its IRB.

10. See 42 United States Code 241(d), which provides the U.S. Secretary of Health and Human Services with authority to grant researchers the right to protect the privacy of research subjects

> by withholding from all persons not connected with the conduct of such research

the names or other identifying characteristics of such individuals. Persons so authorized to protect the privacy of such individuals may not be compelled in any Federal, State, or local civil, criminal, administrative, legislative, or other proceedings to identify such individuals. [42 USC 241(d)] (Note: USC = United States Code)

11. For details of IRB suspensions at several institutions, see Campbell (1999a, 1999b).

12. See also the review provided by Israel and Hay (2006).

13. "The disproportionate attention to problems that can be easily addressed, such as counting signatures, filing forms, refining consent forms over and over, and editing proposals for typos, means that complex ethical questions on which people of good will can disagree may get short shrift" (Center for Advanced Study, 2005, p. 12).

14. Feeley (2007) and other authors raised these points. The Illinois White Paper also notes that "knowledge-generating" activities undertaken by historians and social critics, "driven by the aims of public service as a critic, a gadfly, or a public watchdog," may need to answer to a higher authority than the IRB (Center for Advanced Study, 2005, p. 10).

15. See Tolich and Fitzgerald (2006) for a critique of IRB operations under positivist worldviews.

16. The Center for Advanced Study (2005) referenced, among others, Citro, Iglen, and Marrett (2003); Institute of Medicine (2001, 2002); Levine (2001); and Office of Inspector General (1998).

17. Recent activity within the American Psychological Association suggests that just this type of engagement is proceeding (Munsey, 2007).

♦ References

Amdur, R., & Bankert, E. (Eds.). (2002). *Institutional review board: Management and function.* Boston: Jones & Bartlett.

Campbell, P. W. (1999a, April 30). U.S. examines human-subject research at 3 veterans hospitals. *Chronicle of Higher Education, 45*(34), A32. Retrieved April 16, 2008, from http://chronicle.com/weekly/v45/i34/34a03203.htm

Campbell, P. W. (1999b, May 28). Government restores Duke U.'s right to conduct research on humans. Normality returns after suspension at the medical center, but officials at other institutions are reviewing their research programs. *Chronicle of Higher Education, 45*(38), A30. Retrieved April 16, 2008, from http://chronicle.com/weekly/v45/i38/38a03001.htm

Center for Advanced Study. (2005). *The Illinois white paper. Improving the system for protecting human subjects: Counteracting IRB "mission creep."* Urbana-Champaign, IL: Author.

Citro, C., Iglen, D., & Marrett, C. (2003). *Protecting participants and facilitating social and behavioral science research.* Washington, DC: National Academies Press.

Dohan, D. (2003). *The price of poverty: Money, work, and culture in the Mexican American barrio.* Berkeley: University of California Press.

Feeley, M. M. (2007). Presidential address. Legality, social research, and the challenge of institutional review boards. *Law and Society Review, 41*(4), 757–776.

Independent Review Consulting. (2002). *Five possible initial review routes.* Retrieved December 4, 2007, from www.irb-irc.com/theirb/3.2.1__Review_Processes.pdf

Institute of Medicine. (2001). *Preserving public trust: Accreditation and human research participant protection programs.* Washington, DC: National Academies Press.

Institute of Medicine. (2002). *Responsible research: A systems approach to protecting research participants.* Washington, DC: National Academies Press.

IRB Forum. (2007). *The institutional review board: Discussion and news forum.* Retrieved December 8, 2007, from www.irbforum.org

Israel, M., & Hay, I. (2006). *Research ethics for social scientists. Between ethical conduct and regulatory compliance*. London: Sage.

Levine, R. J. (2001). Institutional review boards: A crisis in confidence. *Annals of Internal Medicine, 134,* 161–163.

Munsey, C. (2007). Fixing the institutional review board system: An APA task force is examining what has become a murky process. *Monitor on Psychology, 38*(9), 50.

National Commission for the Protection of Human Subjects of Biomedical and Behavioral Research. (1979, April 18). *Ethical principles and guidelines for the protection of human subjects of research (The Belmont Report)*. Retrieved December 4, 2007, www.hhs.gov/ohrp/humansubjects/guidance/belmont.htm

Office for Human Research Protections. (2006). *OHRP fact sheet*. Retrieved December 5, 2007, from www.hhs.gov/ohrp/about/ohrpfactsheet.htm

Office for Human Research Protections. (2007). *Secretary's Advisory Committee on Human Research Protections (SACHRP)*. Retrieved December 4, 2007, from www.hhs.gov/ohrp/sachrp/index.html

Office of Inspector General, Department of Health and Human Services. (1998). *Institutional review boards: A time for reform* (No. OEI-01-97–00193). Washington, DC: Government Printing Office.

Penslar, R. L. (1995). *Research ethics*. Bloomington: Indiana University Press.

Public Responsibility in Medicine and Research. (2007). *About us*. Retrieved December 5, 2007, from www.primr.org/AboutUs.aspx?id=32&linkidentifier=id&itemid=32

Ripley, E. B. D. (2006). A review of paying research participants: It's time to move beyond the ethical debate. *Journal of Empirical Research on Human Research Ethics, 1*(4), 9–20.

Shamoo, A. E., & Resnik, D. B. (2003). *Responsible conduct of research*. New York: Oxford University Press.

Steneck, N. H. (n.d.). *ORI [Office of Research Integrity] introduction to the responsible conduct of research*. Rockville, MD: U.S. Department of Health and Human Services.

Tolich, M., & Fitzgerald, M. H. (2006). If ethics committees were designed for ethnography. *Journal of Empirical Research on Human Research Ethics, 1*(2), 71–78.

Trials of war criminals before the Nuremberg Military Tribunals under Control Council Law No. 10. (1949). Retrieved December 4, 2007, from www.hhs.gov:80/ohrp/references/nurcode.htm

U.S. Department of Health and Human Services. (2005). *Title 45, Public welfare, Code of federal regulations. Part 46, Protection of human subjects*. Retrieved December 5, 2007, from www.hhs.gov/ohrp/humansubjects/guidance/45cfr46.htm

9

RESEARCHING OURSELVES BACK TO LIFE

Taking Control of the Research Agenda in Indian Country

◆ Joan LaFrance and Cheryl Crazy Bull

> Here comes the anthros.
> Better hide your past away.
> Here come the anthros on another holiday.
> And the anthros bring their friends to see the circus watch the show
> And when their pens are dried they pack their things and away they go
>
> —Floyd Red Crow Westerman[1]

More than 30 years ago, a well-known husband and wife anthropologist team noted that in their profession they had studied American Indians more than any other group in the world

---

AUTHORS' NOTE: This chapter is partially supported by the National Science Foundation Grant No. 0438720 to the American Indian Higher Education Consortium. Any opinions expressed in this chapter are those of the authors and do not necessarily reflect the views of the National Science Foundation.

(Swisher, 1993). The myriad of research done by social, health, and medical researchers is problematic to many American Indian people whose tribes and families have suffered from a long history of intrusive studies that have built the reputations of anthropologists and other researchers but brought little more than the loss of cultural ownership and exploitation to Indian people. Vine Deloria Jr. (1969), in his trail-blazing book, *Custer Died for Your Sins*, was among the first to denounce the invasion of arrogant researchers pursuing their own agendas and using Native peoples to promote their careers. His chapter on "Anthropologists and Other Friends" inspired Floyd Red Crow Westerman's song "Here Come the Anthros." However, as tribes assert their authority and lay claim to their own agendas, it is no longer a "holiday" for researchers in Indian Country.

In this chapter, we discuss this changing landscape and ethical considerations that need to be taken into account given the shift toward tribal control over what research is done and how it is done. We briefly outline the movement to take control of research agendas and describe the various processes being used in tribal communities to review and regulate research in Indian Country. However, ethical and culturally responsive research requires more than attending to regulatory dictates. Throughout the chapter, we share the experience and reflections of both Indigenous and non-Indigenous scholars regarding lessons learned in conducting research that is respectful of Native cultural mores and responsive to community priorities. We conclude our discussion by examining how research practice informed by Indigenous ways of knowing challenges Western epistemologies and methodologies (in which most of us have been trained). Our discussion focuses primarily on tribal communities in the United States as that is our direct experience.[2]

Although most of our discussion describes our experience in the United States, the history of exploitation and abusive research practices is not unique to American Indians. Nor is the growth of formalized processes to guide research among Indigenous peoples limited to the United States. In Canada, researchers must submit their proposals to Research Ethics Boards that follow the "Tri-Council Policy Statement" (TCPS) for research. Section 6 of the TCPS directs researchers to a number of documents that outline ethical guidelines for working with First Nations and Aboriginal communities. Noting that in Canada, and elsewhere, Indigenous peoples have "distinctive perspectives and understandings embodied in their cultures and histories," the policy statement "recognizes the international consensus that has developed over recent decades that Aboriginal Peoples have a unique interest in ensuring accurate and informed research concerning their heritage, customs and community" (Canadian Institutes of Health Research, 2005, sec. 6, p. 6.2).

In 1998, the Health Research Council of New Zealand issued *Guidelines for Researchers on the Health Research Involving Maori*. The guidelines are intended to inform researchers about when consultation is necessary and processes to use to initiate consultation with Maori. The document notes that one of the purposes of the guidelines is to "ensure that the research outcomes contribute as much as possible to Maori health and well-being, while the research process maintains or enhances mana Maori" (Maori authority or power; Health Research Council of New Zealand, 1998, p. 3).

In an address to the Canadian Evaluation Society, Marlene Brant-Castellano, co-Chair of the Royal Commission on Aboriginal Peoples (RCAP), told a story of her experience at a special meeting of the RCAP to solicit feedback on the content of a proposed research program. The entire first session was spent facing criticisms of research, with many echoing the statement, "We have been researched to death." An elder who listened for a long time, offered the following observation: "If it is true that we have been researched to death, maybe it is time we started researching ourselves back to life again" (Brant-Castellano, 1997, p. 1). The elder's wisdom reveals the importance of research in our communities while recognizing the essentialness of self-determination. It is in this spirit of "researching ourselves back to life" that we write this chapter.

♦ Arguing for Change

Research in Indigenous communities faces the challenge of whose voice is speaking with authority about Aboriginal experience and in the validity of information—both the reporting of facts and their interpretation (Brant-Castellano, 1997). Over the years, Indigenous writers have argued the importance of building capacity among Indigenous researchers and shifting research agendas. In 1977, Joseph Trimble, a Lakota researcher, described himself as a "sojourner," a lone voice attempting to sort through the American Indian community needs and the agendas of researchers. In a review of articles on Indian educational research, he found that most of the literature concentrated on problems centered on the investigator's interest and not on those of the tribal people from whom the data were obtained. Often these research studies depicted Indians in a naive or negative light (Trimble, 1977). LaFromboise and Plake (1983) noted the need to increase the number of American Indian researchers and expand community participation in research. In 1991, the *American Indian Quarterly* dedicated an issue to research in Indian Country. Wax (1991) described many of the ethical problems inherent in conducting research in Indian communities, including the incompatibility of worldviews; the varying views of ethics and science; and issues of membership and individual autonomy, and disclosure and informed consent. V. Deloria (1991) argued that researchers needed to focus on real needs in Indian communities and minimize useless research. In a 1993 interview published in the *Tribal College Journal of American Indian Education*, John Red Horse, Professor of American Indian Studies at the University of Minnesota, described the need for stronger control over research conducted in Indian communities (Boyer, 1993). In 1999, in her foundational work on decolonizing methodologies, Linda Tuwahi Smith addressed imperialism, research, and knowledge while also offering guidance to those who aspire to do respectful and ethical work with Indigenous peoples. Her framework for a research agenda that honors and builds the cultural life of a people also serves as a guide for tribes seeking to establish their own guidelines for community-based research.

With the development of tribally controlled K–12 and postsecondary schools, there has been a rise in the national discussion regarding Native-led research agendas and in the development of research capacity among tribal people and their institutions. The National Indian Education Association joined forces with other national Indian organizations in the mid-1990s to develop an Indian education research agenda that remains at the forefront of education initiatives. Other national groups such as the Association of American Indian Physicians supported similar initiatives.

As a growing number of Indigenous scholars were calling for research agendas that were responsive to tribal needs and respected community cultural values, in the United States the *Belmont Report* (1979) outlined the "Ethical Principles and Guidelines for the Protection of Human Subjects Research," which fueled the development of institutional review boards (IRBs) within governmental agencies and institutions of higher education to protect individuals from abusive research practices. Regulations and processes were instituted to foster respect for persons—recognizing their "self-determination" to consent to be subjects of research, to at a minimum "do no harm" and to the extent possible maximize benefits, and to strive for fairness in distribution of both the burdens and the benefits of research (National Commission for the Protection of Human Subjects of Research, 1979). Certainly, these protections extend to all people, including Indians who are subjects of research studies. However, given the long and often negative legacy of being subjects of research, and a number of issues that emerged in Indian Country despite IRB processes of federal agencies and universities, tribal communities have become increasingly aware of the need to protect not only tribal individuals but also tribal and community reputations, culture, and heritage.

◆ When Human Subjects Protection Fails to Protect

Despite the carefully drawn prescriptions for research approval developed by governmental agencies, colleges, and universities, a number of tribal communities continued to experience humiliations and repercussions from poorly conducted or reported research findings. The early research into the outbreaks of the 1993 hantavirus pulmonary syndrome in the Four Corners area fueled newspaper headlines describing the "Navajo Flu." Sensational reporting resulted in Navajo people being denied services in local restaurants and children having to present health certificates to attend summer camps (Kciji, 1993, *Indian Country Today*). The Barrow Alcohol Study issued a premature press release of limited results of a survey that led to headlines describing Barrow as a city of alcoholics. Noe et al. (2006) reported that the negative reporting led Standard and Poor's to lower the city's bond rating, which affected financing for a number of community projects.

IRB processes have not prevented the misuse of research data. The Havasupai encouraged researchers at Arizona State University (ASU) to study the high rates of diabetes among tribal members. In 1990, tribal members began to provide blood samples, with an understanding that they were for diabetes-related research. In 2003, a member of the tribe was surprised to learn at a dissertation defense that a graduate student had used the blood samples to illustrate how an isolated and intermarried group of people had migrated from Asia.[3] Samples of the blood drawn for the diabetes study also have been used to study the incidence of schizophrenia among the tribe. The dispute about the use of the blood samples and whether proper consent was obtained by the researchers is the subject of a major civil lawsuit (Rubin, 2004). Regardless of the judicial outcome of the suit, the case had a profound effect on tribes, especially in the Southwest, with some placing temporary moratoriums on research.

Inherent in the experience of Native people with research is the recognition that all aspects of Native lives are fodder for someone else's desire to own "intellectual property." This can range from capturing their tribal stories for children's storybooks to mapping their DNA for the wealth of information buried in their genes about human origins, evolution, and diversity. The experience of Native people with research such as that conducted by the Human Genome Organization, partially supported by the National Institutes of Health (which also oversee the establishment and regulation of IRBs), is representative of that experience. A component of the Human Genome Project that seeks to collect and eventually map the DNA of vanishing people targets Indigenous people at the heart of their identity. For tribes such as the Lakota of the Northern Plains, who believe their DNA to be closely tied to their origins as buffalo people and with the buffalo, this is the ultimate infringement on who they are. What appears innocuous to outside researchers is profoundly intrusive within the Lakota sense of themselves as a People. Recently, a *New York Times* article (Rother, L. In The Amazon, Giving Blood but Getting Nothing, June 20, 2007, from online NYT archives Web search) shared the experience of Indigenous tribes in Brazil providing blood samples to scientists on the promise of medicine and other help, only to later find that the samples were being sold over the Internet along with their DNA.

These incidents of the failure of human subjects protection have reinforced the importance of direct tribal engagement in the review of and approval of research as well as issues related to the ownership of data and reporting of findings. Tribes realize that they have a responsibility to protect the interest of individual members as well as the community as a whole. Most formal nontribal IRB processes do not account for community interests or protections. In the following section, we describe the different ways in which research authority is or could be exercised through tribal review processes and their influence on research.

◆ Claiming the Research Agenda

Few Americans fully appreciate the political status of American Indians and Alaskan Natives.[4] In Indian country, sovereignty expresses the recognition of and respect for tribal governance and nationhood. Treaties between Indian Nations and the United States established a unique federal/tribal relationship.

Recent federal laws have encouraged tribal self-determination and self-governance. As a result, many tribes now operate their own economic development, infrastructure, educational, health, and welfare programs through funding relationships with the federal government and through their own economic relationship. Programs operating on Indian reservations operate within a civil structure unfamiliar to most Americans. Tribes are governmental units separate from state and local governments. In many tribes, the governing bodies include a General Council, which is composed of all tribal citizens of age 18 and above, and an elected business council, which is usually called the Tribal Council. Other tribes have more traditional forms of governments based on historical leadership patterns (LaFrance, 2004). In addition to running a number of business enterprises, tribes construct and manage housing programs, dispense welfare through tribal Temporary Assistance to Needy Families programs, provide employment training services, operate their own health clinics through contracts with the Indian Health Service (IHS), and operate their own day care centers, Head Start, K–12 schools, and tribal colleges and universities.

It is not surprising that as tribes take over the delivery of services to their members, they are also reclaiming their right to determine what research will be done in their communities. In their guide for tribes regarding how to develop a research code, The American Indian Law Center (1999) explained the importance of tribal self-determination regarding research.

Indian tribes, in addressing the question of regulating research in the Indian community, are in fact defining for themselves the degree to which they wish to make themselves available as subjects. While they may and probably should feel a responsibility as members of the human community to participate in some kinds of research and assume a fair share of the risks inherent in research which will benefit society as a whole, they must define this responsibility for themselves, and they should not feel that the value systems of research professions are of universal validity, binding on them for all purposes. (p. 5)

Although tribes in the United States have the authority to establish formal research review procedures, only a few have developed their own IRB processes. Bowman (2006) estimated that less than 1% of tribes have their own review boards, although many rely on those established by federal agencies such as the IHS or their own institutions of higher education. Regardless of whether a tribal government has developed a formal IRB or alternative review processes, research, especially in any health-related area, is now subject to tribal approval either through the IHS or, in some cases, a tribal college.

♦ Indian Health Service IRB

Any research that is conducted in an IHS facility must be approved by either the national IHS review board, or any of the 10 IHS service area IRBs. In addition to standard IRB protections for human subjects, the guidelines for review require that formal written approval from appropriate tribal governments must be submitted with the research proposal. They further state that any publications or presentations with findings about specific tribes must be accompanied by approval from the relevant tribal government(s), even if the tribes are not named in the manuscript. If a tribe has its own IRB, the research project must have the approval of both the tribal and IHS IRBs. However, if a tribal IRB is registered with the Office of Human Research Protection and has a Federal-Wide Assurance (FWA), then the tribal IRB process is sufficient (U.S. Department of Health and Human Services, Indian Health Service, 2007).

♦ Tribal College IRB

In 2004, the *Tribal College Journal* dedicated an issue to research at Tribal Colleges and Universities (TCUs), and described the importance of establishing a TCU IRB. According to Hernandez (2004), TCUs are increasingly adopting review procedures that serve as gatekeepers for research in tribal communities. He reported on a survey in 2002 that found that only 9 of the 35 tribal colleges had IRBs. In June 2007, the American Indian Higher Education Consortium polled its membership of 34 TCUs and found that 11 reported having their own IRBs, although some of these partner with a tribal IRB, and 2 colleges are partnering with an institute of higher education's IRB. Tribal colleges can choose to register with the federal Office of Human Research Protection (OHRP) and be designated as having an FWA, which allows the college to receive federal funds to conduct research themselves.

Dr. William Freeman, the former chair of the national IHS IRB and currently on the faculty of Northwest Indian College, has provided extensive training to TCUs regarding the steps involved in establishing an IRB (W. Freeman, personal communications, June 28, 2007). He encourages the development of IRBs that are flexible and can be shaped to fit the needs of the student population and the communities served by the college. When a tribal college receives a request for research that is limited to using only their students as participants, or only using student data within the control of the college, it may or may not request a review by a tribal government or an entity of the tribe. However, whenever the research has potential to influence tribal culture or community, Freeman recommends that the college formally engage the tribe in the review. He cited an example of a request to research a college's Native language program. Although the research would be working only within the college language program, the Culture Committee of the tribe was formally consulted in the review processes.

Although IRBs do not exist in all the tribal colleges, many of them have research policies that oversee the conduct of research in their institution and serve as a resource for local tribal research relationships. This development arose naturally out of the increasingly educated Native population now returning to tribal communities.

♦ Tribal IRB

The National Congress of American Indians (NCAI)[5] commissioned a study regarding research regulation options for tribes (Sahota, 2007). The paper outlines various approaches that are being used or could be considered by tribes to control research in

American Indian and Alaskan Native communities and presents advantages and disadvantages for each. The following list illustrates the various ways in which tribes are implementing or can consider policies to regulate research.

- *Contracting with entities that have IRBs:* Tribes can contract to use IRBs such as those developed by the IHS or by tribal colleges on the reservation or another institution of higher education. Obviously, partnering with an existing IRB is an attractive option for smaller tribes that lack the infrastructure and personnel to oversee research. Tribes that have a small demand from outsiders for research would also benefit from partnering with an existing IRB. However, tribes have less control over research decisions, especially if they partner with an outside institution of higher education.

- *Creating a tribal IRB:* In choosing to establish a tribal IRB, tribes exercise their sovereignty and have control over decisions related to research in their community. A tribe can form a formal IRB that is approved by OHRP and has an FWA, or it can develop a research review process tailored to its own community. Sahota lists seven tribes that have IRBs—Cherokee Nation, Chickasaw Nation, Choctaw Nation, Ho-Chunk Nation, Navajo Nation, the California Rural Indian Health Board, and the Three Affiliated Tribes of North Dakota. In addition to exercising sovereignty, tribal IRBs lend legitimacy to research in their communities. The disadvantage is the time and money required to staff the IRB and train board members.

- *Using community advisory boards or other forms of research review committees:* One alternative to a formal IRB is the establishment of a community advisory board (CAB). The board can be established to oversee and advise a particular research project, or the tribe might create a CAB to oversee all research. CABs are more closely involved with research than IRB members. They generally work in partnership with the researchers and review and discuss all aspects of the research project as it is being implemented. This continuing relationship with the research is an advantage of CABs. However, as an advisory group, they have less formal authority; however, a tribe can establish a CAB as part of its governing structure and in its laws or codes, establish enforcement procedures. Tribes can establish other forms of review boards that are not IRBs or CABs but perform similar functions. CABs are also a good option for urban Indian organizations that wish to oversee research programs that recruit research subjects from their memberships or programs participants.

- *Using existing committees:* In some cases, a tribe may use an existing committee within their tribal governmental structure to serve as a review board. For example, the Health and Social Services Committee could be assigned to review research proposals relative to its services. Or a Tribal Culture Committee can review research related to cultural practices and language.

Not only do tribes have to be responsive to federal guidelines in the establishment of an IRB, they frequently have to build the capacity of the community to evaluate research opportunities and to create a framework by which not only can research be regulated, but also the tribe can be assured of the benefits of the research. Native scholars exist throughout Indian Country—individuals who are not formally trained in Western methodologies but who conduct research in culture, language, natural resources, and community issues. These individuals can serve as key participants in the research review process. IRBs have requirements regarding who must serve as board members and regarding the formality of the process. Community individuals often require training and special support to fully contribute as participants.

The NCAI article illustrates the wide range of review processes that may affect researchers in Indian Country. Some tribes may engage in a combination of processes, such as initiating the formal IRB through the tribal college and also asking the researcher to work with a tribal cultural committee or advisory board. Researchers need to pay careful attention to the policies in place or emerging among tribes and communities and are advised to make these inquiries well in advance of defining research goals and developing proposals. It is no longer sufficient to rely only on a university IRB process to ensure that research can be conducted in a tribal or Indian community.

◆ Impact of Taking Control of Research Agendas

IRBs and related review processes are mostly regulatory in nature, establishing procedural processes to ensure responsive and respectful research. However, non-Indian researchers who have navigated through the new terrain of regulations and procedures are learning that more significant than the procedures are the relationships that are being developed that enhance not only tribal benefits but also researchers' cultural competence and understanding of community-based research practices. In the emerging literature describing research experience in the shifting environment toward tribal control, non-Indian researchers describe a growing appreciation for issues of time, community engagement, reporting findings, and ownership.

Most researchers note that the tribal IRB movement definitely slows down the review process. Researchers seeking approval on a large reservation with subgovernmental units such as chapters or districts often have to make personal visits at meetings to discuss their research proposal and get approval from these units before seeking a formal tribal IRB. Projects that span a state or region will require approval from all the tribes in the geographic area (J. Baldwin, 2007, personal interview; McDonald, Peterson, & Betts, 2005; Sobeck, Chapleski, & Fisher, 2003). However time-consuming, the process itself builds strong connections at the community base and deepens the sense of partnership between the community and researchers. One researcher reported that she thought she understood and practiced community-based research; but only after working through a challenging tribal review process and learning how to fully engage tribal people in the research did she realize the full potential and power of community-based research (J. Baldwin, 2007, personal interview).

Tribal review processes have stimulated development of research teams that include members of the community and outside researchers. Often, it is imperative that a tribal member or employee of a tribal program serve as a co–principal investigator to facilitate the local research processes (J. Baldwin, 2007, personal interview). In a number of studies of social and health concerns in the Great Lakes area, Sobeck et al. (2003) learned that "tribal members themselves must be part of the decision-making if the research project is to beneficial to all actors involved, including tribal organizations and tribal members" (p. 74). They have learned to appreciate tribal values for cooperation, involvement in process, and respect, noting that, in their experience, everyone in a community research team is considered an expert. They caution tribes to encourage community participation and not delegate review responsibility only to their own bureaucratic units.

Community participation is frequently cited as essential in the descriptions of lessons learned from various case studies and articles regarding successful practices in doing research in Indian Country. Mohatt and Thomas (2006) described a collaborative research model aimed at building fully equitable community-investigator partnerships. Over the course of four years, a widely representative group of Alaskan Natives worked with researchers to collaboratively answer questions regarding every step of the research from considering whether common ground existed (the issue is understood similarly from Native and researchers' points of view) to responsibility for disseminating research results. Noe et al. (2006) set out to study empirically the factors that would influence American Indians to participate as subjects in health research. Their findings supported tribal review processes and community based research practices. They found that communities are more responsive to research when a tribal college or Indian organization conducts the research and the community is actively involved in the designing the study. They also found that research is supported when it addresses serious concerns of the tribe and has the potential to bring money into the community. Compensation and anonymity were also factors that increased the likelihood of worthwhile participation.

Tribal review processes require sharing research findings within the tribal community. Densely written research reports are not appropriate vehicles to meet this requirement. Researchers and their community partners have used various means to inform the community through newsletters, presentations at community meetings, and tribal schools. The Navajo Nation sponsors a biannual conference for researchers to present outcomes of their research on the reservation and to discuss research processes. The conference is open to students, government and tribal personnel, and any other interested individuals.

Access to technology has allowed the posting of research findings and often the storage of data at readily accessible tribal sites. The Research Policy Center of the National Congress of American Indians, the American Indian Higher Education Consortium, the National Indian Education Association, and other national and international groups increasingly provide opportunities at tribal gatherings to share community-based tribal research.

A key issue emerging from the growing interest among tribes to approve and control research is the ownership of data. Tribal review processes force upfront discussion of ownership of data and the role of tribal approval of any publication of findings. As tribes become more sophisticated in the regulation of research, expertise in tribal legal departments will increasingly become part of any research review process. In their advice to Cooperative Extension Professionals, McDonald et al. (2005) noted that tribal concerns over data ownership might require consultation with university legal departments. The researchers had different experiences doing community assessments: In one case, they worked out an informal agreement regarding community ownership; however, in another project, they entered into a more formal agreement with a tribal IRB that allowed the university to retain the rights to use data for noncommercial teaching and research purposes, although the tribal board could review any proposed dissemination of information.

Control of data at the tribal or IHS level and subjecting research publications to tribal or IHS prior review counters the deeply held value of academic freedom and the culture of using peers in one's field to determine the worthiness of articles for publication. However, tribes have their own sense of appropriate storytelling and the importance of presenting information in ways that protect the community's reputation. Shared authorship of publications is one means of overcoming tribal concerns about research use and the "story" that is told. Joint negotiation of how a story is told is a critical ethical concern when working in Indian Country, despite the values that American researchers place on intellectual freedom and the government's limit on their ability to regulate or prohibit research. Indian tribes are subject to the Indian Civil Rights Act of 1968, which protects free expression. When exercising their right to review and approve of publications, tribal governments in both their legislative and judicial branches should justify their actions through balancing protection of the community with individual free expression (American Indian Law Center, 1999).

Researchers are finding that despite the challenges involved in regulatory requirements for research in Indian Country—issues of time, negotiation of ownership, and shaping research to fit tribal priorities—there are many rewards in working in partnership with tribal people. However, there are a number of issues that are not easily resolved through procedural processes, negotiated agreements, or community-based partnerships. Research is not culturally neutral, and Western conceptions of knowledge and research methodologies can bump up against tribal values and worldviews that are contrary to standard academic research practices. In the next section, we discuss ethical issues arising from different cultural orientations.

♦ Alternative Epistemologies and Value Systems

Increasingly, Indigenous scholars have engaged in a discourse on indigenous knowledge as it is viewed and experienced within a non-Western way of knowing. Brant-Castellano (2000) described three categories of Aboriginal knowledge:

- *Traditional knowledge:* This knowledge is handed down from generations—creation of stories, origins of clans, encounters between ancestors and the spirit world. This can also be knowledge based on the stories and experiences of the people. This knowledge reinforces values and beliefs.

- *Empirical knowledge:* This is gained through careful observation from multiple vantage points over an extended time.

- *Revealed knowledge:* This knowledge is acquired through dreams, visions, and spiritual protocol.

B. Deloria, Foehner, and Scinta (1999) noted that "the old people experienced life in everything." Knowledge itself has life and moral purpose. The energy or spirit permeating throughout the universe forms connections and "participates in the moral content of events, so responsibility for maintaining the harmony of life falls equally on all creatures" (pp. 49, 52). Making connections to Indigenous ways of knowing, Deloria explained that Western science and the wisdom of traditional knowledge differ:

> The old Indians were interested in finding the proper moral and ethical road upon which human beings should walk. All knowledge, if it is to be useful, was directed toward that goal. Absent in this approach was the idea that knowledge existed apart from human beings and their communities, and could stand alone for "its own sake." In the Indian conception, it was impossible that there could be abstract propositions that could be used to explore the structure of the physical world. Knowledge was derived from individual and communal experiences in daily life, in keen observation of the environment, and interpretive messages that they received from spirits in ceremonies, visions, and dreams. (p. 44)

Native scholars in mainstream and tribal communities are exploring the issues of "Native voice" in both the research experience and in the writing and publication of research. Leading Indian intellectuals discuss this in journals and books intended for Native and non-Native audiences. Elizabeth Cook-Lynn (1998), noted Dakota author and critic, characterized these experiences as the difference between the voice of the Native experience arising from "within a communal, tribally specific indigenous past" (p. 135) and the experience of the objective, that is, scientific approach. It is the difference between having research based in Native life and research based in European or Western culture. Researchers who benefit both professionally and personally from their tribal research experience accept that the Indigenous worldview that is informed by this knowledge is inherently different from their personal or professional experience as informed by their "mainstream" experience. In Native communities, deeply held cultural beliefs and their related practices form the basis of an understanding that requires an acceptance of ceremony and spiritual activities as a source of that understanding. This is far from the experience of most Western trained practitioners who must not only distance themselves from their subjects but also ignore any hint of a spiritual or creation-based source of knowledge.

Recognition of often contradictory views about creation, practice, and geographic place honors the tribal view that each group of people or tribal nation has their own relationship with the spiritual forces that govern the universe and the purpose of their unique tribal view is to explain relationships as they apply to that tribe (V. Deloria, 1995). Knowledge is also highly personal and based on experience. Contradictory perceptions of knowledge can be accepted as valid because they are unique to the individual, and collective wisdom results through a process of putting minds together (Brant-Castellano, 2000).

These views of knowledge or knowing underscore the importance of approaching research projects in a highly collaborative manner that honors the views and perceptions of cultural values and does not reinforce Western notions of hierarchy and privilege. For example, in tribal community aspects of knowledge are privileged and not viewed as accessible only for the asking. In Native cultures, teachers must determine whether a learner is ready to learn; learners must demonstrate readiness. Therefore, not all information shared by tribal informants, especially elders, can be recorded and reproduced (Brant-Castellano, 2000). An Indigenous researcher faced this ethical dilemma when interviewing an elder in her community as part of her dissertation research. Although she was viewed as worthy and ready for the story she was given, she had to explain to the elder that once she wrote it down in her dissertation, she could not control who would have access to the information.

Issues of credit for stories or information are also problematic. Mohatt and Thomas (2006) explained that noting yourself, your family, and homeland are important in Native cultures. Yet researchers are trained to maintain a distance, to think of participants as subjects with identifying numbers. Confidentiality is critical. Yet in their gathering of stories from Alaskan Natives, many wanted to have their names attached to their stories. They considered their story of resilience in maintaining a sober life should be part of the communities' collective knowledge. It took a negotiation with IRB regulations to allow participants to choose whether or not they wanted to attach their names to their stories. When the participants were assured that all the data for the research project would be destroyed in five years, many objected as they did not understand why their story would not be shared and become part of the accumulated knowledge of community. On the other hand, Sobeck et al. (2003) described problems using community members for data collection because participants would be known and their confidentiality threatened. These competing value stances—between an Indigenous valuing of naming the story as part of a community's shared experience and the Western tradition of confidentiality—need to be negotiated and mediated at the level of personal interactions, within community research teams, and with the regulatory strictures of review processes.

Informed consent processes can be problematic in a culture that values relationships over roles and position. Signing a paper may not be perceived as a trustworthy practice, especially in communities with a history of broken treaties and "paper"-based promises. Consent is based on the credibility of the person, not on the project itself. Smith (1999) noted that asking for consent to be interviewed can be perceived as quite rude in Indigenous communities; consent is based on trust and is a dynamic relationship and not a static decision. Alternatives to written consent forms are important considerations when working in Indigenous communities. Oral consent may be more appropriate and when gathered within the context of trustworthy relationships, consent should be viewed as ongoing as well as reciprocal. For example, consent should not only be sought when seeking information but also when interpreting information by sharing how a person's information is used in any final report (American Indian Higher Education Association [AIHEC], in press; Christensen, 2002).

Indigenous researchers must comply with the same regulatory demands of approval and review processes (those of the academy as well as within tribal communities) as non-Indigenous researchers. However, the Indigenous researcher is continually challenged to sort out ethical considerations somewhat differently than non-Native researchers. Native researchers positioned as "insiders" have to follow similar processes as non-Indians in terms of gaining approval, working in partnership, and being respectful and responsive. However, Smith (1999) also argued that they have to be humble, "because the researcher belongs to the community as a member with a different set of roles, status and position" (p. 139). Expertise gained through higher education may be appreciated within the community but will not supersede the need to fulfill traditional roles and responsibilities. The young woman described above who was given a story during her dissertation research has to negotiate through her responsibilities to honor cultural traditions, while also meeting the dictates of Western research institutions.

More generally, Native researchers are obligated to continually and critically reflect on the foundations of their formal research discipline (such as anthropology, sociology, education), while also confronting the legacy of colonialism that shapes research experience (Menzies, 2001). They must continually confront complexities in negotiating across boundaries of Western research standards and traditional notions of what type of knowledge is valued. For example, positivist research designs focusing on Western notions of external validity encourage experimental or quasi-experimental designs requiring manipulation and isolating variables that are viewed as critical in determining causality. This framing of knowledge creation is antithetical to beliefs forming the foundation for Indigenous ways of knowing—beliefs that view knowledge as arising out of observation within context, place, and community. Tribes are essentially ethnocentric. They are less concerned about whether a program is "generalizable" across communities. Rather, they want to understand what works and why it works within their own community.

The current push for "evidence-based" research and evaluation driven by positivist epistemologies are problematic within a cultural framing that believes knowledge does not exist apart from context and community and does not stand alone for its own sake (AIHEC, in press). Indigenous researchers and evaluators must negotiate through conflicting worldviews and run the risk of having their work dismissed if it does not conform to Western notions of rigor or robustness. On the other hand, using "objective" methodologies based on a narrow range of measurement and comparison are viewed as flawed in a tribal cultural context that values forming relationships, connecting with community, and honoring a sense of place (Smith, 1999).

The sorting of dilemmas and contradictions resulting from culturally divergent views of research provides rich opportunities for development of transformative processes that are robust enough to accommodate and value different "ways of knowing," while also contributing to the development of high-quality and sustainable research in Indian and Alaskan Native communities. As Indigenous scholars navigate the shifting sands of crossing boundaries between tribal and academic worlds and non-Indigenous researchers build bridges to tribal communities through responsive research, the setting is ripe for creative tensions that can lead to new ways of considering research practice and ethical guidelines.

◆ Sitting by the Fire

Tribal people want research and scholarship that preserve, maintain, and restore tribal sovereignty, traditions, culture, and language (Crazy Bull, 1997). For research to be complete in its context and content, it must be viewed by the participants as inherently valued and trustworthy (Arlee, 1996; Marker, 1996). As Indigenous people explore ways to revitalize their languages and cultures and to overcome generations of poverty and its attendant social ills, research can be a useful tool in that restoration. Translating traditional practices and experiences into contemporary settings and institutions is part of the contribution that researchers can make to tribal communities. The damage that has been done to the inherent right of tribes to preserve their identity and cultural practice is being undone in Indigenous communities throughout the country. Research responsive to research agendas, done in collaboration with tribal partners and adhering to the self-governance authority of tribes through policies and regulations including IRBs, helps rebuild tribes.

In writing this chapter, we hope to encourage both Indian and non-Indian researchers to continue to share their experiences and tell their stories. It is from reflecting on our experience both from the inside out and the outside in (Symonette, 2004) and through the sharing of our actual day-to-day experience and engagement as researchers in Indian Country that competence is developed. It cannot be found in reading a book about Indians or in watching the latest film intended to portray the Indian experience or in meeting each element of a regulatory process. It is found sitting around the campfire listening to the stories and telling our own stories as well.

◆ Notes

1. From the song "Here Come the Anthros," written and recorded by Floyd Red Crow Westerman.

2. Throughout this chapter, various terms are used to represent Indigenous Peoples. We do not believe that there is any one correct term since no words can truly capture the specific names of Peoples who are indigenous to the lands in which they live. Native American and American Indian, Indian Country, Nations, or Tribes are used to describe tribal people of the United States. Aboriginal and First Nations are used for the peoples of Canada. Specific names of Indigenous groups are used as appropriate for reference. In using various terms, we honor the way in which those who wrote articles referenced in the chapter used the terms of description and our own preferences.

3. Havasupai cultural beliefs, like those of most tribes in the United States, do not support the "Bering Straits" theory of migration. The tribe claims that it would not have sanctioned this avenue of research if it had been properly informed (Rubin, 2004).

4. Our discussion of sovereignty focuses on the legal status of American Indians and Alaskan Natives. Although Hawaiian Natives are not formally included in the U.S. government's trust responsibility toward tribes on the mainland, we note that they have faced a similar legacy with research and that they are also developing their own IRB processes.

5. Founded in 1944, the National Congress of American Indians serves as a major tribal government organization with 250 member tribes from throughout the United States. NCAI is positioned to monitor federal policy and coordinated efforts to inform federal decisions that affect tribal government interests.

◆ References

American Indian Higher Education Association (AIHEC). (in press). *Indigenous evaluation framework: Telling our story in our place and time.* Unpublished manuscript.

American Indian Law Center, Inc. (1999). *Model tribal research code.* Unpublished manuscript.

Arlee, J. (1996, Summer). *Salish Kootenai College culture leadership program.* Paper presented at the Native Research and Scholarship Symposium, Orcas Island, WA.

Bowman, N. (2006, June). *Tribal sovereignty and self-determination through evaluation.* Paper presented at the meeting of the National Congress of American Indians, Sault Sainte Marie, MI.

Boyer, P. (1993). The utility of scholarship: An interview with John Red Horse. *Tribal College Journal of American Indian Higher Education, 4,* 18–19.

Brant-Castellano, M. (1997, May). *Partnership: The key to ethical cross-cultural research.* Speech presented to the Canadian Evaluation Society, Ottawa, Ontario, Canada.

Brant-Castellano, M. (2000). Updating aboriginal traditions of knowledge. In G. J. Sefa Dei, B. L. Hall, & D. Goldin-Rosenberg (Eds.), *Indigenous knowledge in global contexts: Multiple readings of our world* (pp. 21–36). Toronto, Ontario, Canada: University of Toronto Press.

Canadian Institutes of Health Research, Natural Sciences and Engineering Research Council of Canada, Social Sciences and Humanities Research Council of Canada. (2005). *Tri-council policy statement: Ethical conduct for research involving humans.* Retrieved July 2, 2007, from http://pre.ethics.gc.ca/english/policystatement/policystatement.cfm

Christensen, R. (2002, April). *Cultural context and evaluation: A balance of form and function.* Workshop proceedings of the Cultural Context of Educational Evaluation: A Native American Perspective. Arlington, VA: National Science Foundation.

Cook-Lynn, E. (1998). American Indian intellectualism and the new Indian story. In D. A. Mihesuah (Ed.), *Natives and academics: Researching and writing about American Indians* (pp. 111–138). Lincoln: University of Nebraska Press.

Crazy Bull, C. (1997). A Native conversation about research and scholarship. *Tribal College Journal of American Indian Higher Education, 9,* 17–23.

Deloria, B., Foehner, K., & Scinta, S. (Eds.). (1999). *Spirit and reason: The Vine Deloria, Jr. reader.* Golden, CO: Fulcrum.

Deloria, V., Jr. (1969). *Custer died for your sins.* New York: Macmillan.

Deloria, V., Jr. (1991). Commentary: Research, redskins, and reality. *American Indian Quarterly, 15,* 457–468.

Deloria, V., Jr. (1995). *Red earth, white lies.* New York: Scribner.

Health Research Council of New Zealand. (1998). *Guidelines for researchers on health research involving Maori 1998* (ISBN 0-9583396-7-8). Auckland, New Zealand: Author.

Hernandez, J. (2004). Blood, lies, and Indian rights. *Tribal College Journal of American Indian Higher Education, 16,* 11–12.

Kciji, T. (1993, November 3). Newspapers insensitive in labeling disease 'Navajo Flu. *Indian Country Today* from Knight Ridder Tribune. Retrieved April 17, 2008, from www.highbeam.com/doc/1G1-14288433.html

LaFrance, J. L. (2004). Culturally competent evaluation in Indian Country. *New Directions in Evaluation, 102,* 39–50.

LaFromboise, T. D., & Plake, B. S. (1983). Towards meeting the research needs of American Indians. *Harvard Educational Review, 53,* 45–51.

Marker, M. (1996, Summer). *Indian education in the Pacific Northwest.* Paper presented at the Native Research and Scholarship symposium, Orcas Island, WA.

McDonald, D. A., Peterson, D. J., & Betts, S. C. (2005). More tips: What if a cooperative extension professional must work with Native American Institutional Review Boards. *Journal of Extension, 45,* Article 5TOT1. Retrieved March 6, 2007, from www.joe.org/joe/2005October/tt1.shtml

Menzies, C. R. (2001). Reflections on research with, for, and among Indigenous Peoples. *Canadian Journal of Native Education, 25,* 19–35.

Mohatt, G., & Thomas, L. R. (2006). I wonder, why would you do it that way: Ethical dilemmas in doing participatory research with Alaskan Native communities. In J. Trimble & C. Fisher (Eds.), *The handbook of ethical research with ethnocultural populations and communities* (pp. 93–115). Thousand Oaks, CA: Sage.

National Commission for the Protection of Human Subjects of Research. (1979). *Ethical principles and guidelines for the protection of human subjects of research.* Washington, DC: Department of Health and Human Services. Retrieved April 17, 2008, from www.hhs.gov/ohrp/humansubjects/guidance/blemont.htm

Noe, T., Manson, S., Croy, C., McGough, H., Henderson, J., & Buchwald, D. (2006). In their own voices: American Indian decisions to participate in health research. In J. Trimble & C. Fisher (Eds.), *The handbook of ethical research with ethnocultural populations and communities* (pp. 77–92). Thousand Oaks, CA: Sage.

Rother, L. (2007, June 20). In the Amazon, giving blood but getting nothing. *The New York Times.* Retrieved from www.nytimes.com/2007/06/20/world/americas/20blood.html

Rubin, P. (2004, May 27). Indian givers. *Phoenix New Times.* Retrieved from www.phoenixnewtimes.com/2004-05-27/news/indian-givers/

Sahota, P. (2007). *Research regulation in American Indian and Alaskan Native communities: Policy and practice considerations.* Unpublished manuscript, National Congress of American Indians, Policy Research Center, Washington, DC. Retrieved April 17, 2008, from www.ncaiprc.org/pdf/1196282550Research_Regulation_final_paper_110607.pdf

Smith, L. T. (1999). *Decolonizing methodologies: Research and indigenous peoples.* London: Zed Books.

Sobeck, J. L., Chapleski, E. E., & Fisher, C. (2003). Conducting research with American Indians: A case study of motives, methods, and results. *Journal of Ethnic and Cultural Diversity in Social Work, 12,* 69–84.

Swisher, K. G. (1993). From passive to active: Research in Indian Country. *Tribal College Journal, 4,* 4–5.

Symonette, H. (2004). *Walking pathways towards becoming a culturally competent evaluator: Boundaries, borderlands, and border crossings* (New Directions in Evaluation, No. 102, pp. 95–109). San Francisco: Jossey-Bass.

Trimble, J. E. (1977). The sojourner in the American Indian community: Methodological issues and concerns. *Journal of Social Issues, 33*(4), 159–174.

U.S. Department of Health and Human Services, Indian Health Service. (2007). *Human research participation protection in the Indian Health Services.* Retrieved July 3, 2007, from www.ihs.gov/medicalprograms/research/irb.cfm

Wax, M. L. (1991). The ethics of research in American Indian communities. *American Indian Quarterly, 15,* 431–456.

10

ETHICAL PRACTICES IN QUALITATIVE RESEARCH

◆ Yvonna S. Lincoln

It must be remembered that ethics and values, like scientific findings, are not statements that come from an invariant source. They do not reside in a world of abstract ideals. Rather, ethics (like all plans of action) consists of symbolic meanings subject to the most complex political arguments.

—N. K. Denzin, 1989, p. 256

All human effort—including theorizing—is done by beings whose knowledge is incomplete, whose insights are imperfect, and whose understanding is often blinded by tentativeness.

—C. G. Christians, 2007, p. 441

Next to the flowering of epistemologies—philosophies concerning the ways in which we come to know (Belenky, Clinchy, Goldberger, & Tarule, 1986; Butler, 1993; Donovan, 1985; Hill Collins, 2000; hooks, 1984; Plummer, 2001; Reed-Danahay, 2001; Skeggs, 2001)—perhaps the most fertile proposals for qualitative research are shifts in the ethical practices of research and researchers. Emerging primarily from the real-life encounters of qualitative researchers trying to practice phenomenologically oriented research within a new ethical framework, contemporary proposals for revised ethical practice are largely grounded in deep reflection, consistent reflexivity around field experiences, and sophisticated understandings of the limits of current federal law regarding research ethics (Cannella & Lincoln, 2007a, 2007b; Guba & Lincoln, 1989). Researchers are also beginning to question the limits of institutional review boards (IRBs) in monitoring ethical practices, whether in the United States or in Europe or Canada (which maintain ethical regulatory bodies similar to those in the United States, with similar regulatory provisions for the ethical treatment of research participants), or, more importantly in contexts where there are no regulatory bodies governing research with human participants (American Anthropological Association [AAA], 1998; Cannella & Lincoln, 2007a, 2007b).

In situations such as the latter, professional organizations have stepped up well in advance of federal legislation, outlining ethical practice with respondents, particularly in the developing world. The AAA, the American Historical Association (AHA), the American Sociological Association (ASA), the International Communications Association, the American Evaluation Association (AEA), the Canadian Evaluation Society, the Austral-Asian Evaluation Society, and the American Educational Research Association (AERA), in particular, have engaged experienced field researchers and mature inquirers in task forces to create professional standards for ethical practice, with the AAA taking the lead with ongoing discussions of ethical practice in its newsletter, *Anthropology Today*. The most extensive work thus far has been done with regard to the human rights and protections of U.S. and international indigenous peoples, but the effects of that work, alongside work done in Western contexts on research and evaluation ethics, have taken the dialogue on ethics and the protection of human subjects to new and extremely sophisticated dimensions.

For example, rather than speaking simply of the protection of human subjects, researchers have begun to speak of social justice (Cannella, 1997; Christians & Traber, 1997), theories of justice (see, e.g., Rawls, 1971), theories of caring (Noddings, 1984, 2005a, 2005b; Tronto, 1987, 1993), and ethical theories of intention (Gillies & Alldred, 2002). Thus, the discussion has expanded rather dramatically and now anchors its dialogues not within U.S. federal guidelines, which are deemed narrow and less than serviceable for a globalized research context, but in philosophical discourses of ethical systems of justice, caring, reciprocity, communitarianism, intentionality, politics, marginality, hybridity, democracy, and egalitarianism (see, e.g., Denzin & Lincoln, 2005, 2008). In general, ethical issues have arisen around four major frameworks: (1) the ethical treatment of those *with* whom, *on* whom, and *for* whom (on whose behalf) we conduct research; (2) ethical considerations of the contexts in which research is conducted; (3) ethical considerations for a globalized ethnographic practice, for the debate over ethics has moved far beyond the West and Western institutions and academies; and (4) ethical considerations surrounding data and the preparation of reports, especially in the question of for whom reports are created. While these issues should primarily concern Western researchers—because the West dedicates more funding to social science than most developing countries and has been more avid and adventurous about moving beyond national boundaries to understand peoples from other lands, readers should understand that the debate and dialogue have spread far beyond the West and now involve a plenitude of indigenous and non-Western voices. Resisting marginalization, non-Western peoples have begun to formulate their own terms of engagement with Western social science, most of it around the four topics above, although there are other issues as well. The following discussions, however, will revolve around the four issues mentioned above.

♦ Shifts in the Treatment of Participants

Perhaps nowhere is the ethical dialogue more profound than in the treatment of human subjects,[1] or, more appropriately, human research participants. It would be a source of great pride to claim that the dialogue around ethics was both initiated and substantially developed by Western researchers, but this is only partially true. In fact, the dialogue is genuinely two-sided, with Western researchers elaborating a set of ethical practices decidedly and deliberately surpassing those of federal legislation, while at the same time, indigenous peoples have been very carefully drawing up their own policy and legislative statements about how, when, and under what circumstances research may be pursued in their midst and with their own peoples (see, e.g., Battiste, 2008; Grande, 2008; Lincoln & Denzin, 2008; Smith, 1999).

U.S. federal guidelines call for four protections to be provided when conducting research with human participants, whether in the United States or abroad (a situation that provokes its own set of ethical dilemmas): (1) participants should be fully informed regarding the nature of the research and the potential consequences of participating, known as *informed consent*, including the right to withdraw from the study at any time prior to publication; (2) *deception*, when it occurs as a part of the research design, must be accompanied by a full debriefing at the end of the study, to include all participants who have been duped or otherwise deceived; (3) participants must be guaranteed that they will not be identified by name or otherwise, referred to as *anonymity or confidentiality*; and (4) personal records will not be opened without the express consent of research participants, frequently referred to via the shorthand "Buckley amendment rights," or *rights to privacy* (Lincoln & Guba, 1989). These rights have been laid out both in the so-called *Belmont Report* (1978) and in subsequent clarifications throughout the *Federal Register*.

The Belmont Report Commission members were not unaware of the philosophical implications of their work. They considered three principles derived from ethical considerations that should frame researchers' efforts: (1) beneficence, or the maximization of "good outcomes for science, humanity and the individual research participants" while risk to human subjects, harm, or outright wrong were to be minimized; (2) respect, by which they meant treating human participants with respect, dignity, courtesy, and agency; and (3) justice, or "ensuring ... those who bear the risk [as research participants] are [those] who benefit from it," as well as ensuring that the procedures are "reasonable, nonexploitative, and carefully considered" as well as "fairly administered" (Mertens, 1998, p. 24). Furthermore, the Belmont Commission spelled out six norms of scientific research that should act as guidelines for the conduct of research, including: (1) the use of a valid research design, as free of flaws as possible to make it; (2) a researcher competent to conduct the research; (3) the identification of the consequences of the research, principally for research participants; (4) the appropriate use of sample selection; (5) the assurance of voluntary informed consent, "without threat or undue inducement"; and (6) information to research participants as to whether harm will be compensated (National Commission for the Protection of Human Subjects in Biomedical and Behavioral Research, 1978; Mertens, 1998, p. 24).[2]

In a philosophical sense, discussions surrounding research ethics almost inevitably return to issues of power: power between persons and power relations connected to institutions, historical circumstance, economics, gender, social location, race, class, sexual orientation, cultural backgrounds and experiences, actual location, and what Weems (2006) termed a "market logic of relations." Consequently, the proposal for a revised ethics of research for qualitative, phenomenological, constructivist, interpretivist, and critical inquirers frequently means deconstruction of the particular frameworks that constrain relations and that act to restrain the power of one group against that of another. Such frameworks (perhaps there are others) include the frameworks inherent in paradigms, the frameworks inherent in face-to-face relations, the framework of institutions that sponsor and support research (primarily, but not exclusively, the academy in the West), and the framework of an emerging globalization of research—one of the meanings we might take from Lisa Weems's "market logic of relations." (The market logic of relations also references, unfortunately, the explosive commodification and corporatization of knowledge as well as knowledge workers, but it is this same impulse that non-Western and indigenous peoples have tried to counter with extremely elaborate and knowledgeable ethical principle statements, very tightly legally drawn, to safeguard their own populations, cultures, land, rights, artifacts, human remains, and intellectual property.)

♦ Paradigmatic Frameworks for Ethics

Among the first calls for a revised ethics for qualitative and phenomenological research was a call issued around paradigmatic concerns, where *paradigm* was defined as a metaphysical system of beliefs about the nature of the world and what and how we can know about it. With John K. Smith's challenge (personal communication, 1985) to develop criteria for judging alternative paradigm (i.e., naturalistic or constructivist) inquiry *on its own terms*, Egon Guba and I attempted to do so, finding as we thought through "criteria for rigor" that the criteria were framed in light of revised researcher-researched relationships (Guba & Lincoln, 1989) rather than strictly methodological purity. Thus, the criteria for judging the adequacy and trustworthiness of alternative paradigm inquiry, particularly interpretivism and constructivism, were as much ethical criteria as they were adequacy or rigor (or validity) criteria. While positivist inquiry rests its arguments for rigor and validity on method, phenomenological inquiry rests its arguments for trustworthiness on both method and data (trustworthiness criteria) and its arguments for authentic alternative paradigm inquiry on self-Other relations, especially in the move toward engaging participants as co-constructors of research methods and interpretations. Although they were originally developed for practitioners of alternative paradigm evaluation, it quickly became clear that the "authenticity" criteria—criteria developed solely from referent axioms of constructivist and phenomenological inquiry and "authentic" to that paradigm alone, rather than referencing positivist paradigm rigor criteria—were equally applicable to all forms of disciplined inquiry proceeding from phenomenological models (including many forms of critical theorist research; see, e.g., Kincheloe & McLaren, 2000; Lather, 1991; Lincoln & Guba, 1985, 2000).

The principles for authenticity (Guba & Lincoln, 1989) included five fundamental dimensions: balance, or fairness; ontological authenticity; educative authenticity; catalytic authenticity; and tactical authenticity. A brief description of the criteria will serve to illustrate their ethical essence. *Fairness*, or balance, references the researcher's strenuous efforts both to locate all stakeholders in the inquiry and to persuade them to become full partners in nominating issues of interest that should be investigated. Not all stakeholder groups will consent to become involved in the inquiry effort, through no fault of the researcher; but such an attempt is a *bona fide* effort to escape the synoptic "managerialism" of earlier evaluation (and other inquiry) efforts. Fairness imposes constraints on the researcher's abilities to focus findings for the benefit of funders, program managers, administrators, local governmental officials, and others who hold fiscal or political power over research participants and mandates that systematic endeavors will be directed toward garnering input and participation from all stakeholders, from design stages to interpretation and publication stages.

Ontological authenticity references the ability of the inquiry's (and inquirer's) activity, particularly data collection and interpretation, to elicit from respondents constructions that they were unaware that they held. Readers know that from time to time they find themselves making a statement and then realizing that they were "unaware that they felt that way!" This particular form of authenticity refers specifically to that *mental awakening*—the recognition that feelings, attitudes, beliefs, values, or other mental dispositions never were expressed previously, even to oneself. Studs Terkel tells the story of one individual he was interviewing. The man made a statement, then asked for the audiotape to be played back to him. The interviewee notes with some bemusement and fascination that he was unaware that he ever felt that way until he heard himself making that particular statement on tape (Wolf, 1984). Ontological authenticity connotes the capacity of phenomenological inquiry to bring new levels of awareness to individuals of their own mental constructions. Since some, or much, of what we know exists at the tacit, rather than the propositional, level, one function of the involvement as a participant in research is engaging the possibility that some tacit knowledge will become propositional to individuals and stakeholder groups. Heightened awareness and knowledge of our own social constructions and mental models is the first step toward taking meaningful action; it is a part of the process of *conscientizacion*, a term introduced by Paolo Freire to suggest that coming to know is a powerful part of changing one's historical circumstance.

Educative authenticity refers to the mandate among phenomenological, qualitative, and interpretivist inquirers to make others aware of the social constructions of all stakeholder groups. In strict positivist inquiry, respondent constructions (or other forms of data) are withheld from other respondents; only the researcher fully understands where congruences and conflicts lie, or how respondents report differently on the same phenomenon. In alternative paradigm inquiry, however, researchers make every effort, through portrayals, interim oral reports, interviews, and other means, to inform all stakeholding groups of each others' (group) constructions. In this way, all stakeholders have access to all data (reported in ways that preserve confidentiality); data are not restricted to a small body of funders, researchers, and managers who engage in "corporatized" decision making. Information, in the form of social constructions, and data, frequently in the form of tables, charts, and quantitative summaries, become the property of the entire community, creating a more informed, sophisticated, and communitarian decision-making community. Data, formerly restricted to those already holding significant power and authority, are now shared assets, to be debated and acted on transparently and democratically.

Research data, however, have no impact if individual and group stakeholders are indifferent to them or if interpretations are those that the community of stakeholders had already recognized for themselves. Findings not only must shed new light on a phenomenon of interest, they must also engender sufficient interest, consequence, and weightiness to prompt stakeholders to some positive action. This prompt to action is termed *catalytic authenticity*. As the *Belmont Report* makes clear, insignificant research questions are a misuse of time and resources. Fulfilling the norms of scientific inquiry means that questions should be of compelling interest, as well as holding promise of some beneficence for stakeholders. The likelihood of some beneficence, as well as the possibility of redressing some injustice (e.g., redistributing health care services so that traditionally underserved populations will have access to more equitable medical treatment), should serve to catalyze stakeholders to take action on their own behalf (or on behalf of some nonautonomous populations, e.g., their children, the elderly, those with handicapping conditions).

Having moved research participants to action, however, does not ensure that action will be taken. In some instances, participants in the research will be unable or unwilling to take action for themselves, for a variety of reasons. The most likely reason will be inexperience with encounters with power and authority figures. One of the most compelling examples comes from my own experience in "the Valley"—the Rio Grande border between Texas and Mexico. Residents of the *colonias*, a series of virtual shantytowns along the border, are frequently undocumented and, therefore, considered illegal immigrants. Nevertheless, their children are entitled, under state law, to attend school and to receive some form of medical and health services. But asking for such services and requesting that schools strive to meet the needs of the residents of the *colonias* is a daunting task, especially when neither the children nor the parents are English-speaking.

Thus, the final task of authenticity criteria, and one heavy with overtones of ethical professional behavior, is the training of research participants to speak on their own or on their children's behalf. This criterion is termed *tactical authenticity*, for its purpose is to train participants on how to "speak truth to power" and how to utilize recognized policies and procedures to make their wishes known to those in authority. It does little good for social science to inform and educate if those now in possession of the additional sophistication do not know how to deploy it toward any positive ends. Leaving research participants with sound findings but no strategies for utilizing their new knowledge is, for all intents and purposes, unethical.

There are, however, additional ethical dimensions of self-Other relations. There is no way to catalog them all, but included among them might be neighborliness (Savage, 1988), reciprocity, reflexivity, mutuality, empathy, and genuine (as opposed to created, posed, or pretended) rapport, although rapport itself is a contested concept in fieldwork, especially in critical ethnography, where authors suggest that "in all ethnographic settings, *but especially in those inspired by a critical orientation* [italics in original], a new way of thinking about rapport, *perhaps even discarding the notion altogether* [italics added], is unavoidable" (Springwood & King, 2001b, p. 408). Neighborliness, reciprocity, mutuality, empathy, and rapport all are evidences of caring relationships, especially those with a basis in genuine exchange, interdependence, mutual responsibility, and communitarianism.

A word of caution is in order here. While my personal stance is one of striving for rapport in the somewhat traditional ethnographic sense—that is, of attempting to "connect" with the informant/respondent/participant by active listening with the intent of entering her or his world, however briefly and incompletely, neither I nor others should remain unaware of the particular critiques that have been mounted by Springwood and King (2001a, 2001b), George Marcus (1986), Marcus and Fischer (1986), Rosaldo (1989), Wong (1998), and others. In these critiques and others, reflexivity and rapport are interrogated as tending to "(re)produce interpretive knowledge that locates cultural critic[s] as ones with greater power of analytical acuity than informants." While this kind of positioning is likely repugnant to more sophisticated research participants and respondents, and, indeed, is the oft-repeated criticism of constructivists by action and participatory researchers (although we believe it is an unwarranted criticism), it is sometimes the end result of "researchers openly attempt[ing] to complicate and desanctify their authority and enter into dialogic relationships with informants" (Springwood & King, 2001b, p. 409). The inner tension, the ethnographic versus the ethical dilemma, however, is clear when Springwood and King (2001b) pointed out that

> on the one hand, then, more and more ethnographers are developing projects that seek to reveal how the complicated, empowered practices of their informants structure a global system of disadvantage and displacement.... On the other hand, ethnographers are practicing within the timely legacy of a significant reflexive ethnographic orientation that demands a mature inventory of their own positioning and biases in relation to the people and the landscapes of activity they are engaging....
>
> The difficult question is, How do researchers, writers, feminists, activists, or critics *ethnographically engage* those folks who are implicated in the [re]production of those *very* sites they seek to excavate, deconstruct or reconstruct, and perhaps challenge and eliminate? Wherein is rapport? Mutual collaboration? (pp. 409–410)

This tension is not readily resolvable, nor is there any particular essential advice on what must be our legitimate stance on rapport. Certainly, critical ethnographers have mounted a reasonable argument regarding the inutility of rapport in some instances (Lerum, 2001; Marcus, 2001; Wood, 2001) or its sabotaging effects on a critical theoretical project. It does seem useful, however, to recommend that rapport be one ethical commitment to which is always applied the situational question: Is rapport the right stance, given my project, given who my respondents are, given the particular landscape and context in which I am operating? Rapport may well be appropriate in some circumstances (home territory) but inappropriate in others (international territory), or rapport—or the choice to enact attempts at rapport—may depend profoundly on the contradictory landscapes of "sometimes colliding voices" (Springwood & King, 2001b, p. 409).

To return to the very feminized aspects of ethics (Noddings, 1984)—reciprocity, mutual responsibility, a sense of community, empathy, it can well be argued that such conceptions of ethical behavior act as a corrective to the distanced stance of experimental research, where such a stance is presumed to ensure objectivity on the part of the researcher and truthfulness on the part of research respondents. Clearly, these interpersonal qualities of ethical behavior both correspond to and at the same time induce a vastly different mindset and approach from researchers toward those with whom they research and work. This stands in sharp contrast to the "rape model" of research Reinharz described as the typical social science stance. These communitarian, feminized characteristics of ethical behavior bespeak authentic engagement with participants, a sense of humanity, some notion of a human community, a profound respect for respect, and a refusal to objectify or to "monumentalize" (Rosaldo, 1989)—to treat cultures and peoples as though they were rigid, fixed, museum-like, static, unchanging. More specifically, communitarian and caring ethical stances support a classical liberal democratic egalitarianism.

If caring, reciprocity-oriented, egalitarian, and empathetic exchanges characterize the emerging ethics of qualitative researchers in self-Other relations, there remain stances toward communities that bespeak yet another level of ethical theorizing: communities and cultures.

◆ Shifts in Community-Oriented and Communitarian Ethical Frameworks

Just as there are relational criteria for self-Other transactions, there are also smaller (i.e., personal) and larger (i.e., community-wide) ethical frameworks that guide our practice as social scientists. Two emerging, and sometimes (viewed as) competing, philosophical scaffolds include theories of justice, derived from the work of Lawrence Kohlberg (1976, 1981) and Daniel Levinson (1978), and theories of caring and relation, derived from the work of Carol Gilligan (1982) and Nel Noddings (1984, 2003, 2005a, 2005b).

Gilligan's (1982) work begins with a critique of theories of moral development extant at the time of her own research. She appeared to understand decades ago that theories of justice were incomplete without theories of personal relations and caring, taking account of the differences in the ways men and women develop morally. Today, theories of caring merge readily with many strands of feminist theory and the theorizing of women of color, especially with the latter's emphasis on community, sharing, giving, personal responsibility, and shared decision making. Ethical frameworks derived from theories of caring stress "sensitivity to the needs of others and the assumption of responsibility for taking care [that] lead[s] women to attend to voices other than their own and to include in their judgment other points of view" (p. 17) and the certain knowledge that "we are, by virtue of our mutual humanity, already and perpetually in potential relation" (Noddings, 1984, p. 86; see also Ellis, 2007).

Theories of justice, on the other hand, stress rights, "the legal elaboration of rules and the development of fair procedures for adjudicating conflicts" (Gilligan, 1982, p. 10), responsibilities, "separation, autonomy, individuation, and natural rights" (Gilligan, 1982, p. 23). The two philosophical scaffolds theorizing moral development in humans are primarily noted for their emphasis on differences in moral development between men and women, and thus theories of justice are characterized as masculine in orientation and theories of caring and relation are characterized as a feminine model of moral development. While it is both easy and fashionable to claim for oneself one position or another, one theoretical bent or another, it is likely more useful to pay attention to Gilligan's (1982) own advice, cited earlier, on what it might take to create more fertile theories.

There are criticisms of the work of both Noddings and Gilligan, particularly their "feminizing" of the ethic of care (Tronto, 1987) and their earlier tendency to ignore issues that are pressing for persons of color, non-Western peoples, indigenous cultures, and other marginalized groups. Consequently, writers have tried to enlarge the concepts of care to encompass discourses on marginalization, hybridity, recognition of cultural rights, issues of citizenship (Sevenhuijsen, 1998), and the politics and moral dilemmas of caring (Tronto, 1993). In fact, Tronto (1987, 1993) is firmly against a "women's morality" since its boundaries are too limiting from the political and epistemological viewpoints. Rather, she suggested that we expand the "moral terrain" to an ethic of caring that moves beyond the rather simplistic and gendered notions of a "women's morality" to a larger political and ethical concern—namely, that human beings care for others all the time and that caring should be embodied in our political as well as our spiritual and moral existences.

In our relations with research participants, for instance, theories of caring can and should subsume federal ethics legislation, with respect, dignity, and courtesy afforded to individuals and groups and beneficence being the guiding principle. As communities, however, we might wish to focus on theories of justice, particularly social justice and just social relations, when deconstructing the historical, class, race, gender, economic, and social antecedents to clear cases of injustice in the distribution of goods and services, to poverty, and to all manner of oppression. As Noddings (2003, 2005a, 2005b) made clear in her later work, a theory of caring always underlies a sound theory of justice, and therefore, theories of caring precede theories of justice. Both work together to create a more just, ethical, and desirable world. It is not an either-or proposition, nor is it a matter of opting for either the "feminine" or the "masculine"(although my choice is to emphasize precisely those characteristics of caring that have been criticized as overly feminized: connection, a sense of community, other-concerned, respect for the voices of many); rather, it is a matter of balancing between the two, choosing the contexts of application with a highly refined sense of "moral discernment" guided by "the moral dimension of everyday life" (Christians, 2007, p. 443). "Only when life-cycle theorists divide their attention and begin to live with women as they have lived with men will their vision encompass the experience of both sexes and their theories become correspondingly more fertile" (Gilligan, 1982, p. 23).

◆ Shifts in Institutional Frameworks for Ethics

Just as there are ethical frameworks for relationships with individuals, individual respondents, and communities and cultures, there are likewise ethical responsibilities and frameworks for institutions and organizations. Some of those ethical considerations and debates are explored in the following sections.

INSTITUTIONAL REVIEW BOARDS

Although researchers are frequently frustrated with their own IRBs, and there are those who feel that IRBs overstep their mandated boundaries at times (Rambo, 2007), IRBs exist, in part, to oversee the "protection of human subjects" and are therefore at one node of the researcher-researched-context ethical review apparatus. While IRBs cannot make all judgments regarding appropriate design and cannot specify with any accuracy appropriate methodological procedures (although many are trying to do so; see Lincoln & Tierney, 2004, for actual case examples, and also Gunsalus et al., 2007, on "mission creep"), they assuredly can and do ask questions about whether any given design ensures adequate safeguards for humans potentially participating in the research.[3] Researchers bear some obligation to be as clear and straightforward about their designs as possible, specifying procedures and practices in terms that are not oblique and striving to make clear that they themselves have given serious consideration to ethical issues that might possibly arise.

When conflicts arise between IRBs and individual researchers, researchers bear some responsibility for educating board members, explaining the particular contours of their research and being frank, open, and honest about the particular kinds of research in which they are engaged. Qualitative researchers appear to be having more difficulty recently with IRBs, and it is likely that this new circumstance has arisen because of the likelihood that IRBs are experiencing a new and different sense of the "accountability culture" arising as a result of a larger politically conservative pendulum swing around research design and what constitutes evidence more broadly, and consequently have adopted a more activist stance. Rather than approving proposed research on review of its methods, sampling, and procedures for adequate safeguard of human subjects, IRBs are now electing to question the designs themselves (Lincoln & Tierney, 2004) and to make suggestions and even demands regarding how research should be restructured and redesigned, regardless of the researcher's intent or the nature of the fit between research problem and methodology.

When they work well, however, IRBs serve as a watchdog community to ensure that fundamental ethical considerations—those outlined in federal law and regulations—are weighed carefully and that adequate provisions are in place to meet or exceed the requirement of legal protections. IRBs, however, are not the only professional communities directed to police ethical considerations and ensure that federal standards are met and even exceeded.

PROFESSIONAL DISCIPLINARY NETWORKS

A number of professional associations have created codes of ethics for their members' practices, and although compliance is voluntary among the associations' members, there is considerable monitoring by members of each other and by standing ethics committees. The AERA (2002), the American Psychological Association (2002), the ASA (1999), the AAA (1998), the AEA (Joint Committee on Standards for Educational Evaluation, 1981, and subsequent editions; 1988) and the AHA (2005), as well as others, have all created extensive codes of ethics and professional standards for their members. In several of these codes of ethics, the federal mandates are clear, but the ethical statements go much farther in specifying the kinds of ethical dilemmas that professionals might encounter and advising against entering certain relationships. The AAA even goes so far as to specify that no harm should come to nonhuman primates and that these species are to be treated with dignity as if they were human. It is of major interest to note that the AAA is a strong supporter of (and helped frame) the new United Nations Declaration of the Rights of Indigenous Peoples (2007). They were likewise instrumental in helping to frame the United Nations Convention on the Rights of the Child (1987) as well as the 1983 United Nations Convention on the Elimination of All Forms of Discrimination Against Women. Thus, as a professional and disciplinary association, they have been, for more than 20 years, at the forefront of helping to set ethical standards for dealing with groups and cultures.

More important, these professional associations are quite clear regarding the ethical obligations toward younger scholars who are being mentored, toward graduate students, and with respect to publication rights when junior scholars and graduate students have contributed to intellectual work in a substantive way. Each of the codes mentioned above (as well as others) takes up the issue of intellectual property and publication, recognizing the role of publication in advancement in the academy, and therefore, casting it as an ethical issue. As much of the work done by historians, sociologists, evaluators, and anthropologists is ethnographically oriented, their statements on ethical standards, taken together, provide strong guidelines for qualitative researchers of all stripes, even though the intellectual problems may be framed differently from discipline to discipline.

◆ Shifts in Globalized Frameworks for Ethical Relations With Indigenous Peoples: Performing Culture Ethically

Anthropologists and other ethnographic and qualitative practitioners are now beginning to realize that culture does not exist apart from those who enact it (Conquergood, 1985). As Norman Denzin (2003) put it, "We inhabit a performance-based, dramaturgical culture. . . . and culture itself becomes a dramatic performance" (p. 10). Culture does not precede the individuals who share it. Rather, culture is created by those same individuals, "on the fly," as symbols, signs, material culture, and other artifacts and performances are exchanged across a social landscape contoured by globalization, corporatization, neocolonialism, postindustrialism, and postmodernism. The forces of a market economy shape and are shaped by the political economy of culture, rites, rituals, multiple and shifting identities, and linguistic turns across an ideological pidgin vocabulary of terrain under conflict and contention. Into this terrain, ethnographers enter at their own peril but also, unfortunately, at the peril of their proposed participants.

CULTURE AS PERFORMATIVE AND INDIGENOUS ETHICS

It is into this terrain that indigenous peoples have marched also, not to research but rather to constrain the power of researchers to create representations that foreground the "status" of indigenous peoples as disadvantaged in one or more ways. As Smith (1999) made plain, indigenous peoples are beginning to derive their own culturally bound codes of ethics. They are "being promulgated.... as a sheer act of survival" (p. 119), primarily to fend off the predations of researchers with their own, Western notions of how to "fix" what ails the tribe/culture/people. These codes of ethics are written into charters (Smith, 1999)

> that refer to collective, not individual, human rights. These rights include control and ownership of the community's cultural property,[4] its health and knowledge systems,[5] its rituals and customs, the culture's basic gene pool, rights and rules for self-determination, and an insistence on who the first beneficiaries of indigenous knowledge will be. (Denzin, 2003, p. 257)

(The case of the Maori is a special case, and their status is quite different from, say, that of the Native Americans in the United States or the aboriginal peoples in Australia and is rather more similar to the First Nations status in Canada.) In other cases, indigenous charters call for rights to traditional lands, including who may fish, harvest, or hunt, and demand rights to control both access by nonindigenous peoples and the extraction of resources and/or minerals. In this way, indigenous peoples have carved out an ethics that not only protects and preserves their own cultural heritage, artifacts, and sites but also is deeply implicated in the ethics of environmental protection. Many indigenous peoples are deeply connected to the land and see no reason to permit rapacious corporations to denude forests, strip minerals, or hunt protected wildlife. Thus, not only do these charters provide an indigenous ethical code to which outsider researchers must closely adhere, but they additionally stave off the more predatory instincts of all manner of corporate "harvesters."

Ethnographers and other qualitative researchers wishing to conduct research in arenas where tribes and cultures have created their own statements of ethics are not free to engage in whatever research they believe to be appropriate. Rather, the cultural group decides, often in concert, whether such researchers will be admitted and under what circumstances. In many instances, researchers must be assigned a native researcher, a collaborator who accompanies the outsider on every foray the researcher undertakes. The native researcher is not only a gatekeeper but also the ethics informant, notifying the outsider immediately when he or she is in danger of trespassing in ways that are neither culturally appropriate nor permitted. Research in a globalized world is neither as easy nor as necessarily friendly as it was in the past. Indigenous peoples around the world—on their own, with the help and advice of the United Nations, or even with the (sometimes problematic) aid of the World Bank—are setting rules and regulations for entry into their cultures. Furthermore, many of these charters and statements of research ethics demand rights to edit the representations that are made from the fieldwork. Tribes and cultures recognize that the portraits that have been painted of them in the past have been unfortunate, and they have no wish to repeat that saga. The gaze of the voyeur can be neither as lingering nor as prurient as it once was (see Lincoln & Denzin, 2008, for a more extensive discussion of these new limits to the privileges of Western researchers).

The ethics that are emerging from this set of indigenous demands[6] are described by Smith (1999), Bishop (1998), Christians (2000), and Denzin (2003) as communitarian; rooted in the feminist ethics of caring as well as the theory of social justice; and grounded in personal accountability, sharing, knowledge as a community and collective entity rather than as an individual possession, reciprocity, relationality, a commitment to community solidarity, and neighborliness. They "embody a dialogic ethic of love and faith grounded in compassion" (Denzin, 2003, p. 247) and frequently are grounded in "four interpretive research processes," outlined by Smith (1999), including "decolonization.... transformation.... healing.... and mobilization [to action]" (Denzin, 2003, p. 246).

Clearly, this is a very different set of ethical principles from those outlined in the *Belmont Report*, which presumes a very different view of the individual human being as well as a very different view of "community," the *Report*'s *community* being the community of Western scientists. The "rational individual" assumed in Western science is replaced in indigenous ethics with the dialogic community, with well-developed deliberative processes for arriving at truth and knowledge. Truth evolves as a function of group hearing, community and individual transformation, and ultimately healing.

CULTURAL CONTINUITY

There is another, critical, ethical dimension to the globalized and/or the indigenous, what Christians (2007) called "cultural continuity." Christians labeled this cultural continuity an "imperative," arguing that while contemporary Western codes of ethics are built on the principle that human beings are first and foremost rational beings (Christians, 1997), interpretive social science rather "understands the human in radically different terms.... as cultural beings" (Christians, 2007, p. 439). Entertaining a vision of humans as cultural beings rather than merely rational beings permits the contemplation of a new research ethics "controlled by the norm of cultural continuity" (Christians, 2007, p. 440). For Christians (2007)—as well as for those of us who engage in work around the world amid the "ruins" of globalization—cultural continuity "works...within the general morality" (p. 443), but its outlines and foundational tenets are readily visible: human flourishing, research as a "catalyst for critical consciousness," cultural recognition, the recognition of "cultural groups politically" (p. 442). In the end, Christians asserted, the research act should enhance relationality, as well as reflecting "moral discernment" (p. 443).

Given the profound interest of indigenous peoples in achieving political recognition and at the same time maintaining cultural continuity within their own group in ways that grant and preserve the dignity of persons, the ethical mandate that research "must 'comport well' with the controlling norm of cultural continuity" and enhance "cultural formation" (Christians, 2007, pp. 441–442) seems a sound fit with a revised ethics of research for an interpretivist, ethnographically oriented social science, most especially with indigenous peoples but equally well with other cultural groups (e.g., various groups of Hispanic-language and Hispanic-descent peoples, Japanese Americans, and Hmong children, to name three such distinct lingual and cultural communities).

◆ Shifts in the Treatment of Data and Reports

Data, always recognized by U.S. and other Western nations' federal law as belonging to the individuals who provided it, has nevertheless been treated heretofore as though it were the private possession of the researchers who collected it. Increasingly, that will no longer be true, as research participants request to see the reports that are being written about them, ask for and are granted the rights to coauthorship, and demand some say in the representations made therein. An ever-increasing number of researchers—particularly action researchers, participatory action researchers, and many interpretivist paradigm practitioners—already involve research respondents as coresearchers in defining the research questions of interest, designing data collection methods that are culturally and situationally appropriate, collecting data, analyzing data, and interpreting findings, as well as participating in framing and perhaps even writing the report, acting as coauthors with academy-based professionals. Furthermore, the commitment to sharing data widely, rather than holding it as "secret" or providing it only to those with power and authority, shifts the balance of power strongly toward the community context rather than toward the managerial, funder, or corporate context.

Perhaps the most important shift has been in the ethical imperative to publish outside the academy—that is, to publish in languages other than English and in journals and other media outlets that may not be included in Western rankings of prestigious scholarly journals (González y González & Lincoln, 2006, 2007; Lincoln & González y González, 2007). The ethics of such work revolve about the recognition of communities as collections of individuals with agency and the rights to self-determination. Indeed, where Western researchers have failed to recognize these rights, indigenous people have sometimes framed their own codes of ethics to preserve their rights and to outline the responsibilities of foreign social scientists who seek to conduct research within the indigenous community.

♦ Shifts in the Treatment of Contexts

INDIGENOUS PEOPLES DEVELOPING THEIR OWN CODES

As mentioned in a previous section, indigenous peoples now sometimes create statements of principles, including ethical principles, that will guide the practice of social scientists (and sometimes medical practitioners) in their midst. These statements of principles for First Nations or indigenous peoples often very tightly specify who may conduct research, with whom, with which accompanying local researcher/gatekeeper, and at what times; what kinds of questions will be entertained; and who gives approval for such outsider work. Researchers do not now, as they did in the past, come and go freely in indigenous contexts; the rules have changed, and even where local cultures do not have such statements of principles, professional and disciplinary organizations maintain a running dialogue regarding ethics and the rights of indigenous peoples. The AAA in its newsletter, *Anthropology Today*, maintains such a dialogue, perhaps the most insightful dialogue anywhere in the world on field ethics, publication ethics, and the ethical principles of cultural encounters. Coincidentally, the principle of "cultural continuity" argued by Christians (2007) and referenced earlier is quite consonant with the emerging issues and principles that are the foci of that ongoing dialogue.[7]

INDIGENOUS SYMBOLS, MYTHS, RITUALS, RITES, AND ART

In the same vein, indigenous groups are reclaiming their rights to cultural symbols and artifacts—including bones from ancient digs and archaeological excavations, sometimes even arguing in the courts that white researchers and others have no legal rights to employ or deploy tribal symbols as advertising or for any other purposes not approved by tribes or cultural groups. The recent battle at the University of Illinois over the University's use of "Chief Illiniwek" as their team and university mascot is a good case in point. Native American groups objected strenuously to the objectification of a Native American (albeit an imaginary one) as a mascot, a symbol, and sometimes a commercial product. The University has now taken the representation off their letterhead, and slowly but surely, this symbol is being expunged from the University's official communications and performances. While many alumni, as well as current students, aggressively argued for the maintenance of this symbol as a reference to courage, strength, bravery, and other powerful emotional and psychological assets, it would seem that the Chief will, over time, disappear from contemporary and future university history (see Denzin, 2003, for a fuller story on this matter; see also various articles on this subject published over time in the *Chronicle of Higher Education*, 1994–2004). The single point to be made here is that native peoples over the world are increasingly seeking to control the representations made of themselves, explaining that such representations come complete with associations, many of which are unfavorable and pejorative. For native and indigenous peoples, as well as for other cultural groups, representation *is* an ethical issue.[8] Increasingly, cultural groups are regaining control of some of the most exploitive of those representations.

◆ Conclusion

If there is ever to be a rapprochement between positivists, phenomenologists, and critical theorists, it will not proceed from the methodological issues of "mixed methods" but rather from the issues of fieldwork and research ethics (Mauthner, Birch, Jessop, & Miller, 2002) reporting research (i.e., the form that research reports take), and social justice. As interpretive and qualitative researchers revise and revisit fieldwork ethics, whether on their home turf or in far places, there is a growing awareness of the limits of Western rationalism and its failure in the face of new geopolitical and geo-cultural realities. Intercultural competence is simply not enough.

Self-Other relations are undergoing scrutiny in virtually every camp: feminists, poststructuralists, interpretivists, border theorists, critical theorists, and theorists of race and ethnic studies. Stalwart norms of fieldwork practice such as reciprocity are hotly argued (Denzin, 2003; Weems, 2006), as is reflexivity (Downe, 2007), and even narrative research (Barone, 2007; Connolly, 2007; Hendry, 2007; Rosiek, 2007). Researchers call forth autoethnographic narratives to explore who they are as researchers, as multiple and shifting identities in the field and back home, as a means for interrogating their own practices, including ethical practices with their informants and respondents.

Researchers are exploring, too, what it means to practice community-building and communitarian ethics, rather than accepting the Enlightenment metanarrative of the autonomous individual possessing a pure, single, core identity. A more sweeping understanding of the meaning of community, and of how communities hold, gather, and pass on collective, rather than individual, knowledge, is reshaping ethnographers' and ethnography's consciousness of just what it is they are seeking to re-present. The ethics emerging from a reconfigured sense of community and solidarity is reshaping the consciousness of the social sciences.

Interpretive researchers feel, too—whether they conduct research outside of the West or not—the effects of a postmodern, postindustrial, globalized, knowledge economy and understand that the rules of the game have changed substantially and irrevocably, as cultural groups achieve political recognition and a measure of autonomy and self-determination. Indigenous peoples now speak for themselves and frequently utilize tribal charters or statements of principles to govern their relationships with researchers from "outside." It is the ethnographer who is now the Other; it is the gaze of the cultural group that is turned toward researchers and their research. And it is indigenous peoples' first call on knowledge produced in their community, not the academy's. These altered self-Other relations produce ripples even back to home territory, as researchers try to sort out where ethical pitfalls might lie.

The crisis of representation, too, has passed from the hands of anthropologists and ethnographers into the hands of culturally savvy groups. No longer content to let the West represent them, frequently unfavorably, cultural groups and indigenous peoples wrest from would-be researchers the editing rights for the portraits researchers prepare, sometimes collaborating as coauthors and at other times acting as approval bodies for publications. Representations are recognized as having ethical overtones, since they may bring about further disadvantage, oppression, mistreatment, or misunderstanding. Indigenous peoples argue, too, for the rights to their cultural symbols, rites, rituals, and artifacts and even their dead. The claims cultural groups make on Western science are less concerned with science's rationalistic portraits than with reclaiming a lost patrimony and uncovering and reinvesting with power cultural signs and symbols as legitimate cultural capital. As a corporatized developing world avidly collects cultural signs for the spiritually impoverished purposes of commercialization and advertising or for the aesthetic enrichment of wealthy elites, the ethics of preserving indigenous peoples' rights to such signs, symbols, and artifacts, as well as the simple right of determining access, becomes somewhat clearer.

Intertwined with all the other ethical dilemmas are the dilemmas of how data are treated, how reports are written, as well as who writes them. The encouragement to utilize locals as coauthors can now be a mandate. Furthermore, the necessity of producing bilingual texts—that is, one text in the researcher's language and one parallel text in the language of the local context—may no longer be a matter of choice, since some indigenous groups insist that knowledge produced on-site is for the use, first, of those who provided the data, the indigenous peoples themselves. With or without this contract, however, it is unethical to withhold data and information from those who provided it, particularly since sharing such data widely may have a positive impact on many ethical dimensions: community formation, mobilization to action, the raising of a critical consciousness among research participants, and so on.

All these dimensions interact with each other. While individual scholars may deal with one issue or another in any given work, all the issues nevertheless are complexly interconnected. Furthermore, they may act as "triggers," one issue prompting another, one conflict raising another, one compromise creating another ethical conundrum. While it is true that no single researcher can, with sanity, pursue all these ethical domains at once, it is useful to know and understand what some of their contours and topographies might be. If even one shameful ethical *contretemps* is sidestepped, one painful ethical fieldwork misadventure avoided, it would have been worth considering.

◆ Notes

1. There is still ample reason to believe that the use of the term *human subjects* is indirectly pejorative, and my preference remains *research participants*. As Robert L. Wolf pointed out many years before his death, *subject* derives from the Latin *subjugo*, to go under the yoke, or to become a slave or a thrall of another.

2. Readers might notice, with careful scrutiny, that there are minor and major differences between the norms of scientific research set out by the framers of the *Belmont Report* and the framers of the, more recent, "Scientific Research in Education," the National Research Council's Committee on Scientific Principles for Education Research (2002). Major differences would include the latter's emphasis on posing "significant questions that can be investigated empirically," which is later explained to be with primarily quantitative methods, usually via a design that is a randomized field experiment; linking "research to relevant theory," although some of the more significant research, particularly on women, on race, and on handicapping

conditions, has been undertheorized, and therefore, little, if any, "relevant theory" actually exists or can be brought to bear; "replicat[ing] and generaliz[ing] across studies," although the philosophical and scientific objections to the possibility of generalization from human contexts militate against and undermine the likelihood of observing this particular norm, particularly the generalization criterion; and disclosing "research to encourage professional scrutiny and critique" (pp. 3–5). With regard to the latter criterion, it is difficult to understand why any researcher would not wish to disclose research; the pressures on publishing one's research as a means to advancement throughout the academy means that virtually no one need consider this admonition as anything more than an afterthought. The National Research Council's six principles bear little resemblance to the six, far broader and more inclusive, scientific norms originally written into the *Belmont Report*. It should be noted here, as a framing device, that the biomedical and behavioral commission that prepared the *Belmont Report* represented a far broader constituency of the scientific community that normally works with human populations than did the Committee of the National Research Council, which consisted of a very narrow (and relatively smaller) group of educational researchers only. It should also be noted that the framers of the *Belmont Report* included several nationally and internationally known medical and social science ethicists, which the National Research Council's group did not.

3. As some researchers have reported, the issues that have come up recently have been major misunderstandings between researchers and IRBs over paradigm issues, with IRB members insisting on strict positivist designs even when they are inappropriate for the kinds of research proposed (Gunsalus et al., 2007). This has been an especially troublesome issue for social scientists and, more recently, for doctoral dissertation students. A variety of techniques have been utilized for getting around intransigent and/or unknowledgeable IRBs, including declaring ethnographic work to be "oral history," a designation now regarded as "exempt" from IRB review, or having the student perform the research for another agency (e.g., a school district or mental health agency) and then declare the data collected as "archived." Both tactics are successful but raise ethical issues in and of themselves. In some instances, efforts to educate IRBs regarding phenomenological work have been successful, and in other instances, they have been maddeningly unsuccessful. It is no wonder that strategies for end-runs around unknowledgeable boards have been devised and are being pursued around the country.

4. There is a battle ongoing even now with respect to symbols reflecting tribal heritages and whether Westerners can appropriate such symbols, although they belonged to an earlier people. Tribal elders are litigating to have the symbols removed from national park structures. The issue is clearly a tangled one but is closely tied to the larger argument of whether cultures "own" intellectual property rights to signs, symbols, artifacts, and other material and symbolic significations of their culture or of a predecessor culture. For a more extended discussion of this issue, see, for instance, Coombe's (1998) *The Cultural Life of Intellectual Properties* and Allen's (2002) *Blood Narrative: Indigenous Identity in American Indian and Maori Literary and Activist Texts*, especially on emblematic figures (141ff.), as well as Zerner's (2003) edited volume, *Culture and the Question of Rights*, in particular the strong Introduction by Zerner. Perhaps the most accessible, but also the most complete from a legal standpoint, is Kembrew McLeod's (2007) excellent text *Owning Culture: Authorship, Ownership and Intellectual Property Law*.

5. An Indian informant tells me that the Indian government just went online with 40,000 pages of health, herbal, and other types of knowledge, to prevent Western companies from "copyrighting" native and indigenous knowledge concerning healing, herbal medicines, various foodstuffs, and biological and genetic varieties. The lessons learned in other developing countries regarding the copyrighting of various genetic and plant material that had been a part of the indigenous food chain for millennia by U.S. corporations has been a dramatic and tragic story; India was not going to let that happen.

6. Unfortunately, not all indigenous peoples have such charters, nor have they developed

statements that deal with the relations with outsiders that they will tolerate.

7. Those columns on ethics were recently collected and assembled into notebooks for IRB board members on my campus. The then chair of the campuswide IRB, an interpretivist, critical, poststructural feminist researcher, was quite concerned that the board was acting with a set of ethics far more relevant to 1950 than to 2000 and sought to engage in continuing education of the board on issues of ethics, especially in international work and work with intact cultural groups here and abroad.

8. Another good example would be the advertising use of a Chihuahua dog, with a strange and rather broad accent, to sell Taco Bell. Hispanic, Latino, and Mexican American individuals protested loudly and threatened with enough boycotting power for the ads to be withdrawn.

◆ References

Allen, C. (2002). *Blood narrative: Indigenous identity in American Indian and Maori literary and activist texts*. Durham, SC: Duke University Press.

American Anthropological Association. (1998). *Code of ethics of the American Anthropological Association*. Retrieved June 1, 2007, from www.aaanet.org/committees/ethics/ethicscode.pdf

American Educational Research Association. (2002). *Ethical standards*. Retrieved June 21, 2007, from www.aera.net/uploadedFiles/About_AERA/Ethical_Standards/EthicalStandards.pdf

American Historical Association. (2005). *Statement on standards of professional conduct*. Retrieved June 1, 2007, from www.historians.org/pubs/Free/ProfessionalStandards.cfm4

American Psychological Association. (2002). *Ethical principles of psychologists and code of conduct*. Retrieved June 18, 2007, from www.apa.org/ethics/code2002.html

American Sociological Association. (1999). *Code of ethics and policies and procedures of the ASA Committee on Professional Ethics*. Retrieved June 18, 2007, from www.asanet.org/galleries/default-file/Code%20of%20Ethics.pdf

Barone, T. (2007). A return to the gold standard? Questioning the future of narrative construction as educational research. *Qualitative Inquiry, 13*(4), 454–470.

Battiste, M. (2008). Research ethics for protecting indigenous knowledge and heritage: Institutional and researcher responsibilities. In N. K. Denzin, Y. S. Lincoln, & L. T. Smith (Eds.), *Handbook of critical and indigenous methodologies* (pp. 497–509). Thousand Oaks, CA: Sage.

Belenky, M. F., Clinchy, B. M., Goldberger, N. R., & Tarule, J. M. (1986). *Women's ways of knowing: The development of self, voice and mind*. New York: Basic Books.

Bishop, R. (1998). Freeing ourselves from neocolonial domination in research: A Maori approach to creating knowledge. *International Journal of Qualitative Studies in Education, 11*, 199–219.

Butler, J. (1993). *Bodies that matter: On the discursive limits of "sex."* New York: Routledge.

Cannella, G. S. (1997). *Deconstructing early childhood education: Social justice and revolution*. New York: Peter Lang.

Cannella, G. S., & Lincoln, Y. S. (2007a). IRBs and qualitative research [Special issue]. *Qualitative Inquiry, 13*(3).

Cannella, G. S., & Lincoln, Y. S. (2007b). Predatory ethics vs. dialogic ethics: Constructing an illusion, or ethical practice as the core of research methods. *Qualitative Inquiry, 13*(3), 315–335.

Christians, C. G. (1997). The ethics of being in a communications context. In C. Christians & M. Traber (Eds.), *Communication ethics and universal values* (pp. 3–23). Thousand Oaks, CA: Sage.

Christians, C. G. (2000). Ethics and politics in qualitative research. In N. K. Denzin & Y. S. Lincoln (Eds.), *Handbook of qualitative research* (2nd ed., pp. 133–155). Thousand Oaks, CA: Sage.

Christians, C. G. (2007). Cultural continuity as an ethical imperative. *Qualitative Inquiry, 13*(3), 437–444.

Christians, C. G., & Traber, M. (Eds.). (1997). *Communication ethics and universal values.* Thousand Oaks, CA: Sage.

Connolly, K. (2007). Introduction to Part 2: Exploring narrative inquiry practices. *Qualitative Inquiry, 13*(4), 450–453.

Conquergood, D. (1985). Performing as a moral act: Ethical dimensions of the ethnography of performance. *Literature in Performance, 5*(1), 1–13.

Coombe, R. J. (1998). *The cultural life of intellectual properties: Authorship, appropriation and the law.* Durham, SC: Duke University Press.

Denzin, N. K. (1989). *The research act: A theoretical introduction to sociological methods* (3rd ed.). Englewood Cliffs, NJ: Prentice Hall.

Denzin, N. K. (2003). *Performance ethnography: Critical pedagogy and the politics of culture.* Thousand Oaks, CA: Sage.

Denzin, N. K., & Lincoln, Y. S. (Eds.). (2005). *The Sage handbook of qualitative research* (3rd ed.). Thousand Oaks, CA: Sage.

Denzin, N. K., & Lincoln, Y. S. (Eds.). (2008). *The handbook of critical and indigenous methodologies.* Thousand Oaks, CA: Sage.

Donovan, J. (1985). *Feminist theory: The intellectual traditions of American feminism.* New York: Frederick Ungar.

Downe, P. J. (2007). Strategic stories and reflexive interruptions: Narratives of a "safe home" amidst cross-border sex work. *Qualitative Inquiry, 13*(4), 554–572.

Ellis, C. (2007). Telling secrets, revealing lives: Relational ethics in research with intimate others. *Qualitative Inquiry, 13*(1), 3–29.

Gillies, V., & Alldred, P. (2002). The ethics of intention: Research as a political tool. In M. Mauthner, M. Birch, J. Jessop, & T. Miller (Eds.), *Ethics in qualitative research* (pp. 32–52). London: Sage.

Gilligan, C. (1982). *In a different voice: Psychological theory and women's development.* Cambridge, MA: Harvard University Press.

González y González, E. M., & Lincoln, Y. S. (2006). Decolonizing qualitative research: Non-traditional reporting forms in the academy. *Forum Qualitative ozialforschung (International e-Journal of Qualitative Research), 7*(4), Article 1. Retrieved June 21, 2007, from www.qualitative-research.net/fqs-texte/4-06/06-4-1-e.pdf

González y González, E. M., & Lincoln, Y. S. (2007, April 10–14). *Decolonizing methodologies further: Authorial intentions, reader response, and the uses of qualitative research.* Paper presented at the annual meeting of the American Educational Research Association, Chicago, IL.

Grande, S. (2008). Red pedagogy: The unmethodology. In N. K. Denzin, Y. S. Lincoln, & L. T. Smith (Eds.), *Handbook of critical and indigenous methodologies* (pp. 233–254). Thousand Oaks, CA: Sage.

Guba, E. G., & Lincoln, Y. S. (1989). *Fourth generation evaluation.* Newbury Park, CA: Sage.

Gunsalus, C. K., Bruner, E. M., Burbules, N. C., Dash, L., Finkin, M., Goldberg, J. P., et al. (2007). The Illinois white paper: Improving the system for protecting human subjects: Counteracting IRB "mission creep." *Qualitative Inquiry, 13*(5), 617–649.

Hendry, P. M. (2007). The future of narrative. *Qualitative Inquiry, 13*(4), 487–498.

Hill Collins, P. (2000). *Black feminist thought: Knowledge, consciousness and the politics of empowerment.* New York: Routledge.

hooks, b. (1984). *Feminist theory: From margin to center.* Boston: South End Press.

Joint Committee on Standards for Educational Evaluation. (1981). *Standards for evaluations of educational programs, projects, and materials.* New York: McGraw-Hill.

Joint Committee on Standards for Educational Evaluation. (1988). *The personnel evaluation standards: How to assess systems for evaluating educators.* Newbury Park, CA: Sage.

Kincheloe, J. L., & McLaren, P. (2000). Rethinking critical theory and qualitative research. In N. K. Denzin & Y. S. Lincoln (Eds.), *The handbook of qualitative research* (2nd ed., pp. 279–314). Thousand Oaks, CA: Sage.

Kohlberg, L. (1976). Moral stages and moralization: The cognitive-developmental approach. In T. Lickona (Ed.), *Moral development* and behavior: Theory, research and social issues (pp. 346–378). New York: Holt, Rinehart & Winston.

Kohlberg, L. (1981). *The philosophy of moral development*. San Francisco: Harper & Row.

Lather, P. (1991). *Getting smart: Feminist research and pedagogy with/in the postmodern*. New York: Routledge.

Lerum, K. (2001). Subjects of desire: Academic armor, intimate ethnography, and the production of critical knowledge. *Qualitative Inquiry, 7*(4), 466–483.

Levinson, D. J. (1978). *The seasons of a man's life*. New York: Alfred A Knopf.

Lincoln, Y. S., & Denzin, N. K. (2008). Epilogue: The lions speak. In N. K. Denzin, Y. S. Lincoln, & L. T. Smith (Eds.), *The handbook of critical and indigenous methodologies*. Thousand Oaks, CA: Sage.

Lincoln, Y. S., & González y González, E. M. (2007, April 10–14). *Decolonizing evidence: The politics of bilingual data*. Paper presented at the annual meeting of the American Educational Research Association, Chicago.

Lincoln, Y. S., & Guba, E. G. (1985). *Naturalistic inquiry*. Beverly Hills, CA: Sage.

Lincoln, Y. S., & Guba, E. G. (1989). Ethics: The failure of positivist science. *Review of Higher Education, 12*(3), 221–240.

Lincoln, Y. S., & Guba, E. G. (2000). Paradigmatic controversies, contradictions, and emerging confluences. In N. K. Denzin & Y. S. Lincoln (Eds.), *The handbook of qualitative research* (2nd ed., pp. 163–188). Thousand Oaks, CA: Sage.

Lincoln, Y. S., & Tierney, W. G. (2004). Qualitative research and institutional review boards (IRBs). *Qualitative Inquiry, 10*(2), 219–234.

Marcus, G. E. (1986). Contemporary problems of ethnography in the modern world system. In J. Clifford & G. Marcus (Eds.), *Writing culture* (pp. 165–193). Berkeley: University of California Press.

Marcus, G. E. (2001). From rapport under erasure to theaters of complicit reflexivity. *Qualitative Inquiry, 7*(4), 519–528.

Marcus, G. E., & Fischer, M. K. (1986). *Anthropology as cultural critique: An experimental moment in the human sciences*. Chicago: University of Chicago Press.

Mauthner, M., Birch, M., Jessop, J., & Miller, T. (Eds.). (2002). *Ethics in qualitative research*. London: Sage.

McLeod, K. (2007). *Owning culture: Authorship, ownership and intellectual property law*. New York: Peter Lang.

Mertens, D. M. (1998). *Research methods in education and psychology: Integrating diversity with quantitative and qualitative approaches*. Thousand Oaks, CA: Sage.

National Commission for the Protection of Human Subjects of Biomedical and Behavioral Research. (1978). *The Belmont report: Ethical principles and guidelines for the protection of human subjects of research* (DHEW Publication No. OS 78–0012). Washington, DC: Government Printing Office.

National Research Council, Center for Education, Division of Behavioral and Social Sciences and Education. (2002). *Scientific research in education* (Report by the Committee on Scientific Principles for Education Research, R. J. Shavelson & L. Towne, Eds.). Washington, DC: National Academy Press.

Noddings, N. (1984). *Caring: A feminine approach to ethics and moral education*. Berkeley: University of California Press.

Noddings, N. (2003). *Caring: A feminine approach to ethics and moral education* (2nd ed.). Berkeley: University of California Press.

Noddings, N. (2005a). Caring in education. In *The encyclopedia of informal education*. Retrieved December 21, 2007, from www.infed.org/biblio/noddings_caring_in_education.htm

Noddings, N. (2005b). *The challenge to care in schools: An alternative approach to education*. New York: Teachers College Press.

Plummer, K. (2001). The call of life stories in ethnographic research. In P. Atkinson, A. Coffey, S. Delamont, J. Lofland, &

L. Lofland (Eds.), *Handbook of ethnography* (pp. 395–406). London: Sage.

Rambo, C. (2007). Handing IRB an unloaded gun. *Qualitative Inquiry, 13*(3), 353–367.

Rawls, J. (1971). *A theory of justice.* Cambridge, MA: Belknap Press/Harvard University Press.

Reed-Danahay, D. (2001). Autobiography, intimacy and ethnography. In P. Atkinson, A. Coffey, S. Delamont, J. Lofland, & L. Lofland (Eds.), *Handbook of ethnography* (pp. 407–425). London: Sage.

Rosaldo, R. (1989). *Culture and truth: The remaking of social analysis.* Boston: Beacon Press.

Rosiek, J. (2007). Introduction to Part 1: Horizons of narrative inquiry. *Qualitative Inquiry, 13*(4), 447–449.

Savage, M. C. (1988). Can ethnographic narrative be a neighborly act? *Anthropology and Education Quarterly, 19,* 3–19.

Sevenhuijsen, S. (1998). *Citizenship and the ethics of care: Feminist considerations on justice, morality and politics.* London: Routledge.

Skeggs, B. (2001). Feminist ethnography. In P. Atkinson, A. Coffey, S. Delamont, J. Lofland, & L. Lofland (Eds.), *Handbook of ethnography* (pp. 426–442). London: Sage.

Smith, L. T. (1999). *Decolonizing methodologies.* London: Zed Books.

Springwood, C. F., & King, C. R. (Eds.). (2001a). Coming to terms: Reinventing rapport in critical ethnography [Special issue]. *Qualitative Inquiry, 7*(4).

Springwood, C. F., & King, C. R. (2001b). Unsettling engagements: On the ends of rapport in critical ethnography. *Qualitative Inquiry, 7*(4), 403–417.

Tronto, J. C. (1987). Beyond gender difference to a theory of care. *Signs: Journal of Women in Culture and Society, 124,* 644–663.

Tronto, J. C. (1993). *Moral boundaries: A political argument for an ethic of care.* New York: Routledge.

Weems, L. (2006). Unsettling politics, locating ethics: Representations of reciprocity in postpositivist inquiry. *Qualitative Inquiry, 12*(5), 994–1011.

Wolf, R. L. (Interviewer/Producer). (1984). Interview with Studs Terkel [Videotape]. Bloomington: Indiana University.

Wong, L. M. (1998). The ethics of rapport: Institutional safeguards, resistance and betrayal. *Qualitative Inquiry, 4*(2), 178–199.

Wood, W. W. (2001). Rapport is overrated: Southwestern ethnic art dealers and ethnographers in the "field." *Qualitative Inquiry, 7*(4), 484–503.

Zerner, C. (Ed.). (2003). *Culture and the question of rights: Forests, coasts and seas in Southeast Asia.* Durham, SC: Duke University Press.

11
ETHICAL PERSPECTIVES IN PROGRAM EVALUATION

◆ Amanda Wolf, David Turner, and Kathleen Toms

Evaluation may be distinguished from other social research by its goal of providing usable information to support decisions about program or policy operations and effectiveness. This emphasis on actionable information, with consequences for the wider society, raises ethical issues that go beyond issues of good research practice. These broader considerations arise from program evaluators' exercise of professional judgment in maintaining social relationships and serving various social expectations. Practicing evaluators have a range of guidance to consult as they work, but there is limited empirical research into how they approach ethics in their day-to-day work practices. This chapter describes new research conducted among a group of evaluators—applied social researchers—in both North America and Australasia (Australia and New Zealand). The research suggests that evaluators share an emerging practice perspective about their use of research methods and the attendant ethical considerations in that use, but exhibit an array of views on the purposes of evaluation and their own relationships and responsibilities to clients, program participants, groups within society, and the public at large.

◆ *Evaluation as a Profession Based in Social Research*

Evaluation is widely held to involve the systematic application of social research methods to assess the strengths and weaknesses of social interventions, including programs, policies, personnel, products, and organizations. It is designed to aid in decisions about the effectiveness, efficiency, and/or appropriateness of interventions and their implementation and management (Alkin, 2004; American Evaluation Association [AEA], n.d.; Australasian Evaluation Society [AES], 2002; Kellogg Foundation, 1998; Rossi, Lipsey, & Freeman, 2004). Thus, evaluation differs from research in its explicit, indeed required, determination of the merit, worth, or value of that which is researched (Scriven, 1991). This focus leads some writers to emphasize elements of evaluation that extend beyond an "academic research" focus, such as its "relevance and usefulness" to program practitioners (Kellogg Foundation, 1998), its adaptation to political and organizational environments with an explicit purpose to "inform social action to improve social conditions" (Rossi et al., 2004), and its democratizing processes (Ryan & DeStefano, 2000). In aiding decisions by determining value, evaluators borrow theory, concepts, and methods from many disciplines. Evaluations are multidisciplinary investigations involving judgment and oriented by decision requirements.

Ethics, as it concerns principles of moral behavior and their application, clearly extends from evaluation activities—notably evaluators' uses of research methods—to its purposes, believed by at least some evaluators to reach far into society at large. Moreover, evaluators are *professionals*, with a "social contract" for services to the public, and its attendant ethical obligations. The contract may be construed to entail either providing information relevant to decisions that potentially affect the public or engaging directly with stakeholders to facilitate their improved understanding of the challenges they face (Schwandt, 2007).

Evaluation developed as a distinct field in the 1960s and 1970s (Stevahn, King, Ghere, & Minnema, 2005). Like their kindred policy analysts, who also emerged as professionals around the same time, evaluators are not licensed or formally credentialed to practice, as are members in professions such as accounting, nursing, or engineering. Yet many have undertaken significant education and training. They have acquired theoretical and practical skills that other evaluators recognize. They identify themselves as members of a profession, by joining associations of evaluators and holding jobs with evaluation titles. Both research ethics as it concerns evaluators' methods and practice ethics as applied to the conduct of evaluation in a day-to-day context are covered in significant depth and richness in the literature. Not surprisingly, pockets of difference may be found, but mainly in contrast with a core consensus.

At the level of evaluation *activity*, then, there is little to separate evaluation from *applied social research*. Notwithstanding the fact that both evaluation and social research encompass a vast range of methods, addressed to an equally vast range of problems, both evaluators and social researchers are bound by formal rules or informal norms covering matters associated with the collection and use of information from people. It is not uncommon for individuals to consider themselves both researchers and evaluators, especially when their work consists of assignments of both types. However, when people define themselves as evaluators, and a particular exercise as evaluation, we need to look to the *purposes* or aims of their activities to find in what ways evaluation as practice differs from other forms of social research, and hence in what ways evaluation ethics is specific to evaluation practice. Evaluation ethics as it pertains to the evaluator as a professional is still emerging. We lack a clear consensus on principles associated with the social accountability or public responsibility that is specific to evaluators as members of a discrete professional body.

The next section of this chapter reviews relevant literature on research, practice, and professional ethics. We look at the ways in which evaluation associations promote the ethical use of research methods in evaluation practice through standards, guidelines, and principles of evaluation practice. Based on that review and the aspects of those documents noted, the discussion is then broadened to include more recent consideration of practice ethics and professional ethics for evaluation. Ethics in evaluation, however approached, continues to be a lively topic of focused attention, as evidenced by conference sessions and special journal sections. As befits a field of emerging practice, new ideas, disagreements, and consensus intermingle. Sensing this dynamism, we were encouraged to undertake some novel exploratory research on evaluators' own views of the relative importance of aspects of the ethical practice of evaluation in light of the open questions about ethics being debated by evaluators. We were further encouraged to take the unusual step of presenting these findings in this *Handbook*, a step that fully acknowledges that the articulation of ethics in evaluation is a fast-moving exercise currently engaging the energies of many dedicated evaluators.

♦ Evaluation Activity: Its Practice and Ethics

Evaluators work across public sectors (such as health, education, and justice). They may be employed or contracted by public agencies (including legislative bodies; organizations such as the Government Accountability Office in the United States, which operates as the evaluative arm of Congress; and local-level school district or transportation boards), nonprofit organizations, or universities. Originally trained in a variety of disciplines, such as educational psychology, statistics, or sociology, evaluators use an extensive range of qualitative, quantitative, or mixed research methods. In addition, because evaluators in public policy and public administration provide information relevant to public decisions, they use methods appropriate to assessing the political context and value conflicts prominent in many public policies and programs. Relevant context and values may be determined by public sector agencies, participants in evaluated policies and programs or other affected individuals, various academic or professional experts, or the wider society (Simons, 2006). Thus, the activities of evaluation are multifaceted, with the evaluator personally interacting with, or affected by, the ethically relevant features of tasks, relationships, and social expectations.

Individual evaluation projects may target ongoing process improvement or may assess the results of public activities. Some evaluations are conducted with the cooperation or full engagement of policy stakeholders, and others seek to restrict interactions to narrow study questions. Evaluation may be quickly conducted on a shoestring budget or may consume significant resources over several years. Such contextual factors are among the many that impinge on the scale and scope of evaluation activity and so, too, are potentially ethically relevant.

Many evaluation associations, such as those in France, Germany, Canada, the United States, the United Kingdom, Australia, and New Zealand, have developed national standards or guides to evaluation practice that are significantly geared to ethical matters (Picciotto, 2005). The AEA's *Guiding Principles for Evaluators*, most recently reviewed and ratified in 2004, lists five principles: (1) systematic inquiry, including maintaining high technical standards and ensuring an appropriate match between questions and methods; (2) competence, including skills, abilities, and cultural competence; (3) integrity/honesty; (4) respect for people, covering widely recognized principles of research ethics; and (5) responsibilities for general and public welfare, including taking into account stakeholder perspectives and interests and the broad assumptions, implications, and potential side effects of an evaluation. The AES's *Guidelines for the Ethical Conduct of Evaluation*, republished in 2006, traverse much of the same ground.

The five principles of this document apply to commissioning and preparing for an evaluation (ensuring informed and reasonable expectations and involving all potentially affected persons so that they have a say in identifying and reducing the risks in an evaluation) and designing, conducting, and reporting an evaluation (covering general research ethics, and fair and balanced reporting).

Typically, these guiding documents have evolved over the course of years, with significant member involvement. More recent codes, such as that of South Africa, build on existing documents (Picciotto, 2005). Hence, the final products enjoy wide, if incomplete, consensus. By intention and by virtue of the very process of engagement and consensus building, the guidelines tend to be high level and nonprescriptive. Preambles and caveats make clear the need for evaluators to make decisions case by case regarding the applicability and appropriate balance of the principles of applied use of research methods. Others note that the principles themselves are open to interpretation (Goodyear, 2007; Schweigert, 2007).

A large scholarly and practitioner-focused literature attempts to apply some order to the great variety of ethical principles captured and implied by the standards evaluators are encouraged to follow. In one effort, Picciotto (2005) examined the core functions of evaluation and developed normative arguments for the standards of propriety, transparency, independence, integrity, competence, quality, comprehensiveness, efficiency, utilization, and governance, but he did not address the matter of pragmatic trade-offs. An intriguing tack by a Finnish scholar starts with the main "aggregates" in any evaluation and deduces a key principle for each. The four aggregate-principle pairs are the evaluator (the principle of truth), the object of evaluation ("justness"), the process (ability), and the community (responsibility; Laitinen, 2002). Stevahn et al. (2005) sought order and conciseness through a taxonomy of evaluator competencies. While a thorough assessment of these and other ways to define a comprehensive, yet tractable, set of principles of good and right behavior is outside the scope of this study, all such efforts confirm that the ethical in evaluation includes the ethical conduct of research, or research-like activities, as well as some ethically influenced social and relational practices and objectives.

Against this background, ongoing guideline development activities reflect a clear shift in emphasis from technical issues of competent research practice to wider social and professional considerations. Program evaluation standards published by the Joint Committee on Standards for Educational Evaluation, under revision in 2007 (www.wmich.edu/evalctr/jc), illustrate a wider view of evaluator responsibilities. Propriety standards direct evaluators to be responsive to stakeholders and to provide their results in ways that are complete and balanced. Utility standards note that evaluators should make their purposes and values clear and should show concern for the consequences of their work. The standards reflect interest in issues surrounding the commissioning of evaluation and the nature of stakeholder involvement in setting the evaluation parameters (a development noted some years ago by Newman, 1995) and concerns about how evaluation results are used and how they fit into the "bigger picture" of social change. That is, evaluation is said to contribute to the "further development of politics and society" (Beywl, 2006, p. 10; Newman, 1995). An illustration of this development is the increasing focus on cultural issues, particularly involving indigenous groups. The AES has devoted increasing attention to indigenous issues, as has the AEA. The AEA has topical interest groups for indigenous peoples, multiethnic issues, and international and cross-cultural evaluation. These developments are not uniquely focused on ethics, nor is attention to indigenous issues in applied research, for example, unique to evaluation. However, they clearly signal a widespread expansion of the ambit of evaluation ethics beyond research ethics conceived as a relationship between evaluator and *individual* participant. They signal a refined attention to the ethics of public responsibility, by focusing at the level of evaluator-*group* interactions. Finally, though implicitly, these developments acknowledge a multiplicity of evaluator values and identities—a far cry from an evaluator-as-researcher who speaks in a universal language of science.

In sum, guidelines and codes of ethics share attention to the use of research tools and exhibit sensitivity to varied practical constraints in the application of these tools. Given the broadly consultative manner of their development, revised standards reveal an incipient consensus that ethics in evaluation has multiple meanings. Ethics is surely something more than the competent use of research tools, with competence a matter of good or bad skills, or what Schwandt (2005) recently described as practice-as-science. Practice, Schwandt continued, may also be construed as "pedagogy," helping others to inform themselves. In addition, in the practice of evaluation, with its emphasis on value identification and clarification, and the need to work within other public constraints, evaluators function professionally, with the added accountabilities and ethical implications entailed. Voluntary standards and codes of practice such as those used in evaluation assist the public to trust the competency of the profession as a whole. When compared with the ethical codes of other professions, however, these evaluation guides are more standards of competent practice than codes of professional ethics.

Evaluators, like researchers, occasionally push beyond the parameters established for the use of research methods and must make professional judgments about the ethics of their choices. These judgments, tempered by evaluators' social contract, and the purposes evaluation serves in relation to society at large, may also be guided by an ethics of professional practice. Thus, while evaluators, in common with all professionals, are limited in how they ethically justify their decisions, it remains open to question the manner in which professional norms contain one or more emerging ethical perspectives.

♦ Evaluation Practice: Toward Professional Ethics?

Most of the academic or practitioner-academic literature on evaluation ethics falls into one of three categories. First, specific challenges or dilemmas are examined, drawing on a range of theories and examples and providing overall assessments about the nature of satisfactory resolutions. For example, Mathison (1999) examined the ethical challenges facing internal and external evaluators. She found that the key distinction stems from the different communities they occupy and not from the nature of ethical challenges. Datta (1999), in another example of this strand of literature, considered arguments for and against evaluator neutrality and advocacy. The second main category of literature on ethics as it applies to evaluation stems from specific cases and concentrates on research ethics and dilemmas that arise from conflicting or differently interpreted principles. A regular feature in the *American Journal of Evaluation*, "Ethical Challenges," examines ethical dilemmas and offers alternative views on cases exhibiting both classical and newer challenges (see also Morris, 2007). Finally, there is a limited literature reporting primary research on evaluators' ethical challenges. Again, this focuses mainly on research ethics. For instance, members of evaluation societies have been surveyed to ascertain the issues they encounter and believe to be most serious (Morris & Cohn, 1993; Turner, 2003). Morris (1999) reviewed primary research on the extent and types of ethical challenges evaluators face. Overall, issues concerning evaluator competence, independence, treatment of research participants, and use of findings loom large in this strand of research.

Despite widespread assertions that evaluation is a distinct profession, this view is rarely argued explicitly. Clearly, the literature shows that evaluation is not simply a skilled occupation in which practitioners are expected to perform a set of skills in more or less regular tasks, with limited scope for independent decision making. At the same time, evaluation does not exhibit the full set of classic professional benchmarks (notably a requirement that evaluators pass a standard licensing-type examination or otherwise become accredited by a governing professional organization). However, evaluators do display the fundamental *characteristics* of professional practice, including the requirement to think, function, and learn across a series of "new" instances. Professionals blend together experience, knowledge, and a certain disposition or "feel" in their work. Their work provides a service to society and is valued by society for its contribution to the public good.

Evaluation, then, is professional due primarily to its relationship with the society that it serves, rather than by any narrowly defined "typical" practice. Professional ethics concerns the moral issues that arise when individuals draw on specialist knowledge to provide services to the public (Chadwick, 1998). It follows, we believe, that as a professional practice, evaluation has its own unique ethical considerations, held in reference to its "social contract." As is true for any profession, the "rightness" of professional practices *and* societal consequences are central to evaluators' contract. Whether done ethically or not, evaluations often have a wide and direct influence in society through their influence on debate and decision. Many other professionals exert their influence more indirectly—for example, by addressing individual "cases" guided, more or less, by prescriptive codes of conduct and accumulated "best practices." In contrast, public scrutiny of evaluation may include heightened attention to design choices, such as whose views are included or excluded, how findings are checked for accuracy, and how results are reported, when compared with more researcher-directed studies.

Evaluators have responsibilities to evaluation commissioners to conduct quality work and to treat the beneficiaries and participants in evaluations programs with respect. They are trained and encouraged to consider and aspire to maintain the rightness of their own practices: to strike the balance between what is in the best interest of their clients and what is in the best interest of society. As Schweigert (2007) noted, "Because the situations of evaluation are inevitably complex and various, often involving conflicts between principles as well as among aims or claims of stakeholders, evaluators need an interpretive framework to clarify the issues at hand and open the way to workable—and just—solutions" (p. 396). Schweigert went on to propose such a framework, asserting that none currently operates effectively.

Evaluators may also have obligations toward the future well-being of communities, to the health of democratic debate, and to the evaluation profession itself. Toms (1993) conducted the evaluation field's initial study into professional ethical practices in Canada and the United States using in-depth interviews of federal evaluators in the two countries. Toms found that both a "communitarian ethic and an ethical individualism" were joined in evaluators' operating reality. This intrinsic ethical disposition, and its orientation to some notion of the "good," is re-expressed by Picciotto (2005), who noted, "the primary responsibility of the evaluator in a democratic society is to enhance accountability, tell truth to power, illuminate policy options, promote public involvement and contribute to the transparency of decisions taken in the public interest" (p. 35). In New Zealand, evaluation is central to the government's "managing for outcomes" framework. As a result, evaluators are pushing out their focal depth, from immediate effects to enduring changes in social variables. A parallel expansion of design, purpose, and scope is evident among professional researchers. Feminist research methods, for example, have evolved over the past decade to formalize the input of research participants not only into the honest reflection of their contribution to the answers to researcher questions but also into the very formulation of the researchers' questions (Mertens, 2004). Evaluation and research blend together in practice. Indeed, while answering a question at the AEA conference in 2004 regarding her experiences from compiling the *Encyclopedia of Evaluation*, Sandra Mathison (2004) stated that she has come to view "evaluation as the broader area, so that I see research as a form of evaluation rather than evaluation as a form of research" (personal notes).

Summarizing the state of empirical information in light of current themes of interest in the literature, we have some evidence from surveys on what ethical principles guide evaluators generally and some case-based studies to see how the principles are accommodated in challenging reality. Even taken together, however, we still have a limited understanding of how various preferences and trade-offs combine in evaluators' day-to-day ethical orientations or in evaluators' own views of the relative importance of aspects of ethical practice.

♦ New Research on Ethical Perspectives in Evaluation

In 2005, we used Q methodology to explore and understand better the ethical orientations of practicing evaluators in North America and Australasia toward ethics in practice and to compare their holistic perspectives with each other and with themes evident in the literature. Q methodology is a systematic way to discover and assess the judgmental and subjective elements of people's attitudes and beliefs. In our case, those beliefs are about ethics in evaluation covering personal, situational, professional, and societal dimensions. Subjectivity in Q methodology refers to "communication behavior," or, simply, what people say to themselves and others about some topic at hand (Brown, 1980; Brown, Durning, & Selden, 2008; McKeown & Thomas, 1988; Stephenson, 1953). Unlike surveys, Q methodology captures views as a whole, as a snapshot of what is on a person's mind, and compares each snapshot with all others. Individuals' points of view are treated as variables. The statistical procedures of correlation and factor analysis serve to identify patterns among seemingly disparate views. Thus, Q methodology is similar to qualitative studies, in which the whole of a person's experience is examined. However, unlike qualitative analysis, the use of quantitative procedures to highlight similarities and differences constrains the researchers' interpretations to what the data numerically support.

In a preliminary exercise, subscribers to the AEA and AES electronic discussion lists were invited to submit views on what constitutes "ethical practice" of evaluation and what principles or rules guide them day-to-day. This exercise was akin to dipping a bucket in to the ever-evolving "talk" about ethics in evaluation as it flows like a river in evaluators' conversations. The scoop returned some 400 discrete "statements" from 91 respondents. From these, 56 representative statements were selected. This sample of statements expresses a range of views relating to paying clients, program beneficiaries or participants, the community and society, the evaluation profession, and personal values. Some statements in each of these thematic categories express views about technical aspects of practice and others emphasize the service, purpose, or value elements of practice. Since the sample statements were provided by both AEA and AES members, grammar and spelling were Americanized.

Next, 23 AEA and 17 AES members completed Q sorts, in which they sorted the statements into a quasi-normal distribution ranging from −5 to +5 according to the degree to which they agreed or disagreed with each statement concerning ethics in evaluation. In the process of Q sorting, participants impart their own meaning to the terms in the statements and to the statements themselves. Brief written comments explaining strong choices were invited. Using *PQMethod* (2002) software, we intercorrelated the sorts and factor analyzed the resulting correlations. Statistical analysis identified factors that represent underlying commonality among a group of participants (based on the Q sort each provided as a snapshot of their views). Finally, we examined each factor's weighted-average Q sort, based on the individual sorts that were statistically significant on a factor, to develop an interpretation of the distinctiveness of the factor and then to draw out the implication of these findings as an emerging perspective on ethics in evaluation.

We undertook three analyses, first examining the combined data and then focusing on the disaggregated AEA and AES data. When all 40 sorts were combined, one unrotated factor explained 37% of the variance among sorts. All sorts loaded significantly on this factor at $p < .05$. The composite evaluator captured by this factor values integrity and independence. This evaluator is not overly swayed by the interests of paying clients, believes in and relies on codes of ethics and their articulation of rights and responsibilities, and upholds the use of best practice in research methods. The common characteristics also emphasize respect for the evaluated community, rejection of a "value-free" premise, apparent wariness of potential for bias to arise in the relationship with a paying client, and belief in evaluation's role in the larger process of social change. In short, we detect clear evidence that evaluators see themselves as practitioners of well-conducted research, where this activity is intimately bound to a client's needs and those of the program participants, as well as to a larger process in society. Practice ethics extends beyond a conventional research-as-discovery.

In many respects, this portrait aligns well with the main competencies assembled by Stevahn et al. (2005), which were shown in a comparative analysis to be largely captured in guidelines by North American evaluation associations. Therefore, having found strong similarities in the views of participating evaluators from both countries, we sought to isolate fine-grained differences, both within and between regions. To facilitate this interpretation, varimax rotation was used because it maximizes the variance between clusters of points of view and therefore served this study's objectives of discovery and comparison.

Using this finer sieve to accentuate differences, we found four AEA factors and three AES factors. The interpretations are summarized in Table 11.1. Consistent with much reporting in Q methodology, each factor is given an evocative label. The descriptions project "portraits" suggested by the component statement scores for the factors. It should be noted that the portraits are composites, not pigeonholes into which real people slot neatly. The factors, in other words, are points of view that real people may identify with to some degree or another. However, the phenomena of interest are the viewpoints, not the people who hold them. For this reason, the findings from this Q study could be used to design follow-up research to gauge the relative prevalence of different points of view.

To interpret the factors, we sought to develop pictures of the hypothetical individuals whom the factors perfectly represented, using scores showing how the given statements were ranked. To illustrate this process, consider one statement, with rankings for the four AEA factors in parentheses:

Accountability for conducting the evaluation according to ethical standards rests in the hands of the evaluator (5 –2 2 0).

This statement contributes to the overall interpretations for all factors. First, it supports a picture of a client-centered professional (AEA 1) as an individual with unique expertise and the willingness to accept accountability demanded by the social contract. With change agents (AEA 2), the statement's ranking fits with their sense of

Table 11.1   Factor Descriptions and Representative Statements

American Evaluation Association

AEA 1: The client-centered professional. Evaluators are not agents of change, but practice is community embedded, culturally influenced, and able to be done with client involvement. Methods should be appropriate, reports balanced. Evaluators should guide clients toward asking the right questions and should thoroughly apply standards in their work. *I have a relationship with clients, stakeholders, and program users as full partners. (+4)*

AEA 2: The change agent. These evaluators are client centered, but they are also change agents. Evaluation is not value-neutral. Clients should be trained by the evaluator to participate in evaluations that respect the community and cultural ethos. Evaluation contributes specifically to uncovering benefits and costs in human terms, which informs the "big picture" of social change. *We should actively engage with our clients, cross-train them, and share the risks and outcomes. (+4)*

AEA 3: The practitioner. Personal values guide these evaluators, who use their experiences and "gut" reactions to judge their own practice. With some similarity to AEA1, they seek integrity in their methods and relationships, thus providing independent feedback to their clients. However, they reject absolute objectivity and like AEA 2 are sensitive to the effects of evaluation on people's lives. The ethical evaluator is not a whistle-blower. *Generally speaking, my practice is informed by my own personal values and standards rather than by "ethics standards." (+4)*

AEA 4: The socially constrained technical professional. For these evaluators, codes of ethics serve as a compass to methodological integrity, and their practice is not informed by personal values or beliefs. Evaluation takes place in context of social culture that must be respected and responded to. They believe that participation in evaluation can empower participants. However, evaluators are not change agents. Evaluation would not normally play a role in society's "big picture." *I do not think it is possible to do evaluation without reference to the social and cultural conditions in which the results are to be applied. (+4)*

Australasian Evaluation Society

AES 1: The technical professional. These evaluators strongly agree with the need to have integrity and use appropriate methods in their practice. Ethics concerns principles such as do-no-harm and respect for the rights to privacy and self-determination of their clients. While hands-on client participation is not a problem, they reject the view that evaluations ought to put clients in the best light or make technical decisions predicated on client benefit. They do not see themselves as change agents. *The principles "do-no-harm," the right to privacy, the right to ownership of personal information, and the right to self-determination need to be considered and applied when designing evaluations and when unanticipated situations arise. (+5)*

AES 2: The empowerer. Ethical practice should do no harm and ensure the participants' right to privacy. Appropriate methods should be used, and different perspectives should be balanced. Ethical evaluation is not value-free, cannot be objective, and is influenced by the evaluator's perspective. These evaluators believe that evaluation findings fit into the "bigger picture" of social change, so ethical evaluators must take into account the social and cultural conditions in which results will be applied, respect community, and be "culturally competent." Participatory evaluation is a means to empower participants. *I believe that taking part in participatory evaluations can potentially be an empowering experience for participants, particularly those who do not have a voice or who are often silenced and disempowered as a result of traditional consultation and evaluation processes. (+5)*

> **AES 3: The client-focused change agent.** These evaluators rely on personal ethics and judgments in their work. Evaluators are change agents. They should not keep the clients at arms length, but should work with them, assisting them to ask the right questions. They believe that use of evaluative information is part of the deal and that blatant political use is not acceptable.
>
> *Evaluators are "change agents," and the sooner we come down off the high horse of "objectivity" the more prepared we will be as a profession to more clearly and truthfully articulate our paradigm and its contribution. (+4)*

NOTE: The score associated with each statement shows the average Q-sort ranking of the statement by the significant loaders on the factor. Scores range from +5 to –5.

partnership, of not going it alone, rather than as a denial of their own accountability. Practitioners (AEA 3) gave the statement a positive score, but not as strong as client-centered professionals (AEA 1). People on this factor find principled professionalism important, but not overriding, perhaps due to their more pragmatic orientation. For them, accountability is certainly part of the story, but it is not clear-cut. Perhaps there is some unwillingness to draw attention to the evaluator, who may draw on some ad hoc principles from time to time. Finally, as we began to appreciate the socially constrained technical professional (AEA 4) as a technical expert with a bigger-picture awareness, the 0 score fits. The statement registers in the middle of the distribution due to a canceling-out effect. People like this evaluator portrait may hold a strongly positive attitude toward professional responsibility, like the client-centered professionals (AEA 1). But against this, the socially constrained technical professional (AEA 4) might consider the whole notion of evaluator accountability too narrow given the operation of societal constraints and consequences.

Eventually researchers' provisional understandings, built statement by statement and comparatively across factors, emerged and cohered in an overall sense of each factor, as summarized in Table 11.1. Table 11.2 shows a selection of statements, including one that is distinguishing for each factor.

In one way or another, all participants in this study, as shown by the seven regional factors, emphasized professionalism and ethical research practices. There is compelling evidence that ethics in evaluation entails using appropriate data collection and analysis methods, with an emphasis on quality practices and principles of research ethics. Evaluators who differ in some respects all believe strongly in the need for community respect. These features are compatible with those in the literature.

However, the distinct patterns that emerged from this exploratory research provide rich material for reflection on emerging perspectives on ethics in evaluation practice. Among the key differences between factors are whether evaluators should be "change agents," the relative roles of sets of standards and personal values, and the possibility or desirability of using "objective" methods. The role of the client also varies across factors. Some see the client as a partner sharing the responsibility for evaluation risks and outcomes, whereas others believe it their professional responsibility to maintain established standards at one remove, as it were, from the hurly-burly of everyday relationships. Ethics, in short, cannot be separated from responsibility, but both can be more or less tightly bound to the evaluator.

Some subtle differences in orientation were suggested by the North American and Australasian results. The socially constrained technical professional (AEA 4) and the empowerer (AES 2) both agree strongly, and more strongly than others,

Table 11.2 Selected Statement and Scores for Each Factor, With Distinguishing Scores in Boldface

Statements and Scores on Each Factor	AEA 1	AEA 2	AEA 3	AEA 4	AES 1	AES 2	AES 3
Generally speaking, my practice is informed by my own personal values and standards rather than by "ethics standards."	0	0	**4**	**−4**	−1	**−3**	3
We should actively engage with our clients, cross-train them, and share the risks and outcomes.	2	**4**	**−4**	0	−1	0	**5**
Evaluators are "change agents" and the sooner we come down off the high horse of "objectivity," the more prepared we will be as a profession to more clearly and truthfully articulate our paradigm and its contribution.	**−3**	3	**4**	**−4**	**−4**	1	**4**
I do not think it is possible to do evaluation without reference to the social and cultural conditions in which the results are to be applied.	1	3	1	**4**	2	4	0
I have a relationship with clients, stakeholders, and program users as full partners.	**4**	1	0	0	0	0	**4**
The principles "do-no-harm," the right to privacy, the right to ownership of personal information, and the right to self-determination need to be considered and applied when designing evaluations and when unanticipated situations arise.	3	0	1	3	**5**	3	1
I believe that taking part in participatory evaluations can potentially be an empowering experience for participants, particularly those who do not have a voice or who are often silenced and disempowered as a result of traditional consultation and evaluation processes.	3	2	−1	3	1	**5**	0

that evaluation must consider social and cultural contexts, and that evaluators must respect the community being evaluated. Yet the AES empowerer rejects the notion of value-free evaluation, or objectivity of the evaluator, while the AEA counterpart places much stronger weight on using objective methods to "call it like it is." When the client-centered professional (AEA 1) is compared with the client-focused change agent (AES 3), we find strong agreement on relating to clients and other stakeholders as full partners. But the Australasian factor is again less concerned with independence and standard procedures and more inclined to accept that "reality" constrains the ability to present an objective truth to decision makers when compared with the North American factor.

Overall, the study results in a picture of a multifaceted profession. "Ethics" is not a simple subject. The factors are a contribution to an ongoing discussion among thoughtful and reflective practitioners. Below are three quotations from participants' written comments, illustrating this thoughtfulness, as well as the deep currents running through the concepts of ethics in practice:

> My firm opinion is that, as far as is compatible with objectivity, client

involvement results in a much more useful and worthwhile product. I also consider that one of my responsibilities is to make the practice of evaluation accessible to many, thereby fostering a wider culture and understanding of evaluation practice and use. [Significant on AES 1 (technical professional)]

At base, "ethical practice" is doing right. The focus has to be on goals, objectives and data, not on the client's, or any participant's benefit. Intimate client involvement is unethical . . . the responsibility for the execution of evaluation recommendations is the program's. A "gut feeling" is an inappropriate substitute for being informed about ethical standards. An evaluator has to accept responsibility for his/her actions, including his/her application of ethical standards. If done properly, the evaluation is a means of program improvement and no more. (Significant on both AEA 1 and 4 [client-centered professional and socially constrained technical professional])

Every evaluation is about working closely with the client to clarify the parameters of the work. There are ethical issues to be dealt with in every evaluation, and one needs to work through these as they arise. My role is going into a project in order to assist the key stakeholders to see themselves, and learn from that. . . . Call me pompous if you like, but I am an evaluator because I want to make a difference in the world, and I have a strong improvement "ethic" of wanting to ensure that programmes, policies and initiatives are of the highest possible quality. (Significant on both AES 1 and 2 [technical professional and empowerer])

♦ **Concluding Observations**

The Q research contributes new information to the discussions of ethics by presenting composite pictures of the various ways evaluators think about ethics in their practices. Within evaluation circles, energetic discussion continues concerning the evolving content of various guidelines and sets of standards as they apply to ethics in evaluation. We conclude with some final observations on the ongoing conversation.

Evaluators are all one species, dedicated to providing their varied services to society and the public. The Q study found little to suggest that evaluators are Balkanized in camps with different ethical orientations. Instead, we found stimulating, if often subtle, differences in orientation superimposed on a core set of professionally inflected values. Since evaluators provide direct services to the society that they serve, it is not surprising that they evidence a strong professional relationship with the different definitions of the good across their individual contexts of practice. These differences are likely to account for the marginal differences found between factors and between regions.

Accordingly, we believe that efforts to further develop and enhance evaluation standards and to harmonize such efforts internationally are likely to be productive as long as those efforts take account of differences in ethical orientations between evaluators who align strongly with a view of evaluation service as research, in contrast to those evaluators who emphasize the social aspects of their practice. Put differently, while standards may be marginally improved by refining elements of competency expected of evaluators, significant advances will require explicit attention to issues of ethics in society, where evaluators may hold very different views.

The similarities and differences among the factors discussed in this chapter inform understanding of evaluators' practice. They also shed light on the ethical views of professional social science researchers, as well as on the contemporary content of evaluation's professional ethics, which for the most part have not been empirically examined. This research shows how practicing evaluators view ethics more broadly than as just a technical or procedural issue but look at relationships with clients and the wider community as well. This broadening horizon may be an indicator of evaluation's maturing into a true profession.

Many respondents in the Q methodology study show attachment to objective standards. Yet overall, there is a sense that evaluators are growing more comfortable with a view of ethics that does not make blanket demands. The factors show that differences between evaluation and research influence the response of professional evaluators to ethical issues. A fairly inchoate, but nevertheless pervasive, undercurrent of pragmatism shows in all the factors, and somewhat more so in the AES factors: Evaluators understand that to make progress on the ethical issues that confront them requires developing, adopting, and adapting research methodology and the ethical parameters surrounding its use to the concrete and everyday realities of their varied practices. Evaluators have to work out the issues that confront them to the satisfaction of fellow evaluators and those for whom they work and those on whose behalf they work. As evaluators are frequently called on to exercise their professional judgment, they will be breaking new ground in the old research ethics "standards" as they formally incorporate community voice and ensure public involvement while they protect sources and ensure that findings are as unbiased, rigorous, and honest as possible. And as evaluation is increasingly prominent in democratic decision making, the issues surfaced in this chapter point somewhat optimistically toward further productive refinement and deepening of the theory and practice of evaluation.

Finally, professional ethics concerns the rightness of practices relative to the "common good." However, the *good* is intersubjectively defined by each society. At any moment, each evaluator may be assumed to have an evolving notion of practice as consistent with the common good, based on his or her accumulated experiences and the reflections of those within his or her traditions and communities who have endeavored to define and support the good. While the unifying characteristic of evaluation practice is its use of research methods within an already established framework of their ethical use, evaluators may now be ready to move to the next stage in defining ethical codes of practice. The findings reported here suggest some possible points of discussion toward new consensus and acceptance of differences.

♦ References

Alkin, M. C. (Ed.). (2004). *Evaluation roots: Tracing theorists' views and influences.* Thousand Oaks, CA: Sage.

American Evaluation Association. (2004). *Guiding principles for evaluators.* Retrieved February 1, 2007, from www.eval.org/Publications/GuidingPrinciples.asp

American Evaluation Association. (n.d.). *About us* (Association homepage). Retrieved February 1, 2007, from www.eval.org/aboutus/organization/aboutus.asp

Australasian Evaluation Society. (2002). *Guidelines for the ethical conduct of evaluations.* Retrieved February 1, 2007, from www.aes.asn.au

Beywl, W. (2006, November). The role of evaluation in democracy: Can it be strengthened by evaluation standards? A European perspective. *Journal of MultiDisciplinary Evaluation, 6,* 10–29.

Brown, S. R. (1980). *Political subjectivity: Applications of Q methodology in political science.* New Haven, CT: Yale University Press.

Brown, S. R., Durning, D. W., & Selden, S. C. (2008). Q methodology. In K. Yang & G. J. Miller (Eds.), *Handbook of research methods in public administration* (Public Administration and Public Policy Series, Vol. 134, 2nd ed., pp. 721–763). Boca Raton, FL: CRC Press.

Chadwick, R. (1998). Professional ethics. In E. Craig (Ed.), *Routledge encyclopedia of philosophy.* London: Routledge.

Datta, L. (1999). *The ethics of evaluation neutrality and advocacy* (New Directions for Evaluation, No. 82, pp. 77–88). San Francisco: Jossey-Bass.

Goodyear, L. K. (2007). Editorial: Special issue on ethics in evaluation. *Evaluation and Program Planning, 30,* 392–393.

Kellogg Foundation. (1998). *The W. K. Kellogg Foundation evaluation handbook.* Retrieved February 1, 2007, from www.wkkf.org/Pubs/Tools/Evaluation/Pub770.pdf

Laitinen, I. (2002, June). *Ethics of evaluation: The case of Finnish Evaluation Society.* Presented at the PUMA Expert Group on Government Relations With Citizens and Civil Society, Paris. Retrieved May 6, 2007, from www.finnishevaluationsociety.net

Mathison, S. (1999). *Rights, responsibilities, and duties: A comparison of ethics for internal and external evaluators* (New Directions for Evaluation, No. 82, pp. 25–34). San Francisco: Jossey-Bass.

Mathison, S. (Ed.). (2004). *Encyclopedia of evaluation.* Thousand Oaks, CA: Sage.

McKeown B., & Thomas, D. (1988). *Q methodology: Quantitative applications in the social sciences.* Newbury Park, CA: Sage.

Mertens, D. M. (2004). *Research and evaluation in education and psychology: Integrating diversity with quantitative, qualitative, and mixed methods* (2nd ed.). Thousand Oaks, CA: Sage.

Morris, M. (1999). Research on evaluation ethics: What have we learned and why is it important? In J. L. Fitzpatrick & M. Morris (Eds.), *Current and emerging ethical challenges in evaluation* (New Directions for Evaluation, No. 82, pp. 15–24). San Francisco: Jossey-Bass.

Morris, M. (2007). *Evaluation ethics for best practice.* New York: Guilford Press.

Morris, M., & Cohn, R. (1993). Program evaluators and ethical challenges: A national survey. *Evaluation Review, 17,* 621–642.

Newman, D. (1995). The future of ethics in evaluation: Developing the dialogue. In W. R. Shadish, (Ed.), *Guiding principles for evaluators* (New Directions for Program Evaluation, No. 66, pp. 99–110). San Francisco: Jossey-Bass.

Picciotto, R. (2005, October). The value of evaluation standards: A comparative assessment. *Journal of MultiDisciplinary Evaluation, 3,* 30–59.

PQMethod: Release 2.11 [Freeware, developed by P. Schmolk]. Retrieved November 28, 2002, from www.rz.unibw-muenchen.de/~p4ibsmk/qmethod/pqmanual.htm

Rossi, P. H., Lipsey, M. W., & Freeman, H. E. (2004). *Evaluation: A systematic approach* (7th ed.). Thousand Oaks, CA: Sage.

Ryan, K. E., & DeStefano, L. (Eds.). (2000). *Evaluation as a democratic process: Promoting inclusion, dialogue, and deliberation* (New Directions for Evaluation, No. 85). San Francisco: Jossey-Bass.

Schwandt, T. A. (2005). The centrality of practice to evaluation. *American Journal of Evaluation, 26*(1), 95–105.

Schwandt, T. A. (2007). Expanding the conversation on evaluation ethics. *Evaluation and Program Planning, 30,* 400–403.

Schweigert, F. J. (2007). The priority of justice: A framework approach to ethics in program evaluation. *Evaluation and Program Planning, 30*(4), 394–399.

Scriven, M. (1991). *Evaluation thesaurus* (4th ed.). Newbury Park, CA: Sage.

Simons, H. (2006). Ethics in evaluation. In I. Shaw, J. C. Greene, & M. Mark (Eds.), *The international handbook of evaluation* (pp. 213–232). London: Sage.

Stephenson, W. (1953). *The study of behavior: Q-technique and its methodology.* Chicago: University of Chicago Press.

Stevahn, L., King, J. E., Ghere, G., & Minnema, J. (2005). Establishing essential competencies for program evaluators. *American Journal of Evaluation, 26*(1), 31–42.

Toms, K. (1993). *A Canadian-American cross national study of the personal and professional ethics of evaluators.* Unpublished dissertation, State University of New York at Albany.

Turner, D. (2003, November). *Evaluation ethics and quality: Results of a survey of Australasian Evaluation Society members.* Prepared for the meeting of the AES Ethics Committee, Auckland, New Zealand.

SECTION III

ETHICS AND RESEARCH METHODS

Ethical decision making is intimately intertwined with all phases of the research process (see, e.g., Chapter 22 by Silka, this volume). Beginning with the identification of a research topic, continuing with the choice of methods for studying that topic, and proceeding through each and every aspect of data collection, analysis, presentation, and reanalysis, decisions made feed back into theory development and influence subsequent rounds of research problem identification. Each stage of the research process shares some common ethical issues while, at the same time, each study, basic or applied, is unique.

Section III focuses on the implications of method for ethics and that of ethics for research methods. As with many social science research problems, ethical as well as practical concerns greatly influence the method(s) of choice. For example, in clinical and educational research, we now regard it unethical to withhold services known to be effective from research participants. This ethical imperative would seem to be obvious and self-evident—so much so that it is now considered an ethical rule specifying "a threshold of behavior below which the conduct of research should not fall" (Kitchener & Kitchener, Chapter 1, p. 12, this volume). Yet as historians of social research are well aware, this "rule" was not always so. The Tuskegee study on syphilis is an oft-cited example (see, e.g., Chapters 1, 8, and 25, this volume) that modified experimental research by the substitution of "wait groups" for control groups in a variety of settings.

Similarly, in recent years, Zimbardo's (1972) prison simulation experiment and Milgram's (1974) series of obedience experiments conducted between 1960 and 1963 have been excoriated as demeaning and downright dangerous to participants. Yet at the time they were undertaken, researchers did so without expectation of harm. Indeed, prior to implementation, Milgram conducted an extensive inquiry regarding the likely effect of his procedures on participants. Neither mental health professionals nor lay people expected either obedience or emotional distress. Thus, even if today's more stringent ethical standards were applied to Zimbardo's and Milgram's work using the knowledge base of the 1960s, these studies would most likely be approved by the average Institutional Review Board (IRB). However, Milgram's and Zimbardo's results and those of other researchers, such as Darley and Latane (1968) who investigated helping, changed the social science knowledge base such that today none would gain IRB approval easily—if at all.

The first chapter in this section (Chapter 12) provides further insight into the role of social science research history in shaping ethical standards. A memoir and commentary written by the sociologist of law Richard D. Schwartz, an elder in the social science research community and coauthor with Eugene Webb, Donald Campbell, and Lee Sechrest (1966) of *Unobtrusive Measures: Nonreactive Research in the Social Sciences*, reexamines some classic research, including examples from his long, distinguished research career. In the process, ethical lapses identifiable only in hindsight are examined as Schwartz argues that development of ethical standards is, of necessity, an evolutionary process.

In the second chapter in this section, Melvin Mark and Chris Gamble (Chapter 13) take a close look at randomized experiments and quasi-experiments, looking at embedded ethical arguments for and against these approaches to social science knowledge accumulation. Like Schwartz, they too find that ethical issues are not static but respond both to technical developments in methodology and to historical events. The latter, they argue, not only affect the topics researchers are likely to find of interest but also the values by which they judge both feasibility and ethical considerations.

Picking up where Mark and Gamble left off, Johnson and Bullock's "The Ethics of Data Archiving: Issues From Four Perspectives" (Chapter 14) indicates that even after the original research project is complete, ethical issues remain. One set of issues confronts the original data gatherers; a second confronts the data miners. Still others are the responsibility of data archivists who serve as links between past and future while maintaining ethical standards vis-à-vis the original research participants who also may have ethical issues of their own. Finally, Johnson and Bullock discuss the responsibility of citizens whose particulars might appear in large scale databases and whose tax dollars support research to maintain a watchful eye lest the findings they have supported become proprietary and, as such, removed from public access.

While Mark's work and that of Johnson and Bullock scrutinize approaches that are predominantly quantitative, Anne Ryen's chapter, "Ethnography" (Chapter 15), has a focus that is strictly qualitative. The ethical issues she highlights are profoundly and, at times, intimately personal. Since a hallmark of the ethnographic method is the ongoing relationship(s) the ethnographer develops over often-extended periods of time—in Ryen's case she has worked with the same informant/translator/cultural interpreter/collaborator/friend for well over a decade—questions of ethical consequence can surface and submerge from moment to moment not only as the research evolves but also as interpersonal relations and role shifts occur.

Mary Brydon-Miller's "Covenantal Ethics and Action Research: Exploring a Common Foundation for Social Research" also examines the ethics of interpersonal relationships in a research context. Here, however, the interpersonal relationships involved are complicated by "unapologetic ethical and political engagement and its commitment to working with community partners to achieve positive social change" (Chapter 16, p. 243). The centrality of caring human relationships is to be maintained across research methods, across institutional/organizational alliances, and across individual egos through negotiation of informed consent and ownership, control, and dissemination of research results in the service of a desired end.

The section concludes with the work of Colin Irwin (Chapter 17). Unlike Ryen and Mark and Gamble, who examine experimental, quasi-experimental, and ethnographic research in general, Irwin's chapter, "Research Ethics and Peacemaking," is about a very specific application of a standard quantitative method—polling—to a very specific set of problems, resolving interethnic and international conflict. One key aspect of his work is open archiving of results. Another is its inclusiveness of factions that may share nothing other than their desire to reduce conflict. In this manner, Irwin's chapter places ideas found in each of the other chapters in the section in a global spotlight.

◆ References

Darley, J. M., & Latane, B. (1968). Bystander intervention in emergencies: Diffusion of responsibility. *Journal of Personality and Social Psychology, 8,* 377–383.

Milgram, S. (1974). *Obedience to authority.* New York: Harper Colophon Books.

Webb, E. J., Campbell, D. T., Schwartz, R. D., & Sechrest, L. (1966). *Unobtrusive measures: Nonreactive research in the social sciences.* Chicago: Rand McNally.

Zimbardo, P. G. (1972). Psychology of imprisonment. *Society,* 9, 4–8.

12

ON ETHICS IN SOCIOLEGAL RESEARCH

◆ Richard Schwartz

This *Handbook* covers a wide range of ethics issues. Having done research in sociology of law for many years, I would like to reflect on the ethics questions that have come up in my research. I will present some of those experiences later on. But first, let me try to generalize about the ethics problem.

Do ethics develop in every professional field? We could define a profession as one that has a set of distinctive ethics. In that case, every profession would by definition have ethics. But that kind of circularity would make the analysis too easy. Instead, let's take the professions as conventionally defined and ask about their codes of ethics. Which professions have them? How long have they had them? What are their contents? How do we know what they are? Are they written? Are they learned by neophytes who study for, apply to, and qualify as members of the profession? Are ethical standards enforced? What sanctions are used? Who makes the judgments? In effect, each profession has its own answers to these questions.

Medicine, a field as ancient as civilization, acquired a set of ethics 2,500 years ago and has retained its basic principle throughout the intervening period. The fundamental rule "Above all, do no harm" continues to guide physicians even now. In modern medicine, there are many writings and many procedures that elaborate on this principle, but the principle remains central to the medical profession. Many nondoctors, even if unfamiliar with Latin, recognize the words *Primum, non nocere!*

Enforcement is generally within the profession. In effect, the medical profession says to the state, "Leave this business to us." That is a position that has advantages for both the state and the profession. If medical ethics became law, a burden would fall on the state and would probably be handled clumsily. The medical profession knows better than the state's attorney what physicians ought to do and how to ensure that they do it.

That said, the state is not precluded from a role. Professional ethics do not wholly determine what is permitted in medical practice. Whatever the medical code of ethics might say, physician-assisted suicide is a violation of the law and is subject in most jurisdictions to prosecution as a crime. The point is that the profession and the state are both involved in social control of professional conduct. The state, in this division of labor, handles only those standards that apply to everyone.

Medicine with its long-standing and fully developed ethical code contrasts with other professions. The legal profession has fewer ethical limitations, though how one compares the two is not entirely clear. In any event, law also has its ethical standards that are enforceable by the profession—as well as by the court. Some standards are clear and compelling for lawyers. One rule that is both clear and enforced is the rule against conflict of interest. Taking one side of a case precludes any hint of taking the opponent's case directly or indirectly. Thus, the plaintiff and the defendant cannot be ethically represented by lawyers who are members of the same firm.

One should note that the ethics of judicial conduct are clearer and stricter than the standards applied to lawyers. The role of the judge is defined as nonpartisan in those cases where the judge has the power to decide between conflicting claims. If the judge has an interest such as personal gain in the outcome, judicial ethics requires that the judge withdraw from the case—an action known by the technical term *recusal*. That the term is not well known in the world outside the courtroom is evidence that the judiciary, although drawn from the legal profession, has developed additional ethical standards.

Ethics in medicine and law contrast with ethics in the social sciences. These disciplines are thought of as professions, but their ethical standards have been less definite. Several reasons for this difference come to mind.

The social sciences have not been designated as professions until relatively recently. They generally emphasize the acquisition of new knowledge over the application of established knowledge for the solution of problems. The methods they use vary widely. Some of these methods have not been tried before. New methods devised to generate new knowledge may create side effects that are regrettable, but such effects ususally emerge with experience. Many social scientists prefer to use established methods, but there are always some who seek new ways of generating knowledge. Some of these methods have been criticized, for example, by institutional review boards (IRBs) and fellow professionals. Occasionally such criticism reaches beyond the circle of professionals as seen in reaction to the controversial psychological experiments of Milgram (1963) and Zimbardo, Haney, and Banks (1973).

Neither inside nor outside criticism has so far led to a general set of ethical rules within the social science professions. Perhaps it is too early in the history of these disciplines for distinctive ethics to have emerged. Or the quest for new knowledge may create a justifiable belief in the value of innovative methods that overbalance concerns about harm done as a side effect of the research process. Some have innovated with minimal regard to the harms they might have caused. There has not been, to my knowledge, any instance of harmful effect sufficient to have jolted a particular social science profession into formulating a code that would "outlaw" a given practice within the profession—let alone outlaw it with the laws of the state. But we have, I believe, sometimes come close to the line.

In this light, I want to turn to some of the experiences relevant to ethical questions that I have had as a social science researcher. My method, I suppose, is called *narrative* these days. In an older jargon, it might well have been considered part of a memoir—a very small and selective part to be sure.

Ethics includes things one should do and things one shouldn't do. Within a given profession, a consensus tends to be created consisting of such "yeses," "no-s," and "maybes." In sociology, for a long time, I thought there were many more maybes than there were prohibitions. That tentativeness concerning standards reflected the culture of sociology, a field whose scientific status was asserted by some, questioned by many, and rejected by others.

The development of an ethical code requires more than a committee report or a document. Ethics constitute a set of standards widely accepted by those to whom it applies. Professional ethics constitute standards that are widely accepted within the profession. A consensus on ethics emerges over time, as the profession matures. The nature of that consensus depends on the orientation of its members and on the tasks in which they are engaged. Where those tasks are very diverse, an ethical consensus may be difficult to attain. That diversity has been characteristic of sociology and of the related social sciences. For that reason, among others, there are many ethical issues that have not been settled clearly.

The ethics of a profession depend, of course, on the nature of the task. When the general objective is clear, the ethics are also likely to be clear. The medical profession is an excellent example. Preserving and restoring health is a clear objective of the medical profession. In light of that objective, a fundamental ethical principle emerges: Above all, do no harm.

In the case of the social sciences, though, the objectives are not so clear. In general, the idea of social science is to apply scientific methods to the subject matter of society. We want to know the origins, development, and functioning of human societies. But the methods by which such knowledge can be obtained cover a wide range, and there are conflicts within the social sciences as to which methods are appropriate for obtaining the knowledge. For now, at least, it seems best that each of the social science disciplines develops and publicizes its own ethical standards.

Because of this diversity, ethics of the social science professions have developed slowly and uncertainly. Certain questions have emerged, however, that seem to have become the ethics of the social science professions. Among these, let me suggest the following:

1. Record and validate your data. Make the data available, following its use, to professional social scientists.

2. Cooperate with members of the profession in replication research.

3. Protect the privacy of your subjects and do them no harm.

In the account that follows, I propose to describe some research experiences that relate to these principles. While I hope these principles are emerging as a consensus in the social sciences, they have in my past experience not been especially clear. For example, no one ever told me that one has a duty to validate measures by having more than one observer make judgments independently of another observer. In the example that follows, I just happened to validate mainly because the opportunity to do so made it convenient.

The virtue of validation suggested itself to me in a study of legal evolution (Schwartz & Miller, 1964). The idea of the study was to examine a sample of ethnographies of simple and more complex societies to see whether they had mediation, damages, police, and lawyers. The original judgments were made by a student of mine, James C. Miller. He had been my student when he was an undergraduate, and the work he did for me on the evolution study was done while he was a law student. Because he already knew my ideas from the earlier teaching, I realized that he might be shading his judgments to fit my hypotheses. To offset that possibility, I happened to have the funds to employ another student to read the same ethnographies and to make judgments parallel to those of Miller but completely independent of Miller.

The second student, Robert C. Scholl, had no knowledge of the hypotheses. He was just given a list of societies described in the Human Relations Area Files and asked to determine (yes or no) whether they had mediation, damages, police, and lawyers. When the two sets of results were put side by side they showed more than 90% agreement on their determinations.

These judgments led me to trust the accuracy of the results more than I would have if I had only Miller's judgments to go on. Scholl contributed to the validity of the study *because* he didn't know what the study was all about. That experience helped me see the value of independent validation.

That was not a perfect exercise in validation, of course. Scholl, like Miller, was a law student. So his judgments as to whether, for example, police were present in a given society might have been affected by the kinds of assumptions and definitions that they both would have learned in their first year criminal law course. Suppose validation had been sought from a graduate student in anthropology. Would the judgments have been the same? I don't know and didn't find out. There has to be some reasonable limit as to how extensive the validation process should be. Besides, I didn't have the resources to hire another data coder.

At all events, the study did contain some degree of validation through the independent judgment method. Did that mean that there is an ethical requirement to do so in every study? Yes and no. One should weigh the nature of the study and its amenability to independent validation before deciding what methods to use. Miller's judgments might have been sufficient for that study, especially if they were reported in such a way that they could be checked by others.

It would have been less satisfactory if, for example, the ethnographic data from these societies were not accessible to others for inspection. If, in addition, a researcher kept research records private, notwithstanding a bona fide request, it would lead some to raise the ethical question. In this case, however, the ethnographic reports were available on library shelves and, even better, in the Human Relations Area Files, where they were classified according to topics specified in the Files' Outline of Cultural Materials. Any reader could check the judgments of Miller and Scholl. The data were accessible, and cross validation could be carried out by those who wanted to do so. To follow up the original research in that way would add confidence to the analysis and its conclusions.

Among the social sciences, there are vast differences in validation because the methods for data gathering and reporting vary enormously. The field of ethnography illustrates the validation problem. Where there is only one observer, what method is available to validate the data the ethnographer provides? In the rare cases where a second observer went to the same society, the facts reported have sometimes radically contradicted the first report. Ruth Benedict's (1934) study of the Pueblo Indians made the assessment that they were a nonaggressive and cooperative people. Bennett (1946) found this tendency expressed in his ethnographic data. But he also found that conflict and aggressive behavior arose within this society under certain circumstances. Another example is noted in Oscar Lewis' *Life in a Mexican Villiage: Tepoztlán Restudied*, which revisited Robert Redfield's 1930 publication, *Tepoztlán, a Mexican Village: A Study of Folk Life*.

In ethnography, the results depend on the integrity of the observer. One can check that integrity, I suppose. If a given ethnographer turns out to be a bald-faced liar in other settings, the integrity of the ethnography is called into question. In a field that has not yet developed validation techniques for individual reporting, one is tempted to say that gossip becomes an ethical requirement. Well, let's call it the sharing of views as to how much confidence to accord to a particular reporter.

There have been some cases where ethnographies have been discredited by the waning of confidence in the observer. One ethnographer reported his findings concerning a society that experienced extreme famine. The ethnographer in the case of the Ik, an East African tribe, reported that the adults monopolized the available food and did not feed their children. This ethnography reported a finding so unusual that it led to determined efforts at validation. When that failed, the purported finding tended to be dismissed, along with the professional bona fides of the ethnographer (see Barth, 1974).[1]

Gossip as to character is insufficient, of course, as a way of determining professional performance. The ethnographic method involves the taking of detailed field notes, with manuals specifying how this should be done. Professional training requires that those notes be available. A graduate student seeking a Ph.D. in anthropology will be expected to take detailed field notes that will (or ought to) be subject to examination by the candidate's committee. Once the practice of note taking is established, the ethics of anthropology assumes that the practice will continue in subsequent professional work.

There is still the question as to whether field notes must be preserved and made available on inquiry. That is sometimes a touchy point. I recall an instance in which two sociologists fought vigorously over the availability of records. The case was brought to my attention because I happened to be the chair of the Ethics Committee of the American Sociological Association.

The complainant had been asked by a critic to produce the records of his interviews and other data from a study he had published. The study had a certain amount of emotion attached to it. It reported that people who changed their names from ethnically identifiable ones to typical Anglo-Saxon names were more successful than a comparable group who had not (Broom, Beem, & Harris, 1955). It turned out that the author of the study had changed his own name from Bloom to Broom, giving him allegedly a personal motive to find as he did. His critic, who had not changed his own name, wanted to challenge Broom's findings by examining the data on which Broom had based his conclusions. This conflict was then referred to the Ethics Committee. After due deliberation, the Ethics Committee decided not to take a position on the question. In effect, they decided that in this case at least, it was not necessary for the original researcher to hand over his records to the critic.

The Ethics Committee might have decided, that in principle, records of research ought to be available to be seen by others. As I recall, they did no such thing. On the whole, in sociology as well as anthropology, validation in that way was not required. It may have been seen as desirable, but it was not the kind of ethical requirement that was widely understood and accepted in the social sciences at that time.

Professions clearly vary in their ethical requirements for a host of reasons. In a systematic study of the professions, there is a need for more research findings on the question of how professional ethics have evolved, are evolving, and (as some would-be reformers might put it) should evolve to keep these professions on the straight and narrow or, at least, on how to help professions perform their announced missions ethically and effectively.

Now let's consider another norm that does not seem to have become part of the ethics of social science. It has to do with replication of research. When a novel finding is reported in some fields, especially the natural sciences, others in the field try to replicate it. A scientist may report, for example, that he has found a novel way to clone animals. Another claims that he has generated atomic energy from water. The more remarkable the finding, the greater the inclination to test it. The report of the findings is expected to provide sufficient detail to permit replication, and if the report does not, the original researcher has an obligation to supply whatever significant details may not have been included in the original report. There is no room for evasion of this responsibility.

That, at any rate is my understanding of how the natural sciences generally proceed. In the social sciences, on the other hand, there seems to be no expectation of replication. Generally speaking, a finding is a finding is a finding. The more original and unexpected it is, the more likely it is to be noted. But replication is not a responsibility taught to graduate students or practiced by their teachers. Why not? Are some of the social science fields moving in that direction? And if the instances are rare, is that because it is difficult? Or is it because social scientists are searching for original results more than testing theory or adding to the corpus of findings? For whatever reasons, the social sciences do not emphasize replication as a practice—much less as a requirement.

If replication were emphasized, would that carry ethical implications? Would it be requiring too much to say that there is an ethical obligation to test findings that one suggests are incorrect or phony? One could say that the original researcher has an ethical obligation to inform a would-be replicator about the crucial details of the original study. It clearly would be unethical to try to block replication.

It may be useful here to draw on the field of law to specify potential ethical standards in social research. Law has developed some concepts that might be borrowed in thinking about ethical standards. Let me be clear.

I am not for a moment suggesting that social science ethics ought to be enforceable as a matter of law. It would do major harm to scientific inquiry if research practices were to become issues for the civil courts to decide. Professional ethics should remain a matter for the profession to formulate and enforce.

Rather, the idea I had in mind in suggesting some borrowing of legal ideas concerned the concept of intent. Disciplines in the social sciences, searching for ethical standards, should be able to distinguish between intention and accident, purpose and negligence. While due diligence is always desirable, it makes a difference, ethically, whether the researcher purposely avoided replication or just didn't think about it enough to facilitate it. In a well-spelled-out ethical code, I would expect that distinction to be made.

This brings to mind another research experience, which, unlike the legal evolution study, did not cross-validate in gathering the data. This one involved field research using only one investigator to gather the data. And for a long time after the study was reported and frequently reprinted, I wondered whether that investigator had indeed done all that the directors of the research had asked him to do.

I refer to a study that I did in collaboration with Jerome H. Skolnick. It was called "Two Studies of Legal Stigma" (Schwartz & Skolnick, 1962). The first of the studies in that paper examined the chances for employment of people who had or did not have a criminal record. We found a sample of potential employers in the Catskill region of New York State as the summer season was beginning. We prepared four portfolios giving the record of a fictitious person. The control portfolio described the person. The second portfolio described the same person but said he had just been released following a term in prison where he served time for a nonviolent crime. The third portfolio had the same material as the second but with a letter from the judge who urged potential employers to give the man a job to advance his rehabilitation. The final portfolio described the same man and said that he had been tried for the same nonviolent crime and acquitted.

These portfolios were presented one at a time on a random basis to potential employers. The field researcher recorded the responses of the employers who suggested that the man visit the manager's place of employment to be interviewed for a job. The operative criterion was whether the potential employer requested a follow-up. A positive response would include an indication of interest sufficient so that the employer asks the agent to send the person for an interview.

The results of the study reported by the field researcher were that positive responses were more frequent for the man who had served time, especially if his record included a recommendation of the judge. The responses were less favorable in the case where the man had been accused of a crime and acquitted.

These findings were of interest because they were counterintuitive. The general belief is that acquittal exonerates. The fact that a prosecutor has taken the person to court suggests that a prima facie case existed. Also, given the vagaries of the legal process, plus the standard of innocent until proven guilty beyond a reasonable doubt, the potential employer might well have decided to play it safe.

But my purpose in mentioning that research is primarily to suggest the kinds of ethical considerations that are the subject of this book. There was, in this research, no second researcher at the time. For that reason, the results are not as dependable as in the cross-cultural project reported above. As a result, both authors entertained some doubt as to the validity of the results.

As it happens, those doubts were relieved years later when the basic issue was studied again. In a recently reported study, Pager (2003) investigated the same issue and found similar results. Her work brings to mind the desirability of replication. That practice itself occurs less often than one would like to see. It is not considered an imperative. People should be free to replicate or not, as the opportunity presents itself. What comes closer to the ethical side is that the original researcher should be prepared, if asked, to cooperate with a professional colleague who seeks to replicate the original finding. To that end, the availability of records and description of procedures is a legitimate request.

Another ethical issue is raised by Schwartz and Skolnick's study. The data were generated by asking people whether they were interested in hiring a particular candidate who did not exist. To gather the data, the manager's time was used in an inquiry that was destined to go nowhere. That deception might have been compensated, for example, if the design included an effort to supply a worker comparable with the one pictured. It is not something we did, but on reflection I think we ought to have. Well, it may not have been all that serious ethically to have engaged in a bit of deception, but we as professionals should reflect on the uses of deception. Is it ever justified, and if so, when and why?

One can learn a bit on this subject from the medical profession. In the testing of the Salk vaccine, an experiment was done that involved a placebo inoculation of a randomly selected control group. As described in a talk by Leona Baumgartner, the Health Commissioner of New York City at the time, the vaccine did reduce the frequency of polio in the experimental group, compared with the children who received the placebo. Dr. Baumgartner reported that the experiment was brought to an end when the results were observed. She did, however, meet with those members of the control group who had contracted polio and apologetically explained what had happened. She described a rather remarkable response from the children. They said that they understood the purpose and expressed both forgiveness and pride that the vaccine had worked and that they had been a part of the research effort (Dawson, 2004).

Positive results of this kind are rare and hard to come by. While we hope that the social sciences can generate practical results from our efforts, the use of deception and invasion of privacy are methods that should be considered from an ethical point of view. Another project that I was involved in illustrates the point. This one had to do with factors affecting compliance with federal income tax laws (Schwartz & Orleans, 1967).

The design involved a series of interviews with a sample of taxpayers in the month before the due date for filing income tax returns. Two groups (plus a control) were approached in person by the interviewers who were taking public opinion responses to taxpaying. In one of the experimental groups, emphasis was placed on the positive uses of taxes. They were asked their preferences in public budgeting for parks and recreation, education, and support of hospitals. The other group was asked questions having to do with penalties for violation of the tax laws, emphasizing potential negative consequences.

The purpose of the research was to learn about motives for tax compliance. The research was able to determine the taxpaying behavior of the groups through the cooperation of the Internal Revenue Service. The commissioner at the time agreed to provide us with information about group differences between the experimental groups and the control. (As a matter of law, he could not provide individual returns.) The result showed that for that sample the positive-uses group paid significantly more taxes than the group reminded of their potential punishment for tax evasion. It was a striking result that may or may not turn out to be confirmed by subsequent research.

That research also illustrates an ethical problem. To what extent is the use of deception permissible in the social sciences? The tax research just described did not inconvenience people or lead them to do something they should not have. What could be wrong about getting people to pay the taxes they owed the government?

Even so, the use of deception in any research raises ethical questions. Some designs, such as those employed by Milgram and Zimbardo, arguably represent a greater potential harm than a design that seeks to motivate tax compliance. The questions addressed in this *Handbook* suggest that one should be careful to define unethical conduct clearly and bear in mind the standards when one weighs the legitimacy of research methods against the gain to knowledge that might result from the research.

My focus thus far has been on the need, internal to the social science professions, to validate findings. I have not addressed the matter of how findings will be put to use in the broader society. Although the behavioral sciences have rarely been called to advise on major issues of policy, there are trends in that direction. Some social scientists, economists in particular, are regularly involved in important policy decisions. And that tendency—to advise on policy issues—is likely to grow with the maturation of the social sciences generally.

To preserve the integrity of the disciplines, while rendering needed policy advice, is an important challenge for the social as well as for the natural sciences (see Pielke, 2007). If the findings are uncertain, that fact should be made clear as part of advice given. Value preferences should be specifically disclosed and if possible set aside in using social scientific knowledge to provide policy advice. As society takes the work of social scientists more seriously, social scientists should take their professional responsibility to the society more seriously as well.

♦ **Note**

1. Here, Barth raises questions about the validity of Colin Turnbull's (1972) book, *The Mountain People*.

♦ References

Barth, F. (1974). On responsibility and humanity: Calling a colleague to account. *Current Anthropology, 15*(1), 99–103.

Benedict, R. (1934). *Patterns of culture*. New York: Houghton Mifflin.

Bennett, J. W. (1946). The interpretation of Pueblo culture: A question of values. *Southwestern Journal of Anthropology, 2*, 361–374.

Broom, L., Beem, H. P., & Harris, V. (1955). Characteristics of 1,107 petitioners for change of name. *American Sociological Review, 20*, 33–39.

Dawson, L. (2004). The Salk polio vaccine trial of 1954: Risks, randomization and public involvement in research. *Clinical Trials, 1*(1), 122–130.

Milgram, S. (1963). Behavioral study of obedience. *Journal of Abnormal and Social Psychology, 67*, 371–378.

Pager, D. (2003). The mark of a criminal record. *American Journal of Sociology, 108*(5), 937–975.

Pielke, R. A., Jr. (2007). *The honest broker: Making sense of science in policy and politics*. New York: Cambridge University Press.

Schwartz, R., & Orleans, S. (1967). On legal sanctions. *University of Chicago Law Review, 34*(2), 274–300.

Schwartz, R. D., & Miller, J. C. (1964). Legal evolution and societal complexity. *American Journal of Sociology, 70*(2), 159–169.

Schwartz, R. D., & Skolnick, H. H. (1962). Two studies of legal stigma. *Social Problems, 10*, 133–142.

Turnbull, C. M. (1972). *The mountain people*. New York: Simon & Schuster.

Zimbardo, P. G., Haney, C., & Banks, W. C. (1973). Interpersonal dynamics in a simulated prison. *International Journal of Criminology and Penology, 1*, 69–97.

13

EXPERIMENTS, QUASI-EXPERIMENTS, AND ETHICS

♦ Melvin M. Mark and Chris Gamble

Experiments are a mainstay in many areas of social science research, as well as in other research domains such as medical trials of new treatments. For example, experiments predominate in the leading journals in social and cognitive psychology (Cook & Groom, 2004). Experiments are also relatively commonplace in certain areas of applied social research, such as in experimental trials that are conducted to assess the effects of various psychological, educational, and social interventions (e.g., Greenberg & Schroeder, 1997). As detailed below, experiments can be valuable when it is useful to know whether (and to what extent) one variable causes a difference in another. For instance, experiments can help answer questions such as the following: Does participating in an organization's diversity training lead to improved interactions across racial, ethnic, and gender lines? Does reducing the class size in primary schools in Tennessee stimulate an increase in student performance? Are social support groups for cancer patients effective in reducing stress? Do abstinence-based sex education programs work in terms of reducing the rate of sexual activity and pregnancy?

In social research, experiments are not always feasible, at least not experiments in the technical, random assignment sense of the term shared by many social science researchers. Especially in applied social research, practical considerations may limit the way a variable of interest can be studied. Consider, for instance, a health researcher interested in the effects of increases in cigarette taxes on tobacco consumption. The researcher would not be able to create an experiment in which different people were faced with varying levels of taxes, but could look at the effects of tax hikes on cigarette sales in whichever states happen to raise state cigarette taxes. In addition to pragmatic limits, in both basic and applied social research ethical constraints may preclude experiments, at least of the random assignment variety. For example, researchers may be interested in the health and cognitive consequences of children's exposure to toys with lead paint, but ethical considerations surely should preclude randomly assigning children to exposure (or not) to such toys. Even the basic researcher may face ethical limits, as when a psychologist is interested in the effects of exposure to extreme stressors, and so may choose to assess the consequences of a real-life stressor such as a natural disaster.

This chapter addresses ethical issues in the context of randomized experiments and quasi-experiments. Our examples often come from the evaluation of social programs and policies, but the issues apply to applied social research more generally. We attend to randomized experiments more than quasi-experiments, largely because experiments are more frequently criticized in terms of ethics. In the next section, these two types of studies are defined and illustrated. We examine the rationale for such studies, especially randomized experiments. We do so because this rationale comprises an important part of an argument, detailed in the section that follows, that can be made in favor of the ethicality of randomized experiments in particular circumstances. More generally, in that and the following section of the chapter we summarize major arguments for and against such studies. Subsequently, the chapter focuses briefly on a less common but potentially important position—that the ethical issues we face in actual practice are not fixed. Rather, we suggest that researchers may, by using recently developed or increasingly practiced methodological procedures, find a way out of past ethical quandaries. We also make a related point: The specific values used in making ethical judgments are not fixed, but instead arise (at least in part) from the state of the world in which the study is to take place. We illustrate this point in terms of achievement gaps and global climate change. In the penultimate section, we point to an area where further technical development could help alleviate an important and underrecognized ethical concern about randomized experiments and quasi-experiments. By way of preview, the core idea in that section is that experimental and quasi-experimental researchers need better methods for simultaneously (a) discovering the nuances of where and when treatments work, without (b) giving undue weight to chance findings. We end with brief conclusions.

◆ An Overview of Experiments and Quasi-Experiments

Experiments and their quasi-experimental cousins were developed and systematized because they can help provide answers to one kind of question involving causal inferences. Specifically, these methods allow us to estimate the effect of an already identified, potential cause on one or more outcomes of interest. For instance, an experiment or quasi-experiment might be conducted to assess the effect of school size (the potential causal variable) on children's school readiness and social skills (the outcomes of interest).

Of course, as everyday experience indicates, experiments are not intrinsically required for causal inferences, including inferences about the effect of a potential cause. Indeed, one form of ethical criticism of experiments is that they are not needed in a particular case. One variation on this theme is that, in the particular case at hand, estimating the effect of the treatment was not the most appropriate research question. For instance, in program evaluation an argument might be made that, in the particular circumstances, studying the lived experience of program participants is more valuable than estimating the effects of the program (e.g., Rallis, in press). Although not always framed as an ethical criticism, this implies that resources were squandered and the study had a poor benefit-risk ratio. A second variation on this theme can be sounded when the critic sees the task of assessing the effects of an intervention as appropriate for the investigation at hand. Instead, the criticism is that simpler, less intrusive, and less costly techniques would have sufficed (e.g., Scriven, in press). For instance, *if* the introduction of a new teaching technique next year would lead to a clear and unambiguous improvement in learning relative to past years, then the criticism would be that depriving some students of the new technique for the sake of a randomized experiment would be unethical, and the added costs of the experiment would not be balanced by a greater benefit. (However, an advocate of experiments might counter that an a priori judgment that the technique would lead to a clear and unambiguous improvement is risky in the absence of prior evidence, especially experimental evidence.)

To make sensible judgments about such criticisms, it is important to understand the rationale for experiments and quasi-experiments. Although experimental methods are not necessary for all causal inferences, they can be valuable in certain circumstances. Despite advocates who imply that the randomized experiment is the gold standard needed for every causal inference, we believe that a more defensible position is that experiments (and their best approximations) are especially worthwhile in certain circumstances: when people care about what effects, if any, a possible cause has; when multiple factors are likely to influence the outcome of interest; when change over time can occur in the outcome of interest, due to the effects of factors other than the primary causal variable being studied; when people naturally vary on the outcome of interest; and when an effect is worth knowing about, even if it is not dramatically huge in size (Mark, in press). Put differently, to use a phrasing drawn from the work of Donald Campbell and his colleagues (e.g., Campbell & Stanley, 1966; Cook & Campbell, 1979; Shadish, Cook, & Campbell, 2002), experiments and quasi-experiments may not be important when there are few plausible alternative explanations of an observed effect. For instance, a formal experiment with random assignment is not required to infer the effects of touching a red-hot electric stove burner. Contrast this with questions such as the effectiveness of educational interventions. In estimating the effect of, say, class size on academic achievement, there are several complications that can confound causal inference: Academic achievement is affected by numerous factors other than class size, including factors such as socioeconomic status that may be correlated with naturally occurring variations in class size; academic achievement is characterized both by change over time and differences across individuals, making it difficult (if not impossible, without an adequate research design) to sort out the effects of class size; and people are likely to care about improvements in academic achievement even if they are not absolutely huge and thus unlikely to be visible "to the naked eye."

In randomized experiments, individuals (or other units, such as classrooms) are randomly assigned to treatment conditions. For example, some children could be assigned at random—essentially, with a flip of a coin, or more likely, by a random number table or a computerized equivalent—to be in a small or a regular-sized classroom. As another example, some patients could be randomly assigned to receive a new drug for arthritis pain, while other patients are instead assigned at random to the currently available drug (or, alternatively, to a placebo). The benefits of randomized experiments can be seen in relation to what

Campbell and his colleagues (Campbell & Stanley, 1966; Cook & Campbell, 1979; Shadish et al., 2002) call "internal validity threats." These are generic categories of alternative explanations—that is, ways of accounting for the study results (other than that the treatment made a causal difference on the outcome variable).

Imagine, for example, a researcher who wishes to estimate the effect of a new drug for arthritis pain by measuring pain first before and then again after patients started taking the drug. Other sources of change, that is, validity threats, could easily obscure the true effects of the drug. For example, arthritis pain might typically increase over time (e.g., as aging joints lose cartilage). Campbell labeled this kind of naturally occurring change as *maturation*. If arthritis pain normally increases over time because of maturation, a drug that is actually beneficial could look ineffective in a simple before and after comparison. Imagine alternatively that *statistical regression* rather than maturation is common. This would be the case if arthritis patients tend to visit the doctor when their pain is at its worst, and if they would feel better later even without any medical intervention (much as cold symptoms tend to improve after five to seven days). Such a pattern of statistical regression could make an ineffective medication look good in a simple before and after comparison. For these and other reasons,[1] you often would not get an accurate answer about an intervention's effect simply by measuring the relevant outcome variable (e.g., pain) both before and after the treatment of interest (e.g., the drug).

As another example, imagine an evaluation of the effects of class size on academic achievement. In the absence of random assignment, one might compare the achievement of students in smaller classes with the performance of students in larger classes. Here, the validity threat of *selection* would apply. That is, any observed difference between students in smaller and larger classes could easily have resulted not from the effect of class size but from preexisting differences on any of a number of variables. For example, the schools that tend to have smaller classes may differ from the other schools in terms of the community's economic circumstances, the average educational attainment of the citizens, or a variety of other things related to school budgets. These and other confounds could easily obscure the true effect of class size. Researchers may try to account for known confounds statistically, but conventional approaches to statistical control are based on often-tenuous (and often implicit) assumptions that the relevant differences are known and well measured.

In contrast, random assignment effectively takes care of such selection problems (and, assuming the experiment is conducted successfully, other internal validity threats including maturation). If students (or other units) are assigned to conditions at random, no selection bias will exist. This is not to say that the two groups will be *exactly* equal prior to the treatment, but no systematic bias will exist. Moreover, any random differences between the two groups can be effectively accommodated with familiar hypothesis-testing statistics (Boruch, 1997). The ability to estimate treatment effects without bias (i.e., without the intrusion of selection and other internal validity threats) provides the primary argument for randomized experiments.

Quasi-experiments are approximations of randomized experiments. Unlike randomized experiments, by definition quasi-experiments lack random assignment to conditions. At the same time, like randomized experiments, quasi-experiments involve comparisons across two or more conditions, and they may include before-after and/or other comparisons. Quasi-experiments are advocated when experiments are not feasible for practical or ethical reasons (Cook & Campbell, 1979). In addition, *sometimes* quasi-experiments, even relatively simple ones, can give compelling answers to cause-and-effect questions because plausible alternative explanations are few or can be effectively eliminated by other kinds of evidence (e.g.,

Eckert, 2000). In such circumstances, quasi-experiments presumably suffice (however, it may be challenging to be certain in advance that no plausible alternative explanations will rear their ugly heads).

Numerous quasi-experimental designs and design variants exist, and these are discussed in detail elsewhere (see Mark & Reichardt, in press; Shadish et al., 2002). One relatively simple quasi-experiment, alluded to previously, is the "one-group, pretest-postest design." In this simple quasi-experiment, participants are measured on an outcome variable both before and after the treatment of interest. The researcher's hope is that if the treatment is effective, outcome scores should improve, while scores will hold steady if the treatment has no effect. However, a variety of validity threats exist, including maturation and statistical regression. "Stronger" quasi-experimental designs, such as the so-called regression-discontinuity design and complex interrupted time series designs, generally tend to rule out more validity threats than do "weaker" quasi-experiments such as the one-group, pretest-posttest design. This chapter concerns ethical issues in the context of experiments and quasi-experiments, and thus does not provide detail on the full range of quasi-experimental designs and features. We will, however, provide an overview of the regression-discontinuity (R-D) design, which is one of the strongest quasi-experimental designs in terms of internal validity (Shadish et al., 2002). In addition, as discussed below, this design offers promise of avoiding ethical criticisms of the randomized experiment, with little, if any, loss of internal validity.

♦ Ethics in and About Randomized Experiments and Quasi-Experiments

In writings about randomized experiments and quasi-experiments, discussions of ethics typically start out (and sometimes end) with the same historical and conceptual base as is offered in more general discussions of research ethics. In many such discussions, the historical specter of the research horrors of Nazi Germany and the Tuskegee syphilis study gives way to a summary of the National Commission for the Protection of Human Subjects on Biomedical and Behavioral Research and its *Belmont Report* (Department of Health, Education, and Welfare, 1978). Such discussions of the ethics of experimental and quasi-experimental research (e.g., Boruch, 1997; Shadish et al., 2002) typically highlight the three principles of the *Belmont Report*: beneficence (maximizing good outcomes and minimizing risk), respect for participants (protecting autonomy and ensuring well-informed, voluntary participation), and justice (fair distribution of risks and benefits). In an expansion of the typical analysis of the ethics of randomized experiments, Boruch (1997) also discussed in some detail the legal rationale and standards for treating participants ethically, which lead to a similar set of considerations as the Belmont principles.

The three Belmont principles often inform discussion of a set of familiar topics. These include informed consent; privacy and confidentiality; the provision of incentives for research participation; the debate about deception in research; and considerations that arise when potential research participants cannot themselves autonomously provide consent, as with children (e.g., Fisher & Anushko, 2008; Sieber, in press). These topics, which are thoroughly addressed elsewhere, also arise frequently in writings about research ethics in general or about the ethics of nonexperimental research approaches (as illustrated in several chapters in this *Handbook*). Because these topics are well treated elsewhere, and because there are other ethical issues that arise specifically in the context of quasi-experiments and especially randomized experiments, we do not address them in detail here. Instead, we turn now to arguments, both pro and con, regarding the ethicality of random assignment experiments (returning shortly to quasi-experiments).

♦ *The Ethical Argument for Randomized Experiments*

Several decades ago, advocates of randomized trials in medicine argued that there is an ethical argument for conducting and participating in randomized experiments. A notable and relatively early example was published in *Science* (Gilbert, McPeak, & Mosteller, 1977). In short, the argument that randomized experiments are ethical involves at least two claims. The first claim is that there exists an important need to know about a given cause-effect relationship, because uncertainty prevails about the best course of action. To use a historical example from medicine, it was important to know the effects of radical mastectomy versus the alternative treatment, lumpectomy, for Stage 3 or earlier breast cancer. At the time when Gilbert et al. (1977) wrote, radical mastectomy was the standard treatment, even though it carried considerable costs to the patient, certainly in terms of physical recovery and rehabilitation. On the other hand if, as had been the conventional wisdom of the day, lumpectomy actually led to a lower survival rate, then moving away from radical mastectomies would have created grave costs to patients. Chalmers (1968) reminded us how limited the standard ways of the day were for choosing from among alternative medical treatments: "One only has to review the graveyard of discarded therapies to discover how many patients might have benefited from being randomly assigned to a control group" (p. 910).

A second general claim underlying the ethical argument for randomized experiments is that these methods bring value relative to other ways of addressing the causal questions. This can involve the claim either that randomized experiments are necessary to get the right answer with an adequate level of certainty, or that they will help stimulate action (e.g., creating change in medical practice or in policy making), or both. In arguing that randomized experiments are needed to get the right answer, advocates often make their case in terms of the existence of validity threats that would plausibly bias the findings from other methods (Bickman & Reich, in press; Cook, 2002). For example, if researchers simply compared the survival rate of women who had radical mastectomies with that of women who happened to receive a lumpectomy instead, the threat of selection would loom large (e.g., the women who had lumpectomies might have had less severe cases or different kinds of surgeons). Those making this type of argument (e.g., Cook, 2002) often cite research showing different results from experimental and quasi-experimental studies (for a partial review, see Mark & Reichardt, in press).

In a recent volume on what constitutes credible evidence in evaluation and applied social research (Donaldson, Christie, & Mark, in press), several contributions illustrate well the kind of arguments made by supporters of randomized experiments. For example, Bickman and Reich (in press) highlighted "the cost of making a wrong decision about causality." They indicated,

> We know that there are costs in making the wrong decision. To call a program effective when it is not means that valuable resources may be wasted and the search for other means to solve the problem will be hindered. Some programs may not only be ineffective but harmful. In such cases the costs of a wrong decision would be higher. On the other hand, falsely labeling the program as ineffective would mean that clients who would have benefited from the intervention will not have that benefit.

Bickman and Reich further noted the need for good evidence about program effectiveness, leading them to endorse randomized experiments (though with detailed consideration of their limits). Referring to educational contexts, Gersten and Hitchcock (in press) referred to the need

> to dramatically increase the number of [randomized experiments] in education ... so that professional educators would have an evidence base for making decisions about selecting curricula, intervention programs for students with learning problems, selecting professional development approaches and determining effective structures for establishing tutoring programs.

Henry (in press) referred explicitly to the possible positive consequences of experiments for decision making and accountability in representative democracies. According to Henry,

> public policies and programs are intentional acts undertaken with the coercive force of government behind them. Authoritative bodies such as legislatures make public policy and program choices in most cases. The choices of these bodies are binding on the governed and therefore, to inform citizen's attitudes about which public programs are good or bad and potentially to influence voting decisions, democracies require that the consequences, both intended and unintended, of programs are determined.

Henry further contended that to achieve findings about program consequences that are "as conclusive as possible," the "most conclusive and widely regarded means for producing findings that have these attributes are random assignment experiments." As these comments by Bickman and Reich, Gersten and Hitchcock, and Henry indicate, advocates of experiments, whether or not they are explicitly addressing the ethics of random assignment, refer (a) to the need to get causal answers in the face of uncertainty about the best course of action and (b) to the value of experiments for providing better, actionable answers.

Thoughtful advocates of randomized experiments have presented more detailed variations on these two claims. For example, both Shadish et al. (2002) and Boruch (2005), drawing on the Federal Judicial Center (1981) Advisory Committee on Experimentation in the Law, identify five criteria that should be met to determine that a random experiment is justified. First, the proposed study needs to address an important problem. Put differently, it should first be established that something in society needs to be improved. Second, there needs to be real uncertainty about the best course of action, that is, about which alternative is preferable. In the case of a novel program, for example, its value must be unclear relative to existing programs. Third, it should be likely that alternatives to an experiment would not be equally informative. A stringent version of this criterion is that the researcher should demonstrate that only an experiment would be able to address the question effectively. Fourth, it should be plausible that the study results will be used, for example, to inform discussion about changing the policy, program, or practice in question. Fifth, the experiment should respect participants' rights, for example, by not being coercive and not leaving participants worse off than if they had not been in the experiment.

Less attention has been given to the ethicality of quasi-experiments in relation to these five criteria. Obviously, in terms of the third criterion, a quasi-experiment would be the preferable choice if it would address the causal question as well as a randomized experiment in the case at hand. Not as clear is how to respond to conflicts across the criteria, such as an instance in which a quasi-experiment would alleviate concerns about coercion but might provide less compelling evidence about program effectiveness.

♦ From Criteria to Complexity and Controversy

Drawing on these five criteria and the three Belmont principles, we now move to a handful of more complex and even more controversial issues.

Can randomized trials be used in the service of the good and the just? As indicated by Bickman and Reich (in press), drawing the wrong conclusion about whether a social program is effective can have negative consequences, perhaps severe ones. Both beneficence (the maximization of good outcomes and the minimization of risk) and justice (the fair distribution of risks and benefits) can be negatively affected if methods are used that lead to the wrong conclusion because of uncontrolled biases. This is especially so if one considers not only the participants in the study itself but also potential program participants for years to come. For example, one hypothesis offered in the area of "development aid" is that recipients should have to pay something for goods and services, such as mosquito nets that can help prevent malaria. The reasoning is that people who get the nets for free will be less likely to use them. But if this reasoning is in fact false, and if the practice nevertheless continues because a weak quasi-experimental test inaccurately supported the idea, then the people who need the nets will be disadvantaged for years to come, both financially and in terms of increased risk of malaria. As this and other potential examples (e.g., welfare reform, reading instruction, and minimum wage policies) suggest, greater good may accrue to disadvantaged individuals when better information is generated about treatment effectiveness. Alternatively stated, a case can be made that good ethics justifies the use of research methods that will give the best answer about program effectiveness, as this may increase the likelihood of good outcomes, especially for those initially disadvantaged.

How do we balance the benefits/risks to study participants versus those who follow? The claim that randomized trials can support beneficence and justice is strongest when considering the benefits that would accrue to individuals who may receive the preferable treatment *after the study is over.* This highlights the complex issue of how to weight the benefits and risks that apply to *study participants,* relative to the potential benefits to others who did not participate in the study. For example, if preschool experiments demonstrate the sizable benefits for the poor of certain kinds of preschool experience, generations of children could benefit if the research affects policy—but that would do little to improve the life course of the children who were assigned to the comparison group in the original experiments. Gilbert et al. (1977) noted that a current generation inevitably owes a debt to past ones, and they suggested that a way of paying that debt forward, so to speak, is to participate in experimental trials that will provide better care for those who follow. Others, however, may be less comfortable with the idea that study participants bear the study's risks, while the greatest benefits accrue to others.

Numerous suggestions have been given regarding ways of making the benefit-risk ratio acceptable for study participants, even if they end up being in the less effective treatment group (e.g., Shadish et al., 2002). These include comparing a new treatment option to the best available treatment rather than a no-treatment comparison; offering the more effective treatment to those in the other group after the study is over, when this is practical; and providing participants with benefits that leave them better off than they would have been without participating in the study (e.g., payment for participation, or health services in a study of job training), even if these are unrelated to the primary outcome variable. In assessing the benefit-risk ratio for study participants, we contend that it is appropriate to consider what opportunities would have been present if the study had not been conducted. For example, the Congressionally mandated experimental trial of an Early Head Start program created preschool opportunities for those in the treatment group that would not have existed in the absence of the experiment.

How do we make judgments about the criteria and the Belmont principles? Perhaps the most challenging aspect of assessing the ethicality of a randomized experiment involves the question of how to make judgments about a particular case. Who decides, and how, that the causal question is important, relative to the other questions the researcher might address? And what is the protocol for determining whether an experiment would do better in answering the causal question, relative to alternative methods? The question of who decides, and how, is especially vexing because researchers from different traditions are likely to have quite different views. For example, writing in the same volume as Henry and Bickman and Reich, Greene (in press) acknowledged that the results of randomized experiments can sometimes be valuable, but she characterized the question "Does the program work?" as "one small question." Greene contended that

> questions about the causal effects of social interventions are characteristically those of policy and decision makers, while other stakeholders have other legitimate and important questions.... This privileging of the interests of the elite in evaluation and research is radically undemocratic.

We do not take it as a given that other stakeholders, at least potential program participants, lack interest in the question, "Does the program help?" Nevertheless, the general point is that although the five criteria (and the Belmont principles) appear reasonable, difficulties may arise in practice when trying to decide whether the criteria (and principles) have been met.

A commonly offered procedure for making such judgments, and more generally for making prospective judgments about the ethics of a proposed study, is to rely on institutional review boards (IRBs). We note here simply that (a) a complex set of technical and political judgments is required (e.g., Is a random assignment experiment needed, relative to alternative methods? Is the question of the treatment's effects on possible outcomes sufficiently important, relative to other possible research questions?) and (b) IRB members may not have the requisite skills or may not always receive adequate and unbiased information for making such judgments in a truly thoughtful way.

Is research quality an ethical issue? Methodological quality is usually seen as a technical consideration. For example, in the American Evaluation Association's *Guiding Principles for Evaluators*, technical quality appears in the "Systematic Inquiry" and "Competence" Principles. However, if wrong answers could result in harm to subsequent program participants, and if methodological limits would increase the risk of getting the wrong answer, then methodological shortcomings appear to be an ethical concern (Mark, Eyssell, & Campbell, 1999). After all, as Bickman and Reich remind us, getting the wrong answer can change a study's risks and benefits, sometimes dramatically. A similar claim has been made by other commentators, including Rosenthal (1994): "Bad science makes for bad ethics" (p. 128). However, this is not a position on which consensus exists, as illustrated by Pomerantz's (1994) rejoinder to Rosenthal.

Should the way we think about these questions depend on the study's stakes? In considering the question of whether high methodological quality is an ethical imperative, Mark et al. (1999) suggested a contingent view. Specifically, they posited that in the case of high-stakes studies (e.g., tests of HIV/AIDS prevention studies, where the cost of a wrong answer could be enormous), methodological quality could reasonably be viewed from an ethical lens. In contrast, they suggested that in studies with lower stakes (e.g., a lab-based masters thesis in social psychology), methodological quality might better be viewed from the perspective of competence rather than ethics. Expanding on that position, we suggest that the answers to several if not all the questions in this section, and indeed the very task of applying the five criteria, may simplify when a study's stakes are low. For instance, consider simple lab studies, such as a psycholinguistic study of the effects of prior exposure to nouns versus verbs on the interpretation of an ambiguous statement. The risks to participants are negligible. The research question need not rise to the level of a serious social problem to justify the conduct of a randomized experiment. Of course, in many field-based, applied experiments the stakes will be higher.

◆ Ethical Challenges and Solutions: Changes Over Time With New Techniques and Concerns

In this section, we suggest that the nature of answers to ethical questions regarding experiments and quasi-experiments is not fixed. Some considerations, of course, are relatively enduring, such as the *Belmont Report* principles (though even for these, cultural variations may occur). On the other hand, implementing these general principles in practice depends not only on the details of a particular case but also on the changing landscape of methodological practices available to address ethical concerns. Similarly, as we discuss shortly, the values used to judge the success of a policy or program—and to assess the risks and benefits of a study—may evolve over time.

METHODOLOGICAL IMPROVEMENTS TO ADDRESS ETHICAL ISSUES

One of the criticisms of randomized experiments is that they artificially create a difference in treatments that may disadvantage one group of participants. Especially in the early days of experiments, common practices did not minimize this risk. Power analyses, which estimate the number of participants needed to observe the effect of interest, were rare. As a result, more participants than needed may have been exposed to a less effective treatment. Or there may have been too few participants to observe the effect of interest, reducing the potential benefit of the study. Power analyses have become relatively commonplace, reducing the magnitude of risk.

Stop rules are another technique that can help attenuate risk. In short, stop rules involve an explicit protocol to cease an experiment after a significant treatment effect of a specific magnitude is observed in preliminary analyses. Without stop rules, an experiment typically would continue until a specified number of participants or point in time was reached. Stop rules can reduce risk to participants by reducing the number of participants exposed to the less effective treatment, or by reducing the length of time they received the less effective treatment, or both. Especially in cases in which these participants can then receive the more effective treatment, stop rules can reduce risk and thus contribute to more ethical experimentation. Indeed, especially with stop rules, power analyses, and other procedures such as informed consent to random assignment, experiments may in some cases raise fewer ethical concerns than alternatives, at least if one considers the relative fairness of the implicit rules that otherwise govern assignment to condition. These implicit rules may include the happenstance of location, first come first served, cronyism, and so on.

Another criticism of randomized experiments is that they rely on random allocation to conditions, even in circumstances where some other principle would be preferred. Two ways of addressing this criticism involve methods choices. One is to conduct the randomized experiment, but with a set of inclusion and exclusion criteria that limit all participants to those within an acceptable range. For instance, an experimental evaluation of a compensatory reading program might include as participants only students whose reading performance falls within a certain range.

An alternative is to use the R-D design. This design is well suited when there is a clear preference that the treatment should go to those in greatest need (or, instead, to the most meritorious), and when a suitable measure of need (or merit) is available. In the R-D design, the treatment that participants receive depends on their scores on a prior measure called the quantitative assignment variable, or QAV. People who score above a specific cutoff value on the QAV receive one treatment, and those below the cutoff receive the other treatment. In a study of a compensatory after-school reading program, for example, prestudy reading scores might be the QAV, with students scoring below the cutoff assigned to the compensatory reading program and students above the cutoff to a comparison group. Later, after the program, students would be assessed on the outcome measure, say, postprogram reading scores. For a merit-based intervention, such as merit scholarships, the treatment group would consist of participants scoring above the cutoff, and the comparison group those below. The basic logic of the R-D design is that if the program is effective, there should be a detectable jump in scores at the cutoff. Moreover, generally there are no plausible validity threats that could account for a discontinuity in scores occurring precisely at the cutoff. For an accessible presentation on the logic and analysis of the R-D design, see Mark and Reichardt (in press). Historically, the R-D design has been implemented only rarely (Shadish et al., 2002), but it has received increased attention in recent years, including investigation of alternative analysis approaches (e.g., Hann, Todd, & Van der Klaauw, 2001). Thus, continued enhancements of the quasi-experimental R-D design may increase its acceptability as an alternative to the randomized experiment.

Another recent development, while relying on random assignment, holds considerable promise in avoiding many of the ethical criticisms directed at randomized experiments. In a random encouragement design, participants are not randomly assigned to one condition or another. Rather, some randomly chosen individuals receive extensive recruitment efforts that encourage them to participate in the treatment of interest; in contrast, those in the randomly created comparison group receive no such recruitment. As an example, Wells et al. (2000), using a range of encouragements, including education and reduced fees, solicited patients at a randomly assigned set of clinics to participate in a quality improvement program for treatment of depression. In a random encouragement experiment, statistical methods such as instrumental variables analysis are used in an effort to provide good estimates of the treatment effect (see Schoenbaum et al., 2002, for an illustration of instrumental variables analysis with the Wells et al., 2000, data). In essence, these analyses assume that any effect of encouragement arises only by way of the increased program participation that the encouragement creates; this assumption facilitates statistical estimates of the effect of the program itself. The random encouragement design alleviates ethical concerns that can arise from procedures that restrict participants' access to multiple treatment options. It can reduce concerns about coercion. These ethical benefits *may* occur with little loss of validity, although we believe further experience is needed to demonstrate this conclusively.

Other criticisms of random assignment involve claims that experiment's benefits are limited because they do not reveal why a treatment works (if it does) or aid in broader understanding when and for whom the treatment should be effective. In recent years, a number of procedures that help address these concerns have become relatively common as adjuncts to experiments and quasi-experiments. Three ancillary procedures are especially notable in this regard: implementation assessment, meditational tests, and the study of moderation (see Mark & Reichardt, in press, for an overview).

EVOLUTION OF THE VALUE BASIS FOR MAKING JUDGMENTS

As the discussion of stop rules, random encouragement designs, and the like indicates, methodological developments may reduce risks, increase benefits, and provide more desirable alternatives. Thus, the methodological advances of tomorrow can modify the ethical assessments of today. A similar argument can be made that the very values that underlie judgments about the merit and worth of interventions may change over time (Mark, Henry, & Julnes, 2000). Of interest here is that these same values may also enter into the cost and benefit assessments of proposed studies.

Two brief examples should suffice. First, questions about inequities have become common in certain program and policy areas (Ceci & Papierno, 2005). In education, for example, achievement gaps are a serious concern. In health, considerable attention is given to health disparities. In both cases, the concern is about differential outcomes across racial/ethnic, socioeconomic, and gender categories. All other things being equal, in a community concerned with differential outcomes, a program or policy will be seen as more worthy to the extent it reduces these gaps. More important for this chapter, judgments of the potential benefits of a study will depend in part on the study's capacity to assess whether the program has reduced gaps.

We suggest that the current attention to specific disparities is not inevitable in some logical sense. Rather, certain disparities call for attention because they have been shown to exist and because, for a variety of reasons, people have become more concerned about them over time. Less attention would be given to gender gaps in mathematics achievement if such gaps had not been observed, for example. Looking at the current state of affairs, this may sound rather pedestrian. However, looking forward we tentatively offer a hypothesis that may be less obvious. As global climate change continues, environmental impact may become more important, for example, in program evaluation. It may become a more frequent criterion for assessing the merit and worth of programs and policies, even those not focused primarily on environmental issues. Regarding judgments of research ethics, a proposed study's environmental impact, as well as its capacity to assess the program's environmental impact, may—and, we would argue, should—be considered in terms of judging the study's expected benefits and risks.

◆ Ethical Risks of Focusing on Average Effect Sizes and the Need for Principled Discovery

One potentially important criticism of experiments and quasi-experiments is that their focus on average effect sizes misses a great deal of the action in a world in which causal relations are contingent, or put differently, where the effect of a treatment depends on many interactions (e.g., Greene, in press). In such a world, a program that works for some might have no effect or even be harmful for others. Although this argument is not always framed in terms of research ethics, it has a serious ethical dimension. At the extreme, the experimentalist's focus on average effect sizes runs the risk of violating the Hippocratic dictate, "First, do no harm." That is, a program could be beneficial to most participants, resulting in a significant overall treatment effect, while actually being harmful to a minority of participants. If there is a harmful effect on a subset of participants, and if the experiment fails to detect this, the harmful effects will not be ameliorated and, even worse, the study results could lead to the program being administered universally in the future despite its harmful effects to some. Surely, such a state of affairs would undermine the claim than the experiment is ethical.

Rosenthal (1994) offered an ethical critique of the traditional experimentalist's tendency to focus on average effect sizes. According to Rosenthal,

> Many of us have been taught that it is technically improper and perhaps even immoral to analyze and reanalyze our data in many ways (i.e., to snoop around in the data).... [This] makes for bad science and for bad ethics. (p. 130)

Rosenthal's "bad ethics," we suggest, arises most seriously if the admonition to "do no harm" is violated. (See also Chapter 14, this volume, for further discussion of data reanalysis.)

One response to this ethical concern is to attempt "principled discovery" (Mark, 2003; Mark et al., 2000). In short, the idea is to complement traditional analyses of experimental and quasi-experimental research with iterative analysis procedures, involving both data and conceptual analysis. The goal is to discover complexities, such as unpredicted differential effects across subgroups, while not being misled by chance. Why the concern about chance? Recall that statistical significance means only that a given finding is unlikely to have arisen by chance if there really were no difference—so that doing many exploratory tests creates a risk for chance findings. Stigler (1987) captured the problem pithily: "Beware of testing too many hypotheses; the more you torture the data, the more likely they are to confess, but confession obtained under duress may not be admissible in the court of scientific opinion" (p. 148).

This problem would largely disappear if the relevant theories were developed well enough to guide researchers to specify the most important contingent hypotheses in advance (e.g., that the program effect will be larger for a certain subgroup of participants). But in most areas of applied social research, theory is not so developed. The false confession problem also would be solved if the experimenter could snoop in the data from one study and then, if an important finding emerges (e.g., a program benefits one subgroup and harms another), see if the pattern replicates in another study. Unfortunately, options for replication are limited in many areas of applied social research. For example, some program evaluations take years and cost millions of dollars; so replication is an infeasible strategy relative to the timeline for decision making.

Principled discovery has been offered as a way to try to discover more from the data while not being misled by false confessions. Before starting principled discovery, the researcher would conduct analyses to test the a priori hypothesis (e.g., that the new treatment will lead to better outcomes than the old treatment). The principled discovery that follows involves two primary stages (which may further iterate). In the first stage, the researcher carries out exploratory analyses. For example, an experimental program evaluator might examine whether the program has differential effects by looking for interaction effects using one after another of the variables on which participants have been measured (e.g., gender, race, age, family composition). A wide variety of statistical techniques can be used for the exploratory analyses of this first stage of principled discovery (Mark, 2003; Mark et al., 1998). If the Stage 1 exploratory analyses result in an interesting (and unpredicted) finding (and if replication in another study is infeasible), then in the second stage of principled discovery the researcher would seek one or another form of independent (or quasi-independent) confirmation of the discovery. In many instances, this will involve other tests that can be carried out within the same data set (although data might be drawn from other data sets, or new data might be collected after Stage 1). For example, if a gender effect is discovered in an educational intervention, this might lead to a more specific prediction that boys and girls will differ more after transition to middle school than before. As this example illustrates, Stage 2 of principled discovery includes conceptual analysis as well as data analysis. That is, the second stage of principled discovery will generally require an interpretation of the finding from the Stage 1 exploration. But why does the second stage help alleviate the problem of chance, of tortured data confessing falsely to something? In short, if the original discovery is not real but instead is due only to chance, then there is generally no reason to expect the Stage 2 test to be confirmed. For example, if a gender effect from Stage 1 had arisen solely due to chance, it would be unlikely that the size of the gender difference would be affected by the transition to middle school.

Principled discovery has considerable potential for enhancing emergent discovery in quasi-experimental (and experimental) research, while reducing the likelihood of being misled by chance findings. Despite its potential benefits, important practical limits will often apply to principled discovery. These include the possibility that in some studies data elements will not be available for the second stage of principled discovery, as well as the likelihood that statistical power may be inadequate for some contrasts (Mark, in press). Despite such limits, principled discovery appears to be an approach that can help address some of the practical and ethical objections to randomized and quasi-experimental studies of the effects of interventions in a complex world.

◆ Brief Conclusions

This chapter has addressed ethical issues that arise in the context of randomized experiments and quasi-experiments. We have not addressed all related issues, such as the often complex and indirect pathways through which research findings affect (or fail to affect) policy and practice. Nor have we consistently emphasized an important point about which Tom Schwandt (personal communication, 2007) has reminded us: Research designs do not have an intrinsic ethical value. Ethical judgments regarding experiments, for example, should reside in particular individual cases for which the details matter. However, our sense is that, as in many other areas of human judgment, prejudices and overgeneralizations often override thoughtful judgments about the ethicality of experiments and quasi-experiments in particular cases. We hope that careful consideration of the issues raised in this chapter should aid thoughtful judgments about the ethical status of experiments and quasi-experiments, including consideration of ancillary procedures and alternatives.

◆ Note

1. Among the other reasons, in the language of Campbell and his colleagues, are the validity threats of history, testing, instrumentation, and attrition.

◆ References

Bickman, L., & Reich, S. M. (in press). Randomized control trials: A gold standard with feet of clay. In S. Donaldson, T. C. Christie, & M. M. Mark (Eds.), *What counts as credible evidence in applied research and evaluation?* Thousand Oaks, CA: Sage.

Boruch, R. F. (1997). *Randomized experiments for planning and evaluation.* Thousand Oaks, CA: Sage.

Boruch, R. F. (2005). Comments on "Use of randomization in the evaluation of development effectiveness." In G. K. Pitman, O. N. Feinstein, & G. K. Ingram (Eds.), *World Bank series on evaluation and development: Vol. 7. Evaluating development effectiveness* (pp. 205–231). New Brunswick, NJ: Transaction Books.

Campbell, D. T., & Stanley, J. C. (1966). *Experimental and quasi-experimental designs for research.* Skokie, IL: Rand McNally.

Ceci, S. J., & Papierno, P. B. (2005). The rhetoric and reality of gap closing: When "have nots" gain but the "haves" gain even more. *American Psychologist, 60,* 149–160.

Chalmers, T. C. (1968). Prophylactic treatment of Wilson's disease. *New England Journal of Medicine, 278,* 910–911.

Cook, T. D. (2002). Randomized experiments in educational policy research: A critical examination of the reasons the educational evaluation community has offered for not doing them. *Educational Evaluation and Policy Analysis, 24,* 175–199.

Cook, T. D., & Campbell, D. T. (1979). *Quasi-experimentation: Design and analysis issues for field settings.* Skokie, IL: Rand McNally.

Cook, T. D., & Groom, C. (2004). The methodological assumptions of social psychology: The mutual dependence of substantive theory and method choice. In C. Sansone, C. C. Morf, & A. T. Panter (Eds.), *The Sage handbook of methods in social psychology* (pp. 19–44). Thousand Oaks, CA: Sage.

Department of Health, Education, and Welfare. (1978). *The Belmont Report: Ethical principles and guidelines for the protection of human subjects of research.* Washington, DC: Government Printing Office.

Donaldson, S., Christie, T. C., & Mark, M. M. (Eds.). (in press). *What counts as credible evidence in applied research and evaluation?* Thousand Oaks, CA: Sage.

Eckert, W. A. (2000). Situational enhancement of design validity: The case of training evaluation at the World Bank Institute. *American Journal of Evaluation, 21,* 185–193.

Federal Judicial Center. (1981). *Experimentation in the law* (Report of the Federal Judicial Center Advisory Committee on Experimentation in the Law). Washington, DC: Government Printing Office.

Fisher, C. B., & Anushko, A. E. (2008). Research ethics in social science. In P. Alasuutari, J. Brannen, & L. Bickman (Eds.), *Sage handbook of social research methods* (pp. 96–109). London: Sage.

Gersten, R., & Hitchcock, J. (in press). What is credible evidence in evaluation? The role of the what works clearinghouse in informing the process. In S. Donaldson, T. C. Christie, & M. M. Mark (Eds.), *What counts as credible evidence in applied research and evaluation?* Thousand Oaks, CA: Sage.

Gilbert, J. P., McPeak, B., & Mosteller, F. (1977). Statistics and ethics in surgery and anesthesia. *Science, 198,* 684–689.

Greenberg, D., & Schroeder, M. (1997). *The digest of social experiments* (2nd ed.). Washington, DC: Urban Institute Press.

Greene, J. C. (in press). Evidence as "proof" and evidence as "inkling." In S. Donaldson, T. C. Christie, & M. M. Mark (Eds.), *What counts as credible evidence in applied research and evaluation?* Thousand Oaks, CA: Sage.

Hann, J., Todd, P., & Van der Klaauw, W. (2001). Identification and estimation of treatment effects with a regression-discontinuity design. *Econometrica, 69,* 200–209.

Henry, G. T. (in press). When getting it right matters: The case for high quality policy and program impact. In S. Donaldson, T. C. Christie, & M. M. Mark (Eds.), *What counts as credible evidence in applied research and evaluation?* Thousand Oaks, CA: Sage.

Mark, M. M. (2003). Program evaluation. In S. A. Schinka & W. Velicer (Eds.), *Comprehensive handbook of psychology* (Vol. 2, pp. 323–347). New York: Wiley.

Mark, M. M. (in press). Credible evidence: Changing the terms of the debate. In S. Donaldson, T. C. Christie, & M. M. Mark (Eds.), *What counts as credible evidence in applied research and evaluation?* Thousand Oaks, CA: Sage.

Mark, M. M., Eyssell, K. M., & Campbell, B. J. (1999). The ethics of data collection and analysis. In J. L. Fitzpatrick & M. Morris (Eds.), *Ethical issues in program evaluation* (pp. 47–56). San Francisco: Jossey-Bass.

Mark, M. M., Henry, G. T., & Julnes, G., (1998). A realist theory of evaluation practice. In G. Henry, G. W. Julnes, & M. M. Mark, (Eds.), *Realist evaluation: An emerging theory in support of practice* (pp. 3–32). San Francisco: Jossey-Bass.

Mark, M. M., Henry, G. T., & Julnes, G. (2000). *Evaluation: An integrated framework for* understanding, guiding, and improving policies and programs. San Francisco: Jossey-Bass.

Mark, M. M., & Reichardt, C. S. (in press). Quasi-experimental methods and mindset for applied social research. In L. Bickman & D. Rog (Eds.), *Handbook of applied social research methods* (2nd ed.). Thousand Oaks, CA: Sage.

Pomerantz, J. R. (1994). On criteria for ethics in science: Commentary on Rosenthal. *Psychological Science, 5,* 135–136.

Rallis, S. F. (in press). Considering rigor and probity: Qualitative pathways to credible evidence. In S. Donaldson, T. C. Christie, & M. M. Mark (Eds.), *What counts as credible evidence in applied research and evaluation?* Thousand Oaks, CA: Sage.

Rosenthal, R. (1994). Science and ethics in conducting, analyzing, and reporting psychological research. *Psychological Science, 5,* 127–134.

Schoenbaum, M., Unutzer, J., McCaffrey, D., Duan, N., Sherbourne, C., & Wells, K. B. (2002). The effects of primary care depression treatment on patients' clinical status and employment. *Human Service Research, 37,* 1145–1158.

Scriven, R. (in press). The logic of causal investigations. In S. Donaldson, T. C. Christie, & M. M. Mark (Eds.), *What counts as credible evidence in applied research and evaluation?* Thousand Oaks, CA: Sage.

Sieber, J. E. (in press). Planning ethically responsible research. In L. Bickman & D. Rog (Eds.), *Handbook of applied social research methods* (2nd ed.). Thousand Oaks, CA: Sage.

Shadish, W. R., Cook, T. D., & Campbell, D. T. (2002). *Experimental and quasi-experimental designs for generalized causal inference.* Boston: Houghton Mifflin.

Stigler, S. M. (1987). Testing hypotheses or fitting models: Another look at mass extinction. In M. H. Nitecki & A. Hoffman (Eds.), *Neutral models in biology* (pp. 145–149). Oxford, UK: Oxford University Press.

Wells, K. B., Sherbourne, C., Schoenbaum, M., Duan, N., Merideth, L., Unutzer, J., et al. (2000). Impact of disseminating quality improvement programs for depression in managed care: A randomized controlled trial. *Journal of the American Medical Association, 238,* 212–220.

14

THE ETHICS OF DATA ARCHIVING

Issues From Four Perspectives

◆ David Johnson and Merry Bullock

◆ **Introduction: Setting the Ethical Discussion in Its Context**

Ethics is the study of right actions to achieve good outcomes. When applied to real life, context becomes significant. Actions deemed right by one group or in a particular setting may be deemed wrong by another group or in a different setting. Consider open-source versus proprietary-source code in software engineering. Those who believe that code is a commodity see the free provision of code as criminal. Those who see code as a resource for all look on restricting access as greedy and unethical. Ethics in archiving has such a situational aspect.

AN EXAMPLE FROM EUROPE

For scientists, knowledge is the good outcome from archiving. Easy access is desirable. For those who sell data, profit is the good to be achieved. Restricting access is profitable. The two camps have been at war for years. Proprietary data proponents advanced their ethic in 1995, when the European Union issued directive 96/9/EC on the legal protection of databases. These excerpts summarize the purpose of the directive:

Whereas the unauthorized extraction and/or re-utilization of the contents of a database constitute acts which can have serious economic and technical consequences; Whereas databases are a vital tool in the development of an information market within the Community ... Member States shall provide for a right for the maker of a database which shows that there has been qualitatively and/or quantitatively a substantial investment in either the obtaining, verification or presentation of the contents to prevent extraction and/or re-utilization of the whole or of a substantial part, evaluated qualitatively and/or quantitatively, of the contents of that database. (European Parliament, 1996)

Countries had until January 1998 to enact laws to protect database businesses. Countries had the *option* of providing some use of data from proprietary databases for educational or scientific purposes. The directive was meant to protect databases across the European Union to promote growth of database commerce.

For scientists, however, the result is a bewildering array of provisions that may be described under several emerging themes. One theme is that requests to use databases for science can (and in the case of sensitive data, often must) be submitted to a national authority, such as a data protection authority, for an opinion on whether the research can go forward. The opinion is often accompanied by provisions regarding how the research must be done to guarantee privacy for those (called "data subjects") to whom the data pertain. The circumstances under which the request must be submitted vary. In Greece, Luxembourg, and Portugal, for example, requests must be submitted to the national data protection authority. In France, the Minister of Culture authorizes the scientist to access the data, and the data protection authority specifies safeguards that will be in place as the data are used. Other countries focus on sensitive data. In Sweden, the data protection authority must do a background check if genetic data are to be accessed or if other sensitive data are to be used and the original data subjects are not available to give consent, and an ethics committee has not reviewed the research.

Substantial public interest is a second theme. Scientific analysis in the public interest can be approved because public benefit outweighs data privacy. The concept is important when it comes to sensitive data. In England and Austria, sensitive data can be used only when the public interest is served. Belgium requires full anonymization or encoding of data so they cannot be traced to data subjects. Portugal also favors anonymizing but considers it a procedure requiring permission.

A third theme has to do with distinguishing sensitive from nonsensitive data. If sensitive data are needed, the most common legal requirement is authorization by the data authority, who also often stipulates safeguards to protect data subjects. For nonsensitive data, the laws tend to be more relaxed, usually requiring research plan approval by an ethics committee. Italy and Spain have no safeguards on use of nonsensitive data. In the Netherlands, nonsensitive data use cannot go beyond the stated research purpose. Several countries do stipulate, however, that secondary data analysis may not be used to make decisions that affect data subjects. England adds a consideration of balance: Secondary analysis may not cause damage or distress to data subjects. A thorough discussion of these laws is found in Douwe Korff's (2002) study for the European Commission, *EC Study of Implementation of Data Protection Directive: Comparative Study of National Laws*.

It is worth noting that the European legal approach was presaged in 1980 by the Organization for Economic Co-Operation and Development (OECD) in its *Recommendations of the Council Concerning Guidelines Governing the Protection of Privacy and Trans-Border Flows of Personal Data*. Nineteen European countries in addition to the United States and Canada were members of the OECD in 1980. The implication of these early recommendations is that conceptually, the individual right to privacy came first, and the laws that came after to facilitate database-related commerce had to take account of the privacy principles. There are seven principles of privacy that can be seen as the ethical base on which the European approach to database regulation is built:

1. Data subjects should be notified when their data are being collected.

2. The purpose of data collection should be defined, and the collected data should be used only for the stated purpose.

3. If data are to be disclosed, the data subject should be able to give consent to the disclosure.

4. Steps should be taken to ensure that collected data are secure and that the potential for abuse is minimized.

5. When data are collected, the identity of the data collector should be disclosed to the data subject.

6. Data subjects should have access to their data and also have the ability to correct inaccuracies in the data.

7. Data subjects should have legal means to hold data collectors accountable for complying with the principles.

To date, there has been no nationwide movement in the United States to regulate databases. Scientific use of databases is governed by the same regulations that govern research generally. That is, institutional review boards (IRBs) must review and approve the research. But U.S. legislators watch European legislation closely and have introduced bills that contain nearly the exact text of bills introduced and passed into law in European countries. Database regulation is one area where such emulation is a real possibility because the same business interests that were successful in Europe also push for regulatory protection in the United States and in other countries as well. In 2000, for example, there was an attempt at the World Intellectual Property Organization of the United Nations to craft a treaty (first drafted in 1996) that could have extended European-style property rights to database owners in the 192 countries that are members of the United Nations. The treaty was strongly opposed by scientists and, in the end, failed to move forward.

Legislation to ensure good outcomes from right actions is not equally good for all stakeholders. Database and data sharing laws define situations in which personal privacy can be violated, for example, when potential public benefit outweighs the benefit of privacy. The same laws facilitate the buying and selling of data, a good outcome for commercial interests but an impediment to the use of databases to advance scientific knowledge. The ethical issues that underlie this legislation are consistent across countries even if the positions taken by the countries on the issues they address differ.

The purpose of this chapter is to explore ethical behavior in the case of scientific use of databases, especially in the behavioral and social sciences. This discussion properly takes place against the backdrop of the effort across nations to find a workable balance among the sometimes competing interests of individuals, corporations, and scientists to define the ethical landscape for data archiving. In the remainder of the chapter, we will look at these ethical issues from the vantage points of the four stakeholder groups concerned with the scientific use of databases: primary and secondary researchers, archivists, data subjects, and the public.

♦ Primary Researchers

As countries differ in legislative approaches to archiving, different scientific disciplines take different stances toward the responsibility of primary researchers to archive for the benefit of secondary researchers. At one extreme are applied scientists whose research is essential to new product development and patents. Such scientists are sometimes required by contract or as a condition of employment not to disclose data at least until the patents are in place so that the employer will be able to profit from the scientist's research. Here, ethical considerations have to do with whether, when, how much, and at what level of specificity to archive. The primary researcher's first obligation is to help the company prosper. If shared data allowed a rival company to beat the first company to market, then data sharing would violate the scientist's ethical obligation to promote good outcomes for the scientist's employer. The obligation of the scientist to increase the general store of knowledge is outweighed by the need to behave ethically within the corporation.

At the other extreme are scientists who study group behavior, for example, political scientists, economists, and sociologists. Data archives are so important in these fields that building archives is a discipline-wide activity. In the United States, a large proportion of government funds available for research in several social sciences go toward database development and maintenance. The Inter-University Consortium for Political and Social Research (ICPSR) has, since 1962, been the organization most responsible for maintaining archives for such scientists. Universities and other member organizations pay dues to ICPSR to maintain databases and the infrastructure to make the data accessible. In return, all faculty, staff, and students at a member institution have access to the archives. Many national organizations are ICPSR members—Australia, Japan, Korea, Germany, Israel, Italy, Denmark, and Holland to name a few. ICPSR partners with the Council of European Social Science Data Archives to expand the number of databases available to researchers worldwide. The result of international cooperation is a vast store of databases, standards with respect to data, and policies with respect to use. Because ICPSR has developed policies and practices toward many of the ethical questions we will examine in the remainder of the chapter, we will refer often to the practices as models for emulation (Inter-University Consortium for Political and Social Research, 2007b).

The fundamental archiving question for a primary researcher is whether to archive at all. If the scientist's ethical obligation is to produce knowledge, archiving would seem to be the right action. It increases the likelihood of producing knowledge. ICPSR, however, recognizes that not all data should be archived. It makes no attempt to require archiving of scientists in member universities and organizations. Rather, it encourages scientists to consider the importance of their data for others. If it is judged useful, then the scientist is encouraged to archive. ICPSR staffers search journals and attend scientific meetings to identify data that ought to be archived. They then encourage the scientist to archive. The scientist must then weigh a course of action.

The right response may not always be to archive. There are valid, ethical reasons to hesitate to give data. The researcher may not be finished using the data. The primary researcher has a right to make first use of the data. ICPSR addresses this right by negotiating when data will be disseminated. It preserves an archival copy of the data but does not disseminate until the accepted date. The ICPSR preference is to keep data in this archive-only state for no more than a year, but it makes exceptions. The ICPSR practice is a reasonable balance between the right of the primary researcher to first use of the data and the obligation of the scientific community to derive the greatest knowledge from the data it generates.

Difficulty preserving confidentiality is a second reason to hesitate making data publicly accessible. ICPSR works with primary researchers to minimize this problem. It sometimes anonymizes data to preserve confidentiality. But the utility of some data is decreased by anonymization. Longitudinal data from cohorts of individuals followed over decades is an example. It is important to the analysis of data to know to whom a data set pertains. In such cases, ICPSR makes data available in a nonpublic environment. A researcher must go to ICPSR physically, must sign a promise not to divulge information that can identify specific data subjects, must use the data in a facility monitored by cameras, must use a computer not connected to the Internet, must not bring paper or personal computers into the facility, and must be searched when leaving. The search includes examination of how data are arranged in the cells of the researcher's data analytic framework to ensure that no cluster of data could identify a data subject.

If a researcher breaches confidentiality, ICPSR will ask the researcher's institution to do a scientific misconduct investigation, ban the researcher from further access to confidential data, and ask federal agencies to cease supporting the individual's research. The price of breaching confidentiality could be the researcher's career. The threat is a deterrent. It also increases the confidence of primary researchers that the privacy of their data subjects will not be compromised by secondary users of the data.

If a primary researcher's data are archived, what are the ethical obligations of that researcher to the archivist, the secondary researchers, and the public? We have looked at how the primary researcher can meet his or her obligations to the data subjects. What governs ethical behavior toward the other stakeholders? The answer lies in what unites the stakeholder groups: the greatest production of knowledge from the data resources.

The primary researcher needs to work with the archivist to ensure that the data can be used by secondary researchers. This presents practical difficulties that can be daunting. Researchers who regularly archive can plan from the beginning how data should be arranged for use by others. But most researchers think about how to address their own research questions as they do their work. The result is that it takes additional work generally not covered by one's research grant or recognized by one's institution to make data ready for use by others. Although it helps maximize the return on investment in research, such data preparation is usually not rewarded in tenure or promotion or pay decisions. The professional framework within which researchers work does not, in this instance, facilitate the most ethical behavior on the part of the primary researcher.

The primary researcher needs help to do the right thing and should not be penalized for seeing that data are formatted and that sufficient metadata (information about the data) are provided to make the data useful to others. Lacking support, some researchers have declined to archive. Archiving facility staff can sometimes compensate by consulting with, then processing the data for, the primary researcher. Ideally, however, research institutions should make it easier for the primary researcher to prepare data for archiving. The benefit for advancing knowledge would be large. Increased archiving would benefit even the primary researcher by prompting development of tools and techniques that make it easy to reliably relate and integrate results from a series of one's experiments or studies.

Archiving advocates are attempting to come to the rescue by building templates for ordering, storing, and transmitting data. The effort, known as the data documentation initiative (DDI), is being undertaken internationally by more than 30 universities and other organizations. The aim is to standardize the arrangement of data and its documentation across the social sciences and to make the templates for standardizing available to researchers. The ease with which the Internet can be used to transmit data and the software technology that facilitates this transmission have provided the means to impose this order on data sets. Extensible markup language (XML) is being used to design templates into which researchers will eventually place both data and metadata to facilitate their own data analyses while simultaneously arranging the data for archiving. XML offers this capability because it is a metalanguage, a language for describing other languages. So its utility does not depend on any particular kind of data analytic software. If these templates can be adopted worldwide, a secondary researcher will not need to learn a new way to access and use data each time he or she goes to a different archive. The data formats, means of presenting metadata, and tools for analysis will be the same from archive to archive and country to country. Moreover, primary researchers will have a tool for organizing data that will be compatible with most commonly used data analytic software.

Besides XML, what makes this possible is that the DDI standard is built on a data model rather than a particular software or computing environment. The model is extensible and modular. Extensibility comes from XML, a simplified version of standard generalized markup language, the international standard metalanguage by which the languages of other software are described. Its modularity means that the format can accommodate the simplest to the most complex data sets. So the templates can be used with nearly any data and nearly any research design regardless of the software the primary researcher used to order and analyze the original data. This adaptability is made possible by data type descriptions or DTDs that make it possible for XML to work with the data by identifying its type. The DDI Alliance (2007) expects to submit its standards to the International Standards Organization (ISO) for official recognition. The ISO stamp is the indication that the application in question is the world standard in its domain. The standards embodied in the DDI tools were developed to be compatible with those being established in areas of science other than the behavioral and social sciences. The aim here is to reach standards for data collection, management, archiving, and analysis that are consistent across all of science. And perhaps most important from a human point of view, the Alliance is working continually to improve the user-friendliness of the tools.

Whether using DDI templates or some other means of ordering and explaining data, the primary researcher must provide metadata to secondary users. Data are of little secondary use without metadata, the guidebook to the data. They tell users how the data were collected, under what conditions, what constraints were in place, and what anomalies may have occurred. Secondary analysts are sometimes accused of engaging in an invalid undertaking in that the analyst may not have used analytical methods that respect the statistical requirements imposed by the manner in which the original data were collected. The secondary user does have an ethical obligation to treat the data properly, including the obligation to develop analytic tools that make secondary analyses robust. But the primary researcher has a reciprocal ethical obligation to provide the information about the data that will allow proper secondary analysis of the data.

◆ Archivists

The ethical obligations of the archivist flow back to the primary researchers and data subjects and forward to secondary researchers and the public, including the scientific public. Archivists are like public officials in that they work out and enforce the standards of behavior that help the stakeholders interact to achieve the ethical purpose of archiving, advancement of knowledge.

As we have seen, a primary concern of the public is protection of privacy. The archivist is the agent most directly able to ensure that the privacy of data subjects is maintained during secondary data analysis. One of the "public official" roles assumed by archivists is that of a judge, weighing when it is or is not in the public interest for a researcher to know the identity of data subjects. A body of practice now exists that makes such decisions less difficult than in the early days of electronic databases. Confidentiality decisions fall along four main dimensions.

The simplest is when there is no need to identify data subjects. Data subjects are protected by removing the means to identify the data subject. There are many means: removing identifiers from data sets, removing geographic or place references or describing them generically, inserting dummy data that do not change analytic outcomes but render knowing identities useless, and presenting data at a level of aggregation that obscures individual contributions to the database.

The second dimension has to do with identifiers that need to remain intact if the data are to be analyzed meaningfully. Longitudinal studies following individuals and drug trials in which adverse effects were experienced by only a few individuals are examples of such data. In some cases, the need is to trace what happened to individuals over time. Who the individuals are is less important than keeping an individual's data aggregated. Nonidentifying markers can be substituted for names in these cases. A variation is to associate a number key with the names of the data subjects but to separate the two so that the researcher can access the name key only when required for the data analysis.

In other cases, knowing the data subject's identity is necessary and more elaborate steps are needed to meet the archivist's ethical responsibility toward data subjects. As mentioned earlier, a number of European countries require a compelling public need before the archivist can allow access to identities. When possible, some countries also require the data subject's consent. In the United States, archivists have sought data subject consent, particularly in the case of longitudinal data sets, even though the legal mandate to do so is less clearly drawn than in most European countries.

The mandate in the United States is less clearly drawn in part because data subjects know from the beginning that their data will be used in research. They sign consent forms stating as such. The U.S. debate is over how extensive informed consent should be and whether it can be construed to apply to secondary analysis. The heart of the problem is that even when confidentiality is satisfied, and the ethical action toward data subjects has been taken, the data subject may not have explicitly given permission for secondary analysis. This procedural issue can be resolved by making possible future secondary analysis explicit in the consent form. Archivists should encourage primary researchers to include such a provision. Wider adoption of such provisions could happen if graduate students being taught to write informed consent forms were taught to remember secondary analysis as part of informed consent. Today, in lieu of such a standard provision, the archivist is advised to seek counsel of an objective third party when a difficult decision about confidentiality needs to be made. In the United States, that party is most often the IRB. In Europe, it is usually a country's Data Protection Authority, sometimes supplemented by a university's research review committee.

In any case, the archivist is bound to ensure that data are not misused. Usually, this is done by designating degrees of access. Data accessible online will be aggregated obscuring individual identities. Access to data with intact identifiers happens only after a research proposal has been cleared by an appropriate review board. The cautions that need to be taken at the archiving facility to ensure ethical use of the data were outlined earlier.

There is a third dimension of personal data that has special considerations. These are highly sensitive data needed to protect the public. Examples of these data are personnel errors that led to near accidents on commercial airliners or records of medical errors that could have led to patient death. Understanding what happened can cause changes that improve public safety. But the data could place individuals in danger of criminal prosecution or loss of employment.

Here, the archivist is not in a position to determine right actions in the absence of legal assistance, even though this is an emerging area of archiving ethics.

To obtain the data, privacy has to be protected. No one volunteers information that would result in imprisonment or job loss. There is a growing understanding that these data are important enough to protect them from discovery in civil or criminal cases. That legal protection is not in place yet. The relevant databases are being built through anonymous reporting. Moreover, most such databases are under the management of government agencies that can control access.

The National Patient Safety Agency (2007) of England collects anonymously tendered data on medical mistakes, for example. The English system is modeled on the Aviation Safety Reporting System used for more than 30 years by airline personnel to anonymously report irregularities related to air travel (National Aeronautics and Space Administration, 2007). The latter system is sponsored by the U.S. Federal Aviation Administration (FAA). The National Aeronautics and Space Administration (NASA) is the neutral third party that collects data, removing identifying information from it. The FAA prohibits itself from using information from the system in a disciplinary action. Nevertheless, enough information about an incident can be pieced together to identify probable time, place, and responsible individuals. Assurance of freedom from disciplinary action has been indispensable to data collection. The archivist's role is to maintain the anonymity of the data reporters while providing for timely data analyses and results reporting to authorities in a position to make changes to enhance public safety.

The fourth dimension of privacy protection concerns the possibility of discovering data subject identity by piecing together information from several sources. Here, the archivist's ability to act is limited to checking to see that the researcher does not cluster enough data about a single subject to allow identification from data under the archivist's control and to requiring the researcher not to reveal details about individuals. It is still possible to gather data from several sources to discover details a data subject would not want revealed. The archivist's responsibility has to be limited to making clear that if misuse of data is discovered, the archivist will invoke the same actions as for misuse of data under the archivist's direct control.

Beyond protecting data subjects, the archivist is also responsible for seeing that archives fulfill their primary purpose—to facilitate the growth of scientific knowledge. That responsibility is played out across four domains: collection growth, preservation, utility, and financial stability.

It was mentioned earlier that not every offered data set has archival value, and some unoffered data sets do have such value. In growing an archival collection, the archivist's ethical responsibility is to seek to archive what has the potential to advance knowledge if made available to secondary researchers. The archivist must make value judgments. How should such judgments be made?

With growth in storage media capacity, it is possible to store almost everything. The archivist is challenged to predict what data researchers will want to use, what data they *should* use, even what data should be archived because they are important to a small, specialized group of researchers. Will data that are "hot" today have a long shelf life or become yesterday's fad? What data going unnoticed today will become important? What data are of such historical importance that they should be preserved whether or not researchers use them? These are questions that librarians have faced and toward which they have generated answers that will help archivists.

First, different archives (like libraries) have different roles. Data chosen for archiving should be consistent with the archive's mission but should not be chosen in isolation. Archives interconnect. Archivists should know how their data sets supplement those in other archives. Secondary researchers can link data from several archives to meet a research need. If archives work cooperatively, the utility of the worldwide network of data resources can be maximized.

At most archives, more than one desire on the part of users should be served. The archive should contain bestsellers, classics, material of enduring importance, and material of greater value than users realize initially. Bestsellers are data sets in current high demand. They may not last in popularity, but people want them now. Classics have proven their worth over time and warrant preservation because they have had an impact. Data of enduring importance are those likely to become classics. They spark many new investigations, become the subject of debate in journals, and have the potential to change the thinking of large numbers of researchers. Data that are of greater value than potential users realize are the "sleepers," the data only a few people notice in the beginning. Each data type has its place in the archivist's quest to build a portfolio that will encourage the growth of scientific knowledge.

Archivists should share responsibility for building the archive with the user community. Although expert in their work, archivists need the perceptions of users to ensure that what is chosen for archiving is sufficiently comprehensive. Advisory boards and committees meet this need for a number of archives around the world. The archivist and those who advise the archivist must develop a keen understanding of the current state of knowledge in the domain covered by the archive, including an understanding of gaps that can be filled, important questions that can be asked, and insights that can be deepened if the right data are made available.

Just as gathering data sets randomly does not constitute building a useful archive, simply storing data electronically does not amount to preservation. Archives are not museums. Their worth depends on making data available in forms that facilitate analysis even as analytic tools and storage modes evolve. The archivist's ethical obligations with respect to preservation and utility go hand in hand. Technical advancement ensures that preservation is not a one-time action.

An essential aspect of preservation is migration. It includes both moving data from old to new storage media and converting data to formats that will keep the data accessible as the tools for performing operations on the data change. A graphic illustration of the importance of migration is the case of NASA data from the early days of space exploration. NASA collected much more data than could easily be analyzed as they were collected. So the data were stored on tape. Several years ago, NASA officials discovered that the tapes had deteriorated to the point that the data could not be migrated to a different medium. They were simply lost. Timely migration is needed to prevent such disasters.

Data can come to the archiving facility on a variety of media from paper to floppy disks to compact disks, to files transmitted over the Internet. They can arrive in a variety of formats, from spreadsheets to videos to pdf files. Although archives attempt to set format standards for submission of data, the result is not yet uniformity. Even when data sets coming on a variety of media in a variety of formats are standardized and made available in widely accessible formats, the job is far from done. As technology evolves, archival holdings must be migrated to continue being accessible. The decision of those involved in the DDI to use XML in developing templates is an attempt to slow the need for large changes in formats. XML, a language for describing languages, should outlast any language it subsumes. If archivists can convince researchers to use the templates, the work involved in keeping data sets useful can be substantially diminished.

As is implied by the DDI, the archivist is also called on to view his or her role as preserver and facilitator in a larger context. The archives of the world should be moving toward interactivity. One day, we should be able to work on databases from archives around the world as though they were one archive. Standards are a large part of what will make this possible. The DDI is an important step in that direction. In making XML the documentation language, the DDI establishes a single standard for the archives that are its members. In addition to its position as a metalanguage, XML supports Unicode, the international standard for characters that includes the characters of most of the human languages spoken in the world. These attributes make the XML standard the most universal platform available for archives and brings researchers close to the day when they can use many archives as though they were one archive.

Along with all these responsibilities, the archivist also needs to ensure the financial stability of the archive, though he or she is not alone in meeting this responsibility. The purpose of an archive is lost if it lacks the funds to make data available. But charging users in the way commercial databases charge is not an acceptable practice for scientific archives. Shared knowledge is essential to the advancement of science. Selling data undermines the purpose of scientific data archiving by creating classes of haves and have-nots. Scientists with funds would be able to carry out secondary research and scientists without funds would not be able to do so. That is unconscionable.

How to provide the funds to operate archives without discriminating against scientists in poor countries or poor institutions is a challenge for the archivist. Maintaining an archive is not an inexpensive venture, and funding needs cannot be met by one-time infusions such as from grants. The archivist must look for ways to sustain the effort over time. Understanding the nature of scientific archives provides a means for thinking about how to address the funding problem. The archivist is performing a service for scientists on behalf of the general public in that the knowledge flowing from scientific research is ultimately a public good. In the end, it is the responsibility of the community of scientists and the community at large to support the archives. The archivist's role is to plan a support structure that facilitates the contributions of the scientific community and the general public toward the archive. In practice, there appear to be two main means for facilitating scientific and public support of archives.

In both cases, the principle being honored is to distribute cost across a large base. In the case of scientists, several archives have created a membership structure wherein institutions with scientists who are major users of the resource pay dues to support the archives. Within this group of institutional users, degrees of use are recognized by differences in dues rates. For example, community colleges pay much less than research-intensive universities. To illustrate, for ICPSR, a major research university might pay $15,000 per year for membership, a community college $1,600, and nonmembers an access fee of $500 per data set. Even with graduated rates, some institutions find it hard to pay the dues. Again looking at ICPSR as a model, such institutions can band together and pay a federated membership. This reduces dues by up to 20%. This progressive taxation is a fair way to balance the need to support the archive against differing abilities to pay.

What of the general public? In practice, public support seems to take two main forms: government entities acting as archivists and government agencies giving grants to support archives. Governments collect great volumes of data for various public policy purposes. The collection of such information is beyond the resources of scientists and nongovernment archiving facilities. It represents a tremendous investment in archiving that is borne completely by the general public through taxes. The data contained in these databases are world treasures that should be as open as possible for use by researchers around the world.

As discussed at the beginning of the chapter, however, countries vary in their view of how accessible data should be. In the United States, scientists and the federal government have worked together to promote data availability. Many government databases are open for exploration by researchers at no cost to the researcher. Federal agencies work with scientists to plan and execute data collection in ways that will make the data most useful for research. Archives such as the ICPSR facilitate researchers' combining data from government and nongovernment sources. This burden sharing helps make data available to the broadest number of researchers at the least cost to the researcher.

There are other ways to address the obligation to pay the costs of archives. Iceland, for example, took a controversial path in the late 1990s, when it established a national health data system that contains detailed genetic information about Iceland's entire population and the ancestors of today's citizens as far back as 1,200 years ago (Hlodan, 2000). The data serve citizens in that the genetic information can be used to identify predispositions for a variety of health disorders. This, in turn, facilitates the development of drugs and treatments that will improve the health of Iceland's citizens. But the government awarded an exclusive license to the database to a private genetics research company called deCODE. That company licensed the right to search for genetic links to certain diseases to several pharmaceutical companies. The result is that the database serves the ethical purpose of generating revenue for the company and for Iceland's government in the form of license fees. But scientists find data access limited to too few users. Citizens worry that putting detailed genetic information about themselves in the hands of a private company opens the way for abuses of privacy. (And the prospect of paying a private company to gain access to information about one's own family rankles many.) The ethical obligation of archivists and the public to find the means to support archives is clear enough. As differences between the U.S. and Icelandic approaches show, however, finding the right balance between accessibility and supportability is not easy.

♦ Secondary Researchers

What is the ethical obligation of the secondary researcher? It is to produce knowledge that could not have been generated without the archives. As with the archivist, that obligation carries duties that extend backward to the primary researcher, data subjects, and archivists who make the secondary researcher's work possible and forward to the public, the recipient of the knowledge the secondary researcher produces.

The secondary researcher has the same responsibility as the primary researcher to honor data subject privacy. If the secondary researcher can identify data subjects, that ability must not be used to harm the data subject or to help others identify the data subject.

A reason that primary researchers sometimes give for declining to archive is that other users are likely to use the data incorrectly. It is true that there are many ways to do secondary analysis badly. The secondary analyst is responsible to the primary researcher to do all in his or her power to use the data in ways that yield reliable results. As underscored earlier, however, the primary researcher must provide adequate metadata to enable responsible use of his or her data. To use the data properly, secondary researchers should be well versed in the statistical and analytic methods that have been, and are being, developed for secondary analysis of discontinuous data.

The need for such familiarity is not so great when the databases are large national collections such as the database containing a country's census. These data sets were not produced through experiments, and the data in the archive were collected under similar conditions across collection sites. In a sense, the country's government is the primary researcher. But secondary analysts can safely employ the same data analytic techniques that government scientists used because the analyses are of the same kind as those performed by government analysts.

The real challenge arises when the secondary analyst wishes to analyze data from several experiments done at different times by different researchers using different subjects under different conditions. The challenge is to do valid, reliable analyses of discontinuous data treated as though they were continuous. The statistical methods for such analyses are different from those that can be employed when all the data are collected under the same conditions. Statistical methods exist for comparing discontinuous data. Secondary researchers must know when and how to use these methods to ensure the reliability of their analyses.

Although the issue of comparing discontinuous data is usually raised with respect to secondary analyses, in fact scientists commonly compare discontinuous data. Knowledge about a given phenomenon is built up by many scientists working in different places at different times under different conditions and with different data subjects. If discontinuous data were not comparable, we would have no way of constructing scientific knowledge from the data analyses of a diversity of scientists. The criticisms that have been leveled at secondary researchers for attempting to compare results from a number of independent experiments could just as well be leveled at scientists generally though the literature reviews that are the common means of comparing results across studies are carried out with less rigor than are most secondary data analyses. All scientists have something to learn from the efforts of secondary data analysts to validly aggregate and analyze discontinuous data, and we will return to that notion as we close this chapter.

The obligation of the secondary researcher toward the archivist is to use data with integrity. The secondary researcher should be thoroughly familiar with the metadata for each of the data sets he or she will be using, should be prepared to use data analytic methods that are appropriate to the data, and should be open to discussing research design with data experts at the archive to be assured that the research will yield reliable results.

The obligation of the researcher toward the public is to produce good research and reliable knowledge. The aids in place at archival facilities—the metadata, the data analytic tools, the description of other relevant data sets, and, often, the means to link to these data sets if they are not part of the holdings of the archive—are all meant to facilitate the secondary researcher's work. The secondary researcher must bring to the archive and its helpful tools the expertise to use the data and the tools in ways that will advance understanding rather than mislead the public, including other scientists.

Finally, the secondary researcher should not be simply a user of the work of others. He or she should be involved in improving archives. It was not so long ago that many archives consisted of pieces of paper in boxes or files. Then there were punch cards and reel-to-reel tapes. Then there were hard drives and mainframes. Then there was the Internet. All were advances in the infrastructure to support secondary data analysis. They might not have been used thus if individuals had not exercised vision. Similarly, today's researchers can envision the possible future of archives and help implement that future. Secondary researchers should participate in the creative processes that help archives improve. In doing so, they honor their obligation to make the most of the very large public investment in research.

◆ The Public

It may seem odd to consider the public as having ethical obligations with respect to data archiving, but the public investment in research makes the public a stakeholder. It is in the nature of stakeholding to expect to reap benefits but also to have obligations. At the beginning of the chapter, we looked at how governments have regulated archives. In democratic nations, governments are agents of the public. The laws regarding archiving are measures taken by representatives of the public to ensure ethical use of archives. At the same time, we saw that the public a government represents is far from monolithic. Some governments have opted to make profit the highest good to be achieved through archiving. Other governments have recognized the value of knowledge as a public good and have facilitated scientific uses of archives. In examining the actions of various governments, we have seen that the public has an obligation to protect its members by seeing that confidentiality is respected even while recognizing that there are instances in which confidentiality can be breached if the likely outcome is an important benefit to society.

The public also has an obligation to see that public investment in research pays off. Recognition has come about only gradually that the traditional means of collecting the knowledge yield from research—publications and presentations by individuals or teams of researchers reporting on results from primary research—does not fully tap the potential knowledge that could be gained from research. Publications and presentations will remain tools for communicating scientific knowledge. But the greatest knowledge gain is going to come from pooling data from many sources to ask questions that were not imagined when the individual data sets were generated. The public has an obligation to help create the infrastructure that will make it possible to derive the most knowledge from its investment in research. As representatives of the public, several governments have, indeed, invested in generating data for archives and in financing archives. Federal science agencies such as the National Science Foundation and the National Institutes of Health in the United States require data archiving of certain grantees and have encouraged other grantees to archive or to make data available to researchers who request them. In all these ways, public officials are helping the public obtain the greatest return on its research investment.

University officials also represent a segment of the public—namely, scientists and students whose education at least in the sciences is founded on research. The traditions of educational institutions sometimes change slowly enough to impede the production of knowledge. For example, interdisciplinary research yields many of today's cutting-edge discoveries. But university departments reward scientists when they make contributions within their discipline rather than within science more broadly construed. Senior researchers have become members of campus research centers to work collaboratively, but young scientists are often excluded from these centers because collaborative work takes away from the time they have to do work within the discipline that contributes to promotion and tenure. Similarly, university departments have been slow to recognize archiving and secondary research as valuable enough to reward. In view of their major contribution to the advancement of knowledge, university officials should encourage these activities by giving them weight in promotion and job-security decisions.

The value of archives has come to be understood only gradually. A case in point that shows what one representative of the public did when its members began to appreciate the need for archives suggests a path other public representatives might take to maximize the knowledge yield from worldwide investment in research.

In the 1990s, the National Institute on Aging, one of the U.S. National Institutes of Health reviewed what knowledge decades of research funding by the agency had produced. Officials found that much research had been produced, and results had been reported in the traditional ways. The volume of work was impressive. But in looking at what could be said about aging based on the research, the officials found problems. The agency had concentrated on funding research programs by individual experimenters or by small teams of experimenters. The researchers had little sense of a need to see that their ways of choosing subjects, their research designs, their analytic methods, or other aspects of their research were compatible with or comparable to the research of others. The end effect in terms of knowledge was that results from some studies seemed to contradict results from other studies. There were doubts about the comparability of research results. In general, there was uncertainty about the true state of knowledge on aging.

The result of the agency's taking stock of the effect of its manner of supporting research was a change of direction toward encouraging grantees to stop doing their research in isolation from each other. To help accomplish that end, the National Institute on Aging made funds for building archives and for carrying out secondary data analyses an ongoing part of its granting activity. The agency also provided funding for the National Archive of Computerized Data on Aging or NACDA (Inter-University Consortium for Political and Social Research, 2007a). ICPSR was given the contract for managing the archive, and it is now part of the network of databases available through ICPSR and its affiliates. What the National Institute on Aging hopes to accomplish with these steps is more reliable knowledge about aging. But the actions of the Institute have important implications for the whole of science. The reliability of the knowledge legacy from research is based on consistency of results. When the means to determine consistency—comparable samples, sufficient descriptions of controls, and so forth—are absent, it is difficult to determine with any degree of certainty what the true state of knowledge is in a given area of investigation. Archives impose a discipline on researchers and also provide other researchers through metadata a much more complete description of the parameters of archived research than is available in scientific publications or in oral presentations at meetings. Those who plan from the first to archive data must consider in the research design how to relate the research with confidence to other research in the area. Over time, the result of a general movement toward archiving across the scientific community can be unprecedented robustness in research results and more rapid advances in scientific understanding. This is what the National Institute on Aging hopes to accomplish within its sphere of influence. The Institute's approach is worthy of wide emulation.

♦ References

DDI Alliance. (2007). *Data documentation initiative*. Retrieved February 11, 2008, from www.ddialliance.org/org/index.html

European Parliament. (1996, March 11). *On the legal protection of databases*. Retrieved February 11, 2008, from http://eur-lex.europa.eu/LexUriServ/LexUriServ.do?uri=CELEX:31996L0009:EN:HTML

Hlodan, O. (2000, June). *For sale: Iceland's genetic history*. Retrieved February 11, 2008, from www.actionbioscience.org/genomic/hlodan.html

Inter-University Consortium for Political and Social Research. (2007a). *National archive of computerized data on aging*. Retrieved February 11, 2008, from www.icpsr.umich.edu/NACDA/welcome.html

Inter-University Consortium for Political and Social Research. (2007b). *Policies*. Retrieved February 11, 2008, from www.icpsr.umich.edu/ICPSR/org/policies/index.html

Korff, D. (2002). *EC study of implementation of data protection directive: Comparative study of national laws*. Colchester, UK: University of Essex Human Rights Center.

National Aeronautics and Space Administration. (2007). *Aviation safety reporting system*. Retrieved February 11, 2008, from http://asrs.arc.nasa.gov

National Patient Safety Agency. (2007). *National patient safety agency portal*. Retrieved February 11, 2008, from www.npsa.nhs.uk

Organization for Economic Cooperation and Development. (1980, September 23). *Guidelines on the protection of privacy and trans-border flows of personal data*.

Retrieved February 11, 2008, from www.oecd.org/document/0,2340,en_2649_34255_1815186_1_1_1_1,00.html

World Intellectual Property Organization. (1996, December 2). *Basic proposal for the substantive provision of the treaty on intellectual property in respect of databases to be considered by the diplomatic conference.* Geneva, Switzerland: Author.

15

ETHNOGRAPHY

Constitutive Practice and Research Ethics

◆ Anne Ryen

To define ethnography, I draw on Delamont's (2004, p. 218) description. She defined ethnography as qualitative research by participant observation during fieldwork where participant observation covers a mix of observation and interviewing. When traditional anthropologists move to their field site (Bronislaw Malinowski [1922] to the Triobrand Islands, Margaret Mead [1935] to the Admiralty Island off the North coast of New Guinea, William Foote Whyte [1943/1981] to Chicago, Paul Rabinow [1977] to Morocco), they are associated with total immersion as opposed to sociologists who usually go to the field in the morning and return home in the evening, hence partial immersion (Delamont, 2004, p. 218).

In this chapter, I claim that methodological, analytical, and ethical issues are closely interconnected. However, I will start with some comments about the history of ethnography and how these experiences generated reflections that later came to be associated with research ethics. I then proceed by positioning ethnography within an ethno-informed

AUTHOR'S NOTE: I thank David Silverman, the reviewers, and the editors of the *Handbook* for comments on my first draft. I also thank the Nufu—project on remuneration in Tanzanian businesses—for offering opportunities for more fieldwork.

framework. This is essential to my discussion of research ethics in ethnographic practice where my focus is on ethical dilemmas involved in getting and publishing data (De Laine, 2000; Mauthner, Birch, Jessop, & Miller, 2002) drawing on illustrations from my fieldwork with my main informant. I round off by arguing that seeing both researcher and research subject as members offers an alternative approach to exploring ethical issues in research, but one that does not release the researcher from his or her ethical responsibility. That is, I argue that there is a close link between research paradigm and research ethics. What we come to see as challenges and solutions to dilemmas in research ethics in practice is informed by epistemology.

◆ An Ethnographic Roundtrip

My interest here is the endless flow of questions facing the ethnographer that call for answers in order for the fieldwork to proceed (or not). The textbook version of fieldwork tends to portray it as a semismooth activity with a few obstacles, which the clever researcher manages without too much effort. The nature of fieldwork is, however, like all interactions, situational and contextual and cannot be sketched out in advance. The very reason for choosing any field is to acquire knowledge about it. If we already knew, we would have gone somewhere else. For this reason, although ethics guidelines tell us where we should end up, they quite possibly cannot tell us how to get there. Finally, such guidelines tend to direct themselves to the researcher as if he or she is the conductor orchestrating loyal members of the band. But as Fielding (2004) put it, "Field research is never something we do *to* research subjects, but something one does *with* research subjects. It is co-produced by researcher and subjects" (p. 251). Although in different ways, this is an ongoing activity throughout the project and is closely affiliated with research ethics both in the field and later when writing up our research based on data coproduced in the field. This way, former ethnographic work also has generated reflections now highly relevant to contemporary issues in research ethics.

Vidich and Lyman's (1994) overview of the history of ethnography[1] can work as a good point of departure. Apart from illustrating the territorial move, they also presented us with questions emerging from participating in groups unfamiliar to the ethnographer. Essential here is that some of these questions presuppose or even constitute the background to matters that later came to be categorized as ethical questions. Ethnography partly changed from being an activity exercised by pioneers in geographical areas that for Westerners came to be labeled *exotic*, often ignoring the fact that the classic Western explorers originally entered territories of substantial economic activity (Hall, 1996), to eventually exploring our own Western communities (such as the sociologists of Chicago) and to studies of "the Other" in the West, such as the American Indians and American blacks (for both, see Vidich & Lyman, 1994); the hard to study, such as street-corner boys by Whyte (1981); political extremists by Fielding (2004); and the daily and ordinary by Gullestad (1984). The same ways as these studies generated the puzzle of how to understand people whose values are not our own, these ethnographies have in their own ways generated reflections on research ethics by discourses on otherness, values, voices, and representational and other dilemmas associated with ethnographic research. This has, in particular, been motivated by the quest that preoccupied past researchers and lately also by the institutionalization of research ethics materialized as hurdles we need to overcome. In general, the formula for acceptance has been to meet the range of preset, positivist-informed criteria for ethical research. Less frequently, the spotlight has been directed toward how these requirements or criteria came to be constituted as the "correct" ethical pin code or set of ethical mandates providing guidelines (Denzin & Lincoln, 1994; Haimes, 2002; Ryen, 2004). I will return to this later. Meanwhile, it is worth emphasizing that the latter refers to avoiding uncritically taking the granted for granted (Ryen, in press-b) with reference to alternative perspectives (Denzin, 1997, p. 296; Punch, 1994). This brings us to philosophy as the point of departure to research ethics, though still mostly dominated by Western traditions such as Kant on deontology and Mills on utilitarianism (for both, see Vaags, 2004). However, outside the West, voices have for some decades argued that the problem rests with the claim that Western research is universal rather than contextual (Atal, 1981; Wallerstein, 2004). In the absence of multiple voices as in Asian philosophy, the array of African contexts, and others, we may pose the question whether imperialism also applies to research ethics[2] (Reissman, 2005; Ryen, 2007, in press-b).

I will proceed by focusing on research ethics in ethnography from an ethno-informed approach. A brief introduction to its epistemological background highlights the essential interactional or collaborative aspects of this approach allocating the researcher a position as another "member." This bears particular consequences for research ethics in research practice, which in many ways makes it a delicate field both when it comes to field relations and to publishing data. This is the background to my discussion of research ethics.

◆ Constituting Social Reality

In their book *The New Language of Qualitative Research*, Gubrium and Holstein (1997) wrote about knowledge production in qualitative inquiry (p. 3). To grasp the diversity of qualitative research, they referred to Clifford Geertz's (1997) "idioms" of reality that highlight the way the language of qualitative methods both relate to how researchers view and describe social life and, thereby, shape knowledge of social reality. "Accordingly, each idiom presents a distinctive reality, virtually constituting its empirical horizons" (p. 5). The epistemological diversity materializes in separate guidance for research practice from data collection and field relations to representation of the "facts" of the social world. Denzin and Lincoln (1994) expressed this by claiming that we need to be aware of the differences between paradigms because it is these that generate significant implications at the practical, everyday, empirical level (p. 104). This, as we shall see, also becomes crucial to diversity in ethnographic ethical research practice.

Traditional naturalistic ethnographies have invited the reader into descriptions of "there" by offering citations and stories from the informant and others who, as the local specialists, take us inside to show us what it is like in "there" (whether a local community, a street corner, or a business). The claim that the social world can be discovered by being "there," as in traditional ethnography, has for long been disputed by those who argue that social reality is accomplished rather than experienced.

The object of ethnomethodological inquiry is what Gubrium and Holstein (1997) referred to as "worlding" or "reality construction practices" (p. 39). This does not imply that the existence of reality is contested; rather, in Schutz's (1970, p. 58) words, we "bracket" our belief in it by making members' constituting practices our main focus to analyze how they themselves produce recognizable forms that are treated as real. Then, instead of relating to members' commonsense accounts from everyday life as descriptions of "there," we rather examine how they make "there" into a recognizable social reality (Atkinson & Coffey, 2002). We make their ongoing achievement of the social phenomena they are talking about into the very topic of our research, not using it as a resource (Gubrium & Holstein, 1997, p. 42; Silverman, 2006).

According to Sacks, analyses of talk-in-interaction have shown patterned regularities, and his "apparatus" represents one way of analyzing such talk, illustrating how "participants orient and respond to each other in an orderly, recognizable way" (Gubrium & Holstein, 1997, p. 55). By analyzing how members talk, we can describe the practices they employ to constitute the reality of the phenomenon they make into being. Sacks has developed these regularities into what is called *membership categorization device* (MCD), which "consists of a collection of categories (e.g., baby, mommy, father = family; male, female = gender) and some rules about how to apply these categories" (Silverman, 2006, p. 183), also referred to as "rules of application." According to Sacks, the category-bound activities rule describes how people in everyday life come to hear things the way they do based on assumptions on what people are doing because each of the pairs of MCDs implies common expectations about what sort of activity is appropriate. As an illustration, the collection "parent-child" carries with it parental responsibility that qualifies for the label "a standardized relational pair" (Silverman, 2006, p. 141).

To analyze the complexity of daily life's constitutive practices, we need to get close to get detailed data, but without getting engrossed as in naturalism. This differentiation between topic and resource relates to what Garfinkel and Sacks (1967) referred to as "ethnomethodological indifference" and implies that the researcher abstains from judgments of value, importance, and so on. As we shall see later, this is crucial to ethical research practice within this approach. Let us now look at some data to illustrate the above and as a point of departure for a discussion of research ethics in ethnography.

◆ Accomplishing Field Relations

My own ethnographic work with my main informant falls somewhere between Delmont's concepts of partial and total immersion in the sense that I organize my fieldwork as sections of total immersion intercepted by leaving the field for my "regular" work. In between these sections, we communicate by mobile phones, a model we have used for about four years. As is often the case, data are collected by both participant observation and interviews. These data work well to illustrate the link between epistemology and research ethics or, more precisely, the implications of exploring constitutive practice to research ethics. In this project, "the inside" is Asian business in East Africa. I have known Mahid, my colleague in this endeavor, for some years now, from his depression after having lost in business, through health problems, sorrow, and until he was financially back in business.

Even in ethno-informed fieldwork, we face the traditional two classic challenges of getting access to the field and staying in the field (Ryen, 2002), whether to tape natural talk (Silverman, 2006, p. 201) or to tape talk when participating in the field ourselves. Then, after entering the field, we need to unveil the finely grained interactional aspects of being in the field. This calls for being cautious when we put categories to our data. The focus is on participants' mundane practices, where we explore both process (social reality as a collaborative accomplishment) and context (talk is situated).

Let me present a few examples of paired identities invoked by Mahid and myself through excluding the traditional and obvious researcher-researched. The important aspect is that when we alter the way we come to see field relations, this has, as we later shall see, crucial implications for issues relating to research ethics in ethnographic practice.

MAN-WOMAN

Early in the project during a trip to one of Mahid's many projects, we were talking about doing interview studies in the region. The first two extracts below are taped talk from sitting in the car at one of his business projects. The car had become an arena where we spent a considerable amount of hours driving in the region. As such it blended with Emerson, Fretz, and Shaw's (1995) recommendation that ethnographers should look for the ordinary rather than the exceptional. At times stopping for elephants, crossing national borders, or jumping on a plane have become part of the ordinary as well as driving for hours on the way to somewhere. Here are a couple of extracts where we constitute a paired identity as man-woman talking about doing interviews with businesspersons:

Extract 1

A: How should I respond do you think? What would be expected from her [the female researcher]?

M: Now you are trying to interview, and you are trying to get what is in their heart. Right?

A: Yeah!

M: No, if you respond in a very, . . . draw the line you'll never get what they feel. You'll never get it out. Your job becomes very difficult. All right, then you have to make a leeway. It is like I was telling you earlier when you throw a hook at the sea, eh eh, the river and you're fishing and the fish grabs the bite. All right? You just don't start pulling them. You let the fish go wander around in different directions till the fish is totally exhausted so it makes the job very easy to pull it, roll it out, come on, come on baby, come on

(Uganda, 2003)

Extract 2

A: Would you accept me if I came to your office asking?

M: Why not? (a bit aggressive). Would I accept you? (warm)

A: As an interviewer.

M: No, you know, I won't; if you came to my office and said you wanted to interview me, I'd say, Why? (aggressive) Don't you know enough of me? (warm) (both laughing)

(Uganda, 2003)

Careful analysis of my tapes also shows another paired identity.

PATIENT-COUNSELOR

In the intercept between our first and second meeting, Mahid had experienced close to an economic collapse and suffered from an ever-upcoming depression. In these periods, he used to call me rather frequently stating that he simply wanted me to be available when he needed someone to listen. Rather than this explanation, we should look at how we do being Mahid and me:

Extract 3

M: I was so depressed this morning. You were not here when I needed you the most.

A: I am so sorry.

M: I tried calling you again and again, and I must have sent you six sms.

M: I don't know what you have done to me. . . . You are so different.

A: What do you mean? In what ways am I different?

M: Your generosity. Nobody else has been like that. They take what they want and then fuck off, but with you I can talk. When I am depressed, I need someone to listen. . . . This part is so important to me.

(mobile, August 2003)

Other times we do friendship.

FRIEND-FRIEND

One morning, I found that Mahid had sent me a text message on my mobile in the middle of the night, when his son died from cancer:

Extract 4

Mahid's sms:

Hi got a bad news [my son] passd away i am in shock wil talk 2morow.

(May 29, 2005)
(I have anonymized the name of his son)

Next morning, I called him and offered to call back. He was explicit that he would appreciate my phone calls with reference to need of emotional support. The last is a member's explanation, whereas our focus here is how we constitute our field relationship.

Doing friendship may take different forms also, including humourous situations such as when he thought of visiting my country and I told him he could join my husband training before the hunting season:

Extract 5

A: You'll hit the clay pigeons or me?

M: I'll probably hit you.

A: Yes, you're safe, not me. (both laughing)

(mobile, December 25, 2004)

Or here, in another moment of what might be seen as depression, when he is asking me what I would do when he is gone:

Extract 6

A: I will not even know when you're gone . . .

M: Someone will contact you after one to three months and let you know. What will you do?

A: I will go to your grave, sit down with my tape recorder, and play it over again. We'll have some lo-ong, good talks, and maybe a few conflicts, but we'll sort them out.

M: (laughing)

(mobile, December 19, 2004)

These finely grained ongoing processes moving between such paired identities show field relations to be flexible, dynamic, and complex and less limited to the classic and fixed roles of researcher-researched. However, the ultimate aim here is not the analyses themselves but the ethical implications embedded in this ethno-informed approach.

◆ Research Ethics in Ethnographic Practice: A Delicate Field!

Research ethics make us see what Fielding (2004) referred to as "something noble—sociology's aspiration to be a moral discipline" (p. 249). It also prompts less euphoric reflections. Let me refer to three of these.

The first relates to images of the field motivated by the interview prescriptions to follow middle-class manners in field relations (be polite, nice, emphatic, show interest, etc.), supplied by examples of deviations from this standard, most frequently exiled to the attachments of the report rather than in the text itself. Later, we get more stories telling us that field relations can be complex (Dua, 1979; Rabinow, 1977), problematic (Fielding, 2004; Pandey, 1979), exhausting (Crehan, 1991; Srinivas, 1979), and absorbing (Davis, 1986; Thurnbull, 1986). The point, however, is that such challenges often portrayed as exceptions in fieldwork, rather should be regarded *part of the fieldwork* itself (Ryen, 2005, p. 121), reflecting the ordinary everyday life in which we as ethnographers are supposed to participate (Emerson et al., 1995).

Second, this leads to a paradox in that the possible harm discussed within certain social science disciplines most probably is relatively modest compared with the potentials of other (academic) groups, such as economists (e.g., what happened to all the unskilled women who lost their jobs due to the World Bank's Structural Adaptation Programme in Tanzania?), the medical professions (e.g., side effects of medical treatment or for various reasons lack of treatment), or engineers (e.g., road accidents and lifelong handicaps are guaranteed). Yet social scientists with social interaction as their explicit main focus are one of the groups most eagerly looking for the nuts and bolts of correctness in research. The connotation of opening our fairly modest bag of doubts and worries may be that this is seen as a risky activity calling for external control and protection.

Adler and Adler (2002) offered a historical background to the American situation and pointed to the unintended and unhappy effects this may have caused by researchers now shying away from certain topics (at times, even the question "protecting who?" may have become unclear). Alternatively, we may worry that the effects of local institutional hurdles to make sure our projects are ethical, push some projects over to NGOs and other nonuniversity organizations. Does that imply that the good becomes the best's worst enemy? Will this generate a niche for groups less dependent on (big) corporations for funding?

This takes us to my third point, deriving from Fielding's (2004) reference to the messiness of field relations. He referred to the researchers' own timidity about entering groups of the hard to study or groups resisting being researched. The effect is large variations in knowledge about groups. This is why we know very much about the poor, to whom he referred as too powerless to resist research, and relatively little about the powerful or elites. No code of ethics can overcome this dilemma—another ethical problem partly reflecting researchers' (trained?) incapacity (Veblen, 1953) in handling gross or subtle resistance or even hostility.

The next section departs from the very message of the first, that field relations are complex. It invites the reader to the essence of my chapter, the interpenetration of ethical, methodological, and analytical issues. This makes the question of research ethics in ethnographic work even more complicated and adds to the researcher's responsibility—easily caught up somewhere between paradigm-specific codes or a pluralist model where we get lost in alternatives.

Let me structure my further discussion into two sections, one on getting data and the other on publishing data. For each, I focus on a few ethical dilemmas in ethnography.

♦ Getting Data

The above extracts show how we as researcher and research subject both take part in constituting our relationship in ethnographic research. Mahid and I do this across contexts in the car, during business dinners with third parties, in the office or on the mobile, and across time from morning till evening. However, rather than solving old ethical dilemmas, this tends to introduce more. When borders get blurred, old categories dissolve, and new ones are accomplished, ethical responsibility may become vague. The old perspectives get less relevant and need to be replaced by new perspectives on intricate matters related to dynamic and flexible relations, co-accomplishing data, and a feeling of reality constituted in the ongoing relationship face-to-face or communicated by (new) technology (e.g., mobiles). Let me use a couple of illustrations from ethnographic practice, both well-known dilemmas. The first refers to the professional-private dilemma and the second to truth or, rather, bluff.

THE PROFESSIONAL-PRIVATE DIVIDE

There are numerous examples in my data of my informant narrating long stories (up to three hours in the car) about how he used to catch women's attention—such as the American stewardess or the two Australian women, and so on. In these contexts, the array of our paired identities was initially supplemented by the hero-troublemaker pair. Waiting for linkages to business (some women were heading international NGOs and could provide contracts), I used to listen patiently for some time. When the stories seemed to take off in another direction, I tried to signal my lack of interest by what I saw as indirect cues, such as looking out of the car window away from him (and the tape recorder off). The second time I did this, he got angry in the same way as he did after a long narrative about an Icelandic woman:

Extract 7

M: She would have prepared dinner back home with candles, and I said, "I can't, you come with me." She would not complain. She was nice; also, she would talk to people but be silent when we discussed business. Now she is getting married.

A: Good for her.

(Uganda, November 2003)

He told me that she later got a new boyfriend but was asking him first:

Extract 8

A: What happened to him?

M: Later, he left.

A: Of course, no man will be stand in to the first priority.

(Uganda, November 2003)

My informant got furious, shouting at me and making the two German guests at the neighboring table stop talking, just watching. I made no comments but decisively moved to another table, taking up my book and drinking my coffee. Later, he came back, inviting me over to see a buffalo walking right outside, and we sat together for dinner. He was silent and morose; I felt the atmosphere stifling. Back in the city, he claimed he was quitting the project and decided to get drunk in the bar. My effort to talk together eventually worked well; he mellowed down and eventually apologized.

The narratives are many, and Mahid is an excellent storyteller. We may see the above narrative and the aftermath in different ways that diverge as to research ethics. My lack of interest may be seen as ethically correct by avoiding going private. The dilemma is simultaneously rejecting his masculinity. This way the professional-private dimension gets problematic. On the other hand, the incident can also be seen as a performed event in a context—historical, political, biographical—that shapes the different understandings we bring to and experience during the performance (now as text). All the women in the narratives are cooperative, admiring him, never opposing him, and always sexually available. Also, they are all white (for a discussion of whiteness, stereotypes of the sexuality of the ethnic Other, and ethnic differences, see Nagel, 2003). However, if the performance referred to the historically problematic relationship between ethnicity and gender in the region, the performance in situ could convey transcending of the old colonial ethnic power relations by bonding with the audience—two white German men—by exercising power over the white woman. This is also a good illustration of pain, discomfort, and complexity in the field. Rather than regarding conflicts, temper, or topics as ethically problematic, the ethnomethodological nonjudgmental attitude may rather constitute these as data that may contribute to the ethnographer's central purpose of producing a critical discourse about the worlds we explore.

GETTING LOST IN NICENESS?

These related incidents refer to some problematic ethical dilemmas. First, honesty can cost dearly. Not being so nice (e.g., showing no interest) makes field relations vulnerable and may hold us back from more "natural," less controlled reactions and thereby deprive the informant of responses he or she would have gotten elsewhere. On the other hand, concealment is as much part of our lay repertoire of mundane practices as any other interactional device. (Fine, 1993, claimed that we could rather talk about layers of honesty.) There is a professional worry here. If we want the fieldwork to resemble "natural" situations (as in Silverman's, 2006, quest for "natural data," p. 44), we should also accept disputes. (I have left Mahid's car in anger when he has been too grumpy.) Our problem then is the risk of the informant withdrawing from the project. At this stage in my project, withdrawal would have been extremely inconvenient. However, later when this risk changed (I had plenty), I decided to accept more "temper" from both sides. This opened up stories on the problematic side in running businesses and information on projects I did not know about. It also provided data on categories applied in particular contexts—for example, insight into what he portrays as acceptable or not, stories about people breaking contracts, when his lawyer is getting involved, corruption among staff, and so on. Eventually, we have come to make our mutual levels of energy into humor—for instance, "Wow, I never knew you had that much energy" (Mahid) or "No worries, you are too stubborn to die yet" (Anne, when he is worrying about his health).

Here, we are back to the ethno-informed approach where the imminent danger is failing to explore how members constitute the phenomenon they collaboratively accomplish, but rather just taking it for granted. "Privacy" is a good example. Participating with Mahid and his colleagues has made me notice how they introduce topics and stories that to me would be private (such as sexual activities), whereas there are others (such as corruption) that tend to be more silenced.

The ethical problem is twofold: balance and alertness. We need to manage the balance between the acceptable and the not acceptable. Second, alertness: Stake and Jegatheesan (2006) referred to this in their reference to "zones of comprehension and privacy." When we reduce the interpersonal distance, our comprehension rises—hence the importance of rapport, but at some point we may intrude into that person's zone of privacy. However, it took me three days of mending to restore rapport when I had withdrawn my capacity to be a good listener. This means that at least we could notice who initiates and retreats to simply listening to rather than follow up certain topics. However, no prescriptions or external control mechanisms can solve these ethical dilemmas (see Table 15.1 in Ryen, 2004, p. 244, for an overview of values and ethics in some contemporary paradigms).

This means that we as researchers need to be alert. When categories get blurred, things may also come out of control, as it sometimes happens when fieldwork gets gendered (researcher or woman? private or professional?; see Ryen, in press-a). By taping hours of talk, spending even more hours transcribing the tapes, and then working back and forth analyzing the data, I have gotten close enough to explore the resources or practices members use. This is how we gain access to indigenous meaning and eventually recognize local contexts that may call for being alert to or managing the blurredness of field relations compared with the structural approach.

This is a different way of approaching research ethics and one that demands a capacity to carefully listen to and look for detailed interaction in our communication. Going back to the stories, at times they may be metaphors rather than stories from "there." When stories also come to deal with delicate matters, they also raise a more profound ethical dilemma as to the balance between closeness and detachment. However, "delicate stories" is a cultural category, and only by accepting to listen can we explore rather than take for granted that this is a universal category. By being good listeners, we get access to local perspectives, including phenomena such as "medicine men," which eventually in one of my "African" studies introduced me to the differentiation between real and fake medicine men.

Methodological and ethical issues are closely entangled. We assume that a good capacity to listen brings us closer to indigenous meaning. This situates us as foreigners. The paradox then is that still we import our own categories about delicate issues to guide our attention. Here, we are close to Oakley's (1981) old feminist criticism of patriarchy in methodology. Furthermore, ethnographic practice can be seen as dealing with going into someone's life but withholding the right to decide on and to pick and choose the meaty parts, leaving the rest behind. So Mahid's temper can be seen as a sanction on the researcher violating how we generally do relationships or friendships and possessing rather than sharing the conductor's place.

I have come to accept his stories, even to join him in laughing, though they are less frequent now, and Mahid is fully back in business and out of his depression. This is to say that I am more relaxed as to the ethical dilemma associated with the balance issue. So, over the course of our long association, Mahid and I have become more relaxed with each other. We are now familiar with each other's linguistic codes. Getting to this point has been messy, as Fielding (2004) put it, and thorny, but we are each now able to initiate expressions of concern for the other at, for example, times of illness.

This takes us to my next point, which shows that relating to the referential aspect of language is highly problematic. Maybe there was no Icelandic woman but just a story meant as a subtle (and elegant) metaphor for a too eager Nordic ethnographer, hence his temper.

TRUTH, BLUFF, AND LANGUAGE

Questions about truth used to be the standard in data collection. However, truth and lies are cultural categories that we should not analyze with the same categories that have produced the very same phenomena. Rather we need to explore them. No doubt, ethnographic work can be painful (when people you trust lie to you), annoying (when people trap you), and an exercise in patience (at times it can pay off to control aggression, and since data are confidential we cannot share with others to get comfort). Still, ethnographic practice also offers stories and data to explore "truth."

One evening after dinner, during my fieldwork, Mahid was calling someone. Returning from the lady's room, I came to follow this conversation, where I assume this is what "someone" is saying:

Extract 9

Someone: How are you doing? What did you do last night?

Mahid: Ok. We went dining at Speake.

Someone: Who did you go with?

Mahid: I went with Mark and Philip, and then Kirit joined in.

(Kampala, Uganda, May 2004)

When Mahid later told me that he had been talking to his wife, we can conclude that both activity (dinner) and place (name of hotel) do refer to an external reality. However, my name had been substituted by "Mark and Philip," so I clearly came to hear it as a classic lie. The interest, however, is with how I came to hear it this way. Knowing their identities, wife and husband, they themselves make a paired relational category. As such, the original extract will be heard by his wife as an uncomplicated story of yesterday's activities. If we then refer to Sacks' (Silverman, 2006, p. 186) definition of category-bound activities, of what activities members in such categories may be assumed to do, wives are likely to hear the category "husband–foreign woman," quite disquieting compared with "husband–Mark and Philip." By playing with paired relational categories, my informant simply draws on members' competence in everyday life. In this case, he avoided upsetting his wife's standardized rights and obligations. Rather than distribute moral labels, our task as researchers is to analyze members' mundane practices in constituting "bluffs" or "truth." This is in line with ethnomethodology being characterized by moral nonjudgment (Ryen, 2004, p. 244, Table 15.1). This way, membership categorization allows people to make sense of people and events (Silverman, 2006, p. 146). If any, the interest is rather with what easiness the researcher was admitted into the story as a loyal member (or audience).

Acquiring an awareness of our mundane practices offers an insight we as researchers can draw on to manipulate relationships in the field. At times, I actively draw on this competence, which sometimes makes Mahid comment, "You know how to handle me." I see this as a lay competence I legitimately can employ (especially to handle stress or other messy contexts) without moral troubles given that it is not used to harm people. On the other hand, moral nonjudgment does not release the researcher from his or her moral responsibility, as we shall see below.

♦ Publishing the Data

When it comes to publishing our data, issues where members diverge may come to the fore. Examples would be questions such as whose data these are and what are the consequences of the answer (whatever it may be). Are the implications of a process consent always understood (see Ryen, in press-b)? Can the informant invite other people to share the/my/our data, or can the informant withdraw from the project and demand all data to be destroyed before your publications are out? What consequences does this have for negotiating the project contract? Should research be a money- and lawyer-free zone? If your book is a best-seller (very rare), whose money is it? Whyte's (1981) *Street Corner Society* represents the classic example, including some controversies on this issue. Lately, journalist Åsne Seierstad's (2003) *The Book Seller of Kabul,* which was based on observations while staying in and being with the bookseller and his family during parts of the war in Afghanistan, was taken to court. The Afghanistan family had no information about the book project and reacted against having their family life becoming public. The court settled the conflict, but without exact information to the public about how money from this success would be shared between the journalist and the bookseller Shah Mohammad Rais. However, the bookseller later wrote his own book, *Det var en gang en bokhandler i Kabul* (*Once Upon a Time There Was a Bookseller in Kabul,* Rais, 2006). Whyte's classic sociological book and this new example, both based on being with people in the field, are different books (research vs. journalism), different processes (open vs. masked), and different outcomes (only Seirerstad's book was taken to court by the victim, or main character). Later the bookseller's second wife also took the author to court.

All these issues have been on the agenda of my project willingly or not. Mahid has for a long time wanted me to write a book on his life, but so far our book projects have not overlapped, a familiar situation for many fieldworkers.

However, when he once decided to step out of the project, he asked me to delete all tapes (I pretended this made no impression on me though realizing a potential conflict). His reintroduction made this irrelevant but made me speed up publications. When he later suggested that the data would be great for his children, there are reasons why this complicates a researcher's professional life. Some reasons refer to the ownership of ideas, others to the costs and the efforts that have materialized into these hours of taped talk and notes. Also, he has consented to the project. As I have described elsewhere, Mahid insisted on an oral contract due to the situation in that region (Ryen, 2007). What seemed to be a reasonable suggestion may still turn out not to be so, though the outcome of any court in East Africa may take years to settle.

Later, we have reintroduced the book project. (He tries to discipline me by referring to a journalist he claims already is on the job, though he would reserve the job for me if I can start it soon.) Now, confidentiality is on the agenda. With reference to his health, where he claims his life is soon coming to an end, he claims he has no worries. For me, there is still a family and relatives who may have a voice. Our last discussion topic has been money or potential surplus. His claims have changed in accordance with his financial situation, and the suggestion so far is to set aside some money for a regional NGO.

All these aspects introduce research and research outcomes to the market by pointing to rights, compensations, and monetary outcomes from the product, whose ideas, data, and final products are all part of the researcher's project materialized by external funding. If we then still see data as a collaborative outcome, it may be an ethical dilemma that we now switch back to the researcher's authority. My approach has been patience and more talk without agreeing willingly to give away my data until after publication. Rather, I would be interested in producing alternative publications for different audiences. When we last met, we developed an outline for a book, and our discussion seemed to settle down now replaced by enthusiasm that allowed for a serious discussion of the ethical dilemmas referred to.

◆ Conclusions

Evidently, ethical dilemmas are endemic to ethnographic research. Claiming social reality as collaboratively constituted introduces an alternative approach to how we come to see our activities. First, this illustrates the severe shortcomings of our traditional, dominating research ethics guidelines. Second, making the researcher into a member as in an ethno-informed approach puts further responsibility on his or her shoulders. Rather than making life simpler, it introduces new and other dilemmas and challenges in ethnographic work made apparent when we move from the field to getting our data published. This is closely linked with also allocating a more prominent place for the researched.

This way, we end up with different layers we need to uncover when debating research ethics. First, we have for long accepted that the methods we use inflict on our data. Second, reasonably, they are also crucial to the ethical dilemmas we confront along the research process. And third, what dilemmas we come to see and categorize as "ethical" partly reflect the paradigm, method talk, or interpretive framework we as researchers operate within. So exploring the same field, drawing on the same field relations, and analyzing the same data extracts may offer alternative outcomes. As argued above, it is this interweave or lace of ethical, methodological, and analytical situation that poses the biggest ethical challenge to the research community in general and to the active researcher in particular. Rather than stricter regulations, the answer will be related to a high awareness of the complexity of social science research.

◆ Notes

1. This overview works well for our purpose despite the fact that it is an overview that works

better for the United States than for some other countries (Ryen, 2005).

2. Which for obvious reasons cannot be referred to as "ethical imperialism."

♦ References

Adler, P. A., & Adler, P. (2002). The reluctant respondent. In J. F. Gubrium & J. A. Holstein (Eds.), *Handbook of interview research: Context and method* (pp. 515–536). Thousand Oaks, CA: Sage.

Atal, Y. (1981). The call for indigenization. *International Social Science Journal, 33*(1), 189–197.

Atkinson, P., & Coffey, A. (2002). Revisiting the relationship between participant observation and interviewing. In J. F. Gubrium & J. A. Holstein (Eds.), *Handbook of interview research: Context and method* (pp. 801–831). Thousand Oaks, CA: Sage.

Crehan, K. (1991). Listening to different voices. In M. N. Panini (Ed.), *From the female eye: Accounts of women fieldworkers studying their own communities* (pp. 99–106). New Delhi: Hindustan.

Davis, D. (1986). Changing self-image: Studying menopausal women in a Newfoundland fishing village. In T. L. Whitehead & M. E. Conaway (Eds.), *Self, sex and gender in cross-cultural fieldwork* (pp. 240–261). Urbana: University of Illinois Press.

De Laine, M. (2000). *Fieldwork, participation and practice: Ethics dilemmas in qualitative research*. London: Sage.

Delamont, S. (2004). Ethnography and participant observation. In C. Seale, G. Gobo, J. F. Gubrium, & D. Silverman (Eds.), *Qualitative research practice* (pp. 217–229). London: Sage.

Denzin, N. K. (1997). *Interpretive ethnography: Ethnographic practices for the 21st century*. Thousand Oaks, CA: Sage.

Denzin, N. K., & Lincoln, Y. S. (1994). *Handbook of qualitative research*. Thousand Oaks, CA: Sage.

Dua, V. (1979). A woman's encounter with Arya Samaj and untouchables: A slum in Jullundur. In M. N. Srinivas, A. M. Shaw, & E. A. Ramaswamy (Eds.), *The fieldworker and the field: Problems and challenges in sociological investigation* (pp. 115–126). Bombay, India: Oxford University Press.

Emerson, R. M., Fretz, R. I., & Shaw, L. L. (1995). *Writing ethnographic field notes*. Chicago: University of Chicago Press.

Fielding, N. (2004). Working in hostile environments. In C. Seale, G. Gobo, J. F. Gubrium, & D. Silverman (Eds.), *Handbook of qualitative research practice* (pp. 248–260). London: Sage.

Fine, G. A. (1993). Ten lies of ethnography: Moral dilemmas in field research. *Journal of Contemporary Ethnography, 22*(3), 267–294.

Garfinkel, H., & Sacks, H. (1967). On the formal structures of formal actions. In J. C. McKinney & E. A. Tiryakian (Eds.), *Theoretical sociology: Perspectives and developments* (pp. 337–366). New York: Appleton-Century-Crofts.

Gubrium, J. F., & Holstein, J. A. (1997). *The new language of qualitative research*. New York: Oxford University Press.

Gullestad, M. (1984). *Kitchen-table society: A case study of the family life and friendship of young working-class mothers in urban Norway*. Oslo, Norway: Universitetsforlaget.

Haimes, E. (2002). What can the social sciences contribute to the study of ethics? Theoretical, empirical and substantive considerations. *Bioethics, 16*(2), 89–113.

Hall, R. (1996). *Empires of the monsoon: A history of the Indian Ocean and its invaders*. London: HarperCollins.

Malinowski, B. (1922). *Argonauts of the Western Pacific*. London: Routledge.

Mauthner, M., Birch, M., Jessop, J., & Miller, T. (2002). *Ethics in qualitative research*. London: Sage.

Mead, M. (1935). *Sex and temperament in three primitive societies*. New York: Morrow.

Nagel, J. (2003). *Race, ethnicity and sexuality*. New York: Oxford University Press.

Oakley, A. (1981). Interviewing women: A contradiction in terms. In H. Roberts (Ed.),

Doing feminist research (pp. 30–61). London: Routledge.

Pandey, T. N. (1979). The anthropologist-informant relationship: The Navajo and Zuni in America and Tharu in India. In M. N. Srinivas, A. M. Shaw, & E. A. Ramaswamy (Eds.), *The fieldworker and the field: Problems and challenges in sociological investigation* (pp. 246–265). Bombay, India: Oxford University Press.

Punch, M. (1994). Politics and ethics in qualitative research. In N. K. Denzin & Y. S. Lincoln (Eds.), *Handbook of qualitative research* (pp. 83–97). Thousand Oaks, CA: Sage.

Rabinow, P. (1977). *Reflections on fieldwork in Morocco*. Berkeley: University of California Press.

Rais, S. M. (2006). *Det var en gang en bokhandler i Kabul* [Once upon a time there was a bookseller in Kabul]. Oslo, Norway: Damm.

Reissman, C. K. (2005). Exporting ethics: A narrative about narrative research in South India. *Health: An Interdisciplinary Journal for the Social Study of Health, Illness and Medicine, 9*(4), 473–490.

Ryen, A. (2002). Cross-cultural interviewing. In J. F. Gubrium & J. A. Holstein (Eds.), *Handbook of interview research: Context and method* (pp. 335–354). Thousand Oaks, CA: Sage.

Ryen, A. (2004). Ethical issues. In C. Seale, G. Gobo, J. F. Gubrium, & D. Silverman (Eds.), *Handbook of qualitative research practice* (pp. 230–247). London: Sage.

Ryen, A. (2005). Metodiske og etiske utfordringer i tverrkulturell forskning. In S. Oltedal (Ed.), *Kritisk sosialt arbeid* (pp. 105–135). Oslo, Norway: Gyldendal.

Ryen, A. (2007). Exporting ethics: The West and the rest? In I. Furseth & P. Leer-Salvesen (Eds.), *Religion in late modernity* (pp. 201–218). Trondheim, Norway: Tapir Academic Press.

Ryen, A. (in press-a). Crossing borders? Doing gendered ethnographies of third-world organizations. In B. Jegatheesan & R. E. Stake (Eds.), *Access: A zone of comprehension, and intrusion*. Holland: Elsevier.

Ryen, A. (in press-b). Do Western research ethics work in Africa? A discussion about not taking "the taken-the-granted" for granted. In D. M. Mertens (Guest Ed.), *Mosenodi*. University of Botswana, Gaborone, Botswana.

Schutz, A. (1970). *The phenomenology of social relations*. Chicago: University of Chicago Press.

Seierstad, Å. (2003). *The book seller of Kabul* [Bokhandleren i Kabul]. Oslo, Norway: Cappelen.

Silverman, D. (2006). *Interpreting qualitative data*. London: Sage.

Srinivas, M. N. (1979). The fieldworker and the field: A village in Karnataka. In M. N. Srinivas, A. M. Shaw, & E. A. Ramaswamy (Eds.), *The fieldworker and the field: Problems and challenges in sociological investigation* (pp. 19–28). Bombay, India: Oxford University Press.

Stake, R., & Jegatheesan, B. (2006). *Prospectus: Advances in program evaluation*. Urbana: University of Illinois at Urbana-Champaign.

Thurnbull, C. M. (1986). Sex and gender: The role of subjectivity in fieldwork. In T. L. Whitehead & M. E. Conaway (Eds.), *Self, sex and gender in cross-cultural fieldwork* (pp. 17–27). Urbana: University of Illinois Press.

Vaags, R. H. (2004). *Etikk*. Bergen, Norway: Fagbokforlaget.

Veblen, T. (1953). *The theory of the leisure class: An economic study of institutions*. New York: New American Library.

Vidich, A. J., & Lyman, S. M. (1994). Qualitative methods: Their history in sociology and anthropology. In N. K. Denzin & Y. S. Lincoln (Eds.), *Handbook of qualitative research* (pp. 23–59). Thousand Oaks, CA: Sage.

Wallerstein, I. (2004). Social sciences and the quest for a just society. In P. N. Mukherji & C. Sengupta (Eds.), *Indigeneity and universality in social science: A South-Asian response* (pp. 66–82). New Delhi: Sage.

Whyte, W. F. (1981). *Street corner society*. Chicago: University of Chicago Press.

16

COVENANTAL ETHICS AND ACTION RESEARCH

Exploring a Common Foundation for Social Research

◆ Mary Brydon-Miller[1]

Action research takes many forms, from community-based researchers helping poor women in Tanzania to develop income-generating strategies (Swantz, Ndedya, & Masaiganah, 2001), to teachers working to form closer bonds with at-risk students (Meyer, Hamilton, Kroeger, Stewart, & Brydon-Miller, 2004), to indigenous communities in Guatemala working together to address the impact of state-sponsored violence (Lykes, 2001), to senior employees and members of management in a Norwegian industrial setting working together to address the concerns of older workers (Hilsen, 2006). But despite distinct differences in terms of location, age, and educational attainment of participants, and the issues facing them, each of these examples illustrates a central aspect of action research: It is an inherently and explicitly values-imbued practice. Rather than espouse the doctrine of value neutrality and objectivity demanded in conventional, positivist-inspired research, action research is defined by its unapologetic ethical and political engagement and its commitment to working with community partners to achieve positive social change. This moral positioning of our research practice demands a reexamination of the ways in which we understand and enact research ethics, a reconceptualization that not only shapes the practice of action research but also offers a new perspective on the question of ethics in all forms of social research.

In this chapter, I argue for a fundamental reconsideration of the basic terms by which we understand and evaluate research ethics, suggesting that rather than approach the determination of ethics using the current contractual discourse that regards research as commodity and ethics as a legalistic exchange, we adopt a covenantal ethics founded on the establishment of caring relationships among community research partners and a shared commitment to social justice.

I begin by outlining the fundamental value system that undergirds the practice of action research. This articulation of an embedded ethical position leads to a discussion of the notion of immanent[2] versus imposed ethics as a strategy for distinguishing action research from more conventional research methods. Acknowledging this tension and building on the participatory and socially engaged nature of action research, I then introduce the concept of covenantal ethics—that is, an ethical stance enacted through relationship and commitment to working for the good of others that is an inherent component of action research—and contrast this with the system of contractual ethics, which typifies other research methods and is exemplified by current systems of human subjects review in which the terms of interactions are externally defined and monitored.

This shift to a system of covenantal ethics reflects many of the same concerns raised in discussions of feminist ethics as well as guidelines developed to inform researchers working in indigenous and minority communities and drives a reconfiguration of major components of the research process from the initial definition of the research question to decisions regarding the distribution of research results.

After considering some of the key shifts in practice precipitated by this reframing of our basic notions of research ethics, I conclude with a brief discussion of the ways in which covenantal ethics might inform the development of new strategies for teaching and mentoring ethical research, the establishment and maintenance of community partnerships, and the creation of a more equitable and sustainable agenda for social research in the future.

♦ Comparing the Core Values of Action Research and Conventional Research Models

The core values of action research have been defined as "a respect for people and for the knowledge and experience they bring to the research process, a belief in the ability of democratic processes to achieve positive social change, and a commitment to action" (Brydon-Miller, Greenwood, & Maguire, 2003, p. 15). Reflecting a similar understanding of the basic ethical stance of action research, Reason and Bradbury (2001) described it as "a participatory, democratic process concerned with developing practical knowing in the pursuit of worthwhile human purposes" (p. 1). And Greenwood and Levin (1998) noted that action research "promotes broad participation in the research process and supports action leading to a more just or satisfying situation for the stakeholders" (p. 4) and suggested that it "aims to increase the ability of the involved community or organization members to control their own destinies more effectively and to keep their capacity to do so" (p. 6).

R. Tandon (2005), whose work across India and throughout Asia has provided a model of effective community-based research for over a quarter century, reflected a similar moral framework for defining what he termed participatory research,[3] observing that "its articles of faith include a commitment to collective participation, and empowerment of the ordinary people in having and knowing their world; in envisioning a new society; and in playing their collective roles in that process of transformation" (p. 213). Also using slightly different language to identify their practice, community-based participatory researchers (Israel, Eng, Schulz, & Parker, 2005) nonetheless articulate the same basic set of values. Minkler and Wallerstein (2003), for example, while acknowledging that there is a broad range of practices that fall within the general category of community-based participatory research, suggested that it is the "emancipatory end of the continuum" (p. 7) that should be seen as the goal. And Hall (2003), in his foreword to Minker and Wallerstein's volume, *Community-Based Participatory Research for Health*, encouraged researchers to

> take part in the alternative global movements of the majority world, and support the struggles for justice and democracy in your own communities. The choices you make about the work you do and the life you lead are important and powerful. (p. xiv)

As noted above, authors use different terms to identify similar socially engaged forms of scholarship, and not all practices calling themselves action research reflect the same radical social justice stance defined above, but to a large extent this commitment to open and transparent participation, respect for people's knowledge, democratic and nonhierarchical practices, and positive and sustainable social change forms a common core of values among those within the action research community. Thus, action research might be considered to reflect a set of immanent ethics, a set of values that serve to define the practice itself and to provide a common discourse by which those engaged in this practice can guide their own work and evaluate the contributions of others.

This contrasts sharply with more conventional approaches to research in which the role of the researcher is that of the objective and disinterested observer of a tightly defined and circumscribed set of actions on the part of a group of naive subjects with no expectation that the research will contribute in any direct way to addressing specific concerns of the participants or their communities.[4] This general framework, reflecting the biomedical model of research, functions reasonably well in the settings for which it was originally developed—for example, in the systematic assessment of the risks and benefits of new drug therapies. The problem arises when this same model is generalized as the only scientifically supportable approach to all research with human subjects.

While this assumption of an exclusive claim to all credible processes of knowledge generation may be more explicitly stated in quantitative research, it has also permeated much of qualitative research. As Moss (1992) suggested in describing the role of the ethnographer, the goal "is to interfere as little as possible with the daily routines in the community" (p. 158). And rather than respect for the knowledge and experience of community participants, the attitude of researchers can be downright dismissive. "But if our 'subjects' happen to be wrong or confused or resistant in what they are thinking, then adding their voices to our research may contribute little of importance to the knowledge developing in the field" (MacDonald, 1998, p. 114). Of course, many qualitative researchers do articulate research methods that honor the voices of participants and that raise critical social issues (Brabeck, 2000; Denzin & Lincoln, 2005; Tolman & Brydon-Miller, 2001), positions consistent with those defined within a system of covenantal ethics and the more engaged forms of scholarship that such an ethical stance implies.

These more engaged forms of research notwithstanding, the overall dominance of the biomedical model with its assumptions regarding the necessity of objectivity, distance, and value neutrality has also been reflected in the development of policies and procedures of institutional review boards. Beginning with this understanding of research as without an internal moral compass and reacting to examples of horrific research, such as the medical experiments of Nazi doctors (Lifton, 1986/2000) or the Tuskegee Syphilis Study (Jones, 1993; Thomas & Quinn, 1991), documents such as the Helsinki Declaration on an international level (Human & Fluss, 2001) and the *Belmont Report* in the United States (Sales & Folkman, 2000) attempt to impose a set of ethical requirements on a practice that is otherwise regarded as unequipped to generate any kind of inherent moral framework. It is from efforts such as these that the current human subjects review processes with their catalog of requirements and ever-lengthening compliance documents are created in an attempt to instill ethical values on otherwise amoral research practice.

◆ Contrasting Contractual and Covenantal Ethics

The outcome of this process has been the development of the legalistic, contractual system of practitioner credentialing and project oversight currently reflected in the human subjects review processes in place at most universities and required of most granting organizations.[5] The problem is not in the existence of such systems nor in the individuals who serve on these boards, the vast majority of whom are highly trained professionals dedicated to performing what is most often a thankless task, but it is instead in the all too common belief that simple adherence to the specifications of such documents ensures that the resulting research will be ethical. Rather than consider the broader ethical and moral implications of research, such systems narrow our focus to a minute examination of the precise language of consent forms and a somewhat perverse fascination with whether or not these forms are secured under lock and key for a specified time period. The broader questions of how power relationships frame the discourse of validity in social research, of what real contributions are made to the overall welfare of the community, and of who owns research results and how this information is made available to the public are largely deemed to be outside the realm of the review board's charge and, as a result, too often escape attention altogether. Such concerns place the entire research enterprise more starkly within the broader economic and political systems which favor an individualistic, entrepreneurial relationship to research that emphasizes grantsmanship, the patenting of specific products and processes, and a capitalist approach to knowledge generation quite at odds with the collaborative, egalitarian, social change focus of action research. Placed within this broader economic context, even the seemingly altruistic efforts to bring new, more effective drug therapies to the market are understood as driven by the economic interests of large pharmaceutical companies and the importance of reenvisioning a research ethics truly designed to support the common good rather than common greed becomes all the more apparent.

It is also the case that, based on this unquestioning belief in the importance of objectivity and distance, the very aspects of action research that make it most meaningful and most effective in achieving its goal of positive social change—the relationships among the research participants and the deep and sustained commitment to working together to address important problems—are instead viewed with suspicion and seen as liabilities (liability in a literal sense, given the concern over litigation that governs much of the deliberation of review bodies) rather than as vital mechanisms that strengthen our ability to understand and address important social issues in ethically defensible ways.

In this way, the long-term commitment of action researchers to working with community partners is redefined as coercion and deemed an ethical problem rather than recognized as a powerful form of moral engagement.

If conventional research methods and existing systems of human subjects review dictate a contractual definition of research ethics, action research can best be understood by adopting a model of covenantal ethics,[6] "the unconditional responsibility and the ethical demand to act in the best interest of our fellow human beings" (Hilsen, 2006, p. 27). Hilsen based her discussion of covenantal ethics on the work of William F. May (1980, 1984, 2000) and her broader investigation of the ethical demands of action research on the contributions of the Danish philosopher Knud Ejler Løgstrup (1956/2000). She operationalized this approach to ethics in three specific practices—the acknowledgement of human interdependency, the cogeneration of knowledge, and the development of fairer power relations—paralleling the basic values of action research. The development of trust, both in the sense of developing trusting relationships among research participants as well as helping our community partners develop an ability to "trust in their own powers of action and decision" (Hilsen, 2006, p. 28) is a fundamental imperative of such covenantal ethics. Hilsen went on to suggest that "action research's commitment to promote social justice makes it even more of an ethical demand to take responsibility for the social consequences of the research and make it *explicit* both in our practice and our communications about that practice" (p. 32).

This notion of covenantal ethics and the specific practices of action research are mirrored in the challenges to conventional research raised by feminist scholars.[7] The commitment to grounding our understanding of ethics within the context of human relationships as suggested by covenantal ethics is captured in Meara and Day's (2000) discussion of feminist virtue ethics and in particular in "the other-regarding virtue of respectfulness" (p. 260; see also MacIntyre, 1984; May, 1984). Kitchener (2000) likewise reflected a recognition of the importance of respectfulness and included in her discussion of feminist virtues trustworthiness, the willingness to take responsibility, and caring and compassion, all of which resonate with the values underlying covenantal ethics and action research (see also Noddings, 1999).

The call to move from observation to action likewise is reflected in feminist ethics. "Feminist ethics go beyond moral awareness of particulars, ethical principles, and knowledge of the good to advocate for action to achieve social justice" (Brabeck & Ting, 2000, p. 12). As Kirsch (1999) suggested,

> Researchers must begin to collaborate with participants in the development of research questions, the design of research studies, and the interpretation of data if they want to ensure that feminist research contributes toward enhancing—and not interfering with—the lives of others. Moreover, researchers need to find ways to invite participants to study their own communities and to represent their own voices, values, and lives in public and academic discourse. (p. x)

Feminist action researchers have long advocated such a rapprochement, insisting that "action research and feminism are mutually implicated because action research involves collaboration among all the legitimate stakeholders, the valuation of all knowledge, and the enhancement of fairness, justice, healthfulness, and sustainability—all values that underlie feminism" (Greenwood, 2004, p. 158; see also Brydon-Miller, Maguire, & McIntyre, 2004; Maguire, 1987).

This emphasis on understanding our identity as researchers from the perspective of our relationships with our community partners and on locating our research practice within the context of a shared commitment to social change has been central to explorations of research ethics from the perspective of indigenous and minority communities as well (see, e.g., Cram, Chapter 20, and Chilisa, Chapter 26, this volume, for insightful examinations of this issue). Building on culturally grounded systems of ethics, many of these discussions reflect similar concerns regarding existing frameworks to those raised here, and the ethical systems they offer as solutions often closely parallel the basic tenets of action research. As Hermes (1999) has noted in describing the development of a First Nations' methodology,

> A well-articulated "ethic" that legitimates community-generated research questions and culturally appropriate research behaviors and holds researchers accountable to these standards would displace the current system of research projects that are accountable only to institutions of higher education or funding sources. (p. 87)

Covenantal ethics, with its focus on relationships, respect, and responsibility thus provides a broad framework that addresses many of the issues raised by feminist, minority, and indigenous scholars. Having outlined this new framework for understanding the basic nature of research ethics, how then do these distinctions between immanent and imposed, covenantal and contractual ethics inform the ways in which specific issues facing researchers might be understood? This reconfiguration of our understanding of research ethics has profound implications for the entire research process, from the generation of the research question to the development and distribution of results. In the following discussion, I consider the ways in which this shift might affect practice by focusing on two key points in the research process—the negotiation of informed consent and the question of ownership and control of research results.

♦ Beyond Autonomy and Informed Consent: Negotiating Participation and Defining the Terms of Engagement in the Research Process

A key ethical principle enshrined in current human subjects review processes is the concept of autonomy, reflected within the review process by informed consent procedures. As noted in the *Belmont Report* (Sales & Folkman, 2000),

> Respect for persons requires that subjects, to the degree that they are capable, be given the opportunity to choose what shall or shall not happen to them. This opportunity is provided when adequate standards for informed consent are satisfied. (p. 201)

Reflecting the system of contractual ethics,

> informed consent includes a clear statement of the purposes, procedures, risks, and benefits of the research project, as well as the obligations and commitments of both the participants and the researchers. The resulting explicit agreement is in most cases documented through the use of a written consent form, which should be clear, fair, and not exploitative. (Fischman, 2000, p. 35)

This description suggests a straightforward and transparent agreement between the researcher and the research subject.

However, one troubling aspect of the existing model of human subjects review is the potential for the process itself, and in particular the ritual of the consent form, to contribute to what Newkirk (1996) has referred to as an "act of seduction" (p. 3) on the part of researchers toward their research subjects. As he described the process, "The measures devised to protect those being studied often aid the researcher in the seduction... Typically these forms provide a very brief and often vague description of the project, and then provide a number of assurances" (p. 4); "the form helps to reinforce the impression of the researcher's solicitousness" (p. 4) and "heighten the sense of importance of the study about to be undertaken" (p. 5). After being lulled into a false sense of security and encouraged by the expressed interest and engagement of the researcher to reveal their most deeply felt beliefs and most cherished experiences, subjects are then at the mercy of the researcher, whose selections, interpretations, and judgments of those revelations—which may or may not reflect well on the subjects or truly capture their understandings of events—are received as the voice of superior intellect and perception. This is the part of the process Newkirk referred to as "the betrayal."

In challenging this mode of operation, Newkirk makes three important recommendations: first, that the consent process acknowledge the potential for negative interpretations to be made public; second, that subjects themselves have an opportunity to contribute to the process of interpretation; and third, where concerns exist, that researchers have the obligation to contribute whatever expertise and resources they have toward ameliorating the problem. In this, Newkirk actually outlines a process very close to that of action research and, in emphasizing the relational nature of all social research, suggests solutions that reflect the same basic values as those of covenantal ethics. His final warning is relevant to all of us conducting research with human subjects: "Ultimately, those of us in the university must question the automatic belief in our own benevolence, the automatic equation between our own academic success and ethical behavior. For the stakes are high" (Newkirk, 1996, p. 14).

Boser (2006) raised a concern with the informed consent process related specifically to the practice of action research, but with broader implications for the human subjects review process in general. Noting that action research is a cyclical process involving ongoing negotiation and dialogue among all participants, she observed that "participants cannot give informed consent to research activities in advance, because the full scope of the process of the research is not determined in advance by one individual" (p. 12). She suggested that a more effective means of ensuring that such research is ethical is to develop iterative processes of reconfirming consent that are embedded within the context of the research itself. Furthermore, she noted that differences in power among participants and between researchers and their community partners must be considered and recommended that researchers remain mindful of the potential barriers to participation and open to alternative forms of gathering and disseminating input from community partners. "Integrating consideration of ethical issues into the research cycle, and guiding this consideration through examination of the potential for risk and asymmetrical patterns of power, will promote democratic practices and support realization of the action research potential" (p. 19).

One strategy for reconfiguring the informed consent process that is both more consistent with the notion of covenantal ethics and mindful of the power dynamics noted by Boser is to develop mechanisms for the mutual negotiation of informed consent (Khanlou & Peter, 2005). Such a strategy is articulated by Fisher and Ball (2002) in their description of the tribal participatory research model, in which ongoing review of the research process is explicitly placed under the control of community-based oversight committees. Recounting the devastating impact of governmental programs of relocation of American Indian and Alaskan Native (AIAN) families from their communities and the policy of forcing children to attend boarding schools where AIAN children were forbidden to speak their own languages or practice their own religion, these authors make clear the deep suspicion with which native communities might regard researchers coming in from outside. In many ways, this legacy of exploitation of an oppressed community and the resulting distrust of researchers among AIAN communities parallels the response of African Americans to the Tuskegee Syphilis Study (Thomas & Quinn, 1991), another infamous example of research carried out as a thinly veiled mechanism for maintaining oppression.

Challenging this, the Family Wellness Project described by Fisher and Ball (2002) includes clear tribal oversight, the training and employment of native researchers, and culturally grounded intervention and assessment strategies, including mechanisms such as videos and regular meetings designed to disseminate the results of the research within the communities themselves. As the authors noted, this emphasis on community oversight "is germane to all communities that experience oppression and discrimination" (p. 239).

One central aspect of action research and of covenantal ethics reflected in these studies is the centrality of human relationships and the commitment to working alongside our community partners to bring about positive social change. This should translate more concretely into the creation of community-based review boards, as outlined by Fisher and Ball, whose charge is to ensure that all research being conducted within the community has direct benefits to its members. At the same time, it is vital that researchers recognize that regarding any community as an unproblemmatically homogeneous entity fails to acknowledge the hierarchies of power that exist within any group of humans, privileging some while oppressing others.[8] One of the challenges to shifting the control of review processes to communities, whether you define this as communities of practice or as local communities in a geographic sense, is to develop mechanisms for ensuring broad participation by all factions within a community while respecting the community's own culture and traditions regarding leadership and decision making.

In addition to raising concerns regarding informed consent, the shift from contractual to covenantal ethics can be examined through a second critical aspect of the research process, the determination of ownership, control, and dissemination of the results. In most research settings, the disconnect between the original subjects of research and the final analysis of the information they provide to researchers as well as the lack of understanding on the part of those being studied as to where and how the research will be used contribute to the potential for researchers to take advantage of the situation by furthering their own agendas while overlooking the interests of those taking part in their studies.

◆ *Beyond Anonymity: Negotiating Ownership and Defining the Terms of Distribution of Research Results*

"Nothing about us without us." This motto of the disability rights movement (Charlton, 2000; see also Brydon-Miller, 1993) captures the dilemma of representation and control that marks the question of ownership of research data and decisions regarding where and how research results are distributed. In conventional models of research, these responsibilities are clearly defined as being under the control of the academic researcher. "Respect for privacy and confidentiality is at the heart of the conduct of ethical research with human participants" (Folkman, 2000, p. 49). The common assumption in conducting research with human subjects is that clear mechanisms must be put in place to safeguard the identity of participants in the research process and that this protection is clearly articulated in the informed consent and ensured through strict attention to guarding the confidentiality of research data. In fact, most human subjects review protocols call for any identification of research subjects to be excised from the data and for all research-related materials to be kept in a locked storage facility under the control of the researcher, a stipulation that is now subject to verification by review board staff. Once the data have been analyzed and the results rendered into academic language, the research is published in a peer-reviewed journal or academic volume or presented at a professional conference, which further distances the original owners of the knowledge—the research subjects—from its ultimate destination.

The commodification of the research process is clear in terms of the rewards systems in place, which recognize individual scholars for such publications and presentations, while the universities themselves profit from the funds brought in by large research grants and granting agencies, both public and private, maintain the power to control the way in which knowledge is then translated into policy and product. In general, none of these rewards, despite the rhetoric of human subjects review processes, directly benefit the subjects themselves. In fact, the inclusion of specific monetary incentives for research subjects is regarded as coercive by review boards, and any substantial individual benefit for participation is generally not permitted.

There are actually two related issues in question here. The first is the way in which the knowledge collected during the research process is interpreted and represented, and the second is how that knowledge is then distributed. The question of voice and representation has been widely discussed by scholars from multiple points of view, including feminist, postcolonial, and critical race theorists. Critical race theorists, for example, suggest the use of counter-storytelling—that is, accounts challenging the dominant narrative—as a mechanism for addressing systemic racism (Delgado, 2000). Similarly, postcolonial theorists draw on the concepts of subalternity (Spivak, 1988) to explore questions of voice and agency within marginalized communities. But too often this rhetoric of representation is unaccompanied by any specific mechanisms for taking action or for making the knowledge gained through the research process available and accessible to members of those communities (Williams & Brydon-Miller, 2004).

Reflecting the basic tenets of caring and commitment central to covenantal ethics, action researchers, on the other hand, have developed collaborative strategies for gathering, organizing, and presenting the results of their community-based research. This attention to participation in all phases of the research process provides opportunities for community partners to develop their own interpretations of the materials they create and maximizes the usefulness of this information to the participants in the research process and other members of their community. One such methodology, for example, developed specifically for action research projects is photovoice, a process in which community participants themselves take photographs representing some critical issue or aspect of their lives and then engage in a collaborative process of interpretation of the resulting images (Brydon-Miller, 2006; Lykes, 2001; McIntyre & Lykes, 2004; Meyer et al., 2004; Wang, 1999). These representations, often accompanied by a coauthored explanatory text, can then be used by their creators to develop a more nuanced shared understanding of the issue within the community itself, to educate the broader community about important concerns, and to advocate for change. Working with Mayan women serving as community health care workers, Lykes and her community partners (2001) created photovoice projects that provided opportunities for the participants to "develop individual and collective stories that had heretofore been silenced or spoken only privately to outside researchers or human rights workers" (p. 369). These stories and the community dialogue that resulted from them led to the development of a variety of initiatives intended to improve the lives of local community members and to support the interests of the indigenous population of Guatemala at broader national and international levels as well.

The development and dissemination of materials that more effectively communicate the results of collaborative research efforts is an especially important aspect of action research. Kelly, Mock, and Tandon (2001), for example, in their collaborative investigation with African American community leaders in the city of Chicago, developed a quote book, a training manual, videos, and a graphic representation of their findings to help illustrate their findings regarding strategies for leadership development within the community. As the authors noted, their strategy of including community participants in all stages of the research process marks a shift in power that "clearly validates the indigenous knowledge and experience of community members. However, this shift must be accompanied by providing community members with skills, competencies, and knowledge necessary to design effective programs and policies" (S. D. Tandon, Kelly, & Mock, 2001, p. 215).

This research, as well as the photovoice projects described above, are fine exemplars of covenantal ethics in that they demonstrate respect for the community members who serve as coresearchers, emphasize the critical role of participation and community control, and directly challenge social injustice. It is also important to note that such projects typically take place over an extended period of time, providing an opportunity for the development of genuinely trusting, respectful relationships among all research participants, another key element of covenantal ethics.

The work of the Highlander Research and Education Center, which has for over 75 years been addressing issues of community ownership and control of knowledge, provides another excellent exemplar of the way in which the ideals of covenantal ethics can be put into practice (Horton, 1993; Lewis, 2001). Founded in 1932, Highlander has led the way in the development of community-based examinations of environmental issues, union reform, civil rights training and advocacy, and a variety of other issues. Unaffiliated with any university, Highlander has maintained its independence and hence its ability to address the concerns of community partners without having to bow to the economic and political pressures that face those of us working within more traditional academic settings.

Merrifield's (1993) description of a series of Highlander-sponsored studies of environmental and occupational health illustrates how community researchers can use sophisticated data-gathering techniques, generally believed to be the sole territory of highly trained and credentialed scientists, to address environmental degradation resulting from industrial pollution and other serious health-related problems. These studies as well as other research in areas as diverse as community health (Krieger, Allen, Roberts, Ross, & Takaro, 2005; Schulz, et al., 1998), land ownership and tax reform movements (Horton, 1993), and public policy regarding grandparents providing foster care (Minkler, 1999) demonstrate that action research and covenantal ethics can apply to quantitative studies just as readily as they do to qualitative research.

Finally, any discussion of the question of intellectual property and the development of new, more open systems of knowledge distribution must, of course, acknowledge the immense potential impact of new technologies.[9] The potential impact of social networking tools, auto-publishing, and open access sources has already begun to challenge the traditional bastions of information gathering and distribution, but it remains to be seen whether these new outlets will remain open and active and continue to grow in influence or whether the hierarchical system that has heretofore controlled access to research will find new ways to reassert its control.

♦ Covenantal Ethics as a Common Foundation for Social Research

With its focus on the development of caring and committed relationships, on respect for people's knowledge and experience, and on working with community partners to achieve positive social change, covenantal ethics clearly provides a framework more consistent with the values underlying action research than the existing contractual model. But shouldn't all social research share these aspirations? This is not to say that other forms of both quantitative and qualitative research do not make important contributions to our understanding of social phenomena or that action research is the only means of achieving these goals. Research that expands our understanding of the world in any way should be valued, and it is this very diversity of ways of generating knowledge that allows us to deepen our understanding of social issues and to develop effective strategies for addressing common concerns. That said, if rather than relying on the existing system of imposed contractual ethics as the primary mechanism for assessing research ethics, all scholars began with a grounding in covenantal ethics, we might find that our combined efforts to bring about positive social change are more effective and our own personal sense of fulfillment in our work enhanced.

This is also not to suggest that the existing system of contractual ethics be entirely dismantled. Rather, contractual ethics should be understood as serving the broader demands of covenantal ethics under certain well-defined circumstances. As noted earlier, this system was initially developed to ensure that participants in controlled biomedical studies were fully informed about possible side effects, and in this regard it continues to work fairly well. The shift to covenantal ethics would, however, reframe this review process in fundamental ways. For example, as suggested in the earlier discussion of informed consent, the initial question of which studies should be undertaken, who would participate, and how the research would be conducted would be developed in consultation with community partners. Review processes would also include questions regarding dissemination of research results, requiring scholars to articulate specific plans for making the knowledge gained through their research accessible to members of the public.

If such a reframing of the review process and, indeed, of our fundamental understanding of research ethics sounds overly idealistic and naive, what are the practical considerations of such a shift? Certainly, building trusting relationships with community partners takes time, especially when working in communities in which trust has been betrayed by researchers in the past. It also demands that researchers develop a new set of skills focused on effective communication, consensus building, mediation, and negotiation. And it requires that universities, academic publishing concerns, and funding agencies embrace this new ethical framework as well and respond by reconfiguring systems to reflect this new set of expectations (Brydon-Miller & Tolman, 2001). I conclude this discussion by beginning to examine some of the systemic changes that will be required to support this shift to covenantal ethics.

♦ Anticipating the Broader Implications of the Shift to Covenantal Ethics

The shift to a system of covenantal ethics reframes our understanding of the research process in fundamental ways, not only affecting the nature of the individual research endeavor itself but also demanding changes in the systems of training, monitoring, and evaluating researchers; the development and maintenance of community partnerships; and the very way we understand and value our practice as researchers.

The current emphasis in providing training in research ethics focuses on helping students negotiate the specific demands of human subjects review boards. As part of its bid to win national accreditation for its overall review process, the human subjects review board of my own institution recently instituted an online testing system developed by an outside corporation whose business it is to develop such licensing systems, emphasizing again the entrepreneurial nature of the entire system of academic research. Both faculty and students must demonstrate that they have successfully passed this test before their proposals to the review board will receive consideration. Like so much of current educational practice, it all seems to have come down to achieving a particular score on the test. At conferences and among students and faculty at my own institution, a great deal of the discussion I've heard seems to focus on how to finesse the system rather than on any substantive examination of the deeper ethical imperatives of human subjects research.

When I present the topic of research ethics to my own students, I begin by asking them to reflect on their personal value systems and how this might inform their research practice. We do this through the use of first-person action research projects (Chandler & Torbert, 2003; Torbert, 2001), in which the focus of the inquiry is on the researcher's own practice. The dialogue that results from this process allows for a much more meaningful exploration of the issues of trust, commitment, and social change central to covenantal ethics. This same focus on the ongoing ethical challenges of engaged forms of research must be maintained throughout the student's program and should be supported not only by coursework related to research ethics but also by establishing mentoring relationships and opportunities for institution-wide dialogue in which the ethical issues of research are revisited on a regular basis.

Rather than maintaining what is often an adversarial relationship between institutional review boards and faculty and student researchers, this shift to covenantal ethics includes working within the system to develop more effective mechanisms for ensuring that research involving human subjects reflects the values of caring and commitment in substantive ways. It would be naive to assume that simply invoking a system of covenantal ethics will resolve all ethical problems. Instead, a new form of review, one that recognizes the unique contributions and ethical challenges of multiple forms of research and that engages community partners as informed and empowered contributors to the process, must be developed. Here, Boser's (2006) recommendations regarding iterative cycles of negotiation of the research process and Fisher and Ball's (2002) discussion of local review boards provide important directions for more informed community involvement. Ongoing and inclusive opportunities for discussions of the ethical implications of community-based research held in venues familiar to community partners would help ensure that such research addresses critical social issues as these are defined by community members themselves. At the same time, it is imperative that rather than using the rhetoric of citizen participation to maintain existing systems of oppression (Arnstein, 1969), such dialogue reflect a critical awareness of issues of power and representation among all participants in the process so that the resulting research truly challenges inequality and fosters genuine social change.

Finally, moving away from a contractual definition of research ethics to a covenantal understanding of our deep and abiding responsibility to act in the interest of others shifts our current identification of research as commodity to a system in which *all* research, not simply action research, is regarded as a source of common good. The covenant includes ourselves, our universities, our funding sources, and our communities. And it extends beyond local interests to embrace the problems facing people around the globe, recognizing the most critical ethical imperative—that we dedicate ourselves to working together to address issues of community development, environmental sustainability, and social justice.

◆ Notes

1. I am indebted to my colleagues Anne Inga Hilsen, Annulla Linders, Helen Meyer, Beth Moore, and Bronwyn Williams as well as two anonymous reviewers for their helpful comments on earlier drafts of this chapter.

2. Other authors, including Fromm, Derrida, Foucault, and Baudrillard, have used the phrase *immanent ethics* or some variation of this notion. My use of the term refers specifically to the area of research ethics and the notion that particular values might be a fundamental and defining aspect of research approaches such as action research.

3. Other terms that have been used include *participatory research, participatory action research*, and *community-based research*. Each reflects a distinct genesis, and there are distinctions among these practices in terms of their histories, disciplinary foundations, and so on. The most inclusive term, *action research*, is used here to indicate this range of participatory, socially engaged practices. For more detailed discussions of these various contributions, see Khanlou and Peter (2005), Reason and Bradbury (2001), and Brydon-Miller, Greenwood, and Maguire (2003).

4. There is, of course, a set of values underlying this approach as well. The assumption that there is a scientific truth that can be uncovered and that it is through science that human problems will be solved and the valuing of expert knowledge over other forms of knowing, for example, all reflect a particular value system.

5. Institutional review boards are the standard mechanism for ensuring ethical oversight in the United States and many other countries. However, this system is not universal. Norway, for example, has instituted human subjects review processes through legislation (A. I. Hilsen, personal communication, April 12, 2008).

6. While this notion of covenantal ethics originates in the Judeo-Christian concept of the covenant between God and humankind, I use the term in a more secular sense to suggest a solemn and personally compelling commitment to act in the good of others.

7. It is clearly impossible given the constraints of space and the overall focus of this chapter to do justice to the many variants of feminist theory and their implications for framing our understanding of research ethics. Interested readers are encouraged to see Brabeck (2000) and Kirsch (1999) for more fully developed discussions of this topic.

8. See Catherine Campbell's (2003) volume *"Letting Them Die": Why HIV/AIDS Prevention Programmes Fail* for a stark and compelling examination of the role of power and privilege in a community-based action research project.

9. For an interesting and well-informed discussion of the intersection of intellectual property issues, new technologies, and research ethics, see Carla Shafer's discussion in Greenwood, Brydon-Miller, and Shafer (2006).

◆ References

Arnstein, S. R. (1969). A ladder of citizen participation. *Journal of the American Institute of Planners, 35*(4), 216–224.

Boser, S. (2006). Ethics and power in community-campus partnerships for research. *Action Research, 4*(1), 9–21.

Brabeck, M., & Ting, K. (2000). Introduction. In M. M. Brabeck (Ed.), *Practicing feminist ethics in psychology* (pp. 3–15). Washington, DC: American Psychological Association.

Brabeck, M. M. (Ed.). (2000). *Practicing feminist ethics in psychology*. Washington, DC: American Psychological Association.

Brydon-Miller, M. (1993). Breaking down barriers: Accessibility self-advocacy in the disabled community. In P. Park, M. Brydon-Miller, B. Hall, & T. Jackson (Eds.), *Voices of change: Participatory research in the United States and Canada* (pp. 125–143). Westport, CT: Bergin & Garvey.

Brydon-Miller, M. (2006). Photovoice and Freirean critical pedagogy. In G. H. Beckett & P. C. Miller (Eds.), *Project-based second and foreign language education: Past, present, and future* (pp. 41–53). Greenwich, CT: Information Age.

Brydon-Miller, M., Greenwood, D., & Maguire, P. (2003). Why action research? *Action Research, 1*(1), 9–28.

Brydon-Miller, M., Maguire, P., & McIntyre, A. (Eds.). (2004). *Traveling companions: Feminism, teaching, and action research.* Westport, CT: Praeger.

Brydon-Miller, M., & Tolman, D. (2001). Making room for subjectivities: Remedies for the discipline of psychology. In D. Tolman & M. Brydon-Miller (Eds.), *From subjects to subjectivities: A handbook of interpretive and participatory methods* (pp. 319–327). New York: New York University Press.

Campbell, C. (2003). *"Letting them die": Why HIV/AIDS prevention programmes fail.* Bloomington: Indiana University Press.

Chandler, D., & Torbert, B. (2003). Transforming inquiry and action: Interweaving flavors of action research. *Action Research, 1*(2), 133–152.

Charlton, J. T. (2000). *Nothing about us without us: Disability oppression and empowerment.* Berkeley: University of California Press.

Delgado, R. (2000). Storytelling for oppositionists and others: A plea for narrative. In R. Delgado & J. Stefancic (Eds.), *Critical race theory: The cutting edge* (pp. 60–70). Philadelphia: Temple University Press.

Denzin, N. K., & Lincoln, Y. S. (2005). *The SAGE handbook of qualitative research* (3rd ed.). Thousand Oaks, CA: Sage.

Fischman, M. W. (2000). Informed consent. In B. D. Sales & S. Folkman (Eds.), *Ethics in research with human participants* (pp. 35–48). Washington, DC: American Psychological Association.

Fisher, P. A., & Ball, T. J. (2002). The Indian family wellness project: An application of the tribal participatory research model. *Prevention Science, 3*(3), 235–240.

Folkman, S. (2000). Privacy and confidentiality. In B. D. Sales & S. Folkman (Eds.), *Ethics in research with human participants* (pp. 49–57). Washington, DC: American Psychological Association.

Greenwood, D. J. (2004). Feminism and action research: Is "resistance" possible, and, if so, why is it necessary? In M. Brydon-Miller, P. Maguire, & A. McIntyre (Eds.), *Traveling companions: Feminism, teaching, and action research* (pp. 157–168). Westport, CT: Praeger.

Greenwood, D. J., Brydon-Miller, M., & Shafer, C. (2006). Intellectual property and action research. *Action Research, 4*(1), 81–95.

Greenwood, D. J., & Levin, M. (1998). *Introduction to action research: Social research for social change.* Thousand Oaks, CA: Sage.

Hall, B. (2003). Foreword. In M. Minker & N. Wallerstein (Eds.), *Community-based participatory research for health* (pp. xiii–xiv). San Francisco: Jossey-Bass.

Hermes, M. (1999). Research methods as a situated response: Toward a First Nations' methodology. In L. Parker, D. Deyhle, & S. Villenas (Eds.), *Race is . . . race isn't: Critical race theory and qualitative studies in education* (pp. 83–100). Boulder, CO: Westview Press.

Hilsen, A. I. (2006). And they shall be known by their deeds: Ethics and politics in action research. *Action Research, 4*(1), 23–36.

Horton, B. D. (1993). The Appalachian land ownership study: Research and citizen action in Appalachia. In P. Park, M. Brydon-Miller, B. Hall, & T. Jackson (Eds.), *Voices of change: Participatory research in the United States and Canada* (pp. 85–102). Westport, CT: Bergin & Garvey.

Human, D., & Fluss, S. S. (2001, July 24). *The World Medical Association's Declaration of Helsinki: Historical and contemporary perspectives* (5th draft). Paris: World Medical Association. Retrieved December 11, 2005, from www.wma.net/e/ethicsunit/helsinki.htm

Israel, B. A., Eng, E., Schulz, A. J., & Parker, E. A. (Eds.). (2005). *Methods in community-based participatory research for health.* San Francisco: Jossey-Bass.

Jones, J. H. (1993). *Bad blood: The Tuskegee syphilis experiment* (Rev. ed.). New York: Free Press.

Kelly, J. G., Mock, L. O., & Tandon, S. D. (2001). Collaborative inquiry with African American community leaders: Comments on a participatory action research process. In P. Reason & H. Bradbury (Eds.), *Handbook of action research: Participative inquiry and practice* (pp. 348–355). London: Sage.

Khanlou, N., & Peter, E. (2005). Participatory action research: Considerations for ethical review. *Social Science & Medicine, 60,* 2333–2340.

Kirsch, G. E. (1999). *Ethical dilemmas in feminist research: The politics of location, interpretation, and publication.* Albany: State University of New York Press.

Kitchener, K. S. (2000). Reconceptualizing responsibilities to students: A feminist perspective. In M. M. Brabeck (Ed.), *Practicing feminist ethics in psychology* (pp. 37–54). Washington, DC: American Psychological Association.

Krieger, J., Allen, C. A., Roberts, J. W., Ross, L. C., & Takaro, T. K. (2005). What's with the wheezing? Methods used by the Seattle-King County healthy homes project to assess exposure to indoor asthma triggers. In B. A. Israel, E. Eng, A. J. Schulz, & E. A. Parker (Eds.), *Methods in community-based participatory research for health* (pp. 230–250). San Francisco: Jossey-Bass.

Lewis, H. M. (2001). Participatory research and education for social change: Highlander Research and Education Center. In P. Reason & H. Bradbury (Eds.), *Handbook of action research: Participative inquiry and practice* (pp. 356–362). London: Sage.

Lifton, R. J. (2000). *The Nazi doctors: Medical killing and the psychology of genocide.* New York: Basic Books. (Original work published 1986)

Løgstrup, K. E. (2000). *Den etiske fordring* [The ethical demand]. Oslo, Norway: J. W. Cappelens Forlag. (Original work published 1956)

Lykes, M. B. (with the Association of Maya Ixil Women, New Dawn, Chajul, Guatemala). (2001). Creative arts and photography in participatory action research in Guatemala. In P. Reason & H. Bradbury (Eds.), *Handbook of action research: Participative inquiry and practice* (pp. 363–371). London: Sage.

MacDonald, S. P. (1998). Voices of research: Methodological choices of a disciplinary community. In C. Farris & C. M. Anson (Eds.), *Under construction: Working at the intersections of composition, theory, research and practice* (pp. 111–123). Logan: Utah State University Press.

MacIntyre, A. (1984). *After virtue.* Notre Dame, IN: University of Notre Dame Press.

Maguire, P. (1987). *Doing participatory research: A feminist approach.* Amherst: Center for International Education, University of Massachusetts.

May, W. F. (1980). Doing ethics: The bearing of ethical theories on fieldwork. *Social Problems, 27*(3), 358–370.

May, W. F. (1984). The virtues in a professional setting. *Soundings, 67,* 245–266.

May, W. F. (2000). *The physician's covenant: Images of the healer in medical ethics* (2nd ed.). Louisville, KY: Westminster John Knox Press.

McIntyre, A., & Lykes, B. (2004). Weaving words and pictures in/through feminist participatory action research. In M. Brydon-Miller, P. Maguire, & A. McIntyre (Eds.), *Traveling companions: Feminism, teaching, and action research* (pp. 57–77). Westport, CT: Praeger.

Meara, N. M., & Day, J. D. (2000). Epilogue: Feminist visions and virtues of ethical psychological practice. In M. M. Brabeck (Ed.), *Practicing feminist ethics in psychology* (pp. 249–268). Washington, DC: American Psychological Association.

Merrifield, J. (1993). Putting scientists in their place: Participatory research in environmental and occupational health. In P. Park, M. Brydon-Miller, B. Hall, & T. Jackson (Eds.), *Voices of change: Participatory research in the United States and Canada* (pp. 65–84). Westport, CT: Bergin & Garvey.

Meyer, H., Hamilton, B., Kroeger, S., Stewart, S., & Brydon-Miller, M. (2004). The unexpected journey: Renewing our commitment to students through educational action research. *Educational Action Research, 12*(4), 557–573.

Minkler, M. (1999). Intergenerational households headed by grandparents: Contexts, realities, and implications for policy. *Journal of Aging Studies, 13*(2), 199–218.

Minker, M., & Wallerstein, N. (Eds.). (2003). *Community-based participatory research for health.* San Francisco: Jossey-Bass.

Moss, B. J. (1992). Ethnography and composition: Studying language at home. In G. Kirsch & P. Sullivan (Eds.), *Methods and methodology in composition research* (pp. 153–171). Carbondale: Southern Illinois University Press.

Newkirk, T. (1996). Seduction and betrayal in qualitative research. In P. Mortensen & G. E. Kirsch (Eds.), *Ethics and representation in qualitative studies of literacy* (pp. 3–16). Urbana, IL: National Council of Teachers of English.

Noddings, N. (1999). Care, justice and equity. In M. S. Katz, N. Noddings, & K. A. Strike (Eds.), *Justice and caring: The search for common ground in education* (Vol. 1, pp. 7–20). New York: Teachers College Press.

Reason, P., & Bradbury, H. (2001). Introduction: Inquiry and participation in search of a world worthy of human aspiration. In P. Reason & H. Bradbury (Eds.), *Handbook of action research: Participative inquiry and practice* (pp. 1–14). London: Sage.

Sales, B. D., & Folkman, S. (Eds.). (2000). *Ethics in research with human participants.* Washington, DC: American Psychological Association.

Schulz, A. J., Parker, E. A., Israel, B. A., Becker, A. B., Maciak, B. J., & Hollis, R. (1998). Conducting a participatory community-based survey for a community health intervention on Detroit's East Side. *Journal of Public Health Management and Practice, 4*(2), 10–24.

Spivak, G. C. (1988). Can the subaltern speak? In C. Nelson & L. Grossberg (Eds.), *Marxism and the interpretation of culture* (pp. 271–313). Basingstoke, UK: Macmillan Education.

Swantz, M. L., Ndedya, E., & Masaiganah, M. S. (2001). Participatory action research in Southern Tanzania, with special reference to women. In P. Reason & H. Bradbury (Eds.), *Handbook of action research: Participative inquiry and practice* (pp. 386–395). London: Sage.

Tandon, R. (2005). Social transformation and participatory research. In R. Tandon (Ed.), *Participatory research: Revisiting the roots* (pp. 203–215). New Delhi, India: Mosaic Books.

Tandon, S. D., Kelly, J. G., & Mock, L. O. (2001). Participatory action research as a resource for developing African American community leadership. In D. L. Tolman & M. Brydon-Miller (Eds.), *From subjects to subjectivities: A handbook of interpretive and participatory methods* (pp. 200–217). New York: New York University Press.

Thomas, S. B., & Quinn, S. C. (1991). The Tuskegee Syphilis Study, 1932–1972: Implications for HIV education and AIDS risk programs in the black community. *American Journal of Public Health, 81*(11), 1498–1505.

Tolman, D. L., & Brydon-Miller, M. (Eds.). (2001). *From subjects to subjectivities: A handbook of interpretive and participatory methods.* New York: New York University Press.

Torbert, W. R. (2001). The practice of action inquiry. In P. Reason & H. Bradbury (Eds.), *Handbook of action research: Participative inquiry and practice* (pp. 250–260). London: Sage.

Wang, C. (1999). Photovoice: A participatory action research strategy applied to women's health. *Journal of Women's Health, 8*(2), 185–192.

Williams, B. T., & Brydon-Miller, M. (2004). Changing directions: Participatory-action research, agency, and representation. In S. G. Brown & S. I. Dobrin (Eds.), *Ethnography unbound: From theory shock to critical praxis* (pp. 241–257). Albany: State University of New York Press.

17

RESEARCH ETHICS AND PEACEMAKING

◆ Colin Irwin

The critical ethical challenge for the social scientist/peacemaker is to reconcile the divergent interests of the parties to a conflict. In the context of applied social science, Donald Campbell pointed to the solution to this problem through full disclosure and the participation of *adversarial stakeholder(s)* in both the design of experiments and the interpretation of results. By applying these principles to public opinion research in Northern Ireland, political parties from across the political spectrum were able to generate a program of prenegotiation problem solving and public diplomacy that helped secure the Belfast Agreement. These methods have been successfully reproduced in Macedonia, Bosnia-Herzegovina, Kosovo and Serbia, and Cyprus. Comparisons are made between this body of work and polls run by the U.S. State Department, Organization for Security and Co-operation in Europe (OSCE), British Home Office, and others in Northern Ireland, the Balkans, Israel, Palestine, Cyprus, Muslim World, and in the United Kingdom with respect to the "War on Terror." The political and methodological difficulties predicted by Campbell are identified and analyzed in terms of failed negotiations and ineffective peacemaking. The global implications of these failures require a global response. From the perspective of research ethics, this can be done by extending the proposition that "people make peace with their enemies" to an operational moral code that "social scientists must make peace research with their adversarial stakeholders."

Introduction

Peacemaking is arguably one of the most important tasks anyone can undertake. However, in practice, it is also one of the most difficult endeavors a social scientist can engage in, given the conflicts of interest between the parties involved. The key ethical challenge for the researcher is to reconcile these divergent interests with questions of justice while maintaining the confidence and safety of their informants and themselves. This is not easy, but it must be done if the imperative of peacemaking is to be taken forward as a subject of practical enquiry.

I have been involved in programs of applied social research and peacemaking in Northern Ireland, the Balkans, Cyprus, Israel, Palestine, and the emergent global conflict between the West and the Muslim World. The work completed in Northern Ireland was a great success, so I shall begin there and then look at some of the other conflicts and their research failings concluding with some methodological/moral principles that, if adopted, could help bring peace where there is now war. First, however, the critical problem of "conflicts of interest" needs to be addressed and resolved as a theoretical concern.

Reconciling Conflicts of Interest

Donald Campbell (1986) believed political power within the scientific community and social-ideological commitments (national, political, religious, economic self-interest, etc.) to be major obstacles to the achievement of an objective social science. He also believed that applied social science was even more problematic, almost to the point of being impossible where matters of policy are concerned (Campbell, 1984). Among a list of such difficulties he noted the following:

> A second difference between applied social science and laboratory research is that the still greater likelihood of *extraneous, nondescriptive interests and biases* entering through the inevitable discriminatory judgemental components that exist in all science at the levels of data collection, instrument design and selection, data interpretation, and choice of theory. As we move into the policy arena, there is much less social-system-of-science control over such discretionary judgement favouring descriptive validity, and there are much much stronger nondescriptive motives to consciously and unconsciously use that discretionary judgement to, so to speak, break the glass of the galvanometer and get in there and push the needle one way or the other so that it provides the meter reading wanted for non-descriptive reasons. (Campbell, 1984, p. 315)

Campbell (1986) went on to note that "since scientists have to live in the larger society and are supported by it in their scientific activity, it becomes probable that science works best on beliefs about which powerful economic, political, and religious authorities are indifferent" (pp. 108–135). Clearly, quite the opposite is the case when dealing with matters of state, waging war, and making peace. In these circumstances, all too frequently, both domestic electoral imperatives and powerful international economic, political, and religious interests are at work. Fortunately, however, Campbell provided us with some solutions to these difficult problems of political interests and questions of methodology. In addition to all the usual recommendations for open, transparent, multimethod, multiteam research, he suggested that

> there should be *adversarial stakeholder* participation in the design of each pilot experiment or program evaluation, and again in the interpretation of results. We should be consulting with the legislative and administrative opponents of the program as well as the advocates, generating measures of feared undesirable outcomes as well as promised benefits. (Campbell, 1984, p. 328)

This, with some modifications appropriate to the needs of negotiations, public opinion research, and public diplomacy, is essentially what was done as part of the Northern Ireland peace process. And having successfully replicated the Northern Ireland methods in a number of other states, it is now possible to say what the most important characteristics of a "peace poll" are (Irwin, 2006a):

1. All the parties in a conflict should draft and agree to all the questions.

2. All the communities and peoples in the conflict should be asked all the questions.

3. All the results should be made public.

These principles of polling and public diplomacy in conflict settings may appear to be very simple. Perhaps they are. But, regrettably, this is rarely done.

♦ The Northern Ireland "Peace Polls"

After nearly 30 years of terrorist actions, the transfer of regional power to London and numerous failed political initiatives to find a solution to the "Irish question," the Forum for Peace and Reconciliation in Northern Ireland was established in 1996. Critically, a system of proportional representation was used to elect representatives to the Forum, which ensured participation from all sections of the Northern Ireland community. Ten parties thus gained the right to nominate representatives to the negotiations on the future of Northern Ireland along with the British and Irish Governments, all under the chairmanship of Senator George Mitchell of the United States.

Perhaps the single most important feature of the Northern Ireland "peace polls" was the participation of the parties to these negotiations in their design and, in particular, their collective agreement to the questions being asked. The value of the public opinion surveys was a direct function of the care and attention given to asking the right questions, and it was to this end that the greatest resources were applied. Running a poll would normally take several weeks while the design of the questionnaire would often take as many months. In practice, the work undertaken to produce an acceptable draft questionnaire went through the following stages:

1. A letter was sent out to all the parties inviting them to participate in the design and running of a public opinion poll in support of the peace process.

2. At an initial meeting with party officers, a party negotiator would be assigned to the task and issues relating to methods, topics, timing, and publication would be discussed.

3. An outline or "first draft" questionnaire would be sent out to the party contacts for discussion purposes with a covering letter that summarized the views of parties with regard to methods, topics, timing, and publication. This letter would also contain a list of the party contacts so that they would be free to discuss any matters arising with each other.

4. The second and subsequent meetings with party representatives would review the draft questionnaire to register party requests for changes and additions.

5. The third and subsequent letter and draft questionnaire noted all requests for changes and additions. For the sake of clarity, footnotes would be removed relating to previous drafts so that all notes referred only to current alterations.

6. When the questionnaire started to "stabilize" it would be sent out for pretesting to identify fieldwork difficulties relating to problems of

comprehension and length. The parties were notified that this stage in the work had been reached and that they should identify any final changes they might like as well as indicating which questions could possibly be left out to be dealt with in a later poll, if so required.

7. Final changes were made by those running the poll on the evidence of objective fieldwork tests. These changes were noted in the final draft that was sent to all the parties with a covering letter detailing the survey research schedule and publication date.

8. From this point onward, parties were not permitted to interfere in any way with the program of research, analysis of data, and publication. However, they did receive full statistical reports and were free to make criticisms of the findings if they wished so.

Thus, in accordance with Campbell's exacting standards for applied social science research, parties from across the political spectrum representing loyalist and republican paramilitary groups, mainstream democratic parties, and center cross community parties, all agreed the questions to be asked, the research methods to be used, the timing, and mode of publication. The first two polls dealt with procedural or "shape of the table" issues, the third poll explored all the major elements of a comprehensive settlement, the fourth poll tested that settlement against public opinion, and the last four polls dealt with problems of implementation.

This program of research is described in considerable detail in my book *The People's Peace Process in Northern Ireland* (Irwin, 2002a), where all aspects of methodology from questionnaire design to report writing and dissemination are dealt with in considerable detail, so I shall not say much more about that here.[1] However, I would like to add some comments about the politics of the research not mentioned in the book. The British and Irish governments were opposed to this independent program of research. They did not wish to participate in the writing of any of the questions, designing the research, or acting as funders. They even raised objections to my presence in the building where the parties were provided with office space but were overruled by the parties at a meeting of their business committee. The two governments had their own plans for a settlement and did not want those plans disturbed too much by either the will of the parties or the people of Northern Ireland. Fortunately, Senator Mitchell and his U.S. staff understood the benefits of the independent research and supported it. So the program of public opinion polling went ahead, the Belfast Agreement was concluded, and the parties knew they could win a referendum before the referendum was run. Seventy seven percent of the Northern Ireland electorate said "yes" to the Agreement when it was tested against public opinion (Irwin, 1998) and that support only dropped to 71% in the referendum proper. Our program of applied social research was both successful and, as these things go, quite accurate. Other questions of research ethics relating to issues of confidentiality, independence, transparency, and safety were dealt with as follows:

1. All discussions with the parties were confidential so that they could explore issues for which they might have been called a "traitor" in public. For similar reasons, no papers were signed or written permissions given. Everything was done on trust.

2. In the preamble to every questionnaire, the person being interviewed was told who was doing the research and why, who was paying for it and where, and how all the results would be made public. Their confidentiality was assured and they were free to participate or not.

3. The independent Joseph Rowntree Charitable Trust covered most of the bills.
4. All the results were published in the local press, in reports to the parties, the negotiations chairperson, and the two governments. Also, when the Internet became available they were posted on the project Web site www.peacepolls.org.
5. My contacts in the parties with paramilitary associations (IRA [Irish Republican Army], UVF [Ulster Volunteer Force], UFF [Ulster Freedom Fighters]) provided me with their mobile telephone numbers. If any of the interviewers had problems, then that problem was promptly sorted out with a few phone calls.

I would be the first to admit that working with up to 10 political parties and getting them all to agree to a common program of research is not easy. It requires considerable patience, but the benefit of building a political consensus supported by a majority of the electorate is well worth the effort. It brings stability through agreements that are clearly seen to have the support of the people.

◆ Macedonia

The Centre for Democracy and Reconciliation in South East Europe (CDRSEE) had taken a keen interest in my Northern Ireland work since I met one of their directors at a conference on the future of Cyprus in Istanbul in December 1998. Subsequently, in April 2000, they invited me to Thessaloniki in Greece to address a group of young parliamentarians from the Balkans and in 2002, when there appeared to be a real possibility of war breaking out between Macedonians and Albanian insurgents, they asked me to run a poll in the former Yugoslav Republic of Macedonia to analyze the problem from the local point of view, and hopefully identify some solutions. Meetings were held in Skopje and Tetrovo with representatives from a broad cross section of society and the major ethnic groups. Building on the Northern Ireland experience informants were asked what they thought the major problems were and what could be done to resolve them.

Interestingly, the results for the "problems" question were very similar to results gained for equivalent questions run in Northern Ireland (Irwin, 2004a), and perhaps that is why, when I showed the Northern Ireland work to Macedonians and Albanians they were most enthusiastic about doing a similar piece of research for themselves. Cooperation with the local people was never a problem once they knew the issues that they raised would be properly addressed and that all the results would be put into the public domain.

Inevitably, in the "solutions" question, each community placed items at the top of their "wish lists" that dealt with their particular community's "problems." Remarkably, a "state-funded university in Albania" came in at the very top of the Albanian list at 85% "essential" and at the very bottom of the Macedonian list, at only 1% "essential." Such polarization was indicative of deep social divisions that needed to be addressed. But both Albanians and Macedonians also put "free and fair elections" near the top of both of their lists at 80% and 72% "essential," respectively. On this point, they shared a common concern, so when this issue was explored in much more detail with a range of measures that could be taken to ensure free and fair elections, a series of policies were identified that would gain the support of all sections of society.

The international community took note, appropriate actions were taken, the forthcoming elections were a success, and Macedonia, not for the first time, avoided being drawn into a war that had been so disastrous for her neighbors (Irwin, 2002c). Given the degree of ethnic tensions present in Macedonian society, the First President, Kiro Gligorov, must take much credit for keeping his people out of the Balkans war. I had an opportunity to spend an hour with him going through the draft questionnaire before it was run. He took a very keen interest in it and remarked how thorough and relevant he thought the questions were when compared with the surveys he had been used to seeing prepared by the contractors for the U.S. State Department. Later that year, when I had an opportunity to raise this point with European Union (EU) staff in Brussels one senior diplomat remarked that he had once sat on the lawn of the U.S. Ambassador's residence in Skopje drinking cocktails while composing such questions for inclusion in such polls. This methodology clearly does not meet the standards for engagement by interested parties recommended by Campbell, refined for public opinion purposes in Northern Ireland, and now replicated in Macedonia. Additionally, unlike the State Department polls, all the results were published in the local press to stimulate critical discussion and maximize their public diplomacy impact. Finally, the results were also published as a review "Forum" article (Engstrom, 2002; Irwin, 2002b, 2002c; Troebst, 2002) in *The Global Review of Ethnopolitics* so that Campbell's standards for "adversarial . . . interpretation of results" could also be met (Campbell, 1984). Public opinion polls, in particular, seem to lend themselves to this most creative of academic formats (Hancock, 2003; Irwin, 2003a, 2003b; Kennedy-Pipe, 2003; Noel, 2003).

◆ Bosnia and Herzegovina

Following the success of the Macedonian poll, the CDRSEE teamed up with the BBC World Service Trust to undertake a program of public diplomacy and good governance in Bosnia and Herzegovina. Using the same "problems" and "solutions" methodology employed in Northern Ireland and Macedonia, detailed results were obtained for literally hundreds of policies that could be implemented to strengthen and consolidate their peace and move the country forward along the path to EU membership. Subjects covered included the causes and consequences of the war, problems with the Dayton Agreement, political culture and elections, interethnic relations, public corruption and the criminal justice system, the economy, education, the role of women in society, the media, domestic governance, and the role of the international community. With only a few exceptions, there was a great deal of agreement about what the major problems were and what needed to be done by government and the international community to remedy the situation (Irwin, 2005a).

The peace agreement "hammered out" in Dayton, in November 1995, was designed to bring an end to the war by rewarding the military and political leaderships of the Bosniak, Serb, and Croat factions with a share in federal power and administrative control over their respective enclaves. The result was an unstable peace with ultimate authority resting in the hands of the Office of the High Representative, a constitution that few understood, and a system of government that, for the most part, simply did not work. Although the Dayton Agreement stopped the violence, it could not also be the legal foundation on which to build an efficient, modern, and economically sound state ready to take its place as a new member of the EU. The people of Bosnia-Herzegovina understood this very well and knew what had to be done to put matters right.

In Northern Ireland, *The Downing Street Declaration* (1993) and *The Framework Documents* (1995) outlined many of the central features later found in the Belfast Agreement, completed in 1996. People knew what was coming. Similarly, numerous reports heralded the need for reform in Bosnia-Herzegovina, and this opinion poll suggested that the people were ready to make the necessary changes. However, following the publication of the poll, the High Representative, Paddy Ashdown, while echoing some of the main conclusions of the survey, also squarely placed the responsibility for such reform with the people and their politicians:

> The Dayton Agreement was not designed for state building but to end a war. It ought to be changed, perhaps, but that is not the business of the international community. This issue will be decided by the citizens of Bosnia-Herzegovina because it is their country. (Ashdown, 2005)

Their country, "yes" but not altogether their constitution, and like the people of Northern Ireland, they may well need some help. The OSCE Democratization Department run an extensive program of public opinion polling in Bosnia-Herzegovina in support of reform, and although I was given access to much of their recent work when I was there, a senior manager pointed out that a great deal of it was not published and they did not undertake research projects in partnership with local politicians. However, the manager thought that this might now be a good idea. I can only hope that this has been done as the results of this poll suggest that, as in Northern Ireland, such engagement can be used to explore and define the steps that need to be taken to achieve reform with, critically, strong support from the general public.

♦ Kosovo and Serbia

I was first asked if I would be undertaking a poll in Kosovo when I was in Macedonia in 2002. The Albanians living there thought it would be a good idea but the opportunity did not arise until the CDRSEE were able to secure funding for such a project in 2005 as a prelude to the negotiations for the "final status" of Kosovo. This project was technically more difficult than the previous projects as it entailed running two simultaneous polls: one in Kosovo for Kosovo Albanians, with a booster sample for the remaining Serbs, and one in Serbia for Serbs, with a booster sample for Serb IDPs (internally displaced persons) from Kosovo. It was also more politically difficult given the strength of mistrust and ill feeling between the two communities who had to be separated and/or protected by NATO forces. This reality was reflected in the poll under the now familiar headings of "problems" and "solutions," which dealt with topics relating to Serb and Albanian relations, security, how negotiations should proceed, what might happen if negotiations failed, and Kosovo's "final status" (Irwin, 2005b).

All the questions on matters of security and relations between Kosovo Albanians and Serbs indicated that the ideal solution of complete safety, choice of citizenship, and full equality was at best an aspiration that could be strived for. It was a dream that would take at least a lifetime to achieve, if ever. But what could be achieved was real progress toward this ideal in terms of social and political reform in combination with suitable constitutional arrangements that would go as far as such arrangements could to ensure security for all. By bringing together the most workable elements of all the questions reviewed in the solutions half of the report, this could be done and must be the objective of negotiations. Implementation, however, will take time. Fortunately, both Kosovo Albanians and Serbs welcome the involvement of the international community, particularly the EU, whose influence in the region was on the rise.

This program of research had been undertaken with input from politicians, academics, and journalists, and from staffers in the presidents offices on down, in both Pristina and Belgrade. They all got the reports, including the UN negotiating team, and I was delighted to see all the relevant parties at the press conferences held in Pristina and Belgrade in October 2005. Of course, I thought this program of research should be taken forward as part of the negotiations process and when I was in Washington later that year, the Academy for Educational Development (AED) informed me that they had been asked to do this. Unfortunately, they also informed me that they had been told by the U.S. Mission in Pristina that they were not allowed to include track one politicians in their project. I explained to AED that if such interference in the independence of their work was imposed on them, then their project would most likely fail just as surely as the recent Cyprus negotiations (reviewed later in this chapter), and I recommended they bring this fact to the attention of the U.S. Mission in Pristina. I do not know, but can only hope that the AED was subsequently given a free hand to undertake their program of research with input from the local politicians who must make the peace and ultimately take responsibility for it.

♦ Israel and Palestine

Following the conclusion of the Belfast Agreement in 1998 and the "Mitchell Review" of the Agreement in 1999, Atlantic Philanthropies awarded me a two-year fellowship in 2000 to explore the possibilities of applying the methods developed there internationally. With the assistance of this grant, I made arrangements to visit Jerusalem in 2002, and it soon became clear that a group of suitable people could be brought together to design and run polls similar to those undertaken in Northern Ireland. Naomi Chazan, who was then the Deputy Speaker of the Knesset and a past Director of the Truman Institute for the Advancement of Peace, as well as Ghassan Khatib, Director of the Jerusalem Media and Communication Centre and who later became the Minister of Labor in the Palestinian Authority cabinet, both expressed a keen interest in such a project.

The Director of the Palestinian Academic Society for the Study of International Affairs, Mahdi Abdul Hadi, was particularly interested in running a poll that explored the possibilities for elections in the Occupied Territories. Some questions were drafted, and with the support of the French government, he was to fly to Paris to examine these issues further. But when his colleagues were stopped at Israeli checkpoints and prevented from joining him at the airport, the project was brought to a close and elections were not held until after Arafat's death in 2004. Freedom of association and freedom of expression is a minimum requirement for this kind of peace research, and this condition could not be met at that time.

Regrettably, the public opinion polling and peace research is not as well coordinated between the two communities in Israel and Palestine as it needs to be, or even between the academics and the politicians within each community. These omissions lead to results that fail to realize their full potential by frequently examining only one side of what may be a common problem and/or leaving out what may be the most critical or important questions that need to be addressed. For example, the results of Segal's (1999) public opinion poll and analysis on the future of Jerusalem was largely dismissed by Palestinians because it failed to test his proposals for dividing the city against their preferred option for an open shared city. Similarly, when Shikaki (2003) tested various options for dealing with the problems of Palestinian refugees and their right of return, his results were largely dismissed by their refugee agencies because they felt his questions did not properly address their concerns (Nashashibi, 2003; Sitta, 2003). And finally, although Hermann and Yuchtman-Yaar's (2002) excellent analysis of Israeli public opinion clearly demonstrates that support for Barak's peace proposals were very problematic, they ignore comparable Palestinian data that showed Arafat was in a very similar situation. In this case, unfortunately,

Campbell's *adversarial stakeholder(s)* did not cooperate to jointly participate "in the interpretation of results." If peace negotiations are to be successful, then realism is required on both sides and all parties need to know where everyone's red lines are.

Although cooperation between public opinion and peace researchers in Israel and Palestine has improved in recent years, the research is not done as an ongoing collaborative enterprise with party negotiators in an effort to pin down the details of an acceptable accommodation. The "people" are not brought along in and with negotiations in a proactive public way so that when deals are attempted, they tend to fail for lack of public preparation. Regrettably, President Clinton's efforts may have failed because of this lack of prenegotiation problem solving and "stage setting," and it seems very likely that future efforts may similarly fail if negotiating practices are not changed (Klein, 2002).

With this point in mind, after presenting a paper on this topic in Jerusalem in May 2006, I asked the major Palestinian and Israeli polling and peace research organizations, if they would like, to engage in a joint project to introduce best practice from Northern Ireland into their work. All the Palestinian organizations welcomed such an opportunity, some even offered funding, but all the Israeli institutions declined. Negotiations, of any kind, it would seem, were not then part of their agenda. In June, Israel invaded Gaza, and in July they invaded Lebanon.

An official from the U.S. Consulate in Jerusalem once asked me what I do when I get the wrong results. I tried to explain that it was not possible to get a wrong result if the questionnaire covers all the issues fairly and if the sampling is accurate. He was a little surprised that I publish everything. He did not seem to understand. He wanted to put his finger in Campbell's galvanometer and "cherry pick" the meter reading he desired. This approach to public opinion and peace research does not work and must be abandoned. Cyprus was another sad example of this kind of failure.

◆ Cyprus

Following meetings and lectures at the Nobel Institute and Peace Research Institute in Oslo (PRIO), I was invited to attend a meeting of the Greek-Turkish Forum in Istanbul in December 1998. The meeting was organized by PRIO and the Norwegian Foreign Ministry with Richard Holbrooke, President Clinton's Special Envoy for Cyprus in the Chair. I made a presentation of my Northern Ireland work to the Greek and Turkish Cypriots present and explained how it was used to help build a consensus around the Belfast Agreement. They subsequently decided they would like to undertake a similar program of research in Cyprus and even settled on the subject for the first poll, the full range of confidence-building measures being discussed at the Forum. We expected strong positive responses to all the matters being raised, and from there we intended to go on to deal with the more difficult political issues that would have to be addressed to find a solution to the Cyprus problem in later polls. We had a plan of action.

Unfortunately, the U.S. State Department took over the plan and substituted a program of confidential polls of their own that mixed up questions about the future of Cyprus with questions that analyzed political support for local politicians and U.S. foreign policy. These polls did indicate that a solution to the Cyprus problem would be easier to achieve than the Northern Ireland settlement (Irwin, 2006b). Regrettably, however, the results of these polls were not undertaken as part of a proactive program of public diplomacy and were therefore of little value as an aid to the Cyprus peace process. Indeed, these polls may have done more harm than good. When I eventually got to Cyprus in 2002, the U.S. Embassy staff believed that they were dealing with an intractable problem that was almost impossible to solve because the type of questions that ended up in the media were frequently biased toward the "problems" and away from the "solutions."

The public diplomacy dangers of allowing these kinds of questions to be run in separate media polls on the island were brought to the attention of the U.S. Embassy staff in Nicosia, U.S. government officials in Washington, and members of the UN negotiating team in Cyprus. I also pointed out that the U.S. program of polling was relatively undeveloped when compared with the Northern Ireland work and that a lot more could be done with it to make a positive contribution to the Cyprus peace process. But those responsible for the U.S. polling did not seem to understand or just simply did not want to understand, so the Greek-Turkish Forum invited me back to the island later that year to talk directly to members of the Greek and Turkish Cypriot negotiating teams as well as representatives of civil society. Although the Greek Cypriot negotiators wanted to go ahead with a poll, the Turkish Cypriot government did not. However, the Turkish Cypriot opposition parties (who are now in power) did want to proceed, but in the end, without U.S. support, no polls were undertaken and without the benefits of an effective program of public diplomacy, both the negotiations and subsequent referendum failed in April 2004, and Cyprus remained divided.

Given their special responsibilities for Cyprus, the Foreign Affairs Committee (FAC) of the U.K. House of Commons launched an investigation into the failure of these negotiations and referendum. Fortunately, in the meantime, Alexandros Lordos, a Cypriot psychologist, frustrated by these same failures undertook his own program of public opinion research to examine why the UN plan had been rejected by the Greek Cypriots. It should be pointed out that he did this at his own expense. His poll and analysis clearly demonstrated that an agreement could have been reached if better adjusted to the needs of both communities (Lordos, 2004). The FAC (2005) recognized this fact in their report. Lordos (2005) then undertook another poll, but this time, in the Turkish Cypriot North, and he then presented the results of both polls to the Wilton Park conference on *Cyprus: The Way Forward* in February 2005. Wilton Park is an Executive Agency of the U.K. Foreign and Commonwealth Office and they concluded as follows:

> The importance of regular opinion polling was underlined at the conference to indicate public opinion on a range of issues at different stages of the negotiations before the public are asked to vote on the whole package. Experience elsewhere has shown that there is often much more flexibility on the part of the public than politicians believe. (Wilton Park Conference, 2005, para. 30)

Subsequently, on June 22, 2005, the same point was made to the UN Security Council by Sir Kieran Prendergast as follows:

> Mr. President . . . There are some important positives to acknowledge. All parties wish to see some sort of resumption of active UN good offices. All parties accept that the UN plan should serve as the document on which negotiations would resume. Political figures on both sides in Cyprus are maintaining cordial contacts with each other in an effort to promote mutual understanding. There are useful contacts at other levels too, whether among experts on particular subjects or among ordinary people now that they are able [to] cross to the other side. And I was interested to learn that an independent bicommunal survey that polled attitudes to potential changes to the UN plan found the encouraging result among grass roots opinion on both sides that it might be possible to make certain

changes that would secure majority support for the plan in both communities. (Prendergast, 2005, para. 20)

If the Greek and Turkish Cypriots who had wanted to undertake a program of public opinion research and public diplomacy in 1998 had been encouraged in this enterprise instead of being discouraged, then it seems very likely that the Cyprus problem could have been solved in 2004. The FAC and Wilton Park reports detail the failures of simply "doing deals behind closed doors" very well indeed and, unfortunately for the people of Cyprus, stand as a prime example of how NOT to undertake negotiations in the modern world of informed electorates, a free press, adherence to democratic principles, and referenda. Fortunately, no one has died as a result of these failures in recent years and the international community can now make good on their omissions. But the same cannot be said of relations between the West and the Muslim World and what is called the "War on Terror." Across the Middle East and around the world, the death toll mounts.

♦ The Muslim World and the "War on Terror"

The U.S. Department of State presently undertakes an average of two polls a year in most countries where they have a mission (General Accounting Office [GAO], 2003). But the primary purpose of these polls is to gather information on local party political strengths and weaknesses, local social and political issues, and international relations with an emphasis on the United States and U.S. foreign policy. A June 2003 Pew Research Center 20-nation public opinion survey found extremely unfavorable attitudes toward the United States in the Muslim World (Pew, 2003), and U.S. government efforts at public diplomacy to turn the tide met with only mixed success (William K. Fung Multidisciplinary Workshop, 2003). With a view to making U.S. public diplomacy more effective in their dealings with the Muslim World, the 2003 reports of both the U.S. GAO (2003) and the Council on Foreign Relations (CFR, 2003) advocated much greater use of public opinion polls. However, the CFR observed that

> the imperative for effective public diplomacy now requires much wider use of newer channels of communication and more customized, two-way dialogue and debate as opposed to "push-down," one-way mass communication. (p. 6)

> U.S. foreign policy is too often communicated in a "push-down" style that does not take into account the perspectives of the foreign audience or open the floor for dialogue and debate. (p. 30)

The research methods developed in Northern Ireland and successfully reproduced in the Balkans and Cyprus clearly do not make this mistake, and in an effort to achieve the kind of balanced dialogue sought as an ideal by the Council on Foreign Relations, I was invited to make recommendations to the U.S. State Department in October 2003 at a seminar arranged for this purpose by the Yaffe Center for Persuasive Communication (2003) at the University of Michigan. Participants included public opinion experts, social psychologists, journalists and media specialists, advertising and public relations executives, political scientists, and area studies specialists with a focus on, for example, Middle East public attitudes (Tessler, 2003) as well as public diplomacy policymakers from the U.S. State Department. Remarkably, all these experts told the State Department essentially the same thing and that was to listen to what the target audience had to say and to take their views "on board" when formulating policies and communicating programs of remedial action.

Regrettably, this advice has not been followed up with adequate effect. Applications made by myself (Irwin, 2004b) and with colleagues (Irwin & Guelke, 2004) to the U.S. Institute of Peace, U.K. Economic and Social Research Council (ESRC), and appropriate U.S. and U.K. government departments, to critically examine public opinion research as it relates to Muslim communities and the Muslim World, were all turned down in 2004. Disappointingly, the work that has been done falls far short of the standards for applied social research set by Campbell and, as such, fails to detail adequate solutions to the problems of establishing good relations with and between Muslim peoples and their states. In Northern Ireland, similar omissions led to a failure to properly understand the causes of Catholic alienation in the 1970s (Guelke, 1968) resulting in two more decades of insurgency and civil war. The United States, the United Kingdom, and the Muslim World cannot afford to repeat these mistakes again. But the limited polling that has been done in Britain since the London bombings on July 7 and 21, 2005, do point to the dangers that should have been properly researched and identified following the events of 9/11, 2001.

The primary responsibility for monitoring such attitudes, values, and relevant dependent and independent variables rests with the U.K. Home Office. They started their Citizenship Survey in 2001 with a national sample of 10,000 and minority ethnic booster sample of 5,000. Initially, this very extensive poll was run once a year but it was increased to twice a year in 2003. Data from these surveys are fed into the Home Office Civil Renewal Unit, Active Community Unit, Race Equality Unit, and Community Cohesion Unit. Unfortunately, none of the questions in these surveys dealt directly with support and/or justification for terrorist activity. In particular, there were no questions on attitudes toward the foreign policy of the United Kingdom and her allies in the Middle East (Smith & Wands, 2003) and, perhaps in part due to these obvious biases in data collection, the Home Affairs Committee's Inquiry into Terrorism and Social Cohesion drew no conclusions about either the extent of radicalization among the British Muslim population or the full range of grievances that might lay at the heart of their alienation. In their Sixth Report published in April 2005 the Home Affairs Committee concluded,

> We believe that the analysis in the Cantle report remains valid. Key issues in the report, such as the importance of leadership, especially at a local level, the need to overcome segregation, the role of schools and the importance of opportunities for young people and the need for clarity over what it means to be British, are central to the problems discussed in this inquiry. The threat of international terrorism brings a new dimension to existing issues, and perhaps makes their resolution even more pressing—it does not change them. (Home Affairs Committee, 2005, para. 13)

But political analysts have concluded that British involvement in Iraq has increased Britain's vulnerability to terrorist attacks (Gregory & Wilkinson, 2005) and Al-Quaeda has attributed the cause of the London bombings directly to the UK's actions in the Middle East (Ayman al Zawahiri, 2005).

> Hasn't Sheik Osama bin Laden told you that you will not dream of security before there is security in Palestine and before all the infidel armies withdraw from the land of Muhammed. (Ayman al Zawahiri, 2005)

Not surprisingly then, following the London bombings, independent polls undertaken by YouGov for the *Daily Telegraph* (King, 2005) and by Communicate Research (2005) for *Sky News* addressed these politically sensitive issues directly (see also *The Sun*/MORI 2005 poll). In the CommunicateResearch poll, 2% of 462 Muslims interviewed on July 20/21 "agreed" or "strongly agreed" with what the suicide bombers did on July 7 and in the YouGov poll conducted between July 15 and 22, 6% of 526 Muslims interviewed said the bombings were justified.

Perhaps influenced by the results of these polls, Dominic Grieve, the opposition Conservative Party shadow Attorney General, expressed the view that the London suicide attacks were "totally explicable" because of the deep anger felt by British Muslims over Iraq. Hazel Blears, the Home Office minister, much to the annoyance of many leaders in the Muslim community, strongly rejected this analysis (Morris & Brown, 2005).

In this case, the failure of the Home Office research can best be characterized in terms of Campbell's *adversarial stakeholder(s)* not being allowed or encouraged to explore "measures of feared undesirable outcomes" in terms of alienation and radicalization in the context of British foreign policy in the Middle East. Unlike Cyprus, however, this failure has not contributed to a failed negotiation and referendum, but to a failure of intelligence, resultant bombings, and deaths.

◆ Conclusion

Unfortunately, across the full spectrum of applied peace research, the problems of conflicting interests are no less acute with disastrous results for all concerned. "Dead wrong in almost all of its prewar judgments" was the damning conclusion of the nine-member bipartisan commission set up by the U.S. President to critically examine the failure of the U.S. intelligence community to accurately assess Iraq's chemical, biological, and nuclear weapons capabilities (The Commission on the Intelligence Capabilities of the United States Regarding Weapons of Mass Destruction, 2005). Lord Butler's report reached similar conclusions with regard to the failings of the British intelligence community although the language used was far more circumspect (Butler, 2004). Should anyone have been surprised? Donald Campbell would not have thought so. Indeed, he might have been more surprised if the U.S. and U.K. intelligence communities had got things right and supported the findings of the UN inspectors in opposition to the political agendas of their respective governments. How can this problem be solved?

The observation that "people make peace with their enemies" provides us with an ethical principle on which to build an operational moral code. By extension, "social scientists must make peace research with their adversarial stakeholders." If they do this, they can become peacemakers. Wars could be avoided, lives could be saved, and the world would be a much, much better place. Conversely, if they work for the narrow interests of one government alone, then they run the risk of placing their hands in that state's spilt blood.

◆ Note

1. There are separate chapters on both quantitative and qualitative methods in the book, which are also summarized in my (Irwin, 2001) paper "How public opinion polls were used in support of the Northern Ireland peace process," which is freely available on the Internet at www.ethnopolitics.org and www.peacepolls.org (see also Irwin, 1999, 2004a).

◆ References

Ashdown, P. (2005, January 18). Interview in *Nacional* (Zagreb).
Ayman al Zawahiri. (2005, August 4). *al Jazeera* [video tape].
Butler, Lord of Brockwell. (2004, July 14). *Review of intelligence on weapons of mass destruction.* Report of a Committee of Privy Counsellors to the House of Commons. London: Her Majesty's Stationery Office.

Campbell, D. (1984). Can we be scientific in applied social science? In R. Conner, D. G. Altman, & C. Jackson (Eds.), *Evaluation studies review annual* (Vol. 9, pp. 26–49). Reprinted in E. S. Overman (Ed.). (1988). *Methodology and epistemology for social science: Selected papers Donald T. Campbell* (pp. 315–334). Chicago: University of Chicago Press.

Campbell, D. (1986). Science's social system of validity-enhancing collective belief change and the problems of the social sciences. In D. W. Fiske & R. A. Shweder (Eds.), *Metathory in social science: Pluralisms and subjectivities* (pp. 108–135). Chicago: University of Chicago Press.

Council on Foreign Relations. (2003). *Finding America's voice: A strategy for reinvigorating U.S. public diplomacy.* Report of an Independent Task Force: Peter G. Peterson, Chairman. New York: Author.

The Commission on the Intelligence Capabilities of the United States Regarding Weapons of Mass Destruction. (2005, March 31). *Report to the President of the United States.* Washington, DC.

CommunicateResearch. (2005, July). *Sky News poll.* Retrieved August 6, 2006, from www.communicateresearch.com/poll.php?id=61

The Downing Street Declaration. (1993, December 15). Formally titled The Joint Declaration on Peace issued by John Major, then British Prime Minister, and Albert Reynolds, then Taoiseach (Irish Prime Minister), on behalf of the British and Irish Governments.

Engstrom, J. (2002, September). The common ground. *The Global Review of Ethnopolitics,* 2(1). Retrieved August 6, 2006, from www.ethnopolitics.org/ethnopolitics/archive.html

The Framework Documents. (1995, February 22). A New Framework for Agreement. A shared understanding between the British and Irish Governments to assist discussion and negotiation involving the Northern Ireland parties.

Gregory, F., & Wilkinson, P. (2005, July). Riding pillion for tackling terrorism is a high-risk policy. In *Security, Terrorism and the UK* (ISP/NSC Briefing Paper 05/01, pp. 2–4), London: Chatham House.

Guelke, A. (1968). *The age of terrorism and the international political system.* London: IB Tauris.

Hancock, L. E. (2003, March/June). Pushing for peace and stability: Some observations on Colin Irwin's polls. *Global Review of Ethnopolitics,* 2(3/4). Retrieved August 6, 2006, from www.ethnopolitics.org/ethnopolitics/archive.html

Hermann, T., & Yuchtman-Yaar, E. (2002). Divided yet united: Israeli-Jewish attitudes toward the Oslo process. *Journal of Peace Research,* 39(5), 597–613.

Home Affairs Committee. (2005, April). *Sixth Report, House of Commons, London.* Retrieved August 6, 2006, from www.publications.parliament.uk/pa/cm200405/cmselect/cmhaff/165/16502.htm

House of Commons Foreign Affairs Committee. (2005). *Cyprus, second report of session 2004–05.* London: Stationary Office.

Irwin, C. J. (1998, March 31). Majority say yes to the search for settlement. *Belfast Telegraph.*

Irwin, C. J. (1999). The people's peace process: Northern Ireland and the role of public opinion polls in political negotiations. *Security Dialogue,* 30(3), 105–117.

Irwin, C. J. (2001, September). How public opinion polls were used in support of the Northern Ireland peace process. *The Global Review of Ethnopolitics,* 1(1), 62–73. Retrieved August 6, 2006, from www.ethnopolitics.org/ethnopolitics/archive.html

Irwin, C. J. (2002a). *The people's peace process in Northern Ireland.* Basingstoke, UK: Palgrave Macmillan.

Irwin, C. J. (2002b, September). Forum Macedonia: An opinion poll and its implications. *The Global Review of Ethnopolitics,* 2(1). Retrieved August 6, 2006, from www.ethnopolitics.org/ethnopolitics/archive.html

Irwin, C. J. (2002c, September). Forum Macedonia: Reply—Making dreams come true. *The Global Review of Ethnopolitics,* 2(1). Retrieved August 6, 2006, from www.ethnopolitics.org/ethnopolitics/archive.html

Irwin, C. J. (2003a, March/June). Devolution and the state of the Northern Ireland peace process. *The Global Review of Ethnopolitics,* 2(3/4). Retrieved August 6, 2006, from www.ethnopolitics.org/ethnopolitics/archive.html

Irwin, C. J. (2003b, March/June). International negotiation best practice: A reply to Hancock, Noel and Kennedy-Pipe. *The Global Review of Ethnopolitics,* 2(3/4). Retrieved August 6, 2006, from www.ethnopolitics.org/ethnopolitics/archive.html

Irwin, C. J. (2004a). Using public opinion polls to support peace processes: Practical lessons from Northern Ireland, Macedonia, Cyprus, Israel and Palestine. In A. Guelke (Ed.), *Democracy and ethnic conflict: Advancing peace in deeply divided societies.* Basingstoke, UK: Palgrave Macmillan.

Irwin, C. J. (2004b, Spring). *Improving relations with, and within, the Muslim World: Applying lessons of public diplomacy from Northern Ireland.* Application to U.S. Institute of Peace (USIP), Washington, DC.

Irwin, C. J. (2005a, September). A people's peace process for Bosnia and Herzegovina? *Ethnopolitics,* 4(3), 1–18. Retrieved August 6, 2006, from www.ethnopolitics.org/ethnopolitics/archive.html

Irwin, C. J. (2005b, October). *Coming to terms with the problem of Kosovo: The peoples' views from Kosovo and Serbia.* Retrieved August 6, 2006, from www.peacepolls.org

Irwin, C. J. (2006a). The Northern Ireland "Peace Polls." *Irish Political Studies,* 21(1), 1–14.

Irwin, C. J. (2006b, May 22–23). *Public opinion and the politics of peace research: Northern Ireland, Balkans, Israel, Palestine, Cyprus, Muslim World and the "War on Terror."* Palestinian Centre for Policy and Survey Research and the Harry S. Truman Research Institute for the Advancement of Peace Joint Conference: Public Opinion, Democracy and Peace Making, Notre Dame of Jerusalem Centre, Jerusalem.

Irwin, C. J., & Guelke, A. (2004). *A critical analysis of public opinion research and support for peace processes.* Application to ESRC, New Security Challenges Programme.

Kennedy-Pipe, C. (2003, March/June). The story from the polls: Some reflections. *The Global Review of Ethnopolitics,* 2(3/4). Retrieved August 6, 2006, from www.ethnopolitics.org/ethnopolitics/archive.html

King, A. (2005, July 23). One in four Muslims sympathises with motives of terrorists. *Daily Telegraph,* London.

Klein, M. (2002, November 22). Bar-Ilan University, Israel, *Failed Israeli and Palestinian Interactions,* Royal Irish Academy.

Lordos, A. (2004). *Can the Cyprus problem be solved? Understanding the Greek cypriot response to the UN peace plan for Cyprus.* Retrieved August 6, 2006, from www.help-net.gr/download.htm

Lordos, A. (2005). *Civil society diplomacy: A new approach for Cyprus?* Retrieved August 6, 2006, from www.help-net.gr/download.htm

MORI. (2005, July 23). *Attitudes of British Muslims.* Retrieved August 6, 2006, from www.mori.com/polls/2005/s050722.shtml

Morris, N., & Brown, C. (2005, August, 3). Senior Tory says that suicide attacks are "totally explicable." *The Independent.* Retrieved August 6, 2006, from http://www.independent.co.uk/news/uk/crime/senior-tory-says-that-suicide-attacks-are-totally-explicable-501240.html

Nashashibi, I. M. (2003, August 25). Member Arab Media Watch and US Director of Deir Yassin Remembered, *Shikaki's rigged survey: Palestinians and the right of return.* Retrieved August 6, 2006, from www.counterpunch.org/nashashibi08222003.html

Noel, S. (2003, March/June). Public opinion and the peace process in Northern Ireland: A comment. *The Global Review of Ethnopolitics,* 2(3–4). Retrieved August 6, 2006, from www.ethnopolitics.org/ethnopolitics/archive.html

Pew. (2003). *Views of a changing world 2003, Pew Global Attitudes Project,* Pew Research Center, Washington, DC. Retrieved August 6, 2006, from http://pewglobal.org/reports/display.php?ReportID=185

Prendergast, K. (2005, June, 22). Briefing to the Security Council on the Secretary-General's Mission of Good Offices in Cyprus.

Segal, J. M. (1999, December 13–15). *A Solution for Jerusalem Grounded in the reality of the Attitude of the Israeli and Palestinian Publics,* The International Conference on Jerusalem, The Royal Institute of International Affairs (Chatham House), London.

Shikaki, K. (2003, January–June). *Results of PSR Refugees' Poll in the West Bank/Gaza Strip, Jordan and Lebanon on Refugees' Preferences and Behavior in a Palestinian-Israel Permanent Refugee Agreement. Palestinian Centre for Policy and Survey Research.* Retrieved August 6, 2006, from www.pcpsr.org/survey/polls/2003/refugeesjune03.html

Sitta, S. A. (2003). President Palestine Land Society (London), Right to return of Palestine refugees, *Al-Ahram Weekly,* September 2, 2003, and *Al-Ahram Weekly English,* August, No. 651, pp. 14–20. Retrieved August 6, 2006, from http://weekly.ahram.org.eg/2003/651/op11.htm

Smith, P., & Wands, S. (2003, March). *Home Office Citizenship Survey 2001, Technical Report.* Prepared for Home Office, BMRI Social Research. Retrieved August 6, 2006, from www.homeoffice.gov.uk/rds/pdfs04/hocstechreport.pdf

Tessler, M. (2003, October 16–17). Director, Center for Political Studies, University of Michigan, "Middle East Attitudes and Opinions," *Communicating with sceptical audiences: Challenges and solutions,* The Yaffe Center, Ann Arbor, MI.

Troebst, S. (2002, September). The great divide. *Global Review of Ethnopolitics,* 2(1). Retrieved August 6, 2006, from www.ethnopolitics.org/ethnopolitics/archive.html

U.S. General Accounting Office. (2003, September). *U.S. Public Diplomacy, State Department expands efforts but faces significant challenges* (GAO-03–951). Report to the Committee on International Relations, House of Representatives.

William K. Fung Multidisciplinary Workshop. (2003, October 16–17). *Workshop on communicating with sceptical audiences: Challenges and solutions.* Yaffe Center for Persuasive Communication, University of Michigan, Ann Arbor. Retrieved August 6, 2006, from www.yaffecenter.org/yaffe.nsf/0/A30E7D70C2E0A68085256DBD000D6223?OpenDocument

Wilton Park Conference. (2005, February 7–10). *Cyprus: The way forward.* Report on Wilton Park Conference WPS05/24, Larnaca, Cyprus.

SECTION IV

ETHICAL ISSUES IN RESEARCH PRACTICE

This section addresses what the Kitcheners in Chapter 1 refer to as intermediate-level ethics, the ethics of particular cases. Researchers' ethical thought, decision making, and action at this level are, of necessity, heavily informed by their situational knowledge and, to the extent that decisions must be made on an ad hoc basis during the normal research process, highly dependent on each researcher's ordinary moral sense. As such, employment of higher-order ethical thought will only occur to the extent that researchers are socialized into and have internalized the ethical code(s) of their discipline(s), any legal issues pertaining to the specific research effort, and any taboos or demands made by the culture of the research setting. Ethical principles underlying development of those codes/laws/customs, even if known, may or may not be invoked. Ethical theory and metaethics, if involved at all, are only likely to be applied analytically after the fact.

How does the researcher, seeking to be ethical, shape his or her ordinary moral sense such that, without thinking about it as an ordinary instrument to be taken from the research toolkit as an object of reflection, it comes, instead, as reflex, to be incorporated in his or her work seamlessly? Are there ways in which the responsible researcher can consciously increase the likelihood that his or her ordinary moral sense can be relied on to come unbidden to the fore when ethical challenges are encountered?

Hazel Symonette's "Cultivating Self as Responsive Instrument" (Chapter 18), which opens this section provides a persuasive response. "Know Thyself!" Although a researcher's topics and settings may change substantially over the course of a lengthy career, the researcher's sense of abiding self remains, at core, a constant. And a part of that constant is the ordinary moral sense. American English speakers, for example, recognize that one person has "a heart of gold" and that another is "rotten to the core." Similarly, in the unwritten Mina language of West Africa, one person may be recognized as "ahmay gnoin," beautiful inside, and another as "ahmay gnignon," rotten meat. Symonette reminds us that, as the popular saying repeats, "Wherever I go, there I am," and, thus, in addition to self-knowledge awakening the individual's moral sense, self-knowledge also is a prerequisite to knowing the specifics of a research situation and to being able to be both authentic and culturally responsive within it. She highlights the influence on ethical practice of the specifics of any situation inclusive of the researchers' attitudes, expectations, relationship skills, knowledge base, and methodological strengths and weaknesses.

At the same time, Peggy Gabo Ntseane, in Chapter 19, "The Ethics of the Researcher-Subject Relationship: Experiences From the Field," reminds us that, no matter how globalized, for most of the planet's people, there is a specific geography called "home" in which one must mind one's manners, consult with traditional authority, and give a good accounting of oneself as a member of the community. Ntseane's home, Botswana, is one that few readers have experienced. Nevertheless, it is likely that most of us will be able to empathize with her frustrations as she returns to Botswana for her doctoral research after training in the United States, where she has learned conformity to professional ethical codes, processes, and procedures that are at best irrelevant to the concerns of her community and, at worst, antithetical to it. For all of us, our ordinary moral sense is sometimes at odds with our professional training. This chapter and, indeed, several others in this section challenge the reader to rethink the situatedness of ethical problem solving.

Like Ntseane's chapter, Fiona Cram's (Chapter 20) is strong in its sense of place. However, the struggle depicted in "Maintaining Indigenous Voices" is not one of how, in a practical sense, one might reconcile the demands of seemingly incommensurable systems, but, rather, as an indigenous person, she reflects on the way in which the Maori people of her homeland Aoteroa (New Zealand) have been misused and misrepresented by colonization and by research completed by people who, even if well meaning, are ignorant of indigenous beliefs, lifestyles, skills, values, and sensibilities. Using the metaphor of "shoes that don't fit," she illustrates how nonindigenous researchers have marginalized and continue to marginalize the Maori and calls for Kaupapa Maori research (research in the Maori way), research review, and self-depiction as a means of decolonization, knowledge building, and empowerment. The implications of Maori values are translated into guidelines for ethical research.

David Matsumoto and Caroline Jones (Chapter 21) engage in cross-cultural research that does not evoke a single place, but spans a multiplicity of cultures. Their chapter, "Ethical Issues in Cross-Cultural Psychology" discusses issues of design, sampling, handling of sensitive topics, data management, and interpretation of findings in the context of cross-cultural comparison. Since it is not possible for an individual researcher to have site-specific expertise in the as many as 30 or more cultures and 50 or more languages that might be involved in a cross-cultural study, this chapter also introduces the ethics of cross-cultural collaboration.

Linda Silka's "Partnership Ethics" (Chapter 22) also brings the reader into situations in which social science researchers collaborate. Partnerships may occur across universities, research centers, community agencies, organizations, and interest groups. They may occur across institutions within the same community, across communities, and even cross-nationally. Partnerships confront not only many of the same cultural challenges as those Matsumoto and Jones describe, but also may entail working together over long periods of time and across evolving research interests. As in postcolonial situations as described by Cram, partnerships, too, are brought face-to-face with issues of power and status. While every partnership is different, each shares a common pattern. Cyclical concern with control of funding, of process, of access, and of information predictably provoke ethical dilemmas that commonly recur over the lifetime of any and all.

One specific area Silka identifies as a source of possible contention and of ethical dilemmas is that of data presentation. This topic is also addressed in the final two chapters of the section, Julianne H. Newton's "Visual Representation of People and Information: Translating Lives Into Numbers, Words, and Images as Research Data" (Chapter 23) and Bruce Brown and Dawson Hedges' "Use and Misuse of Quantitative Methods: Data Collection, Calculation, and Presentation" (Chapter 24).

Newton and Brown and Hedges emphasize that to be an ethical researcher, one must keep one's skills honed and tools both up to date and sharpened. Graph or photograph, meta-analysis or factor analysis, the ethical researcher knows the strengths and limitations of his or her tools and makes no misleading claims either out of ignorance or by intent. However depicted, in words, numbers, or images, data representation has consequences for those whose lives and whose experiences are represented, for those who seek to understand, for those who chose to act on the basis of the information, and for those whose lives may be affected by their actions. Both Newton and Brown and Hedges provide suggestions that will increase the likelihood of fair representation fairly understood. And both ground that likelihood in the researcher's self-knowledge, skill, professionalism, and ordinary moral sense.

In sum, this section tells us that to be ethical, social science research is site specific *and* it is global, that these two realities challenge us to reevaluate the limits of individuals' ordinary moral sense, professional codes of ethical conduct, and the ethical values tied to specific time and place. It also tells us that, in the end, it is in the researcher herself or himself and his or her ordinary moral sense that contradictions can be recognized and labeled, if not resolved.

18

CULTIVATING SELF AS RESPONSIVE INSTRUMENT

Working the Boundaries and Borderlands for Ethical Border Crossings

◆ Hazel Symonette

Culture and context are critical shapers of social research processes, interpretations, and judgments. Ethical practice and excellence in research are intimately intertwined with orientations toward and responsiveness to diversity, and most importantly, one's boundary-spanning capacities for authentically engaging diversity. Diversity includes those consequential dimensions of human difference that have socially patterned influences on interpersonal relations and the nature of the interface with organizations, institutions, and other aspects of social structure: notably, human differences that make a substantive difference for access, process, or success. Because cultures and contexts are dynamic and ever changing, this is a lifelong process. It calls for ongoing personal homework in expanding and enhancing one's portfolio of multicultural or intercultural resources and other boundary-spanning competencies.

Too often, we researchers—from our privileged standpoints—look but still do not see, listen but do not hear, touch but do not feel. As Kaylynn TwoTrees (2003) aptly put it, "privilege is a learning disability." We do violence to others' truths when we fail to develop and refine the self as an open, diversity-conscious and expansively learning-centered, responsive instrument. Without vigilant attention, our work suffers greatly from such excellence-eroding burdens. Honoring these considerations summons us to expand our understandings of the self in dynamically diverse contexts within power and privilege hierarchies at a single point in time and also our understandings of the contexts embodied in the self across time.

Effectively doing this self-development work requires that we prioritize our focus on human differences that make a socially patterned difference—most notably, those associated with privileged social identities. Consequently, we need to hold in high consciousness the fact that privilege is a feature of a social system and not an intrinsic attribute of individuals.

> People have or don't have privilege depending upon the system they're in and the social categories other people put them in. . . . Privilege exists when one group has something that is systematically denied to others not because of who they are or what they've done, but because of the social category they belong to. (Johnson, 2001, p. 38)

Researchers, especially in applied research and evaluation contexts, have been one of the privileged authorities because their roles typically confer social powers to define reality and make impactful judgments about others:

> Privilege grants the cultural authority to make judgments about others and to have those judgments stick. It allows people to define reality and to have prevailing definitions of reality fit their experience. Privilege means being able to decide who gets taken seriously, who receives attention, who is accountable to whom and for what. (Johnson, 2001, p. 33)

In "Vision, Privilege and the Limits of Tolerance," Cris Cullinan (1999) succinctly characterized the implications and operational dynamics embodied in privileged social identities. With those identity markers come the presumption of competence, the presumption of worthiness, and the presumption of innocence (e.g., honesty, good will, good intent). In contrast, nonprivileged social identities must instead actively make the case and "prove" competence, worthiness, and innocence. As privileged authorities, how are researchers embodying normative expectations and acting on the trust conferred via their social role as respectful, trustworthy answer seekers and answer makers?

In this chapter, I explore the role of the *self* in research: how our most valuable instrument may be calibrated and cultivated, how empathy may be gained, and how responsively self-aware and ethical practices call for extensive cultural and contextual groundings. In addition to embracing these considerations as an essential professional development pathway for excellence, researchers have an ethical responsibility to proactively assess and address the ways in which our personal repertoire of perceptual and interpretive resources may ignore, obscure, or distort more than illuminate.

♦ Self-Calibration, Reactivity, and Validity

The work of social scientists has at least some measure of ethical implications given their potentially impactful involvement in people's lives. Such impacts are especially salient in more applied research approaches such as action research and evaluations. Social research ethics speak to the morally responsible ways in which we should conduct ourselves as we design and engage in systematic inquiry, analysis, interpretation, and dissemination processes vis-à-vis individuals, groups, organizations, communities, and so on. Ethical practice is reflected in the extent to which researchers conduct themselves and their research in ways that are respectful, are fairly representative (accurate and just), and ideally leave persons better off—or at least minimally, "does no harm." These should be collaboratively deliberated and negotiated judgments and not simply unilateral decisions based on the researcher's intent, beliefs, and judgments.

In addition to these ethical considerations, quality imperatives demand serious examination of factors that may erode as well as enhance validity. Conventional definitions of validity speak to the extent to which a measurement instrument/process accurately captures and represents with fidelity that which it purports to measure. For example, Messick (1989) offered this well-established test-related validity definition: "The appropriateness or correctness of inferences, decisions, or descriptions made about individuals, groups, or institutions from test results" (p. 13). Validity assessments, however, relate more broadly to the full spectrum of instrumentation and systematic inquiry and inference methodologies. Foundational instrumentation issues include the uses of self-as-instrument. *Who* is conceiving, designing, engaging, implementing, and inferring during systematic inquiry processes with *Whom* in what ways toward what ends. Who decides? Who judges?

To what extent is what manifests perceived and received as both *appropriate* and *effective*:

- *Appropriate*: Behaviors and initiatives that are congruent with the expectations, demands, and codes of engagement in a particular situational, relational, or spatial/geographic context
- *Effective*: Behaviors and initiatives that yield the intended or desired outcomes

These criteria undergird a "both/and" agenda even though the effectiveness dimension is too often privileged and given consideration at the expense of the other dimension. Such myopic practices undermine long-term effectiveness since perceived appropriateness is often a critical prerequisite for moving beyond expedient compliance toward generative commitment and sustainability. Assessments of validity ultimately reside in an instrument's/methodology's intended purpose, use, and application.

Honoring ethical and quality imperatives summons researchers' capacities to fully hear and heed the voices of key stakeholders—their needs and challenges as well as their assets and resources. In social research, ethical considerations start with a focus on the WHO: Who is researching/evaluating whom based on what, when, and where? Who are we as knowers, inquirers, and engagers of others? Who are we and what perceptual, conceptual, and interpretive orientations and experiences do we bring that exert critical influences on the research processes we design and implement? This occurs whether intended or desired or not. What matters most is interpersonal *impact* not personal *intent*. Expanding one's self-awareness is especially crucial when engaging and working across diversity divides—notably, salient human differences that make a socially patterned difference in access, process, and success. Such interpersonal relations vary widely in their impacts on the quality, accuracy, and trustworthiness of observations and interpretations.

◆ Demystifying Data

Data are neither self-evident nor do they speak for themselves. The same data can conjure up dramatically different meanings and interpretations depending on where one stands and sits and, thus, what one brings as relevant perspectives, tools, techniques, and orientations. More specifically, what can and does one look and listen for, actually see and hear, and, then, meaningfully discern?

DYNAMIC MULTILEVEL SCANNING, TRACKING, AND FANNING: SELF-TO-SELF, SELF-TO-OTHERS, SELF-TO-SYSTEMS

Increase diversity-grounded awareness of the need for continuous assessment/evaluation of one's own conceptual, perceptual, and meaning-making/meaning-shaping prisms and the particular ways they are informed and shaped by multiple social identities and sociopolitical roles, diverse life paths, sociocultural, and other experiences.

- Perceptual prism: Who and what *matters* when and where?
  - *Lenses*: The sensing portals through which researchers connect with the physical, social, and spiritual world—*What is the nature of* researchers' *pathways for perceiving and receiving the "VOICES" as well as other data?*
  - *Filters*: The sifting and winnowing processes and protocols based on researchers' operational definitions of what is *substance* and worthy of attention ("signal") versus *noise* and extraneous variation—*What does the researcher look at and actually see, listen to and actually hear, touch and actually feel versus not fully and accurately seeing, hearing, or feeling? To what extent would which stakeholders agree with one's self-assessment?*
- Interpretive prism: Why, how, and how much "it" matters?
  - *Frames*: The meaning-shaping/meaning-making resources and "infrastructure"—*What are the researcher's personal thinking and feeling practices, perspectives, and processes, that is, the constellation of relevant values, beliefs, attitudes, orientations as well as social-structure locations vis-à-vis what the context (situational, relational, spatial/geographic) is calling for from the researcher?*

Researchers are not empty vessels, blank slates, or inanimate "tools"—notably, robots for data gathering, analysis, interpretation, and dissemination. Ethical praxis summons us to start with the presumption that default predispositions exist so one needs to commit to discovering, excavating, and taking account of the ways in which they may hinder or enhance one's work in a given context.

WHY BOTHER?

Focusing on the WHO in research humanizes what is too often a set of sterile, routinized tasks. Clearly, the *what* and *how* questions are important—the purpose, methods, and processes—but the human systems dynamics and social relations (the *who*) are foundational prerequisites for excellence and ethical practice. Researchers need to mindfully attend to and engage the many-faceted WHO and the contested terrain often associated with diverse views and vantage points. This will increase prospects for accuracy and validity as well as engaged participation in research, planning, improvement, and accountability processes. The extent to which stakeholders perceive and receive the researcher as trusting and trustworthy, as respectful and respectable and, most important, as fairly working in their best interests affects the form and levels of their engagement. These perceptions also determine the quality, depth, and trustworthiness of the data that they are willing to share.

Researchers need to proactively attend to these issues and regularly question the extent to which they can hear and engage the full spectrum of stakeholders in full voice—notably, discerning their hopes, expectations, and experiences. Appropriately responsive choices of methods can create and maintain a *grace space* for multiple stories to be told in full voice and for multiple truths to gain a respectful hearing. This is one of the most powerful contributions that researchers can make through recognizing that "so long as we participate in a society that transforms difference into privilege, there is no neutral ground" (Johnson, 2001, p. 131). The compelling watchwords are multipartiality and intersubjectivity, not the more distant and elusive impartiality and objectivity.

Our social positioning and, thus, our sociocultural lenses and filters exert critical influences on the research processes we design and implement and, ultimately, our interpretations and judgments regarding what is substantive and worthy of study and what is noise and extraneous variation. These issues relate to what Karen Kirkhart designated *"interpersonal validity"* in her 1994 presidential address at the American Evaluation Association annual conference: Notably, "the soundness and trustworthiness of understandings emanating from personal interactions.... the skills and sensitivities of the researcher or evaluator, in how one uses oneself as a knower, as an inquirer" (Kirkhart, 1995, p. 4). Who we are as knowers, inquirers, and engagers of others matters. We need to understand who we are as researchers and how we know what we believe we know about ourselves and others.

◆ The Self, Social Relations, and Data Quality

Ultimately, the nature of social relations will determine the quality and trustworthiness of the data collected, the soundness of the meaning making and possible interpretations, and the prospects for research processes that facilitate grounded understandings and "inclusive excellence."* Culturally and contextually responsive research processes summon all stakeholder groups to step forward in full voice to authentically communicate their truths. Research typically occurs in social contexts, so reactivity abounds whether recognized, intended, or not. Reactivity concerns typically focus on "artificial effects" related to research instruments and strategies, but they also have direct relevance for the WHO—the person who administers the instruments and designs the strategies. This multilateral process is shaped in varying degrees by all parties involved within and across diversity divides. That some voices and views are neither heard nor heeded does not mean they are not present and operative despite the seeming silence. Reactivity abides and resides in the nature of the social relations constructed as well as emergent among the parties involved. Its existence is not solely controlled by the determinations of the researcher (see Table 18.1).

To maximize accuracy, validity, and excellence, researchers must mindfully monitor and address this inevitable reactivity in order to develop authentic insights and understandings of the persons whom they seek to research. How does one mindfully address the ways in which one's presence may introduce nonrandom variation—bias/contamination/invalidity—as well as random variation (noise)? We can address our own limitations only with deep multilateral self-awareness, commitment, and initiative. Through ongoing efforts, we can cultivate our capacities to move from within our own sociocultural/sociopolitical boundaries into the shared space of borderlands and perhaps even across the borders into others' spaces as an *inside-outsider*: an effective border-spanning communicator and perhaps even a respectful border-crosser.

---

*Inclusive Excellence: The Association of American Colleges and Universities, with support from the Ford Foundation, spearheaded a research agenda that spotlights the integral interconnections among diversity and educational quality initiatives. It places these intersections at the center of campus planning and practice. The *Making Excellence Inclusive* project is designed to help colleges and universities fully integrate these efforts and embed them into the core of academic mission and institutional functioning: "Through this initiative, AAC&U re-envisions diversity and inclusion as a multilayered process through which we achieve excellence in learning; research and teaching; student development; institutional functioning; local and global community engagement; workforce development; and more."

Table 18.1 Potential Sources of Invalidity Related to Human Systems Dynamics

"WHO"-Centered Social Relations	
On-Stage Effects	
Extraneous Variables	*Alternative Explanations*
Social desirability	Subject may be saying what he or she "should" believe
Evaluation apprehension	Subject may be trying to impress someone judging "mental health," intelligence, etc.
Faking bad/Faking good	Subject may be trying to sabotage or help research
Demand characteristics	Subject may be doing what he or she thinks researcher wants
More Persistent Changes Caused by Research	
Extraneous Variables	*Alternative Explanations*
Placebo effect	Subject may be changing because he or she expected to
Researcher expectancy (self-fulfilling prophecy)	Researcher may subtly communicate an expectancy that subject acts to fulfill
Personal relationship effect	Subjects may perform differently because of nature of relationship with researcher
Reflexivity problems	Responses may be due to researcher's personal characteristics or behavior with subjects
Data Access and Representation Issues	
Extraneous Variables	*Alternative Explanations*
Incomplete access	Researcher may have selective access to only a subset of the potentially relevant data, so key unobserved factors may explain the research issue/question
Researcher selectivity	Events are due to causes that the researcher's theory considers unimportant or to causes someone in the researcher's social position cannot discern
Researcher distortion or bias	Researcher's evaluation of data may be colored by preconceptions/predispositions

SOURCE: Adapted from P. Stern and L. Kalof, *Evaluating Social Science Research,* 1996, excerpts from tables 3.1 and 3.2.

♦ Embracing Lifelong Responsive Self-Development

Cultivating *self-as-responsive-instrument* is a developmental journey without end because cultures and contexts are dynamic and ever changing. Responding to this lifework agenda requires ongoing personal homework, notably, ever-deepening awareness and knowledge of self-in-context as a lifelong project. So what are the necessary and sufficient conditions for embarking on and sustaining oneself during an often turbulent learning and reflective-practice journey? Among other things, this complex and often-convoluted journey involves the following processes.

- *Mapping the social topography:* Proactively survey the shifting sociocultural and sociopolitical terrain—diverse socially patterned ways of knowing, being, doing, thinking, and engaging in the context of power and privilege structures and flows. In what ways does the social landscape manifest itself in social boundaries, borderlands, and intersections? Identify from multiple stakeholder perspectives the salient differences that make a difference in access, process, and success. More specifically, who gains entry? For and with whose rhythms and ways of being, doing, and engaging is the "system" congruent—a mirror versus a window experience? Who benefits?

- *Multilevel dynamic scanning:* Continuously assess and refine one's own sociocultural antennae for monitoring, understanding, and engaging in social relations embedded within contexts of power, privilege, and other social structures while remaining aware of one's own sociopolitical location within that social topography. Cultivate flexible micro/macro zoom control powers—responsively zoom in for relevant intrapersonal and interpersonal details and zoom out for the big-picture social structural context.

- *Cultivating empathic perspective taking:* Develop one's capacity to imaginatively stand in others' perspectives and to live by its moral imperative, the *Platinum Rule*—treat others as they want to be treated (or at least be aware of what that is)—as a bridging complement to the *Golden Rule*, treating others as we want to be treated (Bennett, 1998). To maximize ethical practice and excellence, cultivate and regularly polish multifaceted lenses, filters, and frames that can more fully and accurately inform one's perceptions and meaning-making reflections and interpretations. Discover what they illuminate and, even more important, what they ignore, obscure, or distort. Given these realities, expand one's capacity to transform ambiguity and uncertainty into curiosity while productively working the frequent tensions between personal *intent* and interpersonal *impact*.

Engaging in these processes helps one to slow down, monitor, and interrupt default flows and potentially problematic leaps: *Because I perceive X, I know what X means and why it is/should be valued or not.* Through mindfully tracking, we are better able to honor and embrace a foundational intercultural/cross-cultural communications model—*Description-Interpretation-Evaluation (D-I-E)*—which explicitly decouples processes that are often conflated (Lustig & Koester, 2002, p. 76). Failure to mindfully address the ethnocentric "presumption of similarity and single reality theories" (Bennett, 1998, p. 207) leads evaluators—as well as other practitioners—to often overlook, if not explicitly dismiss, many diversity patterns as extraneous nuisance variation and noise. When not dismissible in such oversimplifying ways, socioculturally grounded differences are often defined as problematic targets for amelioration and correction. Difference tends to be almost automatically interpreted as deficient and deviant. Not surprisingly, then, patterns of sociocultural diversity have become intimately intertwined with systemic processes of asymmetric power relations and privilege.

◆ Empathic Perspective Taking: Ethnorelative Commitment to Excellence

To authentically and accurately answer the questions posed earlier calls for a diversity-grounded capacity to mindfully stand in one's own perspective while consciously shifting and responsively standing in others' perspectives. More specifically, doing self-as-instrument work summons us to deliberately engage in *cognitive frame shifting* (border-crossing in one's head) and *affective frame shifting* (border crossing in one's feelings). This requires knowing and anchoring in one's own center—core values, beliefs, expectations—while knowingly extending one's borders, that is, the boundaries of the self. With expanded intercultural and other cross-boundary awareness and understandings, one can demonstrate *appropriate and effective behavioral code switching: doing the right things right from multiple vantage points.*

Milton Bennett, Director of the Intercultural Communications Institute, provides useful frameworks for exploring and guiding this capacity-building self-development agenda. Based on extensive research highlighted in "Overcoming the Golden Rule: Sympathy and Empathy," he outlines a comprehensive model and six-step process for developing empathy—"the imaginative intellectual and emotional participation in another person's experience"—versus sympathy—"the imaginative placing of ourselves in another person's position" (Bennett, 1998, p. 207). In contrast to sympathy, empathy starts with the presumption of difference and multiple reality theories as opposed to presumed similarity and single reality. This foundational presumption represents Step 1. This capacity-cultivating process works from the inside-out so Step 2 is *Knowing Self*:

> The preparation that is called for is to know ourselves sufficiently well so that an easy reestablishment of individual identity is possible. If we are aware of our own cultural and individual values, assumptions, and beliefs—that is, how we define our identities—then we need not fear losing those selves. We cannot lose something that can be re-created at will. The prerequisite of self-knowledge does not eliminate the possibility of change in ourselves as a result of empathizing. It merely makes such change a chosen option rather than an uncontrollable loss. (Bennett, 1998, p. 210)

A very critical, ongoing "Knowing-Self" task involves exploring the contours, parameters, and dynamics of one's own life space: notably, the nature of one's *comfort zone* versus *stretch zone* versus *panic zone*. How do these zones show up and operate within and around each of us?

Step 3, *Suspending Self*, calls for a temporary expansion of the boundary between self-identity and the rest of the world, including other people: "Suspension of the self-boundary is facilitated by knowing where the boundary is (self-knowledge), but *only* if one first has a self-reference assumption of multiple-reality which presumes difference" (p. 210). *Allowing Guided Imagination* represents Step 4:

> In the extended state, we can move our attention *into* the experience of normally external events rather than turning our attention *onto* those events, as we usually do. This shifting of awareness into phenomena not normally associated with self can be called "imagination." (p. 210)

For accurate interpersonal empathy to occur, Bennett argues that in Step 5—*Allowing Empathic Experience*—we must allow our imagination to be guided into the experience of a specific other person: "If we are successful in *allowing* our imagination to be captured by the other person, we are in a position to imaginatively participate in that person's experience." The last critical task—Step 6, *Reestablishing Self*—involves reconstituting our boundaries by "remembering the way back to ourselves." (p. 211)

Empathy is a foundational prerequisite for authentic intercultural/multicultural communications and engagement—that is, ethnorelative versus ethnocentric social relations and development work. Developing essential border-crossing bridge-building competencies—and being so perceived by relevant others—requires the empathic skills associated with cognitive and affective frame shifting and behavioral code switching. Having such competencies would place one at ethnorelative Stage 5 of Milton

Bennett's *Developmental Model of Intercultural Sensitivity*—"Adaptation to Intercultural Difference." In contrast, many well-intentioned educators, evaluators, and other service professionals operate at ethnocentric Stage 3—"Minimization of Intercultural Difference." Unlike Stages 1 and 2—"Denial of Intercultural Difference" and "Defense Against Intercultural Difference," this highest ethnocentric stage does recognize differences but judges them to be trivial and ephemeral vis-à-vis similarities and commonalities (Bennett, 1986). Recognition of differences is surely necessary but woefully insufficient for excellence in communication and much less for excellence in education and evaluation.

◆ Decentering Pathways in Operationalizing WHO Matters: An Example

Wherever there is sociocultural diversity, there very likely is some diversity in the expected and preferred research processes and practices and the associated quality judgment criteria. Whose ways of being, doing, thinking, knowing, and engaging define the "mainstream" rules, roles, and normative expectations that undergird conventional research processes and practices? Researchers—especially in the applied domains of action research and evaluation—must mindfully monitor and expand the diversity of their own ways of being, doing, thinking, knowing, and engaging that inform and shape their choices among research processes, practices, and products. Such choices differ significantly in the extent to which various stakeholder groups must look through *windows* versus looking in a *mirror*, notably, their responsiveness to and congruence with diverse lived experiences. Like the power and privilege realities of other social processes and practices, the burdens of dissonance from *window-gazing* versus *mirror-gazing* are nonrandom and typically socially patterned along power and privilege divides. Openness to these decentering realities and complexities of diversity is foundational to maximize accuracy, appropriateness, respect, and excellence.

For example, Edward Hall's (1976) high- and low-context model, a major taxonomy of societal variations in cultural patterns (beliefs, values, norms), provides some useful illustrative insights. The dominant sociocultural structures and processes in the United States are low context so conventional research training and practices have also had a low-context orientation. Note, however, that there are many high-context cultural communities within the United States: for example, Native American, Japanese American, African American, and Mexican American. When *low-context* data collection and interpretation strategies are used in *high-context* sociocultural settings, much meaning-making content may be mangled or lost—notably, where one focuses literally on the words versus on those words embedded in a multifaceted web of nonverbal communication modalities:

> A high context (HC) communication or message is one in which most of the information is either in the physical context or internalized in the person, while very little is in the [linguistically] coded, explicit, transmitted part of the message. A low-context (LC) communication is just the opposite; i.e., the mass of the information is vested in the explicit code. (Hall, 1976, p. 91)

While high-context transactions feature "preprogrammed information in the receiver or in the setting," most of the information must be in the transmitted low-context message to make up for what is missing in the context (Hall, 1976, p. 101). High-context listening challenges us to move beyond simple ear listening to full-body listening (like a Satellite dish). The Chinese ideograph for listening—Ting—embodies this.

Table 18.2   Some Examples of Low/High-Anchor Attributes

Low-Context Cultural Orientation		High-Context Cultural Orientation
Low nonverbal use	← O →	High nonverbal use
Message explicit	← O →	Message implicit
Direct communications	← O →	Indirect communications
Low relational commitment	← O →	High relational commitment
Task focused	← O →	Process focused
Monochronic/chronological	← O →	Polychronic/relational time
Space territorial	← O →	Space communal

SOURCE: Lustig and Koester (2002).

Table 18.2 gives some common high-context versus low-context cultural contrasts in communications messages based on the extensive research of anthropologist Edward Hall (Lustig & Koester, 2002, pp. 111–114).

Think of such contrast pairs as anchors characterizing a continuum range. Given your typical orientation and preferences, where would you place yourself on these continua? Where would you place the persons, groups, organizations, and/or communities that you usually research? Where would you place your most common research instruments, protocols, strategies? For example, written questionnaires are low context while in-depth individual and group interviews tend to be higher-context tools. They provide more channels for messaging communications than words alone.

To what extent are these profiles congruent? In what ways do they significantly diverge and what implications might that have for the quality and responsiveness of your communications and your work generally? More specifically, to what extent do the persons that you engage discern and experience your research processes, protocols, practices, and products as accurately representing and reflecting the fullness of their lived realities? To what extent are their internal sociocultural structures and rhythms honored—experiential validity? Potential disconnects are critical because they may inadvertently introduce confounding variation and noise into data collection, analysis, and interpretation processes—notably, sources of *invalidity*. The questions raised here cannot be simply answered secondhand or at a distance.

Too often, research involves the unacknowledged and unresolved collision of differing worldviews given dramatic divergences in the living "rules" of being, knowing, doing, thinking, and engaging for those who are evaluated versus those who evaluate. None of us is born multicultural, so we each must consciously and conscientiously put ourselves in decentering situations that fire up our awareness of our own sociocultural prism: lenses, filters, and frames. Most important are our often havoc-wreaking *blind spots* (don't know that don't know) in addition to the many *blank spots* that we already know that we don't know. As a result, many cluelessly, and sometimes recklessly, "cross borders" without invitation, visa, or passport; and then—especially among the "privileged"—they often do so without consciousness or any personal consequence.

Bottom line, let us normalize the experience of sitting in *both/and* tensions and commit to staying engaged in spite of being bumped out of one's *comfort zone* and plunged into the *stretch zone*, and sometimes even the *panic zone*.

♦ Key Resources in the Journey Toward Ethical Practice and Inclusive Excellence

Effective self-presentation and appropriate uses of the self vis-à-vis others are critical pathways toward ethical practice and inclusive excellence—especially in communications-based professions such as social research, evaluation, and education. Bringing a well-endowed professional toolkit is surely necessary but not sufficient. Even if top of the line, it is all for naught if not complemented by interpersonal validity-enhancement work and is, thus, eclipsed by problematic perceptions of the person. So who do the persons that you seek to communicate with and engage perceive you as being? These questions are at the heart of bridge-building border crossings, which over time and adaptive praxis culminate in one becoming a more fully endowed border-crossing bridge builder and excellence-grounded ethical researcher.

A critical challenge involves recognizing and working with the frequent tensions between your own self-image and others' image of you. Regardless of the truth value of others' perceptions, they still rule until authentically engaged in ways that *speak-into-their-listening*. Of course, knowing others' images of who they think we are does not compel us to embrace and own such views. Nevertheless, we need full awareness of such views since they inform and influence how people relate to us, or not. This is particularly critical for the accuracy and integrity of research, and especially evaluative research processes, because such awareness determines prospects for gathering "good" and relevant data to make sound and trustworthy interpretations and judgments about merit, worth, value, significance, congruence, and so on.

Understanding how others perceive us requires moving beyond unilateral self-awareness into multilateral self-awareness to enhance authenticity, productivity, and excellence. Such images and judgments are culturally and contextually conditioned so the figure-ground examination of self in context is crucial. Culture is one critical context that reflects diverse socially patterned ways of knowing, doing, being, thinking, and engaging. Doing this work challenges each of us to engage in dynamic assessment and evaluation at multiple levels—micro/macro scanning, monitoring, and responsive discovery and adaptation processes at the intrapersonal, interpersonal, and organizational/institutional levels. Doing so moves one toward cultural competence that is much more a stance than a status, much more about one's orientation toward diversity than facts and figures about diverse places, spaces, and peoples. Moreover, cultural competence is not simply a matter of who one perceives oneself as being and what one believes one brings to any given situation—unilateral self-awareness. Even more important for the viability, vitality, productivity, and trust-building capacity of a transaction and relationship cultivation is multilateral self-awareness: self in relational and situational context and self as pivotal instrument.

SELF AS INSTRUMENT PORTFOLIO

What are the strengths/gifts, vis-à-vis the limits/constraints, of the perceptual, conceptual, and interpretive prism that you bring into a particular situational, relational, or spatial/geographic context? This self-calibration question represents a starting point within a given context, not an endpoint. We each need to create a comprehensive generic, as well as context-specific, *self as instrument portfolio*. It will serve as a resource for mapping out what one personally has to work *with* versus work *on* in a given research setting. It is worth investing some time brainstorming and listing your salient social roles, identities, and orientations—both from your vantage point and also the vantage points of others in a particular context. To move beyond swift auto-pilot assessments, complete such an inventory as a foundation for more mindfully identifying and exploring attributes that may have important implications for one's data collection, analysis, and interpretation work as a researcher. Together, these constitute your "forcefield of preparedness" for the tasks at hand.

What can you call upon from your self as responsive instrument portfolio for both *appropriate* and *effective* engagement and professional practice? Let us invest quality time in the ongoing development of our "self as instrument portfolios" as an essential complement to our professional research toolkits. Each of us can start with a listing of our salient social roles and identities—both from our own vantage points and also the vantage points of relevant stakeholders in a given research context.

Most important is the extent to which our meaning-making transactions and interpretations resonate with lived realities, (experiential validity) and, thus, are perceived as appropriate by others. Those who stand and sit on the privilege- and power-connected sides of diversity divides typically have not a clue regarding neither diverse perceptions nor their implications for social relations and outcomes. In contrast, those not so situated within a power-privilege hierarchy maintain high consciousness given its survival-framing consequences, that is, abridged life-chance opportunities for access and success. Such divergent realities often manifest in persons vigorously talking past each other even when seeming to use the same words.

JOHARI WINDOW AS A SKILLS-BUILDING RESOURCE

The dynamic insights and potential wisdom embodied in the *Johari Window* communications model offers a resource for pulling many of these disparate pieces together. This long-established communications model offers a useful developmental framework for cultivating multilateral self-awareness. It uses a four-paned window metaphor to facilitate processes for proactively giving and soliciting feedback to reduce the "hidden" and "blind" domains (Luft, 1982, p. 34).

> We can think of this model in two ways: as a window through which we look inward to see ourselves more clearly, and as a window through which others observe us. Through looking inward and disclosing to others what we perceive in ourselves, and through inviting feedback from them about what they notice in us, we gain in self-awareness. (Bell, 2001. p. 1)

Disclosing *personal intent* and simultaneously seeking insights into the frequent blind spots of *interpersonal impact* helps interrupt nonproductive default responses. Left unchecked, defensive responses erode prospects for continuous learning, for personal responsibility, and for commitment to change. This model can be flexibly used to increase the "open window" of communications between and among individuals, groups, organizations, and so on. It can be used to facilitate more authentic border-spanning communications that more effectively discern, navigate, and negotiate salient "diversity divides." The Johari Window is a powerful resource for skill-building as a bridge-building border crosser.

TRUST BUILDING AND QUALITY

Much research is grounded in social relations and trust is the glue and fuel for cultivating viable and productive social relations. Researchers need to mindfully attend to *trust building* as a foundation for quality research because their roles and responsibilities often automatically engender fear and mistrust, especially in evaluation-oriented research. Lack of trust erodes the prospects for full access to important data and networks and undermines the perceived value and utility of research processes and findings. In what ways and to what extent do one's communications and research processes, practices, and products enhance versus erode trust? Answering this question calls for the triangulation of ongoing multiway dialogues with key stakeholders, especially with those who are being researched. Dennis Reina and Michelle Reina[1] (1999), in *Trust and Betrayal in the Workplace*, have provided a comprehensive and highly nuanced framework for trust-building work along with a battery of assessment instruments for individuals, teams, organizations, and internal/external customers. Among their three major types of trust—intrapersonal, interpersonal, and transformative—the Transactional (interpersonal) Trust components are especially relevant: Contractual Trust (trust of character), Competency Trust (trust of capability), Communication Trust (trust of disclosure).

♦ In Search of an Integral Researcher-Self as Responsive Instrument

Ethical practice and inclusive excellence in research commands us to deepen our awareness of *"interpersonal validity"* as a critical complement to the more conventional *methodological validity*. This includes the soundness and trustworthiness of understandings warranted by one's uses of the *self vis-à-vis* one's uses of research tools, techniques, and strategies. A productive starting point for a research project involves dynamically scanning, monitoring, and reading the relational, situational, and spatial/geographic contexts. Doing so calls for more than "facts and figures" knowledge or do's-and-taboos checklists. Like other social relations, it matters *Who* is carrying *What* and *How* in determining the extent to which research processes will be embraced as a resource, rejected, or suspiciously tended to in perfunctory ways. Dynamic awareness and knowledge of the social topography *vis-à-vis* one's own and others' boundaries lay the groundwork for working the borderlands (free-flow zone) and ultimately for engaging in appropriate border crossings.

The most important challenges involve identifying salient and impactful diversity dimensions in a given context and implementing processes that will *appropriately and effectively* engage the full spectrum of stakeholders and, thus, responsively shape research processes and practices. To what extent are you hearing and heeding the voices of all stakeholders in full voice and to what extent would which stakeholders agree?

This chapter closes with a glimpse of a holistic researcher model of the self as responsive instrument. Crafted from the vantage point of an individual researcher, the model builds on Ken Wilber's Integral

Table 18.3 Calibrating and Cultivating an Integral Researcher-Self as Responsive Instrument

Agent/Actor Vantage Point/Stance	Interior Environment	Exterior Environment
Individual — Standing in one's own vantage point/perspective (self-empathy)	**Inside/In** Self-to-Self/Inward *** Self-Awareness *** • What is my vision of who I be/am becoming calling for from me—unilateral self awareness? • How am I showing up in my own intrapersonal world of self? • WHO AM I? *** Subjective *** *** Cultural *** **WE**	**Inside/Out** Self-to-Self/Outward *** Research Task Management *** • What is the situational context—the research agenda—calling for from me? • How am I showing up in that world of work and other tasks? • WHAT MATTERS? **I IT** *** Behavioral *** **ITS * Social Systems ***
Collective — Standing in the perspectives/vantage points of multiple relevant collectives and reference groups	**Outside/In** Self-to-Others *** Social Awareness *** • What is the relational context calling for from me—multilateral self-awareness? • How am I perceiving others as perceiving/receiving me showing up in a world of many We's and They's? • What cues and clues telegraph the message "one of us" versus "not one of us"—however, US-ness is defined? • WHO BELONGS?	**Outside/Out** Self-to-Systems *** Relationship/Process Management *** • How is the researcher interfacing and engaging with the collective intentions and diverse sociocultural orientations organized and manifesting in the world in ways that impact their implementation of the research agenda? • For and with whose rhythms and ways of being, doing, and engaging is the system congruent—a mirror versus a window experience? • WHO MATTERS—AUTHORIZES/ DECIDES—AND HOW?

Quadrant Model (2007, p. 2). I have focused on the most underdeveloped and untended dimensions of an integral model: notably, the interconnections among interior environments, both the individual and the collective. In Table 18.3, I have mapped many of the chapter concepts across the four quadrants, for example, unilateral self-awareness in the upper left quadrant and multilateral self-awareness in the lower left.

This model offers a framework of sensitizing concepts and questions for mindfully scanning, tracking, and monitoring WHO factors—notably, the human systems dynamics. These items speak to the multiple dimensions of diversity that live in the interpersonal interface among human beings: the researcher and those who are researched, the data seekers, and the data providers. As you move into a new research context, the sensitizing concepts and questions associated with each quadrant provide a comprehensive self-assessment framework, with heads-up alerts, for checking in with ourselves. What are the relevant assets and resources in your researcher portfolio—professional, intercultural, interpersonal, intrapersonal—as well as your needs, challenges, blank spots, and blind spots? What is the status of your force field of preparedness and readiness for the sociocultural context as well as the tasks embodied in the research questions and agenda? Who says so and how do I know?

◆ Connecting the Dots: Data → Information → Insights

To move beyond *data-land* isolation to the expansively interconnected and engaging *world of insights* calls for empathic perspective-taking: that is, the ability to manifest, facilitate, and foster border-spanning communications and actions via flexibly multifaceted lenses, filters, and frames. Such skills are demonstrated, for example, through *speaking-into-the-listening* from multiple vantage points. Through empathic speaking and doing, disembodied data can be transformed, for many, into interlinked information that is intrapersonally embraced, embedded, and unleashed as insights. Using appropriate diverse codes of engagement allows one to speak and behave in ways that are perceived and received as trustworthy, respectful, competent, credible, compelling, and so on. These skills inform and undergird how we craft data-grounded pathways through information fields enroute to insights: notably, generative provocative possibility thinking, being, and doing.

With vigilance and clear-eyed honesty, let us continually assess our empathic perspective-taking skills *vis-à-vis* the ways we are aided versus hindered by our own voice, social identities, experiences, and orientations. Who we are as knowers, inquirers, and engagers of others matters. This integral researcher model can help us mindfully tend to these considerations in order to move beyond flattened, disembodied social research approaches toward more full-bodied ones that foster ethical praxis and inclusive excellence.

◆ Note

1. See Dennis Reina and Michelle Reina's trust Web site (www.trustinworkplace.com) and book (1999) for more information.

◆ References

Bell, L. A. (2001, May). *Self-awareness and social justice pedagogy*. National Conference on Race and Ethnicity in Higher Education presentation handout, Seattle, WA.

Bennett, M. (1986). Towards ethnorelativism: A developmental model of intercultural sensitivity. In M. Paige (Ed.), *Cross-cultural orientation*. Lanham, MD: University Press of America.

Bennett, M. (1998). Overcoming the Golden Rule: Sympathy and empathy. In M. J. Bennett (Ed.), *Basic concepts of intercultural communication: Selected readings* (pp. 191–214). Yarmouth, ME: Intercultural Press.

Cullinan, C. (1999, Spring). Vision, privilege and the limits of tolerance. *Electronic Magazine of Multicultural Education, 1*(2). Retrieved October 8, 2007, www.eastern.edu/publications/emme

Hall, E. T. (1976). *Beyond culture*. New York: Anchor Books.

Johnson, A. (2001). *Privilege, power and difference*. Mountain View, CA: Mayfield.

Kirkhart, K. (1995). Seeking multicultural validity: A postcard from the road. *Evaluation Practice, 16*(1), 1–12.

Luft, J. (1982). The Johari Window. In L. Porter & C. R. Mills (Eds.), *Reading book for human relations training* (pp. 205–209). Arlington, VA: National Institute for Applied Behavioral Science.

Lustig, M. W., & Koester, J. (2002). *Intercultural competence: Interpersonal communication across cultures* (4th ed.). New York: Allyn & Bacon.

Messick, S. (1989). Validity. In R. Linn (Ed.), *Educational measurement* (pp. 13–103). New York: Macmillan.

Reina, D. S., & Reina, M. L. (1999). *Trust and betrayal in the workplace*. San Francisco: Berrett-Koehler.

Stern, P., & Kalof, L. (1996). *Evaluating social science research* (2nd ed.). New York: Oxford University Press.

TwoTrees, K. (2003). *7 directions practice*. Retrieved May 5, 2001, from www.7dp.org/seven/index.html

Wilber, K. (2007). The integral approach. *Integral life*. Retrieved June 8, 2007, from www.integralinstitute.org/public/static/abtapproach.aspx

19

THE ETHICS OF THE RESEARCHER-SUBJECT RELATIONSHIP

Experiences From the Field

◆ Peggy Gabo Ntseane

Researchers and educators are aware of both methodological challenges and ethical practices that must be adhered to in conducting social research. However, based on my practical experiences with research methods in the field, interactions with respondents, and the insider/outsider researcher dilemmas in a Third World context, it is timely that the question "Do standards of research ethic protocols work across contexts?" is posed for research discourse. In an attempt to respond to this question, I argue in this chapter that ethical dilemmas experienced in researching "the other," namely non-Western social contexts, are illustrative of the fact that some standard conventional ethical considerations and practices do not work across contexts. The chapter examines instances in which ethical protocols can contradict the social knowledge construction and acquisition of society's common understandings as prescribed by Indigenous Knowledge systems.

The chapter starts with an overview of the general theories and arguments for ethics in social research as an effort to identify gaps based on the author's experiences in data collection in Botswana (Africa). This reflection demonstrates the importance of considering social diversity in social research ethics, especially in qualitative research that is influenced by alternative knowledge construction paradigms. The chapter also discusses subtle ethical issues that arise when the author "turns the camera to self" for a critical self-reflection. Qualitative field work ethical dilemmas are identified to illustrate that the role of the researcher in the researcher-researched relationship can be complex. Lessons from this methodological reflection are used to argue for a continued reflection revision, reformulation, and rethinking of those aspects of traditional Western-oriented ethics that devalue or even marginalize other social context experiences.

The chapter ends by arguing that, in the age of globalization, it is important to continue strengthening the conventional ethical focus by considering ethical values from diverse contexts. The African collective ethic is perceived as a critical addition because while it does not dismiss other contributions, it offers a unique emphasis. For example, the ethical issue of "consent" in the African context embraces cultural beliefs of consensus, respect, and uplift of one another.

Given the reality that African values of knowledge construction and knowledge acquisition research methods have historically been devalued, marginalized, or ignored by international researchers due to the experience of colonialism (Q. Mkabela, 2005; Ntseane, 2006), there is need for ethical research processes that contribute to transformational healing (see Chapter 26, this volume). An example is the African's remembrance of the time in their history in which they were asked to "sign" documents even though they lived in an oral society in which writing was foreign to them. The colonizers allowed the Africans to either use their thumbprints or they made an "X" on documents that they could not read, resulting in their great grandparents losing their lands. The effect of this oppressive use of power is still evidenced in many Africans being unwilling to sign their names to give consent in research, as is commonly expected under Western ethical norms. These are the wounds that need to be healed by African researchers who have to deal with these legacies of colonialism, in addition to care of the social research participants as individuals.

◆ Overview of the Social Research Ethical Frameworks

Scholars have identified several frameworks in an attempt to understand field relations. This section analyzes social research ethical explanations and identifies the gaps in their contribution. Three different theories, namely, the conventional, feminist, and Afrocentric theorizing arguments on research ethics, are discussed.

CONVENTIONAL ETHICAL ISSUES

An overview of the literature (Berg, 2004; Creswell, 1998; Hertz, 1996; William & Heikes, 1993) on qualitative research concurs that researchers have an obligation to their colleagues, their study population, and the larger society. Given that social researchers intrude in the social lives of human beings, they must ensure that rights, privacy, and welfare of the people and communities involved in the study are protected. According to Punch (1994), authors of this literature stress that concern about research ethics should revolve around various issues of avoiding harm, informed consent, and protection of privacy, as well as confidentiality and/or anonymity of the participants who provide data. Conventional ethical issues also require researchers to ensure voluntary participation and avoid deception of participants. For example, most social researchers would agree that potential research participants should be provided with clear information on the purpose of the study and how it will be carried out, including duration as well as anticipated risks and benefits not only to society but also to participants. However, in spite of all these good intentions, the reality is that there are practical practices that demonstrate the violation of this conventional ethical code across time, space, and culture (Chilisa & Preece, 2005).

Qualitative researchers who critique the conventional emphasis of ethics conclude that the relationship between researcher and participants in qualitative research is very different from quantitative approaches; hence most conventional procedures for informed consent and protection of human participants are irrelevant and, at best, amount to little more than ritual (Bogdan & Biklen, 1992). This is so because, in qualitative research, the relationship between the researcher and the participants is frequently ongoing and evolving. Although conventional ethical frameworks speak about anonymity, qualitative research frequently includes visuals such as photographs of people and communities as data and in research dissemination products such as reports. Furthermore, pseudonyms of town names in a report that has pictures of the towns could actually compromise the ethical efforts. Consent that requires participants to sign a contract is irrelevant when dealing with illiterate participants or in oral contexts such as those we find around the world. As can be seen from these few examples, conventional or standard ethical procedures are not always relevant in certain research contexts, especially with qualitative research topics.

While a lot has been written about ethics in social research, it was not until late in the 1990s that debates on the interaction between the researcher and the participants began to appear in the research literature. For example, Williams' discussion with her respondent Cathy (cited by Lundsford & Ray, 1996) reminds researchers that scrutiny of the lives of participants can have negative consequences for them in spite of the researchers' good intentions. Newkirk (1996) also argued that there is "seduction and betrayal in qualitative research" when he questioned acceptance of the "automatic equation between our own academic success and ethical behavior" (p. 3). Furthermore, a closer look at conventional ethical issues reveals that the focus of these generic standards is on how to do research, the utilization of research findings, quality versus quantity in data analysis, and ethically appropriate practices in doing research. Omission of reflecting on fieldwork experience from this list is unfortunate because it hides the conflicts and tensions that all researchers inevitably face and learn from.

FEMINIST ANALYSIS

Feminist standpoint theory argues that one's point of view is important in gaining knowledge and understanding people, particularly women (for more on feminist theories, see Chapter 3, this volume). Researchers should realize that they also are the "other" in participants' communities and therefore subject to observation and analysis. Patai (1991) argued that due to inequalities based on race and class, ethical research is not possible regardless of researchers' good intentions because social researchers do use others for their own ends. She pointed to the inherent hierarchy and inequalities between First World feminist researchers and Third World participants and asked, "Is it possible to write about the oppressed without becoming one of the oppressors?" (p. 659). Commenting on collaborative research and ethical dilemmas, Wolf (1992) also asked, "Can we truly offer the view from below when we are far above it, looking down? Can middle class women actually drop down even temporarily?" (p. 28). As can be deduced from these questions, feminist theory introduces the element of power relations in social research ethics.

The standpoint theory of feminists and other scholars introduced issues of hierarchy, exploitation, appropriateness, and empowerment in fieldwork and argued that these are not only important at the beginning of the fieldwork, but their relevance continues with issues of authority, authorship, and representation of the other. In fact, the feminist standpoint theorists' suggestions on how to deal with ethical dilemmas emphasize the need to care for social research participants. For instance, they advocate for engaging in acts of reciprocity (Smith, 1999); the use of oral histories, or life histories, (Behar, 1993; Patai, 1991) and activist research (i.e., returning research to the community; Heshusius, 1994).

It is important to mention that, in general, gender theories have been criticized. An important example is their insensitivity to African contexts where African men are recognized as partners in the struggle against gender because of their unique experiences with colonialism, imperialism, and the variable race (Asante, 1995). African scholars argue that the identified ethical problems of authorship, authority, and representation of the other by feminist theorists are not enough for African researchers who also grapple with questions about ownership of the data. This is so because African researchers who participate in collaborative research are marginalized because of contract agreements that privilege Western researchers in this matter. The challenges for African researchers are to confront research individualism, multiple differences and borders, the way in which research agendas are established and funded, writing and representation, and ways of engaging African research participants.

In spite of the general picture of the marginalization of other cultures' Indigenous Knowledge systems as discussed earlier, it is important to acknowledge that some Western researchers, especially those conducting qualitative research have started to reflect critically on their ethical experiences and thus have also questioned the applicability of universal codes in certain situations (Wilkinson & Kitzinger, 1996). For example, feminists maintain that "others" by definition are oppressed and marginalized by the dominant culture, and consequently, their cultures and traditions are typically represented as inferior or pathological. The next section presents the Afrocentric paradigm that argues for research processes that value diverse partnerships.

THE AFROCENTRIC PARADIGM

An Afrocentric orientation to research started with Asante in the late 1970s who began speaking about the idea that Africans and persons of African descent must be seen as proactive subjects within their history rather than as passive objects of Western perceptions about African people's history (Asante, 1990). The Afrocentric paradigm argues that research should be approached as a negotiated partnership that allows indigenous communities to define for themselves the degree to which they wish to make themselves available as social research participants. According to Mazama (2001), Afrocentricity contends that Africa's main problem is the unconscious adoption of Western worldviews and perspectives; hence, Africans always find themselves and their experiences relegated to the periphery or the margin of Western experience.

The Afrocentric paradigm is opposed to theories that "dislocate" Africa in the periphery of human thought and experience. As a research method, Afrocentricity focuses on Africa as the cultural center of the study of African experiences and interprets research data from an African perspective. As Mazama (2001) put it, "The Afrocentric idea rests on the assertion of the primacy of the experience of African people. In the process, it also means viewing the European voices as just one among the many and not necessarily the wisest one" (p. 388). Flaherty (1995) observed that because communities have felt excluded from policies, research is often viewed as a "colonial intrusion" or a use of power by the powerful. Questions of who sets research priorities and agendas, what gets done, and who benefits from it are often on the minds of the researched in Africa. According to Q. Mkabela (2005), this paradigm "promotes the notion that relevant research output is achieved when it could satisfy not only material needs of people, but also their intellectual, spiritual and cultural needs" (p. 184). Another critical attribute of the Afrocentric paradigm is that knowledge is not produced for the sake of knowledge but always for the sake of African people's liberation. For example, if participation in research is to be of any use to African researchers and their African subjects, it has to activate our consciousness to African values and methods of knowledge construction and knowledge acquisition.

It is important to mention here that there is evidence of considerable misunderstanding of the Afrocentric paradigm in the academic world; hence, the literature shows multiple definitions of Afrocentricity. For example, there are scholars who argue that what makes one Afrocentric is the participation in a "core African value system coupled with the experience of oppression" (Collins, 1991, p. 206). This is misleading because to be African is not necessarily to be Afrocentric. As Mazama (2001) observed, "Afrocentricity stresses the importance of cultivating a consciousness of victory as to dwelling on oppression" (p. 389). Another striking example of total misunderstanding of Afrocentricity is provided by Adams (1993) thus: "The purest form of Afrocentricity places Africa at its center as the source of the World's people and its most fundamental ideas and intervention" (p. 34). Again this is not because Afrocentricity places African people at the center, but because it stresses that all people are entitled to practice and celebrate their own culture as long as it does not interfere with the collective being. As the Afrocentric literature shows, "All people have a perspective which stems from their centers—while Eurocentrism imposes itself as universal; Afrocentrism demonstrates that it is only one way to view the world" (Asante, 1988, pp. 87–89).

Scholars who contribute to postcolonial theory agree that colonization must be understood not only as geographic domination but also as colonization of the mind; hence, the current methods of teaching and research remain Western in non-Western contexts (Dube, 2000). An indigenous epistemology commands a way of life cognizant of the traditional peoples' philosophy prior to colonization in Africa. The missionaries who came to Africa during the colonial period found Indigenous Knowledge systems that they dismissed, destroyed, and replaced with Western-derived knowledge systems. The word *indigenous* refers to traditional ways of doings things. Indigenous epistemology on the other hand refers to ways of knowing and knowledge construction that are resident within society and passed on from generation to generation. Ntseane (2006) observed that Indigenous Knowledge or cultural knowledge do not base their reality on any scientific knowledge: "The learning from the ways of life or culture, the source of such knowledge is never identified or known, but the knowledge is respected without question" (p. 222). The African renaissance also underlines the imperative that educational research that excludes indigenous ways of knowing is most likely to fail to speak to or produce research results that can enhance the quality of life of the researched communities. Failure to work with the framework and language of the researched means that life and death matters are either not understood or take a long time before they are understood. This is unfortunate because as Bailey (1994) noted, it is unethical to provide partial information, present facts out of context, or provide misleading information. In agreement, Chilisa (2005) observed that "postcolonial societies still ignore, marginalize and suppress other knowledge systems and ways of knowing" (p. 669).

Although not recognized, a collective sense of responsibility is a strong orientation of African values. For example, in southern Africa, there is an interconnected relationship between the individual, community, and other forces such as nature and ancestral spirits. In fact, even national development agendas embrace cultural concepts that reinforce this value, namely, *Ubuntu* in South Africa and *Botho* in Botswana. These concepts encompass "ideas of respect for human life, mutual help, generosity, cooperation and respect of older people, harmony and preservation of the sacred" (Avoseh, 2001, p. 481). For instance, although as a young person, I was converted to my denomination (Catholic), my understanding of what it means to be human is still influenced by my culture of a connectedness to the earth (*Lefatshe*) and all its inhabitants (birds, animals, plants) and the ancestral spirits (*Badimo*). The connectedness of the living and the dead is embraced through totems, taboos, and survival practices. For example, in the case of ailments, it is believed that when all medical processes fail to cure a disease, healing is sent from the spirits of the ancestors through ritual practices such as *phekolo* and *go kgwa-kgaba* meaning to appease the ancestral spirits. This is done by calling the ancestors names and begging them to give the patient a good life or to take him to heaven with them if that will please them. Thus, collective ethics in an African context recognizes that survival derives from group harmony and all actions are within a collective context (N. Q. Mkabela & Luthuli, 1997). Collective ethics grows where individuals are also linked to one another through multiple bonds in a holistic relationship.

Based on the three theoretical arguments (conventional, feminist analysis, and Afrocentric paradigm) above, it can be concluded that conventional research ethics protocols fail to protect the researched from methodological flaws in non-Western contexts. Research ethics in less-developed countries are affected by cultural, social, and economic conditions affecting both researchers and the population. As Chilisa (2005) observed, this can be explained by the fact that ethics is narrowly defined and it emphasizes protection of the individual, while ignoring the researched's ownership of knowledge and respect for communities. Many ethical questions still need to be asked and answered, especially on the role of the relationship between the researcher and the participants in the scientific research processes and outputs. Thus, lessons from the field cannot continue to be ignored because of the recognition of the need for researchers to balance engagement and disengagement when interacting with participants. The next section presents a case study of the author's practical experiences with conventional ethical practices during fieldwork in an Africa context.

♦ Practical Experiences With Conventional Ethical Issues: Tales From the Field

As a doctoral student who was studying in the United States but, at the same time, a research practitioner in Africa, I was allowed to collect data for my Ph.D. dissertation back home, namely, in Botswana. This privilege gave me the opportunity to work across two distinct cultures in terms of knowledge construction and acquisition. This section of the chapter presents both the methodological challenges and the ethical dilemmas encountered due to the status of being both an insider and an outsider, not only in my original context (Botswana) but also in the Western cultural notions of social research objectivity. The first thing that struck me was the Human Research Subjects (HRS) consent form that had to be approved at my university prior to my departure to Africa.

CONSENT

The process of obtaining informed consent by the use of the HRS form from the university violates the cultural way of soliciting consent in Africa. In the Botswana context, consent is obtained by going through the following hierarchical steps:

- *Community consultation through the local leadership ('Go ipega'). Step 1:* Before interacting with any member of the community, the culture mandates that the visitor present himself or herself to the village leadership (Chief), who will then consult other local leaders. *Step 2*: If necessary, the local leadership will call a community meeting where the visitor will be introduced to the rest of the community members. *Step 3*: In the case of a researcher, the visitor (researcher) will be given the opportunity to introduce their research objectives and the methodological approaches to be used. *Step 4*: The community local leadership and the community will then give the researcher their "public or general consent." This is very critical, because without this public consent, the researcher cannot even get into the community to talk to individuals. *Step 5*: Having obtained the general consent from the community through the local leadership, this gives the researcher leeway to solicit informed consent from the targeted group in the community.

- *Consent of the target group:* Since I was interested in interviewing small businesswomen, at this level of consent I went to the businesses sampled to request their participation. To my surprise, all business owners suggested a meeting with all employees where I would introduce my study fully for them to decide whether their business should participate. Again, permission was granted at this level. It was interesting for me to learn that once the interest group had agreed, the researcher was then free to approach any individual to represent the business as long as that was in line with the study's objectives/focus. However, I still had to get permission at the individual level.

- *Individual-level consent:* This was also another eye-opener because I learned that individual employees were also members of families and their consent required their family's approval.

After successfully going through all the steps of the culturally accepted consent process, the recommended HRS process seemed to undermine the cultural way of soliciting informed consent. In fact, some expressed the wish to not sign the consent form because they believed that a cultural "oral agreement" was more binding. For example, when I asked the participants to sign the consent form, they were surprised and uncomfortable. Others even said, "aaah! I thought I had agreed, now why do I have to sign papers?" "Why do I have to sign, don't you believe me when I say I agree to participate in your study?" said another with disbelief. Statements like these are a good indicator of an existing contradiction between indigenous and conventional ways of soliciting consent. After this field experience, I asked myself: If informed consent is what is critical, why does it have to be written? Does having it written prove its validity, and if so, in whose context?

ANONYMITY AND CONFIDENTIALITY

This is another ethical practice that posed challenges. I was dealing with successful small businesswomen. When I asked for pseudonyms for their businesses, it soon became very clear that my respondents wanted their business names to be used, not pseudonyms. Some of the names meant a lot to their business success because they were names of beloved family members who had played a critical role in supporting the business. This is how some of the research participants expressed this point:

> I want the name of my business to go into the book that you are going to write.

> I am not educated but one day my children or even grandchildren will be educated and able to read books at the university, so they should be able to read about the family business that gave them the opportunity to get the education.

Based on such powerful comments, I could not help but ask myself questions such as, What is the difference between acknowledging somebody's contribution in the literature sections of scientific reports and the acknowledgment that these research respondents were asking for? These research participants simply wanted to be acknowledged in writing for the work they are doing for their communities. As an African feminist myself, I am an advocate of the view that voices of people without privileges in the reporting and dissemination stages of the research should be honored.

THE USE OF TECHNOLOGY

To address issues of credibility, rigor, and trustworthiness of my qualitative research findings, I agreed with my committee members and wrote in black and white that data from the interview would be tape-recorded. This proved to be another challenge in an oral society. The following comments attest to this:

> I have not heard my voice on the machine before, what if it does not come out right?
>
> I thought we were going to have a woman to woman talk, now why the machine, I don't want my voice taken to the national radio station.
>
> If you have to tape-record this conversation, then I have to consult my family first, I thought this was going to be a normal interview.

Based on the above comments, it is clear that the use of technology in qualitative research fieldwork such as tape-recording responses can compromise quality of the data especially in situations where people have to be cautious of what they say.

THE INSIDER/OUTSIDER DILEMMA

This was another experience from my field relations that brought both challenges and frustrations. As an insider (i.e., born and raised in Botswana and a woman interviewing other women), respondents expected me to be both a researcher and an interviewee. For instance, I was perceived as the author of their book (i.e., my dissertation). This proved to be an advantage because it ensured their commitment, thus openness. As one put it, "For a change our views are going to be written correctly, so we can afford to be open and tell it to one of us."

However, the insider position was also a disadvantage because it was difficult to get responses for questions that women considered to be trivial or commonsense knowledge to me. For example, they made statements such as, "Aah!! You have the answer to that question, why are you asking me questions that you know answers for, we want real, important or serious questions." So I constantly had to switch hats and put on the outsider status. I often had to remind participants that the information from the trivial questions was for my American professors who did not know about our culture and so they needed confirmation from them.

INDIVIDUAL VERSUS COLLECTIVE INTERVIEWING

Although the unit of analysis for this study was the individual (viz., business owner), in many situations during data collection, what started as an individual interview usually ended as a group interview. This came about due to several cultural practices including the following:

> *The business management style*: For businesses where teamwork is valued, the business owner preferred to have other supervisors around. This is how one explained it, "You see I may be the owner of the business but I am not responsible for everything that goes on here. So it will not be proper to speak about what other people do when they are here to speak for themselves."

Family setup: Where the household head is usually a man, he may occasionally ask the wife or older children to participate in the interview even if they have not given consent. In this culture, individual's actions (good or bad) are perceived as owned by the family.

Cultural practice: In the Setswana oral culture, people do not receive knowledge or give information alone. In fact, there are proverbs to support and reenforce this practice such as, "*se tshwara ke ntsa pedi ga se thata.*" Although the literal translation is "to be held by two dogs is not difficult," the proverb means that "if there is a task and people work on it collectively, there is always success."

This collective approach to everything including research proved to be an ethical challenge during fieldwork. It meant that the family or group contributes to the interview and has access to confidential information. How does that relate to confidentiality and anonymity issues as understood from the conventional ethical perspective?

♦ Turning the Camera to Self: A Researcher's Critical Self-Reflection

In this section, I base my comments on seven years experience with qualitative research and my view of ethics from my training at a Western university that aligns with the ethics usually associated with experimental research and postpositivism. This emphasis of ethics is not reflective of other ethical stances that have emerged from constructivism (see Chapter 10, this volume) or the transformative paradigm (see Chapter 6, this volume). I have been in situations where my obligations as a researcher and as a citizen have conflicted, thus raising numerous methodological challenges/dilemmas that are not easily resolved by conventional codes of ethics in research. The questions that still confront me are the following: What is the responsibility of the researcher in situations where the expectations of the participants contradict the ethical guidelines of the profession or conventional research processes? What are ethical questions and do they only reside in how the researcher should behave in the field or can ethics be understood in terms of the researcher's obligation to the people who have touched their lives in the course of being a qualitative researcher? Is there a need to consider social diversity in social research because of experiences from the field in other contexts? The desire to answer these questions and my unique interactions with qualitative research participants in an African context motivated me to turn the camera to myself as a researcher. The encounters and interactions with human research participants of my qualitative study on "an understanding of the transition of how semiliterate women moved themselves from poverty in the rural areas to owning successful small businesses in urban areas of Botswana" brought both achievements and challenges that are presented next as ethical dilemmas illustrating my struggles and attempts to be an ethically responsible researcher.

- *Insider/outsider: Cooption/resistance.* One of the outcomes of my self-reflection as a qualitative researcher in an African context is the extension of the insider/outsider dilemma to include cooption/resistance ethical dilemma issues. For example, as an academic researcher, one is expected, or even coerced, to comply with Western notions of objectivity and ethics if one is to be published. But, on the other hand, one is also an insider participating in the marginalization of participants' realities as attested to by my field relations in this chapter's sections on issues of consent and confidentiality.

- *Traditional reality of knowledge acquisition and knowledge construction versus Western notions of research objectivity*. This self-reflection exercise also reveals the conflict between knowledge systems, that is, Western notions of research objectivity and African context notions of reality, both acquired by the researcher. In my African context, knowledge production is communally owned and is disseminated to the rest of the community by indigenous intellectuals through songs, plays, poems, dance, theatre, and storytelling. Chilisa and Preece (2005) showed how poems and songs are an illustration of the way African communities have collected data, and analyzed, deposited, retrieved, and disseminated information. Dube (2000) has also discussed "divining" as an ethical method of reading in Africa. In the context of the divining and the client, there is no absolute knowledge because the diviner, the set of bones symbolizing divine power, evil power, foreign power (good or bad), elderly, men and women, young and old, homesteads, family, life and death, and ethnic groups (that include white people), and the visitor construct knowledge together. This worldview challenges the positivist view of knowledge as absolute, the researcher as the sole objective constructor of knowledge, and the researched as a passive object. This dilemma contributes to ethical questions of loyalty.

- *Collaborative research ethics versus collective ethics.* If collaborative and cooperative research is done on behalf of the community and individuals within a community, then the African collective paradigm should be embraced. The current ethical dilemmas of collaborative research such as marginalization of both the Third World researchers and their researched communities should not be allowed to continue. Scholarly literature acknowledges that ethical research is likely to be achieved in the African context if the community itself influences and shapes the research methods (Cunningham & Durie, 1998; Q. Mkabela, 2005). This implies that research ethics codes are culturally defined and need to include indigenous values that are likely to shed light on current collaborative research problems experienced by researchers from less-developed countries.

The next section draws lessons learned from both the practical experiences with recommended conventional ethical practices and the author's critical self-reflection about the roles of fieldwork relations and how these can inform research methodologies and representation of the research findings.

◆ Field Relations Experiences: Contributions to Theory and Practice of Ethical Social Research

Based on analysis of the field experiences above, the following methodological lessons are drawn for social research ethics theory and practice. Ethical dilemmas associated with *informed consent* discussed in this chapter indicate that there is a disparity between the conventional and the indigenous ways of soliciting consent. In this particular African context, consent is not only understood at the "I and We" level but is also understood at different levels of relationships, namely, individual, collective interest group, and community levels. In relation to issues of "oral agreements" versus "written agreements," this experience reveals that African researchers have a responsibility for researching on traditional issues of consent and ensuring that those that are appropriate are not marginalized in the scientific research process. Similarly, researchers have to be sensitive to contextual ethical issues. For example, when dealing with illiterate research subjects in contexts where people are going through a process as a result of legacies of colonialism and marginalization due to other social factors such as gender inequality, apartheid, racism, power relations, class, sexuality, and so on. During the colonial period, land was taken using written agreements that were not explained or even understood by Africans, most of who could not read and write at the time. It is therefore ethical that informed consent for an African researcher has to be sensitive to the expectation of honesty and loyalty to the African people. While written consent among the literate participants might not be resisted; however, for the not-so-literate, researchers have to approach the issue of written consent with far more sensitivity.

In relation to anonymity and confidentiality standards, it can be inferred from the experience shared that while ethical values/norms are essential in protecting the research participants, it is equally important to recognize the voices of the researched. For example, in this particular experience, participants are requesting that their contributions to scientific research be openly acknowledged in the literature. The use of a pseudonym in the case of a participant who would love to be acknowledged openly should be avoided. This calls for social research ethics theory and practices that are context specific. It is encouraging to realize that there is a move even among Western researchers such as the postpositivist, the constructivist, and transformative researchers to push for conventional notions of ethics that are more accommodative of other ways of knowledge construction. In particular, contemporary feminists have argued for what they call "an ethic of involvement" as an effort to avoid dominant representation of the "other" and in fact, some are committed to documenting and celebrating the survival skills, the inherent strengths, and the positive cultures and traditions of the "other" (Gilligan, 1982).

In the past decade, we have seen the growth of the use of technological innovation in social research, such as audio and visual Internet, digital cameras, and microtape recorders, to mention a few. It seems as if the introduction of these technological innovations in the data collection process was done without prior assessment of their relevance to cultural realities. Although conventional research methodology recognizes the researcher as the key instrument, especially in qualitative research, it fails to recognize the impact of the interaction between the researcher and the researched on the quality of the data. In the African context, *Ubuntu* (humanness in humanity), the "I/We" relationship is limited because the African cultural value emphasizes that the individual must not only be accepted but also be respected. In other words, there is need to preserve the individuality and the collective in research presentations.

Since the experience discussed in this chapter reveals the existing dynamics of the cultural context, social research ethical standards should be revised to accommodate this diversity. For example, an attempt should be made to revise, reformulate, or rethink those aspects of traditional Western ethics that depreciate or devalue other social context experiences. This chapter illustrates that while the African ethical context does not dismiss other contributions, it is different from the feminist standpoint theory because, in addition to an emphasis on *care* of the research participants, it is also concerned with healing and transformation. For example, sensitivity to certain ethical concerns is necessary in African ethics because of the unique experience of marginalization that is characterized by the tragedy of imposing foreign frameworks and alienating students from their cultures, worldviews, environments, and continents. Chilisa (2005) revealed that the thinking of black Africans is "circular and therefore complex and multiple, reflecting the interconnectedness that people have with the environment, the spirits, ancestors and everything around them" (p. 661).

♦ Summary

This chapter started by giving an overview of ethical theoretical frameworks in an effort to acknowledge contributions of different ethical contexts as well as to identify gaps. Using the author's practical fieldwork experiences in an African context, additional ethical dilemmas specific to that context included the varied levels of informed consent (i.e., individual, target group, and community relationships); anonymity and confidentiality; the use of technology; the insider/outsider dilemma; and individual versus collective interviewing. Based on these fieldwork ethical dilemmas, an analysis of the critical self-reflection on the role of the researcher reveals that the interaction of the researcher and human participants can also generate data that should be analyzed to inform social research ethics. In this particular context, the researcher's internal dilemmas reveal that in other contexts, the insider/outsider dilemma expands to issues of cooption/resistance; traditional reality of knowledge acquisition and knowledge construction versus Western notions of research objectivity; and collaborative research ethics versus collective ethics.

Overall, the analysis of the field experience with conventional social research ethics confirms the existence of the disparity between theory and practice in protecting the research participants due to diversity in cultural contexts. Qualitative research participants' responses to some ethical practices reveal their quest for being given autonomy. Finally, it was argued while the constructivist and transformative paradigms in the West give hope of reconciling some of the ethical problems identified in the chapter, an attempt needs to be made to revise, reformulate, or rethink those aspects of traditional Western ethics that depreciate or devalue other social context experiences. The African collective ethics was singled out as appealing because, while it does not dismiss other contributions, it also offers new methods of data analysis and interpretation that involves the researched in the validation of research processes and the findings.

♦ References

Adams, R. (1993). African-American studies and the state of the art. In M. Azeveto (Ed.), *Africana studies: A survey of Africa and the African Diaspora* (pp. 25–45). Durham: North Carolina Academic Press.

Asante, M. (1988). *Afrocentricity.* Trenton, NY: African World Press.

Asante, M. (1990). *Kemet, Afrocentricity and knowledge.* Trenton, NY: African World Press.

Asante, M. K. (1995). *Afrocentricity: The theory of social change.* Retrieved September 15, 2004, from http://64.233.187.104/search?q=cache:Vrrntf9t3DsJ:www.africawithin.com/asante/social_change.htm+Afrocentricity:+The+theory+of+social+change&hl=en&ie=UTF-8

Avoseh, M. B. M. (2001). Learning to be active citizens: Lessons of traditional Africa for lifelong learning. *International Journal of Lifelong Education, 20*(6), 479–486.

Bailey, K. D. (1994). *Ethical standards in research: Contextualizing guidelines to fit ethnographic needs.* Thousand Oaks, CA: Sage.

Behar, R. (1993). *Translated woman: Crossing the border with Esperanza's story.* Boston: Beacon.

Berg, B. L. (2004). *Qualitative research methods for the social sciences* (5th ed.). Boston: Pearson Education.

Bogdan, R. C., & Biklen, S. K. (1992). *Qualitative research in education: An introduction to theory and methods.* Boston: Allyn & Bacon.

Chilisa, B. (2005). Educational research within postcolonial Africa: A critique of HIV/AIDS research in Botswana. *International Journal of Qualitative Studies, 18*(6), 659–684.

Chilisa, B., & Preece, J. (2005). *Research methods for adult educators in Africa.* Cape Town, South Africa: Pearson Education.

Collins, P. (1991). *Black feminist thought.* New York: Routledge.

Creswell, J. W. (1998). *Qualitative inquiry and research design: Choosing among five traditions.* Thousand Oaks, CA: Sage.

Cunningham, C. W., & Durie, M. H. (1998). *A taxonomy and a framework for outcomes and strategic research goals for Maorie research and development.* Paper presented at the meeting of Foresight participants. New Zealand: Massey University.

Dube, M. W. (2000). *Postcolonial feminist interpretation of the Bible.* St Louis, MO: Chalice Press.

Flaherty, M. (1995). Freedom of expression or freedom of exploitation. *The Northern Review, 14,* 178–185.

Gilligan, C. (1982). *In a different voice.* Cambridge, MA: Harvard University Press.

Hertz, R. (1996). Introduction, ethics, reflexivity and voice. *Qualitative Sociology, 19,* 3–9.

Heshusius, L. (1994). Freeing ourselves from objectivity: Mapping subjectivity or turning toward a participatory mode of consciousness? *Educational Researcher, 23*(3), 15–22.

Lundsford, A. A., & Ray, R. E. (1996). Ethics and representation in teacher research. In P. Mortensen & G. E. Kirsch (Eds.), *Ethics and representation in qualitative studies of literacy* (pp. 287–301). Urbana: National Council of Teachers in Education.

Mazama, A. (2001). The Afrocentric paradigm. *Journal of Black Studies, 31*(4), 387–405.

Mkabela, N. Q., & Luthuli, P. C. (1997). *Towards an African philosophy of education.* Pretoria, South Africa: Kagiso Tertiary.

Mkabela, Q. (2005). Using the Afrocentric method in researching indigenous African culture. *Qualitative Report, 10*(1), 178–189.

Newkirk, T. (1996). Seduction and betrayal in qualitative research. In P. Mortensen & G. E. Kirsch (Eds.), *Ethics and representation in qualitative stidues of literacy* (pp. 3–16). Urbana: National Council of Teachers in Education.

Ntseane, P. G. (2006). Western and indigenous African knowledge systems affecting gender and HIV/AIDS prevention in Botswana. In S. Merriam, B. C. Courtenay, & R. M. Cerviro (Eds.), *Global issues and adult education: Perspectives from Latin America, Southern Africa and the United States* (pp. 219–230). San Francisco: Jossey-Bass.

Patai, D. (1991). Sick and tired of scholars nouveau solipsion. *Chronicle of Higher Education, 40*(25), A52.

Punch, M. (1994). Politics and ethics in qualitative research. In N. K. Denzin & Y. S. Lincoln (Eds.), *Handbook of qualitative research* (pp. 83–98). Thousand Oaks, CA: Sage.

Smith, L. T. (1999). *Decolonizing methodologies: Research and indigenous peoples.* London: Zed Books.

Wilkinson, S., & Kitzinger, C. (Eds.). (1996). *Representing the other: A feminism and psychology reader.* London: Sage.

William, C., & Heikes, E. J. (1993). The importance of the researcher's gender in the in-depth interview: Evidence from two studies of male nurses. *Gender and Society, 7,* 280–291.

Wolf, M. (1992). *A thrice-told-tale: Feminism, postmodernism, and ethnographic responsibility.* Stanford, CA: Stanford University Press.

20

MAINTAINING INDIGENOUS VOICES

◆ Fiona Cram

At the age of 21 Deborah Cheetham met her real family and found that by birth she was Aborigine. Up until that moment she had believed herself to be a part of her affluent, white, Baptist family. She describes the resentment of people who react negatively to her reclaiming her Aborigine heritage after she has experienced the privileges of assimilation: "This whole 'privileged' thing is like being given a pair of shoes that are one size too small. Everybody says 'Look at those shoes, you're so lucky! You should be so grateful . . . ' but you're still walking around in shoes that don't fit and it hurts. Eventually, you get scars."

—*Sunday Star Times* (July 18, 1999, p. D2)

In this chapter, the "shoes that don't fit" are the representations that have been imposed on indigenous peoples. These representations speak back to us, in someone else's voice, about who we are, where we belong, and what we should strive to become. They are the annihilation, assimilation, and/or integration agendas of colonial governments faced with indigenous peoples whose indigenous feet cling too tightly to land that is required for newcomer settlement. And they are the "civilization" that is forced on us, courtesy of god, education, and science.

These representations have invariably been about how indigenous peoples are different from, and deficient when compared with, the newcomer, nonindigenous peoples. This, in turn, justifies the marginalization of indigenous peoples from their lands, cultures, and families, and from having a say in their futures. And often, the people complicit in evidencing these representations have been, and continue to be, scientists. But this chapter does not purport to speak on behalf of all indigenous peoples for, while our experiences at a broad level may have similarities, the intimate details of the hurts and injustices experienced prevent grand generalizations being made (and this may apply to even those generalizations that opened this chapter). Rather, this chapter is about "writing what you know" and so begins and ends with the experience of Māori, the indigenous peoples of Aotearoa[1] New Zealand. And even at this level, there is caution about generalizing—to the point where this chapter describes what one Māori woman, with roots within the tribe of Ngāti Kahungunu, has been thinking about. So, with those provisos, I encourage you to "think along with me . . . take what is useful and leave the rest" (Hampton, 1993, p. 261).

This chapter looks first, and briefly, at the experience of colonization and then asks how research has aided the colonial agenda. Breaking the links between research and colonization begins with the recognition that the two are intertwined, followed by the active decolonization of research and the recognition of the rights of Māori and other indigenous peoples to define and represent ourselves. In the second section, the UN Declaration of the Rights of Indigenous Peoples is previewed, alongside other declarations of indigenous rights to indigenous identities, indigenous knowledge, and the means of knowledge production. These declarations add strength to calls from Māori for *Kaupapa Māori* research (i.e., research done the Māori way).

What then follows is an exploration, through seven cultural values, of a "community-up" approach to defining researcher conduct (Cram, 2001; L. T. Smith, 1999, 2006). These cultural values underscore a Kaupapa Māori research "relationship ethic." It is acknowledged that this work may resonate with the desires of other peoples to make research processes and outcomes more supportive of the emancipatory goals of their own group; for example, feminists (e.g., Lather, 1991), African Americans (e.g., hooks, 1984), and people with disabilities (see Barnes, Chapter 29, this volume). Again, at a broad level, we are all committed to the displacement of oppressive knowledge. At a local level, Kaupapa Māori addresses the oppression of Māori in our own land and the breaches of the Treaty of Waitangi guarantees of *tino rangatiratanga* (sovereignty). In this way, it is unique.

♦ Colonization and Research

When Captain James Cook arrived on the shores of Aotearoa ("Land of the long, white cloud") in 1769, he encountered a people who thought of themselves as ordinary, as *tangata maori* (Orange, 1987). Cook's descriptions of these people could be said to attest to his admiration for them, for example, "The Natives of this Country are strong, raw boned, well-made, Active people rather above the common size" (Beaglehole, 1968, p. 278). Looking back from the shore, and from *waka* (canoes), our ancestors knew that the newcomers were different from them, that these white people were the "other." And so the scene was set for many encounters, both friendly and unfriendly (Salmond, 1991).

After Cook came whalers, sealers, and traders. Timber and flax were important trading items and several shore stations were established. The early European settlers respected the control of the Māori and a relationship was forged based on interdependence and economic advantage. Then, in 1814 the first missionaries arrived—contributing European agricultural technologies, a written version of the Māori language (essential for spreading the "good word"), and Christian and Victorian morality (see, e.g., Barrington & Beaglehole, 1974; Walker, 1990). During these times, the price of contact with the newcomers was paid for in Māori deaths from introduced infectious diseases. Charles Darwin's visit in 1935 reinforced a belief that these deaths were a natural outcome of an inferior people (Māori) living alongside a superior people (non-Māori newcomers; (Desmond & Moore, 1991). And this belief held firm as the Māori population declined by a third or more during the 19th century.

By 1840, there were 2,000 newcomers in this country and an estimated 200,000 to 500,000 Māori (Durie, 1994). From this dominant position, Māori chiefs entered into a treaty, *Te Tiriti o Waitangi* (the Treaty of Waitangi), with the newcomers that guaranteed Māori the rights of British subjects, alongside continued sovereignty and control over their possessions. This treaty is the constitutional code that created this nation and it signaled the willingness of Māori to share this land (A. Mead, 1999). However, this treaty was not honored by the newcomers and, within a few short decades after its signing, Māori were the ones who were the "other" (Orange, 1987; Walker, 1990), pushed to the margins in our own lands (see McIntosh, 2005).

Ward Churchill (1996) wrote that the process of colonization rests on the dehumanization of indigenous peoples and the belief that their rights are lesser than those of the newcomers. This process incorporates a mix of science, cultural arrogance, and political power (see L. T. Smith, 1999). Colonization transforms the economic, political, demographic, and social order of a society as the power and resources of the indigenous inhabitants are redistributed to the newcomers (Jackson, 1996). Systems that are established by the newcomers then ensure that this redistribution continues to occur until colonization is explicitly acknowledged and addressed (Teariki & Spoonley, 1992). In this way, social inequalities and racism are concealed and the position of the newcomers is secured.

Wade Nobles's exploration of political and scientific colonialism is helpful in understanding the drivers behind colonization and the role research plays (see Table 20.1). Just as political colonialism lays claim to products in the colonies that have commercial value, scientific colonialism is about the belief that information can be accessed and created as a right by newcomer scientists. Within Aotearoa New Zealand scientific colonialism has its roots in the Darwinian mythology of Māori inferiority. Māori have been, and continue to be, constructed within colonial worldviews and ways of knowing with the result that the mainstream "commonsense" is one of Māori deficit (Cram, 1997). Ngahuia Te Awekotuku (1991) described this as "many decades—even centuries—of thoughtless, exploitative, mercenary academic objectification" (p. 12).

As a result, we have found ourselves in "minoritized spaces," dislocated from "white," "normalized," "majoritized space" (Laguerre, 1999), with this reflected in poor health, social, and economic outcomes (Robson & Harris, 2007). The experiences of other indigenous peoples are similar (Harry, 2001; Janke, 1988).

As a result of the colonization of Aotearoa, Māori now live in two lands (Reid & Cram, 2004). In one land, Aotearoa, we remain *tangata maori*, ordinary. Within many Māori gatherings and in places where being Māori is normal we find ourselves, our knowledge, and our ways of knowing accepted and validated. Within Aotearoa, a positive discourse around Māori values and beliefs is a taken-for-granted commonsense. It is not unusual to hear Māori talk about the comfort and safety they are able to find in Māori situations where they do not have to explain what being Māori is about and why being Māori

Table 20.1	Comparative Colonialisms	
Colonialism Manifested by	Political Colonialism	Scientific Colonialism
1. Removal of wealth	Exportation of raw materials and wealth from colonies for the purpose of "processing" it into manufactured wealth and/or goods.	Exporting raw data from a community for the purpose of "processing" it into manufactured goods (i.e., books, articles, wealth).
2. Right of access and claim	Colonial power believes it has the *right of access* and use for its own benefit anything belonging to the colonized people.	Scientist believes he or she has unlimited *right of access* to any data source and any information belonging to the subject population.
3. External power base	The center of power and control over the colonized is located outside the colony itself.	The center of knowledge and information about a people or community located outside of the community or people themselves.

SOURCE: Nobles (1991, p. 296, table 1).

is okay—because everyone knows. (This is not to be naïve or romantic about the other issues and tensions that exist within these forums.)

The other land, New Zealand, is often the place Māori have to go for education, employment, health care, and welfare assistance. Many Māori occupy this place more or less permanently and have become accustomed to it, whereas for others it is like a pair of ill-fitting shoes that are hurriedly pushed off on their return to Aotearoa. The challenge of Kaupapa Māori (a Māori way, see section Kaupapa Māori) is to reclaim New Zealand as Aotearoa, for Māori and for whomever else wants to share this place on our terms. These terms are not difficult to locate as they are in the Māori text of *te Tiriti o Waitangi*. The guarantee of *tino rangatiratanga* is the affirmation of our sovereignty and our right to determine our own destiny. It is the guarantee of our right to be Māori on our own terms. And just as research has played a role in our colonization, research that is done under Kaupapa Māori, or supporting a Māori kaupapa, can assist in this decolonization project.

♦ Reclaiming and Decolonizing Research

The Declaration on the Rights of Indigenous Peoples by the United Nations (2007) recognizes that indigenous peoples have been deprived of human rights and fundamental freedoms during the course of our colonial histories and that colonization has prevented indigenous peoples "from exercising, in particular, their right to development in accordance with their own needs and interests" (p. 1). The Declaration contains 45 articles that acknowledge critical issues for indigenous peoples, including the right to our identity, to name ourselves, to self-determination and the maintenance of our traditions and languages, and to our intellectual and cultural properties. These are reinforced by our rights to be protected from further dispossession and from propaganda directed against us.

The principles embodied within the Declaration also run through many of the statements made by indigenous peoples about their rights as guardians of their own heritage, as well as the producers of new knowledge and representations about themselves. The Alaska Native Knowledge Network (1995) defined the heritage of indigenous peoples as being composed of "all objects, sites and knowledge the nature or use of which has been transmitted from generation to generation, and which is regarded as pertaining to a particular people or its territory" (p. 11). This also encompasses future objects, knowledge, and works. Likewise, the Mataatua Declaration on Cultural and Intellectual Property Rights of Indigenous Peoples (1993) calls on state, national, and international agencies to "recognize that indigenous peoples also have the right to create new knowledge based on cultural traditions" (p. 2.2), alongside their guardianship of customary knowledge.

These reassertions of indigenous rights to indigenous knowledge, both traditional and contemporary, have rippled through the research world. Some of the first steps taken in the decolonizing of indigenous research were by nonindigenous social scientists working in conjunction with indigenous communities. They recognized that different ways of engaging with, and researching, indigenous people needed to be found if the research was to be valid as well as "useful" to the communities. Common recommendations made were for more collaborative research, conducted by culturally sensitive researchers (Moewaka Barnes, 2000; World Health Organization, 1997).

Many guidebooks and ethical protocols have emerged over the past 10 to 20 years that speak on how nonindigenous peoples should conduct themselves when doing research with indigenous peoples. Now, many of these even state that the research should be *for* rather than merely *on* indigenous groups (e.g., Health Research Council, 1998). The involvement of nonindigenous researchers in indigenous research is now expected to be more collaborative, "within the framework of mutual respect, equity, and empowerment" (Indigenous Research Protection Act 1.6, Indigenous People's Council on Biocolonialism). "Mutual understanding and trust" is the comparable phrase used by the Association of Canadian Universities for Northern Studies (ACUNS) Council in its Ethical Principles for the Conduct of Research in the North. The term *partnership ethic* has also been coined by the ACUNS Council, emphasizing "the need to create meaningful relationships with the people and communities affected by research" (ACUNS Council, 1997).

At the same time as the development of a new research ethic for nonindigenous researchers, there has been a growth in the capacity of indigenous peoples to conduct their own research. In this country, non-Māori researchers are instructed to share their skills with their Māori collaborators, and many funding agencies have instigated training and scholarship opportunities for Māori interested in research careers. In Hawai'i, programs such as "Imi Hale—Native Hawaiian Cancer Network" are striving to build Native Hawaiian health research capacity (Tsark & Braun, 2004). According to the World Health Organization (1997), "the increasing numbers of indigenous peoples who have slowly taken the initiative in their own research . . . have turned the bogeyman of 'otherness' on its head. They now seek to determine the agenda of research about themselves, what to study, how, and who will do the research" (p. 10).

◆ Kaupapa Māori

In Aotearoa New Zealand, the development of Kaupapa Māori has set the scene for research that is "by Māori, for Māori, with Māori."[2] Kaupapa Māori is literally "a Māori way" (Taki, 1996). According to Graham Smith (1997), Kaupapa Māori is underpinned by Māori philosophies and has a vision of Maori cultural, social, and economic well-being. Kaupapa Māori informs practice, research, and policy within many disciplines (e.g., education, health, social services) and within mainstream (where Māori groups operate) Māori and Iwi (tribal) contexts (see, e.g., Pihama, Cram, & Walker, 2002). For example, Kaupapa Māori programs and services that are developed by Māori providers, for Māori communities, encompass Māori cultural values and practices and so connect with, and serve, their communities well (Pipi et al., 2002).

Kaupapa Māori research[3] is prescribed for Māori researchers in cultural terms (Te Awekotuku, 1991) and makes "cultural and moral sense" (Durie, 1996). Our ancestors existed within a research culture whereby knowledge was refashioned "as part of ongoing information management practices" (Reid, 1999, p. 61), and Kaupapa Māori is about reclaiming this. It is about a reflexive cycle of evolving, growing, and updating our knowledge base, sourced from within our own values and beliefs (Henry & Pene, 2001). Kaupapa Māori research can facilitate the revitalization of traditional constructions as well as the formation of new constructions of what it means to be Māori within Aotearoa and within New Zealand. The role of researchers is therefore twofold: the affirmation and validation of Māori worldviews (the Aotearoa component) and the critique of Pākehā/colonial constructions of Māori (the New Zealand component).

While the protocols guiding research with indigenous communities largely target nonindigenous researchers and emphasize a "partnership ethic," Kaupapa Māori research stresses a "relationship ethic" (Ormond, Cram, & Carter, 2006). It is the relationship connections between those involved that guide the way the research is conducted. These connections are made by "identifying, through culturally appropriate means, your bodily linkage, your engagement, your connectedness . . . [to] people" (Bishop, 1996, p. 152). For example, my colleagues and I have found that people's agreement to participate in research is often based as much on the trust they have in us as members of the same tribe as it is on our capabilities as researchers (Cram et al., 1997). The "community-up" approach initiated by Linda Smith acknowledges that the key accountabilities that indigenous researchers have is to their own people within a relationship ethic, and offers guidance for researchers that is drawn from seven Māori cultural values. These are explored next.

◆ A "Community-Up" Approach

Initially, Linda Smith (1999) introduced the notion of a code of conduct for Kaupapa Māori research and proposed seven practices to guide the behavior of Māori researchers. These were expanded on by Cram and colleagues (Cram, 2001; Pipi et al., 2004) and then featured in L. T. Smith (2005, 2006; see Table 20.2). Other Māori researchers have also reflected on the practices (e.g., Jones, Crengle, & McCreanor, 2006). There are many overlaps between (as well as layers within) these practices. However, it is useful here to explore them in turn.

AROHA KI TE TANGATA

Aroha ki te tangata is about researchers having respect for the people who are their research collaborators and participants. Within Māori culture, there are ways of showing respect that are based on common understandings of how two peoples come together to accomplish a task. "Rituals of first encounter" bridge the multiple ways in which people are separated spatially and spiritually (Irwin, 1994). These rituals may involve the observation of quite formal protocols or may be less formal. At their heart these rituals are about relationship building and strengthening, and the establishment of genealogical connections, which may include "relationships to non-kin persons who have become like kin through shared experiences" (H. M. Mead, 2003, p. 28). Elders who are knowledgeable about

Table 20.2 "Community-Up" Approach to Defining Research Conduct

Cultural Values (L. T. Smith, 1999)	Researcher Guidelines (Cram, 2001)
Aroha ki te tangata	A respect for people—allow people to define their own space and meet on their own terms
He kanohi kitea	It is important to meet people face-to-face, and to also be a face that is known to and seen within a community
Titiro, whakarongo . . . kōrero	Looking and listening (and then maybe speaking)—develop understanding to find a place from which to speak
Manaaki ki te tangata	Sharing, hosting, being generous
Kia tupato	Be cautious—be politically astute, culturally safe, and reflective about insider/outsider status
Kaua e takahia te mana o te tangata	Do not trample on the *"mana"* or dignity of a person
Kia mahaki	Be humble—do not flaunt your knowledge; find ways of sharing it

SOURCE: Adapted from L. T. Smith (2006, p. 12, diagram 1).

genealogy are important to this process as they are able to make connections between people, and also advise about proper processes and formalities.

These rituals also orient visitors to the ways in which the local people conduct themselves which, in turn, has implications for the ways in which researchers should conduct themselves. Such rituals may be important even if the researchers and the local people are closely related as a discussion about conduct with respect to a "research relationship" might not have taken place before. When researchers are well-known within their communities they may be able to move quickly while still adhering to tribal protocols (cf. Pipi et al., 2004).

Genealogical connections may gain a researcher entry to a community and the support and guidance of elders (also see subsection *Kia tupato*), and they may assist in the recruitment of participants, but ultimately it is the researcher's professional conduct that will transform these opportunities into research realities.

HE KANOHI KITEA

The source of this guideline is the *whakatauki* (traditional saying), "He reo e rangona, engari, he kanohi kitea," translated as "A voice may be heard but a face needs to be seen." *He kanohi kitea* is often taken to mean that meetings between the researcher and the community, including research participants, should occur face-to-face as this "allows the people in the community to use all their senses as complementary sources of information" (Pipi & Cram, 2000, cited in Pipi et al., 2004, p. 146). Māori research often begins with *hui* (meetings) between researchers and community stakeholders to negotiate permission for, and the parameters of, a research project (e.g., Glynn, Berryman, Grace, & Glynn, 2004; Waldon, 2004).

He kanohi kitea is also about the relationships that are built between the researchers and the research community (before, during, and after the research project), so that the researcher is someone who is known to, and seen around, the community. Research that includes local people as, for example, interviewers, *kaiawhina* (support people), or coordinators, has the added advantage that these people live in, and are seen in, the community (Jones et al., 2006; Pipi et al., 2004).

In this technological age, new research methods are available to us that may challenge the idea of face-to-face engagement with research participants throughout the research process and the notion that a researcher is a "known" face becomes more important. So, for example, interviews may be conducted over the telephone or via an e-mail exchange without necessarily being culturally inappropriate. Suzanne Pitama conducted a focus group with Māori weavers by teleconference; a method that was made possible by the participants all knowing one another and "knowing" the researcher because they had met her or because they knew how she was related to one of their colleagues (Cram et al., 2002).

TITIRO, WHAKARONGO... KŌRERO

Titiro, whakarongo... kōrero is the fine art of watching, listening, and then, sometime later, talking. In this way, a researcher can soak in what people are saying and observe their actions without the pressure to contribute until they have a good understanding of the context for, and the content of, what they are seeing and hearing. This helps build trust between researcher and research participants as the researcher is showing his or her respect for the people who are contributing. This practice has its roots in a Māori language learning school known as *Ataarangi*: Pupils are initially encouraged to acquire the language through looking and listening, and letting their Māori world grow inside their worldly knowledge.

Within group interactions, Moana Jackson (1988) described this process as *whakawhitiwhiti kōrero* or shared thoughts. This is akin to the "mutual thinking" that Sheryl Te Hennepe (1993) described as an outcome of the time taken within a relationship to discover the intricacies of one another.

Within a research setting this is about making sure that research participants are truly understood so that a researcher is able to be guided by them throughout the research process and is capable of representing them well within the research outputs. It is also about listening and looking from a strengths-based perspective that seeks to challenge mainstream understandings and explicate Māori versions of reality.

MANAAKI KI TE TANGATA

Manaaki ki te tangata is about looking after people. Within research it encompasses the ways in which the researcher gives back to the community, through gifts and other forms of reciprocity that acknowledge the time and energy research participants and communities have committed to a research project. It is now accepted practice that research participants receive a small *koha* (gift; Jones et al., 2006). Other forms of reciprocity such as training, networking, and access to the researchers for community-initiated projects are also important.

Throughout their research process, the Māori health research centre, *Te Rōpū Rangahau a Eru Pōmare*, have been in the community "consulting, liaising, researching, giving feedback on research results, teaching research methods, and doing all manner of odd jobs" (Cram et al., 1997). This reciprocity, or *utu* in Māori terms, is not bounded by time and extends beyond the "end" of a research project—such is the nature of a relationship ethic (Bevan-Brown,

1998). If there is no reciprocity, then the community's resources have been diminished by the research (Fullilove & Fullilove III, 1993; also see subsection *Kia mahaki*).

KIA TUPATO

Kia tupato literally means "be careful." Within a research setting, this is about researchers and participants being culturally safe. For Hirini Mead (2003), being *tika* (right) is about being guided by *tikanga* (cultural rules and protocols). Similarly, Kathy Irwin (1994, p. 27) wrote that culturally safe research happens when "Māori institutions, principles and practices are highly valued and followed." For example, in one epidemiological study, personnel records were blessed by a *kaumatua* (elder) prior to them being accessed by the researchers. This ensured the safety of the researchers as some of the records were of people who had passed away (Keefe et al., Cram, & Purdie, 1999).

The genealogical connections made by a researcher also provide an assurance of safety and support. As Arawhetu Peretini (1992) pointed out, "the system of guardianship is an extremely old and cherished concept in *Te Ao Māori* [the Māori world], with many of the roles of guardians being to act as caretakers, mentors, teachers, protectors" (p. 12). It is only a short step to see the role that such guardians can play in Māori research. In their reflections on research interviews conducted with Māori families that had lost a baby to Sudden Infant Death Syndrome (SIDS), Edwards, McManus, and McCreanor (2005) stressed the important role played by the Māori SIDS Prevention (MSP) care workers who were present during the interviews. The MSP care workers were on hand to offer expert support and comfort to participants during and after the interviews, and their presence helped participants maintain their composure while talking about this grief-laden topic.

KAUA E TAKAHIA TE MANA O TE TANGATA

Kaua e takahia te mana o te tangata translates as not trampling the *mana* (authority) of the people. While all the practices explored here are in some way about upholding the *mana* of those involved in a research project, the particular focus here is on the analysis and reporting of research findings. One complaint often heard from Māori communities is that they have not received feedback on the findings of research they have been involved in. When this occurs, they are not only left unformed about findings, they are unable to judge whether the researcher has represented them well (Cram, 2006).

To be faithfully represented within research may involve a journey of healing for those who participate. In these circumstances, the need to uphold participants' *mana* in any account of the research findings is especially highlighted. For example, the Davis Inlet People's Inquiry (Labrador, Canada) was sparked by the deaths of six children in a house fire on February 14, 1992. The children died because there was confusion about whether they were in the house and because there was no water to put out the fire. The whole community was involved in the inquiry and the resulting report, "Gathering Voices," was seen by the community "as a tool to help us to solve our problems on our road to recovery." In the acknowledgments of the Innu Nation and Innu Band Council's report on the Davis Inlet People's Inquiry (1995), "Gathering voices," David (Tepit) Nui, Katie (Kiti) Rich, and Tshenish Pasteen describe the motivations behind the inquiry: "We hope this gathering of voices has broken the silence of a forgotten people. We hope also that it will continue to help our true spirit and strength, as well as dignity to plan our future" (p. xi).

The *mana* of this community rested and was maintained by the way their stories were represented. Within Kaupapa Māori research, there is a focus on the representation of Māori research findings from a strengths base, rather than the victim blaming, deficit base that we have seen so often in mainstream research. As "insiders,"[4] Māori researchers may be at an advantage as they can "hear" the commonsense of their communities; they understand the reality of the lives of the people they are researching (cf. Bishop, 1996) and so can represent them well. At the same time, this positioning—this grounding in a Māori worldview—does not preclude Māori researchers from being rigorous, systematic, ethical, and scientific (L. T. Smith, 1995).

KIA MAHAKI

Kia mahaki is about being humble; sharing knowledge and seeking to empower the community through research. Empowerment is the facilitation of opportunities and possibilities for people to actively control their own lives (cf. Rappaport, 1981). To be real, the community itself must decide what is empowering for them (Durie, 1996), with the researcher able to contribute by "de-powering" themselves (Huygens, 1993). This de-powering involves the sharing of knowledge, expertise, networks, and so on with a community so that, for example, they are better placed to access research findings and put them to use for the community's own ends (also see subsection *Manaaki ki te tangata*). Margaret Mutu (1998) wrote about the importance of sharing in this process:

> Shared knowledge . . . is one of the key tools for empowering the people and providing controls to prevent the misuse and abuse of power. . . . the results of research are of little use to the people if they are not then made available to form part of the knowledge base of the people and to help them make decisions. (p. 51)

Empowerment can happen at a variety of levels, for example, individual, *whānau* (families), community, and society. Fullilove and Fullilove III (1993, p. 129) suggested ways of giving back to a research community, which are about empowerment: sharing knowledge about research so that the community becomes less reliant on researchers, sharing the results of the research with the community, and involving the community as a coproducer of research.

Research might result in people feeling empowered because they have been represented by "one of their own"; a Māori researcher, one of their relations, has understood them and been able to tell their stories in ways that uplifts them and does not trample on their *mana*. Or the representations of them by a researcher might change their explanations from their own circumstances from ones based on personal deficit to ones emphasizing the denial of rights (Kidder & Fine, 1986). This may empower communities to challenge deficit, victim-blaming practices and policies and thereby reclaim Aotearoa piece by piece.

◆ Conclusions

This chapter has presented an overview of one framework for organizing Māori researcher roles and responsibilities within a relationship ethic. The aim of doing so is to add to the dialogue about how to undertake research, "so that in the end everyone who is connected with the research project is enriched, empowered, enlightened and glad to have been part of it" (H. M. Mead, 2003, p. 318). As researchers, we practice with a vision that our research will change the world but, at the same time, we want to do our best to ensure that if change does not happen overnight, then at least our communities will be better off in some small ways for having engaged with us.

Research guidelines have eased the entry into our communities of non-Māori researchers by assisting them with passwords and ideas about collaboration within a "partnership ethic." For Māori researchers, and other indigenous peoples around the world, such guidelines may not be enough as the people we do research with are our relations and our children's children need to know that there is a place for them in our communities, that we have not spoiled their *turangawaewae* (home ground) for them through our unethical research. Our responsibilities are therefore greater, and longer lived, than those of our non-indigenous colleagues. The "community-up" approach described here offers some insight into how Māori strive to achieve this. Its validity for other indigenous peoples will be in if, and how, it resonates with, or helps promote, their own models of research practice with their relations.

Research is one tool Māori use to recenter ourselves as "ordinary." To do this, we aim to ensure that research serves us better, that it allows our stories to be both told and heard, and that it destabilizes "existing power structures that hold us in the margins" (L. T. Smith, 2006). This is not to say that we are naïve. Research is a political endeavor; it is not knowledge that is power, rather it is those in power who dictate what is and what is not "valid" knowledge and often this validity is about maintaining the status quo. When Māori use research and other tools to push back from our position of marginalization, this is a threat to the status quo and so those at the center will, and do, push back. Our research will continue to be interrogated by those in power. And we will continue to be committed to decolonizing research so that it facilitates the decentering of "whiteness as ownership the world forever and forever" (DuBois, 1920, cited in Myers, 2004, p. 8). Our very survival may well depend on this happening.

◆ Notes

1. While Aotearoa is used here as the Māori name for our country, we [I] must apologize to those in the tribe of Ngai Tahu who consider that "Aotearoa" relates solely to the North Island.

2. Linda Smith (1999) argued that while non-Māori researchers cannot do Kaupapa Māori research, they can support a Māori Kaupapa (see also Cram, 1997).

3. Within Kaupapa Māori research, we have adopted a critical stance that reflects on both our research methodology and method. By methodology, we mean the philosophical approach that determines the way we undertake research, including, for example, our relationship with participants and the communities in which we work and live. In this case, Kaupapa Māori theory has informed our approach and our research practice. Methods, on the other hand, are tools that can be used to produce and analyze data, for example, in-depth interviewing, questionnaires, and so on.

4. Within a relationship ethic, researchers need to acknowledge and negotiate the multiple ways in which they will be insiders and outsiders to a community they are doing research with; for example, they may live away from "home," have academic qualifications, be male or female, young or old, and so on. And because researchers need to maintain a professionalism that makes themselves and their research practice safe for their community, they will of necessity be looking "in from the outside while also looking out from the inside" (Minh-Ha, 1991, p. 74). Graham Smith (1997, p. 31) used the phrase *organic intellectual*, after Gramsci, to describe his position on the "outside" as a Māori academic who speaks from the "inside" about Māori aspirations with respect to Māori education.

◆ References

ACUNS Council. (1997). *ACUNS ethical principles for the conduct of research in the North*, revised document approved by ACUNS Council, 28 November 1997. Retrieved September 16, 2002, from www.yukoncollege.yk.ca/~agraham/ethics.htm

Alaska Native Knowledge Network. (1995). *Principles and guidelines for the protection of the heritage of indigenous peoples*. Alaska Native Knowledge Network, University of Alaska, Fairbanks. Retrieved

March 4, 1999, from www.ankn.uaf.edu/protect.html

Barrington, J. M., & Beaglehole, T. H. (1974). *Māori schools in a changing society*. Wellington: New Zealand Education Research Council.

Beaglehole, J. C. (1955–1974). *The journals of Captain James Cook on his voyages of discovery* (4 Vols.). Cambridge, UK: Cambridge University Press.

Bevan-Brown, J. (1998, July 7–9). *By Māori, for Māori, about Māori: Is that enough?* Paper presented at the Te Oru Rangahau Māori Research and Development Conference Massey University, Palmerston North, Auckland, New Zealand.

Bishop, R. (1996). Addressing issues in self-determination and legitimation in Kaupapa Maori Research. In B. Webber (compiler), *He paipai korero* (pp. 143–160). Wellington: New Zealand Council for Educational Research.

Churchill, W. (1996). *From a Native Son: Selected essays on indigenism, 1985–1995*. Boston: South End Press.

Commission on Human Rights. Sub-Commission on Prevention of Discrimination and Protection of Minorities. (1993, June 12–18). *Mataatua Declaration on Cultural and Intellectual Property Rights of Indigenous Peoples*. Formulated at the First International Conference on the Cultural and Intellectual Property Rights of Indigenous Peoples, Whakatane, Aotearoa, New Zealand. Retrieved February 11, 2004, from www.aotearoa.wellington.net.nz/imp/mata.htm

Commission on Human Rights. Sub-Commission on Prevention of Discrimination and Protection of Minorities, Forty-fifth session (1993, August). *Draft declaration on the rights of indigenous peoples. Discrimination against indigenous peoples*. Report of the working group on indigenous populations on its eleventh session. Chairperson: Ms Erica-Irene A. Daes (Annex 1). Geneva, Switzerland: Author. Retrieved February 11, 2004, from the Native Law Centre of Canada, University of Saskatchewan Web site: http://www.cwis.org/drft9329.html

Cram, F. (1997). Developing partnerships in research: Māori research and Pākehā researchers. *SITES, 35*, 44–63.

Cram, F. (2001). Rangahau Maori: Tona Tika, Tona Pono. In M. Tolich (Ed.), *Research ethics in Aotearoa* (pp. 35–52). Auckland, New Zealand: Longman.

Cram, F. (2006). Talking ourselves up. *Alternative: An International Journal of Indigenous Scholarship* (Special Suppl. 2, *Marginalisation*), 28–45.

Cram, F. (with Henare, M., Hunt, T., Mauger, J., Pahiri, D., Pitama, S., & Tuuta, C.). (2002). *Maori and science: Three case studies*. (A report prepared for the Royal Society of New Zealand). Auckland, New Zealand: IRI.

Cram, F., Keefe, V., Ormsby, C., Ormsby, W., & Ngāti Kahungunu Iwi Inc. (1997). Memorywork and Māori health research: Discussion of a qualitative method. *He Pukenga Kōrero, 3*, 37–45.

Desmond, A., & Moore, J. (1991). *Darwin*. London: Penguin Books.

Durie, M. (1994). *Whaiora: Maori health development* (1st ed.). Auckland, New Zealand: Oxford University Press.

Durie, M. H. (1996, February). *Characteristics of Māori Health Research*. A paper presented at the Hui Whakapiripiri: Hongoeka, Department of Māori Studies, Massey University, Palmerston North, New Zealand.

Edwards, S., McManus, V., & McCreanor, T. (2005). Collaborative research with Māori on sensitive issues: The application of tikanga and kaupapa in research on Māori Sudden Infant Death Syndrome. *Social Policy Journal of New Zealand, 25*, 88–104.

Fullilove, M. T., & Fullilove, R. E., III. (1993). Understanding sexual behaviours and drug use among African-Americans: A case study of issues for survey research. In D. G. Ostrow & R. D. Kessel (Eds.), *Methodological issues in AIDS behavioural research* (pp. 117–132). New York: Plenum Press.

Glynn, T., Berryman, M., Grace, H., & Glynn, V. (2004). Activating whānau (extended family) processes within a community and school literacy partnership. *Journal of Māori and Pacific Development, 5,* 14–30.

Hampton, E. (1993). Toward a redefinition of American Indian/Alaska Native education. *Canadian Journal of Native Education, 20*(2), 261–310.

Harry, D. (2001). Biopiracy and globalization: Indigenous peoples face a new wave of colonialism. *Splice, 7*(2/3). Retrieved April 24, 2008, from www.ipcb.org/publications/other_art/globalization.html

Health Research Council. (1998). Guidelines for researchers on health research involving Māori. Retrieved May 15, 1999, from the HRC Web site: www.hrc.govt.nz/maoguide.htm

Henry, E., & Pene, H. (2001). Kaupapa Māori: Locating indigenous ontology, epistemology and methodology within the academy. *Organisation, 8,* 234–242.

hooks, b. (1984). *Ain't I a woman: Black women and feminism.* Boston: South End Press.

Huygens, I. (1993). A letter, an idea. *New Zealand Psychological Society Bulletin, 76,* 22–25.

Innu Nation & Innu Band Council. (1995). Gathering voices: Finding strength to help our children. In C. Fouillard (Ed.), *Report on the Davis Inlet People's Inquiry.* Foreword by David (Tepit) Nui, Katie (Kiti) Rich, and Tshenish Pasteen (p. xi). Vancouver, British Columbia, Canada: Douglas & McIntyre.

Irwin, K. (1994). Māori research methods and processes: An exploration. *SITES, 28,* 25–43.

Jackson, M. (1988). *The Māori and the criminal justice system: A new perspective: He Whaipaanga Hou.* Wellington, New Zealand: Department of Justice.

Jackson, M. (1996). Māori health research and Te Tiriti o Waitangi. In Te Rōpū Rangahau Hauora a Eru Pōmare, *Hui Whakapiripiri: A Hui to discuss strategic directions for Māori health research* (pp. 8–10). New Zealand: Te Rōpū Rangahau Hauora a Eru Pōmare, Wellington School of Medicine.

Janke, T. (1998). *Our culture: Our future. Report on Australian indigenous cultural and intellectual property rights.* Sydney, Australia: Micheal Frankel.

Jones, R., Crengle, S., & McCreanor, T. (2006). How tikanga guides and protects the research process: Insights from the Hauora Tāne project. *Social Policy Journal of New Zealand, 29,* 60–77.

Keefe, V., Ormsby, C., Robson, B., Reid, P., Cram, F., & Purdie, G. (1999). Kaupapa Māori meets retrospective cohort. *He Pukenga Kōrero, 5,* 12–17.

Kidder, L. H., & Fine, M. (1986). Making sense of injustice: Social explanations, social action, and the role of the social scientist. In E. Seidman & J. Rappaport (Eds.), *Redefining social problems* (pp. 52–61). New York: Plenum Press.

Laguerre, M. (1999). *Minoritized space: An inquiry into the spatial order of things.* Berkeley: University of California, Institute of Governmental Studies Press.

Lather, P. (1991). *Getting smart: Feminist research and pedagogy with/in the postmodern.* New York: Routledge.

McIntosh, T. (2005). Māori identities: Fixed, fluid, forced. In J. H. Liu, T. McCreanor, T. McIntosh, & T. Teaiwa (Eds.), *New Zealand identities: Departures and destinations* (pp. 38–51). Wellington, New Zealand: Victoria University Press.

Mead, A., Te. P. (1999, May, 8). *Speaking to Question 6. How are the values of Maori going to be considered and integrated in the use of plant biotechnology in New Zealand?* Presented at the talking technologies conference on Plant Technology, Wellington, New Zealand.

Mead, H. M. (2003). *Tikanga Māori: Living by Māori values.* Wellington, New Zealand: Huia.

Minh-Ha, T. (1991). *When the moon waxes red: Representation, gender and cultural politics.* New York: Routledge.

Moewaka Barnes, H. (2000). Collaboration in community action: A successful partnership between indigenous communities and researchers. *Health Promotion International, 15,* 17–25.

Mutu, M. (1998, July 7–9). Barriers to research: The constraints of imposed frameworks. In Te Pūmanawa Hauora (Ed.), *Proceedings of Te Oru Rangahau Māori Research and Development Conference* (pp. 51–61). Palmerston North, Auckland, New Zealand: Massey University.

Myers, C. (2004). Differences from somewhere: The normativity of whiteness in bioethics in the United States. *American Journal of Bioethics, 3*(2), 1–11.

Nobles, W. (1991). Extended self: Rethinking the so-called negro self-concept. In R. L. Jones (Ed.), *Black psychology* (3rd ed., pp. 295–304). Berkeley, CA: Cobb & Henry.

Orange, C. (1987). *The treaty of Waitangi*. Wellington, New Zealand: Allen & Unwin.

Ormond, A., Cram, F., & Carter, L. (2006). Researching our relations: Reflections on ethics. *Alternative: An International Journal of Indigenous Scholarship* (Special Suppl. 2, Marginalisation), 180–198.

Peretini, R. (1992). *Cervical screening, Maori women and our Whanau: Report of the Maori women's working group on the cervical screening register*. Unpublished report. Wellington, New Zealand: Ministry of Health.

Pihama, L., Cram, F., & Walker, S. (2002). Creating methodological space: A literature review of Kaupapa Māori research. *Canadian Journal of Native Education, 26*, 30–43.

Pipi, K., Cram, F., Hawke, R., Hawke, S., Huriwai, TeM., Keefe, V., et al. (2002). *Māori and Iwi provider success: A research report of interviews with successful Iwi and Māori providers and government agencies*. Wellington, New Zealand: Te Puni Kokiri. Retrieved January 13, 2007, from the Te Puni Kōkiri Web site: www.tpk.govt.nz/publications/research_reports/mps_report.pdf

Pipi, K., Cram, F., Hawke, R., Hawke, S., Huriwai, TeM., Mataki, T., et al. (2004). A research ethic for studying Māori and Iwi provider success. *Social Policy Journal of New Zealand, 23*, 141–153.

Rappaport, J. (1981). *Redefining social problems*. New York: Plenum Press.

Reid, P. (1999). Te pupuri i te ao o te tangata whenua. In P. Davis & K. Dew (Eds.), *Health and society in Aotearoa New Zealand* (pp. 51–62). Auckland, New Zealand: Oxford University Press.

Reid, P., & Cram, F. (2004). Connecting health, people and country in Aotearoa/New Zealand. In K. Dew & P. Davis (Eds.), *Health and society in Aotearoa New Zealand* (2nd ed., pp. 33–48). Auckland, New Zealand: Oxford University Press.

Robson, B., & Harris, R. (2007). (Eds.). *Hauora: Māori standards of health IV, 2000–2005*. Wellington, New Zealand: Te Rōpū Rangahau Hauora a Eru Pōmare, University of Otago.

Salmond, A. (1991). *Two worlds: First meetings between Maori and Europeans 1642–1772*. Auckland, New Zealand: Viking.

Smith, G. H. (1997). *The development of Kaupapa Māori: Theory and praxis*. Doctoral dissertation, Faculty of Education, University of Auckland, New Zealand.

Smith, L. T. (1995, August). *Re-centering Kaupapa Māori research*. Paper presented at Te Matawhanui conference, Massey University, Palmerston North, Auckland, New Zealand.

Smith, L. T. (1999). *Decolonising methodologies: Research and indigenous peoples*. Otago, New Zealand: Otago University Press.

Smith, L. T. (2005). On tricky ground: Researching the native in the age of uncertainty. In N. K. Denzin & Y. S. Lincoln (Eds.), *The Sage handbook of qualitative research* (3rd ed., pp. 85–108). Thousand Oaks, CA: Sage.

Smith, L. T. (2006). Researching in the margins: Issues for Māori researchers—A discussion paper. *Alternative: An International Journal of Indigenous Scholarship* (Special Suppl. 2, Marginalisation), 4–27.

Taki, M. (1996). *Kaupapa Māori and contemporary Iwi resistance*. Unpublished M.A. thesis, Education Department, University of Auckland, New Zealand.

Te Awekotuku, N. (1991). *He tikanga whakaaro: Research ethics in the Māori community*. Wellington, New Zealand: Manatu Māori.

Te Hennepe, S. (1993). Issues of respect: Reflections of first nation students' experiences in postsecondary anthropology classrooms. *Canadian Journal of Native Education, 20,* 193–260.

Teariki, C., & Spoonley, P. (with Tomoana, N.). (1992). *Te whakapakari te mana tangata. The politics and process of research for Māori.* Auckland, New Zealand: Department of Sociology, Massey University.

Tsark, J., & Braun, K. L. (2004). Na Liko Noelo: A program to develop Native Hawaiian researchers. *Pacific Health Dialog, 11,* 225–232.

Waldon, J. (2004). Oranga kaumātua: Perceptions of health in older Māori people. *Social Policy Journal of New Zealand, 23,* 167–180.

Walker, R. J. (1990). *Ka whawhai tonu matou.* Auckland, New Zealand: Penguin Books.

World Health Organization. (1997). *Toward a comprehensive approach to health guidelines for research with Indigenous peoples.* Report of the Working Group on Research, November 29-December 1, 1995. Washington, DC: Division of Health Systems and Services Development World Health Organization, Pan American Health Organization.

21

ETHICAL ISSUES IN CROSS-CULTURAL PSYCHOLOGY

◆ David Matsumoto and Caroline Anne Leong Jones

Cross-cultural psychology is the branch of psychology that attempts to test the boundaries of knowledge about human behavior by comparing it in two or more cultures. Cross-cultural psychology is a research method, a statement of scientific philosophy, and an attitude that blends inquisitive critical thinking with curiosity and interest in culture. As such, cross-cultural psychology can be an exciting and motivating adventure; but it can also be one that presents the researcher with a number of significant ethical issues and practical challenges.

In this chapter, we discuss some key ethical issues, dilemmas, and challenges associated with conducting cross-cultural research. We organize our discussion around four sections: the design of cross-cultural studies, sampling, sensitive topics, and dealing with data and the interpretation of findings. Many of the issues and challenges that cross-cultural researchers are confronted with are, in actuality, quite similar to those we are faced with when conducting monocultural research. Many ethical considerations that all researchers must make—regardless of whether they are conducting a multinational study involving 30 countries and 50 languages or a simple study using a convenience sample of American college students—are somewhat universal in nature. Thus, we refer interested readers to the American Psychological Association's current guidelines on Principle Ethics (www.apa.org/ethics/code2002.html#general), which outlines five ethical principles for the conduct of psychologists: beneficence and nonmaleficence, fidelity and responsibility, integrity, justice, and respect for people's rights and dignity. Moreover, these issues are discussed in depth elsewhere in this volume (Chapter 8, this volume). Thus, instead of reiterating many of the same points made elsewhere by others, we strive to discuss here ethical issues unique to cross-cultural research that may not be covered elsewhere, all the while acknowledging that many of the same principles and guidelines discussed elsewhere are applicable here as well. As there are only very few resources on this topic, we consider our work a living document, the start and definitely not the end of a dialogue, on this issue.

♦ Ethical Issues in the Design of Cross-Cultural Research

As with all properly structured and internally reliable research, issues related to design are fundamental and must be considered before contact is initiated with human participants and data are collected. One of the biggest ethical dilemmas facing cross-cultural researchers today is the potential for the findings from their studies to be used to vindicate powerful stereotypes about cultural groups. In our view, vindication is quite different from testing the accuracy of stereotypes. The latter involves researchers' conscious knowledge of stereotypes and their efforts to test their validity and boundaries; presumably such conscious knowledge would also inform researchers of the need to be aware of their potential influence on the process of research. Vindication refers to researchers' ignorance of such stereotypes, and thus their potential lack of awareness of how these stereotypes may affect their decisions about research unconsciously. Thus, it is incumbent on researchers to understand how this can be the case, and to use research designs that can minimize this possibility. We begin an exploration of these issues by discussing the limitations related to interpretations from cross-cultural comparisons.

POTENTIAL DANGERS OF CROSS-CULTURAL RESEARCH

Cross-cultural research is comparative, that is, it requires the collection of data from members of two or more cultures and the comparison of their data. One of the most fundamental issues cross-cultural researchers face, therefore, concerns their operationalization of culture. A perusal of the literature would show very quickly that there is a great diversity in these operationalizations among researchers. Many, for instance, operationalize culture by country; others use race, ethnicity, sexual orientation, or disabilities to operationalize culture.

Researchers should be aware that their choice of operationalization of culture in comparative research may have important consequences, and may be associated with possible ethical dilemmas. For example, when making decisions concerning how to operationalize cultural groups, researchers often believe that differences exist between them (which is why they are conducting the study in the first place), and conduct their studies to demonstrate that those differences actually do exist. Of course, one of the major goals of cross-cultural comparison is to examine whether or not such differences exist so that the boundaries of knowledge can be tested and elucidated. One consequence of this process, however, is those very differences that are documented can be used to help perpetuate stereotypes of differences by consumers of that research. It is fairly easy, for example, to take research findings documenting differences between Americans and South Koreans, or European Americans and African Americans, and to make statements that overgeneralize those findings to all members of those groups, essentially pigeonholing individuals into the social categories and applying those findings to them. That is, cross-cultural research (or more precisely, the incorrect application and interpretation of cross-cultural research) can be used to ignore the large degree of individual differences that exist in human behavior, and cross-cultural researchers need to be aware of this potential when designing their studies.

For instance, Iwata and Higuchi (2000) compared Japanese and Americans using the State-Trait Anxiety Inventory (STAI) and reported that Japanese were less likely to report positive feelings, and more likely to report higher state and trait anxiety, than Americans. They wrote,

> In traditional Japan, a typical collectivistic society, individual psychological well-being is subordinate to the well-being of the group; that is, maintenance of social harmony is one of the most important values (Iwata et al., 1994). The healthy collectivist self is characterized by compliance, nurturance, interdependence, and inhibited hedonism (P. J. Watson, Sherbak, & Morris, 1998). The inhibition of positive affect seems to represent a moral distinction and reflect socially desirable behavior in Japan (Iwata et al., 1995). For this reason, the Japanese are taught from childhood to understate their own virtues and avoid behaving assertively (Iwata et al., 1994). *Because of this socialization, the Japanese seem less likely to generate positive feelings and more likely to inhibit the expression of positive feelings* [italics added]. (Iwata & Higuchi, 2000, p. 58)

Unfortunately, there are many assumptions that underlie this interpretation of the data, none of which were empirically linked to the differences. These include the ideas that (a) Japan is a collectivistic society; (b) individual psychological well-being is subordinate to the well-being of the group; (c) maintenance of social harmony is one of the most important values; (d) Japanese selves are characterized by compliance, nurturance, interdependence, and inhibited hedonism; (e) the inhibition of positive affect represents a moral distinction and is socially desirable; (f) the Japanese underestimate their own virtues; and (g) the Japanese avoid behaving assertively. Based on this simple, two-country comparison, however, it is easy to generate such interpretations, and for them to be used to justify stereotypes of cultural differences that may not be true (Matsumoto, 2002).

The findings from cross-cultural comparisons can also be used in a negative way to oppress members of certain groups. If we conducted a study about cognitive ability and found significant differences in test scores for Sunni and Shiite populations—what would the implications of our findings be? Is it possible that we would add to ethnocentric and/or stereotypic beliefs? Certainly, similar findings concerning African American differences in IQ have spurred a great debate on such issues in the past 40 years (Jacoby, Glauberman, & Herrnstein, 1995; Jensen, 1969). Researchers, thus, need to be aware that findings could be used in these ways and have the obligation of taking active steps to avoid misuse of their findings. This starts with the tempered and nuanced interpretation of their findings in their own writings, incorporating information not only about between- but also about within-group differences in their data (e.g., through the use of appropriate effects size statistics and interpreting data in relation to these statistics; Matsumoto, Grissom, & Dinnel, 2001; Matsumoto, Kim, Grissom, & Dinnel, in press). This obligation also extends to correcting misinterpretations of one's findings by other researchers who cite one's research.

LIMITATIONS OF CROSS-CULTURAL COMPARISONS

Cross-cultural comparisons that document the existence of differences between groups constitute the core of the majority of cross-cultural psychological research. These studies are methodologically quasi-experimental in which cultural group is the independent variable and psychological variables are dependent variables. As mentioned above, most often the cultural groups are national groups (i.e., countries), although ethnic, language, and racial groupings have also been studied. Also, as mentioned above, they are important because they test the boundaries of the traditional American monocultural research of the past.

One of the limitations of these types of comparisons, however, is that they do not allow for empirically justified interpretations about the source of group differences. When group differences have been found, researchers have typically concluded that those differences have a cultural, racial, or ethnic source, when in fact the mere documentation of between-group differences does not justify such interpretations. There are many ways in which two or more countries, ethnic groups, or racial groups may differ. Some of these ways are cultural, and some are not. The problem in inferences occurs when researchers attribute the source of group differences to culture without being empirically justified in doing so. And even if the source of observed differences is indeed culture, it is not exactly clear what cultural variables produce the differences and why. Campbell (1961) referred to this type of error of interpretation in inference as the ecological fallacy, and in the case of cross-cultural studies, this is known as the *cultural attribution fallacy*—the inference that something "cultural" about the groups being compared produced the observed differences when there is no empirical justification for this inference (Matsumoto & Yoo, 2006). This limitation exists partly because of the ways cultures are sampled (country, ethnic, or racial groups) and partly because many cross-cultural studies involve comparisons of only two or a small handful of groups. The groupings used, however, are not necessarily cultural. The resulting cultural attribution fallacy does, undoubtedly, lead to findings that can be considered stereotypical.

For example, in the Iwata and Higuchi (2000) studies described above, none of the assumptions that underlie their interpretations of the findings were actually measured and empirically linked to their findings. Part of this limitation starts with the recognition that the differences researchers observe in cross-national, racial, or ethnic group comparisons are "country," "racial," or "ethnic group" differences rather than "cultural" differences per se. That is, country, race, and ethnicity are not culture. And we believe that interpretations of differences from cross-country, racial, or ethnic group comparisons without an incorporation of culture are doomed to be based on stereotypes, in which country, racial, or ethnic group differences are merely interpreted to have occurred "because of" some kind of stereotypic differences between the groups. This is unfortunate, because one of the goals of such research should be the elucidation of those stereotypes—where they are true, where they are not, and their limitations in understanding human behavior. Stereotypes are not inherently bad; but when cultures are reduced to stereotypes and these stereotypes are inflexibly used as a basis to interpret group differences without empirical justification, this is clearly an extremely limited way of doing research and understanding the relationship between culture and psychological processes. Yet the way we do cross-cultural research may, in fact, be facilitating these very limited ways.

DEFINING CULTURE

One of the reasons why stereotypic interpretations of the findings from cross-cultural research are easy is because of the limitations inherent in the ways in which cross-cultural researchers operationalize culture. As mentioned above, researchers typically operationalize culture according to nationality, race, ethnicity, or some other social categories. These social groups may indeed be associated with cultural differences, but they beg the question of exactly what is culture in the first place.

In our work, we define culture as a unique meaning and information system that is shared by a group and transmitted across generations, and that allows the group to meet basic needs of survival, pursue happiness and well-being, and derive meaning from life (Matsumoto, 2007; Matsumoto & Juang, 2007). This definition is important because it allows us to go beyond the mere documentation of differences between countries, racial or ethnic groups, and other social categories, and to search for the differences in the meaning and information systems of these groups that contribute to the observed differences. In this way, research can be designed to isolate the source of country, racial, or ethnic group differences in cultural variables, thus reducing the chance that such findings be used to perpetuate stereotypes. In contemporary cross-cultural psychology, these are known as unpackaging studies.

UNPACKAGING STUDIES

Unpackaging studies are extensions of basic cross-cultural comparisons, but they include the measurement of a variable that assesses the active cultural ingredients that are thought to produce the differences on the variable(s) being compared across cultures. That is, in unpackaging studies, culture as an unspecified variable is replaced by more specific variables to truly explain cultural differences. These variables are called context variables and should be actually measured in the study to examine the degree to which they account for cultural differences. The underlying thought to these studies is that cultures are like onions, where layer after layer needs to be peeled off until nothing is left. Poortinga, Van de Vijver, Joe, and van de Koppel (1987) expressed the view this way:

> In our approach culture is a summary label, a catchword for all kinds of behavior differences between cultural groups, but within itself, of virtually no explanatory value. Ascribing intergroup differences in behavior, e.g., in test performance, to culture does not shed much light on the nature of these differences. It is one of the main tasks of cross-cultural psychology to peel off cross-cultural differences, i.e., to explain these differences in terms of specific antecedent variables, until in the end they have disappeared and with them the variable culture. In our approach culture is taken as a concept without a core. From a methodological point of view, culture can be considered as an immense set of often loosely interrelated independent variables. (p. 22)

When measured on the individual level, researchers then examine the degree to which the context variables statistically account for the differences in the comparison, typically by mediation or covariance analyses (Baron & Kenny, 1986; MacKinnon, Lockwood, Hoffman, West, & Sheets, 2002). If they do, then researchers are empirically justified in claiming that that specific aspect of culture, that is that context variable, was linked to the differences observed. If they do not, then researchers know that that specific context variable did *not* produce the observed differences. In either case, researchers are empirically justified in making claims about which aspects of culture are related to the variables of interest.

A number of different types of variables can be used as context variables, and unpackaging studies can be conducted in a number of different ways. In one of the first unpackaging studies (Singelis, Bond, Sharkey, & Lai, 1999), for example, country differences in self-construals unpacked country differences in embarrassability; that is, because self-construals can be considered a cultural variable, the findings allowed for an interpretation that group differences in embarrassability was empirically linked to cultural differences in self-construals. There are other research designs that allow for the empirical linking of the active cultural ingredients that produce group differences with those differences, such as experiments and multilevel analyses. One important type of research in this genre, for instance, is studies that prime participants to behave in individualistic or collectivistic ways (Hong, Morris, Chiu, & Benet-Martinez, 2000), and show differences in the same individuals primed differently. Space limitations prohibit us from describing all these more fully here; interested readers are referred to other sources for detailed accounts of them (Matsumoto & Yoo, 2006; Van de Vijver & Matsumoto, in press).

ETHICAL ISSUES REGARDING THEORIES AND HYPOTHESES TO BE TESTED

One issue that cross-cultural researchers need to face is the question of whether or not their research question is worthy enough of being studied in the first place. Just because a question can be asked does not necessarily mean that it should be asked. An excellent example of this can be found in the notorious Tuskegee experiment on the disease course of untreated syphilis. Surely medical science could have done without the information gained in that "investigation" (especially since a cure for the disease was discovered before the completion of the study), not to mention the ethical misconduct of having a vulnerable population unwittingly involved in the experiment. It is also necessary to consider if the suffering involved is worth the potential knowledge. For example, even though the U.S. Army might be curious to understand how their soldiers react to feelings regarding their own mortality by designing a study that actually *evokes* these intense emotions in human participants—they might have to leave this question unanswered. The diligent researcher, however, will most likely try to operationalize their variable of interest. For example, the Army could consider using the experience of a soldier's first parachute jump, or some other naturally occurring experience (if one happens to be, in this example, a soldier in the Army). It is reasonable that most soldiers jumping out of a plane for the first time are experiencing some form of fear that is similar to a fear of death—although the ethical difference is that they are jumping out of the plane by *choice* and not by coercion.

ECOLOGICAL- VERSUS INDIVIDUAL-LEVEL ANALYSES

Although most hypothesis-testing cross-cultural research uses individual participants as the unit of analysis, ecological-level studies use countries or cultures as the unit of analysis. Data may be obtained on the individual level, but subsequently aggregated into averages or overall scores for each culture. These new summaries or averages are then used as data points for each culture (Matsumoto & Juang, 2007). One of the ethical issues that arises when interpreting the results from ecological-level studies is related to the fact that relationships among variables measured at one level do not necessarily translate to the same relationships at another level. A positive correlation based on ecological-level data can be positive, negative, or zero when individual-level data are analyzed. The classic work in this field is Robinson's (1950), who demonstrated that, even though a small, positive correlation (0.118) existed between foreign birth and illiteracy when individual-level data were analyzed, strong negative correlations were obtained when data were aggregated across individuals by region (–0.619) or state (–0.526). Similar types of differences in findings have been obtained in studies of the relationship between socioeconomic status and childbirths (Entwisle & Mason, 1985), attachment and acting out behaviors (Bond, 2004), person perception and behavior intention (Bond & Forgas, 1984), and cultural values, social beliefs, and managerial influence strategies (Fu et al., 2004).

One of our recent studies highlights the major potential difference between ecological- and individual-level correlations. On the individual level, for instance, the effects of emotional suppression on mental health and adjustment is well documented (Butler et al., 2003; Gross & John, 2003; Gross & Levenson, 1993); individuals who are more expressive are generally better adjusted than those who suppress their emotions. On the cultural level, however, suppression is not only correlated with less positive adjustment and well-being; but is also negatively correlated with negative adjustment indices such as country-level indices of depression and anxiety; smoking, alcohol, and drug abuse; and crime rates. Thus, the ecological-level relationship between suppression and negative adjustment is exactly the opposite of that which is found on the individual level, highlighting the fact that researchers cannot make inferences about individual-level processes from cultural-level data.

◆ Issues Regarding Sampling, Recruitment, and Consent

Sampling methodology lies at the core of research involving human subjects—and can most often be the issue from which stems all sorts of ethical considerations. How do we know, in the case of sampling, that the participants who represent our target cultures of interest are a "good" representation of that culture? In the most basic cross-cultural studies, data are collected from a sample of people from one culture and then compared with the data obtained from a sample of people from another culture (or known values from another culture). Let's say, we decided to run a cross-cultural study that used the scores of 100 Americans. What if all the Americans in our sample were from the same small town in the middle of South Dakota? What if they were all naturalized citizens living in San Francisco? What if they all had the same ethnic background or all came from upper-class, dual-income families? What are the criteria that we have decided to use to define what our "American" sample is? What does it mean to be enculturated as an "American"? What is "American" culture? These are all issues that we, as cross-cultural researchers, must pay special attention to when conducting our research. They are potentially problematic, and related to ethics, because of the assumption of homogeneity among group members, researchers, and their methods. Statistics testing group differences, for instance, do not care about the specific composition of those groups; that is a methodological issue that only researchers can control. Yet the findings will be applied as if they are true for those who comprise the groups being tested and have the potential to perpetuate stereotypic impressions and interpretations or create them (Matsumoto & Juang, 2007).

Issues concerning sampling adequacy and sampling equivalence are discussed in detail elsewhere (Matsumoto & Juang, 2007; Van de Vijver & Matsumoto, 2007). In this section, we will focus predominantly on two issues of sampling that may need special ethical consideration: informed consent and participant recruitment.

INFORMED CONSENT

In the United States, it is impossible to conduct research involving human participants without first receiving approval from an institutional review board (IRB), and most IRB guidelines require that researchers obtain consent from the participants before collecting data. These procedures, however, do not exist in most countries outside the United States. In fact, in most places outside the United States, not only is submitting a research proposal for review unnecessary but obtaining consent from human participants is unnecessary, as well. This raises ethical dilemmas for researchers: Do we obtain consent from participants in cultures in which it is not necessary to obtain consent, or even frowned upon? Will all participants understand the concept of "consent" in the same way? What does "consent" mean in different cultures and who is authorized to give and obtain "consent"? Furthermore, if we *do* obtain consent from our participants, how do we obtain it? Many participants in many cultures will likely view consent documents with skepticism or fear. Will they understand such a process and feel comfortable about giving consent?

Regardless of whether obtaining consent is necessary or not, we believe that researchers should always strive to ensure that (a) informed consent is obtained and understood by the participant, (b) invasion of privacy is minimized, and (c) consent will be obtained only in a manner that minimizes coercion or undue influence. How can this process be done in a culturally competent manner?

In our experience, many of the same consent procedures can be used around the world, if delivered in a skillful and culturally competent manner by the research team. This manner involves the truthful and honest description of the procedures of the study, its risks and benefits, combined with a genuine interest in the participant and his/her welfare. If written consent is required, forms need to be translated in a competent and culturally appropriate manner. Involving cultural informants as collaborators or experimenters can help ensure that researchers are making the most diligent of efforts in this difficult ethical area of research.

RECRUITMENT

In the United States, participants in most psychology studies are recruited from an undergraduate psychology participant pool of students, mostly from introductory psychology classes, who view descriptions of studies and sign up for them voluntarily and of their free will. In many cases, this process is administered by software that can be accessed by any computer connected to the Internet, in which case participants have minimal intervention by anyone else asking for their participation. Participation in research is a well-known process to many students in many universities in the United States.

In other countries and cultures, however, this is not necessarily the case. Many countries do not have an undergraduate participant pool as we do in the United States. Thus, different procedures are often required to recruit participants. In many instances, course instructors request that their students participate. In many situations, however, students may feel compelled to participate in a study that they would otherwise not choose of their own volition, because of the perceived status of the researcher or possible ramifications for noncompliance to the requesting instructor. This compelling force may border on coercion or undue influence and presents an ethical dilemma. We believe that researchers should avoid any recruitment procedures that involve actual or perceived coercion to participate in the studies.

♦ Sensitive Topics

When conducting cross-cultural research, it's important to be aware of the fact that there are some topics and issues that are sensitive to study and raise interesting ethical problems for researchers. We mention three of them briefly here, to raise awareness of them: sex and sexuality, human rights issues, and deception.

SEX AND SEXUALITY

The United States and much of Western and Northern Europe are cultures in which sex and sexuality issues can be discussed relatively openly and freely in everyday discourse. For that reason, conducting research on sex and sexuality is relatively much easier in those cultures. In many other cultures of the world, however, these topics are taboo, especially among youth or women. Thus, researchers must exercise caution when conducting research on these topics in cultures in which they are taboo.

For example, in some cultures of the world, homosexuality is a severe taboo, punished in some societies by social isolation, physical punishment, and in some cases, even death. A researcher studying homosexuality in such cultures may be subject to the same kinds of repercussions, which strongly prohibits the generation of much useful research information about homosexuality in those cultures. Additionally, it would be very difficult for individuals to volunteer to participate in such studies, for fear of their safety and lives. In such cultures, there may be the added anxiety that the research project itself is part of an organized activity, either by activist groups or government, to identify homosexual individuals. Such concerns exist not only for people who live in those cultures but also for individuals who emigrate to other countries; they still may fear for their lives. Thus, it may be difficult to conduct such a study on homosexual immigrants in the United States for the same reasons. We have conducted such studies (Mireshghi & Matsumoto, 2006), and they raise interesting and important questions concerning recruitment and consent, as described above.

Even if issues concerning sex and sexuality are not a direct focus of the study, they may be indirectly related because of questions concerning these issues on standard personality questionnaires. For example, two items on the Intercultural Adjustment Potential Scale, a scale designed to assess the potential to adjust to a multicultural environment (Matsumoto, Yoo, & LeRoux, 2007), are "sex education is a good thing" and "when a man is with a woman he is usually thinking of sex." Despite the fact that these, and many other, items are designed to indirectly tap personality constructs and are imbedded within literally tens or hundreds of other items, they may be taboo in other cultures. We have conducted studies in which cultural informants have reviewed the items and recommended or required deletion of a number of these, and those that ask about attitudes toward things such as drugs, in our protocols.

HUMAN RIGHTS ISSUES

Cultures differ considerably on many practices and issues that U.S. Americans often find difficult to understand and even offensive. These include abortion attitudes and practices, circumcision or female genital mutilation, and the punishment of women accused of premarital sex or extramarital affairs. (Conversely, many cultures find many U.S. attitudes and practices offensive, too.) Clearly, these are important social issues that are worthy of study and documentation; yet, like with issues concerning sex and sexuality, they may be taboo and difficult, if not impossible, to study in other cultures, and even in the United States.

Another human rights issue to consider is the track record of countries—in which researchers wish to work—with regard to human rights issues. Many countries in the world have been accused in the past and present of human rights violations, and how these have been and are dealt with may, in some cases, form part of an important context within which research in those countries may occur. It behooves researchers to know of these issues, and to gauge the degree to which they may affect the research and findings, and whether it is wise to do the research in the first place.

DECEPTION

Deception is used in many studies in the United States, and when it is used, it must pass muster at the level of the IRB so that its use does not introduce undue risks to the participants, and participants are fully debriefed about it at the end and give their informed consent to use the data. That is, there are complex and important checks on the use of deception in the United States. Because IRBs do not exist in many other countries, however, such checks therefore do not exist; there are, however, other ways in which such checks are done. Thus, it becomes easier to conduct research that involves deception. Such ease, however, comes with the greater obligation to exercise caution. We do not believe that all research involving deception should be outright banned in countries with no IRB procedure; but we do believe that such research needs to be conducted with additional care and caution, by engaging cultural informants as collaborators who can gauge the necessity of the deception, and by enacting procedures that ensure the full debriefing of the participants and obtaining of consent to preserve individual participant integrity.

METHODS, SENSITIVITY, OR ETHICS?

The topics we raise in this section blend together issues concerning methodology, cultural sensitivity, and ethics. Clearly, studying sensitive topics in a culturally insensitive manner is likely to yield invalid results, thus posing a methodological dilemma. But cultural insensitivity in methodology also has the potential to treat participants and cultures in a disrespectful manner, and this clearly is an ethical problem at the same time. To be sure, we do not argue for a ban on research on sensitive topics. We do, however, suggest that such research must be undertaken with care, precision, and sensitivity for the topics studied vis-à-vis the cultures in question. Involving cultural experts as collaborators in the research, recruiting participants who participate without coercion with full informed consent, and interpreting findings in a culturally relevant manner are steps by which researchers can make progress in studying difficult topics.

◆ Dealing With Data and the Interpretation of Findings

ANALYZING DATA

When analyzing cross-cultural data, researchers typically rely on inferential statistics that test for group differences, such as analysis of variance, chi-square, t tests, and the like. The major problem with these types of statistics is that they only test for whether group means are different from each other but not the degree to which they are different, nor how individuals in those groups are different from each other. Thus, relying solely on such statistical procedures to analyze data makes it easy for researchers and consumers of research to draw rather stereotypical interpretations of the group differences, because all the statistics demonstrate whether or not group differences exist.

Statistically significant group differences in means, however, may or may not be practically significant in terms of understanding differences among people in those groups. To make such interpretations concerning practical meaningfulness, researchers who deal with quantitative data need to engage with a class of statistics known as effect size statistics. There are, in fact, many different types of effect size statistics, all of which are computed differently, serve a different purpose, and tell researchers a different thing about the group differences. Space restrictions prevent us from discussing these in detail; interested readers are referred to other sources for detailed accounts of them (Grissom & Kim, 2005; Matsumoto et al., 2001; Matsumoto et al., in press). Our point here is that researchers who deal with quantitative data should make use of this class of statistics to make more accurate and less stereotypic interpretations of the differences observed. Researchers should also consider using statistics related to dispersion more comprehensively in their reports and interpretations of the data (see Chapter 24, this volume).

CULTURAL BIASES IN INTERPRETATIONS

Just as culture can bias formulation of the research questions in a cross-cultural study, it can also bias the ways researchers interpret their findings. Most researchers will inevitably interpret the data they obtain through their own cultural filters, and these biases can affect their interpretations to varying degrees. For example, if the mean response for Americans on a rating scale is 6.0 and the mean for Hong Kong Chinese is 4.0, one interpretation is that the Americans simply scored higher on the scale. Another interpretation may be that the Chinese are suppressing their responses. This type of interpretation is common, especially in research with Asian samples. But how do we know the Chinese are suppressing their responses? What if it is the Americans who are exaggerating their responses? What if the Chinese mean response of 4.0 is actually the more "correct" one and the American one is the one that is off? What if we surveyed the rest of the world and found that the overall mean was 3.0, suggesting that both the Chinese and the Americans inflated their ratings? In other words, the interpretation that the Chinese are suppressing their responses is based on an implicit assumption that the American data are "correct." One of us has made this sort of ethnocentric interpretation of research findings in a study involving American and Japanese judgments of the intensity of facial expressions of emotion, without really giving much consideration to other possibilities (Matsumoto & Ekman, 1989). In later research (Matsumoto, Kasri, & Kooken, 1999), we were able to show that, in fact, the Americans exaggerated their intensity ratings of faces, relative to inferences about subjective experience of the posers—the Japanese did not suppress.

Anytime researchers make a value judgment or interpretation of a finding, it is always possible that this interpretation is bound by a cultural bias. Interpretations of good or bad, right or wrong, suppressing or exaggerating, important or not important are all value interpretations that may be made in a cross-cultural study. These interpretations may reflect the value orientations of the researchers as much as they do the cultures of the samples included in the study. As researchers, we may make those interpretations without giving them a second thought—and without the slightest hint of malicious intent—only because we are so accustomed to seeing the world in a certain way. As consumers of research, we may agree with such interpretations—when they agree with the ways we have learned to understand and view the world—and we will often do so unconsciously and automatically.

CULTURAL INFORMANTS

As we have mentioned throughout this chapter, the involvement of cultural informants, at least on the level of advisers and at best on the level of collaborators, is a must in cross-cultural research. While we have listed this section here toward the end of this chapter, we strongly believe that these cultural informants/collaborators should be engaged from the very beginning of any study, providing needed advice and guidance about whether or not to conduct the study in the first place, the appropriateness of the theory and hypotheses to be tested, and the adequacy and appropriateness of the research design.

The involvement of cultural informants can help avoid cultural bias in interpreting results, such as those described immediately above. We strongly encourage researchers to seek out such informant/collaborators at the earliest stages of their studies, and to work collaboratively with them throughout the research process. Most scientific organizations such as the American Psychological Association have guidelines or criteria for authorship, and we encourage researchers to ensure that informants contribute their share of intellectual material to the research to gain authorship.

CONFIDENTIALITY

In the United States, we have many rules, regulations, and guidelines concerning the need to maintain confidentiality of any data sources. Such rules do not exist in many other countries, and many other collaborators or cultural informants may not be aware of such need or procedures. We believe that even though a country may not have such rules or regulations that data need to be kept confidential, with access only to the research team. Many participants in many other countries may worry about who has access to their data, especially if they have made statements about issues that are politically, socially, or morally sensitive in their cultures. Sometimes data have to be smuggled out of a country because of this worry (e.g., Scherer & Wallbott, 1994). Clearly, participants in research should be free of such anxiety concerning the use of their data when they provide it and afterward, researchers should take extra precautions to ensure that this is indeed the case.

IMPACT OF RESEARCH ON THE COMMUNITY

A focus on the ecology of lives approach and designing research and interventions at the community level suggest a long-term commitment to the locale as part of the research process. "One-shot" or "safari" approaches to community-based research should be discouraged, including the low probability that such an approach would leave a positive residual after the project ends or the grant money runs out. Researchers doing work in other countries and cultures should be attuned to how research can make positive impacts on the lives of the community, because many other countries do not have the reciprocal cycle of access → benefit that we do in the United States.

We must also take heed to avoid actions, procedures, interactive styles, and so on that violate local customs and understandings of the community. Our goals are for understanding and learning to occur—not unnecessary cultural faux pas as a result of our own lack of education of a culture outside our own. Incidences of this nature can be tempered by positive learning interaction with our cultural expert and a research of customs and norms on our own. At every phase of research, including the consent process, sensitivity and attention should be given to the cultural *ethos* and *eidos* of the community.

♦ Conclusion

In this chapter, we have raised many ethical issues concerning cross-cultural psychological research with regard to design, sampling, sensitive issues, and dealing with data. Undoubtedly, we have raised more questions than provided answers, and this may be inevitable, because in many cases the answers for many of the issues raised reside in local cultural communities, not in a one-size-fits-all approach to the ethical conduct of research in different cultures. Our purpose has been first and foremost to raise awareness of the sometimes very difficult issues that face cross-cultural researchers. As mentioned in the introduction, we sincerely hope that the issues raised here serve as the start, not end, of a dialogue concerning ethics in cross-cultural research.

♦ References

Baron, R. M., & Kenny, D. A. (1986). The moderator-mediator variable distinction in social psychological research: Conceptual, strategic, and statistical considerations. *Journal of Personality and Social Psychology, 51*(6), 1173–1882.

Bond, M. H. (2004). Culture and aggression: From context to coercion. *Personality and Social Psychology Review, 8,* 62–78.

Bond, M. H., & Forgas, J. P. (1984). Linking person perception to behavior intention across cultures: The role of cultural collectivism. *Journal of Cross-Cultural Psychology, 15,* 337–352.

Butler, E. A., Egloff, B., Wlhelm, F. H., Smith, N. C., Erickson, E. A., & Gross, J. J. (2003). The social consequences of expressive suppression. *Emotion, 3*(1), 48–67.

Campbell, D. T. (1961). The mutual methodological relevance of anthropology and psychology. In F. L. Hsu (Ed.), *Psychological anthropology* (pp. 333–352). Homewood, IL: Dorsey.

Entwisle, B., & Mason, W. M. (1985). Multilevel effects of socioeconomic development and family planning programs on children ever born. *American Journal of Sociology, 91*(3), 616–649.

Fu, P. P., Kennedy, J., Tata, J., Yuki, G., Bond, M. H., Peng, T.-K., et al. (2004). The impact of societal cultural values and individual social beliefs on the perceived effectiveness of managerial influence strategies: A meso approach. *Journal of International Business Studies, 35,* 284–305.

Grissom, R., & Kim, J. J. (2005). *Effect sizes for research: A broad practical approach.* Mahwah, NJ: Lawrence Erlbaum.

Gross, J. J., & John, O. P. (2003). Individual differences in two emotion regulation processes: Implications for affect, relationships, and well-being. *Journal of Personality and Social Psychology, 85*(2), 348–362.

Gross, J. J., & Levenson, R. W. (1993). Emotional suppression: Physiology, self-report, and expressive behavior. *Journal of Personality and Social Psychology, 64*(6), 970–986.

Hong, Y. Y., Morris, M., Chiu, C.-Y., & Benet-Martinez, V. (2000). Multicultural minds: A dynamic constructivist approach to culture and cognition. *American Psychologist, 55,* 709–720.

Iwata, N., & Higuchi, H. R. (2000). Responses of Japanese and American university students to the STAI items that assess the presence or absence of anxiety. *Journal of Personality Assessment, 74*(1), 48–62.

Jacoby, R., Glauberman, N., & Herrnstein, R. J. (1995). *The bell curve debate: History, documents, opinions* (1st ed.). New York: Times Books.

Jensen, A. R. (1969). How much can we boost IQ and scholastic achievement? *Harvard Educational Review, 39,* 1–123.

MacKinnon, D. P., Lockwood, C. M., Hoffman, J. M., West, S. G., & Sheets, V. (2002). A comparison of methods to test mediation and other intervening variable effects. *Psychological Methods, 7*(3), 83–104.

Matsumoto, D. (2002). *The new Japan.* Yarmouth, ME: Intercultural Press.

Matsumoto, D. (2007). Culture, context, and behavior. *Journal of Personality, 75*(6), 1285–1319.

Matsumoto, D., & Ekman, P. (1989). American-Japanese cultural differences in intensity ratings of facial expressions of emotion. *Motivation & Emotion, 13*(2), 143–157.

Matsumoto, D., Grissom, R., & Dinnel, D. (2001). Do between-culture differences really mean that people are different? A look at some measures of cultural effect size. *Journal of Cross-Cultural Psychology, 32*(4), 478–490.

Matsumoto, D., & Juang, L. (2007). *Culture and psychology* (4th ed.). Belmont, CA: Wadsworth.

Matsumoto, D., Kasri, F., & Kooken, K. (1999). American-Japanese cultural differences in judgments of expression intensity and subjective experience. *Cognition & Emotion, 13,* 201–218.

Matsumoto, D., Kim, J. J., Grissom, R. J., & Dinnel, D. L. (in press). Effect sizes in cross-cultural research. In F. J. R. Van de Vijver & D. Matsumoto (Eds.), *Cross-cultural research methods in psychology.* New York: Oxford University Press.

Matsumoto, D., & Yoo, S. H. (2006). Toward a new generation of cross-cultural research. *Perspectives on Psychological Science, 1*(3), 234–250.

Matsumoto, D., Yoo, S. H., & LeRoux, J. A. (2007). Emotion and intercultural communication. In H. Kotthoff & H. Spencer-Oatley (Eds.), *Handbook of applied linguistics, Vol. 7: Intercultural communication* (pp. 77–98). Berlin: Mouton de Gruyter.

Mireshghi, S., & Matsumoto, D. (2006). *Cultural attitudes toward homosexuality and their effects on Iranian and American homosexuals.* Manuscript submitted for publication.

Poortinga, Y. H., Van de Vijver, F. J. R., Joe, R. C., & van de Koppel, J. M. H. (1987). Peeling the onion called culture: A synopsis. In C. Kagitcibasi (Ed.), *Growth and progress in cross-cultural psychology* (pp. 22–34). Berwyn, PA: Swets North America.

Robinson, W. S. (1950). Ecological correlations and the behavior of individuals. *American Sociological Review, 15*(3), 351–357.

Scherer, K. R., & Wallbott, H. (1994). Evidence for universality and cultural variation of differential emotion response-patterning. *Journal of Personality & Social Psychology, 66*(2), 310–328.

Singelis, T., Bond, M., Sharkey, W. F., & Lai, C. S. Y. (1999). Unpackaging culture's influence on self-esteem and embarassability. *Journal of Cross-Cultural Psychology, 30*, 315–341.

Van de Vijver, F. J. R., & Matsumoto, D. (in press). *Cross-cultural research methods in psychology.* New York: Oxford University Press.

22

PARTNERSHIP ETHICS

◆ Linda Silka

Research partnerships have become subjects of great interest as past research practices have come under renewed scrutiny and criticism. Books, monographs, and reviews have begun to appear that promote research partnerships (Bringle & Hatcher, 2002; Brugge & Hynes, 2005; Israel, Schulz, Parker, & Becker, 1998; Minkler & Wallerstein, 2002; Silka, 2006). Various commissions have called for partnerships as solutions to problems with past research practices (Kellogg Commission, 1999). Many funders, including the Centers for Disease Control, the Environmental Protection Agency, the National Institutes of Health, the Kellogg Foundation, and the Robert Wood Johnson Foundation, have begun calling for more partnership-based research (Green & Mercer, 2001; O'Fallon & Dearry, 2002; Shepard, Northridge, Prakash, & Stover, 2002). Various journals, including *Environmental Health Perspectives, Journal of Higher Education Outreach and Engagement, Journal of Urban Health, Progress in Community Health Partnerships Research*, and *Gateways: International Journal of Community Research and Engagement*, now solicit partnership research. And international organizations such as Community-Campus Partnerships for Health (www.ccph.info) have emerged to support the many efforts now being made to build community-university partnerships.

These groups see research partnerships as antidotes to the problems of individual investigator-led research, problems that include the lack of community control and community say in the conduct of research. But partnerships raise their own ethical concerns. This chapter highlights some of these ethical concerns by situating them within the stream of activities and decisions that occur in research partnerships. The chapter introduces and uses the *Research Cycle Framework* to highlight the steps to partnership research and the ethical dilemmas associated with these steps. This framework helps pinpoint the particular ethical concerns that emerge at the beginning, middle, and ends of a cycle of research. As we shall see, partnerships can anticipate a range of ethical dilemmas that research partners will face at various stages in their work together.

♦ Defining Research Partnerships

A working definition of research partnerships is in order. Research partnerships are ways of doing research in which one or more researchers come together with others (e.g., an organization, community, or tribal nation) to carry out a joint program of research. Partnership research differs in important respects from the more traditional individual investigator-led research; in the latter, the scientist typically controls all aspects of the research agenda (i.e., selects the research focus, recruits the "subjects," controls the data analysis and interpretation, and determines the means by which the findings will be disseminated). In partnership research, the partners seek to carry out all these steps within equitable, power-sharing arrangements. Research partnerships generally extend across time and involve multiple studies; in this way, they also contrast with individual, one-shot investigations that are generally of short duration.

Examples of research partnerships abound. Loyola University of Chicago developed the highly touted Center for Urban Research and Learning through which researchers and community groups develop joint research projects on a broad range of topics (Nyden, 2006). The frequently cited University of Michigan's Detroit Academic-Urban Research Center exemplifies the kind of research partnership built around a core set of partnership agreements, with the research agenda emerging through shared decision making about which topics will be investigated and how they should be studied (Israel, Lichtenstein, Lantz, & McGranaghan, 2001). Not all partnerships begin fully formed or occur between large groups; some start as a single scientist working with a few community members. The widely cited research partnership between the Concerned Citizens of Tillery North Carolina and the University of North Carolina epidemiologist Steve Wing is an example of a research partnership in which one scientist took the step of changing the relationships that typify academic approaches to research (Grant & Wing, 2004; Wing, Grant, Green, & Stewart, 1996). Some research partnerships are longstanding, while others are newly emerging: The largely immigrant community of Lawrence, Massachusetts, located near Boston's research universities has been inundated with requests from researchers wishing to use this impoverished community as a laboratory in which to test their hypotheses. In response, the city has begun to develop a set of principles and practices for research partnerships (Silka, Cleghorn, Grullon, & Tellez, in press).

As these examples indicate, research partnerships are far from identical. They vary in their origins, size, and the length of time in which they have been in existence. They can be local, national, or even international in scope. Regardless of these differences, in all cases of partnerships they hold the promise of addressing the ethical problems of research being done *to* communities rather than *with* communities. Research partnerships are more likely to focus on the problems of interest to those who are affected, to ensure that participants in research have a say in how the investigations are conducted, and to ensure that the results are available to groups outside the scientific community.

♦ Research Partnerships Raise Complex Ethical Questions

What ethical questions emerge in the partnership approach to research and where can partnerships look for guidance? For all the promise of research partnerships, they raise thorny ethical issues for which current ethical standards—narrowly focused as they are on institutional review board (IRB) guidelines and informed consent—provide at best, limited guidance. Current ethical guidelines focus on the individual research study and how it can be ethically conducted (i.e., Are the subjects treated fairly in the conduct of the study? Are their rights observed? Are they made aware of what they will be asked to do in the study? Are they told that they can choose to end their participation at any point?). Important as such guidelines are, they offer little help in identifying ethical dilemmas in partnership, about who decides what research should be done or what steps should be taken once the data are collected (i.e., will the focus be on using the results, however partial they may be, or will the focus be on continued scientific investigations?). Research partnerships—because they involve shared decision making and extend over time—often struggle with complex ethical questions having to do with how the focus of study will be selected, how the data will be collected, who owns the data, and how the data will be used (Nyden & Wiewel, 1992; Wing, 2002).

These ethical dilemmas arise in all research partnerships, yet new partnerships are often ill-prepared when they encounter these obstacles, and many partnerships struggle to come up with their own makeshift solutions. The issues are strikingly similar across partnerships and emerge at predictable points in each partnership. What has been missing has been a shared language or framework that enables partnerships to anticipate the ethical problems that emerge and to communicate with each other about these problems.

♦ The Need for a Framework for the Ethics of Research Partnerships

The articulation of a set of overarching ethical principles—principles such as that all power should be shared or that all decisions should be made jointly—is frequently the way new partnerships are given advice about how to carry out research ethically within a partnership. But abstract advice insufficiently prepares partnerships for the kinds of difficulties they will encounter as they try to carry out research together. Abstract advice does little to help partnerships as they struggle with the actual circumstances under which ethical dilemmas about power sharing and decision making arise. What is needed is a guiding framework that puts all the information together (Silka & Renault-Caragianes, 2007). In this chapter, we use a simple framework to show when partnerships can expect to encounter various ethical issues.

The ethical problems with which partnerships struggle, it turns out, are tied to daily partnership experiences (e.g., at what point in the research process do data ownership issues come up and what stands in the way of the easy resolution of these issues between researchers and communities?). Ethical issues are not separate from the steps of partnership research, but instead arise at predictable points in the cycle of research and are a part of these steps. The *Research Cycle Framework* described herein situates many of the ethical issues within the activity cycles that move a partnership forward in its research. This framework is designed to be useful for different kinds of partnerships addressing different kinds of research problems while at the same time allowing individual partnerships to communicate with each other and learn from each others' experience.

◆ Ethical Issues at Different Points in the Research Cycle

Partnership research is best understood as a cycle with beginning, middle, and end stages, and these stages occur and reoccur as the partnership develops a program of research that grows and extends over time. Each stage in a cycle of research creates ethical dilemmas with which the partners struggle. At *initial stages,* many of the struggles concern ethical questions about who controls the selection of the research topics and who decides the focus that the research will take. During the *middle stages* of a cycle of research, partnerships struggle with questions about how the research design should be implemented and whose interpretation of the data will hold sway. At *final stages* of a cycle of research, partnerships can expect to face difficult questions about data ownership, dissemination, and use. Examples are used below to indicate the kinds of ethical issues that research partnerships will grapple with at beginning, middle, and final stages of their programs of research (Figure 22.1).

ETHICAL CONCERNS AT INITIAL PARTNERSHIP STAGES

The primary task at initial stages of a research partnership is to decide on the focus of research. The ethical approach is said to be one in which the researcher and the community make all decisions about the research agenda together. Thus, the partnership between researchers and the community should first be formed and only then are decisions made about particular focus (childhood lead poisoning as opposed to, for example, youth gang violence).

So if shared decision making on all elements of the research agenda is the ethical approach, why is this joint decision making so hard to achieve and what can be learned from these difficulties? It turns out that in the real world of partnerships, these pronouncements of what should be done (like many such exhortations) misconstrue who is at the "research table" at early stages and why they are there. Consider the researcher. What a researcher typically brings to a research partnership is expertise on a particular topic. Thus, a researcher with expertise in lead poisoning would be involved only if lead is the focus of the partnership. In the abstract, a partnership could study anything and the partners could decide together what they will study, but in the real world, a particular research partner lends

Figure 22.1 Research Cycle Partnership: What Issues Emerge at Each Stage?

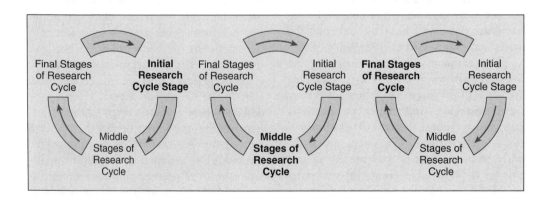

his or her skills to a mere handful of research topics. If individual researchers are the ones to initiate the request for partnership, he or she is already mindful of what their work suggests is in need of study before they make contact with community partners. Thus, the need at early stages for shared decision making cannot be met by mandating that partners must be made to come together with a clean slate and decide everything from scratch. The dilemma in early stages is how to achieve the ethical goal of partners meeting on equal terms without assuming that everything is open to discussion and joint decisions.

Or consider this in another way. Outsiders to the partnership process can assert that the only ethical approach to the initial stages is one in which all parties have equal say over all aspects of the research agenda. Such a blanket assertion about what should be done does little to help us understand why this early stage is so difficult for many partnerships. It turns out that researchers and their community partners are often not even aware of where and how they disagree about research practices. Researchers with an extensive background in some topic (e.g., researchers who are experts on childhood lead poisoning) may simply take as a given that they are in the best position to make the decisions about what the next line of research on lead poisoning ought to be. Community leaders, on the other hand, aware as they are of the costs to the community of problems such as childhood lead poisoning, may assume that they are best positioned to know which research is most urgently needed. These differences are not idle; they speak of issues that will need to be negotiated within a partnership to ensure that rigorous research meets the goal of ameliorating community problems.

Each partner is an expert and therein lies the challenge. The researcher is usually an expert of great depth on a very specific topic. Community members are often experts on their neighborhoods. Neighborhood residents are likely to hold a nuanced understanding of the complicated ways that local people spend their lives: how and when children play on the ground in local parks that might be lead contaminated, what kinds of cooking utensils families use that might be lead contaminated, or where neighbors with small yards tend to plant gardens and whether these vegetable growing areas are underneath lead-painted windows. Community members and researchers generally lack experience in asking about each others' expertise or finding ways to converse about them, understand them, and blend their different skills.

Initial stages of a research cycle are the points at which these and other ethical dilemmas related to research partnerships begin to emerge. The initial stages raise questions, for example, of whether the research partnership should focus on solving a problem *or* on understanding that same problem at its most basic level. Again, communities and researchers often have different goals with regard to the purpose of the research. Communities might see a problem that is greatly affecting the health of the children in their community, and these community members are urgently seeking ways to address this problem. Researchers are trained to see "getting to the bottom of things" as crucial and to focus on eliminating any and all alternative explanations that could explain a particular finding. These differences in goals fundamentally affect choices of research direction and allocations of research time.

Other issues related to the focus of the research (and, therefore, the ethics of who controls the research agenda) also regularly arise at the initial stages of a research cycle. These include the question of whether the purpose of the research is to gain general knowledge (with the individual "subjects" serving just as a means to that knowledge) or to gain knowledge intended to be useful to the specific individuals or groups who participate in the research. It is not unusual for researchers to talk about the local community where they do their research as "the laboratory." For the researcher, a community nearby is a convenient place to test out hypotheses; those researchers might have little interest in ameliorating the problems in that same community. Community members may be concerned about whether the results speak directly to problems in their community; they may be less concerned about the generalizability of the findings.

These difficulties at the initial stages—difficulties linked to decisions about what research will be done, who will make this determination, and whether the research will be basic or applied—point to the importance of partnerships devoting early attention to how the research will be carried out. These initial problems in community-university research partnerships were vividly captured by Loretta Jones (2006) in her keynote address to the Community Campus Partnerships for Health Conference. Jones likened community-campus research partnerships to a bus journey in which people use the bus to go to different places. She pointed out that researchers and community members often envision vastly different destinations for their "journey": the researchers might be focused on science, whereas the community might be intent on ensuring that the findings result in more than an academic publication.

The metaphor of the shared bus journey can serve as a kind of shorthand to make the problems in collaborations explicit. By using the metaphor of the bus journey together with the research cycle framework, partnerships can raise issues that are otherwise difficult to discuss (that researchers have already decided which problem will be studied before the community is consulted, that the researchers failed to ask communities *how* they thought that the problem should be investigated, or that the researchers focus only on studying a problem without giving attention to how the findings would help solve the problem or what benefits will be left behind in a community).

ETHICS ISSUES AT MIDDLE STAGES OF A RESEARCH CYCLE

The middle stages are those that occur after the partners have already come together and decided on the problem that will be the focus of research. Just as vigilance is called for in preparing for the kinds of ethical issues that arise at the initial stages of a research partnership, so too awareness is needed in partnerships of the problems that often make themselves felt at these middle stages.

Many of the middle stage problems concern data (i.e., what data should be collected, how should these data be collected). Concerns may be raised about the selection of the methods that will be used to answer research questions. Although such questions might be assumed merely to be ones of methodology or of scientific rigor, they, in fact, go to the heart of ethical conduct of partnerships. These questions concern issues of who decides what will be the correct way to collect information to answer the research question. That is to say, who will decide what is credible? And credible to whom? Quigley (2001) has reported on the problems with research done under the auspices of the Nuclear Regulatory Agency that examined exposure in tribal communities to above ground nuclear testing. Researchers who carried out the studies argued that according to their models, the exposure levels were simply too low to have created significant risks for tribal community members. But when community members looked at how the research was done, they expressed great concern at the failure of the scientists' model to include key exposure vectors such as large dietary intake of small mammals that browse on contaminated land. This example illustrates why at these middle stages partnerships need to find ways to bring together their knowledge so that comprehensive and informed data collection can occur.

The middle stages also often raise questions about research protocols and their implementation. The researchers might be focused on following a research protocol with exactitude. The community might know that an idealized protocol as laid out by researchers, who are unfamiliar with the community, cannot be followed in the "on the ground" circumstances in which the research will actually be done. Our environmental justice partnership in Lowell, Massachusetts, investigated urban environmental threats faced by Cambodian and Laotian households (Coppens, Silka, Khakeo, & Benfey, 2000). The study protocol called for visiting a representative sample of Southeast Asian households in the community and then interviewing heads of household at those locations. Once our team arrived at the homes, it quickly became apparent that the planned protocol with its focus on "head of household" was not consistent with family expectations. Everyone in families wanted to participate, wanted to talk over the questions, and wanted to decide together on the answers that best captured their shared views. The research protocol as planned by researchers was not appropriate. In other partnerships, the issues about research design might be different from that given in this example, but whatever these concerns, they need to be talked about by the partnership, and decisions need to be made in ways that integrate scientific rigor and community knowledge.

A related set of questions threaded throughout the middle stages is, "When is enough known?" "When has enough research been done?" Many underserved communities have experienced what they describe as being "studied to death." Studies continue to be done *on* them despite the fact that there is little to show in the way of benefits to the community. How then does the research partnership decide that sufficient information is now in place and that the focus should turn to interventions rather than to the continued collection of data? Who makes this decision and how will these decisions be made within a partnership? Elsewhere (Silka, 2003), we point to the value of partnerships closely scrutinizing the problems when academic journals are the sole way that knowledge about partnership research is accumulated. Important as such academic publication outlets can be, they create problems for communities because so much more research is carried out (and takes up the time and resources of communities) than is ultimately published. The result is that communities may experience a continuing stream of researchers eager to do the investigations, but the researchers are oblivious to the fact that largely the same studies have already been carried out.

ETHICAL DILEMMAS AT THE FINAL STAGES OF A RESEARCH CYCLE

And what of the final stages? At the final stages of the research cycle, many of the questions again concern the data: Who owns the data? Who controls the release of the data? How will the data be used? If studies investigate contamination levels of lead in the blood of a community's young children, for example, does the community own the data? The researcher? The partnership? Community partners have described cases where data samples—such as blood—are used by researchers in ways that are vastly different from uses originally envisioned or agreed on by the community.

Partnerships are struggling with questions such as whether the community partner should be able to approve research findings before they are submitted for publication. Calls for community prepublication oversight are becoming more common. The Akwesasne Tribal Nation in upstate New York learned only through published journal articles that researchers had discovered high level of contaminated breast milk among women in the tribal nation. The researchers did not meet with the tribal nation to discuss the results prior to their publication. Many researchers, however, struggle with calls for the community to give their approval before findings can be submitted for publication. Researchers sometimes interpret such calls as "prior restraint." Communities are often puzzled that researchers fail to understand the need for careful consideration of how the results will be described and how the community is portrayed. Thus, the researchers sometimes see the issue as scientific freedom whereas the communities see the issue as fundamentally one of respect and power sharing.

As the above examples indicate, the final stages of a cycle of research within a partnership are likely to raise a host of ethical issues that might not have been apparent at initial stages unless attempts are made to anticipate them. IRB protocols do not yet provide the nuanced guidance that will allow partnerships to sort out these issues. The use of the research cycle framework is one means of allowing partnerships to anticipate these issues so that previous relationship building is not undone by misunderstandings at the end.

ETHICAL ISSUES THAT RECUR THROUGHOUT THE RESEARCH CYCLE

The *Research Cycle Framework* points out the importance of partnerships being particularly vigilant in recognizing the kinds of ethical problems that will create difficulties for the partnership when particular tasks in the research are being carried out (see Table 22.1). The cycle—because it points to research as taking time and as happening across time—can also help partnerships be aware that certain issues recur throughout the research cycle or are of concern at all points.

The press of time is an example of just such an issue. Anyone who has been involved in research partnerships is familiar with comments from the community *and* from researchers about how long the partnership research process takes to bear fruit. Yet this shared concern about time masks significant differences between groups about *when* lengthy delays or intensive time commitments are seen as problematic. Both groups—community members and researchers—express frustration about how long things take, but the two differ in whether those delays are seen as partnership related (e.g., bringing people together) or research related (waiting for approval from a journal for publication of the results). For example, researchers frequently comment on how long it takes to build trust with a community so that research can be begun; many researchers, particularly those who are untenured, conclude that they can ill-afford to become involved in efforts that take such a long time to "pay off." Yet those same researchers often find long time delays unproblematic when the substantial time delays are due to the need to collect still more data, to test an alternative explanation, or to wait for a research manuscript to undergo peer review. As in all partnership matters, time issues emerge at every stage, but the implications of these issues and what to do about the conflicting perspectives among partners with regard to these issues is at the heart of the ethical challenges raised by attempts to do research in partnership.

If research partnerships are to overcome the ethical challenges associated with each stage of a cycle of research—challenges that have been illustrated throughout this section—steps will need to be taken to prepare partners for this new approach to research. The next section takes up this issue.

◆ Preparing People for Involvement in Research Partnerships

In the classic article "Should the Philosophy of Science be Rated 'X'?," Brush (1974) raised the question of whether information about the complications of research, if broached too early, might discourage people from undertaking a research career. In Brush's case, he was raising the question of whether graduate students would become disenchanted with science if they are exposed too early to the difficulties and ambiguities of science as actually practiced. We might ask the same question about the dangers of focusing on the difficulties of research within a partnership. If people are made aware of the problems of partnerships—such as those described in this chapter—might people too readily give up on this emerging approach? The

Table 22.1 Research Cycle Model Issues

- **Steps in the research partnership:** The importance of efforts in research partnerships lies not just in the particulars of *what* we do (trying to address a particular hypothesis) but *when* we do it. For example, if the researcher decides on the area of study before consultation with the community, this is a problem even if the particular hypothesis is one with which the community might agree.
- **Who decide on the research agenda and research questions?** Researchers and their community partners often disagree about who should set the research agenda. Researchers with a detailed background in a particular area (e.g., the causes of lead poisoning in children) often assert that they should make the decisions about the agenda. Community members, aware of the health costs to the community of a health problem, often assert that they should make the decisions about the research agenda. *How can these differences be negotiated so that rigorous research is carried out that is helpful in addressing problems and answering basic research questions?*
- **The importance of solving a problem versus understanding the problem at a basic level:** Communities and researchers often have different goals for the collection of data. Communities may see a problem that is devastating their children and need to find a way to eliminate the problem. Researchers are often trained to try to get to the bottom of things and to leave no alternative explanation in place that could account for a problem. These differences in goals can fundamentally affect the partnership.
- **When is enough known?** When has enough research been done: Many underserved communities have experienced being "studied to death." They keep being studied and yet there is little to show in the way of benefits to the community. *How does one decide that there is sufficient information to focus on interventions as opposed to collecting more data? Who makes this decision?*
- **Who owns the data?** Research generally results in data. Questions are increasingly emerging about who owns these data. *If studies investigate contamination levels of lead in the blood of a community's young children, does the community own the data? The researcher? Both?*
- **The pressure of time:** Everyone involved in research partnerships talks about the need for things to get done quickly; they are worried about how long research takes. Often the difference is where people seem to think it is reasonable for delays to occur. For example, researchers talk about how long it takes (and how effortful it is) to get a community on board in planning for research. Many researchers will say that as a consequence they can't afford to get involved in community-researcher partnerships. On the other hand, researchers think it is acceptable for delays to result from the need to get IRB approval, the need to do another study, or the need for a research manuscript to be reviewed for publication in a journal. Both groups worry about time and talk about being frustrated by how long things take. What differs is which delays seem bothersome.
- **Who speaks for the community?** Researchers have been called to task for assuming that anyone who lives or works in a community is qualified to speak for that community. Such may not be the case. Individuals may promote themselves as leaders but may not be viewed as leaders by those in the community. An informal or unseen structure may determine who in the community is best qualified to provide leadership.
- **Is the purpose of the research to gain general knowledge or to gain knowledge that is intended to be useful to those who participate in the research?** Many researchers talk about individual communities as "laboratories." For the researcher, a community near to his or her university is a place to test out hypotheses, but those researchers might have relatively little interest in ameliorating the problems in that same community. Community members, on the other hand, may be very concerned not about the generalizability of the findings but about whether the findings speak directly about the kinds of problems in their community and what should be done about those problems.

(Continued)

Table 22.1 (Continued)
• **Should the community be able to approve research findings before they are submitted for publication:** Many researchers struggle with calls from the community to give their approval before findings can be submitted for publication. Many communities are puzzled by the researchers not understanding the need for careful consideration of how results are described and how the community is portrayed. Researchers sometimes see the issue in terms of prior restraint of publication whereas communities sometimes see the issue as one of respect and power sharing.

SOURCE: From Silka Online Workshop "Building Strong Community University Research Partnerships." (www.researchethics.org/brochureMarch.doc)

research cycle framework articulated here is intended to forestall this by linking problems with ideas for how those problems can be addressed. So ultimately, how do we prepare key groups to engage in partnerships? In the next sections we lay out some of these issues for IRBs, students, colleagues, and communities.

PREPARING IRBs FOR EVALUATING THE ETHICS OF RESEARCH WITHIN PARTNERSHIPS

As noted earlier, the rules that guide the work of IRBs are not designed to call attention to the ethical dilemmas within partnerships (Collaborative Initiative for Research Ethics in Environmental Health, 2005). Instead, most of the ethical questions that IRBs are asked to adjudicate are directed at safeguarding individual participants and evaluating the ethics of what they will be asked to do in the proposed research. The researcher must explain in detail the likelihood that an individual could be harmed through participation in a research project. The focus is on ensuring anonymity and confidentiality. Partnership ethics raise a different set of questions: What happens when a whole community is the focus of the research, when community researchers might be collecting data about people with whom they are familiar, or on questions of the ethics of who owns the data and how the data will be used?

Much is now being written about the problems that research partnerships are encountering in receiving approval for partnership research. IRBs are prepared to evaluate the ethics of one-shot studies, studies in which a clear separation exists between the roles and responsibilities of investigators and subjects. The review boards generally expect that the plans for research are completely fixed; review boards seem taken aback at the possibility that research plans might change as partners discuss preliminary findings or as the partnerships deepen. As roles, responsibilities, and approaches become blurred, the boards become increasingly wary of approving the proposals. Research partnerships find that they cannot direct their IRBs to a set of guidelines that speak directly to this research practice.

IRBs will need guidance and training on research partnerships, if these review boards are to have the background resources that they need to envision the ethical dilemmas that could arise within a program of planned partnership research. Even a cursory examination of the content currently required to pass the test to obtain the research certificate of National Institutes of Health shows that current requirements do little to prepare researchers to address questions of partnership ethics. Any training to educate IRBs about research partnerships will need to be done within the preexisting framework of IRBs in which likely benefits are weighed against possible costs. IRB members will need to be informed about the characteristics of partnership research, be provided with examples such as those included in this chapter, and be given information about the kinds of risks and benefits that arise in partnership research.

PREPARING STUDENTS FOR PARTICIPATING IN RESEARCH PARTNERSHIPS

Graduate students who are training to be researchers will also need instruction in the ways in which partnership research differs from individual investigator-led research. At present, students in most fields receive little training on research partnerships. Partnership research is not highlighted in most research methods classes, and to the extent that partnership models are introduced at all, they are presented late in the curriculum, often long after students have formed their opinions of what constitutes good research practice. We should be unsurprised, then, that students often regard partnership research as scientifically compromised.

Students' views are not neutral about entering into partnerships or sharing authority on research decisions; what students have been taught works against collaborating with nonresearchers. In large part, the training to be a scientist emphasizes the process of learning to design research and to rely on the academic literature of knowledge. To have succeeded at one's training is to have mastered the literature that the leading scientists in one's field see as the source from which new research questions should emerge. Other views on what should be studied—the views of community partners, for example—may seem unsophisticated by comparison. Often, there is little room for community views in the model that students learn of how research questions are to be arrived at.

If we are to prepare students for the future world of partnership research, various changes will be needed in how students are trained. Students will benefit from courses that provide extended information on and experience with research partnerships. At University of Massachusetts Lowell (UML), we have begun to develop such courses, including a full semester graduate course on the ethics of research partnerships (Silka, 2005). This course has been taught both face-to-face and online, and in both formats, the research cycle framework has served as the orienting focus throughout. An experiential approach has been used in this course that included practice and grounding in real examples across many contexts, many research problems, and many disciplines. The voices of participants in this research were emphasized. Participants reported the course to be very helpful. Information about the course is available in the Web site www.Researchethics.org.

REACHING ACADEMIC COLLEAGUES WITH THE IDEA OF DOING RESEARCH WITHIN PARTNERSHIPS

As many have discovered, one's colleagues are often hesitant to adopt partnership approaches to research. It is worth considering what might lie behind the widespread reluctance of researchers to adopt partnership approaches. Although it is easy to conclude that academics are simply reluctant to change, the muted enthusiasm may in fact reflect deeper concerns that will need to be addressed.

Research done in partnership with the "subjects" undermines basic assumptions about the research enterprise. To carry out research within a partnership is to be forced into the disquieting position of reevaluating many long-held assumptions about research. Partnership approaches go against much of what we have learned about our craft as researchers: the importance of being in charge, the need to design research that is well-structured and elegant and that can withstand alternative explanations, the need to direct our efforts toward academic audiences and to publish in highly regarded academic journals. And the years we have devoted to refining a traditional approach to research can often make it difficult to consider alternative methods of investigating research questions. Some might liken doing research by partnership to trying to write a coherent novel by a group. Novels cannot be written by more than one person without losing focus, and those who argue against partnership research might say the same. One needs to be prepared to address these objections by showing how research partnerships have been effective in collecting data to address long-standing problems.

For different reasons, junior and senior faculty can each see partnership research as problematic. Senior faculty have invested many years in traditional approaches to research and so may not be open to partnership approaches. Many junior faculty, because of their concerns over tenure, may be wary of staking their academic future on an approach not accepted as mainstream. In short, many obstacles stand in the way of successfully leading one's colleagues to consider partnership approaches to research.

So what works in overcoming some of the faculty objections to partnership research? We have used several strategies. One we have used with success at our university (UML) is to highlight the ways in which research universities such as the University of Michigan (at their Center for Community and Academic Urban Research) effectively use partnership-based approaches. We also point to the many funders that now support research programs when it is partnership based, and we introduce our colleagues to the many emerging peer-reviewed journals that seek partnership-based research.

We have also found it helpful to customize the approach that we use with individual faculty members. We look for research problems that particular researchers are struggling with that lend themselves to a partnership approach. Investigators, for example, might be concerned that their research (e.g., pediatric asthma) will fail to lead to policy changes. Their interest in partnership research can be piqued if they are shown how research pursued through partnerships has resulted in policy change. Still other colleagues may have trouble in achieving access to populations of interest (e.g., new immigrants). Illustrating how access has opened up for other researchers through partnership can be helpful in showing these colleagues the value of partnerships. With still others, we have shown how important hypotheses have emerged within partnerships that would have gone unarticulated if the academic literature was the sole basis for ideas. In this way, academic colleagues begin to see that rich questions emerge from partnerships and not merely from the academic literature.

In our experience, some approaches do not work. We have little success touting ethics, that is, in trying to make the case for partnership research by pointing out that such an approach is ethically more supportable (e.g., that it is ethically right to share power) than is investigator-controlled research. Telling academics that it is ethical to share power does not work. As academics, we often think that we *are* equitably sharing power—sometimes, even when we are fully controlling the research agenda. Our verbal fluency makes it easy for us to assert control. At many a partnership conference, we have observed that faculty monopolize the decision making without ever realizing the extent to which decision making was not being shared. Alternative approaches will be needed if more faculty are to begin to carry out their research within partnerships.

INVOLVING COMMUNITIES IN PARTNERSHIP RESEARCH

A few years ago at a technical assistance workshop on health disparities sponsored by the Centers for Disease Control, I was asked to give a presentation to community members on improving working relationships within community-university research partnerships. In preparing this talk (Silka, 2004), I found myself giving a great deal of thought to trying to make sense of all the times in which good intentioned partnerships end in frustration and conflict. In many of these cases, things went awry as partners worked with unexpressed but powerful metaphors about the other that created all sorts of misunderstandings. The assumptions are powerful. As noted earlier, Jones (2006) used the metaphor of a bus journey, where the community and university may have different destinations, to capture some of the problems in partnerships. This metaphor was very generative: audience members pointed to problems of who climbed aboard the bus, how to get unwanted people off the bus, how to ensure that the bus was going in the right direction, and so forth. Audience members were able to use the metaphor to formulate new ways to solve some of the long-standing problems within their research partnerships. As consideration is given to involving community partners in collaborative research, perhaps an important starting point will be simply to bring to light the metaphors and analogies that communities and universities use to influence and shape the others' behavior. For example, insight into how universities behave as partners can be gained by considering the ways in which they are, in fact, like various other entities: In my talk, I suggested that we look at universities as "tiny, little nations," "sport franchises," or "high tech" firms. Tiny, little nations are always worried about not being taken seriously on the world stage; they are forever trying to find ways to increase their stature and visibility. In a similar fashion, universities and their faculty often act like tiny, little nations with their own laws, rules, and boundaries; universities are easier to work with when one understands that they are chronically more worried about their ranking relative to other universities than whether their research meets community needs. Sport franchises are known for their high visibility stars and are always trying to find ways to be more competitive through these stars; universities, likewise, have their high profile, high status faculty who generate large grants and many publications but may or may not be good partners. Universities, when viewed as high tech firms, can be understood as knowledge focused enterprises. High tech firms often have multiple, independent knowledge production projects going on at one time and a single high tech firm may, in actuality, be an assortment of separate entrepreneurial enterprises all going in different directions that happen to occur under the auspices of a single company. Universities are decentralized in the same way and as a result are often difficult as partners. Each of these analogies captures something about universities as challenging research partners. Metaphors and analogies for the community partner can be equally telling of course. The point is that effective training for partnerships has to build language, whether research cycle language or the language of shared metaphors, that helps partners understand and anticipate how the perspective of the other is likely to shape, enlarge, or limit actions at various steps in the research partnership.

ENGAGING IN PARTNERSHIP ETHICS EVEN WHEN A PARTNERSHIP DOES NOT YET EXIST

Groups sometimes simply fall into working together on research and may not view themselves as a partnership. A formal partnership may not yet have been established or perhaps is not even contemplated. Even where the relationship is tentative, much can be gained by these informal networks becoming familiar with the ethical issues that loom on their horizon. Indeed, there is much to be gained if informal alliances start to envision their planned research activities in partnership terms. By doing so, nascent relationships may be able to avoid some of the pitfalls that have sidetracked other promising collaborations.

The research cycle framework also serves as a useful tool for making ethical issues visible as a part of the planning activities that typically occur when groups come together. By "trying on" a partnership framework, groups can start to envision the kinds of ethical issues that they are likely to have to deal with at various points in the future. They can see that when they work together, they will come face to face with issues of ownership, with issues of choices of methods, or with issues of how data will be analyzed. They can see that they will need a plan for how these issues will be addressed. They will need rules for shared decision making. By using the framework, they have the opportunity to think through these things before all goes awry.

◆ Conclusion: Moving Forward on the Ethics of Research Partnerships

Research partnerships are becoming transformative as they emerge in many different disciplines and focus on an increasingly broad range of topics. They resolve long-standing ethical issues and create new opportunities for research to affect difficult societal problems. But as this chapter has suggested, even as research partnerships become a means for addressing past ethical problems resulting from unequal distributions of power, this partnership approach also raises new ethical issues and challenges. As noted in this chapter, the new issues and challenges are tied to various steps in the partnership approach to research. Within a partnership, new strategies may now be needed, for example, for maintaining confidentiality, strategies that are different from those used when a single investigator fully controlled the research project. When communities analyze data from their own community, issues of confidentiality and anonymity become more complicated than when a technician without ties to the community assumes this data role. The relative weighting of internal and external validity also becomes more complicated. What is taken to be effective, meaningful research may become more complex when as much emphasis is placed on community judgments of external validity as on researcher assessments of internal validity. All these issues and a host of others can be approached, as we have seen, through a framework of partnership research that lays out how particular ethical issues come to the forefront at predictable points in a cycle of research.

Ultimately, partnership research raises larger questions about the enterprise of research than can be dealt with in a single chapter. The partnership approach blurs the boundaries between research and other endeavors. If research is an activity carried out not just by researchers but by partnerships, and if all partners can weigh in on how that research should be done, people may well ask how research differs from other ways of making meaning in the world. Is it reasonable to accord research a privileged place as a truth-gathering activity? Questions about the value of research are starting to emerge about many kinds of research but perhaps they are more pronounced in the case of partnership research. No consensus has yet emerged on these questions, but we should remain open to the discussions of these important questions.

What lies ahead for research partnerships? Will they become a common way to carry out research? Research partnerships came about in part to solve ethical problems that were not easily addressed in any other way. Partnerships have been seen as a way to ensure that researchers do not control the research agenda in ways that the research fails to address urgent community concerns or transgresses on the rights of communities and individuals. But in the midst of pursuing research partnerships, new sets of problems have been uncovered and these problems often make partnerships hard to be successful. The difficulties of being successful at partnership research raise the concern that, unless these problems are addressed, any large-scale movement toward doing research by way of partnerships is likely to be short lived. Without careful attention to these problems, people may decide that partnerships are not worth it. This chapter suggests some of the ways that these problems can be addressed head on so that the movement toward doing research within partnerships will continue to grow.

◆ Further Readings

Community campus partnerships for health principles of good community-campus partnerships. Available at www.ccph.info

Israel, B. A., Eng, E., Schulz, A., & Parker, E. A. (2005). *Methods in community-based participatory research for health*. New York: Jossey-Bass.

Protocols for Lawrence, Massachusetts Research Partnership. Available from Linda Silka at Linda_Silka@uml.edu

Research ethics tip sheets for partnership research. Available in English, Khmer, and Spanish at www.uml.edu/centers/cfwc/community.htm##research

◆ References

Bringle, R. G., & Hatcher, J. A. (2002). Campus-community partnerships: The terms of engagement. *Journal of Social Issues, 58*(3), 503–516.

Brugge, D., & Hynes, H. P. (Eds.). (2005). *Community research in environmental health: Studies in science, advocacy and ethics*. London: Ashgate.

Brush, S. (1974). Should the history of science be rated X? *Science, 183*, 1164–1172.

Collaborative Initiative for Research Ethics in Environmental Health. (2005). Retrieved July 29, 2006, from http://researchethics.org/articles.asp

Coppens, N. M., Silka, L., Khakeo, R., & Benfey, J. (2000). Southeast Asians understanding of environmental health issues. *Journal of Multicultural Nursing and Health, 6*(3), 31–38.

Grant, G. R., & Wing, S. (2004). Hogging the land: Research and organizing put a halt to swine industry growth. *Race, Poverty, and Environment: A Journal for Social and Environmental Justice*. Retrieved July 29, 2006, from http://urbanhabitat.org/node/164

Green, L. W., & Mercer, S. L. (2001). Can public health researchers and agencies reconcile the push from funding bodies and the pull from communities? *American Journal of Public Health, 91*(12), 1926–1929.

Israel, B. A., Lichtenstein, R., Lantz, P. M., & McGranaghan, R. (2001). The Detroit Community-Academic Urban Research Center: Development, implementation and evaluation. *Journal of Public Health Management and Practice, 7*(5), 1–19.

Israel, B. A., Schulz, A. J., Parker, E. A., & Becker, A. B. (1998). Review of community-based research: Assessing partnership approaches to improve public health. *Annual Review of Public Health, 19*, 173–202.

Jones, L. (2006, May 31 to June 3). *Walking the talk: Achieving the promise of authentic partnerships*. Address given at ninth annual Community Campus Partnerships for Health Conference, Minneapolis, MN.

Kellogg Commission on the Future of State and Land-Grant Universities. (1999). *Returning to our roots: The engaged institution*. Washington, DC: National Association of State Universities and Land-Grant Colleges. Retrieved July 29, 2006, from http://www.nasulgc.org/NetCommunity/Page.aspx?pid=305&srcid=751

Minkler, M., & Wallerstein, N. (Eds.). (2002). *Community-based participatory research for health*. New York: Jossey-Bass.

Nyden, P. (2006). The challenges and opportunities of engaged scholarship. In L. Silka (Ed.), *Scholarship in action: Applied research and community change*. Washington, DC: U.S. Department of Housing and Urban

Development. Retrieved July 29, 2006, from www.oup.org/files/pubs/scholarship.pdf

Nyden, P., & Wiewel, W. (1992). Collaborative research: Harnessing the tensions between researcher and practitioner. *The American Sociologist, 23*(4), 43–55.

O'Fallon, L. R., & Dearry, A. (2002). Community-based participatory research as a tool to advance environmental health sciences. *Environmental Health Perspectives, 110*(2), 155–189.

Quigley, D. (2001). *Ethical considerations in research methodologies for exposure assessment of toxic and radioactive contaminants in native communities.* Retrieved March 9, 2007, from researchethics.org//uploads/word/toxic.doc

Shepard, P. M., Northridge, M. E., Prakash, S., & Stover, G. (Eds.). (2002). Advancing environmental justice through community-based participatory research [Entire issue]. *Environmental Health Perspectives Supplements, 110*(Suppl. 2).

Silka, L. (2003, Spring). Community repositories of knowledge. *Connection: Journal of the New England Board of Higher Education, 71,* 61–64.

Silka, L. (2004, October). *Strengthening community-university partnerships.* Presented at REACH2010 Technical Assistance Workshop: Foundations for Sustainability Addressing Disparities Amidst Change, Atlanta, GA.

Silka, L. (2005). Can we teach research ethics? On line? When the research is with diverse communities? *Qualitative Research Journal, 4*(2).

Silka, L. (Ed.). (2006). *Scholarship in action: Applied research and community change.* Washington, DC: U.S. Department of Housing and Urban Development. Retrieved July 29, 2006, from www.oup.org/files/pubs/scholarship.pdf

Silka, L., Cleghorn, G., Grullon, M., & Tellez, T. (in press). Creating community-based participatory research in a diverse community: A case study. *Journal of Empirical Research on Human Research Ethics.*

Silka, L., & Renault-Caragianes, P. (2007). Community-university research partnerships: Devising a model for ethical engagement. *Journal of Higher Education Outreach and Engagement, 11*(2), 171–183.

Wing, S. (2002). Social responsibility and research ethics in community-driven studies of industrial hog production. *Environmental Health Perspectives, 110,* 437–444.

Wing, S., Grant, G., Green, M., & Stewart, C. (1996). Community based collaboration for environmental justice: South-east Halifax environmental reawakening. *Environment and Urbanization, 8*(2), 129–140.

23

VISUAL REPRESENTATION OF PEOPLE AND INFORMATION

Translating Lives Into Numbers, Words, and Images as Research Data

◆ Julianne H. Newton

Figure 23.1 $x^2 + y^2 + z^2 = 1$ (Videotaped by Susan Lakin). Lakin explores psychological pain by videotaping "primeval screams of transvestites" with flash fired in complete darkness. "In my portraits, the image of Larry is juxtaposed to his female persona, Gina," Lakin (2007) wrote. She added, "Although the details of his physical appearance are not present in either image, gender coding identifies them as male and female. The images, therefore, raise questions about how we identify cultural symbols as they relate to representations of gender" (para. 4).

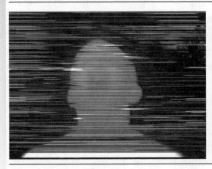 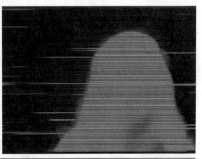

SOURCE: Used with permission of the artist. Original in color.

AUTHOR'S NOTE: The author would like to thank the editors and anonymous reviewers for their excellent critiques of earlier versions of this chapter.

If I could do it, I'd do no writing at all here. It would be photographs; the rest would be fragments of cloth, bits of cotton, lumps of earth, records of speech, pieces of wood and iron, phials of odors, plates of food and of excrement. . . . A piece of the body torn out by the roots might be more to the point.

—James Agee (Agee & Evans, 1941/1969, p. 13)

There is no mystery regarding the question of where images come from. Images come from the activity of brains and those brains are part of living organisms that interact with physical, biological and social environments.

—Antonio Damasio (1999, p. 322)

A person is a poem written in a language uniquely her or his own. At best, a translation communicates an equivalent—a reasonably faithful representation of the original. The translation will approach equivalence only to the extent that the translator (1) understands the original and (2) can communicate that understanding to others. Fundamental to that translation/communication process in social research is visual fluency: the ability to *perceive* clearly at the moment of interaction, to *translate* authentically during the moment of analysis, and to *frame* a reasonably equivalent mode at the moment of re-presentation. At each step in the process, *visual ethics* matter.

This chapter examines visual ethics issues that confront social science researchers when gathering, examining, and, ultimately, presenting information visually. The chapter first outlines key concepts underlying the interdependent dynamic of visual perception, translation, and framing as literal and figurative terms for research processes and meaning making. The chapter then reviews primary methodological and epistemological concerns of representation in the context of visual ethics theory, focusing on the researcher's power *to make visible* or *invisible, to facilitate* or *confound understanding,* and *to honor the trust imparted to the researcher from the initial interaction through the final representation.* Finally, the chapter recommends steps for visually ethical practice.

Given the complexities of human perception, the power of the visual to convey and evoke is both blessing and bane in research with human beings. Although social researchers long ago shifted their understanding of their abilities from supposedly omniscient observers to intersubjective meaning makers, we still debate the appropriate role of personal point of view in their work. In no area is this challenge more daunting than when one considers visual components of data gathering and reporting. The power of the visual to mislead or focus researcher, participant, and viewer/reader perception underscores the significance of understanding ethical implications of representing research with human beings. The ethics of visual representation also reach beyond truth to include how one interacts with another, the extent to which one works to understand the complexity of the other, and sensitivity to issues of privacy as one reveals information to various audiences.

In social research, the variety of visual methods employed has expanded along with technologies of seeing and analyzing. At one time, methods relied on ocular observation, writing, and drawing, either freehand or with aids such as the camera *obscura* and camera *lucida*.[1] The invention of photography in the second quarter of the 19th century answered increased desire for realistic representation of the external world, leading to research such as Hugh Diamond's investigations of mental illness. The growth of the social sciences paralleled the development of both photography and moving images as tools for exploring social and natural worlds, facilitating observation and representation of motion, gesture, and the nuances of human expression. Early proponents of light-writing technologies assumed that the tools ensured transparent objectivity. However, perceptual complexities were evident as early as the first fixed image in 1826, and photographs were staged, composited, manipulated, and misused in the 19th century as well. Although a few astute early social researchers recognized the influence of their presence on behavior of research participants, it was the middle of the 20th century before most fields began synthesizing concerns about the influences of point of view, moment, location, and other situational factors on data collection and subsequent representation. Not until the development of digital imaging, with its easily altered pixels, did the general public begin to understand the many ways an image could be manipulated—both while photographing and later at the computer. Today, computer software makes possible the quick transformation of photographs into print or Internet formats and of other data forms, such as numbers and words, into charts, graphs, and tables. Simulation of scenarios as well as people can be created through virtual reality software and social networks, such as Facebook. We conduct interviews by e-mail and through blogs, surveys online, and ethnographies in virtual communities.

Some social researchers believe all pictures lie because they frame parts of reality and can be perceived in multiple ways. That is like saying all researchers lie—for any observation, recording, translation, analysis, or dissemination inherently carries the "view" of the maker. In this way, method and tool, seer and transcriber, content and medium intertwine. How one collects an image, for example, and what one does with an image directly influence the meaning that image will convey, in turn directly influencing, though not controlling, the meaning a perceiver will derive from the representation.

These issues fall into two overarching but overlapping areas: *methodology* and *epistemology* (Newton, 1984). Methodological concerns encompass issues of *process*—how one goes about gathering, analyzing, and reporting visual data, and the tools one uses to conduct research. Epistemological concerns encompass issues of *meaning*—what one says one knows and means as a result of gathering, analyzing, and reporting visual data. These concerns include the forms of communication chosen for discourse about the research. Process and meaning are necessarily intertwined; process and meaning form the symbiotic core of knowing. Visual knowing, based on what an individual researcher or participant perceives, records with camera or pen, and represents with pictures, sounds, written words or numbers, is foundational to social research.

◆ Visual Ethics Theory

In this chapter, *ethics* comprise a process of conducting research with personal and professional integrity toward goals of truth and beneficence. *Visual ethics* refers to "the study of how images and imaging affect the ways we think, feel, behave, and create, use, and interpret meaning, for good or for bad" (Newton, 2004, p. 433). The *theory of visual ethics* articulates and analyzes fundamental issues in visual communication through a synthesis of physiological and environmental influences on human visual behavior. The concept of *human visual behavior* derives from the *vision instinct*, the hard-wired tool by which humans survey their environments in the interest of surviving (Newton, 2001). Human visual behavior refers to all the ways human beings use and create images, including dreams, imagination, and memory; perception of external stimuli; gestures, facial expressions, bodily movements, and clothing; and extensions of self through language, art, literature, and mass media. A thread unifying these ways of knowing and expressing is the *visual*—defined here as (1) ocular stimuli communicated via the part of the electromagnetic spectrum that humans can see, (2) one of the forms of stimuli we perceive that result in *images*, or (3) mental activity that results in images. The *human visual system* comprises the imaging processes through which humans interpret, store, remember, make meaning, and convey and respond to information. Perception researchers believe that at least 75% of all information humans take in is visual. Research indicates that people who do not possess physical sight also organize perceptual stimuli and neural information in image form (Sacks, 2003). Whether you are reading this chapter visually, reading it in Braille, or hearing it read aloud, your brain is responding with visual patterns assembled to help you make sense of what you read.

Through this process of perceiving, image making, and cognition, we translate the external world into forms we use as mental equivalents for meaning making and communication. In research practice, methodological routines and biases frame our translations of the perceived stimuli into what and how we present to others—who then work through their own processes of perceiving, translating, and framing. In social research, our translations of people become the frames through which readers/viewers come to know those people and their lives.

Consider the *eye*, just one part of the human visual system and that part of the body through which we collect light rays reflected from and refracted through the material world via the electromagnetic spectrum. The eye is a significant tool of the sighted social researcher. When the eyes gather light rays, convert them into electrical impulses, and send them quickly to the thalamus for further distribution to the amygdala and the visual cortex, humans believe they are seeing directly and immediately. However, when they look at something with their own eyes, what they think they see actually is the result of a slightly delayed response to ocular stimuli; the delay is necessary for the brain to organize information and make meaning of what we see. In that way, all visual information is mediated; indeed it is important to remember that all information humans perceive is mediated by the brain before meaning is derived.

Further complicating visual response is the fact that the thalamus first sends a rough schema of what is seen to the amygdala, which determines whether the body's defense mechanisms should be set into motion. Consider what happens when a person suddenly sees a snake; a common response is to jump away. Without that quick, nonconscious response, humans probably would not have survived as a species. In the meantime, the thalamus sends a second, more detailed image of what is seen to the visual cortex. The visual cortex gathers information from both the thalamus and the amygdala for further processing. Only then does conscious thought have an opportunity to play a role in the human visual system's use of the stimuli conveyed via neural pathways of the brain.

Beyond immediate responses to external visual stimuli, the mind thinks in images. Cognitive neuroscientist Antonio Damasio (1999) explained that not all mental images are visual in the usual sense of the term; he used the term *image* as a synonym for *mental pattern*. "Images can be conscious or nonconscious" and have "a structure built with the tokens of each of the sensory modalities—visual, auditory, olfactory, gustatory, and somatosensory" (p. 318). Particularly pertinent is Damasio's clarification of the term *representation*:

> The problem with the term representation is not its ambiguity, since everyone can guess what it means, but the implication that, somehow, the mental image or the neural pattern represents, in mind and in brain, with some degree of fidelity, the object to which the presentation refers, as if the structure of the object were replicated in the representation... I make no such suggestion... whatever the fidelity may be, neural patterns and the corresponding mental images are as much creations of the brain as they are

products of the external reality that prompts their creation. (p. 320)

Damasio's (1999) attention to the concept of *fidelity* resonates with our concern that data representation be *valid* (does a representation communicate in an authentic manner what was studied and what we think it does?) and *reliable* (would we represent the same data in the same way in repeated studies under the same circumstances—and do readers/viewers understand the data the way we do?). The extent to which research data are faithful to the research participants and to the meanings derived from the research requires more than verisimilitude. Seeking fidelity in social research encompasses one of the researcher's classic ethical paradoxes: embracing the self-imposed challenge to enhance knowledge while realizing that research data can at best present a close approximation to the human lives and activities examined. All knowers hold within them the power to see or ignore, to make visible or invisible. Furthermore, although some of that power is conscious, much is not.

Philosopher William May (1980) conceptualized the relationship a researcher establishes with fieldwork participants as engendering a *covenantal ethic*—a reciprocal and authentic exchange between researcher and participant that transcends conventional notions of contract. Visual ethics theory asserts that the covenant extends beyond the actual research process (perceptual stage) to include the analysis (translation stage) and presentation (framing stage) of the information derived from the exchange.

Cognitive theory supports this extension of the covenantal ethic. Damasio (1999) stressed the relational aspects of image creation:

> When you and I look at an object outside ourselves ... the image we see is based on changes which occurred in our organisms—when the physical structure of the object interacts with the body ... Thus, the images you and I see in our minds are not facsimiles of the particular object, but rather images of the *interactions* [italics added] between each of us and an object which engaged our organisms, constructed in neural pattern form according to the organism's design. (pp. 320–321)

For Damasio, an object can be a person, place, or toothache—things we engage "from the outside of the brain toward its inside"—or things we reconstruct "from memory, from the inside out, as it were" (pp. 318–319). The key point is that we construct images "when we engage objects" (p. 318). In regard to engaging people, Martin Buber (1923/1970) said it this way: "When we walk our way and encounter a [person] who comes toward us, walking [her] way, we know our way only and not [hers]; for [hers] comes to life for us only in the encounter" (p. 124).[2] Even if a researcher achieves a true encounter through which genuine understanding of the other occurs, the challenge of representation has just begun. When we translate people into representational formats, we conceptualize them—that is, we describe them in words as authentic sources of knowing, we show photographs of them as objects of viewing, or we condense and consolidate them into numbers for a chart or table. In this way, we translate people through a process of relating into mental patterns we can use for constructing (or framing) meaning that we might choose to present as images or as data. The most difficult challenge is to transcend what Buber termed *I-It* when encountering and representing people. Applying Buber's concepts of "I" and "Thou" (though the Kaufmann, 1970, translation is "I" and "You"), Lake and Newton (2007) explained,

> Knowing oneself and knowing another person arises from the encounter between oneself and another. In the process, both self and other transform from Its to Yous,

fostering wisdom through sacred, mutual respect and deep understanding—what we might call the ultimate form of communication but consists of multiple truths. (p. 6)

In this sense, translation becomes *transformation* and requires understanding of self-images as well as other images.

Damasio (1999) explained the process with an example of words on the pages of his book:

> The words I am using to bring these ideas to you are first formed, however briefly and sketchily, as auditory, visual, or somatosensory images of phonemes and morphemes, before I implement them on the page in their written version. Likewise, those written words now printed before your eyes are first processed by you as verbal images before they promote the activation of yet other images, this time nonverbal, with which the "concepts" that correspond to my words can be displayed mentally. In this perspective, any symbol you can think of is an image, and there may be little leftover mental residue that is not made of images. Even the feelings that make up the backdrop of each mental instant are images . . . The obsessively repeated feelings that constitute the self in the act of knowing are no exception. (p. 319)

Damasio's thoughts about something as relatively simple (yet learned) as reading the words on a page emphasizes the complexity involved not only in representing (framing) people and their lives as forms of data but also in the original derivation (perceiving) of information during the research process and analysis (translation/transformation) of the information for presentation. The final representations (frames), whether in the form of photographs, survey numbers, hanks of hair, shards of bone, or memories, affect what meanings viewers/readers of the research perceive. Visual ethics theory supports social research through a focus on roots of observation and representation in the human visual system.

♦ Foundations of Ethical Visual Representation in Social Research

PROCESS: VISUAL TOOLS AND METHODS

Among the visual tools a researcher can use are the body (includes the human visual system of eye/brain/memory); electromagnetic spectrum; stylus/canvas; camera (still and moving); and/or computer. A social researcher—herself an instrument, as Pink (2004) noted—needs every tool at her disposal to be an ethical and effective observer. Awareness of the capabilities and limitations of each tool is key to comprehending the ethical complexity of the role of the visual in social research.

The most basic tool is the body, the original multimedium, capable of moving, seeing, hearing, smelling, touching, and tasting to varying degrees, depending on the physical abilities of a particular individual's body. In the opening scene to the film *Kinsey*, the famed researcher of human sexuality coaches a new interviewer about hiding personal responses to interviewees in order to minimize interpersonal influences. When to present a "straight face" and when to respond honestly is but one of the visual behaviors a social researcher must master. Furthermore, he must master the ability to be consciously sensitive to the behavior of others while also tending to his own. While conducting a telephone survey, for example, a researcher may form an image of the respondent in her mind (and vice versa) that can affect tone of voice or pacing, in turn affecting responses.

Researchers extend their bodies through pencil, paper, canvas, tape recorder, camera, telephone, and computer as aids to perception. Even simple doodling as a way of thinking, drawing plans of a house or neighborhood, or sketching expressions and landscapes can enhance not only the moment of observation but also subsequent translation and representation. Obviously, the level of skill and talent involved affect the quality of the visual data collection; a drawing will look realistic only to the extent that the researcher's eye and hand can make it so.

Whatever the tool/method of observation and recording, each carries its own set of ethical issues. For example, when conducting fieldwork and using a pad and pencil to aid observation, does one write and draw while in the field, or only in private, after interaction? Making notes and drawings while interviewing can enhance data collection through immediacy of records, and many individuals better attend to and remember what they see and hear if they simultaneously translate the observations onto paper. In turn, observing a researcher at work with pen and pad can assure a participant of the researcher's care in recording information accurately. On the other hand, it can make a participant feel self-conscious or intimidated. These issues are alternately enhanced and magnified when a more complex tool, such as a camera or tape recorder, is used. Not only does the perceived presence of the researcher alter behavior, but the perceived presence of a tool, particularly one with "eyes" or "ears," also can affect participant response and, thus, the quality of the data received (Buss, 2001; Milgram, 1977). As with all social research, the comfort/discomfort of participants, accuracy of data collection, and potential effects on the translation and framing stages of research are ethical concerns. The ease with which nonconscious visual aspects of such concerns can go unnoticed is particularly worrisome, however.

Each visual tool/method used—whether eye, memory, pen/pencil/paper, camera, computer—involves specific literacies for all involved; the more literate the user, the better the opportunity for good perception, data collection, and representation. This is a matter of ethics directly rooted in visual and other types of perception. Although performative aspects of the visual in social research undergird other aspects (see Goffman, 1973), researchers often fall back on methodological routines and traditional practices for assurance that their practices are ethical. Meditation, journaling, constant questioning of meanings derived, and seeking information from participants, other researchers, and even readers/viewers can enhance the potential for the researcher to transcend the It of the Self as well as the It of the Other. In this way, the data-gathering experience is more likely to become one of deep knowing and understanding, thus maximizing the potential for congruent translation and representational framing. With a solid foundation of self-aware, ethical practice in the field or laboratory (or whatever the environment), the researcher can proceed to conscious, self-aware translation of material gathered. When the self-reflection process continues, the researcher has the opportunity to draw on the nonconscious processes of the mind to identify biases while translating into words, numbers, and images for analysis and presentation. Visual communication supports all aspects of social research—from the original conceptualization of the project, to the situation and manner in which the participant is first contacted, to the physical appearance and structure of a questionnaire or interview, and so on through the physical appearance and conditions under which the research is presented and accessed.

At each step of the process, images, as mental patterns and part of the human visual system, serve and result from the rational and intuitive, conscious and nonconscious cognitive processes of the mind (Williams & Newton, 2007). In the snake example described earlier in the chapter, after the brain's initial nonconscious response to seeing the snake, the viewer has the conscious opportunity to assess the extent of danger. In social research, the "snake" might be an initial misinterpretation of data. On reflection, the misinterpreted information and erroneous mental patterns can be recontextualized and corrected.

Examples

How might this visual system actually work when conducting research? Imagine for a moment that you are doing fieldwork with at-risk youth. A 16-year-old girl draws a knife on you. A normal response would be fear and preparation for self-protection (as in the snake example). Your experience will influence your response. Depending on whether you're an old hand at unpredictable situations with troubled teens or a novice researcher, you most likely will quickly assess the circumstances and either talk your way out of the situation, fight for your life, or run away. Your quick response—and perhaps your life—depends to a large extent on your brain's quick, largely nonconscious assessment of the visual stimuli indicating danger and possible options for enhancing the likelihood of survival. Your experiences and instincts are part of the resources on which your mind draws to protect you.

Now, imagine a less-dangerous situation, one in which you're interviewing an elderly woman as part of a study of end-of-life care. Your eyes meet hers in a locked gaze. Your perception of her will depend not only on the circumstances but also on the subtle twinkle of life still left in her eyes, the determined jutting of her chin as she tells you how she has been treated in the hospital, your memory of holding your grandmother's hand as she died, the woman's response to the subtle flinching of your facial muscles as your compassion and memory are unwittingly expressed, and the extent to which you have grown to care for this person. If you are an experienced researcher, you may be able to continue meeting the woman's gaze, consciously imbuing your own gaze with understanding and compassion. If you are inexperienced, you might turn away, uncomfortable with the intimacy of the moment. Either way, journaling and reflecting on the experience later via your visual memory will enhance your interpretation and subsequent representation.

These examples describe only a few of the possible range of research experiences that rely on visual perception for personal protection, interaction, and analysis. The dangerous situation may be relatively easy to record, decode, and write about. The second situation may require more self-reflection to sift perceptual memories and select appropriate representational modes for a research report.

In both cases, research data will include descriptive information, most often translated from visual observation into verbal notes; data may include drawings, still or moving image recording, and the eventual folding of information about your perceptions into coded themes, summary numbers, statistics, or charts. The quality of the research data and how you report that data depend directly on the accuracy, authenticity, and fairness of your observations, responses, records, memories, analyses, and reports.

A photograph or drawing may come closest to relaying the characteristics of the girl or the woman to someone who did not experience them directly. Graphic artist Joe Sacco (2007), who calls himself a "subjective journalist," believes that his successive minimalist panels can convey the atmospheres he observed while conducting intensive first-person research in Palestine, Bosnia, and Iraq. "The reader will see the background details subconsciously, experiencing them much as I did," Sacco said. The human nervous system is so astute at perceiving external information it encounters that the width or arc of a line in a chart or the shading used to distinguish bars in a graph can communicate nuances of meaning the researcher may or may not have intended.

MEANING: CONTENT AND DISCOURSES

The form in which a researcher presents, or re-presents what was seen, whether in the field or the laboratory, carries as much ethical responsibility for authenticity and accuracy as did the process of gathering the data. The representation can be only as good—and ethically produced—as the method used and data collected. Nevertheless, solid methods and solid data can be misused, miscommunicated, misrepresented, and poorly or inappropriately disseminated, thereby resulting in misperceptions. Representational forms range from memories to verbal descriptions, drawings, charts, photographs, films, videos, animations, X-rays, functional magnetic resonance imaging, positron emission tomography, and CT scans. Each form requires expertise for appropriate use.

A chart, for example, even one prepared by top scientists, can easily misrepresent research data through inaccurate scaling. Edward Tufte (1997) cited the now-famous example of a poorly crafted chart that led to the ill-informed decision to launch the space shuttle Challenger despite temperatures that threatened proper functioning of O rings on the solid rocket booster joints. Consider another example: a pair of illustrations representing quantitative and qualitative data from a study of race, gender, and class as portrayed in newspaper photographs (Newton, Dunleavy, Okrusch, & Martinez, 2004). The study assigned five values for the overall category of class, with 1 as lower and 5 as higher, and coded class according to wealth, status, and power.[3]

Figure 23.2 Representation of How Coders Quantitatively Interpreted Fall 2001 Front-Page Photographs From Two Oregon Newspapers in Terms of Class

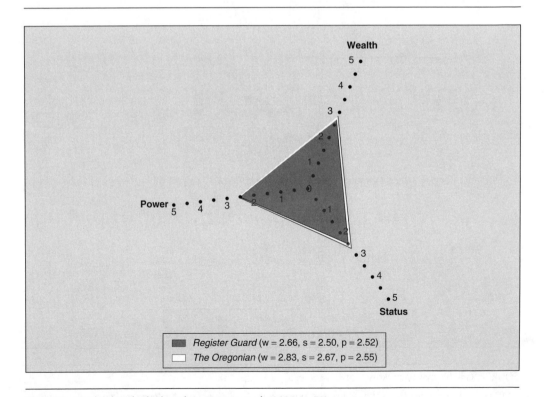

SOURCE: Graphic by Chad Okrusch in Newton et al. (2004, p. 72).

NOTE: Class was defined by wealth, status, and power, with 1 = *lower class*, 2 = *lower middle class*, 3 = *middle class*, 4 = *upper middle class*, and 5 = *upper class*.

Rather than rely on assumptions of race based on visual perception, the researchers coded for shade of skin, with a scale ranging from 1 for lighter and 5 for darker. Significant at the .01 level were correlations between wealth and status, wealth and power, status and power, wealth and skin shade, and power and skin shade. In Figure 23.2, the illustration of statistical data conveys a relatively clean set of conclusions. Figure 23.3, the illustration of qualitative data, conveys the amorphous results that so often characterize qualitative data in social research. Representing the data only as Figure 23.2 leads to the misleading conclusion that complex concepts are easily categorized and discerned. Figure 23.3 portrays a sense of the nuances of perception.

Another example of ethical challenges to representation is an image of photojournalism that was misread and miscaptioned, erroneously going down in public memory as the moment Christa McAuliffe's family saw the Challenger space shuttle explode. Two sharp visual journalists who were on the scene—and were careful observers with the experience and skill ethical visual researchers need—caught the error. Arthur Pollock of the Boston Herald watched the family closely while photographing the liftoff. When he saw a photograph captioned as the moment of the explosion, he checked it against his own still images and contacted video journalist Edward Dooks to compare visual data (Dooks, 2004). Their research was conclusive. The image

Figure 23.3 Representation of How Coders Qualitatively Interpreted Fall 2001 Front-Page Photographs From Two Oregon Newspapers in Terms of Class

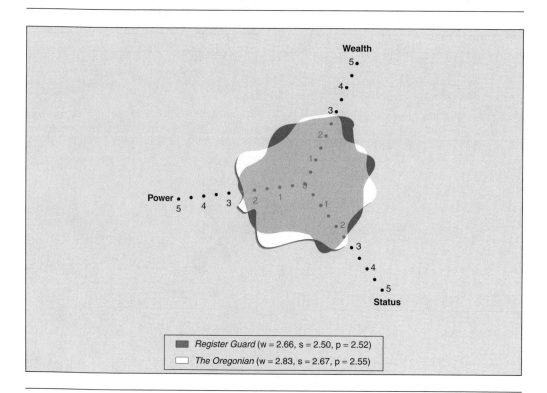

SOURCE: Graphic by Chad Okrusch in Newton et al. (2004, p. 73).

NOTE: Class was defined by wealth, status, and power, with 1 = *lower class*, 2 = *lower middle class*, 3 = *middle class*, 4 = *upper middle class*, and 5 = *upper class*.

of McAuliffe's family emblazoned in public memory as the moment of the explosion was actually an image of the family looking upward in awe and worry as they watched the liftoff. Although the period of time in question was a matter of seconds, the family's responses shifted from uplifted awe/concern (at the point of liftoff) to downcast confusion (at the point of explosion). Two professional observers challenged published assumptions to put forward the most authentic visual truth with correct contextualizing captions in subsequent national publications.[4]

The forms of disseminating images continue to expand. They range from a piece of paper hand drawn by a child (as with images from Darfur distributed by Human Rights Watch) and then scanned for distribution via the Internet, to scholarly journals and books, to art museums and university galleries, to theatrical performances and films, to poems and novels, to shopping malls, cell phones, T-shirts, and video games. Again, each form carries ethical advantages and disadvantages. A child's drawing connotes an innocent, unfiltered eye, yet important details may be lacking or questioned. Scholarly reports can offer profound insight into culture and behavior but usually emanate from a particular intellectual tradition that can shade translation and framing. Reports framed as art can evoke strong empathy from viewers or delegitimize work as merely personal expression. Representations distributed via the Internet or popular artifacts can get information quickly to large audiences or be discredited as commodities of popular culture or as violations of research participant trust.

Seeking responses to the representations, a kind of "market research," can greatly enhance the quality of representations ultimately published. Although peer review is one indicator of how representations will be perceived, seeking responses from those outside the field as well as from participants can be quite revealing. At this point, a social researcher might consult a graphic designer, for example, to determine if numerical data are represented effectively. Issues include determining whether the representation is indeed representative, or merely appealing; significant truth leading to understanding or partial representation leading to misunderstanding; balanced presentation or decontextualized material leading to misperception.

Representations themselves are performances, productions rehearsed and framed for acting out on private, public, scholarly, and popular stages. When a viewer/reader perceives the presentations, she enters a form of research practice, entering the world of the particular researcher and participant made manifest beyond their original interaction via representations of various kinds.

◆ Interplay of Process and Meaning in Research Representations

What follows is a mind experiment intended to exemplify the interplay of visual ethics issues involving process and meaning when using photographic and verbal images. Consider a set of two photographs taken as part of a social research project.

A MIND EXPERIMENT

At this point, please do not look at the images that follow. Just read these words:

The first image shows a woman and a man standing in the shadow of a concrete-block structure, which has an open door and a window with bars. The light is soft on the people in the shade but bright to the left side and in the background. A chair and bundle can be seen between the two people, who stand apart, and structures can be seen in the background. The woman, who is in the middle left of the scene, has medium-toned skin and back-lit white hair, cants her head, looks off to the side and clasps her hands to her chest. She wears a short-sleeved, mid-calf-length dress, a flowered-print apron, and shoes. The man, who is in the right foreground and leans against a stack of wood, has medium-toned skin and wears a straw cowboy hat, white shirt with sleeves rolled up, slacks, and a belt. He looks into the camera with a slight smile, a bit of gray hair shows beneath the hat, and he holds a cigarette between the first two fingers of his left hand.

Before reading further, please stop and try to envision the scene in your mind's eye. Try drawing the scene—stick figures are fine for this exercise. Then move on to this set of words:

The second image shows a woman and a man standing inside a fairly large room, which has smooth walls, a window with bars and shutters, a cracked concrete floor and a slanted, wooden, beamed ceiling; two beds, two chairs, a suitcase, a flower-decorated frame on a dresser, and a flowered-cloth-covered piece on which stand a framed picture, an image of the Virgin de Guadalupe, and flower arrangements. Both people, who stand just to the right of center in the scene, look into the camera and smile. The woman, who has medium-toned skin and white hair, has her arms folded in front of her, and is shorter than the man. She wears a dark sweater over a print, knee-length dress, and dark stockings and shoes. The man, who has light-toned skin and short, gray hair, holds his right arm around the woman. He wears a short jacket over a face-imprinted T-shirt, wrinkled pants, and shoes. He holds a cigarette between the first two fingers of his left hand.

Before reading further, *please stop again and try to envision the scene in your mind's eye. Once again, try drawing the scene. Then, continue reading.*

Now, picture the two images in your mind and focus your attention on your visualizations of the people.

Pause to reflect a moment.

What kind of relationship do the individuals in each image have? Are the people the same individuals in each image? What do you feel toward the people who are described in the words and who now are the basis of images in your mind? Does any kind of narrative involving the two people come to mind? Do colors, smells, sounds, textures, tastes come to mind?

At this point, go ahead and look at Figures 23.4 and 23.5 at the end of this chapter.

How similar or different are your mind's-eye images from the two photographs? If you study the photographs, do you begin to interpret the two people's gestures, body positions, gazes, relationship to each other, social and economic status, race, nationality, ages? What if you learn more about the people in the images—that the people in both photographs are the same, that they are in their 70s, married, and live with their daughter (who cleans the school across the street for a living) and her two teenaged children in a small town in Northern Mexico, that in Figure 23.4 they are standing in sweltering heat and the woman is reacting to something her husband said? In Figure 23.5, it is winter, and the couple is standing in their newly remodeled bedroom.

In Figure 23.4, the photographer felt comfortable making a quick, unposed photograph because she had a relationship with the couple and they had seen and talked about other photographs she had taken of them. In Figure 23.5, taken about a year after the first photograph, the couple has responded to the question, "How and where would you like to be photographed?" With both the photographs and verbal context, you can begin to formulate a clearer understanding of the two individuals, what their lives might be like, and even what their relationship with the photographer was like.

Words, numbers, graphics, and photographs represent and evoke images in different ways. Together, they communicate more than each can alone. The Gestalt psychologists put forward the perceptual principle that the whole is greater than the sum of its parts. What this means for the representation of people and information in social research is that the parts a researcher selects and how she puts the parts together can vary to the extent that the meaning derived from the research can vary. The frame one puts around one's work—whether the frame be chart or table, words or photographs, article or book, exhibition or performance—will cue the reader/viewer nonconsciously to perceive the parts ordered within that frame in a particular manner. Also important to consider is how including visual evidence of the researcher (a photograph of the researcher with a participant, for example) in data representation can cue the reader/viewer to recognize the realities of the research process, lessening the likelihood that data will be perceived transparently. The relatively new trend of representing ethnographic research via a theatrical performance is an excellent way to cue viewers to perceive the narrative with intuitive understanding of the subjective, human interaction that produced the narrative. Presenting statistically valid results via an analysis of variance table may cue viewers to conclude that the data are valid and reliable, regardless of whether they are.

At this point, it is helpful to use Figures 23.4 and 23.5 as examples for applying steps that can enhance the likelihood that research data are handled ethically and with congruity of process and meaning.

1. *Knowledge of self:* As do most researchers, the researcher began the project with the best of intentions: respecting subjects and community, spending as long as possible in the field, carrying cameras for a while before using them, giving participants copies of photographs, journaling throughout, and keeping ethical interactions foremost.

2. *Knowledge of tools and methods:* An experienced journalist, the researcher had extended her abilities by studying visual social science, research interviewing techniques, social documentary, and photography.

3. *Practice with tools and methods:* The researcher conducted a pretest in her own neighborhood, seeking to document life of her neighbors in pictures and words. Practicing the multiple-level process of gathering, analyzing, and presenting a 46-image picture/word report using eye, pen and pad, camera, and tape recorder helped the researcher prepare for the larger Mexico project.

4. *Use multiple tools, methods, and discourses:* Where possible, the researcher used a variety of means to gather, analyze, and present information in a variety of forms. The researcher had added photography to her reporting and writing skills in order to maximize forms of gathering and presenting data.

5. *Obtain IRB approval:* Although this was not required at the time this project was conducted, the researcher took every effort to inform participants of the purposes of the research, of their rights to consent or to refuse participation, and of how data would be used. Throughout the project, participants referred to the work as "el estudio."

6. *Involve research participants in all stages of research process:* Where possible, the researcher worked with participants—not only in the data gathering but also in the analysis and representation stages. The first pictures taken were made in a public park as positive/negative Polaroids so the researcher could give copies to participants. Thousands of photographs were given to participants, who were then asked for their feedback and suggestions. An exhibit of photographs also took place in the community. An example of the success of this process is a photograph of a mother and child in which the mother looked (to the researcher) quite haggard. On seeing the photograph, however, the mother was not concerned about how she looked; she focused on how the light portrayed her infant son. Discussion of the image led

to a deepened understanding of how the woman saw herself, how she saw her role as a mother, and how easily the researcher could have misinterpreted the significance of visual information in the photograph. In regard to Figures 23.4 and 23.5, the researcher had discussed the purposes of the project with Doña Margarita and Don Pedro[5] at every opportunity. Both seemed to take delight in being part of a study that would help communicate how people in a small town in Northern Mexico felt about education and life. Doña Margarita asked to be photographed almost every time the researcher met her. Nevertheless, she always expressed dismay about how she looked in the images when she saw them. She saw herself as dark and old. On several occasions, the researcher told her how beautiful she was, how important she was to her family and to the researcher, and how important it was for people outside her community to know what her life was like. Both she and Don Pedro received copies of the two photographs and talked with the researcher about how they felt being photographed (she felt a little nervous, he was fine), about the photographs ("well, that's what we look like"), and about the researcher's showing the photographs to other people. When Doña Margarita would complain about how she looked in the pictures, her daughter would tell her, "Mamá, Julie's camera doesn't lie."

7. *Obtain feedback about visual representation in research reports:* In addition to showing the photographs to participants, the researcher sought feedback from a range of photographers and scholars to help her edit and interpret the visual data.[6]

8. *Continue the process of enhancing self-awareness:* It was some time before the researcher felt comfortable showing the photographs from this project to others because the people who participated had become like family to her. She was extremely protective of them because they had opened themselves completely to her and because she felt the balance of power lay in her hands. Continued journaling about the process, theoretical reflection, and opportunities for dialogue with participants when the researcher returned to the research community helped the researcher uncover several important insights: (1) that whenever possible, the researcher gave imaging power to participants because of her agreement with William Stott's (1973) theory that the way people want to be seen may very well be the "best truth" and in order to minimize the influence of her own filters on their realities; (2) she gave participants every possible opportunity to give her feedback about the work; (3) she came to realize that she had access to and rapport with women and children more than men and boys, resulting in more content about females than about males; (4) that in seeking older women to photograph and work with, she was dealing with her grief about the loss of her grandmother. These are issues that can help contextualize the work and inform image selection for representation. Ultimately, social researchers need to consider ethical responsibilities to self, participant, research community, the project at hand, the field of study, and society at large (Newton, 1984). No one can cover all these concerns perfectly; but the effort to do one's best to address these concerns can result in the most reasonable—and ethical—representation and perception of research truths that humans can achieve.

♦ Conclusion

This review highlights issues of visual ethics in social research. Visual research methods are so complex that they occupy a 1,700-page, four-volume set (Hamilton, 2006) addressing classic essays, visual objectivity, visual technologies, and the visual as method. A great deal of theory building remains to be done to apply visual ethics thoroughly to social research. Issues range from photo-elicitation protocols, to the ethics of giving children cameras to photograph their home lives, to ownership of visual data, to the influence of IRB consent requirements on subsequent observed behavior. A number of significant readings that enlighten various aspects of visual research are included in the chapter reference list.

Researchers are good at planning the design of their methods for gathering information. However, representation of that information also requires *design*, in every sense of the term. "Design is choice," wrote Tufte (1983). He continued,

> Most principles of design should be greeted with some skepticism, for word authority can dominate our vision, and we may come to see only through the lenses of word authority rather than with our own eyes.
>
> What is to be sought in designs for the display of information is the clear portrayal of complexity. Not the complication of the simple; rather the task of the designer is to give visual access to the subtle and the difficult—that is, [author's spacing]
>
> the revelation of the complex. (p. 190)

Ethics of mind and ethics of vision are inseparable. Both motivate and manifest through behavior and both underlie research practice. In many ways, research is the fundamental human activity. Early humans surveyed their environment for food, safety, and shelter. Contemporary humans survey the globe, the galaxy, and even the universe for the food, safety, and shelter of knowledge. Humans rely on seeing as a primary way of knowing, using the eyes as extenders and receivers of the gaze, as windows for the mind. Through the six million or so years of human history, we have developed ways to extend the mind's knowing through sound, gesture, facial expression, writing, drawing and painting, sculpting, photographing, filming, videotaping, digital imaging, and electronic media disseminated via the electromagnetic spectrum (of which sighted humans see only a small part with the naked eye).

Ethical visual research grounds its methods and meanings in the fundamental principles of visual perception at each stage. Humans see to know, but what they think they see are the products of brains that have evolved to perceive mental patterns, images formed in response to interaction with others and with objects. In this way, we construct conscious and nonconscious stories of the self and others. The brain interprets visual information and guides behavior on nonconscious levels before the conscious mind is aware of the seeing and knowing. Research in cognitive neuroscience suggests that even the most advanced levels of creativity, problem solving, and decision making are rooted in the nonconscious imaging of the brain. The carefully reasoned, conscious thinking on which we believe we base most of our decisions and behavior is a secondary response to a primary intuitive form of knowing based on nonconscious mental patterning.

Thus, the significance of the role of the human visual system, which operates on largely nonconscious levels, in research cannot be overstated. No matter how systematic, cautious, sensitive, or aware the observer, the nonconscious mind interprets and reacts to what it sees, even when the conscious mind might choose to act differently had it the opportunity (and time) to make itself aware. At any given moment, we can be conscious of only a fraction of what we perceive. Trying to discern and represent people and their lives through images can result in "almost-like-this" status at best, or "not-at-all-like-this" status at worst. The goal of research is to find and convey the best truth one can, and that can indeed be a *reasonable,* as-close-as-I-can-get, though-not-perfect, *truth*—the best truth a human can perceive, translate, and frame at any given moment (Newton, 2001). Attending to issues of visual ethics can reduce the level of potential distortion and enhance the transparency of the research process to facilitate effective perception of the research report.

The most significant measure of ethical representation of visual data is conscious observation of oneself as a researcher while collecting, analyzing, and constructing forms through which to communicate information. Meditation, visualization, and reflection can enhance this observation by accessing and integrating conscious, rational thought, with nonconscious, intuitive perspectives and ways of knowing. Issues of gender, race, sex, age, or disability are communicated (or presumed) quickly in visual, intuitive ways. Representations of such information—if good—will resonate with something of the characteristics of those represented. Just as a well-turned phrase can convey and evoke the subtleties of an idea, even more can a well-created visual representation convey and evoke the substance of research data, engendering a sense of the experience of the researcher and participant as they collaborate. An ethical representation of their interaction will be one that conveys as much about the context of the interaction and as much detail as possible while also synthesizing the information into a readable/viewable form with the best likelihood for intended perception. Ethical visual research processes can help produce more ethical visual representation of people and their lives through careful, nuanced perception, translation, and framing of the interactions of researcher and person encountered and the data they created together through the research covenant.

Figure 23.4 Doña Margarita and Don Pedro Outside Their House (Photograph by Julianne Newton)

Figure 23.5 Doña Margarita and Don Pedro in Their Bedroom (Photograph by Julianne Newton)

Were a person a poem, how best to translate the person poem for others to encounter, to know? Visual ethics in social research are about making wise choices for all concerned to enhance knowledge. Ethical representation of that knowledge begins with ethical research of self in the encounter with the other.

♦ Notes

1. See Rosenblum (1997) for historical and technological details about photography.

2. To honor gender inclusiveness, "man" has been changed to "person" in Buber's quotation. In the Buber quotation, "his" has been changed to "her" and "hers." Male and female references are alternately applied throughout the chapter.

3. Please refer to the published report for theoretical and operational definitions of these complex concepts and for details of results.

4. See Hariman and Lucaites (2004a, 2004b), Pollock (2004), and Dooks (2004) for documentation and complete details of this recurring misrepresentation.

5. Names were changed to protect participants.

6. See Newton (1983) for a full report and analysis of the study.

♦ Further Readings

Babbie, E. (1986). *Observing ourselves, essays in social research*. Belmont, CA: Wadsworth.

Ball, M. S., & Smith, G. W. H. (1992). *Analyzing visual data*. Newbury Park, CA: Sage.

Banks, M. (1998). Visual anthropology: Image, object and interpretation. In J. Prosser (Ed.), *Image-based research: A sourcebook* for qualitative researchers (pp. 9–23). Philadelphia: Falmer Press.

Banks, M. (2001). Visual methods in social research. London: Sage.

Barnes, S. B. (2002). Computer-mediated communication: Human-to-human communication across the Internet. Boston: Allyn & Bacon.

Barry, A. M. (1997). Visual intelligence. Stony Brook: State University of New York Press.

Behar, R. (1996). The vulnerable observer: Anthropology that breaks your heart. Boston: Beacon Press.

Chaplin, E. (1994). Sociology and visual representation. London: Routledge.

Collier, J., Jr., & Collier, M. (1986). Visual anthropology: Photography as a research method. Albuquerque: University of New Mexico Press.

Denzin, N. K. (1997). Interpretive ethnography: Ethnographic practices for the 21st century. Thousand Oaks, CA: Sage.

Gazzaniga, M. (2005). The ethical brain. New York: Dana Press.

Gilman, S. L. (Ed.). (1976). The face of madness: Hugh W. Diamond and the origin of psychiatric photography. New York: Brunner/Mazel.

Gross, L., Katz, J. S., & Ruby, J. (Eds.). (1988). Image ethics, the moral rights of subjects in photographs, film, and television. New York: Oxford University Press.

Gross, L., Katz, J. S., & Ruby, J. (2003). Image ethics in the digital age. Minneapolis: University of Minnesota Press.

Harper, D. (2002). Talking about pictures: A case for photo elicitation. *Visual Studies, 17*(1), 15–26.

Harper, D. A. (1982). Good company. Chicago: University of Chicago Press.

Hope, D. S. (Ed.). (2006). Visual communication: Perception, rhetoric, technology. Cresswell, NJ: Hampton Press.

Humphreys, L., & Messaris, P. (2006). Digital media: Transformations in human communication. New York: Peter Lang.

Kaufmann, W. (1970). I and you: A prologue. In M. Buber, *I and thou* (W. Kaufmann, Trans.). New York: Scribner. (Original work published 1923)

Lassiter, L. E. (2005). The Chicago guide to collaborative ethnography. Chicago: University of Chicago Press.

Lester, P. M., & Ross, S. D. (2003). Images that injure: Pictorial stereotypes in the media (2nd ed.). Westport, CT: Praeger.

LeDoux, J. (1996). The emotional brain. New York: Simon & Schuster.

Lutz, C. A., & Collins, J. L. (1993). Reading National Geographic. Chicago: University of Chicago Press.

Maharidge, D., & Williamson, M. (1989). And their children after them (Foreword by C. Mydans). New York: Pantheon Books.

Mead, M., & Bateson, G. (1977). Margaret Mead and Gregory Bateson on the use of the camera in anthropology. *Studies in the Anthropology of Visual Communication, 4*, 78–80.

Messaris, P. (1994). Visual "literacy": Image, mind and reality. Boulder, CO: Westview Press.

Messaris, P. (1997). Visual persuasion: The role of images in advertising. Thousand Oaks, CA: Sage.

Meyer, P. (1995). Truths & fictions: A journey from documentary to digital photography (Introduction by J. Fontcuberta). New York: Aperture.

Moriarty, S. (1994). Visual communication as a primary system. *Journal of Visual Literacy, 14*(2), 11–21.

Newton, J. H. (2004). A visual method for visual research: Exploring ethical issues in pictures by applying a typology of visual behavior. In K. Smith, G. Barbatsis, S. Moriarty, & K. Kenney (Eds.), Handbook of visual communication (pp. 459–477). Mahwah, NJ: Lawrence Erlbaum.

Nichols, B. (1981). Ideology and the image: Social representation in the cinema and other media. Bloomington: Indiana University Press.

Pink, S. (2001). Doing visual ethnography: Images, media and representation in research. London: Sage.

Prosser, J. (Ed.). (1998). Image-based research: A sourcebook for qualitative researchers. Philadelphia: Falmer Press.

Prosser, J. (2000). The moral maze of image ethics. In H. Simons & R. Usher (Eds.), *Situated ethics in educational research* (pp. 116–132). London: Routledge.

Roberts, L. (2006). *Good: An introduction to ethics in graphic design*. Lausanne, Switzerland: AVA.

Ruby, J. (Ed.). (1982). *A crack in the mirror: Reflexive perspectives in anthropology*. Philadelphia: University of Pennsylvania Press.

Ruby, J. (2000). *Picturing culture: Explorations of film & anthropology*. Chicago: University of Chicago Press.

Smith, C. Z., & Whitney, S. (2002, Autumn). Living with the enemy: Reflections from those who know. *Visual Communication Quarterly, 9*(4), 4–14.

Smith, K., Moriarty, S., Barbatsis, G., & Kenney, K. (2004). *Handbook of visual communication*. Mahwah, NJ: Lawrence Erlbaum.

Stanczak, G. C. (Ed.). (2007). *Visual research methods: Image, society, and representation*. Thousand Oaks, CA: Sage.

Tagg, J. (1988). *The burden of representation: Essays on photographies and histories*. Basingstoke, UK: Macmillan.

Wagner, J. (Ed.). (1979). *Images of information: Still photography in the social sciences* (Preface by H. S. Becker). Beverly Hills, CA: Sage.

Wheeler, T. (2002). *Phototruth or photofiction? Ethics and media imagery in the digital age*. Mahwah, NJ: Lawrence Erlbaum.

Williams, B. (1985). *Ethics and the limits of philosophy*. Cambridge, MA: Harvard University Press.

Williams, R. (2003). Transforming intuitive illiteracy: Understanding the effects of the unconscious mind on image meaning, image consumption, and behavior. *Explorations in Media Ecology, 2*(2), 119–134.

Worth, S. (1981). *Studying visual communication* (Edited, with an introduction by L. Gross). Philadelphia: University of Pennsylvania Press.

Worth, S., & Adair, J. (1997). *Through Navajo eyes: An exploration in film communication and anthropology* (Foreword, afterword, and illustrations by R. Chalfen). Albuquerque: University of New Mexico Press.

Zelizer, B. (2000). *Remembering to forget: Holocaust memory through the camera's eye*. Chicago: University of Chicago Press.

Zillmann, D., & Gibson, R. (1999). Effects of photographs in news-magazine reception on issue perception. *Media Psychology, 1*, 207–228.

◆ References

Agee, J., & Evans, W. (1969). *Let us now praise famous men: Three tenant families*. Boston: Houghton Mifflin. (Original work published 1941)

Buber, M. (1970). *I and thou* (W. Kaufmann, Trans.). New York: Scribner. (Original work published 1923)

Buss, A. (2001). *Psychological dimensions of the self*. Thousand Oaks, CA: Sage.

Damasio, A. (1999). *The feeling of what happens*. New York: Harcourt Brace.

Dooks, E. (2004). Letter to the editor. *Visual Communication Quarterly, 11*(3/4), 25.

Goffman, E. (1973). *The presentation of self in everyday life*. New York: Overlook Press.

Hamilton, P. (Ed.). (2006). *Visual research methods*. Thousand Oaks, CA: Sage.

Hariman, R., & Lucaites, J. (2004a). Correction to photo of McAuliffe family. *Visual Communication Quarterly, 11*(3/4), 26–27.

Hariman, R., & Lucaites, J. (2004b). Modernity's gamble. *Visual Communication Quarterly, 11*(1/2), 4–16.

Lake, H., & Newton, J. H. (2007, May 2–5). *The value of one (or two) in qualitative research*. Paper presented to the third annual International Congress of Qualitative Inquiry, Institute for Communication Research, University of Illinois, Urbana-Champaign.

Lakin, S. (2007, October 17–November 18). $x^2 + y^2 + z^2 = 1$. Rochester Contemporary Art Center's Sibley Window, Rochester, New York.

May, W. (1980). Doing ethics: The bearing of ethical theories on fieldwork. *Social Problems, 27*(3), 358–370.

Milgram, S. (1977). *The individual in a social world: Essays and experiments.* Reading, MA: Addison-Wesley.

Newton, J. H. (1983). *The role of photography in a social science research project in northern Mexico: A matter of ethics.* Unpublished master's thesis, University of Texas at Austin.

Newton, J. H. (1984, Spring). Photography and reality: A matter of ethics. *Photo-Letter, 5,* 36–44.

Newton, J. H. (2001). *The burden of visual truth: The role of photojournalism in mediating reality.* Mahwah, NJ: Lawrence Erlbaum.

Newton, J. H. (2004). Visual ethics. In K. Smith, G. Barbatsis, S. Moriarty, & K. Kenney (Eds.), *Handbook of visual communication* (pp. 429–443). Mahwah, NJ: Lawrence Erlbaum.

Newton, J. H., Dunleavy, D., Okrusch, C., & Martinez, G. (2004). Picturing class: Mining front-page photographs for clues to the formation of accidental communities of memory. In D. Heider (Ed.), *Class and news* (pp. 61–83). Lanham, MD: Rowman & Littlefield.

Pink, S. (Ed.). (2004). *Working images: Visual research and representation in ethnography.* London: Routledge.

Pollock, A. (2004). Response. *Visual Communication Quarterly, 11*(3/4), 25–26.

Rosenblum, N. (1997). *A world history of photography.* New York: Abbeville Press.

Sacco, J. (2007, May 18). Presentation to Program in Comparative Literature Witnessing Genocide Colloquium, Lewis Lounge Law School, University of Oregon, Eugene.

Sacks, O. (2003, July 28). The mind's eye: What the blind see, a neurologist's notebook. *The New Yorker, 79*(20), 48–59.

Stott, W. C. (1973). *Documentary expression and thirties America.* New York: Oxford University Press.

Tufte, E. R. (1983). *The visual display of quantitative information.* Cheshire, CT: Graphics Press.

Tufte, E. R. (1997). *Visual explanations: Images and quantities, evidence and narrative.* Cheshire, CT: Graphics Press.

Williams, R., & Newton, J. H. (2007). *Visual communication: Integrating media, art and science.* London: Taylor & Francis.

24

USE AND MISUSE OF QUANTITATIVE METHODS

Data Collection, Calculation, and Presentation

◆ Bruce L. Brown and Dawson Hedges

Social science research in the 21st century is a broad field, touching on a number of academic disciplines as well as a wide variety of professions. It ranges from political science and sociology on the one hand to cognitive neuroscience and experimental psychology on the other; from behavioral medicine and the mental health professions to business, economics, and organizational behavior; and from social theory and philosophy to family science. The kinds of data in this broad array of fields and endeavors are highly diverse, and the ethical questions bearing on the use and presentation of data are similarly varied and far reaching.

Any discussion of ethical issues in the use of quantitative methods and practices of data presentation must be highly selective—a mere sampling of the data ethics issues in the diverse subdisciplines and a few representative principles. This chapter focuses primarily on less well-explored issues. It will be enough to merely mention the commonly encountered and well-known works on ethical issues in data presentation, such as Huff's (1954) classic *How to Lie With Statistics*. This is the most widely read statistics book in history, selling more than 500,000 copies in the

English edition (Steele, 2005). It is well-known for its lucid examples of intentionally or unintentionally deceitful data presentation practices. Perhaps one could say that the popularity of the work is evidence that Huff has hit a nerve. Apparently, there is suspicion, if not antagonism, in the public mind with respect to unethical data presentation practices. In the remainder of the chapter, it will be demonstrated that such suspicion is not entirely unjustified.

The celebrated work of Tufte (1983, 1990, 1997) is also well-known but in the more positive light of presenting compelling and impressive examples of best practices in the visual display of quantitative information. He is described by *The New York Times* as "the Leonardo da Vinci of Data." There is, however, also an ethical aspect to the work of Tufte that parallels the work of Huff in identifying "worst practices," such as his discussion of "chartjunk" (graphical embellishments that add nothing to the information of a chart), his discussion of misleading uses of rectangular areas within certain types of histograms and bar charts, or his criticisms of the ubiquitous inane intrusions of PowerPoint into the world of otherwise rational scientific dialogue (Tufte, 2003). Therefore, even though Tufte's primary focus is on examples and principles of best practices in data presentation, one can also find a strong current of identifying and criticizing malignant practices that fall somewhere along a spectrum ranging from unclear and misleading to intentionally deceptive and unethical. The work of these two titans of data presentation is obviously relevant to the topic of this chapter, but their work is sufficiently well-known (as well as being focused primarily on only data presentation) that neither their seminal works nor the continued work by others in this area will be rehearsed in any detail here. Rather, the focus is on broader data issues, examples, and questions that have not been so extensively explored.

In preparation for the remainder of the chapter, a simple taxonomy is first proposed of two major types of data (experimental and correlational) and two major divisions of research (fundamental science and applied research). These form the framework for discussion of data ethics issues. The first examples of data-related ethical issues come from the applied science of mental health care research. Next will be a discussion of data computation and presentation issues that apply to significance tests (experimental methods) followed by some that apply to latent variables (holistic correlational methods). An exploration of several ethical conflicts with respect to publication and data sharing then takes center stage, followed by a discussion of the ethical implications of ontological biases, hidden assumptions, and their relation to a workable philosophy of science.

♦ Classification of Types of Research and Types of Data

In setting the taxonomic stage for the rest of the chapter, a classification framework is drawn from the history of psychology. In some ways, psychology is a microcosm of the broader social sciences given its wide diversity of subject matter and methodological approaches, making it a reasonably good exemplar of the ethical issues of data analysis and presentation in the social sciences as a whole.

In his presidential address to the American Psychological Association, Cronbach (1957) classified psychological research as either experimental or correlational. Experimental methods are particularly strong in isolating cause and effect, in providing careful control, and in testing hypotheses with precision. Correlational methods excel in providing context, in holistically dealing with many variables, and in establishing the total pattern of relationships. Experimental data usually comes from carefully controlled experiments in a laboratory setting, and correlational data usually comes from research involving questionnaires, surveys, and attitude measurement.

The second dimension of classification used in this chapter is the contrast between basic science research and applied research. These two binary classification schemes, experimental versus correlational and applied research versus fundamental science, are not necessarily orthogonal to one another. That is, it would seem that the application of tightly controlled experimental methods to create scientific data would be most easily achieved within the laboratory in the investigation of fundamental basic science, whereas such control would be more difficult to achieve in applied settings, where one would expect to see broad and holistic but less well-controlled correlational methods. However, the examples of the following section involve rigorous experimental methods in an applied context—medical and mental health care clinical trials research using double-blind, placebo-controlled studies.

♦ Ethics in Mental-Health Care Applications

In the medical, clinical, and mental-health care areas, data falsification can arguably have life and death consequences, but so can the more innocent but equally dangerous errors that result from incompetence and erroneous data decision practices. In such serious matters, the line of demarcation between ethics and best practices is not always clear. Methodological rigor is closely related to ethical vigilance: When research, statistical calculation, and data presentation can be done better and more accurately, they should be. That is, there is an ethical imperative to demand and use the highest standards of research and data presentation. More broadly, there is an ethical imperative for researchers and readers of research to acquire and maintain a deep understanding of methodological advances and their limitations. The first area of data ethics to be considered is that of the application of careful experimental methods in the investigation of treatments for psychological disorders.

CLINICAL DRUG TRIALS FOR PSYCHOLOGICAL DISORDERS

Since mandates from the U.S. Food and Drug Administration that new drugs must show superiority to placebo before approval (Healy, 2004), double-blind, placebo-controlled, randomized clinical trials have become the standard methodology for evaluating the efficacy and safety of drugs for a variety of disorders. Used widely in psychopharmacology, the methodology of double-blind, placebo-controlled, randomized clinical trials has also been adapted to efficacy studies of psychotherapy. Despite the advantages of this methodology, including a standardization of research protocols and potential to reduce bias in interpreting the results, the methodology of double-blind, placebo-controlled trial has come under increased scrutiny in a variety of areas (Moncrieff, 2002). An ethical obligation exists on both the part of the authors and on the readers of papers reporting the results of clinical trials to be aware of methodological problems with clinical trials lest inappropriate weight be given to clinical trials in implementing clinical, standards-of-care, and public health decisions and policy, as can be illustrated by several examples.

One area of scrutiny is the potential for publication bias (Moncrieff, 2001), in which trials reporting negative findings, particularly if involving a small number of participants, may have a reduced chance of publication. The end result is a potential for published literature to be weighted on the side of positive studies, even though the actual research though largely unpublished may be much less available than studies that have shown more favorable results. As such, publication bias potentially represents an ethical problem not only for researchers but also for editors of journals, peer reviewers for journals, and readers of peer-reviewed journals. Despite the tremendous advantages of the peer-review process, presented findings in psychopharmacology and other clinical fields including psychotherapy may be tainted by publication bias, a problem with ethical overtones that affects the entire clinical research population and patients alike.

By resulting in the so-called negative studies not being published, any publication bias carries the potential of inflating reported effect sizes of the drugs, or treatment, under investigation, possibly reducing the drug-placebo difference and making either the treatment appear more effective than it really is or making the placebo response seem weaker than it is, or both. Because the results from clinical trials are important not only in guiding clinical practice (De Angelis et al., 2004) but also in supporting and even driving theory, any potential source of error in determining actual effect sizes in clinical trials requires careful scrutiny. Failure to do so is arguably not only a scientific issue but also an ethical one as well. In fact, the International Committee of Medical Journal Editors wrote, "Honest reporting begins with revealing the existence of all clinical studies, even those that reflect unfavorably on a research sponsor's product" (De Angelis et al., 2004, p. 1250). Similarly, Drazen and his colleagues maintained that

> once a clinical trial is mounted, the sponsor has an ethical obligation to publicly acknowledge the contribution of the participants and the risk they have taken by ensuring that information about the conduct of the trial and its principal results are in the public domain. (Drazen, Morrissey, & Curfman, 2007, pp. 1756–1757)

The International Committee of Medical Journal Editors argues that every clinical trial should be registered and its details made publicly available (De Angelis et al., 2004), and in 2007 the U.S. Food and Drug Administration Revitalization Act required registration of all clinically directive trials in a public database (Drazen et al., 2007). While the mandatory registration of clinical trials is an important ethical step, it only pertains to clinical trials; other research results may continue to languish unpublished and unscrutinized, potentially skewing the cumulative effect sizes of published studies. Studies of psychotherapy efficacy, for example, may not be as readily available as are medication trials.

Still other ethical issues involving publication bias confront researchers. Under pressure to publish, researchers may alter the very design of their work and methods or choose a topic that deliberately maximizes the likelihood of obtaining positive, and hence publishable, results. This unnoticed source of bias could have major effects on the integrity and fidelity of the underlying science of a wide variety of crucial applied areas.

META-ANALYSIS AND PUBLICATION BIAS

The widespread use of meta-analysis in a number of disciplines presents several areas of interest to an examination of ethical issues in data presentation. Combining as it does findings from several studies, meta-analysis offers the powerful advantage of increasing the generalizability of any one individual study, as well as the possibility of identifying previously unnoticed aspects of the problem in question. To combine data from several studies, meta-analysis requires the calculation of effect sizes from each of the source studies comprising the meta-analysis. The effect sizes are then pooled together, and the summary effect size takes into account all the effect sizes from the component studies.

Despite the solid advantages of meta-analysis, ethical issues in data presentation from meta-analysis occur at several points. During the entire process of doing a meta-analysis, potentially massive amounts of data are used, and failure whether purposeful or inadvertent to properly abstract and analyze the findings can lead to erroneous results. Inasmuch as researchers conducting meta-analysis can use rigorous and accurate methods of data collection, analysis, and presentation, they should, even though such an imperative merges methodological and ethical issues into an often complex mixture requiring intellectual and ethical rigor and transparency.

While the meta-analyst may use the most rigorous of meta-analytic techniques, the final effect-size estimate depends on the quality of the studies used in the analysis. Source studies can vary widely in quality, and the meta-analyst can be confronted with the often daunting problem of determining which studies to include in the analysis. A discussion of the techniques to choose among studies is beyond the scope of this chapter, but the important ethical point here is that the process of study inclusion and exclusion must be clearly described; otherwise, the eventual reader of the study has no context by which to interpret the final effect size. The use of elaborate tables and statistics in a published meta-analysis may lend the appearance of credibility, but unless the criteria for study inclusion and exclusion are described and have been adhered to by the authors, the final effect sizes amount to little more than a statistical mirage. While the calculation of effect sizes is the sine qua non of a meta-analysis, different techniques of calculation can greatly affect the actual effect size, all of which may be perfectly legitimate statistically. Again, the ethical point here is the necessity of transparency in describing calculations of effect sizes.

Funnel plots generated from meta-analyses enable an estimation of how much data are unpublished, and even an approximation of the missing effect sizes. Because of this property, funnel-plot techniques are often used in meta-analysis in an attempt to estimate publication bias, providing a correction of sorts to the reported effect sizes (Whitehead, 2002). While there are different methods by which funnel plots can be constructed, a funnel plot most simply involves a plot of effect size on the X-axis and the associated sample size on the Y-axis. Accordingly, effect sizes can be calculated from published studies and shown in a funnel plot with the sample sizes from which the effect sizes were taken (Whitehead, 2002). Unlike statistical significance, true effect size is independent of sample size. Therefore, the mean effect size is expected to remain invariant regardless of sample size, but the variance of effect sizes in a collection of studies varies inversely with the size of the study samples. There is more variance in small sample sizes simply due to a decreased chance of having the sample mean equal the population mean. In a funnel plot, therefore, the observed effect sizes from the larger sample sizes tend to converge around the true effect size, while reported effect sizes from the smaller and hence more inconsistent studies diverge more broadly both to the left and right of the true effect size. The resulting shape of the graph is an inverted funnel, with the true effect size found in the middle of the funnel (Whitehead, 2002; see Figure 24.1).

If studies, particularly smaller ones, with small and statistically insignificant effect sizes are withheld from publication, the resulting funnel is complete and symmetrical at the top, but shows only the right half of the funnel at the bottom, the asymmetry indicating that the visible effect size may be an overestimation. In this case, the actual effect size might be closer to that of the placebo group than the reported studies indicate. Conversely, if the funnel plot is indeed shaped like a symmetrical funnel, it is more likely that all studies have been properly taken into account. Other explanations are possible for asymmetrical funnel plots in addition to publication bias. Most important, heterogeneity in the published studies also results in asymmetrical funnel plots, but asymmetry in this circumstance is also a cause for caution when interpreting the effect sizes from published studies.

Funnel-plot analysis and its related techniques serve as methods of bias detection,

Figure 24.1 Funnel Plot

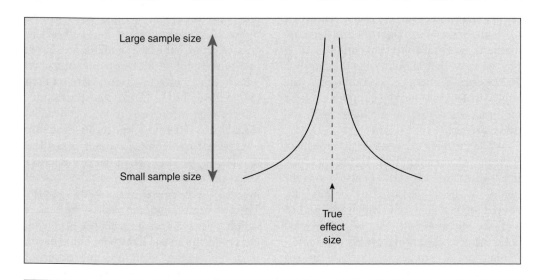

indirectly describing a problem that has ethical overtones. This again illustrates the theme that the use of appropriate analytical techniques in addition to being a methodological issue becomes an ethical one as well. Funnel plots can be constructed for effect sizes for both active-treatment groups and also for placebo groups. While missing data from the left side of funnel plots drawn from the treatment groups indicate publication bias, asymmetry from missing data on the right side of a funnel plot constructed from placebo groups also would suggest publication bias, again artificially enhancing the statistical separation between active-treatment groups and placebo groups.

♦ Fundamental Social Science and Behavioral Science Methods

We now turn to a consideration of some of the fundamental data calculation and presentation methods that are used in basic science as well as applied research contexts. First, we will consider the evolution over the past half century in the way data from experiments are calculated and presented and see that what starts out as an identification of best practices can evolve into ethical expectation.

COHEN'S TRIUMPH: THE EVOLUTION OF EFFECT SIZE REPORTING

In his now classic textbook about advanced statistical methods, William L. Hays (1963) introduced methods for calculating effect sizes. Certainly, others had noticed the rather cynical observation that the alternative hypothesis is essentially always supported if the sample size is large enough. That is, since the standard error becomes smaller and smaller with increasing sample size, with a large enough N, even very weak relationships will be statistically significant. To quote from Hays, "virtually any study can be made to show significant results if one uses enough subjects, regardless of how nonsensical the content may be" (p. 326). A year earlier, Cohen (1962) used power analysis to demonstrate that many published (and statistically significant) results do not necessarily represent strong relationships. What set Hays and to some extent Cohen apart from others who had noticed this problem in the past was their proposed solutions. Cohen provided power analyses to complement the reported statistical test results, and Hays presented several indices of effect size and strength of relationship, suggesting that they be used in connection with traditional significance tests as a way of indicating that a result is not only statistically significant but also practically significant.

In the 30 years following the publication of Hays's text, Jacob Cohen (1962, 1969, 1988, 1990, 1994) took the lead in developing procedures for effect size estimation and power analysis and advocated their inclusion in the process of null hypothesis significance testing (NHST). In accord with these and other similar recommendations, and in response to growing criticisms of NHST and calls for statistical reform in a wide variety of disciplines, the American Psychological Association Board of Scientific Affairs appointed in 1996 a Task Force on Statistical Inference (TFSI). The report of the task force (Wilkinson & TFSI, 1999) for the most part agreed with the growing criticism of traditional approaches to NHST. In the section titled "hypothesis tests," they emphatically stated

> It is hard to imagine a situation in which a dichotomous accept-reject decision is better than reporting an actual p value or, better still, a confidence interval. Never use the unfortunate expression "accept the null hypothesis." *Always provide some effect-size estimate when reporting a p value.* (p. 599 [italics added])

In the following section, titled "effect sizes" they advised,

> We must stress again that reporting and interpreting effect sizes in the context of previously reported effects is *essential to good research* [italics added].... (p. 599)

Undoubtedly, in the minds of many, the issue of reporting effect size has moved from being recommended practice to becoming a matter of data ethics. It would seem that at least some panel members of the TFSI share that feeling, as illustrated by the moral tone of the phrase "essential to good research." Another indication of increased moral force is the growing number of journals mandating effect size reporting. In 1994, *Educational and Psychological Measurement* became the first journal to require that effect size be reported with NHST (Thompson, 1994), and a number of other journals (including several APA journals) have followed suit. One can also see the change in that decade from the fourth edition of the *Publication Manual of the APA* (APA, 1994) and the fifth edition. In the fourth edition, the statement on effect size reporting was "you are encouraged to provide effect-size information . . ." but immediately followed by the moderating clause "although in most cases such measures are readily obtainable whenever the test statistics and sample sizes are reported" (APA, 1994, p. 18). In the fifth edition, "*failure to report effect sizes*" is listed under the heading "Editors find in submitted papers the following kinds of *defects in the design and reporting* [italics added] of research" (p. 5).

Many advocates of NHST reform watched carefully as the fifth edition of the *Publication Manual of the APA* came to publication (APA, 2001) to see how well the TFSI recommendations were supported and advocated. This is a huge issue for the reform movement, since the *Publication Manual* has a profound effect on editorial practice in a broad array of psychology-related fields. As stated in the manual itself (APA, 2001), "There are now 27 APA primary journals. And at least a thousand other journals in psychology, the behavioral sciences, nursing, and personnel administration use the *Publication Manual* as their style guide" (p. xxi). Many advocates felt that the new edition of the manual fell far short of what was needed. Fiona Fidler

(2002) quoted Roger Kirk, one of the chief reform advocates, from personal communication as saying "They didn't go nearly far enough. I'm very disappointed, very disappointed" (p. 749). Even though Fidler admitted that "like the TFSI report, the manual includes recommendations to report effect sizes, CIs (confidence intervals), and graphics," she followed up by saying, "unlike the TFSI report, it stops short of endorsing statistical reform in any general way" (p. 752). In particular, the manual has been criticized for "not following through on its own recommendations to include effect sizes" (p. 752). That is, although there are some fairly strong advocating passages in the text of the manual, the example paper on pages 306 to 320 (which many researchers follow directly without reading the manual) does not include effect sizes with its reports of statistical significance. Although the glass is half full, for staunch advocates it is still half empty. The manual may not have satisfied the ethical imperative in their view, but, clearly, substantial progress has been made since the early work of Cohen (1962) and Hays (1963). The camel's nose is in the tent.

A BRIEF NOTE ON THE ETHICS OF UNDERPOWERED STUDIES

One of the lessons to be learned from all the fuss about effect sizes and power analysis is that once we have some idea of what effect size we are trying to detect, it is very possible to solve these equations backward in order to determine what sample size will be necessary to detect that effect. Why should we do this? For ethical reasons. If the study does not have sufficient power to produce publishable results, we have wasted time and effort. As Oransky (2007) put it, "Why are we subjecting people to be poked and prodded when the study is doomed to fail from the start?" (p. 6). Besides being true to the trust of those who submit to our research procedures, there are other issues as well. An underpowered negative study can be difficult to interpret (Oransky, 2007), making study design an ethical issue in a second way. Underpowered studies still involve financial and human costs but carry a high risk of producing results that are difficult to interpret, thus not fulfilling our intended purpose of moving knowledge forward.

LATENT VARIABLES ANALYSIS METHODS AT 100: CAN THEY BE TRUSTED?

Factor analysis and other latent variable models represent the highest level of correlational data analysis. They are exemplary in their quantitative sophistication and conceptual elegance, and highly useful in capturing the holistic pattern of multiple variables. They have become the method of choice in the contemporary guise of confirmatory factor analysis, structural equation modeling, and so-called causal modeling, or, more generally, latent variables analysis methods. Cudeck and MacCallum (2007) in an edited book celebrating 100 years of factor analysis and latent variables referred to it as "one of the great success stories" of statistics in the social sciences.

With equal alacrity, it can be argued that factor analysis is responsible for more than 100 years of unfounded ontological claims, with statements such as "the personality scale was factor analyzed and four factors emerged." Brown, Hendrix, and Williams (2003) have shown that when the target data set has the usual amount of measurement error, factor analysis methods cannot correctly determine the number of latent variables, nor can it correctly establish the structure of the latent variables. At commonly encountered levels of reliability for individual variables, factor analysis methods cannot separate error from structure.

Hays (1963) and Cohen (1962) identified a way of improving the reporting of experimental data (with effect sizes), and it eventually acquired ethical overtones. This may turn out to be larger. If the simulation results reported by Brown et al. (2003) stand the test of peer review, counterclaims, and rebuttal, they have direct ethical implications, and could lead to a reconsideration of a century of research based on inadequate quantitative modeling.

◆ Publication, Data Sharing, Conflicts of Interests, and the Greater Good

There are many stakeholders to be considered in the research enterprise, and their claims must be carefully taken into account when examining the ethical issues in data analysis and presentation. There must be a fair and judicious consideration of often competing claims. Tenure and professional advancement hang in the balance, but so does the fidelity and integrity of science as the best possible reflection of how things actually are. The standards of reviewers and editors, the interests of participants in the studies, who have expended effort and perhaps even endured some pain to help create the scientific data, the creative exertion and intellectual property of authors and coauthors—all these must be taken into account.

The ethical issues connected with publication, authorship, a willingness to share data, and the accompanying conflicts of interest are myriad. A sampling will suffice. Data sharing and the enabling of secondary analysis is really an "efficient-markets" issue. Many eyes looking at the same data could potentially make a substantial increase in our return on investment from the research process, but there are "restraining forces," not the least of which is competition for visibility and for resources. Peer-reviewed publications are the coin of the realm and the key to winning professional advancement, the respect of one's colleagues, and a thriving career. To open one's data to secondary analysis requires a certain measure of unselfishness and concern with the greater good of not only a discipline but also humanity at large.

In a classic example of understatement, Zamiska (2006) pointed out that "scientists around the world collect important samples and data, but they don't always want to make them public, because sharing the information could jeopardize their chances of publishing papers and promoting their careers" (p. B1). This kind of competition and independence is understandable, but it comes at a high cost. Chase (2006) described the situation well: "Even as AIDS researchers around the world strive toward a common goal, they do so largely independent of one another due to a mix of commercial interests, bureaucratic jostling and personal rivalries" (p. B1).

However, there are now beginning to be strong countercurrents, at least in the high-stakes areas of research. The push for data sharing is increasing, particularly in dealing with life and death issues. This is well illustrated by a news article in *The Wall Street Journal* (Chase, 2006) announcing that "Bill Gates is tying his foundation's latest, biggest AIDS-vaccine grants to a radical concept: Those who get the money must first agree to share the results of their work in short order." In a related article in *The Wall Street Journal* a month later, Zamiska (2006) pointed to initial success in a worldwide movement to build interlab cooperation to deal with the potentially devastating avian flu crisis. He noted that "the effort led to the publication of a letter in the journal *Nature* in which 70 scientists—including six Nobel laureates—committed themselves to share data more quickly and openly" (p. B1).

In these high-stakes areas of medical concern, strong driving forces for cooperation and data sharing are beginning to offset the almost irresistible restraining forces of personal interest and professional rivalry, as reflected in recommendations from the American Medical Association for data sharing and availability (AMA Manual of Style, 2007). However, most areas of the social and behavioral sciences do not deal with such immediately grave issues, and predictably, there is much inertia and even resistance that blocks interlaboratory cooperation. In a footnote to a methodological evaluation paper on factor analysis, Fabrigar, Wegener, MacCallum, and Strahan (1999) gave a clear indication of the magnitude of the problem:

> when we contacted authors to request their data, we found that a relatively small proportion of them agreed to our request. In the majority of cases, authors did not answer our request even after reminder letters were sent. In other cases, authors indicated that the data were no longer available. Finally, in a few cases, authors indicated that they would send the data but did not or directly refused to send the data at all. This last situation is particularly interesting given that current APA ethical guidelines specify that authors publishing in APA journals must make their data available to third parties for a period of 5 years following publication. (footnote 13, p. 293)

Another major ethical issue in the arena is the opposite kind of problem—the tendency to hide one's light under a bushel. Even though it is obviously in one's interest to publish, there is also much inertia and resistance in this area, and it also has ethical implications. Research involves cooperation and investment of time from multiple people: subjects/respondents, colleagues, support staff, and so on. Sometimes such efforts are directly compensated and sometimes not, but always the effort is expended with the intent and the expectation that it will help move our collective knowledge forward. It is a breach of one's ethical responsibility to coworkers to let a paper sit in one's drawer unpublished. Continuing on until the paper reaches publication is an ethical responsibility for those committed to a career in scholarly work. Besides the responsibility to coauthors, participants, and one's institution of employment, there is also the question of being true to one's self. Presumably, one goes into academics with the intent to do research, publish, and help move science forward: a dancer dances and a scholar publishes.

The process of creating and publishing peer-reviewed work is usually difficult and perhaps often discouraging, but as Harnad (1986) has pointed out, virtually every paper can be published if one is determined and persistent. Persistent authors can start at the top of the journal hierarchy and work their way down until the paper finds its level, often with a considerable amount of knowledge gained from the criticism of peer reviewers along the way. The top of the journal hierarchy is obviously much to be preferred over publication in a "pay journal" or vanity press journal, but one should do what one can with each paper. Invited chapters can be of much value to the discourse and dialogue within the discipline, but perhaps are generally recognized as more of a duty of citizenship than an avenue of highly rewarded scholarship. Peer-reviewed publications are clearly the most rewarding and rewarded avenues of publication, and the pursuit of them in the best possible journals is the ethical responsibility of one who is committed to a life of scholarship.

◆ *Ethics, Assumptions, Ontological Biases, and Philosophy of Science*

ETHICS AND PHILOSOPHY OF SCIENCE

Kuhn's (1962) well-known sociological analysis of the actual human process of science reminds us that science is, after all, a human endeavor. We are not angels, and there is much of politics and even intrigue, the managing of appearances, and the protection of turf in scholarship. However, Kuhn's work seems to also have the deeper implication that not only is science a human process of politics, of influencing and convincing others, but it also *should* be. No one person is clever or wise enough to set the canons of science for all time that others should follow—scientific endeavor should always have to prove its mettle to the scrutiny of critical eyes and the superior wisdom of consensus over time. However, the Kuhnian consensus fails us and fails the interests of truth if there is a muzzling of the dissenting voice. Popper's concept of science as self-correcting by falsification likewise requires scientists of strong ethical mettle if not good will, who are willing to admit when they are mistaken. Science has come to be trusted because of the gatekeeping function that bars the door to local crackpots and hare-brained assertions, but as editorial power is wielded to maintain orthodoxy, the entire enterprise of science is jeopardized.

ETHICS, ASSUMPTIONS, AND BIAS

Perhaps a deeper level of ethics in the presentation of scientific data is the question of underlying philosophical and scientific assumptions of any particular author. Basic and often unexamined assumptions affect directly the phenomenon studied, the interpretation of results (Hedges & Burchfield, 2005a), and, ultimately, the presentation of the findings. Whether an investigator reports data from the perspective of materialistic, dualistic, or any other set of assumptions, the presented findings will contain echoes of those assumptions, often significantly constraining the presented data and blinding the reader to alternative interpretations (Hedges & Burchfield, 2005a). In this regard, "ideologies and dogmas are the jailers" (Changeux & Ricoeur, 2000, p. 173), and, as such, a fully ethical presentation of scientific data requires an understanding on the part of author and reader alike of the assumptions that gird the research and findings. An awareness of the assumptions driving research findings enables researchers and readers alike to better nuance the findings than would be possible without an understanding of the supporting assumptions. Because data from the social sciences are a public affair having the potential to influence theory, public policy, and clinical treatment, an awareness of assumptions becomes an ethical issue in that philosophical sloppiness may lead to a faulty interpretation of research findings. Inasmuch as researchers and readers have the capability to examine their assumptions and potential biases, they have the obligation to do so. As a simple example, the placebo effect is often assumed to be an embarrassing or even fabricated phenomenon that simply interferes with the interpretation of clinical-trial results (Hedges & Burchfield, 2005b), when, in fact, it is possible that the placebo response "may be nature's way of providing clues to fundamental aspects of the healing process..." (Kupfer & Frank, 2002, p. 1854). A basic assumption that all mental illness is biologically determined, for instance, may lead a researcher to emphasize a small but statistically significant difference between drug and treatment arms in a clinical trial, whereas a researcher with more holistic assumptions about the nature of mental illness may focus on the placebo response itself. Either presentation carries the potential to influence readers' interpretations of the findings, which in turn may affect clinical practice and guide future research. Regardless of the true nature of the placebo response, an author's assumptions when reporting on the placebo response can greatly affect its presentation in the literature.

◆ Conclusion

To the extent that science has come to be respected as trustworthy because of its capacity to rigorously test and challenge truth claims, the continued use of methods that have been adequately demonstrated to be indefensible moves across the line of best practices into the area of ethics. The peer-review process is the fundamental mechanism for weighing such claims and the challenges and counterclaims that result.

Science is only as good as the collection, presentation, and interpretation of its data. The philosopher of science Karl Popper argues that scientific theories must be testable and precise enough to be capable of falsification (Popper, 1959). To be so, science, including social science, must be essentially a public endeavor, in which all findings should be published and exposed to scrutiny by the entire scientific community. Consistent with this view, any errors, scientific or otherwise, in the collection, analysis, and presentation of data potentially hinder the self-correcting nature of science, reducing science to a biased game of ideological and corporate hide-and-seek.

Examples from clinical trial research, meta-analysis, significance testing, and latent structure analysis illustrate the broad theme of interaction between methodology and ethical practice. In short, if a better or a best method of data collection or analysis is available, then an ethical imperative exists to incorporate that method, instead of relying on outdated or inferior practices. In some cases, however, such as in the calculation of effect sizes in meta-analysis, no one method may be clearly superior, even though different calculation methods may produce vastly different results. In these cases, the ethical injunction lies in methodological transparency—the clear exposition of exactly what was done, thus providing readers with a context in which to interpret the findings.

For Popper's conceptualization of the scientific method to work fully, researchers must present their data to the scientific and lay community at large. Any bias in the presented data from unpublished studies, outdated or inaccurate statistical analysis, or unexamined assumptions can significantly hinder the public self-correction of science. Any hindrance to the collection, analysis, or publication of data, such as inaccessible findings from refusal to share data or not publishing a study, should also be corrected for science to fully function. While mistakes will occur, a researcher who knows or should know better is engaging in the misuse of data. At this level, methodology requires an ethical check at every step to ensure the proper generation, use, publication, and interpretation of research findings.

◆ References

American Medical Association. (2007). *AMA manual of style: A guide for authors and editors* (10th ed.). New York: Oxford University Press.

American Psychological Association. (1994). *Publication manual of the American Psychological Association* (4th ed.). Washington, DC: Author.

American Psychological Association. (2001). *Publication manual of the American Psychological Association* (5th ed.). Washington, DC: Author.

Brown, B. L., Hendrix, S. B., & Williams, R. N. (2003). Deconstructing psychology's quantitative heritage: The "new look" of visual parables. In N. Stephensen, H. L. Radtke, R. J. Jorna, & H. J. Stam (Eds.), *Theoretical psychology: Critical contributions* (pp. 78–89). Concord, Ontario, Canada: Captus University.

Changeux, J. P., & Ricoeur, P. (2000). *What makes us think? A neuroscientist and philosopher argue about ethics, human nature, and the brain.* Princeton, NJ: Princeton University Press.

Chase, M. (2006, July 20). Gates won't fund AIDS researchers unless they pool data. *The Wall Street Journal*, pp. B1, B4.

Cohen, J. (1962). The statistical power of abnormal-social psychological research: A review. *Journal of Abnormal & Social Psychology, 65*, 145–153.

Cohen, J. (1969). *Statistical power analysis for the behavioral sciences.* New York: Academic Press.

Cohen, J. (1988). *Statistical power analysis for the behavioral sciences* (2nd ed.). Hillsdale, NJ: Lawrence Erlbaum.

Cohen, J. (1990). Things I have learned (so far). *American Psychologist, 45*, 1304–1312.

Cohen, J. (1994). The Earth is round ($p < .05$). *American Psychologist, 49*, 997–1003.

Cronbach, L. J. (1957). The two disciplines of scientific psychology. *American Psychologist, 12,* 671–684.

Cudeck, R., & MacCallum, R. C. (2007). Preface. In R. Cudeck & R. C. MacCallum (Eds.), *Factor analysis at 100: Historical developments and future directions.* Mahwah, NJ: Lawrence Erlbaum.

De Angelis, C., Drazen, J. M., Frizelle, F. A., Haug, C., Hoey, J., Horton, R., et al. (2004). Clinical trial registration: A statement from the International Committee of Medical Journal Editors. *New England Journal of Medicine, 351,* 1250–1251.

Drazen, J. M., Morrissey, S., & Curfman, G. D. (2007). Open clinical trials. *New England Journal of Medicine, 357,* 1756–1757.

Fabrigar, L. R., Wegener, D. T., MacCallum, R. C., & Strahan, E. J. (1999). Evaluating the use of exploratory factor analysis in psychological research. *Psychological Methods, 4,* 272–299.

Fidler, F. (2002). The fifth edition of the *APA Publication Manual*: Why its statistics recommendations are so controversial. *Educational and Psychological Measurement, 62,* 749–770.

Harnad, S. (1986). Policing the paper chase. *Nature, 322,* 24–25.

Hays, W. L. (1963). *Statistics.* New York: Holt, Rinehart & Winston.

Healy, D. (2004). *Let them eat Prozac: The unhealthy relationship between the pharmaceutical industry and depression.* New York: New York University Press.

Hedges, D., & Burchfield, C. (2005a). The assumptions and implications of the neurobiological approach to depression. In B. D. Slife, J. S. Reber, & F. C. Richardson (Eds.), *Critical thinking about psychology: Hidden assumptions and plausible alternatives* (pp. 99–120). Washington, DC: American Psychological Association.

Hedges, D. W., & Burchfield, C. M. (2005b). The placebo effect and its implications. *Journal of Mind and Behavior, 26,* 161–179.

Huff, D. (1954). *How to lie with statistics.* New York: Norton.

Kuhn, T. (1962). *The structure of scientific revolutions.* Chicago: University of Chicago Press.

Kupfer, D. J., & Frank, E. (2002). Placebo in clinical trials for depression: Complexity and necessity. *Journal of the American Medical Association, 287,* 1853–1854.

Moncrieff, J. (2001). Are antidepressants overrated? A review of methodological problems in antidepressant trials. *Journal of Nervous and Mental Disease, 189,* 288–295.

Moncrieff, J. (2002). The antidepressant debate. *British Journal of Psychiatry, 180,* 193–194.

Oransky, I. (2007). Why size matters: So just how big should a study be before you pay attention to it? *CNS News, 9,* 6.

Popper, K. R. (1959). *The logic of scientific discovery.* New York: Harper.

Steele, J. M. (2005). Darrell Huff and fifty years of *How to Lie With Statistics. Statistical Science, 20,* 205–209.

Thompson, B. (1994). Guidelines for authors. *Educational and Psychological Measurement, 54,* 837–847.

Tufte, E. R. (1983). *The visual display of quantitative information* (2nd ed.). Cheshire, CT: Graphics Press.

Tufte, E. R. (1990). *Envisioning information.* Cheshire, CT: Graphics Press.

Tufte, E. R. (1997). *Visual explanations: Images and quantities, evidence and narrative.* Cheshire, CT: Graphics Press.

Tufte, E. R. (2003). PowerPoint is evil. *Wired, 11,* 1059–1028.

Whitehead, A. (2002). *Meta-analysis of controlled clinical trials.* West Sussex, UK: Wiley.

Wilkinson, L., & APA Task Force on Statistical Inference. (1999). Statistical methods in psychology journals: Guidelines and explanations. *American Psychologist, 54,* 594–604.

Zamiska, N. (2006, August 31). A nonscientist pushes sharing bird-flu data. *The Wall Street Journal,* pp. B1, B7.

SECTION V

ETHICS WITHIN DIVERSE CULTURAL GROUPS

Ethics concerns the morality of human conduct (Edwards & Mauthner, 2002). In relation to research, it refers to the moral deliberation, choice, and accountability of the researcher throughout the research process. Contemporary society is characterized by social diversity. As implications of cultural diversity become more salient and researchers are urged to become more reflective, ethical dilemmas are set to increase (Birch, Miller, Mauthner, & Jessop, 2002). This presents both ethical and methodological issues for researchers who find themselves working in culturally complex communities with diverse groups who may experience various forms of marginalization. Sieber (1992) noted a need for increased cultural sensitivity, collaboration, respect, and tailoring of the research procedures to the population being studied. Because of the difficulty of becoming a community insider in a "foreign" culture, the researcher can choose to collaborate with community leaders and organizations, such as churches and schools. While Sieber wrote of the need to have an honest desire to communicate effectively, respect the community members, and share the decision making, the authors in this section extend the concepts inherent in ethical work in culturally complex communities based on their experiences.

Katrina Bledsoe and Rodney Hopson, in their chapter "Conducting Ethical Research and Evaluation in Underserved Communities" (Chapter 25), explore notions of ethics in research embedded in research standards and principles, arguing that these notions are fundamental to the conceptual and operational balance of the field. This chapter explores "inappropriate theoretical and methodological perspectives" used historically (and in the present) to study underserved communities, especially with African Americans (and also Africans); the need for appropriate research questions, methods, design, and analysis; and some suggestions for amelioration (Chapter 25, p. 393).

Bagele Chilisa (Chapter 26) criticizes the application of values and assumptions about the nature of knowledge and reality that inform research paradigms embedded in the First World's history, culture, and social context to other settings. She illustrates how the application of First World research processes and ethical standards in sub-Saharan Africa all too often distorts reality; perpetuates stereotypes about the "other"; shows disrespect for local participants, communities, and culture; and violates indigenous research ethics. She contrasts these processes with *Ubuntu*, an African value system that privileges an I/we relationship in contrast to the Western concept of the I/you individualistic perspective (Khoza, 1994; Louw, 2001) and is part of the African contribution to extending our understanding of the meaning of ethical research.

Divya Sharma (Chapter 27), writing about research ethics in the context of sensitive behaviors, describes Hawala, a traditional underground economy that operates outside the legal structure in ways that are taken for granted by participants and by some governments, including that of India. In the United States, in contrast, the same practices are regarded as criminal acts. Therefore, ethical issues involved in the study of the underground economy and those who participate in it differ greatly from one site to the other. The contrasts in this example highlight special ethical considerations that affect research into sensitive behaviors, in this case, the transfer of funds outside the traditional banking system. During field research, researchers may observe a Hawala transaction that would make them a witness to a legal or illegal activity. The Hawala dealer or user being observed may not be aware of the researcher's concern with regard to legality and this raises ethical issues about subjects' voluntary participation and informed consent. With Hawala being a multilayered concept, it is not easy to distinguish criminal from noncriminal behaviors.

In postcolonial societies, there are hierarchical divisions based on historical positioning and on privilege associated with wealth, race/ethnicity, and other factors. Often overlooked by social science researchers, this lack of recognition constitutes an ethical issue in itself and, when explored, has additional ethical implications. Helen Moewaka Barnes, Tim McCreanor, Shane Edwards, and Belinda Borell (Chapter 28) contribute to the theme of "studying up" in this volume by scrutinizing the colonial system that regulates research and practices in Aotearoa (New Zealand). Research that challenges the oppression of Maori plays a key role in informing policy and action in the areas of resource management, environmental protection and sustainability, health service provision and promotion, and Maori development in general. The authors contrast the demands of university ethical review boards and the fundamental ethical principles reflected in Maori culture.

Colin Barnes continues the exploration of ethical implications of cultural diversity in his chapter "An Ethical Agenda in Disability Research: Rhetoric or Reality?" (Chapter 29). He describes the shift from explaining disability solely in terms of individual pathology to the ways in which environmental and cultural barriers effectively exclude people with disabilities from everyday life. This sociopolitical or social model of disability approach has stimulated the adoption of an emancipatory research paradigm that draws explicitly on disabled people's collective experience and so challenges directly the widespread social oppression of disabled people. Advocates of emancipatory disability research have concentrated on participant validation that involves disabled people in identifying research questions, collecting and analyzing data, and disseminating findings. The notion of taking fieldwork data back to respondents for verification is generally regarded as a key criterion for determining the ethicality of the research.

Sarah-Jane Dodd (Chapter 30) examines ethical issues related to research in the lesbian, gay, bisexual, transsexual, and queer (LGBTQ) communities. Once regarded as suffering from psychiatric disabilities, the LGBTQ population has emerged from consignment to the category of the ill and gained a voice within North American society. Nevertheless, this place is not secure. LGBTQ youth remain more vulnerable to suicide and premature departure from school as well as to forced treatment alleged to "set them straight" at the behest of parents or guardians and those who provide treatment the effectiveness of which is, at present, unsubstantiated by social science research. The import of this chapter extends well beyond the focus population as it takes on the question surrounding social science's ethical obligations with regard to interventions (psychoeducational treatment, in this case) of unsubstantiated efficacy, as well as the tensions faced by researchers as they attempt to balance the desire to increase visibility of sexual minorities and gender queer individuals while minimizing participation risk. It also considers the particular ways in which standard aspects of ethical research practice, such as informed consent, confidentiality, and protection from harm may vary for LGBTQ individuals. The chapter culminates with suggestions for best practices to consider when conducting social science research.

In chapters that depart from issues of diversity based on culture, the next two focus on issues of diversity based on age. Luis Vargas and Margaret Montoya (Chapter 31) explore the moral and legal implications of informed consent for research with children, focusing on the minors' decision making in social and clinical research, with special attention to cultural issues. Institutional review board practice regarding informed consent has "resolved" the problem of obtaining informed consent from children by use of dual consent forms, informed *consent* signed by a parent or guardian, and informed *assent* from children able to write their names. Is this practice satisfactory from an ethical point of view? The fundamental premise of their chapter is that legal, ethical, and psychological approaches to decision making among children who participate in research are culturally embedded. The implications of culture include concerns about the imposition of dominant cultural ideas about both child development and ethics on members of nondominant cultures.

At the other end of the life span, given the longer lives of those in technologically advanced societies, a host of new issues are arising with regard to social science research regarding aging and the aged. Karen Szala-Meneok (Chapter 31) examines ethical implications in research with those experiencing cognitive impairments of aging, including informed consent. Respect for older persons involves paying attention to their dignity. This includes facilitating their autonomy in making decisions, enhancing voluntarism, avoiding coercion, and assuring privacy and confidentiality. Beneficence involves protection for persons with diminished capacity and the maximization of benefits and minimization of risks for all participants. Szala-Meneok includes many practical suggestions for ethically conducting research with older people, such as having them sign advanced directives with regard to participation in social science research as they do with regard to physical interventions. Her chapter, though focused on the aged living in affluent societies, also has implications for research involving anyone who may be ill or experiencing diminished or diminishing capacity.

♦ References

Birch, J., Miller, T., Mauthner, M., & Jessop, B. J. (2002). Introduction. In M. Mauthner, M. Birch, J. Jessop, & T. Miller (Eds.), *Ethics in qualitative research* (pp. 1–13). London: Sage.

Edwards, R., & Mauthner, M. (2002). Ethics and feminist research: Theory and practice. In M. Mauthner, M. Birch, J. Jessop, & T. Miller (Eds.), *Ethics in qualitative research* (pp. 14–31). London: Sage.

Khoza, R. (1994). *African humanism*. Diepkloof Extension, South Africa: Ekhaya Promotions.

Louw, D. J. (2001). *Ubuntu: An African assessment of the religious order*. Retrieved September 27, 2001, from www.bu.edu/wcp/papers/Afrlouw.htm

Sieber, J. (1992). *Planning ethically responsible research*. Newbury Park, CA: Sage.

25

CONDUCTING ETHICAL RESEARCH AND EVALUATION IN UNDERSERVED COMMUNITIES

◆ Katrina L. Bledsoe[1] and Rodney K. Hopson

◆ *Overview of the Issue of Ethical Concerns in Research in Underserved Communities*

Underserved communities, such as those that have been considered historically disadvantaged due to social class, ethnic background, gender, disability, and the like, have received secondary consideration in their involvement in the *process* of research and evaluation. By process, we mean the manner in which the research is conducted, from research question development to utilization of results. We carefully make the distinction between *process* and *content* because issues that concern underserved communities have been discussed at length in the literature. For instance, there is a plethora of research on ethnic communities, their purported perspectives, and cultural practices (e.g., Hall, 2001; Smith, 1999; Stanfield

AUTHORS' NOTE: The authors have greatly benefited from the editorial comments of the volume editors, Donna Mertens and Pauline Ginsberg, and our anonymous reviewers. Acknowledgements also go to Mark Bailey of Trenton Central High School, and Dolores Bryant, and Donna Pressma of Children's Home Society in Trenton, New Jersey.

& Dennis, 1993). However, when the process of how data regarding such perspectives and practices have been obtained is articulated, we find that in some cases these were not easily or willingly disclosed (e.g., Molyneux, Wassenaar, Peshu, & Marsh, 2005).

Researchers have long discussed the issues that confront underserved and historically disadvantaged groups in research (e.g., Guthrie, 2003). For instance, in the classic psychology book *Even the Rat Was White* (Guthrie, 2003[2]), it was acknowledged that African Americans had not been included in the process, which in turn contributed to misunderstanding and misinterpretation of the culture itself.

In the 21st century, the battle cry for incorporating diverse perspectives and for cultural competency in research settings reached a deafening din (e.g., Harper, 2006; Rogers, 2004). Yet researchers and evaluators have not extensively considered the manner in which they need to be inclusive and competent in the research *process*, from inception to conclusion. Participants and communities recount in case after case, for example, a disturbing lack of accountability in relaying results to communities, a failure to include researched groups in the distribution and dissemination of results to larger audiences, and a lack of consideration for the long-term utilization of results within underserved communities. A telling comment from the first author's experience working with an African American community-based organization focusing on women's issues perhaps best illustrates this lack of accountability:

> We've had large organizations with prestige come in here, gather data, leave, and then we never hear from them again. . . . So we need to know that you're not going to "helicopter in," swooping in and getting personal information, and then "helicopter out" never to be seen again. (Program Director, 2002)

Unfortunately, community upon community tell similar stories of researchers' intentional and unintentional failure to implement a research process that is uniquely designed in conjunction with those who are the focus of the research and the subsequent recipients of the possible benefits and costs of the findings (e.g., Harper, 2006; Washington, 2007). Finally, researchers may be uninformed or may not consider the ethical violations entailed by the inappropriate use of theoretical and methodological perspectives that accurately represent neither the community nor its situation (Bledsoe, 2005b). Such discussions have long been at the forefront of debate in ethnographic research circles. Famed anthropologist Margaret Mead (as cited in Freeman, 1999) has sustained prolonged critique concerning the methodology used in what is still considered a groundbreaking study concerning Samoan culture. Specifically, the ethics of Mead's ethnographic study of the sexuality of Samoan girls, which was based on four case studies and presented Samoan women as highly sexualized prior to engaging in marriage and family, has been questioned. For example, Freeman (1999) asserted that Mead's work was highly subjective and presented to American society an inaccurate, if not biased, perspective of sexuality in Samoan culture tinged with Mead's own personal agenda. Yet Freeman has sustained a similar critique in his own interpretation of the same research. These debates serve to illustrate that when there is a lack of accountability in theory and method, misinterpretations and misperceptions can occur. Such occurrences can open the door for inaccurate assessment and reporting.

The focus of this chapter is on conducting ethically sound research with *underserved and disadvantaged communities*. We believe the need for this emphasis is because, being less powerful than other groups who may also be at risk, underserved and disadvantaged communities are most at risk of being denied access to appropriate services and opportunities due to inaccurate assessment and reporting (e.g., Bledsoe, 2005b). Such communities often do not have the resources (e.g., money, political clout, and representation) to challenge inaccurate and prejudicial findings. Thus, it is important for researchers and evaluators to consider and diminish the disparity in the power dynamic that often exists between researcher and participant.

In this chapter, we discuss the consequences of inappropriate theoretical and methodological perspectives, and why their use not only violates ethics in the social sciences but also violates norms of social justice and human rights. Additionally, we underscore the necessity of capacity and relationship building as part of the social responsibility of researchers. Thus, our discussion centers on the following: developing appropriate community relations, determining appropriate research questions, using representative methodology, accurately reporting results, assisting in the appropriate use of results, and considering the researcher/evaluator as social justice advocate. Finally, in understanding the ethics associated with conducting research in underserved communities, we seek to broaden the view of ethics and research participation within these communities.

◆ A Brief Background of Ethics in Social Science Research

Others in this *Handbook* (e.g., Kitchener & Kitchener, Chapter 1, this volume) have sought to provide a historical context for research ethics in general, and for governmental (Mabry, Chapter 7, this volume) and institutional oversight (Speiglman and Spear, Chapter 8, this volume); thus, this section rests on the assumption that the reader is reasonably familiar with ethical regulation and established professional codes for conducting research in the social sciences. Despite these codes and the general knowledge of them, historical documentation illustrates a legacy of lax attention to ethical treatment of research and evaluation study participants over an extended period of time (e.g., Carbonell, 2002; Washington, 2007).

We acknowledge that some of the more frequently documented ethical violations have occurred, not in social science research, but in clinical trial studies such as the infamous *Tuskegee Study of Untreated Syphilis in the Negro* (Washington, 2007). The study, which was focused on the effects of syphilis, was to last a few months. However, it lasted 40 years, with researchers deliberately refusing to provide proper medication, information, or treatment of the disease. Only when the story was leaked to the news media in 1972 was the study discontinued. Yet the damage had already been done: A scant 74 of the 600 participants were remaining. Several had died from the disease; many died with complications associated with the disease; family members were infected; and the number of congenital syphilis births skyrocketed.

Despite the development of institutional review boards (IRBs), which were formed in response to unethical medical experimentation under the Nazi regime (Cozby, 2007), the violation of ethics continues, such as coercion to participate in study procedures[3] and not obtaining consent in classroom settings. This continued trend illustrates that despite documented principles for conducting ethical research, within each discipline and subspecialty (e.g., American Educational Research Association [AERA], 2008; American Evaluation Association [AEA], 2008; American Psychological Association [APA], 2008), questionable ethical research practices and violations continue to occur. Although the codes seem to clearly articulate the responsibility of the researcher to the participant, when they are carefully analyzed, it is arguable that the ethical principles are more concerned with the responsibility of the *researcher* in a leadership position rather than the egalitarian *relationship* that should exist between researchers and participants (see also Chapter 6, this volume). Nowhere is this gap in ethics more apparent than in underserved communities.

The major questions are then, (a) for whom is the research process designed and

(b) who benefits most from current sets of ethical principles? We might argue that much of social science research is designed to answer questions in the manner most beneficial to the researcher and, perhaps, in response to some organizational or community political agenda (e.g., the needs of dominant culture-resourced community) rather than addressing the needs of underserved communities. What are the erroneous assumptions? And what else is needed to ensure accurate research development and reporting for socially compromised communities such as communities of color and those of low socioeconomic status? We explore these issues in the following sections.

◆ Ethical Issues in Working With Underserved Communities: The Assumption of Homogeneity

To understand the limitations of established ethical principles in the social sciences, especially as they relate to the needs of underserved and historically disadvantaged groups, the assumption of universality (the belief that all groups and communities inherently share similar characteristics and values) in research must be explored. Universality is the principle on which most research in the social sciences rests (e.g., Guba & Lincoln, 1989).

The scientific method itself assumes objectivity, neutrality, and rationality. The "realist" and "rational" positions (most often associated with control) provide an illusion of all-knowing objectivity concerning what should be the fate of the participant, if any. This generalized view can be conceived of as based on a white male-dominant culture perspective that purports to be participant and community focused but may also reflect a paternalistic outlook. Such a perspective also assumes that ethical practice will be based on a generalized belief that respect for the human condition and social justice is similar in every cultural setting (Guba & Lincoln, 1989). Yet historical debacles such as the Tuskegee Syphilis Study (Washington, 2007) dispute this assessment: The general prejudices and segregation concerning African Americans during Jim Crow were instrumental in the ethical violations that occurred. Additionally, the lack of cultural competence, and a general denial of "other" perspective provided a venue for which disregard of alternative perspectives could and did occur.

Finally, this realist perspective does not take into consideration that the assumption of homogeneity ultimately distances the researcher from the methodology chosen to ascertain "truth" for a specific group, the kinds of relationships that one will and can develop with participants, the dissemination of results, and the care for the participants. Such a universal and control-focused perspective (e.g., Lane, 2005) precludes the fact that the concept of universality itself is culturally determined by those of the dominant culture and is shaped by the myth that all are afforded the same rights as those who conceived of this universal perspective. Factors that challenge this universality such as cultural background, social class, and the participant's experiences within society are diminished or dismissed (e.g., Berry, Poortinga, Segall, & Dasen, 1992; Lane, 2005).

Mertens (2007); Greene, Millet, and Hopson (2004); and others (e.g., Bledsoe, 2005b; Hopson, Greene, Bledsoe, Villegas, & Brown, 2007) suggested that this perspective of research is exclusive, without consideration of moderating factors such as the abovementioned. Mertens (2007) further suggested that, by extension, what is considered ethical practice in the realist perspective is skewed because ethical practice varies from context to context.

Harper (2006), in her article focusing on ethical multiculturalism, argued that researchers should consider three perspectives in terms of ethics. On one end, *fundamentalism* views ethics as universal and assumes participants and communities share more basic similarities than differences. On the opposite end of the spectrum is *multiculturalism*, which holds that ethical principles are culturally bound and context dependent (Harper, 2006). Finally, the emergence of a midpoint would be *ethical multiculturalism* perspective, which purports to combine both a *fundamentalist* and a *multiculturalist* perspective. Harper suggested that much of the biomedical and social sciences have a stake in an *ethical multiculturalism* that addresses issues such as, but not limited to, cultural awareness, knowledge, sensitivity, and beneficence. Nonetheless, the struggle to maintain this perspective is difficult, and issues such as the reporting of race and ethnicity in research continue to illustrate the fundamentalist perspective (e.g., continued reliance on "collapsed" categories that focus on race, particularly in data analysis and interpretation).

Hall (2001) argued further that cultural factors and beliefs influence the participation of participants, as do misperceptions and misconceptions of research. Additionally, participants who may be more "collective" rather than "individualistic" in orientation may not participate (Markus & Kitayama, 1991) or may provide data that are only partially representative of the context, based on thoughts of the outsider or observer. For instance, in some distinct Asian cultures, the value of "collectivism" might preclude individualized consent and subsequent participation, without first considering the issues that might affect the family or community at large (Markus & Kitayama, 1991).

The authors here do not dispute that there are shared similarities across cultures.[4] But should it be taken for granted that all communities, and hence, future participants, underserved or not, fit under the same Western-dominated perspective of research and ethics? We suggest that in considering research from a holistic perspective (e.g., considering issues related to contextual factors and shared relationships), we consequently encourage ethical practice.

◆ The Role of Ethics in Social Science Research With Underserved Communities

Although there are many shared ethical principles in conducting research across researchers and evaluators, perhaps none is more shared than the principle of undertaking research that ultimately serves the human good. For instance, the preamble of *Ethical Principles for Psychologists and Code of Conduct* states,

> Psychologists are committed to increasing scientific and professional knowledge of behavior and people's understanding of themselves and others and to the use of such knowledge to improve the condition of individuals, organizations, and society. (APA, 2008, p. 2)

Other disciplines, such as education, espouse similar rhetoric:

> Education, by its very nature, is aimed at the improvement of individual lives and societies. Further, research in education is often directed at children and other vulnerable populations. A main objective of this code is to remind us, as educational researchers that we should strive to protect these populations. (AERA, 2008, p. 3)

Similar principles are embraced by the AEA:

> Evaluators have obligations that encompass the public interest and good. These obligations are especially important when evaluators are supported by publicly-generated funds; but clear threats to the public good should never be ignored in any evaluation. Because the public interest and good are rarely the same as the interests of any particular group (including those of the client or funder), evaluators will usually have to go beyond

analysis of particular stakeholder interests and consider the welfare of society as a whole. (AEA, 2008, p. 1)

Despite these declarations, however, the manner in which research is conducted generally serves the researcher, and the ethical standards essentially are directed toward the researcher collecting data in a distanced manner so as not to disturb the natural setting in which behaviors, programs, and phenomena occur. We contend that such a process and, hence, the ethical standards on which the codes rest, may not be appropriate in working with underserved communities. Furthermore, we assert that issues of profound importance to understanding underserved communities that are often considered as confounds in research and evaluation such as history of the communities' experiences, self versus community orientation, culture, and literacy, must be considered. For example, in a study focusing on obesity prevention, assumptions concerning the rationale behind perceived high rates of obesity among urban high school students were based on high-level stakeholder (e.g., teachers, researchers, community partners) program theory that was loosely informed by the literature. This theory emphasized an individual deficit model that was anchored by variables such as low self-esteem, poverty, and educational deficiency. Yet pre-research design discussion groups with students identified contextual factors such as cultural identity and cultural socialization to determine one's views of nutrition and body esteem (Bledsoe, 2005).

MODERATING ISSUES OF HOMOGENEITY

Across disciplines, research studies share similar processes both methodologically and ethically. Common practices include what we refer to here as "compassionate objectivity"[5]: maintenance of professional relationships with participants, accurate and unbiased data collection and the use of reliable and valid instrumentation, appropriate compensation for research, and proper and responsible utilization of results. Yet this perspective does not consider aspects such as close relationships between the researcher and participants, values of communities, and the general context in which potential participants reside. Consideration of contextual and relationship factors, including socioeconomic status, respect, and partnerships between researcher and participants, will likely generate more accurate data.

PERSPECTIVES TOWARD HUMAN CONDITION ISSUES WITHIN UNDERSERVED COMMUNITIES

Generally, social and medical issues in Westernized communities tend to be viewed from an individual deficit model perspective (Treloar & Holt, 2006). For example, it has been documented that certain cultures may consider mental illness as a natural progression in life, one that is not worthy of worry (e.g., Walker, 2001). Although one could consider using a more mainstream definition of mental illness, it may be more appropriate to consider how disease and mental illness and subsequent treatment are viewed in the society. Hall (2001) noted that there was little evidence that empirically supported therapies (ESTs), which were developed and based on dominant culture definitions of mental illness, are effective with minority and underserved populations.

HISTORY OF THE PARTICIPANTS AND THEIR CONTEXT

For many communities, consideration of the history of the community and its context is essential for designing the appropriate research to answer key questions. For example, in one evaluation research study, service providers attempted to encourage participants to participate in a community-based prenatal program in New Jersey. The participant turnout was unusually low. On further investigation of the city's socioeconomic and cultural history, the researchers found a substantial history of racism among general medical practitioners and service providers within the city, dating back from the late 1960s. Thus, when the sponsoring organization designed an intervention to combat the city's high rate of sudden infant death syndrome (SIDS) among African American women (the rate was 1 out of every 2 infants who died from SIDS; Division of Family Health Services, 1998), they had little response. Researchers later found that African American mothers were less likely to seek services due to perceived discrimination based on race and, instead, relied on family members to provide needed advice about care. This example underscores the need for understanding historical and contextual factors within community settings.

CONSIDERATION OF CULTURE

Hall (2001) noted that conducting research in underserved communities requires more than simply making sure that these communities are reflected numerically in sampling. Inclusion alone is not likely to yield significant information on the relevance of theories and interventions as there is much heterogeneity among categorized ethnic groups on issues such as socioeconomic status, acculturation, and the like (Hall, 2001). Additionally, the use of broad terms such as *ethnic minority* is too often considered a euphemism for "deficit" in comparison with the dominant cultural group.

Beiser (2003) suggested that culture not only shapes the nature of the problem and the community's view of it, it also shapes the structure of the research paradigm and one's interpretation of how best to approach it. Thus, culture may have a significant effect on the variables chosen and how to best measure those variables. MacQueen and Buehler (2004) found in their research with HIV-positive participants that it is difficult to divorce the variables of stigma, poverty, discrimination, and other social issues from the epidemiology of the disease. Rather than focus on measurement of these issues as moderating factors, the variables should be considered in the research design itself in terms of types of methodology used, data collected, and relationships developed. For example, methods such as storytelling or community groups can be used to flesh out rich contextual information on issues such as discrimination and political factions within the community.

CONSENT OF THE COMMUNITY

In accordance with the IRB guidelines, researchers attempt to define what the risks may be for respondents and communities to participate in a research study, and this definition appears to be based on the *researchers'* general knowledge of the costs and benefits to the individual. But it is difficult to consider hidden factors that may render the situation as more egregious for individuals who are connected to, for example, a collectivist community in which the tribe, clan, or family takes precedence over individual concerns. For instance, Molyneux et al. (2005) found in their study with Kenyan participants that community leaders made decisions about participation in research. Thus, in the case of working with a collectivist community, consultation with community members regarding potential risks and benefits of specific research can provide enhanced benefits and legitimacy (e.g., Mertens, 2007).

Consider the case for the most basic aspect of the research process, that of informed consent. The APA's principle of informed consent states,

(a) When obtaining informed consent as required in Standard 3.10, psychologists inform participants about (1) the purpose of the research, expected duration, and procedures; (2) their right to decline to participate and to withdraw from the research once participation has begun; (3) the foreseeable consequences of declining or withdrawing; (4) reasonably foreseeable factors that may be expected to influence their willingness to participate such as potential risks, discomfort, or adverse effects; (5) any prospective research benefits; (6) limits of confidentiality; (7) incentives for participation; and (8) whom to contact for questions about the research and research participants' rights. They provide opportunity for the prospective participants to ask questions and receive answers. (APA, 2008, p. 8)

Yet, in contrast, Dawson and Kass (2005) noted that many groups and communities do not make decisions about participation in research in a vacuum. In some cases, individual participants consider factors not related to the preservation of the self, but instead to the preservation of the larger community. Dawson and Kass suggested that rather than assuming that informed consent is negotiated at the individual level, instead, relationships need to be formed with whole communities and oftentimes on more than one occasion. Such communities influence the participant's decision-making process; therefore, it is reasonable to assume that informed consent should be an intertwined process (see also Chapter 19, this volume.) Finally, researchers must also consider the possibility that in some communities, signing an informed consent is not necessary, if the bond with the researchers is developed, respected, and maintained (see also Chapters 9, 19, 26, and 27, this volume).

CONSIDERATION OF LITERACY

Literacy continues to be one of the greatest challenges in conducting research with underserved communities. For instance, Dawson and Kass (2005) noted in their research, with 387 participants conducting research in international collaborative research, almost half of those surveyed acknowledged that the informed consent forms were highly technical, hard to read, and not useful to those who had limited literacy in the language, or not at all. Additionally, they felt that the language related to literacy of informed consent should also consider dialect.

THE NOTION OF RESPECT

Although ethical standards in the social sciences generally focus on respect for the participant, respect does not specifically consider aspects such as trust within the community. Weijer (1999) suggested that a new principle of respect for communities should be included and that respect does not negate the individual's right to decision making in this context. Dawson and Kass (2005) echoed this sentiment: Just because the focus is on gaining trust of the community within the research setting, this does not negate or necessarily influence the individual's right to make self-preserving decisions.

SOCIAL RESPONSIBILITY AS A FACTOR IN WORKING WITH UNDERSERVED COMMUNITIES

It is arguable that social responsibility of the researcher and evaluator is generally associated with maintaining the integrity of the ethical principles of disciplines. However, we propose that in working with underserved communities, social responsibility may need to be conceptualized beyond a fundamentalist/realist paradigm (which ensures that one maintains a logical and rational perspective). If we redefine the meaning behind social responsibility in underserved communities, we need to consider it less in terms of maintaining the established ethical principles and consider it in the exact denotative sense: that contribution to the welfare of society would include the building and maintenance of relationships so that the achievement of a common goal can be obtained (*Webster's Dictionary*, 2008).

♦ The Researcher as an Invested Relationship Partner in Underserved Communities

Although ethical principles across the social sciences acknowledge a relationship between the researcher and the participant (e.g., AEA, 2008; AERA, 2008; APA, 2008), the relationship seemingly falls into one of two categories: that of the paternal parent, in which the researcher/evaluator determines the parameters of the research based on superordinate knowledge or informed judgment (e.g., Scriven, 1991), or that of the respectful observer, who is not necessarily invested or connected to the participants and their community but is an intrigued visitor (e.g., Scriven, 1991). Although ethically, these relationships seem to maintain the integrity of the data collected, we consider the usefulness of developing close relationships with participants and stakeholders and inviting them to make an equal investment in the research development and process (e.g., Greene et al., 2004; Mertens, 2007). By building relationships in which researchers, stakeholders, and participants are all equally invested, we encourage and foster inclusion and, in turn, generate data that best represent the context, community, and its situation.

BUILDING COMMUNITY RELATIONS BETWEEN RESEARCHER AND PARTICIPANTS

The concept of relationship building with participants is not new and has evolved throughout history[6] (e.g., Cozby, 2008). Yet in underserved communities the recall of broken relationships between researcher and community seems continuous, and the trust level underwhelming. Two questions researchers and evaluators often address are (a) what amount of time they plan to stay and (b) in what community agenda (if any) they are invested. Such questions are not unusual. Similar to a love relationship, communities who feel they have much to lose, may consider the relationship in terms of social equity: What are the costs and benefits to investment in the "love relationship" (i.e., research program), and what will be received in return for that investment (Walster, Walster, & Berscheid, 1978)?

Researchers and evaluators such as Mertens (2007), House and Howe (2000), and Greene et al. (2004) most notably have discussed the importance of relationship building in the research setting, especially with those communities that are often disenfranchised or unheard. For instance, Mertens (2007) noted that inclusiveness is a cornerstone to beginning meaningful relationships and to generating data reflective of the context and the situation. Mertens' inclusive evaluation, within the transformative paradigm, assumes that knowledge and, hence, behaviors and programs are not neutral but instead reflect the power structure and interests of society. Therefore, inclusiveness provides the opportunity to offer a voice to those who would otherwise be rendered voiceless by the research process (e.g., Bledsoe, 2005b) and to equalize the power structure.

House and Howe (2000) have discussed the issue of democracy in evaluation research, both democratic evaluation and deliberative democratic evaluation, as a mechanism to promote equity and inclusion in research for participants that might otherwise be passive in the process. In deliberative democratic evaluation, dialogue is the foundation to reconciling the values and desires of all stakeholders, including those who are yet to be identified. Such a dialogue can assist in establishing a superordinate agenda in which all, including the researcher, are invested (House & Howe, 2000).

IDENTIFYING UNDESERVED STAKEHOLDERS

As in any research and evaluation process, identification of affected stakeholders is necessary to target populations and communities. In many cases, identification of the stakeholders, even within advantaged communities falls to those who can be easily communicated with and to those who are the most vocal or visible community members (e.g., Bledsoe & Graham, 2005). This is even more pronounced in underserved communities (Scriven, 1991). We contend that the blueprint for working ethically in underserved communities is to fully identify even those who are not originally specified as stakeholders. Identification of who is considered an unintended stakeholder is important primarily because that person will likely be a recipient of the interventions or programs that may be instituted based on identified stakeholders. Only in asking all possible stakeholders to participate and in attempting to address the values and issues most important to them in a deliberative, inclusive manner can a representative perspective of the community, its context, beliefs, and values be generated (e.g., Bledsoe, 2005a).

As an example, let us return to our earlier discussion concerning the prenatal program developed to specifically target African American women in a small city in New Jersey. Program-level stakeholders noted that they did not understand why low-income African American women who had complained about the lack of services available to them were not taking part in the program. When potential clients were asked to articulate the reasons they did not take part in the services provided, several enlightening perspectives emerged. First, participants noted that the city's history of racism made it difficult to obtain services; second, participants noted that the medical community's history of racism toward African Americans essentially reflected the city's attitude thereby making it difficult to get reliable trustworthy care; third, potential participants noted the use of what were considered effective home remedies and solutions that were passed from healthy family members and finally, participants also noted the "see-saw" nature of the provision of program services: Here today, gone tomorrow, often under mysterious circumstances.

This example demonstrates that by not including all stakeholders (and perhaps the most important ones), several critical contextual aspects had not been recognized. Hence, data that would be generated in this situation would produce inaccurate judgments about the values and circumstances of the most underserved (e.g., "inappropriate" values of African Americans and low socioeconomic status community members; Fitzpatrick & Bledsoe, 2007). If African American stakeholders are not asked about their attitudes, then the reasons for nonuse of services would not have been known and community members' motivation would have been misunderstood.

One of the concerns of researchers is *how* to effectively identify underserved stakeholders. Possible venues include attending community gatherings and organizations, schools, home visits, and important community milestones. In these cases, more convenience/availability/haphazard/snowball sampling might be more likely to provide access to hard-to-reach community members.

We acknowledge that using these sampling methodologies essentially increases the risk of bias in realist circles (e.g., Lipsey, 1989). Much of the purported "gold standard" in research implies that a fundamentalist perspective that looks at averages across groups (e.g., comparisons by collapsed racial/ethnic groups) is the best way to determine causality and program effectiveness. But excluding whole groups of community members who may need programming or research results may not be feasible or ethical (e.g., Dawson & Kass, 2005). Additionally, the realist/fundamentalist perspective assumes that (a) heterogeneity does not exist between populations and (b) confounding and extraneous factors such as racism, discrimination, gender, low socioeconomic status, and the like have no effect on the participants and the type of information they will provide or the questions they might answer.

Finally, we believe that researchers must consider that the realist perspective is not necessarily valued by the participants themselves. One of the frequent research assumptions is that communities will immediately see the value of what is being accomplished. Such valuing only occurs when a history of trust between the researcher and community has been developed.

◆ **Ethical Research With Underserved Communities: The Research Process and Outcomes**

In this section, we consider the research process, including the determination of research questions, methodology, analyses, and utilization of results and capacity building.

DETERMINATION OF APPROPRIATE RESEARCH QUESTIONS

There is little dispute among researchers residing anywhere on the philosophy of science continuum that appropriate questions are necessary for research (Morgan, 2007). However, the determination of such questions largely depends on the researchers themselves or, at the very least, on high-level stakeholders such as funding agencies. (For another point of view, see Chapter 22, this volume.) These questions are often determined in a vacuum with little input at the formative or implementation stages from potential participants and/or communities and often reflect the values of the researchers and powerful others. Additionally, the questions developed are often considered objective, rational, and representative of the "universal." Yet as House (as cited in Hopson et al., 2007) has noted, researchers and evaluators are imbued with their own beliefs and values. Thus, such biases are apparent in the development of research questions. When communities are asked to participate, they are largely asked to react rather than develop. Such reaction without ownership or agreement of the purpose of the research can foster inaccurate research questions leading to, in the long run, inaccurate results and assessment of those results.

Greene et al. (2004) and Hopson et al. (2007) have demonstrated that democracy and inclusion in the research process can produce applicable and measurable questions. For example, in a project that included an intervention to reduce obesity among urban black and Latino adolescents in New Jersey (Bledsoe, 2005b), the evaluation team was asked to participate not as objective and distanced researchers, but as community stakeholders that included the school district, the state government department of health, and local community-based organizations. Each stakeholder was asked to address personal interests in the project, how those interests might benefit the community, and in what ways. Thus, as invested stakeholders, the evaluation team had to assume responsibility to provide truthful, invested interest beyond the need to provide credible scientific evidence.

When the high-level stakeholders (including the researchers) had established questions in tandem with one another, the team then asked the student participants for feedback as to the kind of questions they felt should be considered. Since these were high school students, the most feasible way for dialogue and discussion to take place was through focus groups. In this case, focus groups allowed for the creation of a bond with the students who began to feel (a) that they had some control about what they would be asked to disclose and in what manner and (b) that they had ownership in the development of the project itself.

DETERMINATION OF APPROPRIATE RESEARCH METHODOLOGY AND DESIGN

Much of social science research has debated the effectiveness of quantitative versus qualitative methodologies (e.g., Guba & Lincoln, 1989; Morgan, 2007). Since the focus of some research is on demonstrating causality (rather than correlation, which is more tentative and allows for the introduction of factors beyond the control of the researcher; Davidson, 2000), the belief in experiments as the most appropriate way to determine exact factors that define the human condition and, by extension, the environment is strong (e.g., Cozby, 2008; Lipsey, 1989). Yet belief in the objectivity, rationality, and logic of experimental design can be inappropriate in underserved communities. For instance, the randomized control trials (RCTs) often recommended in educational research do not always account for contextual factors such as culture or social class. Due to the need to isolate and/or hold constant variables (often for the sake of determining effectiveness of an intervention), the RCT might miss moderating variables such as the abovementioned. Therefore, an RCT may be able to identify differences in performance among these groups but it may not be able to provide answers beyond this finding (e.g., Hall, 2001). Researchers such as Beiser (2003) have found that, in many cases, experimental research designs, purportedly making use of what are considered validated and reliable instruments are neither competent nor sensitive enough to pick up information that truly represents the situation. In these cases, it is the inappropriate use of the design that fails to generate information that describes the context, again, often due to the need to hold constant factors that may confound the results. Beiser (2003) admitted that aspects such as culture can influence the manner in which questions are answered on seemingly universal issues. For instance, for the obesity prevention project, ethnic identity questions from supposedly reliable and validated measures by Phinney (1992) and Oyserman, Gant, and Ager (1995) were interpreted by student participants as being racist and dominant culture focused, although this was not the intention.

How is the abovementioned alleviated? In her work evaluating a family literacy program, Bledsoe (2007) found it best to first consider the historical context of the situation as well as the psychological perspectives of the communities who were the focus of the evaluation. Understanding the historical context (and by context, we mean considering aspects such as the history of racism and discrimination in the area and state), as well as understanding the impact of that context on the program staff and consumers, helped in the development of a more accurate and useful design. Specifically, Bledsoe (2005b) chose to expand the use of qualitative methodology to accommodate the general cultural milieu of storytelling. Finally, understanding the historical perspective allowed the research team to tailor surveys and other quantitative assessments to better capture the environment and community setting.

DETERMINATION OF APPROPRIATE ANALYSES

The determination of the kind of analyses that should be conducted is inherently tied to the kind of methodology that is used and how the results generated by that methodology will be used (Morgan, 2007). As mentioned previously, in many underserved communities, storytelling and context are instrumental to understanding the situation, and statistical analyses may not represent the true nature of the data. Additionally, it may limit the kind of information provided by participants. The first author recalls a conversation with a student participant concerning physical measurements that were being taken to indicate a reduction in obesity, and by extension, unhealthy eating habits.

> What will that tell you? Do those numbers tell you that in the last three months, my grandmother and I have been eating good food like vegetables, fruit, and skinless baked chicken? She's calmer, so am I; and I know I'm doing better. But those numbers, it makes it look like I'm not. (Student participant, 2005)

In this case, if the reliance were solely on numerics, the true answer to one of the main research questions, which was, "Is the program effective in reducing obesity and encouraging good health?" would have been missed. Despite this aspect, there is a tendency of researchers to diminish the use of qualitative data in the interpretation of findings, especially with underserved populations (Bledsoe, 2005b). In some manner, there seems to be a general distrust in participants being able to provide information that is not positively biased and self-serving (Miller & Ross, 1975).

UTILIZATION OF RESULTS AND CAPACITY BUILDING

In many cases, communities are unaware of how the research will be used and to what end (e.g., Bledsoe, 2005b). Earlier we established that basic ethical principles encourage researchers to use their results for the betterment of the human condition and for those who might be most affected by them (AEA, 2008; AERA 2008; APA, 2008). Indeed, it is hoped that such results will provide the foundation for communities to build capacity to maintain, sustain, and thrive. But what is the personal responsibility of the researcher to ensure the utilization of results in a manner that is conducive to improving the lives of the participants and community? We contend that championing the use of results in a manner that encourages and uplifts the environment must be a cornerstone in working with underserved communities.

Many communities are reluctant to use results because of the belief that the interpretations of those results will be pathologized, thereby confirming observer stereotypes of its members (Hall, 2001). In the first author's work with a leadership program for African American managers, the research team was asked to assume an advocacy role to assist in encouragement of the utilization of results by the organization, its constituents, and its membership at large. Such a request assumed that (a) the evaluators were as invested in the research as the participants, (b) they were willing to provide long-term advice and consultation, and (c) they were interested in becoming spokespersons on behalf of the community, participants, and/or organization. The question is, Did this encourage bias, rendering the researcher/evaluator powerless in truth-telling? The team believed it did not, because it had developed a partnership and provided an arena that allowed for truth-telling both positive and negative within the context of the research.

♦ Concluding Thoughts

We have discussed why the perspective of a universalist/realist approach to researcher is not always the most appropriate for working with underserved communities. Yet, in some cases, this perspective is considered the most appropriate for establishing issues such as causality and for demonstrating accountability (e.g., Davidson, 2000). We wish to note, however, that larger and sometimes global concerns present an interesting quagmire for researchers. For instance, concerns such as educational accountability through the No Child Left Behind Act of 2002 in the United States puts pressure on researchers to determine a "gold standard" of best practices (and by extension, ethics) that provide the most bulletproof method of determining what works.

We write this chapter not with the intention to discredit the research and ethics of the fundamental and realist perspectives; we uphold the belief that researchers are dedicated to conducting rigorous and honest research. The chapter serves to illustrate that the ethical principles we use are inherently tied to the methodology we value and use (e.g., Guba & Lincoln, 1989; Hopson et al., 2007; Mertens, 2007). In admitting this, we suggest several plausible strategies in working with underserved communities. First, although we do not insist on abandoning more quantitative/realist perspectives, we do encourage the continued more consideration of qualitative approaches in working with underserved communities. The nature of the term *underserved* means, in many situations, being underserved in the information provided and underserved in one's right to determine the design of the research. We also encourage consideration of some nonconventional questions. When might a community-focused consent be most appropriate? When is it appropriate to be the advocate, or to stand by as a respectful but supportive and invested observer? We hope that researchers will not associate the consideration of these questions with abandonment of conducting good research.

The acknowledgement of expanding ethical principles and research approaches signals that research, and the way in which we conceptualize the researcher and participant relationship, is representative of a much more global and larger issue: that society, with its vast and diverse populations, must broaden its perspectives on how it will treat its citizens and the manner in which it will contribute to the betterment of these communities.

♦ Notes

1. Comments concerning this chapter should be sent to the first author via e-mail: katrina.bledsoe@gmail.com, or via land mail: P.O. Box 41495, Arlington, VA 22204.

2. Second edition. The first edition was published in 1998.

3. The Stanford Prison study continues to be the most often cited (Cozby, 2008). Zimbardo's study (1971, as cited in Cozby, 2008) created a climate of coercion for participants involved in a study focusing on the perils of prison life. Participants continued in the study despite growing emotional instability. Additionally, researchers became so immersed themselves that they were reluctant to release participants in a timely manner.

4. We use the term broadly here, rather than as a solo reference to race and ethnicity.

5. The authors define compassionate objectivity as a perspective that allows the researcher to empathize with the participants while still using the tools often associated with the universalist perspective such as judgment and conclusions based only on observable phenomena, and not influenced by one's emotions, values, or personal biases.

6. The terminology to define the researcher/participant relationship has evolved over time. Participants have previously been referred to as experimentees, volunteers, and subjects. The term *participant* is used to denote the collaborative relationship between the participant and the researcher (Cozby, 2008).

♦ References

American Educational Research Association. (2008). *Standards for reporting on Empirical Social Science Research in AERA publications*. Retrieved August 25, 2008, from www.aera.net/opportunities

American Evaluation Association. (2008). *Guiding principles for evaluators*. Retrieved August 22, 2008, from www.eval.org/Publications/GuidingPrinciples.asp

American Psychological Association. (2008). *Ethical principles for psychologists and code of conduct.* Retrieved August 25, 2008, from www.apa.org

Beiser, M. (2003). Why should researchers care about culture? *Canadian Journal of Psychiatry, 48,* 154–160.

Berry, J. W., Poortinga, Y. H., Segall, M. H., & Dasen, P. R. (1992). *Cross-cultural psychology: Research and applications.* Cambridge, UK: Cambridge University Press.

Bledsoe, K. L. (2005a, Fall). Trenton Central High School Obesity Prevention Program: Democracy through inclusion. *Harvard Family Research Project Evaluation Exchange, 9*(3), 17.

Bledsoe, K. L. (2005b). Using theory-driven evaluation with underserved communities: Promoting program development and program sustainability. In S. Hood, R. H. Hopson, & H. T. Frierson (Eds.), *The role of culture and cultural context: A mandate for inclusion, the discovery of truth and understanding in evaluative theory and practice. Evaluation and Society Series* (pp. 175–196). Greenwich, CT: Information Age.

Bledsoe, K. L. (2007). Summary of the Fun With Books Program. *American Journal of Evaluation, 28,* 522–524.

Bledsoe, K. L., & Graham, J. A. (2005). Using multiple evaluation approaches in program evaluation. *American Journal of Evaluation, 26,* 302–319.

Carbonell, S. L. (2002). Exploring disparity in mental health services through cultural psychology and narratives of Latina psychologists. *Dissertation Abstracts International, 63*(3-B), 1260.

Cozby, P. C. (2008). *Methods in behavioral research* (9th ed.). New York: McGraw-Hill.

Davidson, E. J. (2000). *Ascertaining causality in theory-based evaluation* (New Directions for Evaluation, No. 87, pp. 17–26). San Francisco: Jossey-Bass.

Dawson, L., & Kass, N. E. (2005). Views of US researchers about informed consent international collaborative research. *Social Sciences & Medicine, 61,* 1211–1222.

Division of Family Health Services. (1998). *Blue Ribbon Panel.* Trenton, NJ: Division of Health of Family Services.

Fitzpatrick, J. L., & Bledsoe, K. L. (2007). Evaluation of the fun with books program: An interview with Katrina Bledsoe. *American Journal of Evaluation, 28,* 522–535.

Freeman, D. (1999). *The fateful hoaxing of Margaret Mead: A historical analysis of her Samoan research.* Boulder, CO: Westview Press.

Greene, J. C., Millet, R. A., & Hopson, R. K. (2004). Evaluation as a democratizing practice. In M. T. Braverman, N. A. Constantine, & J. K. Slater (Eds.), *Foundations and evaluation: Contexts and practices for effective philanthropy* (pp. 96–118). San Francisco: Jossey-Bass.

Guba, E., & Lincoln, Y. (1989). *Fourth generation evaluation.* Newbury Park, CA: Sage.

Guthrie, R. V. (2003). *Even the rat was White* (2nd ed.). New York: Allyn & Bacon.

Hall, G. C. N. (2001). Psychotherapy research with ethnic minorities: Empirical, ethical, and conceptual issues. *Journal of Counseling and Clinical Psychology, 69,* 502–510.

Harper, M. G. (2006). Ethical multiculturalism: An evolutionary concept analysis. *Advances in Nursing Sciences, 29,* 110–124.

Hopson, R. K., Greene, J. C., Bledsoe, K. L., Villegas, T., & Brown, T. (2007). A vision for evaluation in urban educational settings. In W. T. Pink & G. W. Noblitt (Eds.), *International handbook of urban education* (pp. 306–316). Berlin: Springer.

House, E. R., & Howe, K. R. (2000). *Deliberative democratic evaluation checklist.* Retrieved August 25, 2007, from www.wmich/.edu/evalctr/checklist/dd_checklist.htm

Lane, H. (2005). Ethnicity, ethics, and the deaf-world. *Journal of Deaf Studies, and Deaf Education, 10,* 291–310.

Lipsey, M. W. (1989). *Design sensitivity: Statistical power for experimental research.* Newbury Park, CA: Sage.

MacQueen, K. M., & Buehler, J. W. (2004). Ethics, practice, and research in public health. *American Journal of Public Health, 9,* 928–931.

Markus, H. R., & Kitayama, S. (1991). Culture and the self: Implications for cognition, emotion, and motivation. *Psychological Review, 98,* 224–253.

Merriam Webster. (2007). *Webster's dictionary.* Retrieved August 22, 2007, from www.dictionary.com

Mertens, D. M. (2007). Transformative considerations: Inclusion and social justice. *American Journal of Evaluation, 28,* 86–90.

Miller, D. T., & Ross, M. (1975). Self-serving biases in the attribution of causality: Fact or fiction? *Psychological Bulletin, 82,* 213–225.

Molyneux, C. S., Wassenaar, D. R., Peshu, N., & Marsh, K. (2005). "Even if they ask you to stand by a tree all day, you will have to do it (laughter). . . . !": Community voices on the notion and practices of informed consent for biomedical research in developing countries. *Social Science and Medicine, 61,* 443–454.

Morgan, D. L. (2007). Paradigms lost and pragmatism regained: Methodological implication of combining qualitative and quantitative methods. *Journal of Mixed Methods Research, 1,* 1–32.

Oyserman, D., Gant, L., & Ager, J. (1995). A socially contextualized model of African American identity: Possible selves and school persistence. *Journal of Personality and Social Psychology, 69,* 1216–1232.

Phinney, J. (1992). The Multigroup Ethnic Identity Measure: A new scale for use with adults from diverse groups. *Journal of Adolescent Research, 7,* 156–176.

Rogers, W. A. (2004). Evidence based medicine and justice: A framework for looking at the impact of EBM upon vulnerable or disadvantaged groups. *Journal of Medical Ethics, 30,* 141–145.

Scriven, M. (1991). *Evaluation thesaurus.* Newbury Park, CA: Sage.

Smith, L. T. (1999). *Decolonizing methodologies: Research and indigenous peoples.* London: Zed.

Stanfield, J. H., II, & Dennis, R. M. (1993). *Race and ethnicity in research methods.* Newbury Park, CA: Sage.

Treloar, C., & Holt, M. (2006). Deficit models and divergent philosophies: Service providers' perspectives on barriers and incentives to drug treatment. *Drug and Alcohol Rehabilitation, 3383,* 33.

Walker, C. A. (2001). Native illness meanings: Depression and suicide. *Dissertation Abstracts International, 62*(04), 1334A.

Walster, E., Walster, G. W., & Berscheid, E. (1978). *Equity: Theory and research.* Boston: Allyn & Bacon.

Washington, H. A. (2007). *Medical apartheid. The dark history of medical experimentation on Black Americans from Colonial times to the present.* London: Doubleday.

Weijer, C. (1999). The IRB's role in assessing the generalizability of non-NIH-funded clinical trials. *IRB: A Review of Human Subjects Research, 20,* 2–3.

26

INDIGENOUS AFRICAN-CENTERED ETHICS

Contesting and Complementing Dominant Models

◆ Bagele Chilisa

> *It is all very good for you white men to follow the Word of God, . . . God made you with straight hearts like this—holding out his finger straight; but it is a very different thing with us Black people. God made us with a [circular] heart like this—holding out his bent finger. Now suppose a Black man tells a story, he goes round and round—drawing a number of circles on the ground; "but when you (white people) open your mouth your tale proceeds like a straight line"*
>
> —Mackenzie (1971) as cited in Bennet (1997, p. 47)

In this chapter, I discuss ethics informed by Afrocentrism, a worldview that "seeks to uncover and use codes, paradigms, symbols, motifs, myths and circles of discussion that reinforce the centrality of African ideas and values as a valid framework for acquiring and examining data" (Asante, 1990, p. 6). The chapter discusses the ethical principles of justice, respect, and honesty, which are commonly known as duty ethics principles or deontology (Edwards & Mauthner, 2002) from an

Afrocentric perspective. The chapter further explores the application of contextual or situational ethics (Edwards & Mauthner, 2002) in former colonized, historically oppressed societies with particular reference to African experiences with research. Examples of ways of addressing honesty and justice using African value systems and practices (Reviere, 2001) are presented. An African-centered ethics framework informed by Afrocentrism and the value of *Ubuntu* is also discussed.

Ubuntu is an African value system that privileges an I/we relationship in contrast to the Western concept of the I/you individualistic perspective (Khoza, 1994; Louw, 2001). *Ubuntu* means humanity or humanness and informs how we should relate with others. It informs how researchers from developed countries should relate with researchers from former colonized societies and how researchers from all over the world should relate with the researched. *Ubuntu* underscores an I/we relationship where there is connectedness with living and nonliving things; there is brotherhood, sisterhood, guesthood, and community togetherness. Consequently, relationships are not linear but involve circular repetitive, back and forth movements. For indigenous African communities, circular, back and forth movements allow us (speaking as an indigenous researcher) to go back into the past and invoke metaphors from our culture that help us build ethics protocols that promote social justice and respect for postcolonial/indigenous communities. We go back and forth to the humiliation of colonialism, slavery, and imperialism, to deconstruct and decolonize the archival knowledge that continues to masquerade as "common sense knowledge" and "facts" about us as lesser peoples. We go back to reclaim preserved bodies such as that of El Negro[1] that were stolen and served as illustrations for researchers seeking to promote their agendas and bury the bodies in an effort to rebuild our dignity. To be ethical for us is to face the challenge of questioning and challenging contemporary literature that continues to circulate what Bhaba (1994) called "colonial nonsense about the other." It is to recognize that "researchers are cultural beings with the authorization to 'bless' or 'damn'" (Thomas, 1985, p. 329). It is to acknowledge that

> researchers are knowledge brokers, people who have the power to construct legitimating arguments for or against ideas, theories or practices. They are collectors of information and producers of meaning which can be used for, or against indigenous interests. (Cram, Ormond, & Carter, 2004, p. 158)

Thus, introspection and retrospection according to Asante (1990) must be used to locate the Afrocentric place from where inquiry is conducted. The chapter goes further to discuss six principles that guide introspection and retrospection located in the Afrocentric place of research inquiry and the value of *ubuntu*. The six ethical principles discussed are as follows:

- The responsibilities of researcher as a transformative healer
- Ethics built on a deep respect for spirituality, religious beliefs, and the practice of others
- Ethics that underscores the importance of agreement and consensus
- Ethics built on dialogue, particularity, individuality, and historicity
- Ethics built on an iterative process that involves many circles of dialogue and negotiation, cooperation and solidarity
- Ethics that promote self-determination and rebirth

The chapter begins with an overview of scientific colonialism and a critique of dominant ethics principles from an Afrocentric perspective. The chapter then discusses the Afrocentric approach and the various ethical principles that are informed by Afrocentrism and the African value of *Ubuntu*.

◆ Scientific Colonization

Formerly colonized societies were invaded, conquered, and subjected to external rule by the colonizers. In Africa, the culmination of this subjugation came in 1884 when the European powers, namely, Britain, Belgium, France, Germany, Italy, Portugal, and Spain, met at the Berlin conference and divided Africa among themselves. This marked the process of colonization. Colonialism is a process marked by the shifting of wealth from the colony to the colonizer. Under colonialism, the colonizer has the right of access and claim to anything belonging to the colony, and it is the center of power and control (Cram, 2004). Writers differentiate between different types of colonialism, namely, political and scientific colonialism. Scientific colonialism speaks directly to the production of knowledge and ethics in social science research. Scientific colonialism has been described as imposition of the positivist paradigm approach to research on the colonies and other historically oppressed groups. Scientific colonialism gave the researchers the right to export data from the colonies for purposes of processing into books and articles. There was also the belief that the researchers had unlimited rights of access to any data source and information belonging to the population (Cram, 2004). With these unlimited powers, researchers went out to collect data and write about the one reality that they understood. In the social sciences, the disciplines of psychology, anthropology, and history mapped theories, formulae, and practices that continue to dictate how former colonized societies can be studied and written about. Psychology, for instance, placed itself, its conceptions, and formulations as the standard by which all people of the world are to be understood, and today researchers from all over the world, molded to accept oppressive perspectives as the norm, find it difficult to operate differently (Ramsey, 2006).

The continued assault on postcolonial identities and their social realities have resulted in conflicts between researchers from developed countries and researchers and the researched from former colonized societies. The conflict has become more apparent as researchers from developed countries increasingly become involved in research in less developed countries.

◆ Collaborative Research Between Researchers in Developing and Developed Countries

There is currently an increase in the volume of collaborative research between researchers in universities from developed countries and those from developing countries—university researchers or independent researchers from developed counties with communities, industries, and governments in developing countries. Caballero (2002) gave the following reasons for the increasing volume of research:

- National and international efforts to provide assistance to researchers in developing counties
- International agencies such as the United Nations Children's Fund; United Nations Educational, Scientific and Cultural Organization (UNESCO); World Health Organization; United States Agency For International Development; Department For International Development; and Canadian International Development Agency providing opportunities for researchers from the developed countries to work and to specialize in research questions specific to developing countries

- The increasing value of indigenous knowledge to the global economy and the need to involve the experts in the communities
- The increasing role of industry in the production of knowledge

In response to these developments, there has been a parallel plethora of ethical guidelines for human research. Caballero (2002) noted, for example, that the U.S. National Bioethics Advisory Commission found more than 90 documents from government, in-government, and international organizations that provided ethical guidelines for human research. Developing countries and indigenous communities have also come up with their own ethics review boards and ethical guidelines. The Maori, for instance, have Guidelines for Research and Evaluation with Maori (Ministry of Social Development, 2004); in Australia, the Aborigines have the Mi'kinaw Research Principles and Protocols (Aboriginal Research Centre, 2005; see also Barnes, McCreanor, Edwards, & Borell, this volume; Cram, this volume).

♦ Gate Keeping and Ethical Review Boards: Erasing the Other's Voice

The plethora of ethics review boards, each operating with its own ethics guidelines, has given rise to conflict over which ethics guidelines should be used—especially, where there is partnership or collaborative research between researchers from developed countries and those from former colonized societies. Some researchers from developed countries, still operating with colonial tools of manipulation and power to access, control and own all types of data from the former colonies, write over, erase, and relegate to marginal and irrelevant the ethical guidelines from former colonized societies. Still others are compelled by research funding agencies, many of them international and national corporations based in developed countries, to enter into contract agreements that privilege Euro-Western ethical frameworks.

In collaborative research, there are contract agreements between the partners outlining roles and responsibilities, how disputes should be settled, collection of data, evaluation of research reports, their dissemination and copyrights. An analysis of contract agreements between the University of Botswana and partners from the developed countries revealed instances where partners from the developed countries expected their laws to apply in cases where there were disputes and ethics guidelines from their institutions to be applied during the research process (Chilisa & Koloi, 2007). In some instances, there are expectations that any publications in a local or international journal arising from the research have to be approved by partners from the developed countries who also claim ownership and copyrights to the data and report emanating from the research conducted in the partner country. In one of the contract agreements for which I was one of the researchers doing collaborative research with researchers from a university in a developed country, the contract agreement read as follows:

> Any and all intellectual property including copyright in the final and other reports arising from the work under agreement will be property of the University of "X" [from a developed country]. (Department for International Development, 2000, as cited in Chilisa, 2005, p. 676)

In another collaborative research with researchers from the developed countries, I found myself co-opted into dominant deficit thinking and theories that sought to construct the researched as the problem. I was uncomfortable with a statement in the draft report that reads,

A high acceptance of multiple sexual partners both before marriage and after marriage is a feature of Botswana society. Given the high priority and status given to sexual pleasure and fathering children, condoms are not popular especially with regular partners. (Chilisa, 2005, p. 676)

The sentences conflicted with what I considered to be the valued norms of the communities I was brought up in. The researchers from the developed country argued that the statements were informed by a review of literature. Elsewhere (Chilisa, 2005), I ask the question, "Which literature, generated by which researchers, using which theoretical frameworks?"

In some cases, the conflict is with publishers and other gatekeepers of knowledge over what can be said. In another instance, I was a writer theorizing on African-centered research methodologies. One of the reviewers of my manuscript had difficulties in opening space for research methodologies informed by African worldviews. The reviewer noted,

> There are difficulties in getting Africans in the theorising and building of knowledge on ways of conducting research. You have to address questions such as how do you test the validity of your findings ... by African or Western standards. What language do you use to build a research community and how do you research, store and transmit the accumulated knowledge? Arguably, the whole idea of research belongs to the north/western paradigm, so probably some Africanness will have to be sacrificed in the process.

This reviewer's comments show that some pockets of scientific colonialism with its assumption of a colonizer who is the center of power and who reserves the right to decide which ethics guidelines should be used, the right to know and to name, the right to ownership of all the data, and the ownership of the outcome of research in the form of reports and books still remain. These remnants of scientific colonialism raise many challenges to how ethics should be conceptualized and ethical principles applied in former colonized societies. The colonial and marginalizing hegemonies call for a decolonizing assessment of the universalized ethical models from a postcolonial/indigenous perspective. A decolonizing assessment calls on indigenous communities to resist and critique colonial and marginalizing hegemonies that have been normalized and to envision other ways that see the world differently. To decolonize the research methodologies is

> to argue that people must enter the world of scientific and scholarly analysis from the path of their historically and culturally developed perspectives. These perspectives are not counter to the universal truth, but simply access the universal through the window of one's particular worldview. (Akbar, 1991, p. 248, as cited in Ramsey, 2006)

What follows is a discussion of the Afrocentric paradigm (Asante, 1987, 1988, 1990) and how it has informed an Afrocentric research methodology (Mkabela, 2005; Reviere, 2001).

♦ The Afrocentric Paradigm

Afrocentricity is a paradigm whose origin is attributed to Asante's work *Afrocentricity* (1988), *The Afrocentric Idea* (1987), and *Kemet, Afrocentricity and Knowledge* (1990). It places the African ways of perceiving reality, ways of knowing, and value systems on equitable footing with other scholarly examinations of human experience. It is an African-centered worldview that establishes a conceptual framework for how the world is seen and understood. It is culturally specific and draws on African philosophical and theoretical assumptions and serves Africans just as classical Greek civilization serves as a reference point for Europe (Diop, 1978). Drawing from the Afrocentric paradigm, Asante (1990) came up with three basic beliefs that guide the research process. Reviere (2001) has summarized these as follows:

- Researchers must hold themselves responsible for uncovering hidden, subtle, racist theories that may be embedded in current methodologies.
- Researchers must work to legitimize the centrality of African ideals and values as valid frames of reference for acquiring and examining data.
- Researchers must maintain inquiry rooted in strict interpretation of place.

Reviere (2001) argued that the insistence on a clear definition of space is the central distinguishing characteristic. An Afrocentric inquiry must be executed from a clearly defined Afrocentric place and must include a clear description of this location (Reviere, 2001). Mkabela (2005) added that an African-centered methodology focuses on Africa as the cultural center for the study of African experiences and interprets data from an African perspective. She went on to say that Afrocentrists argue for pluralism in philosophical views without hierarchy. All cultural centers are to be respected, and thus, the diversity that is characteristic of Africa is accommodated as the researcher shifts from one cultural space to another. Baugh and Guion (2006) argued that the Afrocentric method suggested for use with Africans, and people of African descent, can also serve as a reference for research with other marginalized indigenous groups because it addresses issues pertinent to most former colonized societies. The Afrocentric method and methodologies in former colonized and indigenous societies requires researchers to develop relationships with the researched and reaffirm those relationships, use methods that may not be conventional for use with white populations and is collaborative, allowing the community to participate and provide input during all stages of the research process (Baugh & Guion, 2006).

♦ Culture and the Afrocentric Method

The Nile Valley Civilization is considered to be the geographic and historical foundation of cultural commonalities derived and shared among the continent's approximately 6,000 tribes and countless descendants (Ramsey, 2006). Asante (1987, 1990) is credited with identifying *Ma'at* and *Nommo* extracted from the Nile Valley Civilization as the two principles intrinsic to African cultures. *Ma'at* is the quest for justice, truth, and harmony and, in the context of research, refers to interrogating the manner in which the research process is in harmony with the culture of the people and pursues issues of truth and justice. *Nommo* describes the creation of knowledge as a vehicle for improvement in human life and human relations (Reviere, 2001, p. 711). From *Ma'at* are derived seven cardinal virtues—namely, truth, justice, rightness, propriety, harmony, order, and balance and reciprocity (Karenga & Carruthers, 1986).

Contemporary African scholars, like Oruka (1990), Kaphagawani (2000), Mamdani (1999), Prah (1999), and Chilisa and Preece (2005), discussed how African philosophies and theoretical perspectives inform African ways of seeing and knowing reality and value systems. Former colonized societies struggle with identity questions, and for them, the reality they seek to define, understand, and have others understand is the ontological question of what a person is or what human existence is. Conceptions of the social reality that is investigated can be understood in relation to our understanding of what human existence is. Such conceptions of reality also inform ways in which the conventional ethics principles should be adapted to address the interests and needs of the researched and ways in which to design ethics protocols sensitive and empathetic to the researched. What follows is a discussion of the nature of human existence and how the African value system of *Ubuntu* informs this human existence.

Most African communities, with particular reference to Bantu people of southern Africa for instance, view human existence in relation to the existence of others. Among views of "being," for instance, is the conception that *"nthu, nthu ne banwe"* (*Ikalanaga/Shona version*). According to Goduka (2000, p. 71), an English translation that comes close to the principle is, "I am we; I am because we are; we are because I am." A person is because of others. Communality, collectivity, human unity, and pluralism are implicit in this principle. The principle is in direct contrast to the Eurocentric view of humanity of I think, therefore, I am, which was expressed by Descartes. The latter, Goduka (2000, p. 71) observed, expresses a concept of self that is individually defined and "is in tune with a monolithic and one-dimensional construction of humanity." *Ubuntu* is a worldview. Chikanda (1990) explained it as African humanism that involves "alms-giving, sympathy, care, sensitivity to the needs of others, respect, consideration, patience and kindness." Also explaining the ontological question of what is a person, Asante (1987) noted that among people of African heritage, human nature assumes all elements of the universe both living and nonliving, both human and nonhuman. It is a human nature that is spiritual.

◆ Religiosity

Spirituality is therefore an important component of *Ubuntu*. Desmond Tutu, explaining *Ubuntu*, notes that *Ubuntu* is an organic relationship between people such that when we see another we should recognize ourselves and God in whose image all people are made. Elsewhere, I note that our understanding of humanness or reality in Botswana, for example, is influenced by our connectedness to the earth (*lefatshe*) and all its inhabitants, including animals, birds, plants, and the spirits (*Badimo*; Chilisa, 2005). This connectedness is embraced and celebrated through taboos and totems. For instance, my totem is *Kwena* (crocodile), an animal that remains sacred to me and my relatives. In this way, I remain connected to the crocodiles and care about their preservation. Botswana sees the human and physical world as one, and self and world as one, and separating them from these, their traditional conceptions of God, can deprive them of their source of knowledge as a people (Tournas, 1996, p. 40). The existence of being and behavior is not easily separated from the supernatural and nature. It is not a simple existence made up of hierarchies, but it is a web of relations and interconnectedness that extends to nonliving things. Understanding this type of reality requires a back and forth movements that connect to this web of relations (Table 26.1).

◆ Ubuntu *and Respect for Self and Other Through Consensus Building*

In the *ubuntu* context, to exist is to respect others and oneself. *Ubuntu* embraces the importance of agreement and consensus (Louw, 2001). In African traditional culture, when there is an issue to be discussed at the *Kgotla* (community meeting), although there may be a hierarchy of importance among speakers, every person gets an equal chance to speak up until some kind of agreement, consensus, or group cohesion is reached. The role of the people in consensus building is etched in the language that guides the discussion. In Botswana, for example, participatory democracy is encouraged through the sayings,

> Mumua lebe o a bo a bua lagagwe gore monalentle a ntshe la gagwe (everyone

| Table 26.1 | A Contrast of an I/You With an I/We Relationship |

I/You Relationship	I/We Relationship
Relations between people seen in hierarchy	Relations are multiple and interconnected and include relations between people and nonliving things. The being is not only related to other beings but also to nature
Guided by individualism of political social philosophy that places high value on freedom of the individual and generally stresses the self-directed, self-contained, and comparatively unrestrained individual or ego (Khoza, 1994, p. 3)	Guided by the I/we relationship where emphasis is on self-respect and respect for others, care for oneself and the others, the community, nature in general, and compassion, empathy, patience, and openness
People are the measure of things and thereby implying the elimination of the supernatural to explain the why, the what, and how of things which in Western worldviews should be directed by people's reliance on observation, logic, and reason	*Ubuntu* is religious, expansive, transcendental, and centrifugal

has a right to a say, for even what might appear like a bad suggestion helps people to think of better ideas)

Mongwe le mongwe o latlhela thware legonyana (everybody throws in a word)

Mafoko a kgotla a mantle otlhe (every contribution has a value in a gathering)

Agreement and consensus should however not be confused

With outmoded and suspect cravings for an oppressive universal sameness... True Ubuntu takes plurality seriously. While it constitutes personhood through other persons, it appreciates the fact that other persons are so called precisely because we can ultimately never quite stand in their shoes or completely see through their eyes. When an Ubuntist reads solidarity and consensus, s/he therefore also reads alterity, autonomy and cooperation. (cited in Louw, 2001, p. 6)

♦ Ubuntu *and the "Other": Respect for Particularity, Individuality, and Historicity*

Ubuntu respects particularity, individuality, and historicity (Louw, 2001). In the *ubuntu* ethical framework "we expose ourselves to others to encounter the difference of their humanness so as to inform and enrich our own (Sindane, 1994, pp. 8–9). *Ubuntu* incorporates dialogue, preserving the

other in her otherness, in her uniqueness without letting the other slip into distance. It embraces the perception of the "other" that is never fixed or rigidly closed but adjustable or open-ended. When the *Ubuntu* read consensus, s/he also reads open-ended-ness, contingency and flux. (cited in Louw, 2001, p. 11)

♦ Self-Determination and Rebirth

Ubuntu has survived colonialism and cultural imperialism and suffers marginalization by dominant Western discourses tied to market profits in a capitalist world economy. *Ubuntu*-informed ethics in research in this context is a long process of going back and forth to question subversive research practices that continue the violence and oppression of postcolonial/indigenous communities. The "we" in the I/we relationship is emphasized to facilitate a rebirth of a people relegated to the lowest scale in the Euro-Western scale of human hierarchy and Fourth world in the global market economy. In ethics, the "we" allows us to invoke the concept of African renaissance and Africanization in research.

> The African renaissance is a unique opportunity for Africans to define ourselves and our agenda according to our realities and taking into account the realities of those around. It's about Africans being agents of history and masters of our destiny. Africa is in a transformative mode. The renaissance is about African reflection and African redefinition. (Makgoba, Shope, & Mazwai, 1999, p. xii)

Ubuntu is inbuilt in our rebirth; thus, we define our "agenda taking into account the realities of those around us. Africanisation refers to a process of placing the African worldview at the centre of analysis" (Teffo, 2000, p. 107). Validating this view, Prah (1999) noted,

> We cannot in all seriousness study ourselves through the eyes of other people's assumptions. I am not saying we must not know what others know or think of us. I am saying we must think for ourselves like others do for themselves. (p. 37)

These assertions further raise the questions, "For whom are proposed ethics meant?" "Who is the audience for this chapter?" The questions blend into other questions that have been asked such as who should do research among former colonized, historically colonized societies and indigenous communities, or research in culturally complex societies. Porsanger (2004), for example, noted that there have been some extreme opinions that only indigenous researchers may conduct research "on, with, and about indigenous people." Porsanger rejected this extreme view observing that indigenous scholars and indeed those scholars from former colonized societies cannot be privileged on the basis of their background because there are a great variety of insider views, some of which may not be sensitive and responsive to the needs and the interest of the indigenous communities. The "I am we" *Ubuntu* principle makes provision for

> the rationale, modulation and interconnectedness of the categories of race, class, gender, ethnicity and their respective isms ... all those things which Europeans and westerners see as either or opposites binaries or dichotomous thinking. (cited in Goduka, 2000, p. 29)

From this perspective, researchers from all over the world are called to, first, see themselves as related and connected by the same goals of commitment to build harmony among communities that they research, to reciprocate by giving back to communities for what they take, and to strive for truth, justice, fairness, and inclusiveness in the construction of knowledge. An African-centered ethical framework, thus, requires researchers to contextualize conventional ethics principles, taking into consideration the history of colonialism and its effects on the formerly colonised, the culture of the African people based on *Ma'at* and *Nommo*, and the seven cardinal principles of truth, justice, rightness, propriety, harmony, order, and balance and reciprocity that emanate from *Ma'at* and contemporary African theorizing on Africanization and

Ubuntu. What follows is an ethical framework that focuses on researchers' and researched's relationships and responsibilities of researchers. The framework is informed by the *Ubuntu* principles of "I am we, I am because we are," *Ubuntu* principles of religiosity, respect for Self and Other through consensus building, and respect for particularity, individuality, and historicity.

♦ The Responsibilities of Researcher as a Transformative Healer

Ubuntu informs our construction of harmony, justice, and reciprocity as much as it is informed by *Ma'at* and *Nommo*. In discussing the relationship between the researchers and the researched and the responsibilities of a researcher, one has, therefore, to go back and forth to invoke the seven virtues of *Ma'at* to explain the application of *Ubuntu*-based ethical relationships between them. According to Ramsey (2006), the application of the seven virtues of *Ma'at* as a point of reference constructs the social scientist researcher as a transformative healer. The role of a transformative healer involves self-reflection and self-questioning on the researcher's responsibilities and the relationship with the other and others, nonliving and living. The meaning of a transformative healer, however, has to be understood in the African context from which it emerges. In the African context, before a healer could be allowed to perform classical healing rites, he or she had to undergo intensive study of self, understand how self is unique yet related to the whole and identify his or her life purpose. The healer had to be a living example of how to resolve crises, challenges, and difficulties (Ramsey, 2006). I have outlined the following as challenges that a transformative healer needs to reflect on and question:

1. Researcher as colonizer, researched as colonized

2. Researcher as knower/teacher and researched as object/subject/known/pupil

3. Researcher as redeemer, researched as the problem

4. Ethical responsibilities of researchers in the application of theoretical frameworks and literature review to inform the research process

I look at how each of these challenges is manifest in the research process and the questions that researchers who assume the responsibilities of a transformative healer need to ask themselves in order to carry out research in an ethical manner.

♦ Researcher as Colonizer, Researched as Colonized

Postcolonial/indigenous researchers who embrace ethical responsibilities as healers, seeking to bring about transformation in their societies, strive to expose the modern discursive practices, pervasive and nearly invisible strategies that facilitate the marginalization, oppression, and disregard of human rights of postcolonial/indigenous communities. The colonizer/colonized, researcher/researched relationships can be a starting point to begin to review events and practices in the research process so that the ethical responsibility of a healer engaged in a transformative journey is not compromised. Researchers as producers of knowledge make assumptions about the power relations between themselves and the researched and are consciously or unconsciously guided by these assumptions. These assumptions inform the researchers' interactions with the researched, the kind of knowledge that can be produced, and how it can be produced. The colonizer/colonized relationship interrogates power relations with regard to researchers as privileged elites researching with and operating with Western models of thought. The concern is on Eurocentrism as a science that privileges Western ways of knowing and perceiving reality. In this framework, the indigenous/postcolonial researchers can assume many identities. They can operate at the level of colonizer co-opted by the dominant Western discourse on methodology that uses Euro-Western standards as universal truths against which the "other" former colonized societies marginalized by globalization are researched and written about. At another level, they can operate as healers, challenging and resisting the blind Euro-Western application of methodologies across all cultures. At this level, they are members of the former colonized, marginalized, written about, and rewriting what has been written about the "other," "others," and themselves. These multiple positions require knowledge production approaches that are multiple, interconnected, and sensitive and engaging the researcher with ethical issues that position the researcher as healer where healers need to heal themselves before they can assist others to heal. The researcher needs to ask the following questions:

1. Whose side am I on?
2. Do I challenge and resist dominant discourses that marginalize those who suffer oppression?
3. Who am I writing about? Self or "Other" or both?
4. What needs to be rewritten?

♦ Researcher as Knower/Teacher and Researched as Object/Subject/Known/Pupil

At another level, the power relations operate within spaces of researched as subject/object and researcher as knower. Researchers act as knowledge imperialists and colonizers when they claim authenticity of description, interpretation and dissemination of results under the guise of scholarship, and authority in the area of study. The researched become objects and "passive onlookers." In this objectification and "thingification of people" (Loomba, 2001), researchers do not ask the researched if they agree in the way their lives are described and interpreted. bell hooks (1991) noted that in such instances, the researcher becomes the authoritative author who is not sensitive to the voices of the researched but is more interested in his or her standing as an authority in the subject he or she writes in which the researched cannot participate. A transformative healer reflects and raises the following questions:

1. Do the researched own a description of themselves?
2. Have the voices of the researched been captured in a way that the researched recognize themselves, know themselves, and would like others to know them?

Elsewhere (Chilisa, 2005), I describe an ethical method of data collection and interpretation etched in the *dingaka* (diviners) practices. According to Dube (2001), *dingaka* use a set of as many as 60 bones symbolizing divine power, evil power, foreign spirits (good or bad), elderly men and women, young and old, homesteads, family life or death, and ethnic groups that include *Makgoa* (white people) to construct a story about the consulting client's life. The pieces represent experiences, networks, and relationships of people and the environment. In constructing a story, the diviner consults the patterns of the divine set as the client throws them to the ground. The diviner asks the client to confirm the interpretation of the set as a true story about his or her troubled part of life. In the process, neither the set nor the diviner has exclusive knowledge. The client is invited to talk freely about his or her life and to reject the constructed story if it does not tally with her or his life experiences (Chilisa, 2005). I have suggested three ways in which the consultation process contributes to an ethical research process as follows:

1. In the context of the diviner and the client, there is no absolute knowledge; the three, that is the diviner, the set, and the visitor, construct knowledge together.

2. Context is complex, expansive, and infinite since there is no claim to an identified description of context. Context is, however, brought to the consciousness of both the diviner and the client through symbolic representations of the surroundings.

3. The story in whatever form is read and agreed on. No interpretation occurs in the absence of any one of the three (Chilisa, 2005, p. 680).

The premises of the diviner's knowledge construction method promote community-centered ways of doing research that respect the "other," offering alternative ways in which researchers may work with communities to theorize and build models of research designs that restores the dignity and integrity that has been violated through scientific colonization.

Reviere (2001, p. 711) has, in addition to the conventional procedures that should form the criteria against which research should be judged for the accuracy of the lived experiences of the researched, proposed five canons located in an African space. These five canons, namely *Ukweli* (truth), *Kujitoa* (commitment), *Utulivu* (justice), *Uhaki* (harmony), and *Ujamaa* (community) are derived from the seven cardinal African virtues of truth, justice, rightness, propriety, harmony, order, and balance and reciprocity. The five canons speak to procedures and strategies for establishing rigor in research and establishing credibility, trustworthiness, and dependability or validity and reliability as commonly known in quantitative research. *Ukweli* seeks for truth grounded in the people's experience. The canon of *Ukweli* shifts emphasis from objectivity to truth, fairness, and honesty and how these can be achieved. *Ukweli* requires researchers to establish whether the conclusions that they reach are representative of only their own position or whether they represent a consensus of the researched and other opinions. *Kujitoa* requires the researcher to emphasize how knowledge is structured and used over "the need for dispassion and objectivity" (Reviere, 2001, p. 716). *Utulivu* requires that the researcher actively avoids creating, exaggerating, or sustaining divisions between or within communities but, rather, strives to create harmonious relationships between and within groups. *Ujamaa* requires that theory and practice be informed by the aspired aspirations and interests of the community, while *uhaki* requires the encouragement and maintenance of harmonious relationships between communities and groups. In addition to the conventional methods that establish procedures that enable the researched to recognize the descriptions and interpretations of human experiences as accurate are, among others, prolonged and substantial engagement, peer debriefing, member checks, triangulation, and reflexivity (Creswell, 1994; Krefting, 1991). Reviere (2001) has proposed an African-centered procedure informed by the five canons of *ukweli, uhaki, utulivu, ujamaa,* and *Kujitio.*[2] The procedure is as follows:

- Involve a group of self-identified Afrocentric research scholars who meet once or twice per month to discuss relevant issues uncovered by the inquiry and provide feedback on whether the inquiry and the researcher's interpretation of the data embody the principle of Afrocentrism as understood in the Afrocentric research community.

- Use the Internet and e-mail system to solicit views and critiques of African scholars worldwide.

- Initiate direct correspondence with well-established scholars, including those of Afrocentric orientation, to dialogue on the ideas and findings generated by the inquiry.

- Analyze the data from an Afrocentric perspective using the Afrocentric canons and own experience to the subject of inquiry as well as consulting with the wider community for interpretation of data.

♦ Researcher as Redeemer, Researched as the Problem

Researchers are also implicated in the imperialist agenda when they participate in the "othering" of the researched through deficit discourses, theories, or literature that construct the researched as the problem. Elsewhere (Chilisa, 2005), I problematize my position as a researcher co-opted into the dominant Western deficit discourse on the historically colonized, resisting this discourse and failing because of the overwhelming literature that has normalized and constructed as facts and "common sense" a deficit discourse about the "Other." Common among these deficit discourses is the normalized thinking that blames the devastating epidemic of HIV and AIDS on a "permissive female sexuality," a thinking perpetuated by a colonial discourse on sexuality that equated African women with animals (Chilisa, 2006; Collins, 1990). This deficit thinking and constructions about the Africans should propel researchers to review, critique, and think afresh the steps in carrying out research.

The golden rule for novice researchers is that they should always read the literature to assist the researcher in choosing a researchable topic, focus the research questions, provide theoretical basis for analyzing findings, legitimize a researcher's own assumptions, and give credit and acknowledge the strength of previous findings. One major limitation of this approach is that the concepts, the theories, and the research studies conducted and the literature in general have been written on former colonized societies by missionaries, travelers, navigators, historians, anthropologists, and so on who, in most cases, looked on the researched as objects with no voice to add to the way they wanted to be written about. This literature and body of knowledge continues to inform our research practices.

As Western educated scholars researching former colonized societies, we need to ask ourselves the following questions:

1. What psychological harm, humiliation, embarrassment, and other losses if any have these theories and body of knowledge caused the researched?

2. What is the body of indigenous knowledge of the former colonized societies that we researchers can use to counter theories and the body of knowledge that may cause humiliation and embarrassment to the researched?

These questions make it increasingly important for researchers to familiarize themselves with colonial epistemologies and their social construction of former colonized and historically oppressed groups in order to understand the theoretical landscape and literature within which the international community of researchers are encouraged and coerced to operate. Healer/transformative researchers should debate these theories and literature to expose the possible psychological harm and loss of whatever kind that has occurred over the years because of these theories. Postcolonial theories provide an important framework through which Western educated researchers can explore the possible biases in the literature we read, identify the knowledge gaps that have been created because of the unidirectional borrowing of Euro-Western literature, and bring to a halt the continuing marginalization of other knowledge systems that occur because of the dominant Euro-Western research paradigms and their discourses on what can be researched and how it can be researched. A transformative healer needs to reflect and raise the following questions:

1. What assumptions, prejudices, and stereotypes informed the review of literature?
2. How do the literature and theories reviewed portray the researched?
3. Is there any deficit thinking or theorizing in the literature reviewed?
4. What evidence is there to bring to question the literature reviewed?
5. What are the gaps in the literature?

Ethics for researchers researching in historically oppressed, former colonized societies should involve going back and forth to retrieve marginalized and dominant literatures to review, analyze, and challenge colonizing and deficit theorizing and interpretations and to create counter narratives that see the past differently and envision a transformative agenda for the researched. It also involves defining what literature and theorizing in the context of former colonized societies is. Literature is our language, proverbs, cultural artifacts, legends, stories, practices, songs, poems, dances, tattoos, lived experiences such as our fight against HIV/AIDS, and personal stories and community stories told in weddings, funerals, celebration, wars, ritual songs, and dance and silence. Youngman (1998) and Omolewa, Adeola, Adekanmbi, Avoseh, and Braimoh (1998), for instance, used proverbs to provide an indigenous concept of lifelong learning and literacy. Chilisa and Preece (2005) showed how the Botswana legend on the origin of humankind can be used as a reference point in countering Western theorizing on gender relations and Western perceptions on African tradition and gender. In the study of gender, for instance, the asymmetrical relationship between men and women in African societies is traced back to tradition. Oral traditions on the story of origin would, however, defy this worldview and open another space to interrogate the gender relations. According to the Tswana story of origin, the people came from the hill of Lowe. When they came out, men and women were walking side by side, driving sheep, goats, and cattle. This story defies explanations that justify inequalities on the basis of tradition and reveals other ways of viewing gender relations based on tradition.[3] In an ongoing study to examine sociocultural, family, and social influences on Botswana adolescents' sexual behaviors, researchers collected metaphorical language/sayings such as proverbs, popular legends, community stories, songs, rituals, myths, and taboos that communicate messages on sex, sexuality, and gender relations. The collection is to provide baseline literature that enables the researchers to include African indigenous voices in framing the issues on gender relations, sexuality, and adolescent behavior.

As more and more scholars from former colonized societies begin to make choices on what they research and delve into areas that colonial epistemologies dismissed as sorcery, researchers who assume their responsibilities as healers will be confronted by the realities of the limitation of Western hegemonic ethical standards such as the principle of informed consent of the researched. A transformative healer will seek to go beyond Euro-Western research issues of power that mainly focus on the "I" (the researcher) and the "you" (the researched) to more involving I/we relationships that see reality differently.

◆ Ethics Built on a Deep Respect for Religious Beliefs and the Practices of Others

How do we study or come to understand a reality that does not separate the physical from the nonphysical and the I from the you? Data collection both quantitative and qualitative always begins with biographical information of the researched. Often, however, information is sought based on an I/you relationship where emphasis is on the individual. *Ubuntu* ethical protocols would embrace biographical information that includes the researched's lineage and totemism, as they relate to the topic of inquiry. Totemism embraces religion and spirituality.

Ubuntu requires that the knowledge production is conducted with care, love for one another, empathy, and compassion that are derived from an understanding of a human nature that embraced all as created by God. Swanson (2006) reveals how the concept of *I am because we are, I am we, and we are because I am* served as a point of reference in applying the conventional concept of reflexivity in researching school mathematics among a poor community in postapartheid Africa. *Ubuntu,* she argued, allowed her to disrupt and decolonize dominant meanings and deficit thinking by promoting compassion, care, togetherness, empathy, and respectful ways of doing research that allowed the researchers to see themselves in the researched. *Ubuntu* from this perspective is an African contribution to any researcher's reflexivity and critical journey of the researcher and the researched into each other's lives. Laible (2000) called this way of knowing "a loving epistemology." She explained it as a way of knowing where the production of knowledge should include a journey of the researcher and the researched into each others' lives.

◆ Ethics That Underscores the Importance of Agreement and Consensus, Dialogue, and Particularity

Under African eyes, an I/we relationship emphasizes respect for the self, the other, and others and implies a unification of the self with the environment. The deontological and consequential ethical framework based on the Western mode of individualism places emphasis on a one-on-one contractual agreement where relationships between the researchers and the researched are entered through signed consent forms. Nyamnjoh (2006) questioned the assumption that when researchers have passed their research proposal through ethics review boards, the research will be conducted in an ethical way that is sensitive to human rights and is respectful to the integrity and dignity of the researched. They also questioned the consent agreement made by the researched. What is the researched, for instance, giving consent to?

Ubuntu invites us to further ask the following questions: Whose consent is asked? Is it consent from the I, the "other," or others? Consent to do what? Is it consent to write and describe the other and then to extrapolate or generalize the written story to the rest of the community unspoken to? The consent under Euro-Western eyes carries with it a desperate hidden desire to make the I speak for those whose consent has not been sought. In the I/we relationship, if it is made known to the researched that the consent includes allowing the researcher to use the researched to speak for others, the story I believe would be different for it would be told from multiple perspectives.

In the I/we relationship, consent agreements would invoke consensus arrived at through circles of discussion where membership in the circle of discussion is informed by the intricate web of connections that is the basis of relationships based on *Ubuntu* principles. In Botswana, for example, even after an institutional review board gives consent that research can be carried out, the researcher has to consult with the chief of the village who, in turn, calls the people to a village council to deliberate on an issue and reach a consensus. If a researcher is allowed to do the research, then she or he may visit households to interview the identified key informants and still have to ask for individual and group consent. In an African setting, a husband may seek the views of his wife and children before he can consent to speak. In most cases, he will decline to speak on behalf of family members, preferring everyone in the family who may be affected to participate in the dialogue (see Ntseane, this volume). From the I/we relationship emanate four types of consent: individual consent, community consent, group consent, and collective consent. Mkabela (2005) referred to the process as collective ethics and concluded that when collective ethics is translated into the research process it would include the following:

- An appreciation of the importance of individuals in the research group

- An understanding that research is part of a very complex (community) whole

- The respect of heritage authority

- The inclusion of elders and cultural committees in the research process

- An understanding of the interconnectedness of all things (including the spiritual) and required long-term perspective in dealing with research issues

- An understanding that researchers must act in an appropriate and respectful way to maintain the harmony and balance of the group (community)

Researchers can, for example, employ cultural symbols to show respect for the researched peoples' values and to build relations with the people. Ellis and Earley (2006) showed how she was able to use *Aseema* (tobacco), a cultural symbol used by the Anishambe, one of the indigenous people of North America, for thanking people, asking for help, praying for information, and sharing stories to gain access to the indigenous people "while being of non-indigenous roots." Earley observed that *aseema* was used, not as a technique to persuade the interviewee to reveal more and be more honest in his or her responses (Fontana & Frey, 2005), "but rather as a culturally relevant means of establishing consent in the context of empathising with a worldview other than their own" (Ellis & Earley, 2006, p. 8). Ellis and Earley (2006) advised that "researchers must attempt to find the most culturally relevant modes of establishing consent even if that entails challenging the signed informed consent IRB protocol" (p. 7). Clearly then, employing indigenous cultural symbols assists to interpret and apply universal ethics principles in the context of the worldviews and practices of former colonized and historically oppressed and silenced societies. Former colonized societies, it should be pointed out, are actively engaged in developing guidelines for carrying out research that is culturally sensitive and responsive to the communities researched. The Working Group on Indigenous Minorities in Southern Africa has for instance worked on research policies that seek to protect the San of Southern Africa from the unethical practices of some researchers (Chilisa & Preece, 2005).

◆ Conclusion

Ethical frameworks from a Euro-Western perspective invariably center on the relationship between the researcher and the researched. This conceptualization is narrow, because it ignores the hierarchies of power between researchers from different nations who may be involved in collaborative research. It also ignores the normalized hierarchies of knowledge systems that affirm and privilege Euro-Western knowledge systems relegating to irrelevant other knowledge systems. The dominant ethical frameworks still take as a starting point an accumulative process of knowledge production that, in most cases, affirms and privileges deficit literature, theories, and thinking about former colonized societies.

Ethics from African-centered perspectives begin with researchers from all over the world assuming roles of transformatives/healers with responsibilities to heal self and then reflect, question, and take action on colonizer/colonized relationships that still embrace scientific colonization with its assumption of colonial powers that still have the right of access and ownership to the data from former colonized societies. *Ubuntu* ethics promote a cyclic process of researcher/researched relationship where consent to carry out research is sought at individual level, community level, and group level and where consent is a collective decision. *Ubuntu* is an important African contribution to researcher reflexivity and the critical journey of the researcher and the researched into each other's lives.

◆ Notes

1. Chilisa and Preece (2005) argued that the worst violation of consent ethics in Africa was during the colonial era when various types of specimens to illustrate scientific discourses were stolen by explorers and researchers alike. They illustrated stealing as a violation of consent ethics through a case study of El Negro. El Negro is the remains of a chief whose body was stolen from its grave on the night it was buried and taken to France in 1830 where it was exhibited in the museum in Banyole in the north of Barcelona. It was removed from public exhibition in 1997 after protests by Africans and people of African ancestry and repatriated to Africa where it was buried in Gaborone, the capital of Botswana, in 1997.

2. According to Reviere (2001), *ukweli* loosely translated from Swahili means truth, *utulivu* means justice, *uhaki* means harmony, *ujamaa* means community, and *kujitoa* means commitment.

3. For more examples of indigenous sources of literature see Chilisa and Preece (2005).

◆ References

Aboriginal Research Centre. (2005). *Mi'knaw research centre and protocols*. Retrieved May 10, 2006, from http://mrc.uccb.ns.ca/prinpro.html

Asante, M. K. (1987). *The Afrocentric idea*. Philadelphia: Temple University Press

Asante, M. K. (1988). *Afrocentricity*. Trenton, NJ: Africa World Press

Asante, M. K. (1990). *Kemet, Afrocentricity and knowledge*. Trenton, NJ: Africa World Press.

Baugh, E. J., & Guion, L. (2006). Using culturally sensitive methodologies when researching diverse cultures. *Journal of Multidisciplinary Evaluation, 4*, 1–12.

Bennet, B. S. (1997). Suppose a black man tells a story; the dialogues of John Mackenzie the Missionary and Sekgoma Kgari the King and Rainmaker. *Pula: Botswana Journal of African Studies, 11*(1), 42–57.

Bhaba, H. (1994). *The location of culture*. New York: Routledge.

Caballero, B. (2002). Ethical issues for collaborative research in developing countries. *American Journal of Clinical Nursing, 76*, 717–720.

Chilisa, B. (2005). Educational research within postcolonial Africa: A critique of HIV/AIDS research in Botswana. *International Journal of Qualitative Studies, 18*(6), 659–684.

Chilisa, B. (2006). Sexuality education: Subjugated discourses and adolescent voices. In C. Skelton, B. Francis, & L. Smulyan (Eds.), *Gender and education* (pp. 241–261). London: Sage.

Chilisa, B., & Koloi, O. (2007, October). *The politics and ethics of collaborative research*. Seminar Series on Responsible Conduct of Research, Office of Research and Development, University of Botswana, Gaborone.

Chilisa, B., & Preece, J. (2005). *Research methods for adult educators in Africa*. Cape Town, South Africa: Pearson/UNESCO.

Chikanda, N. E. (1990). *Shared values and Ubuntu*. Unpublished conference paper read at the Human Science Research

Council (HSRC) conference KONTAK on nation building, Pretoria, South Africa.

Collins, P. (1990). *Black feminist thought*. London: Hammersmith.

Cram, F. (2004). *Theories, practices, models analyses*. Paper presented at the Evaluation workshop in Hawaii.

Cram, F., Ormond, A., & Carter, L. (2004, June 10–12). *Researching our relations: Reflections on ethics and marginalization*. Paper presented at the Kamhameha schools Research Conference on Hawaiian Well being, Honolulu, Hawaii.

Creswell, J. W. (1994). *Research design: Qualitative and quantitative approaches*. Thousand Oaks, CA: Sage.

Diop, C. (1978). *The cultural unity of Black Africa*. Chicago: Third World Press.

Dube, M. W. (2001). Divining Ruth for international relations. In M. W. Dube (Ed.), *Other ways of reading the Bible* (pp. 179–198). Geneva: WCC.

Edwards, R., & Mauthner, M. (2002). Ethics and feminist research: Theory and practice. In M. Mauthner, M. Birch, J. Jessop, & T. Miller (Eds.), *Ethics in qualitative research* (pp. 14–31). Thousand Oaks, CA: Sage.

Ellis, J. B., & Earley, M. A. (2006). Reciprocity and constructions of informed consent: Researching with indigenous populations. *International Journal of Qualitative Methods, 5*(4). Retrieve May 7, 2008, from www.ualberta.ca/~iiqm/backissues/5_4/html/ellis.htm

Fontana, A., & Frey, J. (2005). The interview: From political stance to political involvement. In N. Denzin & Y. Lincoln (Eds.), *The Sage handbook of qualitative research* (pp. 695–727). Thousand Oaks, CA: Sage.

Goduka, I. N. (2000). African/indigenous philosophies: Legitimizing spiritually centred wisdoms within the academy. In P. Higgs, N. C. G. Vakalisa, T. V. Mda, & N. T. Assie-Lumumba (Eds.), *African voices in education* (pp. 63–83). Lansdowne, South Africa: Juta.

hooks, b. (1991). *Yearning: Race, gender, and cultural politics*. London: Turnaround.

Kaphagawani, D. N. (2000). What is African philosophy? In P. H. Coetzee & A. P. J. Roux (Eds.), *Philosophy from Africa* (pp. 86–98). Cape Town, South Africa: Oxford University Press.

Karenga, M., & Carruthers, J. (1986). *Kemet and African worldview: Research, rescue and restoration*. Los Angeles: University of Sankore Press.

Khoza, R. (1994). *African humanism*. Diepkloof Extension, South Africa: Ekhaya Promotions.

Krefting, L. (1991). Rigor in qualitative research: The assessment of trustworthiness. *American Journal of Occupational Therapy, 45*, 214–222.

Laible, J. C. (2000). A loving epistemology: What I hold critical in my life, faith and profession. *Journal of Qualitative Studies in Education, 13*(6), 683–692.

Loomba, A. (2001). *Colonialism/postcolonialism*. London: Routledge.

Louw, D. J. (2001). *Ubuntu: An African assessment of the religious order*. Retrieved September 27, 2001, from www.bu.edu/wcp/papers/Afrlouw.htm

Makgoba, M. W., Shope, T., & Mazwai, T. (1999). Íntroduction. In M. Makgoba (Ed.), *Africa Renaissance: The new struggle* (pp. i–xii). Cape Town, South Africa: Mafube & Tafelberg.

Mamdani, M. (1999). There can be no African renaissance without an African-focused intelligentsia. In M. Makgoba (Ed.), *African Renaissance: The new struggle* (pp. 125–134). Cape Town, South Africa: Mafube & Tafelberg.

Ministry of Social Development. (2004). *Ngau Ara Tohutohu Rangahau Maori Guidelines for research and evaluation with Maori*. Centre for Social Research and Evaluation with Maori, Te Pokapu, Rangahau Arotake Hapori.

Mkabela, Q. (2005). Using the Afrocentric method in researching indigenous African culture. *Qualitative Report, 10*(1), 178–189.

Nyamnjoh, F. (2006). Responsible ethics. In R. Apollo & F. B. Nyamnjoh (Eds.), *Challenges* and responsibilities of social science research in Africa: Ethical issues (pp. 1–7). Addis Ababa, Ethiopia: OSSREA.

Omolewa, M., Adeola, O. A., Adekanmbi, G. A., Avoseh, M. B. M., & Braimoh, D. (1998). *Literacy, tradition and progress: Enrollment and retention in an African rural literacy programme.* Hamburg, Germany: UNESCO Institute for Education.

Oruka, O. (1990). *Sage philosophy: Indigenous thinkers and modern debate.* Nairobi, Kenya: Nairobi University Press.

Porsanger, J. (2004). An essay on indigenous methodology. *NORDLIT, 15,* 105–120.

Prah, K. K. (1999). African renaissance or warlordism? In M. Makgoba (Ed.), *African Renaissance: The new struggle* (pp. 37–61). Cape Town, South Africa: Mafube & Tafelberg.

Ramsey, G. (2006). Ethical responsibilities of an African-centred research. In R. Apollo & F. B. Nyamnjoh (Eds.), *Challenges and responsibilities of social research in Africa: Ethical issues* (pp. 167–171). Addis Ababa, Ethiopia: OSSREA.

Reviere, R. (2001). Toward an Afrocentric research methodology. *Journal of Black Studies, 31*(6), 709–727.

Sindane, J. (1994). *Ubuntu and nation building.* Pretoria, South Africa: Ubuntu School of Philosophy.

Swanson, D. (2006). *Humble togetherness and Ubuntu: An African contribution to a reflexive, critical, narrative journey.* Paper presented at the Second International Congress of Qualitative Inquiry, University of Illinois, at Urbana-Champaign.

Teffo, L. J. (2000). Africanist thinking: An invitation to authenticity. In P. Higgs, N. C. G. Vakalisa, T. V. Mda, & N. T. Assie-Lumumba (Eds.), *African voices in education* (pp. 103–117). Lansdowne, South Africa: Juta.

Thomas, C. (1985). Social science research: Some implications for Afro-American scholars. *Journal of Black Studies, 15*(3), 325–338.

Tournas, S. A. (1996). From sacred initiation to bureaucratic apostasy: Junior secondary school-leavers and the secularization of education in southern Africa. *Comparative Education, 32*(1), 27–43.

Youngman, F. (1998). *Old dogs and new tricks? Lifelong education for all-the challenges facing adult education in Botswana.* Inaugural lecture, University of Botswana, Gaborone.

27

RESEARCH ETHICS AND SENSITIVE BEHAVIORS

Underground Economy

◆ Divya Sharma

The September 11, 2001, attacks on the United States created an urgent need to understand means of terrorism funding. This, in turn, brought into focus Hawala,[1] a form of informal value transfer system[2] (IVTS) that allows people to transfer money from one country to another without going through the formal banks and other financial institutions. It has been used for legal, illegal, and criminal purposes. In a typical Hawala transaction, the sender will approach the Hawala dealer, for instance, in New York, and give him money that he wants to send to someone in Delhi, India. He will also provide the recipient's name and contact information. At the end of the day, the Hawala dealer will fax or e-mail the list to his counterpart in India. The dealer in India will then make payments in local currency within 24 hours. It is possible for the dealer to make payments because of the locally available large cash pool, some of which may be generated through illegal and criminal activities including, but not limited to, tax evasion, drug trafficking, and extortion. The local cash pool that facilitates these transactions is the least explored aspect of Hawala.

♦ Hawala and Hundi

The literal meaning of Hawala in Arabic is "transfer," and in Hindi it means "reference." It is an offshoot of the system of Hundi that was integral to India's indigenous banking system that predates the Western banking system (Jain, 1929; Kashyap, 2002); immigrants from South Asia and the Middle East use it extensively.

Hundi is one of the oldest known bills of exchange. Its documented history is about 2,000 years old, and Indian merchants and traders used it both as debit and credit cards within India, as well as while traveling to East Africa and other foreign locales for trading clothes and spices (Markovits, 2001). Hundis were drawn in all amounts. For example, in 1030 AD, two brothers Vastupal and Tejpal drew a Hundi in the amount of $2.2 million (approximate, based on current exchange rate of a U.S. dollar to Indian rupees[3]) to build Dilwara temples in Rajasthan, India. On the other hand, there is an example of Hundi being drawn in the amount of 42 rupees (just about 1 U.S. dollar) in the 17th century (Kashyap, 2002). Lakhani (n.d.) noted, as in the case of modern-day traveler's checks, there were provisions to replace lost or damaged Hundis. The British East India Company also used Hundis to carry out trade transactions with Indian merchants and traders for about 200 years. By the early 1800s, the British had established their own banking networks across India, and it is around the 1830s that they declared it illegal to use Hundis. It is then that the Hundi system went underground only to reemerge as Hawala in early to mid-1900s. Today, it has become synonymous to Hawala and is used in Pakistan and Bangladesh for Hawala-like operations.

Figure 27.1 is an example of a typical Hawala transaction (Sharma, 2005).

There are instances when Hawala transactions have been completed in less than four hours. There are also cases where dealers have used their courier persons to deliver money at the doorstep especially in the towns and villages where people may not have access to banks or transportation or need money on short notice. Hawala transactions are therefore cheaper and faster than bank transactions, and Hawala dealers provide a better exchange rate.

In addition to Hawala, fei ch'ien (Flying Money), Undiyal, casa de cambio (stash house), phoe kuan (message houses), Chop Shop, and Chits are some other well-known forms of IVTS. Undiyal was extensively used in the aftermath of the Tsunami in 2004 in parts of Southeast Asia and provided money to the locals in parts of Sri Lanka days before the government agencies and nongovernment organizations could reach them. One of the features of these IVTS is that there is no paper trail, making it a preferable means of money transfer for criminal elements.

Figure 27.2 shows legal, illegal, and criminal dimensions of Hawala.

The larger picture of Hawala includes more noncriminal uses than criminal ones. As is the case of any news event, however, it is not a newsworthy story if someone receives money earned legitimately for groceries, rent, or marriage, but it is a newsworthy story if Hawala is used to send or receive money generated through or for criminal activities. Because of the bias generated by the type of events involving Hawala that receive news coverage, researchers and the larger community in general have to guard against overgeneralizing the criminal component. Hawala gained particular global notoriety after the 9/11 attacks due to news reports about its use by terrorists to receive funds from the Middle East. Although many of these news reports have not been substantiated[4] and the investigations revealed that the 9/11 terrorists had received part of the money through wire transfers, credit cards, and formal banks, it still brought to attention

Figure 27.1 A Typical Hawala Transaction

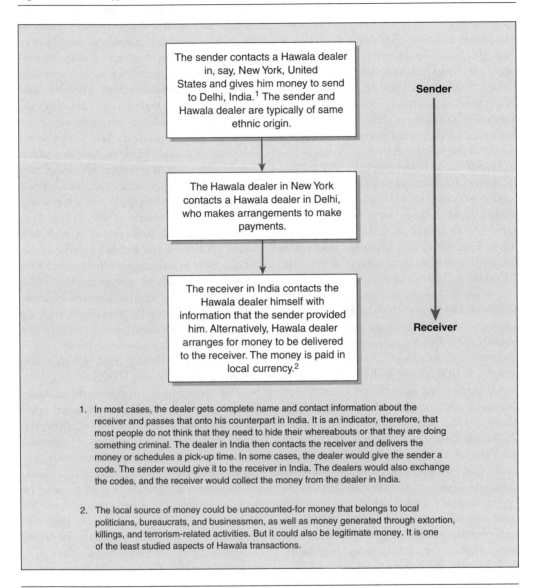

1. In most cases, the dealer gets complete name and contact information about the receiver and passes that onto his counterpart in India. It is an indicator, therefore, that most people do not think that they need to hide their whereabouts or that they are doing something criminal. The dealer in India then contacts the receiver and delivers the money or schedules a pick-up time. In some cases, the dealer would give the sender a code. The sender would give it to the receiver in India. The dealers would also exchange the codes, and the receiver would collect the money from the dealer in India.

2. The local source of money could be unaccounted-for money that belongs to local politicians, bureaucrats, and businessmen, as well as money generated through extortion, killings, and terrorism-related activities. But it could also be legitimate money. It is one of the least studied aspects of Hawala transactions.

the abuses of IVTS in committing transnational crimes and generated research interest in understanding the system itself that, in return, has furthered the growth of qualitative research in the field of criminal justice.

◆ Research Interest in Hawala After September 11, 2001

Studies of Hawala in the immediacy of the 9/11 attacks were scarce and often contained partial or even misinformation about the system. Heightened fear levels due to terror attacks have also come to serve as a justification for violating research ethics in the name of the benefits of doing research on this topic. There was increased political pressure[5] on countries such as India to close down and/or regulate Hawala, and the 9/11 Commission Report (2004) and the PATRIOT Act of 2001 (U.S. Congress, 2001) stressed the importance of investigating Hawala. This created an environment where, even in the research community, Hawala

Figure 27.2 Legal, Illegal, and Criminal Dimensions of Hawala

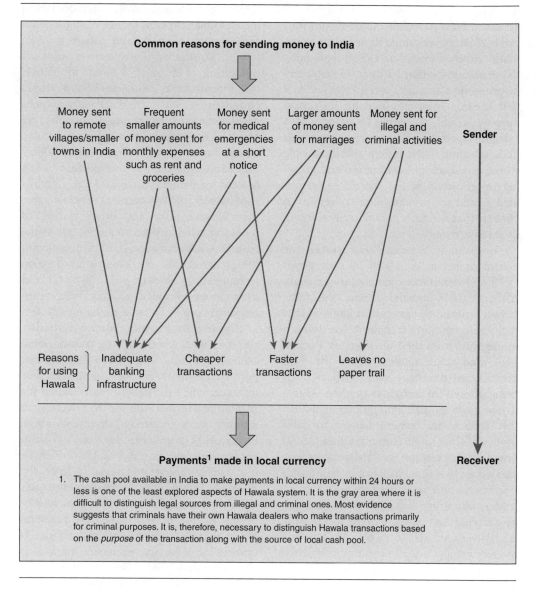

was treated as any other criminal enterprise. It has been equated with money laundering and called *Islamic banking* and *terrorists' banking system*. Pohit and Taneja's (2000) study on informal trade between India and Bangladesh notes that traders "relied a great deal (60% to 100%) on Hawala" to make payments. They contended that "the uniqueness of this system is that there is no physical transfer of currency" (p. 15). This is an inaccurate interpretation; instead, it is one of the similarities between formal and informal banking. In another instance, the news media had experts talking about the system of *Halawa*, a sweet, instead of Hawala.

According to Passas (2003), there has been little to no evidence to serve as a basis for most of the articles and reports on Hawala. Instead, information on Hawala has primarily been gathered through secondary sources such as the Internet. Owing to interest in studying Hawala, any incident even now is picked up by all media outlets and repeated all day long in the 24 × 7 media culture. The press, both in India and the United States, focuses on criminal abuses of Hawala, while hundreds of thousands of people continue to use it for legitimate purposes (Sandhu, 1998). This adds to the perception that Hawala is exclusively or primarily a criminal enterprise. The fact that Hawala is largely used for legitimate purposes could, therefore, be baffling to a foreign researcher and requires a thorough understanding of the system and the people who use it. Lack of information and growing misinformation has, therefore, generated a need for primary data collection on Hawala that is largely possible only through qualitative means.

For example, after the 9/11 attacks, the United States made a call to shut down IVTS and remittance agencies, particularly Al-Barakaat in Somalia. It was one of the largest remittance agencies in Somalia that facilitated money transfers for Somali immigrants from the United States, Persian Gulf, and other regions. After the 9/11 attacks, Al-Barakaat was suspected of being abused for terrorism funding. Many, if not most, Somali immigrants relied on this agency and others like it to send money to their home country. Omer (2002) noted, "The closure of Al-Barakaat has created a crisis of confidence in remittance operations and it is predicted that more traders will utilize informal channels, such as carrying suitcases of cash, to conduct trade overseas" (p. 18). This also hurt the already fragile Somali economy. Similarly, for many people in South Asia and the Middle East, Hawala is the only secure, fast, and reliable means of receiving or sending money. But with an increasing number of criminals, including terrorists, using Hawala and other IVTS, there are safety concerns, especially in the Western countries, about large-scale use of IVTS for criminal purposes. Most governments in South Asia and the Middle East feel that Western concerns have been exaggerated and shutting down IVTS is not only impossible but could also create problems especially due to inadequate banking in many of these countries.

In May 2002, the United Arab Emirates (UAE) government invited national and international experts, money changers, law enforcement officials, and others to Abu Dhabi, to discuss constructive ways of regulating Hawala. Again, in 2004, the International Monetary Fund (IMF) collaborated with the UAE government for the second International Conference on Hawala. It concluded that public awareness of remittance issues and more data collection and analysis are important steps toward regulating it (IMF, 2005, p. v). Most experts and law enforcement officials agree that Hawala, like any other system of money transfer, is open to abuse, but as the Abu Dhabi Declaration (UAE Government, 2002) noted, the challenge is to develop techniques to identify possible blood and drug money without disrupting the communities that use IVTS for legitimate purposes.

Research on Hawala requires an understanding that, when studying transnational crimes, legal and illegal behaviors are not perceived similarly across communities. For instance, while the United States called for regulating Hawala, the Indian government recently decriminalized it, despite its abuse by terrorists in India. Under India's Foreign Exchange Regulation Act of 1973 (FERA), it was criminal to use Hawala. In 1999, the Foreign Exchange Management Act (FEMA) replaced FERA (Government of India, 1999). FEMA aimed to facilitate external trade and promote orderly development of a foreign exchange market. It also decriminalized Hawala, bringing it under the purview of civil law. The maximum penalty was reduced from five times of the sum involved to twice the sum. This was a rational response because many people receive money through Hawala for medical emergencies, marriage expenses, house renovations, and also to meet their day-to-day needs (K. Bhargava,[6] personal communication, July–August, 2002). There are cases where elderly people were receiving small but frequent amounts of money from their sons working in the Gulf region. It would, therefore, be problematic to treat all these people the same as those involved in criminal and terrorism-related activities. Bhargava believes that most Hawala dealers are involved in noncriminal activities and argues that the only way for law enforcement agencies to avoid net widening is to infiltrate criminal enterprises and/or specifically look for Hawala dealers who work for criminals. Passas (1999) suggested that criminal laws appear to be the least effective way of dealing with IVTS, remarking that it would be more effective to address some of the key issues such as government overregulation, discrimination, and political and economic crimes, high taxes, and inefficient and nonexistent banking services (p. 5). Therefore, despite numerous calls to regulate Hawala, clearly it would be impossible to do so without understanding the complex history and nature of the system itself, along with the cultural, economic, political, and legal context within which it operates. This could be best achieved through primary data collection in the field.

With no defined population and no sampling frame, researchers have been challenged to use qualitative methods to study Hawala. Although "traditionally social science publications have tended to focus more on discussions of the findings and practicalities of undertaking research than on researchers' own personal experiences" (Sampson & Thomas, 2003, p. 184), it is all the more pertinent to explore the personal experiences of researchers, in particular the ethical dilemmas and challenges, especially when studying transnational crimes.

This raises a number of concerns especially with reference to research on human subjects and the code of ethics as laid down by the American Sociological Association (ASA). Chambliss and Schutt (2003) noted that researchers must abide by the standard ethical guidelines "concerning the treatment of human subjects," but that it is not always possible to follow these in watertight compartments (p. 43). Singer (1993) acknowledged ethics as a necessary component in all human interactions and noted that the need to abide by certain ethical guidelines is heightened when a researcher interacts with another culture that has different sensibilities and conceptual interpretations of behavior than one's own.

◆ Qualitative Data Collection, Generalizability, and Ethics

ASA ethical guidelines emphasize that research cause no harm to subjects, that subjects' informed consent to participate is voluntary, that researchers disclose their identity, that subjects' anonymity and confidentiality should be maintained unless explicitly waived, and that the benefits of research should outweigh the foreseeable risks. The following discussion highlights ethical issues associated with these guidelines arising from studying IVTS such as Hawala in the field.

Most researchers investigating Hawala start with the perception that it is largely a criminal system. This is primarily due to the media coverage of Hawala in criminal contexts only. For instance, Howard (2003), while explaining the financing of terrorism, calls Hawala an "Islamic banking (Hawala) system" (p. 78), but in fact, the system is far more broad and has long existed in predominantly non-Islamic regions as well as being extensively used for noncriminal purposes (Passas, 2003; Sandhu, 1998; Sharma, 2006). Howard also repeated Pohit and Taneja's contention that Hawala is a unique system due to no "actual money movement" (p. 78), thus not only committing the same error in understanding Hawala but also authenticating misinterpretation through repetition. It is all due to limited and one-dimensional information available on Hawala.

Misinformed researchers may cite the urgent need to understand a "criminal" and "dangerous" system as a reason to compromise some of the ethical guidelines. There are great concerns about doing so in field-based research. Given the nature of Hawala, one cannot simply put together questions and put them in the mail to Hawala dealers or customers. Since there is no sampling frame, researchers must resort to use of nonprobability methods such as theoretical and snowball sampling. Using these methods further limits generalizability, often posing the danger of ecological fallacy where findings could very easily have a negative impact on policy making as in the case of Al-Barakaat and Somali refugees discussed earlier.

In the case of studies of Hawala done by outsiders, access is further limited due to cross-cultural environments. It is possible that researchers will get very limited information and may not be able to anticipate the extent and all possible means of information for cultural, including linguistic, reasons. As noted earlier, one of the functional necessities of a system such as Hawala is trust. That is a lot more difficult to establish in the case of any foreign researcher, especially one without the language and sociocultural context.

FIELD RESEARCH AND WITNESSING HAWALA TRANSACTIONS

In recent years, researchers have started interviewing and observing Hawala dealers in person. It is easier to do so in parts of the Middle East and most of the South Asian countries, than in the United States, as most people, including law enforcement officials, are aware of noncriminal uses of Hawala rooted in its sociocultural and historical origins as well as being influenced by economic factors such as inadequate banking infrastructure.

During field research, a Hawala dealer, conducting usual business, may make a transaction in the presence of a researcher, therefore, he or she may be a witness to an illegal and/or criminal activity, raising an ethical issue about subjects' voluntary participation and informed consent. It is a second issue if the researcher only believes that he or she has witnessed a crime and reports it, thus violating the ethical guideline of not only maintaining subjects' confidentiality but also putting subjects at risk. If Hawala were a criminal banking system, then researchers might justify compromising ethical imperatives. But with Hawala being a multilayered concept, it is not easy to distinguish legal from illegal behaviors. Another issue is that a researcher may witness criminal behavior, but believe that it is not a crime, and put himself or herself at risk.

LINGUISTIC COMPETENCE, CULTURAL CONTEXT, AND VOLUNTARY PARTICIPATION

With tens of languages and thousands of dialects, it is nearly impossible for a nonindigenous researcher to get complete information. For instance, in India, states such as Maharashtra, Gujarat, Delhi, Punjab, and Andhra Pradesh are the hub of Hawala dealings. Many businessmen from Gujarat rely on Hawala because of ethnic community ties. They converse in Gujarati language especially for informal banking transactions. Similarly, there is anecdotal evidence about parallel bookkeeping for Hawala and the diamond trade in Mumbai that is often used to clean the blood diamonds from African nations. Here, researchers can collect data if they know Hindi and English, but if they want to get more in-depth information, knowledge of the Marathi language is a must. Many Hawala dealers and customers also share ethnic bonds, making it difficult for a researcher who is an outsider to find and/or approach them. In my own fieldwork on Hawala, due to my limited knowledge of languages in these parts of India, I could only focus my research in parts of Delhi and Punjab where Hindi, English, Punjabi, and Urdu are most common. The problem is more pronounced for foreign researchers who have to rely on the use of interpreters.

One of the surest means for foreign researchers to contact Hawala dealers in countries such as India is through law enforcement officials who do not hesitate to assist as interpreters. These officials not only have access to the setting but also provide safe cover to the researcher. It does, however, raise an ethical concern about coerced participation. Despite common knowledge of noncriminal uses of Hawala among law enforcement officials, a police officer is a symbol of authority and when he takes a researcher to the respondent, it creates a power equation where the respondent must participate. Crigger, Holcomb, and Weiss (2001) noted that a researcher would be seen as less of an authority figure if he or she takes part in the setting as compared to when he or she approaches it as an expert. The use of law enforcement officials in studying Hawala therefore could be seen as a gray area in terms of coerced participation.

BALANCING SAFETY AND ACCESS

Recent studies on Hawala include researchers using semistructured interviews with those Hawala dealers and their customers who do not see anything wrong with their activities. Hawala dealers and customers often share an informal relationship and normally know each other and conduct business through word of mouth (Sharma, 2006; Zagaris, 2007). Most Hawala dealers also have their regular businesses such as video stores, sweets shops, or clothing and do Hawala transactions as a side business. Criminals, however, use their own Hawala dealers who are not as accessible to researchers. Yet based on their concerns about safety and access and a mainly criminal perception of Hawala, most foreign researchers approach law enforcement officials to study *criminal* aspects of Hawala. It may restrict data collection to fewer locations and respondents and put field research itself in jeopardy.

A common (and sometimes not unrealistic) justification that researchers provide for their methods is the sense of fear and lack of security that they have while doing fieldwork about Hawala in foreign territories. On the other hand, because of the nature of research on Hawala, it is not easy to access respondents without local officials and contacts. It is not uncommon for investigative journalists[7] to unwittingly cross this line to study important issues in depth; but there are more limitations put in place for a researcher in an academic setting, because their method of study is more transparent and visible. Their findings could also have an impact in developing regulatory policies. Although codes of ethics ensure respondent and researcher safety, it may also limit access to fuller understanding of Hawala especially in foreign environments.

Marshall and Batten (2004) noted that it is important to train researchers for cross-cultural studies with a realistic understanding of the respondents' culture, history, language, and expectations. Nonetheless, even if well trained, it would be difficult for a foreigner to develop contacts in a short period of time to study Hawala. Although in their study of residential burglars, Wright, Decker, Redfern, and Smith (1992) noted that they avoided using police and probation officers as that could give the impression of there being some sort of a sting operation, in studying Hawala, the situation is different. In both studies, officials are easily available links and most law enforcement officials are aware of where persons of interest might be found.

NOTE TAKING, INFORMED CONSENT, AND ETHICS

Welland and Pugsley (2002) noted that it is not always possible to plan ethical means of informed consent, especially when working overseas. Informed consent implies that the respondents are informed about the research and their consent is formally obtained, but Tuckman (1999) argued that it needs further and often different interpretation in a cultural or ethnic context as ethical conduct is fluid and subjective (see also Chapters 19 and 28, this volume). Similarly, Larossa, Bennett, and Gelles (1981) while doing their research on family, raised questions about ethical concerns,

"Do the subjects in the research fully understand what participation in the project entails and have they given their consent to participate?" (p. 304). This is one of the most debatable ethical issues while studying Hawala. The problem is multifold while dealing with different languages as each language has its own cultural ethos.

In most studies on Hawala, respondents are unwilling to sign, including a consent form, for their voluntary participation. In the West, it is a common practice (even required) to get written consent to conduct most research on human subjects. While studying Hawala in India, researchers run into difficulties of, first, finding someone to do an adequate translation of a consent form and, then, into questions about why a respondent should sign anything if he or she is ready to talk to the researcher anyway. These objections mostly come from respondents themselves who feel uncomfortable in signing anything for a foreigner especially on the issue of Hawala. Even law enforcement officials suggest avoiding getting anything on paper from respondents who technically are involved in illegal activity and even though law enforcement officials overlook it.

There are also a few examples where researchers (more commonly foreigners) have requested to take notes. Most Hawala dealers are not comfortable about it, but some do agree. Where they do not agree, there have been examples of researchers using hidden audio/video recorders in pens and PDAs (personal digital assistants) to get interviews on the record. It is done not to be unethical, but to avoid memory gaps and to double check translations. A common justification is that, in most cases, Hawala dealers may not be able to provide thorough information in English. Even interpreters have been found to use their own judgment in translating materials instead of translating every bit of information. The interpreter may think something is repetitive and/or irrelevant, but it might be useful information for a researcher.

A researcher may also be concerned about leaving the setting without adequate information and therefore make an on-the-spot decision to use recording devices. In doing research on Hawala, it is extremely rare for a researcher to go back to the same dealers, so once a researcher has access to the setting, he or she wants to make full use of it. This does not justify violating ethical guidelines about informed consent but presents an issue that is common in cross-cultural field studies. One way researchers justify this is that they will prevent revealing the identity of respondents by destroying audio/video data when collected without an informed consent.

The guideline about informed consent is also open to interpretation when doing cross-national field research. The sociocultural sensibilities of respondents are different depending on who the researcher approaches and talks to and where. Whether written permission is obtained or not, there is a possibility of abuse of privacy and confidentiality where some respondents' actual names may not appear in news reports and articles/papers published, but the way their business areas are described, it is easy for a local resident to figure out who the respondent is.

The use of written consent clearly does not work while studying Hawala in India where many respondents agree to talk to the researcher, but get suspicious at the very mention of paperwork. It could also explain why even at many universities in India, researchers prefer not to go through any IRB-like (institutional review board) controls that may put off the respondents. There is certainly a need to find a middle ground. For that matter, a number of people who use Hawala to send money home sometimes refuse even to call it Hawala due to the fear of repercussions especially in the United States. It is improbable to get them to put their names on anything that is remotely associated with Hawala. Therefore, with the growing environment of ethnic profiling and stigmatization, it would be difficult to study the extent of Hawala in the United States except when dealing with already identified criminal abuses of Hawala. This further criminalizes the system and stigmatizes the ethnic communities that use Hawala and other similar IVTS for legitimate purposes.

The above discussion brings a number of ethical concerns and cultural issues to the fore in situations where a person may be at ease spending hours talking about his Hawala dealings, but would not sign a consent form or allow note taking. It also limits the number of interviews that a researcher could successfully conduct in a day. It may be relatively easier for an indigenous researcher who knows the local language to remember most of the information, but it could be difficult for a foreigner especially when relying on an interpreter.

LANGUAGE, CONSENT, AND CULTURAL CONTEXT

As noted earlier, most Hawala dealers do not like to sign anything no matter what kind of assurances about confidentiality are provided. Written consent therefore is almost impossible to get. While working as a research assistant in India, I often carried a letter explaining my role and sought verbal consent only, because the very reference to anything written on paper generated suspicion and limited my access to respondents. It is ironic for them to leave a paper trail for the study of a system that boasts of leaving no paper trail.

The existing evidence also suggests that errors may occur due to words that are in a certain dialect and cannot be translated. For example, in one case a researcher concluded that a big family enterprise had Hawala transactions all over the state of Maharashtra and Dubai. Although it could be a possibility, the red flag that the researcher had identified incorrectly was the use of the term *bhai* that literally translates into brother. But in a cultural context, it is a commonly used term among friends across India. In a criminal context, it is also commonly used for local goons. So depending on the context, the term has a different meaning altogether. It cannot be stressed enough therefore that in the study of transnational crimes, training and education of researchers, as well as collaboration with local researchers, is critical. It also implies that researchers from various cultural environments would bring different and necessary local, cultural sensibilities toward such studies and add to the validity of qualitative data.

ETHICAL CONCERNS ABOUT RESEARCHER'S SUBJECTIVITY

As in the case of any qualitative methods, there is a concern about spending too much time and overidentifying with respondents, that is, with those whose basic survival depends on the money received through Hawala and other IVTS. It is one thing for a researcher to be sympathetic to respondents' situations to the point where greater understanding is generated, but it could become a concern when a researcher starts identifying with the causes and concerns of the respondents to the point of losing objectivity. Along with hampering validity, it would also create ethical concerns. On a few occasions, researchers have openly discussed a Hawala dealer's identity and location because they (researchers) are convinced of Hawala being a necessary means of money transfer in many communities, thus leading to violations of confidentiality and potentially putting the dealer at risk. Similarly, in forums where researchers present their findings and discuss Hawala as a perfectly legitimate system, it is not uncommon for some audience members to volunteer unsolicited information of the Hawala dealings that they are aware of, again, putting individuals who have not given their informed consent at risk and also tempting researchers to include unverified hearsay in their studies.

Thousands of people who use Hawala for legitimate purposes have a sense of altruism toward Hawala dealers. For example, Rahim Bariek was born in Afghanistan, came to the United States in 1989, and became a U.S. citizen in 1994. He wanted to send money to his father-in-law in Pakistan and approached a local branch of Chevy Chase Bank to wire the money. The bank official told him that there was no guarantee that money would be wired safely because of high levels of corruption in Pakistan. Bariek sent a money order but that was stolen in the mail. Eventually, he went to a Hawala dealer. "It was safe, faster and cost less" (Bariek, 2001, Prepared Statement). Later, Bariek opened his own money transfer agency where his customers would normally send $20 to $400 to their families in Pakistan to buy food or pay rent. Infrequently, they would send larger amounts between $1,000 and $5,000 for marriage-related expenditure. Like Hawala operators in India, Bariek also added that in Afghan culture, a Hawala dealer is seen as an honest person without whom many people have no other way of supporting their families.

In another case, in Jalandhar (Punjab, India), a Hawala dealer worked mostly for a local grocer and sometimes managed to get in touch with other small businessmen who provided him with cash to make local Hawala payments. The dealer felt that there was nothing wrong about his actions as he was merely helping. The families that receive money through dealers treat them as one of their own. Some dealers have received money for families that they have known for years prior to doing Hawala transactions for them. In such cases, many Hawala dealers do not charge them any commission for receiving money for them. The common argument is that they are like a family. It adds to the sense of altruism that many Hawala dealers exhibit.

On the surface, researchers' support for Hawala may appear nothing more than a sense of empathy with those involved in Hawala transactions, especially Hawala customers, but there could be concern that a researcher may start overlooking the criminal aspects altogether, just as there is concern regarding the opposite. It is therefore a difficult balance that a researcher must maintain while exploring the complete spectrum. This balance could be partially achieved through guarding against overreaching in any instance, whether criminal or noncriminal. It is easier for a researcher to get carried away when the law enforcement officials also sit and joke around with Hawala dealers. During my field research in India, more than a few law enforcement officials joked that it is the United States that fears Hawala while many in India rely on it for daily needs. There is also a degree of cynicism that the United States did nothing to curb Hawala transactions especially during the 1980s at the height of Sikh militancy and the Kashmiri struggle that eventually turned into full-blown terrorism, but it has started to study the system after the 9/11 attacks and the suspicion that Hawala may have been used. Many law enforcement officials in India, therefore, believe that the interest in studying this system will soon die down or at least remain limited to its criminal connotation only.

Another ethical concern while doing field research on Hawala is using information that a researcher receives outside the structured research process. For example, there are scores of legal and illegal immigrants in the United States who use Hawala and other IVTS to send money to their home countries. Many refugee populations, H1 work visa holders, and students on F1 visas fall in this category. Students on F1 visas, for instance, are allowed to work for 20 hours per week, but many of them take up other jobs that pay in cash and send that money to India through Hawala. It is cheap labor to many ethnic small businesses and an easy way to make some extra money for the students.

Within the ethnic community, there is little to no criminality associated with Hawala and therefore people do not mind talking freely about it. For instance, at a social gathering, I heard about a small businessman from India who made about $800 per month (approximately 32,800 Indian rupees) in India. Going by the cost of living and buying power in India, it would mean making about $3,000 to 4,000 per month in the United States. In other words, he was financially secure and was placed in the upper middle-income group in India. Then, he decided to come to the United States and started working as a waiter and a cook in an Indian restaurant. With no documents to support his stay in the United States, he received cash payments. At nights, he worked at a gas station where again he was paid in cash. He was making about $1,800 per month that is just above 73,000 Indian rupees per month. It was more than double the amount that he was earning in India. In addition, he paid no tax on this income. Initially, he was planning to work for three to four years in the United States, live with basic minimum expenses, save up some quick money, and leave. From time to time, he used Hawala to send money home with a list of latest gadgets that his family could buy to live a better life. He had come to the United States on a short-term business visa but ended up staying for years. It is not uncommon for people to share such information in ethnic gatherings where a researcher is only a participant in a cultural event, but ends up with information on Hawala and sees it as useful enough to include in a study. But with increased emphasis on criminal aspects of Hawala, the ethics of doing so are suspect, especially with more and more focus on certain ethnic neighborhoods.

Hawala, like any other system, is open to abuse, but to focus on its one aspect only leads to inadequate policies about regulating it as well as creating social and cultural alienation among immigrant (legal and illegal) groups especially of lower socioeconomic status. This is why law enforcement agencies in India are more interested in differentiating between criminal and noncriminal Hawala transactions and replaced FERA by FEMA. It is also a common belief in India that criminals can use any formal banking system as well as Hawala. It is no secret that drug dealers have long used formal banks and even funded terrorism through formal bank channels. Citibank, for example, took one step in identifying possibly criminal money by putting a limit on the amount of money that could be transferred per transaction through its online banking system such as CitiNRI.[8] But all that it means is that instead of making one big transaction, customers can easily make multiple smaller transactions, especially when they need to send a large amount for medical emergencies. For those who use formal banks for legitimate purposes, it only added another layer of bureaucracy in sending or receiving money. Dialogue with people who are affected by formal and informal money transfer systems is thus critical in finding an adequate and relatively longer-lasting solution that could be aided through qualitative exploratory research.

◆ Concluding Remarks

The preceding discussion identifies some of the key ethical concerns related to use of qualitative research in situations where the legality of the behavior under study is in question. It has always been a complex process and carries even more complications when studying transnational systems like Hawala that are multifaceted. As law enforcement agencies begin to tackle cross-national crimes, it is necessary to understand social structures within which these crimes take place. To approach Hawala from an exclusively criminal perspective could end up alienating ethnic communities and further push people to use criminal organizations in the absence of access to formal banking means. Overemphasis on criminal aspects of Hawala also stigmatizes age-old money transfer practices within ethnic communities that may be rooted in ethnohistorical habit as well as bigger problems such as inadequate banking infrastructure in many developing countries. It is important therefore to sensitize researchers about on-the-ground realities in other countries as well as about the ethnic behaviors and cultural practices in the immigrant communities in the United States.

Qualitative methods provide a productive first step in the direction of exploring various behaviors associated with Hawala, but also present a number of ethical issues. Punch (1986) acknowledged that while doing qualitative research one of the hurdles is the lack of consensus within the research community. Academic conventions and peer control might be effective means of making judgment calls, but disagreements within the community about ethics have always presented gray areas. The question of what benefits of a particular research topic could outweigh its risks is a subjective one. It is more vigorous when using qualitative methods because many arguments and counterarguments are built *after* the data collection, making it difficult to judge risk and benefit of every incident that required on the spot decision making.

Research on Hawala in the current atmosphere of urgency and fears related to terrorism further increases ethical concerns. But the research in this field is of critical value because of the impact on the United States and Indian criminal justice policies to identify and respond to criminal activity while distinguishing it from the legitimate uses of Hawala. Inadequate banking infrastructure and other factors rooted in the socioeconomic reality are as critical to understand as criminal funding. As in the case of other transnational influences, to develop effective means of regulating legal and illegal behaviors, it is important to identify and understand the context within which these behaviors exist. It is common knowledge that most successful policies in the criminal justice system are the ones that people support. By focusing on criminal aspects of Hawala, there could be a problem of net widening where it appears that the criminal justice system throws a net and gets as many people in its net as possible. It is important to recognize that like any other banking system, Hawala is also prone to criminal abuses.

ETHICS OF FUNDING

One related problem about looking at the big picture could be tied with the funding available for research on such issues. In most instances, there is money available to study use of Hawala in terrorism funding and human and drug trafficking. It is necessary that the federal, state, and local funding agencies see the utility of understanding Hawala as a whole to develop better, more effective regulatory policies without alienating any groups.

By developing a more thorough understanding of Hawala, it would also be easier for law enforcement agencies across nations to collaborate. In many instances, law enforcement officials in India have pointed out both reluctance and inability to approach these problems from the United States' perspective. One of the common arguments is that Hawala is a consequence of a number of factors and as long as those factors exist, people will continue to use Hawala. Therefore, instead of stigmatizing the use of Hawala, it could be more useful to identify and tackle those factors. For instance, after the Abu Dhabi conference, one of the recommendations was to provide support to developing countries to improve their banking infrastructures as well as encourage government transparency. There are instances where politicians, bureaucrats, and businesses have used Hawala to launder money, but due to political corruption and a lethargic criminal justice system, many people with higher socioeconomic status get away with little to no punishment. It is difficult to change people's perceptions about Hawala in such environments and would be more beneficial to provide incentives to improve the criminal justice system in many of these countries. This is not to suggest that criminals do not abuse Hawala system, but only that there are a number of people who use Hawala for noncriminal purposes. People's perceptions and behaviors can be influenced gradually, but by approaching the situation from an outright criminal angle it may create more cynicism toward the law enforcement agencies in the environments where Hawala dealers are considered altruistic, while political institutions have very little legitimacy in people's opinion.

◆ Notes

1. Hawala is also spelled as havala, hawalla, and havallah.
2. Passas (2002, p. 8) defined IVTS as any network or mechanism used to transfer funds or value from place to place either without leaving a formal paper trail of the entire transaction or without going through regulated financial institutions.
3. The current exchange rate is about 1 U.S. dollar = 41 Indian rupees.
4. It has been reported that Mohamed Atta, the ring leader of the 9/11 attacks received money through interbank wire transfer to Sun Trust bank in Florida. It is alleged that the money was wired from Egypt or UAE. Adam Cohen (2001, October 1), CNN.
5. In early 2002, the Deputy Secretary of the U.S. Treasury, Kenneth Dam, visited India and urged the then Finance Minister of India, Yashwant Sinha, to regulate Hawala transactions on the Indian side.
6. Kuldip Bhargava was at the time working as the Special Director of the Enforcement Directorate (ED), Central Bureau of Investigation, New Delhi, India. ED is the key investigating agency in India, looking into the incidents of Hawala, corruption, and terrorism funding.
7. Daniel Pearl, a reporter with *The Wall Street Journal*, was interested in studying Hawala and its abuse for terrorism funding, with particular focus on links between Pakistan's Inter-Services Intelligence, Al-Qaeda, and shoe bomber Richard Reid. He was kidnapped and killed by terrorists in Karachi, Pakistan, in 2002. Among other things, the incident also raised questions about safety of investigative reporters as well as how far one could go in trying to understand the complete picture with regard to any issue. There are more and more researchers and reporters who want to study various issues in depth instead of presenting a superficial picture and therefore ethical and safety concerns about field research, especially in other countries, gain momentum.
8. CitiNRI is a service specifically targeted at nonresident Indians (NRIs) who have family members in India. They get ATM cards to operate their Citibank accounts in the United States as well as India. In most cases, NRIs would give one card to their family members in India. It also saves the trouble of physically carrying money to India. One can simply deposit the money in his or her account in the United States in dollars and withdraw in India, in Indian rupees.

◆ References

The 9/11 Commission Report. (2004). *Final report of the national commission on terrorist attacks upon the United States*. New York: W. W. Norton.
Bariek, R. (2001, November 14). *Prepared statement of Mr. Rahim Bareik. Hearing on Hawala and underground terrorist financing mechanisms*. Washington, DC: Subcommittee on International Trade and Finance, U.S. Senate Committee on Banking, Housing and Urban Affairs. Retrieved May 1, 2008, from http://banking.senate.gov/01_11hrg/111401/bariek.htm
Chambliss, D. F., & Schutt, R. K. (2003). *Making sense of the social world: Methods of investigation* (2nd ed.). Thousand Oaks, CA: Pine Forge Press.
Cohen, A. (2001, October 1). *Following the money. Freeze! How the U.S. plans to attack terror by shutting down its financial supply lines*. CNN. Retrieved November 19, 2007, from http://www.cnn.com/ALLPOLITICS/time/2001/10/08/money.html
Crigger, N. J., Holcomb, L., & Weiss, J. (2001). Fundamentalism, multiculturalism, and problems conducting research with populations in

developing nations. *Nursing Ethics, 8*(5), 459–469.

Government of India. (1999). *The Foreign Exchange Management Act, 1999 (FEMA)*. New Delhi, India: Author. Retrieved August 17, 2007, from http://finmin.nic.in/the_ministry/dept_revenue/fema_directorate/index.html

Howard, R. D. (2003). Understanding Al Qaeda's application of the new terrorism: The key to victory in the current campaign. In D. H. Russell & L. S. Reid (Eds.), *Terrorism and counterterrorism* (pp. 75–85). New York: Guilford Press.

International Monetary Fund. (2005). *Regulatory frameworks for Hawala and other remittance systems*. Washington, DC: IMF Publication Services, Monetary and Financial Systems Department.

Jain, L. C. (1929). *Indigenous banking in India*. London: MacMillan.

Kashyap, N. (2002, Summer). Hundi system (bill of exchange) in amber during the seventeenth century. *Studies in Humanities and Social Sciences, IX,* 1. Indian Institute of Advanced Technology, Shimla, India.

Lakhani, D. (n.d). *Income tax statute: Definitions of Hundis*. Retrieved August 17, 2007, from www.incometaxindia.gov.in/circulars/1977/Cir221.asp

Larossa, R., Bennett, L. A., & Gelles, R. J. (1981). Ethical dilemmas in qualitative family research. *Journal of Marriage and the Family, 43*(2), 303–313.

Markovits, C. (2001). The global world of Indian merchants, 1750–1947. In *Cambridge Studies in Indian History and Society: Vol. 6*. Paris: Centre National de la Recherche Scientifique.

Marshall, A., & Batten, S. (2004, September). Researching across cultures: Issues of ethics and power. Forum: Qualitative Social Research. *Online Journal, 5*(3). Retrieved June 29, 2007, from http://www.qualitative-research.net/fqs-texte/3-04/04-3-39-e.htm

Omer, A. (2002). *A report on supporting systems and procedures for the effective regulation and monitoring of Somali Remittance Companies (Hawala)*. Somalia: United Nations Development Program. Retrieved May 6, 2008, from http://mirror.undp.org/somalia/Remittance/ssp-hawala.pdf

Passas, N. (1999). *Informal value transfer systems and criminal organizations: A study into so-called underground banking networks*. The Hague: The Netherlands Research and Documentation Centre (WODC), The Hague by the Ministry of Justice.

Passas, N. (2002). *Informal value transfer systems, money laundering and terrorism*. Unpublished Interim report to Financial Crimes Enforcement Network. The Hague: The Hague, Netherlands (FinCEN) and the National Institute of Justice (NIJ).

Passas, N. (2003). Hawala and other informal value transfer systems: How to regulate them? *Journal of Risk Management, 5*(2), 49–59.

Pohit, S., & Taneja, N. (2000). *India's informal trade with Bangladesh: A qualitative assessment*. Center for International Private Enterprise, Washington, DC. Retrieved November 24, 2002, from www.cipe.org

Punch, M. (1986). *The politics and ethics of fieldwork*. Beverly Hills, CA: Sage.

Sampson, H., & Thomas, M. (2003). Risk and responsibility. *Qualitative Research, 3*(2), 165–189.

Sandhu, H. S. (1998). Hawala: A good old vehicle for the movement of bad money. *Laundering News, 2,* 2.

Sharma, D. (2005, November). *Problems in regulating Hawala*. Paper presented at the annual conference of American Society of Criminology, Toronto, Ontario, Canada.

Sharma, D. (2006). Historical traces of Hundi, socio-cultural understanding and criminal abuses of Hawala. *International Criminal Justice Review, 16*(2), 99–121.

Singer, P. (1993). *How are we to live? Ethics in an age of self-interest*. Melbourne, Australia: Text Publishing.

Tuckman, B. W. (1999). *Conducting educational research* (5th ed.). Orlando, FL: Harcourt Brace.

UAE Government. (2002, May 16). *Abu Dhabi Declaration on Hawala*. Presented at the

First International Conference on Hawala at Abu Dhabi, UAE.

UAE Government & International Monetary Fund (2004, April 5). *Abu Dhabi Declaration on Hawala*. Presented at the Second International Conference on Hawala at Abu Dhabi, UAE.

U.S. Congress. (2001). The Uniting and Strengthening America by Providing Appropriate Tools Required to Intercept and Obstruct Terrorism (USA PATRIOT Act) Act of 2001, *Public Law* 107–56. Washington, DC: Author. Retrieved November 29, 2005, from http://news.findlaw.com/cnn/docs/terrorism/hr3162.pdf

Welland, T., & Pugsley, L. (Eds.). (2002). *Ethical dilemmas in qualitative research*. Burlington, VT: Ashgate.

Wright, R., Decker, S. H., Redfern, A. K., & Smith, D. L. (1992). A snowball's chance in hell: Doing fieldwork with active residential burglars. *Journal of Research in Crime and Delinquency, 29*(2), 148–161.

Zagaris, B. (2007). Problems applying traditional anti-money laundering procedures to non-financial transactions, "parallel banking systems" and Islamic financial systems. *Journal of Money Laundering Control, 10*(2), 157–169.

28

EPISTEMOLOGICAL DOMINATION

Social Science Research Ethics in Aotearoa

◆ Helen Moewaka Barnes, Tim McCreanor, Shane Edwards, and Belinda Borell

In Aotearoa, now widely known as New Zealand, the sovereign territory of indigenous Maori, explored and colonized by Britain and other Western nations from the 1800s onward, the ongoing impacts of the processes of illicit and unjust domination continue to reverberate (Reid & Cram, 2005). There have been profound consequences in terms of damage to Maori economy and culture (especially from land confiscation and alienation), to population health and well-being and the loss of potential and actual development. In turn, these have had a negative impact on social cohesion, justice, and equity against a background of serious disparities on all social indicators (Ajwani, Blakely, Robson, Tobias, & Bonne, 2003; Durie, 2004; Ministry of Social Development, 2006; Spoonley, Macpherson, & Pearson, 2004; Te Puni Kokiri, 1999; Walker, 1990).

On the other hand, the social agenda in this country has been substantially influenced by resurgent Maori development that has sought redress and culture change from the paternalistic colonial roots of our contemporary society. From the earliest encounters and as embodied in the Treaty of Waitangi,[1] Maori have operated from an ethic of self-determination that has historically, and in the contemporary setting, fuelled tensions between Maori and non-Maori over what form that sovereignty should take (Orange, 1987; Sharp, 1990). By warfare, diplomacy, petition, protest action, via the courts and the Waitangi Tribunal,[2] through the development of affirmative policy agendas across the spectrum of social concern, through initiatives in indigenous education and development, Maori have battled for shared power and a more equitable social order. These challenges have not been allowed to pass unimpeded by entrenched settler[3] interests. A raft of mainstream measures, in the military, legal, political, and ideological domains have been enacted to maintain colonial domination (Durie, 2004).

The tension between renaissance and resistance has been obvious in the field of social research, where the past two decades have seen an efflorescence of work in Maori theory, epistemology, and research (Bishop, 1996; Cram, 2001; Jahnke & Taiapa, 1999; Moewaka Barnes, 2000; Smith, 1999). Huge effort has gone into shifting Maori knowledge and research from the status of invisible, derogated folklore to authoritative and valued understandings that can be used in policy development and implementation, legal settlement of historical injustices (especially land claims), and in support of Maori innovation and development. Established systems of ethics regulation and monitoring, from legitimating overarching paradigms to the conduct of research, remain an impediment in the struggle to articulate and enact Maori ways of knowing, research practices, knowledge creation, and transfer.

In this chapter, we examine how Maori ways of finding out about and knowing the world have been subordinated to Western/settler epistemological traditions. By scrutinizing emergence of a particular set of ethical paradigms and practices and the ways in which these are imposed, we highlight the irony that, in this branch of epistemological endeavor, which is so concerned with sensitivity and safety, Maori approaches are still an adjunct to a rationalist model, the main purpose of which is sustaining the status quo. We provide a brief sketch of the political economy of Maori/Pakeha[4] relations in Aotearoa, outline the history of ethics in this context, and provide narratives from our research experience to illustrate ways in which dominance is created and reproduced. We refer to the importance of mundane, microlevel research processes and practices as well as tensions within the broader field of social science research ethics (Cram, McCreanor, Smith, Nairn, & Johnstone, 2006) and a wider agenda for social change within New Zealand society (Dew & Davis, 2004; Kelsey, 2002; Spoonley et al., 2004). Our conclusions draw these together to argue for strong recognition of the contributions Maori research and ethical approaches are making to social equity here and to call for change and development in ethical practices.

◆ Research Ethics in Aotearoa New Zealand

We begin with a brief account of the development of social science ethics in Aotearoa, which contextualizes the concerns we have about how Maori research ethics have been marginalized. It also contributes to the theme of "studying up" in this volume by scrutinizing the colonial system that regulates our research and practices.

In Aotearoa, Government responses to Maori claims for more involvement in decision making and resource allocation have been to engage in diverse processes of consultation. However, there is a perception that such exercises are mainly about being seen to be behaving appropriately rather than changing behavior toward more equitable power sharing (Walker, 1990). As a result, pressure has grown for fairer and more progressive engagements between Maori and Pakeha in areas such as resource management, environmental protection and sustainability, health service provision and promotion, and Maori development in general. Research has been a key mechanism for informing policy and action in these areas.

In Aotearoa, we have a very strong and complex network of health and social ethics committees that work to apply national and uniform standards (Ministry of Health, 2006) to the conduct of research in a wide range of fields (Campbell, 1995; Goodyear-Smith, Lobb, Davies, Nachson, & Seelau, 2002; McNeil, 2002). Their early roots lie in the efforts of hospital committees, modeled on the British system (Richmond, 1977). The contemporary system has arisen out of concern with emerging medical technologies in fertility and genetics in the mid-1980s (G. Jones & Telfer, 1990), but especially out of a major inquiry (the Cartwright inquiry) into informal, unregulated cervical cancer research at National Women's Hospital in Auckland. This research involved observing the effects of nonintervention in women with abnormal cervical histologies. It resulted in preventable deaths from cervical cancers, illnesses, and disabilities (Cartwright, 1988; Coney, 1988; McNeil, 1989), required support and compensation for those who suffered, and brought strong censure on the researchers involved. The inquiry gave rise to a set of national ethical standards that effectively shifted practice toward the more systematic (and litigation conscious) American model (Gillett, 1989) and has reverberated throughout university, research, legal, professional, and political communities ever since (Campbell, 1991, 1995; Daniels, 1989; Poutasi, 1989; Rosier, 1989).

As research ethics emerged onto the national agenda in the early 1990s, the academy, both funders and providers, began to invest in ethical requirements and processes, motivated by a need to manage risk to researchers, to participants, and to institutions themselves. Research proposals must now address potential risks that had hitherto been a matter of unscreened professional practice. Universities and hospitals require that research be vetted by committees that apply implicit and explicit standards. In practical terms, requirements include written participant information and consent forms, complaint processes, and provision of supports for participants in the case of possible trauma (including psychological distress) arising from the research.

There are currently three broad systems of ethical committees that may be used by researchers depending on the focus and scope of their projects: university, area health board, and the National Health and Disabilities Ethical Committees. Ethical approval is now a requirement for release of funding from external bodies and critical to career advancement of researchers. Both experience and research show some discontent with these requirements among researchers (Harris, 1988; Mitchell et al., 1994; Neutze, 1989; Paul, 1988, 2000). However, there is also general acceptance of these processes, and it is fair to say that research ethics represent an important and developing strand within social science research (Campbell, 1995; Edwards, McManus, & McCreanor, 2005; Park, 1994; Tolich, 2002).

In national ethical guidelines, Maori interests are represented via a focus on broad principles derived from institutional and legal readings of the Treaty of Waitangi that attempt to enact partnership, participation, and protection for Maori and Maori communities. Overall, the guidelines require that research relating to Maori be undertaken "in a culturally sensitive and appropriate manner" (Ministry of Health, 2006) that emphasizes consultation, inclusion, and knowledge sharing, and may specifically provide for the use of *te reo Maori, tikanga*, relevant Maori theoretical frameworks, and Maori concepts of well-being (e.g., Durie, 1994; Pere, 1991).

The disjuncture between Maori frameworks and the rationalist Western/settler epistemological system is stark. Maori epistemological and ethical schemata are essentially other and, despite advances and ambiguities, remain add-ons, widely seen as politically forced rather than critical and vital alternatives to the status quo.

The medical origins of the research ethics system in Aotearoa in part explain the mismatch with Maori research practices. Biomedical models of health operate from within positivist scientific traditions of the West (Antonovsky, 1996; Beaglehole, 2002), evoking the power relations of the objective observer operating within an impeccable methodology that ensures realist, generalizable truths. Such rationalist methodologies are incommensurable with, and intolerant of, other approaches and theories of knowledge creation and accumulation. Traditions, approaches, and methods from outside the Western epistemological frame are regarded with skepticism and hostility and are regulated, undermined, and marginalized.

Most social science research in this country is conducted within positivist frameworks with a minor deviation due to theoretical poststructuralism permitting a brittle endorsement of certain qualitative styles (Braun & Clarke, 2006; Park, 1994). At a national *hui* of Maori social scientists convened in 2006, it was clear that, while there are a number of vital nodes of Maori social science activity, they are underresourced, overworked, and fragmented (Whariki, 2007) and, therefore, not strongly positioned to join and carry debates over issues of research ethics in the face of resourced, legislated, and established settler theory and practice (S. Clarke, 2005; Gillett, 2005; Moore, 2004).

There are multiple examples, before, during, and following first European contact, of innovative Maori development from within their own cultural resources and epistemologies that could be cited here. The point is that strengths eroded by colonial processes, particularly if provided with resources and support, are available for application to many contemporary issues of importance to Maori and the public good. In critiquing settler practices, our aim is to further open a space already spoken to by many Maori thinkers and writers to encourage wider debate and understanding of Maori contributions to social science research ethics development for Aotearoa. The rationale for this analysis turns on political considerations around self-determination of indigenous peoples, a principled support for epistemological diversity, the need for equity and justice in our social order, and a broadly pragmatic approach that seeks to ensure the best possible outcomes of research through ensuring that the ethical issues are dealt with in culturally appropriate ways.

◆ Tikanga and Research

Partially in response to the National Women's Hospital scandal, Te Awekotuku (1991) stressed the importance of research responsibility and accountability to the Maori communities that it works within, warning that breakdowns would result in findings of dubious validity and jeopardize future studies.

Despite the challenges and developments led by Maori and the movement and intent shown by Pakeha, powerful mechanisms of ethical control and guidance fall well short of embracing Maori epistemologies despite having encompassed the need to shift beyond rationalist, positivist practice. This tension has some important implications for ethics and conventional ethical procedures. Both ethics committee and research funder application forms are designed from the perspective that the research design, processes, analysis, and dissemination will not be controlled by Maori but will involve Maori in some way. Applicants are asked for detailed information about specific population groups aside from Pakeha, including consultation processes, the research team's knowledge and proficiency in relevant languages and customs, ongoing involvement of groups consulted, and dissemination practices. For Maori, the perception is that these requirements are intended to engage non-Maori researchers in efforts to make their practices safe for Maori and other groups they might work with.

As a result of this emphasis, Maori members on ethics committees work within particular paradigms and references that are not necessarily very meaningful or relevant to a Maori research ethic. These dominant ethical epistemologies are not only applied to non-Maori working with Maori but also to Maori working with Maori.

What speaks to how indigenous people should conduct themselves and whose realm this is? In the climate of research ethics development described above and through the theorizing of Kaupapa Maori research[5] (Smith, 1995, 1999), a number of Maori concepts have been articulated and incorporated into Maori research practice. Contributing to these discussions, Cram (Chapter 20, this volume) outlines a number of areas that Maori may consider to be central to a Maori research ethic. Several papers (Edwards et al., 2005; R. Jones, Crengle, & McCreanor, 2006) point out the implications of these approaches for researchers and participants, arguing for processes to protect both parties.

Through the practice of research, ethical processes are evaluated by Maori and non-Maori. In a Maori worldview, many of the non-Maori practices (and in some cases also Maori) are evaluated as unethical, and it is not uncommon for us to start a research relationship by trying to rebuild some of the trust that has been lost. Although all researchers are evaluated by the people they work with, non-Maori working with Maori usually have more choice about what level of evaluation they accept from Maori and the level of detachment they feel from this evaluation.

An overriding understanding among Maori is that, if indigenous researchers do not conduct themselves with accountability to Maori ways of operating, the comeback will be much greater and more devastating than any censure that an ethics committee could deliver. As Cram concludes and we illustrate in our stories from the field, transgressions can reverberate throughout families and through generations.

As Maori, we are used to walking in at least two worlds—the diverse environments that stem from Maori worldviews and the world of the colonizer, which surrounds us. As researchers, we negotiate these worlds and the spaces between them. Meeting institutional ethical requirements is about fitting into the dominant processes, knowing what is required, and ensuring that when we come to carry out the research we will not be hamstrung by these requirements. This means that we often fill in ethics proposals in ways that keep our options open; we can then act appropriately in the Maori world without being limited by what we have written on the ethics form.

In Maori worlds, we carry out research with many ethics requirements acting as a kind of *white noise*. We work in ways that we know to be appropriate for Maori but still make sure that we fulfill institutional ethics requirements. We acknowledge that areas ethics committees focus on are useful to think through, but the processes that are central to institutional ethics are rarely of central concern to Maori.

When carrying out research, the first information that we give as Maori is who we are and where we are from, that is, our affiliations, tribal and otherwise, including our research organization. Maori who we engage with generally want to know the purpose of the research, who owns and benefits from the information, and what the dissemination processes are. The purpose of the research is also an important institutional requirement, but, for Maori, it is seen as more than what the researchers want to know and encompasses why the researchers are doing the research; what their agendas are and whether they are to be trusted (see also Cram, Chapter 20, this volume).

An example of the different importance placed on ethical processes is attitudes toward informed consent and confidentiality. Maori (researchers and participants) frequently view consent forms as a known requirement of universities; "something we fill in for Pakeha," independent of any expectations that the participant has about the acceptability of the research process. Expectations about the research relationship and our communication and accountability processes are separate and may be unspoken. This relationship-based ethic may clash with an ethics committee approach, for here relationships are in an ongoing process of negotiation, rather than a one-off decision.

Maori understand these differences and negotiate them with regular monotony acutely aware of the difference that, attaches. But, when you are of the dominant culture, there is little need to question your own worldview or sometimes even to acknowledge that you have one. The pragmatic approach that Maori take to gaining ethics approval and then acting ethically (not necessarily the same thing) enables the system to function and apparently work for Maori—Maori researchers carry out projects and regularly gain ethics approval for them. As such, it presents few challenges to the dominant way of viewing ethics.

Our experiences as a Maori research group reflects the importance of processes and building relationships over time. Research proposals are often developed over many years of engagement, informal and formal. However, since community connection and involvement in research including design, implementation, and dissemination are built into the ongoing practices of our research group, we do not fit with funder expectations and requirements, despite strongly meeting ethical obligations. Proposal forms from the Health Research Council (HRC) of New Zealand (2006) ask for evidence and documentation of consultation and networking with Maori as well as descriptions of the cultural skills and competencies of researchers. First, our immersion in Maori communities means that the dynamics do not lend themselves to such documentation. Second, we are only able to undertake the work we do because of these competencies while non-Maori researchers are able to proceed (with negative or unknown impacts) by meeting the instrumental requirements of an ethics committee. Non-Maori groups are not required to provide equivalent credentials for knowledge of English language or specific Pakeha cultural practices.

The following stories from the field illustrate ways in which the glacial pace of change affects Maori social research practice. From these examples, we have learned much about the ethics apparatus and can discern a number of states that prevail, including blocking and falling short of Maori ethical requirements. Responding to Maori challenges, we draw these insights together in our conclusions.

♦ Stories From the Field

LESSONS FROM THE FIELD: EDWARDS

In a Maori sudden infant death syndrome (SIDS) study (Edwards et al., 2005; McManus, Abel, & McCreanor, 2005), we carried out the requirements of the funder (HRC) and host institution (Auckland University), committing to the standard provisions of informed consent and confidentiality. However, we were acutely aware that gathering data from the Maori parents who had lost a baby to SIDS required far more. The project was driven by completely different concerns that turned on the safety and well-being of the researchers and our participants who, apart from their obvious loss, were frequently subjected to grueling and adversarial police and coronial inquiries that in many cases cast the tragedy as a crime to be solved, damagingly disrupting and prolonging grief processes and resolution (E. Clarke & McCreanor, 2006).

From the outset, the project was developed as a partnership between the researchers and members of the National Maori SIDS Prevention Team (MSPT; Everard, 1997; Tipene-Leach, Abel, Haretuku, & Everard, 2000) to understand the contexts in which Maori SIDS occurs so as to strengthen prevention efforts. We based our approach firmly in Maori ethical practices that considered the inherent sacredness of the objectives (to reduce preventable loss of babies) and the significant affects on the well-being of parents. These orientations to the situation and the *mana* of the people involved arose from MSPT praxis and the values of Maori research team members and guided the development of the research design and implementation.

MSPT care workers discussed possible contributors from within their caseloads and made selections based on their perceptions of readiness of the bereaved parents to give interviews and on sample diversity criteria. Care workers approached possible participants with whom, as a matter of established MSPT practice, they had firmly established and ongoing relationships, in a staged process, a minimum of 18 months after the death of the baby. Where parents agreed to participate, the individual care workers set up the meetings, attended the interviews, and provided follow-up to encompass any reactions and distress arising from revisiting the trauma.

A number of participants commented that they achieved a kind of closure through provision of a safe, secure environment in which to tell their own story from beginning to end without interruption, pressure, or deflection from investigative authorities or family members with different perceptions of events. We obtained data of the highest quality about the social and environmental antecedents of Maori SIDS and its sequelae and disseminated widely through *hui*, reports (McManus et al., 2005), and publications (Edwards et al., 2005; Edwards, Tipene-Leach, & McCreanor, in press) locally and internationally; the study has significantly contributed to understanding determinants of indigenous SIDS.

LESSONS FROM THE FIELD: EDWARDS AND MCCREANOR

"*Hauora Tane: Health of Maori Men*" was another HRC-funded project that involved authors Edwards and McCreanor. In the face of entrenched health disparities that saw Maori men, as a group, experiencing worse health than other demographic subgroups within Aotearoa, we sought to understand the social determinants of these outcomes through life story data gathered as individual interviews (Jones et al., 2006).

The university ethics committee required the usual provisions for confidentiality and informed consent. In practice, we found that these forms were at best irrelevant "red tape" and, at worst, a source of suspicion, disrupting the expected Maori processes of research and evoking questions about what would happen to the forms and who really controlled the research.

The impetus for the study arose from the work of Maori researchers who had carried out a replication of *Rapuora*, a national survey of Maori women's health (Murchie, 1984), in partnership with the Maori Women's Welfare League (MWWL). They were challenged to carry out an equivalent study of the health and well-being of Maori men and the funded research included capability building and skills development among Maori men in recognition of the low profile of the issue on official horizons and the scarcity of Maori male researchers. We knew that the issues around Maori men's health would be sensitive and not easy to articulate. We therefore adopted an approach that relied on matching interviewers and participants on both geographic and gender variables and also drew strongly on *tikanga* to guide and manage the project. Through the MWWL, we recruited men with *whakapapa* or community connections, most of whom had no research training or experience, to gather the data within each of the League's administrative regions. We provided live-in training at *marae* in Auckland, regular e-mail contact and mentoring while they were in the field, and gatherings to debrief and discuss data analysis. We engaged the male researchers we had trained to pilot test a national survey that was developed from the qualitative research and made use of the established networks to facilitate the return of the research findings to audiences in each of the districts as well as a major report (R. Jones et al., 2007) and published paper (R. Jones et al., 2006).

Because the project was set against the background of a well-regarded study, responded to Maori calls for research, and was conducted through Maori networks and processes, it was able to proceed and collect data of outstanding quality. Initial suspicion of the project, which threatened participation, was able to be allayed, not through institutional ways of proceeding with the research, but in spite of the institutional requirements that had given rise to the suspicion in the first place.

LESSONS FROM THE FIELD: MOEWAKA BARNES

In the late 1990s, I put in an ethics research proposal to a university committee, covering evaluation of Maori projects in several communities, run by four Maori service providers. We had been selected by the providers and were working with them throughout the evaluation as well as jointly appointing and supporting community researchers. Evaluation plans had been worked through and agreed to by each of the providers. This was detailed in the ethics proposal.

One comment from the ethics committee was that we could not telephone and make arrangements to carry out interviews with Maori participants; our process should be to ring, introduce ourselves, make an appointment to visit, and further explain the project. If the participant agreed, make an appointment to return to carry out an interview. These processes had not been suggested for another project we were working on with mainly non-Maori participants. This requirement was mentioned at a *hui* where we were discussing evaluation processes. A Maori researcher from another university said that they had been told the same thing and had told the committee that this is what they would do, even though they were unsure whether this would work in practice. Our response had been to write a detailed letter to the ethics committee explaining why this process would not necessarily be appropriate.

We explained that the researchers were selected in collaboration with their *iwi* and would follow appropriate processes for each situation. For example, it is not uncommon to interview someone and then be told who you are going to interview next. One elder said to me, "You should talk to our *kaumatua* down the road. I'll ring and see if he's home, then I'll take you down." Under set rules of encounter, this approach would not be possible. The prescribed ethical approach would take precedence over the wishes of these two *kaumatua*. This is not to say that flexibility is not acceptable to ethics committees, it is more that ethics forms guide one to write in a particular way, filling in set sections with set practices. It is simpler and easier to say to ethics committees "this is how we will do it" (as our *hui* participant did) rather than to explain that there will be a range of ways, and we may not be able to describe the full list of possibilities. Our explanation was accepted by the committee.

At a later date, and to another ethics committee, we filled in an ethics form in a way that left the research process open for communities and participants to have their *tikanga* needs met. This was a time-consuming process, and it would have been much simpler to fill in the form in a straightforward, one-size-fits-all approach.

Each section required some detail and an open range of possibilities. For example, to refer to the issue in the previous story, in the section asking who would make the initial approach to participants, we wrote,

> This will depend on the entry point into the research project. Some will already be involved through the collaborating *iwi* groups, some will attend the *hui* and some will be suggested by others ... some participants will directly contact

the researchers. The researchers are known in their communities. If an approach is to be made to someone who has been suggested, then the most appropriate way of contacting this person/*whanau* will be determined.... We will very much follow a process that is appropriate for the situation, for the potential participant and for their role in the community.

Issues of confidentiality also required some explanation. We wrote that we would discuss these issues in the consultation and collaboration processes and would develop protocols for identifying what information is of a more sensitive and locational nature. We undertook to look at different levels of knowledge sharing; some information could be held by the *iwi* in each site and decisions made as to what is *iwi* owned and held and what and how information is to be dispersed to wider audiences. Although confidentiality is often a cornerstone of ethics, we suggested that, in some cases, it might be unethical not to name or identify some organizations; for example, if there are particular issues that a *marae* group has with their *whenua*, the research may be used to highlight and develop strategies to deal with the issue.

In other sections, the way in which various *hui* and discussions would guide the *tikanga* were detailed. The information and consent sheets provided multiple options, to be selected at a later date, depending on the process to be followed. However, the ethics proposal also stated that written consent might be seen as inappropriate or some participants might wish to provide oral consent as a point of *tikanga*. We described how we wanted to be able to offer a range of consent options to each community and to work within their *tikanga*, consistent with the principles outlined by our university.

These principles included partnership, respect, and individual and collective rights. We felt this directed researchers to be flexible and responsive in working with Maori, rather than following a set way of conducting the research. An aside to this story is that, when working with a non-Maori researcher who was requested by a *hapu* group to carry out research using their particular *tikanga* practices, the non-Maori researcher's response was that this breached ethics. This researcher was following the preordained, individual process that had been described in the proposal, rather than one that was respectful of participants' collective approaches. In this example, it is possible to see how one set of ethics directly challenges another.

It was uncertain how the ethics committee would view our proposal. To their credit, they were very positive, and the proposal was accepted. It is likely that their trust in the process was due to some particular circumstances—the people on the committee, previous proposals by the applicant, and the applicant being known to the committee and having discussed ethics, Maori, and the Treaty with them on their invitation. Since implementation, one of the *iwi* groups we were working with wanted to incorporate the project as part of a wider strategic research direction. Because our ethics proposal had built these types of processes and possibilities into the project, we were able to be responsive and develop this direction with minimal problems. A straightforward notification to the university ethics committee followed.

One further comment on this project came from a funding committee, which felt that we had not thought through the ethical implications fully enough. This was despite the fact that this was a joint proposal put forward by researchers and *iwi* who had worked together for a decade. We had explained our longstanding *whakapapa* and research connections, our process of working together through negotiation and individual and collective decision making, but we did not have a predetermined ethical standard. Thinking through the implications would be integral and ongoing as the research progressed; it was our perception that this reliance on a relationship ethic, rather than a procedural ethic, saw our approach judged as unthought through.

A related story, illustrating the serious way we as Maori view transgressions, came about in my role as a support person for a Ph.D. student. In my master's program, the student had developed a trusting relationship with a Maori person of high *mana* who had contributed to the student's thesis. The student had found much wisdom in their conversations (interviews) and was planning to further discuss the subject for the doctorate, when the *kaumatua* died. The student sought the permission of the family to include the previous material, outlining possible processes.

The family response was supportive; they understood that there was a trusting relationship and also noted that the student would need to heed the *mana* of the deceased in any use of the data. The ethics committee would, because of institutional requirements, need to give approval before the processes could be implemented.

On the face of it, this might seem a relatively straightforward situation, but the student was aware of deep implications. To refer to our previous point about transgressions, any inappropriate use on the student's part could bring censure from the committee. This is negligible, however, in the face of what it would mean in the Maori world, where the *wairua* of the student, the student's family, and even wider could be affected for generations. To include this information is a daunting prospect, but not to include it can be unethical; the knowledge was given to be shared, in the hope of others learning and benefiting. The task with which the researcher is charged is to do it, fully understanding these issues and responsibilities.

These experiences highlight a tension between filling out a proposal in the commonly expected way and following principles such as the ones in the Treaty of Waitangi, which lead the research process to be a more flexible, iterative one.

It could be argued that confidentiality is not necessarily a Maori issue. However, confidentiality issues are illustrative of where worldviews and concepts may clash.

There is a pervasive standard of anonymity in mainstream research. In ethics forms, a researcher doesn't have to ensure anonymity but needs to explain any departure from this assumed standard. Anonymity and identity are interlinked and are a complex matter for Maori. In some *hui* (e.g., *Hui Whakapiripiri*), Maori have described anonymity as unethical and a nonstandard practice; being able to front up, face-to-face, and having stories attributed is the standard. If research is going to make a difference, then anonymity may be counterproductive—how do you tell the story of your *hapu* and colonization if you can't name and identify yourself?

If *tikanga* is about processes, then the main role of external groups such as ethics committees is to safeguard the *tikanga* of others, rather than prescribing what *tikanga* is and how it is applied in advance, implying that there is a universal right or wrong way of doing things. *Tikanga* is about ensuring that relationships and processes are in place to enable the research to follow paths that work for each participant and for each situation, many of which cannot be anticipated. The more closely that researchers are involved with the researched, the more likely it is that they will need to be responsive and adaptable and the greater the likelihood that they will be able to do so; close relationships with the local community, for example, can ensure that the appropriate people will be on board and able to provide expertise, endorsement, and guidance for the research. In this way, prescribing a right and wrong way of carrying out research may not be ethical for the participants involved.

In relation to ensuring ethical ways of conducting research and ethical implications, if we live within a Maori worldview, how *could we* as researchers transgress without serious reverberations? The care and respect (and bravery) that is needed to tread these paths is at the forefront of our minds, possible censure by the academy is truly white noise by comparison.

LESSONS FROM THE FIELD: EDWARDS

Tikanga, described as wise action and thought, draws on theory and practices validated by Maori. The most interesting and challenging ethical dilemmas are not where right and wrong are clear but rather where they are conflicted.

The following example arose in the context of a doctoral study that required university ethics approval. My research practice is informed by my personal ethics; what is wisest given my knowledge level of particular situations. The greatest concern I had was the effects that my activities would have for all concerned, on the *mana* of my participants, my people, and myself. In Maori communities that I am familiar with, the consequences to the individual and their *whanau* can remain for generations.

My personal ethics were informed by my knowledge of my own tribal (*Ngati Maniapoto*) context, having resided, watched, listened, and practiced over years of inclusion and involvement. The knowledge of the potential effects on long-term collective and personal *mana* and responsibility, together with the shame that would touch my family possibly well into the future, was foremost in my mind.

In my doctoral research, I am recording and studying the extant knowledge of elders with whom I share *whakapapa* connections. These kinships have been forged into relationships over many years and many interactions. Interestingly, actions of earlier ancestors that neither I nor the participants have known resonated through these relationships with vividness and clarity during the course of our (re)connections. The scope of our relationships meant that, as well as the topics of the research, the elders regularly discussed my development as part of their care for, and of, me and my family. Perhaps unsurprisingly, this resulted in high levels of mutual trust and my elders were supportive of me engaging in the study; when I talked to them about the possibility of interviewing them, all agreed.

However, having received my elders' ethical approval to engage in this research, enrolling in a course of doctoral study at a university meant that I was also required to apply for research ethics approval via that system; I effectively needed two sets of ethical approval. As part of my ethics application to the university, I was keen to maintain a *Ngati Maniapoto* epistemological approach consistent with my cultural grounding and the theme of my research.

Te reo Maori is one of the official languages of Aotearoa, and I wrote my ethics application in *te reo Maori* and answered the questions concisely. For the ethics committee viewing the application, this was challenging as it was believed to be the first application they had received in *te reo Maori*; translation was required. Even so members not familiar with the Maori world were left with more questions than answers and I met with the full committee to discuss the application. I explained to them in English what I was doing; although they were happy with that, they said they needed to have something for their records. Once the discussion ended, the Chair of the committee said that my discussion had greatly enhanced their understandings. Members commented that they were clearly dealing with two different systems; for me it was two different worldviews and two different ideologies. At the conclusion, the Chair requested that I write my verbal iterations up and the committee would be happy to accept the application. I pondered for a minute and asked if I might be allowed to do so orally as this was the best way I could express myself and that it was exactly what my research was arguing for. Some members of the committee felt excited by this, with a lawyer member saying that, since oral evidence is acceptable in court, oral ethics should be given the same space. The Chair, on behalf of the committee, agreed, after requesting that I speak in English to expedite approval decisions. I agreed but informed him that it would not be as relevant and contextual in English, as regards my *hapu* and *iwi* and our epistemologies. Ethical approval was granted after the Chair of the Ethics Committee had heard my tape.

We have since heard from a colleague that an ethics application in Maori to another committee was required to be resubmitted in English (J. Gavala, personal communication, June 10, 2006).

To be able to articulate something of what it means for me to work within Maori approaches, I developed a conceptual schema that encapsulates the ethical framework guiding my research. I suggest a set of *matapuna* (principles) and *uara* (values) that can be applied to Maori contexts and may have wider relevance for other settings. The three *matapuna* I propose are *tika*, *pono*, and *aroha*, terms often referred to in Maori settings. They are the researchers accountabilities to *hapu* and *whanau*,[6] namely, to act in a manner that does not detract from, but maintains or enhances the mana of the *whanau* or *hapu*. Actions are based on correctness, truthfulness, honesty, and transparency, for the benefit of the research participants and, at times of conflict, the overriding responsibility for the researcher is to focus on others.

I also suggest a set of *uara* that detail the researcher's responsibilities, first to the participants and second, the researcher's *whanau* and *hapu*. Broadly speaking, the *uara* cover relationships, communication, reciprocity (benefits and hospitality), ongoing connections, bonds and interactions, mutual respect, the researcher's place, and their spiritual and physical well-being.

◆ Conclusions

Contrasting views exist on ethical theory and practice between Maori and non-Maori and within and between different groups of Maori. Acknowledging and enabling approaches that reconcile diverse worldviews is a challenge for this generation and those to come. Reconciliation lies in the negotiation of ambivalence and contestation that is always present in journeys of development. This ambivalence and contestation is common to minority peoples who share histories where the "dominance of certain types of cultural form have had to be negotiated continually in the process of liberation and reclamation" (Ashcroft & Ahluwalia, 1999, p. 12).

These few stories plus the accumulated wisdom of the Maori literature in this area suggest that conventional ethical requirements are alien and alienating to Maori researchers and communities, and cannot provide or understand the kinds of protection and guidance needed for the successful and more equitable conduct of social research.

Ethics for Maori research takes many flexible forms and a variety of ethics frameworks and guides present themselves for consideration. These range from Western epistemologically based ethics proposals to frameworks developed by Maori, usually very strongly relationship based.

The stories that we have presented demonstrate that one size does not fit all, even within Maori research approaches. What they have in common is the commitment to honoring relationships and being guided by the researched in recognition that *tikanga* (ethics) lies with participants. This is in contrast to the dominant epistemological approach, which vests ethics with the researcher and is largely determined by preset requirements. What this lends itself to is the domination of one epistemology over another (e.g., non-Maori vs. Maori), the subordination of evolving ethical processes that would enable greater decision making and power to sit with participants and, lastly, the tendency to tread safe and preset paths rather than diverse journeys (between and within cultures).

For these reasons, some suggest separate ethics committees or processes for Maori; this is not an unlikely scenario. However, a change in focus for mainstream ethics approval may benefit both non-Maori and Maori. A greater focus on relationships, power, decision making, and intentions would lead researchers to address more underlying ethical considerations that guide processes. Evidence of relationships and processes to guide ethics and *tikanga* is a legitimate basis for ethical approval, as is the understanding that Maori are being judged and evaluated within an incredibly powerful and relevant framework.

It is acknowledged that some actions are in themselves a cause for alarm and that a shift in focus would present those vested with approving research protocols with the tension of having enough information about actions to feel that the researcher understands safety and conduct issues while not requiring so much set detail that the ethics protocols are immutable. Currently, this balance is weighted on the side of prescribed action where participants' greatest power is the refusal to participate.

♦ Maori Words Used in This Chapter

Maori	English
Aroha	love, empathy
Hapu	kinship group of multiple whanau
Hui	meeting or gathering
Iwi	tribe
Pakeha	people of European origin
Marae	gathering places
Matapuna	principles
Kaumatua	respected elder, male or female
Mana	inherited or earned prestige
Pono	honest, true, transparent
Te reo Maori	Maori language
Tika	right, correct
Tikanga	Maori practices or processes
Uara	values
Wairua	spiritual
Whakapapa	line of descent from ancestors
Whanau	extended family

♦ Notes

1. The Treaty of Waitangi is an agreement between the British Crown and Maori signed progressively between 1840 and 1841. Contested interpretations range between cession and guarantee of Maori sovereignty.

2. This is a commission set up specifically to deal with historical and other grievances (Byrne, 2005; Orange, 1987) between Maori and the New Zealand Government.

3. Following Bell (2004), we adopt the term *settler* to encompass the wide range of European (mainly British) cultural groups who have colonized Aotearoa since 1840.

4. Definitions of terms are included at the end of the chapter.

5. *Kaupapa Maori* research is a theory of research and practice based in Maori worldviews.

6. In this context, *whanau* refers also to a group that shares a common identity or belonging, for example, a group of researchers working under the banner of a university.

♦ References

Ajwani, S., Blakely, T., Robson, B., Tobias, M., & Bonne, M. (2003). *Decades of disparity: Ethnic mortality trends in New Zealand 1980–1999* (Public Health Intelligence Occasional Bulletin No. 16). Wellington, New Zealand: Ministry of Health and University of Otago.

Antonovsky, A. (1996). The salutogenic model as a theory to guide health promotion. *Health Promotion International, 11*, 11–18.

Ashcroft, B., & Ahluwalia, P. (1999). *Edward Said: The paradox of identity*. London: Routledge.

Beaglehole, R. (2002). Overview and framework. In R. Detels, J. McEwen, R. Beaglehole, & H. Tanaka (Eds.), *Oxford textbook of public health* (4th ed., Vol. 1, pp. 83–87). Oxford, UK: Oxford University Press.

Bell, A. (2004). Cultural vandalism and Pakeha politics of guilt and responsibility. In

P. Spoonley, C. Macpherson, & D. Pearson (Eds.), *Tangata, Tangata: The changing ethnic contours of New Zealand*. Southbank, Victoria, New Zealand: Dunmore Press.

Bishop, R. (1996). *Whakawhanaungatanga: Collaborative research stories*. Palmerston North, New Zealand: Dunmore Press.

Braun, V., & Clarke, V. (2006). Using thematic analysis in psychology. *Qualitative Research in Psychology, 3*(2), 77–101.

Byrne, B. (2005). Nation and identity in the Waitangi Tribunal Reports. In J. Liu, T. McCreanor, T. McIntosh, & T. Teaiwa (Eds.), *New Zealand identities: Departures and destinations*. Wellington, New Zealand: Victoria University Press.

Campbell, A. (1991). Ethics after Cartwright. *New Zealand Medical Journal, 104*(905), 36–37.

Campbell, A. (1995). Ethics in a bicultural context. *Bioethics, 9*(2), 149–154.

Cartwright, S. (1988). *The report of the committee of inquiry into allegations concerning the treatment of cervical cancer at National Women's Hospital and other related matters*. Auckland, New Zealand: Government Printing Office.

Clarke, E., & McCreanor, T. (2006). He wahine tangi tikapa . . . : Statutory investigative processes and the grieving of Maori families who have lost a baby to SIDS. *Kotuitui: New Zealand Journal of Social Sciences Online, 1*, 25–43.

Clarke, S. (2005). Two models of ethical committees. *Journal of Bioethical Inquiry, 2*(1), 41–47.

Coney, S. (1988). *The unfortunate experiment*. Auckland, New Zealand: Penguin Books.

Cram, F. (2001). Rangahau Māori: Tona Tika Tona Pono. In M. Tolich (Ed.), *Research ethics in Aotearoa: Concepts, practice, critique* (pp. 35–52). Auckland, New Zealand: Longman.

Cram, F., McCreanor, T., Smith, T., Nairn, R., & Johnstone, W. (2006). Kaupapa Maori research and Pakeha social science: Epistemological tensions in a study of Maori health. *Hulili, 3*(1), 41–68.

Daniels, K. (1989). The Cartwright Report and its implications for social work. *Social Work Review, 2*(4), 8–13.

Dew, K., & Davis, P. (Eds.). (2004). *Health and society in Aotearoa New Zealand*. Auckland, New Zealand: Oxford University Press.

Durie, M. (1994). *Whaiora: Maori health development*. Auckland, New Zealand: Oxford University Press.

Durie, M. (2004). *Race and ethnicity in public policy: Does it work?* Paper presented at the Social Policy Research and Evaluation Conference, Wellington, New Zealand.

Edwards, S., McManus, V., & McCreanor, T. (2005). Collaborative research with Maori and sensitive issues: The application of tikanga and kaupapa in research on Maori Sudden Infant Death Syndrome. *Social Policy Journal of New Zealand, 25*, 88–104.

Edwards, S., Tipene-Leach, D., & McCreanor, T. (in press). Love your woman cause it ain't nobody's fault: Maori men's grief around death of an infant from SIDS. *Journal of Death Studies*.

Everard, C. (1997). Managing the New Zealand cot death study: Lessons from between the rock and a hard place. *Journal of Community Health and Clinical Medicine for the Pacific, 4*(2), 146–152.

Gillett, G. (1989). Medical ethics: New ethical committees, their nature and role. *New Zealand Medical Journal, 102*(870), 314–315.

Gillett, G. (2005). Bioethics and cara sui. *Journal of Bioethical Inquiry, 2*(1), 24–33.

Goodyear-Smith, F., Lobb, B., Davies, G., Nachson, I., & Seelau, S. (2002). International variation in ethics committee requirements: Comparisons across five nations. *BMC Medical Ethics, 3*(E2), 1–8.

Harris, E. (1988). The Cartwright Report and consent. *New Zealand Medical Journal, 101*(865), 671.

Health Research Council. (2006). *GA207 Application form*. Retrieved November 10, 2006, from www.hrc.govt.nz/assets/doc/0809GA207form.doc

Jahnke, H., & Taiapa, J. (1999). Maori research. In C. Davidson & M. Tolich (Eds.), *Social* science research in New Zealand (pp. 39–50). Auckland, New Zealand: Longman.

Jones, G., & Telfer, B. (1990). National bioethics committees: Developments and prospects. *New Zealand Medical Journal, 103*(884), 66–68.

Jones, R., Crengle, S., & McCreanor, T. (2006). How Tikanga guides and protects the research process: Insights from the Hauora Tane Project. *New Zealand Journal of Social Policy, 29,* 60–77.

Jones, R., Crengle, S., McCreanor, T., Aspin, C., Jansen, R., & Bennett, K. (2007). *Hauora o nga Tane Maori: The health of Maori men.* Auckland, New Zealand: Tomaiora Maori Health Research Group, University of Auckland.

Kelsey, J. (2002). *At the crossroads: Three essays.* Wellington, New Zealand: Bridget Williams Books.

McManus, V., Abel, S., & McCreanor, T. (2005). *SIDS Report.* Auckland, New Zealand: Maori SIDS Prevention Unit, Auckland University.

McNeil, P. (1989). The implications for Australia of the New Zealand "Report of the Cervical Cancer Inquiry": No cause for complacency. *Australian Medical Journal, 150*(5), 264–271.

McNeil, P. (2002). Ethics committees in Australia and New Zealand: A critique. *Politeia, 18*(57), 113–119.

Ministry of Health. (2006). *Operational standards for ethics committees. Updated edition.* Wellington, New Zealand: Author [government report, no specific author].

Ministry of Social Development. (2006). *The Social Report 2006.* Wellington, New Zealand: Author [government report, no specific author].

Mitchell, E., Hassall, I., Scragg, R., Taylor, B., Ford, R., & Allen, E. (1994). The New Zealand cot death study: Some legal issues. *Journal of Paediatric and Child Health, 28*(1), S17–S20.

Moewaka Barnes, H. (2000). Kaupapa Maori: Explaining the ordinary. *Pacific Health Dialog, 7,* 13–16.

Moore, A. (2004). New Zealand's Ethics Committees. *New Zealand Bioethics Journal, 5*(2), 3.

Murchie, E. (1984). *Rapuora: Health and Maori women.* Wellington, New Zealand: Maori Women's Welfare League.

Neutze, J. (1989). A standard for ethical committees. *New Zealand Medical Journal, 102*(863), 111.

Orange, C. (1987). *The treaty of Waitangi.* Wellington, New Zealand: Allen & Unwin.

Park, J. (1994). Reflections on project design: Experience with the "Place of Alcohol in the lives of New Zealand Women" project. *Sites, 28,* 44–54.

Paul, C. (1988). The New Zealand cervical cancer study: Could it happen again? *British Medical Journal, 297*(6647), 533–539.

Paul, C. (2000). Health researchers' views of ethics committee functioning in New Zealand. *New Zealand Medical Journal, 113*(1111), 210–214.

Pere, R. (1991). *Te Wheke: A celebration of infinite wisdom.* Gisborne, New Zealand: Ao Ake Global Learning.

Poutasi, K. (1989). An analysis of the key recommendations of the "Report of the Cervical Cancer Inquiry 1988." *New Zealand Health Review, 8*(3), 3–6.

Reid, P., & Cram, F. (2005). Connecting health, people and country in Aotearoa New Zealand. In K. Dew & P. Davis (Eds.), *Health and society in Aotearoa New Zealand* (pp. 33–48). New York: Oxford University Press.

Richmond, D. (1977). Auckland Hospital ethics committee: The first three years. *New Zealand Medical Journal, 86*(591), 10–12.

Rosier, P. (1989). The speculum bites back. *Reproductive and Genetic Engineering, 2*(2), 121–132.

Sharp, A. (1990). *Justice and the Maori: The philosophy and practice of Maori claims in New Zealand since the 1970s.* Auckland, New Zealand: Oxford University Press.

Smith, L. (1999). *Decolonizing methodologies: Research and Indigenous Peoples.* London: Zed.

Smith, L. T. (1995, February). *Towards Kaupapa Maori research*. Paper presented at the Matawhanui Conference: Maori University Teachers Conference, Palmerston North, New Zealand.

Spoonley, P., Macpherson, C., & Pearson, D. (Eds.). (2004). *Tangata Tangata: The changing ethnic contours of New Zealand*. Southbank, Victoria, New Zealand: Dunmore Press.

Te Awekotuku, N. (1991). *He Tikanga Whakaaro research ethics in the Maori community*. Wellington, New Zealand: Ministry of Maori Affairs.

Te Puni Kokiri. (1999). *Progress towards closing the social and economic gap between Maori and Non-Maori*. Wellington, New Zealand: Te Puni Kokiri.

Tipene-Leach, D., Abel, S., Haretuku, R., & Everard, C. (2000). The Maori SIDS Prevention Programme: Challenges and implications for Maori health service development. *Social Policy Journal of New Zealand, 14*, 65–77.

Tolich, M. (2002). Pakeha "paralysis": Cultural safety for those researching the general population of Aotearoa. *Social Policy Journal of New Zealand, 19*, 164–178.

Walker, R. (1990). *Ka Whawhai Tonu Matou*. Auckland, New Zealand: Penguin Books.

Whariki Research Group (2007). Report to the BRCSS management group on the first National Maori Social Science Hui, Rotorua, 16–17 November, 2006. Auckland, New Zealand: Te Ropu Whariki, Massey University.

AN ETHICAL AGENDA IN DISABILITY RESEARCH

Rhetoric or Reality?

◆ Colin Barnes

Over recent years, there has been a growing interest in the ethics of social research (Hammersley, 1999). This is especially pertinent to studies that are considered overtly politically motivated and challenge conventional notions of objectivity, the elimination of bias, and academic freedom (Humphries, Mertens, & Truman, 2000, p. 3). A particular case in point is disability research.

Inspired by the writings of disabled activists and scholars in the 1980s and 1990s, the emancipatory turn in social research has had a particularly important influence on disability researchers in the United Kingdom. The emergent critique of conventional wisdom and ways of theorizing disability was extended to mainstream social research. The shift from explaining disability solely in terms of individual pathology to the ways in which environmental and cultural barriers effectively exclude people with accredited impairments[1] from everyday life was especially influential. Indeed, this sociopolitical or social model of disability approach has stimulated the adoption of a more justifiable emancipatory research paradigm that draws explicitly on disabled people's collective experience and so challenges directly the widespread social oppression of disabled people.

This chapter will review key issues in the emergence of emancipatory disability research with particular reference to the British literature. It begins with a brief discussion of research ethics in relation to the emergent critique of traditional ways of researching disability, particularly its theoretical standpoint and the disempowering role of research experts. Second, attention centers on the key features of ethical or emancipatory disability research in line with a social model framework (Oliver, 1992). This stresses an avowed commitment to the empowerment of disabled people through a process of political and social change while also informing the process of doing disability research. The third section addresses claims that the emphasis on political partiality deflects attention away from important debates about the choice of methodology and data collection strategies and their implementation when undertaking disability research.

I argue against recently expressed cynicism that openly partisan disability research has little or no meaningful emancipatory outcomes and therefore is little more than an "impossible dream" (Oliver, 1997). I suggest that research that adheres to emancipatory principles is a crucial element in the ongoing struggle for a less disabling society.

♦ Ethics and the Challenge to Traditional Disability Research

Research ethics cover those questions about what ought and what ought not to be done by researchers when undertaking social research. For Martyn Hammersley (1999, 2000), a preoccupation with ethics, or "ethicism," along with empiricism, instrumentalism, and postmodernism has become a major concern in contemporary social research. He maintains that this tendency often results in a neglect of research technique—good as opposed to poor research practice when doing social research and the type of knowledge it generates. For Hammersley, ethicism is the outcome of instrumentalism: The idea that research should have policy or practical implications and the growing scepticism or "irony" in social research commensurate with the emergence of postmodernism. This, he maintains, has led to a downplaying of the importance of the detailed analysis of the complexity of knowledge.

While Hammersley's argument may have a considerable appeal among some sections of the research community concerned primarily with the generation and exploration of the nuances of knowledge production for its own sake, it has little resonance among the general population. It may also be responsible for the growing disillusionment with much social research over recent years as it inevitably generates the question what is the point of doing social research if it is of no practical use or benefit to those being researched. This is certainly the case with reference to the bulk of social research on disability until the 1990s as it rarely involved disabled people in the research process. Moreover, the knowledge generated was overly complex, generally couched in academic and technical language and, therefore, accessible to research experts only. Hence, it had little or no relevance to disabled people and their organizations. Moreover, as most of it was founded on individual medical or deficit explanations of disability, it also served to reaffirm traditional negative assumptions about disabled people and the causes of disablement. In doing so, it helped compound disabled people's individual and collective disadvantage (Barnes, 1996; Barnes & Mercer, 1997; Barnes, Oliver, & Barton, 2002; Oliver, 1992; Stone & Priestley, 1996). The ethics of these approaches have been seriously questioned by disabled writers and critics.

Until recently, disability was equated almost exclusively with undesirable difference and individual functional limitations eased only by medical and professional rehabilitation. Hence, condemned as "second-class citizens" (Beckett, 2007, p. 15), disabled people experienced widespread social exclusion from mainstream society and were often segregated into residential institutions. Criticism of this conventional wisdom emerged in Europe and the United States in the 1960s. In the United Kingdom, the Union of the Physically Impaired Against Segregation (UPIAS) initiated a credible redefinition and sociopolitical analysis of disability (UPIAS, 1976) that resonated around the world following its adoption by Disabled People's International in 1981 (Driedger, 1989). This approach highlights the impact of disabling social and environmental barriers on people with accredited impairments or long-term health problems and, more specifically, nondisabled experts' roles in the disablement process.

The need to extend this critique to mainstream social researchers is evidenced by the experiences of disabled residents at the Le Court Cheshire Home in the South of England during the 1960s. A group of disabled residents at the Home asked academic researchers at the Tavistock Institute to investigate their living conditions stimulated by the anticipated benefits of applying social psychological insights into residential living (E. J. Miller & Gwynne, 1972, chap. 2). Little did the residents realize how severely their hopes would be dashed.

The trigger for the invitation was a dispute with management that began in the late 1950s over residents' attempts to counter the constraints of institutional living. Nursing staff in the home operated a fairly rigid regime in terms of resident's bedtimes, mealtimes, and leisure activities. Consequently, they wanted greater control over their lives. This included choosing their own bedtimes and TV programs, whether they could go to the pub or enjoy sexual relationships in their rooms. Their attempts to introduce a more liberal regime that involved them in the running of Le Court were repeatedly confounded by changes in senior staff (Mason, 1990).

Indeed, some staff and management committee members welcomed the restoration of discipline into the running of the home and a downgrading of regular consultation with the residents. The researchers were fascinated by the research issues raised in this clash of perspectives on residential life.

It was not until 1966 that funding from the Ministry of Health was obtained to conduct a pilot study. There followed an intensive investigation of attitudes and behavior in five different residential institutions, with an action research component to follow through the implementation of changes of policy and practice (E. J. Miller & Gwynne, 1972, p. 22). Le Court was placed at the center of this phase, although the research was affected by periodic "crises" with changes in senior staff and continuing concerns about consultation over how the home was run. The fieldwork at Le Court was completed at the end of 1967.

In concluding the project, the researchers, Eric Miller and Geraldine Gwynne, stressed that their role as researchers was to maintain a balanced and objective outlook and to avoid being captured by a permanent bias that appeared to take sides in the conflicts between the residents and management. Therefore, while they recognized and sympathized with the aspirations of the residents, these were considered unrealistic because of the assumed limitations of their impairments. Instead, they recommended that control within the homes should remain with the nursing staff but that they should adopt an "enlightened guardianship" approach that took greater account of the needs and ambitions of inmates (E. J. Miller & Gwynne, 1972).

Perhaps unsurprisingly, the residents concluded that Miller and Gwynne had sided with their oppressors and were simply looking after their own professional and career interests. One of the inmates, Paul Hunt, a principal architect in the research initiative, and founder of the UPIAS, bitterly condemned the researchers describing them as "parasite people." They described the researchers' primary aim was to make repressive institutions "work a little better" (Hunt, 1981, p. 40). In short, the "research experts" could not see beyond an individualistic medical approach to disability in which "the root cause of the whole problem is in our defective bodies and not in the social death sentence unnecessarily passed on us" (Hunt, 1981, p. 41).

This trenchant attack on academic research consultants for reinforcing existing prejudices and discrimination against disabled people became a central reference point for later writers exploring a new direction for disability research (Barnes & Mercer, 2006). An approach that is considered more ethically justifiable emerged from a series of seminars funded by the Joseph Rowntree Foundation titled "Researching Disability" in 1992 (Disability, Handicap and Society [DHS], 1992). To counter the disabling tendencies of conventional disability research, emancipatory disability research requires researchers to fully involve disabled people and their representative organizations in all aspects of the research process. Its primary aim is to explore and deconstruct widespread and commonsense assumptions that disablement is the inevitable outcome of physical, sensory, or cognitive impairments.

Echoing the views of Howard Becker (1967), the disabled scholar Mike Oliver (1992), in particular, expanded on this theme in specifying the following stark choice: "Do researchers wish to join with disabled people and use their expertise and skills in their struggles against oppression or do they wish to continue to use these skills and expertise in ways in which disabled people find oppressive?" (p. 102).

Until the mid-1990s, research on disability may be divided into two main areas. First, large-scale national surveys were conducted by the Office for Population Censuses and Surveys (OPCS; Harris, Cox, & Smith, 1971; Martin, Meltzer, & Elliot, 1988) and as part of a study of poverty in the United Kingdom (Townsend, 1979). These studies have documented the prevalence of impairments within the general population and the difficulties associated with such conditions in key areas of daily living. They were designed to inform discussions around possible policy changes, particularly in the social security system and social "care"[2] services so as to reduce the number of people living in poverty. Second, there has been a considerable amount of small-scale, mostly academic research into chronic illness and disability by sociologists and psychologists. These concentrated on how individuals experience and cope with their illness or impairment and its symptoms and functional limitations (Barnes, Mercer, & Shakespeare, 1999; Bury, 1997). In general, both approaches did not involve disabled people or representatives of their organizations, were based on individual deficit models of disability, and downplayed or ignored the impact of disabling physical and social environments, and their impact on policy has been negligible (Abberley, 1992; Barnes & Mercer, 1997; Oliver, 1992).

There are exceptions though; examples include Mildred Blaxter's (1976) *The Meaning of Disability* and Peter Townsend's (1979) *Poverty in the United Kingdom.* Both studies highlight the link between impairment, poverty, and the wholly inadequate service support for disabled people. It is notable, however, that the link between impairment and poverty was first brought to the nation's attention by the Disablement Incomes Group (DIG) formed in 1965 by two disabled women (Barnes & Mercer, 2003). Also, Townsend joined DIG in the late 1960s and was involved in detailed discussions with UPIAS concerning the root causes of disability in 1975 (UPIAS, 1976). But disabled people were not involved in the gestation, development, or dissemination of either of these projects, and there is scant reference in both studies of the activities of disabled people's organizations such as DIG and the UPIAS. The former is mentioned only once in the two reports and the latter not at all.

Furthermore, most of these projects affirmed their attachment to scientific ideals of objectivity and neutrality. All of which are contestable concepts (Barnes, 1996). In contrast, disability writers took their lead from critical social theory (Oliver, 1992; Rioux & Bach, 1994). In the most widely cited contribution in Britain to establishing the credentials of an emancipatory paradigm for doing disability research, Mike Oliver (1992) located it firmly within critical theory. This included anti-imperialist/racist and feminist attacks on positivist and, to a lesser degree, interpretive research on the grounds that these had failed to challenge orthodox wisdom on the causes of disability and the systematic exclusion of disabled people from everyday life.

Doing disability research from an emancipatory standpoint entails the adoption of a social model or sociological understanding of disability as a form of social oppression (Barnes et al., 1999). Notwithstanding that given recent controversies surrounding the social model of disability (Shakespeare, 2006; Shakespeare & Watson, 2001), it is important to stress that the social model "involves nothing more fundamental than a switch away from the physical limitations of particular individuals to the way the physical and social environments impose limitations upon certain categories or groups of people" (Oliver, 1981, p. 37).

Therefore, it is not a theory but provides the starting point for several sociological theories of disability (Priestley, 1998). Nor is the social model a rejection of appropriate medical or rehabilitative interventions. It is simply a tool that can be applied to the situation of all disabled people regardless of the nature of their impairment to further their empowerment (Oliver, 2004).

Researchers are therefore openly committed to advancing disabled people's political struggles by seeking to give voice to their experience and acting generally to eradicate disabling barriers in society. The early emphasis was on "conscious partiality" (Mies, 1983, p. 122) by the researcher and granting epistemological privilege to a specific social group. This praxis orientation requires researchers to become actively engaged in political struggles and function as a catalyst for exploring relations between theory, practice, and action (Touraine, 1981).

As noted above, the value-free approach has been dismissed as "politically naïve and methodologically problematic" (Back & Solomos, 1993, p. 182). This view corresponds with the assertion that disability research should strive to produce a radical critique of the disabling society. However, this position invites criticism that politically committed researchers reveal or confirm little other than their existing perception of social reality and in so doing exclude from the outset, other perspectives, actions, and beliefs (Silverman, 1998, 2001). In response, disability researchers argue that the same could be said of all social research and acknowledge instead the significance of stating clearly their ontological (the character of social reality) and epistemological (how the social world is known) positions and strive to ensure that their choice of research methodology and data collection strategies are rigorous and open to scrutiny (Barnes & Mercer, 2004). This is especially important as research projects that address politically sensitive issues are often subject to the most careful and intense scrutiny. Consequently, any flaw in the research process may be used to undermine findings and policy implications.

This is not to suggest that they are unaware that "objective partisanship" (Gouldner, 1965, 1971) is not without difficulties or contradictions but that they must address potentially counterfactual data or explanations as and when they appear within the research process.

◆ Doing Emancipatory Disability Research

Clearly then, the social model of disability lies at the heart of emancipatory disability research. It focuses on the environmental, cultural, and social barriers that exclude people with an accredited impairment from mainstream society and prioritizes disabled people's knowledge and experience (Oliver, 1990).

Nonetheless, the social model has been criticized for oversimplifying differences in the experience of oppression within the disabled population. Initially, a "standpoint" position prevailed in which disabled people's experiences and knowledge claims were generalized across all groups, but more recently, the research spotlight has shifted to explore differences in the experience of oppression, particularly on the basis of age, gender, ethnicity, and race, thus, undermining the notion of a homogeneous category of privileged knowers and turning the spotlight onto competing discourses, voices, and experiences within the disabled population (Corker, 1999). Additionally, the presumed commonality in experience and knowledge claims have been challenged by specific groups such as Deaf people, people with "learning difficulties,"[3] and mental health system users and survivors (Beresford & Wallcraft, 1997). Here, capitalizing "Deaf" refers to individuals with a "severe" hearing impairment who self-define as a distinct linguistic and cultural group (Davis, 1995). All of which is to be welcomed as it has served to enhance our understanding of the complexity and extent of the oppression encountered by different sections of the disabled population.

Furthermore, the early focus on structural and cultural forces led to criticism that social model–influenced disability research should widen its ontological gaze from "public" barriers to incorporate the feminist maxim that the "personal is political" to encompass private concerns including the experience of impairment (Morris, 1992; Shakespeare, 2006; Thomas, 1999, 2007). Notwithstanding that any discussion of disabled people's experiences remains contentious where it does not concentrate on a critical analysis of the "inner workings of the disabling society" (Finkelstein, 1999, p. 861). This is because of the danger that they become entrapped in limited or restrictive service provider agendas that focus almost exclusively on cure or care solutions that implicitly if not explicitly reinforce a personal tragedy view of disability (Barnes & Mercer, 2003, 2004, 2006).

The impetus for emancipatory disability research is to expose disabling barriers as part of the wider politicization and empowerment of disabled people (Finkelstein, 1999) and the achievement of meaningful gain (Oliver, 1997). Therefore, political outcomes are elevated to center stage when judging disability research. Oliver specifically downgrades his own work on the experience of spinal cord injury, *Walking Into Darkness* (Oliver, Zarb, Silver, Moore, & Salisbury, 1988), precisely because of its lack of a definite impact on service provision. Yet the reasons why local and national policymakers accept research findings and recommendations are diverse and rarely within the control of the researchers (Maynard, 1994). In practice, research may succeed or fail at different levels, or have an unintended impact, with any judgment liable to variation over time, or well after the research project has been completed (Barnes, 2003; Barnes & Mercer, 2004, 2006).

Emancipatory research should be judged on whether it facilitates the self-empowerment of disabled people in terms of "individual self-assertion, upward mobility and the psychological experience of feeling powerful" (Lather, 1991, p. 3). Here, empowerment and emancipation are used interchangeably and defined in terms of revealing social barriers, changing perceptions of disability, and generating political action. Alternatively, a recent tendency among some disability researchers such as Mike Oliver (1997), for example, is to suggest that the chief beneficiaries of social research are researchers themselves. This is because social researchers are accorded a particular status and are often well paid in comparison with research participants. Vic Finkelstein (1999, p. 863) referred to such confessions as "Oliver's gibe."

Further problems may arise with attempts to create a research balance sheet detailing the particular strengths and weaknesses of emancipatory disability research. Even for those pursuing a social barriers approach, the definition of oppressor and oppressed and their respective gains are not always clear-cut. Consequently, it can never be a zero-sum contest with one winner and loser; while among the winners and losers some gain more than others. Again, oppressors and oppressed are not always easily distinguished, and stable categories across different social contexts may change over time, and the former may include some disabled people in selected social situations (Barnes & Mercer, 2006). Such difficulties might only be addressed through disability researchers' protracted involvement with research participants and/or representatives of the disabled population.

Indeed, a key feature of emancipatory disability research is that it should be accountable to disabled people. The preferred option has been to ensure that control is vested in a small group led by representatives of disabled people's organizations. Thus, the emancipatory credentials of the British Council of Disabled People's (BCODP[4]) antidiscrimination project rested on its design within a social model approach and accountability to disabled people through an advisory group in which disabled people and members of organizations controlled by disabled people were in the majority. This group met every two months to review progress. The first five months were spent discussing the aims and objectives of the research with key figures in Britain's disabled people's movement, while data analysis and drafts of chapters were circulated to the advisory group and representatives of disabled people's organizations. Comments and recommendations for amendments were discussed at advisory group meetings and mutually agreed amendments were included in the final draft (Barnes, 1991, pp. xi–xix).

A further aspect to accountability is the wide-ranging dissemination of the research products in a variety of accessible formats to stimulate campaigns and legislative action. The BCODP project produced various articles in journals, magazines, and the popular press and an eight-page summary leaflet—produced in Braille and on tape for people with visual impairments. In this way, the research contributed to the further politicization of disabled people. The distribution of this and similar material added considerable weight to the arguments for antidiscrimination legislation at both the grass roots and national levels. Britain's first Disability Discrimination Act entered the statute books in 1995 (Barnes, 2003). Similarly, research sponsored by the BCODP (Barnes, 1993; Zarb & Nadash, 1994) helped stimulate the clamor among disabled people for the legalization of Direct Payments to enable them to purchase their own support services. The Community Care (Direct Payments) Act became law in 1996 empowering local authorities to provide funds to disabled individuals with which to employ personal assistants (Barnes & Mercer, 2003, 2006).

Emancipatory disability researchers have stressed the significance of transforming the interactions between researcher and research participants and the material relations of research production such as the reliance on external funding bodies (Lloyd, Preston-Shoot, Temple, & Wuu, 1996; Oliver, 1992, 1997; Zarb, 1992). All too often, the expectations and constraints from funding agencies and academic orthodoxies reinforce traditional research hierarchies and values (Barnes, 1996; Moore, Beazley, & Maelzer, 1998).

The emancipatory potential of disability research is equated with disabled people being "actively involved in determining the aims, methods and uses of the research" (Zarb, 1997, p. 52). This requires that researchers abandon traditional claims to autonomy. However, some disability writers have expressed alarm that there are signs of a new breed of disability research experts who adopt an approach similar to that of other disabling professionals

(Finkelstein, 1999). The fear is that some disability researchers claim to speak for disabled people without meaningful consultation or involvement with disabled people and their organizations. The aspiration to break down the established hierarchy and ensure researcher accountability to disabled participants raises a number of key questions about the nature of control and how it is implemented:

- Who controls what the research will be about and how it will be carried out?

- How far have we come in involving disabled people in the research process?

- What opportunities exist for disabled people to criticize the research and influence future directions?

- What happens to the products of the research? (Zarb, 1992, p. 128)

In consequence, a continuum spanning weak to strong involvement is evident. Indeed, instances of disabled participants assuming full control of research projects are rare but increasing, and this is evident in research studies involving groups of mental health users and survivors (Chamberlain, 1988) and people with learning difficulties (Goodley & Van Hove, 2005). A useful example is the Strategies for Living project, a user-led program of work supported by the Mental Health Foundation, which produced six local user-led research projects between 1998 and 2000. The main concern of many of these projects "is on alternative and self-help approaches to mental health." This focus developed out of extensive nationwide consultation with "mental health" system user groups complemented by a U.K.-wide Strategies for Living study in which 71 key informants were interviewed about their experiences of dealing with emotional distress. Each of the six reports demonstrates an innovative example of "mental health" research that is articulated, designed, and carried out by mental health systems user and survivors.

The projects distributed around England and Wales were supported through small grants (for costs), training in research skills and ongoing support to the researchers during the main period of the research. The combination of topics and research approaches has been highly innovative and had the advantage of being independent of existing statutory mental health services and thus the particular agenda attached to those services. (Nicholls, 2001, p. 3)

Examples of the projects undertaken include *An Investigation Into Auricular Acupuncture* by Carol Miller (2001) and *Research Project Into User Groups and Empowerment* by Sharon Matthew (2001).

Another notable example is the work conducted by Shaping Our Lives, a national research and development project run by service users, including disabled people, older people, people with "learning difficulties," "mental health" systems users and survivors, and support services. Formed in 1996, Shaping Our Lives has conducted extensive user-led research on service users' experiences of "social care" services (e.g., Turner, 2003).

Moreover, other work has developed around "coresearchers and cosubjects" cooperation, indicating a reflective dialogue with neither side dominating the other (Lloyd et al., 1996). Some believe that participatory options are the most realistic aspiration in the present political and economic context (Ward, 1997; Zarb, 1997), but these offer something far less than full control by disabled people (Oliver, 1992).

It is important, however, to remember that not all lay participants have the time or inclination, even if politically aware, to take control of research production. John Swain (1995) illustrated the more general experience of many researchers whereby participants tend to defer to the "research experts." This is especially so where technical matters such as devising research questions, collecting data, and analyzing data are concerned. For Swain, rather than seeking a reversal of the social relations of research production, disabled participants sought to build a "working partnership" that would generate "mutually beneficial outcomes" (Priestley, 1997, pp. 104–105).

Nonetheless, greater participant or user involvement has been given a major boost by the active support of the Joseph Rowntree Foundation, which has been a long-term major supporter of social and disability research (examples include Barnes, 1991; Morris, 1993; Zarb & Nadash, 1994). More recently, the Big Lottery's Health and Social Research Fund has also prioritized user participation in its research program and a similar focus has been developed in research programs funded by the NHS (National Health Service; Barnes & Mercer, 2006). Nonetheless, the structural constraints and inequalities between researcher and researched are not easily eliminated, particularly if the researchers are not used to having their authority challenged (Lloyd et al., 1996; Moore et al., 1998). Furthermore, some disability researchers have been reticent to acknowledge power relations and hierarchies within research teams, mostly by assuming that a consensus position is inevitable (Barnes & Mercer, 2006).

Moreover, while the use of Braille, large print, and computer disks for people with sensory impairments has become widespread, equivalent support for people with learning difficulties has been far less widely recognized (Goodley & Moore, 2000; Ward, 1997). This has been raised by studies involving people from this section of the disabled population where some of the most imaginative attempts to develop collaborative approaches have been implemented. Indeed, research has moved a considerable distance since the early 1990s toward recognizing informant's reliability as the "best authority on their own lives, experiences, feelings and views" (Stalker, 1998, p. 5). This has generated a number of innovative methodological approaches, often adopting "advocacy" models, with people with learning difficulties acting as research advisers through to conducting their own research with researcher support. Recent examples include Chappell (2000); Walmsley and Johnson (2003); and Williams, Simons, and Swindon People First Research Team (2005).

◆ Methodology and Methods

Here, methodology refers to a theory of how research should be conducted—positivist, interactionist, participatory, and emancipatory—and methods comprise the specific techniques for data collection, such as surveys or participant observation and analysis (Harding, 1987). Early explorations of emancipatory disability research tended to conflate methodology and data collection strategies and treat both as subsidiary, technical matters. In view of the complexity of the research process, whether emancipatory or otherwise, it is useful to recognize that discussions of "methodology matters" (Stanley, 1997) and warrants more than a vague commitment to pluralism, whether of methodologies or methods.

Rather than retreat into a relativist stance, the methodological criteria advocated for evaluating disability, or indeed, all social, research varies considerably between paradigms. For positivists, the emphasis is on

> internal validity (isomorphism of findings with reality), external validity (generalisability), reliability (in the sense of stability), and objectivity (distanced and neutral observer) . . . (while those within the interpretive paradigm stress) . . . the trustworthiness criteria of credibility (paralleling internal validity), transferability (paralleling external validity), dependability (paralleling reliability), and confirmability (paralleling objectivity). (Guba & Lincoln, 1994, p. 114)

More recently, the same authors have supplemented their account by noting the recent concern with achieving "authenticity" in both interpretive and poststructuralist accounts (Lincoln & Guba, 2000).

This warrants a commitment to make the entire research process transparent from design through data collection, analysis, disseminations, and recommendations. The aim is to produce an accessible and convincing account of the research procedure that is understandable to research participants and lay audiences (Maynard, 1994; Mies, 1983; Stanley & Wise, 1993). However, the use of formal tests of quality control promoted by mainstream social researchers has often hidden disablist assumptions that rarely acknowledge the specific circumstances of researching disability (Sample, 1996; Stalker, 1998).

In contrast, advocates of emancipatory disability research have concentrated on participant validation. That is, the involvement of disabled people in identifying research questions, collecting data, analyzing, and disseminating findings. The notion of taking fieldwork data back to respondents for verification is generally regarded as a key criterion, whereas collectivizing the whole process of data collection and analysis, except perhaps to a small advisory group, is infrequently practiced. Not least, achieving full participation requires additional time and resources if it is to prove effective. Only 2 of the 30 key activists who provided in-depth interviews for Campbell and Oliver's (1996) study of disability politics took up the offer to "validate" interview transcripts or read the draft manuscript. Oliver candidly admitted "we neither had the time, energy or money to make it a wholly collective production" (Oliver, 1997, p. 19). This option may result in substantial changes in the research agenda and possibly its funding, something institutions are reluctant to sanction (Barnes & Mercer, 2004, 2006; Mercer, 2002).

A further measure is the feminist assertion that the validity of their research methods can be judged effectively by the quality of their relations with research participants. Friendliness, openness, and general close rapport with participants have acquired a confirmatory status. Researchers record how their disabled participants expressed their appreciation that their views were taken seriously, and they were encouraged to express their "real" feelings (Mercer, 2002). However, such narratives cannot be considered an adequate indication of quality assurance. Also, exploiting an individual's willingness to discuss their private thoughts and/or relationships to enhance the quality of research raises important ethical considerations that are not easily resolved. This suggests much greater sensitivity to how researchers directly and indirectly influence the research process (Davies, 2000; Lloyd et al., 1996). But the problems arising from how to balance methodological concerns and political goals are rarely discussed in depth in much of the disability literature.

Conversely, researchers adhering to emancipatory principles have been keen to devise new ways of collecting, processing, and analyzing their data (Mercer, 2002), including innovative studies with disabled children (Ward, 1997; Watson et al., 1999). Some disability researchers have particularly stressed the importance of choosing a disabled person as interviewer or the equivalent (Vernon, 1997), but what little discussion has taken place has not reached agreement about how far this matching process should be extended to cover, for example, age, social class, and type of impairment. Hence, it is useful to note that

> having an impairment does not automatically give someone an affinity with disabled people, nor an inclination to do disability research. The cultural gulf between researchers and researched has as much to do with social indicators like class, education, employment and general life experiences as with impairments. (Barnes, 1992, pp. 121–122)

Therefore, it may not be a necessary prerequisite for researchers to have an impairment to do emancipatory disability research. Neither Gerry Zarb nor Pamela Nadash was disabled when working on the BCODP-sponsored *Cash for Care* project mentioned earlier. Nonetheless, the merits of employing nondisabled researchers are disputed. It is rare though for anyone to contend, like Humphrey (2000), that research knowledge may be improved by their involvement.

There have also been few attempts to involve research participants, beyond a small advisory committee, in collectivizing the processing and analysis of data. The exceptions are mainly restricted to small-scale, interview-based studies but it remains unclear how far participants defer to researcher expertise (Vernon, 1997). More generally, disciplinary and theoretical perspectives exacerbate the division between participants and researchers by influencing what the researcher records and how it is interpreted. This includes a decision about how far researchers will go in re-presenting or re-authoring lay accounts by making inferences, selecting, abstracting, and reformulating what people said or really meant (Corker, 1999; Shakespeare, Gillespie-Sells, & Davies, 1996; Vernon, 1997).

Initially, exponents of emancipatory disability research expressed uncertainty about the relative merits of different quantitative and qualitative research methods. Oliver (1997) said, "I am not sure whether interviews, questionnaires, participant observation, transcript analysis, etc., are compatible or incompatible with emancipatory research" (p. 21).

Subsequently, the majority has emulated the general trend in social research by utilizing more qualitative procedures and data. This is justified on the grounds that quantitative methods are inherently exploitative of research participants and produce less authentic data in comparison with the qualitative emphasis on intersubjectivity and nonhierarchical relationships. Even though there are some notable counterexamples, including Miller and Gwynne's (1972) much derided study of life in a residential home, a generally dismissive attitude to the quantifying method has prevailed. It was forcibly expressed by critics of the OPCS surveys who charged that reliance on postal questionnaires and structured interviews reinforced the division between research experts and lay disabled respondents (Abberley, 1992; Oliver, 1990).

Nevertheless, mainstream quantitative research has been widely exploited by emancipatory researchers to expose the extent of disabling barriers (Barnes, 1991). Furthermore, large-scale surveys were employed in the Zarb and Nadash (1994) study on direct payments and more recently on research into user-led disability service providers sponsored and sanctioned by national agencies controlled and run by disabled people; the BCODP and the National Centre for Independent Living (Barnes & Mercer, 2006). Moreover, even within feminism, there have been growing claims that experiential studies have done much less than quantitative studies to document women's social oppression (Oakley, 2000). Indeed, the "qualitative turn" in social research in general, and disability research in particular, has tended to discourage researchers from devising participant-centered structured interviews and surveys that could facilitate resistance to disabling barriers and attitudes. Again, specific methodological issues such as sampling, data processing, and constructing concepts and explanations have generated little serious debate (Mercer, 2002).

As many advocates have demonstrated (Barnes & Mercer, 2004; Mercer, 2002; Moore et al., 1998; Stone & Priestley, 1996), the process of doing emancipatory disability research throws up many unexpected issues. One of the most significant is the degree to which presumptions of objectivity and detachment remain common within the academy, while the alternative assertions of emancipatory disability research are largely unknown or contested (Barnes et al., 2002).

♦ Conclusion

This chapter has chronicled how an ethical or emancipatory research paradigm has been adopted as a distinctive approach to doing disability research by researchers in the United Kingdom. It is an approach that is rooted in the redefinition of the cause of disabled people's individual and collective disadvantage by disabled people themselves, generally known as the social model of disability, a broad-based accountability to disabled people and their representative organizations, and a commitment to social research that challenges the social exclusion of disabled people from mainstream society. Inevitably, however, its emergence has generated a range of criticisms from the increasingly diverse theoretical traditions that now engage with disability and disability research; many of which arise from the problems associated with the often difficult and controversial task of transforming these broad principles into research policy and practice. As a consequence, recent debates on data collection strategies within the disability research literature are limited and sometimes contradictory. All of which has given rise to concerns that doing emancipatory disability research is proving to be an "impossible dream" (Oliver, 1997).

Nevertheless, if such rhetoric is not to become an unwelcome reality, disability research must be judged by its capacity to facilitate the empowerment of disabled people. This is not an easy option as there are no universally agreed epistemological or methodological guidelines. In addition, the disabling tendencies of postmillennial environments and cultures will not succumb easily to individual emancipatory projects. However, the argument presented here suggests that when directly linked to disabled people's ongoing struggle for change, doing emancipatory disability research can have a meaningful impact on their empowerment, the policies that affect their lives, and the ongoing struggle for a more equitable and just society.

♦ Notes

1. The phrase *accredited impairment* is used here in recognition that impairments are both biologically and culturally determined. Many impairments such as baldness in women do not impede an individual's ability to function but result in social disadvantage or, from a social model perspective, disability.

2. The concept care is a contested concept within the disability studies literature in the United Kingdom as it implies social services users are somehow inadequate and dependent on the benevolence of nondisabled people and the state (see Barnes & Mercer, 2003).

3. The term *learning difficulties* is the preferred term used by organizations controlled and run by people who have been diagnosed with cognitive or intellectual impairments or disabilities such as People First. However, the term is also widely used to refer to people with a diverse array of conditions to include people with dyslexia and those with multiple impairments with complex support needs.

4. The British Council of Disabled People (BCODP) was renamed the United Kingdom's Disabled People's Council (UKDPC) at its annual general meeting in October 2006.

♦ References

Abberley, P. (1992). Counting us out: A discussion of the OPCS disability surveys. *Disability, Handicap and Society,* 7(2), 139–156.

Back, L., & Solomos, J. (1993). Doing research, writing politics: The dilemmas of political intervention in research on racism. *Economy and Society,* 22(2), 178–199.

Barnes, C. (1991). *Disabled people in Britain and discrimination.* London: Hurst (in association with the British Council of Organisations of

Disabled People [Renamed the British Council of Disabled People in 1997 to accommodate individual members]). Retrieved July 22, 2007, from www.leeds.ac.uk/disability-studies/archiveuk/index.html

Barnes, C. (1992). Qualitative research: Valuable or irrelevant? *Disability, Handicap and Society, 7*(2), 115–124.

Barnes, C. (1993). *Making our own choices.* Derby, UK: British Council of Disabled People. Retrieved from www.leeds.ac.uk/disabilitysstudies/archiveuk/index.html.

Barnes, C. (1996). Disability and the myth of the independent researcher. *Disability and Society, 11*(1), 107–110. Retrieved July 22, 2007, from www.leeds.ac.uk/disability-studies/archiveuk/index.html

Barnes, C. (2003). What a difference a decade makes: Reflections on doing "emancipatory" disability research. *Disability and Society, 18*(1), 3–17.

Barnes, C., & Mercer, G. (Eds). (1997). *Doing disability research.* Leeds, UK: Disability Press. Retrieved July 22, 2007, from www.leeds.ac.uk/disability-studies/archiveuk/index.html

Barnes, C., & Mercer, G. (2003). *Disability.* Cambridge, UK: Polity Press.

Barnes, C., & Mercer, G. (2004). Introduction. In C. Barnes & G. Mercer (Eds.), *Implementing the social model: Theory and research* (pp. 1–17). Leeds, UK: Disability Press.

Barnes, C., & Mercer, G. (2006). *Independent futures: Creating user led disability services in a disabling society.* Bristol, UK: Polity Press.

Barnes, C., Mercer, G., & Shakespeare, T. (1999). *Exploring disability.* Cambridge, UK: Polity Press.

Barnes, C., Oliver, M., & Barton, L. (2002). Disability, the academy and the inclusive society. In C. Barnes, M. Oliver, & L. Barton (Eds.), *Disability studies today* (pp. 250–260). London: Polity Press.

Becker, H. (1967). Whose side are we on? *Social Problems, 14,* 239–247.

Beckett, A. E. (2007). *Citizenship and vulnerability: Disability and issues of social and political engagement.* London: Palgrave.

Beresford, P., & Wallcraft, J. (1997). Psychiatric system survivors and emancipatory research: Issues, overlaps and differences. In C. Barnes & G. Mercer (Eds.), *Doing disability research* (pp. 67–87). Leeds, UK: Disability Press.

Blaxter, M. (1976). *The meaning of disability.* London: Heinemann.

Bury, M. (1997). *Health and illness in a changing society.* London: Routledge.

Campbell, J., & Oliver, M. (1996). *Disability politics: Understanding our past changing our future.* London: Routledge.

Chamberlain, J. (1988). *On our own.* London: MIND.

Chappell, A. L. (2000). Emergence of participatory methodology in learning difficulty research: Understanding the context. *British Journal of Learning Disabilities, 28,* 38–43.

Corker, M. (1999). New disability discourse, the principle of optimisation and social change. In M. Corker & S. French (Eds.), *Disability discourses* (pp. 192–209). Buckingham, UK: Open University Press.

Davies, J. M. (2000). Disability studies as ethnographic research and text: Research strategies and roles for promoting change? *Disability and Society, 15*(2), 191–206.

Davis, L. (1995). *Enforcing normalcy: Disability, deafness, and the body.* New York: Verso.

Disability Handicap and Society. (1992). Researching disability [Special issue]. *Disability, Handicap and Society* (renamed *Disability and Society* in 1993), 7(2).

Driedger, D. (1989). *The last civil rights movement.* London: Hurst.

Finkelstein, V. (1999). Doing disability research. *Disability and Society, 14*(6), 859–867. Retrieved July 22, 2007, from www.leeds.ac.uk/disability-studies/archiveuk/index.html

Goodley, D., & Moore, M. (2000). Doing disability research: Activist lives and the academy. *Disability and Society, 15*(6), 861–882.

Goodley, D., & Van Hove, G. (Eds.). (2005). *Another disability studies reader: Including people with learning difficulties.* Leuven, Belgium: Garant.

Gouldner, A. (1965). *Applied sociology: Opportunities and problems.* New York: Free Press.

Gouldner, A. (1971). *The coming crisis of Western sociology.* London: Heinemann.

Guba, E. G., & Lincoln, Y. S. (1994). Competing paradigms in qualitative research. In N. K. Denzin & Y. S. Lincoln (Eds.), *The handbook of qualitative research* (pp. 105–117). Thousand Oaks, CA: Sage.

Hammersley, M. (1999). Some reflections on the current state of qualitative research. *Research Intelligence, 70,* 15–18.

Hammersley, M. (2000). *Taking sides in social research.* London: Routledge.

Harding, S. (1987). Introduction. Is there a feminist method? In S. Harding (Ed.), *Feminism and methodology: Social science issues* (pp. 1–14). Milton Keynes, UK: Open University Press.

Harris, A., Cox, E., & Smith, C. (1971). *Handicapped and impaired in Great Britain* (Vol. 1). London: HMSO.

Humphrey, J. C. (2000). Researching disability politics, or some problems with the social model in practice. *Disability and Society, 15*(1), 63–85.

Humphries, B., Mertens, D. M., & Truman, C. (2000). Arguments for an "emancipatory" research paradigm. In C. Truman, D. M. Mertens, & B. Humphries (Eds.), *Research and inequality* (pp. 3–23). London: UCL Press.

Hunt, P. (1981). Settling accounts with the parasite people: A critique of "A Life Apart" by E. J. Miller and G. V. Gwynne. *Disability Challenge, 1*(May), 37–50. Retrieved from July 22, 2007, www.leeds.ac.uk/disability-studies/archiveuk/index.html

Lather, P. (1991). *Getting smart: Feminist research and pedagogy with/in the postmodern.* New York: Routledge.

Lincoln, Y. S., & Guba, E. G. (2000). Paradigmatic controversies, contradictions, and emerging confluences. In N. K. Denzin & Y. S. Lincoln (Eds.), *The handbook of qualitative research* (2nd ed., pp. 163–188). Thousand Oaks, CA: Sage.

Lloyd, M., Preston-Shoot, M., Temple, B., & Wuu, R. (1996). Whose project is it anyway? Sharing and shaping the research and development agenda. *Disability and Society, 11*(3), 301–315.

Martin, J., Meltzer, H., & Elliot, D. (1988). *OPCS surveys of disability in Great Britain: Report 1—The prevalence of disability among adults.* London: HMSO.

Mason, P. (1990). *The place of Le Court residents in the history of the disability movement.* Unpublished manuscript. Retrieved July 22, 2007, from www.leeds.ac.uk/disability-studies/archiveuk/index.html

Matthew, S. (2001). *Research project into user groups and empowerment.* London: Mental Health Foundation.

Maynard, M. (1994). Methods, practice and epistemology: The debate about feminism and research. In M. Maynard & J. Purvis (Eds.), *Researching women's lives from a feminist perspective* (pp. 10–26). London: Taylor & Francis.

Mercer, G. (2002). Emancipatory disability research. In C. Barnes, M. Oliver, & L. Barton (Eds.), *Disability studies today* (pp. 228–249). London: Polity Press.

Mies, M. (1983). Towards a methodology for feminist research. In G. Bowles & R. D. Klein (Eds.), *Theories of women's studies* (pp. 117–139). London: Routledge & Kegan Paul.

Miller, C. (2001). *An investigation into auricular acupuncture.* London: Mental Health Foundation.

Miller, E. J., & Gwynne, G. V. (1972). *A life apart.* London: Tavistock.

Moore, M., Beazley, S., & Maelzer, J. (1998). *Researching disability issues.* Buckingham, UK: Open University Press.

Morris, J. (1992). Personal and political: A feminist perspective on researching physical disability. *Disability, Handicap and Society, 7*(2), 157–166.

Morris, J. (1993). *Independent lives? Community care and disabled people.* Basingstoke, UK: Macmillan.

Nicholls, V. (2001). Foreword. In S. Matthew (Ed.), *Research project into user groups and empowerment* (pp. 3–4). London: Mental Health Foundation.

Oakley, A. (2000). *Experiments in knowing: Gender and method in the social sciences.* Cambridge, UK: Polity Press.

Oliver, M. (1981). A new perspective for social workers. In J. Campling (Ed.), *The handicapped person in the community* (pp. 25–59). London: RADAR. Retrieved July 22, 2007, from www.leeds.ac.uk/disability-studies/archiveuk/index.html

Oliver, M. (1990). *The politics of disablement.* Basingstoke, UK: Macmillan. Retrieved July 22, 2007, from www.leeds.ac.uk/disability-studies/archiveuk/index.html

Oliver, M. (1992). Changing the social relations of research production? *Disability, Handicap and Society, 7*(2), 101–114.

Oliver, M. (1997). Emancipatory research: Realistic goal or impossible dream. In C. Barnes & G. Mercer (Eds.), *Doing disability research* (pp. 15–31). Leeds, UK: Disability Press. Retrieved July 22, 2007, from www.leeds.ac.uk/disability-studies/archiveuk/index.html

Oliver, M. (2004). If I had a hammer: The social model in action. In J. Swain, S. French, C. Barnes, & C. Thomas (Eds.), *Disabling barriers: Enabling environments* (pp. 7–12). London: Sage.

Oliver, M., Zarb, G., Silver, J., Moore, M., & Salisbury, V. (1988). *Walking into darkness: The experience of spinal injury.* Basingstoke, UK: Macmillan.

Priestley, M. (1997). Who's research? A personal audit. In C. Barnes & G. Mercer (Eds.), *Doing disability research* (pp. 88–107). Leeds, UK: Disability Press. Retrieved July 22, 2007, from www.leeds.ac.uk/disability-studies/archiveuk/index.html

Priestley, M. (1998). Constructions and creations: Idealism, materialism and disability theory. *Disability and Society, 13*(1), 75–97.

Rioux, M., & Bach, M. (Eds). (1994). *Disability is not measles: New research paradigms in disability.* Toronto, Ontario, Canada: Roeher Institute.

Sample, P. L. (1996). Beginnings: Participatory action research and adults with developmental disabilities. *Disability and Society, 11*(3), 317–322.

Shakespeare, T. (2006). *Disability rights and wrongs.* London: Routledge.

Shakespeare, T., Gillespie-Sells, K., & Davies, D. (1996). *The sexual politics of disability: Untold desires.* London: Cassell. Retrieved July 22, 2007, from www.leeds.ac.uk/disability-studies/archiveuk/index.html

Shakespeare, T., & Watson, N. (2001). The social model of disability: An outmoded ideology? *Research in Social Science and Disability, 2,* 9–28. Retrieved July 22, 2007, from www.leeds.ac.uk/disability-studies/archiveuk/index.html

Silverman, D. (1998). Research and social policy. In C. Seale (Ed.), *Researching society and culture* (pp. 59–69). London: Sage.

Silverman, D. (2001). *Interpreting qualitative data: Methods for analysing talk, text and interaction* (2nd ed.). London: Sage.

Stalker, K. (1998). Some ethical and methodological issues in research with people with learning difficulties. *Disability and Society, 13*(1), 5–19.

Stanley, L. (1997). Methodology matters! In V. Robinson & D. Richardson (Eds.), *Introducing women's studies* (pp. 198–219). London: Macmillan.

Stanley, L., & Wise, S. (1993). *Breaking out again: Feminist ontology and epistemology.* London: Routledge.

Stone, E., & Priestley, M. (1996). Parasites, pawns and partners: Disability research and the role of non-disabled researchers. *British Journal of Sociology, 47*(4), 699–716.

Swain, J. (1995). Constructing participatory research: In principle and in practice. In P. Clough & L. Barton (Eds,), *Making difficulties: Research and the construction of special educational needs* (pp. 75–93). London: Paul Chapman.

Thomas, C. (1999). *Female forms: Experiencing and understanding disability.* Buckingham, UK: Open University Press.

Thomas, C. (2007). *Sociologies of disability and illness: Contested ideas in disability studies and medical sociology.* London: Palgrave.

Touraine, A. (1981). *The voice and the eye: An analysis of social movements.* Cambridge, UK: Cambridge University Press.

Townsend, P. (1979). *Poverty in the United Kingdom.* Harmondsworth: Penguin Books.

Turner, M. (2003). *Shaping Our Lives: From outset to outcome.* London: Shaping Our Lives.

Union of the Physically Impaired Against Segregation. (1976). *Fundamental principles of disability.* London: Author.

Vernon, A. (1997). Reflexivity: The dilemmas of researching from the inside. In C. Barnes & G. Mercer (Eds.), *Doing disability research* (pp. 158–176). Leeds, UK: Disability Press. Retrieved July 22, 2007, from www.leeds.ac.uk/disability-studies/archiveuk/index.html

Walmsley, J., & Johnson, K. (2003). *Inclusive research with people with learning difficulties: Past, present and futures.* London: Jessica Kingsley.

Ward, L. (1997). Funding for change: Translating emancipatory disability research from theory to practice. In C. Barnes & G. Mercer (Eds.), *Doing disability research* (pp. 32–48). Leeds, UK: Disability Press.

Watson, N., Shakespeare, T., Cunningham-Burley, S., Barnes, C., Corker, M., Davis, J., et al. (1999). *Life as a disabled child: A qualitative study of young people's experiences and perspective: ESRC research report.* Retrieved February 5, 2007, from www.leeds.ac.uk/disability-studies/projects/children/report.rtf

Williams, V., Simons, K., & Swindon People First Research Team. (2005). More researching together: The role of nondisabled researchers in working with People First members. *British Journal of Learning Disabilities, 33*(1), 6–14.

Zarb, G. (1992). On the road to Damascus: First steps towards changing the relations of research production. *Disability, Handicap and Society, 7*(2), 125–138.

Zarb, G. (1997). Researching disabling barriers. In C. Barnes & G. Mercer (Eds.), *Doing disability research* (pp. 49–66). Leeds, UK: Disability Press. Retrieved July 22, 2007, from www.leeds.ac.uk/disability-studies/archiveuk/index.html

Zarb, G., & Nadash, P. (1994). *Cashing in on independence.* Derby, UK: British Council of Disabled People. Retrieved July 22, 2007, from www.leeds.ac.uk/disability-studies/archiveuk/index.html

30

LGBTQ

Protecting Vulnerable Subjects in All *Studies*

♦ Sarah-Jane Dodd

The purpose of this chapter is to explore the issue of ethical research practice from the perspective of lesbian, gay, bisexual, transgender, and queer[1] (LGBTQ) individuals. The inclusion of a chapter on LGBTQ individuals within a volume such as this shows just how far both research ethics and LGBTQ rights have come in the past 30 years. There has been a somewhat parallel process between the significant improvements in our attention to, knowledge of, and protection of human subjects and the simultaneous social and political improvements for LGBTQ persons.

This chapter explores the impact of social context on both macro- and micro issues surrounding ethical research practices. It highlights the tension faced by researchers as they attempt to balance the desire to increase visibility of sexual minorities and gender queer individuals while minimizing participation risk. It also considers the particular ways in which standard aspects of ethical research practice, such as informed consent, confidentiality, and protection from harm may vary for LGBTQ individuals. The chapter culminates with suggestions for best practices to consider when conducting social science research.

Throughout this chapter, it is hoped that we can learn from the mistakes of the past where studies involving LGBTQ individuals did not adhere closely to ethical research principles (e.g., Bremer, 1959;

Humphreys, 1970; Owensby, 1941). And, it is also hoped that we can learn from the numerous excellent examples of researchers who are working hard to address the ethical issues that arise out of their work with LGBTQ samples, both during and after their projects (many references are available, but a few include Carrier, 1999; Elze, 2003b, 2005; Hooker, 1993; James & Platzer 1999; Platzer & James, 1997; Valentine, Butler, & Skelton, 2001; Woodman, Tully, & Barranti, 1995). Consequently, this chapter highlights the areas where LGBTQ persons may be especially vulnerable in research situations and where careful consideration by the researcher is essential to protect the human subjects involved.

Statistically, it is likely that *any* research involving a sample of the general population will include some subjects who overtly or covertly identify as lesbian, gay, bisexual, transgender, or queer. For example, in a national sample of members of the American Psychological Association and the National Association of Social Workers, 14% identified as gay, lesbian, or bisexual (Crisp, 2005). While in a sample of 1,940 women with co-occurring disorders and a trauma history drawn from nine sites across the United States, 6% identified as lesbian and 11% as bisexual (Savage, Quiros, Dodd, & Bonavota, 2007). Therefore, this chapter also offers some best practices for all research involving human subjects regardless of the focus of the study.

It is important to acknowledge the limits of using the term *LGBTQ* as an abbreviation to represent distinct and diverse groups as it does not honor the significant differences that exist both within the separate groups and between the groups. For example, transgender individuals have enjoyed far less progress in terms of protection from discrimination and have largely remained invisible both within the larger social context and within social science research. However, since in general many of the points raised throughout apply to all marginalized groups, especially sexual minorities, in the interest of space and for the purposes of simplicity within this chapter the groups are addressed as a whole.

♦ Social and Historical Context

Sieber (2004) pointed out that social and behavioral research occurs in a "social milieu" (p. 398), one that influences all aspects of the research process. This idea is crucial when considering research about sensitive subjects or with stigmatized groups. In fact, it has been argued that the cultural milieu and the marginalization, stigmatization, and discrimination that LGBTQ populations face makes their risk of harm even greater than for other individuals when participating in a research project (James & Platzer, 1999). These heightened risks may be exacerbated further if the study involves socially controversial behaviors, including alcohol and drug use, involvement with the criminal justice system, partner violence, and HIV/STD sexual risk behaviors (Martin & Meezan, 2003).

Society is not static; the norms and values of society are constantly evolving. Indeed, social science research plays a key role in influencing the norms and values of society as well as of identifying shifts when they have occurred. Therefore, the social context in which research occurs is vital from an ethical perspective since it has the potential to influence many aspects of the research process, from problem formulation to the theories available, which influence the framing of the question, access to (or avoidance of) subjects, the interpretation of results, and the impact of the results on programs and policy. Overlaying a social context of marginalization, stigmatization, and discrimination creates a range of potential ethical concerns throughout the research process.

In the United States, the gay civil rights movement has as its foundation the

Stonewall Riots of 1969, when gay men and lesbians resisted arrest for gathering together at a small club in New York City's Greenwich Village. Prior to the riots, narrow stereotypes of gay men as effeminate and lesbians as very masculine women prevailed. For both gay men and lesbians, their same-sex attractions were thought to be rooted in pathology (Friedman & Downey, 2002), and bisexual and transgender persons were almost completely invisible. It was believed that lesbian and gay individuals were suffering from a psychiatric illness and attempts at treatment focused on "reparative therapy," a shifting of sexual identity, or at least sexual behavior, from homosexual to heterosexual (Nicolosi, 1991).

Having gained momentum from Stonewall and scientific support from Evelyn Hooker (1957, 1958), gay activists were successful in challenging the medical and psychiatric establishment for their role in supporting the "sickness theory," which helped maintain cultural and systemic prejudices and oppression of gay and lesbian people (Gould, 1995, p. 4). In 1973, the American Psychiatric Association (APA) removed homosexuality from the *Diagnostic and Statistical Manual of Mental Disorders* (*DSM*). And, in 1975, the American Psychological Association adopted a resolution stating that "homosexuality per se implies no impairment in judgment, stability, reliability, or general social or vocational capabilities" (Conger, 1975, p. 633). Gender identity disorder still remains as a category in the fourth edition of *DSM* (*DSM IV-TR*, APA, 2000).

However, while LGBTQ persons have gained some voice in North American society, there are vast geographic differences as to the volume, safety, and security of that voice. Individuals whose sexual orientation or gender identity does not conform to societal norms are ostracized and even victimized. As a result, LGBTQ youth remain more vulnerable to suicide and other mental health issues (Elze, 2002; Roberts, Grindel, Patsdaughter, Reardon, & Tarmina, 2004), victimization in school (Elze, 2003a; Gay, Lesbian and Straight Education Network [GLSEN], 2006), lower academic achievement, and lower college attendance (GLSEN, 2006) than their non-LGBTQ peers. In addition, both LGBTQ youth and adults receive strong negative social and political messages about their sexual orientation, with some being encouraged or even forced to undergo "conversion" therapies designed to "set them straight."

Similarly, there is global unevenness for gay rights and transgender protection. So while some countries and municipalities have passed laws allowing gay marriage, including Canada, Holland, South Africa, and Spain, as well as Massachusetts in the United States, other countries still view homosexual activity as a criminal offence punishable by imprisonment or even the death penalty (e.g., Afghanistan, India, Kenya, Malaysia, Nepal, Pakistan, Singapore, Sri Lanka, Saudi Arabia, and Sudan). The difficult ethical responsibility of researchers is protecting their subjects from risk while also being mindful of the potential global ramifications of any study involving LGBTQ persons. For example, research determining genetic markers for LGBTQ individuals may be used to promote discrimination and even punishment in some parts of the world.

◆ Homophobia, Heterocentrism, and Heterosexist Bias

Homophobia is always associated with negative attitudes toward homosexuals or homosexuality and is often associated with discomfort, fear, anger, and disgust (Crisp, 2006; DiAngelo, 1997; Gonsiorek, 1988). Exploring the relationship between homophobia and heterosexism, DiAngelo (1997) defined homophobia as the "fear and/or hatred of gays, lesbians, and same-sex closeness, and heterosexism as the social and institutional power that supports homophobia and enforces heterosexual superiority" (p. 6). Heterosexist bias is rooted in the cultural assumption that "heterosexuality is normative and that nonheterosexuality is deviant and intrinsically less desirable" (Berkman & Zinberg, 1997, p. 320). Heterocentrist bias expands the notion of heterosexism to all aspects of behavior, not just sex. Given the pervasive prevalence of heterosexist and heterocentrist bias within Western culture, it is logical to assume that heterosexist bias is currently the norm in social science research. This bias affects research ethics for LGBTQ individuals in three ways, by biasing the research lens, creating invisibility, and filtering out relevant LGBTQ studies.

♦ A Distorted Lens

A heterocentrist cultural bias ensures that all problem formulations, theories, research questions, and hypotheses, even when generated by LGBTQ researchers, have an underlying heterocentrist bias to overcome, especially when researching LGBTQ-specific topics. It has been argued that research on sexual orientation cannot be "value-neutral," since all countries where sexual orientation research is conducted still have some degree of homophobia (Schuklenk, Stein, Kerin, & Byne, 1997). So, for example, when exploring the long-term relationships of gay men, the dominant cultural heterosexual norm of monogamous relationships affects every part of the research process, including the researcher's and the reader's interpretation of results. Similarly, reflecting the power structure and social context in which they exist, traditional psychoanalytic models equate healthy development with heterosexuality and therefore regard homosexual behavior as a form of developmental arrest (Deutsch, 1995). As a result, research based on these theories of human behavior and human development tends to pathologize positions on homosexuality.

Heterocentrist bias may also act as a filter for what is an "appropriate" area of study. Guided by social norms, key areas may remain unstudied, as is the case with "developmental and educational researchers [who] have overlooked the development of sexual orientation among adolescents and youth" (D'Augelli & Grossman, 2006, p. 35).

♦ The Danger of Invisibility

The second danger of heterocentrist bias is that it ensures that any study not specifically engaging questions of sexual orientation or gender identity is unlikely to consider sexual orientation or gender identity in the construction of documents, protocols, instruments, or analysis. This omission is substantiated by Boehmer (2002) who conducted a content analysis on 20 years of *MEDLINE* articles (English language only) and found that only 0.1% addressed LGBT issues. This oversight leads to distinct problems for the LGBTQ population. As Boehmer (2002) illustrated, even when researchers and funders focus particular attention on a topic, the needs of LGBTQ individuals are not a specific part of the consideration. For example, in her *MEDLINE* study, a search for "breast cancer" found 26,554 articles, but only six of those considered LGBT individuals as a separate part of their analysis. The widespread neglect of LGBTQ individuals in public health research has devastating consequences for the health of the LGBTQ community. Similar to when health care research and drug trials focused on men and generalized the results to women, the exclusion of sexual orientation as a variable of study prevents the identification of lower or higher prevalence rates of particular diseases among LGBTQ individuals. A potentially catastrophic example of omission was evident in a 28-page special issue of *Morbidity and Mortality Weekly Report* (*MMWR*—a publication of the Centers for Disease Control; Kadour, 2005). The issue focused on suicidality, and despite considerable consensus about the potential for gay youth to be at risk for suicide, there was no mention of sexual orientation in the special report (Kadour, 2005). As Kadour (2005) pointed out, "Data are a cornerstone of any public health system, and the lack of data on sexual minorities correlates with the failure of public health to address this group's needs" (p. 31). When studies do not ask their subjects about their sexual orientation or their gender identity, they are eliminating the opportunity for the particular needs of those individuals to be identified. Studies on intimate partner violence, school bullying, or cardiovascular disease that omit sexual orientation and gender identity can be used to justify programming for the issues in general but not to justify the particular need for programs specifically for LGBTQ individuals when appropriate or when warranted by the data (Kadour, 2005).

Invisibility within studies should be of serious concern to social science researchers, but also creates an area of tension for researchers to resolve. If a researcher conducting any study is asking questions about gender or relationship status, then inclusive language should always be used when asking questions (see Best Practices Arising From the Field section for specific examples). But the researcher has to make an active decision whether or not to include a question on sexual orientation, which balances the tension between the need to increase visibility, knowledge, and understanding of LGBTQ individuals and limiting the risks posed by research participation. If a researcher adds a question about sexual orientation or gender identity to a "benign" study about obesity or sleep habits, there are instantly increased safety and risk issues, which may vary depending on geographic region and study context. Once sexual orientation is added, institutional review boards (IRBs) are more cautious about the context, for example, whether it is a work-based study. How public or private the study location is will also be a consideration to make sure that a potentially vulnerable question is not asked on a public street corner. Methodology questions will also be raised since surveys offer more privacy than in-person interviews, and focus groups create even greater vulnerability than interviews. It is important therefore to be aware that the inclusion of sexual orientation or gender identity as a variable in a study creates an added layer of complexity to social science research on any topic and may shift the need for protections around privacy and confidentiality and even methodology.

◆ The Ethical Responsibility of Gatekeepers

The third concern is that within a heterocentrist perspective research gatekeepers (e.g., IRBs, journal editors, and funding agencies) may be biased against LGBTQ studies. After all, "researchers and ethics committees do not work within an ideological vacuum" (de Gruchy & Lewin, 2001, p. 867). Historically, human subject committees have rejected socially sensitive proposals at twice the rate of nonsensitive ones (Ceci, Peters, & Plotkin, 1985). When no ethical violation was present in the socially sensitive protocol, then methodological and even sociopolitical concerns were raised as reasons for nonapproval. It is not clear whether such bias continues to exist since more recent studies are not available. However, a similar experience of the IRB as gatekeeper is documented by de Gruchy and Lewin (2001). They wanted to conduct a study on "human rights abuses of gay men and lesbians in the South African Defense Force by health professionals during the apartheid era" (p. 865). The IRB rejected their proposal and as in the Ceci, Peters, and Plotkin (1985) study, methodological reasons for rejection were cited. The "rejected" authors recommended that "when heterosexism or homophobia exists, it should be openly discussed rather than hidden behind a facade of debate on scientific validity" (de Gruchy & Lewin, 2001, p. 867).

The fact that sociopolitical considerations appear to play a role in IRB decision making can have a profound impact on a researcher's choice of research topic, methodology, recruiting, and sample. Sieber and Stanley (1988) noted that "although there is nothing that forbids research on sensitive topics, there are powerful forces working against the conduct of such research" (p. 50). Researchers may avoid some research topics completely or make compromises aimed at ensuring IRB approval. This was the case for Randal Donelson who described his process of "refining" his research question and methodology because of concerns from his dissertation committee around getting IRB approval for a study proposing to explore "discourse related to homosexuality in a primary (school) classroom" (Donelson & Rogers, 2004, p. 132). In an effort to combat potential IRB concerns, the subsequent study used narrative rather than naturalistic observations. While obtaining parental consent for naturalistic classroom observations on any topic may be difficult, the concern raised was specifically around the study's focus on homosexuality (Donelson & Rogers, 2004).

IRBs are not the only research gatekeepers. Funding agencies also play a key role as gatekeepers of acceptable research and, therefore, by default decide what is important to study (Ceci et al., 1985). Similarly, journal editors serve a filtering function deciding what research is worthy of publication and dissemination (Ceci et al., 1985; Herek, Kimmel, Amaro, & Melton, 1991). For academics who rely on funding and publication for promotion, these actual or perceived biases against particular subject areas can be influential in determining choice of study topics.

♦ Potential to Do Harm? Conversion Therapy

Within a heterocentrist context, it makes sense that one area of research interest is around "correcting" homosexual behavior. Studies have focused on attempting to change a person's sexual orientation through various forms of "conversion," "reparative," or "reorientation" therapies. Early conversion therapies involved very limited samples and invasive techniques. One historical account describes studies that used "electric shock to the hands and/or genitals, or nausea-inducing drugs, which would be administered simultaneously with the presentation of homoerotic stimuli" (Haldeman, 2002, p. 260) to try to reduce or eliminate same-gender sexual desires. Specific examples include studies that investigated the efficacy of metrazol (Owensby, 1940) and pharmacological shock (Owensby, 1941) in converting homosexuality based on the premise that homosexuality was symptomatic of underdeveloped schizophrenia. And another example is Bremer's (1959) study of castration, which found that it did reduce sex drive but did not change sexual orientation.

Less invasive, though not necessarily less controversial, "conversion therapy" research used psychotherapy (Bieber et al., 1962). While Bieber et al.'s study caused no direct harm, Martin and Meezan (2003) contended that the study may have caused participants psychological harm by "encouraging them to maintain futile efforts towards changing their sexual orientation, and by reinforcing guilt and shame regarding their sexual feelings" (p. 183).

The issue of reparative therapy creates a tangled web because it is a highly charged topic that engages the scientific, political, and religious communities simultaneously. The controversy continues despite a 1998 position statement from the American Psychological Association (1998) denouncing reparative therapy and similar statements from other mental health organizations. On one side of the debate is the assertion that research and practice of reparative therapy is an ethical imperative out of

(a) respect for the self-determination and autonomy of persons, (b) respect for valuative frameworks, creeds and religious beliefs and values regarding the moral status of same-sex behavior, and (c) service provision in response to a clinical problem based on available scientific research. (Yarhouse & Throckmorton, 2002, p. 66)

On the other side is the assertion that it is unethical to use (or study) these reparative therapies "that cause harm, that are based on faulty and specious assumptions, and that incorporate societal prejudice" (Schreier, 1998). Furthermore, it is ethically inappropriate since "homosexuality per se is not an illness and does not require treatment" (Halpert, 2000, p. 19).

There are often passionate methodological critiques of studies that do claim reparative therapy led to a shift in sexual orientation. In one case, Spitzer's (2003) assertions about the efficacy of reparative therapy led to an edited volume of 26 commentaries asserting methodological limitations and refuting the claims (Drescher & Zucker, 2006). Others have leveled complaints that many of the findings in support of reparative therapy are published in non-peer-reviewed journals, where publication is secured through payment (Christianson, 2005). Social science researchers need to consider carefully the ethical implications of engaging in research on conversion therapy and other interventions of unsubstantiated efficacy, weighing the potentially harmful psychological consequences of "failed" conversion efforts against the potential benefits of "successful" efforts.

◆ Potential to Do Harm: The Ethics of Genetic Research on Sexual Orientation

It is not uncommon for genetic research to be controversial "depending on the social meaning and significance of the behavior under study" (Schuklenk et al., 1997). It is, therefore, not a surprise that the idea of a "gay gene" has been very popular in the press or that studies in support of this theory have received widespread media attention, even when there were methodological concerns and a failure to duplicate results. For example, there was considerable media attention from the popular press when Dean Hamer, Hu, Magnuson, Hu, and Pattatucci's (1993) study identified a link between DNA markers on the X chromosome and male sexual orientation. And, although the DHHS (Department of Health and Human Services) Office of Research Integrity found no misconduct in Hamer et al.'s study (Kaiser, 1997), the findings have not been duplicated even when similar methodology has been employed (Schuklenk et al., 1997). The difference in media attention paid to findings related to the identification of a gay gene and those that fail to identify a gay gene is informative.

In his very comprehensive book on "Gay Science," Murphy (1997) argued that it is not gay gene research itself but rather its application that is of concern. He supports social and political interventions aimed against discrimination and toward promoting positive views about homosexual activity as opposed to limiting gay gene research. In contrast, others raise concerns that in a predominantly homophobic world, the consequences of such research could have serious negative ramifications (Schuklenk et al., 1997), as findings could be used either to promote acceptance or to justify discrimination. It is conceivable that if a genetic connection to sexual orientation was identified, it would support the idea that sexual orientation is not a "choice," but a characteristic, similar to eye color, hair color, and gender. Such a finding may lead to a reduction in discrimination and an increase in legal protection and equality for gay men and lesbians. Unfortunately, the flip side of the possible responses is quite alarming. If a gene related to sexual orientation is discovered, then the potential discriminatory uses for the findings are many. For example, prenatal testing may be used to determine sexual orientation, which may lead to the aborting of fetuses believed to be gay, lesbian, or bisexual. Unfortunately, even if the likelihood of the misuse of genetic testing is questionable in the United States, it would certainly have the potential for use in countries where no legal protections are afforded to LGB persons. It is conceivable that such efforts may lead to a reduction in the number of LGB persons in the world, and may contribute to their further marginalization and stigmatization. In addition, the utilization of a sexual orientation gene as a way to identify individuals (especially children) who may be LGB may be especially troubling. There is the potential for the gene to be used to identify individuals who are required to go to "treatment," and perhaps worse in countries where homosexuality is illegal.

♦ Avoiding Coercion and Exploitation: Generating Fully Informed Consent

One of the most commonly noted examples of research used to justify the need for IRBs is Humphreys' (1970) ethnographic study *Tearoom Trade: Impersonal Sex in Public Places,* which involved the deception of men who were engaged in same-gender sexual activity. The researcher posed as a "lookout" for men who were engaged in public sexual activity and then used DMV (Department of Motor Vehicles) records to trace their identities and home addresses through their car license plates. A year later, the researcher went to the men's homes and recruited them to be participants in an interview under the guise that it was a community health survey.

Given this history, the issue of fully informed consent is particularly sensitive for LGBTQ individuals. Understanding this context can help researchers to approach obtaining informed consent in a sensitive and open manner. Researchers should take great care to ensure that participants fully understand the purpose of the project, the researcher's role, the level and type of participation required, and the intended plan for dissemination of findings. The fact that recruitment may occur in informal settings with "party-like" atmospheres, such as at gay pride events, gay bars, or gay-specific health fairs, should not preclude taking time to ensure that participants have not been swept along with the crowd, but rather are fully informed prior to participation.

The recruitment process and informed consent procedures should not be tainted by inappropriate or excessive incentives for participation in the study. While it is important to appropriately honor individuals for the time that they devote to a study, using excessive incentives can lead to coercion, especially for individuals with limited resources or a low income. The potential sampling pool of LGBTQ individuals can be very small and hard to recruit even in urban areas and is especially small for transgender individuals. If incentives are high enough, research participation can be a potentially lucrative endeavor; therefore, it has been suggested that job discrimination and the high cost of surgery may make transgender individuals particularly vulnerable to agreeing to participate in studies that they are not completely comfortable with (Martin & Meezan, 2003).

Privacy and confidentiality are perhaps even more precarious when researching LGBTQ youth. However, given the high suicide rates, the high dropout rates, the potential for mental health concerns, and the need for social support (Elze, 2005; GLSEN, 2006; Illingworth & Murphy, 2004; Roberts et al., 2004), research on gay youth is vital to support the development of appropriate interventions. Valentine et al. (2001) documented the lengths they went to in their U.K.-based study to ensure that they created a safe, private space when interviewing gay youth. They did not conduct interviews in schools or at family homes where interviews may have been seen or overheard. Instead, they chose community centers and other community-based settings, which offered more discreet and private spaces. They also found e-mail a useful mode of communication (Valentine et al., 2001), but caution should be taken to ensure that no record of the transaction could be located by family members.

Research on youth usually requires informed assent from the young people choosing to participate in the study, as well as informed consent from their parent or guardian. For LGBTQ youth who are not out to their parents or who experience unsupportive or even violent homes requesting parental consent for a research study involving LGBTQ issues could pose a serious risk. In such cases, a researcher may request that an independent adult advocate, who has an existing relationship with the youth through a social service agency or school, be used to establish informed consent (Elze, 2003b) or that the sponsoring agency be judged in loco parentis and therefore provide informed consent (Martin & Meezan, 2003).

♦ Confidentiality and Privacy Issues

Evelyn Hooker has discussed the lengths to which she went to protect the confidentiality and privacy of her sample in her pioneering studies of the prevalence of mental health issues in gay men. She took pains to devise coding systems to keep interview data and identities separate and to ensure that all interview locations were extremely discreet. She would not acquiesce to those who demanded that the interviews be conducted on the university campus, but instead chose to use a private entrance to her personal home. The legal and social ramifications for disclosure of participant's sexual orientation were immense, and from a pragmatic standpoint, she knew that if she wanted to generate a meaningful sample then she had to foster the trust of participants who would then contribute additional subjects to her snowball sample. But she also recognized that it was her ethical responsibility to provide her subjects with these protections (Hooker, 1993). Although the legal ramifications of sexual orientation or gender identity disclosure have diminished since her studies in the 1950s, 1960s, and 1970s, the social and familial consequences remain a significant threat for many. It is for this reason that confidentiality and privacy are especially crucial aspects of research involving LGBTQ individuals. Disclosure of sexual orientation or gender identity may have a negative impact for the individuals involved as subjects risk job discrimination, strained or severed family relationships, and possibly even violence. For example, James and Platzer (1999) noted in their study about nursing care provided to gay men and lesbians in England that many participants feared that disclosure of their sexual orientation would have a negative impact on the nursing care they received.

The issue of confidentiality can be complicated for LGBTQ individuals and researchers given the potentially small social community to which they belong. It is not uncommon for researchers and participants to have social encounters or overlapping roles, which can magnify issues of confidentiality (Woodman et al., 1995). Recognizing the possibility of such nonstudy interactions, researchers should discuss the possibility with participants as part of the informed consent process. Researchers also have to exercise extra vigilance in disguising the identity of subjects when disseminating findings, since many participants may be known to each other (Woodman et al., 1995). Similar care should be taken when working with LGBTQ youth, since disclosure may lead to bullying at school from both teachers and peers as well as having potentially catastrophic consequences at home (Elze, 2003a; GLSEN, 2006; Illingworth & Murphy, 2004).

◆ Best Practices Arising From the Field

Research on sexual orientation and gender identity is highly charged and highly personal, which make it vulnerable to bias and predetermined opinions. The potential for legal, cultural, and social repercussions of study results, both locally and globally, makes it crucial to follow ethical guidelines carefully. For just this reason, Martin and Knox (2000) recommended that researchers with strong personal beliefs either supporting or opposing LGBTQ individuals should refrain from engaging in research on the topic, since the degree of bias may be difficult to protect against.

The following steps are suggested to protect LGBTQ research subjects. As with all ethically sound research protocols, follow good research guidelines such as making sure that all study documents use inclusive language, are written at appropriate reading levels, and are available in different languages as applicable. Survey questionnaires and interview schedules should be pilot tested to ensure the appropriate nonoffensive use of language and labels, such as queer, dyke, transgender, boi, butch, femme, stud, and so on (Martin & Meezan, 2003).

When inclusive language is used in all studies, it reduces the invisibility of LGBTQ individuals and increases the level of specificity of findings. If researchers are asking a question about gender, then it should be fully inclusive with the gender response option either left blank for self-definition or with categories that always include transgender, gender queer, and other as an option. Similarly, in questions asking individuals about their relationship status, inclusive options should be provided. Categories may include single (or no partner), same-gender partner, opposite gender partner, transgender or gender queer partner, more than one partner, and other. Information about cohabiting or legal recognition of their relationships can be separate, for example, asking if an individual is married, in a domestic partnership, in a civil union, divorced (opposite gender), divorced (same gender), divorced (transgender), widowed (opposite gender), widowed (same gender), widowed (transgender), and other.

Protecting confidentiality requires that a coding system be used to ensure that all data (surveys, interview tapes, transcripts, etc.) be kept in a locked location separate from all identifying information. In addition, any voice or e-mail message should have no sensitive references. This includes the e-mail address used, the subject line, and the *body* of the message, which is automatically revealed in many e-mail programs. With the participant's permission, sensitive material may be included as an attachment. As an extra precaution, participants may be encouraged to delete any e-mail responses to the researcher from their "outbox" or "sent mail" file but should be warned that responses may still be traceable. When using snail mail, the return postal address should not include any disclosing information. Usually, the researcher's name and address is sufficient, unless the researcher is well-known in that community or nationally as an advocate for LGBTQ issues or research.

An additional layer of confidentiality protection may be achieved by obtaining certificates of confidentiality, which protect identifying information from subpoena for legal proceedings. Certificates of Confidentiality provide protection against "compelled disclosure of identifying information about subjects enrolled in sensitive biomedical, behavioral, clinical, or other research. The protection is not limited to federally supported research" (Office for Human Research Protections, HHS, 2003). On their helpful Web site aimed to encourage the appropriate use of certificates of confidentiality, the National Institutes of Health

(NIH) suggest that the certificates are granted when disclosure of study information "could have adverse consequences for subjects or damage their financial standing, employability, insurability, or reputation" (NIH, 2002). One study of researchers at the University of California San Francisco reported that the certificates, although occasionally cumbersome to obtain, were generally regarded as favorable by the researchers who used them (Wolf & Zandecki, 2006). Wolf and Zandecki (2006) also noted that the certificates had held up against challenges from legal proceedings for disclosure. Utilizing Certificates of Confidentiality may enhance protection of subjects who reveal sensitive data and may encourage increased participation from subjects reluctant to disclose information with potentially adverse legal consequences.

When studying LGBTQ youth, the issues of informed consent and confidentiality become even more complex. Valentine et al. (2001) and Elze (2003b, 2005) noted that in certain cases achieving parental consent may not be safe for some youth under 18 years of age. In these cases, assent from the youth, when secured following the ethical guidelines of achieving assent or consent, must be considered adequate to avoid either jeopardizing the participating youth or rendering the achievement of a representative sample impossible. Depending on the IRB, either the whole study may receive universal approval to substitute assent for parental consent or each individual case may require separate assessment, an advocate may be appointed on behalf of the youth or the sponsoring agency may act in loco parentis and provide consent when appropriate (Elze, 2003b; Martin & Meezan, 2003).

A diverse, representative committee, often referred to as a Community Advisory Board (CAB) or a Research Advisory Committee (RAC), should be formed for all research projects to advise the research process throughout, and to ensure cultural competence and sensitivity. Gathering a diverse range of advisors can ensure that the research project not only protects all vulnerable subjects but may ensure the successful completion of the project as well. Advisory boards may be especially useful when conducting qualitative research, given that the dynamic and evolving nature of the research may make it difficult to fully assess the risks in advance. Studies that are not LGBTQ specific should consider including one or more representatives from the LGBTQ community on their CAB/RAC, since most samples are going to include some representatives from that community.

Similar to CABs and RACs, it is also suggested that the composition of IRBs should have greater diversity to be more reflective of society in general, including laypersons and individuals with diverse characteristics (de Gruchy & Lewin, 2001). Consultation with an expert in the field of LGBTQ studies may also be useful for IRBs considering specific studies. IRBs should also be trained in guidelines for assessing socially sensitive research to ensure that personal and political biases are discussed in an open format. In fact, de Gruchy and Lewin (2001) recommended that the IRBs "discuss socially sensitive research with the research team in an open and constructive manner, with a view to facilitating the research rather than preventing it" (p. 867). It is essential that IRB members do not mistake their own discomfort with a research topic as indication of ethically questionable methodology but rather focus on the appropriateness and robustness of the protections in place for the human subjects involved.

Out of respect for research participants, once a study is complete there is an ethical obligation to disseminate the findings back into the community and to make policy recommendations if appropriate (Martin & Knox, 2000). It is important that researchers are not seen as using the community to secure a grant or tenure without giving back. Many years ago, Walsh-Bowers and Parlour (1992) conducted a review of 351 articles on homosexuality that were published between 1974 and 1988. They found that authors rarely reported providing feedback to subjects and seldom used data to promote social action. While it is possible that those actions were taken but not reported, and it is hoped that progress has been made in the past two decades, their study still raises the important ethical obligation that researchers have to ensure appropriate utilization of findings to minimize subjects' alienation from the research process.

◆ Thoughts for the Future

Given the representation of LGBTQ individuals within society, it is likely that they will be represented in the samples of the majority of social science research endeavors. As such the ethical imperatives highlighted within this chapter not only apply to LGBTQ-specific research but to *all* ethically sound social science research. In particular, the need for inclusive language, confidentiality, and fully informed consent are essential. Similarly, participatory action committees for any social science study should be reflective of the population from which the sample is drawn, including LGBTQ individuals where appropriate. "The social and behavioral sciences have an important role to play in increasing society's knowledge about and understanding of lesbians, gay men, [transgender, queer] and bisexual people" (Herek et al., 1991, p. 957). Even though the inclusion of sexual orientation or gender identity as a variable in a study may add a layer of complexity to the research process, researchers have a responsibility to generate comprehensive knowledge that does not further marginalize LGBTQ individuals.

Social scientists from different disciplines are bound by different ethical codes but with common themes. As technology, research methodology, and the sociopolitical climate continue to evolve social science researchers will face new and increasing ethical challenges related to LGBTQ individuals. It is important to continue an open and honest dialogue, to engage the difficult questions, to collaborate across disciplines, and to anticipate the challenges that might arise in order to conduct ethically sound inclusive social science research.

◆ Note

1. Queer, which has historically been used pejoratively against LGBT individuals, has more recently been proudly reclaimed by the LGBT community. Queer is usually used in reference to sexual orientation, while gender queer is used in reference to gender identity. In its most general use, queer refers to "any person who transgresses traditional categories of gender or sexuality" (Burdge, 2007, p. 244). For example, gender queer may be used by individuals who identify in some part with both genders or with neither gender.

◆ References

American Psychiatric Association. (2000). *DSM IV-TR—Diagnostic and statistical manual of mental disorders*. Washington, DC: Author.

American Psychological Association. (1998). Resolution on the appropriate therapeutic responses to sexual orientation. *American Psychologist, 53*, 882–935.

Berkman, C., & Zinberg, G. (1997). Homophobia and heterosexism in social workers. *Social Work, 42*(4), 319–332.

Bieber, I., Dain, H., Dince, P., Drellich, M., Grand, H., Gundlach, R., et al. (1962). *Homosexuality: A psychoanalytic study*. New York: Basic Books.

Boehmer, U. (2002). Twenty years of public health research: Inclusion of lesbian, gay, bisexual, and transgender populations. *American Journal of Public Health, 92*(7), 1125–1130.

Bremer, J. (1959). *Asexualization: A follow-up study of 244 cases*. New York: Macmillan.

Burdge, B. (2007). Bending gender, ending gender: Theoretical foundations for social work practice with the transgender community. *Social Work, 52*(3), 243–259.

Carrier, J. (1999). Reflections on ethical problems encountered in field research on Mexican male homosexuality: 1968 to present. *Culture, Health & Sexuality, 1*(3), 207–221.

Ceci, S., Peters, D., & Plotkin, J. (1985). Human subjects review, personal values, and the regulation of social science research. *American Psychologist, 40*(9), 994–1002.

Christianson, A. (2005). A re-emergence of reparative therapy. *Contemporary Sexuality, 39*(10), 8–17.

Conger, J. (1975). Proceedings of the American Psychological Association for the year 1974: Minutes of the annual meeting of the Council of Representatives. *American Psychologist, 30*, 620–651.

Crisp, K. (2005). Homophobia and use of gay affirmative practice in a sample of social workers and psychologists. *Journal of Gay and Lesbian Social Services, 18*(1), 51–70.

Crisp, K. (2006). The gay affirmative practice scale (GAP): A new measure for assessing cultural competence with gay and lesbian clients. *Social Work, 51*(2), 115–126.

D'Augelli, A., & Grossman, A. (2006). Researching lesbian, gay, and bisexual youth: Conceptual, practical, and ethical considerations. *Journal of Gay and Lesbian Issues in Education, 3*(2/3), 35–56.

de Gruchy, J., & Lewin, S. (2001). Ethics that exclude: The role of ethics committees in lesbian and gay health research in South Africa. *American Journal of Public Health, 91*(6), 865–868.

Deutsch, L. (1995). Out of the closet and on to the couch: A psychoanalytic exploration of lesbian development. In J. Glassgold & S. Iasenza (Eds.), *Lesbians and psychoanalysis: Revolutions in theory and practice* (pp. 19–37). New York: Free Press.

DiAngelo, R. (1997). Heterosexism: Addressing internalized dominance. *Journal of Progressive Human Service, 8*(1), 5–21.

Donelson, R., & Rogers, T. (2004). Negotiating a research protocol for studying school-based gay and lesbian issues. *Theory Into Practice, 43*(2), 128–135.

Drescher, J., & Zucker, K. (2006). *Ex-gay research: Analyzing the Spitzer study and its relation to science, religion, politics, and culture*. Binghamton, New York: Haworth Press.

Elze, D. (2002). Risk factors for internalizing and externalizing problems among gay, lesbian and bisexual adolescents. *Social Work Research, 26*(2), 89–100.

Elze, D. (2003a). Gay, lesbian, and bisexual youths' perceptions of their high school environments and comfort in school. *Children and Schools, 25*(4), 225–239.

Elze, D. (2003b). 8,000 miles and still counting. . . . Researching gay, lesbian and bisexual adolescents for research. *Journal of Gay and Lesbian Social Services, 15*(1/2), 127–145.

Elze, D. (2005). Research with sexual minority youths: Where do we go from here? *Journal of Gay and Lesbian Social Services: Issues in Practice, Policy & Research, 18*(2), 73–99.

Friedman, R., & Downey, J. (2002). *Sexual orientation and psychoanalysis*. New York: Columbia University Press.

Gay, Lesbian and Straight Education Network. (2006). *The 2005 National School climate survey: Executive summary of a report from the Gay, Lesbian and Straight Education Network*. New York: Author.

Gonsiorek, J. (1988). Mental health issues of gay and lesbian adolescents. *Journal of Adolescent Health Care, 9*(2), 114–122.

Gould, D. (1995). A critical examination of the notion of pathology in psychoanalysis. In J. Glassgold & S. Iasenza (Eds.), *Lesbians and psychoanalysis: Revolutions in theory and practice* (pp. 3–17). New York: Free Press.

Haldeman, D. (2002). Gay rights, patients rights: The implications of sexual orientation conversion therapy. *Professional Psychology: Research and Practice, 33*(3), 260–264.

Halpert, S. (2000). If it ain't broke don't fix it: Ethical considerations regarding conversion therapies. *International Journal of Sexuality and Gender Studies, 5*(1), 19–35.

Hamer, D., Hu, S., Magnuson, V., Hu, N., & Pattatucci, A. (1993). A linkage between

DNA markers on the X chromosome and male sexual orientation. *Science, 261,* 321–327.
Herek, G., Kimmel, D., Amaro, H., & Melton, G. (1991). Avoiding heterosexist bias in psychological research. *American Psychologist, 46*(9), 957–963.
Hooker, E. (1957). The adjustment of the male overt homosexual. *Journal of Projective Techniques, 21,* 18–31.
Hooker, E. (1958). Male homosexuality in the Rorschach. *Journal of Projective Techniques, 22,* 33–54.
Hooker, E. (1993). Reflections of a 40-year exploration. *American Psychologist, 48,* 450–453.
Humphreys, L. (1970). *Tearoom trade: Impersonal sex in public places.* Chicago: Aldine Press.
Illingworth, P., & Murphy, T. (2004). In our best interest: Meeting moral duties to lesbian, gay, and bisexual adolescent students. *Journal of Social Philosophy, 35*(2), 198–210.
James, T., & Platzer, H. (1999). Ethical considerations in qualitative research with vulnerable groups: Exploring lesbians' and gay men's experiences of health care—a personal perspective. *Nursing Ethics, 6*(1), 73–81.
Kadour, R. (2005). The power of data, the price of exclusion. *Gay & Lesbian Review,* Jan/Feb, 31–33.
Kaiser, J. (1997). No misconduct in "gay gene" study. *Science, 275*(5304), 1251.
Martin, J., & Knox, J. (2000). Methodological and ethical issues in research on lesbians and gay men. *Social Work Research, 24*(1), 51–59.
Martin, J., & Meezan, W. (2003). Applying ethical standards to research and evaluations involving lesbian, gay, bisexual, and transgender populations. *Journal of Gay and Lesbian Social Services, 15*(1/2), 181–201.
Murphy, T. (1997). *The ethics of sexual orientation research.* New York: Columbia University Press.
National Institutes of Health. (2002). *NIH announces statement on Certificates of Confidentiality.* Release Date: March 15, 2002. Notice: NOT-OD-02-037. Retrieved February 19, 2007, from www.grants.nih.gov/grants/policy/coc

Nicolosi, J. (1991). *Reparative therapy of male homosexuality.* Northvale, NJ: Jason Aronson.
Office for Human Research Protections (U.S. Department of Health and Human Services). (2003). *Guidance on certificates of confidentiality.* Retrieved February 19, 2007, from www.hhs.gov/ohrp/humansubjects/guidance/certconf.htm
Owensby, N. (1940). Homosexuality and lesbianism treated with metrazol. *Journal of Nervous and Mental Disease, 92,* 65–66.
Owensby, N. (1941). The correction of homosexuality. *Urological & Cutaneous Review, 45,* 494–496.
Platzer, H., & James, T. (1997). Methodological issues conducting sensitive research on lesbian and gay men's experiences of nursing care. *Journal of Advanced Nursing, 25,* 626–633.
Roberts, S., Grindel, C., Patsdaughter, C., Reardon, K., & Tarmina, M. (2004). Mental health problems and use of services of lesbians: Results of the Boston Lesbian Health Project II. *Journal of Gay and Lesbian Social Services, 17*(4), 1–16.
Savage, A., Quiros, L., Dodd, S. J., & Bonavota, D. (2007). Building trauma-informed practice: Appreciating the impact of trauma in the lives of women with substance abuse and mental health problems. *Journal of Social Work Practice in the Addictions, 7*(1/2), 91–116.
Schreier, B. (1998). Of shoes, and ships, and sealing wax: The faulty and specious assumptions of reorientation therapies. *Journal of Mental Health Counseling, 20*(4), 305–315.
Schuklenk, U., Stein, E., Kerin, J., & Byne, W. (1997). The ethics of genetic research on sexual orientation. *The Hastings Center Report, 27*(4), 6–13.
Sieber, J. (2004). Empirical research on research ethics. *Ethics & Behavior, 14*(4), 397–412.
Sieber, J., & Stanley, B. (1988). Ethical and professional dimensions of socially sensitive research. *American Psychologist, 43*(1), 49–55.
Spitzer, R. (2003). Can some gay men and lesbians change their sexual orientation? 200

participants reporting a change from homosexual to heterosexual. *Archives of Sexual Behavior, 32*(5), 403–417.

Valentine, G., Butler, R., & Skelton, T. (2001). The ethical and methodological complexities of doing research with "vulnerable" young people. *Ethics, Place & Environment, 4*(2), 119–125.

Walsh-Bowers, R., & Parlour, S. (1992). Research patient relationships in journal reports on gay men and lesbian women. *Journal of Homosexuality, 23*(4), 93–112.

Wolf, L., & Zandecki, J. (2006). Sleeping better at night: Investigators' experiences with certificates of confidentiality. *IRB: Ethics & Human Research, 28*(6), 1–7.

Woodman, N., Tully, C., & Barranti, C. (1995). Research in lesbian communities: Ethical dilemmas. *Journal of Gay and Lesbian Social Services, 3*(1), 57–66.

Yarhouse, M., & Throckmorton, W. (2002). Ethical issues in attempts to ban reorientation therapies. *Psychotherapy: Theory/Research/Practice/Training, 39*(1), 66–75.

31

INVOLVING MINORS IN RESEARCH

Ethics and Law Within Multicultural Settings

◆ Luis A. Vargas and Margaret E. Montoya[1]

The issue of minors' rights in research continues to generate much debate among researchers, attorneys, policymakers, clinicians, and child advocates. Among the areas of concern are the social value of the research, the minor's ability to consent or assent, the beneficial or nonbeneficial aspect of the research,[2] the importance of having representative participant samples, and the importance of sampling varied cultural, social, and situational contexts of minors' lives. This chapter addresses the issue of minors' decision making in social and clinical research involving culturally diverse populations in the United States. The chapter presents a brief overview of the sociolegal and cultural context of minors' decision making as pertains to participation in social and clinical research, a discussion of cognitive and moral development in minors' decision making, a brief discussion of the empirical studies on children's competence for assent/consent, and a description of a contextual-interactional approach to understanding informed consent or assent in culturally diverse populations of minors. A fundamental underlying premise throughout this chapter is that legal, ethical, and psychological approaches to decision making in children participating in social and clinical research are culturally embedded. Cultures develop and exist in conditions of subordination and dominance; members of the dominant culture usually have different ideas about ethics and different concepts of right and wrong than members of nondominant cultures.

◆ Sociolegal and Cultural Context of Decision Making

The concept of decision making in minors must be understood within the context of culturally based beliefs, values, and laws. A society's beliefs about children's physical, cognitive, moral, and social development will vary depending on historical, cultural, and social context. Legal propositions on which rights are based reflect core beliefs, values, and attitudes of a particular society—a particular culture within a particular place at a given time. A corollary relevant to this chapter is that, as a society becomes multicultural, legal and ethical decision making becomes ambiguous, fluid, and challenging.

LEGAL PROPOSITIONS

Should minors have legal rights or should the rights attach to those, such as parents or legal guardians, who presumably have the best interests of the minor in mind? Opinions are divided between those who believe that minors should have rights, such that they could consent to participate in research, and those who do not believe they should have rights, such that they can only assent (agree) to participate in research and their parents or guardians bear the right to consent for them. At the center are those who believe that minors should have certain rights but not others. Sociolegal conceptualizations on rights lead to different strategies for dealing with decision making in minors.

One conceptualization distinguishes between the will, or choice, theory that views rights as the exercise of choices that are so important that they must be protected, and the welfare, or interest, theory that views a right as an interest that is so important that it must be protected (Archard, 2006). According to Archard, the will theory fits rights that pertain to doing certain things, or actions (e.g., right of freedom of speech or right to associate with anyone of a person's choosing) and interest theory fits rights that pertain to being the recipient of certain benefits (e.g., right to receive health care) or being protected from certain untoward actions by others (e.g., right not to be tortured). This choice-interest distinction parallels the division observed in child advocacy between those who focus on recognizing children's autonomy and privacy and those who focus on supporting their care and protection (Melton, 1983, 2005b).

As is probably obvious, these two theories on rights have different implications for minors. The will theory makes it more difficult to conceptualize minors as having rights. Here, the challenge to minors having rights would be to demonstrate that minors are capable of exercising choice. Thus, the need for minors' assent to participate in research is perhaps more easily understood within a choice theory. The interest theory might make it easier to conceptualize minors as having the right to consent as participants in research to the extent that the duty adults have to protect important interests of children is seen as directly relating to the rights that minors are given. What theory might prevail probably depends, in major part, on the cultural views and values of a particular society toward children.

In recent years, there has been a renewed interest in children's rights, in large part spurred by the ratification of the UN Convention on the Rights of the Child (CRC) by the General Assembly on November 20, 1989. As noted by Silver (2006), the CRC includes several choice rights: "the right to freedom of expression, including the freedom to seek, receive, and impart information and idea of all kinds . . ." (Article 13); "the right to freedom of thought, conscience and religion" (Article 14); "the right to freedom of association" (Article 15); "the right to privacy" (Article 16); and "the rights to be free from all forms of physical and mental violence" (Article 19). These choice rights have raised concerns among some scholars about protecting parental liberty in a child-centered legal system, which some believe that the CRC advocates. Silver (2006) argued that family autonomy, or parental authority, is the best way to ensure diversity in a free society. She stated,

> There is no surer way to preserve pluralism than to allow parents maximum latitude in rearing their own children. Conversely, there is no surer way to threaten pluralism than to terminate the rights of parents who contradict officially approved values imposed by reformers empowered to determine what is in the "best interests of the child." (p. 3)

Only two countries have failed to ratify the CRC, Somalia and the United States (Melton, 2005a). The United States's failure to ratify the CRC, in part, is based on one potent cultural force in the United States—the Religious Right, which viewed the CRC as potentially weakening the family's autonomy as well as parental authority and was concerned about the CRC's potential impact on issues such as home schooling, corporal punishment, and abortion rights of pregnant minors (Melton & Wilcox, 2001). This cultural force is evident both in laws and ethical standards in the United States that continue to preserve parents' authority to make decisions for their minor children, including the minors' participation in research, and that minimize the voice that minors have in making decisions about their participation in research.

Melton (2005a) offered a different perspective from that of Silver on the CRC: "The CRC (1989) . . . goes beyond kiddie-lib and child-saving orientations to ensure that the entitlements necessary for children's development as members of community are provided in a manner consistent with their status as persons" (p. 920). The CRC has particular relevance to the ability of minors to make decisions about participating in research. Article 12 is noteworthy in its relevance to informed consent and culturally responsive ethical practice. Article 12.1 states,

> Parties shall assure to the child who is capable of forming his or her own views the right to express those views freely in all matters affecting the child, the views of the child being given due weight in accordance with the age and maturity of the child. (p. 4)

From the perspective of culturally responsive practice, it is not difficult to see how this article might facilitate (and perhaps even require)

- the creation of an informed consent process for minors in research that would give the minor the right to make decisions about participation in research, thereby, requiring informed consent within contextual and developmental parameters, rather than assent in isolation of context and development and

- how such an informed consent process could be tailored to local communities and their cultures to provide for a broader conceptualization or spectrum of consent that includes extended family and community participation in a child's choice.

Of particular note is that the CRC moves from an arbitrary age limit for obtaining the right to consent to an appreciation of what

Melton and Wilcox (2001) called "the structures and processes that actually promote children's growing participation in community life" (p. 6). The view of minors in the CRC represents a cultural shift from a relatively fixed age to one that is more flexible and contextual. In other words, there has been a shift from the legal binary view of minors in the United States that has relied on the assumed intrinsic abilities and decontextualized behavior and characteristics of a minor, where a minor's status is directly linked to a specific age.

JURISDICTIONAL CONTEXT

Jurisdictional issues must be considered in making determinations about a minor's decision-making rights. The federal constitutional context in the United States lends some uniformity in a certain set of considerations. On the other hand, state constitutions, common law, statutes, and regulatory schemes vary and reflect regional cultural and political differences. Thus, whereas in California, minors may be presumed to have the capacity to consent to outpatient mental health treatment without the consent of a legal guardian if they are 12 years or older; in New Mexico, minors are not presumed to have such capacity until they are 14 years or older. In certain parts of the United States, there is yet another set of jurisdictional issues that have to be taken into account for American Indian and Alaska Native children, namely Tribal Law, which will vary, sometimes considerably, from tribe to tribe (see Fraser, 2000). To further complicate matters, these jurisdictional structures often overlap.

LEGAL INTERESTS AND ETHICAL STANDARDS

The perspective on minors' decision making is influenced by the legal values placed on children's statuses (e.g., emancipated minors and mature minors[3]) and various interests (e.g., interests of parents or guardians, the state's interest as *parens patriae*, and the interests of American Indian/Alaska Native Tribal governments). State laws vary on the degree to which they grant minors' adult status, as either emancipated minors or mature minors, and some states do not have such provisions. Some researchers believe that mature minors should be given the right to informed consent for certain types of social and clinical research, such as research that provides a specific treatment or that examines their reasons and reactions as pertains to seeking this treatment (Fisher, 2004; Fisher et al., 2002; Fisher, Hoagwood, & Jensen, 1996).[4]

Psychologists conducting research must respond to both ethical principles and legal mandates. To comply with the American Psychological Association Ethical Principles of Psychologists and Code of Conduct ("APA Ethics Code"), parents or guardians must give explicit permission, not just passive or implicit permission (APA, 2002; Fisher, 2004), as in the case of sending parents or guardians forms requesting response only if they do not want their child or ward to participate in the research. However, the APA Ethics Code provides the following caveat:

> If this Ethics Code establishes a higher standard of conduct than is required by law, psychologists must meet the higher ethical standard. If psychologists' ethical responsibilities conflict with law, regulations, or other governing legal authority, psychologists make known their commitment to this Ethics Code and take steps to resolve the conflict in a responsible manner. If the conflict is unresolvable via such means, psychologists may adhere to the requirements of the law, regulations, or other governing authority in keeping with basic principles of human rights. (p. 1062)

The doctrine of *parens patriae* grants the power and authority of the state to protect persons who are legally unable to act on their own behalf, such as in the treatment of minors, persons with mental disorders, and others who are legally incompetent to manage their own affairs (Clark, 2000; *Steele v. Hamilton County Mental Health Board*, 2000). This doctrine provides for state courts to have the inherent power to intervene to protect the best interests of children whose welfare is jeopardized. In the case of American Indians/Alaska Natives, the tribe may act under the doctrine of *parens patriae*, as has been accepted by the Eighth, Ninth, and Tenth Circuits and several Federal District Courts, although without published analysis (Fraser, 2000).

In conducting social and clinical research with American Indians/Alaska Natives on reservations, the researcher must seek the tribe's approval for the research (Indian Child Welfare Act, 1978) and where there is no established protocol, at minimum, the researcher must provide notice to the tribe about the research. In cases in which the state has custody of an American Indian/Alaska Native minor, the state may not have a legal obligation to obtain consent of the tribe but we would contend that it is the ethical obligation of the researcher to also obtain consent from the child's tribe, or at least provide notice to the tribe.

♦ The Law, Ethics, and Children's Development

Legal and ethical obligations regarding the participation of children in research often extend beyond substantive content of the law. Beliefs about cognitive and moral development form the basis for the way a society constructs its laws and social policies and, in turn, those laws and social policies serve to maintain those beliefs. Furthermore, the type of reasoning used in crafting law and ethical standards is determined by culturally rooted values and worldviews.

HOW LAW'S BINARY THINKING DISTORTS ETHICAL DECISION MAKING

Legal and ethical decisions are influenced by culture in some not so obvious ways, such as in the way we reason, or more specifically, in the narratives, premises, and rules that we construct to guide our reasoning. Laws in the United States have been heavily influenced by standard logic, which is based on two Aristotelian concepts: the law of the excluded middle (Aristotle, 1999; Suber, 1997) and Aristotle's rule of justice articulated as "Treat likes alike and treat unalikes unalike" (MacKinnon, 2007, pp. 6–7). Russell (1997) described the law of the excluded middle very succinctly: "Everything must either be or not be" (p. 72). The use of an age cutoff for the age at which someone can give informed consent is based on these Aristotelian concepts. A person is either, say, 18 years old or not. Legal and ethical decision making is thus made unambiguous and made to appear much less complicated. But "What are the consequences of this type of culturally rooted reasoning?" and "Is decision making based on this type of reasoning valid or justifiable?"

Taking a social constructionist perspective, King (1991) followed Luhmann's (1989) theory in proposing that law is a closed social system and has a normative social function, that is, a function to organize people's expectations for the purpose of managing and controlling social conflict. The law does this by the use of binary thinking; for example, something is either legal or illegal, or right or wrong, or even male or female. King (1991) postulated that, because this closed social system is faced with other versions of reality, contributions by, say, psychological science, must be reconstructed to make it fit with the law as a closed-system. From this perspective, law promotes those aspects of the contribution of other disciplines (such as psychology) which are compatible with its closed-system nature leading to a hybrid between law and science, justice and child welfare. He concluded,

> If the analysis set out in this article proves correct, the result at one level will be the continuing coding of issues concerning complex human relationships into categories of right and wrong, lawful and unlawful and, at another level, in the perpetuation of a system of "abuse-promoting child protection." (p. 320)

By this he means that child welfare knowledge will be subjugated to the law and will be used to serve institutional legal goals that fail to reflect such values as autonomy and respect.

From a constructionist perspective, James (1992) critiqued King's (1991) proposition in line with Teubner (1989) that there need not be the type of hybriding described by King (1991) because the state of affairs only represents different discipline-based constructions of reality. Thus, for James (1992), the legal system need only be aware of its tendency to be a closed system "as a means of defending and perpetuating its traditional hegemony, in the face of competing discourses which seek to question its hitherto unquestioned competence to deal with such complex human and social issues as the welfare of children" (p. 282). In a way, James's view shows how a legal system can accommodate to other forms of logic or reasoning and other forms of knowledge that address the complexities of situations and cannot provide the certainties that the legal system expects. As noted earlier, we are seeing a shift, as a result of newer theories of development, from stage-oriented theories that have been the basis for a fixed chronological age for age of majority to theories that allow a more flexible standard and integrate the contextual complexities of children's and adolescents' decision making.

Because of the tendency of law and ethics to defend and protect institutional and professional power and perogatives, it is important in a pluralistic society like the United States that a process of examining, challenging, and modifying legal and codified ethical standards be maintained. This involves adopting an ethos of self-examination of professional practices as well as giving power and voice to those who may be excluded in a system's or profession's policy making and systematic self-examination. As pertains to minors, particularly minors of color, participation in research, we believe that it is imperative that the voices of these minors *and* the voices and viewpoints of their families and communities be given much more weight than they are currently given in law, institutional review boards (IRBs),[5] and ethical standards of professions.

HOW THEORIES OF DEVELOPMENT AFFECT LAW AND ETHICS

Legal concepts about the age of majority and about what abilities a minor does or does not possess often reflect predominant developmental theories within a society. Developmental stage theories that postulate that children progress through stages of development and, on average, develop certain abilities at certain ages have influenced, and provided the basis for, laws that establish a fixed age of majority (Miller-Wilson, 2006). Stage theories have been useful in examining legal propositions about age-related abilities. For example, one study (Nannis, 1991) showed that third grade (8- to 9-year-old) students were less likely to understand the purpose of the research than fifth graders (10- to 11-year-olds), while most children regardless of grade level believed that they had some or complete input about whether to participate in the research.

These types of studies suggest that children go through stages of development whereby they attain certain abilities in a step-wise fashion during their maturation and provide a sound basis for the crafting of laws and ethical standards that impose fixed-age restrictions for certain rights and legally sanctioned actions, such as in giving informed consent versus assent. These types of theories are conducive to binary thinking in law and ethical standards; that is, either a youth is a minor or not, or either the youth on the basis of chronological age has or does not have the requisite abilities for decision making. A danger here is that binary reasoning may lead to overly simplistic, although practical, laws or ethical standards for decision making.

With the advent of ecological/contextual developmental and social constructionist theories, we have seen greater attention by legal, psycholegal, and ethics scholars on contextual factors in the conceptualization of minors' decision making. In ecological/contextual and constructionist theories of development, the emphasis is on how context affects a child's ability. For example, research by ecologically or contextually oriented investigators has shown that a child may demonstrate a higher ability in one situation (e.g., in a familiar setting in the presence of supportive parents or extended family members) but not in another (e.g., in an unfamiliar setting in the presence of strangers). Specifically, a youth's decision-making ability varies according to context. This perspective complicates legal and ethical decision making as pertains, for example, to decisions about a youth's ability to give informed consent.

Different developmental theories raise different legal and ethical questions. Stage-based developmental theories ask *when and if* a youth has the requisite abilities. Contextual and constructionist developmental theories ask *under what conditions* a youth can demonstrate the requisite abilities. While contextual and constructionist theories of development may provide a more individualized and contextualized assessment of a child's or adolescent's decision-making capacity, they also place a greater burden of responsibility on those conducting research with children and adolescents to adequately examine the optimal conditions for each child to demonstrate requisite abilities regarding his or her decision to participate in a research project. Current research based on contextual and constructionist developmental theories challenges the assumptions in the law based on simplistic, although practical, dichotomous decisions based on chronological age (Miller-Wilson, 2006).

One line of reasoning in jurisprudence, the feminist postmodern view, examines law under the assumption that the construction of laws is temporally, spatially, and culturally situated and must, therefore, be analyzed in context. From this perspective, laws can be examined for ways in which they demonstrate implicit and detrimental assumptions about gender, along with race, class, sexual orientation, and so on that reflect the historically and culturally situated circumstances in which the laws were enacted and the power differentials between different groups affected by the law (Levit, 2002). Contextual and constructionist developmental and feminist approaches to jurisprudence are now leading to the understanding and appreciation of the importance of considering the circumstances and interactions, rather than developmental stages, that can lead to the participation of children in decision making. We suggest that, in the case of children in research, consent should involve the minors in the context of their abilities, their families, and communities.

In a narrative review summarizing the empirical studies on children's competence for consent and assent in psychological literature, Miller, Drotar, and Kodish (2004) noted that research about children's competence to consent to research or treatment has lacked a structure that can guide researchers' hypotheses and interpretation of results. They described fundamental approaches used in informed consent as (1) legal versus ethical or psychological approaches, (2) autonomy versus best interests, (3) child- versus family-centered, and (4) consent versus assent. While current state and federal laws frame competence in a binary (either competent or not competent) fashion, ethical or psychological approaches increasingly have used broader conceptualization of competence that consider developmental, situational, and interactive aspects of children's decision making. An ethical and psychological approach to children's decision making regarding participation in research is more likely to address *the child-in-context* (i.e., considering developmental, situational, and interactive influences). As pertains to autonomy versus best interests approaches, Miller et al. believe that the autonomy-based approach fails to appreciate that children may not be able to exercise meaningful autonomy. In the case of a child's participation in research, the autonomy-based approach looks at what is the best decision for a particular child, whereas the best-interest approach looks at whether the child should make the decision to participate in the research. In the child-versus family-centered approaches, the focus on children's rights often means that the role of parents is minimized, if not ignored. Yet parents play an important role in fostering and supporting children's autonomy and emerging abilities related to competent decision making. Miller et al. noted that parents often have not been included in the empirical research on children's competence to consent or assent.

Most of the empirical studies reviewed by Miller et al. did not make clear distinctions between consent and assent and all but three focused on children's competence to consent. What is lacking are conceptual models not only to guide research on children's decision making abilities as pertains to participation in research but also, and perhaps more importantly to guide researchers conducting any type of research in which children, particularly those who do not share the researcher's background or worldview, are participants in order to ensure that consent and assent are obtained in a developmentally and culturally responsive manner.

Noting that the CRC has an implicit children's rights focus on social and clinical research and leaning toward the support of children's rights, Melton (2005b) offered a framework that addresses contextual and processual aspects of children's participation in research. Joffe (2003) argued for shared decision making between children and parents in any discussion about children's assent to participate in research. The Institute of Medicine (IOM, 2004) described an approach that promotes the idea that children should have varied levels of involvement in research depending on their level of cognitive ability, emotional maturity, and psychological state. The IOM made specific recommendations to obtain assent from children and adolescents in clinical research. Miller et al. (2004) presented a conceptual model to guide future research on children's decision making as participants in research that includes consideration of (1) predisposing factors (cognitive development, prior experience with decision making, parents' belief about child autonomy, family's cultural and religious values, attitudes and beliefs, and language; (2) child factors (preference for involvement, emotional state, prior experience with decision making, health and physical status, and current cognitive functioning); (3) parent factors (facilitation of child's involvement/support, parental understanding of consent, and coercive influence); (4) clinician/researcher factors (facilitation of child's involvement/support, communication behaviors, and coercive influence); and (5) situational factors (e.g., time constraints, type of decision, stress of decision, complexity of decision, and coercive influence such as the setting).

◆ A Contextual-Interactional Approach to Children's Decision Making in Research With Culturally Diverse Populations

Although the narrative review of empirical studies on children's competence for assent and consent by Miller et al. (2004) is intended to address the current state of affairs in research into children's competence as participants in research, the model they present provides a useful framework for addressing and understanding children's decision making as participants in clinical and social research with culturally diverse populations. The approach outlined below borrows heavily from the work of Miller et al. to describe a contextual-interactional approach to understanding children's decision making in culturally diverse research participants.

CONSIDERATION OF CONTEXTUAL FACTORS AND INSTITUTION/COMMUNITY INTERFACE OF THE RESEARCH SETTING

Assessment of contextual factors requires a consideration of the institutions and communities involved, issues of power and privilege, and the potential for overt or covert coercion of children and their parents in (1) the interaction between institutions and the community/parents; (2) the timelines and requirements for participants; (3) the timelines and requirements for the researchers in conducting the research; (4) the career benefits, including tenure, salary increases, and research grants (all of which are rarely disclosed), that flow to researchers from the participation of parents and children; and (5) the nature of the decisions that need to be made (e.g., whether to participate in a study on the relationship between family functioning and delinquent behavior or in a survey of youth drug abuse and suicidality). One of the objectives of IRBs is to provide a review of the potential safety and harm of the proposed research and to comply with federal law, CFR Title 45 (Public Welfare) Subtitle A (Department of Health and Human Services) Part 46 (Protection of Human Subjects). Ideally, an IRB would review how a principal investigator is considering these potential sources for overt or covert coercion of children and their parents. However, IRBs are often part of universities or large institutions heavily invested not only in conducting research but also in ensuring that researchers in their universities or institutions seek and get funding for their research projects. Although IRBs usually have public members, most of the IRBs are composed of research-active faculty members, and researchers and the public members may have little familiarity with the populations and communities from which participants are recruited. Thus, there is a potentially inherent bias in the IRB review process.

To see how far situations can go awry, we might consider *Ericka Grimes v. Kennedy Krieger Institute, Inc.* and *Myron Higgins, a minor, etc. v. Kennedy Krieger Institute, Inc.* (2001). In these cases, an IRB approved a nonbeneficial research project by a prestigious research institute associated with Johns Hopkins University that involved determining the effectiveness of varying degrees of lead paint abatement procedures on children, who, with their parents, were unaware of the danger to the children. The Maryland Court of Appeals overruled the trial court that had ruled that the corporation conducting the research did not have a duty to warn minor volunteer participants and/or their legal guardians about the dangers of the study when the researcher knew of the potential for harm and the participants were not made aware of the danger prior to their decisions about participation.

These cases, while very dramatic and rare, underscore the need for researchers to engage in a genuine and impartial assessment of the contextual factors of their research. These cases also highlight the responsibility of researchers to provide sufficient information to the IRB about the cultural, social, economic, and historical contexts of the participant populations to ensure that the IRB has the necessary information to allow for an adequate review of the research project. For example, researchers in a survey study of alcohol use among adolescents may take a very different tack in obtaining parental consent and minor assent for participants in an upper-middle-class European American community than in an isolated rural American Indian reservation that has struggled with alcoholism and alcohol-related deaths for many generations and where most of the families live well below the poverty level. To further complicate matters, the historical perspective of many members of the reservation to the survey research could be,

> Here is another curious white man/woman coming in to study how the alcohol the white man gave us has damaged us and our children. When they get what they want, they'll go, leave us to continue to struggle on our own without ever offering any help.

Understanding and appreciating a community's values, beliefs, attitudes, and experiences with research is essential to carrying out research in which the community, parents, and children have an active and clearly acknowledged role in the decisions that the community and parents make for their children's participation in research. Prior to beginning or even formulating the research plan, the investigators might consider openly discussing with the research team and community stakeholders the possible impact of timelines and requirements for participants and researchers, the specific career benefits and/or risks for the investigators from the proposed research, and the nature of the decisions that need to be made by participants and community stakeholders to collaboratively evaluate the potential for biases or coercion of the child participants and their parents.

A number of scholars have addressed problems that relate to more specific, microcontexts of research using culturally diverse and/or disadvantaged minors. For example, one scholar (Alta Charo, 1993) noted that most of the patients in one study of terminal cancer patients were African Americans and were referred to as "charity patients." Another scholar (Ross, 1997) reported that there are serious inequities in research, noting that the poor and less educated "bear most of the research burden" and better educated and higher socioeconomic status individuals are less likely to participate in most research. Thus, it is incumbent on the researcher who is recruiting and obtaining permission from culturally diverse and disadvantaged populations to closely examine these types of processes and potential biases that operate at both the broader institutional, economic, and political levels and at the more specific, or micro, interactional level of recruiting participants for social and clinical research.

Research conducted in schools, mental health centers, or hospitals may have considerable inequities in rates of participation by various groups of children. Each research setting and the targeted participant pool present unique challenges for the researcher. For example, undocumented immigrant parents may have very different rates of consent for their children's participation in a research study as compared with U.S. citizens or documented residents. An undocumented parent's consent and a child's assent may be motivated by fear of antagonizing the teacher or treatment provider, concern about calling attention to the child's and/or parent's undocumented status and/or need for translation services, or worry that the child might lose certain benefits or services if the parent refuses to give consent. An immigrant parent who is learning English may not be able to advocate for her or his child should a concern arise about the child's participation during the course of the research study. Researchers have to be careful to ensure that they are taking an ethical approach to recruitment of participants. For example, in a school-based research study, care must be taken to make sure that neither parents nor children feel obliged to participate because other students have agreed or because a teacher exerts undue pressure on the students or parents because she or he does not want to be viewed by the administration or the researchers as being unsupportive of the research.

FORMATION OF COMMUNITY-RESEARCHER PARTNERSHIPS

There has been increasing attention paid to the need for researchers to collaborate with communities from which the participants are recruited to find better ways to develop and carry out research that effectively balances good scientific design and optimal compliance with ethical practices and legal requirements (see Fisher et al., 2002; Melton, 2005a). In other words, it is not sufficient for the researcher to ensure compliance with IRB and federal requirements, institutional policies, professional ethical standards, or even personal norms. It is important to understand and appreciate the unique situations, contexts, and community ties of the participants. As Fisher et al. (2002) and Melton (2005a) have stressed, it is important that researchers develop partnerships with community stakeholders, parents, and minors that encourage and facilitate the exchange of information that not only allows for culturally responsive consent procedures for parents and assent procedures for minors but also leads to culturally responsive and meaningful research methods and designs and the establishment of mutual respect among researchers, participants, and community stakeholders.

Researchers working with American Indian/Alaska Native communities are familiar with the distrust, if not antagonism, toward researchers. These communities, in particular, have been the subject of considerable maltreatment during and after research. For example, from the late 1940s to the mid-1980s, the Navajo miners were exposed to radiation without their knowledge (*Begay v. United States*, 1984/1985). Disempowered ethnic minority groups have tended to bear the brunt of particularly insensitive research. For instance, in the Tuskegee Syphilis Study, which ran from 1932 to 1972 and was intended to study the terminal effects of syphilis, African American men infected with the disease were intentionally left untreated and consequently left to die and to infect their spouses and children (Ruffins, 1998). Although not involving children, this study is widely known to have made African Americans highly skeptical toward health providers and researchers generally.

A group of national leaders in bioethics, multicultural research, and ethnic minority mental health convened by the American Psychological Association, National Institute of Mental Health, and the Fordham University Center for Ethics Education (Fisher et al., 2002) described how some American Indian and Alaska Native communities now have ordinances or covenants that prohibit researchers from conducting research without the explicit approval of tribal or village councils. The group offered some very helpful ideas for developing researcher-community collaborations. They noted that hiring independent support staff from the local communities from which the participants are being recruited may help researchers better respond to method, design, or procedural issues and to concerns expressed by prospective participants. It may also help having the principal investigator more present and visible during the course of the research and more communicative with the community after the research results have been made public. Consultation with prospective participants and their parents and with community stakeholders will also facilitate the researchers' understanding and appreciation of the cultural aspects that are necessary to consider in soliciting consent from parents and assent from minors from particular cultures.

Following and elaborating on the recommendations made by Hillabrant (2002) pertaining to research in Indian reservations, we suggest the following. The researchers may want to hire community or tribal members to assist in the research projects, beginning with the development of the research proposal, including decisions about sampling strategy and participant recruitment, instruments and methods, design, statistical analyses, and proposed presentation and publications of results. In addition, the researchers may want to engage in collaborative decisions about how the informed consent form is written and explained and how informed consent from parents, possibly involving extended family members and the community or tribe, and assent from minors will be obtained. The researchers may want to have meetings with community leaders and stakeholders to jointly plan how confidentiality or anonymity will be preserved. Researchers may want to wait to publish research results until after they meet with community or tribal leaders and obtain their input on the results, what they mean to the community or reservation, and how and to whom the results will be disseminated.

CONSIDERATION OF PREDISPOSING FACTORS

Informed consent and assent is sometimes obtained in a perfunctory manner that follows a standard template that meets federal regulations and IRB requirements. From an ethical vantage point, one might argue that this is antithetical to engaging in a meaningful dialogue with research participants and to creating a researcher-participant relationship that optimizes the reliability and validity of a study's results. A meaningful informed consent and assent procedure must be carried out in a context that considers the knowledge base of the participants and their families; the experiences that the participants, families, or prior generations have had with research; the language and customs of the participants, families, and communities; and the parents' views about values such as independence and collectivism as pertains to their children. It also requires that researchers understand and appreciate their own positions of power and privilege and that they learn ways of mitigating these aspects so as not to behave in ways that are unintentionally coercive.

CONSIDERATION OF PARENTAL AND EXTENDED FAMILY FACTORS

It often seems ironic that, in research involving culturally diverse and/or disadvantaged children, researchers assume that the parents *can* give informed consent just by the nature of being adults. This is analogous to assuming that any adult can drive a car regardless of her or his prior experience with driving a car. Potential ability is not actualized ability. Parents and the community stakeholders/leaders may need to be provided with information about what the research involves, what the children's participation will mean in terms of time commitments to *both* children and parents, the impact of participation on home or community activities, obligations on both children and parents, and financial burdens on the children and parents. If a researcher or research assistant is planning to make home visits, the researcher might want to address the efforts that they can take to make these visits minimally disruptive or intrusive on the participants' and other family members' activities. Researchers must be prepared to answer practical questions that parents may have in the course of the study. (Does my child have to miss the big soccer tournament because the research assistant can only come at that time? Does the medicine need refrigeration? Do I need to take time off from work to give my permission for my child to participate in the research?) Researchers also must be prepared to address issues that are not brought up but which affect the consent process: Can the parents read or truly understand the consent forms and procedures? What is the level of the parents' education? Is the consent form written in a way that is readily understandable? Are the consent and assent forms written in the language of the parents and children? Writing informed consent or assent forms includes using the type of language suitable for the population of interest and using the idioms understandable to that population. Translating a consent form in Spanish used in Puerto Rico may present problems for immigrant parents from rural Northern Mexico whose children are the target population of the study.

Researchers must be prepared to delve further into cultural values and norms. What are the cultural views of the parents pertaining to the autonomy of their children? How do these views compare with those of our professional, legal, and ethical standards in our mainstream society? The level of autonomy expected for a rural American Indian or Latino American child may be very different from that expected for a middle-class, urban, European American child. The researcher who places great importance on encouraging and supporting the child's voice and autonomy may be acting in ways that run counter to the cultural values in that community. The CRC has emphasized "the rights of the child" in ways that some scholars believe jeopardizes family autonomy and parental authority. Historically, the legal system in the United States has placed great importance on the nuclear family and the rights of biological parents to the exclusion of extended family members and/or the tribe who, in some cultures, may have important roles in protecting and caring for children and, consequently, in making decisions about children. In traditional American Indian families and less assimilated Latino families, grandparents, godparents, and/or uncles and aunts can have a major role in making decisions about a child.

In conducting research in communities, researchers must consider the views of the parents and their community toward the research and the researchers. Should researchers be content to simply meet the ethical and legal obligation of our U.S. system or do researchers have an ethical obligation to allow the parents of the research participants to consult with those who in their culture have an important and socially sanctioned role in making decisions for the child? How does the researcher or research assistant who tries to be culturally responsive in these ways negotiate the pressures that she or he may feel to get consents quickly so as to meet the necessary timelines? In the case of treatment research, do the parents truly understand that there will be no negative consequences for their children who may already be receiving some form of treatment if they or the children do not give consent or assent? In the case of informed consent, it is as important to consider not just what is said but what is *not* said. What is not said can lead to erroneous assumptions of potentially negative consequences for the parent and child.

Incentives, particularly monetary ones, given to parents for their children's participation in social and clinical research must be carefully considered to ensure that they do not have a coercive or exploitative quality. Incentives targeting parents who must give consent rather than the children who are the actual participants may lead to conflicting interests. For families whose income barely covers basic necessities, a seemingly token amount of $25 may have much greater value when it means helping pay for a recent repair of the family's only car. In this case, a parent may be more prone to give consent and/or strongly encourage the child to assent not because the parent sees potential merit of the research and has fully understood the risks (if any) and inconveniences to the child but because the incentive can help the family. We suggest that decisions about the use and type of incentives for parents and/or children, including the amount of money when money is the incentive, be made in collaboration with the community or tribal leaders and stakeholders.

In cases in which most parents do not have prior experience with giving consent for social or clinical research, the researchers might consider partnering with community educators to provide a preconsent education session either jointly to the potential child participant and her or his parents or to groups of parents and children who constitute potential participants. Conducting this type of session may be a first step in conveying the notion that obtaining consent must involve an equal partnership among the researcher, family (parent + child), and community and clear and direct communication characterized by mutual respect.

CONSIDERATION OF CHILD FACTORS

If the researcher intends to treat children, and by extension their family and community, with respect and convey a genuine sense of care and concern for their safety and well-being, one child cannot be treated like any other child. The researcher must recognize the uniqueness of each child in her or his ability to make decisions about participation in social and clinical research. This intention carries a responsibility to consider the child's level of cognitive, language, and moral development; prior experience in decision making; beliefs, views, and attitudes about parental or extraparental authority (e.g., extended family or tribal council); cultural beliefs, views, and values concerning the child's personal autonomy in making decisions, such as those related to participating in social or clinical research; religious beliefs and values (as in the case of a survey about sexual activity, drug use, or suicidality); current mental and physical health status; the child's or family's values about privacy and bodily boundaries; and her or his preference about getting involved in the research. The researcher must assess how well the child understands the notions of record keeping, confidentiality, disclosure requirements (e.g., as in the case of a child's admission of suicidal ideation and intent), and potential risks of the research being made public, along with the child's views about the value and validity of the research and about the degree to which the child should be self-disclosing (as in a survey about personal sexual activity or personal or family substance use). In obtaining assent, the researcher might want to consider the optimal conditions for the child to give assent. For example, what is the context in which the child might demonstrate her or his optimal abilities (at home with her or his parents, at school with her or his teacher of choice present, etc.). The determination of what constitutes the best context will inevitably require that parents and community/school stakeholders be consulted.

As described in the case of using incentives for parents, the use of incentives with minors, especially monetary ones, to encourage participation must also be carefully considered. In one study of adolescent and parent perspectives on ethical issues in youth drug use and suicide survey research (Fisher, 2003), researchers found both gender and ethnic differences. Male students were more likely than female students to think that monetary incentives might prevent participants from complaining if they thought that researcher did something wrong. Hispanic and African American adolescents were more likely than East Asians and European American adolescents to be concerned that monetary incentives would be coercive for adolescents who needed the money.

CONSIDERATION OF RESEARCHER FACTORS

Researchers should consider how they are viewed by the parents, children, and community or tribal stakeholders and how these views affect participation rates. In cultures, such as in some Asian and Latino cultures, researchers may be viewed as strong authority figures and a high value may be placed on deference to and conformity with those, such as the researchers, with ascribed authority or power. In some Latino communities, researchers may be viewed as having immigration control functions and, thus, to be avoided. Researchers need to take particular care in obtaining consents from parents and assents from minors from cultures that have these or other unique values (Fisher et al., 2002). Researchers have an obligation to examine their roles, behaviors, and social responsibilities in the context of the communities in which they are conducting their research to decrease the possibility of subtle forms of coercion and exploitation.

Researchers should consider their style of communication, not just in the consent and assent process but in the instruments and forms they use. For example, Stevenson, De Moya, and Boruch (1993) noted that the use of structured tests in which some items were repeated may be viewed in some African American communities as reflecting a lack of interest in the participants and a lack of respect for the participants' experiences and feelings. Or consider a consent form about a study that examines the relationship of family functioning on delinquent behavior in an isolated American Indian reservation and uses questionnaires that ask about the family's participation in formal church services, the child's participation in Sunday school, or participation as a family in activities such as summer vacations with the nuclear family. Potential participants may see a study that uses such questionnaires as out of touch with their actual life experiences where spirituality is much more intertwined with all aspects of life and the extended family has a significant role in a child's life.

The group of national leaders described in Fisher et al. (2002) noted that decisions about disclosing confidential information to protect ethnic minority minors require special consideration for a number of reasons: (1) studies of minors from ethnic minorities are more likely to investigate, and gather sensitive material about, maladaptive rather than normative developmental processes (see also Scott-Jones, 1994); (2) use of assessment instruments that have not been validated on ethnic minority children, along with institutional biases, may lead to an under- or overrepresentation of problem behaviors that fall under laws mandating disclosure and reporting; and (3) poorer ethnic minority families may be more available to researchers studying psychological and social problems because of their greater use of public medical, mental health, social, and legal services (see also Ross, 1997; Scott-Jones, 1994). This group also cited research to indicate increasing evidence that shows that Asian, Latino, and African American adolescents often expect researchers to assist them in getting help for problems revealed in the course of the study to which their parents have consented and to which they have assented.

◆ Conclusion

Involving children and adolescents in social and clinical research in diverse cultural settings is a journey along which we are likely to learn that our seemingly clear convictions and ethical standards are challenged by the complexities of different and even conflicting beliefs, values, and attitudes of the cultures of our research participants, their families, and their communities. But the context for this learning depends on recognizing the interlocking dynamics that affect ethical considerations, such as the varying power and prerogative of the individual researcher, institution-based IRBs that prescribe to the researcher various aspects of her or his conduct, and professional organizations that set the ethical standards by which the researcher must abide. Unless the researcher, along with the IRB and professional organizations, are acutely sensitive to their power and prerogatives and to the fact that they are all products of culture, it will be difficult to give voice to children and adolescents being studied in diverse cultural contexts and to obtain valid and reliable results from research with this population and in diverse cultural contexts. The failure of the United

States to ratify the CRC reveals that the leaders in our country have not reached a consensus about supporting the rights of minors. The suggestions provided in this chapter may seem impractical and overly complicated, particularly because they often put the responsibility on the individual researcher to examine and respond to children's and adolescents' decision-making abilities after examining the contexts, both interpersonal and environmental, in which these abilities are best demonstrated. To quote O'Neill (2005) in his Canadian Psychological Association presidential address on ethics and problem definition, "At the end of the day, psychology is the sum of the choices made by individual psychologists" (p. 19). Accordingly, it is not a matter of whether we can afford the time and expense to engage in the ethical practices we suggest; we believe that in a pluralistic country such as the United States we cannot afford not to.

♦ Notes

1. We would like to thank the editors, Donna Mertens and Pauline Ginsberg, for their very helpful review and direction in writing this chapter and two anonymous reviewers for their very thoughtful and helpful reviews of an earlier draft of this chapter.

2. Beneficial research, also referred to as therapeutic research, refers to research that may have a direct benefit to the participant (e.g., as in the case in clinical research that involves one condition in which one group receives a treatment condition that may benefit the participant). Nonbeneficial research, also referred to as nontherapeutic research, refers to research that does not have direct benefit to the participant but may have some benefit to society by the knowledge gained. Much of social research and some clinical research are of this type.

3. Emancipated minors are those who have been granted adult legal status (the age of majority) by state law because they have assumed adult responsibilities (e.g., self-support). The rights granted to legally emancipated minors can include the ability to sign legally binding contracts, own property, and keep one's own earnings. States have different laws governing emancipated minors and some states have no laws regarding emancipation. Mature minors are those who have not reached the age of majority but who, by state law, are allowed to be treated as adults for specific purposes (e.g., to give consent for certain types of treatment, such as for drug abuse or mental disorders).

4. In the case of minors who are neither emancipated nor mature minors by federal law, 45 CFR 46 Subpart D defines "children" as "persons who have not attained the legal age for consent to treatments or procedures involved in research, under the applicable law of the jurisdiction in which the research will be conducted." "Assent" is defined as "a child's affirmative agreement to participate in research" and the law further states, "Mere failure to object should not, absent affirmative agreement, be construed as assent." "Permission" is defined as "the agreement of parent(s) or guardian to the participation of their child or ward in research."

5. In the United States, an institutional review board is a group of individuals, including researchers, clinicians, and public members, formally designated by an institution, and empowered by the Food and Drug Administration, to approve, monitor, and review biomedical and behavioral research involving human participants in order to protect the participants' rights and welfare.

♦ References

Alta Charo, R. (1993). Protecting us to death: Women, pregnancy, and clinical research trials [Electronic version]. *St. Louis University Law Journal, 38,* 135.

American Psychological Association. (2002). Ethical principles of psychologists and code of conduct. *American Psychologist, 57,* 1060–1073.

Aristotle. (1999). *The metaphysics* (H. Lawson-Tancred, Trans.). London: Penguin Books.

Begay v. United States, 591 F. Supp. 991 (D. Ariz. 1984), aff'd, 768 F.2d 1059 (9th Cir. 1985).

Clark, N. L. (2000). Parens patriae and a modest proposal for the twenty-first century: Legal philosophy and a new look at children's welfare. *Michigan Journal of Gender and Law, 6*(2), 381–448.

Ericka Grimes v. Kennedy Kreiger Institute and Higgins, a minor, etc. v. Kennedy Kreiger Institute, 366 Md 29; 782 A. 2d 807; 2001 Md. Lexis 496 (2001).

Fisher, C. B. (2003). Adolescent and parent perspectives on ethical issues in youth drug use and suicide survey research. *Ethics & Behavior, 13*(4), 303–332.

Fisher, C. B. (2004). Informed consent and clinical research involving children and adolescents: Implications of the revised APA Ethics Code and HIPAA. *Journal Clinical Child and Adolescent Psychology, 33*(4), 832–839.

Fisher, C. B., Hoagwood, K., Boyce, C., Duster, T., Frank, D. A., Grisso, T., et al. (2002). Research ethics for mental health science involving minority children and youths. *American Psychologist, 57*(12), 1024–1040.

Fisher, C. B., Hoagwood, K., & Jensen, P. (1996). Casebook on ethical issues in research with children and adolescents with mental disorders. In K. Hoagwood, P. Jensen, & C. B. Fisher (Eds.), *Ethical issues in research with children and adolescents with mental disorders* (pp. 135–238). Mahwah, NJ: Erlbaum.

Fraser, C. (2000). Protecting Native Americans: The tribe as parens patriae. *Michigan Journal of Race and Law, 5*, 665–694.

Hillabrant, W. (2002). *Research in Indian country: Challenges and changes* (Report No. RC 023 925). East Lansing, MI: National Center for Research on Teacher Learning. (Eric Document Reproduction Service No. ED473271)

Indian Child Welfare Act, 92 Stat. 3069, 25 U.S.C. 1901–1963 (1978).

Institute of Medicine. (2004). *The ethical conduct of clinical research involving children.* Washington, DC: National Academies Press.

James, A. L. (1992). An open or shut case? Law as an autopoeitic system. *Journal of Law and Society, 19*(2), 271–283.

Joffe, S. (2003). Rethink "affirmative agreement," but abandon "assent." *American Journal of Bioethics, 3*(4), 9–11.

King, M. (1991). Child welfare within law: The emergence of a hybrid discourse. *Journal of Law and Society, 18*(3), 303–322.

Levit, N. (2002). Theorizing the connections among systems of subordination [Electronic version]. *University of Missouri-Kansas City Law Review, 71*, 227.

Luhmann, N. (1989). Law as a social system. *Northwestern University Law Review, 83*, 136–150.

MacKinnon, C. A. (2007). *Sex equality* (2nd ed.). New York: Foundation Press.

Melton, G. B. (1983). *Child advocacy: Psychological issues and interventions.* New York: Plenum Press.

Melton, G. B. (2005a). Building humane communities respectful of children: The significance of the Convention on the Rights of the Child. *American Psychologist, 60*, 918–926.

Melton, G. B. (2005b). Treating children like people: A framework for research and advocacy. *Journal of Clinical Child and Adolescent Psychology, 34*(4), 646–657.

Melton, G. B., & Wilcox, B. L. (2001). Children's Law: Toward a new realism. *Law and Human Behavior, 25*(1), 3–12.

Miller, V. A., Drotar, D., & Kodish, E. (2004). Children's competence for assent and consent: A review of empirical findings. *Ethics & Behavior, 14*(3), 255–295.

Miller-Wilson, L. S. (2006). Law and adolescence: Examining the legal and policy implications of adolescent development research in the child welfare, juvenile justice, or criminal justice systems. *Temple Law Review, 79*(2), 317–324.

Nannis, E. D. (1991). Children's understanding of their participation in psychological research: Implications for issues of assent and consent. *Canadian Journal of Behavioural Science, 23*(2), 133–141.

O'Neill, P. (2005). The ethics of problem resolution. *Canadian Psychology, 46*(1), 13–20.

Ross, L. (1997). Children as research subjects: A proposal to revise the current federal regulations using a moral framework [Electronic version]. *Stanford Law & Policy Review, 159,* 164.

Ruffins, P. (1998). *The Tuskegee Experiment's long shadow.* Retrieved May 8, 2007, from Black Issues in Higher Education Web site: http://findarticles.com/p/articles/mi_m0DXK/is_1998_Oct_29/ai_53257761/pg_4

Russell, B. (1997). *The problems of philosophy.* New York: Oxford University Press.

Scott-Jones, D. (1994). Ethical issues in reporting and referring in research with low-income minority children. *Ethics & Behavior, 4,* 97–108.

Silver, C. (2006). *Family autonomy and the Charter of Rights: Protecting parental liberty in a child-centered legal system* (Discussion paper # 3). Retrieved April 28, 2007, from Centre for Cultural Renewal Web site: www.culturalrenewal.ca/downloads/sb_cuturalrenewal/discussion3.pdf

Steele v. Hamilton County Mental Health Board, 90 Ohio St.3d 176, 736 N.E.2d 10 (2000).

Stevenson, H. C., De Moya, D., & Boruca, R. F. (1993). Ethical issues and approaches in AIDS research. In D. G. Ostrow & R. C. Kessler (Eds.), *Methodological issues in AIDS research* (pp. 19–51). New York: Plenum Press.

Suber, P. (1997). Legal reasoning after postmodern critiques of reasoning. *Legal Writing, 3,* 21–50.

Teubner, G. (1989). How the law thinks: Toward a constructivist epistemology of law. *Law and Society Review, 23,* 728–257.

UN Convention on the Rights of the Child. (1989). *General Assembly Resolution 44/25, U.N. GAOR Supp.* 49 at 165, U.N. Doc. A/44 736.

ETHICAL RESEARCH WITH OLDER ADULTS

◆ Karen Szala-Meneok

Research with older adults can contribute valuable knowledge about the aging process and enhance the well-being of older people and society in general. In North America, persons 65 years and older are considered aged. However, advances in preventive medicine are leading to greater longevity with more people living to 100 years and beyond. With an age range of 40 years, differing backgrounds and experience, and varying capacity, the elderly are a highly diverse group. Nevertheless, in general, the older the participants included in a study, the frailer they are likely to be.

Qualitative research is generally not something *done to* participants but rather *something that transpires between* researchers and participants. Research techniques include listening, observing behavior, and examining material culture. In contrast to experimental research, it usually poses no greater risk of physical harm or discomfort than that encountered in daily life. Nevertheless, qualitative research with vulnerable older adults can require special protection.

In the spirit of justice and a commitment to collecting quality data, the researcher should not automatically exclude individuals from research because of age or health deficits. Although it may take more time to recruit older persons and more creativity to collect data from them, the rewards will better reflect and *respect* the study population. Project time lines should accommodate the special needs of the elderly and budgets factor in any additional time, research staff, or technology required to support consent and data collection.

Working with older people on topics related to aging presents intriguing ethical questions. It is particularly important to weigh the risks of doing research with vulnerable groups against the potential benefits of knowledge gained. Particular ethical challenges include selecting participants equitably and ensuring free and informed consent. In consultation with review boards, researchers need to determine whether consent safeguards such as anticipatory decision-making mechanisms or prospective authorization are required.

This chapter covers a broad spectrum of disciplines and methodological techniques used in qualitative research that either is about the aging process or includes elderly people. It is hoped that there will be something of value for new and seasoned scholars within these pages.

◆ Ethical Principles

Ethical principles should guide all stages of the research enterprise from defining the research question to publishing the results. Broad ethical principles include respect for persons, beneficence, and justice. Certain operational concepts related to these principles are particularly relevant to the study of the elderly. Respect for older persons involves paying attention to their dignity. This includes facilitating their autonomy in making decisions, enhancing voluntarism, avoiding coercion, and assuring privacy and confidentiality. Beneficence involves the protection for persons with diminished capacity and the maximization of benefits and minimization of risks for all participants. Justice requires that benefits and risks be distributed fairly. Provided it is feasible, elderly persons should be involved in studies that would benefit them. Researchers may decide to leave them out of some studies that would theoretically be of benefit because of methodological challenges involved or concerns about participant burden. However, it is their responsibility to recognize and address the limitations of these studies.

Attention to these general principles is required during study design, when sample selection occurs and instruments are created and chosen. The process of obtaining consent warrants particular care. Special attention should be given to consent protocols in studies that involve long-term participation. Data collection requires attention to interactive style and empathic skills as well as to formal techniques.

◆ Research Design

In selecting participants, researchers are faced with two related questions. Does their research require the inclusion of the elderly, and if so, what are the criteria for including participants? Balancing the possible gains from a study with concerns about nonmalfeasance (doing no harm) when working with vulnerable participants can be challenging.

When research poses little risk, sample selection is straightforward. Researchers in anthropology, sociology, and geography often select older persons as informants because they are repositories of cultural information or can shed light on the social, economic, political, or physical process of aging. When researchers approach participants as experts, the latter feel respected and perhaps empowered. In contrast, stringent criteria for sampling must be set up when greater than minimal risk is involved, especially if participants are not likely to benefit from the findings. For example, participation in studies about elder mistreatment, suicide, or depression may be extremely stressful. Researchers need to ask themselves hard questions about benefits, risks, and respect when selecting subjects.

Mental health issues are an important consideration in sample selection. While cognitive impairment (CI) is not an inevitable consequence of aging, its incidence increases dramatically beyond the eighth decade (*Diagnostic and Statistical Manual of Mental Disorders*, 4th ed., American Psychiatric Association, 1994). CI includes dementia, acquired brain injury, developmental disabilities, or other psychopathologies. Some people experience progressively diminished capacity to consent to research, while others have fluctuating capacity as a result of schizophrenia, delirium, or depression. Research on these conditions is vital, but conducting research with people whose decisional capacity is compromised challenges ideals such as voluntarism, justice, beneficence, and respect for participants. Nevertheless, it is vital to create a sampling framework that serves both the purpose of the study while minimizing harm to the participants.

In the past, persons with diminished decisional capacity were sometimes sampled for reasons of convenience. In 1963, the Jewish Chronic Disease Hospital case in New York City revealed that chronically ill but cancer-free patients were injected with live liver cancer cells to observe the human transplant rejection process. Patients were not informed about the nature of the experiment (Faden & Beauchamp, 1986). Today, researchers must provide compelling reasons for including persons with compromised decisional capacity in their studies. It is generally accepted that these individuals should not be recruited unless they are the only source of data (Alzheimer's Association, 1997). The study's invasiveness, the level of risk, the potential for benefit, and the severity of cognitive impairment are issues to be addressed when creating criteria for sample selection.

Because of its interactive approach, it is unlikely that persons with severe CI will be able to participate actively in qualitative research. However, social scientists have conducted studies with persons with mild cognitive impairment (MCI). Frank et al. (2006) conducted focus groups with persons with mild dementia to explore the impact of learning in the diagnosis of Alzheimer's disease. Lingler et al. (2006) conducted in-home semistructured interviews with persons with MCI and elicited rich personal narratives about their lived experience. Without talking to persons with CI, they would not have been able to learn about the effects of this disease from an insider perspective. In another study, qualitative researchers wanted to understand end-of-life cancer care issues for persons with MCI dying in hospice. The ethical issues were greater in this study because the participants experienced risks and discomforts but few or no benefits. However, although participant observation and in-depth interviewing of hospice staff and family members could provide valuable insights for improving patient care (Kayser-Jones, 2002), their own experiences provided the most reliable data. In cases such as this, capacity assessment may be warranted before participants are enrolled but managed with sensitivity.

Observational research of individuals with severe CI is a possibility but would require the use of alternative consent strategies as well as the consent of individuals providing care who would also be observed. Sample selection must take into account the context of the potential participant's life as well as care for their dignity and privacy.

Researchers planning to include older persons in their studies should familiarize themselves with health and other issues relevant to this population. When the elderly, particularly the frail elderly, are study participants, selection of research assistants requires particular attention—the greater the risk, the more need for care. Ideally, those working with the frail elderly should have some knowledge of, or experience, working with this population and exhibit sensitivity in interpersonal relations. As granting agencies increasingly expect student training to be included in research programs, investigators must be vigilant in the supervision of undergraduate or graduate research or when study staff include students. Orientation and training of all study staff should address ageist assumptions. Expenses and additional time required for modifications to accommodate the needs of the elderly are best integrated into time lines and budgets during the design stage of the project.

◆ Tools and Techniques

Once the decision has been made to include older persons in a study, the researcher's next step is to consider issues relevant to accessing this group and managing their recruitment. For the older persons in good mental and physical health, recruitment strategies need not be different from those for adults in general. Specific strategies depend on the type of research envisaged. Common techniques include direct or indirect contact by letter, telephone, or e-mail. However, if there is a possibility that a sample may include vulnerable elderly people, researchers must prepare strategies to protect them.

When cold calling is planned, the effect of the call on a potential participant must be considered. Loneliness should not be exploited to reach a recruitment quota. Some older people living alone welcome the chance to talk to interviewers. They may not be interested in the study itself but consent to achieve social contact. It is important that researchers and their staff be sensitive to the possibility that older subjects may find it difficult to say "no." Verbal and nonverbal cues can reveal ambivalence. When participants only marginally match the selection criteria for the study, data quality can be compromised. When first contact is by telephone, interviewers may wish to screen individuals for cognitive impairment. One strategy is to prepare inclusion questions that ask the interviewee to explain to them key elements from the consent script. If comprehension is in doubt, the interviewer can thank interviewees for their time and move on to the next call. Similar strategies can be used for face-to-face interviews.

For studies focusing on older people, approaching individuals through third parties may be beneficial to both researchers and participants. Initial contact with people with severe sensory deficits could be channeled through experts such as health care providers, patient advocates, or family members who can assess risk to potential participants. Many older adults are wary of con artists who prey on trusting or cognitively impaired seniors. When conducting research in a large metropolitan area, seniors on our advisory team urged us to make presentations to seniors groups and the "Senior's Support Officer" at the local police department. When our telephone interviews began, seniors did call these services as well as the research ethics board and the study office to make sure we were "legitimate."

Researchers are encouraged to conduct preliminary background research on groups they intend to include in their sample and become familiar with factors that may limit their participation. At times, the necessity of working through third parties can be problematic. The recruitment of institutionalized persons is usually brokered through clinical or social service staff or family members who assume the role of "gatekeeper." Wenger (2001) noted that as frailty increases, more persons become part of decision making and the equitable and just selection of subjects may be compromised. For example, drawing samples from long-term care facilities can pose challenges. Administrators and staff are responsible for caring for residents and protecting their privacy. They may hinder access even to residents without CI or serious health problems because they may be burdened with existing responsibilities, they fear for the patient, or because they anticipate disapproval from family members. Planning for and allocating sufficient time to work with administrators and staff can facilitate research and ensure that when appropriate, residents are able to participate.

Learning about age-related health changes such as sensory and physical deficits is an important prerequisite for preparing appropriate strategies and research materials for older study participants. Visual, auditory, and communication deficits influence how a person understands recruitment information about a study (Philpin, Jordan, & Warring, 2005) and their willingness or ability to participate. Appropriate tools and strategies to accommodate these deficits contribute to effective recruitment, good rapport between researcher and participant, and just and respectful research.

Modifying documents for the visually impaired is essential. In their recent evidence-based module on enhancing legibility and readability of documents, Russell-Minda, Jutai, and Strong (2006) reported that font size should be 16 to 18 point Times New Roman or Arial or similar serif or sans serif fonts. Attention should be paid to contrast, font heaviness and color, and line and letter spacing. Areas of white space and nonglossy paper also contribute to clarity. Sutton (2002) provided further recommendations to increase accessibility. Participants should have adequate time to read study materials and be given the option of having printed materials read to them. For individuals with vision or hearing impairments that are not age related, researchers should pursue alternate communication modalities such as Braille or sign language.

Recruitment using oral presentation together with written materials usually works well with hearing impaired older persons. Written communication is the most reliable means of eliciting consent. Some persons habitually speak loudly to all older persons whether they are deaf or not. This patronizing approach does little to develop rapport with potential participants. Interviewers can show consideration and enhance understanding by speaking distinctly, minimizing background noise, and inquiring whether they should speak louder. Speaking slowly and facing the participant can enhance understanding if the latter is lipreading. The Internet has become an important tool for some deaf persons and may facilitate online recruitment. Devices that amplify telephone volume or caption phones will make recruitment more effective but not all persons with hearing impairments have access to these devices. The National Institute on Deafness and Other Communication Disorders (1999) has developed guidelines to assist researchers for obtaining consent.

Individuals who have suffered a stroke or traumatic brain injury may have aphasia—difficulty in speaking or understanding language. They may also have difficulty reading. Giving interviewees time to recall words and form sentences and corroborating what was said are useful techniques. If aphasics cannot communicate, qualitative researchers are unlikely to recruit them because of the interactive nature of this research. However, some important advances are being made in research with this group. Stein and Brady Wagner (2006) described their use of a "patient-selected helper" who facilitates communication in supported conversations but leaves final decisions to the participant. Researchers also have devised alternatives to standard consent forms that include shortened text and a combination of words and pictures (Kagan & Kimelman, 1995).

Although it is important to accommodate potential participants with sensory deficits, particular strategies sometime backfire. Obtaining feedback from community members or researchers experienced with the population can catch issues before they become a problem. An example occurred when I worked with a group of active and outspoken seniors (Szala-Meneok & Lohfeld, 2005). They confronted me about why university researchers were sending them materials on yellow paper. They explained that this was offensive to them because the color yellow was associated with cowardice. Even after I explained that people with vision problems find it easier to read black font on yellow paper than other formats, they suggested that seniors would prefer larger font on plain white paper. Reading over documents *with* participants (regardless of visual acuity) ensures that points are covered and questions answered.

◆ Consent Strategy

Designing an appropriate consent strategy is vital. Participants themselves recognize this when they joke about "signing their lives away." A core tenet in research ethics is that for consent to be free, it must be informed. The researcher's responsibility is to craft consent documents or use other strategies to explain to participants, what they will be asked to do, what risks and benefits they may encounter, their rights as participants, and how confidentiality will be safeguarded. It is also the researcher's responsibility to ensure that participants understand the implication of consent.

CRAFTING CLEAR DOCUMENTS

In designing consent documents, researchers aim to achieve the "3Cs" of consent: being comprehensible, comprehensive, and concise. The purpose of consent forms and other study documents is to inform not to impress. Academic terminology is better left to scholarly manuscripts. Most older participants are intelligent lay persons, who require complete study information in clear prose. Plain language is not a form of condescension or elder-speak (baby talk) sometimes used with older adults (Williams, Kemper, & Hummert, 2004). Just as overzealous protection is paternalistic, overly simplistic language is disrespectful. When creating comprehensible documents, the researcher may find it helpful to write an initial draft in their usual writing style, then complete one or two plain language iterations. Asking a group of older persons to pilot consent and other documents for clarity and appropriate tone is valuable.

ALTERNATIVE FORMS OF CONSENT

Written consent is considered the ideal method for documenting willingness to participate; but people need not be excluded from a study because they have sensory deficits, limited education, poor literacy skills, or suffer from arthritis or other conditions that prevent them from reading or signing forms. Obtaining written consent might be inappropriate or impractical in some circumstances, for example, with telephone interviews or Internet surveys or in some societies. Verbal consent can take a variety of forms. Computer-assisted telephone interviews (CATI), for example, may begin with a script that introduces prospective older participants to the study and "walks" them through a verbal consent process. In these instances, a log is maintained to record that consent was obtained. Alternately, some researchers audiotape the participant's verbal consent, note the date, and state their own name as the witness.

RE-CONSENT

Re-consent ensures free and informed consent throughout longitudinal studies or long-term ethnographic fieldwork. Built-in re-consent means that older participants, whose patterns of politeness or keeping one's word may make it difficult for them to withdraw, know from the beginning that "they have an out." Re-consent procedures may include strategies for monitoring verbal and nonverbal cues for participant stress, loss of interest, disinclination to continue, or problems with understanding study activities. They also help the researcher broach potentially sensitive issues of ending a person's involvement because of participant burden or changes to health or cognitive status. Scheduled re-consent sessions can serve to arrange a graceful exit that respects the participant and enhances study management.

CAPACITY TO CONSENT TO RESEARCH: AN EMERGING AREA OF RESEARCH

Some 10 assessment tools (Dunn, Nowrangi, Palmer, Jeste, & Saks, 2006) are currently under evaluation to determine their ability to assess capacity to consent to research participation. These instruments, which differ from tools that focus on capacity to consent to medical treatment, assess understanding, appreciation, reasoning, and choice (Dunn et al., 2006). While assessment tools should be used for protocols that involve more than minimal risk, there is no consensus on what tools are appropriate in which circumstances or for what population or about what makes a study greater than minimal risk. As the acceptance and use of these tools increases, review boards may begin to expect their use. There is a danger that they may be used too widely.

Problems related to cognitive assessment are problematic for both researchers and potential participants. First, administering psychometric tests requires specific skills and an appropriate team member must be recruited. Second, persons with MCI or no impairment may feel stigmatized or be anxious about taking the test. I would not blame an older person for feeling insulted by having to "pass a test" to be part of my study, particularly if it were minimal risk research. When one consent assessment tool was tested, some participants became frustrated and upset and decided not to participate (Resnick et al., 2007). Ensuring the capacity of people to give informed consent should not outweigh the need for respect. By inappropriately screening for capacity to consent, would-be "protectors" may actually increase risk to participants. If researchers work with review boards to establish policies to handle assessment results and avoid participant distress, they may avoid this situation.

Assessment tools elicit information about understanding, appreciation, reasoning, and choice. A review of capacity assessment tools suggests that short item instruments with 3 to 5 questions show most promise for identifying comprehension issues (Palmer et al., 2005). Social scientists conducting minimal risk research may not need a capacity assessment tool but employing minimal assessment questions might be useful. After initial discussion, qualitative researchers might test individuals who they suspect lack consent capacity. Asking prospective participants to explain the study's purpose, risks, and benefits may be sufficient to determine capacity.

OTHER CONSENT SAFEGUARDS

Social scientists, particularly those working in the health science fields, should consider familiarizing themselves with additional consent safeguards. As well as capacity assessment tools, these include anticipatory decision-making strategies such as advanced directives for research (ADRs), the appointment of substitute decision makers (SDMs), and the use of subject advocates who monitor verbal or physical assent. SDMs cannot enroll an individual in a study but can withdraw participants with diminished decisional capacity (Alzheimer's Association, 2004; National Bioethics Advisory Commission, 1999).

Becoming familiar with anticipatory decision-making mechanisms helps ensure study participants are protected. Another reason is that if proposals are submitted to boards that review primarily greater-than-minimal-risk biomedical research, there may be an expectation that research with older populations should automatically have these safeguards in place. Qualitative researchers should be prepared to consider their use or provide adequate rationales for not using them. In addition, researchers and review boards should familiarize themselves with current state or provincial laws regarding capacity assessment and the use of SDMs and ADRs (Bravo, Paquet, & Dubois, 2003; Smyer, 2007).

♦ Data Collection

The data collection techniques employed with the elderly resemble those used with other adults. Social scientists use participant observation, interviews, and questionnaires. In some qualitative studies, participants are sometimes asked to construct a geneology, tell stories, or demonstrate a skill. Multidisciplinary teams studying the ageing process often use qualitative techniques such as questionnaires, open-ended or closed-ended one-on-one interviews, and CATI. Similar accommodations are required for the frail elderly or those with disabilities as were identified for the section on the consent process. Offering participants choices, giving them enough time to complete a study task, and being mindful of ageist assumptions are essential in qualitative research whether one is working with seniors in an urban high rise or on an island in the Pacific. One should protect but not disenfranchise.

THE TEMPORAL DIMENSION

As with all research, it is important to be sensitive to the level of burden for participants. Time is valuable to study participants as well as to researchers. It is important not to assume that because people are retired, they have limitless time. Some older persons prefer to break up their participation into a number of sessions. Moreover, with the frail elderly, it is important to be aware of the possibility of fatigue. Opportunities to collect data from people with diminished or fluctuating capacity may be limited and the researcher will need to be flexible to benefit from their input.

Many social scientists collect data over months and even years during repeated field trips. Rapport building lays the groundwork for evolving trust and contributes to the generation of high-quality data. Some social scientists have grown old alongside their study participants, having weathered milestones such as marriage, parenthood, and work, the loss of parents, sickness, disappointments, and accomplishments. Sharing their lives contributes to the researcher's understanding of society in general and the aging process in particular. Researcher/participant relationships often evolve into friendship; however, the researcher must remain mindful that it could be difficult for a participant to say "no" to a friend.

PRIVACY AND GIVING CREDIT

Elderly people live alone, with partners, in a variety of extended family types, or in institutionalized care. In North America and many other developed countries, the ideal is to foster independent living, *aging in place*, until frailty, deteriorating physical health, or cognitive functioning warrant assisted living or institutionalization. The best location for data collection depends on the participant's circumstances. While it is often convenient for both researchers and participants to collect data at the participants' home, these settings may not provide the privacy required during discussion of sensitive matters. However, when older people have mobility problems, it is not always possible to arrange an alternative venue. Sometimes privacy can be achieved through careful scheduling. Many elders living alone rely on family or personal support workers to assist with daily living. Researchers can try to schedule their sessions around their visits. When caregivers and recipients live together, sensitivity to the needs of both is important. Collecting data on older caregivers, Szala-Meneok and Lohfeld (2005) discovered that understanding the latter's needs involved information about the recipients of their care. It was essential to protect each member of the caregiver/care receiver dyad from overhearing confidential remarks about the other. Sending transcriptions for member checking or study findings was problematic when both had access to mail. Anticipating and planning for these and similar scenarios will mitigate risks. When caregiver/care recipient dyads participate in the same studies briefings about protecting their own and each other's privacy may be helpful.

It is very difficult to safeguard the privacy of elderly people living in institutions. Most facilities take pains to preserve privacy but activities usually considered private are relatively public in these settings. Because many ward residents share a room with several people, researchers may need to locate alternate spaces to conduct confidential interviews. While long-term care facilities are the homes of residents, that home is no longer a "bastion of privacy."

Although it is usually important to protect the anonymity of the participants, individuals who provide expert knowledge or personal experiences may desire acknowledgement. Beyond altruism, they may wish to be recognized as sources of important information. Naming these participants recognizes the value of their intellectual property and enriches the data.

AUTONOMY, VOLUNTARISM, AND COERCION

When older persons speak a different language from the interviewer, a translator is needed. In these circumstances, accuracy may best be served by bilingual research assistants. In circumstances where family members are asked to translate, the researcher should be aware that the interviewee may feel unable to talk freely or that the translator may modify the interviewee's words to protect either the interviewee or the family. Ensuring the autonomy of older study participants with diminishing capacity is a challenge. Their decision whether to participate in research can be threatened when SDMs are involved, or when participants live with overprotective or controlling spouses or an adult child.

Voluntarism is critical to any research but is sometimes difficult to safeguard among the institutionalized elderly. Researchers may be seen as authority figures. If potential participants hear the researcher addressed as doctor, they may think that deciding not to participate could influence their care even if the researcher is not an M.D. Voluntarism may also be an issue when a participant wishes to withdraw. Participants may feel compelled to take part in the research for reasons of social desirability, fear of repercussions if they do not participate, or losing social contact with the researcher.

ISSUES ARISING DURING RESEARCH

Researchers should develop strategies for dealing with suspected elder abuse. They should identify their legal responsibilities in these circumstances and investigate what legal protection is available for reporters of suspected abuse. Their own moral perspective will guide their response, particularly when research is conducted in societies where there are no formal laws dealing with elder mistreatment.

♦ Conclusions

Researchers must treat all study participants with respect, minimizing the possibility of harm. However, research with the elderly requires particular vigilance. Additional safeguards are needed to maintain autonomy while guarding against paternalism. Research on capacity assessment is an emerging area of interest in ethics especially in greater-than-minimal risk research. Social scientists should carefully monitor developments in this area to determine that they remain current and can anticipate new expectations by review boards. Emerging best practices (Kon & Klug, 2006) for greater-than-minimal risk research with persons with compromised decisional capacity suggest that greater care should be taken to ensure comprehension of consent materials. This new focus may lead to changes in the review and eventual conduct of minimal risk research with older adults. Revised standards will most likely affect research conducted in health science settings with the most vulnerable older persons. The level of safeguards should ultimately be proportionate to the level of risk and vulnerability of the population. To protect vulnerable persons, we generally focus on the risks of doing research—sometimes we have to worry about the risk to participants of not doing research.

◆ References

Alzheimer's Association. (1997). *Ethical issues in dementia research*. Retrieved October 31, 2007, from www.alz.org/national/documents/statements_ethicalissues.pdf

Alzheimer's Association. (2004). Research consent for cognitively impaired adults: Recommendations for institutional review boards and investigators. *Alzheimer Disease and Associated Disorders, 16*(3), 171–175.

American Psychiatric Association. (1994). *Diagnostic and statistical manual of mental disorders* (4th ed.). Washington, DC: American Psychiatric Association,

Bravo, G., Paquet, M., & Dubois, M.-F. (2003). Knowledge of the legislation governing proxy consent to treatment and research. *Journal of Medical Ethics, 29*(1), 44–50.

Dunn, L. B., Nowrangi, M. A., Palmer, B. W., Jeste, D. V., & Saks, E. R. (2006). Assessing decisional capacity for clinical research or treatment: A review of instruments. *American Journal of Psychiatry, 168*(8), 1323–1334.

Faden, R., & Beauchamp, T. (1986). *A history and theory of informed consent*. New York: Oxford University Press.

Frank, L., Lloyd, A., Flynn, J. A., Kleinman, L., Matza, L. S., Margolis, M. K., et al. (2006). Impact of cognitive impairment on mild dementia patients and mild cognitive impairment patients and their informants. *International Psychogeriatrics, 18*, 151–162.

Kagan, A., & Kimelman, M. D. Z. (1995). Informed consent in aphasia research: Myth or reality? *Clinical Aphasiology, 23,* 65–75.

Kayser-Jones, J. (2002). The experience of dying: An ethnographic nursing home study [Special issue]. *The Gerontologist, 42*(3), 11–19.

Kon, A., & Klug, M. (2006). Methods and practices of investigators for determining participants' decisional capacity and comprehension of protocols. *Journal of Empirical Research on Human Research Ethics,* 61–66.

Lingler, J. H., Nightingale, M. C., Erlen, J. A., Kane, A. L., Reynolds, C. F., Schulz, R., et al. (2006). Making sense of mild cognitive impairment: A qualitative exploration of the patient's experience. *The Gerontologist, 46*(6), 791–800.

National Bioethics Advisory Commission. (1999). *Research involving persons with mental disorders that may affect decision-making capacity commissioned papers by the national bioethics advisory commission* (Vol. 2). Retrieved October 31, 2007, from www.bioethics.gov/reports/past_commissions/nbac_mental2.pdf

National Institute on Deafness and Other Communication Disorders. (1999). *Guidelines on communicating informed consent for individuals who are deaf or hard-of-hearing and scientists*. Retrieved October 31, 2007, from www.nidcd.nih.gov/news/inform/printready.htm

Palmer, B. W., Dunn, L. B., Applebaum, P. S., Mudaliar, S., Thal, L., Henry, R., et al. (2005). Assessment of capacity to consent to research among older persons with Schizophrenia, Alzheimer Disease, or Diabetes Mellitus: Comparison of a 3-item questionnaire with a comprehensive standardized capacity instrument. *Archives of General Psychiatry, 62,* 726–733.

Philpin, S. M., Jordan, S. E., & Warring, J. (2005). Giving people a voice: Reflections on conducting interviews with participants experiencing communication impairment, *Journal of Advanced Nursing, 50*(3), 299–306.

Resnick, B., Gruber-Baldini, A. L., Pretzer-Aboff, I., Galik, E., Buie, V. C., Russ, K., et al. (2007). Reliability and validity of the evaluation to sign consent measure. *The Gerontologist, 47*(1), 69–77.

Russell-Minda, E., Jutai, J., & Strong, G. (2006). Clear Print: An evidence-based review of the research on typeface legibility for readers with low vision, module five. *Vision Rehabilitation Evidence-Based Review.* London: Canadian National Institute of the Blind. Retrieved October 31, 2007, from www.cnib.ca/en/services/accessibility/text.clearprint/Clear%20Print%20Full%20Review.doc

Smyer, M. (2007). Contexts of capacity: Local and state variations in capacity assessment: Commentary on assessment of decision-making in older adults. *Journal of Gerontology, 62B*(1), 14–15.

Stein, J., & Brady Wagner, L. C. (2006). Is informed consent a "yes" or "no" response? Enhancing the shared decision-making process for persons with aphasia. *Topics in Stroke Rehabilitation, 13*(4), 42–46.

Sutton, J. (2002). *A guide to making documents accessible to people who are blind or visually impaired.* Washington, DC: American Council of the Blind. Retrieved October 6, 2007, from http://acb.org/accessible-formats.html

Szala-Meneok, K., & Lohfeld, L. (2005). The charms and challenges of an academic qualitative researcher doing participatory action research (PAR). In D. Pawluch, W. Shaffir, & C. Miall (Eds.), *Doing ethnography: Studying everyday life* (pp. 52–650). Toronto, Ontario, Canada: Canadian Scholar's Press.

Wenger, G. C. (2001). Interviewing older people. In J. F. Gubrium, & J. A. Holstein (Eds.), *Handbook of interview research: Context and method* (pp. 259–278). Thousand Oaks, CA: Sage.

Williams, K., Kemper, S., & Hummert, M. L. (2004). Enhancing communication with older adults: Overcoming elder-speak. *Journal of Gerontological Nursing, 30*(10), 17–25.

SECTION VI

CONCLUSIONS AND FUTURE DIRECTIONS

This final section of the *Handbook* contains chapters that look to the future of research ethics in a broad context. The first of these resituates social science research ethics in a broader, world context of globalization. The second looks toward the future because it relates to ethical preparation of the next generation of social science researchers. The third examines the relationship between social research and public policy as a moral imperative. Finally, the editors abstract lessons from the *Handbook* as a whole. The overarching goal of this section is to leave readers with a sense of history, of growth, and of the challenges ahead as social science researchers engage in ethical thought and practice.

Robert Stake and Fazal Rizvi's "Research Ethics in Transnational Spaces" (Chapter 33) describes the ethical challenges social researchers face in light of pressures of the discriminatory social benefits of global trade, increasing international economic and refugee migration, increasing levels of poverty, irretrievable environmental problems, major health concerns such as AIDS, increasing civil strife in Asia and Africa, the so-called clash of civilization between Western and Islamic worlds, high rates of youth unemployment, increasing income gaps between rich and poor nations, and within nations, the drifting apart of socioeconomic classes. To a greater or lesser extent, as a result of globalization, space has been compressed and stretched at the same time, leading to the expansion of social relations, activities, and networks. There has been an intensification and acceleration of social exchanges, accompanied by profound ethical dilemmas for researchers in terms of working with communities with no fixed geographic boundaries in the context of power differentials that span the globe. Social researchers inevitably need to make judgments about attaching priority to some issues and not others, necessitating the making of ethical choices at each step in the process, from design to interpretation and dissemination. In transnational contexts, there is likely to be a greater range of interests and perspectives that need to be negotiated.

Nicholas C. Burbules' chapter, "Privacy and New Technologies: The Limits of Traditional Research Ethics" (Chapter 34), reminds us that however well we know (or think we know) our research topics and specific research settings, the broader research context is undergoing rapid change. He proposes a fundamentally different approach to ethics in our increasingly uncertain, globalized, interdependent, ubiquitously networked environment. "Networked ethics" introduces the concept of "moral luck" and challenges the notion that researchers might be able to anticipate the dissemination and effects of their own work.

Celia B. Fisher, Frederick J. Wertz, and Sabrina J. Goodman remind readers of their obligation to prepare the next generation of ethical researchers in Chapter 35, "Graduate Training in Responsible Conduct of Social Science Research: The Role of Mentors and Departmental Climate." They discuss a variety of strategies to enhance the responsible conduct of research, such as providing examples of ethical behavior in their own work as well as mentoring students at their institutions. Professional success requires awareness and understanding of professional standards, regulations, and ethical values of the scientific community that can be transmitted to trainees either explicitly or implicitly through the mentoring process. Complex issues rise to the surface concerning the preparation of the mentors, effective mentoring strategies, and transference of ethical principles from the mentor relationship to application in research.

Kenneth R. Howe and Heather MacGillivary's chapter, "Social Research Attuned to Deliberative Democracy" (Chapter 36), takes a proactive stance with regard to the ethical implications of conducting research and evaluation, and using the implications of deliberative democratic political theory for social research methodology as a means to influence public policy. They examine the change in the roles of researchers and evaluators when they are working with communities with a conscious purpose of influencing public policy with the results of their research. The ethical responsibility associated with a stronger linkage between research and public policy serves as a critique and also provides a basis for discussion of ethical implications when researchers adopt a proactive stance with regard to public policy.

Concluding the *Handbook of Social Research Ethics*, editors Pauline E. Ginsberg and Donna M. Mertens provide a summary of the ethical issues addressed, the tensions identified, ongoing challenges in ethical thought, and indications of future directions in the development of social science research ethics. Meant to stimulate further dialogue, Chapter 37, titled "Frontiers in Social Research Ethics: Fertile Ground for Evolution," pulls from the past and offers a glimpse into the future as portrayed by the *Handbook*'s contributors.

33
RESEARCH ETHICS IN TRANSNATIONAL SPACES

◆ Robert Stake and Fazal Rizvi

Wilmslow Road runs by the campus of the Manchester Metropolitan University in England, at an interface between academia and commerce. It is where students shop, meet their friends, and hang out. Is this the same place where one of us—Fazal—used to shop when he was a graduate student more than 30 years ago? In one sense, it clearly is—many of the buildings are the same and it is still a center of vibrant commercial activity. In terms of its location, its physical geography has not changed.

In another sense, however, Wilmslow Road has been totally transformed. Its social geography is now differently configured, with shops and their signs tended by people with roots in a range of different cultural origins. Saris and samosas are sold where once there were only fish and chips shops. The ubiquitous McDonald's and Starbucks compete for business with South Asian restaurants. And even in cooler temperatures, people sip their café latte alfresco, while talking on their cell phones and wireless computers with family and friends who perhaps live and work on the other side of the world. But even these overt changes do not entirely capture the ways in which Wilmslow Road has changed.

Certainly, where the occupants of a neighborhood change, its culture changes far more drastically than if the buildings were replaced with new ones. Many of these cultural changes occur rapidly but in the shadows. Television views private nooks and crannies but often obscures the cultural landmass, now significantly affected by the processes of globalization. Given the instant flows of fashion, art, and information, the same music inhabits the iPods of the young in Karachi and Kensington, and professionals wear the same brands of blue jeans. In this sense, Wilmslow Road is now connected to various parts of the world through the global mobility of its inhabitants and their capacity to remain constantly in touch with people and communities elsewhere. As they move, their money, ideas, and cultural tastes and aspirations do as well.

Of course, these interconnectivities are not new. There have always been people who have moved, suburbs that have been culturally diverse. Migration is as old as the world itself. But there is something new about the ways in which places like Wilmslow Road are now culturally constituted. The scale of mobility and diversity has clearly altered its demography, but more important, it is the capacity of its new inhabitants to remain interconnected across borders that has transformed the cultural economy of Wilmslow Road. Where the communication between people was once irregular, it is now not only highly regularized but also instant. People shopping in Wilmslow Road and their relatives and friends in other parts of the world are engaged in each other's lives on a daily basis. This has converted Wilmslow Road into what might appropriately be described as a transnational space.

Wilmslow Road is of course not an exception. Communities around the world are similarly becoming interconnected with each other in ways that are unprecedented. The villages in Pakistan that now have access to television and mobile phone and depend for their subsistence on remittances from their families working in New York, London, or Dubai are no less implicated in the global logic of capital and are also experiencing significant cultural shifts, not because they necessarily want to but because of the impact of global forces about which they probably know very little. In this sense, their communities too are becoming transnational spaces, albeit in ways that are significantly different from metropolitan places like Manchester.

Indeed, it is difficult now to imagine places that remain unaffected by the mobility of people, money, ideas, and ideologies. Transnational connectivity and interdependence have become a norm, and as researchers, we can no longer assume self-contained communities whose inhabitants are not linked, in ways both direct and indirect, to people and places a long way from where they live and work. We need to attend, therefore, like never before, to the dynamics of global networks and patterns of global communication affecting the localities that are the object of our research and whose borders are now considerably stretched.

Of course, this interconnectivity does not occur in a space that is symmetrical. All social transformations take place within particular configurations of power. Different people and communities experience and interpret interconnectivity differently because issues of unequal power relations define social relations. The movie and rock stars, star athletes, and Starbucks are able to enjoy the transnational spaces in ways in which the poor, the refugees, and the developing communities cannot, giving rise to new faces, and possibly to a new structure, of ethical issues that can hardly be avoided by social researchers.

Yet social research remains ethically clouded, due in no small part to pressures of the discriminatory social benefits of global trade, increasing international economic and refugee migration, increasing levels of poverty, irretrievable environmental problems, major health concerns such as AIDS, increasing civil strife in Asia and Africa, the so-called clash of civilization between Western and Islamic worlds, high rates of youth unemployment, increasing income gaps between rich and poor nations, and within nations, the drifting apart of socioeconomic classes.

In this chapter, we reflect on the challenges of conducting social research in transnational spaces in ways that are ethically informed. The first part of this chapter presents a discussion of the notion of transnational space, as a way of highlighting a range of problems, both theoretical and practical, that are potentially raised in conducting social research in the era of globalization and in dealing with issues of research ethics. We then claim that the traditional ways of addressing ethical issues in social research are the starting point. Transnational situations will complicate the recognition of ethical problems, but we start with what we know deserves ethical respect. We then consider technologies of monitoring ethical conduct in social research such as codes of ethics and institutional reviews and argue that these are insufficient for meeting the complexities of doing research in transnational spaces. We conclude that ultimately ethical responsibility must reside with the researchers themselves.

◆ Transnational Spaces

The idea of transnational space has been widely used by recent social theorists to describe how the contemporary processes of globalization are transforming the places in which we live and work. While most people continue to identify themselves as belonging to particular localities, it is equally true that these localities are increasingly becoming integrated into larger global networks of social relationship. They are deeply affected by shifting demographic profiles, economic realities, political processes, and communication systems. High levels of immigration, for example, have changed the character of urban spaces in particular, requiring us to engage with a new politics of cultural difference.

Increasingly fluid and porous economic, political, and cultural borders are changing the ways in which many people think about their sense of belongingness. The modernist project of a neat fit between territory, language, and social identity can no longer be taken for granted. Border thinking (Mignolo, 2000) has become more important than ever before. As Suárez-Orozco and Qin-Hilliard (2004) pointed out, "external and internal borders are increasingly becoming noisy and conflictive where cultural communication and miscommunication play out in schools, communities, places of work and worship" (p. 3).

The noise across borders is both facilitated and driven by the new information and communication technologies, enabling people and organizations to interact with each other across vast differences and in ways that are often instantaneous. These technologies are changing the nature of work, leisure, and learning as well as patterns of interpersonal relationships. The constraints of time and space are no longer insurmountable, speeding up the circulation of new images, information, and ideologies.

As a result, there is something new about the manner in which people now belong to a particular locality. Migrants, for example, often wish to and are able to retain links to their country of origin and develop new global networks across the diaspora (Cohen, 1997) through which they now derive cultural meaning and make sense of their identity. This view departs significantly from the traditional models of migration as a nonrecurring and unidirectional relocation, requiring policies of cultural integration. It suggests instead that, increasingly, migration is a continuous "coming and going" process that involves familial and nonfamilial networks that link economic exchange and cultural practices across various boundaries.

Furthermore, those who move and those who do not are now equally able to use the new media to remain in touch with each other and develop new relationships. In this way, mobility is not merely physical but also virtual, with the potential of playing an equally significant role in the formation of social identities and cultural practices (see Aneesh, 2006). Of course, the possibilities of mobility are not only available to migrants but also to others who can forge new social networks to pursue their economic and political interests. These changes have the potential of transforming entire systems of cultural meaning, practices, and institutions—in short, reconstituting the social space.

In recent years, critical geographers such as Massey (2005) and Soja (2000) have argued against a naturalistic understanding of space as a self-evident container of objects and activities. They have suggested that the boundaries of space are never clear and are always contestable. Space is much more than an objectively structured grid within which objects are located and events occur. According to Pile and Thrift (1995), space is a much more complex notion that describes the interrelationship between people and place as well as the elaborate and dynamic patterns of human settlement and interaction. Indeed, Crang and Thrift (2000) argued that an essentialized conception of space can paradoxically reduce the world to "spaceless abstraction" (p. 2).

In contrast, these critical geographers propose a relational view of space that invokes a more complex understanding of how space is constituted and given meaning through human endeavors and social networks. Space is continuously produced, they argue, through sociospatial relations. The relationship between space, spatial forms, and behavior is thus no longer assumed to follow orthogonal directions and distance functions. Instead, space is better conceived as a product of political and economic interactions that are represented in cultural images, desires, and aspirations. In this way, space is not merely a place but a social experience constituted through shared meaning, cultural symbols, and negotiated social relations, as well as material practices (Massey, 2005).

This does not mean that space is entirely a social construction. In a very helpful analysis, Soja (2000) distinguished between space and spatiality, suggesting that while not all space is socially produced, all spatiality is. Soja's analysis emphasizes both the symbolic construction of space at the level of social imaginary and also its more concrete articulation in the landscape. In this way, a university, for example, can be interpreted as a spatial allocation that has a physical form but needs to be understood also as a complex phenomenon given meaning through certain myths and rituals, partly defined in terms of its socially defined arrangements that express its changing purposes, range of relationships, and processes.

What this brief discussion of space suggests, then, is that all localities are produced through various processes of spatialization and that the ever-increasing level of global mobility and exchange deeply affects the ways in which our spatial experiences are constituted and represented. To a greater or lesser extent, as a result of globalization, space has been compressed and stretched at the same time, leading to the expansion of social relations, activities, and networks. There has been an intensification and acceleration of social exchanges.

According to Steger (2004) these shifts have involved "the creation of new and the multiplication of existing social networks and activities in recent decades that increasingly overcome traditional political, economic, cultural and geographical boundaries" (p. 9). More significantly, these shifts have not occurred merely at an objective and material level, but they have also transformed our consciousness about the growing manifestations of social interdependence, leading us to make decisions and choices that were once unrealizable. In this way, the idea of a transnational space makes perfect sense because it draws attention to the links people are now able to forge across national boundaries and from which they can derive social meaning.

♦ Researching the Transnational

Now if this account is even partially accurate in describing how localities around the world are becoming *transnationalized*, then its implications for social research may involve deep ethical concerns. How do we, for example, research spaces that do not have any clear boundaries and where social relations potentially span vast distances? How do we take into account the distribution and dynamics of power whose contours potentially involve the entire globe? How do we provide accounts of social meaning when these are not linked to any specific community? How do we study social inequalities when its causes do not necessarily reside within the community that is the object of our research? In other words, how do we address the conceptual difficulties that inevitably arise in social research when the very constitution of *the social* cannot be easily defined?

Social research has traditionally involved the collection and analysis of information about how people relate to each other—how they make social meaning—within some specified locality or organization. This implies that research almost inevitably occurs within an assumed space, be it a social organization like a school or a community marked by deep, familiar, and cooperative ties between its members and defined by its geographical borders. While social research can, of course, have many purposes—to provide an account of social identities; to understand how people make meaning of their lives; to explain social, economic, and political relations; to reveal patterns of inequality and power; to determine deep structural barriers to the realization of objectives; and so on—it always takes place within a space. We cannot therefore ignore the issues of how, in the era of globalization, space is constituted and how its boundaries are drawn.

Of course, space is never constituted in a uniform and consistent manner. Not all spaces are transnationalized in the same way or, indeed, to the same extent. Some spaces, like global cities (Sassen, 1995) such as Chicago and London, have become transnationalized to a greater extent than isolated rural communities in Africa, for example. In this sense, transnationalization may be viewed as an ongoing dynamic social process affected by changing forms of connectivity between the global and the local, between a community's interior and its exterior. At a conceptual level, however, the notion of a transnational space would seem to undermine any meaningful distinction between the inside of a space and its outside, long regarded as central to social research. If such traditional naturalistic distinctions as the inside and outside of a community or an organization cannot be easily maintained, then many new questions emerge for social research.

In recent years, numerous ethnographers have pointed out, for example, that in the emerging global context, both the ideas of *ethno* and *graphic* have become problematic. The relationship between the ethnographer and the people he or she studied was already complex, but in transnational spaces, new questions arise around key terms such as *othering* and *authorial* control, leading to what Wittel (2000) called a "crisis in objectification" (p. 1). With respect to the idea of *ethno*, a culture can no longer be treated as a coherent entity, unique from and unaffected by its engagement with other cultures. Through enhanced mobility of capital, people, and ideas, cultural contact has become a norm, leading Clifford (1997) to suggest that human location is now constituted by displacement as much as by statis.

With the deterritorialization, pluralization, and hybridization of cultures, the notion of *the field* as a geographically defined research area has also become more complex. As Marcus and Fischer (1986) pointed out, the transnational, political, economic, and cultural forces that now shape localities have undermined the traditional notion of the field. Gupta and Ferguson (1997) therefore suggested the need to redefine the notion of the field, by *decentering* it in ways that deny any clear-cut distinction between *the here* and *the elsewhere*.

If people and objects are increasingly mobile, then Gupta and Ferguson (1997) argued, ethnography has to engage these movements and, with them, the ways in which localities are a product of the circulations of meanings and identities in time-space. Social research is becoming embedded self-consciously with the world systems, shifting its focus from single sites and local situations to become multisited and multilocal, responsive to networked realities.

Castells (1996) has drawn our attention to the ways in which our communities are becoming globally networked. A *network society*, for Castells, is an open structure, able to expand without limits and in ways that are dynamic. It consists of a set of nodes and connections across the nodes, characterized by flows and movement. The Internet is a good example of how its ubiquitous uses are reshaping our everyday practices, affected as they are by the ways in which information flows across various nodes of networks, in spaces that are highly mediated and interactive. These nodes are often transnational and deeply connect us to social networks that do not necessarily reside within a specific territory.

Transnational spaces are difficult to research because they are characterized by greater levels of displacement, dynamism, contingency, plurality, and complexity. They challenge some of the most taken-for-granted categories in social research and potentially demand new theoretical and methodological resources. In recent years, social theorists in a host of disciplines have sought to develop these resources. However, considerably less attention has been paid to the issues of ethics in transnational social research. In what follows, we ask whether transnational research demands new conceptions of research ethics or simply involves recognition of old issues in a new complexity.

♦ Research Ethics: Different but With a Fundamental Core

Traditionally, ethics has been viewed as the sum of human aspiration for honor in interpersonal life, for respect in face-to-face encounters, and fairness in the collective treatment of people. Professional ethics requires social researchers to be open with regard to their aims, methods, criteria, findings, and limits of competence; to safeguard the interests of constituents and clients; and to work toward human dignity and social justice. These aspirations have always been difficult to achieve, but they call for extra thinking in transnational spaces.

Given the globally stretched nature of our communities, it has become more difficult to identify the constituents of transnational research. How might their wide-ranging and often conflicting interests be taken into account? What indeed might be the scope of a transnational researcher's field of ethical concern? To what extent should the ethical issues relating to those who are closer to us be given priority?

Ethical behavior is individual and collective. Culture is the carrier of ethics. As to what is good and proper in research, we agree largely with others of our culture and less with those we consider outsiders. But cultures are dynamic and, in the context of globalization, ever more so. So not only do social researchers inevitably confront issues of multiplicity of cultural traditions, they also face the problem of cultural changes now occurring at an unprecedented rate (Kitchener, 1984).

Social researchers inevitably need to make judgments about attaching priority to some issues and not others. In this way, ethical choices are built into the ways in which research is designed, well before the stage of interpreting the collected data. In transnational contexts, there is likely to be a greater range of interests and perspectives that need to be negotiated. Within a familiar context, these mostly intersect with each other, but in transnational contexts, there is often a greater possibility of fundamental conflict in values and even worldviews.

From a distance, choices are either institutional or personal, but close-up, even institutional choices have a personal dimension. If one of the purposes of social research is to work toward human dignity and justice, then personal choices intervene inevitably. But when even the most local of circumstances are potentially linked to issues of global justice, then it is not clear to what extent researchers can be expected to take these issues into account, without making research totally unfocused.

Many world changes happen without allowing citizens or researchers discernable choice. World trade, global warming, war, poverty, youth malaise, fleeing across borders, poor distribution of medicine, and youth unemployment now seem constants of transnational spaces. And while they violate our sense of justice and our ethos for living, they are background, seldom foreground, for the ethics of research. Stress and malevolence increase the likelihood of ethical plight, raising the question of the extent to which and how researchers might seek to take action in a world that is becoming increasingly more interconnected and interdependent. Equally problematic is the issue of which of the many ethical issues the researchers should foreground.

It could be argued that the problems calling for ethical behavior in research are little different in our chaotic world than they were in bordered spaces. Those problems may occur with greater frequency and greater danger, but they are the same problems. Most happen not because we are researchers but because we are humans engaged in research. We have injured others through infidelity, intimidation, misuse of power, misappropriating intellectual property, methodological limitations, time and budget constraints, and misrepresentation. (There is probably no limit to the possibilities.) Injury may have occurred by accident or intent, but it is injury nevertheless.

Invariably the same problems of disrespect, lying, breaking promises, putting people at risk, squandering, and cheating arise in most, if not all, contexts of research. In transnational settings, however, the question arises as to the extent to which these indiscretions have the same meaning in terms of ethical significance in all cultures. And if they do not, then how should researchers deal with cultural difference and misunderstanding, on one hand, and neglect on the other? The search for ethical injury still starts with recognition of neglect, but neglect itself is not easily recognizable if its consequences manifest themselves in communities distant from, and perhaps unknown to, the researcher.

Ethical challenges are, of course, different from legal problems, not marked by formal charges and presumptions of innocence. Ethical problems are more pervasive, often defy explication, and are less amenable to authoritative judgment. Furthermore, they are not incomprehensible in most circumstances. They may be dressed and valued differently in different cultures, but they are often recognizable in all. If such were not so, then ethical debate across cultural traditions would not be possible.

In the practice of transnational social research, we may be more likely to encounter political and ideological disagreement, difficulty in identifying and representing all stakeholder interests, and client resistance when reports are unfavorable. Programs are unique, ethical difficulties unpredictable, and ethical codes and principles necessarily general—all of which ensure that few studies avoid trouble. There may be a greater potential for ethical trouble in transnational research and less possibility of knowing it.

But the greater potential for ethical trouble should not in itself deter us from both conducting research in transnational settings and addressing ethics issues that arise. Ethical accountability should still be expected. It should be assumed that many of the ethical issues in transnational contexts will be the same, but the possibility of the emergence of new ethical problems in particular contexts should not be discounted. A commitment to identify and debate ethical transgressions across cultural traditions and consider facts of global interconnectivity and interdependence should come to occupy a more important place in our deliberations about research design and treatment of information, as should the need to be self-reflexive about the epistemic assumptions that inevitably inform our research judgments and ethical choices.

♦ Codes of Ethics and Ethical Accountability

To what extent are the traditional technologies of ethical accountability adequate for these tasks? Do codes of ethics help? One key problem with codes of ethics is that their standards provide categories that are too broad and principles that are too general. When provided, the illustrative examples connect poorly with real problems. And thus, codes and transgressions can be too easily dismissed, especially in the contexts of the more complex and difficult cross-cultural issues that arise in transnational spaces.

In recent years, many codes have been drawn up. Let us note briefly the one provided in 2003 by the Social Research Association (SRA), a British group. Their *Code of Ethics* (SRA, 2003) mainly points to professional literature papers dealing with ethical issues. It identifies four summary obligations, emphasizing the groups placed at risk by unethical practices.

1. *Obligations to society:* If social research is to remain of benefit to society and the groups and individuals within it, then social researchers must conduct their work responsibly and in light of the moral and legal order of the society in which they practice. They have responsibility to maintain high scientific standards in the methods employed in the collection and analysis of data and the impartial assessment and dissemination of findings.

2. *Obligations to funders and employer:* Researchers' relationship with and commitments to funders and/or employers should be clear and balanced. These should not compromise a commitment to morality and to the law, and to the maintenance of standards commensurate with professional integrity.

3. *Obligations to colleagues:* Social research depends on the maintenance of standards and of appropriate professional behavior that is shared among the professional research community. Without compromising obligations to funders/employers, subjects, or society at large, this requires methods, procedures, and findings to be open to collegial review. It also requires concern for the safety and security of colleagues when conducting field research.

4. *Obligations to subjects:* Social researchers must strive to protect subjects from undue harm arising as a consequence of their participation in research. This requires that subjects' participation should be voluntary and as fully informed as possible, and no group should be disadvantaged by routinely being excluded from consideration (Reamer, 1982).

As the SRA authors acknowledge, these are abstract and require reading of the explanatory detail, and then further into the literature. What they say here is that researchers should be responsible, moral, legal, scientific, clear and balanced, open, safe, protective, and nondiscriminatory. It says little about what they should *not* do. Nor do they mention the responsibilities to humanity and the broader global community that the social researchers might have, beyond the society, colleagues, subjects, and employers with whom they are more directly and immediately associated.

This may imply that ethics are situational and not likely to be violated if ordinary practice is followed. But just as is the case with the concept of common sense, while it has powerful rhetorical merits, the notion of ordinary practice may be interpreted differently in different contexts. More important, in globalizing contexts, new research practices are constantly demanded to better reflect the shifting realities of transnational spaces. Among these realities is the fact that the society to which researchers are expected to have certain obligations now represents a space that may be globally stretched.

Much of social research is designed to provide descriptive and normative information useful for improving social services

(House, 1991). Many codes of ethics specifically call for research that promotes, for example, social determination and social justice. There is the National Association of Social Workers (NASW, 1996) in the United States drawing attention to the need to eliminate sexual harassment and do good things for youth. In this way, the NASW code does not tell us what to do but reminds us to question what we are doing.

This is particularly the case in advocacy research (Mabry, 1995). This kind of research invariably conflicts with at least some of the principles articulated in codes of ethics for social researchers and frequently involves a leaning toward the well-being of one set of clients and away from another. Ensuring accuracy of reporting may conflict with the more general ethical principle of protecting vulnerable clients. More proactive, political advocacy, no matter how well-meant, submerges the role of the researcher beneath that of social agent.

A common ethical dilemma is whether to include information in the research report that will trouble the host organization. Perhaps too often, our interpretations are tailored separately for the manager's ears, for the governing board, for the external collaborators, and for the public. In spite of MacDonald's (1977) advice to have no private conversations with any client or stakeholder, thus to have but one report for all, it is often almost impossible to avoid conversations unique to different clients, data sources, and those who inquire about our reports. We would like anyone reading our final report to be confident that we are identifying all the major issues and explaining as best as we can the dominant phenomena. So is it possible for researchers to be honest about their obligations to funding agencies and employers, as the SRA code of ethics suggests, and be confident still that the obligations to the potentially limitless number of stakeholders are also met?

What this suggests is that the principles articulated in codes of ethics are relevant but do not take us very far. We recognize our obligation for full disclosure. We want to treat all parties equitably. And we want to protect an institution that is challenging social injustice. The three cannot be served simultaneously. We are caught between these three principles. In such a situation, ethical behavior is not so much a matter of following principles as of balancing competing principles. So, for example, disclosure may have to be tempered to achieve social justice, and the institution may need to receive criticism to protect deserving individuals.

In spaces characterized by stretched boundaries, different cultural traditions, and competing interests, it may be more useful to have multiple codes, expressing ethical concern from different perspectives, to illuminate actual problems.

Codes express professional aspiration but offer little in the way of problem solving. As Newman and Brown (1996) suggested, "These principles and criteria do not lead to the resolution of ethical dilemmas through application of a formula. . . . They help us think about ethical issues; they do not resolve the issues for us" (p. 54).

A single code, a single orientation, is insufficient. With multiple codes expressed in different ways and emphasizing different values, we can better recognize the ethical situation and better reflect on our activities and judgments. And, in transnational contexts, it may be that the ethical responsibility of the researcher cannot be identified a priori but needs to be developed from multiply relevant sources. In an increasingly globally interconnected world, codes can never be sufficient to solve actual ethical dilemmas that now arise with greater frequency and intensity.

◆ Research Ethics and the Question of Privacy

Apart from codes of ethics, various administrative structures for ethical review have been developed over the past few decades. To consider how they may deal with ethical issues in transnational research let us look at a concrete example of personal privacy. The ethical review committees set up in the United States in recent years as institutional review boards (IRBs) regard participant protection as a major ethical requirement of any proposal to conduct social research.

With transnational research, the issue of personal privacy and the nature of consent are likely to be seen differently in different cultures, sometimes differently within the same family, and across time as well (see, e.g., Chapters 19 and 26, this volume). IRBs maintain that privacy needs to be maintained throughout a research project. What do researchers do that increases the likelihood that deeply personal information will not be revealed? Highly planned and protected collections of private information may be ethical, but unreviewed plans and casual personalistic inquiry, sooner or later, are not. The ethical dilemma frequently becomes one of balance between privacy and advocacy.

Personal privacy protects the mind, body, property, and reputation that would keep the persons researched secluded. Especially in changing times, a person is differently vulnerable at different times, and our boundaries of privacy need resetting. Some people don't mind telling strangers something they would rather not tell someone close. Privacy is greatly situational. The issue of researcher intrusion is not only a personal matter but is also a professional and societal one. A single researcher's indiscretion casts a shadow on the research community. The world is a poorer place if, as a people or profession, we regard personal privacy as worth protecting only if the person expresses a need for it. How much the U.S. Constitution, for example, guarantees personal privacy is debated. It grants explicit protection from search of homes. But nothing is said about intimate stories. Beyond tradition and law, how should intrusion be constrained?

A colleague was observing in homes of immigrant families. They expressed openness to questions, any questions. When alone, a mother volunteered a family secret: A member had had a child out of wedlock. The father had not acknowledged the birth and seemed sure to be troubled by his wife's revelation. Should the researcher have heard this secret? It seems that except in special circumstances, a researcher should not know what any member of the family does not want known.

Early anthropologists were vocal about earning the trust of the islanders and gave the impression that ethical choice was protected and granted to those with secrets. If not overly pressed, it was claimed, the islanders would tell the anthropologist only what they wanted to tell. The anthropologists prided themselves on waiting for the propitious time (Erickson, 2006).

But that is not good enough for transnational research today. Ethically, the researcher should not hear what the secret holder fails to protect. The researcher often expects to protect secrets by distancing the story from the storyteller. The researcher promises, "I'll carefully sort through the stories and delete or anonymize the problematic things." Careful review and confidentiality are important vows, not to be made casually or without scrutiny of colleagues. But those are not protection enough. The researcher is aware that a well-anonymized anecdote may be easily recognizable to a family member. And a reader may link an early page to a later one, linking what was intended to appear unlinked. Editing and anonymizing are weak protections, but they remain useful. We think that researchers have a responsibility to dissuade participants from sharing information that is potentially harmful to others—and if the participant cannot be dissuaded, the researcher has at least the responsibility to listen without hearing.

Think of a researcher studying Internet use by children. He or she may legitimately ask whether or not parents have set rules but may not ask if a parent threatens punishment. Parent rules are a researchable topic but probably incidental to a study of Internet use and intrusive. The researcher has no ethical grounds for asking about child control without laying a firm groundwork of intent and parental (and sometimes the child's) consent.

When researchers find that the talk puts persons in jeopardy, they should demur. The respondent may resist suggestions to stop. The researcher should withdraw, saying something like, "I really cannot listen further," detouring to high-priority topics and lamenting the shortness of time. Of course, that may be rude. It may seem important for the respondent to talk about the private matter for any number of reasons. Shutting down that topic of conversation may lead to loss of other information. It often seems unattractive to the researcher to terminate the storytelling.

But the transnational ethical position should consider that revealing any privacy is a loss of privacy, whether or not the information is passed further. A secret known by one person is not the secret it was before. The perception of the secret by the secret holder is sometimes changed by revelation even to a stranger. It may then hold a different value. It may then awaken a different anxiety. Privacy is less a matter of information transfer than of personal security. And what of the privacy requirement when the researcher learns that the researched is engaged in conversations on the Internet with groups identified by the state as a threat to national security?

This suggests the need for researchers to ensure that their position is comprehensible. It is not wrong for a secret to be told, but it may be unethical for a secret to be heard by a researcher. Hearing it endorses the idea that secrets may be told without hurt. Secrets can be good or bad, but a researcher should not hear them without weighing in advance and on the spot the costs and benefits of the revelation. Institutional review is little assurance. It is the ethical responsibility of the individual researcher to withdraw from intrusion, even when the respondent feels no violation.

Informally or formally, researchers have a contract with the respondent. The contract cannot explicate all the possibilities, but it should indicate generally what we want to know and how we will use it. Changes should be cause for renegotiation. The forms for such contracts are a part of research ethic and institutional review and always need rethinking and restating. Research practice cannot be adequately covered by standardized contracts and codes. Protection against intrusion into privacy remains greatly the responsibility of the individual researcher, partly created on the spot, sentence by sentence.

This suggests that the realization and resolution of ethical conflict come largely from within. It is personally dismaying to recognize that efforts to be honorable, respectful, and fair will sometimes be obstructed. Sometimes, conflict is brought to our attention by others, but this is usually as a particular instance rather than violation of a general principle. Researchers with little integrity can identify some ethical principle to justify the violation of other principles—conscience is an essential voice from within. Ultimately, researchers are forced to rely on personal, situational judgment. Codes and institutional reviews cannot protect them from the need to address ethical dilemmas that arise in transnational spaces with greater complexity, diversity, and perhaps, even intensity. And it is to this lonely coastline our train of thought has been inexorably chugging.

◆ Other Obstacles to Simple Good and Bad

Many studies of social process are exercises in ambiguity, with each of the components only partially defined. The phenomena themselves have vague boundaries, unspecified connections, and internal inconsistencies. Many a well-meaning researcher sets out to clarify the variables and conditions (Worthen, Sanders, & Fitzpatrick, 1997, p. 86), and sometimes this helps, but the nature of the social research remains partially obscured, with previous misperception of it only partially resolved and ever constructed and reconstructed by its constituencies. Viewed in the context of our earlier statement that ethical behavior is not so much a matter of following principles as of balancing competing principles, these ambiguous conditions invite individual, unique interpretations of studies. As paintings are often interpreted with iconically different eyes, the art of social research is often interpreted from ethically different sides.

Preparing a roster of the stakeholders in a study often results in hierarchical ambiguity. Directors of a public service may precisely identify their clients but can do little more than list constituencies and potential audiences. To some extent, the risks to the stakes and to the stakeholders remain vague.

For one purpose or another, the roles and responsibilities of the cross-cultural researcher will not be adequately clarified. In addition to providing new information and organizational feedback, as mentioned above, researchers are measurers of productivity, impact, and effectiveness; portrayers of process; comparers of options; advisors to clients; and often, administrators (Schwandt, 1989; Scriven, 1991). Roles change as the research progresses. The contract-negotiating parties may go out of their way to clarify what is expected and allowed on the part of the researcher, but the definitions remain ambiguous in their minds and even more so to stakeholders outside the negotiations (Newman & Brown, 1996, p. 50; Stake, 1976, p. 31).

Ambiguity is inevitable. Programs, audiences, and roles defy sharp definition. Uncertainties are seldom insurmountable. Nevertheless, basing ethical standards on clarification is shortsighted and unrealistic. Routines for redefining scope and thrust are desirable not only for developing a high-quality report but also for managing role shifts and unanticipated situations. Many of the phenomena of social service are too complex to be spelled out adequately in any contract, design, or final report. Transnational researchers should try to describe those matters from multiple perspectives, some views more credible (and compelling) than others.

It is important to realize that reality can be ill formed (Spiro, Vispoel, Schmitz, Samarapungavan, & Boerger, 1987). Weak form may not be a matter of poor acuity. A veridical representation cannot be better formed than the original. The researcher who intentionally leaves out the obscure, the ill formed, and the inconsistent to make a handsome or credible portrayal violates a standard of accuracy.

The values manifold of an entity, too, should not be presumed to be a simpler structure than the phenomenon. Presentation of simple, summary indicators of value for complex entities should not escape the scrutiny of those concerned about ethical practices. Oversimplification is little discouraged by codes of ethics. The inappropriateness of overly simplistic and falsely vivid representation is not to be found there.

We are troubled by deliberate efforts to simplify the representation of complex international programs. A simple interpretation or conclusion even when the program is complex gets no protest from most codes. Neither do the final synthesis procedures proposed by Scriven (1994) that appear to endorse at least occasional oversimplification of program merit (Stake et al., 1996). We should not object to having codes or scriptures or laws or standards just because they fail to mention all possible wrongs. We should look beyond those standards for grounds for resolving ethical conflict.

Many teachers are protected under an ethic of academic freedom to teach unpopular views of social systems, history, and most visibly today, Darwinian theory. Supporters believe that it is in the best interest of learners to encounter alternative views and the fact that respected academics differ. Even when the official course guide favors another perspective, teachers are encouraged by professional organizations to explain to students how they might see things otherwise. This freedom seldom extends to omission of content specified in the guide. There is a literature on academic freedom (Epstein,1995), but little is written, or possibly could be written, identifying how far that freedom extends, for it is a contextual matter as well as contentious.

Many researchers are protected under a similar ethic to study more or less what they choose and to choose which facets to examine and which to ignore. Researchers studying pedagogy may examine learning theories, histories, and most visibly, student motivation but often choose not to examine the issues important in finance, teacher selection, and professional development. Supporters of this ethic argue that schooling will be better understood if the researcher, rather than those who commission research, decides what is worth studying and what he or she is most capable of understanding. Clearly, the public and system administrators have an obligation to pose research questions and to oppose research deemed intrusive and already headed toward misleading the public. But some of an investigation regularly and wisely goes beyond the proposal toward what the researcher finds needing examination. And an ethic of research freedom should continue.

This ethic is hampered by current IRBs that, intending to prevent risk to human subjects, require stating in advance all that will be studied and how. It is reasonable to suppose that IRB procedures will continue to mature so that research designs may evolve without jeopardizing the study of human subjects (Denzin, in press; Chapter 8, this volume).

What may be tolerable neglect for an individual researcher is not necessarily tolerable neglect for a research field. If all pedagogy research were to fail to examine fiscal issues, then the research would be biased and incomplete. If the composite research were to examine only popular issues, or only unpopular issues, or only fundable issues, then the research community would violate research ethics. According to an ideal code of ethics, the community as a whole should be able to examine all discernable aspects of the phenomenon or entity. Furthermore, the individual citizen should be able to know something of the completeness of coverage in the research field and to advocate greater coverage. To balance competing ethical principles while retaining academic freedom in research, our research community should respect the need for knowledge of social service practices.

Communities, too, expect to be free to decide what they will study. All organizations have obligations to behave ethically, including in cross-cultural matters, which have the potential to harm individuals and the society. In some ways, each member adds to the construction of meanings of organizational work, but certain individuals and groups consciously or unconsciously have control and should bear greater ethical responsibility. Working with many organizations, individual researchers will extend and limit the responsibility of research, also shaping the ethical tone for it. Still, the responsibility is usually set by directors, trustees, business managers, shareholders, and general staffs. It is especially important to express the ethical obligations for research in ways that can be seen to apply to organizations as well as to individuals.

Transnational considerations are more apparent at the organization level than at the individual level. In Manchester, there was need for examining the influence of Islamic extremists (including those halfway around the world) on the youth of local Pakistani families. It was little recognized as a responsibility of local school agencies, the Home Office, and community organizations. These organizations, like individuals, try to protect their choices of activities to monitor. But ethically, they should not be free to ignore the extracurricular learnings of children of the community. Doing so, of course, infringes on the privacy of some citizens.

Whenever people of different experiences, personalities, and cultures mix, there will be a variety of ways of looking at social relationships. Activities and concerns will be seen differently. Evidence will be valued and interpreted differently. Transnational spaces increase the diversity of thinking styles and appeals to authority.

Researchers tend to presume that even as cultures differ, one form of logic and one synthesis of findings will be superior. In particular, many favor a report that takes numerous variables into consideration rather than one or two. Circumstances that seem needing portrayal as shades of color to the researcher will still appear to some thoughtful people as matters of black and white. It may be a misrepresentation, perhaps an imposition, even an undemocratic act, for the researcher to present the findings of a study as a matter more complex than it is in the eyes of constituents. Fastidious fieldwork and analysis followed by triangulation and ethical review are our aim, but the view into particular transnational spaces should neither be simplistic nor portrayed to be as complicated as the researcher can make it.

It would be unwarranted to declare that disposition toward a highly conditional and situated worldview is an unethical act. But lack of consideration of the social act as discrete and absolute could be one-sided and unfair. Rejection or omission of a simplistic explanation of problems may only express a preference among epistemologies. It can be argued that a researcher, to be fully ethical, should present (or clearly allude to) multiple, even contradictory, views or views that are simple as well as those that are multicultured and/or complex, especially if repeatedly encountered in the field.

That is not to say that all views are equally respectable or that the preferred view should be the most popular. It is to say that the researcher has an ethical responsibility to recognize phenomena as various people see them and reason them through. A preference for the most complex syntheses of evidence may fare well in some conversations among intellectual and cultural peers, but ethical responsibility should limit the bias they have against thinking simple.

♦ Toward a Greater Ethic of Personal Responsiblity

Returning one last time to our initial assertion, ethical behavior is not so much a matter of following principles as of balancing competing principles. It is useful to have multiple codes, holding one up against the other, not so that we can find one to justify what we want to do anyway but so that we can, in a multicultural world, recognize different manifestations of ethical value and better deliberate their implications. Deliberation is as much served by recall, storytelling, and intuition as by measurement of criteria. Ethical conflict is resolved, not without but within.

Much as we need a research literature that includes codes and rules and principles, we should not rely on simple strictures that translate poorly into real situations. The diversity and particularity of practical issues and dilemmas ensure that compendia of ethics will be general and that their generality will limit their utility. The National Council of Teachers of Mathematics (1989) gave us an important example in creating standards by treating them as an aspiration rather than as a restraint. The standards we have cited also suggest an aspiration but greatly understated. Much more we need personal, situational elaboration of the ethical points. More research on ethics in research needs to be initiated by researchers, sometimes self-funded, sometimes funded by professional organizations, and clearly sometimes by disinterested parties.

From all transnational spaces, from Pakistanis in Islamabad and Pakistanis on Wilmslow Road, from all advancements and retreats, we need stories, deliberations, and personal experiences of researchers facing ethical dilemmas. We need to ponder cultural situations. As part of our search for understandings, we need to present the cases to surrogate audiences, seeking perspectives, sometimes from specially appointed panels. We need cases that illustrate obstacles to fairness, respect, and honor.

As a matter of transnational practice, it should be the responsibility of every researcher to discuss ethical problems with fellow professionals and thoughtful clients. It should be the responsibility of professional organizations to facilitate and reward members for the use of panels and collaborative sharing of experience. Ethical problems are seldom matters of simply breaking a code. They are usually matters of finding the least hurtful balance among ethical principles. Ultimately, these will be matters of professional judgment that draw from both personal and cross-cultural experience.

♦ References

Aneesh, A. (2006). *Virtual migration: Programming of globalization*. Durham, NC: Duke University Press.
Castells, M. (1996). *The rise of the network society*. Oxford, UK: Blackwell.
Clifford, J. (1997). *Routes: Travel and translation in the late twentieth century*. Cambridge, MA: Harvard University Press.
Cohen, R. (1997). *Global diasporas: An introduction*. London: UCL Press.
Crang, M., & Thrift, N. (Eds.). (2000). *Thinking space*. London: Routledge.
Denzin, N. K. (in press). IRBS and the turn to indigenous research ethics In B. Jegatheesan (Ed.), *Access, a zone of comprehension, and intrusion: Vol. 11. Advances in program evaluation. Advances in program evaluation*. London: Emerald Group.
Epstein, R. A. (1995). *Simple rules for a complex world*. Cambridge, MA: Harvard University Press.
Erickson, F. (2006). Studying side by side. Collaborative action ethnography in educational research. In G. Spindler & L. Hammond (Eds.), *Innovation in educational ethnography: Theory methods, results* (pp. 235–257). Mahwah, NJ: Lawrence Erlbaum.
Gupta, A., & Ferguson, J. (1997). *Culture, power and place: Explorations in critical anthropology*. Durham, NC: Duke University Press.
House, E. (1991). Evaluation and social justice: Where are we? In M. W. McLaughlin & D. C. Philips (Eds.), *Evaluation and social justice: At quarter century, 19th yearbook of the National Society of the Study of Evaluation* (p. 233). Chicago: University of Chicago Press.
Kitchener, K. (1984). Intuition, critical evaluation and ethical principles: The foundation for ethical decisions in counseling psychology. *The Counseling Psychologist, 12*(3), 43–56.
Mabry, L. (1995). *Advocacy in evaluation: Inescapable or intolerable?* Paper presented at the annual meeting of the American Evaluation Association, Vancouver, British Columbia, Canada.
MacDonald, B. (1977). A political classification of evaluation studies. In D. Hamilton (Ed.), *Beyond the numbers game* (pp. 224–227). London: Macmillan.
Marcus, G., & Fischer, M. (1986). *Anthropology as cultural critique: An experimental moment in the human sciences*. Chicago: University of Chicago Press.
Massey, D. (2005). *For space*. London: Sage.
Mignolo, W. (2000). *Local histories/global designs*. Princeton, NJ: Princeton University Press.
National Association of Social Workers. (1996). *Code of ethics*. Washington, DC: Author.
National Council of Teachers of Mathematics. (1989). *Curriculum and evaluation standards for school mathematics*. Reston, VA: Author.
Newman, D., & Brown, R. (1996). *Applied ethics for program evaluation*. Thousand Oaks, CA: Sage.
Pile, S., & Thrift, N. (1995). Mapping the subject. In S. Pile & N. Thrift (Eds.), *Mapping the subject: Geographies of cultural transformation* (pp. 3–28). London: Routledge.
Reamer, R. (1982). *Ethical dilemmas in social service*. New York: Columbia University Press.

Sassen, S. (1995). *The global city: New York, London and Tokyo.* Princeton, NJ: Princeton University Press.

Schwandt, T. (1989). Recapturing the moral discourse in evaluation. *Educational Researcher, 35,* 11–16.

Scriven, M. (1991). *Evaluation thesaurus* (4th ed.). Newbury Park, CA: Sage.

Scriven, M. (1994). The final synthesis. *Evaluation Practice, 15,* 367–382.

Social Research Association. (2003). *Ethical guidelines.* Retrieved December 7, 2007, from www.the-sra.org.uk/ethical.htm

Soja, E. (2000). *Postmetropolis: Critical studies of cities and regions.* Oxford, UK: Blackwell.

Spiro, R. J., Vispoel, W. P., Schmitz, J. G., Samarapungavan, A., & Boerger, A. E. (1987). Knowledge acquisition for application: Cognitive flexibility and transfer in complex content domains. In B. C. Britton (Ed.), *Executive control processes* (pp. 177–199). Hillsdale, NJ: Erlbaum.

Stake, R. (1976). *Evaluating educational programmes: The need and the response.* Paris: Organisation for Economic Co-operation and Development.

Stake, R., Migotsky, C., Davis, R., Cisneros, E., DePaul, G., Dunbar, C., Jr., et al. (1996). The evolving syntheses of program value. *Evaluation Practice, 18,* 89–103.

Steger, M. (2004). *Globalization: A very short introduction.* Oxford, UK: Oxford University Press.

Suárez-Orozco, M., & Qin-Hilliard, D. (Eds.). (2004). *Globalization: Culture and education in the new millennium.* Berkeley: University of California Press.

Wittel, A. (2000). Ethnography of the move: From field to net to internet [Electronic version]. *Qualitative Social Research, 1*(1). Retrieved May 6, 2006, from http://qualitative-research.net/fqs-texte/1-00/1-00wittel-e.htm

Worthen, B., Sanders, J., & Fitzpatrick, J. (1997). *Program evaluation* (2nd ed.). New York: Longman.

34

PRIVACY AND NEW TECHNOLOGIES

The Limits of Traditional Research Ethics

♦ Nicholas C. Burbules

In this chapter, I want to contrast two ways of thinking about the ethical challenges presented by the uses of new information and communication technologies in research, one derived from a more traditional research ethics perspective and one suggesting an alternative perspective that frames ethical issues in networked contexts in a fundamentally different way. I want to call this alternative perspective, not *network ethics*, that is, familiar ethical categories and principles *applied to* the networked domain, but *networked ethics*, a rethinking of how one makes ethical judgments in an environment that is structured by a complex, interdependent, and rapidly changing set of relations, as these new technologies are.

Whereas, for example, traditional analyses of threats and protections to privacy are generally derived from a rights-based account, I believe that we need to approach the problem today with a different vocabulary and set of assumptions. Indeed, it may turn out that over a broad range of concerns "protections" of privacy, as such, are simply no longer possible. Networked ethics, as I am calling it, poses a serious challenge to what traditional philosophical ethics has sought to provide in terms of clear distinctions of right and wrong, or good and bad; or clear-cut ways of adjudicating conflicts over social responsibilities and obligations. In networked contexts, "moral luck" and an increased intermingling and interdependency of "good" and "bad" effects appears to be the norm.

In the context of research ethics, I will argue, many of the elements of typical human subjects review (privacy, anonymity, the right to "own" information about one's self) need to be rethought; as do the procedures by which the well-being of research subjects is, we hope, to be served. I hope to indicate the enormity of the challenges we face today and even greater challenges to come.

The first step in this argument is changing the way we think about these new technologies. Many analyses of new information and communication technologies, and the global network that ties them together, regard them as simply a new medium for interaction, more complex and powerful than others we have known for a while, but in fundamental ways just the same. The Internet is a big encyclopedia; a cellular phone is just a portable phone; e-mail is electronic letter writing; a computer is a very fast calculator or word processor; data collection and analysis are speeded up, but changed only quantitatively, not qualitatively. This is, I think, a misunderstanding. The media of communication *influence* content, and do not merely carry it from one person to the next (Burbules, 2007). Information sharing and knowledge construction proceed by very different processes in this new collaborative space, that is, a place where people work together to create knowledge. Their ability to work together is a function of this networked environment and its capacity to (a) bring people together from disparate locations, (b) gather information from a range of sources and actively integrate it in a form that is accessible to all, (c) represent that information simultaneously and dynamically, and (d) allow participants to interact in relation to that information, to act on it, to modify it in a continuously changing manner. This relation among participants, between them and the information, and among them *through* the information commonly available to them, often described as the "Web 2.0" phenomenon, represents a dynamic with important implications for many social knowledge activities, including the doing of research.

◆ The Changing Meanings of "Privacy"

In addition to these new social relations, new analytical tools—particularly powerful mechanisms for data mining, modeling, and simulation building—create a transformed research environment that in many cases is changing the nature of disciplines themselves. But here I want to focus on a changed perspective toward the relationship between human activities and the representation and study of those activities through research. As William Bogard argues, the processes of surveillance and the processes of simulation have merged: The capacity to build extremely complex models based on massive and diverse databases, increasingly sophisticated focus group and survey methods, and demographic sampling allow for increasingly accurate predictions about individual actions and choices (Bogard, 1996; see also Burbules & Callister, 2000; Warnick, 2007). The methods have enabled market researchers, pollsters, and others to become increasingly adept at developing audience or consumer profiles and predicting the preferences of persons before they have even considered the choices themselves. Such highly effective social science and psychological techniques are used for everything from helping to identify potential "terror" suspects in a post-9/11 era, to marketing breakfast cereals or movies, to helping politicians select the homes and neighborhoods on which to focus their "get out the vote" efforts. Such methods of profiling and prediction are not new, of course; but through the use of various digital technologies they have become much more sophisticated and effective, and extend through more and more areas of our lives (e.g., when marketing researchers can analyze the patterns of our purchases at the grocery store).

It is sobering to think that when one likes a movie, a television show, a politician, or breakfast cereal, it is often because a demographically accurate test audience of people very much like us previewed the product and advised the producers on how to change it so that they (and we) would enjoy it even more. The product is a simulation designed to fit the audience's expectations; the audience are already-examined subjects whose preferences and reactions have been predicted and shaped in advance. We seem to be making a free choice as consumers (or as voters, etc.), but it is a choice that was prepared for us to make—of course, we like it, *it was made for us to like*. Furthermore, as these choices are prepared for us, our tastes and attitudes are also changed by them. The link between taste, choice, research, and the design of products is not linear, but circular: Our tastes are changed by the choices we make, and not only vice versa. These "public" incursions by researchers and marketers predict and shape many of our actions even in the "private" sphere (what we read, what we eat for breakfast); they are partly constitutive of the people we are.

Indeed, if one pushes this argument a bit further, the very notion of private, personal, anonymous activities and choices becomes attenuated. At a literal level, such research and prediction methods may not identify us as individuals, but through models and simulations they touch on our activities and choices, anticipate them, and to a significant degree shape them. They constitute us as objects of knowledge and intervention even when they do not directly and specifically study *us*. In that sense, even some of our most personal and secret choices, preferences, and activities are known. Nor, as we will see, is this only an aspect of marketing research or similar activities; it is coming to be true of other areas of research as well.

Furthermore, across an increasing range of our daily activities, the processes of data collection occur not through voluntary choice and certainly not through informed consent; they are automatic consequences of those activities—making a purchase, browsing the Internet, watching certain television shows, working in an office where employee behaviors are monitored and recorded, visiting a bank or ATM, and so on. The increasing use of Enterprise Systems in workplace and other settings has accelerated this automatic collection of data. In these cases, the amassing of digital data is not an additional step in the process, but is inherent in those activities themselves (every time you swipe your card, for example)—and in more and more cases it is not possible to "opt out," certainly not without considerable conscious effort and inconvenience. The growth of so-called ubiquitous technologies—mobile, ever present, and increasingly networked together—situates us almost continuously in a data-gathering environment, the apotheosis of Jeremy Bentham's (and later, Michel Foucault's, 1977) "panopticon." The attendant growth of very large databases, and the increased power of data mining tools for analyzing them, has created a boon for academic and other researchers; and while conventional human subjects protections are intended to protect private or individual information, the kinds of modeling techniques and methods I have described can make many of those protections moot. And, of course, there are other researchers who are not subject to even those safeguards.

Educational institutions are increasingly implicated in these same processes. Student computer use is regularly monitored. Few individuals are as continuously measured as are school students: Test scores and other performance factors are now collected as a matter of course at the classroom, school, district, and state levels. These are used externally for government reporting purposes and internally for classifying and sorting students. Increasingly, we are going to see these databases, at least at an aggregate level, used for research purposes as well. What Bogard wants us to see is how such processes—common practices in schools and elsewhere—are simultaneously acts of surveillance and simulation: They create knowledge, they create categories and norms, they create identities and subject positions, and they constrain and direct human behavior. They are privacy issues not only because the information, once gathered, might be misused; they are privacy issues because, even when used "properly," they survey and constitute the identities that students carry with them throughout their lives, in school, at home, and at play, and because they represent attempts to shape, through modeling and prediction, the horizons of possibility within which people act. As I have tried to show, seemingly personal or individual choices are often made from among a range of choices that have already been defined in advance.

This argument represents a case study in how quantitative change can yield qualitative differences. The volume of digital information, the sheer speed of access to and transmission of information, creates a substantially new knowledge environment. When questions and replies, searches and discoveries, analytical and sorting functions, and so on, build on one another, each yielding a variation on the one before, they become parts of an ongoing interactive cycle, and not simply the beginning and end of a single, epistemically complete or self-sufficient process. The Internet, within which more and more data about people can be found—and through which more and more data are collected every minute we are using it—amplifies this new relation between public and private information. The nature of a Web 2.0 world is that the use of, and participation in, online resources is also automatically an informational contribution to them. For example, although it is not my main topic here, the use of blogs and social networking sites by many young people clearly reflects a very different (and dangerous) understanding of what kinds of "personal" information they are prepared to share with others, and poses deep dilemmas for researchers who might want to access and use this information, assuming a tacit consent by the people who post it for others to see. If I put something on my Facebook site, do I realize that I am making it public? Do I need to be warned about the ways in which it may be used by researchers, legal authorities, future employers, and so on?

Another factor that blurs matters of form and content is the hypertextual character of the Internet; when material is interlinked in complex and unlimited ways, the very notion of discrete "information points" or "facts" is altered. Every element or idea can be seen immediately in its relation to, and dependence on, others. This relation is not just a conceptual hypothesis, but is often expressed concretely in hypertextual links; hyperlinks *show* us these interdependencies and *lead* us to make new associations because they are navigational paths and not just conceptual artifacts. By making links to others, and being linked to by others, a kind of publicity is created for the particular and the personal, whether one chooses that or not.

Finally, another factor, one especially pertinent to this essay, is how the design of these information and communication spaces blurs matters of *is* and *ought*. Countless choices made in the structure of these environments, choices that in turn guide or direct or discourage future choices, get locked in implicitly as the technologies are built. Some of these consequences may be anticipated, if unintended; and sometimes they are intended; but most often they are recognized only with hindsight, as actual patterns of use reveal the biases and constraints built into the design.

♦ A Networked Ethics

The basic pieces are in place now to build an argument about networked ethics. What

I have tried to show, first, is how new information and communication technologies, and how they are linked together in networked systems, represent a radical and not just an incremental change to the ways in which we need to deliberate about knowledge and value. Many traditional philosophical distinctions and categories do not fit this rapidly changing environment very well. Second, I have explored more specifically how data gathering, storage, and analytical methods that depend on these new networked technologies create a new and more complex relation between action and prediction, between voluntary agent and subject of knowledge, and between public and private availability of information.

Next, I want to push this argument further. Networked environments such as the Internet, which are of educational, cultural, economic, and political significance, cannot be understood simply as media for carrying information or communication content. They are, as I have discussed, a space—a space with specific features that transform the very terms of ethical analysis. This space is characterized by at least five important dimensions:

COMPLEXITY

Networked information and communication technologies are problematic from an ethical standpoint, first, because they are unfathomably complex. To be sure, life is complex. But the networked environment joins together a world of lives, resources, experiences, and interactions; and by joining all these, gives rise to a new second-order set of phenomena, namely, the ways in which these elements influence and are influenced by each other. The scope and reach of these interactions increases by a multiple factor as the networked domain expands.

Ethical judgments have always derived their clarity and sense of finality by delimiting the relevant factors, both in number and by temporal constraints. Questions of the form, "Should one do X or do Y?" can only be analyzed or resolved as such when X and Y are imagined to be the only options, when most of the factors impinging on X and Y can be taken into account, and when the likely consequences of X and Y can be traced out in a relatively straightforward way. Perhaps this is never completely true in the real world, although it is the form of many dilemmas posed as examples in moral philosophy. ("Your family is hungry. Should you steal bread to feed them?") Yet even if one can imagine situations that are relatively bounded in this manner, it is a very poor model for decisions we face in networked environments. Here there are always several options, multiple constraining and enabling factors, and unanticipatable consequences. Because it is networked, every choice has many contingencies, and these in turn have contingencies, ad infinitum. Choose, one must, in partial or complete ignorance of these contingencies; but we should not allow ourselves to imagine that we are the masters of this environment or of the effects of our interventions in it. The ethics of complexity indicate that we can never anticipate or control all the effects of what we do.

UNCERTAINTY

Networked information and communication technologies are problematic from an ethical standpoint, second, because they confront every choice with a horizon of uncertainty. Complexity is one part of this uncertainty. But another part of it is the rapidly changing nature of this environment. Even given an analysis of the relatively proximate effects of one's actions, one can never know for sure how that choice is impinged on by the choices of countless others who are making choices at just the same moment, and within the same networked environment. This is the paradox of the commons, with a vengeance. And because the number of networked connections is growing, beyond our awareness or control, at an extremely rapid rate, even one's attempts to survey the field of options and likely consequences will often miss the mark because the terms of decision are changing, in real time, even as one is attempting to understand them. Future changes to the system are even more difficult to foresee. The ethics of uncertainty indicate that we can never know, beyond a very narrow horizon, the interaction effects and unintended consequences of our choices.

GLOBALIZATION

Networked information and communication technologies are problematic from an ethical standpoint, third, because they occur within a global context, one that is both the condition for these new networks and, in part, a product of them. Because this environment is global, the numbers of people involved in, and affected by, changes to the networked system is vastly greater than those involved in or affected by most human actions and choices. These numbers contribute to the complexity and uncertainty already discussed. But there is another important dimension of this issue: Because this population is global, it is also enormously diverse. The perspectives and interests of these participants carry all the differences of their gender, race, sexuality, social class, nationality, ethnicity, and religion. There is no reason to believe that they will agree or have shared views on any substantive matter before them. They will often have very different moral sentiments and ways of judging situations as they are expressed online. One need not be a relativist to find it problematic to assume that any single way of adjudicating an ethical problem will be acceptable to all, or that those acting and choosing, and those affected by those actions and choices in a networked environment, will have symmetrical, or even compatible, understandings of them. The ethics of globalization indicate that singular moral judgments will always be problematic, viewed from some perspective, and that as a result someone involved in, or by, those judgments will feel that a wrong has been done to them.

UBIQUITY

Networked information and communication technologies are problematic from an ethical standpoint, fourth, because they are becoming ubiquitous, even if they are frequently invisible to users. As the network we call the Internet is tied into the structure of homes, into consumer products, into schools, into automobiles and transportation systems, into clothing and personal items, even into our bodies (through pacemakers, prosthetic devices, corrective or enhancing sensory assistants, etc.), the science fiction dream (or nightmare) of an efficient, interactive, and seamless coordination of many life activities and concerns will be achieved. Judge this as one will, it is already happening to a significant degree. This ubiquity blurs the divide between activities online and those not online, or the public and the private, because one is almost always implicated in the network, not only when one has switched on the computer, the cell phone, the handheld digital assistant, or the television (or the newer devices that are incorporating all these functions). Ubiquity invests online choices and actions with all the quotidity of daily life, and vice versa (Burbules, in press). Ethical deliberation about a problematic situation assumes, subtly, that there is a respite from that situation—that inaction or withdrawal from it is at least conceivably an option before taking action. But the ethics of ubiquitous computing indicate that there *is* no outside to these situations, and that decision making is usually part of a seamless ongoing involvement with it, in which the terms of one's choices and actions are already changing even as one reflects on them.

INTERDEPENDENCE

Networked information and communication technologies are problematic from an ethical standpoint, fifth, because they are completely and dynamically interdependent with one another—and because the factors described here are interdependent with one another. One of the most perplexing and troubling aspects of this environment is that it is impossible to pick and choose the aspects of it one wishes to interact with, and the aspects one does not; within a microcontext, this selectivity might make some sense, but viewed from a networked perspective such choices and actions are in fact implicated in the whole—not in an abstract, vague way, but in many immediate, concrete, and specifiable ways. For example, one may choose not to visit pornographic sites on the Internet, but visiting any sites at all provides information about one's self and one's browsing preferences that are used for a whole host of marketing and design purposes, including the development of pornographic sites. And, as we know from much of our "spam" e-mail, exposure to what we neither ask for nor want is no longer simply a matter of choice. Here, as in my other examples, there is a limit to how knowledgeably one can trace the ramifications of one's choices and actions, given that other users are partly acting on these choices and actions with their own purposes and interests in mind. Their actions might contradict, reinforce, modify, exploit, or frustrate one's best efforts to act directly and purposefully toward a given end. Sometimes, they can be turned to exactly contrary purposes. The ethics of interdependent computing indicate that every choice and action can be acted on by others in such a manner that their intended effects can be negated or reversed, with or without one's knowledge. The fact that most participants in the networked environment we call the Internet are benign, and that most of one's choices and actions are not worth the time and trouble it would take for others to interfere with them, does not mean that any choice or action is free from such influences; once you go online you give others the tools to use against your purposes.

And so I am tracing two simultaneous and seemingly paradoxical trends to life and action online: As the indeterminacy and limited scope of individual knowledge or control over the ramifications of personal choice and action online increase, so do the capacities for surveillance and study of personal choice and action by third parties, based on the analysis of massive, aggregated databases and other methods. In many of these circumstances, others have better knowledge of the patterns and consequences of our choices and actions than we do.

This tension, and the ethical factors I have traced here—complexity, uncertainty, globalization, ubiquity, and interdependence—are characterized in my account by their technological dimensions. But it must be said that these are not solely (or even fundamentally) *technological* changes; they reflect, and interact with, a much wider set of social, institutional, and political shifts. Perhaps those are the primary factors—cause and effect here is difficult to analyze in any simple way. Similarly, contemporary theoretical trends, such as poststructuralism, have questioned traditional views of ethics and argued for the general uncertainty of ethical foundations for reasons that only partly relate to the reasons I am giving here. I am not a technological determinist, and I do not mean to suggest that changes to technology are the only factors at work.

♦ Privacy Today

In the case of an issue such as privacy, the problem cannot, I think, any longer be viewed as basically "protecting" something that one has a "right" to, which is threatened by "invasions" from others. One has compromised one's privacy the moment one ventures online or participates in the digital universe. Because of the essential publicness of any bit of digital information (even when people may try to protect it or limit access to it), we create privacy problems through our everyday choices and actions. Moreover, most people *want* their digital information to be widely available: They merely want it available only to the proper parties, or those of their choosing. The increasing utility of applications, which analyze and predict our activities and preferences (Amazon's feature of recommending books based on the pattern of our previous purchases—and those of others similar to us; the coupons we get sent through physical mail or e-mail; the profiles that determine whether we are rushed through airport security or picked out for extra scrutiny) have, in most people's minds, moved from novelties to expectations.

In this context, an "invasion" of privacy is not normally the way violations happen; more often it involves an authorized holder of our information who uses it in a way we would not have agreed to, if we had been asked (which is why they often do not ask us), or who sells or provides the information to others (including the government) who use it themselves for still other purposes. In many cases, in fact, we never even find out that this has taken place; witness the present debate on warrantless surveillance in which telecommunications companies were secretly giving the government information they were legally prohibited from sharing. Just recently, a government official said,

> "Privacy no longer can mean anonymity," says Donald Kerr, the principal deputy director of national intelligence. Instead, it should mean that government and businesses properly safeguard people's private communications and financial information . . .
>
> Millions of people in this country—particularly young people—already have surrendered anonymity to social networking sites such as MySpace and Facebook, and to Internet commerce. These sites reveal to the public, government and corporations what was once closely guarded information, like personal statistics and credit card numbers.
>
> "Those two generations younger than we are have a very different idea of what is essential privacy, what they would wish to protect about their lives and affairs. And so, it's not for us to inflict one size fits all," said Kerr, 68. "Protecting anonymity isn't a fight that can be won. Anyone that's typed in their name on Google understands that."
>
> "Our job now is to engage in a productive debate, which focuses on privacy as a component of appropriate levels of security and public safety," Kerr said. "I think all of us have to really take stock of what we already are willing to give up, in terms of anonymity, but (also) what safeguards we want in place to be sure that giving that doesn't empty our bank account or do something equally bad elsewhere" (Hess, 2007).

To complicate the case even further, it is far from clear whether people would agree about which of these unauthorized uses is pernicious and which ones might be beneficial. Many would consider consumer profiling, for example, as a way to develop products and policies to better serve them; clearly, there are strongly different views about the proper scope of government surveillance, data mining, and screening of information during a time of "homeland security" concerns. "Privacy," then, mainly pertains to those of one's information and activities that one prefers to make available *only* to others one chooses and only for purposes one explicitly agrees to. It very rarely means complete and insulated secrecy. The problem is that in the networked context I have described, those personal preferences only carry limited weight. This provides a very different analysis of the moral problem of privacy, I believe. The idea that personal information is a kind of property that one "owns" (and which therefore cannot be collected or gathered without explicit permission) sounds good in principle, but would in practice be so cumbersome to achieve today that even someone inclined to protect themselves in this way would eventually decide that it is simply too much trouble. And this, I think, is the subtle way in which profound and irreversible social changes often happen; not through overt choices, but with a shrug, a moment of suspicion or resentment, and then the conclusion that making an issue of it is more of a hassle than letting it go. This is not the end of the autonomous agent, by any means; but it is the recognition of an agent whose choices are ringed in by contingencies and consequences that are increasingly beyond one's knowledge or control.

What then *is* a networked ethics? Thinking about moral choices and actions online needs to begin with a recognition of the complex, uncertain, global, ubiquitous, and interdependent dimensions of these decisions. As I said, these changes have both theoretical and wider social and institutional roots. I have argued that this way of thinking means not artificially delimiting or simplifying the factors influencing one's decision, nor pretending that its consequences can be mapped out with greater certainty than they can. Obviously, in practice, there is a limit to what can be thought about; and taken to an extreme the perspective argued for here could lead to a kind of moral paralysis or radical cynicism—that what one chooses does not matter, or that since anything can go wrong there is no point in worrying too much about it. On the contrary, judgments and choices must be made; but they are highly contingent, constrained judgments and choices. It is a valuable corrective to begin with the assumption that whenever one imagines that the main factors in a moral judgment or choice have been anticipated, there are almost certainly others to be considered; that a special burden applies in this domain to try to learn more about the unexpected dimensions and circumstances of one's choices and actions; and that putatively autonomous agents must depend in a profound way on gaining from the knowledge and perspectives of others—that in the same way that the networked environment is a collaborative knowledge space, it is also a collaborative moral space.

This greater modesty, caution, and sensitivity to the perspectives of others creates a different framework for moral reflection and adjudication, I am arguing. It depends less on notions of rights to be protected, and more on fostering the conditions of mutually informed choices and actions. It depends less on material and spatial metaphors such as property, a zone of privacy, or bounded personal spaces, to be protected, and more on the dynamic adjudication of differences with others in an ongoing process of reasoned engagement. (And here, too, the Internet as a networked digital environment offers some productive resources.) It depends less on explicit formal principles, and more on developing better capacities for recognizing, and reflecting on, morally problematic situations. Finally, it depends less on a utilitarian calculus of goods and harms based on weighing the consequences of choices and actions, and more on trying to learn, retrospectively, from the unanticipated, and often unanticipatable, effects of decisions gone wrong. In each of these shifts, I am trying to replace an impersonal moral perspective that seeks to generalize what is right and wrong, or good and bad, with a *learning* perspective that focuses on how agents actively, and collectively, think about these problems and try to learn from others what might be beyond their ken.

Most of all, a valuable moral capacity is fostered just by the recognition that in certain contexts—and this is one of them—there are implicit norms and values operating through the form and organization of a system, to which one subscribes as soon as one participates in it. These are neither neutral nor unproblematic. They may in specific cases be challengeable, or changeable. But, on the whole, they are tacit conditions of participation at all—they have effects whether one intends them or not. And even challenging or changing them means participating in them in ways that will sometimes have effects directly opposite to those one intends. This is a moral outlook that is less about perfectionism and more about accepting tacit culpability and implication even in some things one finds objectionable. If this recognition makes us more humble, more cautious, and less self-righteous, that might be a better moral starting point anyway. And this moral outlook, I am suggesting here, ought to inform the perspective of the social researcher.

♦ A Way of Thinking About Research Ethics

Finally, then, I return to the question of research ethics. A networked perspective on ethics grows out of the capabilities and dispositions of participants to that environment, and out of the learning relations they forge among themselves. As I have argued, the circumstances of a complex, uncertain, global, ubiquitous, and interdependent networked system resist analyses based on traditional moral precepts. There cannot be externally formulated principles or rules that can be enforced to direct it, nor can there be an entirely blameless way of acting within it; it is a fundamentally compromised and compromising environment, and one enters it inevitably with a culpability for its larger workings (Williams, 1982). What does research ethics mean, then, under these circumstances, and how can education help promote it? My project here is not to provide a new outline for ethical research conduct; of course, I doubt whether that is possible or even desirable. But I do want to sketch out a way of thinking about ethical matters in this and other contexts. I will discuss this way of thinking in relation to the five characteristics of the networked environment, sketched earlier.

First, research ethics under networked conditions means recognizing the complexity, and hence indeterminacy, of this ethical sphere. It shapes a view of ethics based less on clearly distinguishing right from wrong, and more on trying to sort out from all this complexity a set of choices and actions that, to the extent possible, serve good ends and minimize harms. There will never be a single right way to do this, and different approaches will balance these considerations in different ways. But in order to do this, participants will need to learn more about the complexities of the network and the implications of what they do. This is an educational project. And because this complexity will always exceed our capacity to understand it, and because these consequences and interactions are continually changing, this educational project is unending.

Second, research ethics under networked conditions means recognizing the uncertainty of this ethical sphere. Acting under conditions of uncertainty means that in many cases a clear tracing out of consequences and effects may not be possible in a useful way; at such times, we are thrown back on much more proximate considerations in determining what to do. Sometimes, it will involve trusting one's moral intuitions about what seems decent, fair, or helpful under the circumstances; in the larger scheme of things, it may turn out to be otherwise in its effects, but continually doubting this would simply immobilize our choices and actions. Such an approach places a great deal of emphasis on the reliability of those intuitions about what is decent, fair, or helpful, and here again we are part of an educational endeavor. Learning from moral examples or role models, from studying works of literature, or from shared moral conversation, are all ways to cultivate a better sense of how what we do affects others, and strengthens our resolve to do well (Warnick, 2005). Beyond this, there are no guarantees.

Third, research ethics under networked conditions means recognizing the global character of this ethical sphere. This means developing a better understanding of diverse others, and a recognition of the ways in which global systems affect different participants asymmetrically. It means learning to imagine situations from other perspectives and trying to see how the effects of one's choices and actions might be viewed by others. Finally, it means acknowledging the reciprocity of online relations; that the complexly linked nature of networked systems ties all participants into a common set of obligations that need to be respected—respected not because of external norms applied to it, but because successful participation at all means granting to others the same sorts of considerations one would want one's self. Here again we confront an educational project: to learn about diverse others and to improve our capacity to view matters from other perspectives.

Fourth, research ethics under networked conditions means recognizing the ubiquity of this ethical sphere. This means that in many respects the networked ethics we have sketched here is in fact part of a broader ethics since nearly all of our choices and actions will be "networked" in one sense or another. It is crucial to see that the effects of online interactions are not limited to online consequences or to affecting people only when they are online. As people carry out their work, serve their material needs, develop friendships, care for their own well-being, and so on, through online activities, disruptions to that domain spill over in their effects. At the same time, people bring to their online activities their larger concerns, needs, and interests, and this raises the stakes for what happens there. A networked research ethics means learning to listen to others when they tell us what they want and care about; it means fostering a certain wisdom about what matters in people's lives; it means developing a certain amount of patience and tolerance for choices and actions that might be different from ours (Burbules & Smeyers, 2003). There is no moral rule or precept that, taken as an absolute measure, will not sometimes lead us badly. There is no moral virtue or trait of character that, in extreme or exaggerated forms, does not become a vice. There is no capacity for moral thought and reflection that cannot be turned to bad purposes as well as good; the same insights into others that allow us to care for them and respond to them sympathetically are also insights that can be used to manipulate them. And so on. Here again we find an educational project: If there are no guarantees in any form of moral socialization or instruction, then learning to be moral comes down to, more than anything else, learning to *want* to be moral. This inclination is the only reliable guide to unforeseen circumstances, in which we truly do not know what to do; and it is the underlying trait that supports the processes of reflection and reconsideration that keeps our moral judgment flexible in response to changing conditions. In networked contexts, for reasons I hope to have made clear, it is the sole constant—wanting to be moral—even as we recognize the impossibility of ever being completely so.

Fifth, research ethics under networked conditions means recognizing the interdependence of this ethical sphere. In the sense I mean it here, this refers to the inseparability of good and bad elements in this environment, and the impossibility of keeping one's hands completely clean. For one thing, this recognition should, as I have noted, make us more humble, more cautious, and more aware of our need for the perspectives and support of others in deciding what to do. This ongoing process of negotiation means learning from the experiences of others, to watch their choices and actions, as possible guides to our own; it also means actively negotiating with others, in specific instances, a course of action that will be acceptable to all—it still might turn out badly, but at least the participants have granted some assent to it. At the same time, the persistence of bad or dangerous or harmful dimensions to the networked environment means that we are always navigating, not in the sense of steering a straight course for a safe port, but in continually reacting to events, turning to avoid danger, minimizing risks to ourselves and others (Burbules, 2004). These sorts of capacities, *negotiating* and *navigating,* are the kinds of dispositions, strange as it may sound, on which a networked research ethics depends. They are learned, practiced, and improved on by experiences, including mistakes, gained within the sphere of activity, and not only in preparation for it. They are expressions of situational judgment, not of moral rectitude. They are relatively nonspecific in their direction or intent, because they must remain flexible to react to changing conditions—to say that they need to be guided by a spirit of good will is about as deep as one can go.

Many will find these proposals too lacking in substantive moral content; but I have tried to show that anything more strict will not be able to cope with the complexity, uncertainty, globalism, ubiquity, and interdependence of networked activities and relations. Anything more directive will lead to moral error or confusion as often as moral good: Do no harm? Very well, tell me how to avoid that, with any degree of confidence.

In the context of research ethics, this suggests a severe limit to the value of human subjects review procedures, as they are typically practiced (Gunsalus et al., 2005). These procedures, I would argue, should not be seen as methods for protecting the *rights* of subjects; rather, they should be conceived basically as educational experiences for the researchers—educational in the broad sense described here. The current trend of institutional review boards (IRBs) in universities is to demand even more paperwork, more detail, and more levels of approval. It is reaching a point of diminishing returns, both in the unbearable workload IRBs are making for themselves and also the growing resentment and resistance from the researchers these processes are supposed to be helping.

Instead, I believe there needs to be broader latitude given to the researcher's range of judgment and discretion, and then consequences and accountability for cases where those are abused. I believe that formal codes of conduct are, at best, useful as educational guides and heuristics; often, they are counterproductive in perpetuating in many people's minds a view of ethics that needs to be questioned. I believe that there needs to be less effort in trying to anticipate every possible way in which a research project could go wrong, and more attention to helping research subjects make realistic and informed choices about their participation (though here too there is a horizon of what can be known or anticipated). Risk cannot be eliminated, even in an ideal case. The honest question, then, becomes, What kinds of risk are worth tolerating, and who gets to decide whether it is worth it or not? Finally, if my argument in this paper holds at all, there needs to be greater recognition of the fine line, if even that, between appropriate and inappropriate uses of information for research purposes, and between an absolute "private space" of information and activities that can be protected in a digital era, versus a "public space," which we voluntarily enter and act within.

I realize that this essay has done no more than to sketch the outlines of what this thing, a "networked research ethics," might be. It is a networked endeavor itself, relying on communicative relationships and communities of mutual questioning and support. I have tried to argue for why this is preferable as a way of thinking about the new environment of networked information and communication systems, and have tried to show, using the example of privacy, how it leads in very different directions from traditional ethics. Speaking broadly, it leads more toward a virtue ethics approach, I would argue. A further investigation would need to go into greater detail about what these moral capacities actually look like, and what is required to help them take hold in people. But one implication of this argument is that the procedures of human subjects review ought to be approached less as a process of fulfilling bureaucratic paperwork for compliance purposes, and more as an *educational* process in which the guidelines, the application and review processes, and participation on review committees are all conceived from the standpoint of developing better and more informed moral sensibilities among the community of researchers and research subjects.

This argument also implies that, in the socialization of novice researchers, the separation of research "methods" courses from courses on research ethics (if those latter courses are even offered at all) is artificial and counterproductive. Many of the deepest and most problematic issues in research ethics are inherent in the questions of method themselves. And, finally, as those methods become more powerful the ethical questions, I have argued here, become even more disturbing and intractable because of the effects these research methods and their results can have in reconstituting and shaping the very people and social situations they set out to study.

♦ References

Bogard, W. (1996). *The simulation of surveillance: Hypercontrol in telematic societies.* New York: Cambridge University Press.

Burbules, N. C. (2004). Navigating the advantages and disadvantages of online pedagogy. In C. Haythornthwaite & M. M. Kazmer (Eds.), *Learning, culture, and community in online education: Research and practice* (pp. 3–17). New York: Peter Lang.

Burbules, N. C. (2007). Networks as spaces and places: Their importance for educational research collaboration. In P. Smeyers & M. Depaepe (Eds.), *Educational research: Networks and technologies* (pp. 43–54). Dordrecht, The Netherlands: Springer.

Burbules, N. C. (in press). The meanings of ubiquitous learning. In B. Cope & M. Kalantzis (Eds.), *Ubiquitous learning.* Urbana: University of Illinois.

Burbules, N. C., & Callister, T. A., Jr. (2000). Privacy, surveillance, and classroom communication on the Internet. In *Watch IT: The promises and risks of information technologies for education* (pp. 121–136). Boulder, CO: Westview Press.

Burbules, N. C., & Smeyers, P. (2003). Wittgenstein, the practice of ethics, and moral education. In S. Fletcher (Ed.), *Philosophy of education 2002* (pp. 248–257). Urbana, IL: Philosophy of Education Society.

Foucault, M. (1977). *Discipline and punish: The birth of the prison.* New York: Vintage.

Gunsalus, C. K., Bruner, E. M., Burbules, N. C., Dash, L., Finkin, M., Greenough, W. T., et al. (2005). *Improving the system for protecting human subjects: Counteracting IRB "Mission Creep."* University of Illinois, Urbana-Champaign White Paper. Retrieved May 5, 2008, from www.law.uiuc.edu/conferences/whitepaper/

Hess, P. (2007, November 11). Intel official: Expect less privacy. *AP News Story.* Retrieved November 12, 2007, from http://talkingpointsmemo.com/news/2007/11/intel_official_expect_less_pri.php

Warnick, B. R. (2005). *Learning from the lives of others: A social analysis of human exemplarity and imitation.* Unpublished doctoral dissertation, Department of Educational Policy Studies, University of Illinois, Urbana-Champaign.

Warnick, B. R. (2007). Surveillance cameras in schools: An ethical analysis. *Harvard Educational Review, 77*(3), 317–343.

Williams, B. (1982). *Moral luck.* New York: Cambridge University Press.

35

GRADUATE TRAINING IN RESPONSIBLE CONDUCT OF SOCIAL SCIENCE RESEARCH

The Role of Mentors and Departmental Climate

◆ Celia B. Fisher, Frederick J. Wertz, and Sabrina J. Goodman

Over the past 20 years, a consensus has developed that the responsible conduct of research (RCR) is vital for the continued health of the scientific enterprise (National Academy of Sciences [NAS], 1992; Public Health Service [PHS], 2000). RCR encompasses adherence to the rules, regulations, norms, and practices of science. In the social sciences, RCR is embodied by a commitment to intellectual honesty and personal responsibility for the rights and welfare of research participants. Several government reports have asserted that practices and values underlying scientific integrity are the responsibility of individual faculty and their institutions (Ryan Commission on Research Integrity [CRI], 2003; NAS, 2002; PHS, 2000). These include the Department of Health and Human Services (HHS) requirements for education of principal investigators and research supported staff in RCR (PHS, 2000, 2001), increased federal funding for and success of research advances, increased public awareness of the impact of basic and clinical trials research on public health policy and practices, and a number of highly publicized cases involving charges of scientific misconduct (CRI, 2003; Eisen & Berry, 2002).

Renewed discourse on ethical values in social science has followed a parallel path (Fisher & Anushko, 2008). Until recently, discourse on research ethics in the social sciences has focused almost exclusively on the ethics of deception research (Baumrind, 1964; Fisher & Fyrberg, 1994; Milgram, 1963, 1964; Sieber, 1982). Social-behavioral research has witnessed increased visibility as it has expanded into the public health and mental health science arenas. There have also been a number of highly scrutinized cases of misconduct and ethics controversies (Needleman, 1992; Salter, 1998; Sprague, 1993). In response to this sea change, in recent years several disciplinary organizations have revised ethical standards relevant to research. Australia, for instance, in revising their 1999 *National Statement on Ethical Conduct in Research Involving Humans*, has drafted a new set of guidelines specifically for social scientists highlighting principles such as research merit and integrity, justice, beneficence, and respect (NHMRC, 2007). In the United States, the American Psychological Association (APA) has updated its volume on *Research Ethics with Human Participants* (Sales & Folkman, 2000) and revised its *Ethical Principles of Psychologists and Code of Conduct* (APA, 2002; Fisher, 2003) to be more consistent with federal regulations for human subjects research. The APA's model of having specific enforceable standards for research has been adapted by other social sciences, including the American Anthropological Association (1998), the American Sociological Association (1999), and the Canadian Psychological Association (2000).

◆ RCR Training

Several government reports have endorsed the concept that training a new generation of investigators in the practices and values underlying scientific integrity is the responsibility of individual faculty and their institutions (CRI, 2003; NAS, 2002; PHS, 2000). At the individual level, mentoring is considered a core aspect of RCR education. Mentors and trainees should be aware of their mutual responsibilities in doctoral training programs, and how to resolve mentor/trainee conflicts and competition, work collaboratively, and avoid and recognize mentor/trainee abuse (PHS, 2000). Graduate departments also play a critical role in facilitating or inhibiting RCR graduate education. According to *Integrity in Scientific Research: Creating an Environment That Promotes Responsible Conduct* (NAS, 2002), since the individual scientist (mentor) is the most influential yet unpredictable variable in RCR training, constants must come from an institutional climate that provides consistent and effective training and education, policies and procedures, and tools and support systems. The Ryan Commission (CRI, 2003) also noted the importance of an institutional climate that does not penalize members for identifying those who violate research ethics and recommended that HHS expand existing institutional assurances to require that research institutions provide research integrity education for all individuals supported by PHS research funds.

In summary, graduate programs are the primary training ground for learning the values and ethical practices of one's scientific discipline. Through the direct influence of faculty mentors and the indirect influence of departmental policies, graduate programs create the climate in which research integrity flourishes or flounders. Yet research ethics education has not been a formal aspect of graduate education in the sciences in general and psychological science in particular. The small but growing literature on RCR mentoring and departmental climate has focused on science training broadly defined, with few studies or position papers focusing on the social sciences in particular. The purpose of this chapter is to highlight features of RCR mentoring and departmental climate that have been identified as potentially facilitating or creating obstacles for student socialization into the RCR and to recommend future steps that can help bring this knowledge to graduate training in the social sciences.

◆ Mentoring RCR

The mentoring literature addresses important definitional issues and brings out a key distinction between "mentoring" and "advising." In a recent report, the NAS (1997) concluded that mentoring is more than advising because its main function is to help the protégé become a competent professional and to become socialized into the discipline. The report also concludes that mentoring is a personal as well as professional relationship that develops over time to meet the student's changing needs. Bird (2001) argued that while the terms *mentor* and *thesis advisor* (or research supervisor) are often used interchangeably, the responsibilities associated with these roles are distinct, even when they overlap.

The Acadia Institute's Project on Professional Values and Ethical Issues in the Graduate Education of Scientists and Engineers includes 78 in-depth interviews with doctoral students and faculty in chemistry, microbiology, sociology, and civil engineering at three research universities (Swazey & Anderson, 1996). Some faculty and students saw mentoring as a faculty member's legacy to his or her students. Others reported that mentors with large laboratories often instituted a labwide student-student mentoring process, and if faculty lacked the time to mentor themselves, they would assign mentoring functions to postdocs. Students were more likely than faculty to see distinctions between the advising and mentoring role.

Others have also proposed broader definitions of mentoring. The Council of Graduate Schools (1995) adopted a definition of mentors as people with career experience willing to share their knowledge and provide feedback on protégé performance, give emotional and moral encouragement, provide career opportunities, and model what an academic should be. In a survey of clinical psychology graduate students, it is defined as follows:

> Mentoring is a personal relationship in which a more experienced (usually older) individual acts as a guide, role model, teacher, and sponsor of a less experienced (usually younger) protégé. A mentor provides the protégé with knowledge, advice, challenge, counsel and support in the protégé's pursuit of becoming a full member of a particular profession. (Clark, Harden, & Johnson, 2000, p. 263)

Swazey and Anderson (1996) also emphasized the direct and personal nature of the mentor role as distinguished from *advisors* who perform more narrow technical functions and have relatively little contact with trainees and from *role models* who may play an informal, passive role in trainees' professional socialization.

◆ Functions of Mentoring

Definitions of mentoring incorporate assumptions regarding mentor functions. Mentoring can facilitate student career advancement by guiding the directions of the student's work, evaluating the work from various standpoints including both scientific and social, sponsoring attendance at professional meetings, providing professional visibility for their work, and challenging them to achieve professional goals. Mentoring can fulfill psychosocial functions such as enhancing protégés' sense of competence, values, identity, and work-role effectiveness through acceptance, support, confirmation, counseling, and friendship. Through role modeling, mentors can offer protégés firsthand examples of achievement, success, and professional competence.

Swazey and Anderson (1996) derived three categories of mentor functions from their large-scale survey of students. The first function, *teacher-coach*, trains students for specific activities they will perform on completion of the degree by providing specific information relevant to the student's work, helpful criticism, assistance in writing presentations and publications, and teaching good research practice and proposal writing. The second mentor function, the *sponsor role*, helps students get established in professional networks by writing letters of recommendation, helping with financial support, introducing students to colleagues, and identifying employment opportunities. The third function, *counselor*, expresses continuing interest in the student's progress, provides emotional support, and helps students learn the art of survival in his or her field. The Acadia study found significant differences among four disciplines in the frequency of the three types of mentoring functions, with microbiology students reporting the most and sociology students the least amount of mentoring functions. There were no consistent gender, citizen-race categories, or length of time in program effects on mentoring functions across disciplines. There was some suggestion that in microbiology and sociology, U.S. minority students perceive greater mentor support.

FORMAL VERSUS INFORMAL MENTORING

Informal mentoring has been described as the "hidden curriculum" in scientific research in which "lessons are taught implicitly, through role models, institutional leadership, peers, and during the course of practice" and where trainees discover "how it really works" (Fryer-Edwards, 2002, p. 58). Stern and Elliot (1997) have argued that informal modeling of responsible conduct in research, if effective, only teaches students what to do, but not why they are doing it. Without understanding the whys of RCR, graduates are ill equipped to generalize RCR decision making to new research contexts (Eisen & Berry, 2002). Measures designed to assess formal and informal RCR mentoring in psychology graduate programs have found them to be overlapping, yet distinct factors (Fisher, Fried, Goodman, & Germano, in press).

MENTORSHIP PHASES

In psychology, as in other science fields characterized by formal mentoring, dissertation mentorship is a temporal relationship that begins with formal or informal mentor-protégé discussions regarding a proposed area of doctoral research, proceeds through the dissertation design, proposal, implementation, interpretation, and defense stages, and ends with a redefinition of a collegial peer relationship (Swazey & Anderson, 1996). These phases have been described as (a) the Initiation phase in which protégé and mentor begin to enjoy a relationship characterized by attraction, potential, and synergy; (b) Cultivation phase characterized by stability and essential mentor functions; (c) Separation phase during which a protégé completes graduate school and exits the active relational phase of mentoring; and (d) Redefinition phase defined as an indefinite period when mentorship ends altogether or is redefined as a collegial friendship (Chao, 1997). Adequate mentorship needs to be sensitive to these various phases.

◆ Effective Mentor Characteristics

What personal characteristics are associated with effective mentoring? The NAS (1997) has identified 10 core ingredients for effective mentorship in science. Interpersonal qualities include patient listening, relationship building, and nurturing self-sufficiency. Professional modeling includes demonstrating fair authorship practices, providing introductions to esteemed colleagues, and offering constructive criticism. Bird (2001) has suggested that effective mentors need to have enthusiasm for the field, a positive outlook for the protégé's career choice, an ability to articulate and address sensitive issues, high standards and expectations, a willingness to expend time and effort, nondiscriminatory beliefs about who can do science, an open mind, and an appreciation of diversity. In psychology, mentors have been described as available and invested, altruistic, ethical, and intentional role models (Gilbert, 1985; Kitchener, 1992; Wilson & Johnson, 2001).

INTERPERSONAL SKILLS

Graduate education is often a period characterized by stress, insecurity, and hypervigilance marked by student reports of anxiety, instability in identity, and sense of being an imposter in the graduate program (Bruss & Kopala, 1993). A survey of 610 faculty members across 49 different departments at a research-oriented university found that a mastery-oriented research climate (an educational and cooperative climate) in the professor's own laboratory was related to a more supportive approach to mentoring than an outcome research climate (a competitive and rivalry-oriented lab; Roberts, Kavussanu, & Sprague, 2001). Mentoring in psychology graduate programs is often marked by emotional intensity and informality that leaves the mentor responsible for safeguarding the relationship on an interpersonal level without peer review or consultation (Johnson & Nelson, 1999). Psychologists often stress the interpersonal nature of mentoring, with the mentor providing knowledge, counsel, emotional, and career support, overseeing both the protégé's professional and personal development (Johnson & Nelson, 1999). Schlosser and Gelso (2001) developed the Advisory Working Alliance Inventory (AWAI) to measure the graduate advising relationship. They identified three factors—rapport, apprenticeship, and identification-individuation. Higher scores on the AWAI were related to higher scores on students' sense of research self-efficacy, positive attitudes toward research, and positive perceptions of the advisor expertness, attractiveness, and trustworthiness.

NORMATIVE STANDARDS

Psychology and other disciplines have recognized that RCR must be grounded in a widely accepted consensus that there are good moral reasons for such conduct (Camenisch, 1996; Fisher, 2003). Professional success requires awareness and understanding of professional standards, regulations, and ethical values of the scientific community. This information is transmitted to trainees either explicitly or implicitly through the mentoring process (Bird, 2001; Fisher et al., in press). Swazey and Anderson (1996) and Swazey, Anderson, and Louis (1993) reported cause for concern about the preparation of trainees in normative standards for the conduct of research that are informally and formally transmitted. The APA identifies beneficence and nonmaleficence, fidelity and responsibility, integrity, justice, and respect for people's rights and dignity as the major aspirational moral principles underlying the ethical science and practice of psychology (APA, 2002). Kitchener (1992) and Johnson and Nelson (1999) adapted these ethical principles into normative standards for mentoring in psychology: (a) Autonomy—How can I strengthen my protégés' knowledge, maturity, and independence? (b) Beneficence/nonmaleficence—How can I contribute to my protégés' development and avoid harm? (c) Justice—How do I ensure equitable treatment of my protégés regardless of gender, ethnicity, or age? and (d) Fidelity—How can I be honest and remain loyal to my protégés?

GENDER AND ETHNICITY IN MENTORING

The increasing gender, ethnic, and cultural diversity of academia challenges mentors to be sensitive to individual differences in how the values of RCR are best transmitted. From 1984 to 1994, the percentage of female and ethnic minority faculty members in psychology departments increased from 22% to 37% and from 6% to 11%, respectively (Gehlmann, Wicherski, & Kohout, 1995). In the period between 1999 and 2000, women and ethnic minorities represented 70% and 18% of first-year doctoral students, respectively (APA, 2002). Although women now make up the majority of psychology graduate students, most faculty members, particularly senior faculty, are men (Pion et al., 1996). Similarly, while the number of ethnic minority students in psychology has increased over the past, the numbers are still very small (APA, 2000; Atkinson, Neville, & Casas, 1991; Pion et al., 1996).

Some have reported that women and minority students typically have less access to mentoring and that good mentoring may help them gain advantages more frequently afforded to members of majority groups (Bogat & Redner, 1985; Cohen & Gutek, 1991; Gilbert & Rossman, 1992; Sambunjak, Strauss, & Marusic, 2006; Wilson & Johnson, 2001). Dixon-Reeves (2003) found that mentoring helped African American sociology doctorates advance successfully through the academic ranks. Others have reported that women in academic settings are just as frequently mentored and just as satisfied with their mentorship as their male colleagues (Clark et al., 2000; Fried et al., 1996), that ethnic minority students report greater satisfaction with their mentors than their white counterparts (Mintz, Bartels, & Rideout, 1995), and that male and female mentors are equally capable and equally limited in providing for their protégés' career and psychosocial needs (Clark et al., 2000; Hollingsworth & Fassinger, 2002; Nelson & Holloway, 1990). Ortiz-Walters and Gilson (2005) found that although African, Hispanic, and Native American protégés reported more support and satisfaction from mentors of color than from white mentors and from mentors with more similar values, interpersonal comfort and commitment play a mediating role in the relation of these factors and outcomes.

The small but growing literature on RCR mentoring suggests that a positive mentor-protégé relationship is a critical means of socializing students to the values, norms, attitudes, and specialized knowledge and skills of the discipline (Baird, 1996). However, in a large-scale, multidiscipline, multiuniversity study, only one third of students rated the advisor/mentor relationship as very important in shaping their professional values and preparing them to deal with ethical issues in their field (Swazey & Anderson, 1996), and a smaller study found that mentors were rated by graduate students eighth in a list of nine factors (Sprague, Daw, & Roberts, 2001). In the next section, we look at potential barriers to RCR mentoring that may help shed light on these findings.

♦ Barriers to RCR Mentoring

There are historical, individual, and institutional factors that can impede effective RCR mentoring. Mentors can impede professional socialization through inaccessibility, over- or undersupervision, critical focus on trainee inadequacies, and other behaviors associated with "toxic" mentoring (Swazey & Anderson, 1996). The percentage of dysfunctional mentorship relationships is low, partly because people can terminate such relationships; however, a substantial proportion of mentors may be "marginal," defined as limited in the scope or degree of mentoring functions provided (Ragins, Cotton, & Miller, 2000). In addition, some graduate students work on mentors' research projects in which appropriate or inappropriate behaviors are modeled (Leatherman, 1996).

MENTOR KNOWLEDGE OF RCR

Given the historical tradition of informal mentoring in RCR, few mentors have themselves received any formal ethics instructions and many are more comfortable serving as a role model for research methods than for ethical behavior (Eisen & Berry, 2002). Bebeau and Davis (1996) found that dental investigators were more likely to rate as serious misconduct practices that undermine the trustworthiness of science (falsifying or fabrication of data, retaliation, failure to present negative results, lack of transparency in conflicts of interest, plagiarism) and less serious those practices considered disrespectful of the work of others (gift authorship, citing references without reading them, dividing a project into small units, failure to correct misinterpretation of data or refusal to share data). This study suggests that across disciplines students may not be exposed to issues of scientific integrity that their mentors perceive as unimportant.

MENTOR MISCONDUCT

The ability to recognize, reason about, and effectively implement ethical action plans requires practice (Bebeau, 1994; Rest & Narváez, 1994). Therefore, less-experienced faculty and those who themselves were not mentored in RCR may not have the experience needed to effectively socialize students in responsibly conducting research. Lack of experience and education in RCR can also result in mentoring in the irresponsible conduct of research. In a survey by Clark et al. (2000), 5% of psychology graduate protégés responded that their mentors took credit for their work. In response to open-ended questions, 2% of protégés reported that their mentors published questionable findings, altered research to support the hypothesis, or offered the protégé financial incentive to alter results. Goodyear, Crego, and Johnson (1992), using the critical incident technique to study research supervision, found reports of incompetent and inadequate supervision, intrusion of supervisor's values, encouragement to fraud, and lack of guidelines and questionable handling of authorship issues. In view of this important but limited evidence, some have proposed that mentor leadership training should precede teaching research ethics to ensure that RCR can be sustained at the institutional level (Motta, 2002).

TRADITIONAL SCIENCE VALUES

Another type of barrier results from the traditionally strong scientific ethos, such as the belief that basic scientific tenets such as replication of results will ultimately reveal data falsification or fabrication and that in many instances, scientific misconduct does not result in observable participant harm (Eisen & Berry, 2002). The assumption that science, with its empirical-factual nature, is value free or value neutral, and the belief that research is "pure," without practical impact on society, may have unintentionally led to the "ghettoization of ethics" in science curricula (Fisher, 1999). RCR regulations or disciplinary codes of conduct are presented as tangential or an obstacle to good science (Richman, 2002).

LARGE INSTITUTIONAL RESEARCH

Multisite and multi-investigator collaboration in many scientific fields may also impede mentor-protégé socialization. For example, students working in large laboratories may find it difficult to develop a close working relationship with a faculty member. In such contexts, faculty members sometimes create "secondary mentoring networks, where advanced students and postdoctoral investigators act as mentors" (NAS, 2002). Within the context of these barriers it is not surprising that Stern and Elliot (1997) concluded that across a number of surveys at major research institutions, approximately 90% of graduate students reported little or no guidance in RCR irrespective of whether mentors were perceived as generally supportive. Alternative models have been used, for instance, drawing mentors from new faculty (Jacelon, Zucker, Staccarini, & Henneman, 2003) and peers (Bussey-Jones et al., 2006), with reported success in building strong relationships and a supportive community, but their effectiveness in engendering RCR has not been investigated.

THE COMPLEXITY OF ACADEMIC INSTITUTIONS

In their large-scale study of scientific integrity in academia conducted by the Acadia Institute, Swazey and Anderson (1996) concluded that obstacles to mentoring include the increasing size and complexity of academic and research organizations, the reward system for grants and publications and travel time away from the institution to obtain such rewards, institutional demands on faculty time, and few rewards for dedicated and effective teaching. In addition, few institutions provide training or guidance for the mentoring role (Council of Graduate Schools, 1991). In the next section, we turn to the influence of graduate departments on RCR socialization.

◆ Departmental Climate and RCR Socialization

There is an increased recognition of the effect of institutional factors on individual moral behavior (Power, Higgins, & Kohlberg, 1989). The ethical climate is an important source of information about what constitutes ethical behavior, moral obligations, and codes or regulations that should be applied in the workplace. Victor and Cullen (1988) defined ethical climate as "the prevailing perceptions of typical organizational practices and procedures that have ethical content" (p. 101). In their view, organizations are social actors and are in part responsible for the ethicality of employees' conduct. There is increasing national attention to the role that graduate programs play in RCR socialization, very little is known about the actual departmental policies and practices that influence students' research values and training.

ENVIRONMENTS PROMOTING RCR

The Institute of Medicine National Research Council (NAS, 2002) report titled *Integrity in Scientific Research: Creating an Environment That Promotes Responsible Conduct* focused on the critical role that institutions play in creating a stable, unambiguous work climate in which the expectations and consequences of scientific conduct for mentors and students is clear. Report recommendations relevant to social science departments include encouraging respect and promoting productive interactions between trainees and mentors; adopting a code of conduct, procedures to investigate allegations of scientific misconduct and appropriate sanctions; and monitoring and evaluating the institutional environment supporting integrity in the conduct of research and use this knowledge for continuous quality improvement. The report also recommends offering educational opportunities for RCR training. At present, when research ethics are included in departmental curricula, it often plays a minor role in course outlines devoted to fuller coverage of research-relevant topics. Departmental curricula can be an effective environmental means of transmitting institutional values that compliment values transmitted through mentoring. For example, Tryon (2002) asked 233 school psychology doctoral students, "How prepared are you to obtain informed consent and assent from parent, adolescent, and child participants for your dissertation and/or other research?" The percentage of students who had taken an ethics course who felt prepared for obtaining consent for research was 83.3%. The percentage of students who had not taken an ethics course but responded similarly to this item was 67.3% ($N = 76$; total: $M = 4.16$, $SD = 1.08$). Tryon's study suggests that ethics course requirements at the departmental level are an important institutional resource for student RCR learning.

ASSESSING THE ACADEMIC ETHICAL CLIMATE

The Acadia Institute Project on Professional Values and Ethical Issues in the Graduate Education of Scientists and Engineers (Swazey et al., 1993) surveyed 2,000 doctoral candidates and 2,000 faculty about their experiences with 15 different types of ethically questionable behavior from 99 departments in chemistry, civil engineering, microbiology, and sociology. They found that actual misconduct was rare; 6% to 9% of students and faculty reported having direct knowledge of misconduct. Faculty in civil engineering and sociology detected plagiarism among graduate students at higher levels than microbiology and chemistry faculty. Across disciplines, reports of questionable research practices among faculty were far more common than misconduct: 42% reported inappropriate use of university resources; 33% inappropriate authorship assignment; 22% overlooking sloppy use of data; and 15% failure to include in research summaries data not supporting an investigator's previous research. Inappropriate authorship was most commonly reported in sociology. Between 7% and 23% of faculty and students had firsthand observations of misuse of research funds, unauthorized use of privileged information, and failure to disclose conflict of interest, with sociologists observing the least of these behaviors. A total of 20% reported observing lack of compliance with research regulations involving human subjects, animal care and use, and biosafety. Fisher et al. (in press) found that graduate psychology student perceptions of the RCR departmental climate were associated with their self-evaluations of RCR preparedness and their attitudes toward the integrity of the psychology profession.

These findings raise concerns about departmental climate and faculty modeling of subtle, but no less damaging forms of failure to adhere to research ethics standards. Perhaps not surprisingly, whereas a majority of faculty believes that they should have collective responsibility for their colleagues and students, only 27% and 55% judge that they and their departmental colleague actually share such responsibility for students and colleagues, respectively. Louis, Anderson, and Rosenberg (1995) found disciplinary differences in faculty attitudes and behaviors with higher concordance between idealized and actual practice in chemistry and microbiology, compared with civil engineers and sociologists.

◆ Limitations of Current Knowledge: Challenges

Empirical examination of how knowledge and attitudes about the responsible conduct of social research develop is at a nascent stage. How knowledgeable are social science faculty in the ethics of their discipline? Can mentors who did not receive sufficient guidance in the RCR transmit appropriate and comprehensive research ethics knowledge to their mentees? What kind of training and experience on the part of mentors is necessary to prepare them to transmit best practices in RCR? To what degree do professors discuss research ethics in classroom courses, labs, and research apprenticeships? How do tenure and promotion policies support or discourage faculty from focusing on ethics in their own research and that of their students? And finally, how does the larger academic environment, including institutional regulations, policies, and practices facilitate or impede effective mentoring of RCR?

Another challenge to understanding how to develop effective RCR mentoring and departmental practices is developing methods to assess outcomes of RCR training at the attitudinal and behavioral level. Informal or short-term training in techniques of research ethics may increase RCR knowledge and a sense of preparedness to comply with specific regulations, but formal, long-term training that develops reasoning appears necessary to create changes in moral reflection, ethical decision making, and willingness to engage in ethical practices (Bebeau & Thoma, 1994; Kalichman & Friedman, 1992). Moreover, a second important distinction suggests that neither technical proficiency nor even highly developed ethical reasoning necessarily assures actual ethical conduct in later research activities; group discussions of case studies improves moral reasoning (Bebeau & Thoma, 1994) but may not change future behavior (Kalichman & Friedman, 1992).

♦ The Unique Role of Social Science in RCR

The philosophy of science and critical thought within the social sciences has broadened our understanding of the meaning of "good science" through the 20th century. Research is viewed less as an unbiased discovery of reality and increasingly as a socially constructed practice that entails subjectivity, values, and power relations that require acknowledgment, critical evaluation, and possibly reform. Social scientists realize that science is power, that there is no value-free inquiry, and that the responsible scientist recognizes research participants as moral agents whose values and goals must infuse scientific practice if it is to be fully responsible (Fisher, 1999, 2000, 2002; Fisher & Fyrberg, 1994). Social scientists are increasingly acknowledging the full social network of persons affected by the research, from its original identification of research problems to the interpretation, dissemination, and utilization of research findings (Fishman, 1999). The responsible scientist is learning accountability to the nonscientist; good science involves dialogue that treats those with a stake in the research as partners, equals.

As social scientists recognize that familiarity with federal and disciplinary codes of ethics are a small part of socialization into the RCR, they are focusing on the moral self as the center of values, relational qualities, and personhood (Atkins, Hart, & Donnelly, 2004; Power, 2004). Research trainees are persons whose work cannot be separated from who they are, including their interests, aspirations, social commitments, and identities. Traditional research values may need to evolve to encompass the values of an increasingly diverse student population. Castro, Caldwell, and Salazar (2005), for example, discussed the need for a reevaluation of research socialization as the number of female and ethnic minority graduate students continues to increase (see also Humble, Solomon, Allen, Blaisure, & Johnson, 2006; Koro-Ljungberg & Hayes, 2006). Others focus on how reconsideration of pluralistic values may help advance a social science more responsive to the diverse populations about which it aims to generate knowledge (Hesse-Biber, 2007; Williams, Brewely, Reed, White, & Davis-Haley, 2005). Ponce, Williams, and Allen (2005) have observed that most academic programs do not possess vigorous mentoring cultures because of a mastery philosophy that underplays social relations and may even inadvertently stigmatize students from underrepresented populations. They suggested the cultivation of academic communities in which mentors learn from their protégés as well as vice versa.

Federal regulations and formally adopted ethics codes delineate a number of different areas in which responsibility is crucial in the conduct of research. By their very nature, federal regulations are broadly written. Each science discipline therefore is responsible for operationalizing for its members and trainees the particulars of goodly practiced science. Mentoring is a particularly powerful means of educating students in the normative standards of the discipline not only through instruction but through role modeling, institutional leadership, and direct hands-on collaborative practice with student researchers. In the generational transition toward increasing ethical concern and competency, mentors themselves have not had formal ethical education and may not recognize the importance of this area of mentoring, may not feel comfortable and confident, and may transmit irresponsible practice. Mentoring, which itself can embody and therefore realize the mutually accountable kind of relationship in which the ethically responsible self takes shape, has the potential to encourage a range of individual differences on the part of individuals whose previously marginalized values, sensibilities, and social commitments have been excluded from scientific research and thereby to enrich the identities and responsibilities of research scientists.

The social sciences are in a unique position to contribute to the understanding and enhancement of student socialization into the RCR. Social scientists can apply their expertise for examining and measuring individual behavior and attitudes, interpersonal communication, and environmental factors on the ways in which research values and practices are communicated through mentors and departments and how such communications affect students' sense of RCR preparedness, actual competence, and their attitudes toward the integrity of the profession (Fisher et al., in press). The challenge of such efforts is to employ the wealth of knowledge that has emerged concerning the requirements and features of good, responsible scientific research as they are learned through mentor-protégé relationships in educational settings.

◆ References

American Anthropological Association. (1998). *Code of ethics of the American anthropological association.* Retrieved March 10, 2006, from www.aaanet.org/committees/ethics/ethicscode.pdf

American Psychological Association Ethics Committee. (2000). Report of the Ethics Committee, 1999. *American Psychologist, 55,* 938–945.

American Psychological Association Ethics Committee. (2002). Report of the Ethics Committee, 2001. *American Psychologist, 57,* 650–657.

American Sociological Association. (1999). *Code of ethics.* Washington, DC: Author. Retrieved March 10, 2006, from www.asanet.org/galleries/default-file/Code%200f%20Ethics.pdf

Atkins, R., Hart, D., & Donnelly, T. M. (2004). Moral identity development and attachment. In D. K. Lapsley & D. Narvaez (Eds.), *Moral development, self, and identity* (pp. 65–82). Mahwah, NJ: Lawrence Erlbaum.

Atkinson, D. R., Neville, H., & Casas, A. (1991). The mentorship of ethnic minorities in professional psychology. *Professional Psychology: Research and Practice, 22,* 336–338.

Baird, L. L. (1996). Documenting student outcomes in graduate and professional outcomes. *New Directions for Institutional Research, 92,* 77–78.

Baumrind, D. (1964). Some thoughts on ethics of research: After reading Milgram's "Behavioral study of obedience." *American Psychologist, 26,* 887–896.

Bebeau, M. J. (1994). Influencing the moral dimension of dental practice. In J. R. Rest & D. F. Narváez (Eds.), *Moral development in the professions: Psychology and applied ethics* (pp. 121–146). Hillsdale, NJ: Lawrence Erlbaum.

Bebeau, M. J., & Davis, E. L. (1996). Survey of ethical issues in dental research. *Journal of Dental Research, 75,* 845–855.

Bebeau, M. J., & Thoma, S. J. (1994). The impact of a dental ethics curriculum on moral reasoning. *Journal of Dental Education, 58,* 684–692.

Bird, S. J. (2001). Mentors, advisors and supervisors: Their role in teaching responsible research conduct. *Science and Engineering Ethics, 7,* 455–468.

Bogat, G. A., & Redner, R. L. (1985). How mentoring affects the professional development of women in psychology. *Professional Psychology: Research and Practice, 16,* 851–859.

Bruss, K. V., & Kopala, M. (1993). Graduate school training in psychology: Its impact upon the development of professional identity. *Psychotherapy, 30,* 685–691.

Bussey-Jones, J., Bernstein, L., Higgins, S., Paranjape, A., Genao, I., Bennett, L., et al. (2006). Repaving the road to academic success: The IMeRGE approach to peer mentoring. *Academic Medicine, 81*(7), 674–679.

Camenisch, P. F. (1996). The moral foundations of scientific ethics and responsibility. *Journal of Dental Research, 75,* 824–831.

Canadian Psychological Association. (2000). *Canadian code of ethics for psychologists* (3rd ed.). Retrieved April 25, 2008, from www.cpa.ca/aboutcpa/boardofdirectors/committees/ethics/ethicalguidelines/

Castro, C., Caldwell, C., & Salazar, C. F. (2005). Creating mentoring relationships between female faculty and students in counselor education: Guidelines for potential mentees and mentors. *Journal of Counseling and Development, 83*(3), 331–336.

Chao, G. T. (1997). Mentoring phases and outcomes. *Journal of Vocational Behavior, 51,* 15–28.

Clark, R. A., Harden, S. L., & Johnson, W. B. (2000). Mentor relationships in clinical psychology doctoral training: Results of a national survey. *Teaching of Psychology, 27,* 262–268.

Cohen, A. G., & Gutek, B. A. (1991). Sex differences in the career experiences of members of two APA divisions. *American Psychologist, 46,* 1292–1298.

Council of Graduate Schools. (1991). *The role and nature of the doctoral dissertation: A policy statement.* Washington, DC: Author.

Council of Graduate Schools. (1995). *A conversation about mentoring: Trends and models.* Washington, DC: Author.

Dixon-Reeves, R. (2003). Mentoring as a precursor to incorporation: An assessment of the mentoring experience of recently minted PhDs. In Race in the academy: Moving beyond diversity toward the incorporation of faculty of color in predominantly white colleges and universities [Special issue]. *Journal of Black Studies, 34*(1), 12–27.

Eisen, A., & Berry, R. M. (2002). The absent professor: Why we don't teach research ethics and what to do about it. *American Journal of Bioethics, 2,* 38–49.

Fisher, C. B. (1999). Relational ethics and research with vulnerable populations. Reports on research involving persons with mental disorders that may affect decision-making capacity Vol. II (pp. 29–49). *Commissioned Papers by the National Bioethics Advisory Commission.* Rockville, MD: National Bioethics Advisory Commission. Retrieved August 31, 2005, from www.bioethics.gov/reports/past_commissions/nbac_menta12.pdf

Fisher, C. B. (2000). Relational ethics in psychological research: One feminist's journey. In M. Brabeck (Ed.), *Practicing feminist ethics in psychology* (pp. 125–142). Washington, DC: American Psychological Association.

Fisher, C. B. (2002). Participant consultation: Ethical insights into parental permission and confidentiality procedures for policy relevant research with youth. In R. M. Lerner, F. Jacobs, & D. Wertlieb (Eds.), *Handbook of applied developmental science* (Vol. 4, pp. 371–396). Thousand Oaks, CA: Sage.

Fisher, C. B. (2003). *Decoding the ethics code: A practical guide for psychologists.* Thousand Oaks, CA: Sage.

Fisher, C. B., & Anushko, A. (2008). Research ethics in social science. In P. Alasuutari,

L. Bickman, & J. Brannen (Eds.), *The handbook of social research* (pp. 95–109). Thousand Oaks, CA: Sage.

Fisher, C. B., Fried, A. F., Goodman, S. J., & Germano, K. K. (in press). Measures of mentoring, department climate, and graduate student preparedness in the responsible conduct of psychological research. *Ethics & Behavior*.

Fisher, C. B., & Fyrberg, D. (1994). Participant partners: College students weigh the costs and benefits of deceptive research. *American Psychologist, 49*(5), 417–427.

Fishman, D. (1999). *The case for a pragmatic psychology.* New York: New York University Press.

Fried, L. P., Francomano, C. A., MacDonald, S. M., Wagner, E. M., Stokes, E. J., Carbone, K. M., et al. (1996). Career development for women in academic medicine. *Journal of the American Medical Association, 276,* 898–905.

Fryer-Edwards, K. (2002). Addressing the hidden curriculum in scientific research (2002). *American Journal of Bioethics, 2*(4), 58–59.

Gehlmann, S., Wicherski, M., & Kohout, J. (1995). *Characteristics of graduate departments in psychology: 1993–94.* Washington, DC: American Psychological Association.

Gilbert, L. A. (1985). Dimensions of same-gender student-faculty role model relationships. *Sex Roles, 12,* 111–123.

Gilbert, L. A., & Rossman, K. M. (1992). Gender and the mentoring process for women: Implications for professional development. *Professional Psychology: Research and Practice, 23,* 233–238.

Goodyear, R. K., Crego, C. A., & Johnson, M. W. (1992). Ethical issues in the supervision of student research: A study of critical incidents. *Professional Psychology: Research and Practice, 23*(3), 203–210.

Hesse-Biber, S. N. (2007). *Handbook of feminist research: Theory and praxis.* Thousand Oaks, CA: Sage.

Hollingsworth, M. A., & Fassinger, R. E. (2002). The role of faculty mentors in the research training of counseling psychology doctoral students. *Journal of Counseling Psychology, 49,* 324–330.

Humble, A. M., Solomon, C. R., Allen, K. R., Blaisure, K. R., & Johnson, M. P. (2006). Feminism and mentoring of graduate students. *Family Relations: Interdisciplinary Journal of Applied Family Studies, 55*(1), 2–15.

Jacelon, C. S., Zucker, D. M., Staccarini, J. M., & Henneman, E. A. (2003). Peer mentoring for tenure-track faculty. *Journal of Professional Nursing, 19,* 335–338.

Johnson, W. B., & Nelson, N. (1999). Mentor-protégé relationships in graduate training: Some ethical concerns. *Ethics & Behavior, 9,* 189–210.

Kalichman, M. W., & Friedman, P. J. (1992). A pilot study of biomedical trainees perceptions concerning research ethics. *Academic Medicine, 67,* 769–775.

Kitchener, K. S. (1992). Psychologists as teacher and mentor: Affirming ethical values throughout the curriculum. *Professional Psychology: Research & Practice, 23,* 190–195.

Koro-Ljungberg, M., & Hayes, S. (2006). The relational selves of female graduate students during academic mentoring: From dialog to transformation. *Mentoring and Tutoring: Partnership in Learning, 14*(4), 389–407.

Leatherman, C. (1996). Graduate students' relations with mentors are often tense. *The Chronicle of Higher Learning, 9,* 26–27.

Louis, K. S., Anderson, M. S., & Rosenberg, L. (1995). Academic misconduct and values: The department's influence. *Review of Higher Education, 18,* 393–422.

Milgram, S. (1963). Behavioral study of obedience. *Journal of Abnormal and Social Psychology, 7,* 371–378.

Milgram, S. (1964). Issues in the study of obedience: A reply to Baumrind. *American Psychologist, 19,* 848–852.

Mintz, L. B., Bartels, K. M., & Rideout, C. A. (1995). Training in counseling ethnic minorities and race-based availability of graduate school resources. *Professional Psychology: Research and Practice, 26,* 316–321.

Motta, M. M. (2002). Mentoring the mentors: The Yoda factor in promoting scientific integrity. *American Journal of Bioethics Online Peer Commentaries, 2,* w1–w2.

National Academy of Sciences. (1992). *Responsible science: Ensuring the integrity of the research process, Vol. 1*. Washington, DC: National Academies Press.

National Academy of Sciences. (1997). *Advisor, teacher, role model, fried: On being a mentor to students in sciences and engineering*. Washington, DC: National Academies Press.

National Academy of Sciences. (2002). *Integrity in scientific research: Creating an environment that promotes responsible conduct*. Washington, DC: National Academies Press.

National Health and Medical Research Council, Australian Research Council [NHMRC]. (2007). National statement on ethical conduct in human research. Retrieved July 19, 2008, from http://www.nhmrc.gov.au/publications/synopses/_files/e72.pdf

Needleman, H. L. (1992). Salem comes to the National Institutes of Health: Notes from inside the crucible of scientific integrity. *Pediatrics, 90*, 977–981.

Nelson, M. L., & Holloway, E. L. (1990). Relation of gender to power and involvement in supervision. *Journal of Counseling Psychology, 37*, 473–481.

Ortiz-Walters, R., & Gilson, L. L. (2005). Mentoring in academia: An examination of the experience of protégés of color. *Journal of Vocational Behavior, 67*(3), 459–475.

Pion, G. M., Mednick, M. T., Astin, H. S., Hall, C. C. I., Kenkel, M. B., Keita, G. P., et al. (1996). The shifting gender composition of psychology: Trends and implications for the discipline. *American Psychologist, 51*, 509–528.

Ponce, A. N., Williams, M. K., & Allen, G. J. (2005). Toward promoting generative cultures of intentional mentoring within academic settings. *Journal of Clinical Psychology, 61*(9), 1159–1163.

Power, C. (2004). The moral self in community. In D. K. Lapsley & D. Narváez (Eds.), *Moral development, self, and identity* (pp. 47–64). Mahwah, NJ: Lawrence Erlbaum.

Power, C., Higgins, A., & Kohlberg, L. (1989). *Lawrence Kohlberg's approach to moral education*. New York: Columbia University Press.

Public Health Service. (2000). *Policy on instruction in responsible conduct in research*. Retrieved April 25, 2008, from http://ori.dhhs.gov/html/programs/congressionalconcerns.asp

Public Health Service. (2001). *Responsible conduct in research education policy suspended*. Retrieved April 25, 2008, from http://ori.hhs.gov/policies/RCR_Policy.shtml

Ragins, B. R., Cotton, J. L., & Miller, J. S. (2000). Marginal mentoring: The effects of type of mentor, quality of relationship, and program design on work and career attitudes. *Academy of Management Journal, 43*(6), 1177–1194.

Rest, J., & Narváez, D. (1994). *Moral development in the professions: Psychology and applied ethics*. Hillsdale, NJ: Lawrence Erlbaum.

Richman, K. A. (2002, Fall). Responsible conduct of research is all well and good. *American Journal of Bioethics, 2*, 62–63.

Roberts, G. C., Kavussanu, M., & Sprague, R. L. (2001). Mentoring and the impact of the research climate. *Science and Engineering Ethics, 7*, 525–530.

Ryan Commission on Research Integrity. (2003). *Integrity and misconduct in research*. Report of the CRI to the Secretary of HHS. Retrieved April 25, 2008, from http://ori.dhhs.gov/documents/report_commission.pdf

Sales, B., & Folkman, S. (2000). *Ethics in research with human participants*. Washington, DC: APA Books.

Salter, A. C. (1998). Confessions of a whistleblower: Lessons learned. *Ethics & Behavior, 8*(2), 115–124.

Sambunjak, D., Strauss, S. E., & Marusic, A. (2006). Mentoring in academic medicine: A systematic review. *Journal of the American Medical Association, 296*(9), 1103–1115.

Schlosser, L. Z., & Gelso, C. J. (2001). Measuring the working alliance in advisor-advisee relationships in graduate school. *Journal of Counseling Psychology, 48*, 157–167.

Sieber, J. E. (1982). Ethical dilemmas in social research. In J. E. Sieber (Ed.), *The ethics of social research: Surveys and experiments* (pp. 1–30). New York: Springer-Verlag.

Sprague, R. L. (1993). Whistleblowing: A very unpleasant avocation. *Ethics & Behavior, 3*, 103–133.

Sprague, R. L., Daw, J., & Roberts, G. C. (2001). Influences on the ethical beliefs of graduate students concerning research. *Science and Engineering Ethics, 7,* 507–520.

Stern, J. E., & Elliott, D. (1997). *The ethics of scientific research: A guidebook for course development.* Hanover, NH: University Press of New England.

Swazey, J. P., & Anderson, M. S. (1996). *Mentors, advisors, and role models in graduate and professional education.* Washington, DC: Association of Academic Health Centers.

Swazey, J. P., Anderson, M. S., & Louis, K. S. (1993). Ethical problems in academic research. *American Scientist, 81,* 542–553.

Tryon, G. S. (2002). School psychology students' beliefs about their preparation and concern with ethical issues. *Ethics & Behavior, 11,* 375–394.

Victor, B., & Cullen, J. B. (1988). The organization basis of ethical work climates. *Administrative Science Quarterly, 33,* 101–125.

Williams, M. R., Brewely, D. N., Reed, R. J., White, D. Y., & Davis-Haley, R. T. (2005). Learning from each other: Black female graduate students share their experiences at a White Research I institution. *Urban Review, 37*(3), 181–199.

Wilson, P. F., & Johnson, W. B. (2001). Core virtues for the practice of mentoring. *Journal of Psychology & Theology, 29,* 121–130.

36

SOCIAL RESEARCH ATTUNED TO DELIBERATIVE DEMOCRACY

◆ Kenneth R. Howe and Heather MacGillivary

Working out the relationship between social research and democracy dates at least to the efforts of John Dewey in the early 20th century. One of the fundamental principles Dewey (1927/1954) put forth is that social research should not be applied "*to* human concerns" but "*in* them." Among the important implications of this principle are first, that moral-political content is *internal* to the conduct of social research, not something that can be culled and dealt with exclusively by people in roles other than social researcher; and second, that social research should be used to contribute to the formation of intelligent public opinion, not to manipulate public opinion to serve more narrow financial or political interests.

The political theory in which Dewey's view of social research is embedded is nowadays referred to as *deliberative democracy*. Following a relatively long eclipse, deliberative democracy has reemerged to become very visible in contemporary political theory and practice, particularly in the United States. So far, however, not much effort has been devoted to investigating the implications of deliberative democratic political theory for social research methodology. That is the general task undertaken in this chapter.

It should be emphasized here at the outset that this chapter focuses on the *ought* of social research methodology[1] rather than the *is*. We only speculate briefly about whether the deliberative democratic approach might, in fact, become more prominent.

The chapter consists of four general sections. The first section provides a brief characterization of the deliberative conception of democracy, including how it may be distinguished from its primary competitor, the "aggregative," or "emotive," conception. The second section examines three conceptions of the relationship between social research and democracy and advances Deliberative Democratic Social Research (DDSR) as the most adequate. It also explicates the three central political-cum-methodological principles of DDSR: inclusion, dialogue, and deliberation. These two sections primarily revise and update the view developed by House and Howe (1999) in *Values in Evaluation and Social Research* in light of important work in deliberative democratic theory that followed its publication. The third section examines the scope and limits of the conception put forward in the second section by examining three empirical studies in terms of the DDSR ideal. This section also provides a brief discussion of DDSR and the ethics of social research. The last section provides some brief observations regarding the future of DDSR.

♦ A Sketch of Deliberative Democratic Theory

In its literal sense, democracy is simply "rule by the people." In contemporary democratic theory, the foundation of democratic political forms has both moral and epistemological features, which are related. Morally, human beings should be respected as autonomous agents, who live life from the "inside." Epistemologically, life is marked by uncertainty and infinitely varied experiences such that disagreement between groups and individuals, including moral, is one of its permanent features. Communal decisions, which bind all members of the community despite their differences, are best justified in terms of democratic procedures that can accommodate both the moral and epistemological features described above.

Democracy involves both a negative and positive obligation vis-à-vis respect for autonomy. On the negative side, associated with political liberty, individuals and groups should be impeded as little as possible from living life in terms of their autonomous choices. On the positive side, associated with political equality, individuals and groups should be provided with the opportunities to develop their autonomy and to exercise it in democratic forums.

Among conceptions of democracy, deliberative theory places special emphasis on inclusive and fair participation in the political process. It requires participants to respect one another's autonomy by engaging in good faith critical dialogue, whereby they (1) use "public reason" by avoiding reasoning that others could not find acceptable, for example, sectarian reasoning and (2) are open to revising their initially preferred policies and practices as a result of deliberating with others. The ideal goal of the process is to reach conclusions that will be accepted as reasonable (not necessarily correct) by all concerned.

This conception of democratic decision making contrasts sharply with the conception associated with "aggregative democracy" (e.g., Gutmann & Thompson, 2004). The aggregative conception takes initial preferences as given and exempts them from the need for justification. In contrast to a process of critical dialogue that characterizes deliberative democracy, democratic decision making consists in merely aggregating preferences to produce collective decisions.[2]

To the extent that dialogue is a part of the process in aggregative democracy, it is *strategic* rather than *deliberative*; it is a process whereby individuals and groups attempt to win assent to their initial preferences using whatever gambits prove successful. The idea of subjecting initial preferences to critical evaluation and being open to revising them, central to deliberative democracy, is altogether foreign to the aggregative conception of democratic decision making.

Deliberative democratic theorists make three general criticisms of aggregative democracy. First, basing decisions on the outcome of aggregated preexisting preferences, while holding them largely immune from criticism and revision, serves to entrench preexisting unjust distributions of goods such as income, education, health care, and employment, as well as political power (e.g., Young, 2000). Second, such unjust distributions preclude the possibility of "effective participation" in the democratic process on the part of many citizens. Finally, the aggregative conception is not the self-evidently best way to construe what democratic decision making ought to exemplify. An argument is thus required that has available the cognitive tools necessary to *evaluate* preferences (beliefs, judgments, arguments)—including about democratic procedures—and that doesn't merely take the aggregative conception as given (e.g., Young, 2000). In this connection, the aggregative conception has no tools available to provide a credible response to the first two criticisms above, regarding its shortcomings with respect to justice and democracy, respectively.

Deliberative democracy is also at odds with liberal egalitarianism, albeit in a less fundamental way than with aggregative democracy. Liberal egalitarianism heavily weights patterns of distributions of societal goods (such as income, education, health care, and employment) relative to political participation. Thus, as in John Rawls' (1971) landmark liberal egalitarian treatise, *A Theory of Justice*, working out principles of justice eclipses working out democratic procedures.

The "distributive paradigm" (Young, 1990) of justice exemplified by thinkers such as Rawls has been challenged by deliberative theorists for paying far too little attention to the structures of domination and oppression to be found in the social, cultural, and political dimensions of how goods are distributed. The claim by deliberative theorists (e.g., Benhabib, 2002; Young, 2000) is not that distributional patterns are unimportant, but that they are much more enmeshed in the presence or absence of opportunities for individuals and groups to engage in effective political participation than the distributive paradigm recognizes. Explicating the complicated and nuanced conversation that has taken place regarding these matters over the last several decades is beyond the scope of the chapter. Sufficient for our purposes in the chapter is a brief description of the "paradigm change" (Benhabib, 2002) in political theory that has occurred over the last several decades, in which acknowledgment of the centrality of the problem of political participation became widespread.

For various individuals and groups to effectively participate in political decisions, they obviously must be included in the process. Indeed, Iris Marion Young (2000) placed inclusion at the center of her deliberative democratic theory.[3] Young distinguished two types of inclusion: "external" and "internal." External inclusion is *formal*, for example, as in the extension of the right to vote to African Americans and women or making special efforts to ensure that marginalized groups are included in local face-to-face democratic forums. External inclusion is clearly a necessary condition of genuinely democratic procedures. But it is not sufficient. It does not, by itself, ensure that individuals from marginalized groups will be able to effectively participate in democratic dialogue. In addition to external inclusion, internal (or *substantive*) inclusion is required to ensure that, once admitted to the dialogue, individuals are taken seriously—afforded "recognition"[4]—rather than ignored, dismissed, patronized, or outmaneuvered by those with greater power, including the power associated with knowing better the rules of the discourse.

♦ Deliberative Democracy and Social Research

Anders Hanberger (2006) provided a useful scheme of democratic orientations to social research that consists of three general types: elitist, participatory, and deliberative (or discursive).[5] In this section, we describe each. Although we borrow heavily from Hanberger's characterizations, our characterizations sometimes depart from his. We begin with the deliberative orientation and then use it to critically evaluate the participatory and elitist orientations.

THE DELIBERATIVE ORIENTATION

DDSR rejects the value neutrality associated with aggregative conceptions of democratic decision making and, accordingly, rejects the notion that social research provides a neutral "analytic filter" for informing social policy making. Central to DDSR is the premise that values are *internal* to the conduct of social research, precluding the possibility of value neutrality.

First, the quasi-technical concepts researchers employ often have a significant value dimension, as in "literacy," "mental health," "achievement," or "wealth," for example. In turn, such concepts are typically contained in the potential relationships under investigation, as in "Stricter teacher accountability leads to increased student achievement." Social researchers thus routinely introduce the values of certain subcommunities of researchers, policymakers, program designers, and so on, into the very heart of social research.[6]

Second, the values are not only a part of the descriptive vocabulary of social research. The scope and complexity of prospective interventions are determined by what is taken as given, or "fixed,"[7] and thus off the table, which infuses values into the design of social research. For example, where existing socioeconomic status (SES) stratification is construed as part of the fixed background against which AIDS prevention programs are implemented, it is beyond the purview of social researchers to investigate the causes of SES stratification and to determine means of eliminating it. The task of researchers under these conditions is to determine means within the maneuver space created by existing social-political-economic conditions. In contrast, where SES stratification is not taken as part of a fixed background but is included among the causes of the outcomes to be investigated, a different array of methods is required, typically including qualitative data and nonexperimental designs. We by no means intend to suggest that a straightforward and simple relationship exists between social research methodology and political assumptions, but moral-political assumptions of *some* kind are unavoidable in the conduct of social research, whatever research methods are employed.

Third, social research unavoidably assumes *some* stance toward its role in democratic decision making in virtue of unavoidably assuming *some* stance toward stakeholders regarding who qualifies for participation, what their roles should be in relation to researchers, and what their needs for and rights to information might be. In our view, stakeholder participation ought to be self-consciously aligned with democratic politics.

Motivated by its commitment to the furthering of the democratic function of social research, DDSR is characterized by three central principles: inclusion, dialogue, and deliberation (House & Howe, 1999). Each is a component of deliberative democratic theory per se, though the degree to which they are foregrounded relative to other principles varies. They are particularly well-suited for the purpose of working out a deliberative democratic conception of social research because they double as normative political principles as well as methodological principles.

Inclusion

As a normative political principle, inclusion may, as indicated above, be formal or substantive. Substantive inclusion is the ideal appropriate to deliberative democracy because such a full-fledged form of inclusion is required for persons to be afforded the opportunity to effectively participate in democratic forums. In its most expansive sense, the principle of inclusion may be construed as encompassing the normative principles of dialogue and deliberation.

Inclusion also may be construed as the methodological principle of representative sampling. Accurately describing the views and behaviors of a given cultural or social group requires including its members in the sample to be investigated and, all other things equal, representativeness is a methodological virtue.

Dialogue

As a normative principle, dialogue is an aspect of substantive inclusion. Typically, research participants who are members of marginalized groups will not have their perspectives well understood, much less taken seriously, if they are not able to express their perspectives for themselves and able to engage in back-and-forth dialogue to clarify them.

As a methodological principle, dialogue, like inclusion, facilitates descriptive accuracy. In particular, obtaining an accurate description of the *insider's perspective* requires that researchers engage participants in some form of dialogue. The dialogue may be *elucidating,* whereby the aim is limited to describing participants' perspectives (House & Howe, 1999), or it may go beyond this to engage participants in *critical* give-and-take.

Deliberation

Deliberation rounds out the normative principles of DDSR. Deliberation in the intended sense is a kind of dialogue in which, as suggested above, participants engage in good faith give-and-take in the interest of reaching the most warranted conclusions. Participants must be prepared to entertain the justifications that others give for competing views and be open to changing their own views if warranted on the basis of reason and evidence.

As a methodological principle, deliberation aspires to what Sandra Harding (1993) called *strong objectivity.* In contrast to what might be called a *correspondence* conception of objectivity, in which objectivity rests on establishing that claims correspond to or "mirror" reality, strong objectivity is *procedural.* The degree to which objectivity is achieved in a given case is determined by the number and adequacy of the procedures implemented to reduce bias. These procedures include conventional canons of social research methodology. In DDSR, they also include testing the claims and counterclaims of social researchers by entering them into critical dialogue with those whose perspectives are informed by relevant lived experience.

THE PARTICIPATORY ORIENTATION

In this chapter, we adopt Hanberger's (2006) conception of "participatory." Given this usage, the participatory orientation toward democratic social research (PDSR) differs from DDSR with respect to each of the principles of inclusion, dialogue, and deliberation. Inclusion is more selective for PDSR; it is limited to groups of individuals with a shared goal of advancing some interest, including their own empowerment. Dialogue likewise aims to further the interests and goals of a group, and for this reason, the dialogue exemplified by PDSR need not be deliberative in the sense required by DDSR. Rather it may be, and often is, strategic.

PDSR is often associated with promoting justice for groups that have been subjected to domination. As we suggest later, supporters of DDSR need have no objection to this kind of activity. On the contrary, PDSR often aspires to give effective voice to the very same groups to which DDSR would be especially attuned under the unjust political conditions that so often prevail. As such, PDSR may be underpinned by a normative political theory, as in Cousins and Whitmore's

(1998) conception of "transformative" participatory evaluation.

As a stand-alone normative orientation toward social research, however, PDSR is problematic, for it provides no principled means by which to distinguish participatory evaluation from partisan advocacy. Imagine that an evaluator is hired by the Colorado League of Charter Schools. The avowed mission of the League is to expand the number of charter schools, and, in point of fact, the enrollment in Colorado's charter schools is disproportionately white, higher income, and high achieving. There is nothing to preclude the evaluator from employing a PDSR model to evaluate the success of the League in its activities and from thereby promoting the interests of the League. And there is no reason for the evaluator to subject the accomplishments of the League to the test of whether they are defensible vis-à-vis the public interest in providing equal opportunity for minority and lower-income children. That PDSR lacks the requirement to determine the relative legitimacy of competing interests renders it vulnerable to the charge of being a species of partisan advocacy, sometimes in support of the interests of the powerful.

THE ELITIST ORIENTATION

The elitist orientation toward democratic social research (EDSR) is technocratic. Social researchers are seen as technical experts for whom it is inappropriate to engage in judgments of value about the objects of study. Their role vis-à-vis values is restricted to "descriptive valuing" (e.g., Shadish, Cook, & Leviton, 1995), that is, aggregating the values of the population of interest and conveying the summary/analysis to policymakers and implementers. This is in stark contrast to DDSR, in which researchers create the conditions for and engage in value-laden deliberation with research participants, and PDSR, in which researchers engage in value-laden deliberation as advocates for the interests of research participants. Substantive inclusion is limited to policymakers and implementers, and thus it is only they who engage in dialogue and deliberation. The targets of the policies are included only formally, not as *research participants* but as *research subjects*.

EDSR is fatally flawed from the perspective of deliberative democracy. It is vulnerable to three criticisms that parallel those advanced against aggregative democracy. First, merely aggregating the preferences of research subjects, holding them largely immune from criticism and revision, serves to entrench the current unjust distributions of goods and powers. Second, such unjust distributions preclude the possibility of "effective participation" in the research process on the part of many citizens and thus the possibility of getting their voices heard in policy making and program development. Finally, the technocratic conception of social research embraced by EDSR is not self-evidently best. On the contrary, the idea of the value neutral social researcher has become increasingly dubious in the wake of the downfall of positivism (Howe, 2003). As indicated earlier, values, including moral-political, unavoidably permeate both the descriptive vocabulary and the methodology of social research. It is impossible for social researchers to avoid taking *some* stance on the relationship between their work and democracy (if only implicitly) in deciding on the uses to which they intend their findings to be put.

♦ Scope and Limits of DDSR

The concern with democracy is most salient in social research that aims to evaluate and improve social policy and programs, as distinct from social research that aims to contribute to knowledge to social science disciplines. To be sure, no hard-and-fast line can be drawn here, particularly in disciplines such as economics and sociology, for instance. However, the intended uses and audiences combined with the technical nature of the dialogues associated with disciplinary social research remove it a considerable distance from democratic decision making. Thus, the scope of DDSR is limited to evaluative social research.

Deliberative democracy, unlike "political liberalism" (associated with the "distributive paradigm" described earlier), assigns an important role to the "unofficial public sphere" in addition to the role of "official public sphere" (Benhabib, 2002). The unofficial public sphere may be roughly identified with civil society; the official public sphere, with institutions of government.

Instances of DDSR are themselves forums for democratic deliberation that fall primarily within unofficial public sphere; they are subject to the methodological requirements of DDSR but not to official democratic procedures. DDSR may engage with the official public sphere in virtue of accountability tied to publicly funded DDSR and when the results of DDSR are introduced into deliberative forums within the official public sphere.

DDSR functions as a normative methodological ideal. It does not provide a formula for designing and conducting democratic social research, and trade-offs must be made such that its requirements can only be approximated. In what follows, we discuss three examples of social research in terms of DDSR to illustrate how it applies in practice. The first two self-consciously employed DDSR. We contrast them to illustrate how different circumstances call for different adaptations of DDSR. The third employed PDSR. We use it to help define the boundaries of DDSR and to explore how DDSR and PDSR are related, particularly vis-à-vis their democratic grounding. We end the section with several observations about DDSR and the ethics of social research.

EXAMPLE 1: A STUDY OF THE BOULDER VALLEY SCHOOL DISTRICT CHOICE SYSTEM[8]

Background

Boulder Valley School District (BVSD) is centered in Boulder, Colorado, home to the main campus of the University of Colorado. BVSD enrolls approximately 27,000 students. Whites comprise approximately 80% and Latinos, the largest racial/ethnic minority by far, comprised approximately 12%. In 1999, BVSD commissioned a study of its school choice system following five years of its rapid, unplanned expansion. During this time, the community had become polarized regarding whether school choice was harmful or beneficial but had no evidence to go on beyond anecdote.

School choice began with the inception of BVSD in 1961, but its scale significantly increased in the mid-1990s. Between the 1994 and 1995 and the 1999 and 2000 school years, the number of choice schools increased from 5 to 21 (of 57 total) and enrolled more than 20% of the district's students. Whereas the original choice options emphasized diversity, integrated learning, bilingual education, or some combination, half of the 16 new options emphasized academic rigor and college preparation. The new options were spurred by a group of parents who believed that BVSD, particularly its middle schools, placed too little emphasis on academic achievement. The rationales of increasing parental autonomy and using market competition to drive improvement were also in play.

The start of the study coincided with the launch of a community "deliberative process" that had been undertaken by BVSD in collaboration with the Kettering Foundation and the Colorado Association of School Boards. The subject of the deliberative process was also school choice, particularly in connection with school closures.

The leaders of the process formed a committee that was to negotiate the most important issues and then discuss them with various groups across the district.

This appeared to be a situation tailor-made for DDSR: The researchers could bring existing empirical research to the table, undertake empirical investigations of issues that were identified on the local scene, and actively participate in the deliberative process from start to finish. District officials rejected this approach, however, on the grounds that for the study to be credible, it would have to be carried out independent of the district and the school board. From the outset, then, the DDSR ideal had to be adjusted to the political context, particularly the level of distrust toward district officials and the school board that affected the study they had commissioned.

Inclusion

The principle of inclusion was applied rather straightforwardly. Parents, students, citizens, teachers, and school administrators were identified as the stakeholders whose voices needed to be heard. Except for students, for whom informed consent requirements were often an obstacle, a reasonably representative sample of each group was obtained via surveys and focus groups with "school improvement teams" across a range of levels (elementary, middle, and high) and types of district schools (choice vs. neighborhood). A random telephone survey, stratified by race/ethnicity, was conducted of parents who were not active in the school district or their children's schools.

Dialogue

The primary forums for dialogue were the focus groups in individual schools, in which participants were probed for their perspectives on how the school choice system had affected their schools and what they believed to be the benefits and harms of school choice for the district overall. The form of dialogue was almost exclusively "elucidating." Only on rare occasions did the researchers leading the focus groups challenge what participants had to say and engage them in "critical" dialogue.[9]

There were two logistical reasons for this approach. First, given the time constraints on the study, it would have been very difficult to elicit the variety of stakeholder views if truly critical dialogue were pursued. Second, the political context described earlier hampered dialogue. Suspicion of the study came from both sides: Certain critics of the choice system accused the researchers of doing "market research" on behalf of choice schools, whereas certain supporters of the system accused them of doing a "push poll" to make choice schools look bad. The advice of BVSD officials for the researchers to remain independent proved to be wise.

Deliberation

Within DDSR, critical dialogue shades into and underwrites the more general process of deliberation. But because little by way of critical dialogue occurred during the process of the evaluation, little by way of deliberation occurred. Deliberation occurred only after the evaluation report was completed, and its findings and recommendations were disseminated. They served as grist for the mill of deliberation in forums often not led by the researchers, such as school board meetings and the pages of several local newspapers. The findings of the study were reported on the front page of the Boulder paper the day following the release of the report and was followed in the subsequent weeks and months by a lengthy summary written by the researchers, periodic stories by journalists, and exchanges among citizens in the letters to the editor section. Several problems identified by the study have resulted in policy changes or continue to be deliberated, including increased racial stratification in the district overall, lack of transportation to facilitate choice, unequal fundraising among schools, and poor dissemination of information to parents.

Discussion

The BVSD study was relatively successful in meeting DDSR's aim of contributing to public deliberation about policy, and the principles of inclusion and dialogue were instrumental in this. The study engaged a representative group of the major stakeholders—primarily parents, teachers, and principals—in dialogue about the pros and cons of the district's school choice system. The findings and recommendations were thus grounded in the beliefs and interests, both pro and con, of those with firsthand experiences of the system. Those who disagreed with the findings or recommendations could not do so on the grounds that their views had been not been heard and examined, and, in point of fact, they didn't.

The DDSR ideal was limited by the fact that face-to-face deliberations with stakeholders proved unworkable, a limitation that, as indicated earlier, resulted from time constraints and the polarization surrounding the school choice policy. In this way, the principle of deliberation was detached from the principles of inclusion and dialogue: The study's role in deliberation about the choice policy was largely limited to providing critical analysis via the study report—itself grounded in inclusion and dialogue—which then served as grist for the mill of public deliberation.

EXAMPLE 2: MONITORING THE ENGLISH LANGUAGE ACQUISITION PROGRAM IN DENVER PUBLIC SCHOOLS[10]

Background

Denver Public School District (DPS) has a history of racial tension. In the landmark *Keyes* case, the Congress of Hispanic Educators filed suit against DPS for segregation and the result was court-ordered bussing. By the late 1990s, the bussing order had ended but DPS was put under court order to provide a native language instructional program, the English Language Acquisition program (ELA), for students who did not understand English. The program was "transitional" rather than "maintenance." Its aim was to prepare students for the transition into mainstream classes, taught exclusively in English, not to preserve their native language. The court order was accompanied by a requirement that the implementation of the instructional program be monitored for compliance and effectiveness. In 1999, Ernest House assumed that role.

The ELA was targeted at the approximately 15,000 students (21% of the total enrollment of DPS) who could not speak English well enough to receive instruction in mainstream classes. These student were overwhelmingly Spanish speaking and many were undocumented. The ELA fed into tensions between Latinos and Anglos in Colorado. Colorado adopted English as its official language in the late 1980s and is home to the vocal anti-immigrant Congressman Tom Tancredo, a 2008 candidate for the Republican Party nomination for president. Colorado had an initiative to ban bilingual education similar to those of California and Massachusetts. Although it failed, it was divisive and will likely appear on the ballot again.

Inclusion

House included three primary groups: one combined representatives of DPS with representatives of the co-plaintiffs in the suit against DPS, the U.S. Justice Department, and the Congress of Hispanic Educators (we call this group the "monitoring committee," our label, not House's); staff members of the ELA working in various schools; and other community groups and individuals on both sides of the issue, including the most militant. The monitoring committee met twice yearly over the six-year duration of the monitoring activity, the ELA group met periodically, and the other groups and individuals met on request. House (2006) "turned down no one wanting to offer views about the program" but decided against open public meetings, fearing they would "degenerate into shouting matches" (p. 13). He also agreed with the monitoring committee's request that he not talk to the news media because of the political volatility of the issues.

Dialogue

The dialogues with the community groups and individuals were more elucidating than critical. Although House did not accept the various claims he encountered at face value, neither did he directly challenge them. His interest was including the variety of views from across the community. He placed a premium on maintaining the transparency of his actions and avoiding being identified as allied with one side or the other. This perception would have been very difficult to achieve if he had critically challenged the views of those with whom he had little opportunity to establish trust.

His dialogues with the monitoring committee and ELA staff members exemplified a more critical form. He elicited the groups' views on a variety of issues, including the instrument he used to measure compliance and the accuracy of his periodic reports to the court. House (2006) then engaged them in critical give-and-take, in which they "hashed out disagreements" (p. 8), or at least tried to. The forums were characterized by transparent and fair procedures, in which principles and values, not just groups interests, were put on the table. As indicated previously, this kind of critical dialogue shades into the ideal of deliberation aimed for in DDSR.

Deliberation

The House-led deliberations with the monitoring committee and the ELA staff members count as a successful implementation of DDSR with respect to establishing a rather direct relationship between social research (evaluation research, more precisely) and decision making about the instructional program. In reflecting this success, he added the proviso that DDSR emphasizes stakeholder participation, not decision-maker participation. In this connection, he regretted that the role of the general public in deliberation was virtually nonexistent. He was unable to figure out how this could have been avoided in light of his agreement to refrain from talking to the news media.

Discussion

Both the DPS and BVSD studies were conducted in polarized political climates that reduced trust and required adapting the DDSR ideal. In BVSD, the study was detached from policy/program deliberations. Rather, its results and recommendations were infused into deliberations of the school board and became a topic of debate in the local press. In DPS, in contrast, there was a close connection between the unfolding results and recommendations produced by House and decisions about the instructional program, which exemplified the kind of critical dialogue—deliberation—associated with DDSR. But the scope of the deliberation was quite limited compared with BVSD, for it included only the monitoring committee and the ELA staff.

There will always be a trade-off between how inclusive deliberation can be and how rich it can be in terms of critical give-and-take. Two factors that complicated things in the DPS and BVSD studies vis-à-vis deliberation were the respective agreements to avoid talking to the news media and to detach the study from policy/program deliberations. Even had these obstacles not existed, probably the closest approximation to the ideal of DDSR that can be attained is a combination of the two kinds of deliberation that were achieved in the DPS and BVSD studies: A "thick" form associated with local publics combined with a "thin" form associated with wider publics.

EXAMPLE 3: EVALUATING SUPPORTED HOUSING FOR PSYCHIATRIC CONSUMER-SURVIVORS

Background

The historical oppression of people with chronic psychiatric disabilities (henceforth referred to as "consumers," short for "consumers of psychiatric services") has created major obstacles to integrating them into the community post-deinstitutionalization. The example in this section analyzes social research involving a project to help remedy this problem: the Waterloo Regional Homes for Supported Housing project. A community-based research organization and the local university partnered with the nonprofit organization in the effort. (Detailed accounts can be found in Nelson, Ochocka, Griffin, & Lord, 1998, and MacGillivary & Nelson, 1998.)

As indicated earlier, this is an example of PDSR as opposed to DDSR. We employ it to help better define DDSR. We will also suggest how PDSR might be interpreted so as to be consistent with the general deliberative democratic framework embraced by DDSR.

Inclusion

Participants in the Waterloo study included consumers, their family members, project staff, and the researchers. In contrast to the dictates of DDSR, this study involved no attempt to include stakeholders who did not necessarily agree with the mission of the project. Although participants in the process sometimes disagreed about the best means (e.g., group home, independent living, or temporary institutionalization), permanent reinstitutionalization was not on the table as an option. In this context, effective dialogue would have been impossible had there been voices advocating permanent institutionalization.

Clearly, not all stakeholders had the resources necessary to participate equally. To create a forum exemplifying substantive inclusion, an evaluation steering committee was formed whose membership was more than half consumers. Among additional measures taken by the researchers to help ensure consumers' inclusion was substantive included providing emotional supports, supplying transportation, arranging convenient meeting times, and hosting between meeting debriefings.

Consumers were included as part of the paid research team. This is a common practice in PDSR, where the general mission of given projects is shared by the various participants. This practice is by and large unworkable in DDSR, which makes it a point to include clashing perspectives in deliberations about policy and practice. Consider the Boulder and Denver examples. It would have been disastrous in either study for stakeholders to be included as members of the research team. The stakeholder participants would have had to have been either selected from only one of several contending factions, undermining credibility of the research team, or selected so as to balance stakeholder representation, undermining the research team's ability to function.

Dialogue

The Waterloo project exemplified dialogues characterized by the kind of give-and-take associated with the critical form of dialogue described previously. Consumers brought their lived experiences to the table, which often involved sharing personal narratives of how the psychiatric system had exposed them to negative social stigma. Researchers brought broader, research-based knowledge to the table, acknowledging its limitations vis-à-vis the "life worlds" of the consumers. A forum was created in which consumers had space to behave in ways that would not be considered acceptable in professional settings, while researchers were forgiven their own kind of improprieties. For example, when a researcher used the term *crazy* to describe one of her friends, she was gently reminded of the connotations of this label for the consumer community.

The dialogues were not free of tensions. Project staff worried that the findings of the study could negatively affect their performance reviews. Consumers worried that the study might not incorporate preserving their independence and dignity as essential to the services to be provided to them. Family members expressed anxiety about losing sight of the encompassing aim of promoting the health and well-being of their loved ones. These tensions were largely overcome by first, creation of supportive and trusting relationships overall, and second, inclusion of consumers on the research team. The two combined to create an environment in which the various stakeholders, and particularly the consumers, were empowered to participate in meaningful dialogue. Indeed, in subsequent work by these researchers, psychiatric consumer-survivors have had sole authorship in publications about the research (Reeve, Cornell, D'Costa, Janzen, & Ochocka, 2002).

The dialogues in the Waterloo study were guided by a shared commitment to integrating consumers into the community, which is what makes it an instance of PDSR rather than DDSR. Consistent with limiting the scope of the principle of inclusion to stakeholders with a prior commitment to integration, the Waterloo study restricted the scope of the principle of (critical) dialogue so as to take the question of the wisdom of the commitment to integration off the table.

Deliberation

The design of the evaluation and subsequent research instruments took more than six months, but the end product had buy-in from all stakeholders. This buy-in allowed for swifter deliberation about the results and recommendations. Without this upfront involvement, deliberation about results could legitimately have been obstructed by questions about design and method. In retrospect, the long process of developing relationships and shared trust was a critical element of the deliberation process. Most members on the evaluation committee agreed about the findings of the evaluation since they had been so involved in the process. When these results were presented to other consumers, family members, and staff, difficult questions were posed. However, since the committee members were well-connected with their communities, they were able to explain the rationale for critical decisions along the way.

Discussion

The researchers involved in Waterloo study had over a decade of experience partnering with consumers in participatory research. This long-standing relationship provided a solid foundation on which to build an authentic deliberative forum and underscores a key element of successful deliberation with marginalized populations: forging solidarity (Nelson, Prilelltensky, & MacGillivary, 2001).

Therein lies a tension between PDSR and DDSR. Giving effective voice in the deliberative process to groups who have been subjected to domination and oppression requires building relationships on a foundation of shared values. But this puts researchers in the role of partisans, which is fatal to DDSR. But if researchers do not partner with and serve as advocates for marginalized groups, per DDSR, the voices of marginalized groups will continue to be silenced.

This tension, though real, need not put PDSR at loggerheads with DDSR. As indicated earlier, DDSR seeks to empower marginalized groups in democratic deliberations and, accordingly, is quite sensitive to how mere formal inclusion in deliberative forums does not guarantee that the marginalized will be afforded an effective voice. One of the ways of dealing with the limitations of formal inclusion is by supporting the *subaltern counterpublics* that form to articulate and defend the interests of marginalized groups. Nancy Fraser (1990), who coined the term, described subaltern counterpublics as possessing a "dual character." They function as "spaces of withdrawal and regroupment" as well as "training grounds" for participation in the wider democratic forums. The Waterloo study enhanced the deliberations of a subaltern counterpublic of consumers in the first way described by Frazer and, to a lesser degree, in the second way as well. The methodology of the Waterloo study is thus quite consistent with the more encompassing deliberative democratic framework associated with DDSR, which has as its overriding ideal enabling all to effectively participate in the democratic process. Whether all instances of PDSR might also be grounded in this way we can't say. Examples such as the Waterloo study, however, show that the commitment to deliberative democracy erects no general barrier separating PDSR from DDSR.

DDSR AND THE ETHICS OF SOCIAL RESEARCH

DDSR is subject to the same ethical constraints under the two broad categories—the protection of human subjects and research misconduct—that apply to social research generally. Under the protection of human subjects category, DDSR implies additional constraints.

The protection of human subjects is traditionally conceived in terms of the negative obligation vis-à-vis autonomy described earlier, namely, to avoid impeding persons from acting in accord with their autonomous choices. Thus, the requirement to obtain informed consent is meant to ensure that persons have the information they need to make an autonomous choice of whether or not to participate in a given research project, consistent with their existing values and beliefs. DDSR is more demanding. For it also requires embracing the positive obligation vis-à-vis autonomy to arrange the conditions of deliberation so as to equalize power and to, as appropriate, transform existing values and beliefs by challenging them with competing views through a process of "critical dialogue."

The 18th-century German philosopher Immanuel Kant is credited with formulating the famous dictum *ought implies can*. Given this dictum, a nonswimmer is not morally required to dive into water over her head to save a drowning man, for it would provide no help and would be suicide. As indicated earlier, DDSR is a normative methodological ideal, not a formula for democratic social research. The Boulder and Denver studies described above show that the ideal is very difficult to achieve fully. What social researchers *ought* to do in the name of deliberative democracy has to be judged in terms of what they *can* do.

◆ Concluding Remarks

The widespread adoption of DDSR as the model for public policy research faces two daunting obstacles, at least in the United States. First, a resurgent "experiment*ism*" (Howe, 2005)—a technocratic, nondeliberative approach—has found a comfortable home in a state-sponsored "methodological fundamentalism" that significantly undermines the critical role of social research in the evaluation and formulation of public policy (House, 2003). Second, aggregative democracy is the framework that best describes how democratic politics in fact work. The tendency of dominant groups to strategically pursue their self-interests threatened both the BVSD and DPS studies and limited the degree to which they could achieve the deliberative ideal. In the case of the Waterloo study, it prompted the researchers to withdraw from the wider public domain.

On the more optimistic side, the United States has witnessed a resurgence of deliberative democracy in the 1990s—a "renaissance" according to Gastil and Keith (2005). The resurgence has been impelled by the need to adapt democracy to increasing culture diversity, which has been coupled with a renewed civic spiritedness. These general cultural trends have manifested themselves in increased charitable giving and volunteerism, as well as in the proliferation of nongovernmental organizations whose aim is to foster more robust democratic deliberation. Such organizations include the Kettering Foundation, the Pew Charitable Trusts, the Deliberative Democracy Consortium, the National Coalition for Dialogue and Deliberation, the Public Conversations Project, America Speaks, and Information Renaissance (Gastil & Keith, 2005).

Contemporary theorists of deliberative democracy have paid rather close attention to what has been happening at the level of political practice and have adjusted their theories accordingly (e.g., Benhabib, 2002; Gutmann & Thompson, 2004; Young, 2000). Among their claims is that it is a mistake to everywhere identify deliberative democracy with the idea that citizens must actively participate in face-to-face deliberations about policy matters, particularly the kinds of policy matters addressed by their elected representatives pertaining to the nation and the globe. Rather, democratic practice is "decentered" (Young, 2000); it occurs across a diversity of forums, many of which do afford opportunities for face-to-face interactions and the results of which can have an influence on elected representatives. As indicated earlier, DDSR may be seen as one such forum, typically located in the "unofficial public sphere." Should the general interest in expanding forums for democratic deliberation continue to grow, so, too, should interest in DDSR.

◆ Notes

1. We include the field of program evaluation under the rubric social research. Indeed, we make liberal use of scholarship from this field.

2. What is here called "aggregative democracy" corresponds quite closely to what House and Howe (1999) called "emotive democracy" in *Values in Evaluation and Social Research*.

3. Other deliberative theorists make other principles central. We do not, in a general sense, find Young's emphasis on inclusion to necessarily be the best way to develop a deliberative democratic theory. For reasons that should become clear in Section "Deliberative Democracy and Social Research," however, we do find Young's approach particularly well suited to the task of working out the relationship between social research and democracy.

4. Charles Taylor (1994) made the concept of recognition prominent with his seminal *The Politics of Recognition*. It remains a central concept, even as deliberative theorists such as Benhabib and Young challenge Taylor's analysis of it, which, they believe, too sharply divorces the recognition of cultural identity from matters of distribution.

5. Hanberger's focus is evaluation, which in our view, is straightforwardly applicable to social research. Much social and policy research not identified as "program evaluation" is nonetheless evaluative, if only implicitly.

6. For a more elaborate discussion of the evaluative dimension of the vocabulary of social research, see Howe (2003).

7. We borrow this concept from Root (1993).

8. See Howe and Ashcraft (2005) for a much more comprehensive discussion of this case.

9. For an amplification of the distinction between "elucidating" and "critical" dialogue, see House and Howe (1999).

10. See House (2006) for a much more comprehensive discussion of this case.

◆ References

Benhabib, S. (2002). *The claims of culture*. Princeton, NJ: Princeton University Press.

Cousins, J., & Whitmore, E. (1998). *Framing participatory evaluation*. (New Directions for Evaluation, No. 80, pp. 5–23). San Francisco: Jossey-Bass.

Dewey, J. (1927/1954). *The public and its problems.* Chicago: Swallow Press.

Fraser, N. (1990). Rethinking the public sphere: A contribution to the critique of actually existing democracies. *Social Text, 25/26,* 56–80.

Gastil, J., & Keith, W. (2005). A nation that (sometimes) likes to talk. In J. Gastil & P. Levine (Eds.), *The deliberative democracy handbook* (pp. 3–19). San Francisco: Jossey-Bass.

Gutmann, A., & Thompson, D. (2004). *Why deliberative democracy?* Princeton, NJ: Princeton University Press.

Hanberger, A. (2006). Evaluation of and for democracy. *Evaluation, 12*(1), 17–37.

Harding, S. (1993). Rethinking standpoint epistemology: What is "strong objectivity"? In L. Alcoff & E. Potter (Eds.), *Feminist epistemologies* (pp. 49–80). New York: Routledge.

House, E. (2003). Bush's Neo-Fundamentalism and the new politics of evaluation. In O. Karlsson (Ed.), *Studies in educational policy and educational philosophy* (p. 2). Sweden: Uppsala University. Retrieved April 26, 2008, from www.upi.artisan.se

House, E. (2006). *Evaluation politics in Denver: An example.* Unpublished manuscript.

House, E., & Howe, K. (1999). *Values in evaluation and social research.* Thousand Oaks, CA: Sage.

Howe, K. (2003). *Closing methodological divides: Toward democratic educational research.* Dordrecht, The Netherlands: Kluwer.

Howe, K. (2005). The question of education science: Experimentism versus experimentalism. *Educational Theory, 55*(3), 307–322.

Howe, K., & Ashcraft, C. (2005). Deliberative democratic evaluation: Successes and limitations of an evaluation of school choice. *Teachers College Record, 7*(10), 2274–2297.

MacGillivary, H., & Nelson, G. (1998). Partnerships in mental health: What is it and how do you do it? *Canadian Journal of Rehabilitation, Special Issue on Community Partnerships, 12*(2), 71–83.

Nelson, G., Ochocka, J., Griffin, K., & Lord, J. (1998). "Nothing about me, without me": Participatory action research with self-help/mutual aid organizations for psychiatric consumer/survivors. *American Journal of Community Psychology, 26,* 881–912.

Nelson, G., Prilelltensky, I., & MacGillivary, H. (2001). Partnerships with disadvantaged people: Values, stakeholders, contexts, processes, and outcomes. *American Journal of Community Psychology, 29*(5), 649–677.

Rawls, J. (1971). *A theory of justice.* Cambridge, MA: Belknap Press.

Reeve, P., Cornell, S., D'Costa, B., Janzen, R., & Ochocka, J. (2002). From our perspective: Consumer researchers speak about their experience in a community mental health research project. *Psychiatric Rehabilitation Journal, 25*(4), 403–408.

Root, M. (1993). *Philosophy of social science.* Cambridge, MA: Blackwell.

Shadish, W., Cook, T., & Leviton, L. (1995). *Foundations of program evaluation.* Thousand Oaks, CA: Sage.

Taylor, C. (1994). The politics of recognition. In A. Gutmann (Ed.), *Multiculturalism: Examining the politics of recognition* (pp. 25–74). Princeton, NJ: Princeton University Press.

Young, I. M. (1990). *Justice and the politics of difference.* Princeton, NJ: Princeton University Press.

Young, I. M. (2000). *Inclusion and democracy.* New York: Oxford University Press.

37

FRONTIERS IN SOCIAL RESEARCH ETHICS

Fertile Ground for Evolution

◆ Pauline E. Ginsberg and Donna M. Mertens

There is substantial agreement that, except in the most abstract of concepts such as the general imperative, to behave as one would have others do, social science research ethics evolve in response to developments in the philosophical substrate, in social science methodology, in cultures and cross-cultural contacts, and in response to interest groups and local, regional, tribal, national, and world history (see also Kitchener & Kitchener, Chapter 1; Schwartz, Chapter 12). The pace and direction of this evolution is not steady; rather, ad hoc ethical "solutions" to problems that emerge in specific situations only sometimes make their way into the realm of societal debate and subsequent general acceptance or rejection. There are many variables/factors that affect the process. In evolutionary terms, new conceptualizations or modifications to approaches to ethical problem solving occur often—those which survive are those which do not unduly inhibit the research process and do not attract censure from (e.g., are not edited out by) formal or informal regulatory and professional bodies. Those that thrive and may, indeed, displace earlier practices are those that advance the research process and those that gain a place within customary, regulatory, and professional frameworks.[1]

Kitchener and Kitchener (Chapter 1) provide an organizational model by which it is possible to classify the current state of ethical thought by level of abstraction. They present a five-level model of ethics in social science research: particular behavior (case specific as informed by the researcher's personal moral sense); ethical rules, including professional codes and involving topics such as informed consent and confidentiality; ethical principles such as beneficence (do good), nonmaleficence (do no harm), respect for persons (individuals should be treated as autonomous agents), justice (be fair), and fidelity (be honest); ethical theory (e.g., utilitarianism and deontology) that functions as an heuristic aid in reflecting on ethical principles; and metaethics that asks questions about the meaning of ethical words, the logic of justifying moral decisions, and the reality of moral properties.

While Kitchner and Kitchner (Chapter 1) state that the province of social science research ethics lies in applied ethics, rather than metaethics, nonetheless, the process of reflecting on the meaning of ethics in social science research is the metaethical underlying purpose of this *Handbook*. Hence, we compose this final *Handbook* chapter assuming a reflective reader who is contemplating the meaning of ethics, examining ethical theories and principles as a critical means of assessing rules and codes, and using this reflective process as a basis not only to make contextually specific ethical decisions but also to contribute to the evolution of thought in terms of social science research ethics writ large. Making use of the Kitcheners' model, we identify recurrent themes and tensions that surface in the *Handbook* chapters, using them to extend and challenge the Kitcheners' structural depiction of ethics, to suggest pathways to enhance ethical theory and practice, and to highlight provocative questions and suggestions of frontiers that have the potential to provide fertile ground for evolution and understanding of social research ethics.

♦ Foundations of Social Science Research Ethics

In Western philosophical tradition, the question of whether one should or should not engage in research (or, indeed, whether or not one might learn from that process) was once the key ethical (and practical) issue. In recent history, the positivist paradigm regarded research as a scientific, social, and moral imperative in and of itself. However, a growing number of instances in which the ethical value accorded knowledge accumulation per se clashed, sometimes cataclysmically, with concurrent philosophical and everyday views of morality have brought research ethics into the spotlight (see, e.g., Mabry, Chapter 7; Speiglman & Spear, Chapter 8; Vargas & Montoya, Chapter 31). At the same time, developments in philosophical thought that came to be termed *postmodernism* also called into question the value of research itself. Whereas positivist thought supported the belief that social science research results, like those from the natural sciences, might be generalized from the particular to the general, postmodernism challenges that assumption, emphasizing that all research is context specific and understandable (if at all) as a snapshot of one time, one place, and one set of particulars. Patton, in his role as a *Handbook* advisory board member, extended this line of thinking:

> It might be worth noting that these are endpoints of a continuum where one extreme is that only generalizations matter and the other extreme is that generalizations about humans are inherently impossible and undesirable. The fertile area for sensitive ethical evolution is between these absolutist extremes where we move from absolutes to negotiation, situational sensitivity and responsiveness. (M. Q. Patton, personal communication, February 1, 2008)

Whether or not a researcher accepts this basic postmodern premise, a primary contribution of the postmodern philosophical lens to research ethics is recognition that "every research activity is an exercise in research ethics, every research question is a moral dilemma, and every research decision is an instantiation of values" (Clegg & Slife, Chapter 2, p. 24). What is more, although there may be basic agreement regarding ethical generalities (e.g., treat research participants with respect), differences in basic belief systems, be they cultural, philosophical, paradigmatic, methodological, or personal, lead to different positions in terms of what is considered ethical behavior in social research. What constitutes "respect," after all, may differ greatly from one culture to the next. As an example, Vargas and Montoya (Chapter 31) discuss the issue of respect in the context of whether adolescents should be able to consent to participate in research or whether ability to consent should be limited to the parents. They argue that the answer to this question must depend on the cultural norms of the adolescent in question's community.

Thus, the axiological assumptions (e.g., underlying beliefs about the nature of ethical behavior) of each individual researcher are likely to vary somewhat, but that variation will take on some regularity related to the research paradigm he or she finds most comfortable. For example, Mertens, Harris, and Holmes (Chapter 6) describe the axiological assumption of the transformative paradigm wherein the furtherance of social justice is given priority as the value that underlies such social research. A researcher adhering to the transformative paradigm must, therefore, ask with regard to each and every research decision from the framing of the research question to the presentation of findings: "How can my research at this time and place contribute to social justice?" It is a question that requires a certain amount of prescience regarding the use of the researcher's findings and one that will take precedence over values that take precedence in other paradigms such as the positivist valuing of knowledge for its own sake without the requirement that the researcher know where and how the information he or she gains will be used (see Brown & Hedges, Chapter 24).

In addition to providing a structure for consideration of ethical issues, Kitchener and Kitchener (Chapter 1) indicate that there are two fundamental ethical questions that guide researchers regardless of paradigm and that further exploration of the implications of specific axiological assumptions.

Their questions are as follows:

1. What is the ethically proper way to collect, process, and report research data?

2. How should social scientists behave with respect to their research subjects?

A third question is suggested by the work of various contributors to this *Handbook*.

3. What ethical considerations are imposed by the preexisting social context in which any specific piece of research is contemplated?

This third question is likely to be interpreted differently depending on researchers' choices of paradigm, research focus, population, or research methodology. For example, as previously noted, Mertens et al.'s (Chapter 6) positioning within the transformative paradigm leads them to an analysis of preexisting social contexts that involve specific attention to conditions of injustice. For Silka (Chapter 22), a proponent of community partnerships, identification of ethical issues will involve attention to inclusiveness. Brydon-Miller (Chapter 16) advocates for participatory action research. In so doing, ethical concerns will include the usefulness of research to its participants. Others, for example, Cram (Chapter 20); LaFrance and Crazy Bull

(Chapter 9); Moewaka Barnes, McCreanor, Edwards, and Borell (Chapter 28); Chilisa (Chapter 26); and Bledsoe and Hopson (Chapter 25) are concerned with issues of particular concern to indigenous peoples and/or those who are disadvantaged or underserved. Vargas and Montoya (Chapter 31) examine who can and should make decisions about research participation for children, and both Sullivan (Chapter 5) and Barnes (Chapter 29) examine issues of inclusion with regard to the disability community. All these researchers propose models of community involvement in the determination of the research content, purpose, and questions. Some of them, for example, Mertens et al. (Chapter 6), Sullivan (Chapter 5), and Vargas and Montoya (Chapter 31), do so explicitly within the context of furthering human rights. Researchers engaged in repeated contact with small numbers of participants such as ethnographers (e.g., Ryen, Chapter 15) are concerned with the ethical issues evoked by intensive day-to-day interaction and the degree and manner in which contributors prefer to be identified (e.g., Ntseane, Chapter 19). Those whose methods are less personal, involving only brief contact with participants or, as in the case of Internet-based research, none at all, are far more likely to focus on uniform protection through strategies to preserve participants' anonymity (see Matsumoto & Jones, Chapter 21; Burbules, Chapter 34).

Handbook authors may employ either an intimate or a broad perspective in terms of being responsive to contextual variations. For example, feminist researchers Brabeck and Brabeck (Chapter 3) describe a focused study limited to women of Mexican origin who experienced partner abuse. These same women who informed both the research questions and study design in addition to being study participants also had personal relationships with each other and with one of the authors. In contrast, Sullivan's (Chapter 5) approach to the topic of disability is panoramic, including historical shifts in the disability community that turned the lens of research toward a structural analysis of the disabling society that created dependency-maintaining services institutionalizing very high rates of unemployment, poverty, homelessness, and marginalization as contrasted with the disability rights movement's struggle for civil and individual rights.

◆ Power and Ethics

The third question identified above, "What ethical considerations are imposed by the preexisting social context in which any specific piece of research is contemplated?" is broad in that the term *social context* might encompass such dimensions as culture, class, aspects of the relationship between the researcher and researched (stranger, acquaintance, authority figure, etc.), or even the demand characteristics of the location in which data are collected. And, indeed, there are many variations in the way in which social context is treated by the authors of this *Handbook*.

Yet despite their many differences, an essential theme emerging from the ethical concerns reflected by this third question is intimately connected to consciousness of power dynamics in research situations. Power differentials surface in many guises. These include (at least) determination of what is to be researched, how the research will be carried out, and to whom the results will be disseminated. Power differentials may be reflected in and related to language, nationality, age, ethnicity, socioeconomic status, culture of origin, level of community involvement, access to and control of funding, and dissemination and ownership of data. While the scope of this *Handbook* reaches in many directions, among its diverse authors, there is near consensus that social research ethics must delve into the complexities of power to advance thinking and understanding. Many of the authors of this *Handbook* do not characterize their work as postmodern; however, the postmodernists' promotion of the need to participate in discussions of power by challenging even the underlying assumptions inherent in naive conceptions of science provides useful guidance. In particular, postmodernist contributions to discussions of power are captured in this statement: "There is a kind of monolithic power inherent in the universalism of the scientific mythos, and a postmodern understanding of research ethics would likely begin in the deconstruction of that power" (Clegg & Slife, Chapter 2, p. 30).

Researchers conceptualize power in multifaceted ways, interpersonally and/or culturally. A few examples of one of the ways, the gatekeeping function, will suffice. Mabry (Chapter 7) and Speiglman and Spear (Chapter 8), in the section of the *Handbook* devoted to ethical regulation, discuss in depth the control exhibited by government, professional associations, and institutional review boards (IRBs). These topics also arise in nearly every chapter of the *Handbook*. Discussions include both descriptive and historical information as well as concerns regarding the propensity of ethical codes and review boards to diverge from their overarching goal, protection of research participants, to take on other roles such as protectors of institutional or professional reputations, or to become arbiters of research methodology. Dodd (Chapter 30), Mabry (Chapter 7), and Sullivan (Chapter 5) raise power-related ethical questions about the gatekeeping function of public and private institutions, agencies, and corporations that fund research. These authors stress the importance of looking gift horses squarely in the mouth. The ethical researcher is advised to inquire: Who are the funders? Why are they funding this particular research at this time? Who will profit from which potential research findings? What is the likely effect of doing this research on funder, researcher, and researched? Mabry (Chapter 7) also questions the ethical implications of funding agencies dictating research methods. Brown and Hedges (Chapter 24), in contrast, turn a wary eye toward the gatekeeping function of journal editors and other publishers of social science research. Because publication in peer-reviewed journals and receipt of external funding help determine salary, rank, and tenure for those researchers affiliated with academic institutions, the actual or perceived biases of journal editors, like funders, for and against particular approaches or subject areas can be influential in determining an academic's choice of study topics and research methods. Not only is it incumbent on the researcher, funder, and journal editor to be aware of these potential effects and to evaluate their ethical impact on the research and the researcher, but also, according to Vargas and Montoya (Chapter 31), it is an ethical imperative to disclose what the researcher has to gain on a personal level to research participants. Only then can research participants truly weigh the costs and benefits of their contributions.

From this short sampling of topics alone, one might conclude that social science research ethics is solely about power: who ought to have it and how it ought to be used. There is general consensus that there are roles for governments (and perhaps even for intergovernmental organizations), for communities (however construed), for professional organizations, research institutes, universities, funders, both private and public, and for those that keep the gates of academe. But there is little consensus regarding the role of each of these entities and, perhaps, even less regarding the relationships among them. The *Handbook* does not offer such an integrated analysis of the relationship between social science research and the political process; thus, this is one of those fertile areas for ethical evolution. Segmented approaches, however, have been provided by Howe and MacGillivary (Chapter 36) with regard to deliberative democracy, Sullivan (Chapter 5) with respect to the disability community, Thomas (Chapter 4) with regard to critical race theory, Brabeck and Brabeck (Chapter 3) with regard to women, LaFrance and Crazy

Bull (Chapter 9) with regard to American Indians, and Cram (Chapter 20) with regard to the Maori.

In addition, there is little consensus regarding the appropriate ethical role of the researcher with regard to issues of power and control in the research setting. Experimental social science researchers hold that, once a research question has been identified and has undergone external review, power *must* rest in the hands of the principal investigator. It is the responsibility of the researcher to control all identifiable extraneous variables by holding them constant or to manage them through randomization, sampling, and statistical manipulation. The goal is to obtain generalizable knowledge, and failure to do so as a result of imperfect research design is regarded as a breech of ethics. With regard to experimental or quasi-experimental research on or evaluation of any hypothetical treatment or intervention, Mark and Gamble (Chapter 13, p. 205) write "a case can be made that good ethics justifies the use of research methods that will give the best answer about program effectiveness." Citing Rosenthal (1994), they add, "Bad science makes for bad ethics" (p. 206, this volume).

Qualitative researchers and those using mixed methods (e.g., Bledsoe & Hopson, Chapter 25; Brydon-Miller, Chapter 16; Lincoln, Chapter 10; Mertens et al., Chapter 6; Newton, Chapter 23; Ryen, Chapter 15; Sharma, Chapter 27; Silka, Chapter 22) neither expect nor seek to obtain such power and control. For them, control of the "tools of the trade" means personal power through self-knowledge, introspection, and the ability to form relationships and monitor the ongoing research process (Ryen, Chapter 15; Symonette, Chapter 18), through interviewing and note-taking skills and, as needed, through mastery of statistical and/or visual techniques (Brown & Hedges, Chapter 24; Newton, Chapter 23).

Regardless of method, once the data have been collected and analyzed, researchers would generally agree that, in so far as knowledge is power, it is the researchers' ethical responsibility to share power—that is, to communicate the results of their efforts. Yet they differ greatly with regard to how this might (and ought to) be done. Irwin's chapter (Chapter 17) on the ethics of peace research highlights a method of polling that can be integrated into the process of peacemaking and depends on the widest possible dissemination of poll results among all parties to a conflict. In this instance, result sharing, hence power sharing, is, in fact, the raison d'etre of the research itself. Hence, at minimum, not only do all parties to a conflict participate in formulating the questions the poll will ask, but also newspaper publication of complete results of all polls and their posting on Irwin's Web site make them available to any literate individual with newspaper access or Internet capacity. Irwin (Chapter 17) argues that in order for the researcher to provide information acceptable to all parties and pertinent to effective peace making, the information obtained must be as openly available as the process of obtaining it. Brown and Hedges's (Chapter 24) argument for the ethical necessity of publishing is quite different. They regard publication in the most prestigious journals possible as a primary ethical responsibility to the community of scholars. The power to be shared here, as in the work of Johnson and Bullock (Chapter 14) advocating data archiving, is power among scientific peers.

This rationale, however, would be lost on researchers with a "by us, for us, with us" orientation as reflected in the writings of many indigenous scholars (e.g., Barnes, Chapter 29; Cram, Chapter 20; Moewaka Barnes et al., Chapter 28). In its extreme form, this view of the researcher's first ethical responsibility is not that of a member of a broad international, multicultural research community, many, if not most, of whose members he or she will never meet in person, but, rather, as a member of a primary group in which face-to-face encounters are those that matter. Such face-to-face encounters and the ethical necessity of communicating solely (or, in less extreme form, primarily) with those who have participated in the research matter particularly to researchers who are from indigenous, postcolonial, and minority communities where there is a long, sad history of knowledge—or supposed knowledge—of the community held by oppressors and used in the service of further oppression. (For a wealth of examples, see Bledsoe & Hopson, Chapter 25; Brabeck & Brabeck, Chapter 3; Chilisa, Chapter 26; Cram, Chapter 20; Dodd, Chapter 30; LaFrance & Crazy Bull, Chapter 9; Matsumoto & Jones, Chapter 21; Moewaka Barnes et al., Chapter 28; Ntseane, Chapter 19; Thomas, Chapter 4; Vargas & Montoya, Chapter 31.)

There is, of course, much space between these extreme positions. Researchers commonly hold both professional and community identities. Researchers who take an emancipatory (Barnes, Chapter 29) or transformative stance (Mertens et al., Chapter 6) and those who engage in community partnerships (Silka, Chapter 22) or participatory action research (Brydon-Miller, Chapter 16) are, like indigenous researchers working in their own communities, particularly likely to emphasize power sharing at all stages of a research enterprise, including communication of results. Newton (Chapter 23) depicts the researcher's power this way: "The researcher's power *to make visible* or *invisible, to facilitate* or *confound understanding,* and *to honor the trust imparted to the researcher from initial interaction through final representation*" (p. 354). That it is the researcher's ethical responsibility to honor participant trust through a true and honest final representation of the research is a generalization that would apply in many research contexts.

Yet even contributors who support community empowerment also recognize that researchers' impulses toward power sharing are not always carried out for a variety of reasons, only some of them theory based and others practical. Sullivan (Chapter 5) recognizes the ethical dilemma that arises, for example, when funding agencies do not agree to community involvement at all levels of a project and insist, instead, on researcher control; when communities are diverse and there is neither an obvious group who unequivocally could (or should) hold the reins of power nor a means of negotiating equitable power sharing; or when shared power has the potential to jeopardize researchers' integrity. Do such conditions necessarily entail an all or nothing resolution to the avoidance/avoidance conflict between unethical research and no research at all? Shakespeare (2006, as cited by Sullivan, Chapter 5) resolves the dilemma by placing the researcher squarely between its horns and suggesting that researchers be responsible only to their own consciences. Sullivan (Chapter 5) sees in the transformative paradigm another way out: If "there is an element of the researcher being a 'bit of a provocateur' who 'recognizes inequalities and injustices,' 'possesses a shared sense of responsibility' and works humbly with the community to transform its situation" (pp. 77–78), he or she need not engage in formal power sharing and can still lay claim to participation in a transformative approach that emphasizes social justice for minorities and a "together with" climate in which structures of power can be challenged in order to transform lives.

What are the consequences associated with ignoring ethical questions around power? Stanfield (1999) contended that when determination of the research focus and questions is made without consideration to issues of power (as opposed to actual power sharing), there is a tendency for the more powerful to depict the less powerful in a negative light. Studies of failure of African Americans or Native Americans in the school system support his position. However, research with a goal of improving the condition of community members who experience discrimination and oppression includes the often overlooked strength in communities that are rising to the challenge of addressing seemingly intransigent problems. When theoretical perspectives such as resilience theory and positive psychology are used to frame a study, then a deliberate and conscious design can reveal the positive aspects, resilience, and acts of resistance needed for social change (Bledsoe & Hopson, Chapter 25; Mertens et al., Chapter 6) even when actual power remains in the hands of the researcher. Ludema, Cooperrider, and Barrett (2001) argued, however, that research and evaluation have largely failed as instruments for advancing social-organizational transformation because they maintain a problem-oriented view rather than focusing on the strengths of a community.

This is not meant to imply that researchers solely focus on "problems." The question is, "Do good intentions and strengths-based research make a positive change in power positions in the absence of actual empowerment during the research process?" We are not sure of the answer to this question. However, it could, in theory, make a positive change or a negative one regardless of the researcher's intent or adherence to a transformative or emancipatory paradigm. It is not, after all, necessary to adhere to such a paradigm in order to believe in collaboration and power sharing whenever possible.

In actuality, researchers' approaches to ethical decision making under real-world pressure are less likely to depend on paradigmatic considerations and more likely to rely on the individual moral sense, the most basic component of the Kitcheners' structural model (Chapter 1), to which we now turn.

◆ Structural Model for the Study of Research Ethics

Having introduced the two basic ethical questions identified by Kitchener and Kitchener (Chapter 1) and elucidated the third contextual question by illustrating its relationship to power, we now turn to the Kitcheners' structural model for the study of research ethics. We do so because the model provides a laddered approach to organizing our thoughts, starting with the most specific level of our personal moral sense, and moving to the most abstract levels of ethical theories and metaethics.

PARTICULAR CASES, ETHICS, AND THE ORDINARY MORAL SENSE

In the Kitcheners' analysis, while the ordinary moral sense, encompassing an individual's moral character, beliefs about personal ethical responsibility, and knowledge of the situation, is indispensable to routine and ongoing research activities, it is not sufficient for numerous reasons. Perhaps the most important of these is that there is a subtle but basic difference between "morals" and the "moral sense" of what is right and wrong and "ethics" that implies a more reasoned or systematic process. In Kitcheners' words "not everyone has moral intuitions that lead to defensible ethical choices" (Chapter 1, p. 11). Moreover, during the research process unanticipated situations may arise that call for such quick action and/or are so unique that they are outside the scope of common morality. Although, with experience, Kitchener and Kitchener allow, a researcher's ordinary moral sense may be expected to gain sophistication, even the mature researcher is unlikely to be able to rely solely on his or her common morality. Symonette (Chapter 18) explores the individual researcher/evaluator's personal journey through self-awareness to cognizance of oneself in relation to community. She suggests that the sense of ethics and morality with which we are born and raised needs critical examination in wider cultural terms. While Fisher, Wertz, and Goodman (Chapter 35) would likely agree that common morality is unlikely to resolve all conceivable ethical dilemmas, these authors report social science research that graduate level training and, more critically, mentoring are strategies that can and should enhance development of an ethical sense in entry level practitioners. In behaving as teacher/coach, sponsor, and counselor, a skilled and ethical mentor can, in theory, foster ethical maturation in trainees through multiple mechanisms including rapport, apprenticeship, support, and more. Yet, as Fisher et al. note, evidence of success is equivocal. Some studies of student perception of mentor influence show little perceived importance (p. 555) and studies of graduate institutions reveal many "barriers to mentoring" (pp. 555-557) although they also indicate that clear institutional expectations regarding ethical behavior have a positive effect and that students who have "taken an ethics course" (p. 558) have more knowledge of ethical norms. Research continues regarding how to develop the moral self within a research context while, at the same time, research among practitioners shows some degree of balance between the individual's ordinary moral sense and professional codes in approaching ethical dilemmas (Wolf, Turner, & Toms, Chapter 11).[2]

In Western psychological tradition, there is considerable support for the notion that the capacity to develop a moral sense is innate and that actual moral sensitivities of individuals accrue developmentally, influenced by life experience, most importantly, within the family. Freud's (1917/1958) theory, in particular, links childrearing practices, both cultural and familial, prior to 5 years of age with adult moral and ethical behavior. The mechanism by which Freud postulates that ethics develop, identification with the parental figure,[3] is one of those to which Fisher et al. (Chapter 35) refer in suggesting mentorship as a route to research ethics. Kohlberg's (1976) theory, involving a cognitive component without negating Freud's insights, is far more supportive of the possibility of lifelong learning and moral maturation, but has been criticized, particularly by feminists (e.g., Gilligan, 1982), for its overreliance on abstract, rule-based ethical decision making based on logic and neglect of subjective, context-based ethical decision making based on empathy.

Brabeck and Brabeck (Chapter 3) explore a feminist concept of ethics in which empathy is an integral part and applies that concept to a specific example of feminist research. For the Brabecks

(m)oral adequacy, . . . depends upon paying attention to the particularities of individuals' and a community's narratives while examining these particularities in light of their unique sociocultural contexts; entering into their perspectives; and asking, How is a person's life affected by bigotry, prejudice, and other distortions? (p. 46)

To discover whether this might be a component of the ordinary moral sense sufficient for conducting ethical research, we need to discover whether the ability is present in all humans (males and researchers included) and, if not, whether it can be learned intentionally or whether it is something that only accrues to some people by virtue of life experience (e.g., being female, being oppressed) and to others not at all. Brabeck and Brabeck indicate that standpoint theory suggests that learning is possible, at least for women, and earlier intensive research into empathy training (e.g., Carkhuff, 1970; Truax & Carkhuff, 1967) would support the claim regardless of gender.

Contributors to the *Handbook* from non-Western cultures describe processes similar to those associated with the Western concept of ordinary moral sense. Maori contributors from New Zealand (Cram, Chapter 20; Moewaka Barnes et al., Chapter 28) and African contributors from Botswana (Chilisa, Chapter 26; Ntseane, Chapter 19) refer to ethical behavior that they absorbed as members of their communities and learned to incorporate them into their work as social researchers in much the same way as Western contributors have done. While the processes are almost certainly analogous, specific contents of Maori and African "ordinary" morality are not always so "ordinary" by Western standards and those of the west are not always so "ordinary" by standards of other regions and cultures. By way of illustration, each of the authors cited above refers to experiences in which his or her training in Western social science research methods expected that certain identified behaviors, for example, maintenance of confidentiality, would be a part of his or her "ordinary" moral behavior while, from his or her own cultural perspective, the content of such behavior would be extraordinary indeed—not a sign of consideration for another individual but a sign of disrespect, perhaps, of treating a matter of pride as a matter of shame or of foolish pretense that public knowledge was secret. For social science researchers from non-Western cultures who are trained in Western theories, research methods, and ethics, a clash of cultures with regard to what constitutes accepted "ordinary" morals is typically part of the package. For members of minority populations within the Western tradition, the same may be true but to a lesser degree and more predictably. Researchers sensitive to nuance who wish to collect data cross-culturally will experience at least a hint of difference between what they consider to be ordinary moral behavior, for example, means of showing respect, and that which is considered to be commonplace abroad. Differences will be more noticeable to the degree that the project is long term. Those partnering across cultural boundaries will almost certainly experience a jolt or two (or more) of what is commonly called "culture shock" en route to coming to understand each others' expectations (see Matsumoto & Jones, Chapter 21; Moewaka Barnes et al., Chapter 28; Silka, Chapter 22; Sharma, Chapter 27). Perhaps, for the researchers crossing boundaries, there is no "ordinary" moral sense to be relied on or there is more than one such moral sense and each must be accessed, matched, and/or tailored to different situations.

Cram (Chapter 20) describes much of the Maori way, comprising the basics of Maori ordinary morality. Moewaka Barnes et al. (Chapter 28) provide multiple examples of means by which social science research processes adapt to fit Kaupapa Maori, the Maori way. Chilisa's (Chapter 26) and Ntseane's work (Chapter 19) may be read to similar effect as applied to Botswana. All four of these *Handbook* chapters when considered together speak about the need to incorporate locally relevant ordinary morality into one's research strategy as a means of community acceptance and more useful (however defined) results as well as their being an end in themselves.

While these and other contributors to the *Handbook* vary in the degree to which they would rely on the ordinary moral sense to ensure the ethics of social science research, few see it as sufficient. Thus, Stake and Rizvi (Chapter 33) are in this minority. But they do not place themselves here because of their faith in the underlying goodness of human nature. Rather, their reasons are twofold: pessimism regarding the ability of any code of ethics or set of ethical rules to anticipate ethical issues arising in increasingly complicated transnational research spaces and their conviction that those lacking an internal moral compass will simply use portions of such codes and rules to defend their ethical abuses. The solution, they conclude unhappily ("And it is to this lonely coastline our train of thought has been inexorably chugging," p. 531), is that there is no alternative but to rely on conscience—"an essential voice from within" (p. 531).

We do not share Stake and Rivzi's pessimism. And, so we give the penultimate word on the topic of ordinary morality to Burbules (Chapter 34) who, in his chapter on the limits of traditional research ethics, like Stake and Rivzi, writes about complex transnational (or perhaps a-national) spaces.

> There is no moral rule or precept that, taken as an absolute measure, will not sometimes lead us badly. There is no moral virtue or trait of character that, in extreme or exaggerated forms, does not become a vice. There is no capacity for moral thought and reflection that cannot be turned to bad purposes as well as

good; the same insights into others that allow us to care for them and respond to them sympathetically are also insights that can be used to manipulate them. And so on. Here again we find an educational project: If there are no guarantees in any form of moral socialization or instruction, then learning to be moral comes down to, more than anything else, learning to want to be moral. This inclination is the only reliable guide to unforeseen circumstances, in which we truly do not know what to do; and it is the underlying trait that supports the processes of reflection and reconsideration that keeps our moral judgment flexible in response to changing conditions. (p. 547)

We are unable to give Burbules the last word because we have not yet weighed in with regard to the relevance of the ordinary moral sense to the three salient questions, two from the Kitcheners and one abstracted from other chapters in this *Handbook* that we introduced in the previous section of this chapter: What does the ordinary moral sense or its equivalent have to contribute to the question of how to collect, process, and report research data? What does the ordinary moral sense tell us about how to behave *vis-à-vis* research participants? What does the ordinary moral sense tell us regarding what ethical considerations are imposed by the preexisting social context?

With regard to the first of these questions, the ordinary moral sense tells us little or nothing at all. In the ordinary nonresearch sphere of day-to-day behavior, our collection, processing, and reporting of data are self-serving and meant to answer ordinary questions in which standards of evidence are low and satisficing is routine. For example, in the ordinary sphere, if the question is "Where should I send my child to school?" then as soon as an acceptable school is identified, the data collection ends and the report is made. In formal research, the comparable question, which is the best school for a child with certain characteristics requires an exhaustive search and hence, needs guidance beyond our ordinary moral sense—guidance provided by agreed on ethical rules and codes.

Similarly, the way we treat "participants" in our daily search for answers is likely to rely solely on our personal relationships with them. We ask for personal opinions of friends and expect them to be freely given; we expect responses from public officials commensurate with their public responsibilities; we hire professional consultants and treat them as our employees. The relationship with research participants is rarely similar to any of these. Finally, like fish in water, in our daily lives the social context is only noticeable when it changes. Ethical codes and rules, then, serve to focus our attention on the ways that ordinary life differs from research; and thus, we move onto the second level of the Kitcheners' model.

◆ Ethical Rules, Laws, Administrative Procedures, and Codes of Conduct

Burbules's (Chapter 34) examination of research ethics in cyberspace is in accord with Kitchener and Kitchener's (Chapter 1) analysis: The moral sense is necessary, but not sufficient. One reason for this insufficiency is lack of information about specific situations that a researcher might encounter in practice and how the ordinary moral sense might apply (p. 11). While some such situations are common across researchers as a group, it might take a lifetime or more for an individual researcher to experience even a percentage of these. The role of rules, codes, laws, protocols, and the like is, therefore, to supplement the ordinary moral sense by providing specific guidelines that also use abstract moral principles to common ethical issues encountered in research settings. In Kitchener and Kitchener's words,

For social science researchers, the first resource in evaluating tough ethical decisions ought to be their ethics codes. They attempt to bring together the cumulative wisdom of the profession about acting morally while doing research. Basically, they formulate a set of action guides researchers must follow and ideals which researchers should strive to follow. These rules should provide answers to many ethical questions that social science researchers have and provide a standard against which others both in the profession and outside of it can judge their actions. (pp. 11–12)

This ideal described by the Kitcheners is only partially met. Indeed, they acknowledge that other factors may also enter into the shaping of any specific code. What those factors might be are explored at some length by other authors of the *Handbook*. Mabry (Chapter 7) points out that across time and form of government, "it can be safely said that internal stability and protection from external threats are general aims" and that "(m)any modern governments have pursued (or have claimed to pursue) economic and social benefits for their citizens" (p. 107). To fulfill these goals, governments have an interest in research that, even when it brings benefits to some citizens, rarely benefits all and likely never benefits all equally. Nazi medical experiments and the U.S. Tuskegee syphilis study are particularly dramatic cases in point and are referenced in several chapters of this *Handbook*. Most instances of governmental involvement in research and codes of research are more benign. However, as a general rule, government regulation can be expected to encourage (with varying degrees of subtlety) research and researchers are expected to inform and support government policies even when it does not ban others outright.

Government involvement in monitoring research and research ethics may be direct. Or it may be indirect as is currently the case in the United States where oversight of all federally funded research, and much research that does not receive federal funding, devolves to IRBs, often affiliated with academic or research institutions, that must themselves be approved by an agency of the government. Currently, this agency is the Office for Human Research Protections of the Department of Health and Human Services that also provides training to IRB members and supports both certification of IRB members and credentialing of IRBs, a process also undertaken by two or more independent organizations (Speiglman & Spear, Chapter 8). The first priority of each IRB is to make certain that research is conducted ethically so as to protect participant welfare. In so doing, it examines the researcher's protocol, consent process, and other documents.

The IRB's job is to protect participants by (a) making sure that the research is valid, (b) ensuring that the risks are minimized or balanced by benefits or potential benefits, and (c) ensuring that potential participants are given information relevant to making an informed decision about participating in the research and about the choices involved in doing so. (p. 124)

Other concerns are typically whether documents are culturally appropriate and comprehensible to potential participants, whether recruitment of participants is fair, and whether any compensation for participation constitutes coercion.

Outside the IRB process, as official IRBs located in the community or tribal group, in tandem with outside IRBs, or replacing them altogether, indigenous groups in North America have claimed/are claiming control and monitoring with regard to research with their own people. LaFrance and Crazy Bull (Chapter 9) describe the process by which this has taken place in the United States with the goal of rendering research responsive to the needs of local communities and respectful to cultural mores in a historical (and present-day) context of research by members of the dominant population which have, well-meaning in some cases, not so—even malevolent—in others, lead to misunderstanding and exploitation.

Although in the early stages at least, American Indian control of the research agenda is successful in the realms of greater sensitivity to local practices and needs and is likely to continue to do so as long as it is tied to a community base. We are not, in light of Mabry's research (Chapter 7) regarding governmental regulation generally and Speiglman and Spear's (Chapter 8) investigation of IRBs, altogether optimistic about this being a long-term solution. Over time, issues of self-protection with its accompanying conservatism regarding which topics and methods might be used and related questions about freedom of inquiry are likely to arise. In small communities, local politics may also become a complicating factor. For the present, however, LaFrance and Crazy Bull (Chapter 9) are more than persuasive about the need for local and tribal control.

It is also of interest that, on a less formal basis, there are agencies (e.g., local school districts) and communities not defined by ethnicity, which also claim the right to regulate research and set research priorities with regard to the use of their resources for research purposes. Dodd (Chapter 30), who writes specifically about the gay, lesbian, bisexual, transsexual, and queer communities, suggests forming a community advisory board (CAB) or a research advisory committee for all research projects involving LGBTQ participants

> [as a group] to advise the research process throughout, and to ensure cultural competence and sensitivity. Gathering a diverse range of advisors can ensure that the research project not only protects all vulnerable subjects but may ensure the successful completion of the project as well. (p. 484)

This advice is also appropriate for other groups. Additional models of CABs are contributed by the American Indian experience (Lafrance & Crazy Bull, Chapter 9) and that of the Maori reported by Cram (Chapter 20) and by Moewaka Barnes et al. (Chapter 28).

If rules, regulations, and codes of conduct actually did meet the ideal of distilling and codifying the cumulative ethical wisdom of social science research, we would expect that they would be substantially the same from discipline to discipline, geographic location to geographic location, and, within the United States, IRB to IRB. Mabry (Chapter 7) documents that this is not the case from IRB to IRB. It is likely that this difference is due to differences in perceived self-interest of the IRB membership at each locale. Speiglman and Spear (Chapter 8) indicate that differences in self-interest may be attributable to variation in institutional conservatism and risk management out of fear of financial repercussions in the case of harm coming to a research participant or to public objection to research associated with their institution.

Discipline-based codes of ethics also reveal differences that may be based on perceived self-interest. One might expect that disciplines such as psychology and social work that monitor the admission of members (e.g., National Association of Social Workers and American Psychological Association [APA]) and that hear complaints from peers and members of the public, which can lead to ejection of members for breaches in ethics, would be most self-protective and may, indeed, be more conservative (while also more punitive) in their codes of ethics than discipline-based professional organizations. One example of this difference is found in ethics resolutions regarding participation in and research related to questioning of prisoners during the so-called war on terror by the APA, as compared with the American Sociological Association and the American Anthropological Association. The latter two organizations took a strong stance, condemning not only participation in questioning but also research that would aid and abet such practices. APA, in contrast, rejected stronger resolutions and banned only direct participation.[4]

Stake and Rizvi (Chapter 33) believe that

> It is useful to have multiple codes, holding one up against the other, not so that we can find one to justify what we want to do anyway but so that we can, in a multicultural world, recognize different manifestations of ethical value and better deliberate their implications. (p. 534)

Differences among professional ethical codes not related to the self-protective function of each may reflect genuine historical differences in the ethical issues most commonly encountered by differing social science disciplines during the research process. However, as both professionalism and the variety of potential research venues expand, these variations may become obsolete. Just as Schwartz's chapter (Chapter 12) traces his own and others' evolution in research ethics from past to present, so Burbules (Chapter 34) and Stake and Rivzi (Chapter 33) direct us to contemplate potential futures. One possibility may involve fewer differences across disciplines. For example, cross-cultural psychological research such as that of Matsumoto and Jones (Chapter 21) may be as informed by the ethical thought of anthropology as by that of psychology. Anthropologists working in health care settings may find the ethical thought of psychology illuminating.

A more important immediate concern from the perspective of social science research ethics, however, is the so-called mission creep of IRBs from biomedicine to the social sciences. Quoting the Center for Advanced Study (2005, p. 4), Speiglman and Spear (Chapter 8) note that narrow interpretation of IRB strictures can lead to "imprecision and unreasonable regulatory burden as well as inappropriate regulation and restriction" (pp. 121, 128) such as, for example, insisting on signed consent forms from nonliterate groups and expecting prescience of qualitative researchers regarding, for example, who and how many key informants will be approached. Where advocacy and research intersect, as in participatory, transformative, and empowerment research efforts, strict adherence to codes and/or regulations simply may not be possible. When it is regulations that are concerned, the upshot is that the research itself undergoes prior restraint, must be underwritten and sponsored by individuals or groups outside the normal research process, or completed underground.

Other criticisms of IRB procedures include the likelihood of increasing researcher self-censorship (Mabry, Chapter 7; Speiglman & Spear, Chapter 8) and fear that the amount of trivial documentation that IRBs require may overwhelm serious consideration of ethical issues. Speiglman and Spear write, "Ironically, from Brydon-Miller's perspective, the trajectory to protect human subjects is defined by a highly specific focus on *informed consent* and other documents rather than a more penetrating examination of the ethical implications of the *research itself*" (Chapter 8, p. 131). This is of particular concern to us as we think about the presumed educational role of regulation as a supplement to the ordinary moral sense. Is the novice researcher, the careless one, or the one who is deficient in moral sensibilities likely to confuse a letter from the IRB approving his or her research proposal with a clear bill of ethical health for the lifetime of the project?

Efforts to examine codes of research ethics transnationally since World War II attempt to balance one human right, that is, the right of freedom of expression that underlies researchers' rights of inquiry and dissemination, with another, that is, the right of research participants to be treated lawfully, free of coercion, and as fully informed of the risks and benefits of their participation as possible. Actors in this transnational effort include various arms of the United Nations, including the General

Assembly, World Medical Association, and World Bank (Mabry, Chapter 7). At this point, however, researchers wishing to engage in cross-national research can only adhere to requirements and practices of each of the nations in which they wish to engage (see Matsumoto & Jones, Chapter 21).

Regardless of source—transnational, national, professional, and so on—Mabry (Chapter 7) questions the potential suppression of intellectual curiosity and academic freedom, so essential for researchers, because of the emphasis on compliance. Speiglman and Spear (Chapter 8) share her concern, as do we, but believe that there are modifications to IRB policies and procedures that can maintain the protection of research participants, which was the IRB's manifest intent, without the necessity of relying solely on the ordinary moral sense and a desire for goodness. One of these, one at least partially supported by the differences among professional codes of ethics and the experience of other contributors to this *Handbook* (e.g., Brydon-Miller, Chapter 16; Lincoln, Chapter 10; Moewaka Barnes et al., Chapter 28; Ntseane, Chapter 19; Silka, Chapter 22) would be to separate out and use different formats for qualitative and ethnographic research than for experimental and biomedical research. We are not convinced, however, that the problems can be solved by any simple re-slicing of the pie on the basis of research methodology. Ethnographic research can, after all, be a source of risk and, not unlike biomedical intervention, has an unfortunate history of having been used by some to justify mistreatment of vulnerable people, while experimental research, in addition to its acknowledged misuses, has a long and venerable history of useful findings in sensory research, memory, and other basic psychological processes accrued under conditions of very minimal risk by asking college sophomores to recall word lists, report taste sensations, and complete tasks alone versus in groups.

The personal experiences that Moewaka Barnes et al. (Chapter 28) report in their negotiation with regulatory panels in Aotearoa impress us greatly. Here, issues of culture and methodology, language, custom, and the values of research participants both assured the protection of the latter and the integrity of the research itself. We see this as a potential model though we understand with regret that, in the process of institutionalizing negotiation as must indeed happen when self-protective entities are involved, something will inevitably be lost in translation. We suggest, no rigid code has ever been error-free and none can ever exempt the researcher from employing his or her ordinary moral sense, the experience and advice of peers, and scrutiny in light of abstract principles. Thus, from the standpoint of promoting social science research ethics, the use of ethical codes and regulations is best recognized as (a) an advisory process (b) open to discussion and, (c) where apparently intractable disagreement between researcher and regulator persists, subject to mediation. Guidance at this more complex level of ethical deliberations is provided by a discussion of the third level of Kitcheners' model: ethical principles.

◆ Ethical Principles

Ordinary morality is inadequate to assure ethical social science research due to limitations of researcher motivation, life and research experience, and the speed with which many decisions must be made. Regulations, codes, and procedures can help the researcher prevent, foresee, and prepare to respond to common ethical dilemmas, but institutional and governmental review processes are often insensitive to qualitative modes of inquiry, may be skewed by governmental or institutional self-interest, and also may inhibit free inquiry or conflict with other ethical mandates. These are the two most basic of the processes of ethical judgment. Having found them wanting, we move up to a higher level of abstraction, the critical evaluative level (Kitchener & Kitchener, Chapter 1) of ethical principles such as concern for others' welfare (beneficence) and avoidance of harm (nonmaleficence), and respect for the rights and dignity of individuals, including their ability to make decisions about participation in research, honesty, fairness, and justice.

NONMALEFICENCE AND BENEFICENCE: RESULTS OF RESEARCH

Although the concept of doing good has been used broadly by many of the authors of this *Handbook*, the technical research–based concept exists within the research arena where it is the obverse of nonmaleficence, correctly interpreted as applying within the conduct of the research whereby participants should not be harmed, and any potential for harm to occur must be balanced with other ethical principles (e.g., beneficence). As the Kitcheners remind us, the Preamble of the Ethical Principles of the Psychological Code of Conduct begins with the assumption that the profession will "develop a valid and reliable body of scientific knowledge based on research" and that research is used to "improve the condition of both the individual and society" (p. 13).

What does the principle of beneficence mean when interrogated with the mandate to use research to improve the condition of both the individual and society? Sullivan (Chapter 5) raises questions that focus on the immediate experience of the participant: Is the research intrusive and potentially harmful to the researched? Is there any reciprocity between the researched and the researcher? Is there any payback for the researched as individuals or as a group? Considered more abstractly and along a broader horizon, does this mean that in selection of research topics one is obligated to choose those with the most promise of ameliorating ills and/or providing benefits? Does beneficence dictate specific rules as to how research should be conducted? Mark and Gamble (Chapter 13) and Brown and Hedges (Chapter 24) concur that there is an ethical imperative to abide by the highest research standards, including maintaining up-to-date knowledge of advanced techniques of data analysis and presentation. That done (no mean feat), is it sufficient for researchers to publish their results, thereby advancing knowledge, to be responsive to the principle of beneficence? Brown and Hedges (Chapter 24) suggest an ethical imperative to publish: "Peer-reviewed publications are clearly the most rewarding and rewarded avenues of publication, and the pursuit of them in the best possible journals is the ethical responsibility of one who is committed to a life of scholarship" (p. 382). Johnson and Bullock (Chapter 14) extend Brown and Hedges (Chapter 24) delineation of responsibility by adding the imperative to share at a more basic level by making data available for reuse and reanalysis.

What are the ethical implications of this imperative for applied or action researchers? Do they also have an obligation to publish in order to contribute to knowledge building? And, if they do not have such an obligation, does that suggest that applied and action research is unscientific or lacking potential usefulness to other researchers and members of the broader community? It is our belief that action research is an invaluable adjunct to other forms of research and, while not always having the opportunity to publish in research-oriented journals, action researchers see an ethical imperative in appropriate dissemination of their work. Similarly, other researchers share a responsibility to seek out research that is not necessarily published in scholarly journals as it is relevant to their own work.

While Brown and Hedges (Chapter 24) promote the imperative to publish in academic journals, they also advocate responsibility to participants as well as the scientific community with regard to making findings available and, as such, contribute to consensus among the authors of this *Handbook* that participants' access to the results of their contribution is a basic right and, hence, a matter of justice as well as a potential matter of beneficence. Expanding the concept of language to include visual representation, Newton (Chapter 23) perceives communication of findings as the third of a tripartite set of researcher responsibilities to "*perceive* clearly at the moment of interaction, to *translate* authentically during the moment of analysis, and to *frame* a reasonably equivalent mode at the moment of re-presentation" (p. 354).

Barnes (Chapter 29) extends the communication mandate further still, indicating that another aspect of accountability is the wide-ranging dissemination of the research products in a variety of accessible formats to stimulate campaigns and legislative action.

Do researchers have an ethical imperative for using their research as an instrument of social change? This question does not have a simple answer. Some researchers place themselves squarely in the position of accepting this as a moral imperative. Others reject it for a variety of reasons: that it is outside the scope of the researcher's responsibility, that researchers cannot control the multitude of variables that facilitate or prevent social transformation, or that it is impossible to know the effects of one's research in advance. Because of the question's interest yet its lack of fit with the narrow definition of benevolence/nonmalevolence, we will leave it aside until the conclusion of this chapter.

RESPECT, HONESTY, AND FAIRNESS: BUILDING TRUST

Kitchener and Kitchener (Chapter 1) ascribe specific connotations to respect and trust as ethical research principles. Respect is defined in terms of allowing the research participants to act freely in terms of choosing to participate in and/or withdraw from research and trust as keeping promises and being honest. Other volume contributors define the ethical connotations of respect and trust in cultural terms. For example, Moewaka Barnes et al. (Chapter 28) state that Maori culture views respect in terms of researchers beginning research by explaining who they are and where they are from, that is, their affiliations, tribal and otherwise, including the name of the research organization. They then are obliged to explain the purpose of their research, who owns and benefits from the information, and what the dissemination processes are. Disclosure of the purpose of the research is also an important IRB requirement, but, for Maori, it is seen as more than what the researchers want to know and encompasses the researchers' personal reasons for doing the research; what their agendas are and evidence that they are to be trusted (see also, Cram, Chapter 20).

Moewaka Barnes et al. (Chapter 28) and Cram (Chapter 20) also discuss the ethical importance of developing relationships over time. Proposals are often developed over many years of engagement, informal and formal. The more closely researchers are involved with the researched, the more likely it is that they can be responsive and adaptable. Close relationships with the local community can ensure that the appropriate people will be supportive and able to provide expertise, endorsement, and guidance for the research.

What is the meaning of trust in studies that are conducted in communities that are hostile, acrimonious towards each other, and/or who intend each other harm? For example, suppose a researcher is studying people who do violence to gay men or lesbian women or studying a white supremacist group. What does it mean to understand culture and build trust in such a context? Irwin, writing of peace polling in Chapter 17, indicates that researcher impartiality and openness is the key. Others, such as Mertens et al. (Chapter 6), engaged in transformative work hold that a partial answer comes from an understanding of the notion of privilege and the interrogation of unearned privilege. They cite Kendall (2006) who suggested that researchers focus on studying the societal norms and structures that support discrimination and oppression as a way of revealing how power holders oppress people and working from a multiplicity of vantage points. For those who are white, Kendall instructed that studying "whiteness" as a metaphor for power that oppresses is a necessary part of understanding discrimination and oppression, thereby making visible the tensions associated with relationships between researchers and communities, especially when the research focuses on oppressive societal systems. Hence, rather than focusing on building trust with "oppressors," the researcher focuses on exposing the oppressive structures and, thereby, building trust with those who are oppressed.

Like Irwin (Chapter 17), Howe and MacGillivary (Chapter 36) indicate that researchers develop trust by avoiding perceived bias or favoritism. Thus, they prescribe caution regarding how and to what extent researchers allow community members in the "inner circle" of the research process. In their description of studies using a deliberative democratic framework, they explain that "It would have been disastrous in either study for stakeholders to be included as members of the research team" (p. 575) as the researchers' credibility would be compromised if they were perceived as favoring one faction over another. The deliberative democratic approach used by Howe and MacGillivary "requires embracing the positive obligation vis-à-vis autonomy to arrange the conditions of deliberation so as to equalize power and to, as appropriate, transform existing values and beliefs by challenging them with competing views through a process of 'critical dialogue'" (p. 577).

Several questions serve to stimulate continued thought on the matter of respect, fidelity, and building trust. For instance, "What are the challenges associated with establishing ethical interpersonal relationships in collaborative research?" "What are the ethical strategies for determining ownership of the research data and results?" In some cases, prior negotiations among the researcher partners, participants, and community members can be productive in terms of power and responsibility and means by which those who enter into the relationship with less power can gain support. Silka's (Chapter 22) experience with the cycle of challenges to be met within community partnerships and Brydon-Miller's (Chapter 16) with participatory action research are instructive in this regard. Ryen's (Chapter 15) intimate examination of her shifting relationship with her primary informant and research associate illustrates changes that occur over time as trust is negotiated, given, and earned.

Some of the questions raised above have been concretized by regulations and codes of conduct, and here lie the concerns of most of this *Handbook's* authors and an opportunity to push the margins of our understanding by inquiring as to the relationship between concrete codes and abstract principles, aided by heeding voices that have heretofore not been accurately or adequately represented in formalized ethical codes. Here, too, we have the opportunity to explore the deeper meaning of concepts such as "informed consent," "coercion," "confidentiality," and "anonymity" as they move from abstract to concrete and to promote continued dialogue as to their meaning in different contexts. In the process, Clegg and Slife (Chapter 2), as postmodern theorists, encourage us to question any assumption where there is some independent set of acceptable ethical codes that we might discover by means of this process. They indicate that what we are likely to learn, instead, is more about the singularity of context and about the necessity (and perhaps the joy) of meeting each new situation with full access to our past ethical and professional experience and an open mind.

JUSTICE: ADDRESS DIVERSITY

In Kitchener and Kitchener's (Chapter 1) description of ethical principles, the concept of justice is tied to sharing the burden of participating in research and equitable distribution of the benefits derived from it. They note that codes forbidding discrimination on the basis of characteristics such as age, gender, race, ethnicity, national origin, disability, and religion are in accord with the principle of justice. Based on this principle, Is it sufficient to adopt policies of nondiscrimination or is it incumbent on researchers to address issues of diversity in their studies? If, as we believe, the latter is so, how might that be accomplished? For example, it is common in social science research to "over-sample" from groups such as homeless persons and low-income individuals who are known to be difficult to recruit or who are difficult to contact for follow-up. How does this measure up to the justice principle given that more people from these groups than others are given the opportunity to participate yet fewer are likely to actually do so? As another example, college and university students are overwhelmingly more likely to participate in social science research than any other demographic group. As educated adults, they are also in an advantaged position with regard to being able to access the results of research and any benefits accruing from them. Is this in accord with the justice principle in that those who take the most risk are able to receive the most benefits? Or does the practice of maintaining a university participant pool limited to students perpetuate injustice by denying participation to others?

Having ourselves perhaps oversampled from among applied researchers who are less likely to rely on participant pools than their basic-researcher siblings, the questions above are not questions asked by contributors to this *Handbook*. Rather, their concerns tend to be practical ones faced during research activity in the community.

As feminists, Brabeck and Brabeck (Chapter 3) remind us that within the group of people who identify as women, there are wide variations in age, sexual orientation, socioeconomic status, education, ethnicity, health, and so on. Since no two women are the same, the basis of gender discrimination needs to be addressed in its full complexity. Similarly, disability researchers note the ubiquitous presence of people with complex arrays of disabilities and strengths, each of which may necessitate different approaches, methodologies, and attention to differing subcultures (Sullivan, Chapter 5). Dodd (Chapter 30) and Mertens, Fraser, and Heimlich (2008) query the ethics of oversimplifying questions of gender, asking if categories of gender need to be expanded to include lesbian, gay, transsexual, bisexual, and queer, and being concerned about the injustice of not doing so while, at the same time, being concerned about the risks involved in potential participants "outing" themselves given the potential for harm to come to them.

Language is another critical dimension of diversity with covert and overt ethical implications. Brabeck and Brabeck (Chapter 3), Moewaka Barnes et al. (Chapter 28), Vargas and Montoya (Chapter 31), and Mertens et al. (Chapter 6) discuss power and status issues surrounding choice of language in the context of research with linguistic minorities. Matsumoto and Jones (Chapter 21) and Sharma (Chapter 27) discuss the ethical implications of linguistic and cultural competence when doing research abroad.

To look at the issues with greater abstraction, Mertens et al. (Chapter 6) ask the following questions from their transformative stance:

- What are the important dimensions of diversity to include in research in order to give accurate and appropriate representation to groups who have been pushed to the margins of those with more privilege in society?

- What is the ethical responsibility of the researcher to identify and appropriately address those dimensions of diversity?

- What is the ethical cost of ignoring or inappropriately representing the dimensions of diversity in research? (p. 97)

Their focus on participation and representation is complicated by increasing globalization that renders the traditional categories of culture, nationality, and ethnicity far more complex than in the past (Matsumoto & Jones, Chapter 21; Stake & Rivzi, Chapter 33). As Kitchener and Kitchener (Chapter 1) indicate, however, we are obliged to examine not only the ways in which participants are recruited and depicted but also fairness in the receipt of benefits from research results. Few Handbook contributions do so. One exception is that of Matsumoto and Jones (Chapter 21) who identify as an ethical obligation the postpublication and postpresentation necessity of following up on the uses made of their work such that neither findings nor participants be misrepresented by others who cite their work.

Other exceptions include Brydon-Miller (Chapter 16) who, as an action researcher, feels obliged to take part in action as directed by the findings of her participatory research; Silka (Chapter 22) who, in her ongoing research relationship with a community, senses similar obligations; and indigenous researcher-writers who work in their own community among others with whom they have ongoing personal and lineage relationships entailing obligations to see the implications of their research bear fruit beyond those entailed by the research per se. Finally, Ryen (Chapter 15) discusses her obligations to her primary informant/ participant/research associate/friend beyond the point of completion of any specific research assignment and Brabeck and Brabeck (Chapter 3) and Lincoln (Chapter 10) indicate that participants may make requests of researchers that the latter feel obliged to meet outside the research setting. However, these obligations do not, strictly speaking, fall within the category of benefits of the results of the research itself.

Also, not precisely within the category the Kitcheners limn, but of much interest in codes of researcher conduct, comes the question of researcher's obligation in the case that illegal or quasi-legal behaviors are being studied or are discovered by chance in the process of unrelated research (Sharma, Chapter 27). Practitioner codes of ethics place primary value on anonymity and confidentiality except in cases of danger to a client's self or others and are advised to inform clients that the information that they disclose will be confidential except under those two circumstances and whatever policy guidelines have been set by the provider agency—policies that must be disclosed to the client and discussed with him or her. How differently, if at all, should consideration of the research setting influence the implications of these guidelines? Especially with potentially illegal behaviors, what is the ethical responsibility to be truthful with the participants about the purpose and use of the research findings? Can a case be made that a research participant engaged in illegal or dangerous behavior will be able to benefit from the results of the research? What are the potential ethical conflicts for researchers who witness illegal behavior? Under what conditions, if any, is it ethical to study such behavior at all?

INFORMED CONSENT, AN EXAMPLE OF NONMALEFICENCE AND RESPECT

Obtaining informed consent, according to Western professional codes of ethics, requires that the potential participant understand the risks and benefits of participating, that he or she does not experience coercion, that he or she has the ability to withdraw from the research at any time, and usually, that he or she sign a form that was approved by a review board. Deconstructing this complex concept, we find it entails several aspects that elicit ethical concerns.

The first of these is the signature itself. As Ntseane (Chapter 19), Sharma (Chapter 27), and Moewaka Barnes et al. (Chapter 28) remind us, signing a piece of paper is a very

Western way of documenting consent, and it can be viewed as insulting in cultures where either one's word should be believed or where history has shown that putting one's name on a paper can have disastrous consequences. Moreover, for participants in studies of illegal or criminal behaviors, Sharma questions whether the participants or, for that matter, the researchers truly understand the risks involved. Writing about her experience studying Hawala, a form of informal value transfer system, in India where it is illegal but, unlike in the United States, noncriminal, she writes,

> While studying Hawala in India, researchers run into difficulties of, first, finding someone to do an adequate translation of a consent form and, then, into questions about why a respondent should sign anything if he or she is ready to talk to the researcher anyway. (p. 434)

Similar responses to requests for signed consent are reported among American Indians (LaFrance & Crazy Bull, Chapter 9; Vargas & Montoya, Chapter 31), Africans (Chilisa, Chapter 26; Ntseane, Chapter 19), and undocumented workers (Brabeck & Brabeck, Chapter 3). La France and Crazy Bull (Chapter 9), Vargas and Montoya (Chapter 31), Szala-Meneok (Chapter 32), Sullivan (Chapter 5), and Barnes (Chapter 29) raise questions for those physically unable to sign due to issues of age, infirmity, disability, or literacy status.

The second issue has to do with comprehension of the consent document itself as well as the demands of the research protocol, its risks, and potential benefits. Vargas and Montoya (Chapter 31) emphasize the importance of reading levels and nuanced interpretations of documents to suit geographic language differences when working with Latino or Native American communities (e.g., Spanish is not the same Spanish in Costa Rica and Puerto Rico). The same issues occur with regard to immigrants and linguistic minority communities worldwide. Sharma's (Chapter 27) experience in India where there are hundreds of different languages reminds us that as both a practical and ethical issue, respondents signing consent forms in different languages may not be consenting to exactly the same thing due to linguistic incommensurability. A similar situation is also found in the cross-cultural research experiences of Matsumoto and Jones (Chapter 21). In developing regions, there are individuals and groups who are not only unschooled but whose mother tongue also remains unwritten.

The third issue is that of who needs to be involved in obtaining informed consent. In the West, it is generally assumed that, barring exclusion due to youth or disability, consent is to be obtained solely from each individual participant. Based on I/we relationships of her Botswana home, however, Chilisa (Chapter 26) identifies four types of consent: individual consent, community consent, group consent, and collective consent. Ntseane (Chapter 19), also from Botswana, provides illustrations of these levels in a description of the culturally appropriate consent process that she used for her dissertation. It included talking to and obtaining verbal permission from the tribal chiefs, the community as a whole, specific groups of individuals from whom she wanted to collect data, and their coworkers and families. Vargas and Montoya (Chapter 31) similarly describe the need to recognize cultural consent processes in Native American communities, mentioning the tribe and extended family members who have a major role in making decisions, especially about children. Szala-Meneok (Chapter 32) raises the issue of re-consent in situations of longitudinal design, apparent/potential loss of interest in the research topic, or changes in the physical, developmental, or mental condition of participants. She suggests obtaining consultation and/or outside assessment in the process of re-consent to avoid conflict of interest on the part of the researcher or feeling of coercion on the part of the participant. There is, this suggests, an ethical need to be proactive in assuring participants' understanding of their ability to withdraw at any time.

In the initial recruitment, if a researcher plans to provide compensation to the participants, then ethical tensions surface in terms of what is fair payment and what is coercive. Vargas and Montoya (Chapter 31) suggest the need for critical examination of the issues of power and privilege and the potential for overt and covert coercion both in a general sense and, specifically, when the participant is a young person, whether the compensation should go to the child or the parent. That is, if a young person in a family in poverty is given cash for participation, even as little as $25 can upset the economic balance within the family. Brabeck and Brabeck (Chapter 3) question whether an undocumented mother in an abusive relationship can effectively give fully informed consent to participate in research when the project is associated with a source of assistance. If even a very small amount of money is offered, might this be a form of coercion for women who have no income? If such women agree to participate in the research because they need the money, do they place themselves at additional risk from an abusive partner? Is it ethical to withhold offers of money to such women when similar offers are made to more affluent participants with less scrutiny?

Looking at the issue of coercion from a non-Western stance, we might also ask about a possible conflict between consent and coercion in the context of research in societies where group consent is the norm. When the community gives consent, does that place the individuals from whom a researcher might want to collect data into a coercive situation wherein they cannot refuse to participate?

CONFIDENTIALITY: AN EXAMPLE OF BENEFICENCE AND RESPECT

Codes of ethics and IRB regulations also concretize respect and caring for participants' welfare as confidentiality with regard to the participants' involvement in research. Brabeck and Brabeck (Chapter 3) present the rationale for confidentiality as protection with reference to a study of women who have experienced partner abuse. They hold that, in situations such as this one, the researcher should conceal names even of those participants who express a preference to use their names because of the researchers' deeper understanding of safety issues.

Dodd (Chapter 30) provides an example that points to the tension between the need to increase visibility, knowledge, and understanding of LGBTQ individuals and limiting the risks posed by research participation. The ethical need to protect the anonymity and confidentiality of individual members of a population often targeted for violence is obvious. Less clear would be the situation in which the community as a whole benefits, but segments of the community do not. In another example, "a researcher adds a question about sexual orientation or gender identity to a 'benign' study about obesity or sleep habits, [and] there are instantly increased safety and risk issues, which may vary depending on geographic region and study context" (Dodd, Chapter 30, p. 478). Depending on the results of the study and the context in which they are presented, on the one hand, there are long-term benefits to regularizing members of the LGBTQ community as those who may or may not have problems shared by the rest of the community; on the other hand, there is the risk of adding just one or two more indicators of problems to an already stigmatized group. Here, however, the risk is to the group and not at the individual level.

Other researchers in other contexts raise questions about the established code that places priority on anonymity and confidentiality. For example, Ntseane (Chapter 19) studied women business owners in Africa who were at little risk if their identities were revealed. She indicated that the women she interviewed wanted their names used because it was "their story" and they saw her research as a way of documenting their story for future generations. She raises the question, If researchers use the names of published scholars in their literature reviews, then why not give such specific name recognition to those who provide the data that will be published in the same article? (See p. 302, this volume.)

In Maori culture, a premium is placed on being able to have face-to-face communications that publicly attribute stories to individuals (Moewaka Barnes et al., Chapter 28). Hence, the notion of anonymity and confidentiality is antithetical to their belief that individuals must name and identify themselves. The Maori ethical code is based on a relationship ethic that may "clash with an ethics committee approach" because relationships are an "ongoing process of negotiation, rather than a one-off decision" (p. 447). LaFrance and Crazy Bull (Chapter 9) provide an American Indian example that also prompts questions regarding whether the respect and concern concretized as confidentiality can, in fact, be rightly treated as an all-or-nothing category. As a research participant, one may feel quite differently about whether information about oneself is shared with other participants, with friends and family, with strangers, and in published form.

At the other extreme from Botswana, Native American, and Maori writers, Stake and Rizvi (Chapter 33) argue categorically that researchers need to be both cautious about promising personal privacy and then to take all possible precautions in order to provide it. They write that "ethically, the researcher should not hear what the secret holder fails to protect" (p. 530) and that "except in special circumstances, a researcher should not know what any member of the family does not want known" (p. 530). Using the example of information provided by an individual about a child born out of wedlock, Stake and Rizvi maintain that such information should be kept secret on the principle that family unit should be privileged over the individual. "We think that researchers have a responsibility to dissuade participants from sharing information that is potentially harmful to others—and if the participant cannot be dissuaded, the researcher has at least the responsibility to listen without hearing" (p. 530).

This provocative statement may or may not stand the test of the abstract principle of "respect" for participants in its assumption that it is the researcher who knows what should and should not be told. Yet we join Stake and Rivzi (Chapter 33) in agreement when they take the middle ground between modernism and postmodernism in their stance with regard to ethical principles and the codes that are derived from them, stating,

> the principles articulated in codes of ethics are relevant but do not take us very far. We recognize our obligation for full disclosure. We want to treat all parties equitably. And we want to protect an institution that is challenging social injustice. The three cannot be served simultaneously. We are caught between these three principles. In such a situation, *ethical behavior is not so much a matter of following principles as of balancing competing principles* [italics added]. So, for example, disclosure may have to be tempered to achieve social justice, and the institution may need to receive criticism to protect deserving individuals.
>
> In spaces characterized by stretched boundaries, different cultural traditions, and competing interests, it may be more useful to have multiple codes, expressing ethical concern from different perspectives, to illuminate actual problems. (p. 529)

At the same time, we continue to be grateful to the postmodernists who, as described by Clegg and Slife (Chapter 2) write, "Postmodern thought provides us not with clear-cut answers to the problems of research ethics but, rather, with challenging, instructive, and transforming dialogues that help us think about the ethical implications of research" (p. 27).

While postmodernists urge us to question the clarity of direction provided to researchers by ethical principles such as beneficence and justice, other scholars ask a more fundamental question concerning the universality of the values that underlie these principles.

VALUES: UNIVERSAL OR NOT UNIVERSAL?

And so we turn to this critical and contentious area of thought with important implications for the usefulness of ethical principles related to the universality of the values that underlie the principles (see Ryen, Chapter 15). As we have seen, the principles that Kitchener and Kitchener (Chapter 1) propose are open to a variety of interpretations. Clegg and Slife (Chapter 2) argue that not only are the ethical principles not universal, but it is impossible to conduct research that is "value-free." They contend that the assumptions and philosophies underlying modernist research often involve values that remain unexamined. They suggest that advances in understanding the ethics of research will occur if researchers identify their values as much as possible before, during, and after engaging in research. We would add the necessity of understanding other researchers' values in addition to our own, a particularly crucial endeavor where partnerships are involved.

African scholars write of value systems that contrast with Western understandings and, by doing so, provide non-African researchers a new perspective on the meaning of ethical principles. For example, Chilisa (Chapter 26) describes *Ubuntu* as an African value system that privileges an I/we relationship in contrast to the Western concept of the I/you individualistic perspective (Louw, 2001; Khoza, 1994). Among other implications of *Ubuntu* are the following:

> It informs how researchers from developed countries should relate with researchers from former colonized societies and how researchers from all worlds should relate with the researched. *Ubuntu* underscores an I/we relationship where there is connectedness with living and nonliving things; there is brotherhood, sisterhood, guesthood, and community togetherness. Consequently, relationships are not linear but involve circular, repetitive, back and forth movements. For indigenous African communities, circular, back and forth movements allow us (speaking as an indigenous researcher) to go back into the past and invoke metaphors from our culture that help us build ethics protocols that promote social justice and respect for postcolonial/indigenous communities. We go back and forth to the humiliation of colonialism, slavery, and imperialism, to deconstruct and decolonize the archival knowledge that continues to masquerade as "common sense knowledge" and "facts" about us as lesser peoples. (p. 408)

> A person is because of others. Communality, collectivity, human unity, and pluralism are implicit in this principle. (p. 413)

Having pushed the moral sense to its point of vulnerability in the form of the limitations of any one individual's experience and organization of that sense, and having pushed ethical principles to their limits in terms of their vulnerability to being diverted to other purposes, for example, protection of the institution or profession, and the apparent lack of universality of values, we ask whether it is possible to identify unitary concepts at the next level of abstraction, ethical theory. That is, is there a hypothesis or integrated set of hypotheses regarding the nature of ethics that can enhance the understanding of social science researchers regarding how to behave ethically in the collection, processing, and reporting of data, the ethical treatment of research participants, and how to respond ethically to situations imposed by preexisting social contexts, particularly those involving power differentials?

◆ Ethical Theory

According to Kitchener and Kitchener (Chapter 1), among traditional theories of ethics, candidates for greatest assistance in guiding modern ethicists of social science research include the deontology of Kant's categorical imperative and Ross's "prima facie duties," which are "obligations that can only be overridden by other ethical considerations" (p. 18); virtue theory, which assumes with Aristotle that humans develop innate moral character when placed in a salutary moral environment; contractarianism or contractualism, which assumes a hypothetical agreement in which certain rights are sacrificed in favor of rational universalizability that, if observed by all, would offer protection from a life that, according to the oft-quoted Thomas Hobbes, life would be "solitary, poor, nasty, brutish, and short"; natural law or natural rights theory, which postulates an extant moral order underlying human morality and human rights; utilitarianism, which holds that the morality of actions is assessed on the basis of their outcomes; and the ethics of care, which emphasizes the duty to nurture others.

From among these, Kitchener and Kitchener (Chapter 1) identify utilitarianism as one of the pillars of the 20th century research ethics in its two forms. Action utilitarianism holds that "action is morally right that produces the greatest good for the greatest number of individuals" (p. 17). And a second version, rule-utilitarianism, holds that "action is morally right that is an instance of a general rule, the establishment of which would produce the greatest good for the greatest number of individuals" (p. 17). The other pillar of modern research ethics is deontology as represented by Immanuel Kant and W. D. Ross. Kant's Categorical Imperative (1781/1964) is "always act in such a way that one could will the maxim of one's action to become a universal law of human conduct" (p. 17) and its corollary, "treat humanity, whether others or yourself, always as an end and never merely as a means" (pp. 17–18) are easily detected in regulatory and professional codes' treatment of the relationships between researchers and research participants. Since the 1960s, however, Kitchener and Kitchener (Chapter 1) observe that virtue theory reemerged as a strong candidate for foundational (or pillar) status, only to be followed by multiple competitors. The ethics of care, for example, have been particularly influential among feminist researchers.

Contractarian and utilitarian thought are readily identified in regulatory control of research and in professional codes of research ethics. The idea that the relationship between the researcher and the participant, although not usually monetary, is a contractual one in which the participant makes some sort of sacrifice, giving of his or her (minimally) time and attention based on his or her belief and assurance that the researcher, in turn, will turn that sacrifice to knowledge, which may eventually help the participant directly or indirectly. IRBs buy into this formulation by examining research proposals not only for direct protection of participants from harm but also for protection of participants from frivolous waste of time by approving only those that appear likely to be able to answer the researcher's worthwhile questions. That is, there is an implicit assumption that meritorious research can be identified on the basis of the usefulness of its outcomes. The best research, by extension, is that which helps (or at the IRB level is most likely to help) the most people or, if it helps fewer people, it helps them by a greater amount.

Other ethical theorists have sharpened the focus to more explicitly stimulate ethical thinking in terms of social justice. Simons (2006, cited in Mertens et al., Chapter 6) identifies rights-based and social justice theories of ethics that are commensurate with the transformative axiological assumptions. Rights-based theories, grounded in natural rights philosophy and a democratized Aristotelian belief that assumes innate moral character in all, implies that researchers ought to justify their actions on the basis that every person must be treated with dignity and respect and that the avoidance of harm must be the primary principle. The social justice theory of ethics takes the rights-based theory to a group or societal level (House, 1993) leading to an awareness of the need to redress inequalities by giving precedence, or at least equal weight, to the voices of the least-advantaged groups in society. The implicit goal of inclusion of those who have been denied access to power is an accurate representation of this viewpoint as well as offering support to the less advantaged in terms of their being able to take an active agent role in social change (Mertens, 2009). Rights-based theories are reflected in theoretical positions that shifted the depiction of people with disabilities, women, and people of color from groups with "problems" to a sociocultural understanding of them as groups who were systematically discriminated against in ways that denied members their civil and individual rights (Bledsoe & Hopson, Chapter 25; Brabeck & Brabeck, Chapter 3; Sullivan, Chapter 5; Thomas, Chapter 4). It perhaps follows from a utilitarian point of view that research that helps the disadvantaged is particularly meritorious because any improvement in the conditions of the disadvantaged represents a greater good than improving the conditions of the ordinary person.

But what are we to make of the Categorical Imperative (1781/1964, cited in Kitchener & Kitchener, Chapter 1)? While the admonition to "treat humanity, whether others or yourself, always as an end and never merely as a means" is sufficiently vague (and sufficiently Aristotelian) as to cause no difficulty, that to "always act in such a way that one could will the maxim of one's action to become a universal law of human conduct" is rather problematic and, at the practical level, acting on it is likely to result in major areas of disagreement in research involving actors with differing cultural backgrounds and worldviews. An example from the *Handbook* that is particularly striking is that offered by Vargas and Montoya (Chapter 31) as they puzzle over issues of consent and assent to participate in research as they affect adolescents. The authors consider not only the cognitive developmental capacity of the child, the type of study, and the context in which participants may be recruited but also the customs and mores of the community and the cultural practices of the family. They highlight ethical tensions that arise in situations in which an adolescent is able to understand the potential risks and benefits of a particular piece of research and the parents are, for whatever reason, less able to understand them, in communities with a norm of parental or community control. Should parents make the decision lest family norms be undermined? From the parental point of view, the position of Vargas and Montoya fulfills the categorical imperative. But from the point of view of the adolescent, does it still do so?

While study of the historical process of Western ethical reasoning can place social science researchers' ethical decision making in a context that can save the researcher from repeated reinvention of rhetorical argument, it appears that the answers to standardized ethical dilemmas are only suggestive at best. Moreover, they are bound by time, place, and history. The Kitcheners (Chapter 1) allow that the latter portion of the 20th century and the beginning of the 21st have brought more variation into ethical thought than was present in the preceding period. The prominence of the ethics of care in feminist research ethics and community partnerships is but one manifestation of this phenomenon. We predict that increasing involvement of non-Western researchers in social science will bring yet other ideas and values into the dialogue.

In the interim, we find a wealth of theories, each of which offers thought-provoking and useful ideas, all of which offer an overarching concept regarding the nature of humanity and, hence, a basis for broad application to the ethical problems involved in social science research. However, (and we know this brief summary has not done any theory justice), we also find that none of them appears to have the potential to unify ethical thought in the social sciences across paradigms and that the conceptual distance between theory and day-to-day action in the field is too great to point to specific practices. If we are to search for unity, we must look to the highest level of abstraction in the Kitcheners' model, metaethics; if we are to search for best practices, we must look lower in the Kitcheners' schematic to the personal moral sense. This journey reflects the wisdom of the African view of circularity.

♦ Metaethics

As we approach the topic of metaethics, we come full circle in this journey of reflection on the structure of social research ethics. We have contemplated the need for and limitations of a personal moral sense, codes and regulations, principles, and theories. We see the value of a range of ethical theories that provide insights into the meaning of ethics as they stand in contrast to each other. At times, the insights suggest complementarities; at other times, they reveal conflicts. And so, the train of which Stake and Rizvi (Chapter 33) write, is "chugging along"—but is it, in their words, to a "lonely coast line" or to a realm rich with promise for enhanced understanding and applications in social science research?

Kitchner and Kitchner (Chapter 1) suggest a possible pathway through this complex country side, noting that the standard model for metaethics in social science research ethics is *principlism,* according to which there are several midrange ethical principles that are "'freestanding' and individually warranted—for instance, autonomy and beneficence" (p. 19). "(S)elf-sufficient and not in need of justification by higher-order ethical theory; however, they do justify lower-level ethical rules—for example, confidentiality" (p. 19). The advantage of "ethical theory as a useful heuristic aid in making an ethical decision about how to resolve such a conflict" (p. 19). They warn, however, that "ethical theory does not deductively support a univocal decision about which principle takes preeminence" (p. 19).

The Kitcheners indicate that contemplation of ethics in the social science research context is neither a bottom-up (starting with personal moral sense and moving to metaethics), nor a top-down adventure. It is rather one that is stimulated by movement at all levels of abstraction and, hence, portends intense thought and discussion.

♦ Frontiers of Research Ethics: Evolving Questions

Most of the *Handbook* chapters address tensions rooted in the historical legacy of social science research ethics. However, researchers are faced with many unknowns given the rapidly changing nature of society through globalization, increased linkages between research and public policy, and advances in technology. And so, they find themselves in the position to consider new and, as yet, largely unexplored issues in research ethics that arise because of these new frontiers. They raise questions that range from the abstract to the concrete—questions such as, Are we in a place of greater clarity of ethical principles and theories or are we, as postmodernists claim, in new territory marked by uncertainty, with fewer guideposts, and no clear-cut answers to the problems of research ethics? Do we stand at the frontier armed only with challenging, instructive, and transforming dialogues that help us think about the ethical implications of research (Clegg & Slife, Chapter 2), but do not tell us how to find our way?

When Stake and Rizvi (Chapter 33) take us into the global realm, they ask questions evolving from their view of the emergent global context.

How do we, for example, research spaces that do not have any clear boundaries and where social relations potentially span vast distances? How do we take into account the distribution and dynamics of power whose contours potentially involve the entire globe? How do we provide accounts of social meaning when these are not linked to any specific community? How do we study social inequalities when its causes do not necessarily reside within the community that is the object of our research? In other words, how do we address the conceptual difficulties that inevitably arise in social research when the very constitution of *the social* cannot be easily defined? (pp. 524–525)

Fisher et al. (Chapter 35), who inform us about the preparation of new researchers whose contexts will be at these new frontiers, pose questions about developing moral and ethical sensitivities appropriate to the research context.

How knowledgeable are social science faculty in the ethics of their discipline? Can mentors who did not receive sufficient guidance in the RCR [responsible conduct of research] transmit appropriate and comprehensive research ethics knowledge to their mentees? What kind of training and experience on the part of mentors is necessary to prepare them to transmit best practices in RCR? To what degree do professors discuss research ethics in classroom courses, labs, and research apprenticeships? How do tenure and promotion policies support or discourage faculty from focusing on ethics in their own research and that of their students? And finally, how does the larger academic environment, including institutional regulations, policies, and practices facilitate or impede effective mentoring of RCR? (pp. 558–559)

They also ask how mentors can reinforce the concept of justice by ensuring equitable treatment of their protégés regardless of gender, ethnicity, or age. We would add to their questions: How does a professor, who was trained in the past, mentor students, junior faculty, and research associates, and, indeed, prepare himself or herself to face the issues such as those raised by Stake and Rivzi (Chapter 33), Burbules (Chapter 34), and others that address a very different future of increased Internet connectivity and massive migration?

Howe and MacGillivary (Chapter 36) use the deliberative democratic stance as a platform to argue for inclusion and fair participation in the political process. How, they ask, can researchers demonstrate

> good faith critical dialogue, whereby they (1) use "public reason" by avoiding reasoning that others could not find acceptable, for example, sectarian reasoning and (2) are open to revising their initially preferred policies and practices as a result of deliberating with others. The ideal goal of the process is to reach conclusions that will be accepted as reasonable (not necessarily correct) by all concerned. (p. 566)

And at the same time, they raise issues of the difficulty of demarcating the line between advocacy and research, another piece of fertile ground on which to continue our contemplation of the meaning of ethics. These are provocative questions and deserve careful consideration in the social research community.

The fuzzy boundary between research and advocacy identified by Howe and MacGillivary (Chapter 36) has perhaps the distinction of being the most contentious ethical issue to arise from a thorough reading of the *Handbook*. It entails not only all levels of ethical structure described by the Kitcheners, but also the incommensurability of the modern and postmodern ethical paradigms. In an avowedly simplistic dichotomy, we here explain our understanding of the issues.

According to social science research ethics rooted in the positivist tradition, advocacy is emphatically not a research function. It is the researcher's obligation to approach scientific questions methodically, keeping his or her human passions at bay such that, once collected and analyzed, the data can speak for themselves. The Platonic ideal, though known not to be achievable, is to perceive the shadow on the back of the cave with as much acuity and measurement as necessary in order to construct an accurate representation of reality. Thus, from this perspective, advocacy is seen as being outside the realm of research. Rather, it is in the realm of the citizen. Of course, researchers are also citizens; hence, they are obliged to give serious attention to both these functions. Consensus does not exist with regard to the extent of separation that researchers need to keep between their two roles. From a more positivistic perspective, the closest the researcher ethically comes to advocacy is to point out the degree of likelihood that a specific course of action has the potential to produce a specific effect (as in making recommendations at the end of a research study). To avoid appearances of advocacy, such researchers are encouraged to engage in specific processes and procedures such as self-scrutiny to identify their own biases, keeping process notes, and soliciting rigorous peer review. However, other paradigmatic perspectives suggest that a more activist role on the part of researchers is necessary if they are to consider their work ethical.

In accord with the postmodern paradigm, since the researcher cannot really know anything about his or her subject that is not affected by his or her idiosyncratic view of the problem and any information or context bearing on it, there is no reason not to advocate, as one point of view is as valid or invalid as another. In a democratic context, the researcher's view of what action should be taken competes in the marketplace of ideas with the ideas of others.

Thus, as one example, we might debate the ethical implications of the action of Kenneth and Mamie Clark whose testimony in the Supreme Court case of *Brown v. Board of Education* (1954) resulted in orders to desegregate U.S. schools. The Clarks testified that their research with children asked to identify which of two dolls, identical except for skin color, was nice or bad and pretty or ugly indicated that black children, agreeing that the white doll was the nice and pretty one, showed low self-esteem in African American children. The cause, it was argued, was segregated schooling and the solution proposed was integration. In the Supreme Court, the Clarks' testimony was convincing. Desegregation was ordered and, in hindsight, the benefits of desegregation are far from those envisioned. Results included immediate violence, short-term benefits from the opportunity for African Americans to attend schools that were better equipped and had smaller class sizes, and the opportunity for Americans of European descent to learn with and from people about whose lives they previously had little awareness. In the long term, American public schools are more segregated now than they were in the 1950s (e.g., Paley & Schulte, 2007) and social class segregation has increased.

Recurrent scientific and contentiously political reexamination of the Clarks' research includes claims and counterclaims regarding whether or not their testimony misrepresented or misinterpreted their research results, regardless of whether their subjective assessment of the effects of segregation may have been accurate.[5] Was their research-related behavior ethical? Might our assessment of its ethical qualities be different if they had begun their research with the clear intention of providing advocacy in favor of desegregation and had used methods and/or measures more likely to confirm their subjective assessment? Would our assessment change if they had been investigative reporters rather than psychologists? To what extent are they responsible for the long-term consequences of the failure of desegregation to bring about a just educational system?

With the emergence of voices of indigenous scholars and those who openly advocate for the underserved and underrepresented, the future considerations of research ethics are given more opportunity for critical and deep reflection (e.g., Cram, Chapter 20; LaFrance & Crazy Bull, Chapter 9; Moewaka Barnes et al., Chapter 28; Ntseane, Chapter 19; Vargas & Montoya, Chapter 31). These voices establish a need to be inclusive of questions that go beyond those presented thus far. For example, Chilisa (Chapter 26) expands the list of questions to include the following:

[How do researchers challenge and] resist dominant discourse that marginalize those who suffer oppression? (p. 417)

Have the voices of the researched been captured in a way that the researched recognize themselves, know themselves and would like others to know them? (p. 417)

What psychological harm, humiliation, embarrassment, and other losses if any have these theories and body of knowledge caused the researched? (p. 419)

What is the body of indigenous knowledge of the former colonized societies that we researchers can use to counter theories and the body of knowledge that may cause humiliation and embarrassment to the researched? (p. 419)

Still other *Handbook* contributors (e.g., Bledsoe & Hopson, Chapter 25; Brydon-Miller, Chapter 16; Mertens et al., Chapter 6; Silka, Chapter 22) identify other forms and causes of oppression that are experienced by the less powerful at the hands of the more powerful. Although the lines are not as clearly drawn as these few paragraphs suggest, their philosophical position tends to be commensurate with an emancipatory or transformative stance that emphasizes their obligation to restore social justice as an ethical imperative for the researcher.

♦ Grounds for Further Deliberations

Even as we explore the emergent and evolving frontiers likely to engage social research ethicists in the future, we also recognize that there are many facets of ethics that were not covered in this *Handbook*. These include religion, cultural competence, differentiation of evaluation research from other forms of applied social science research, and research in crisis situations. Religion deserves consideration in this conversation because its proponents (believers) see it as a basis for a personal moral sense, accompanied often by a set of regulations or codes, and established on a set of principles deemed to be of value to those who are part of their own community. There is much richness in the possibilities of holding the notion of ethics and morality as it is portrayed in various religions up to the characterization of ethics in social research. This, however, must remain a topic for some other book as it is too specialized and, at the same time, likely to be too extensive for a volume such as this one. There is, however, another aspect of religion that we wish we had been able to include and that is its role as an example of one of those "hot button" issues, such as gender and ethnicity, all too often avoided by social science researchers for their political incorrectness, just at the time when information about their role in the life experiences of people is most needed.

Although the topic of cultural competence was directly addressed or alluded to in many *Handbook* chapters, it requires additional mention here because of its increased presence in regulation and professional codes of ethics. Many of the professional associations that are mentioned throughout the *Handbook* are trying to decode the meaning of cultural competence for their members and, then, to incorporate that competence as professional requisite. At the same time, administrative bodies such as IRBs and funders such as the U.S. Substance Abuse, Mental Health Administration are also including cultural competency among the requirements for participation in the funding process.

Mertens (2009) maintained that, in the research setting, cultural competency is a critical disposition that is related to the researcher's or evaluator's ability to accurately represent reality in culturally complex communities. Symonette (2004) made explicit the implication that culturally competent researchers and evaluators must understand themselves in relation to the community in question. One major stumbling block to requiring cultural competence is that competence is not a static state. At best, it is a journey in which the researcher/evaluator develops increased understanding of others and of differential access to power and privilege through self-reflection and interaction with members of the community (Sue & Sue, 2003; Symonette, 2004).

Cultural competence in research and evaluation can be broadly defined as a systematic, responsive mode of inquiry that is actively cognizant, understanding, and appreciative of the cultural context in which the research and evaluation takes place; that frames and articulates the epistemology of the endeavor; that employs culturally and contextually appropriate methodology; and that uses stakeholder-generated, interpretive means to arrive at the results and further use of the findings (SenGupta, Hopson, & Thompson-Robinson, 2004, p. 13). The benefits of cultural competency and culturally responsive evaluation approaches include, but are not limited to, the ability to transform interventions so that they are perceived as legitimate by the community (Guzman, 2003), and the researcher/evaluator serves as an agent of prosocial change to combat racism, prejudice, bias, and oppression in all their forms (APA, 2000). To this end, the culturally competent researcher or evaluator is able to build rapport across differences, gain the trust of community members, and self-reflect and recognize one's own biases (Edno, Joh, & Yu, 2003). Through this process of enhanced cultural competency, the end result is a hoped-for increase in the ethics of the research and evaluation because it has the potential to avoid violations of culturally based personal moral sense, values, and principles.

This is an especially important issue as we consider the layers of complexity that are introduced by Stake and Rivizi (Chapter 33) whose warning that culture can "no longer be treated as a coherent entity" as in a globalizing world "a neat fit between territory, language and social identity can no longer be taken for granted" tends to strip the concept of cultural competence from its definitions. If we are to regard Stake and Rivzi's insight as accurate, what is the difference between "cultural competency" and interpersonal competency (see Symonette, Chapter 18) whereby a researcher who knows herself or himself is able to listen accurately and nondefensively to others and to depict them in ways that they would recognize as accurate? (Newton, Chapter 23).

Another area for further deliberation lies in the *Handbook's* lack of conscientious differentiation among basic social science research, applied social science research, and program/policy/project evaluation. The exact lines of demarcation are contested territory. Trochim (2006) indicated that program evaluation draws its distinctiveness from the organizational and political context in which it is conducted, thus requiring management, group, and political skills not always needed in a more generic research setting. Mathison (2008) argued for a distinction based on the development of evaluation as a discipline that began in the

1960s and has an emphasis on the importance of critically examining valuing as a component of systematic inquiry, the development of methodological approaches that prioritize stakeholder involvement, and use of criteria to judge quality that include utility, feasibility, and propriety.

These two contrasting perspectives might be aided by consideration of Scriven's (2003) description of evaluation as a transdiscipline, by which he means,

> because every discipline, profession, and field engages in some form of evaluation, the most prominent example being, perhaps, evaluations of students taking courses and completing disciplinary programs of study, and referred journals in which new research is evaluated by peers to determine if it is worthy of publication. Evaluation is a discipline that serves other disciplines even as it is a discipline unto itself, thus its emergent transdisciplinary status. Statistics, logic, ethics, and evaluation are examples of transdisciplines in that their methods, ways of thinking, and knowledge base are used in other areas of inquiry, e.g., education, health, social work, engineering, environmental studies, and so on. (Scriven, 2005, p. 422)

Evaluation as a discipline or transdiscipline has contributed significantly to understanding how to bring people together to address critical social issues (Mertens, 2009). Mabry (Chapter 7) suggests that evaluation is sufficiently distinct as to need separate regulatory procedures. However, parallel developments in applied social research are also occurring. Practicing evaluators recognize its development as a discipline. However, there is a place at which research and evaluation intersect—when research occurs in the context of provision of information about need for, improvement of, or effects of programs or policies. Hence, much of what is included in this *Handbook* encompasses the territory at the intersection of applied social research and program evaluation.

Finally, we identify what we regard as an important omission in the *Handbook*, the lack of a chapter reporting on ethical issues in disaster situations. In recent years in the United States, we have experienced terrorist bombings that led with unseemly haste into what the editors consider to be an ill-conceived war. In addition, a devastating hurricane in the Gulf states and a tsunami in Southeast Asia revealed that the political and emergency relief systems were unable to ameliorate the effects of the devastation, especially with regard to the poorest people. In these cases, shoddy and/or absent research of many kinds, including social science research, was implicated. We are also reminded that catastrophe, natural and of human manufacture, constitutes the everyday life of people who, even on an especially good day, number in the millions. How can the findings of social science research (and researchers) help prevent catastrophe, ease its immediate pain, and heal the long-term scars? What is more to the point of this *Handbook*, how can that be done while respecting persons as individuals and groups? Are there times when, in the press of the moment, ethical considerations should be sidelined? If so, which ones? Or, are there emerging protocols for ethical behavior under extreme duress? The amazingly rich contributions of the *Handbook* authors lead us to believe that such protocols are possible and at least partially known at this point in time.

♦ Conclusion

Like the *Handbook* itself, this chapter has covered a varied geography. It has mapped some areas in detail and others might as well be labeled as the seas were labeled on European maps when it was believed that the world was flat: "Here there be dragons." In some cases, we have been able to give the presumed dragons names such as

"Ethics in Catastrophe," in others, we have not. Readers who expected of this chapter a neat checklist of ethical behaviors that, if followed like those provided to potential applicants to an IRB, would guarantee ethical research will be greatly disappointed. Those who were, instead, looking for descriptions of rough edges, projections of present-day ethical conundrums evolving into the future, questions to contemplate, and a mix of practical suggestions with speculations, will have found them plentiful. We profoundly hope that you are now contemplating these profound ethical issues and, as you do so, we want to leave you with a gnarly paradox and some words of comfort, both from this volume.

First the paradox: Although a wealth of ethical abuses has been the impetus for regulation of social science research

> a deep ontological issue remains: Regulations and their enforcement create climates of compliance antithetical to the curiosity that drives research and to the freedom that promotes discovery; that is, regulation can obstruct the social value, the raison d'etre, of social science. (Mabry, Chapter 7, p. 118)

And, in closing, a note of hope that was written with regard to cultural competence and partnership across indigenous and nonindigenous groups, but applicable, we believe, to growth in ethics and understanding across the board:

> It is from reflecting on our experience both from the inside out and the outside in (Symonette, 2007) and through the sharing of our actual day-to-day experience and engagement as researchers in Indian Country competence is developed. It cannot be found in reading a book about Indians or in watching the latest film intended to portray the Indian experience or in meeting each element of a regulatory process. It is found sitting around the campfire listening to the stories and telling our own stories, as well. (LaFrance & Crazy Bull, Chapter 9, p. 147)

♦ Notes

1. I am grateful to Donald T. Campbell and the participants in Cazenovia Conference that he hosted in 1981 for some of the language in this paragraph—in particular the editing metaphor (P. E. G.).

2. It is well worth noting, however, that in Wolf et al.'s (Chapter 11) small study, reliance on personal values was more characteristic of members of the American Evaluation Association than of members of the Australasian Evaluation Society. It will be interesting to learn whether or not the difference is robust and whether or not it represents a cultural difference in perceptions of the relative importance of standards and rules versus "gut feelings."

3. For Freud, the parent in question was clearly to be that of the same gender as the child. Present-day studies of mentorship do not make the same gender-based claim.

4. For a history of this issue and frequently asked questions see http://tinyurl.com/ys3fjy.

5. Jackson (2005) and Phillips (2000) are but two examples from a copious bibliography on this topic.

♦ References

American Psychological Association. (2000). *Guidelines for research in ethnic minority communities*. Council of National Psychological Associations for the Advancement of Ethnic Minority Interests. Washington, DC: Author.

Brown v. Board of Education, 347 U.S. 483 (1954).

Carkhuff, R. R. (1970). *Helping and human relations* (Vol. 2). New York: Holt, Rinehart & Winston.

Edno, T., Joh, T., & Yu, H. C. (2003). *Voices from the field: Health and evaluation* leaders on multicultural evaluation. Oakland, CA: Social Policy Research Associates.

Freud, S. (1958). *A general introduction to psychoanalysis*. New York: Washington Square Press. (Original work published 1917)

Gilligan, C. (1982). *In a different voice*. Cambridge, MA: Harvard University Press.

Guzman, B. L. (2003). Examining the role of cultural competency in program evaluation: Visions for new millennium evaluators. In S. I. Donaldson & M. Scriven (Eds.), *Evaluating social programs and problems: Visions for the new millennium* (pp. 167–182). Mahwah, NJ: Lawrence Erlbaum.

House, E. (1993). *Professional evaluation: Social impact and political consequences*. Newbury Park, CA: Sage.

Jackson, J. P. (2005). *Science for segregation: race, law and the case against Brown v. Board*. New York: New York University Press.

Khoza, R. (1994). *African humanism*. Diepkloof Extension, South Africa: Ekhaya Promotions.

Kohlberg, L. (1976). Stage and sequence: The cognitive developmental approach to socialization. In T. Likona (Ed.), *Moral development and behavior* (pp. 31–53). New York: Holt, Rinehart & Winston.

Louw, D. J. (2001). *Ubuntu: An African assessment of the religious order*. Philosophy in Africa. University of the North. Retrieved May 1, 2008, from http://www.bu.edu/wcp/Papers/Afri/AfriLouw.htm

Ludema, J. D., Cooperrider, D. L., & Barrett, F. J. (2001). Appreciative inquiry: The power of the unconditional positive question. In P. Reason & H. Bradbury (Eds.), *Handbook of action research: Concise paperback edition* (pp. 155–165). London: Sage.

Mathison, S. (2008). What is the difference between evaluation and research-and why do we care? In N. L. Smith & P. R. Brandon (Eds.), *Fundamental issues in evaluation* (pp. 183–196). New York: Guilford Press.

Mertens, D. M. (2009). *Transformative research and evaluation*. New York: Guilford Press.

Mertens, D. M., Fraser, J., & Heimlich, J. (2008). M or F? Gender, identity and the transformative paradigm in research methods. *Museums & Society, 3*, 81–92.

Paley, A. R., & Schulte, B. (2007, June 30). Court ruling likely to further segregate schools, educators say. *The Washington Post*, p. A4. Accessed February 5, 2008, from www.washingtonpost.com/wp-dyn/content/article/2007/06/29/AR2007062902134.html

Phillips, L. (2000). Recontextualizing Kenneth B. Clark. *History of Psychology, 3*(2), 142–167.

Scriven, M. (2003). Evaluation in the new millennium: The transdisciplinary vision. In S. Donaldson & M. Scriven (Eds.), *Evaluating social programs and problems* (pp. 19–42). Mahwah, NJ: Lawrence Erlbaum.

Scriven, M. (2005). Transdiscipline. In S. Mathison (Ed.), *Encyclopedia of evaluation*. Thousand Oaks, CA: Sage.

SenGupta, S., Hopson, R., & Thompson-Robinson, M. (Eds.). (2004). *In search of cultural competence in evaluation toward principles and practices: Vol. 102. New directions for evaluation*. San Francisco: Jossey-Bass.

Stanfield, J. (1999). Stepping through the front door: Relevant social scientific evaluation in people-of-color country. *American Journal of Evaluation, 21*, 275–283.

Sue, D. W., & Sue, D. (2003). *Counseling the culturally diverse: Theory and practice* (4th ed.). New York: John Wiley.

Symonette, H. (2004). Walking pathways toward becoming a culturally competent evaluator: Boundaries, borderlands, and border crossings (pp. 95–110). In M. Thompson-Robinson, R. Hopson, & S. SenGupta (Eds.), *In search of cultural competence in evaluation: Vol. 102. New directions for evaluation*. San Francisco: Jossey-Bass.

Trochim, W. M. (2006). *The research methods knowledge base* (2nd ed.). Retrieved February 25, 2008, from www.socialresearchmethods.net/kb/index.php

Truax, C. B., & Carkhuff, R. R. (1967). *Towards effective counseling and psychotherapy*. Chicago: Aldine.

AUTHOR INDEX

Abberley, P., 461, 468–469
Abel, S., 447–448, 456–457
Aboriginal Research Centre, 410, 423
ACUNS Council, 312, 318
Adams, R., 299, 306
Adekanmbi, G. A., 420, 425
Adeola, O. A., 420, 425
Adler, P., 235, 241
Adler, P. A., 235, 241
Agee, J., 354, 371
Ager, J., 402, 406
Ahluwalia, P., 453–454
Ajwani, S., 442, 454
Alaska Native Knowledge Network, 312, 318–319
Alasuutari, P., 212, 561–562
Albertini, J., 93, 100
Alkin, M. C., 171, 182
Alldred, P., 151, 167
Allen, C., 165, 166
Allen, C. A., 252, 257
Allen, E., 444, 456
Allen, G. J., 559, 563
Allen, K. R., 559, 562
Alta Charo, R., 498, 504
Alzheimer's Association, 509, 513, 516
Amaro, H., 479, 485, 487
Amdur, R., 124, 133

American Anthropological Association (AAA), 6, 20, 151, 159, 166, 551, 560
American Educational Research Association (AERA), 166, 393, 395, 399, 402, 404
American Evaluation Association (AEA), 118, 171–172, 178–182, 393, 395–396, 399, 402, 405
American Historical Association, 151, 166
American Indian Higher Education Association (AIHEC), 146, 148
American Indian Law Center, Inc., 139, 143, 148
American Medical Association (AMA), 381, 384
American Political Science Association, 6, 20
American Psychiatric Association, 485, 509, 516
American Psychological Association (APA), 20, 39, 45, 51, 91, 99, 112, 113n17, 118, 159, 166, 379, 384, 393, 395, 398–399, 402, 405, 479, 485, 492, 504, 554–555, 610, 612
American Psychological Association Ethics Committee, 551, 560

American Sociological Association (ASA), 20, 111–112, 118, 151, 159, 166, 551, 560
Anderson, M. S., 552–555, 557–558, 562, 564
Andolsen, B. H., 40, 51
Aneesh, A., 523, 535
Anspach, R. R., 71, 82
Antonovsky, A., 445, 454
Anushko, A. E., 202, 212, 551, 561–562
APA Task Force on Statistical Inference, 379, 385
Applebaum, B., 41–42, 51
Applebaum, P. S., 513, 516
Aristotle, 20, 493, 504
Arlee, J., 147–148
Arnold, B., 44, 52
Arnstein, S. R., 254–255
Asante, M. K., 298–299, 306, 408, 411–413, 423
Ashcraft, C., 578n8, 579
Ashcroft, B., 453–454
Ashdown, P., 265, 271
Aspin, C., 448, 456
Astin, H. S., 555, 563
Atal, Y., 231, 241
Atkins, R., 559–560
Atkinson, D. R., 555, 560
Atkinson, P., 231, 241
Australasian Evaluation Society, 171, 182
Avoseh, M. B. M., 300, 306, 420, 425
Ayman al Zawahiri, 270–271

Bach, M., 462, 472
Back, L., 462, 469
Baier, A., 40, 51
Bailey, K. D., 299, 306
Baird, L. L., 555, 560
Baker, Q., 61, 65
Baldwin, J., 142
Ball, T. J., 249–250, 254, 256
Banerjee, A., 116, 118
Bankert, E., 123, 133
Banks, W. C., 190, 197
Bariek, R., 436, 439
Barnes, C., 75, 77, 80, 82, 82n1, 84, 309, 459, 461–464, 466–470, 469n2, 471–473
Baron, R. M., 327, 334
Barone, T., 163, 166
Barranti, C., 475, 482, 488

Barrett, F. J., 87, 100, 587, 613
Barrington, J. M., 310, 319
Bartels, K. M., 555, 562
Barth, F., 196n1, 197
Barton, L., 459, 468, 470
Batten, S., 433, 440
Battiste, M., 99–100, 152, 166
Baugh, E. J., 412, 423
Bauman, H., 96, 99
Baumrind, D., 551, 560
Bawden, R., 87, 99
Beaglehole, J. C., 309, 319
Beaglehole, R., 445, 454
Beaglehole, T. H., 310, 319
Beauchamp, T., 509, 516
Beauchamp, T. L., 8, 13, 14, 16, 18–20
Beazley, S., 76, 80, 82, 464, 466, 468, 471
Bebeau, M. J., 556, 559–561
Becker, A. B., 252, 258, 337, 351
Becker, H., 461, 470
Beckett, A. E., 460, 470
Beem, H. P., 193, 197
Begay v. United States, 499, 505
Begley, S., 113, 118
Behar, R., 298, 306
Beiser, M., 402, 405
Belenky, M. F., 150, 166
Bell, A., 454–455, 454n3
Bell, D., 58, 65
Bell, D. A., 56, 65
Bell, L. A., 41, 51, 57–58, 290, 293
Belmont Report, 7–8, 16, 18–19, 21, 137, 152
Benedict, R., 192, 197
Benet-Martinez, V., 328, 335
Benfey, J., 343, 351
Benhabib, S., 567, 571, 578
Bennet, B. S., 407, 423
Bennett, J. W., 192, 197
Bennett, K., 448, 456
Bennett, L., 557, 561
Bennett, L. A., 433, 440
Bennett, M., 285–288, 294
Bensman, J., 8, 22
Bentham, J., 17, 21
Benzie, D., 76, 80, 82
Beresford, P., 76, 79–80, 82–83, 463, 470
Berg, B. L., 296, 306
Berkeley, G., 24, 36
Berkman, C., 477, 485

Berliner, D. C., 114, 118
Bernal, Delgado, 95
Bernstein, L., 557, 561
Berry, J. W., 394, 405
Berry, R. M., 551, 556, 561
Berryman, M., 314, 319
Bershcheid, E., 399, 406
Betts, S. C., 142–143, 148
Bevan-Brown, J., 315, 319
Beywl, W., 173, 182
Bhaba, H., 408, 423
Bickman, L., 203, 205–206, 211–213, 561–562
Bieber, I., 479, 485
Biklen, S. K., 297, 306
Bingham, C. R., 86, 99
Birch, J., 387, 390
Birch, M., 163, 167–168, 230, 241, 424
Bird, S. J., 552, 554, 561
Bishop, R., 161, 166, 313, 317, 319, 443, 455
Blaisure, K. R., 559, 562
Blakely, T., 442, 454
Blaxter, M., 461, 470
Bledsoe, K. L., 392, 394, 396, 399–401, 404–405
Blow, F. C., 86, 99
Bochner, A., 29, 37
Boehmer, U., 477, 485
Boerger, A. E., 532, 536
Bogard, W., 538, 549
Bogat, G. A., 555, 561
Bogdan, R. C., 297, 306
Bohman, J., 56, 65
Bonavota, D., 475, 487
Bond, M. H., 327, 328, 334–336
Bonne, M., 442, 454
Borell, B., 442–457
Booth, T., 76, 79, 83
Booth, W., 76, 79, 83
Boruca, R. F., 503, 506
Boruch, R. F., 201–202, 204, 211
Boser, S., 249, 254–255
Boudin, K., 35, 37
Bowe, F., 71, 83
Bowen, I., 35, 37
Bowman, N., 139, 148
Boyce, C., 492, 499, 503, 505
Boyer, P., 137, 148
Brabeck, K., 39–53

Brabeck, M. M., 39–53, 91, 99, 245, 247, 255, 255n7, 257, 561
Bradbury, H., 100–101, 244, 255n3, 257–258, 613
Braddock, D. L., 82n1, 83
Brady Wagner, L. C., 511, 517
Braimoh, D., 420, 425
Brannen, J., 212, 561–562
Branson, J., 96, 99
Brant-Castellano, M., 136–137, 144–145, 148
Braun, K. L., 312, 322
Braun, V., 445, 455
Braverman, M. T., 394, 399, 401, 405
Bravo, G., 514, 516
Bremer, J., 474, 479, 485
Brewely, D. N., 559, 564
Brightbill, N., 54, 67
Bringle, R. G., 337, 351
Brooke, C., 56, 65
Broom, L., 193, 197
Brown, B. L., 380–381, 384
Brown, C., 271, 273
Brown, L., 39, 51
Brown, L. S., 55, 65
Brown, R., 529, 532, 535
Brown, S. R., 176, 182
Brown, T., 394, 401, 404–405
Brown v. Board of Education, 608, 612
Brugge, D., 337, 351
Bruner, E. M., 158, 165, 167, 548–549
Brush, S., 343, 351
Bruss, K. V., 554, 561
Brydon-Miller, M., 43, 52, 131, 187, 243–245, 247, 250–251, 253, 255, 255n3, 255n9, 256–258
Buber, M., 357, 369n2, 371
Buchwald, D., 143, 149
Buehler, J. W., 397, 406
Bullock, M., 214–228
Buie, V. C., 513, 516–517
Burbules, N. C., 158, 165, 167, 538, 547, 549
Burchfield, C., 383, 385
Burchfield, C. M., 383, 385
Burdge, B., 485–486, 485n1
Buriel, R., 44, 52
Burman, E., 35, 37
Bury, M., 83, 461, 470
Buss, A., 359, 371

Bussey-Jones, J., 557, 561
Butler, E. A., 329, 334
Butler, J., 150, 166
Butler, R., 475, 481–482, 484, 488
Byne, W., 477, 480, 487
Byrne, B., 454n2, 455

Caballero, B., 409–410, 423
Cahill, C., 60, 63, 65
Caldwell, C., 559, 561
Caldwell, P., 59, 65
Callister, T. A., 538, 549
Camargo, C. A., 113, 120
Camenisch, P. F., 554, 561
Campbell, A., 444, 455
Campbell, B., 206, 212
Campbell, C., 255n8, 256
Campbell, D. T., x, xivn3, 99, 186–187, 200–202, 204–206, 211–213, 260, 264, 271–272, 326, 335
Campbell, J., 76, 83, 94, 467, 470
Campbell, P. W., 133
Canadian Institutes of Health Research, 136, 148
Canadian Psychological Association, 551, 561
Cannella, G. S., 151, 166
Capaldi, E. G., 26, 37
Carbone, K. M., 555, 562
Carbonell, S. L., 393, 405
Carkhuff, R. R., 588, 612–613
Carrier, J., 475, 486
Carruthers, J., 412, 424
Carter, L., 313, 321, 408, 424
Cartwright, S., 444, 455
Casas, A., 555, 560
Cascardi, M., 47, 52
Castells, M., 526, 535
Castro, C., 559, 561
Catalano, R. F., 87, 100
Ceci, S. J., 209, 211, 478–479, 486
Center for Advanced Study, 126–133, 133n14
Chadwick, R., 175, 182
Chalmers, T. C., 203, 212
Chamberlain, J., 465, 470
Chambliss, D. F., 431, 439
Chandler, D., 254, 256
Changeux, J. P., 383–384

Chao, G. T., 553, 561
Chapleski, E. E., 142, 149
Chappell, A., 80, 83
Chappell, A. L., 466, 470
Charlton, J. T., 250, 256
Chase, M., 381, 384
Chavez, V., 61, 65
Chelimsky, E., 114, 118
Chikanda, N. E., 413, 423–424
Childress, J. E., 8, 13, 16, 18–20
Childress, J. F., 7, 21
Chilisa, B., 92, 97, 99, 248, 297, 299–300, 304–306, 410–413, 417–420, 422–423, 423n1, 423n3
Chiu, C.-Y., 328, 335
Christakis, N. A., 14, 21
Christensen, R., 146, 148
Christians, C., 94, 99, 151
Christians, C. G., 158, 161–162, 166
Christianson, A., 480, 486
Christie, T. C., 200, 203, 211–213
Churchill, W., 310, 319
Cisneros, E., 532, 536
Citro, C., 133, 133n16
Clark, J., 35, 37
Clark, N. L., 493, 505
Clark, R. A., 552, 555–556, 561
Clarke, E., 447, 455
Clarke, S., 445, 455
Clarke, V., 445, 455
Cleghorn, G., 338, 352
Clegg, J. W., 23–38
Clements, C. M., 47, 52
Clifford, J., 525, 535
Clinchy, B. M., 150, 166
Cockram, J., 80, 83
Cocks, E., 80, 83
Coffey, A., 231, 241
Cohen, A., 439, 439n4
Cohen, A. G., 555, 561
Cohen, J., 378–380, 384
Cohen, R., 523, 535
Cohn, R., 174, 183
Colby, A., 41, 52
Cole, E. B., 40, 52
Collaborative Initiative for Research Ethics in Environmental Health, 346, 351
Collins, P., 299, 307, 419, 424
Commission on Human Rights, 319

The Commission on the Intelligence Capabilities of the United States Regarding Weapons of Mass Destruction, 271–272
CommunicateResearch, 270, 272
Coney, S., 444, 455
Conger, J., 476, 486
Conner, R., 271–272
Connolly, K., 163, 167
Conquergood, D., 159, 167
Constantine, N. A., 394, 399, 401, 405
Cook, J. A., 62–63, 66, 88, 100
Cook, T. D., x, xivn3, 198, 200–205, 212–213, 570, 579
Cook-Lynn, E., 144, 148
Coombe, R. J., 165n4, 167
Cooperrider, D. L., 87, 100, 587, 613
Coppens, N. M., 343, 351
Corker, M., 84, 463, 467–468, 470, 473
Cornell, S., 576, 579
Cotton, J. L., 555, 563
Coultrap-McQuin, S., 40, 52
Council of Graduate Schools, 557, 561
Council on Foreign Relations, 269, 272
Cousins, J., 569–570, 578
Cover, J. A., 36–37
Cox, E., 461, 471
Cozby, P. C., 399, 402, 404n3, 405
Cram, F., 99, 248, 309–310, 313–316, 318n2, 319–321, 408–409, 424, 442–443, 455–456
Crandall, R., 5, 21
Crang, M., 523, 535
Crazy Bull, Cheryl, 135–148,
Crego, C. A., 556, 562
Crehan, K., 234, 241
Crengle, S., 313, 315, 320, 446, 448–449, 456
Crenshaw, K., 65, 67
Crenshaw, K. W., 56–58, 65
Creswell, J. W., 296, 307, 418, 424
Crigger, N. J., 433, 439–440
Crisp, K., 475–476, 486
Cromby, J., 63, 67
Cronbach, L. J., 374, 385
Crow, L., 75, 83
Croy, C., 143, 149
Cudeck, R., 380, 385
Cuéllar, I., 44, 52
Cullen, J. B., 557, 564

Cullinan, C., 280, 294
Cunningham, C. W., 304, 307
Cunningham-Burley, S., 467, 473
Curd, M., 36–37
Curfman, G. D., 376, 385

Dain, H., 479, 485
Dale, J., 110, 118
Daly, M., 42, 52
Damasio, A., 354, 356–358, 371
Daniels, K., 444, 455
Danziger, K., 34, 37
Darley, J. M., 186–187
Dasen, P. R., 394, 405
Dash, L., 158, 165, 167, 548–549
Datta, L., 114, 118, 174, 183
D'Augelli, A., 477, 486
Davidson, E. J., 402, 405
Davies, D., 84, 468, 472
Davies, G., 444, 455
Davies, J. M., 47, 52, 76, 467, 470
Davis, D., 234, 241
Davis, E. L., 556, 561
Davis, J., 467, 473
Davis, L., 463, 470
Davis, P., 321, 443, 455–456
Davis, R., 532, 536
Davis-Haley, R. T., 559, 564
Daw, J., 555, 564
Dawson, L., 195, 197, 398, 400, 405
Day, J. D., 247, 257
D'Costa, B., 576, 579
DDI Alliance, 219, 227
De Angelis, C., 376, 385
Dearry, A., 337, 352
Deaton, A., 116, 118
Decker, S. H., 433, 441
de Courtivron, I., 42, 53
DeCuir, J. T., 58, 65–66
de Gruchy, J., 478, 484, 486
deJong, G., 71, 83
De Laine, M., 230, 241
Delamont, S., 229, 241
Delgado, R., 57–58, 66, 251, 256
Deloria, B., 144, 148
Deloria V., Jr., 136, 145, 148
DeMarco, J. P., 9, 21
De Moya, D., 503, 506
Dennis, R., 392, 406

Denzin, N. K., x, xiv, 87, 99, 101, 113, 119, 151–152, 159–160, 163, 166–168, 231, 241–242, 245, 256, 307, 321, 424, 471, 533, 535
DePaul, G., 532, 536
Derrida, J., 27, 49, 52
Descartes, R., 24, 37
Desmond, A., 310, 319
DeStefano, L., 171, 183
Deutsch, L., 477, 486
deVries, B., 41, 53
Dew, K., 321, 443, 455–456
Dewey, J., 25, 579
DiAngelo, R., 476, 486
Diener, E., 5, 21
Dillard, C., 96, 99
Dince, P., 479, 485
Dinnel, D., 332, 335
Diop, C., 412, 424
Disability Handicap and Society, 461, 470
Division of Family Health Services, 397, 405
Dixon-Reeves, R., 555, 561
Dixson, A., 58, 66
Dixson, A. D., 58, 65–66
Dodd, S. J., 475, 487
Dohan, D., 128, 130, 133
Donaldson, S. I., 200, 203, 211–213, 612–613
Donelson, R., 479, 486
Donnelly, T. M., 559–560
Donovan, J., 150, 167
Dooks, E., 369n4, 371
Douglas, M. A., 50, 53
Downe, P. J., 163, 167
Downey, J., 476, 486
The Downing Street Declaration, 264, 272
Drazen, J. M., 376, 385
Drellich, M., 479, 485
Drescher, J., 480, 486
Driedger, D., 460, 470
Drotar, D., 495–497, 505
Dua, E., 59, 66, 234
Dua, V., 234, 241
Duan, N., 208, 213
Dube, M. W., 299, 304, 307, 417, 424
Dubois, M.-F., 514, 516
DuBois, W. E., 66, 318
Dunbar, C. Jr., 532, 536
Duncan, G., 58, 66
Dunleavy, D., 361, 372

Dunn, L. B., 513, 516
Duran, B., 61, 65, 92, 99
Duran, E., 92, 99–100
Durie, M., 310, 313, 319, 442–444, 455
Durie, M. H., 304, 307, 317
Durning, D. W., 176, 182
Duster, T., 492, 499, 503, 505

Earley, M. A., 422, 424
Eckert, W. A., 201–202, 212
Edno, T., 610, 612
Edwards, R., 387, 390, 407–408, 424
Edwards, S., 316, 319, 444, 446–448, 455
Egloff, B., 329, 334
Eisen, A., 551, 556, 561
Eisenhart, M., 114, 119
Eisenstein, H., 40, 52
Ekman, P., 333, 335
Elliot, D., 461, 471
Elliott, D., 553, 557, 564
Elliott, J. R., 86, 100
Ellis, C., 61, 63, 66, 157, 167
Ellis, J. B., 422, 424
Ellsworth, E., 56, 66
Elshtain, J. B., 39, 52
Elze, D., 475–476, 481–482, 484, 486
Emerson, R. M., 233–234, 241
Eng, E., 245, 256–257
Engstrom, J., 264, 272
Enns, C. Z., 40, 52
Entwisle, B., 328, 335
Epstein, R. A., 533, 535
Ericka Grimes v. Kennedy Kreiger Institute and Higgins, a minor, etc. v. Kennedy Kreiger Institute, 497, 505
Erickson, E. A., 329, 334
Erickson, F., 114, 119, 530, 535
Erlen, J. A., 509, 516
Erting, C., 94, 100
European Parliament, 215, 227
Evans, C., 94, 100
Evans, W., 354, 371
Everard, C., 447, 455, 457
Eyssell, K. M., 206, 212

Fabrigar, L. R., 382, 385
Faden, R., 509, 516
Fair, J., 8, 21
Fassinger, R. E., 555, 562

Fay, B., 54, 66
Federal Judicial Center, 204, 212
Feeley, M. M., 127, 129, 133, 133n14
Ferguson, J., 525, 535
Fernandez, S. D., 93, 101
Ferns, T., 50, 53
Feuer, M. J., 114, 119
Fidler, F., 379–380, 385
Fielding, N., 230, 234–235, 238, 241
Fine, G. A., 237, 241
Fine, M., 35–38, 59–60, 66, 68, 237, 317, 320
Finkelstein, V., 75, 82n1, 83, 463, 465, 470
Finkin, M., 167, 548–549
Fischer, M. K., 155, 168, 525, 535
Fischman, M. W., 248, 256
Fisher, C. B., 100, 142, 149, 202, 212, 492, 499, 502–503, 505, 551, 553–554, 556, 558–562
Fisher, P. A., 249–250, 254, 256
Fishman, D., 559, 562
Fitzgerald, M. H., 128, 130, 133n15, 134
Fitzpatrick, J., 531, 536
Fitzpatrick, J. L., 400, 405
Flaherty, M., 298, 307
Flax, J., 27, 37, 41, 52
Flinders, D. J., 110, 119
Fluss, S. S., 246, 256
Flynn, J. A., 509, 516
Foehner, K., 144, 148
Folkman, S., 22, 246, 248, 250, 256, 258, 551, 563
Fonow, M. M., 62–63, 66, 88, 100
Fontana, A., 422, 424
Ford, R., 444, 456
Forgas, J. P., 328, 334
Foucault, M., 27–28, 35, 37, 49, 52, 539, 549
Fowers, B. J., 33, 38
Fox, R. M., 9, 21
Fox-Keller, E., 27, 37
The Framework Documents, 264, 272
Francomano, C. A., 555, 562
Frank, D. A., 492, 499, 503, 505
Frank, E., 383, 385
Frank, L., 509, 516
Frankena, W., 13, 21
Franklin, J., 89, 100
Fraser, C., 492–493, 505
Fraser, J., 598, 613

Fraser, N., 577, 579
Freeman, D., 392, 405
Freeman, H. E., 171, 183
Freeman, W., 140
French, S., 84, 472
Fretz, R. I., 233–234, 241
Freud, S., 612, 612n3
Frey, J., 422, 424
Fried, A. F., 553–554, 558, 560, 562
Fried, L. P., 555, 562
Friedman, M., 109, 119, 476
Friedman, P. J., 559, 562
Friedman, R., 476, 486
Frierson, H. T., 61, 66, 405
Frizelle, F. A., 376, 385
Fryer-Edwards, K., 553, 562
Fu, P. P., 328, 335
Fullilove, M. T., 316–317, 319
Fullilove, R. E., III, 316–317, 319
Fyrberg, D., 551, 559, 562

Gadamer, H. G., 26, 33, 37
Galik, E., 513, 516–517
Gamble, C., 186–187, 198–213
Gant, L., 402, 406
Garcia, L. T., 19, 22
Garfinkel, H., 232, 241
Gastil, J., 577–579
Gay, Lesbian and Straight Education Network, 476, 481–482, 486
Geertz, C., 231
Gehlmann, S., 555, 562
Gelles, R. J., 443, 440
Gelso, C. J., 554, 563
Genao, I., 557, 561
Germano, K. K., 553–554, 558, 560, 562
Gersten, R., 204, 212
Ghere, G., 171, 173, 177, 183
Gibbs, J., 41, 52
Gilbert, J. P., 203, 205, 212
Gilbert, L. A., 554–555, 562
Gillam, L., 61, 66
Gillespie-Sells, K., 76, 84, 468, 472
Gillett, G., 444–445, 455
Gillies, V., 151, 167
Gilligan, C., 14, 21, 40–41, 52, 157–158, 167, 305, 307, 588, 612
Gillon, L., 86, 99
Gilmore, P., 98, 100

Gilson, L. L., 555, 563
Glauberman, N., 325, 335
Glynn, T., 314, 319
Glynn, V., 314, 319–320
Gobo, G., 241–242
Goduka, I. N., 413, 415, 424
Goffman, E., 359, 371
Goldberg, J. P., 158, 165, 167
Goldberger, N. R., 150, 166
Goldman, S. R., 114, 120
Gonsiorek, J., 476, 486
González, G., 44, 52
González y González, E. M., 162, 167–168
Goodley, D., 80, 83, 465–466, 470
Goodman, S. J., 553–554, 558, 560, 562
Goodyear, L. K., 173, 183
Goodyear, R. K., 556, 562
Goodyear-Smith, F., 444, 455
Gordon, B., 95, 100
Gotanda, N., 57, 65, 67
Gould, D., 476, 486
Gouldner, A., 462, 470
Government of India, 430, 440
Grace, H., 314, 319
Graham, J. A., 400, 405
Grand, H., 479, 485
Grande, S., 152, 167
Grant, G., 338, 352
Grant, G. R., 338, 351
Green, L. W., 337–338, 351
Green, M., 338, 352
Greenberg, D., 198, 212
Greene, J. C., 64, 66, 101, 206, 209, 212, 394, 399, 401, 404–405
Greenough, W. T., 158, 165, 167, 548–549
Greenwood, D., 247, 255n3, 255n9, 256
Greenwood, D. J., 244, 256
Grégoire, H., 61, 66
Gregory, F., 270, 272
Griffin, K., 575, 579
Grindel, C., 476, 487
Grisso, T., 492, 499, 503, 505
Grissom, R., 325, 332, 335
Groom, C., 198, 212
Gross, J. J., 329, 334–335
Grossman, A., 477, 486
Gruber-Baldini, A. L., 513, 516–517
Grullon, M., 338, 352
Grushkin, D. A., 98, 100

Guba, E. G., 62–63, 66, 151–153, 167–168, 394, 404, 405, 466–467, 471
Gubrium, J. F., 231–232, 241–242, 510, 517
Gudorf, C. E., 40, 51
Guelke, A., 270, 272–273
Guignon, C. B., 33, 38
Guillemin, M., 61, 66
Guion, L., 412, 423
Guitierrez, K., 114, 119
Gullestad, M., 230, 241
Gundlach, R., 479, 485
Gunsalus, C. K., 165n3, 167, 548–549
Gupta, A., 525, 535
Gustavsen, B., 87, 100
Gutek, B. A., 555, 561
Guthrie, R. V., 392, 405
Gutierrez, K., 114, 119
Gutmann, A., 566, 578–579
Guy-Sheftall, B., 59, 66
Guzman, B. L., 610, 612–613
Guzman, M., 43, 51
Gwynne, G. V., 460, 468, 471

Habermas, J., 56, 66
Hahn, H., 71, 83
Haimes, E., 231, 241
Haldeman, D., 479, 486
Hall, B., 245, 255–257
Hall, C. C. I., 555, 563
Hall, E. T., 287, 294
Hall, G. C. N., 391, 395–397, 402, 405
Hall, R., 230, 241
Halpert, S., 480, 486
Halse, C., 54, 66
Hamer, D., 480, 486
Hamilton, B., 243, 251, 257
Hamilton, P., 366, 371
Hammersley, M., 54, 66, 458–459, 471
Hampton, E., 309, 320
Hanberger, A., 567–569, 578n5, 579
Hancock, L. E., 264, 272
Haney, C., 190, 197
Hann, J., 208, 212
Harden, S. L., 552, 555–556, 561
Harding, S., 42, 52, 466, 471, 569, 579
Hare, R., 9, 21
Hare-Mustin, R. T., 41, 52
Haretuku, R., 447, 457
Hariman, R., 369n4, 371

Harnad, S., 382, 385
Harper, M. G., 392, 394–395, 405
Harris, A., 461, 471
Harris, A. P., 58, 66, 91
Harris, C. I., 58, 66
Harris, E., 444, 455
Harris, R., 85–101, 310, 321
Harris, V., 193, 197
Harry, D., 310, 320
Hart, D., 559–560
Hartsock, N. C., 46, 52
Hassall, I., 444, 456
Hatcher, J. A., 337, 351
Haug, C., 376, 385
Hawke, R., 313–315, 321
Hawke, S., 313–315, 321
Hawkins, J. D., 87, 100
Hay, I., 126–127, 130, 133n12, 134
Hayes, S., 559, 562
Hays, W. L., 378–380, 385
Health Research Council of
    New Zealand, 136, 148,
    312, 320, 447, 455
Healy, D., 375, 385
Hedges, D. W., 383, 385
Heidegger, M., 26, 37
Heikes, E. J., 296, 307
Heimlich, J., 598, 613
Henare, M., 315, 319
Henderson, J., 143, 149
Hendrix, S. B., 380–381, 384
Hendry, P. M., 163, 167
Henneman, E. A., 557, 562
Henry, E., 313, 320
Henry, G. T., 204, 206, 209–210, 212–213
Henry, R., 513, 516
Herek, G., 479, 485, 487
Hermann, T., 266, 272
Hermes, M., 248, 256
Hernandez, J., 140, 148
Heron, J., 95, 100
Herrnstein, R. J., 325, 335
Hertz, R., 296, 307
Heshusius, L., 298, 307
Hess, P., 544, 549
Hesse-Biber, S. N., 559, 562
Higgins, A., 557, 563
Higgins, S., 557, 561
Higuchi, H. R., 325–326, 335

Hillabrant, W., 499, 505
Hill Collins, P., 59, 66, 150, 167
Hilsen, A. I., 243, 247, 255n5, 256
Hintikka, M. B., 42, 52
Hirschheim, R., 56, 66–67
Hitchcock, J., 204, 212
Hlodan, O., 224, 227
Hoagwood, K., 492, 499, 503, 505
Hobbes, T., 16, 21
Hoey, J., 376, 385
Hoffman, J. M., 327, 335
Holcomb, L., 433, 439–440
Hollingsworth, M. A., 555, 562
Hollis, R., 252, 258
Holloway, E. L., 555, 563
Holmes, H., 85–101
Holstein, J. A., 231–232, 241–242, 510, 517
Holt, M., 396, 406
Home Affairs Committee, 270, 272
Honey, A., 54, 66
Hong, Y. Y., 328, 335
Hood, S., 61, 66, 405
Hooker, E., 475–476, 482, 487
hooks, b., 67, 100, 150, 167, 309, 320,
    417, 424
Hopson, R. K., 61, 68, 394, 399, 401, 404,
    405, 610, 613
Horkheimer, M., 54, 67
Horowitz, I. L., 8, 21
Horton, B. D., 252, 256
Horton, R., 376, 385
House, E. R., 89, 100, 112, 119, 399,
    401, 405528–529, 535, 566, 568–569,
    574, 577, 578n2, 578n9, 578n10,
    579, 605, 613
House of Commons Foreign Affairs
    Committee, 268, 272
Houston, B., 41, 52
Howard, R. D., 431, 440
Howe, K. R., 399, 405, 566, 568–570, 578n2,
    578n6, 578n8, 578n9, 579
Hsu, E., 116, 118
Hu, N., 480, 486
Hu, S., 480, 486
Hua, A., 59, 67
Huff, D., 373, 385
Hughes, G. B., 61, 66
Hughes, M., 47, 52, 61
Human, D., 246, 256

Humble, A. M., 559, 562
Hume, D., 41, 52
Hummert, M. L., 512, 517
Humphrey, J. C., 468, 471
Humphrey, L., 8, 21
Humphreys, L., 109, 119, 475, 481, 487
Humphries, B., 458, 471
Humphries, T., 96, 100
Hunt, P., 72–73, 83, 461, 471
Hunt, T., 315, 319
Huriwai, TeM., 313–315, 321
Husserl, E., 26, 37
Huygens, I., 317, 320
Hylton, D., 35, 37
Hynes, H. P., 337, 351

Iglen, D., 133, 133n16
Illingworth, P., 481–482, 487
Independent Review Consulting, 125, 133
Indian Child Welfare Act, 493, 505
Innu Nation & Innu Band Council, 316, 320
Institute of Medicine, 133, 133n16, 496, 505
International Military Tribunals, 115, 119
International Monetary Fund, 430, 440
Inter-University Consortium for Political and Social Research, 217, 227
IRB Forum, 131, 133
Irwin, C. J., 187, 261–265, 267, 269–270, 271n1, 272–273
Irwin, K., 313, 316, 320
Isbister, J., 89, 100
Israel, B. A., 245, 252, 256–258, 337–338, 351
Israel, M., 126–127, 130, 133n12, 134
Iwata, N., 325–326, 335

Jacelon, C. S., 557, 562
Jackson, J. P., 612n5, 613
Jackson, M., 310, 315, 320
Jackson, T., 255–257
Jacoby, R., 325, 335
Jahnke, H., 443, 455
Jain, L. D., 427, 440
James, A. L., 494, 505
James, T., 475, 482, 487
Janke, T., 310, 320
Jansen, R., 448, 456
Janzen, R., 576, 579
Jegatheesan, B., 231, 237, 239, 242, 535

Jensen, A. R., 325, 335
Jensen, P., 492, 505
Jessop, B. J., 387, 390
Jessop, J., 163, 167–168, 230, 241, 424
Jeste, D. V., 513, 516
Joe, R. C., 327, 335
Joffe, S., 496, 505
Joh, T., 610, 612
John, O. P., 329, 335
Johnson, A., 280, 283, 294
Johnson, D., 214–228
Johnson, K., 80, 83, 466, 473
Johnson, M. P., 559, 562
Johnson, M. W., 556, 562
Johnson, R. B., 64, 67
Johnson, W. B., 552, 554–556, 561–562, 564
Johnstone, W., 443, 455
Joint Committee on Standards for Educational Evaluation, 159, 167
Joint United Nations Programme on HIV/AIDS, 115, 119
Jones, C. A. L., 232–336
Jones, G., 444, 456
Jones, J. H., 112, 119, 246, 256
Jones, L., 47, 52, 342, 349, 351
Jones, P. W., 116–117, 119
Jones, R., 313, 315, 320, 446, 448–449, 456
Jones, S. J., 33–34, 37
Jonsen, A., 19, 21
Jordan, S. E., 511, 516
Juang, L., 327–329, 335
Julnes, G., 209–210, 212–213
Jutai, J., 511, 517

Kadour, R., 477–478, 487
Kagan, A., 511, 516
Kagan, J., 28, 37
Kahneman, D., 30–31, 38
Kaiser, J., 480, 487
Kalichman, M. W., 559, 562
Kalof, L., 284, 294
Kane, A. L., 509, 516
Kant, I., 17–18, 21, 26, 37
Kaphagawani, D. N., 412, 424
Karenga, M., 412, 424
Kashyap, N., 427, 440
Kasri, F., 333, 335
Kass, N. E., 398, 400, 405
Katz, J., 7–8, 21

Kaufmann, W., 357, 370
Kavussanu, M., 554, 563
Kayser-Jones, J., 509, 516
Kciji, T., 138, 148
Keefe, V., 313–316, 319–321
Keita, G. P., 555, 563
Keith, L., 75, 83
Keith, W., 577–579
Kellogg Commission on the Future of State and Land-Grant Universities, 337, 351
Kellogg Foundation, 171, 183
Kelly, J. G., 252, 257–258
Kelsey, J., 443, 456
Kemper, S., 512, 517
Kendall, F. E., 95, 100
Kendler, H. H., 32, 37
Kenkel, M. B., 555, 563
Kennedy, J., 328, 335
Kennedy-Pipe, C., 264, 273
Kenny, D. A., 327, 334
Kerin, J., 477, 480, 487
Kershaw, D., 8, 21
Kessler, R. C., 503, 506
Khakeo, R., 343, 351
Khanlou, N., 249, 255n3, 257
Khoza, R., 388, 390, 408, 424, 603, 613
Kidder, L., 36, 37–38
Kidder, L. H., 317, 320
Kim, J. J., 332, 335
Kimelman, M. D. Z., 511, 516
Kimmel, A. J., 5, 21, 479
Kimmel, D., 485, 487
Kincheloe, J. L., 153, 167
King, A., 270, 273
King, C. R., 155–156, 169
King, D., 58, 67
King, J. E., 171, 173, 177, 183
King, M., 493–494, 505
Kirkhart, K., 283, 294
Kirsch, G. E., 247, 255n7, 257, 307
Kitayama, S., 395, 406
Kitchener, K. S., xi, xiv, 5–22, 51n2, 52, 185, 247, 257, 526, 535, 554, 562
Kitchener, R., 5–22, 21, 185
Kitzinger, C., 298, 307
Klein, H. K., 56, 66–67, 267
Klein, M., 267, 273
Kleinman, L., 509, 516
Klug, M., 515–516

Knowlton, M., 79, 83
Knox, J., 483–484, 487
Knox, M., 80, 83
Kodish, E., 495–497, 505
Koester, J., 285, 288, 294
Kohlberg, L., 41, 52, 157, 167–168, 557, 563, 588, 613
Kohout, J., 555, 562
Koloi, O., 410, 423
Kon, A., 515–516
Kooken, K., 333, 335
Kopala, M., 554, 561
Korff, D., 215, 227
Koro-Ljungberg, M., 559, 562
Koski, G., 113, 120
Kovach, H., 116, 119
Krefting, L., 418, 424
Krieger, J., 252, 257
Kroeger, S., 243, 251, 257
Kuhn, T., 25, 37, 382, 385
Kupfer, D. J., 383, 385
Kvale, S., 30, 37

Ladd, P., 99, 100
Ladson-Billings, G., 56, 58, 62–63, 67, 93–95, 100
LaFrance, J. L., 135–148
LaFromboise, T. D., 148
Laguerre, M., 310, 320
Lai, C. S. Y., 327, 336
Laible, J. C., 421, 424
Laitinen, I., 173, 183
Lake, H., 357–358, 371
Lakhani, D., 427, 440
Lakin, S., 353, 371
Lane, H., 94, 100, 394, 405
Lang, H., 93, 100
Lansman, Y., 116, 119
Lantz, P. M., 338, 351
Lapsley, D. K., 560, 563
Larossa, R., 433, 440
Latane, B., 186–187
Lather, P., 153, 168, 309, 320, 463, 471
Lawrence, C. R., 58, 67
Leake, J., 110, 119
Leatherman, C., 556, 562
Lempert, L., 47, 53
Lerner, G., 49, 53
LeRoux, J. A., 331, 335

Lerum, K., 156, 168
Levenson, R. W., 329, 335
Levin, M., 244, 256
Levinas, E., 26–27, 37
Levine, R. J., 133n16, 134
Levinson, D. J., 157, 168
Levit, N., 495, 505
Leviton, L., 570, 579
Lewin, K., 28, 37
Lewin, S., 478, 484, 486
Lewis, H. M., 252, 257
Lewis, O., 192
Lichtenstein, R., 338, 351
Lieberman, M., 41, 52
Lifton, R. J., 246, 257
Lincoln, Y. S., x, xiv, 62–63, 66, 87, 99, 101, 151–153, 158, 162, 166–168, 231, 241–242, 245, 256, 307, 321, 394, 404–405, 424, 466–467, 471
Lingler, J. H., 509, 516
Lipsey, M. W., 171, 183, 400, 402, 405
Lloyd, A., 509, 516
Lloyd, M., 464–467, 471
Lobb, B., 444, 455
Lockwood, C. M., 327, 335
Løgstrup, K. E., 247, 257
Lohfeld, L., 511, 514, 517
Lomborg B., 110, 119
Loomba, A., 417, 424
Lord, J., 575, 579
Lorde, A., 59, 67
Lordos, A., 268, 273
Losen, D., 86, 100
Lott, B., 41, 53
Louis, K. S., 554, 558, 562, 564
Louw, D. J., 388, 390, 408, 413–414, 424, 603, 613
Lucaites, J., 369n4, 371
Ludema, J. D., 87, 100, 587, 613
Luft, J., 290, 294
Luhmann, N., 493, 505
Lundsford, A. A., 297, 307
Lunt, N., 76, 83
Lustig, M. W., 288, 294
Lustig, N., 116, 118, 285
Luthuli, P. C., 300, 307
Lykes, B., 251, 257
Lykes, M. B., 50, 53, 243, 251, 257
Lyman, S. M., 230, 242

Lynn, M., 58, 67
Lyon, E., 47, 52

Mabry, L., 107–119, 393, 529, 535
MacCallum, R. C., 380, 382, 385
MacDonald, B., 529, 535
MacDonald, S. M., 555, 562
MacDonald, S. P., 245, 257
MacGillivary, H., 575–576, 579
Maciak, B. J., 252, 258
MacIntyre, A., 247, 257
MacKinnon, C. A., 493, 505
MacKinnon, D. P., 327, 335
Macklin, R., 14, 21
Macpherson, C., 442–443, 457
MacQueen, K. M., 397, 406
Maelzer, J., 464, 466, 468, 471
Magnuson, V., 480, 486
Maguire, P., 43, 53, 244, 247, 255n3, 256–257
Mahoney, M., 47, 53
Makgoba, M. W., 415, 424
Malinowski, B., 229, 241
Mamdani, M., 412, 424
Manning, P. K., 111, 119
Manson, S., 143, 149
Manzo, L., 54, 67
Marcus, G., 525, 535
Marcus, G. E., 155–156, 168
Marecek, J., 36–38, 41, 52
Margolis, M. K., 509, 516
Mark, M. M., 101, 186–187, 200, 202–203, 206, 208–213
Marker, M., 147, 148
Markovits, C., 427, 440
Marks, E., 42, 53
Markus, H. R., 395, 406
Marrett, C., 133, 133n16
Marschark, M., 93, 100
Marsh, K., 392, 397, 406
Marshall, A., 433, 440
Martin, J., 471, 475, 479, 481–484, 487
Martinez, G., 361, 372
Marusic, A., 555, 563
Masaiganah, M. S., 243, 258
Mason, P., 460, 471
Mason, W. M., 328, 335
Massey, D., 523, 535
Mathison, S., 174, 176, 183, 610, 613
Matsuda, M. J., 58, 67

Matsumoto, D., 325–329, 331–333, 335–336
Matthew, S., 465, 471
Matza, L. S., 509, 516
Mauger, J., 315, 319
Mauthner, M., 163, 167–168, 230, 241, 387, 390, 407–408, 424
Max, A., 110, 119
May, W., 357, 371
May, W. F., 247, 257
Maynard, M., 463, 467, 471
Mazama, A., 298–299, 307
Mazwai, T., 415, 424
McCaffrey, D., 208, 213
McCarthy, J. F., 86, 99
McCreanor, T., 313, 315–316, 319–320, 443–444, 446–449, 455–456
McDonald, D. A., 142–143, 148
McGough, H., 143, 149
McGranaghan, R., 338, 351
McIntosh, T., 310, 320
McIntyre, A., 25, 38, 247, 251, 256–257
McKeown, B., 176, 183
McKie, B., 60, 68
McLaren, P., 153, 167
McLeod, K., 165n4, 168
McManus, V., 316, 319, 444, 446–448, 455–456
McNeil, P., 444, 456
McPeak, B., 203, 205, 212
Mead, A., 310, 320
Mead, H. M., 313, 316–317, 320
Mead, M., 229, 241
Meara, N. M., 247, 257
Mednick, M. T., 555, 563
Meezan, W., 475, 479, 481–484, 487
Melton, G., 479, 485, 487
Melton, G. B., 490–492, 496, 499, 505
Meltzer, H., 461, 471
Menzies, C. R., 146, 149
Mercer, G., 75, 77, 80, 82–84, 337, 459, 461–464, 466–468, 469n2, 470–473
Mercer, S. L., 337, 351
Merideth, L., 208, 213
Merleau-Ponty, M., 26, 31, 38
Merriam Webster, 399, 406
Merrifield, J., 252, 257
Mertens, D. M., 61, 64, 67, 76–77, 83–84, 86, 91, 100–101, 110, 119, 152, 168, 176, 183, 242, 394, 397, 399, 404, 406, 458, 471, 598, 610–611, 613

Meslin, E. M., 7, 21
Messick, S., 281, 294
Meyer, H., 243, 251, 257
Mies, M., 462, 467, 471
Mignolo, W., 535
Migotsky, C., 532, 536
Milgram, S., 21, 111, 119, 186–187, 190, 196–197, 359, 371, 551, 562
Mill, J. S., 17, 21, 110, 119
Miller, C., 465, 471
Miller, D., 96, 99
Miller, D. T., 402, 406
Miller, E. J., 460, 468, 471
Miller, J. B., 41, 53
Miller, J. C., 191–192, 197, 555
Miller, J. S., 555, 563
Miller, T., 163, 167–168, 230, 241, 387, 390, 424
Miller, V. A., 495–497, 505
Miller-Wilson, L. S., 494–495, 505
Millet, R. A., 394, 399, 401, 405
Minh-Ha, T., 318n4, 320
Ministry of Health (New Zealand), 444, 456
Ministry of Social Development (New Zealand), 410, 424, 442, 447, 456
Minker, M., 256, 258
Minkler, M., 67, 245, 252, 258, 337, 351
Minnema, J., 171, 173, 177, 183
Mintz, L. B., 555, 562
Mireshghi, S., 331, 335
Mitchell, E., 444, 456
Mkabela, N. Q., 300, 307
Mkabela, Q., 296, 298–299, 304, 307, 411–412, 422, 424
Mock, L. O., 252, 257–258
Moewaka Barnes, H., 312, 320, 443, 456
Mohatt, G., 142, 145, 149
Mok, M., 80, 83
Molyneux, C. S., 392, 397, 406
Moncrieff, J., 375, 385
Monti-Catania, D., 47, 52
Montoya, M., 489–506
Moore, A., 445, 456
Moore, J., 310, 319
Moore, M., 76, 80, 82–83, 463–464, 466, 468, 470–472
Morgan, D. L., 401–402, 406
MORI, 270, 273
Morris, J., 74–75, 81, 84, 463, 466, 471
Morris, M., 174, 183, 328, 335

Morris, N., 271, 273
Morrissey, S., 376, 385
Mortensen, P., 258, 307
Moss, B. J., 245, 258
Mosteller, F., 203, 205, 212
Motta, M. M., 556, 562
Mounty, J., 86, 101
Mudaliar, S., 513, 516
Munsey, C., 133n17, 134
Murchie, E., 448, 456
Murphy, N., 25, 38
Murphy, T., 480–482, 487
Mutu, M., 317, 320–321
Myers, C., 318, 321
Myklebust, H., 94, 101

Nachson, I., 444, 455
Nadash, P., 464, 466, 468, 473
Nagel, J., 236, 241
Nairn, R., 443, 455
Nannis, E. D., 494, 505
Narváez, D., 556, 560, 563
Nashashibi, I. M., 266, 273
National Academy of Sciences, 550–553, 557, 563
National Aeronautics and Space Administration, 221, 227
National Association of Social Workers, 112, 119, 529, 535
National Bioethics Advisory Commission, 513, 516
National Commission for the Protection of Human Subjects in Biomedical and Behavioral Research, 57, 67, 113, 119–120, 123, 134, 152, 168
National Commission for the Protection of Human Subjects of Research, 137, 149
National Council of Teachers of Mathematics, 534–535
National Health and Medical Research Council, 551, 563
National Institute on Deafness and Other Communication Disorders, 511, 516
National Institutes of Health, 484, 487
National Patient Safety Agency, 221, 227
National Research Council, 164–165n2, 168
Ndedya, E., 243, 258
Needleman, H. L., 551, 563
Nelson, G., 575–576, 579
Nelson, M. L., 555, 563

Nelson, N., 554, 562
Neutze, J., 444, 456
Neville, H., 555, 560
Newell, J. D., 19, 22
Newkirk, T., 248–249, 258, 297, 307
Newman, D., 173, 183, 529, 532, 535
Newton, J. H., 355, 357–359, 361, 366–369, 369n6, 371–372
Nicholls, V., 465, 471
Nicolosi, J., 476, 487
Nielsen, J. M., 42, 53
Nightingale, D. J., 63, 67
Nightingale, M. C., 509, 516
9/11 Commission Report, 428, 439
Nirje, B., 71, 84
Nobles, W., 310–311, 321
Noblitt, G. W., 401, 404–405
No Child Left Behind Act, 114, 120
Noddings, N., 21, 40–41, 53, 151, 156–157, 168, 258
Noe, T., 143, 149
Noel, S., 264, 273
Northridge, M. E., 337, 352
Nowrangi, M. A., 513, 516
Ntseane, P. G., 296–307
Nui, D., 316, 320
Nyamnjoh, F. B., 421, 424, 425
Nyden, P., 338–339, 351–352

Oakes, J. M., 113, 120
Oakley, A., 238, 241–242, 468, 471
Ochocka, J., 575–576, 579
O'Connor, C., 93, 101
O'Fallon, L. R., 337, 352
Office for Human Research Protections, 134, 483, 487
Office of Inspector General, Department of Health and Human Services, 133n16, 134
Okrusch, C., 361–362, 372
O'Leary, K. D., 47, 52
Oliver, M., 72–76, 80–82, 82n1, 83–84, 459, 461–463, 465, 467–471
Omer, A., 430, 440
Omolewa, M., 420, 425
O'Neill, P., 504–505
Ong, A., 62, 67
Onwuegbuzie, A. J., 64, 67
Orange, C., 309–310, 321, 443, 454n2, 456
Oransky, I., 380, 385
Orfield, G., 86, 100

Organization for Economic Cooperation and Development, 215–216, 227–228
Orleans, S., 196, 197
Ormand, A., 313, 321, 424
Ormond, A., 408, 424
Ormsby, C., 313, 316, 319–320
Ormsby, W., 313, 319
Ortiz-Walters, R., 555, 563
Oruka, O., 412, 425
Ostrow, D. G., 503, 506
Owensby, N., 475, 479, 487
Oyserman, D., 402, 406

Pager, D., 195, 197
Pahiri, D., 315, 319
Pain, R., 60, 63, 65, 86
Pais, J., 86, 100
Paley, A. R., 608, 613
Palmer, B. W., 513, 516
Pandey, T. N., 234, 242
Papierno, P. B., 209, 211
Paquet, M., 514, 516
Paranjape, A., 557, 561
Parish, S. L., 82n1, 83
Park, A. H., 43, 53
Park, J., 444–445, 456
Park, P., 255–257
Parker, E. A., 245, 252, 256–258, 337, 351
Parker, L., 58, 67–68
Parlour, S., 484, 488
Parmenter, T. R., 80, 83
Passas, N., 429, 431, 439n2, 440
Pasteen, T., 316, 320
Patai, D., 297–298, 307
Patsdaughter, C., 476, 487
Pattatucci, A., 480, 486–487
Patton, M. Q., 581
Paul, C., 444, 456
Pearson, D., 442–443, 457
Pellauer, M. D., 40, 51
Pellegrino, J. W., 114, 120
Peller, G., 57, 65, 67
Pene, H., 313, 320
Peng, T.-K., 328, 335
Penslar, R. L., 123, 132n4, 134
Pere, R., 444, 456
Peretini, R., 316, 321
Peshu, N., 392, 397, 406
Peter, E., 249, 255n3, 257
Peters, D., 478–479, 486

Peterson, D. J., 142–143, 148
Pew Research Center, 269, 273
Phillips, L., 612n5, 613
Philpin, S. M., 511, 516
Phinney, J., 402, 406
Pica, M., 31–32, 38
Picciotto, R., 172–173, 175, 183
Pielke, R. A., 110, 120
Pielke, R. A., Jr., 196–197
Pihama, L., 313, 321
Pile, S., 523, 535
Pink, S., 358, 372, 401, 404
Pion, G. M., 555, 563
Pipi, K., 313–315, 321
Pitama, S., 315, 319
Pizarro, M., 62, 68
Plake, B. S., 137, 148
Platzer, H., 475, 482, 487
Plotkin, J., 478–479, 486
Plummer, K., 150, 168–169
Pohit, S., 429, 440
Polanyi, M., 31, 38
Polkinghorne, D., 24, 38
Pollock, A., 369n4, 372
Pomerantz, J. R., 206, 213
Ponce, A. N., 559, 563
Poortinga, Y. H., 327, 335, 394, 405
Popper, K. R., 384–385
Porsanger, J., 415, 425
Poutasi, K., 444, 456
Power, C., 557, 559, 563
PQMethod: Release 2.11, 177, 183
Prah, K. K., 412, 415, 425
Prakash, S., 337, 352
Preece, J., 92, 99, 297, 304, 306, 412, 420, 422–423, 423n1, 423n3
Prendergast, K., 268–269, 273
Preston-Shoot, M., 464–467, 471
Pretzer-Aboff, I., 513, 516–517
Priestly, M., 74, 76, 80–81, 84, 459, 462, 466, 468, 472
Prilelltensky, I., 576, 579
Proctor, R. W., 26, 37
Psacharopoulos, G., 116, 120
Public Health Service, 550–551, 563
Public Responsibility in Medicine and Research, 130, 134
Pugsley, L., 433, 441
Punch, M., 231, 242, 296, 438, 440
Purdie, G., 316, 320

Qin-Hilliard, D., 523, 536
Quaye, S. J., 62, 68
Quigley, D., 342, 352
Quinn, S. C., 246, 250, 258
Quiros, L., 475, 487

Rabinow, P., 229, 234, 242
Radan, A., 50, 53
Radeos, M. S., 113, 120
Ragins, B. R., 555, 563
Rais, S. M., 239, 242
Rallis, S. F., 200, 213
Ramaswamy, E. A., 241–242
Rambo, C., 158, 169
Ramsey, G., 409, 411–412, 416, 425
Rappaport, J., 317, 320–321
Rawls, J., 15, 17, 21, 88, 101, 151, 169, 567, 579
Ray, R. E., 297, 307
Raymond, J., 42, 53
Reamer, R., 528, 535
Reardon, K., 476, 487
Reason, P., 95, 100–101, 244, 255n3, 257–258, 613
Reber, J., 28, 38
Redfern, A. K., 433, 441
Redfield, R., 192
Redner, R. L., 555, 561
Reed, C. R., 113, 120
Reed, R. J., 559, 564
Reed-Danahay, D., 150, 169
Reeve, P., 576, 579
Reich, S. M., 89, 203, 205–206, 211
Reichardt, C. S., 202, 208, 213
Reid, P., 310, 313, 316, 320–321, 442, 456
Reid, T., 24, 38
Reina, D. S., 291, 293n1, 294
Reina, M. L., 291, 293n1, 294
Reisch, M., 89, 101
Reissman, C. K., 231, 242
Renault-Caragianes, P., 339, 352
Resnick, B., 513, 516–517
Resnik, D. B., 9, 21, 123, 125, 134
Rest, J., 21, 556, 563
Reviere, R., 408, 411–412, 418, 423n2, 425
Reynolds, C. F., 509, 516
Reynolds, P. D., 5, 21
Rich, K., 316, 320
Richardson, F., 28, 38
Richardson, H. S., 19, 21, 33, 38

Richardson, L., 96, 101
Richman, K. A., 556, 563
Richmond, D., 444, 456
Ricoeur, P., 27, 29, 38, 383–384
Rideout, C. A., 555, 562
Rioiux, M., 462, 472
Ripley, E. B. D., 125, 134
Rivera, L., 44–45, 52
Rizvi, F., 521–536
Roberts, G. C., 554–555, 563–564
Roberts, H., 241–242
Roberts, J. W., 252, 257
Roberts, S., 476, 487
Robinson, W. S., 328, 336
Robson, B., 310, 316, 320–321, 442, 454
Roediger, H., 34–35, 38
Rogers, T., 479, 486
Rogers, W. A., 392, 406
Rogoff, K., 116, 118
Root, M., 578n7, 579
Rorty, R., 25–26, 38
Rosaldo, R., 155–156, 169
Rosenberg, L., 558, 562
Rosenblum, N., 369n1, 372
Rosenthal, R., 206, 209–210, 213, 585
Rosiek, J., 163, 169
Rosier, P., 444, 456
Ross, L., 498, 503, 506
Ross, L. C., 252, 257
Ross, M., 402, 406
Ross, W. D., 13, 17–18, 22
Rossi, P. H., 171, 183
Rossman, K. M., 555, 562
Rother, L., 138, 149
Rousseau, C. K., 58, 66
Rubin, P., 138, 147n3, 149
Ruddick, S., 40, 53
Ruffins, P., 499, 506
Russ, K., 513, 516–517
Russell, B., 493, 506
Russell-Minda, E., 511, 517
Ryan, K. E., 171, 183
Ryan Commission on Research Integrity, 550–551, 563
Ryen, A., 231–232, 234, 237, 239–240, 242

Sacco, J., 360, 372
Sackett, L. A., 47, 53
Sacks, H., 232, 241, 356
Sacks, O., 356, 372

Sahota, P., 140, 141, 149
Saks, E. R., 513, 516
Salazar, C. F., 559, 561
Sales, B. D., 22, 246, 248, 256, 258, 551, 563
Salisbury, V., 463, 472
Salmond, A., 309, 321
Salter, A. C., 551, 563
Samarapungavan, A., 532, 536
Sambunjak, D., 555, 563
Sample, P. L., 467, 472
Sampson, H., 431, 440
Sanders, J., 531, 536
Sandhu, H. S., 430, 440
Sartre, J. P., 26, 38
Sassen, S., 525, 536
Saunders, D. G., 47, 53
Savage, A., 475, 487
Savage, M. C., 155, 169
Sawhney, D. K., 47, 52
Scherer, K. R., 334, 336
Schlosser, L. Z., 554, 563
Schmitz, J. G., 532, 536
Schoenbaum, M., 208, 213
Schreier, B., 480, 487
Schroeder, M., 198, 212
Schuklenk, U., 477, 480, 487
Schulte, B., 608, 613
Schulz, A. J., 245, 252, 256–258, 337, 351
Schulz, R., 509, 516
Schutt, R. K., 431, 439
Schutz, A., 231, 242
Schwandt, T. A., 171, 174, 183, 211, 532, 536
Schwartz, R. D., 186–187, 189–197
Schweigert, F. J., 173, 175, 183
Scinta, S., 144, 148
Scott-Jones, D., 503, 506
Scragg, R., 444, 456
Scriven, M., 183, 399, 406, 532, 536, 610–613
Scriven, R., 200, 213
Seale, C., 241–242
Sechrest, L., 186–187
Seelau, S., 444, 455
Segal, J. M., 266, 273–274
Segall, M. H., 394, 405
Segone, M., 90, 101
Seierstad, Å., 239, 242
Selden, S. C., 176, 182
Seligman, M., 33, 38
SenGupta, S., 61, 68, 610, 613

Sevenhuijsen, S., 157, 169
Shadish, W. R., x, xiv, 183, 200–202, 204–205, 213, , 570, 579
Shafer, C., 255n9, 256
Shakespeare, T., 71, 76–77, 80–81, 84, 461–463, 467–468, 470, 472–473
Shamoo, A. E., 123, 125, 134
Shapiro, H. T., 7, 21
Sharkey, W. F., 327, 336
Sharma, D., 427, 431, 433, 440
Sharp, A., 443, 456
Shavelson, R. J., 114, 119
Shaw, A. M., 241–242
Shaw, L.L., 233–234, 241
Sheets, V., 327, 335
Shepard, P. M., 337, 352
Sherbourne, C., 208, 213
Shikaki, K., 266, 274
Shogan, D., 40, 53
Shohat, E., 59, 68
Shope, J. H., 62, 68
Shope, T., 415, 424
Shoultz, B., 71, 84
Sieber, J. E., 5, 19, 22, 202, 213, 387, 390, 475, 479, 487, 551, 563
Silka, L., 337–338, 343, 345–347, 351–352
Silver, C., 490–491, 506
Silver, J., 463, 472
Silverman, D., 229, 231–232, 237–239, 241–242, 462, 472
Simons, H., 89, 101, 172, 183
Simons, K., 80, 84, 466, 473
Sindane, J., 414, 425
Singelis, T., 327, 336
Singer, P., 431, 440
Sitta, S. A., 266, 274
Skeggs, B., 150, 169
Skelton, T., 475, 481–482, 484, 488
Skolnick, H. H., 194–195, 197
Slater, J. K., 394, 399, 401, 405
Slife, B. D., 23–38
Smeyers, P., 547, 549
Smith, A., 109, 120
Smith, A. J., 50, 53
Smith, C., 461, 471
Smith, D., 62, 68, 98, 100
Smith, D. L., 433, 441
Smith, G. H., 312, 318n4, 321
Smith, J. K., 153

Smith, L., 56, 59, 61–62, 68, 443, 446, 456
Smith, L. T., 97, 101, 145–146, 149, 152, 160–161, 166–169, 307, 309–310, 313–314, 317–318, 318n2, 321, 391, 406, 446, 457
Smith, N. C., 329, 334
Smith, P., 270, 274
Smith, T., 443, 455
Smith-Maddox, R., 64, 68
Smyer, M., 514, 517
Sobeck, J. L., 142, 149
Social Research Association, 528, 536
Soja, E., 523, 536
Solheim, E., 116, 120
Solomon, C. R., 559, 562
Solomos, J., 462, 469
Solórzano, D. G., 57–58, 62, 64, 67–68
Sparks, E. E., 43, 53
Spear, P., 121–134
Speiglman, R., 121–134
Spelman, E., 42–43, 53
Spiro, R. J., 532, 536
Spitzer, R., 487–488
Spivak, G. C., 251, 258
Spoonley, P., 310, 322, 442–443, 457
Sprague, R. L., 551, 554–555, 563–564
Springwood, C. F., 155–156, 169
Srinivas, M. N., 234, 241–242
Staccarini, J. M., 557, 562
Stair, T. O., 113, 120
Stake, R. E., 231, 237, 239, 242, 532, 536
Stalker, K., 466–467, 472
Stanfield, J., 391, 406, 586, 613
Stanley, B., 479, 487
Stanley, J. C., 94, 99, 200–201, 211
Stanley, L., 466–467, 472
Steele, J. M., 374, 385
Steele v. Hamilton County Mental Health Board, 493, 506
Stefancie, J., 57–58, 66, 256
Steger, M., 523, 536
Stein, E., 477, 480, 487
Stein, J., 511, 517
Steininger, M., 19, 22
Steneck, N. H., 123, 125, 134
Stephenson, W., 176, 183
Stern, J. E., 553, 557, 564
Stern, P., 284, 294
Stevahn, L., 171, 173, 177, 183

Stevens, F. I., 61, 68
Stevenson, H. C., 503, 506
Stewart, C., 338, 352
Stewart, S., 243, 251, 257
Stigler, S. M., 210, 213
Stokes, E. J., 555, 562
Stone, E., 74, 80–81, 84, 459, 468, 472
Stott, W. C., 366, 372
Stover, G., 337, 352
St. Pierre, E. A., 96, 101
Strahan, E. J., 382, 385
Strauss, S. E., 555, 563
Strong, G., 511, 517
Suárez-Orozco, M., 536
Suber, P., 493, 506
Sue, D. W., 610, 613
Sullivan, M., 69–84
Sultana, F., 60, 63, 65
Sutton, J., 511, 517
Swain, J., 78, 84, 465, 472
Swanson, D., 421, 425
Swantz, M. L., 243, 258
Swazey, J. P., 552–555, 557–558, 564
Swindon People First Research Team, 466, 473
Swisher, K. G., 135–136, 149
Symonette, H., 147, 149, 279–294, 610, 612–613
Szala-Meneok, K., 511, 514, 517

Taiapa, J., 443, 455–456
Takaro, T. K., 252, 257
Taki, M., 312, 321
Tandon, R., 244, 258
Tandon, S. D., 252, 257–258
Taneja, N., 429, 440
Tarmina, M., 476, 487
Tarule, J. M., 150, 166
Tata, J., 328, 335
Tate, W. F., 58, 67
Taylor, B., 444, 456
Taylor, C., 27, 32–33, 38, 578n4, 579
Teariki, C., 310, 322
Te Awekotuku, N., 310, 313, 321, 445, 457
Teffo, L. J., 415, 425
Te Hennepe, S., 315, 321
Telfer, B., 444, 456
Tellez, T., 338, 352
Temple, B., 464–467, 471
Te Puni Kokiri, 442, 457

Tessler, M., 269, 274
Teubner, G., 494, 506
Thal, L., 513, 516
Thoma, S. J., 559, 561
Thomas, C., 408, 425, 463, 472
Thomas, D., 176, 183
Thomas, K., 65, 67
Thomas, L. R., 142, 145, 149
Thomas, M., 431, 440
Thomas, S. B., 246, 250, 258
Thomas, V. G., 54–68
Thompson, B., 379, 385
Thompson, D., 566, 578–579
Thompson-Robinson, M., 61, 68, 610, 613
Thornton, P., 76, 83
Thrift, N., 523, 535
Throckmorton, W., 480, 488
Thurnbull, C. M., 234, 242
Tierney, W. G., 158, 168
Ting, K., 43, 51, 247, 255
Tipene-Leach, D., 447–448, 455, 457
Tobias, M., 442, 454
Todd, P., 208, 212
Tolich, M., 128, 130, 133n15, 134, 319, 444, 455, 457
Tolman, D., 253, 256
Tolman, D. L., 245, 258
Toms, K., 104, 170–182
Tong, R., 40, 53
Torbert, B., 254, 256
Torbert, W. R., 254, 258
Torre, M. E., 35, 37, 60, 68
Toulmin, S., 19, 21
Touraine, A., 462, 472
Tournas, S. A., 413, 425
Towne, L., 114, 119
Townsend, P., 461, 472
Traber, M., 151, 167
Traustadottir, R., 80, 83
Treloar, C., 396, 406
Treverthan, S. D., 41, 53
Trials of war criminals before the Nuremberg Military Tribunals under control Council Law No. 10, 132n2, 134
Trimble, J. E., 137, 149
Trimpey, M. L., 47, 53
Trochim, W. M., 610, 613
Troebst, S., 264, 274
Tronto, J. C., 151, 157, 169

Truax, C. B., 588, 613
Truman, C., 458, 471
Tryon, G. S., 558, 564
Tsark, J., 312, 322
Tuckman, B. W., 433, 440
Tufte, E. R., 361, 367, 372, 374, 385
Tully, C., 475, 482, 488
Turnbull, C. M., 196n1, 197
Turner, D., 104, 104, 170–183
Turner, L. A., 64, 67
Turner, M., 465, 472
Tuuta, C., 315, 319
Tversky, A., 30–31, 38
TwoTrees, K., 279, 294

UAE Government, 430, 440–441
UAE Government & International Monetary Fund, 441
Ulrich, W., 64, 68
UN Convention on the Rights of the Child, 490, 506
Union of the Physically Impaired Against Segregation, 71, 84, 460–461, 473
United Nations General Assembly, 115–116, 120
United Nations Organization, 89, 90, 101
Unterstaller, U., 47, 52
Unutzer, J., 208, 213
U.S. Congress, 428, 441
U.S. Department of Education, 86, 101, 114, 120
U.S. Department of Health, Education, and Welfare, 113, 120, 202, 212
U.S. Department of Health and Human Services (HHS), 122–123, 134, 140, 149
U.S. General Accounting Office, 269, 274

Vaags, R. H., 231, 242
Valenstein, M., 86, 99
Valentine, G., 475, 481–482, 484, 488
van de Koppel, J. M. H., 327, 335
Van der Klaauw, W., 208, 212
Van de Vijver, F. J. R., 327–329, 332, 335–336
Van Hove, G., 465, 470
Van Maanen, J., 111, 119–120
Vargas, L., 489–506
Veblen, T., 235, 242
Vera, S., 48, 53
Vernon, A., 467–468, 473
Viadero, D., 114, 120

Victor, B., 557, 564
Vidich, A. J., 8, 22, 230, 242
Villegas, T., 394, 401, 404–405
Vispoel, W. P., 532, 536

Wagner, E. M., 555, 562
Waldon, J., 314, 322
Walker, C. A., 396, 406
Walker, L. J., 41, 53
Walker, R. J., 310, 322, 442–443, 457
Walker, S., 313, 321
Wallbott, H., 334, 336
Wallcraft, J., 76, 79–80, 82–83, 463, 470
Wallerstein, I., 231, 242
Wallerstein, N., 245, 256, 258, 337, 351
Walmsley, J., 466, 473
Walsh-Bowers, R., 484, 488
Walster, E., 399, 406
Walster, G. W., 399, 406
Wands, S., 270, 274
Wang, C., 251, 258
Ward, L., 80, 84, 465, 467, 473
Warnick, B. R., 538, 546, 549
Warring, J., 511, 516
Washington, H. A., 392–394, 406
Wassenaar, D. R., 392, 397, 406
Watson, N., 462, 467, 472–473
Wax, M. L., 137, 149
Webb, E. J., 186–187
Weems, L., 152–153, 163, 169
Wegener, D. T., 382, 385
Weijer, C., 398, 406
Weiss, J., 433, 439–440
Welches, P., 31–32, 38
Welland, T., 433, 441
Wells, K. B., 208, 213
Wenger, G. C., 510, 517
Wertz, F. J., 550–564
West, S. G., 327, 335
Whariki Research Group, 445, 457
White, D. Y., 559, 564
White, G., 8, 8, 22
Whitehead, A., 377, 385
Whitehead, A. N., 25, 38
Whitmore, E., 569–570, 578
Whyte, W. F., 229–230, 239, 242
Wicherski, M., 555, 562
Wiewel, W., 339, 352
Wilber, K., 291, 294

Wilcox, B. L., 491–492, 505
Wilhelm, F. H., 329, 334
Wilkinson, L., 379, 385
Wilkinson, P., 270, 272
Wilkinson, S., 298, 307
William, C., 296, 307
William K. Fung Multidisciplinary Workshop, 269, 274
Williams, B. T., 251, 258, 546, 549
Williams, K., 512, 517
Williams, M. K., 559, 563
Williams, M. R., 559, 564
Williams, R., 359, 372
Williams, R. N., 380–381, 384
Williams, V., 466, 473
Willig, C., 63, 68
Wilson, A., 86, 101
Wilson, M., 64, 68
Wilson, P. F., 554–555, 564
Wilton Park Conference, 268, 274
Wing, A. K., 56–57, 59, 68
Wing, S., 338–339, 351–352
Wise, S., 467, 472
Wittel, A., 525, 536
Wittgenstein, L., 24–25, 38
Wolf, A., 104, 170–183
Wolf, L., 484, 488
Wolf, M., 297, 307
Wolf, R. L., 154, 164n1, 169
Wolfensberger, W., 71, 84
Wong, L. M., 155, 169
Wood, W. W., 156, 169
Woodhall, M., 116, 120
Woodman, N., 475, 482, 488
World Bank Independent Evaluation Group, 116–117, 120
World Health Organization, 312, 322
World Intellectual Property Organization, 228
World Medical Association General Assembly, 115, 120
Worthen, B., 531, 536
Wright, H. K., 95, 101
Wright, R., 433, 441
Wuu, R., 464–467, 471

Yarhouse, M., 480, 488
Yee, J. T., 61, 66
Yoo, S. H., 326, 328, 331, 335
Yosso, T. J., 58, 62, 67–68

Young, I. M., 567, 578–579
Youngman, F., 420, 425
Yu, H. C., 610, 612
Yuchtman-Yaar, E., 266, 272
Yuki, G., 328, 335

Zagaris, B., 433, 441
Zamiska, N., 381, 385
Zandecki, J., 484, 488
Zarb, G., 74–76, 80, 84, 463–466, 468, 472–473
Zeber, J. E., 86, 99
Zerner, C., 165n4, 169
Zimbardo, P. G., 8, 22, 186–187, 190, 196–197
Zinberg, G., 477, 485
Zucker, D. M., 557, 562
Zucker, K., 480, 486

SUBJECT INDEX

Academic freedom:
  IRBs and, 129–130
  transnationalism and, 532–533
Acadia Institute's Project on
    Professional Values and Ethical
    Issues in the Graduate
    Education of Scientists and
    Engineers, 552–553, 557–558
Access Alliance Multicultural
    Community Health Centre, 61
Accountability:
  and Aotearoa (New Zealand)
    research ethics, 445–447
  and research ethics for
    transnational spaces, 528–529
Accredited impairment, 469n1
Act-utilitarianism, ethical theory
    and, 17
Advanced directives for research
    (ADRs), 513
Adversarial stakeholders,
    259–260, 266
Advisory working Alliance
    Inventory (AWAI), 554
African-centered ethics:
  and the Afrocentric paradigm,
    411–412
  as built upon dialogue/
    agreement/particularity,
    421–422
  as built upon respect/religion,
    420–421
  and collaborative research
    between
    developed/developing
    countries, 409–410
  culture and, 412–413
  ethics review boards and,
    410–411
  overview, 407–409
  religiosity and, 413
  and researcher as colonizer,
    416–417
  and researcher as knower/
    teacher, 417–419
  and researcher as redeemer
    of problem, 419–420
  and researcher as transformative
    healer, 416
  scientific colonization and, 409
  Ubuntu (self-determination/
    rebirth) and, 415–416
  Ubuntu (self/other respect)
    and, 413–414
Afrocentricity (Asante), 411
Afrocentric paradigm, 295–296,
    298–300
Aged. *See* Older adults and
    research ethics
Aggregative democracy, 566

Alzheimer's disease and older adult research, 508–509
American Anthropological Association (AAA), 6, 20, 151, 159, 166, 551, 560
American Educational Research Association (AERA), 166, 393, 395, 399, 402, 404
American Evaluation Association (AEA), 118, 171–172, 178–182, 393, 395–396, 399, 402, 405
  Guiding Principles for Evaluators, 112, 206
  program evaluation and, 171, 177–180
  psychological research and, 374
  qualitative research issues and, 151
  transformative research/ethics and, 90–91
American Historical Association (AHA), 151, 166
American Indian Higher Education Association (AIHEC), 143, 146, 148
American Indian Law Center, Inc., 139, 143, 148
American Indians:
  and failure of human subject protection, 138–139
  and governmental research agenda, 139
  historical perspectives of research of, 135–137
  impact of controlling research agendas on, 142–144
  and Indian Health Service IRB, 140
  process of research changes for, 137–138
  terminology for, 147n2
  and Tribal College IRB, 140
  and Tribal IRB, 140–142
  value systems/alternative epistemologies and, 144–147
American Medical Association (AMA), 381, 384
American Political Science Association, 20
  and professional code of ethics, 6
American Psychiatric Association, 485, 509, 516
American Psychological Association (APA), 20, 39, 45, 51, 91, 99, 112, 113n17, 118, 159, 166, 379, 384, 393, 395, 398–399, 402, 405, 479, 485, 492, 504, 554–555, 610, 612
  ethical principles of, 323–324
  on informed consent, 397–398
  LGBTQ research and, 475
  and professional code of ethics, 6, 9
  RCR standards and, 554

and regulation of scientific inquiry, 112
Task Force on Statistical Inference (TFSI), 379
transformative research/ethics and, 6, 90–91
American Psychological Association Ethics Committee, 551, 560
American Sociological Association (ASA), 20, 111–112, 118, 151, 159, 166, 551, 560
  Hawala and, 431
  and professional code of ethics, 6
  qualitative research issues and, 151
Anglo-American postmodernism, 25–26
Anthropology Today, 151
Applied ethics, 1–2, 5–6
Applied social research, 171, 610–611
Archivists of data archiving ethics, 219–224
Aroha ki te tangata approach to Māori people, 313–314
Association of Canadian Universities for Northern Studies (ACUNS), 312
Audism, 96. *See also* Deafness
Austral-Asian Evaluation Society (AES), 151, 177–180
Aotearoa (New Zealand) research ethics:
  and accountability of researchers, 445–447
  field accounts of research, 447–453
  historical perspectives of, 442–445
Authenticity criteria and ethics, 153–156
Autonomy, RCR standards and, 554
Average effect sizes, 209–210
Aviation Safety Reporting System, 221
Axiological assumptions of transformative research, 87–92

Balance and authenticity, 153
Balancing approach to ethical theory, 19
Banking system of terrorists. *See* Hawala
Barrow Alcohol Study, 138
Behavioral sciences:
  definition, 7–8
  principlism and, 19
  quantitative research methods, use/misuse and, 378–381
Belfast Agreement, 259
Belmont Report, 8, 16, 18, 113, 116–117, 123, 137, 152, 164–165n2, 202, 206
Bellamy, David, 110
Beneficence:
  ethical principles and, 13–14
  as principle of research ethics, 595–596
  RCR standards and, 554

Beneficial research, 504n2
Bias. *See also* Disability research ethics
  cross-cultural psychology research and, 332–333
  and ethics in underserved communities, 400–401
  heterosexist, 476–478
  mental health care applications and, 367–368
  and reconciling conflicts of interest, 260–261
  value laden resemblances and, 33
Bioethics, principlism and, 19
Biomedical ethics/federal regulations, 7–8
Bogard, William, 538
Book Seller of Kabul, The (Seierstad), 239
Bosnia, peacemaking/ethics and, 264–265
Boulder Valley School District (BVSD), 571–573
Brentano, Franz, 26
Brief Familismo Scale, 44
British Council of Disabled People (BCODP), 463, 468, 469n4
Buckley amendment rights, 152
Butler, Lord of Brockwell, 271

Canadian Evaluation Society, 151
Canadian International Development Agency, 409
Care as concept, 157–158, 243–244, 255n6
Cash for Care project, 468
Casuistry approach to ethical theory, 19
Catalytic authenticity, 153–155
Categorical Imperative of Kant, 17–18
The Center for Advanced Study, 131
Centers for Disease Control (CDC), 337
Centre for Democracy and Reconciliation in South East Europe (CDRSEE), 263–264
Challenger space shuttle, 362–363
Chief Illiniwek, 162–163
Christians, cultural continuity and, 161
CitiNRI, 439n8
Code of Ethics, 112
Coding systems for sensitive material, 482–483, 529
Collaborative research ethics, 304, 404n6
Collective versus individual interviewing, 302–303
Colonization/research of African people, 409, 416–417

Colonization/research of Māori people, 309–312
Common Rule, 123–124, 131
Communication:
  African-centered research ethics and, 421–422
  graduate education and, 554
  Hawala and, 432–433
  networked ethics and, 540–543
  and older adult research, 510–512
  transnationalism and, 535
Communication Trust, 291
Communities, underserved:
  and assumption of homogeneity, 394–395
  historical perspectives of ethics of, 393–394
  minor research ethics and, 498–499
  overview, 391–393
  researcher in, 393, 399–401
  research process/outcomes in, 401–403
  role of ethics in social science research in, 395–399
Community:
  impact of cross-cultural psychology research on, 334
  involvement in research partnership ethics, 348–349
  and researcher partnerships in minor research, 499–500
  transnationalism and, 525
Community advisory boards (CAB), and indigenous communities, 141
Community Care (Direct Payments) Act, 464
Competency Trust, 291
Confidentiality. *See also* Privacy
  in cross-cultural psychology research, 333–334
  and field accounts of Aotearoa research, 449–451
  indigenous peoples and, 145
  IRBs and, 124–125
  LGBTQ research and, 481–484
  and minors in research, 503
  as principle of research ethics, 601–603
  qualitative research issues and, 152
  researcher-self ethics and, 301–302
Conscientizacion, 154
Consent. *See* Informed consent
Contesting research, critical race feminism and, 59–60
Contextual family resemblances, 24, 30–32

Continental European postmodernism, 26–27
Contractarianism, 16
Contractualism, 17
Contractual Trust, 291
Convention on the Elimination of All Forms of Discrimination Against Women, 90
Convention on the Rights of the Child, 90, 159
Conversion therapy for LGBTQ, 479–480
Cook, James, 309–310
Cooption/resistance issues and researcher-subject ethics, 303
Copyright of indigenous knowledge, 165n5
Council of Graduate Schools, 552
Council of National Psychological Associations for the Advancement of Ethnic Minority Interests (CNPAAEMI), 98n1
Covenantal ethics:
  care as concept and, 243–244
  as common foundation for social research, 253
  and distribution of research results, 252–253
  implications of, 253–255
  privacy and, 250–252
  visual representations and, 357
Credibility:
  African canons and, 418
  deliberative democracy and, 575
  informed consent and, 145
  IRBs and, 130
  meta-analysis and, 377
  positivists and, 466
  of resources, 597
  technology and, 302
Critical Legal Studies (CLS), 57
Critical race feminism, 59–60
Critical race theory (CRT):
  ethical research responsibilities of, 62–64
  foregrounding ethical considerations in research, 60–62
  historical perspectives of, 54–55
  philosophical/theoretical roots of, 55–60
Cross-cultural psychology research:
  confidentiality in, 333–334
  cultural bias in interpretations of, 332–333
  cultural informants and, 333
  data analysis in, 332
  deception and, 331–332
  and defining of culture, 326–327
  definition, 323–324
  human rights issues and, 331
  impact on community of, 334
  informed consent and, 329–330
  limitations of comparisons, 325–326
  potential dangers of, 324–325
  recruitment and, 330
  sensitivity and, 332
  sex/sexuality and, 330–331
  theory/hypothesis testing and, 328
  unpackaging studies and, 327–328
Cultural attribution fallacy, 326
Cultural bias, 332–333. *See also* Bias
Cultural competency:
  AEA and, 90
  process/benefits of, 610
  transformative research/ethics and, 97
  underserved communities and, 392
Cultural continuity, 161
Cultural impacts. *See also* Cross-cultural psychology research
  African-centered research ethics and, 421–422
  and ethics in underserved communities, 394–395, 397
  and individual versus collective interviewing, 303
  international/transnational research ethics and, 117–118
  and jurisdictional context of decision-making with minors in research, 492
  and legal interests/ethical standards of decision-making with minors in research, 492–493
  and legal propositions of decision-making with minors in research, 490–492
  performative/indigenous ethics and, 160–161
  of research ethics for transnational spaces, 521–522, 526–527
  and symbols/rituals/art in indigenous peoples, 162–163
  Tribal Culture Committee and, 141
Cultural informants, cross-cultural psychology research, 333
Custer Died for Your Sins (Deloria Jr.), 136
Cyprus, peacemaking/ethics and, 267–269
Cyprus: The Way Forward, 268

Data. *See also* Visual representations
  and older adult research, 512
  Research Cycle Framework and, 342–343, 345
  use/misuse of sharing, 381–382
Data analysis:
  African-centered research ethics and, 419
  in cross-cultural psychology research, 332
Data archiving ethics:
  archivists of, 219–224
  context of, 214–216
  primary researchers of, 216–219
  public and, 225–227
  secondary researchers of, 224–225
Data collection, 235–239
  and coding systems for sensitive material, 482–483
  and older adult research, 514–515
Data documentation initiative (DDI), 218–219, 222–223
Data interpretation, 281–283, 362–363. *See also* Visual representations
Data publishing:
  covenantal ethics and, 252–253
  and ethnography, 239–240
  quantitative research methods, use/misuse and, 381–382
  Research Cycle Framework and, 343, 346
Data treatment, qualitative research issues and, 161–162
Deafness, 79, 91, 93–96, 99n3, 99n4. *See also* Disability community and ethics
Deception, 152, 331–332
Declaration on the Rights of Disabled Persons, 90
Deductivism approach to ethical theory, 19
Deliberative democratic social research (DDSR):
  deliberative orientation and, 567–569
  elitist orientation and, 570
  and ethics of social research, 577
  example: Boulder Valley School District, 571–573
  example: Denver Public School District, 573–574
  example: housing evaluation for psychiatric consumer-survivors, 575–577
  historical perspectives of, 565–566
  participatory orientation and, 569–570
  scopes/limits, 570–571
  theory of, 566–567
Deliberative orientation of social research (DDSR), 567–569
Democracy and social research. *See* Deliberative democratic social research (DDSR)
Denver Public School District (DPSD), 573–574
Deontology, 17
Department For International Development, 409
Descriptive ethics, 1, 5
Dewey, John, 565
Dilthey, Wilhelm, 26
Directive 96/9/EC, 214–216
Disability, Handicap & Society, 73, 75
Disability community and ethics:
  and benefits of research, 81
  and controllers of disability research, 80–81
  disability rights movement in late 20th century, 70–72
  emancipatory disability research and, 73–77
  and invisibility of the disabled in research, 81
  and problem of impairment, 78–80
  social model and disability studies/research, 72–73
  and social research transformation paradigm, 77–78
Disability research ethics:
  emancipatory effects of, 458–459
  emancipatory research methodology/methods, 466–468
  emancipatory research process, 462–466
  traditional disability research, 459–462
Disadvantaged communities. *See* Communities, underserved
Disasters and ethical issues, 611
Discovery, 210–211
Discrimination. *See* Disability community and ethics; Race/racism
Doing Disability Research (Barnes & Mercer), 75–77
Do not harm, 13, 480–481, 548
The Downing Street Declaration, 264–265

Economic impacts on research ethics. *See* Hawala
EC Study of Implementation of Data Protection Directive: Comparative Study of National Laws, 215

Education. *See* Graduate training in RCR
Educational and Psychological Measurement, 379
Educative authenticity, 153–154
Elitist orientation of social research (EDSR), 570
Emancipatory disability research, 73–77, 458–459
Emergent discovery, 211
Empirical knowledge, 144
Empirical social science, 5
Encyclopedia of Evaluation (Mathison), 176
Environmental Health Perspectives, 337
Environmental Protection Agency (EPA), 337
Epistemological assumption of transformative research, 87, 94–96
Epistemology, visual representations and, 355
Ericka Grimes v. Kennedy Krieger Institute, Inc., 497
Ethical egoism, 16
Ethical multiculturalism, 395
"Ethical Principles for Medical Research Involving Human Subjects," 122
Ethical principles of five-level model of ethics, 9, 12–15
Ethical Principles of Psychologists and Code of Conduct, 45, 112, 395, 551
Ethical review boards, 410–411. *See also* Institutional review boards (IRBs)
Ethical rules of five-level model of ethics, 9, 11–12
Ethical theory:
 of five-level model of ethics, 9, 16–18
 transformative research/ethics and, 89
Ethics of care, 18
Ethnic groups. *See* Indigenous communities; Transformative research and ethics
Ethnography:
 data collection for, 235–239
 data publishing for, 239–240
 definition, 229–230
 ethnographic engagement, 156
 and field accomplishments, 232–234
 historical perspectives of, 230–231
 research ethics and, 234–235
 and social reality, 231–232
Ethnomethodological indifference, 232
European Union (EU) and directive 96/9/EC, 214–216
Evaluation. *See* Program evaluation

Even the Rat Was White (Guthrie), 392
Evidence-based research in indigenous communities, 146
Expedited reviews, 125–126
Experimental methodological pluralism, critical race theory (CRT) and, 64
Experiments/quasi-experiments:
 average effect sizes/principled discovery and, 209–211
 complexity/controversy of, 204–207
 criteria for justification of randomized, 204
 ethical challenges/solutions and, 207–209
 ethics concerning randomized, 202–204
 overview, 199–202
Exploitation, and ethical disability research, 79
Extensible markup language (XML), 218–219, 222–223

Fairness and authenticity, 153
Familismo, 44, 48–49
Family resemblances:
 contextual, 24, 30–32
 other, 24, 34–36
 particular, 24, 28–30
 value laden, 24, 32–34
Federal Registry, 152
Federal regulations, social science research and, 7–8
Feminism:
 Continental European postmodernism and, 27
 critical race feminism, 59–60
 deafness and, 94
 ethics of care and, 18
 researcher-self ethics and, 297–298
Feminist perspectives of research ethics:
 attentiveness/subjective knowledge as theme, 43, 46–47
 context analysis/power dynamics as theme, 43, 49–50
 discriminatory critique addition as theme, 43, 47–49
 moral significance of women/experiences as theme, 43–46
 philosophical foundation of, 39–43
 social justice achievement as theme, 43, 50
Fidelity:
 ethical principles and, 14–15
 RCR standards and, 554
 visual representations and, 357

First Nations. *See* American Indians
Five-level model of ethics:
   ethical principles, 12–15, 594–603
   ethical rules, 11–12, 590–594
   ethical theory, 16–18, 604–606
   future evolution of applications for, 581–583
   immediate level of moral reasoning, 9–11
   meta-ethics of, 1, 5, 9, 18–20, 606
   overview, 9–10, 581
Foreign Exchange Management Act (FEMA), 430, 437
Formal mentoring, 553
Forum for Peace and Reconciliation in Northern Ireland, 261–263
The Framework Document, 264–265
Freedoms:
   Indian Civil Rights Act of 1968 and, 143
   IRBs and, 129–130
Freeman, Allen, 57
Frontiers of social research ethics:
   and basic/applied/evaluative research differences, 610–611
   and confidentiality as principle, 601–603
   cultural competence and, 609–610
   disaster situations and, 611
   foundations of, 581–583
   future evolution of, 581, 606–609
   and informed consent as principle, 599–601
   and justice as principles, 597–599
   meta-ethics and, 606
   and nonmaleficence/beneficence as principles, 595–596, 599–601
   and ordinary morality as principle, 594–595
   power and, 583–587
   and respect/trust as principles, 596–597
   and rules/laws/administrative procedures/codes of conduct, 590–594
   structural model for, 587–590
   theory of, 604–606
   and values as principles, 603
Fundamentalism and ethics, 394–395, 400–401
Funding. *See* Institutional review boards (IRBs)
Funnel plots in meta-analysis, 377–378
Future of social research ethics. *See* Frontiers of social research ethics

Gateways: International Journal of Community Research and Engagement, 337
Gelsinger, Jesse, 126

Gender. *See also* Feminist perspectives of research ethics; Lesbian, gay, bisexual, transgender, and queer (LGBTQ) community
   and care as concept, 157–158
   cross-cultural psychology research and, 330–331
   and culturally competent research, 610–611
   Mead's study of Samoan girls, 392
   RCR standards and, 555
   and regulation of scientific inquiry, 111
Geriatric research. *See* Older adults and research ethics
Globalization. *See* Researcher-subject ethics; Transnational spaces and research ethics
The Global Review of Ethnopolitics, 264
Golden Rule, 10
Goodness and randomized experiments, 205
Governmental interest. *See also* Institutional review boards (IRBs)
   and gaps/issues of social science research, 117–118
   informed consent/deception/confidentiality/rights to privacy, 152
   and regulation in social science research, 110–117
   in social science research, 107–110
Graduate training in RCR:
   and current knowledge limitations of RCR, 558–559
   departmental climate and, 557–558
   mentoring barriers, 555–557
   mentoring characteristics, 553–555
   mentoring definitions/functions for, 552–553
   overview, 550–551
   and role of social science in RCR, 559–560
   training for, 551–552
Guidelines for Researchers on the Health Research Involving Māori, 136
Guidelines for the Ethical Conduct of Evaluation, 172
Guiding Principles (American Evaluation Association), 112
Guiding Principles for Evaluators, 172, 206

Hawala:
   data acquisition/informed consent and, 433–435
   definition/typical transaction of, 426–429
   and linguistic competence/cultural context/voluntary participation, 432–433, 435

perceived criminal context of, 431–432, 435–437
post-September 11, 2001 impact on research in, 428–431
researcher's subjectivity and, 435–437
safety/access balance of, 433
transactions, 439n4, 439n7
witnessing transactions of, 432
He kanohi kitea approach to Mäori people, 314–315
Herzegovina, peacemaking/ethics and, 264–265
Hippocratic oath, 13
Historical overview of ethics:
  biomedical ethics/federal regulations and, 7–8
  citizens' rights and, 108
  critical race theory (CRT), 54–55
  and the deaf experience, 96
  deliberative democracy and, 565–566
  and disability rights movement in late 20th century, 70–72, 82n1
  ethnography and, 230–231
  Hawala/Hundi and, 427–428
  internal ethical deliberation and, 8
  LGBTQ research and, 475–476
  philosophical ethics and, 8–9
  of program evaluation, 171
  in underserved communities, 393–394
  and U.S. origin of IRBs, 122–124
Hitler, Adolph. *See* Nazi practices
Holocaust, IRBs and, 128
Homogeneity, and ethics in underserved communities, 394–395
Homophobia. *See* Lesbian, gay, bisexual, transgender, and queer (LGBTQ) community
Homosexuality. *See* Lesbian, gay, bisexual, transgender, and queer (LGBTQ) community
How to Lie With Statistics (Huff), 373
Human Genome Organization, 138–139
Human rights declarations, transformative research/ethics and, 89–90
Human rights issues, cross-cultural psychology research and, 331
Human subject protection, failure of, 138–139
Human visual system, 356
Hundi, 427
Husserlian phenomenology, 26–27
Hypothesis testing, cross-cultural psychology research and, 328

Immanent ethics, 255n2
Impairment vs. disability, 72, 78–80
Inclusion and DDSR, 567–569
Independent ethics committees (IECs). *See* Institutional review boards (IRBs)
Indian Civil Rights Act of 1968, 143
Indian Health Service IRB, 140
Indigenous communities. *See also* African-centered ethics; American Indians
  American Indians and minors in research, 499–500
  Aroha ki te tangata approach to, 313–314
  colonization and research of, 309–311
  and copyright of indigenous knowledge, 165n5
  development of codes in, 162
  He kanohi kitea approach to, 314–315
  Kaua e takahia te mana o te tangata approach to, 316–317
  Kaupapa Mäori and, 312–313
  Kia mahaki approach to, 317
  Kia tupato approach to, 316
  Manaaki ki te tangata approach to, 315–316
  and minors in research, 499–503
  reclaiming/decolonizing research of, 311–312
  researcher-self ethics and, 295–296
  shifts in frameworks for qualitative research of, 159–161
  symbols/rituals/art in, 162–163, 165n4
  Titiro, whakarongo . . . kōrero approach to, 315
Individual versus collective interviewing, 302–303. *See also* Ubuntu
Inductivism approach to ethical theory, 19
Inequality. *See also* Power issues
  covenantal ethics and, 253
  critical race feminism and, 59
  critical race theory (CRT) and, 63
  data collection/analysis and, 525
  and ethics of care, 40
  gender and, 305
Informal mentoring, 553
Informal value transfer system (IVTS), 426, 430–431, 439n2. *See also* Hawala
Informed consent:
  conventional versus indigenous methods and, 304–305
  cross-cultural psychology research and, 329–330

and ethical disability research, 78–79
and ethics in underserved communities, 397–398
and ethics of IRBs, 131
Hawala and, 433–435
LGBTQ research and, 481–482
and older adult research, 512–513
as principle of research ethics, 599–601
researcher-self ethics and, 300–301
Institutional Review Board: Management and Function, 124
Institutional review boards (IRBs):
    academic freedom and, 129–130, 533
    African-centered ethics and, 410–411
    and crisis of confidence (1990s–2000s), 126
    data archiving and, 216, 220
    deception and, 331–332
    and ethics in underserved communities, 393
    and government regulation of research ethics, 113–114
    Indian Health Service IRB, 140–142
    and indigenous communities, 137–138
    LGBTQ research and, 478–479
    as mandated for U.S. funded research, 121–122
    and minors in research, 504n5
    mission creep/net-widening and, 126–130
    National Bioethics Advisory Committee, 132n6
    Norway and, 255n5
    organization/behavior of, 124–126
    problem resolution suggestions, 130–131
    qualitative research issues and, 165n3, 165n5
    randomized experiments and, 206
    research partnership ethics and, 346–347
    shifts in frameworks for qualitative research of, 158–159
    tribal College IRB, 140
    tribal IRB, 140–142
    U.S. origin of, 122–124
Integral Quadrant Model, 291–293
Integrity in Scientific Research: Creating an Environment That Promotes Responsible Conduct, 551, 557
Interest convergence, critical race theory (CRT) and, 58
Internal ethical deliberation, 8
International Committee of Medical Journal Editors, 376
International Communications Association, 151
International Convention on the Elimination of All Forms of Racial Discrimination (1969), 90
International Development Evaluation Association, 90
International Monetary Fund (IMF), 430
International Organization for Cooperation in Evaluation, 90
International/transnational research ethics, 114–117, 214–216
Internet. *See* Technology
Interpersonal trust, 291
Interpersonal validity, 291
Interpretive resemblances. *See* Value laden family resemblances
Inter-University Consortium for Political and Social Research (ICPSR), 217–218, 224, 227
Interviewing, individual versus collective, 302–303
Intrapersonal trust, 291
An Investigation Into Auricular Acupuncture (Miller), 465
Islamic banking, 429
Israel, peacemaking/ethics and, 266–267

Japan, cross-cultural psychology research and, 325
Jewish Chronic Disease Hospital case, 509
Jewish National Hospital cancer study, 7
Joint Committee on Standards for Educational Evaluation, 173
Journalism, IRBs and, 129
Journal of Empirical Research on Human Research Ethics, 132
Journal of Higher Education Outreach and Engagement, 337
Journal of Urban Health, 337
Judgment-making:
    ethnomethodological indifference and, 232
    using value basis, 209
Justice. *See also* Social justice
    ethical principles and, 14–15
    ethics of older adult research and, 508
    as principle of research ethics, 597–599
    RCR standards and, 554
    theories of, 157–158
    transformative research/ethics and, 88–89

Justification of moral issues, meta-ethics and, 5
Justification of randomized experiments, 204

Kaua e takahia te mana o te tangata approach to Māori people, 316–317
Kaupapa Māori, 276, 309, 312–313, 316, 318n3, 446, 454n5
Kellogg Foundation, 337
Kemet, Afrocentricity and Knowledge (Asante), 411
Kennedy Drieger Institute, Inc., Myron Higgins, a minor, etc. v., 497
Kennedy Krieger Institute, Inc., Ericka Grimes v., 497
Kia mahaki approach to Māori people, 317
Kia tupato approach to Māori people, 316
Knowledge:
　Aboriginal, 144
　effect on current RCR, 558–559
　importance of indigenous, 410
　Research Cycle Framework and, 345
　researcher-self ethics and, 303–304
Kosovo, peacemaking/ethics and, 265–266
Kyoto Protocol, 110

Lakatos, Imre, 25
Language. *See also* Communication
　Anglo-American postmodernism and, 25
　coding systems for sensitive material, 482–483
　data archiving and, 218–219
　indigenous peoples and, 162–163
　Māori terms, 454
　and older adult research, 510–512, 514–515
Laws and minors in research, 492–496
Learning difficulties, 469n3
Learning disability, 78–79, 82n2. *See also* Disability community and ethics
Legal studies and ethics. *See* Sociolegal research
Lesbian, gay, bisexual, transgender, and queer (LGBTQ) community:
　best field practices for, 483–485
　confidentiality/privacy issues and, 481–484
　conversion therapy and, 479–480
　and ethics of genetic research, 480–481
　future thoughts for, 485
　and heterocentrist cultural bias, 477–478
　historical perspectives of, 475–476
　homophobia/heterocentrism/heterosexist bias, 476–477
　informed consent and, 481–482
　IRBs and, 478–479
　overview, 474–475
Liberalism, critical race theory (CRT) and, 58
Literacy and research in underserved communities, 398
Lyotard, Jean-Francois., 27

Ma'at, 412–413, 416
Macedonia, peacemaking/ethics and, 263–264
Machismo subscale, 44–45
Manaaki ki te tangata approach to Māori people, 315–316
Māori men's health study, 448–449
Māori people. *See also* Aotearoa (New Zealand) research ethics:
　Aroha ki te tangata approach to, 313–314
　colonization and research of, 309–311
　ethics review boards and, 410
　field accounts of research of, 447–453
　and guidelines for research, 136, 160–161
　He kanohi kitea approach to, 314–315
　Kaua e takahia te mana o te tangata approach to, 316–317
　Kaupapa Māori, 276, 309, 312–313, 316, 318n3, 446, 454n5
　Kia mahaki approach to, 317
　Kia tupato approach to, 316
　Manaaki ki te tangata approach to, 315–316
　reclaiming/decolonizing research of, 311–312
　Titiro, whakarongo . . . kōrero approach to, 315
Māori SIDS study, 447–448
Maturation in experiments, 201
McAuliffe, Christa, 362–363
The Meaning of Disability (Blaxter), 461
Medical practices. *See also* Institutional review boards (IRBs):
　cognitive impairment (CI) and older adult research, 508–509
　and copyright of indigenous knowledge, 165n5
　"Ethical Principles for Medical Research Involving Human Subjects," 122
　and field accounts of Aotearoa research, 447–453
　and genetic research for LGBTQ, 480–481

hantavirus pulmonary syndrome (1993) research, 138–139
historical perspectives of ethics of, 189–190
and Iceland's health data system, 224
indigenous people and health research, 312
mental health care applications and, 375–378
Nazis and, 124, 138, 446
nonmaleficence and, 12–13
Public Responsibility in Medicine and Research (PRIM&R), 130–131
and safeguards in older adult research, 513–514
Tuskegee Study of Untreated Syphilis in the Negro, 7, 122–123, 186, 218, 250, 262, 499
Membership categorization device (MCD), 231
Mental awakenings, 154
Mental health care applications:
   and clinical drug trials for psychological disorders, 375–376
   meta-analysis/publication bias and, 376–378
Mental Health Foundation's Strategies for Living project, 465
Mental health issues:
   ethics of older adult research and, 508–509
   LGBTQ research and, 476
Mentoring for RCR, 552–557
Meta-ethics:
   definition, 1, 5
   of five-level model, 9, 18–20
Methodological assumptions of transformative research, 88, 96–97
Methodological quality, 206–207
Methodological validity, 291
Methodology, visual representations and, 355
Migrants and transnational research ethics, 523–524, 530. *See also* Indigenous communities
Milgram's study of obedience, 8
Minors and research ethics:
   child factors and, 502
   community-researcher partnerships and, 499–500
   decision-making context of, 490–493
   emancipated/mature minors, 504n3
   law/children's development and, 493–496
   overview, 489–490
   parental/extended family factors and, 500–502
   predisposing factors and, 500

   researcher factors and, 502–503
   research setting and, 497–499
Mission creep, 126–127
Mixed methods. *See also* Transformative research and ethics
   critical race theory (CRT) and, 63–64
   methodological assumptions and, 96–97
   and transformative research paradigm, 78
MKUL-TRA studies, 7
Moral reasoning of five-level model of ethics, 9–11
Morbidity and Mortality Weekly Report (MMWR), 477–478
Multiculturalism:
   and child factors of minors in research, 502
   community-researcher partnerships and, 499–500
   and decision-making context of minors in research, 490–493
   ethics and, 394–395
   and law/children's development, 493–496
   and parental/extended family factors of minors in research, 500–502
   and predisposing factors of minors in research, 500
   and researcher factors of minors in research, 502–503
   research setting and minors in research, 497–499
Multiphasic Assessment of Cultural Constructs, 44–45
Muslims, peacemaking/ethics and, 269–271
Myron Higgins, a minor, etc. v. Kennedy Drieger Institute, Inc., 497

National Advisory Health Council, 123
National Aeronautics and Space Administration (NASA), 221–222
National Archive of Computerized Data on Aging (NACDA), 227
National Association of Social Workers (NASW), 475, 529
National Bioethics Advisory Committee, 132n6
National Centre for Independent Living, 468
National Commission for the Protection of Human Subjects in Biomedical and Behavioral Research, 7
National Congress of American Indians, 140–141, 143, 147n5

National Council of Teachers of
   Mathematics, 534
National Indian Education Association, 143
National Institute on Aging, 226–227
National Institutes of Health (NIH),
   122–123, 337
National Patient Safety Agency, 221
National Research Council (NRC), 93
National Science Foundation, 226–227
*National Statement on Ethical Conduct in
   Research Involving Humans*, 551
Naturalism, 24–25
Natural law theory, 16
Natural rights theory, 16
Nazi practices, 7, 17, 108, 113, 115, 122,
   202, 246, 393, 591
Net-widening, 126–127
Networked ethics:
   and changing meanings of privacy, 538–540
   complexity of, 541, 546–547
   and current view of privacy, 543–546
   definition, 537–538
   globalization and, 542, 546
   interdependence of, 542–543, 546–547
   ubiquity of, 542
   uncertainty of, 541–542, 546
   and way of thinking about research ethics,
      546–549
Network society, 526
New Jersey Negative Income Tax program
   (1968–1972), 8
The New Language of Qualitative Research
   (Gubrium & Holstein), 231
New Zealand. *See* Aotearoa (New Zealand)
   research ethics
New Zealand Sign Language, 79
Nile Valley Civilization, 412–413
Nobel Institute and Peace Research Institute in
   Oslo (PRIO), 267
No Child Left Behind, 114
Nommo, 412–413, 416
Nonmaleficence, 12–13, 595–596
Normative ethics, 1, 5
Northern Ireland peace polls,
   peacemaking/ethics and, 261–263
Noumenal reality, Continental European
   postmodernism and, 26
Null hypothesis significance testing (NHST), 379
Nuremberg Code of ethics, 7, 122, 132n1.
   See also Belmont Report

Objectivity, 303–304
Observer as modern other-focus resemblance,
   34–35
Office for Human Research Protection
   (OHRP), 123–124, 126, 130–131, 140
Older adults and research ethics:
   consent strategy for, 512–514
   data collection for, 514–515
   ethical principles of, 508
   overview, 507–508
   research design for, 508–510
   tools/techniques for, 510–512
*Once Upon a Time There Was a Bookseller in
   Kabul* (Rais), 239
Ontological assumption of transformative
   research, 87, 92–94
Ontological authenticity, 153–154
The Open University, 71
Oppression. *See also* Transformative research
   and ethics
   critical race theory (CRT) and, 56–57
   disability terms and, 82n2
   transformative research and, 86
Organization for Economic Co-Operation and
   Development (OECD), 215
Original position, ethical theory and, 17

Paired identities and ethnography, 232–234
Palestine, peacemaking/ethics and, 266–267
Paradigm, defined, 153
Parents and minors in research, 500–502
Participant as modern other-focus
   resemblance, 35
Participatory action research (PAR), 43
Participatory orientation of social research
   (PDSR), 569–570
Particularism:
   African-centered research ethics and, 421–422
   as approach to ethical theory, 19
   particular behavior (action), 9
   particular family resemblances, 24, 28–30
Partnership research ethics:
   academic colleague communication for,
      347–348
   community involvement in, 348–349
   complex questions of, 339
   definition, 337–338
   and definition of research partnerships,
      338–339
   future and, 350–351

IRB preparation for, 346–347
issues at different points of research cycle, 340–346
and need for framework for, 339–340
people preparation (overview) for, 344, 346
in pre-partnership time, 349–350
student preparation for, 347
PATRIOT Act of 2001, 428–429
Peacemaking and ethics:
Bosnia/Herzegovina and, 264–265
conflicts of interest and, 260–261
Cyprus and, 267–269
Israel/Palestine and, 266–267
Kosovo/Serbia and, 265–266
Macedonia and, 263–264
Muslims/War on Terror and, 269–271
Northern Ireland peace polls and, 261–263
overview, 259–260
Peace polls of Northern Ireland, 261–263
Pearl, Daniel, 439n7
Peirce, Charles Sanders, 25
People First, 71
The People's Peace Process in Northern Ireland, 262
Personal tragedy theory, 72
Perspectival resemblances. See Value laden family resemblances
Phenomenology:
Continental European postmodernism and, 26
Husserlian, 31
and postmodern contextual resemblances, 31–32
Philosophical ethics, 8–9
Political colonialism, 311
Postmodernism and ethics, 24–27
Poverty in the United Kingdom (Townsend), 461
Power issues. See also Inequality
future evolution of, 583–587
historical perspectives of, 3
ontological assumption and, 92
transformative research and, 86–87
PQMethod, 177
Prejudice, value laden resemblances and, 33. See also Disability community and ethics; Gender; Older adults and research ethics; Race/racism
Prima facie duties, 17–18
Primary researchers of data archiving ethics, 216–219

Primum non nocere, 12–13
Principled discovery, 210–211
Principlism approach to ethical theory, 18–20
Privacy. See also Confidentiality
archivists and, 219–224
changing meanings of, 538–540
current view of, 543–546
data archiving and, 216
and data archiving and the public, 225–227
and ethical disability research, 79
ethnomethodological data collection and, 239–240
LGBTQ research and, 481–482
networked ethics and, 537–538, 540–543
and older adult research, 514–515
researcher-self ethics and, 296–297
and research ethics for transnational spaces, 529–531
secondary researchers and, 224–225
and way of thinking about research ethics, 546–549
Program evaluation:
as defined by society it serves, 175–176
and differences with basic/applied research, 610–611
new research in, 176–181
practice/ethics of, 172–174
principles of, 173
professional ethics and, 174–176
as a profession in social research, 170–172
Q methodology and, 176–181
Progress in Community Health Partnerships Research, 337
Project Camelot, 8
Psychiatric disability, 79–80. See also Disability community and ethics
Psychological research. See Mental health care applications
Psychology. See Cross-cultural psychology research
Psychology of Deafness, 94
Publications. See also Data publishing
and indigenous communities, 143
peacemaking/ethics and, 267
and publication bias in mental health care applications, 375–376
Public Responsibility in Medicine and Research (PRIM&R), 130–131

Q methodology, 176–181
Qualitative Inquiry (Bochner), 29
Qualitative research:
    critical race theory (CRT) and, 63–64
    emerging change in, 150–152
    Hawala and, 431–437
    paradigmatic ethical framework and, 153–156
    researcher-self ethics and, 297–298
    shifts in communitarian ethical frameworks in, 156–158
    shifts in globalized ethical frameworks (indigenous peoples) in, 159–161
    shifts in institutional ethical frameworks in, 158–159
    shifts in treatment of contexts in, 161–162
    shifts in treatment of data/reports in, 161–162
    and shifts in treatment of human subjects, 152–153
    social relations/self and, 283–284
    terminology for, 164n1
Quantitative assignment variable (QAV), 208
Quantitative research:
    average effect sizes, 209–210
    African-centered research ethics and, 418
    critical race theory (CRT) and, 63–64
    researcher-self ethics and, 297
Quantitative research methods, use/misuse:
    assumptions/bias and, 383
    and classification of research/data types, 374–375
    and clinical drug trials for psychological disorders, 375–376
    meta-analysis/publication bias and, 376–378
    null hypothesis significance testing (NHST), 379
    philosophy of science and, 382–383
    publication/data sharing/conflicts of interest and, 381–382
    social science/behavioral science methods and, 378–381
Quasi-experiments. *See* Experiments/quasi-experiments
Quine, W. V., 25

Race/racism. *See also* American Indians; Critical race theory (CRT)
    achievement gap and, 93–94
    epistemology of indigenous people and, 95–96
    and ethics in underserved communities, 400–401
Randomized experiments:
    average effect sizes/principled discovery and, 209–211
    complexity/controversy of, 204–207
    criteria for justification of, 204
    ethics concerning, 202–204
    and research ethics in underserved communities, 402
Rankings approach to ethical theory, 19
R-D design methodology, 208
Recommendations of the Council Concerning Guidelines Governing the Protection of Privacy and Trans-Border Flows of Personal Data, 215–216
Recruitment, cross-cultural psychology research and, 330
Recusal, 190
Reflexivity, critical race theory (CRT) and, 63
Regulations:
    and gaps/issues of social science research, 117–118
    and government interest in social science research, 107–110
    and government regulation of social science research, 7–8, 110–117
Religion, African-centered ethics and, 413, 420–421
Representation of people/information. *See* Visual representations
Research Cycle Framework, 338–346
Researcher-self:
    as controllers of disability research, 80–81
    and empathic perspective, 285–286
    and ethical practice resources, 289–291
    methodological validity, 291
    as responsive instrument, 284–285
    social relations/qualitative research methods and, 283–284
    sociocultural diversity/qualitative research methods and, 287–289
Researcher-subject ethics:
    Afrocentric paradigm of, 295–298, 412, 416–420
    anonymity/confidentiality and, 301–302
    and coding systems for sensitive material, 482–483
    conventional ethical issues, 296–297
    dilemma of insider/outsider position and, 302
    and ethics in underserved communities, 393, 399–401
    feminist analysis of, 297–298

and field relations' contribution to ethical
  research, 304–305
 Hawala and, 435–437
 individual versus collective interviewing,
  302–303
 informed consent and, 300–301
 and self-reflection, 303–304
 and use of technology, 302
Research ethics frontiers. *See* Frontiers of
 social research ethics
Research Ethics with Human Participants, 551
The Research Policy Center of the National
 Congress of American Indians, 143
Research process, critical race theory (CRT)
 and, 60–62
*Research Project Into User Groups and
 Empowerment* (Matthew), 465
Resemblances. *See* Family resemblances
Respect for persons:
 American Evaluation Association
  and, 112
 Belmont Report and, 113
 and differences in governmental inquiry for
  scientific inquiry, 109–110
 and ethical disability research, 78
 ethical principles and, 14
 and ethics in underserved communities, 398
 international/transnational research ethics
  and, 117–118
 IRBs and, 132n4
 as principle of research ethics, 596–597
Responsible conduct of research (RCR):
 and current knowledge limitations of RCR,
  558–559
 departmental climate and, 557–558
 mentoring barriers and, 555–557
 mentoring characteristics and, 553–555
 mentoring definitions/functions for,
  552–553
 overview, 550–551
 and role of social science in RCR,
  559–560
 training for, 551–552
Revealed knowledge, 144
Review boards. *See* Institutional review
 boards (IRBs)
Rightness of property issues, critical race
 theory (CRT) and, 58
Rights. *See* Human rights declarations,
 transformative research/ethics and
Rights to privacy, 152

Rigor:
 African canons and, 418
 Boulder Valley School District (BVSD)
  and, 571
 disablity studies and, 75
 diverse cultural groups and, 418
 feminist analysis and, 45
 and indigenous evidence-based research, 146
 Kaua e takahia te mana o te tangata
  approach to Maori people and, 316
 mental health care applications and, 375
 meta-analysis and, 377
 paradigmatic criteria for, 153
 quantitative research and, 377
 research cycle issues and, 342–343
 secondary researchers and, 225
 technology and, 302
Robert Wood Johnson Foundation, 337
Royal Commission on Aboriginal Peoples
 (RCAP), 136–137
Rule-utilitarianism, 17
Ryan Commission, The, 551
Ryle, Gilbert, 25

Safety, ethical disability research and, 79
Science:
 Anglo-American postmodernism and, 25–26
 Continental European postmodernism
  and, 26–27
 covenantal ethics/values and, 255n4
 distortion by government, 110
 political influences on, 260–261
 RCR standards and, 556
 scientific colonization, 409
Scientific colonialism, 311
Secondary researchers of data archiving ethics,
 224–225
Selection in experiments, 201
Self. *See also* Researcher-self; Researcher-
  subject ethics
 African-centered ethics/*Ubuntu* and, 413–416
 and empathic perspective, 285–286
 and ethical practice resources, 289–291
 mentor characteristics and, 553–555
 as responsive instrument, 284–285
 social relations/qualitative research methods
  and, 283–284
 sociocultural diversity/qualitative research
  methods and, 287–289
Sensitivity, cross-cultural psychology research
 and, 330–332

Serbia, peacemaking/ethics and, 265–266
Sexism. *See also* Feminist perspectives of research ethics
   critical race theory (CRT) and, 56–57
Sex/sexuality. *See also* Lesbian, gay, bisexual, transgender, and queer (LGBTQ) community; *Tuskegee Study of Untreated Syphilis in the Negro*
   cross-cultural psychology research and, 330–331
   Mead's study of Samoan girls, 392
   Tearoom Trade: Impersonal Sex in Public Places (Humphreys), 480–481
The Sexual Politics of Disability: Untold Desires (Shakespeare, Gillespie-Sells, & Davies), 76
Sign Language, 79, 91, 99n3
Social justice:
   accountability and, 529
   action research and, 247
   American Psychological Association (APA) and, 91
   beneficience and, 92
   critical race theory (CRT) and, 55, 57, 60, 62
   distributive justice and, 88–89
   as factor of emergent ethics, 161
   feminist analysis and, 39, 41–43, 47, 50, 247
   future evolution of, 586
   mixed methods and, 64
   NASW and, 529
   participatory ethics and, 63
   qualitative research and, 157
   rights-based theories and, 604–605
   transformative paradigm and, 77–78, 86, 97, 582, 609
   Ubuntu (self/other respect) and, 408
   underserved communities and, 393–394
   values and, 603
Social relations and data quality, 283–284
Social Research Association (SRA) *Code of Ethics*, 528
Social responsibility and research in underserved communities, 398–399
Social science research. *See also* Transformative research and ethics
   biomedical ethics/federal regulations and, 7–8
   covenantal ethics and, 253
   ethical principles and, 9, 12–15
   ethical rules and, 9, 11–12

   ethical standards and, 191–196
   ethical theory and, 9, 16–18
   ethics of, 5–7
   and five-level model of ethics, 9–10
   gaps/issues and, 117–118
   government interest in, 107–110
   government regulation of, 110–117
   internal ethical deliberation and, 8
   IRBs and, 128
   meta-ethics, 9
   meta-ethics and, 18–20
   moral reasoning and, 10–11
   philosophical ethics and, 8–9
   political influences on, 260–261
   quantitative research methods, use/misuse and, 378–381
   role in RCR of, 559–560
   and role of ethics in underserved communities, 395–399
Sociolegal research, 190–196
Stanford Prison study, 404n3
State-Trait Anxiety Inventory (STAI), 325
Statistical regression in experiments, 201
Strategies for Living project, 465
Street Corner Society (Whyte), 239
Subject as modern other-focus resemblance, 34–35. *See also* Researcher-subject ethics
Substitute decision makers (SDMs), 513, 515
Syphilis study. *See* Tuskegee Study of Untreated Syphilis in the Negro

Tactical authenticity, 153, 155
Task Force on Statistical Inference (TFSI), 379
Tearoom Trade: Impersonal Sex in Public Places (Humphreys), 8, 480–481
Technology:
   African-centered research ethics and, 418–419
   and changing meanings of privacy, 538–540
   and current view of privacy, 543–546
   Hawala and, 434
   networked ethics and, 537–538, 540–543
   researcher-self ethics and, 302
   and way of thinking about research ethics, 546–549
Terrorism. *See also* Hawala
   peacemaking/ethics and, 269–271
   post-September 11, 2001 impact on research in Hawala, 428–431
Thalidomide Drug Tragedy, 7

Theory/hypothesis testing, cross-cultural psychology research and, 328
Theory of Justice (Rawls), 567
Therapeutic research, 504n2
Thesis advisors, 552
Three Seductive Ideas (Kagan), 28
Tikanga, 445–447, 452–454
Titiro, whakarongo . . . kōrero approach to Māori people, 315
Traditional knowledge, 144
Transformative research and ethics:
  axiological assumption of, 87–92
  commensurate theories and, 91
  distributive justice and, 88–89
  epistemological assumption of, 87, 94–96
  human rights declarations and, 89–90
  methodological assumptions of, 88, 96–97
  need for, 85–87
  ontological assumption of, 87, 92–94
  paradigm of, 87–88
  and professional/indigenous codes of ethics, 90–91
  and regulation of scientific inquiry, 110
  regulatory concepts of, 91
  social action, 97–98
  and theories of ethics, 89
Transformative trust, 291
Translations. See Visual representations
Transnational spaces and research ethics:
  ethical accountability for, 528–529
  fundamental core of research ethics for, 526–527
  obstacles/ambiguities of, 531–534
  overview, 521–523
  personal responsibility and, 534–535
  privacy and, 529–531
  researching of, 524–526
  spaces for, 523–524
  underserved communities and, 410
Treaty of Waitangi, 454n1
Tribal College IRB, 140
Tribal College Journal of American Indian Education (Red Horse), 137
Tribal IRB, 140–142
Tri-Council Policy Statement (TCPS), 136
Trust, 291, 596–597
Trust and Betrayal in the Workplace (Reina & Reina), 291
Truth and data collection, 238–239

Tuskegee Study of Untreated Syphilis in the Negro, 7, 122–123, 186, 218, 250, 262, 499. See also Communities, underserved:

Ubuntu:
  definition/principles of, 408
  self-determination/rebirth, 415–416
  self/other respect, 413–414
Underserved communities. See Communities, underserved
Union of the Physically Impaired Against Segregation (UPIAS), 71–72, 460
United Nations (UN). See also Peacemaking and ethics
  Convention on the Rights of the Child, 90, 159
  Declaration on the Rights on Indigenous Peoples, 159, 309
  and ethics in underserved communities, 409
  international/transnational research ethics and, 115–116
  Kyoto Protocol, 110
  transformative research/ethics and, 89–90
United Nations Educational, Scientific and Cultural Organization (UNESCO), 409
United States Agency For International Development, 409
Unobtrusive Measures: Nonreactive Research in the Social Sciences, 186
Unpackaging studies, 327–328
U.S. Department of Health and Human Services (DHHS), 122–124
U.S. Federal Aviation Administration (FAA), 221
U.S. Food and Drug Administration (FDA), 375–376
U.S. Government Accountability Office, 172
U.S. Government Accounting Office, 113
U.S. National Bioethics Advisory Commission, 410
U.S. National Institutes of Health, 226–227
U.S. Public Health Service (PHS), 122
Utilitarian ethics, 110

Validation and social science ethics:
  and empathic perspective, 285–286
  and ethical practice resources, 289–291
  methodological validity, 291
  potential sources of invalidity, 283–284

as responsive instrument, 284–285
social relations/qualitative research methods and, 283–284
sociocultural diversity/qualitative research methods and, 287–289
sociolegal research and, 190–191
Value basis for judgments, 209
Value laden family resemblances, 24, 32–34
Values:
   and action/conventional research model comparison, 244–246
   and contractual/covenantal ethics, 246–250
   and distribution of research results, 252–253
   as principles of research ethics, 603
   privacy and, 250–251
Values in Evaluation and Social Research (House & Howe), 565
VandenBos, Gary, 35
Veil of ignorance, 17
Violence Against Women Act (VAWA), 50
Virtue theory, 17

Visual representations:
   content/discourse meaning for, 360–363
   overview, 353–355
   process/meaning interplay in, 363–366
   visual ethics theory and, 355–358
   visual tools/methods process for, 358–360

Walking Into Darkness (Oliver et al.), 463
War on Terror, peacemaking/ethics and, 269–271
Web 2.0 phenomenon, 538
Wichita Jury Trial (1953), 8
Willowbrook hepatitis study, 7
World Bank, 116–117
World Health Organization (WHO), 409
World Medical Association, "Ethical Principles for Medical Research Involving Human Subjects," 122

XML (extensible markup language), 218–219, 222–223

Zimbardo's prison study, 8

ABOUT THE EDITORS

Donna M. Mertens is a professor in the Department of Educational Foundations and Research at Gallaudet University. She teaches advanced research methods and program evaluation to D/deaf and hearing students. She received the Distinguished Faculty Award from Gallaudet in 2007. The primary focus of her work is transformative mixed-methods inquiry in diverse communities, which prioritizes the ethical implications of research in the pursuit of social justice. A past president of the American Evaluation Association (AEA), she provided leadership in the development of the International Organization for Cooperation in Evaluation and the establishment of the AEA Diversity Internship Program with Duquesne University. She received AEA's highest honor for service to the organization and the field. Her recent books include *Transformative Research and Evaluation* (2009), *Research and Evaluation in Education and Psychology: Integrating Diversity With Quantitative, Qualitative, and Mixed Methods* (2nd ed., 2005), *Research and Evaluation in Special Education* (coauthored with J. A. McLaughlin, 2004), *Parents and Their Deaf Children: The Early Years* (coauthored with K. P. Meadow-Orlans & M. A. Sass-Lehrer, 2003), and *Research and Inequality* (coedited with C. Truman & B. Humphries, 2000). She is widely published in the *Journal of Mixed Methods Research*, *American Journal of Evaluation*, *American Annals of the Deaf*, and *Educational Evaluation and Policy Analysis*. Mertens conducts and consults on evaluations and also leads professional development activities on research and evaluation in many national and international settings. Examples include the United Nations UNIFEM initiative to address the Millennium Goals for women in Africa; cultural exchange programs for D/deaf students between Costa Rica and Gallaudet; mixed-methods research at Fitzwilliam College of Health Sciences, Cambridge University; a nationwide project to improve teaching through the use of technology; a breast cancer screening project for indigenous peoples in Newfoundland; early intervention programs for D/deaf children in Israel for Jewish and Bedouin families; and education for deaf, blind, and mentally challenged students in Egypt.

Pauline E. Ginsberg is Professor Emerita of psychology at Utica College where she taught undergraduates for 23 years. She also taught quasi-experimental design and program evaluation to graduate students at Syracuse University on an adjunct basis. In 1989–1990, she taught psychiatry students at the University of Nairobi and in 2002, as a Fulbright lecturer, she taught counseling psychology students at the same university. Past President of the Eastern Evaluation Association and cofounder of the International and Cross-Cultural Topical Interest Group of the American Evaluation Association, she has had an abiding interest in cross-cultural research ethics and methodology. She has researched public mental health systems in New York, Pennsylvania, Albania, and Kenya. Her monograph, *Public Mental Health Care and Public Policy in Kenya: A Case Study*, was published in 2005. Her current interests include literacy promotion in adolescent immigrants and access to textbooks in developing regions. With a colleague from the University of Nairobi, she is working on a textbook of adolescent development for use in Kenya.

ABOUT THE INTERNATIONAL ADVISORY BOARD MEMBERS AND CONTRIBUTORS

Colin Barnes is Professor of Disability Studies at the University of Leeds. He is a disability activist, writer, and researcher with an international reputation in the field of disability studies and disability research. He is a member of several local, national, and international organizations controlled and run by disabled people. As a committed advocate of disabled people's rights, he has conducted research on various disability issues, published widely, and spoken about the experience of living with impairment in a disabling society to various audiences in a variety of locations, both in Britain and across the world.

Katrina L. Bledsoe is Associate Project Director for the Substance Abuse and Mental Health Administration's Children's Mental Health Services Initiative's National Evaluation, Research Manager at Walter R. McDonald and Associates, Inc., and adjunct assistant professor of psychology at The George Washington University in Washington, D.C. She specializes in applied social psychology, community-based research, theory-driven evaluation, and cultural contexts. Her 13 years of experience researching and evaluating community-based education programs, drug and crime prevention efforts for communities of color, and health issues, add to her knowledge of the factors that are associated with negative and positive health, mental health, and social outcomes for communities of color. She authored articles featured in the *American Journal of Evaluation, Evaluation, Society Book Series,* the *International Handbook of Urban Education,* and work forthcoming in the book *When Research Studies Go Off the Rails: Solutions and Prevention Strategies.*

Belinda Borell is of Ngati Ranginui, Ngai Te Rangi, Whakatohea descent and has lived most of her life in Manurewa South Auckland. She is a senior researcher at Whariki Research Group having recently completed her masters degree on urban Maori youth identities. She is currently leading a major new project investigating privilege—conferred advantage—as a determinant of health and well-being for some population groups, to better understand how systematic disadvantage is maintained in other groups.

Kalina M. Brabeck is a licensed psychologist and an assistant professor in the Department of Counseling, Educational Leadership, and School Psychology at Rhode Island College. Her clinical and research interests include Latino immigrant mental health, violence against girls and women, participatory action research, and feminist practice. She completed her doctoral work in counseling psychology at The University of Texas at Austin and her predoctoral internship at New York University, Bellevue Hospital Center in the Cross-Cultural Track.

Mary M. Brabeck is Dean of The Steinhardt School of Culture, Education and Human Development and Professor of Applied Psychology. She has published more than 90 journal articles and book chapters, and her books include *Practicing Feminist Ethics in Psychology* (2000). She has received numerous awards, including an honorary degree, Doctor of Humane Letters (Honoris Causa), from St. Joseph University in Philadelphia, an Outstanding Achievement Award from the University of Minnesota, a Leadership Award from the American Psychological Association Committee on Women in Psychology, and the Kuhmerker Award from the Association for Moral Education.

Bruce L. Brown is Professor of Psychology and chair of the doctoral program in Applied Social Psychology at Brigham Young University, with his research focus on the developing science of holistic visual display. He currently serves as a member of the Executive Committee of the American Name Society. His publications include applications of visualization methods to behavioral, medical, and social science research, and critical analysis of the claims and practices of popular multivariate statistical methods. He is primary author of *Datamax*, a multivariate graphical analysis system used in manufacturing; *Bibliostat*, a data visualization system used by thousands of libraries in America; and *Metrika*, a publicly available open-source multivariate graphics package (metrika.org).

Mary Brydon-Miller directs the University of Cincinnati's Action Research Center and is Associate Professor of Educational Studies and Urban Educational Leadership in the College of Education, Criminal Justice, and Human Services. She is a participatory action researcher who engages in both community-based and educational action research. Her current scholarship focuses on ethics and action research. Other publications include work on participatory action research methods, feminist theory and action research, refugee resettlement, elder advocacy, disability rights, and academic writing in the social sciences. She teaches courses in action research, the theoretical foundations of urban educational leadership, and research ethics.

Merry Bullock directs the Office of International Affairs at the American Psychological Association (APA), where she serves as APA's point of contact for international academic, research, and policy activities, including APA's UN representation. In addition to APA, she is involved with a number of other international organizations in officer and policy roles. She is associate editor of the *International Journal of Psychology* and former coeditor of the *Journal of Applied Developmental Psychology*. After receiving her undergraduate degree from Brown University and her graduate degrees from the University of Pennsylvania, she has lived, taught, and served in policy, academic, and research positions in Canada, Germany, Estonia, and the United States.

Nicholas C. Burbules is Grayce Wicall Gauthier Professor in the Department of Educational Policy Studies at the University of Illinois. His research focuses on philosophy of education, teaching and dialogue, critical social and political theory, and technology and education. His major current projects include work on ubiquitous technologies in education, virtual reality, and dialogue and "third spaces." His most recent book, *Showing and Doing: Wittgenstein as a Pedagogical Philosopher* (in press), is coauthored by Michael A. Peters and Paul Smeyers. He is also currently the Editor of *Educational Theory*.

Bagele Chilisa is Associate Professor at the University of Botswana where she teaches research methods and evaluation courses to graduate students in the Faculty of Education. One of her main areas of research is on research methodologies that are relevant, context specific, and inclusive of African indigenous ways of knowing and perceiving reality and value systems. She is the first author of two books in this area: (1) *Educational Research: Towards Sustainable Development* and (2) *Research Methods for Adult Educators in Africa*. She also authored a journal article "Educational Research Within Postcolonial Africa: A Critique of HIV/AIDS Research in Botswana" in the *International Journal of Qualitative Studies*, as well as presenting and writing on postcolonial/indigenous ethics. She won an NIH grant to build research capacity using culturally sensitive methodologies that can inform the design of cultural-specific and age-appropriate interventions that can reduce HIV/AIDS infection in adolescents in Botswana.

Clifford G. Christians is the Director of the Institute of Communications Research and head of the Ph.D. in Communications program at the University of Illinois, Urbana-Champaign. He is the Charles H. Sandage Distinguished Professor and a Research Professor of Communications, with a joint appointment as Professor of Media Studies. He was a visiting scholar in philosophy at Princeton University, a research fellow in social ethics at the University of Chicago, and a PEW fellow in ethics at Oxford University. Among other books, he is coauthor of *Media Ethics: Cases and Moral Reasoning* (in 8th edition), *Communication Ethics and Universal Values*, and *Moral Engagement in Public Life: Theorists for Contemporary Ethics*.

Joshua W. Clegg is Professor of Psychology at John Jay College of Criminal Justice, CUNY. His published work focuses on research methodology and philosophy of science, emphasizing the contributions of Continental philosophers such as Emmanuel Levinas and Mikhail Bakhtin, as well as on empirical work in social alienation. He earned his B.S. and M.S. degrees in psychology from Brigham Young University, where he was trained as a phenomenologist and a theoretician, and his Ph.D. in psychology from Clark University, where he was trained as a social psychologist.

Fiona Cram is the Director of a small research, evaluation, and training company, Katoa Ltd., in Wellington. Prior to this, she was variously in the Departments of Psychology and Education at the University of Auckland and a Senior Research Fellow in the International Research Institute for Māori and Indigenous Peoples (IRI), University of Auckland, New Zealand. Most of her work is with Māori and Iwi (tribal) organizations and NGOs. Her research interests are wide ranging and include Māori health (including *whānau* violence, health service provision, and genetics), Māori and community development, and research and evaluation ethics. She is a Ngāti Kahungunu (indigenous tribe of New Zealand) and earned her Ph.D. from the University of Otago. She has a son.

Cheryl Crazy Bull, Sicangu Lakota from the Rosebud Reservation, serves as President of Northwest Indian College, a tribally chartered regional postsecondary institution serving the Pacific Northwest. She is currently a member of the Advisory Board, National Congress of American Indians Policy Research Center. Her focus on reservation-based education and community development includes 22 years in tribal colleges and 4 years as the CEO of a tribal K–12 school. She served three terms as Chair of the American Indian Higher Education Consortium.

Sarah-Jane Dodd is an Associate Professor at the Hunter College School of Social Work and at the City University of New York Graduate Center. She teaches Social Welfare Policy, Research, and Human Sexuality. Her areas of interest include ethical decision making in health care and other social service settings, and issues affecting LGBTQ individuals and their families. She serves as a member of the Hunter College Institutional Review Board Consulting Committee. She is also a consulting editor for the *Journal of Teaching in Social Work*. Along with several book chapters, her articles have been published in a range of journals, including the *Journal of Social Work Education*, *Health and Social Work*, *Nursing Ethics*, and the *Social Policy Journal*.

Shane Edwards is of Ngati Maniapoto descent and works with Te Wananga o Aotearoa at Te Awamutu as Research Director and is also part of Whariki Research Group. He is currently completing his Ph.D. on Ngati Maniapoto identity and knowledge systems, while raising a young family and actively contributing to the development of his community at Kawhia.

Celia B. Fisher, Marie Ward Doty Professor of Psychology and Director of Fordham University's Center for Ethics Education, chairs the Environmental Protection Agency's Human Subjects Research Board. She chaired the American Psychological Association's Ethics Code Task Force. She is a founding editor of the journal *Applied Developmental Science*, author of *Decoding the Ethics Code: A Practical Guide for Psychologists*, and coeditor of seven books. She has more than 100 publications. Her publications and federally funded research focus on scientific and professional ethics and development challenges involving vulnerable populations, including minority youth and families, drug users, college students at risk for drinking problems, and adults with impaired consent capacity.

Chris Gamble is a doctoral student in social psychology at Penn State University. His research focuses primarily on the areas of hindsight bias, counterfactual thinking, and human-nature relations. Although his primary work does not directly address ethics formally, a strong ethical responsibility plays a significant role in shaping his overall research agenda. For example, he hopes that his current and future research will help inform action on issues including climate change. Thus, he is interested in the more general question of the potential contributions of social scientific investigation in facilitating social change, including by serving as a tool to help political decision makers address social issues more effectively.

Sabrina J. Goodman is a doctoral candidate in the clinical psychology Ph.D. program at Fordham University. She is currently a Teaching Associate at Fordham and conducts clinical work and program evaluation research at the Early Childhood Center, a division of the Children's Evaluation and Rehabilitation Center of the Albert Einstein College of Medicine. In addition to her interest in studying the mentoring of ethical research, she is also interested in studying the attachment perceptions and experiences of parents of children with autism spectrum disorders, which is the focus of her dissertation research. She received her master's degree from Fordham in 2005.

Jennifer C. Greene has been an evaluation scholar-practitioner for nearly 30 years. Her evaluation scholarship has broadly focused on probing the intersections of social science method with policy discourse and program decision making, with the intent of making evaluation useful and socially responsible. Greene has concentrated specifically on advancing qualitative, mixed methods, and democratic approaches to evaluation. Her evaluation practice has spanned multiple domains of practice, with an emphasis on the domains of education, community-based family services, and youth development. In 2003, Greene received the American Evaluation Association's Lazarsfeld award for contributions to evaluation theory. In 2007 her book on mixed methods social inquiry was published.

Raychelle L. Harris is a faculty member at Gallaudet University in the Department of Interpretation. Her dissertation study is about the construction of extended discourse in a bilingual ASL (American Sign Language)/English preschool classroom with Deaf teachers and students. Prior to her doctoral studies, she worked as an ASL specialist at New Mexico School for the Deaf, and, as a part of a team, implemented new schoolwide ASL assessment tools and curricula. As a committed advocate of social justice, Harris presents and publishes about the ethics of research within Sign Language communities.

Dawson Hedges is an Associate Professor of Psychology at Brigham Young University and currently serves as the director of the Neuroscience Center at Brigham Young University. His research interests include the effects of stress on brain structure and the neuroanatomy associated with psychiatric illnesses.

Heidi M. Holmes is a doctoral student in the Education Department at Gallaudet University. Her research interests focus on language and literacy among young Deaf children. She works as a Literacy Specialist at the Delaware School for the Deaf preparing professional development for teachers and developing and providing in-service training activities to staff and parents in bilingual ASL (American Sign Language)/English education. She also focuses her research on the topics of research ethics within Deaf communities and social justice.

Rodney K. Hopson is Hillman Distinguished Professor, Department of Educational Foundations and Leadership, School of Education, Duquesne University. With postdoctoral and visiting research and teaching experiences from the Johns Hopkins Bloomberg School of Hygiene and Public Health, the University of Namibia Faculty of Education, and Cambridge University Centre of African Studies, his general research interests lie in ethnography, evaluation, and sociolinguistics. His publications raise questions about the differential impact of education and schooling in comparative and international contexts and seek solutions to social and educational conditions in the promotion of alternative paradigms, epistemologies, and methods for the way the oppressed and marginalized succeed in global societies.

Kenneth R. Howe specializes in professional ethics, philosophy and educational research, and evaluation and policy research. He has conducted research and published more than 50 articles on a variety of topics, ranging from the quantitative/qualitative debate to a philosophical examination of constructivism to a defense of multicultural education. His recent research has focused on the nature of scientific research in education. His books include the *Ethics of Special Education* (with Ofelia Miramontes); *Understanding Equal Educational Opportunity: Social Justice, Democracy and Schooling*; *Values in Evaluation and Social Research* (with Ernest House); and *Closing Methodological Divides: Toward Democratic Educational Research*.

Colin Irwin is a Senior Research Fellow in the Institute of Irish Studies at the University of Liverpool. He was the principal investigator on the project "Peace Building and Public Policy in Northern Ireland" and conducted nine public opinion polls with the political parties elected to negotiate the Belfast Agreement, all of which are reviewed in his 2002 monograph "The People's Peace Process in Northern Ireland." Since then, he has extended his work to include the Balkans, Middle East, Kashmir, and Sri Lanka with analysis, questionnaires, and reports available at www.peacepolls.org. In collaboration with the World Association of Public Opinion Research and support from the Royal Norwegian Ministry of Foreign Affairs, he is now helping to set international standards for "peace polls."

David Johnson is Director of grants and development and former chair of the Department of Mathematics, Science and Computer Science at National Hispanic University, San Jose, California. He held several prior posts: executive vice president of Building Engineering and Science Talent, an organization dedicated to increasing the number of women, members of minority groups, and people with disabilities in science and engineering; senior scientist in the Office of the Chancellor, U.S. Department of Defense, helping defense universities adopt institutional research for planning and decision making; and executive director of the Federation of Behavioral, Psychological and Cognitive Sciences, where he was an advocate for increased archiving of data from psychological research.

Caroline Anne Leong Jones is beginning her Ph.D. in social psychology in the fall of 2008. She plans to finish her master's degree, also in social psychology, from San Francisco State University where she was a member of David Matsumoto's Culture and Emotion Research Lab. Her research interests are foremost in decision making, risk behavior, self-concept, and health, although she finds almost everything to be fascinating. She aspires to be a professor one day, helping and guiding her own students' research endeavors. She holds a bachelor's degree in film production from San Diego State University.

Karen Strohm Kitchener is Professor Emeritus at the University of Denver, where she was previously the head of the Counseling Psychology program for 20 years. She has written extensively on ethics in psychology, including practice, research, and teaching. She was also a member and the chairperson of the APA ethics committee and a member of the committee that revised the APA Ethics Code. Her work has influenced the codes of two professional associations. She has received several awards for her work; the most recent was the Life Time Achievement Award, awarded for the first time by the Colorado Psychological Association.

Richard F. Kitchener, Professor of Philosophy at Colorado State University, specializes in philosophical and theoretical issues at the interface of philosophy and psychology (he has graduate degrees in both fields). He has published several books and anthologies on such issues and is best known for his work on Piaget's genetic epistemology (*Piaget's Theory of Knowledge*, 1986). For several years, he was the editor of the journal *New Ideas in Psychology*. Recently, he received the John Stern Award for Distinguished Professor.

Joan LaFrance is the owner of Mekinak Consulting, which specializes in program evaluation and organizational development work with American Indian tribes and organizations. She has an extensive background in research and evaluation in tribal colleges and organizations as well as experience in program planning and development. Currently, she is working with the National Science Foundation and the American Indian Higher Education

Consortium to develop an indigenous framing for evaluation. She is a member of the Turtle Mountain Band of Chippewa. She has a master's degree in public administration and a doctorate in education.

Yvonna S. Lincoln holds the Ruth Harrington Chair of Educational Leadership and is Distinguished Professor of Higher Education at Texas A&M University. She is the coauthor, editor, or coeditor of more than a dozen books on education, program evaluation, and/or research methods and the author or coauthor of more than 200 journal articles and chapters on various aspects of methods or higher education. She is the former President of the Association for the Study of Higher Education and also the American Evaluation Association and the former Vice President of Division J (Postsecondary Education) of the American Educational Research Association. Her research interests include the future of university research libraries, ethics, and IRB policy in institutions of higher education, and she has also coedited a handbook on critical and indigenous methods.

Linda Mabry is a professor of education at Washington State University Vancouver, specializing in evaluation and the assessment of student achievement. She has served on the Board of Directors of the American Evaluation Association (AEA) and as board liaison to the Ethics and Public Affairs Committees, and she currently serves on the Board of Trustees of the National Center for the Improvement of Educational Assessment. She chaired two AEA task forces, one that produced an organizational response to the U.S. government's proposed (and later adopted) priority for funding certain evaluation designs and another that developed an organizational public statement on educational accountability. She has published empirical examples of case studies and evalutations and on topics of educational measurement, evaluation ethics and philosophy, and qualitative methodology in research and evaluation.

Heather MacGillivary partners with schools and nonprofit organizations to evaluate programmatic interventions using a participatory, strengths-based approach. She has worked in the field of evaluation research for more than 15 years in both the United States and Canada. She has conducted research projects in the areas of out-of-school youth, truancy prevention, charter schools, the juvenile justice system, substance abuse prevention, teen pregnancy, and mental health. She holds an M.A. in community psychology from Wilfrid Laurier University. Currently, she is pursuing her Ph.D. in Education at the University of Colorado at Boulder.

Melvin M. Mark is Professor and Head of Psychology at Penn State University. He has served as President of the American Evaluation Association and as Editor of the *American Journal of Evaluation* (now Editor Emeritus). His interests include the theory, methodology, practice, and profession of program and policy evaluation. Among his books are *Evaluation: An Integrated Framework for Understanding, Guiding, and Improving Policies and Programs* (2000; with Gary Henry and George Julnes) and the coedited volumes *SAGE Handbook of Evaluation* (2006), *Credible Evidence* (in press), *Evaluation in Action: Interviews With Expert Evaluators* (in press), and *Social Psychology and Evaluation* (in preparation).

David Matsumoto is Professor of Psychology and Director of the Culture and Emotion Research Laboratory at San Francisco State University, where he has been since 1989. His books include *Culture and Psychology: People Around the World* (translated into Dutch, Japanese, and Polish), *The Intercultural Adjustment Potential of Japanese* (日本人の国際適応力) (本の友社), *The Handbook of Culture and Psychology* (translated into Russian), and *The New Japan* (translated into Chinese). He is the editor for the *Journal of Cross-Cultural*

Psychology and the culture and diversity section of *Social and Personality Psychology Compass*. He is also the series editor for Cambridge University Press' series on *Culture and Psychology*.

Tim McCreanor is a Pakeha member of Whariki Research Group with a long-standing interest in the use of research, particularly qualitative forms, in stimulating and producing changes in social relations in the direction of social justice. His particular focus has long been on the discursive dimensions of power relations in this country with research domains spanning racism, ageism, and heterosexism.

Janice McLaughlin is Deputy Executive Director and Director of Research at the Policy, Ethics, and Life Sciences (PEALS) Research Centre, Newcastle University. Her research explores disability in family life, in particular exploring the significance of interactions with medical and social care professionals and discourses for articulations of identity and kinship. 2008 will see publication of Families Raising Disabled Children: Values of Enabling Care and Social Justice (with Palgrave), co-authored with Dan Goodley, Emma Clavering and Pamela Fisher. Additionally, Dr McLaughlin publishes in the area of feminist social theory, and published in 2003: Feminist Social and Political Theory: Contemporary Debates and Dialogues (with Palgrave).

Ricardo Millett is an independent consultant to philanthropies and nonprofits and is former President of the Woods Fund of Chicago. Prior to his presidency at the Woods Fund, Ricardo was Director of Program Evaluation for the W.K. Kellogg Foundation. He also served as senior vice president of planning and resource management for the United Way of Massachusetts Bay in Boston, deputy associate commissioner of the Department of Social Services for Massachusetts, and senior analyst at ABT Associates, where he worked on research projects that helped to inform national policy in areas such as day care regulations and housing development in urban areas.

Helen Moewaka Barnes is of Ngati Wai, Ngati Hine, Ngati Manu descent. She is Director of the Whariki Research Group, based at Massey University in Auckland, Aotearoa. Her work covers a mix of quantitative and qualitative research projects across a range of Maori well-being issues. She is particularly interested in identity and the nature of knowledge as well as relationships between the health of people and environments.

Margaret E. Montoya is Professor at the University of New Mexico School of Law with a secondary appointment in the Department of Community and Family Medicine. She has taught torts, contracts, clinical law, and employment law courses. She is licensed to practice law in Massachusetts, New York, and New Mexico. She has worked extensively in civil rights. She has taught in the School of Medicine's cultural competence program and cochairs a task force on cultural competence education. Her articles examine issues of race, ethnicity, gender, and language. She received the prestigious Clyde Ferguson Award, given by law professors of color for accomplishments in scholarship, teaching, and service.

Julianne H. Newton, Full Professor of visual communication, University of Oregon School of Journalism and Communication, is an award-winning scholar, editor, photographer, and teacher. She is author of *The Burden of Visual Truth: The Role of Photojournalism in Mediating Reality* and coauthor of *Visual Communication: Integrating Media, Art and Science*. Her visual ethics publications span scholarly, professional, and public forums, and her documentary photographs have been shown in more than 50 exhibitions in three countries. She was editor of *Visual Communication Quarterly*

(VCQ) 2001–2006 and serves on the editorial boards of the *Journal of Mass Media Ethics, EME* (*Explorations in Media Ecology*), and *VCQ*.

Peggy Gabo Ntseane is an Associate Professor in the Department of Adult Education of the University of Botswana. Her teaching experience includes research methodology with a special interest in qualitative research approaches. She also teaches social context–based courses in Adult Education. Her research interests are gender and development; women and the informal sector; gender and HIV/AIDS; feminist pedagogy and poststructuralist feminism. Her publications include topics such as gender and cultural dimensions of sexuality; women and cross-border trade; gender audit of the Botswana national monitoring and evaluation systems; gender and HIV/AIDS; and women's experiences in experiential and transformational learning. She is trained as an adult educator (Ph.D.), a sociologist (B.S. and M.A.), and a gender expert (Graduate Certificate in Women's Studies).

Michael Quinn Patton earned his doctorate in Sociology at the University of Wisconsin. He is an independent evaluation consultant, former President of the American Evaluation Association and author of *Utilization-Focused Evaluation* (4th ed., 2008) and *Qualitative Research and Evaluation Methods* (3rd ed., 2002). He received the Myrdal Award for *Outstanding Contributions to Useful and Practical Evaluation Practice* and the Lazarsfeld Award for *Lifelong Contributions to Evaluation Theory*. His most recent book on complexity theory applied to social innovation is *Getting to Maybe: How the World is Changed* (Random House, 2007) with Frances Westley and Brenda Zimmerman.

Fazal Rizvi has been a professor in the Department of Educational Policy Studies at the University of Illinois since 2001, having previously held academic and administrative appointments at a number of universities in Australia, including as Pro Vice Chancellor (International) at the Royal Melbourne Institute of Technology and as the founding Director of the Monash Centre for Research in International Education. From 1993 to 2000, he was an editor of *Discourse: Studies in the Cultural Politics of Education*, and in 1996 was the President of the Australian Association for Research in Education. His recent books include *Youth Moves: Identities and Education in a Global Era* (2007), *Globalization, the OECD and Education Policy Making* (2001), and *Education Policy and the Politics of Change* (1996). His new book, *Globalizing Educational Policy*, will be published in 2008.

Anne Ryen is Associate Professor of Sociology at Agder University, Norway, and President of the Research Network *Qualitative Methods* in the European Sociological Association and has been doing research in East Africa for more than 15 years. Her publications include *The Qualitative Interview* (2002), "Cross-Cultural Interviewing" in *Handbook of Interview Research* (edited by J. F. Gubrium & J. A. Holstein, 2002), and "Ethical Issues in Qualitative Research" in *Handbook of Qualitative Research Practice* (edited by C. Seale, G. Gobo, J. F. Gubrium, & D. Silverman, 2004). She is guest-editing special issues of *Qualitative Social Work* (on research ethics) and of the online journal *Qualitative Sociology Review* (on the quality of qualitative research; both in press).

Divya Sharma is currently Assistant Professor of Criminal Justice at Utica College. She earned her doctoral degree in sociology from Panjab University in India. It involved primary data collection in Nairobi, and her dissertation is titled *Ethnicity, Immigration and Identity Crisis: A Study of Indian Immigrants in Nairobi*. As a transnational criminologist, she has been doing research in the field of terrorism funding, flesh trade, and drug trafficking with a strong focus on South Asia. Her other research interests include informal banking systems, transnational crimes, immigration and sociocultural identity, and cultural communication through media. She has been teaching courses in criminology, research methods, terrorism, and victimology.

Lisa Schwartz is the Arnold L. Johnson Chair in Health Care Ethics in the Faculty of Health Sciences at McMaster University. Prof. Schwartz received a Ph.D. in philosophy from the University of Glasgow, and MA and BA in philosophy from McGill University. She has extensive experience in research ethics and ethics review. Her research interests include privacy, access to biosamples, patient advocacy, and measurement and effectiveness of ethics education. She is currently the primary investigator on a qualitative study examining the ethical challenges faced by health care professionals providing humanitarian assistance abroad.

Richard Schwartz is currently a senior research scholar at Yale Law School (after 25 years at Syracuse), working on a book called *Law Not War*. He spent three years as a postdoc at Yale's Institute of Human Relations studying learning theory psychology with Neal Miller and anthropology with Ralph Linton. He brought social science to law by putting together a casebook called *Criminal Law: Theory and Practice*. He later worked with Donald T. Campbell at Northwestern, learning and employing experimental methods in field research. The product was a breezy book by Campbell and others called *Unobtrusive Measures*. He also started the *Law and Society Review* and was the only nonlawyer to serve a full term as dean of a law school. He received his Ph.D. in sociology from Yale.

Linda Silka is Professor in the Department of Regional Economic and Social Development at the University of Massachusetts Lowell. She specializes in community capacity building, program evaluation, refugee and immigrant leadership development, community-university partnerships, community mapping, strategic planning, needs assessment, and community conflict resolution. She is also Director of the Center for Family, Work, and Community at the university and Codirector of the university's Community Outreach Partnership Center. The community-based programs include the Refugee and Immigrant Leadership Training and Development and the Southeast Asian Environmental Justice Partnership.

Helen Simons is Professor of Education and Evaluation at the University of Southampton and Honorary Professor at London Metropolitan and Westminster Universities, UK. She specializes in the theory and practice of program and institutional self-evaluation, qualitative methodologies, and research ethics. In 2000 she was elected an Academician of the Academy of Social Sciences, UK and from 2004–2006 was President of the United Kingdom Evaluation Society (UKES). Helen has actively pursued a democratic approach to the research and teaching of evaluation, case study, and qualitative methodologies, incorporating the creative arts. She has also played a major role in promoting professional research ethics. As ethics convenor of the UKES and the British Educational Research Association, she coauthored the first edition of each society's ethical guidelines and for several years was the chair of the School of Education's Research Ethics Committee. Selected publications on ethics include *Getting to Know Schools in a Democracy*, *Situated Ethics in Educational Research* (with R. Usher), and "Ethics in evaluation" in I. Shaw, J. C. Greene, and M. M. Mark's *The Sage Handbook of Evaluation*.

Brent D. Slife is Professor of Psychology and Chair of the doctoral program in Theoretical and Philosophical Psychology at Brigham Young University. Recently honored with the Eliza R. Snow and Karl G. Maeser awards for Outstanding Scholarship, he was also distinguished as "Teacher of the Year" by the university and "Most Outstanding Professor" by the Psychology Honorary, Psi Chi. He served as the president of the

Society of Theoretical and Philosophical Psychology and on the editorial boards of six journals. He has authored more than 120 articles and books, including *Critical Thinking About Psychology* (2005), *Taking Sides* (2007), *Critical Issues in Psychotherapy* (2001), *Toward a Unified Psychology* (2000), *What's Behind the Research?* (1995), and *Time and Psychological Explanation* (1993).

Patricia Spear was Director of Grants and Contracts Administration and IRB Administrator for the Public Health Institute (PHI) in Oakland, California, for 15 years. (PHI conducts public health–related projects; its research programs are mostly in areas of social and behavioral science.) She is now a member of an institutional review board (IRB) and provides consultation on IRB-related issues.

Richard Speiglman collaborates on research with policymakers, advocates, other researchers, and representatives of philanthropy. The protection of client confidentiality first concerned him during prison research and later when he served as a management analyst for Santa Clara County. Subsequently, he has held research positions at institutions in the San Francisco Bay Area, often working with public agencies to design studies integrating data from surveys, key informant interviews, and administrative data sets concerning HIV and mental health status, alcohol and drug use, treatment utilization, homelessness, welfare receipt, and criminal justice status. He served on the Public Health Institute's institutional review board (IRB) for seven years and has used the services of that and several other IRBs. Currently, he is Managing Partner, Speiglman Norris Associates, Oakland, California, and Senior Research Analyst, Child and Family Policy Institute of California.

Robert Stake is Director of CIRCE at the University of Illinois. A specialist in educational program evaluation, he refers to his approach as *responsive evaluation* and emphasizes use of case studies. His evaluative studies include science and mathematics in elementary and secondary schools, model programs and conventional teaching of the arts in schools, and development of teaching for gender equity. He authored *Quieting Reform*, a book on Charles Murray's evaluation of Cities-in-Schools, and four books on methodology: *Standards-Based and Responsive Evaluation, Evaluating the Arts in Education, The Art of Case Study Research,* and *Multiple Case Study Analysis.*

Martin Sullivan is a Senior Lecturer and Coordinator of the postgraduate program in disability studies at the School of Health and Social Services, Massey University, Aotearoa New Zealand. He has published nationally and internationally on disability. His main area of research is how the interrelations between body, self, and society have an impact on the life chances, life choices, and subjectivity of disabled people, especially people with spinal cord impairment. Martin is a member of the Health Research Council's Expert Panel of People With Disability and has just concluded a six-year term in a ministerial appointment with the National Ethics Advisory Committee on Health and Disability.

Hazel Symonette, senior policy and program development specialist at the University of Wisconsin-Madison, serves higher education as a planning and assessment educator, facilitator, and consultant. She advocates assessment/evaluation as a participant-centered self-diagnostic resource for continuous improvement and is committed to creating authentically inclusive environments that are conducive to success for all. She is the founder and director of the yearlong Excellence Through Diversity Institute. She has offered training on the self as responsive instrument throughout the United States and in Africa, New Zealand, and Australia. After three years as cochairs of the American Evaluation Association's (AEA) Building Diversity Initiative and of the Multi-Ethnic Issues in Evaluation Topical Interest Group, she served as an AEA Board member.

Karen Szala-Meneok is Senior Ethics Advisor and Assistant Professor at the School of Rehabilitation Sciences at

McMaster University. Her work with the Canadian Longitudinal Study on Aging, her research on the function of ethics review boards, and her earlier work on a community-based family caregiver health promotion study contributed to her interest in the ethics of conducting research with older adults. Her expertise in qualitative research methodology was honed through her formal training in social anthropology and her extensive field research in the Canadian subarctic and in urban applied-anthropological settings. She has published in the *Journal of Medical Ethics*, *Healthcare Quarterly*, and the *Journal of Palliative Care*.

Veronica G. Thomas is a Professor in the Department of Human Development and Psychoeducational Studies at Howard University. Her research interests include the psychology of black women, the academic and socio-emotional development of youth placed at risk, and culturally responsive evaluations. She has authored work in scholarly journals such as *New Directions for Evaluation*, *Journal of Black Psychology*, *Family Relations*, *Adolescence*, *Educational Leadership*, *Journal of Adult Development*, *Review of Research in Education*, *Journal of Negro Education*, *Sex Roles*, *Journal of Social Psychology*, *Women and Health*, and *Journal of the National Medical Association*.

Kathleen Toms is currently Executive Director of Research Works, Inc., a private, not-for-profit evaluation and technical assistance company in New York, where she directs evaluation and technical assistance contracts in education, community development, and change management. The role of professional ethics in evaluation practice is her primary research interest. In her spare time, she teaches graduate courses in statistics, research methodology, and evaluation principles and practice. Apart from living for some time in the United Kingdom and receiving her Master's of Philosophy from the University of Manchester, she has lived in Africa and Southeast Asia, where she worked on development projects, an experience that led her to her Ph.D. concentration in evaluation at the University at Albany.

David Turner is currently Director of Research, Evaluation & Modelling in the New Zealand Ministry of Justice. He has had nearly 25 years of experience in program evaluation and other research in both the United States and New Zealand. In New Zealand, he has managed research and evaluation teams in the labor market and crime and justice fields. He is a member of the American Evaluation Association and Australasian Evaluation Society (AES). He chaired the AES ethics committee for three years. He is interested in a range of evaluation tools and techniques, including participative and mixed-methods approaches.

Luis A. Vargas is Associate Professor and juvenile forensic psychologist in the Department of Psychiatry at the University of New Mexico. He was previously the director of the clinical psychology internship program for 14 years. He served 6 years as Chair of the New Mexico Board of Psychologist Examiners. His clinical and scholarly work has focused on providing culturally responsive services to diverse children and adolescents, particularly in Latino communities. He is coeditor (with Joan D. Koss-Chioino) of *Working With Culture: Psychotherapeutic Interventions With Ethnic Minority Children and Adolescents* and a coauthor (with Joan D. Koss-Chioino) of *Working With Latino Youth: Culture, Development, and Context*, both published by Jossey-Bass.

Frederick J. Wertz is Professor and Chair of Psychology, Fordham University. He has received awards for undergraduate and graduate teaching. He is the current editor of the *Journal of Phenomenological*

Psychology and former guest editor of *The Humanistic Psychologist*. He edited *The Humanistic Movement: Recovering the Person in Psychology* and coedited *Advances in Qualitative Research in Psychology: Themes and Variations*. He served as President of the Society of Humanistic Psychology and the Society of Theoretical and Philosophical Psychology, which recently presented him with its Distinguished Service Award. Scholarship focuses on the philosophical foundations of psychology; critiques of theory, methodology, and the scientific status of psychology; and phenomenological research methods. He earned his Ph.D. at Duquesne University.

Amanda Wolf teaches graduate and postexperience courses in policy analysis and research methods and directs the Ph.D. program in the School of Government, Victoria University of Wellington, New Zealand, where she has also served as Chair of a Human Ethics Committee. She researches and publishes on innovative social science methodologies for policy-directed purposes. Other recent research includes work on professional values and role orientations, the policy implications of diversity, and countering misleading statistics. She is the editor of the Q-methodology journal *Operant Subjectivity* and is active in applied cross-cultural research and social science research capability networks in New Zealand.